FIFTH EDITION

Marketing Strategy

O.C. Ferrell
The University of New Mexico

Michael D. Hartline
The Florida State University

SOUTH-WESTERN
CENGAGE Learning

Australia • Brazil • Japan • Korea • Mexico • Singapore • Spain • United Kingdom • United States

SOUTH-WESTERN
CENGAGE Learning™

Marketing Strategy, Fifth Edition
O.C. Ferrell and Michael D. Hartline

Vice President of Editorial, Business:
  Jack W. Calhoun

Editor-in-Chief: Melissa Acuna

Executive Editor: Mike Roche

Developmental Editor: Elizabeth Lowry

Editorial Assistant: Kayti Purkiss

Marketing Manager: Bill Hendee

Marketing Coordinator: Shanna Shelton

Senior MarCom Manager: Sarah Greber

Senior Content Project Manager:
  Diane Bowdler

Production Technology Analyst: Emily Gross

Media Editor: John Rich

First Print Buyer: Miranda Klapper

Production Service: MPS Limited,
  A Macmillan Company

Copyeditor: Jill Pellarin

Compositor: MPS Limited,
  A Macmillan Company

Senior Art Director: Stacy Jenkins Shirley

Internal Design: c miller design

Cover Designer: c miller design

Cover Image: ©iStock Photo

Photo Permissions Acquisitions Manager:
  Deanna Ettinger

Text Permissions Acquisitions Manager:
  Mardell Glinski Schultz

Photography Manager: Deanna Ettinger

Photo Research: Susan Van Etten

For product information and technology assistance, contact us at
Cengage Learning Customer & Sales Support, 1-800-354-9706
For permission to use material from this text or product,
submit all requests online at **www.cengage.com/permissions**
Further permissions questions can be emailed to
permissionrequest@cengage.com

Library of Congress Control Number: 2009943533

ISBN-13: 978-0-538-46738-4

ISBN-10: 0-538-46738-X

South-Western Cengage Learning
5191 Natorp Boulevard
Mason, OH 45040
USA

Cengage Learning products are represented in Canada by Nelson Education, Ltd.

For your course and learning solutions, visit
www.academic.cengage.com

Purchase any of our products at your local college store or at our preferred online store **www.CengageBrain.com**

Printed in the United States of America
2 3 4 5 6 7 13 12

Brief Contents

PART 5—Cases

PART 6—Tools for Developing a Marketing Plan

Contents

CHAPTER 5

Developing Competitive Advantage and Strategic Focus   120

PART 3—Developing Marketing Strategy

CHAPTER 6

Customers, Segmentation, and Target Marketing   152

CHAPTER 7

Product Strategy   191

CHAPTER 8

Pricing Strategy   229

CHAPTER 9

Distribution and Supply Chain Management   263

CHAPTER 10

Integrated Marketing Communications   291

PART 4—Putting Strategy into Action

CHAPTER 11

Marketing Implementation and Control   323

CHAPTER 12

Developing and Maintaining Long-Term Customer Relationships   354

PART 5—Cases

PART 6—Tools for Developing a Marketing Plan

APPENDIX A

Marketing Plan Worksheets   651

APPENDIX B

Example Marketing Plan (VirPharm, Inc.)   663

Welcome to one of the most interesting, challenging, and important topics in your business education. What makes marketing strategy so interesting, challenging, and important you ask? To begin, marketing strategy is interesting because (1) it is inherently people driven, and (2) it is never stagnant. A distinct blend of both art and science, marketing strategy is about people (inside an organization) finding ways to deliver exceptional value by fulfilling the needs and wants of other people (customers, shareholders, business partners, society at large), as well as the needs of the organization itself. Marketing strategy draws from psychology, sociology, and economics to better understand the basic needs and motivations of these people—whether they are the organization's customers (typically considered the most critical), its employees, or its stakeholders. In short, marketing strategy is about people serving people.

For this reason, marketing strategy is interesting because it is never stagnant. The simple fact is that people change. A strategy that works today might not work tomorrow. Products that are popular today are forgotten next week. These truisms are important because truly understanding marketing strategy means accepting the fact that there are few concrete rules for developing and implementing marketing activities. Given the constant state of change in the marketing environment, it is virtually impossible to say that given "this customer need" and "these competitors" and "this level of government regulation" that Product A, Price B, Promotion C, and Distribution D will produce the best results. Marketing simply doesn't work that way. The lack of concrete rules and the ever-changing economic, sociocultural, competitive, technological, and political/legal landscapes make marketing strategy a terribly fascinating subject.

Now that you know why marketing strategy is so interesting, it should be easy to see why it is also challenging. A perfect marketing strategy that is executed flawlessly can still fail. Sometimes, organizations get lucky and are successful despite having a terrible strategy and/or execution. The nature of marketing can make marketing planning quite frustrating.

Finally, the importance of marketing strategy is undeniable. No other business function focuses on developing relationships with customers—the lifeblood of all organizations (even nonprofits). This statement does not diminish the importance of other business functions, as they all are necessary for an organization to be successful. In fact, coordination with other functions is critical to marketing success. However, without customers and marketing programs in place to cultivate customer relationships, no organization can survive.

Our Focus

Given this marketing landscape, *Marketing Strategy, 5th Edition* provides a practical, straightforward approach to analyzing, planning, and implementing marketing strategies. Our focus is based on the creative process involved in applying the knowledge and concepts of marketing to the development and implementation of marketing strategy. Our goal is to encourage students of marketing to think and act like a marketer. By discussing the key concepts and tools of marketing strategy, our emphasis on critical thinking, both analytical and creative, allows students to understand the essence of how marketing decisions fit together to create a coherent strategy.

Our approach in *Marketing Strategy, 5th Edition* is also grounded in the development and execution of the marketing plan. Throughout the text, we provide a comprehensive planning framework based on conducting sound background research, developing market capabilities and competitive advantages, designing integrated marketing programs, and managing customer relationships for the long term. We also emphasize the need for integrity in the strategic planning process, as well as the design of marketing programs that are both ethical and socially responsible. We also stress the integration and coordination of marketing decisions with other functional business decisions as the key to achieving an organization's overall mission and vision. Throughout the text, we offer examples of successful planning and implementation to illustrate how firms face the challenges of marketing strategy in today's economy.

Purpose

We view strategic marketing planning not only as a process for achieving organizational goals but also as a means of building long-term relationships with customers. Creating a customer orientation takes imagination, vision, and courage, especially in today's rapidly changing economic and technological environments. To help meet these challenges, our text approaches marketing strategy from both "traditional" and "cutting-edge" practices. We cover topics such as segmentation, creating a competitive advantage, marketing program development, and the implementation process, with a solid grounding in traditional marketing, but also with an eye toward emerging practices. Lessons learned from the rise, fall, and reemergence of the dotcom sector, recent corporate scandals, and the most recent economic recession illustrate the importance of balancing the traditional and emerging practices of marketing strategy. Our text never loses sight of this balance.

Although our approach allows for the use of sophisticated research and decision making processes, we have employed a practical perspective that permits marketing managers in any size organization to develop and implement a marketing plan. We have avoided esoteric, abstract, and highly academic material that does not relate to typical marketing strategy decisions in most organizations. The marketing plan framework that we utilize throughout the text has been used by a number of organizations to successfully plan their marketing strategies. Many companies report great success in using our approach partially due to the ease of communicating the plan to all functional areas of the business.

Target Audience

Our text is relevant for a number of educational environments, including undergraduate, graduate, and corporate training courses. At the undergraduate level, our text is appropriate for the capstone course or any upper level integrating course such as "Marketing Management," "Marketing Strategy," or "Marketing Policy." At this level, the text provides an excellent framework to use with our included text-based cases, live-client cases, or a computer simulation. At the graduate level, our text is appropriate for courses addressing strategic marketing planning, competitive marketing strategies, or as a supplement for any simulation-based course. A growing segment of the market, corporate training, can utilize our text when educating business professionals interested in developing marketing plans of their own or interpreting and implementing the plans of others.

Each of the 20 cases included in our text describes the strategic situations of real world, identifiable organizations. Because these cases feature real situations, instructors have the option of using the case material as published, or they may give students the opportunity to update the cases by conducting research to find the latest information. In addition to the cases provided in our text, instructors can order customized cases through Cengage Custom Publishing. Many additional resources for students and instructors can be found at our text's companion website, *www.cengage.com/marketing/ferrell*.

Key Features of the 5th Edition

The key features of *Marketing Strategy, 5th Edition* include the following:

- Revised and expanded coverage throughout the text of recent events in marketing practice by well-known global companies.

- Three *Beyond the Pages* features in each chapter. These resources offer vignettes of key issues or current marketing practices at many well-known companies, including Amazon, Ford, Dell, Apple, 3M, Steinway, Tropicana, Nintendo, Sony, Barnes & Noble, Walmart, IBM, Green Mountain Coffee, and 1-800-Flowers. Some of the topics discussed in *Beyond the Pages* include marketing in a weak economy, product and marketing innovation, sustainability, e-waste, data mining, social media, the Chinese market, risk management, customer satisfaction, packaging mistakes, and media fragmentation.

- Six new cases written specifically for our text:
  - Case 2, Monsanto Balances the Needs and Concerns of Multiple Stakeholders, focuses on Monsanto's shift from a chemical company to one focused on biotechnology, and the resulting stakeholder concerns about safety and the environment that come with such a change.
  - Case 3, NASCAR: A Branding Success, looks at NASCAR's marketing and branding successes as it climbed to the top of the motorsports market to become the number one spectator sport in the United States.
  - Case 4, The Indy Racing League (IRL): Driving for First Place, is an excellent companion to the NASCAR case. The case examines the reunification of U.S. open wheel racing and how the new IRL must reconnect with fans to improve its standing in the U.S. motorsports market.

- Case 6, Sigma Marketing: Innovation in a Changing Environment, explores the innovation and market adaptation of this small, family-owned business as it grew from a regional printing company to a global specialty advertising firm.

- Case 12, Hottie Hawg's Smokin' BBQ Embraces Its Future, looks at the phenomenal growth of a regional BBQ catering company after less than one year in business, and the decisions facing the company's current and future operations.

- Case 15, BP Focuses on Sustainability to Repair Its Reputation, considers BP's efforts to improve its corporate reputation and focus on sustainability after a series of ethical and environmental lapses.

- A complete revision of the nine cases that have been carried over from the 4th edition of our text:

   - Case 1, Gillette: Product and Marketing Innovation, examines Gillette's history of product and marketing innovation, and how past success may not be enough to maintain supremacy in the global razor market.

   - Case 5, Blockbuster Fights for Survival Against Intense Competition, describes the ongoing challenges facing Blockbuster as it struggles to maintain relevancy in a changing market for video distribution.

   - Case 7, Mattel: Overcoming Marketing and Manufacturing Challenges, looks at the threats that Mattel faces in its ongoing global operations, including changing customer preferences, competition, product liability, and declining sales.

   - Case 8, New Belgium Brewing (A): Social Responsibility as a Competitive Advantage, shows how a firm can use social responsibility and customer intimacy as key competitive advantages in the highly competitive craft beer market.

   - Case 9, New Belgium Brewing (B): Developing a Brand Personality, explains how New Belgium expanded its branding and communication strategy after the development of its "Brand Manifesto."

   - Case 10, IKEA Looks to Further Penetrate the U.S. Market, discusses how IKEA's strategy of operational excellence may stand in the way of further expansion into the U.S. furniture and home furnishings market.

   - Case 11, *USA Today*: Innovation and Evolution in a Troubled Industry, explores how the nation's largest daily newspaper has used continuous innovation to stay ahead of the technological and sociocultural shifts that threaten the very existence of the newspaper industry.

   - Case 13, FedEx: Building a Global Distribution Powerhouse, reviews the rise of FedEx from a domestic overnight express package delivery service to a one-stop, global transportation and logistics juggernaut.

- Case 14, Mistine: Direct Selling in the Thai Cosmetics Market, explores how Mistine's value-based positioning moved the company to the top of the direct selling cosmetics market in Thailand.

- The inclusion of five new outside cases—two from the Harvard Business School and three from the Ivey School of Business at the University of Western Ontario:
  - eHarmony (Harvard)
  - The Home Depot, Inc. (Harvard)
  - Molson Canada: Social Media Marketing (Ivey)
  - IMAX: Larger than Life (Ivey)
  - Best Buy Inc.—Dual Branding in China (Ivey)

- The inclusion of a brief synopsis at the beginning of each case (except the Harvard and Ivey cases), along with key case themes. These additions allow instructors and students to quickly get a feel for each case, and help identify how cases and individual chapters may be coordinated.

- Our complete case package provides up-to-date coverage of topics that are important and relevant to marketing practice in the twenty-first century. These topics include innovation, social responsibility, sustainability, global sourcing, technology, corporate affairs, and entrepreneurship.

- An updated set of Marketing Plan Worksheets, provided in Appendix A. The worksheets reflect a concise approach to marketing plan development. However, the worksheets are comprehensive in scope to help ensure that students and/or managers do not omit important issues in developing strategic marketing plans.

- A revised example marketing plan (VirPharm, Inc.), provided in Appendix B. This marketing plan, based on a virtual case developed by Dr. Hartline, is our most comprehensive example plan to date. Students will find this plan helpful as it illustrates the format and writing style used in creating an actual marketing plan document.

- A continued user-friendly writing style that covers essential points without heavy use of jargon. Although the text has been completely revised, it remains a friendly 12 chapters in length.

Instructor Resources

The Instructor Resource materials for the 5th edition have been updated. These materials include the following:

- A revised PowerPoint package, available on the Instructor's Resource CD-ROM and our text's website at www/cengage.com/marketing/ferrell.

- An updated website (www.cengage.com/marketing/ferrell) to support the text and cases. In addition to the new PowerPoint package, instructors will find lecture outlines, case teaching notes, and sample syllabi for use in their classes.

- An updated Instructor's Manual, which can also be found on the IRCD and online, includes the following:

  ◦ Lecture outlines for each chapter—These outlines may be used to quickly review chapter content before class or to gain an overview of the entire text. The outlines can also be downloaded from our website so instructors can add their own personal notes and examples before class.

  ◦ Case teaching notes—Our teaching notes use a consistent format to help instructors evaluate cases before use or to assist instructors in leading case analysis and class discussion. These case notes are also available on our website. Although there are many different approaches to using cases, our notes will help instructors identify key issues and alternatives as they relate to the content of the case and corresponding text chapters.

  ◦ Examination materials—These materials include a test bank of multiple choice, true/false, and discussion questions for each chapter.

Student Resources

Our primary student resources are contained within the text. Appendix A includes a detailed set of marketing plan worksheets that assist students in developing marketing plans. Likewise, Appendix B provides a complete example marketing plan to give students an idea of what a finished plan looks like. The remaining student resources can be found online at our website:

- A downloadable Microsoft Word version of the Marketing Plan Worksheets found in Appendix A. The worksheets are designed so students can fill in material and edit the worksheets outside of class.

- A downloadable Microsoft Word version of the lessons from each chapter. This document provides a complete outline of each chapter so that students may add to and edit the lessons outside of class. Alternatively, the file can be used during class as a way to organize note taking.

- Online exercises for each chapter. These exercises allow students to practice the concepts learned in class.

- Online quizzes for each chapter. These quizzes help students prepare for course exams.

- A tutorial on how to perform a case analysis. The tutorial provides a suggested way to conduct cases analyses. Instructors may use this tutorial or provide one of their own.

Acknowledgments

Throughout the development of this text, several extraordinary individuals provided their talent and expertise to make important contributions. A number of individuals have made many useful comments and recommendations as reviewers of this text. We appreciate the generous help of these reviewers:

Lynn Allendorf, *University of Iowa*
Dr. Fazal Ahmed, *University of Pennsylvania*
Julia Cronin-Gilmore, *Bellevue University*
A. Cemal Ekin, *Providence College*
Steven McClung, *Florida State University*
Joseph Ouellette, *Bryant University*
Jeffry Overby, *Belmont University*
Norman Alan Ross, *Northern Arizona University*
Kim Saxton, *Indiana University*
Herbert Sherman, *Long Island University–Brooklyn Campus*
George David Shows, *Louisiana Tech University*
Ziad Swaidan, *University of Houston–Victoria*
Uday Tate, *Marshall University*
Linda Wright, *Longwood University*

We also deeply appreciate the assistance of several individuals who played a major role in developing cases or other materials. Specifically, we thank the following individuals:

Timothy W. Aurand, *Northern Illinois University*
Christin Copeland, *Florida State University*
Leanne Davis, *Florida State University*
Melanie Drever, *University of Wyoming*
Linda Ferrell, *University of New Mexico*
John Fraedrich, *Southern Illinois University–Carbondale*
Kimberly Gaskin, *Florida State University*
Nikole Haiar, *University of Wyoming*
Nuntiya Ittiwattanakorn, *Thammasat University (Thailand)*
Jennifer Jackson, *University of New Mexico*
Keith C. Jones, *North Carolina A&T State University*
Geoff Lantos, *Stonehill College*
Jessie Lee, *Hottie Hawg's Smokin' BBQ, Inc.*
Lameck Lukanga, *University of New Mexico*
Rawadee Mekwichai, *Thammasat University (Thailand)*
Amy Minkewicz, *Florida State University*
Don Roy, *Middle Tennessee State University*
Supishsha Sajjamanochai, *Thammasat University (Thailand)*
Mike Sapit, *Sigma Marketing*
Jennifer Sawaya, *University of New Mexico*
Eve Sieber, *University of New Mexico*
Bryan Simpson, *New Belgium Brewing Company*
Debbie M. Thorne, *Texas State University–San Marcos*
Mandy Walz, *Florida State University*
Ekachai Wangprapa, *Thammasat University (Thailand)*

The editorial, production, and marketing staff at Cengage cannot be thanked enough. With a deep sense of appreciation, we thank Mike Roche, Elizabeth Lowry, and Diane Bowdler at Cengage Learning.

Finally, we express appreciation for the support and encouragement of our families, friends, and our colleagues at The University of New Mexico and The Florida State University.

O.C. Ferrell, Ph.D.

The University of New Mexico

O.C. Ferrell (Ph.D., Louisiana State University) is Professor of Marketing and Creative Enterprise Scholar at the Anderson Schools of Management at the University of New Mexico. He served as the Bill Daniels Distinguished Professor of Business Ethics at the University of Wyoming and was Chair of the Marketing Department at Colorado State University. Prior to his arrival at CSU, Dr. Ferrell was the Distinguished Professor of Marketing and Business Ethics at the University of Memphis. He has also served as a professor at the University of Tampa, Texas A&M University, Illinois State University, and Southern Illinois University. His MBA and B.A. degrees are from Florida State University.

Dr. Ferrell is past president of the Academic Council of the American Marketing Association and former chair of the American Marketing Association Ethics Committee. Under his leadership, the committee developed the AMA Code of Ethics and the AMA Code of Ethics for Marketing on the Internet. He is a Society for Marketing Advances Fellow and the Vice President of Publications for the Academy of Marketing Science. He is a former member of the Board of Governors as a Distinguished Fellow for the Academy of Marketing Science. In addition, he received the first Innovative Educator award from the Marketing Management Association.

Dr. Ferrell has taught a wide variety of courses, including marketing strategy, principles of marketing, marketing ethics, and international marketing, as well as most undergraduate courses in marketing. Annually, Dr. Ferrell teaches a graduate course in competitive marketing strategies at Thammasat University in Bangkok, Thailand.

Dr. Ferrell is the coauthor of 17 books and more than 75 articles. His research is published in the *Journal of Marketing Research*, the *Journal of Marketing*, the *Journal of Business Ethics*, the *Journal of Business Research*, the *Journal of the Academy of Marketing Science*, as well as other journals. His *Marketing: Concepts and Strategies* text, co-authored with Bill Pride, is one of the most widely adopted principles of marketing texts in the world. Furthermore, his *Business Ethics: Decision Making and Cases* text is the leading business ethics text. Dr. Ferrell currently serves as the marketing ethics and values section editor for the *Journal of Macromarketing*.

Dr. Ferrell has served as an expert witness in many high-profile civil litigation cases related to marketing ethics. More recently he has assisted international corporations and worked with state regulatory agencies in modifying marketing programs to maintain compliance with both ethical and legal requirements. He has appeared on the NBC *Today* show and he has been quoted in national papers such as *USA Today*.

Dr. Ferrell and his wife, Linda (also a faculty member at the University of New Mexico), live in Albuquerque. He enjoys golf, skiing, reading, and travel.

Michael D. Hartline, Ph.D.

The Florida State University

Michael D. Hartline (Ph.D., The University of Memphis) is Associate Professor and Chair, Department of Marketing, College of Business, The Florida State University. Prior to joining the FSU faculty in 2001, Dr. Hartline was on faculty at the University of Arkansas at Little Rock, Louisiana State University, and Samford University. His MBA and B.S. degrees are from Jacksonville State University in Alabama.

Dr. Hartline has taught many different courses, but primarily teaches MBA courses in marketing strategy and corporate affairs management, as well as under-graduate courses in services marketing and service operations management. He has won many teaching and research awards and has made many presentations to industry and academic audiences. Dr. Hartline has also served as a consultant to several for-profit and nonprofit organizations in the areas of marketing plan development, market feasibility analysis, customer satisfaction measurement, customer service training, and pricing policy. He most recently worked with Pfizer, Inc., in the corporate affairs, philanthropy, and government relations areas.

Dr. Hartline's research addresses marketing implementation issues in service firms. Specifically, his work examines the role of customer-contact employees and work groups in the effective delivery of quality service to customers. Dr. Hartline's research appears in the *Journal of Marketing*, the *Journal of Service Research*, the *Journal of Business Research*, the *Journal of Services Marketing*, the *Cornell Quarterly*, the *Journal of Relationship Marketing*, the *Journal of Strategic Marketing*, the *Journal of Business Ethics*, and the *Marketing Science Institute Working Paper Series*. He also serves on the editorial review boards of a number of leading marketing journals.

Dr. Hartline and his wife, Marsha, live in Tallahassee with their daughters, Meghan, Madison, and Mallory. They have two dogs, Bella and Chief (both Japanese Chins), and a cat, Snickers. Dr. Hartline is a self-professed electronics and gadget enthusiast who enjoys music, reading, computers, travel, college football (Go Seminoles!), and being a dad.

CHAPTER 1

Marketing in Today's Economy

Introduction

As noted in the opening *Beyond the Pages* story, competing in today's economy means finding ways to break out of commodity status to meet customers' needs better than competing firms. All organizations—both for-profit and nonprofit—require effective planning and a sound marketing strategy to do this effectively. Without these efforts, organizations would not be able to satisfy customers or meet the needs of other stakeholders. For example, having an effective marketing strategy allows Apple to develop popular products, such as the iPhone, iPod, and its MacBook line of notebook computers. Further, effective planning and strategy allows Cola-Cola to continue its leadership in soft drinks and make a key acquisition in its purchase of the Vitamin Water brand, all the while continuing its expansion into the lucrative Chinese market. These and other organizations use sound marketing strategy to leverage their strengths and capitalize on opportunities that exist in the market. Every organization—from your favorite local restaurant to giant multinational corporations; from city, state, and federal governments, to charities such as Habitat for Humanity and the American Red Cross—develops and implements marketing strategies.

How organizations plan, develop, and implement marketing strategies is the focus of this book. To achieve this focus, we provide a systematic process for developing customer-oriented marketing strategies and marketing plans that match an organization to its internal and external environments. Our approach focuses on real-world applications and practical methods of marketing planning, including the process of developing a marketing plan. The chapters of this book focus on the steps of this process. Our goal is to give the reader a deeper understanding of marketing planning, the ability to organize the vast amount of information needed to complete the planning process, and an actual "feel" for the development of marketing plans.

In this first chapter, we review some of the major challenges and opportunities that exist in planning marketing strategy in today's economy. We also review the nature and scope of major marketing activities and decisions that occur throughout the planning process. Finally, we look at some of the major challenges involved in developing marketing strategy.

Beyond the Pages 1.1

WELCOME TO COMMODITY HELL[1]

Welcome to commodity hell, where your product is just like everyone else's, your profit margins are low, and price is the only true means of differentiation that matters to customers. If this scenario sounds far-fetched, it isn't. Many companies today find themselves in this difficult situation. Commoditization is the curse of mature markets whereby products lack real means of differentiation and customers begin to see all competing products as offering roughly the same benefits. When consumers see competing products as commodities, price is the only thing that matters.

Commoditization is a consequence of mature industries, where slowing innovation, extensive product assortment, excess supply, and frugal consumers force margins to the floor. Because firms have few competitive differences, they are unable to increase margins. They must also spend a great deal on promotion to attract new customers. This situation makes firms more vulnerable to the entry of new competitors. Consider the airline industry. Notwithstanding a few minor differences, most air travelers see all airlines as being roughly the same. They all get passengers from point A to point B while offering the same basic customer services. This makes price the driving force in consumer decision making and allows discount airlines such as Southwest and Jet Blue to steal customers away from traditional full-service carriers. This same precarious situation exists in a broad range of industries, including telephone service, hotels, packaged goods, automobiles, household appliances, and retailing.

As might be expected, low price leaders can do quite well in commodity hell. Southwest, for example, was profitable for over 33 years until the economic recession hit in 2008. Walmart and Dell are champions at navigating their way through commodity status. Other firms, however, avoid commodity status through the most basic of marketing tactics: brand building. Here, firms break free from commodity status by developing a distinctive brand position that separates them and

their products from the competition. Firms that come to mind are Apple, Best Buy, Coca-Cola, and Chick-fil-A. By offering compelling reasons for consumers to buy products, brand building allows firms to increase margins.

For example, Starbucks clearly sells one of the most commoditized, ubiquitous products of all time: coffee. Starbucks Chairman Howard Schultz, however, does not accept that his firm is in the coffee business. Instead, Schultz sees Starbucks as a "third place" to hang out (with home and work being no. 1 and no. 2, respectively). Through this mentality, Starbucks offers its customers much more than coffee, including wireless Internet access, music, food, and relaxation. Starbucks' brand was on an unbelievable growth trajectory until two things happened: Other firms—most notably McDonald's—began offering good coffee, and the economic recession occurred. These issues, combined with the fact that Starbucks grew too quickly, began to water down the Starbucks experience and make it more like a commodity. Today, Starbucks is once again using brand building to focus on value through brand promotion, the launch of a $3.95 breakfast combo, and the introduction of Via—a new instant coffee. Schultz hopes these tactics will reinvigorate the company's brand aura.

Getting out of commodity hell is not an easy feat. To do so, firms must give consumers a compelling reason to buy their products over competing products. Ultimately, winning the commodity game is all about innovation. Consider the 10 firms that top *BusinessWeek*'s list of the World's Most Innovative Companies for 2009 (in order): Apple, Google, Toyota, Microsoft, Nintendo, IBM, Hewlett-Packard, Research in Motion, Nokia, and Walmart. Each of these companies offers innovative products, processes, or experiences that stand apart from the competition; yet each competes in mature industries known for commoditization. These companies prove that innovation and good marketing strategy are the antidotes for commodity hell.

The Challenges and Opportunities of Marketing in Today's Economy

Traditional ideas about marketing strategy began to change forever during the mid-1990s. Advances in computer, communication, and information technology forever changed the world and the ways that marketers reach potential customers. The collapse of the dot-com bubble in the late 1990s was followed by a historic collapse of the worldwide economy in 2008. The powerhouse companies of the past have weakened and lost relevance in an economy marked by constant change and consumer skepticism. Consider these fundamental changes to marketing and business practice, as well as to our own personal buying behavior:

- **Power Shift to Customers** Perhaps the single most important change during the last two decades is the shift in power from marketers to consumers. Rather than businesses having the ability to manipulate customers via technology, customers often manipulate businesses because of their access to information, the ability to comparison shop, and the control they have over spending. Individual consumers and business customers can compare prices and product specifications in a matter of minutes. In many cases, customers are able to set their own prices, such as purchasing airline tickets at Priceline.com. In addition, customers can now interact with one another, as merchants such as Amazon and eBay allow customers to share opinions on product quality and supplier reliability. As power continues to shift to customers, marketers have little choice but to ensure that their products are unique and of high quality, thereby giving customers a reason to purchase their products and remain loyal to them.

- **Massive Increase in Product Selection** The variety and assortment of goods and services offered for sale on the Internet and in traditional stores is staggering. In grocery stores alone, customers are faced with countless options in the cereal and soft drink aisles. The growth in online retailing now allows customers to purchase a car from CarsDirect.com; handmade, exotic gifts from Mojo Tree (http://www.mojotree.co.uk); or a case of their favorite wine from Wine.com. Increased transaction efficiency (e.g., 24/7 access, delivery to home or office) allows customers to fulfill their needs more easily and conveniently than ever before. Furthermore, the vast amounts of information available online has changed the way we communicate, read the news, and entertain ourselves. Customers can now have the news delivered to them automatically via RSS feeds (Really Simple Syndication) from hundreds of sources. This radical increase in product selection and availability has exposed marketers to inroads by competitors from every corner of the globe.

- **Audience and Media Fragmentation** Changes in media usage and the availability of new media outlets have forced marketers to rethink they way they communicate with potential customers. Since the advent of cable television in the 1970s, mass media audiences have become increasingly fragmented. Television audiences, for

Consumers have access to an unprecedented selection of goods and services in today's economy.

example, shifted from the big three networks (ABC, CBS, NBC) and began watching programming on ESPN, HGTV, Nickelodeon, and the Discovery Channel. When the growth of the Internet, satellite radio, and mobile communication is added to this mix, it becomes increasingly difficult for marketers to reach a true mass audience. Media audiences have become fragmented due to (1) the sheer number of media choices we have available today, and (2) the limited time we have to devote to any one medium. Today, customers increasingly get information and news from Facebook and Twitter rather than *The New York Times* or CBS. They spend a growing amount of time online or interacting with handheld devices—more time than they spend reading magazines or watching television. As shown in Exhibit 1.1, consumer usage of traditional media is declining, while the usage of nontraditional media such as social networking, podcasting, and mobile media is on the rise. However, despite the challenge of reaching mass audiences today, media fragmentation does have a big advantage: It is easier to reach small, highly targeted audiences who are more receptive to specific marketing messages.

EXHIBIT 1.1	CHANGE IN MEDIA USAGE BY U.S. INTERNET USERS, 2006–2008

	Percent Change
Network TV News	–8.5%
Local TV News	–16.2%
Cable Network News	4.3%
Cable TV News Websites	–18.4%
E-mail Newsletters	5%
Talk Radio	–13.9%
National Newspapers	0%
Local Newspapers	–8.7%
Consumer Magazines	–21.7%
Advice from Coworkers	30.4%
Social Networking Sites	52.9%
Company Websites	18.2%
Shopping Websites	105.9%
Blogs	84.6%
Podcasts	40%
RSS News Feeds	40%
Mobile Media	20%

Source: Ketchum and USC Annenberg Strategic Public Relations Center, "Media Myths and Realities: 2008 Media Usage Survey," January 20, 2009.

- **Changing Value Propositions** Even before "The Great Recession" began in 2008, consumers and business buyers were already facing increasing costs associated with energy, gasoline, food, and other essentials. Then, as the economy weakened, buyers were forced to tighten their belts and look for other ways to lower expenses. This trend actually began after the dot-com collapse as consumers saw for the first time that they could bypass some types of firms and do things for themselves. For example, travel agents and real estate agents have been hit hard by e-commerce. Many customers now turn to Travelocity and Expedia, rather than travel agents, for assistance in booking airline tickets, cruises, or hotel stays. A similar change has taken place in the real estate industry as buyers are moving their house hunting online, while sellers are increasingly taking the "for sale by owner" route. Consequently, many marketers learned a tough lesson: In situations where customers see goods and services as commodities, they will turn to the most convenient, least expensive alternative. Today, many of these same consumers face pay cuts or losing their jobs in addition to increased expenses. These and other economic hardships have forced consumer and business buyers to rethink value propositions and focus on the importance of frugality. The effects on business have been dramatic. For example, Circuit City closed its doors in 2009 in the face of a highly commoditized market and stiff competition from Best Buy, Amazon, and other online merchants. Consumers shied away from Circuit City because they could find lower prices online or better service at Best Buy. There was simply no compelling reason for the firm to exist anymore. A similar shakeout is happening in the book retailing segment. Borders, for instance, has been struggling against fierce competition from Barnes & Noble, Amazon, Walmart, and Target. Likewise, the introduction of Amazon's Kindle and Barnes & Noble's Nook—both wireless e-book readers—sets the stage for further shakeouts in book retailing and book printing. Because books have become highly commoditized, consumers typically search for the lowest prices rather than the fringe benefits offered by traditional bookstores. E-book readers add to that by saving space and paper. This is the essence of being frugal, as customers look for ways to cut spending on unnecessary parts of their lives.

- **Shifting Demand Patterns** In some cases, changes in technology have shifted customer demand for certain product categories. News is one well-known example, where traditional newspapers are slowing disappearing while online and mobile news continue to grow. Now, many newspaper companies have folded and some are on the brink of folding, while others have cut publication to only a few days per week.[2] Another example is the explosive growth in the digital distribution of music and video. The success of Apple's iPod and iTunes, YouTube, and Netflix, along with the continuing integration of television and computers, has dramatically shifted demand for the recording and movie industries. Hollywood film studios are grappling with soft demand in theatres and the declining popularity of DVDs as customers increasingly look for online movie options or for other forms of entertainment such as video games. Further, Blockbuster Video faces an uncertain future after a $374 million loss and a 26 percent decline in mail-order rentals in 2008.[3]

- **Privacy, Security, and Ethical Concerns**   Changes in technology have made our society much more open than in the past. As a result, these changes have forced marketers to address real concerns about security and privacy, both online and offline. Businesses have always collected routine information about their customers. Now, customers are much more attuned to these efforts and the purposes for which the information will be used. Though customers appreciate the convenience of e-commerce, they want assurances that their information is safe and confidential. Concerns over online privacy and security are especially acute with respect to controversial businesses—such as casinos or pornography—and with respect to children. For example, many well-known and respected companies, including Mrs. Fields (cookies), Sony BMG, and Hershey Foods, have been fined for violating the standards of the Children's Online Privacy Protection Act.[4] Sony agreed to pay $1 million for collecting personal information from children under the age of 13 without their parents' permission. Exhibit 1.2 provides an overview of this law and its standards.

- **Unclear Legal Jurisdiction**   When a company does business in more than one country (as many Internet-based firms do), that company often faces a dilemma with respect to differing legal systems. Today, this difference is especially keen for

---

EXHIBIT 1.2   **THE CHILDREN'S ONLINE PRIVACY PROTECTION ACT (COPPA)**

The Children's Online Privacy Protection Act applies to operators of commercial websites and online services that attempt to collect personal information from children under the age of 13. The law explains what must be included in the firm's privacy policy, when and how to seek verifiable consent from a parent or guardian, and the firm's responsibilities to protect children's privacy and safety. Firms cannot evade the law's provisions by claiming that children under 13 cannot visit their sites; nor can they make information optional or ask the visitor's age.

In implementing the provisions of COPPA, the FTC issued the Children's Online Privacy Protection Rule, which is designed to give parents control over the information that is collected from their children. The rule requires a website operator to:

- Post a description of its privacy policy on the site's homepage and any other area where personal information is collected.
- Provide notice to parents about the site's information collection practices. This full disclosure must describe (1) the type of information collected, (2) why the information is being collected, (3) how the information will be used and stored, (4) whether the information will be disclosed to third parties, and (5) parental rights with regard to information content and usage.
- Obtain verifiable parental consent to the collection and use of a child's personal information for internal use. The operator must also give parents the opportunity to choose not to have this information disclosed to third parties.
- Give parents access to their child's information, give them the right and means to review and/or delete this information, and give parents the choice to opt out of the future collection or use of the information.
- Not require that children provide more information than is reasonably necessary to participate in an activity. Children cannot be required to provide information as a condition of participation.
- Maintain the security, confidentiality, and integrity of all personal information collected from children.

Source: United States Federal Trade Commission, Kidz Privacy (http://www.ftc.gov/coppa/).

firms that do business in both the United States and China. Google, for example, faces a difficult situation in dealing with the Chinese government's censorship demands. Though Google is a U.S. firm, it must comply with the Chinese request by operating a completely separate search service that censors information considered sensitive by the Chinese government.[5] Doing business in China is also an issue with respect to protection of intellectual property rights, where Chinese laws do not offer the same protections found in the United States.[6] For example, U.S. software manufacturers lost an estimated $14 billion in sales in 2007 to software piracy in China and other Asian countries.[7]

Another important legal issue involves the collection of sales tax for online transactions. In the early days of e-commerce, most online merchants did not collect sales taxes for online transactions—giving them a big advantage against store-based merchants. In fact, a 1992 U.S. Supreme Court decision exempted out-of-state retailers from collecting sales taxes in states where they had no physical presence. States countered that they were losing millions in yearly tax revenue, but they were poorly organized to mount a collection effort. In 2003, major retailers—including Walmart, Target, and Toys "R" Us—in an agreement with a consortium of 38 states and the District of Columbia, agreed to collect online sales taxes.[8] However, many online merchants still did not charge sales taxes. Today, with most states' coffers reeling from the economic collapse, states are looking for ways to enforce the collection of sales taxes for online transactions. In 2008, New York expanded its physical presence laws to cover online retailers. Many other states are expected to follow suit.[9]

Although the full effect of these challenges will not be recognized for some time, circumstances have forced businesses to move ahead by adjusting their marketing activities at both the strategic and tactical levels. As we review the major marketing concepts and activities in this chapter, we will look at how today's challenges have affected strategic planning in these areas.

Basic Marketing Concepts

Marketing is many different things. Many people, especially those not employed in marketing, see marketing as a function of business. From this perspective, marketing parallels other business functions such as production, research, management, human resources, and accounting. As a business function, the goal of marketing is to connect the organization to its customers. Other individuals, particularly those working in marketing jobs, tend to see marketing as a process of managing the flow of products from the point of conception to the point of consumption. The field's major trade organization, the American Marketing Association, changed the definition of marketing in 2005. From 1985 until 2005, the AMA defined marketing this way:

> *Marketing is the process of planning and executing the conception, pricing, promotion, and distribution of ideas, goods, and services to create exchanges that satisfy individual and organizational objectives.*[10]

In 2005, the AMA changed the definition of marketing to better reflect the realities of competing in today's marketplace:

Marketing is an organizational function and a set of processes for creating, communicating, and delivering value to customers and for managing customer relationships in ways that benefit the organization and its stakeholders.[11]

Notice that the changes in the definition are not merely cosmetic in nature. The new definition stresses two critical success factors in marketing today: value and customer relationships. The notion of value recognizes that customer satisfaction can be derived from many different aspects of the total product offering, not just from having access to high-quality products at a low price. Customer relationships—which grow and thrive on exceptional value—are an absolute necessity in the commodity-driven status of many product markets. Although the former definition of marketing had a decidedly transactional focus, the new definition emphasizes long-term relationships that provide value for both customers and the firm.

A final way to think about marketing relates to meeting human and social needs. This broad view links marketing with our standard of living, not only in terms of enhanced consumption and prosperity but also in terms of society's well-being. Through marketing activities, consumers can buy cars from South Korea and wines from South Africa; and organizations can earn a viable profit, making both employees and shareholders happy. However, marketing must also bear responsibility for any negative effects it may generate. This view demands that marketers consider the social and ethical implications of their actions, and whether they practice good citizenship by giving back to their communities. As exemplified in the New Belgium Brewing case at the end of the text, firms can successfully meet human and social needs through socially responsible marketing and business practices.

Let's take a closer look at several basic marketing concepts. As we will see, ongoing changes in today's economy have forever altered our way of thinking about these foundational aspects of marketing.

What Is a Market?

At its most basic level, a *market* is a collection of buyers and sellers. We tend to think of a market as a group of individuals or institutions that have similar needs that can be met by a particular product. For example, the housing market is a collection of buyers and sellers of residential real estate, whereas the automobile market includes buyers and sellers of automotive transportation. Marketers or sellers tend to use the word *market* to describe only the buyers. This basic understanding of a market has not changed in a very long time. What has changed, however, is not so much the "what" but the "where" of a market; that is, the location of the buyers and sellers. In both consumer markets (like housing and automobiles) and business markets (like replacement parts and raw materials), the answer to the "where" question is quickly becoming "anywhere" as markets become less defined by geography.

Until recently, marketers have considered a market to be a physical location where buyers and sellers meet to conduct transactions. Although those venues (e.g., grocery stores, malls, flea markets) still exist, technology mediates some of the fastest growing markets. The term *marketspace* has been coined to describe these electronic marketplaces unbound by time or space.[12] In a marketspace, physical goods, services, and information are exchanged through computer networks. Some of the largest marketspaces, such as Amazon, eBay, and Monster, are now household names. In fact, Amazon has become the marketspace equivalent of a shopping mall as the company now sells shoes, apparel, jewelry, beauty aids, and sporting goods in addition to its traditional offerings of books and electronics. Marketspaces also exist in the business-to-business realm. The shift from marketplaces to marketspaces has significant ramifications for marketers. The fact that customers can shop, place orders, and exchange information 24/7 means that these businesses must be capable of operating in that same time frame. In effect, marketspace operators never take a break at closing time—they never close. It also means that firms lose some control over the information that is disseminated about their company or products. Through blogs, discussion forums, or even Twitter, customers can exchange information about a marketspace outside the marketspace itself. Furthermore, the substitution of technology for human interaction can be both a blessing and a curse. Some marketspaces, like CarsDirect, are successful because they eliminate the hassle of dealing with another human in the buying process. Many customers, however, have been slow to embrace marketspaces because these venues lack the human element. In these cases, the design and implementation of the online experience is a serious challenge for marketspace operators. Finally, the wealth of information available through today's marketspaces not only makes customers more educated than ever before, it also gives customers increased power through comparison shopping and price negotiation.

Another interesting shift related to markets is the advent of metamarkets and metamediaries. A *metamarket* is a cluster of closely related goods and services that center around a specific consumption activity. A *metamediary* provides a single access point where buyers can locate and contact many different sellers in the metamarket.[13] Assume, for example, that you are engaged to be married. How many different buying decisions will you and your fiancé have to make in the coming months? How many newspaper ads, websites, and magazines will you explore? Although the businesses and decisions are diverse, they all converge on the single theme of wedding planning. This is the driving principle behind a metamarket. Exhibit 1.3 shows examples of common metamarkets and metamediaries. Although customers don't use these terms, they fully understand the concept of finding information and solutions in one place. For example, iVillage (http://www.ivillage.com) has become the Internet's preeminent metamediary with respect to women's issues. One of its most popular sections deals with pregnancy and parenting, which has become the first stop for many anxious parents in need of advice. Metamediaries like iVillage fulfill a vital need by offering quick access and one-stop shopping to a wide variety of information, goods, and services.

EXHIBIT 1.3	COMMON METAMARKETS AND PARTICIPANTS		
	Metamarkets		
	Automotive	Home Ownership	Parenting
Metamediaries	http://www.edmunds.com	http://www.realtor.com	http://parenting.ivillage.com
	http://autos.msn.com	http://realestate.msn.com	http://www.parenting.com
	http://www.carsdirect.com	http://www.bhg.com	
	http://www.kbb.com		
Metamarket Participants	Buyers	Homeowners	Parents
	Manufacturers	Builders	Doctors
	Car dealerships	Real estate agents	Retailers
	Banks	Mortgage companies	Baby supply manufacturers
	Credit unions	Insurance companies	Insurance firms
	Credit reporting services	Home inspectors and	Financial planners
	Insurance firms	appraisers	Educational providers
	Rating services	Pest control services	Toy manufacturers
	Magazines	Magazines	Television programs
	Television programs	Television programs	Movies
	Aftermarket parts/accessories	Retailers	
	Repair services		
	Car rental firms		
	Auction houses		

What Is Exchange?

Closely related to the concept of a market, our ideas about exchange have changed in recent years. *Exchange* is traditionally defined as the process of obtaining something of value from someone by offering something in return; this usually entails obtaining products for money. For exchange to occur, five conditions must be met:

1. **There must be at least two parties to the exchange.** Although this has always been the case, the exchange process today can potentially include an unlimited number of participants. Online auctions provide a good example. Customers who bid on an item at eBay may be one of many participants to the exchange process. Each participant changes the process for the others, as well as the ultimate outcome for the winning bidder. Some auctions include multiple quantities of an item, so the potential exists for multiple transactions within a single auction process.

2. **Each party has something of value to offer the other party.** Exchange would be possible, but not very likely, without this basic requirement. The Internet has exposed us to a vast array of goods and services that we did not know existed previously. Today, not only can we buy a television or stereo receiver from a local merchant, but we also have access to hundreds of online merchants. Furthermore, the ability to comparison shop products and their prices allows customers to seek out the best value.

3. **Each party must be capable of communication and delivery.** The advantages of today's communication and distribution infrastructure are amazing. We can find and communicate with potential exchange partners anywhere and anytime via telephone, computers, interactive television, and smartphones. We can also conduct arm's-length transactions in real time, with delivery of exchanged items occurring in a matter of hours if necessary. For example, you can text message an order to Pizza Hut on your way home from work.

4. **Each party must be free to accept or reject the exchange.** In the online world, this condition of exchange becomes a bit more complicated. Customers have grown accustomed to the ease with which they can return items to local merchants. Easy return policies are among the major strengths of traditional offline merchants. Returning items is more difficult with online transactions. In some cases, the ability to reject an exchange is not allowed in online transactions. Ordering airline tickets on Priceline.com and winning a bid on an item at eBay are contractually binding acts for the customer. In other words, once the actual purchasing process has started, the customer is not free to reject the exchange.

5. **Each party believes it is desirable to exchange with the other party.** Customers typically have a great deal of information about, or even a history with, offline merchants. In online exchange, customers often know nothing about the other party. To help resolve this issue, a number of third-party firms have stepped in to provide ratings and opinions about online merchants. Sites like BizRate.com and Epinions.com not only provide these ratings, they also provide product ratings and serve as shopping portals. eBay and Amazon go one step further by allowing buyers and sellers to rate each other. This gives both parties to the exchange process some assurance that reputable individuals or organizations exist on the other side of the transaction.

The bottom line is that exchange has become all too easy in today's economy. Opportunities for exchange bombard us virtually everywhere we go. Customers don't even have to trouble themselves with giving credit cards or completing forms for shipping information. Most online merchants will remember this information for us if we let them. For example, Amazon's 1-Click ordering feature allows customers to purchase products with a single mouse click.[14] The ease with which exchange can occur today presents a problem in that individuals who do not have the authority to exchange can still complete transactions. This is especially true for underage customers.

What Is a Product?

It should come as no surprise that the primary focus of marketing is the customer and how the organization can design and deliver products that meet customers' needs. Organizations create essentially all marketing activities as a means toward this end; this includes product design, pricing, promotion, and distribution. In short, an organization would have no reason to exist without customers and a product to offer them.

But what exactly is a product? A very simple definition is that a *product* is something that can be acquired via exchange to satisfy a need or a want. This definition permits us to classify a broad number of "things" as products:[15]

- **Goods** Goods are tangible items ranging from canned food to fighter jets, from sports memorabilia to used clothing. The marketing of tangible goods is arguably one of the most widely recognizable business activities in the world.

- **Services** Services are intangible products consisting of acts or deeds directed toward people or their possessions. Banks, hospitals, lawyers, package delivery companies, airlines, hotels, repair technicians, nannies, housekeepers, consultants, and taxi drivers all offer services. Services, rather than tangible goods, dominate modern economies like the U.S. economy.

- **Ideas** Ideas include platforms or issues aimed at promoting a benefit for the customer. Examples include cause-related or charitable organizations such as the Red Cross, the American Cancer Society, Mothers Against Drunk Drivers, or the American Legacy Foundation's campaign against smoking.[16]

- **Information** Marketers of information include websites, magazine and book publishers, schools and universities, research firms, churches, and charitable organizations. In the digital age, the production and distribution of information has become a vital part of our economy.

- **Digital Products** Digital products, such as software, music, and movies are among the most profitable in our economy. Advancements in technology have also wreaked havoc in these industries because pirates can easily copy and redistribute digital products in violation of copyright law. Digital products are interesting because content producers grant customers a license to use them, rather than outright ownership.

- **People** The individual promotion of people, such as athletes or celebrities, is a huge business around the world. The exchange and trading of professional athletes takes place in a complex system of drafts, contracts, and free agency. Other professions, such as politicians, actors, professional speakers, and news reporters, also engage in people marketing.

- **Places** When we think of the marketing of a place, we usually think of vacation destinations like Rome or Orlando. However, the marketing of places is quite diverse. Cities, states, and nations all market themselves to tourists, businesses, and potential residents. The state of Alabama, for example, has done quite well in attracting direct investment by foreign firms. Over the last twenty years, Alabama has landed assembly plants from Mercedes, Honda, and Hyundai, as well as many different parts plants and related firms. It's no wonder that some people think of Alabama as the new Detroit.[17]

- **Experiences and Events** Marketers can bring together a combination of goods, services, ideas, information, or people to create one-of-a-kind experiences or single events. Good examples include theme parks such as Disney World and Universal

Studios, athletic events like the Olympics or the Super Bowl, or stage and musical performances like *The Phantom of the Opera* or a concert by Madonna.

- **Real or Financial Property** The exchange of stocks, bonds, and real estate, once marketed completely offline via real estate agents and investment companies, now occurs increasingly online. For example, Realtor.com is the nation's largest real estate listing service, with over 2.5 million searchable listings. Likewise, Schwab.com is the world's largest and top-rated online brokerage.

- **Organizations** Virtually all organizations strive to create favorable images with the public—not only to increase sales or inquiries, but also to generate customer goodwill. In this sense, General Electric is no different than the United Way: Both seek to enhance their images in order to attract more people (customers, volunteers, and clients) and money (sales, profit, and donations).

We should note that the products in this list are not mutually exclusive. For example, firms that sell tangible goods almost always sell services to supplement their offerings, and vice versa. Charitable organizations simultaneously market themselves, their ideas, and the information that they provide. Finally, special events, like the Daytona 500, combine people (drivers), a place (Daytona), an event (the race), organizations (sponsors), and goods (souvenirs) to create a memorable and unique experience for race fans.

To effectively meet the needs of their customers and fulfill organizational objectives, marketers must be astute in creating products and combining them in ways that make them unique from other product offerings. A customer's decision to purchase one product or group of products over another is primarily a function of how well that choice will fulfill that person's needs and satisfy his or her wants. Economists use the term *utility* to describe the ability of a product to satisfy a customer's desires. Customers usually seek out exchanges with marketers who offer products that are high in one or more of these five types of utility:

- **Form Utility** Products high in form utility have attributes or features that set them apart from the competition. Often these differences result from the use of high-quality raw materials, ingredients, or components; or from the use of highly efficient production processes. For example, Ruth's Chris Steakhouse, considered by many to be one of the nation's top restaurants, provides higher form utility than other national chains because of the quality of beef they use. Papa John's Pizza even stresses form utility in its slogan "Better Ingredients. Better Pizza." In many product categories, higher priced product lines offer more form utility because they have more features or bells and whistles. Cars are a good example.

- **Time Utility** Products high in time utility are available when customers want them. Typically, this means that products are available now rather than later. Grocery stores, restaurants, and other retailers that are open around the clock provide exceptional time utility. Often the most successful restaurants around college campuses are those that are open 24/7. Many customers are also willing to pay more for products available in a shorter time frame (such as overnight delivery via FedEx) or for products available at the most convenient times (such as mid-morning airline flights).

- **Place Utility**   Products high in place utility are available where customers want them, which is typically wherever the customer happens to be at that moment (such as grocery delivery to a home) or where the product needs to be at that moment (such as florist delivery to a workplace). Home delivery of anything (especially pizza), convenience stores, vending machines, and e-commerce are examples of good place utility. Products that are high in both time and place utility are exceptionally valuable to customers because they provide the utmost in convenience.

- **Possession Utility**   Possession utility deals with the transfer of ownership or title from marketer to customer. Products higher in possession utility are more satisfying because marketers make them easier to acquire. Marketers often combine supplemental services with tangible goods to increase possession utility. For example, furniture stores that offer easy credit terms and home delivery enhance the possession utility of their goods. In fact, any merchant that accepts credit cards enhances possession utility for customers that do not carry cash or checks. Expensive products, like a home or a new factory, require acceptable financing arrangements to complete the exchange process.

- **Psychological Utility**   Products high in psychological utility deliver positive experiential or psychological attributes that customers find satisfying. Sporting events often fall into this category, especially when the competition is based on an intense rivalry. The atmosphere, energy, and excitement associated with being at the game can all create psychological benefits for customers. Conversely, a product might offer exceptional psychological utility because it lacks negative experiential or psychological attributes. For example, a vacation to the beach or the mountains might offer more psychological utility to some customers because it is seen as less stressful than a vacation to Disney World.

© Valeria73/Shutterstock

Sporting events deliver psychological utility that goes beyond the actual competition.

The strategic and tactical planning of marketing activities involves the important basic concepts we have explored in this section. Marketers often struggle with finding and reaching the appropriate markets for their products. In other cases, the market is easily accessible, but the product is wrong or does not offer customers a compelling reason to purchase it. The ability to match markets and products in a way that satisfies both customer and organizational objectives is truly an art and a science. Doing so in an environment of never-ending change creates both opportunities and challenges for even the strongest and most respected organizations. As described in *Beyond the Pages 1.2*, Walmart, P&G, and Hulu have found ways to maintain innovative marketing during tough economic times.

Beyond the Pages 1.2

MAINTAINING INNOVATION IN A TOUGH ECONOMY[18]

Innovation has long been considered the lifeblood of business, especially in terms of growth and new market opportunities. Unfortunately, our economy's most recent struggles have made it difficult for companies to maintain the pace of innovation they have enjoyed over the past decade. The reason is purely financial: It is hard to be innovative when you are forced to cut costs, lay off employees, close plants, and maintain market standing. The same is true for consumers as they have reined in spending due to the economy.

Still, some companies have managed to maintain their creativity and innovation even in a down economy. They do so by looking for the new opportunities that come along with changing customer spending patterns. Here are three cases in point:

Walmart

When customers have fewer dollars to spend, they try to make those dollars go farther. In the grocery business, this translates into stronger sales for store brands (private labels). Many of Walmart's store brands are well-known: Great Value, Sam's Choice, Faded Glory, HomeTrends, Ol' Roy, and Equate. To further take advantage of changing shopping patterns, Walmart decided to reinvigorate Great Value—its top-selling private label brand. To do this, Walmart improved the quality of roughly 750 food products, updated the Great Value logo, and freshened the packaging. Industry analysts expect other retailers to adopt the same strategy as customers look for private labels as a way to save money.

Procter & Gamble

One result of the down economy has been that customers forgo buying new cars and instead begin taking better care of the cars they currently own. P&G decided to capitalize on this trend by launching a national chain of franchised car washes under its Mr. Clean brand. To begin, P&G acquired Carnett's—a small car-wash chain. Next, P&G took advantage of lower real estate prices to find suitable locations, and rising unemployment to find talented employees. Because the car-wash industry does not have a dominant national brand, P&G hopes that its Mr. Clean units will capture a good share of the $35 billion industry. Next up for P&G: Tide dry-cleaning shops.

Hulu

When customers have less money to spend on entertainment, they tend to entertain themselves more at home. Hulu.com is perfectly poised to take advantage of this trend. A joint venture between NBC and News Corp., Hulu is an advertising-supported, online video-streaming service that offers prime-time television programming via the Internet. Hulu's growth comes from a growing trend of watching full-length programming via the Internet instead of the television. The trend is especially prevalent among the prized 18- to 44-year-old demographic—a statistic that has advertisers buzzing. Hulu users spend an average of 256 minutes per month watching videos—each one embedded with advertising from mainstream companies like Best Buy, Bank of America, and Nissan. In only two years, Hulu has risen to fourth among video websites and generates over $200 million in revenue. The company expects to begin turning a profit in a few years when it reaches a mass scale and larger audiences.

(continued)

What do these three innovations teach us? First, companies can still be innovative in a down economy. The key is to conduct research to closely follow changing customer preferences and spending. Second, it's not enough to do the research. Good innovation must be accurately timed to the market. Third, to be creative, companies will often have to step outside their comfort zones. P&G is a great example. Who would have thought that a packaged goods company could become a service provider?

The process of planning marketing activities to achieve these ends is the focus of this book. As we turn our attention to an overview of major marketing activities and decisions, we also want to lay out the structure of the text. The chapters roughly coincide with the major activities involved in developing marketing strategy and writing a marketing plan. Although our approach is orderly and straightforward, it provides a holistic representation of the marketing planning process from one period to the next. As we will see, marketing planning is an evolving process that has no definite beginning or ending point.

Major Marketing Activities and Decisions

Organizations must deal with a number of activities and decisions in marketing their products to customers. These activities vary in both complexity and scope. Whether the issue is a local restaurant's change in copy for a newspaper ad, or a large multinational firm launching a new product in a foreign market, all marketing activities have one thing in common: They aim to give customers a reason to buy the organization's product. In this section, we briefly introduce the activities and decisions that will be the focus of the remaining chapters of this book.

Strategic Planning

If an organization is to have any chance of reaching its goals and objectives, it must have a game plan or road map for getting there. A *strategy*, in effect, outlines the organization's game plan for success. Effective marketing requires sound strategic planning at a number of levels in an organization. At the top levels of the organization, planners concern themselves with macro issues such as the corporate mission, management of the mix of strategic business units, resource acquisition and assignments, and corporate policy decisions. Planners at the middle levels, typically a division or strategic business unit, concern themselves with similar issues, but focus on those that pertain to their particular product/market. Strategic planning at the lower levels of an organization is much more tactical in nature. Here, planners concern themselves with the development of marketing plans—more specific game plans for connecting products and markets in ways that satisfy both organizational and customer objectives.

Although this book is essentially about strategic planning, it focuses on tactical planning and the development of the marketing plan. *Tactical planning* concerns itself with specific markets or market segments and the development of marketing programs that will fulfill the needs of customers in those markets. The *marketing plan* provides the outline for how the organization will combine product, pricing, distribution, and promotion decisions to create an offering that customers will find attractive. The marketing plan also concerns itself with the implementation, control, and refinement of these decisions.

To stand a reasonable chance for success, marketing plans should be developed with a keen appreciation of how they fit into the strategic plans of the middle- and upper-levels of the firm. In Chapter 2, we discuss the connection among corporate, business-unit, and marketing planning, as well as how marketing plans must be integrated with the plans of other functions in the organization (financial plans, production plans, etc.). We also discuss the structure of the marketing plan and some of the challenges involved in creating one.

Social Responsibility and Ethics

The role of social responsibility and ethics in marketing strategy has come to the forefront of important business issues in today's economy. Our society still reverberates from the effects of corporate scandals at Enron, WorldCom, and ImClone, among others. Although these scandals make for interesting reading, many innocent individuals have suffered the consequences from these companies' unethical behavior. *Social responsibility* refers to an organization's obligation to maximize its positive impact on society while minimizing its negative impact. In terms of marketing strategy, social responsibility addresses the total effect of an organization's marketing activities on society. A major part of this responsibility is *marketing ethics*, or the principles and standards that define acceptable conduct in marketing activities. Ethical marketing can build trust and commitment and is a crucial ingredient in building long-term relationships with all stakeholders. Another major component of any firm's impact on society is the degree to which it engages in philanthropic activities. Many firms now make philanthropy a key strategic activity.

In Chapter 3, we discuss the economic, legal, ethical, and philanthropic dimensions of social responsibility, along with the strategic management of corporate integrity in the marketing planning process. Although there are occasional lapses, most firms understand their economic and legal responsibilities. However, social and ethical responsibilities, by their nature, are not so clearly understood. Many firms see social responsibility not only as a way to be a good corporate citizen, but also as a good way to build their brands. For example, the Red brand—created by Bono in 2006—has been marketed successfully by firms such as Gap, Apple, Motorola, Armani, Converse, and American Express. These and other companies market Red brand versions of their products, with the aim to donate 50 percent of their profits to the Global Fund to fight AIDS in Africa.[19]

Research and Analysis

Strategic planning depends heavily on the availability and interpretation of information. Without this lifeblood, strategic planning would be a mindless exercise and a waste of time. Thankfully, today's planners are blessed with an abundance of information due to improving technology and the Internet. However, the challenge of finding and analyzing the right information remains. As many marketing planners have found, having the right information is just as important as having the right product.

Marketers are accustomed to conducting and analyzing research, particularly with respect to the needs, opinions, and attitudes of their customers. Although customer analysis is vital to the success of the marketing plan, the organization must also have access to three other types of information and analysis: internal analysis, competitive analysis, and environmental analysis. *Internal analysis* involves the objective review of internal information pertaining to the firm's current strategy and performance, as well as the current and future availability of resources. Analysis of the competitive environment, increasingly known as *competitive intelligence*, involves analyzing the capabilities, vulnerabilities, and intentions of competing businesses.[20] Analysis of the external environment, also known as *environmental scanning*, involves the analysis of economic, political, legal, technological, and cultural events and trends that may affect the future of the organization and its marketing efforts. Some marketing planners use the term *situation analysis* to refer to the overall process of collecting and interpreting internal, competitive, and environmental information.

The development of a sound marketing plan requires the analysis of information on all fronts. In Chapter 4, we address the collection and analysis of internal, customer, competitive, and environmental information. We also discuss the challenges involved in finding the right information from an overwhelming supply of available information. The uncertainty and continual change in the external environment also create challenges for marketers (as the Internet boom and bust have shown us). As we will see, this type of research and analysis is perhaps the most difficult aspect of developing a marketing plan.

Developing Competitive Advantage

To be successful, a firm must possess one or more competitive advantages that it can leverage in the market in order to meet its objectives. A *competitive advantage* is something that the firm does better than its competitors that gives it an edge in serving customers' needs and/or maintaining mutually satisfying relationships with important stakeholders. Competitive advantages are critical because they set the tone, or strategic focus, of the entire marketing program. When these advantages are tied to market opportunities, the firm can offer customers a compelling reason to buy their products. Without a competitive advantage, the firm and its products are likely to be just one more offering among a sea of commoditized products. Apple, for example, has been quite successful in leveraging innovation and the customer experience to maintain a sizable competitive advantage in computers, portable music players, and music and movie distribution. A typical Mac computer costs substantially more than a comparable PC running Windows. However, Apple bundles multimedia software and a top-rated user experience into the mix. As a result, Apple computers continue to command a price premium, where most PC manufacturers engage in price wars.[21]

In Chapter 5, we discuss the process of developing competitive advantages and establishing a strategic focus for the marketing program. We also address the role of SWOT analysis as a means of tying the firm's strengths or internal capabilities to market opportunities. Further, we discuss the importance of developing goals and objectives. Having good goals and objectives is vital because these become the basis for measuring the success of the entire marketing program. For example, Hampton Inn has a goal of 100 percent customer satisfaction. Customers do not have to pay for their stay if they are not completely satisfied.[22] Goals like these are not only useful in setting milestones for evaluating marketing performance; they also motivate managers and employees. This can be especially true when marketing goals or objectives help to drive employee evaluation and compensation programs.

Marketing Strategy Decisions

An organization's marketing strategy describes how the firm will fulfill the needs and wants of its customers. It can also include activities associated with maintaining relationships with other stakeholders, such as employees or supply chain partners. Stated another way, marketing strategy is a plan for how the organization will use its strengths and capabilities to match the needs and requirements of the market. A marketing strategy can be composed of one or more marketing programs; each program consists of two elements—a target market or markets and a marketing mix (sometimes known as the four Ps of product, price, place, and promotion). To develop a marketing strategy, an organization must select the right combination of target market(s) and marketing mix(es) in order to create distinct competitive advantages over its rivals.

Market Segmentation and Target Marketing   The identification and selection of one or more target markets is the result of the market segmentation process. Marketers engage in *market segmentation* when they divide the total market into smaller, relatively homogeneous groups or segments that share similar needs, wants, or characteristics. When a marketer selects one or more *target markets*, he or she identifies one or more segments of individuals, businesses, or institutions toward which the firm's marketing efforts will be directed. As described in *Beyond the Pages 1.3*, marketers increasingly use online social networking as a way to target specific markets.

Advances in technology have created some interesting changes in the ways that organizations segment and target markets. Marketers can now analyze customer-buying patterns in real time at the point of purchase via barcode or RFID scanning in retail stores, and analyzing clickstream data in online transactions. This allows organizations to target specific segments with product offers or promotional messages.[23] Furthermore, technology now gives marketers the ability to target individual customers through direct mail and e-mail campaigns. This saves considerable time and expense by not wasting efforts on potential customers who may not be interested in the organization's product offering. However, these new opportunities for marketers come at a price: Many potential buyers resent the ability of marketers to reach them individually. Consequently, customers and governmental authorities have raised

Beyond the Pages 1.3

TARGETING CONSUMERS VIA ONLINE SOCIAL NETWORKING[24]

Social networking sites on the Internet have proved to be very popular with both users and advertisers. Sites like MySpace, Facebook, LinkedIn, YouTube, Digg, and Twitter allow users to "hang out" in an online equivalent of shopping malls, parking lots, and bars. Most users are teens and young adults who use the sites to trade messages, photos, music, and blogs. The largest of these sites currently is Facebook, which boasts over 300 million active users. MySpace, which was acquired by News Corp. in 2005 for $580 million, has 125 million active users. Other sites like LinkedIn (50 million users) and Twitter (18 million users) are also busy and profitable.

Although social networks are very popular, they have attracted a fair amount of criticism. Many argue that these sites make it easier for predators to reach teens and children through the use of their online profiles. Business experts have been skeptical of the long-term success of social networking as a business model. They argue that younger audiences are fickle and will leave these sites for the next hot thing on the Internet. Others argue that the questionable nature of the content on these sites is a risky proposition when tied to advertising strategies.

Despite these criticisms, online social networking appears to have legs for the long-term—forcing media companies and advertisers to take notice. The reason is simple: The demographic profile of the social networking audience is extremely lucrative. MySpace's audience is primarily in the 12 to 17 age range. Facebook's fastest growing age segment is the 25 and over crowd. LinkedIn has a

different profile of over 30 million members with an average age of 41. Powerful segmentation like this has forced an increasing number of advertisers to consider social networking as a viable media strategy. Target, NBC, Procter & Gamble, Viacom, and Geffen A&M Records are only some of the firms that have run ad campaigns on MySpace.

In addition to the demographic fortune, social networking also allows firms to carefully target promotions to the right audience and collect a striking amount of information about users. For example, Procter & Gamble launched Secret Sparkle to 16- to 24-year-old girls and women using MySpace. These users were not only exposed to ads for the product, but also allowed to participate in a Secret Sparkle sweepstakes. Volkswagen also used MySpace as a part of its "Unpimp Your Auto" campaign for the GTI. The campaign featured Helga, a blond bombshell, and Wolfgang, a German engineer, who both maintained profiles on MySpace. More than 7,500 fans signed up as Helga's friends.

Social networking sites have become so successful that they are beginning to replace Google, Yahoo!, MSN, and AOL as the web portals of choice. In essence, social networking sites have become one-stop shops for communication, information, and commerce. Consumers can buy products without having to leave these sites, and marketers are paying attention. Recently, MySpace revamped its MySpace Music service to allow users to play songs for free, create playlists, and purchase music through Amazon—all from within the MySpace site.

major concerns over privacy and confidentiality. This is especially true with respect to RFID, or radio frequency identification, which uses tiny radio-enabled chips to track merchandise. Because RFID chips can be scanned from distances up to 25 feet, many fear that the technology will allow companies to track consumers even after they leave a store.[25]

Chapter 6 discusses the issues and strategies associated with market segmentation and target marketing. In that discussion, we will examine different approaches to market segmentation and look at target marketing in both consumer and business markets. Effective segmentation and target marketing sets the stage for the development of the product offering and the design of a marketing program that can effectively deliver the offering to targeted customers.

Product Decisions   Earlier in the chapter, we discussed the many different types of products that can be offered to customers today. As one of the basic parts of marketing, the product and the decisions that surround it are among the most important aspects of marketing strategy. This importance hinges on the connection between the product and the customers' needs. Even large corporations fail to make this connection at times. McDonald's, for example, spent over $100 million in the mid-1990s to launch the Arch Deluxe—a hamburger designed for adult tastes. The product failed miserably because it was designed for older customers (not the children who are McDonald's core market), was expensive, and had a very high calorie content. McDonald's customers avoided the Arch Deluxe and the sandwich was eventually discontinued.[26] As this example illustrates, marketing is unlikely to be effective unless there is a solid linkage between a product's benefits and customers' needs.

In Chapter 7, we discuss the decisions that marketers make about products and their total product offering. Product decisions include much more than issues regarding design, style, or features. Marketers must also make decisions regarding package design, branding, trademarks, warranties, new product development, and product positioning. *Product positioning* involves establishing a mental image, or position, of the product offering relative to competing offerings in the minds of target buyers. The goal of positioning is to distinguish or differentiate the firm's product offering from those of competitors by making the offering stand out among the crowd. For example, the mental image that most customers have about Walmart is associated with everyday low prices. Target has a slightly different position, one that emphasizes value with a stronger sense of style and quality.

Pricing Decisions   Pricing decisions are important for several reasons. First, price is the only element of the marketing mix that leads to revenue and profit. All other elements of the marketing mix, such as product development and promotion, represent expenses. Second, price typically has a direct connection with customer demand. This connection makes pricing the most over-manipulated element of the marketing mix. Marketers routinely adjust the price of their products in an effort to stimulate or curb demand. Third, pricing is the easiest element of the marketing program to change. There are very few other aspects of marketing that can be altered in real time. This is a huge plus for marketers who need to adjust prices to reflect local market conditions or for online merchants who want to charge different prices for different customers based on total sales or customer loyalty. Finally, pricing is a major quality cue for customers. In the absence of other information, customers tend to equate higher prices with higher quality.

Pricing decisions are the subject of Chapter 8, where we will discuss buyer and seller perspectives on pricing, pricing objectives, the issue of price elasticity, and strategies for setting profitable and justifiable prices. One of the reasons that pricing is so interesting is that price represents a major point in marketing strategy where buyer and seller motivations come into conflict. Although other elements of the marketing mix are relatively stable, the price can be negotiated. The ease with which buyers can compare prices among competing firms today makes setting the right price even more challenging for marketers.

Distribution and Supply Chain Decisions   Distribution and supply chain issues are among the least apparent decisions made in marketing, particularly with customers. The goal of *distribution and supply chain management* is essentially to get the product to the right place, at the right time, in the right quantities, at the lowest possible cost. *Supply chain* decisions involve a long line of activities—from the sourcing of raw materials, through the production of finished products, to ultimate delivery to final customers. Most of these activities, which customers take for granted, take place behind the scenes. Few customers, for example, contemplate how their favorite cereal ends up on their grocer's shelf or how Dell can have a made-to-order computer at your door in days. Customers just expect these things to happen. In fact, most customers never consider these issues until something goes wrong. Suddenly, when the grocer is out of an item or an assembly line runs low on component parts, distribution and supply chain factors become quite noticeable.

As we will discuss in Chapter 9, distribution and supply chain issues are critical for two major reasons: product availability and distribution costs. The importance of product availability is obvious; customers cannot buy your product if it is not available at the right time, place, or in the right quantities. Distribution decisions, therefore, are closely connected to the issues of time, place, and possession utility that we discussed earlier in the chapter. The importance of distribution costs is tied to the firm's profit margin. No matter how you look at it, distribution is expensive. As a result, firms that take the time to build highly efficient and effective distribution systems can lower their operating costs and create a competitive advantage against rival firms. For large companies, even a fractional decrease in costs can lead to big increases in profits.

Promotion Decisions   Modern marketing has replaced the term *promotion* with the concept of *integrated marketing communication* (IMC), or the coordination of all promotional activities (media advertising, direct mail, personal selling, sales promotion, public relations, packaging, store displays, website design, personnel) to produce a unified, customer-focused message. Here, the term *customers* not only refers to customers in the traditional sense, but also includes employees, business partners, shareholders, the government, the media, and society in general. IMC rose to prominence in the 1990s as businesses realized that traditional audiences for promotional efforts had become more diverse and fragmented. IMC can also reduce promotional expenses by eliminating the duplication of effort among separate departments (marketing, sales, advertising, public affairs, and information technology) and by increasing efficiencies and economies of scale.

As we shall see in Chapter 10, the goals of IMC are the same as those for traditional promotion; namely, to inform, persuade, and remind customers (i.e., all stakeholders) about the organization and its product offerings so as to influence their behavior. Promotional decisions are the most noticeable and among the most expensive of all marketing activities. In today's society, it is virtually impossible to not be exposed to promotional messages. Some of these messages, like Nike's "Just Do It," have become ingrained into modern culture. However, even a good message cannot overcome poor decisions regarding other marketing program elements.

Implementation and Control

Once a marketing strategy has been selected and the elements of the marketing mix are in place, the marketer must put the plan into action. *Marketing implementation*, the process of executing the marketing strategy, is the "how" of marketing planning. Rather than being an add-on at the end of the marketing strategy and marketing plan, implementation is actually a part of planning itself. That is, when planning a marketing strategy, the organization must always consider how the strategy will be executed. Sometimes, the organization must revisit the strategy or plan to make revisions during the strategy's execution. This is where marketing control comes into play. Adequate control of marketing activities is essential to ensure that the strategy stays on course and focused on achieving its goals and objectives.

The implementation phase of marketing strategy calls into play the fifth "P" of the marketing program: people. As we will learn in Chapter 11, many of the problems that occur in implementing marketing activities are "people problems" associated with the managers and employees on the frontline of the organization who have responsibility for executing the marketing strategy. Many organizations understand the vital link between people and implementation by treating their employees as indispensable assets. AFLAC, for example, has been named for 11 consecutive years by *Fortune* magazine to its list of the "100 Best Companies to Work for in America." The Georgia-based company has developed a corporate culture that focuses on caring for employees and providing for their needs.[27] Other companies cited as having good relationships with their employees include Google, Wegman's Food Markets, Adobe Systems, and The Container Store.

Developing and Maintaining Customer Relationships

Over the last decade, marketers have come to the realization that they can learn more about their customers, and earn higher profits, if they develop long-term relationships with them. This requires that markers shift away from transactional marketing and embrace a relationship marketing approach. The goal of *transactional marketing* is to complete a large number of discrete exchanges with individual customers. The focus is on acquiring customers and making the sale, not necessarily on attending to customers' needs and wants. In *relationship marketing*, the goal is to develop and maintain long-term, mutually satisfying arrangements where both buyer and seller focus on the value obtained from the relationship. As long as this value stays the same or increases, the relationship is likely to deepen and grow stronger over time. Exhibit 1.4 illustrates the basic characteristics of transactional versus relationship marketing. Relationship marketing promotes customer trust and confidence in the marketer, who can then develop a deeper understanding of customers' needs and wants. This puts the marketer in a position to respond more effectively to customers' needs, thereby increasing the value of the relationship for both parties.

The principles and advantages of relationship marketing are the same in both business-to-business and consumer markets. Relationship marketing activities also extend beyond customers to include relationships with employees and supply chain

EXHIBIT 1.4	MAJOR CHARACTERISTICS OF TRANSACTIONAL AND RELATIONSHIP MARKETING	
	Transactional Marketing	Relationship Marketing
Marketing Focus	Customer Acquisition	Customer Retention
Time Orientation	Short-Term	Long-Term
Marketing Goal	Make the Sale	Mutual Satisfaction
Relationship Focus	Create Exchanges	Create Value
Customer Service Priority	Low	High
Customer Contact	Low to Moderate	Frequent
Commitment to Customers	Low	High
Characteristics of the Interaction	Adversarial, Manipulation, Conflict Resolution	Cooperation, Trust, Mutual Respect, Confidence
Source of Competitive Advantage	Production, Marketing	Relationship Commitment

partners. In Chapter 12, we discuss these and other aspects of relationship marketing in greater depth. Long-term relationships with important stakeholders will not materialize unless these relationships create value for each participant. This is especially true for customers faced with many different alternatives among firms competing for their business. Because the quality and value of a marketer's product offering typically determine customer value and satisfaction, Chapter 12 will also discuss the role of quality, value, and satisfaction in developing and maintaining customer relationships. Issues associated with quality, value, and satisfaction cut across all elements of the marketing program. Hence, we discuss these issues in our final chapter as a means of tying all of the marketing program elements together.

Taking on the Challenges of Marketing Strategy

One of the greatest frustrations and opportunities in marketing is change—customers change, competitors change, and even the marketing organization changes. Strategies that are highly successful today will not work tomorrow. Customers will buy products today that they will have no interest in tomorrow. These are truisms in marketing. Although frustrating, challenges like these also make marketing extremely interesting and rewarding. Life as a marketer is never dull.

Another fact about marketing strategy is that it is inherently people-driven. Marketing strategy is about people (inside an organization) trying to find ways to deliver exceptional value by fulfilling the needs and wants of other people (customers, shareholders, business partners, society at large), as well as the needs of the organization itself. Marketing strategy draws from psychology, sociology, and economics to better understand the basic needs and motivations of these people—whether they are the organization's customers (typically considered the most critical), its employees, or its stakeholders. In short, marketing strategy is about people serving people.

The combination of continual change and the people-driven nature of marketing makes developing and implementing marketing strategy a challenging task. A perfect strategy that is executed perfectly can still fail. This happens because there are very few rules for how to do marketing in specific situations. In other words, it is impossible to say that given "this customer need" and these "competitors" and this "level of government regulation" that Product A, Price B, Promotion C, and Distribution D should be used. Marketing simply doesn't work that way. Sometimes, an organization can get lucky and be successful despite having a terrible strategy and/or execution. The lack of rules and the ever-changing economic, sociocultural, competitive, technological, and political/legal landscapes make marketing strategy a terribly fascinating subject.

Most of the changes that marketers have faced over the past 20 years deal with the basic evolution of marketing and business practice in our society. One of the most basic shifts involves the increasing demands of customers. Today, customers have very high expectations about basic issues such as quality, performance, price, and availability. American customers in particular have a passion for instant gratification that marketers struggle to fulfill. Some evidence suggests that marketers have not met this challenge. The American Customer Satisfaction Index, computed by the National Quality Research Center at the University of Michigan, indicates that customer satisfaction has only recently recovered since the Center first computed the index in 1994. As shown in Exhibit 1.5, some industries such as newspapers and airlines have suffered large declines in customer satisfaction. Satisfaction in other industries, such as the automotive industry and soft drinks, has remained fairly high and stable.

The decline in satisfaction can be attributed to several reasons. For one, customers have become much less brand loyal than in previous generations. Today's customers are very price sensitive, especially in commoditized markets where products lack any real means of differentiation. Consequently, customers constantly seek the best value and thrive on their ability to compare prices among competing alternatives. Customers are also quite cynical about business in general and are not that trusting of marketers. In short, today's customers not only have more power, they also have more attitude. This combination makes them a formidable force in the development of contemporary marketing strategy.

Marketers have also been forced to adapt to shifts in markets and competition. In terms of their life cycles, most products compete today in very mature markets. Many firms also compete in markets where product offerings have become commoditized by a lack of differentiation (e.g., customers perceive competing offerings as essentially the same). Some examples include airlines, wireless phone service, department stores, laundry supplies, and household appliances. Product commoditization pushes margins lower and reduces brand loyalty even further. To meet this challenge, U.S. firms have moved aggressively into foreign markets in an effort to increase sales and find new growth opportunities. At the same time, however, foreign firms have moved into U.S. markets to meet the challenges of maturing markets in their own countries. It is interesting that while Walmart moved aggressively into China, British retailer Tesco launched a chain of large convenience stores in California.[28] The end result of these changes is that firms around the globe face new competition and new challenges.

In the face of increasing competition and maturing markets, businesses have been forced to cut expenses in order to remain competitive. Some businesses do this by

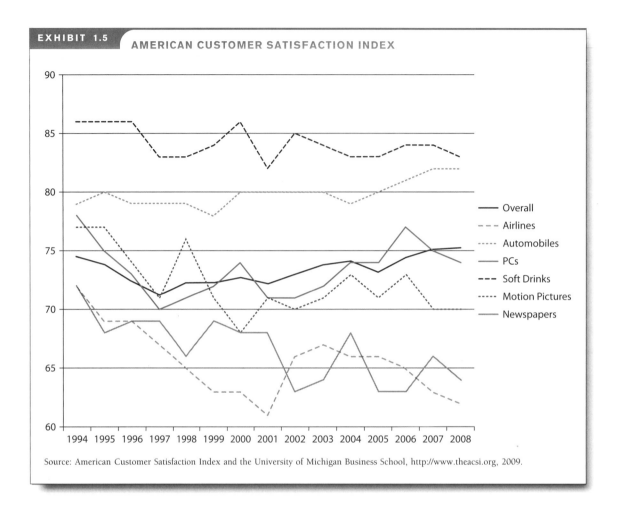

EXHIBIT 1.5

AMERICAN CUSTOMER SATISFACTION INDEX

Legend:
- Overall
- Airlines
- Automobiles
- PCs
- Soft Drinks
- Motion Pictures
- Newspapers

Source: American Customer Satisfaction Index and the University of Michigan Business School, http://www.theacsi.org, 2009.

eliminating products or product lines. General Motors (GM), for example, decided to drop its Saturn and Pontiac divisions—a move similar to its dropping of Oldsmobile and the Hummer H1. Others have maintained their product mix but have aggressively sought ways to lower their distribution costs. The growth in direct distribution (manufacturer to end user) is a result of these efforts. Still other firms have been forced to take drastic measures such as downsizing and laying off employees to trim expenses. This strategy has become all too common after the economic recession that began in 2008.

Needless to say, developing a viable and effective marketing strategy has become extremely challenging. Even the most admired marketers in the world like McDonald's, Procter & Gamble, Anheuser-Busch, and Toyota occasionally have problems meeting the demands of the strategic planning process and developing the "right" marketing strategy. Our goal in this book is not to teach you to develop the "right" strategy. Rather, our approach will give you a framework for organizing the planning process and the ability to see how all of the pieces fit together. Think of it as a mindset or way to think about marketing strategy. The remainder of this text dedicates itself to these goals.

Lessons from Chapter 1

Marketing challenges and opportunities in the new economy include

- A shift in power to customers caused by increased access to information.

- A massive increase in product selection due to line extensions and global sourcing.

- Greater audience and media fragmentation as customers spend more time with interactive media and less time with traditional media.

- Changing customer perceptions of value and frugality.

- Shifting demand patterns for certain product categories, especially those delivered digitally.

- Increasing concerns over privacy, security, and ethics.

- Unclear legal jurisdictions, especially in global markets.

Marketing

- Is parallel to other business functions such as production, research, management, human resources, and accounting. The goal of marketing is to connect the organization to its customers.

- Is defined as an organizational function and a set of processes for creating, communicating, and delivering value to customers and for managing customer relationships in ways that benefit the organization and its stakeholders.

- Has changed in focus over the past 20 years. Today, marketing stresses value and customer relationships.

- Is linked with our standard of living, not only in terms of enhanced consumption and prosperity, but also in terms of society's well-being.

Basic marketing concepts include

- Market—a collection of buyers and sellers.

- Marketplace—a physical location where buyers and sellers meet to conduct transactions.

- Marketspace—an electronic marketplace not bound by time or space.

- Metamarket—a cluster of closely related goods and services that centers on a specific consumption activity.

- Metamediary—a single access point where buyers can locate and contact many different sellers in the metamarket.

- Exchange—the process of obtaining something of value from someone by offering something in return, which usually involves obtaining products for money. There are five conditions of exchange:

    1. There must be at least two parties to the exchange.
    2. Each party has something of value to offer the other party.
    3. Each party must be capable of communication and delivery.
    4. Each party must be free to accept or reject the exchange.
    5. Each party believes it is desirable to exchange with the other party.

- Product—something that can be acquired via exchange to satisfy a need or a want.

- Utility—the ability of a product to satisfy a customer's needs and wants. The five types of utility provided through marketing exchanges are form utility, time utility, place utility, possession utility, and psychological utility.

Major marketing activities and decisions include

- Strategic and tactical planning.

- Social responsibility and ethics.

- Research and analysis.

- Developing competitive advantages and a strategic focus for the marketing program.

- Marketing strategy decisions, including decisions related to market segmentation and target marketing, the product, pricing, distribution, and promotion, which will create competitive advantages over rival firms.

- Implementing and controlling marketing activities.

- Developing and maintaining long-term customer relationships, including a shift from transactional marketing to relationship marketing.

Some of the challenges involved in developing marketing strategy include

- Unending change—customers change, competitors change, and even the marketing organization changes.

- The fact that marketing is inherently people-driven.

- The lack of rules for choosing appropriate marketing activities.

- The basic evolution of marketing and business practice in our society.

- The increasing demands of customers.

- An overall decline in brand loyalty and an increase in price sensitivity among customers.

- Increasing customer cynicism about business and marketing activities.

- Competing in mature markets with increasing commoditization and little real differentiation among product offerings.

- Increasing expansion into foreign markets by U.S. and foreign firms.

- Aggressive cost-cutting measures in order to increase competitiveness.

Questions for Discussion

1. Increasing customer power is a continuing challenge to marketers in today's economy. In what ways have you personally experienced this shift in power; either as a customer or as a business person? Is this power shift uniform across industries and markets? How so?

2. How concerned are you about privacy and security in today's economy? Are you more concerned about online security or about the potential ramifications of RFID technology? Will these issues still be important in 10 years? Explain.

3. The text argues that marketing possesses very few rules for choosing the appropriate marketing activities. Can you describe any universal rules of marketing that might be applied to most products, markets, customers, and situations?

Exercises

1. The pace of change in our economy was frenetic from 1999 to 2001 (the so-called dot-com boom) because of rapidly expanding technology and the growth of the Internet. Shortly thereafter, the bubble burst and many dot-com pioneers disappeared. Conduct some research to determine the reasons for the collapse. Most experts contend that a similar type of shakeout is unlikely today. What is different about today's technology and the Internet that points to this conclusion? How can firms prevent another collapse?

2. Logon to a metamediary in the automobile metamarket (e.g., http://www.edmunds.com, http://www.autos.msn.com, http://www.kbb.com, or http://www.carsdirect.com). What aspects of the car buying experience does the metamediary offer? Which aspects of the experience are missing? How does the metamediary overcome these missing aspects?

3. Think about all of the exchanges that you participate in on a weekly or monthly basis. How many of these exchanges have their basis in long-term relationships? How many are simple transaction-based exchanges? Which do you find most satisfying? Why?

CHAPTER 2

Strategic Marketing Planning

Introduction

The process of strategic marketing planning can either be quite complex or relatively straightforward. As evidenced in *Beyond the Pages 2.1*, strategic planning for a multinational corporation like Ford Motor Company, with its multiple divisions and business units, is more elaborate than planning the marketing strategy of a sole proprietorship. Although the issues differ, the planning process is the same in many ways. Ultimately, the goals and objectives can be quite similar. Large or small, all marketers strive to meet the needs of their customers while meeting their own business and marketing objectives.

One way to think about the marketing planning process is to picture it as a funnel.[1] At the top are important corporate decisions dealing with the firm's mission, vision, goals, and the allocation of resources among business units. Planning at this level also involves decisions regarding the purchase or divestment of the business units themselves. Procter & Gamble's acquisition of Gillette or Delta's merger with Northwest are good examples of the decision-making complexity that is often typical of major corporate decisions. These decisions trickle down the funnel to the business-unit level, where planning focuses on meeting goals and objectives within defined product markets. Planning at this level must take into account and be consistent with decisions made at the corporate level. However, in organizations having only one business unit, corporate and business unit strategy are the same. The most specific planning and decision making occurs at the bottom of the funnel. It is at this level where organizations make and implement tactical decisions regarding marketing strategy (target markets and the marketing mix) as well as marketing plans.

In this chapter, we examine the planning process at different points in this process. We begin by discussing the overall process by considering the hierarchy of decisions that must be made in strategic marketing planning. Next, we introduce the marketing plan and look at the marketing plan framework used throughout the text. We also discuss the role and importance of the marketing plan in marketing strategy. Finally, we explore other advances in strategic planning such as strategy mapping and the balanced performance scorecard.

Beyond the Pages 2.1

FORD MANEUVERS STRATEGICALLY[2]

With the downturn in the economy during 2008–2009, the fate of Detroit's Big Three automakers was far from certain. Consumers–hit hard by higher prices, job losses, and anxious futures–stopped buying new cars in record numbers. The fallout was historic. Chrysler and GM were forced to take massive government bailouts just to maintain operations. Ford Motor Company, however, refused to take the government's money. Ford CEO Alan Mulally insisted that the company had enough cash to survive the meltdown in auto sales.

Ford's ability to weather the storm was based largely on strategic moves that Mulally made shortly after becoming CEO in September 2006. The theme of Mulally's turnaround strategy was to focus squarely on the Ford brand. Mulally's first step was to borrow roughly $24 billion against the company's assets to prepare for the coming economic crisis that he predicted at the time. Mulally then began eliminating the company's luxury brands; first by selling Jaguar and Land Rover to Tata–India's largest carmaker–in 2007, then by looking for a buyer for Volvo. Mulally also worked to better integrate Ford's worldwide operations. For example, in 2010 the company began selling European-developed small cars in the United States. As a part of the focus on core brands, Mulally slowly began eliminating over half of the company's different nameplates–from 97 in 2006 to 40 by 2013.

Part of this effort involved the elimination of the Mercury division and the return of the Taurus nameplate. Finally, Mulally renegotiated agreements with the United Auto Workers to decrease hourly labor costs by 27 percent and paid $2.4 billion to pay down Ford's long-term debt.

One thing that is striking about Mulally's strategy is how it differed from Rick Wagoner's strategy at GM. Since his arrival at Ford, Mulally has not designed or built a single new car, truck, or SUV. Wagoner, on the other hand, introduced a number of new designs at GM including the Saturn Aura and Sky, a redesigned Chevy Tahoe, the Buick Lucerne, the Chevy Equinox and HHR, and many Cadillac offerings. As a part of the government's bailout of GM, Wagoner was forced to resign. GM also planned to drop its Saturn and Pontiac divisions.

Although Ford continues to lose money because of the weakened economy, Mulally's strategy appears to be working. Ford's market share of sales to individual customers has increased. The company is focused on competing in every segment of the industry, with a clearly defined mix of products. Ford also strives to be best in class in terms of quality, fuel economy, and safety. When the meltdown is over, many industry analysts predict that Ford will pick up 25 percent of the sales lost by GM and Chrysler.

The Strategic Planning Process

Whether at the corporate, business unit, or functional level, the planning process begins with an in-depth analysis of the organization's internal and external environments—sometimes referred to as a *situation analysis*. As we will discuss in Chapter 4, this analysis focuses on the firm's resources, strengths, and capabilities vis-à-vis competitive, customer, and environmental issues. Based on an exhaustive review of these relevant environmental issues, the firm establishes its mission, goals, and/or objectives; its strategy; and several functional plans. As indicated in Exhibit 2.1, planning efforts within each functional area will result in the creation of a strategic plan for that area. Although we emphasize the issues and processes concerned with developing a customer-oriented marketing strategy and marketing plan, we should stress that organizations develop effective marketing strategies and plans in concert

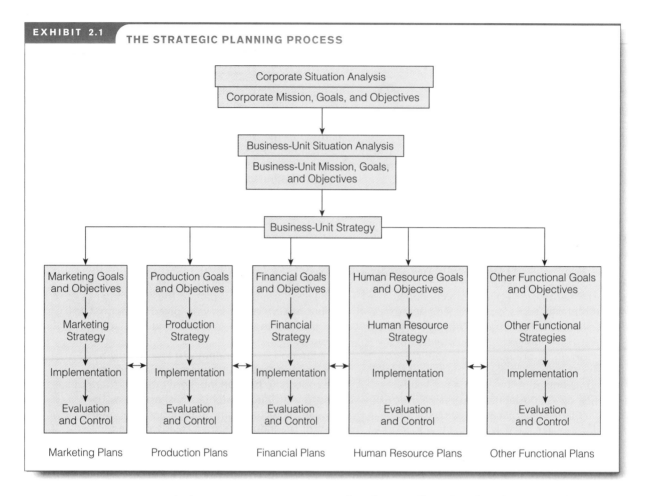

EXHIBIT 2.1   THE STRATEGIC PLANNING PROCESS

with the organization's mission and goals, as well as the plans from other functional areas. Senior management must coordinate these functional plans in a manner that will achieve the organization's mission, goals, and objectives.

In this text, we are interested in a particular type of functional plan—the marketing plan. A *marketing plan* is a written document that provides the blueprint or outline of the organization's marketing activities, including the implementation, evaluation, and control of those activities. The marketing plan serves a number of purposes. For one, the marketing plan clearly explains how the organization will achieve its goals and objectives. This aspect of marketing planning is vital—not having goals and objectives is like driving a car without knowing your destination. In this sense, the marketing plan serves as the "road map" for implementing the marketing strategy. It instructs employees as to their roles and functions in fulfilling the plan. It also provides specifics regarding the allocation of resources and includes the specific marketing tasks, responsibilities of individuals, and the timing of all marketing activities.

Although our focus is on marketing planning and strategy, we cannot emphasize enough that marketing decisions must be made within the boundaries of the organization's overall mission, goals, and objectives. The sequencing of decision stages outlined in the following sections begins with broad decisions regarding the organizational mission, followed by a discussion of the corporate or business-unit strategy. It is within these contexts that marketing goals/objectives and marketing strategies must be developed and implemented.

Organizational Mission Versus Organizational Vision

To adequately address the role of the organizational mission in strategic planning, we must first understand the differences between the organization's mission and its vision. A *mission*, or *mission statement*, seeks to answer the question "What business are we in?" It is a clear and concise statement (a paragraph or two at most) that explains the organization's reason for existence. By contrast, a *vision* or *vision statement* seeks to answer the question "What do we want to become?" For example, Texas Instruments—one of the world's largest technology companies—defines its mission this way: "Texas Instruments Incorporated provides innovative semiconductor technologies to help our customers create the world's most advanced electronics." Compare this to the company's vision: "... to fundamentally change markets and create entirely new ones."[3] Similarly, Google's mission is "to organize the world's information and make it universally accessible and useful." Google's vision is "Never settle for the best." Note that an organization's vision tends to be future oriented, in that it represents where the organization is headed and where it wants to go.

If you ask many businesspeople, "What is your reason for existence?" their response is likely to be "To make money." Although that may be their ultimate objective, it is not their raison d'être. Profit has a role in this process, of course, but it is a goal or objective of the firm, not its mission or vision. The mission statement identifies what the firm stands for and its basic operating philosophy. Profit and other performance outcomes are ends, and thus are out of place and confuse the mission of the firm.

Elements of the Mission Statement   A well-devised mission statement for any organization, unit within an organization, or single-owner business should answer the same five basic questions. These questions should clarify for the firm's stakeholders (especially employees):

1. Who are we?

2. Who are our customers?

3. What is our operating philosophy (basic beliefs, values, ethics, etc.)?

4. What are our core competencies or competitive advantages?

5. What are our responsibilities with respect to being a good steward of our human, financial, and environmental resources?

A mission statement that delivers a clear answer to each of these questions installs the cornerstone for the development of the marketing plan. If the cornerstone is weak, or not in line with the foundation laid in the preliminary steps, the entire plan will have no real chance of long-term success. Exhibit 2.2 outlines several mission statements

EXHIBIT 2.2   THE BEST MISSION STATEMENTS

In their book *Say It and Live It: The 50 Corporate Mission Statements That Hit the Mark*, Patricia Jones and Larry Kahaner identified 50 companies that possess outstanding mission statements. This exhibit lists several of these companies, along with their 1995, 2000, and 2009 mission statements. Remember that these organizations customized their mission statements to fit their own needs and goals, not to match the criteria established in this chapter.

Boeing

1995	To be the number one aerospace company in the world and among the premier industrial concerns in terms of quality, profitability, and growth.
2000	Our mission is bigger and broader than ever. It is to push not just the envelope of flight, but the entire envelope of value relating to our customers and shareholders.
2009	People working together as a global enterprise for aerospace leadership.

Leo Burnett

1995	The mission of the Leo Burnett Company is to create superior advertising. In Leo's words: "Our primary function in life is to produce the best advertising in the world, bar none. This is to be advertising so interrupting, so daring, so fresh, so engaging, so human, so believable and so well focused as to themes and ideas that, at one and the same time, it builds a quality reputation for the long haul as it produces sales for the immediate present."
2000	Our Vision: To be an indispensable source of our clients' competitive advantage. Our Mission: We will work with our clients as a community of star-reachers whose ideas build leadership brands through imagination and a sensitive and deeper understanding of human behavior.
2009	At Leo Burnett our purpose is to be the world's best creator of ideas that truly move people . . . bar none. Together with our partners, we strive to put a meaningful human purpose at the center of our clients' brands, to transform the way people think, feel, and ultimately behave.

Celestial Seasonings

1995	Our mission is to grow and dominate the U.S. specialty tea market by exceeding consumer expectations with the best tasting, 100 percent natural hot and iced teas, packaged with Celestial art and philosophy, creating the most valued tea experience. Through leadership, innovation, focus, and teamwork we are dedicated to continuously improving value to our consumers, customers, employees, and stakeholders with a quality-first organization.
2000	We believe in creating and selling healthful, naturally oriented products that nurture people's bodies and uplift their souls. Our products must be • superior in quality, • of good value, • beautifully artistic, and • philosophically inspiring. Our role is to play an active part in making this world a better place by unselfishly serving the public. We believe we can have a significant impact on making people's lives happier and healthier through their use of our products.
2009	Since day one, Celestial Seasonings has always been about people and passion. The founders hoped to foster the values of beauty and truth through their products and their distinctive packaging. They wanted the tea drinking experience to fulfill all the senses, and committed to featuring specially designed artwork and carefully researched words of wisdom on each package to complement our delicious flavors and aromas. That vision lives on today, even as our product line has extended beyond tea to coffee and culinary spices.

Intel Corporation

1995	Do a great job for our customers, employees, and stockholders by being the preeminent building block supplier to the computing industry.
2000	Intel's mission is to be the preeminent building block supplier to the worldwide Internet economy.
2009	Delight our customers, employees, and shareholders by relentlessly delivering the platform and technology advancements that become essential to the way we work and live.

Source: Patricia Jones and Larry Kahaner, *Say It and Live It: The 50 Corporate Mission Statements That Hit the Mark* (New York: Doubleday, 1995); and the websites of these companies.

considered to be among the best. As you read these statements, consider how well they answer these five questions.

The mission statement is the one portion of the strategic plan that should not be kept confidential. It should tell everyone—customers, employees, investors, competitors, regulators, and society in general—what the firm stands for and why it exists. Mission statements facilitate public relations activities and communicate to customers and others important information that can be used to build trust and long-term relationships. The mission statement should be included in annual reports and major press releases, framed on the wall in every office, and personally owned by every employee of the organization. Goals, objectives, strategies, tactics, and budgets are not for public viewing. A mission statement kept secret, however, is of little value to the organization.

Mission Width and Stability   In crafting a mission statement, management should be concerned about the statement's width. If the mission is too broad, it will be meaningless to those who read and build upon it. A mission to "make all people happy around the world by providing them with entertaining products" sounds splendid but provides no useful information. Overly broad missions can lead companies to establish plans and strategies in areas where their strengths are limited. Such endeavors almost always result in failure. Exxon's past venture into office products and Sears' expansion into real estate and financial services serve as reminders of the problems associated with poorly designed mission statements. Although a well-designed mission statement should not stifle an organization's creativity, it must help keep the firm from moving too far from its core competencies.

Overly narrow mission statements that constrain the vision of the organization can prove just as costly. Early in this century, the railroads defined their business as owning and operating trains. Consequently, the railroad industry had no concerns about the invention of the airplane. After all, they thought, the ability to fly had nothing to do with trains or the railroad business. Today, we know that firms such as American Airlines, Southwest Airlines, and Federal Express, rather than Burlington, Union Pacific, or Santa Fe, dominate the passenger and time-sensitive freight business. The railroads missed this major opportunity because their missions were too narrowly tied to railroads, as opposed to a more appropriate definition encompassing the transportation business.

Mission stability refers to the frequency of modifications in an organization's mission statement. Of all the components of the strategic plan, the mission should change the least frequently. It is the one element that will likely remain constant through multiple rounds of strategic planning.

© Aleiski Markku/Shutterstock

What business does the railroad industry find itself in today?

Goals, objectives, and marketing plan elements will change over time, usually as an annual or quarterly event. When the mission changes, however, the cornerstone has been moved and everything else must change as well. The mission should change only when it is no longer in sync with the firm's capabilities, when competitors drive the firm from certain markets, when new technology changes the delivery of customer benefits, or when the firm identifies a new opportunity that matches its strengths and expertise. As we discussed in Chapter 1, the growth of the Internet and electronic commerce has affected many industries. The importance and role of travel agents, stockbrokers, and car dealers has changed dramatically as customers changed the way they shop for travel, financial products, and automobiles. Organizations in these and other industries have been forced to refocus their efforts by redefining their mission statements.

Customer-Focused Mission Statements   In recent years, firms have realized the role that mission statements can play in their marketing efforts. Consequently, mission statements have become much more customer oriented. People's lives and businesses should be enriched because they have dealt with the organization. A focus on profit in the mission statement means that something positive happens for the owners and managers of the organization, not necessarily for the customers or other stakeholders. For example, a focus on customers is one of the leading reasons for the long-running success of Southwest Airlines. The company's mission has not changed since 1988:

> *The mission of Southwest Airlines is dedication to the highest quality of Customer Service delivered with a sense of warmth, friendliness, individual pride, and Company Spirit.*[4]

The mission statement of cultural icon Ben & Jerry's Ice Cream consists of three interrelated parts, and is a good example of how an organization can work to have a positive impact on customers and society:[5]

> **Social Mission:** *To operate the company in a way that actively recognizes the central role that business plays in society by initiating innovative ways to improve the quality of life locally, nationally and internationally.*
>
> **Product Mission:** *To make, distribute and sell the finest quality all natural ice cream and euphoric concoctions with a continued commitment to incorporating wholesome, natural ingredients and promoting business practices that respect the Earth and the Environment.*
>
> **Economic Mission:** *To operate the Company on a sustainable financial basis of profitable growth, increasing value for our stakeholders and expanding opportunities for development and career growth for our employees.*

The infamous 1982 Tylenol cyanide tragedy illustrated the importance of a customer-oriented mission statement. After several deaths occurred as a result of outside tampering with Tylenol capsules, McNeilab and Johnson & Johnson immediately pulled all Tylenol capsules from the market at a direct cost of $100 million.

When asked about the difficulty of this decision, executives said that the choice was obvious given Johnson & Johnson's mission statement. That statement, developed decades earlier by the firm's founders, established that Johnson & Johnson's primary responsibility is to the doctors, nurses, patients, parents, and children who prescribe or use the company's products. Because the mission dictated the firm's response to the crisis, Tylenol became an even more dominant player in the pain-reliever market after the tragedy.[6]

Customer-focused mission statements are the norm for charities and humanitarian organizations. These nonprofit organizations—just like their for-profit counterparts—strive to fulfill their missions through effective marketing programs. For instance, the mission of the American Red Cross reads as follows:

> *The American Red Cross, a humanitarian organization led by volunteers and guided by its Congressional Charter and the Fundamental Principles of the International Red Cross Movement, will provide relief to victims of disaster and help people prevent, prepare for, and respond to emergencies.*

Unlike other charitable organizations, the American Red Cross holds a key competitive advantage: its Congressional charter. This gives the American Red Cross the authority needed to respond no matter the nature or complexity of the crisis. During the aftermath of Hurricanes Katrina, Rita, and Wilma in 2005, the American Red Cross initiated its single largest disaster response in the organization's history. Through a massive promotional campaign and significant corporate sponsorships, the American Red Cross was able to raise the $2.1 billion needed for relief efforts.[7]

Corporate or Business-Unit Strategy

All organizations need a *corporate strategy*, the central scheme or means for utilizing and integrating resources in the areas of production, finance, research and development, human resources, and marketing, to carry out the organization's mission and achieve the desired goals and objectives. In the strategic planning process, issues such as competition, differentiation, diversification, coordination of business units, and environmental issues all tend to emerge as corporate strategy concerns. In small businesses, corporate strategy and business-unit strategy are essentially the same. Although we use both terms, corporate and business-unit strategy apply to all organizations, from large corporations to small businesses and nonprofit organizations.

Larger firms often find it beneficial to devise separate strategies for each strategic business unit (SBU), subsidiary, division, product line, or other profit center within the parent firm. Business-unit strategy determines the nature and future direction of each business unit, including its competitive advantages, the allocation of its resources, and the coordination of the functional business areas (marketing, production, finance, human resources, etc.). Many organizations manage their differing SBUs in ways that create synergies by providing customers a single-branded solution across multiple markets. Sony, for example, has a number of SBUs and joint ventures, including Sony Electronics (televisions, DVD players, mobile electronics, computers), Sony Music Entertainment (record labels such as Arista, Epic, Columbia, and LaFace), Sony Pictures Entertainment (Columbia TriStar studios, movie distribution), Sony Ericsson (mobile multimedia and cell phones), and Sony Computer Entertainment (the PlayStation family of games and consoles).[8]

An important consideration for a firm determining its corporate or business-unit strategy is the firm's capabilities. When a firm possesses capabilities that allow it to serve customers' needs better than the competition, it is said to have a *competitive*, or *differential*, *advantage*. Although a number of advantages come from functions other than marketing—such as human resources, research and development, or production—these functions often create important competitive advantages that can be exploited through marketing activities. For example, Walmart's long-running strategic investments in logistics allow the retailer to operate with lower inventory costs than its competitors—an advantage that translates into lower prices at retail. The 3M Company is highly regarded for its expertise in research and development. In fact, 3M defines itself as a science company. Their advantage in research and innovation allows its 35-plus business units to excel in six different market and product categories: consumer and office; display and graphics; electro and communications; health care; industrial and transportation; and safety, security, and protection services.[9]

Competitive advantages cannot be fully realized unless targeted customers see them as valuable. The key issue is the organization's ability to convince customers that its advantages are superior to those of the competition. Walmart has been able to convey effectively its low-price advantage to customers by adhering to an everyday low-price policy. The company's advertising plays on this fact by using a happy face to "roll back" prices. Interestingly, Walmart's prices are not always the lowest for a given product in a given geographic area. However, Walmart's perception of offering low prices translates into a key competitive advantage for the firm.

Functional Goals and Objectives

Marketing and all other business functions must support the organization's mission and goals, translating these into objectives with specific quantitative measurements. For example, a corporate or business unit goal to increase return on investment might translate into a marketing objective to increase sales, a production objective to reduce the cost of raw materials, a financial objective to rebalance the firm's portfolio of investments, or a human resources objective to increase employee training and productivity. All functional objectives should be expressed in clear, simple terms so that all personnel understand what type and level of performance the organization desires. In other words, objectives should be written so that their accomplishment can be measured accurately. In the case of marketing objectives, units of measure might include sales volume (in dollars or units), profitability per unit, percentage gain in market share, sales per square foot, average customer purchase, percentage of customers in the firm's target market who prefer its products, or some other measurable achievement.

It is also important for all functional objectives to be reconsidered for each planning period. Perhaps no strategy arose in the previous planning period to meet the stated objectives. Or perhaps the implementation of new technology allowed the firm to greatly exceed its objectives. In either case, realism demands the revision of functional objectives to remain consistent with the next edition of the functional area plan.

Functional Strategy

Organizations design functional strategies to provide a total integration of efforts that focus on achieving the area's stated objectives. In production, this might involve strategies for procurement, just-in-time inventory control, or warehousing. In human resources, strategies dealing with employee recruitment, selection, retention, training, evaluation, and compensation are often at the forefront of the decision-making process. In marketing strategy, the process focuses on selecting one or more target markets and developing a marketing program that satisfies the needs and wants of members of that target market. AutoZone, for example, targets do-it-yourself "shade tree mechanics" by offering an extensive selection of automotive replacement parts, maintenance items, and accessories at low prices.

Functional strategy decisions do not develop in a vacuum. The strategy must (1) fit the needs and purposes of the functional area with respect to meeting its goals and objectives, (2) be realistic given the organization's available resources and environment, and (3) be consistent with the organization's mission, goals, and objectives. Within the context of the overall strategic planning process, each functional strategy must be evaluated to determine its effect on the organization's sales, costs, image, and profitability.

Implementation

Implementation involves activities that actually execute the functional area strategy. One of the more interesting aspects of implementation is that all functional plans have at least two target markets: an external market (i.e., customers, suppliers, investors, potential employees, the society at large) and an internal market (i.e., employees, managers, executives). This occurs because functional plans, when executed, have repercussions both inside and outside the firm. Even seemingly disconnected events in finance or human resources can have an effect on the firm's ultimate customers—the individuals and businesses that buy the firm's products.

In order for a functional strategy to be implemented successfully, the organization must rely on the commitment and knowledge of its employees—its internal target market. After all, employees have a responsibility to perform the activities that will implement the strategy. For this reason, organizations often execute internal marketing activities designed to gain employee commitment and motivation to implement functional plans.

Evaluation and Control

Organizations design the evaluation and control phase of strategic planning to keep planned activities on target with goals and objectives. In the big picture, the critical issue in this phase is coordination among functional areas. For example, timely distribution and product availability almost always depend on accurate and timely production. By maintaining contact with the production manager, the marketing manager helps to ensure effective marketing strategy implementation (by ensuring timely production) and, in the long run, increased customer satisfaction. The need for coordination is especially keen in marketing where the fulfillment of marketing strategy always depends on coordinated execution with other functional strategies.

The key to coordination is to ensure that functional areas maintain open lines of communication at all times. Although this can be quite a challenge, it is helpful if the organizational culture is both internally and externally customer oriented. Maintaining a customer focus is extremely important throughout the strategic planning process, but especially so during the implementation, evaluation, and control phases of the process. Functional managers should have the ability to see the interconnectedness of all business decisions and act in the best interests of the organization and its customers.

In some ways, the evaluation and control phase of the planning process is an ending and a beginning. On one hand, evaluation and control occur after a strategy has been implemented. In fact, the implementation of any strategy would be incomplete without an assessment of its success and the creation of control mechanisms to provide and revise the strategy or its implementation—or both if necessary. On the other hand, evaluation and control serve as the beginning point for the planning process in the next planning cycle. Because strategic planning is a never-ending process, managers should have a system for monitoring and evaluating implementation outcomes on an ongoing basis.

The Marketing Plan

The result of the strategic planning process described in the first portion of this chapter is a series of plans for each functional area of the organization. For the marketing department, the marketing plan provides a detailed formulation of the actions necessary to carry out the marketing program. Think of the marketing plan as an action document—it is the handbook for marketing implementation, evaluation, and control. With that in mind, it is important to note that a marketing plan is not the same as a business plan. Business plans, although they typically contain a marketing plan, encompass other issues such as business organization and ownership, operations, financial strategy, human resources, and risk management. Although business plans and marketing plans are not synonymous, many small businesses will consolidate their corporate, business-unit, and marketing plans into a single document.

A good marketing plan requires a great deal of information from many different sources. An important consideration in pulling all of this information together is to maintain a big picture view while simultaneously keeping an eye on the details. This requires looking at the marketing plan holistically rather than as a collection of related elements. Unfortunately, adopting a holistic perspective is rather difficult in practice.

It is easy to get deeply involved in developing marketing strategy only to discover later that the strategy is inappropriate for the organization's resources or marketing environment. The hallmark of a well-developed marketing plan is its ability to achieve its stated goals and objectives.

In the following sections, we explore the marketing plan in more detail, including the structure of a typical marketing plan. This structure matches the marketing plan worksheets in Appendix A and the sample marketing plan in Appendix B. As we work through the marketing plan structure, keep in mind that a marketing plan can be written in many different ways. Marketing plans can be developed for specific products, brands, target markets, or industries. Likewise, a marketing plan can focus on a specific element of the marketing program, such as a product development plan, a promotional plan, a distribution plan, or a pricing plan.

Marketing Plan Structure

All marketing plans should be well organized to ensure that all relevant information is considered and included. Exhibit 2.3 illustrates the structure or outline of a typical marketing plan. We say this outline is "typical," but there are many other ways to organize a marketing plan. Although the actual outline used is not that important, most plans will share common elements described here. Regardless of the specific outline you use to develop a marketing plan, you should keep in mind that a good marketing plan outline is

- **Comprehensive** Having a comprehensive outline is essential to ensure that there are no omissions of important information. Of course, every element of the outline may not be pertinent to the situation at hand, but at least each element receives consideration.

- **Flexible** Although having a comprehensive outline is essential, flexibility should not be sacrificed. Any outline you choose must be flexible enough to be modified to fit the unique needs of your situation. Because all situations and organizations are different, using an overly rigid outline is detrimental to the planning process.

- **Consistent** Consistency between the marketing plan outline and the outline of other functional area plans is an important consideration. Consistency may also include the connection of the marketing plan outline to the planning process used at the corporate- or business-unit levels. Maintaining consistency ensures that executives and employees outside of marketing will understand the marketing plan and the planning process.

- **Logical** Because the marketing plan must ultimately sell itself to top managers, the plan's outline must flow in a logical manner. An illogical outline could force top managers to reject or underfund the marketing plan.

The marketing plan structure that we discuss here has the ability to meet all four of these points. Although the structure is comprehensive, you should freely adapt the outline to match the unique requirements of your situation.

EXHIBIT 2.3	MARKETING PLAN STRUCTURE

I. Executive Summary

   a. Synopsis
   b. Major aspects of the marketing plan

II. Situation Analysis

   a. Analysis of the internal environment
   b. Analysis of the customer environment
   c. Analysis of the external environment

III. SWOT Analysis (Strengths, Weaknesses, Opportunities, and Threats)

   a. Strengths
   b. Weaknesses
   c. Opportunities
   d. Threats
   e. Analysis of the SWOT matrix
   f. Developing competitive advantages
   g. Developing a strategic focus

IV. Marketing Goals and Objectives

   a. Marketing goals
   b. Marketing objectives

V. Marketing Strategy

   a. Primary (and secondary) target market
   b. Product strategy
   c. Pricing strategy
   d. Distribution/supply chain strategy
   e. Integrated marketing communication (promotion) strategy

VI. Marketing Implementation

   a. Structural issues
   b. Tactical marketing activities

VII. Evaluation and Control

   a. Formal controls
   b. Informal controls
   c. Implementation schedule and timeline
   d. Marketing audits

Executive Summary   The *executive summary* is a synopsis of the overall marketing plan, with an outline that conveys the main thrust of the marketing strategy and its execution. The purpose of the executive summary is to provide an overview of the plan so the reader can quickly identify key issues or concerns related to his or her role in implementing the marketing strategy. Therefore, the executive summary does not provide detailed information found in the following sections, or any other detailed information that supports the final plan. Instead, this synopsis introduces the major aspects of the marketing plan, including objectives, sales projections, costs, and performance evaluation measures. Along with the overall thrust of the marketing strategy, the executive summary should also identify the scope and time frame for the plan. The idea is to give the reader a quick understanding of the breadth of the plan and its time frame for execution.

Individuals both within and outside of the organization may read the executive summary for reasons other than marketing planning or implementation. Ultimately, many users of a marketing plan ignore some of the details because of the role they play. The CEO, for example, may be more concerned with the overall cost and expected return of the plan, and less interested in the plan's implementation. Financial institutions or investment bankers may want to read the marketing plan before approving any necessary financing. Likewise, suppliers, investors, or others who have a stake in the success of the organization sometimes receive access to the marketing plan. In these cases, the executive summary is critical, as it must convey a concise overview of the plan and its objectives, costs, and returns.

Although the executive summary is the first element of a marketing plan, it should always be the last element to be written because it is easier (and more meaningful) to write after the entire marketing plan has been developed. There is another good reason to write the executive summary last: It may be the only element of the marketing plan read by a large number of people. As a result, the executive summary must accurately represent the entire marketing plan.

Situation Analysis   The next section of the marketing plan is the situation analysis, which summarizes all pertinent information obtained about three key environments: the internal environment, the customer environment, and the firm's external environment. The analysis of the firm's internal environment considers issues such as the availability and deployment of human resources, the age and capacity of equipment or technology, the availability of financial resources, and the power and political struggles within the firm's structure. In addition, this section summarizes the firm's current marketing objectives and performance. The analysis of the customer environment examines the current situation with respect to the needs of the target market (consumer or business), anticipated changes in these needs, and how well the firm's products presently meet these needs. Finally, the analysis of the external environment includes relevant external factors—competitive, economic, social, political/legal, and technological—that can exert considerable direct and indirect pressures on the firm's marketing activities.

A clear and comprehensive situation analysis is one of the most difficult parts of developing a marketing plan. This difficulty arises because the analysis must be both comprehensive and focused on key issues in order to prevent information overload—a task actually made more complicated by advances in information technology. The information for a situation analysis may be obtained internally through the firm's marketing information system, or it may have to be obtained externally through primary or secondary marketing research. Either way, the challenge is often having too much data and information to analyze rather than having too little.

SWOT (Strengths, Weaknesses, Opportunities, and Threats) Analysis   *SWOT analysis* focuses on the internal factors (strengths and weaknesses) and external factors (opportunities and threats)—derived from the situation analysis in the preceding section—that give the firm certain advantages and disadvantages in satisfying the needs of its target market(s). These strengths, weaknesses, opportunities, and threats should be analyzed relative to market needs and competition. This analysis helps the company determine what it does well and where it needs to make improvements.

SWOT analysis has gained widespread acceptance because it is a simple framework for organizing and evaluating a company's strategic position when developing a marketing plan. However, like any useful tool, SWOT analysis can be misused unless one conducts the appropriate research to identify key variables that will affect the performance of the firm. A common mistake in SWOT analysis is the failure to separate internal issues from external issues. Strengths and weaknesses are internal issues unique to the firm conducting the analysis. Opportunities and threats are external issues that exist independently of the firm conducting the analysis. Another common mistake is to list the firm's strategic alternatives as opportunities. However, alternatives belong in the discussion of marketing strategy, not in the SWOT analysis.

At the conclusion of the SWOT analysis, the focus of the marketing plan shifts to address the strategic focus and competitive advantages to be leveraged in the strategy. The key to developing strategic focus is to match the firm's strengths with its opportunities to create capabilities in delivering value to customers. The challenge for any firm at this stage is to create a compelling reason for customers to purchase its products over those offered by competitors. It is this compelling reason that then becomes the framework or strategic focus around which the strategy can be developed. As explained in *Beyond the Pages 2.2*, even perennial successes like Dell shift their strategic thinking to stay fresh and competitive.

Marketing Goals and Objectives   Marketing goals and objectives are formal statements of the desired and expected outcomes resulting from the marketing plan. *Goals* are broad, simple statements of what will be accomplished through the marketing strategy. The major function of goals is to guide the development of objectives and to provide direction for resource allocation decisions. Marketing *objectives* are more specific and are essential to planning. Marketing objectives should be stated in quantitative terms to permit reasonably precise measurement. The quantitative nature of marketing objectives makes them easier to implement after development of the strategy.

This section of the marketing plan has two important purposes. First, it sets the performance targets that the firm seeks to achieve by giving life to its strategic focus through its marketing strategy (i.e., what the firm hopes to achieve). Second, it defines the parameters by which the firm will measure actual performance in the evaluation and control phase of the marketing plan (i.e., how performance will actually be measured). At this point, it is important to remember that neither goals nor objectives can be developed without a clearly defined mission statement. Marketing goals must be consistent with the firm's mission, while marketing objectives must flow naturally from the marketing goals.

Marketing Strategy   This section of the marketing plan outlines how the firm will achieve its marketing objectives. In Chapter 1, we said that marketing strategies involve

Beyond the Pages 2.2

DELL'S CONTINUING MAKEOVER[10]

Dell, the one-time bedrock of growth for investors, has struggled a great deal since 2006, when the company first began to fall short of revenue expectations. Although Dell was not losing money, the undisputed king of direct-to-consumer computer sales had lost its way. The reason? Intense competition, deep cost cutting, and declining customer service. Analysts argued that Dell's price cutting went too far and that the company did not invest enough in the "customer experience" as it attempted to maintain margins. Consequently, Dell now finds itself behind HP and Acer in terms of worldwide market share. As the company watched its U.S. and global market shares decline, Dell needed a makeover and it needed it fast.

The first part of Dell's makeover began as an effort to break away from its price-cutting strategy. The company spent $100 million to improve customer service and technical support, and added more than 2,000 workers to cut phone-waiting times by 50 percent. The company also began aggressively pushing its mid- and high-end machines, most notably its XPS line of desktops and notebooks. Part of this strategy was Dell's acquisition of Alienware—a Miami-based PC maker known for its high-end gaming machines and hip styling.

The second part of Dell's makeover began with the reemergence of Michael Dell as CEO in 2007. Shortly after his return, Dell initiated a program of deep cost cutting and layoffs, as well as new low-cost PCs and expanded international operations. Dell also acquired software, storage, and technology service companies in an effort to better diversify the company. The results were positive as Dell's worldwide PC shipments for mid-2008 increased by 21.4 percent. Unfortunately, the company's sales and revenues continued to fall. Many analysts suggested that Dell's focus on market share and sales growth—rather than profit—was to blame. Furthermore, the direct-to-consumer model had lost some of its original luster as competitors had moved to copy the strategy. In fact, rival HP had already moved to make its products available both online and in stores such as Best Buy and Walmart. Dell countered by making some of its products available in Walmart. Dell also launched Adamo—a new line of high-end notebook computers. With a starting price of $1,999, Adamo was designed to compete head-on with Apple's popular MacBook Pro line of notebook computers.

The future of Dell's makeover is somewhat uncertain. In early 2009, Michael Dell began a corporate restructuring to make the company leaner and more cost-efficient. Analysts expect Dell to begin acquiring companies in an effort to build a strong portfolio of computers, software, and services—much like HP and IBM. Many argue that Dell's future lies in supplying infrastructure for corporate data centers rather than low-cost PCs to consumers. Whatever strategy is next for Dell, all agree that the company must focus less on market share and sales, and more on profit like its rivals. Apple (Macs, iPods, iPhones), HP (printers), IBM (software, consulting), and Sony (consumer electronics) all maintain much higher profit margins than Dell. They also do not engage in price wars like Dell is prone to do.

selecting and analyzing target markets and creating and maintaining an appropriate marketing program (product, distribution, promotion, and price) to satisfy the needs of those target markets. It is at this level where the firm will detail how it will gain a competitive advantage by doing something better than the competition: Its products must be of higher quality than competitive offerings; its prices must be consistent with the level of quality (value); its distribution methods must be as efficient as possible; and its promotions must be more effective in communicating with target customers. It is also important that the firm attempt to make these advantages sustainable. Thus, in its broadest sense, marketing strategy refers to how the firm will manage its relationships with customers in a manner that gives it an advantage over the competition.

Frontline employees are important assets in developing and implementing marketing strategy.

Marketing Implementation   The implementation section of the marketing plan describes how the marketing program will be executed. This section of the marketing plan answers several questions with respect to the marketing strategies outlined in the preceding section:

1. What specific marketing activities will be undertaken?
2. How will these activities be performed?
3. When will these activities be performed?
4. Who is responsible for the completion of these activities?
5. How will the completion of planned activities be monitored?
6. How much will these activities cost?

Without a good plan for implementation, the success of the marketing strategy is seriously jeopardized. For this reason, the implementation phase of the marketing plan is just as important as the marketing strategy phase. You should remember, too, that implementation hinges on gaining the support of employees: Employees implement marketing strategies, not organizations. As a result, issues such as leadership, employee motivation, communication, and employee training are critical to implementation success.

Evaluation and Control   The final section of the marketing plan details how the results of the marketing program will be evaluated and controlled. *Marketing control* involves establishing performance standards, assessing actual performance by comparing it with these standards, and taking corrective action if necessary to reduce discrepancies between desired and actual performance. Performance standards should be tied back to the objectives stated earlier in the plan. These standards can be based on increases in sales volume, market share, or profitability; or even advertising standards such as brand name recognition or recall. Regardless of the standard selected, all performance standards must be agreed upon before the results of the plan can be assessed.

The financial assessment of the marketing plan is also an important component of evaluation and control. Estimates of costs, sales, and revenues determine financial projections. In reality, budgetary considerations play a key role in the identification of alternative strategies. The financial realities of the firm must be monitored at all times. For example, proposing to expand into new geographic areas or alter products without financial resources is a waste of time, energy, and opportunity. Even if funds are available, the strategy must be a "good value" and provide an acceptable return on investment, to be a part of the final plan.

Finally, should it be determined that the marketing plan has not lived up to expectations, the firm can use a number of tools to pinpoint potential causes for the discrepancies. One such tool is the marketing audit—a systematic examination of the firm's marketing objectives, strategy, and performance. The marketing audit can help isolate weaknesses in the marketing plan and recommend actions to help improve performance. The control phase of the planning process also outlines the actions that can be taken to reduce the differences between planned and actual performance.

Using the Marketing Plan Structure

In Appendix A, you will find marketing plan worksheets that expand the marketing plan structure into a comprehensive framework for developing a marketing plan. These worksheets are designed to be *comprehensive*, *flexible*, and *logical*. The consistency of this framework with other planning documents will depend on the planning structure used in other functional areas of an organization. However, this framework is certainly capable of being consistent with the plans from other functional areas.

Although you may not use every single portion of the worksheets, you should at least go through them in their entirety to ensure that all important information is present. You should note that the sample marketing plan provided in Appendix B uses this same framework. However, this plan does not match the framework *exactly* because the framework was adapted to match the characteristics of a unique planning situation. You will also find additional marketing plan examples on our text's website.

Before we move ahead, we offer the following tips for using the marketing plan framework to develop a marketing plan:

- **Plan ahead**. Writing a comprehensive marketing plan is very time-consuming, especially if the plan is under development for the first time. Initially, most of your time will be spent on the situation analysis. Although this analysis is very demanding, the marketing plan has little chance for success without it.

- **Revise, then revise again**. After the situation analysis, you will spend most of your time revising the remaining elements of the marketing plan to ensure that they mesh with each other. Once you have written a first draft of the plan, put it away for a day or so. Then, review the plan with a fresh perspective and fine-tune sections that need changing. Because the revision process always takes more time than expected, it is wise to begin the planning process far in advance of the due date for the plan.

- **Be creative**. A marketing plan is only as good as the information it contains and the effort and creativity that go into its creation. A plan developed half-heartedly will collect dust on the shelf.

- **Use common sense and judgment**. Writing a marketing plan is an art. Common sense and judgment are necessary to sort through all of the information, weed out poor strategies, and develop a sound marketing plan. Managers must always weigh any information against its accuracy, as well as their own intuition, when making marketing decisions.

- **Think ahead to implementation**. As you develop the plan, you should always be mindful of how the plan will be implemented. Great marketing strategies that never see the light of day do little to help the organization meet its goals. Good marketing plans are those that are realistic and doable given the organization's resources.

- **Update regularly**. Once the marketing plan has been developed and implemented, it should be updated regularly with the collection of new data and information. Many organizations update their marketing plans on a quarterly basis to ensure that the marketing strategy remains consistent with changes in the internal, customer, and external environments. Under this approach, you will always have a working plan that covers 12 months into the future.

- **Communicate to others**. One critical aspect of the marketing plan is its ability to communicate to colleagues, particularly top managers who look to the marketing plan for an explanation of the marketing strategy, as well as for a justification of needed resources, like the marketing budget.[11] The marketing plan also communicates to line managers and other employees by giving them points of reference to chart the progress of marketing implementation. A survey of marketing executives on the importance of the marketing plan revealed that

    ... the process of preparing the plan is more important than the document itself.... A marketing plan does compel attention, though. It makes the marketing team concentrate on the market, on the company's objectives, and on the strategies and tactics appropriate to those objectives. It's a mechanism for synchronizing action.[12]

Research indicates that organizations that develop formal, written strategic marketing plans tend to be more tightly integrated across functional areas, more specialized, and more decentralized in decision making. The end result of these marketing planning efforts is improved financial and marketing performance.[13] Given these benefits, it is surprising that many firms do not develop formal plans to guide their marketing efforts. For example, a survey of CEOs done by the American Banking Association found that only 44 percent of community banks have a formal marketing plan.[14]

Purposes and Significance of the Marketing Plan

The purposes of a marketing plan must be understood to appreciate its significance. A good marketing plan will fulfill these five purposes in detail:

1. It explains both the present and future situations of the organization. This includes the situation and SWOT analyses and the firm's past performance.

2. It specifies the expected outcomes (goals and objectives) so that the organization can anticipate its situation at the end of the planning period.

3. It describes the specific actions that are to take place so that the responsibility for each action can be assigned and implemented.

4. It identifies the resources that will be needed to carry out the planned actions.

5. It permits the monitoring of each action and its results so that controls may be implemented. Feedback from monitoring and control provides information to start the planning cycle again in the next time frame.

These five purposes are very important to various persons in the firm. Line managers have a particular interest in the third purpose (description of specific actions) because they are responsible for ensuring the implementation of marketing actions. Middle-level managers have a special interest in the fifth purpose (monitoring and control), as they want to ensure that tactical changes can be made if needed. These managers must also be able to evaluate why the marketing strategy does or does not succeed.

The most pressing concern for success, however, may lie in the fourth purpose: identifying needed resources. The marketing plan is the means of communicating the strategy to top executives who make the critical decisions regarding the productive and efficient allocation of resources. Very sound marketing plans can prove unsuccessful if implementation of the plan is not adequately funded. It is important to remember that marketing is not the only business function competing for scarce resources. Other functions such as finance, research and development, and human resources have strategic plans of their own. It is in this vein that the marketing plan must sell itself to top management.

Organizational Aspects of the Marketing Plan

Who writes the marketing plan? In many organizations, the marketing manager, brand manager, or product manager writes the marketing plan. Some organizations develop marketing plans through committees. Others will hire professional marketing consultants to write the marketing plan. However, in most firms, the responsibility for planning lies at the level of a marketing vice president or marketing director.[15] The fact that top managers develop most marketing plans does not necessarily refute the logic of having the brand or product manager prepare the plan. However, except in small organizations where one person both develops and approves the plan, the authority to approve the marketing plan is typically vested in upper-level executives. At this stage, top managers usually ask two important questions:

1. Will the proposed marketing plan achieve the desired marketing, business unit, and corporate goals and objectives?

2. Are there alternative uses of resources that would better meet corporate or business unit objectives than the submitted marketing plan?

In most cases, *final* approval actually lies with the president, chairperson, or CEO of the organization.[16] Many organizations also have executive committees that evaluate and screen marketing plans before submission to the approving executive. In the end, regardless of who writes the marketing plan, the plan must be clear and persuasive to win the approval of the decision makers who make the evaluation. It is also critical that these individuals make efficient and timely decisions with respect to the marketing plan. To give the plan every chance for success, very little time should elapse between the completion of the plan and its implementation.

Once a marketing plan has been approved, it still faces many obstacles before its marketing programs can come to fruition. Exhibit 2.4 outlines some of these obstacles.

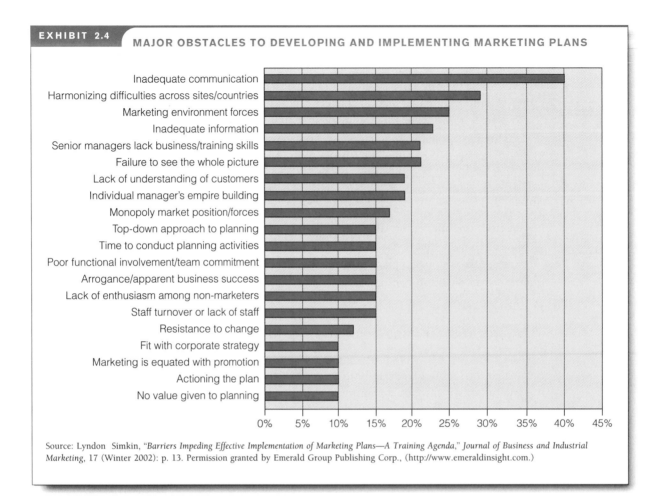

EXHIBIT 2.4   MAJOR OBSTACLES TO DEVELOPING AND IMPLEMENTING MARKETING PLANS

Source: Lyndon Simkin, "*Barriers Impeding Effective Implementation of Marketing Plans—A Training Agenda,*" *Journal of Business and Industrial Marketing*, 17 (Winter 2002): p. 13. Permission granted by Emerald Group Publishing Corp., (http://www.emeraldinsight.com.)

One major hurdle involves the relative time horizon of the organization's key stake-holders, particularly its managers and investors. It is quite common for U.S. firms to ignore long-range strategy and focus on the near term. Typically, this is caused by a compensation structure that rewards executives for short-term financial results such as profit, market capitalization, or stock price. Unfortunately, this mindset can play havoc on many marketing activities—such as advertising to build brand awareness—because their results are only apparent over longer time horizons. Consequently, many firms will shift strategies "midstream" rather than wait for results to emerge.

Maintaining Customer Focus and Balance in Strategic Planning

In the past two decades, many firms have changed the focus and content of their strategic planning efforts and marketing plans. Of these changes, two stand out: (1) renewed emphasis on the customer and (2) the advent of balanced strategic planning. These changes require shifting focus from the company's products to the unique requirements of specific target market segments. Firms have also had to become more astute at linking marketing activities to other functional areas.

Customer-Focused Planning

Focusing on the customer has not been the hallmark of strategic planning throughout history. Early in the twentieth century, planning focused on production ideals such as efficiency and quality. Automobile pioneer Henry Ford has long been credited with the statement that customers could have any color car that they wanted, as long as it was black. This mentality, though it worked well in its day, meant that strategic planning proceeded with little regard for customer needs and wants. Today, cars, trucks, and SUVs come in an array of colors that Henry Ford would have never contemplated. By the middle of the twentieth century, strategic planning focused on *selling* products to customers rather than making products for customers. Marketing strategies during this time concentrated on overcoming customer resistance and convincing them to buy products whether they needed them or not. Today, we no longer see door-to-door sales of vacuum cleaners, brushes, or encyclopedias.

The cornerstone of marketing thought and practice during the mid- to late-twentieth century was the marketing concept, which focused on customer satisfaction and the achievement of the firm's objectives. Having a market or customer orientation meant putting customers' needs and wants first. This shift in thinking led to the growth of marketing research to determine unmet customer needs and systems for satisfying those needs. Today's twenty-first century marketing organizations move one step beyond the marketing concept to focus on long-term, value-added relationships with customers, employees, suppliers, and other partners. The focus has shifted from customer transactions to customer relationships, and from competition to collaboration. As explained in *Beyond the Pages 2.3*, Amazon has created a series of relationships with authors, book publishers, customers, and potential competitors in the creation of the ecosystem for its Kindle e-book reader.

Market-oriented firms are those that successfully generate, disseminate, and respond to market information. These firms focus on customer analysis, competitor analysis, and integrating the firm's resources to provide customer value and satisfaction, as well as long-term profits.[17] To be successful, the firm must be able to focus its efforts and resources toward understanding their customers in ways that enhance the firm's ability to generate sustainable competitive advantages.[18] By creating organizational cultures that put customers first, market-oriented firms tend to perform at higher levels and reap the benefits of more highly satisfied customers. Exhibit 2.5 depicts the difference between a traditional and a market-oriented organizational structure. Where traditional structures are very authoritative, with decision-making authority emanating from the top of the hierarchy, market-oriented structures decentralize decision making.

In a market-oriented organization, every level of the organization has its focus on serving customer needs. Each level serves the levels above it by taking any actions necessary to ensure that each level performs its job well. In this case, the role of the

Beyond the Pages 2.3

AMAZON'S REVOLUTIONARY STRATEGY[18]

Amazon CEO Jeff Bezos has a history of pushing the envelope by expanding into areas that don't seem to fit the mold of an online retailer. Once billed as "Earth's biggest bookstore," Amazon now sells everything from electronics to fishing gear. Always searching for the next revolutionary product or business process, Bezos is no stranger to failure. Amazon's moves into search (with A9), online auctions, and digital music/movie downloads have made little headway in very crowded and competitive markets. However, with the launch of the Kindle, Amazon is poised to truly revolutionize book retailing forever.

On the surface, the Kindle—first introduced in 2007—is a simple e-book reader. Its successor, the Kindle 2, was introduced in February 2009. The Kindle uses an e-ink LCD screen that is very easy to read without causing eyestrain. It offers long battery life and the ability to store 1,500 e-books. Most newly released e-books sell for $9.99, far less than typical hardcover new releases. Newspaper subscriptions are available for about $14.99 per month. However, it's the Kindle's wireless connectivity—termed Whispersync—that sets it apart. The Kindle uses AT&T's high-speed network to allow Amazon's customers to download e-books in 60 seconds or less. Better yet, there are no connection fees for using the network.

The ability to buy an e-book directly from the Kindle without using a computer is poised to completely revolutionize book retailing. Amazon offers over 390,000 e-books through its Kindle Store, with more added every day. That selection, combined with the ease of buying e-books wirelessly, has converted many book purchases into impulse buys. Amazon reports that when a title is available in paper and e-book form, 35 percent of sales are for the e-book version.

With all of its advantages, the Kindle isn't perfect. Its detractors argue that it lacks a color display, smooth web browsing, and it cannot do video. Industry analysts suggest that the Kindle is vulnerable to competition. For example, Barnes & Noble recently launched the Nook—its version of an e-book reader that offers the same features as the Kindle. Future competition is likely to come from Google, Apple, and Sony. Despite the potential for competition, Bezos has stated that he is much more interested in selling e-books than he is in selling Kindles. This explains why Amazon quickly developed an iPhone application and an "iPhone-optimized" Kindle store for the over 37 million iPhones and iPod Touches that have been sold. By contrast, Amazon has sold well over 1 million Kindles since the device first launched. Some experts predict that as much as 20 percent of Amazon's revenue could be realized through the sale of e-books.

Fresh on the heels of the Kindle 2, Amazon launched the Kindle DX—a device with a larger screen that is aimed squarely at the newspaper and textbook markets. At its launch, both *The New York Times* and the *Washington Post* announced programs to subsidize the cost of the DX when customers agree to long-term subscription plans. Several universities also announced plans to test the Kindle DX in the classroom. Although few college textbooks are available in an e-book format, college textbook sales are a $5.4 billion business. Amazon is poised to garner a share of that lucrative market.

CEO is to ensure that his or her employees have everything they need to perform their jobs well. This same service mentality carries through all levels of the organization, including customers. Thus, the job of a frontline manager is to ensure that frontline employees are capable and efficient. The end result of the market-oriented design is a complete focus on customer needs.

In today's business environment, an orientation toward customers also requires that the organization's suppliers and even competitors be customer oriented as well. Though competing firms can continue to serve customers separately, customers can also be served through cooperative efforts that place customers ahead of competitive

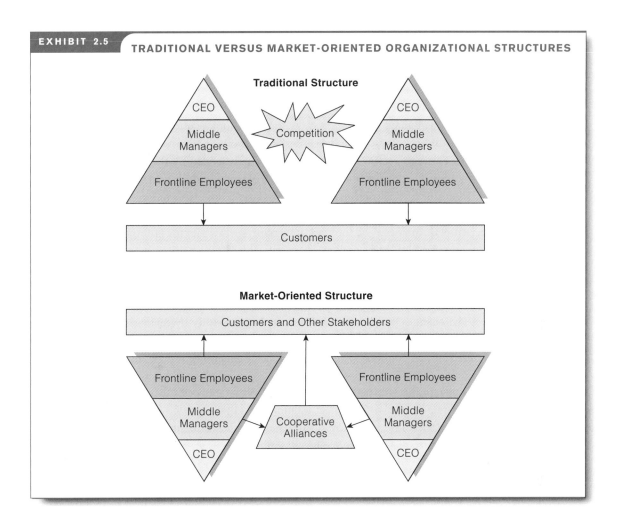

EXHIBIT 2.5

TRADITIONAL VERSUS MARKET-ORIENTED ORGANIZATIONAL STRUCTURES

Traditional Structure

CEO

Middle Managers

Competition

CEO

Middle Managers

Frontline Employees

Frontline Employees

Customers

Market-Oriented Structure

Customers and Other Stakeholders

Frontline Employees

Middle Managers

Cooperative Alliances

Frontline Employees

Middle Managers

CEO

CEO

interests. For example, Toyota has a number of partnerships with rival carmakers, particularly focused on hybrid technology. Nissan is using Toyota's hybrid fuel system in its vehicles, while GM is collaborating with Toyota in developing new fuel-cell technologies. GM and Toyota have a long-standing relationship in the joint production of vehicles including the Toyota Corolla, the Pontiac Vibe, and the Toyota Tacoma. As GM phases out the Pontiac line, it is working with Toyota to develop a replacement vehicle under one of its surviving brands (Chevrolet, Cadillac, Buick, or GMC).[19]

Balanced Strategic Planning

The shift to balanced strategic planning was born out of necessity. As the twenty-first century approached, firms realized that traditional planning and measurement approaches were not able to capture value created by the organization's intangible assets. These assets—including such vital issues as customer relationships, processes, human resources, innovation, and information—were becoming increasingly important to business success, but they were not being reported through traditional financial measures. One solution to this problem was the development of the balanced performance scorecard by Robert Kaplan and David Norton of Harvard University.[20] Their approach to strategic planning is illustrated in Exhibit 2.6.

The basic tenet of the balanced performance scorecard is that firms can achieve better performance if they align their strategic efforts by approaching strategy from four complementary perspectives: financial, customer, internal process, and learning and growth. The financial perspective is the traditional view of strategy and performance. This perspective is vital but should be balanced by the other components of the scorecard. The customer perspective looks at customer satisfaction metrics as a key indicator of firm performance, particularly as the firm moves ahead. Financial measures are not suited to this task because they report past performance rather than current performance. The internal process perspective focuses on the way the business is running by looking at both mission-critical and routine processes that drive day-to-day activity. Finally, the learning and growth perspective focuses on people and includes such vital issues as corporate culture, employee training, communication, and knowledge management.[21]

The balanced scorecard has been used successfully by many public and private sector organizations. Kaplan and Norton found that these successful firms typically adhered to five common principles when implementing the balanced scorecard:[22]

1. **Translate the strategy into operational terms**. Successful firms are able to illustrate the cause-and-effect relationships that show how intangible assets are transformed into value for customers and other stakeholders. This provides a common frame of reference for all employees.

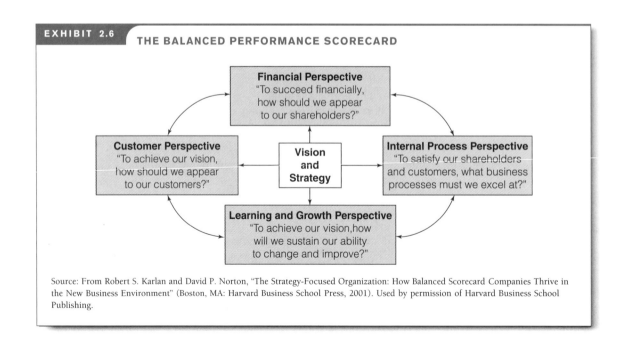

EXHIBIT 2.6   **THE BALANCED PERFORMANCE SCORECARD**

Source: From Robert S. Karlan and David P. Norton, "The Strategy-Focused Organization: How Balanced Scorecard Companies Thrive in the New Business Environment" (Boston, MA: Harvard Business School Press, 2001). Used by permission of Harvard Business School Publishing.

2. **Align the organization to strategy**. Successful firms link different functional areas through common themes, priorities, and objectives. This creates synergy within the organization that ensures that all efforts are coordinated.

3. **Make strategy everyone's everyday job**. Successful firms move the strategy from the executive boardroom to the front lines of the organization. They do this through communication, education, allowing employees to set personal objectives, and tying incentives to the balanced scorecard.

4. **Make strategy a continual process**. Successful firms hold regular meetings to review strategy performance. They also establish a process whereby the firm can learn and adapt as the strategy evolves.

5. **Mobilize change through executive leadership**. Successful firms have committed energetic leaders who champion the strategy and the balanced scorecard. This ensures that the strategy maintains momentum. Good leaders also prevent the strategy from becoming an obstacle to future progress.

The balanced scorecard doesn't refute the traditional approach to strategic planning. It does, however, caution business leaders to look at strategy and performance as a multidimensional issue. Financial measures, though important, simply cannot tell the whole story. One of the major benefits of the balanced scorecard is that it forces organizations to explicitly consider *during strategy formulation* those factors that are critical to strategy execution. We cannot stress this point enough. Good strategy is always developed with an eye toward how it will be implemented. Issues within the balanced scorecard such as employee training, corporate culture, organizational learning, and executive leadership are critical to the implementation of any strategy.

Lessons from Chapter 2

Strategic marketing planning

- Begins with broad decisions, then flows into more specific decisions as the process proceeds through subsequent planning stages.

- Involves establishing an organizational mission, corporate or business-unit strategy, marketing goals and objectives, marketing strategy, and ultimately a marketing plan.

- Must be consistent with the organization's mission and the corporate or business-unit strategy.

- Must be coordinated with all functional business areas to ensure that the organization's goals and objectives will be considered in the development of each functional plan, one of which is the marketing plan.

- Establishes marketing-level goals and objectives that support the organization's mission, goals, and objectives.

- Develops a marketing strategy, which includes selecting and analyzing target markets and creating and maintaining an appropriate marketing program to satisfy the needs of customers in those target markets.

- Ultimately results in a strategic market plan that outlines the activities and resources required to fulfill the organization's mission and achieve its goals and objectives.

The organizational mission

- Answers the broad question "What business are we in?"

- Identifies what the firm stands for and its basic operating philosophy by answering five basic questions:

    1. Who are we?

    2. Who are our customers?

    3. What is our operating philosophy (basic beliefs, values, ethics, etc.)?

    4. What are our core competencies or competitive advantages?

    5. What are our responsibilities with respect to being a good steward of our human, financial, and environmental resources?

- Is not the same as the organization's vision, which seeks to answer the question "What do we want to become?"

- Should not be too broad or too narrow, thereby rendering it useless for planning purposes.

- Should be customer oriented. People's lives and businesses should be enriched because they have dealt with the organization.

- Should never focus on profit. A focus on profit in the mission means that something positive happens for the owners and managers of the organization, not necessarily for the customers or other stakeholders.

- Must be owned and supported by employees if the organization has any chance of success.

- Should not be kept secret but instead communicated to everyone—customers, employees, investors, competitors, regulators, and society in general.

- Should be the least changed part of the strategic plan.

Business-unit strategy

- Is the central scheme or means for utilizing and integrating resources in the areas of production, finance, research and development, human resources, and marketing to carry out the organization's mission and achieve the desired goals and objectives.

- Is associated with developing a competitive advantage where the firm leverages its capabilities in order to serve customers' needs better than the competition.

- Determines the nature and future direction of each business unit, including its competitive advantages, the allocation of its resources, and the coordination of functional business areas (marketing, production, finance, human resources, etc.).

- Is essentially the same as corporate strategy in small businesses.

The marketing plan

- Provides a detailed explanation of the actions necessary to execute the marketing program and thus requires a great deal of effort and organizational commitment to create and implement.

- Should be well organized to ensure that it considers and includes all relevant information. The typical structure or outline of a marketing plan includes these elements:

  - Executive summary
  - Situation analysis
  - SWOT analysis
  - Marketing goals and objectives
  - Marketing strategies
  - Marketing implementation
  - Evaluation and control

- Should be based on an outline that is comprehensive, flexible, consistent, and logical.

- Fulfills five purposes:

  - Explains both the present and future situations of the organization
  - Specifies expected outcomes (goals and objectives)
  - Describes the specific actions that are to take place and assigns responsibility for each action
  - Identifies the resources needed to carry out the planned actions
  - Permits the monitoring of each action and its results so that controls may be implemented

- Serves as an important communication vehicle to top management and to line managers and employees.

- Is an important document, but not nearly as important as the knowledge gained from going through the planning process itself.

- Is most often prepared by the director or vice president of marketing, but is ultimately approved by the organization's president, chairman, or CEO.

Customer-focused strategic planning

- Requires that organizations shift focus from products to the requirements of specific target market segments, from customer transactions to customer relationships, and from competition to collaboration.

- Puts customers' needs and wants first and focuses on long-term, value-added relationships with customers, employees, suppliers, and other partners.

- Must be able to focus its efforts and resources toward understanding customers in ways that enhance the firm's ability to generate sustainable competitive advantages.

- Instills a corporate culture that places customers at the top of the organizational hierarchy.

- Finds ways to cooperate with suppliers and competitors to serve customers more effectively and efficiently.

Balanced strategic planning

- Was born out of necessity because traditional planning and measurement approaches were not able to capture value created by an organization's intangible assets (customer relationships, processes, human resources, innovation, and information).

- Was advocated strongly by Kaplan and Norton with their creation of the balanced performance scorecard.

- Considers traditional financial indicators of performance, but also looks at planning from three additional perspectives: customers, internal processes, and learning and growth.

- Is used successfully by many public and private sector organizations. Successful firms are those that adhere to five principles when implementing the balanced scorecard:

  - Translate the strategy into operational terms.
  - Align the organization to strategy.
  - Make strategy everyone's everyday job.
  - Make strategy a continual process.
  - Mobilize change through executive leadership.

- Does not refute the traditional approach to strategic planning, but it does caution business leaders to look at strategy and performance as a multidimensional issue.

- Forces organizations to explicitly consider *during strategy formulation* those factors that are critical to strategy execution. Good strategy is always developed with an eye toward how it will be implemented.

Questions for Discussion

1. In many organizations, marketing does not have a place of importance in the organizational hierarchy. Why do you think this happens? What are the consequences for a firm that gives little importance to marketing relative to other business functions?

2. Defend or contradict this statement: Developing marketing strategy is more important than implementing marketing strategy, because if the strategy is flawed, its implementation doesn't matter.

3. What are some of the potential difficulties in approaching strategic planning from a balanced perspective? Isn't financial performance still the most important perspective to take in planning? Explain.

Exercises

1. Review each of the mission statements listed in Exhibit 2.2. Do they follow the guidelines discussed in this chapter? How well does each answer the five basic questions? What do you make of the changes or lack thereof in these mission statements over time?

2. Talk with a small business owner about the strategic planning process he or she uses. Does the business have a mission statement? Marketing goals and objectives? A marketing plan? What are the major issues the owner faces in implementing his or her marketing program?

3. Palo Alto Software maintains a website devoted to business and marketing plans. Log on to http://www.mplans.com/sample_marketing_plans/ and take a look at a few of the sample marketing plans available. Do these plans use the same framework discussed in this chapter?

CHAPTER 3

Marketing Ethics and Social Responsibility in Strategic Planning

Introduction

The importance of marketing ethics and social responsibility has grown in recent years, and their role in the strategic planning process has become even more important as many firms have seen their images, reputations, and marketing efforts destroyed by problems in these areas. The failure to see ethical conduct as part of strategic market planning can destroy the trust and customer relationships that are necessary for success. Ethics and social responsibility are also necessary in light of stakeholder demands and changes in federal law. Furthermore, ethical and socially responsible behavior improves marketing performance and profits. Marketing ethics does not just happen by hiring ethical people; it requires implementation of an effective ethics and compliance program.

Motivated by news reports and misconduct, customers have increasingly demanded that businesses behave responsibly. In many cases, ethical behavior and social responsibility have become customer expectations. As a result, some companies are taking social responsibility to a new level. As discussed in *Beyond the Pages 3.1,* corporate use of renewable energy sources and carbon offsetting are becoming increasingly popular among businesses as a way to reduce a company's carbon footprint and to create a positive image among stakeholders.

Other businesses have developed products that combat serious social issues and earn a profit at the same time. For example, Nutriset, a nonprofit organization based in France, has sold food products to combat hunger and malnutrition since 1986. More than 850 million people live in a state of hunger today; hunger kills more people annually than AIDS, malaria, and tuberculosis combined. The company recently launched "Plumpy'nut," a 3-ounce packet with 500 calories that requires no preparation and can be consumed by a child without assistance from an adult. A day's worth of the product costs about $1, and Nutriset has partnered with local entrepreneurs to make the product locally, even using local ingredients when possible. Plumpy'nut has already made great strides in fighting malnutrition. One region in Niger, Africa, for example, had the highest rates of malnutrition in the country until the widespread

Beyond the Pages 3.1

WIND ENERGY HELPS CREATE A RENEWABLE WORLD[1]

The multitude of incentives and renewable energy-related jobs that have increased over the last decade illustrate the sociocultural shift in attitudes about energy. It is common knowledge that finite resources have a relatively short life, but renewable resources such as the sun and wind can be utilized for long-term energy needs. Solar photovoltaic panels use the sun's energy to produce electricity, while solar thermal panels use the sun's energy to produce hot water. Many organizations such as PepsiCo, General Electric, and Toyota are employing renewable energy in their production processes as part of a marketing strategy. For example, Frito-Lay added solar panels to the factory that produces Sun Chips, their green product line, to provide up to 75 percent of energy needs to produce the product.

Despite the growing interest in solar energy, the use of wind energy has been gaining in momentum over the past few years. Wind power accounts for just half a percent of total U.S. energy consumption, but it is the fastest growing renewable energy source with respect to usage and capacity. Thanks to advances in technology, wind power is now much more efficient than before and is available at a cost that is 80 percent lower than in the 1980s. Today's prices hover around 7 cents per kilowatt hour—a price that is competitive with energy produced from fossil fuels such as coal, oil, and gas.

Whole Foods Market is one of the largest buyers of wind energy in the United States. The grocery chain uses solar panels on more than 30 of its stores and also buys wind energy credits to offset 100 percent of its nonrenewable energy use. Between 2006 and 2009, Whole Foods Market purchased 2 million megawatt hours of wind energy credits from wind farms around the country. This is equivalent to the electricity usage of 160,000 homes for 1 year. In 2005, the company became the first Fortune 500 company to offset 100 percent of its nonrenewable energy usage with wind credits. Although the company spends slightly more for wind power, its efforts prevent over 700 million pounds of carbon dioxide pollution each year.

The demand for wind power was growing at a rapid pace until the economic slowdown began in 2008. After that, many firms were forced to cut back on their plans for using wind energy. The use of wind power is very popular in Europe, where wind farms are popping up all over Germany and Britain. Smaller wind farms are also slated to open in a number of western and Midwestern states including Iowa and Wyoming. Worldwide, the United States leads in terms of newly installed wind capacity and controls roughly 27 percent of the worldwide wind market. Worldwide growth is highest in Europe, where 40 percent of all new electricity additions are in wind power versus 35 percent for the United States.

consumption of Plumpy'nut. Nutriset is one of many organizations that have found a way to combine entrepreneurship and social responsibility to earn profits.[2]

In this chapter, we look at ethics and social responsibility, their connection to marketing strategy, and the challenges of ethical behavior. Next we discuss deceptive practices in marketing as well as organizational and self-regulating methods of preventing deception. Finally, we examine the organizational context of marketing ethics, including codes of ethics and the role of ethics and social responsibility in improving marketing performance.

The Role of Ethics and Social Responsibility in Marketing Strategy

In response to customer demands, along with the threat of increased regulation, more and more firms have incorporated ethics and social responsibility into the strategic marketing planning process. Any organization's reputation can be damaged by poor performance or ethical misconduct. However, it is much easier to recover from poor marketing performance than from ethical misconduct. Obviously, stakeholders who are most directly affected by negative events will have a corresponding shift in their perceptions of a firm's reputation. On the other hand, even those indirectly connected to negative events can shift their reputation attributions. In many cases, those indirectly connected to the negative events may be more influenced by the news media or general public opinion than those who are directly connected to an organization. Some scandals may lead to boycotts and aggressive campaigns to dampen sales and earnings. Nike experienced such a backlash from its use of offshore subcontractors to manufacture its shoes and clothing. When Nike claimed no responsibility for the subcontractors' poor working conditions and extremely low wages, some consumers demanded greater accountability and responsibility by engaging in boycotts, letter-writing campaigns, and public-service announcements. Nike ultimately responded to the growing negative publicity by changing its practices and becoming a model company in managing offshore manufacturing.[3] Due to the links between reputation, ethics, and marketing, we explore the dimensions of social responsibility and marketing ethics, examine research that relates ethics and social responsibility to marketing performance, and discuss their roles in the strategic marketing planning process.

Dimensions of Social Responsibility

Social responsibility is a broad concept that relates to an organization's obligation to maximize its positive impact on society while minimizing its negative impact. As shown in Exhibit 3.1, social responsibility consists of four dimensions or responsibilities: economic, legal, ethical, and philanthropic.[4]

From an economic perspective, all firms must be responsible to their shareholders, who have a keen interest in stakeholder relationships that influence the reputation of the firm and, of course, earning a return on their investment. The economic responsibility of making a profit also serves employees and the community at large due to its impact on employment and income levels in the area that the firm calls home. Marketers also have expectations, at a minimum, to obey laws and regulations. This is a challenge because the legal and regulatory environment is hard to navigate and interpretations of the law change frequently. Economic and legal concerns are the most basic levels of social responsibility for good reason: Without them, the firm may not survive long enough to engage in ethical or philanthropic activities.

At the next level of the pyramid, marketing ethics refers to principles and standards that define acceptable marketing conduct as determined by the public, government regulators, private-interest groups, competitors, and the firm itself. The most basic of these principles have been codified as laws and regulations to induce marketers to conform to society's expectations of conduct. However, it is important to understand that marketing ethics goes beyond legal issues: Ethical marketing decisions foster trust, which helps build long-term marketing relationships.

EXHIBIT 3.1

THE PYRAMID OF CORPORATE SOCIAL RESPONSIBILITY

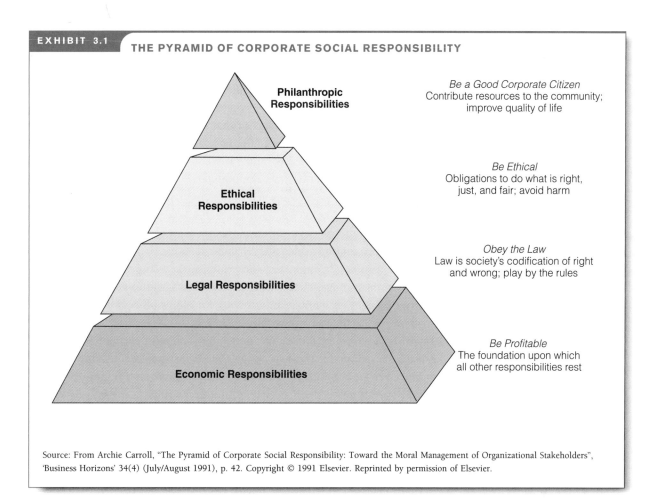

Philanthropic Responsibilities

Be a Good Corporate Citizen
Contribute resources to the community; improve quality of life

Ethical Responsibilities

Be Ethical
Obligations to do what is right, just, and fair; avoid harm

Legal Responsibilities

Obey the Law
Law is society's codification of right and wrong; play by the rules

Economic Responsibilities

Be Profitable
The foundation upon which all other responsibilities rest

Source: From Archie Carroll, "The Pyramid of Corporate Social Responsibility: Toward the Moral Management of Organizational Stakeholders", 'Business Horizons' 34(4) (July/August 1991), p. 42. Copyright © 1991 Elsevier. Reprinted by permission of Elsevier.

Marketing ethics includes decisions about what is right or wrong in the organizational context of planning and implementing marketing activities in a global business environment to benefit (1) organizational performance, (2) individual achievement in a work group, (3) social acceptance and advancement in the organization, and (4) stakeholders. This definition of marketing ethics recognizes that ethical decisions occur in a complex social network within a marketing organization. Marketers are often asked by upper-level management to help make the numbers by reaching almost impossible sales targets. In fact, most marketing misconduct is done to help the organization. Being a team player and bending the rules to make targets may result in a promotion. On the other hand, it has destroyed the careers of some of those willing to do anything that they are asked to do.

Ample evidence shows that ignoring these issues can destroy trust with customers and prompt government intervention. When firms engage in activities that deviate from accepted principles to further their own interests, continued marketing exchanges become difficult, if not impossible. The best way to deal with such problems is during the strategic planning process, not after major problems materialize. For example, Google's plan to scan millions of books into an online database has already met with major conflicts. The goal was to make out-of-print books more readily available to consumers, but Google did not take into account other stakeholder groups. The company had to settle a $125 million lawsuit with book publishers who claimed the actions would infringe on their copyrights. Antitrust regulators are also investigating Google's plan because of concern that Google's control over millions of out-of-print books may give them too much power.[5]

Discussing and addressing these potential problems during the strategic planning process could save a company millions in the long term. As a result, more and more companies have created extensive ethics and compliance programs to identify problems early on. For instance, Lockheed Martin, a technology aerospace manufacturer and global security company, has a comprehensive ethics program. The company has a President and Vice President of Ethics and Business Conduct—positions that are increasingly common in large companies—and publishes a manual explaining its ethics program to both employees and other stakeholders. Lockheed also publishes an Ethics Directory that contains contact information for ethics officers who are responsible for covering each company within Lockheed.[6]

Ethical and socially responsible behavior requires commitment. For this reason, many other firms simply ignore these issues and focus instead on satisfying their economic and legal responsibilities, with an eye toward the overall bottom line of profit maximization. Although the firm may do nothing wrong, it misses out on the long-term strategic benefits that can be derived from satisfying ethical and philanthropic responsibilities. Firms that choose to take these extra steps concern themselves with increasing their overall positive impact on society, their local communities, and the environment, with the bottom line of increased goodwill toward the firm, as well as increased profits.

Many firms try hard to align their philanthropy with marketing and brand image. During major crises, like Hurricane Katrina or the more recent financial meltdown, firms are given an opportunity to make their philanthropic programs more responsive and visible to the public. For example, to help Americans get through the most recent economic downturn, Walmart partnered with Visa to offer reloadable, prepaid Visa cards for $3 instead of the original $9, a move that company officials stated would save their customers over $500 million in service fees. The Walmart Foundation also donated $3.6 million to The United Way and One Economy to help bring free tax preparation and filing services to low- to moderate-income families. Walmart's initiative is not only designed to help its targeted customers, many of whom have low or moderate incomes, but also improves Walmart's image as an increasingly socially responsible company. In fact, during the most recent recession, Walmart was one of the few companies that saw increased sales. As Walmart has demonstrated, socially responsible behavior is not only good for customers, employees, and the community, but it also makes good business sense.[7]

Philanthropic activities make very good marketing tools. Thinking of corporate philanthropy as a marketing tool may seem cynical, but it points out the reality that philanthropy can be very good for a firm. Coca-Cola, for example, partners with the

Erb Institute for Global Sustainable Enterprise at the University of Michigan and the World Wildlife Fund to create internship programs for MBA/MS students. The selected interns work with business and nonprofit leaders to come up with solutions to the challenges of freshwater conservation. Since major corporations have often been at odds with environmental organizations in the past, Coca-Cola's partnership with the World Wildlife Fund markets the fact that it is willing take these stakeholders' concerns seriously to improve the environment for both current and future generations.[8]

Marketing Ethics and Strategy

Marketing ethics includes the principles and standards that guide the behavior of individuals and groups in making marketing decisions. Marketing strategy must consider stakeholders—including managers, employees, customers, industry associations, government regulators, business partners, and special-interest groups—all of whom contribute to accepted standards and society's expectations. The most basic of these standards have been codified as laws and regulations to encourage companies to conform to society's expectations of business conduct. Exhibit 3.2 lists some of the more common ethical issues that occur in marketing.

The standards of conduct that determine the ethics of marketing activities require both organizations and individuals to accept responsibility for their actions and to comply with established value systems. Repeated ethical misconduct in a particular business or industry sometimes requires the government to intervene, a situation that can be expensive and inconvenient for businesses and consumers. Early in the 21st century, many businesses appeared to be cleaning up their acts. However, misconduct in the financial and banking sectors, as well as high-profile failures of companies like GM during the 2008–2009 financial crisis, created a dramatic erosion of consumer confidence. As Exhibit 3.3 indicates, many consumers support increased government regulation of businesses. Not surprisingly, this sentiment peaked during the height of the financial crisis. Marketing deceptions, such as lying or misrepresenting information, were a key reason for the increase in support of government regulation. Such practices increased consumer distrust of some businesses and industries, such as the mortgage industry, and contributed to economic instability during the crisis. Misleading consumers, investors, and other stakeholders not only caused the ruin of established companies like Lehman Brothers, but also led to the arrests of major company officials and the loss of billions of investors' dollars. Without a shared view of appropriate and acceptable business conduct, companies often fail to balance their desires for profits against the wishes and needs of society.

Balancing profits with the wishes of society often leads to major challenges that could require changing a company's marketing strategy. As illustrated in *Beyond the Pages 3.2,* changes, compromises, or trade-offs in marketing strategy are often needed to address public concerns. If a balance is not maintained, more regulation can result to require responsible behavior of all marketers. Therefore, many best practices evolve to ensure ethical conduct that avoids the inflexibility and expense of regulation. Society has developed rules—both legal and implied—to guide firms in their efforts to earn profits through means that do not harm individuals or society at large.

EXHIBIT 3.2   **POTENTIAL ETHICAL ISSUES IN MARKETING**

Overall
- Misrepresenting the firm's capabilities
- Manipulation or misuse of data or information
- Exploitation of children or disadvantaged groups
- Invasion of privacy
- Anticompetitive activities
- Abusive behavior

Product Issues
- Misrepresentation of goods or services
- Failing to disclose product defects
- Counterfeit or gray-market products
- Misleading warranties
- Failure to disclose important product information
- Reducing package contents without reducing package size

Pricing Issues
- Price deception
- Reference pricing claims
- Price discrimination
- Price fixing between competitors
- Predatory pricing
- Fraudulent refund policies

Distribution Issues
- Opportunistic behavior among members of the supply chain
- Exclusive distribution arrangements
- Tying contracts
- Withholding product availability
- Withholding product or promotional support

Promotion Issues
- Bait-and-switch advertising
- False or misleading advertising
- High-pressure salespeople
- False or misleading selling techniques
- Bribery of salespeople or purchasing agents
- Entertainment and gift giving
- Lying
- Stereotypical portrayals of women, minorities, or senior citizens
- Sexual innuendo in advertising
- Fine print in newspaper advertising

When companies deviate from the prevailing standards of industry and society, the result is customer dissatisfaction, lack of trust, and legal action. The economic downturn has caused the public's trust of business to plummet. A survey by Transparency International revealed that 53 percent of respondents view the private sector as corrupt. Another study of 650 U.S. consumers revealed that 32 percent see the financial sector as greedy and impersonal, 26 percent see it as opportunistic, and 22 percent see it as distant.[9] Given that so much of a company's success depends on the public's perceptions of the firm, a firm's reputation is one of its greatest assets. The

EXHIBIT 3.3   **PUBLIC SENTIMENT TOWARD BUSINESS REGULATION**

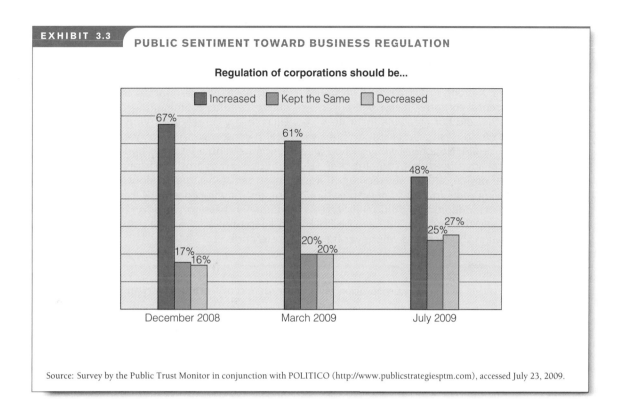

Source: Survey by the Public Trust Monitor in conjunction with POLITICO (http://www.publicstrategiesptm.com), accessed July 23, 2009.

Beyond the Pages 3.2

CEREAL COMPANIES REVAMP IN RESPONSE TO SUGARY CEREAL CRITICISMS[10]

Cereal has long been thought of as a healthy breakfast. Yet in terms of sugar, parents might as well feed their children a cookie to start their day. Some sugary cereals are as much as 50 percent sugar. Honey Smacks, for example contains 15 grams of sugar per serving, which is 3 grams more than is found in a glazed donut. In spite of their poor nutritional profiles, it is often the sweetest cereals that are targeted toward children. In response, many upset parents have filed lawsuits against cereal companies. In order to deal with the backlash and to gain a competitive advantage, companies like Kellogg's have worked to reformulate and reposition their cereals as healthy breakfast choices.

Cereal companies began specifically marketing to children in the 1950s, the same decade in which sugar became a common additive to cereal. As one might imagine, kids gravitated toward these sugary sweets. Cereal companies also introduced cartoon characters to get kids interested in their brands. Tony the Tiger and Trix the Rabbit became beloved child icons. Companies also began placing free toys into cereal boxes. These marketing ploys worked; children craved these fun cereals, making sugary cereals a popular item on the breakfast table for decades.

In 1983, a lawsuit was filed against General Foods, claiming that certain cereal advertisements were deceptive, leading children to believe that by eating certain cereals they could become stronger, happier, or even gain magical powers. The court ruled in favor of the plaintiffs. In 2007, a lawsuit was filed against Nickelodeon and Kellogg's for using cartoon characters from movies and television shows on cereal boxes to attract children. In response, cereal companies stopped co-branding their products, but the parents were not appeased.

(continued)

Sugary cereals were still as popular as ever among children.

In response, Kellogg's took a proactive stance to address parental concerns. It stopped advertising cereals that did not meet the Institute of Medicine and World Health Organization's health guidelines for cereal. No longer will you find a Kellogg's cereal advertised that contains over 12 grams of sugar or 200 calories per serving. It also created guidelines advising consumers to eat sugary cereals in moderation. Additionally, cereals like Special K and the Koshi brand have become popular, although these cereals will never hold the same cache with children as Lucky Charms or Fruity Pebbles. Many major cereal companies are going further to respond to criticism by listing health benefits prominently on cereal labels. Even sugary cereals are trying to appeal to the health-conscious customer, with claims that they contain essential vitamins and minerals. A few brands, such as Frosted Flakes, have even introduced reduced-sugar versions. As long as stakeholders remain concerned, traditional cereal companies have to work to revamp their images to keep up with the public's changing health preferences.

value of a positive reputation is difficult to quantify, but it is very important and once lost can be difficult to regain. A single negative incident can influence perceptions of a firm's image and reputation for years afterward. Corporate reputation, image, and branding are more important than ever and are among the most critical aspects of sustaining relationships with key stakeholders. Although an organization does not control its reputation in a direct sense, its actions, choices, behaviors, and consequences do influence its reputation. For instance, ExxonMobil receives low ratings from the public when gasoline prices spike, as the company has repeatedly set records for all-time-high profits.

Despite corporate governance reforms and a growing commitment to ethics and social responsibility in some sectors, the overall reputation of American corporations continues to slip. According to the Edelman Trust Barometer, only 38 percent of Americans say they trust business, down 20 percentage points from previous years and the lowest since the poll began. American trust in the banking industry is particularly low, with only 36 percent saying that they trust banks. This number is down from 69 percent in previous polls. Reputation is such an important but fragile asset that it may take these industries years to earn back consumer trust.[11]

Some businesspeople choose to behave ethically because of enlightened self-interest or the expectation that "ethics pays." They want to act responsibly and be good citizens, and assume that the public and customers will reward the company for its ethical behavior. Avon, for example, is a company that achieves success, contributes to society, and has ethical management. Andrea Jung, Avon's Chairperson and CEO, operates in the high-risk area of direct selling, without scandals or major ethical issues. In 2008, Jung was named number six among Fortune's 50 Most Powerful Women. Avon markets itself as "the company for women" and engages in many philanthropic activities to benefit women. The Avon Foundation Breast Cancer Crusade has contributed $585 million to 50 countries between 1992 and 2008 and utilizes such high-profile names as actress Reese Witherspoon to broadcast its message. Avon even won approval to conduct direct selling in China—the first approval for a U.S. company since China banned the practice in 1998.[12]

The Challenges of Being Ethical and Socially Responsible

Although most consider the values of honesty, respect, and trust to be self-evident and universally accepted, business decisions involve complex and detailed discussions in which correctness may not be so apparent. Both employees and managers need experience within their specific industry to understand how to operate in gray areas or to handle close calls in evolving areas, such as Internet privacy. For example, how much personal information should be stored on a firm's website without customers' permission? In Europe, the European Union Directive on Data Protection prohibits selling or renting mailing lists—consumers' data cannot be used without their permission.[13] In the United States, firms have more freedom to decide how to collect and use customers' personal data, but advancing technology raises new questions every day. Issues related to personal privacy, unsolicited e-mail, and misappropriation of copyrighted intellectual property cause ethical problems. Protecting trademarks and brand names becomes more difficult as e-commerce has expanded.

Individuals who have limited business experience often find themselves required to make sudden decisions about product quality, advertising, pricing, sales techniques, hiring practices, privacy, and pollution control. For example, how do advertisers know when they make misleading statements as opposed to simple puffery or exaggeration? Bayer claims to be "the world's best aspirin"; Hush Puppies are "the earth's most comfortable shoes"; and Firestone (before its famous recall of 6.5 million tires) promised "quality you can trust."[14] The personal values learned through socialization from family, religion, and school may not provide specific guidelines for these complex business decisions. In other words, a person's experiences and decisions at home, in school, and in the community may be quite different from the experiences and the decisions that he or she has to make at work. Moreover, the interests and values of individual employees may differ from those of the company in which they work, from industry standards, and from society in general. When personal values are inconsistent with the configuration of values held by the work group, ethical conflict may ensue. It is important that a shared vision of acceptable behavior develop from an organizational perspective, to cultivate consistent and reliable relationships with all concerned stakeholders. A shared vision of ethics that is part of an organization's culture can be questioned, analyzed, and modified as new issues develop. However, marketing ethics should relate to work environment decisions and should not control or influence personal ethical issues.

It is imperative that firms become familiar with many of the ethical and social issues that can occur in marketing so that these issues can be identified and resolved when they occur. Essentially, any time that an activity causes managers, employees, or customers in a target market to feel manipulated or cheated, an ethical issue exists regardless of the legality of the activity. Many ethical issues can develop into legal problems if they do not become addressed in the planning process. Once an issue has been identified, marketers must decide how to deal with it. Exhibit 3.4 provides an overview of types of observed misconduct in organizations. All marketers are subject to observing and preventing these types of ethical issues. Although Exhibit 3.4

EXHIBIT 3.4

TYPES OF MISCONDUCT OBSERVED IN ORGANIZATIONS

	2007	2005	Change
Personal Misconduct			
Putting own interests ahead of organization's interests	22%	18%	+4%
Abusive behavior	21%	21%	0%
Lying to employees	20%	19%	+1%
Internet abuse	16%	13%	+3%
Lying to stakeholders	14%	19%	−5%
Discrimination	13%	12%	+1%
Stealing	11%	11%	0%
Sexual harassment	10%	9%	+1%
Improper hiring practices	10%	NA	−
Misconduct That Furthers a Company's Agenda			
Misreporting hours worked	17%	16%	+1%
Safety violations	15%	16%	−1%
Provision of low-quality goods and services	10%	8%	+2%
Environmental violations	7%	NA	−
Misuse of confidential organization information	6%	7%	−1%
Alteration of documents	5%	5%	0%
Alteration of financial records	5%	5%	0%
Bribes	4%	3%	+1%
Using competitors' inside information	4%	4%	0%

Source: From "2007 National Business Ethics Survey: An Inside View of Private Sector Ethics". Copyright © 2007 Ethics Resource Center. Used with permission of the Ethics Resource Center, 2345 Crystal Drive, Suite 201, Arlington, VA 22202, www.ethics.org.

documents many types of issues that exist in organizations, due to the almost infinite number of ways that misconduct can occur, it is impossible to list every conceivable ethical issue. Any type of manipulation, deceit, or even just the absence of transparency in decision making can potentially create harm to others.

Deceptive Practices in Marketing

When a marketing decision results in deception in order to advance individual or organizational interests over those of another individual, group, or organization, charges of fraud may result. In general, fraud is any false communication that deceives, manipulates, or conceals facts in order to create a false impression. It can be considered a crime, and convictions may result in fines, imprisonment, or both. Fraud costs U.S. organizations nearly 1 trillion dollars a year; the average company loses about 7 percent of total revenues to fraud and abuses committed by its own employees.[15] Some of the most common fraudulent activities reported by employees include stealing office supplies and employee shoplifting, claiming to have worked extra hours, and stealing money. In recent years, both marketing and accounting fraud have become major ethical issues and front-page news stories. The negative publicity has taken its toll on public opinion of the marketing profession. Telemarketers, car salespeople, and advertising executives are now among the lowest-ranked marketing professions in terms of the public's perceptions of honesty and ethics.[16]

Deceptive Communication and Promotion

Marketing practices that are false or misleading can destroy customers' trust in an organization. The Federal Trade Commission (FTC) monitors businesses for deceptive practices and takes disciplinary action when needed. It banned American Telecom Services from selling telephones and telephone services through retailers across the nation because the company was not providing promised rebates to tens of thousands of customers.[17] The FTC also required Darden Restaurants, Inc.—owners of The Olive Garden and Red Lobster—to restore fees deducted from consumer gift cards and to prominently disclose fees and expiration dates in all advertising for future gift card offers after the company settled charges that it had engaged in deceptive practices associated with marketing its gift cards.[18] No matter how vigilant, it is difficult for the FTC to catch all forms of deceptive marketing, particularly in the area of advertising.

False and deceptive communication and promotion are the most common and recurring issues in marketing deception. Research has shown that one out of every five advertisements contains misleading information.[19] For example, Burger King staged a taste test that the company claims showed that participants preferred its sandwiches to McDonald's. The problem with claims like these is that they are highly subjective, yet advertisers attempt to make the numbers seem scientific. Other abuses in promotion can range from exaggerated claims and concealed facts to outright lying. Exaggerated claims are those that cannot be substantiated, such as when a commercial states that a certain product is superior to any other on the market. For example, Papa John's International, Inc., invested years and millions of dollars into its "Better Ingredients, Better Pizza" advertising campaign. However, a Texas jury found that the slogan constituted deceptive advertising, and the judge ordered the company to stop using the claim in future advertising. The decision was eventually overturned on appeal and Papa John's still uses the slogan.[20]

Another form of advertising abuse involves making ambiguous statements, in which claims are so weak that the viewer, reader, or listener must infer the advertiser's intended message. Because it is inherently vague, using ambiguous

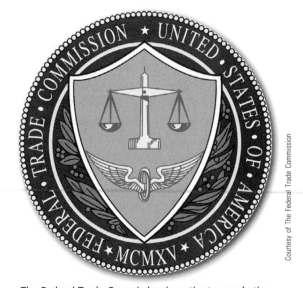

Courtesy of The Federal Trade Commission

The Federal Trade Commission investigates marketing activities to uncover fraudulent and deceptive practices.

wording enables the advertiser to deny any intent to deceive. The verb help is a good example (as in expressions such as "helps prevent," "helps fight," or "helps make you feel"). Consumers may view such advertisements as unethical because they fail to communicate all the information needed to make a good purchasing decision or because they deceive the consumer outright. In another example, the Federal Trade Commission (FTC) and other agencies now monitor more closely the promotions for work-at-home business ventures. Consumers lose millions of dollars each year responding to ads for phony business opportunities such as those promising $50,000 a year for doing medical billing from a home computer.

Another deceptive practice that has become more common is greenwashing, which involves misleading a consumer into thinking that a product or service is more environmentally friendly than it actually is. With customers spending approximately $25 billion a year on green products, businesses are eager to cash in on the green craze. Yet some are willing to cut corners to do so. This generally takes the form of misleading product labels, which can range from making environmental claims that are required by law and are therefore irrelevant (for example, saying that a product is CFC free when CFCs have been banned by the government) to puffery (exaggerating environmental claims) to fraud.[21] Firms need to be careful when using words like green, sustainable, or environmentally friendly so as not to mislead consumers and face potential litigation. The federal government has taken a tougher stand on environmental issues, and as greenwashing becomes more prevalent, it is likely that legal action will increase. Since 2000, the FTC has taken legal action against three companies for greenwashing. Because one-third of consumers rely exclusively on labels to decide whether a product is environmentally friendly, it is important that labels tell the truth.[22]

Some organizations have developed a certification system to help consumers make informed decisions when buying supposedly green products. For example, the Carbon Trust offers a certification that validates claims about reducing carbon output. However, certification organizations are not always trustworthy either. Some of them charge a fee and do not hold products to rigorous standards. For the time being, the best way for consumers to be informed about eco-friendly products is to do their research before going shopping.

Communication in the context of personal selling can also mislead by concealing facts within a message. For instance, a salesperson anxious to sell a medical insurance policy might list a large number of illnesses covered by the policy but fail to mention that it does not cover some commonly covered illnesses. Fraudulent activity has dramatically increased in the area of direct marketing, in which companies use the telephone and nonpersonal media to communicate information to customers, who then purchase products via mail, telephone, or the Internet. Consumers report losses of $1.2 billion annually resulting from fraud, many of them from direct-marketing scams. Of the roughly 1.2 million complaints received by the FTC each year, about 26 percent are associated with identity theft and 9 percent are associated with third-party and creditor debt collection.[23]

Regulating Deceptive Marketing Practices

Many firms attempt to regulate themselves in an effort to demonstrate ethical responsibility and to preclude further regulation by federal or state governments. In addition to complying with all relevant laws and regulations, many firms choose to join trade associations that have self-regulatory programs. Although such programs are not a direct outgrowth of laws, many became established to stop or delay the development of laws and regulations that would restrict the associations' business practices. Some trade associations establish codes of conduct by which their members must abide or risk rebuke or expulsion from the association.

Perhaps the best-known self-regulatory association is the Better Business Bureau (BBB). The BBB's 124 local bureaus across the United States and Canada oversee 3 million businesses and charities, and help resolve problems for millions of consumers each year.[24] Each bureau works to champion good business practices within a community although it usually does not have strong tools for enforcing its rules of business conduct. When a firm violates what the BBB believes to be good business practice, the bureau warns consumers through local newspapers or broadcast media. If the offending organization is a member if the BBB, it may be expelled from the local bureau. The BBB also has a website (http://www.bbb.org) to help consumers identify businesses that operate in an ethical manner. BBB members who use the site agree to binding arbitration with regard to online privacy issues.

Self-regulatory programs like the BBB have a number of advantages over government regulation. Establishment and implementation of such programs are usually less costly, and their guidelines or codes of conduct are generally more practical and realistic. Furthermore, effective self-regulatory programs reduce the need to expand government bureaucracy. However, self-regulation also has several limitations. Nonmember firms are under no obligation to abide by a trade association's industry guidelines or codes. Moreover, most associations lack the tools or authority to enforce their guidelines. Finally, these guidelines are often less strict than the regulations established by government agencies. Still, in many cases, government oversight is absolutely essential to ensure the public's trust. *Beyond the Pages 3.3*, for example, discusses how government intervention during ethical and legal lapses in the financial sector is essential to maintaining trust in our banking system.

Organizational Determinants of Marketing Ethics and Social Responsibility

Although individuals can and do make ethical decisions, they do not operate in a vacuum. Ethical choices in business are most often made jointly in committees and work groups or in conversations with coworkers. Moreover, people learn to settle ethical issues not only using the perspective of their individual backgrounds but also from others with whom they associate in the business environment. The outcome of this learning process depends on the strength of each individual's personal values, the

Beyond the Pages 3.3

STANFORD FINANCIAL BREAKS CONSUMER TRUST[25]

Recently, Ponzi schemes have become all too common, especially in financial circles. A Ponzi, or pyramid, scheme occurs when funds from new investors are used to pay off older investors. What may appear to be a lucrative investment is a scam that pays off only as long as new investors join. Once money stops pouring in, the Ponzi scheme collapses, often with disastrous results.

One alleged Ponzi scheme was committed by R. Allen Stanford, of Stanford Financial, who was accused of operating a $7 billion scheme involving fraudulent CDs–Certificates of Deposit–through a bank on the island of Antigua. Authorities accused Stanford and other executives of using a Ponzi scheme to offer extremely high rates of return. Those investing in Stanford's Antigua bank were promised 9.87 percent compounded annual interest, about six percentage points higher than the U.S. average CD rates at the time. For years many people, including employees and investors, were unclear how Stanford Financial generated such high returns. After inquiring, they were told the information was proprietary and could not be disclosed. Starting in 2003, some people became wary and began to accuse Stanford of running a Ponzi scheme. Stanford was charged with 21 counts of

conspiracy, fraud, bribery, and obstruction of justice, but pleaded not guilty to all charges.

Stanford employees were given high incentives to sell as many CDs as possible, perhaps encouraging them to not ask questions about the investment's high returns. Even the sales staff probably did not know they were participating in a fraud. At the time, the IRS was already investigating Stanford for failing to pay $226.6 million in back taxes. Finally in 2008, Stanford's scheme came to light and investigations subsequently ensued. As in the Bernie Madoff case, the Stanford case begs the question: Why did the Securities and Exchange Commission not spot the Ponzi scheme earlier? The SEC did not file a civil lawsuit against Stanford until 2009, and by then significant damage had been done. Less than 50 percent of the money from the CDs is recoverable, since most of the money never existed in the first place. The Stanford and Madoff cases have added fuel to the fire of those calling for a serious revamping of regulatory bodies' monitoring systems. This is a classic example of white collar crime, where a trusted individual and organization knowingly engages in misconduct and manipulation that damages consumers.

opportunity for unethical behavior, and the exposure to others who behave ethically or unethically. Consequently, the culture of the organization—as well as superiors, peers, and subordinates—can have a significant impact on the ethical decision-making process.

Corporate or organizational culture may be conveyed formally in employee handbooks, codes of conduct, memos, and ceremonies, but it is also expressed informally through dress codes, extracurricular activities, and anecdotes. A firm's culture gives its members meaning and offers direction about how to behave and deal with problems within the firm. The corporate culture at American Express, for example, includes numerous anecdotes about employees who have gone beyond the call of duty to help customers in difficult situations. This strong tradition of customer service might encourage an American Express employee to take extra steps to help a customer who encounters a problem while traveling overseas.

On the other hand, a firm's or industry's culture may also encourage employees to make decisions that others may judge as unethical or it may not discourage actions that may be viewed as unethical. For example, increasing competition in the beer industry has led many firms to use more provocative advertising. Many consumer advocacy organizations have complained that beer industry ads push too hard to attract young consumers who may be under the legal drinking age. After an investigation into beer and alcohol marketing practices, the FTC determined that industry self-regulation works when it comes to beer and alcohol advertising. The investigation found that 92 percent of the industry's ads were acceptable, and only a small percentage of beer and alcohol marketing was truly objectionable. One such case was an Anheuser-Busch campaign that aspired "to connect with fans of many sports" by using college-team colors on Bud Light cans. The FTC had serious concerns with the campaign in that it might promote underage and binge drinking on college campuses. Although there was no formal investigation of Anheuser-Busch, the FTC made it clear that these types of campaigns should not happen again.[26] Many stakeholders, including alcohol and drug policy special interest groups, criticized this ruling as not strict enough.

In marketing, we think of ethical climate as that part of a corporate culture that relates to an organization's expectations about appropriate conduct. To some extent, ethical climate is the character of an organization. Corporate policies and codes, the conduct of top managers, the values and moral philosophies of coworkers, and opportunity for misconduct all contribute to a firm's ethical climate. When top managers strive to establish an ethical climate based on responsibility and citizenship, they set the tone for ethical decisions. Such is the case at the White Dog Café in Philadelphia. Owner Judy Wicks grew her business from a coffee and muffin take-out joint in the first floor of her home to a 200-seat restaurant grossing $5 million annually. Wicks pays a living wage to all restaurant employees, even the dishwashers; however, most employees at the White Dog Café make well above this amount. The restaurant uses 100 percent wind-powered electricity, and 10 to 20 percent of the profits are donated to the affiliated nonprofit, White Dog Community Enterprises, which works to build a more socially just and environmentally sustainable local economy in the greater Philadelphia region. Wicks says she uses "good food to lure innocent consumers into social activism."[27] Thus, the White Dog Café and White Dog Community Enterprises have established an ethical climate that promotes responsible conduct. Ethical climate also determines whether an individual perceives an issue as having an ethical component. Recognizing ethical issues and generating alternatives to address them are manifestations of ethical climate.

To meet the public's escalating demands for ethical marketing, firms need to develop plans and structures for addressing ethical considerations. Some directions for the improvement of ethics have been mandated through regulation, but firms must be willing to have in place a values and ethics system that exceeds minimum regulatory requirements. Although there are no universal standards that can be

White Dog Community Enterprises supports initiatives aimed at creating a local living economy in the greater Philadelphia area.

applied to organizational ethics programs, most companies develop codes, values, or policies to guide business behavior. It would be very naïve to think that simply having a code of ethics would solve any ethical dilemmas a firm might face. In fact, the majority of firms that experience ethical or legal problems usually have stated ethics codes and programs. Often, the problem is that top management, as well as the overall corporate culture, has not integrated these codes, values, and standards into daily decision making.

Codes of Conduct

Most firms begin the process of establishing organizational ethics programs by developing codes of conduct (also called codes of ethics), which are formal statements that describe what an organization expects of its employees. According to a KPMG Integrity Survey, 82 percent of employees reported that their firm has a formal code of conduct such as codes of ethics, policy statements on ethics, or guidelines on proper business conduct.[28] These codes may address a variety of situations from internal operations to sales presentations and financial disclosure practices.

A code of ethical conduct has to reflect the board of directors' and senior management's desire for organizational compliance with the values, rules, and policies that support an ethical climate. Development of a code of conduct should involve the board of directors, president, and senior managers who will be implementing the code. Legal staff should be called upon to ensure that the code has correctly assessed key areas of risk and that standards contained in the code buffer potential legal problems. A code of conduct that does not address specific high-risk activities within the scope of daily operations is inadequate for maintaining standards that can prevent misconduct. Exhibit 3.5 lists the key considerations in developing and implementing a code of ethical conduct.

As a large multinational firm, Texas Instruments (TI) manufactures computers, calculators, and other high-technology products. Its code of ethics resembles that of many other organizations. The code addresses issues related to policies and procedures; government laws and regulations; relationships with customers, suppliers, and

---

EXHIBIT 3.5   KEY CONSIDERATIONS IN DEVELOPING AND IMPLEMENTING A CODE OF ETHICAL CONDUCT

1. Examine high-risk areas and issues.
2. State values and conduct necessary to comply with laws and regulations. Values are an important buffer in preventing serious misconduct.
3. Identify values that specifically address current ethical issues.
4. Consider values that link the organization to a stakeholder orientation. Attempt to find overlaps among organizational and stakeholder values.
5. Make the code of conduct understandable by providing examples that reflect values.
6. Communicate the code frequently and in language that employees can understand.
7. Revise the code every year with input from a wide variety of internal and external stakeholders.

competitors; the acceptance of gifts, travel, and entertainment; political contributions; expense reporting; business payments; conflicts of interest; investment in TI stock; handling of proprietary information and trade secrets; use of TI employees and assets to perform personal work; relationships with government officials and agencies; and the enforcement of the code. TI's code emphasizes that ethical behavior is critical to maintaining long-term success and that each individual is responsible for upholding the integrity of the company. TI's values and ethics statement puts it this way:[29]

> *Our reputation at TI depends upon all of the decisions we make and all the actions we take personally each day. Our values define how we will evaluate our decisions and actions and how we will conduct our business. We are working in a difficult, demanding, ever-changing business environment. Together, we are building a work environment on the foundation of integrity, innovation and commitment. Together, we are moving our company into a new century one good decision at a time. Our high standards have rewarded us with an enviable reputation in today's marketplace: a reputation of integrity, honesty and trustworthiness. That strong ethical reputation is a vital asset, and each of us shares a personal responsibility to protect, preserve and enhance it. Our reputation is a strong, but silent partner in all business relationships. By understanding and applying the values presented here, each of us can say to ourselves and to others, "TI is a good company and one reason is that I am a part of it." Know what's right. Value what's right. Do what's right.*

To ensure that its employees understand the nature of business ethics and the ethical standards that the company expects them to follow, TI offers an "ethics quick test" to help them when they have doubts about the ethics of specific situations and behaviors:

- Is the action legal?
- Does it comply with our values?
- If you do it, will you feel bad?
- How will it look in the newspaper?
- If you know it's wrong, don't do it!
- If you're not sure, ask.
- Keep asking until you get an answer.

TI provides a toll-free number (1-800-33-ETHIC) for employees to call, anonymously, to report incidents of unethical behavior, or simply to ask questions.[30]

Research has found that corporate codes of ethics often have five to seven core values or principles in addition to more-detailed descriptions and examples of appropriate conduct. Six core values are considered to be highly desirable in any code of ethical conduct: (1) trustworthiness, (2) respect, (3) responsibility, (4) fairness,

(5) caring, and (6) citizenship.[31] These values will not be effective without distribution, training, and the support of top management in making them a part of the corporate culture and the ethical climate. Employees need specific examples of how these values can be implemented.

Codes of conduct will not resolve every ethical issue encountered in daily operations, but they help employees and managers deal with ethical dilemmas by prescribing or limiting specific activities. Many firms have a code of ethics, but sometimes they do not communicate their code effectively. A code placed on a website or in a training manual is useless if the company doesn't reinforce it on a daily basis. By communicating both the expectations of proper behavior to employees, as well as punishments they face if they violate the rules, codes of conduct curtail opportunities for unethical behavior and thereby improve ethical decision making. Codes of conduct do not have to be so detailed that they take into account every situation, but they should provide guidelines and principles capable of helping employees achieve organizational ethical objectives and address risks in an accepted manner.

Marketing Ethics and Leadership

There is increasing support that ethical cultures emerge from strong leadership. Many agree that the character and success of the most admired companies emanate from their leaders. The reason is simple: Employees look to the leader as a model of acceptable behavior. As a result, if a firm is to maintain ethical behavior, top management must model its policies and standards. In fact, maintaining an ethical culture is near impossible if top management does not support ethical behavior. For example, in an effort to keep earnings high and boost stock prices, many firms have engaged in falsifying revenue reports. Top executives in these firms encouraged the behavior because they held stock options and could receive bonus packages tied to the company's performance. Thus, higher reported revenues meant larger executive payoffs.

In the realm of marketing ethics, great leaders (1) create a common goal or vision for the company; (2) obtain buy-in, or support, from significant partners; (3) motivate others to be ethical; (4) use the resources that are available to them; and (5) enjoy their jobs and approach them with an almost contagious tenacity, passion, and commitment.[32] Along with strong ethical leadership, a strong corporate culture in support of ethical behavior can also play a key role in guiding employee behavior. Ninety-four percent of respondents to a survey conducted by business consulting firm LRN said it was very important for them to work for an ethical company, with 82 percent saying they would prefer to be paid less if it meant working in an ethical corporate environment.[33] Organizational culture, coworkers and supervisors, as well as the opportunity to engage in unethical behavior, influence ethical decision making. Ethics training can affect all three types of influence. Full awareness of the philosophy of management, rules, and procedures can strengthen both the organizational culture and the ethical stance of peers and supervisors. Such awareness, too, arms employees against opportunities for unethical behavior and lessens the likelihood of misconduct. If adequately and thoughtfully designed, ethics training can ensure that everyone in the firm (1) recognizes situations that might involve ethical decision making, (2) understands the values and culture of the firm, and (3) can evaluate the impact of ethical decisions on the firm in the light of its value structure.[34]

Stakeholders, Market Orientation, and Marketing Performance

One of the most powerful arguments for including ethics and social responsibility in the strategic planning process is the evidence of a link between social responsibility, stakeholders, and marketing performance.[35] An ethical climate calls for organizational members to incorporate the interests of all stakeholders, including customers, in their decisions and actions. Hence, employees working in an ethical climate will make an extra effort to better understand the demands and concerns of customers. One study found that ethical climate is associated with employee commitment to quality and intrafirm trust.[36] Employee commitment to the firm, customer loyalty, and profitability have also been linked to increased social responsibility. These findings emphasize the role of an ethical climate in building a strong competitive position. For example, Burgerville, a regional fast food chain from Washington State, realized significant cost savings, decreased employee turnover, and higher sales after it began to cover 90 percent of healthcare costs for all employees who work over 20 hours per week. Burgerville has found that, while initial costs can be high, being ethical and taking care of its workers does pay off in the end.[37]

As employees perceive an improvement in the ethical climate of their firm, their commitment to the achievement of high-quality standards also increases. They become more willing to personally support the quality initiatives of the firm. These employees often discuss quality-related issues with others both inside and outside of the firm, and gain a sense of personal accomplishment from providing quality goods and services. These employees exhibit effort beyond both expectations and requirements in order to supply quality products in their particular job or area of responsibility. Conversely, employees who work in less ethical climates have less commitment to providing such quality. These employees tend to work only for the pay, take longer breaks, and are anxious to leave every day whether or not they have completed their work.

Market Orientation

An ethical climate is also conducive to a strong market orientation. Market orientation refers to the development of an organizational culture that effectively and efficiently promotes the necessary behaviors for the creation of superior value for buyers and, thus, continuous superior performance of the firm. Market orientation places the customer's interests first, but it does not exclude the interests of other stakeholders. Being market oriented means fostering a sense of cooperation and open information exchange that gives the firm a clearer view of the customer's needs and desires.

Without a strong ethical climate, a competitive workplace orientation can emerge. A competitive orientation encourages personal success, which may come at the expense of openness and cooperation. Internal competition between employees may encourage the achievement of financial performance levels, without regard for their potential effects on other stakeholders both inside and outside the firm. Consequently, employees are unlikely to incorporate the demands and concerns of society, business, or customers in their decisions.

Stakeholder Orientation

The degree to which a firm understands and addresses stakeholder demands can be referred to as a stakeholder orientation. This orientation contains three sets of activities: (1) the organization-wide generation of data about stakeholder groups and assessment of the firm's effects on these groups, (2) the distribution of this information throughout the firm, and (3) the organization's responsiveness as a whole to this intelligence.[38]

Generating data about stakeholders begins with identifying the stakeholders who are relevant to the firm. Relevant stakeholder communities should be analyzed on the basis of the power that each enjoys as well as by the ties between them. Next, the firm should characterize the concerns about the business's conduct that each relevant stakeholder group shares. This information can be derived from formal research, including surveys, focus groups, Internet searches, or press reviews. For example, Accenture utilizes employee surveys to gauge success of their ethics and compliance program in addition to risk assessments and corporate investigations. Caterpillar incorporates an "Annual Assessment and Questionnaire" that is offered in 14 different languages to accommodate employees in over 50 countries.[39] Employees and managers can also generate this information informally as they carry out their daily activities. Purchasing managers know about suppliers' demands, public relations executives about the media, legal counselors about the regulatory environment, financial executives about investors, sales representatives about customers, and human resources advisers about employees. Finally, the company should evaluate its impact on the issues that are important to the various stakeholders whom it has identified.

A stakeholder orientation is not complete unless it includes activities that address stakeholder issues. For example, Gap Inc. reported that although factory inspections are improving, it still struggles to ensure that all its factories are complying with company standards. Gap Inc. admits that it is rare for its factories to fully meet compliance standards, which requires regular factory inspections to ensure safe, fair working conditions. Factory assessors, known as Vendor Compliance Officers, visit factories and assess their performance by rating them on a five point rating system. Gap Inc. recognizes that it is in the company's best interest to work with factories to overcome compliance issues, rather than to simply stop using the factory entirely. However, if an offending factory refuses to change its methods, The Gap will disband its relationship. It has revoked approval of hundreds of factories because they violated vendor codes of conduct. Gap Inc. also partners with the U.K.-based company Historic

Futures, to provide a service to trace materials used in Gap products back to their source (the country of origin and factory). This partnership allows Gap Inc. to be even more aware of labor and environmental conditions in its supply chain. However, The Gap also realizes that it sometimes contributes to problems by making unreasonable demands on factories, such as changing production orders at the last minute. Hence, it continually strives to improve its supply chain decision making so that rush jobs on factories do not occur as often.[40]

The responsiveness of the organization to stakeholder intelligence consists of the initiatives that the firm adopts to ensure that it abides by or exceeds stakeholder expectations and has a positive impact on stakeholder issues. Such activities are likely to be specific to a particular stakeholder group (for example, family-friendly work schedules) or to a particular stakeholder issue (for example, pollution-reduction programs). These responsiveness processes typically involve the participation of the concerned stakeholder groups. Kraft, for example, includes special-interest groups and university representatives in its programs to become sensitized to present and future ethical issues.

A stakeholder orientation can be viewed as a continuum in that firms are likely to adopt the concept to varying degrees. To gauge a given firm's stakeholder orientation, it is necessary to evaluate the extent to which the firm adopts behaviors that typify both the generation and dissemination of stakeholder intelligence and responsiveness to it. A given organization may generate and disseminate more intelligence about certain stakeholder communities than about others and, as a result, may respond to that intelligence differently.

Marketing Performance

A climate of ethics and social responsibility also creates a large measure of trust among a firm's stakeholders. The most important contributing factor to gaining trust is the perception that the firm and its employees will not sacrifice their standards of integrity.[41] In an ethical work climate, employees can reasonably expect to be treated with respect and consideration by their coworkers and superiors. Furthermore, trusting relationships with key external stakeholders can contribute to greater efficiencies and productivity in the supply chain, as well as a stronger sense of loyalty among the firm's customers. A Cone Cause Evolution study revealed that two-thirds of Americans consider a company's business practices when making purchasing decisions, with 85 percent claiming that they would switch products or services should a company be revealed to be unethical. Boycotting a company for ethical misconduct is also a common form of consumer disciplinary action. For example, due to the forest burning practices of palm oil farmers, activists and consumers boycotted Cadbury because of the company's use of palm oil in their chocolate products.[42]

Research indicates a strong association between social responsibility and customer loyalty in that customers are likely to keep buying from firms perceived as doing the right thing. Research by the brand and marketing agency BBMG revealed that about three out of four Americans prefer to buy goods and services from firms that are socially responsible and good corporate citizens.[43] One explanation for this observation may be that good-citizen firms are responsive to customers' concerns and have a sense of dedication to treating them fairly. By gauging customer satisfaction, continuously improving the quality and safety of products, and by making customer information easily accessible and understandable, ethical and socially responsible firms are more likely to serve customers' needs satisfactorily.

Firms that do not develop strategies and programs to incorporate ethics and social responsibility into their organizational cultures will pay the price with potentially poor marketing performance, the potential costs of civil or criminal litigation, and damaging negative publicity when the public discovers questionable activities. On the other hand, firms that do incorporate ethics and social responsibility into their strategic plans are likely to experience improved marketing performance. Unfortunately, because many firms do not view marketing ethics and social responsibility as organizational performance issues, many firms do not believe that these issues need to be considered in the strategic planning process. Individuals also have different ideas as to what is ethical or unethical, leading them to confuse the need for workplace ethics with the right to maintain their own personal values and ethics. Although many corporations and individuals do not fully understand the concept of ethics, and many more do not know how to include it in business strategy, it is possible and desirable to incorporate ethics and social responsibility into the planning process.

Incorporating Ethics and Social Responsibility into Strategic Planning

Many firms integrate ethics and social responsibility into their strategic planning through ethics compliance programs or integrity initiatives that make legal compliance, ethics, and social responsibility an organization-wide effort. Such programs establish, communicate, and monitor a firm's ethical values and legal requirements through codes of conduct, ethics offices, training programs, and audits. Although many firms take considerable time and effort in creating their own codes of conduct, many do not. Krispy Kreme, once a high-flying company, experienced a financial implosion when two executives tried to manage earnings to meet Wall Street expectations. The company's stock, which had traded for $105/share in November 2000 before two-for-one stock splits, fell to $5/share by January 2006.[55] Though Krispy Kreme ousted the corrupt executives and worked to bring its financials up to date, the company suffered significant losses, which only worsened with the 2008–2009 financial crisis. As of 2009, Krispy Kreme Doughnut shares were selling at around $2/share on the New York Stock Exchange, leading analysts to question the future viability of this once popular doughnut chain.[44]

A 2008 poll by Harris Interactive found many scandal-plagued firms at the bottom of its annual survey of perceived corporate reputation, including AIG, Halliburton Company, General Motors Corporation and Washington Mutual. The annual survey measures the sixty most visible corporate reputations on twenty attributes. The Big Three automakers, General Motors Corporation, Chrysler and Ford Motor Company had the largest decrease in credibility scores from the prior year. In addition to the automotive industry's reputation downfall, the financial services industry tied with the tobacco industry for the lowest reputation ranking.[45]

The marketing plan should include distinct elements of ethics and social responsibility as determined by top-level marketing managers. Marketing strategy and implementation plans should be developed that reflect an understanding of (1) the risks associated with ethical and legal misconduct, (2) the ethical and social consequences of strategic choices, and (3) the values of organizational members and stakeholders. To help ensure success, top managers must demonstrate their commitment to ethical and socially responsible behavior through their actions—words are simply not enough. In the end, a marketing plan that ignores social responsibility or is silent about ethical requirements leaves the guidance of ethical and socially responsible behavior to the work group, which risks ethical breakdowns and damage to the firm.

Lessons from Chapter 3

Marketing ethics and social responsibility

- Have grown in importance over the last few years because many firms have seen their image, reputation, and marketing efforts destroyed by problems in these areas.

- Have become necessities in light of stakeholder demands and changes in federal law.

- Improve marketing performance and profits.

- Are important considerations in the development of marketing strategy.

Social responsibility

- Is a broad concept that relates to an organization's obligation to maximize its positive impact on society while minimizing its negative impact.

- Includes the economic responsibility of making a profit to serve shareholders, employees, and the community at large.

- Includes the legal responsibility of obeying all laws and regulations.

- Includes the ethical responsibility to uphold principles and standards that define acceptable conduct as determined by the public, government regulators, private-interest groups, competitors, and the firm itself.

- Includes the philanthropic responsibility to increase the firm's overall positive impact on society, the local community, and the environment.

Marketing ethics

- Contains the principles and standards that guide the behavior of individuals and groups in making marketing decisions.

- Requires that both organizations and individuals accept responsibility for their actions and comply with established value systems.

- Can lead to violations of public trust when ethical standards are not upheld.

- Involves complex and detailed decisions in which correctness may not be so clear-cut.

- Deals with experiences and decisions made at work, which may be quite different from the ethical decisions made away from work.

- Comes into play any time that an activity causes managers, employees, or customers in a target market to feel manipulated or cheated.

Deceptive practices in marketing

- Include fraud, or any false communication that deceives, manipulates, or conceals facts in order to create a false impression.

- Include exaggerated claims or statements about a product or firm that cannot be substantiated.

- Include ambiguous statements in which claims are so weak that the viewer, reader, or listener must infer the advertiser's intended message.

- Include product-labeling issues such as false or misleading claims on a product's package.

- Include selling abuses such as intentionally misleading customers by concealing facts.

- Are typically regulated by the firms themselves or by industry and trade associations.

Ethical decision making

- Is determined not only by an individual's background but also from others with whom the individual associates in the business environment.

- Is affected by the combination of personal values, the opportunity for unethical behavior, and the exposure to others who behave ethically or unethically.

- Is intricately tied to the firm's culture and its ethical climate.

- Can only be improved when a firm develops plans and structures for addressing ethical considerations.

- Is more likely to occur when a strong leader models ethical standards.

A code of ethical conduct

- Is a formal statement that describes what an organization expects of its employees.

- Is not an effective means of controlling ethical behavior unless it becomes integrated into daily decision making.

- Is not truly effective unless it has the full support of top management.

- Must reflect senior management's desire for organizational compliance with the values, rules, and policies that support an ethical climate.

- Should have six core values: (1) trustworthiness, (2) respect, (3) responsibility, (4) fairness, (5) caring, and (6) citizenship.
- Will not resolve every ethical issue encountered in daily operations, but it can help employees and managers deal with ethical dilemmas by prescribing or limiting specific activities.

Marketing ethics and leadership

- Are intricately connected because employees look to the leader as a model of acceptable behavior.
- Become closely intertwined when the leader (1) creates a common goal or vision for the company; (2) obtains buy-in, or support, from significant partners; (3) motivates others to be ethical; (4) uses the resources that are available to them; and (5) enjoys his or her job and approaches it with an almost contagious tenacity, passion, and commitment.

Market orientation

- Is strongly tied to ethics and social responsibility.
- Refers to the development of an organizational culture that effectively and efficiently promotes the necessary behaviors for the creation of superior value for buyers and, thus, continuous superior performance of the firm.
- Means fostering a sense of cooperation and open information exchange that gives the firm a clearer view of the customer's needs and desires.

Stakeholder orientation

- Is strongly tied to ethics and social responsibility.
- Refers to the degree to which a firm understands and addresses stakeholder demands.
- Is composed of three sets of activities: (1) the organization-wide generation of data about stakeholder groups and assessment of the firm's effects on these groups, (2) the distribution of this information throughout the firm, and (3) the organization's responsiveness as a whole to this intelligence.
- Consists of the initiatives that the firm adopts to ensure that it abides by or exceeds stakeholder expectations and has a positive impact on stakeholder issues.

The connection between ethics/social responsibility and marketing performance

- Can cause employees to become more motivated to serve customers, more committed to the firm, more committed to standards of high quality, and more satisfied with their jobs.
- Can cause customers to become more loyal to the firm and increase their purchases from the firm.
- Can lead to increased trust among the firm's stakeholders. The most important contributing factor to gaining trust is the perception that the firm and its employees will not sacrifice their standards of integrity.

- Is so strong that firms not developing strategies and programs to incorporate ethics and social responsibility into their organizational cultures will pay the price with potentially poor marketing performance, the potential costs of civil or criminal litigation, and damaging negative publicity when the public discovers questionable activities.

The connection between ethics and strategic planning

- Is typically done through ethical compliance programs or integrity initiatives that make legal compliance, ethics, and social responsibility an organization-wide effort.

- Is vested in the marketing plan, which should include distinct elements of ethics and social responsibility as determined by top-level marketing managers.

- Is based on an understanding of (1) the risks associated with ethical and legal misconduct, (2) the ethical and social consequences of strategic choices, and (3) the values of organizational members and stakeholders.

- Is manifested in a commitment to ethical and socially responsible behavior through actions—words are simply not enough.

Questions for Discussion

1. Why is marketing ethics a strategic consideration in organizational decisions? Who is most important in managing marketing ethics: the individual or the firm's leadership? Explain your answer.

2. Why have we seen more evidence of widespread ethical marketing dilemmas within firms today? Is it necessary to gain the cooperation of marketing managers to overstate revenue and earnings in a corporation?

3. What is the relationship between marketing ethics and organizational performance? What are the elements of a strong ethical compliance program to support responsible marketing and a successful marketing strategy?

Exercises

1. Visit the Federal Trade Commission website (http://www.ftc.gov). What is the FTC's current mission? What are the primary areas for which the FTC has responsibility? Review the last two months of press releases from the FTC. Based on these releases, what appear to be the major marketing ethical issues of concern at this time?

2. Visit the Better Business Bureau website (http://www.bbb.org). Review the criteria for the BBB Marketplace Torch Awards. What are the most important marketing activities necessary for a firm to receive this award?

3. Look at several print, broadcast, online, or outdoor advertisements and try to find an ad that you believe is questionable from an ethical perspective. Defend why you believe the ad is ethically questionable.

4

Collecting and Analyzing Marketing Information

Introduction

I n this chapter, we begin the process of developing a marketing plan by examining key issues in collecting and structuring marketing information to assist in the formulation of marketing strategies. Managers in all organizations, large and small, devote a major portion of their time and energy to developing plans and making decisions. As shown in *Beyond the Pages 4.1*, continuous tracking of the buying preferences of target consumers over time is critical. However, the ability to do so requires access to and analysis of data to generate usable information in a timely manner. Staying abreast of trends in the marketing environment is but one of several tasks performed by marketing managers. However, it is perhaps the most important task, as practically all planning and decision making depends on how well this analysis is conducted.

One of the most widely used approaches to the collection and analysis of marketing information is the situation analysis. The purpose of the situation analysis is to describe current and future issues and key trends as they affect three key environments: the internal environment, the customer environment, and the external environment. As shown in Exhibit 4.1, there are many issues to be considered in a situation analysis. When viewed together, the data collected during the situation analysis give the organization a big picture of the issues and trends that affect its ability to deliver value to stakeholders. These efforts drive the development of the organization's competitive advantages and strategic focus, as discussed in the next chapter.

In this chapter, we examine several issues related to conducting a situation analysis, the components of a situation analysis, and the collection of marketing data and information to facilitate strategic marketing planning. Although situation analysis has traditionally been one of the most difficult aspects of market planning, recent advances in technology have made the collection of market data and information much easier and more efficient. A wealth of valuable data and information is free for the asking. This chapter examines the different types of marketing data and information needed for planning, as well as many sources where such data may be obtained.

Beyond the Pages 4.1

BABY BOOMERS COME OF AGE[1]

Baby boomers—the 77 million people born between 1946 and 1964—have long been the holy grail of marketers aimed at growing their business. The simple numbers have always made boomers a powerful force and a favored target of marketers for decades. However, today's boomers are reaching a critical milestone: The youngest boomers are now approaching the age of 50. Currently, over half of all baby boomers are over 50, with the oldest boomers now over the age of 60. These numbers are significant because 50 is the typical age at which marketers give up on consumers. Tradition says that by the age of 50, a consumer has developed deeply entrenched buying preferences and brand loyalty that no amount of marketing can undo. Today's marketers, however, are finding that tradition is wrong.

Marketers have rediscovered baby boomers for a number of reasons. One reason is the incredible buying potential. Thanks to better health and longer life expectancies, most boomers plan to continue working well into their 60s in order to shore up their retirement savings. Recent declines in the stock market and the retirement accounts of most boomers have forced them to look for ways to stay in the workforce longer. That extra earning potential makes boomers even more attractive. Today, boomers account for over $1 trillion in spending power every year. A second reason is that today's 50+ consumers are much more active than their parents. Unlike previous generations, boomers are much more likely to change careers, have fewer children, go back to school, remarry, pursue new hobbies, and inherit more money from their parents. Consequently, marketers are finding that boomers' brand preferences and shopping habits are not as entrenched as once thought. Finally, marketers cannot give up on boomers due to the relatively smaller number of Generation X consumers—only 50 million strong—that are following behind them. In the years ahead, marketers must continue to reach out to boomers until the 74 million Generation Y consumers (teens and twenty-somethings) reach their peak earning potential.

Reaching out to boomers has become a challenge for many marketers because they have to throw out their stereotypical ideas about 50+ consumers. Gap, for example, tried to reach out to boomers using advertising featuring well-known boomer celebrities. That strategy backfired, however, because Gap's clothes do not suit boomers' tastes. To solve the problem, the company launched a new chain called Forth & Towne, which sells career wear and causal clothing. Other marketers have found success simply by catering to boomers' ideals and needs. For example, Dove saw its sales increase after it dropped attractive models from its advertising in favor of ordinary, 40-something women. Cover Girl adopted a similar strategy by launching its first line of makeup targeted at older women. Further, Home Depot added renovation services to its mix in addition to its assortment of products for do-it-yourselfers. And even Honda was surprised when it learned that 40 percent of its minivan buyers were older customers who needed to haul grandchildren rather than their own children. As a result, Honda introduced a version of its popular Odyssey minivan to cater to the needs of older consumers.

The picture is not uniformly rosy, however, as real estate developers and makers of luxury products have seen a rapid falloff in both interest and sales among their traditional boomer clients. As their retirement savings have dwindled, boomers today are less interested in buying second homes, cars, vacations, and other luxury items. In fact, some investment analysts question whether boomers will ever be able to retire.

Experts agree that the key to tapping the boomer market is to not assume that they are of one mind. Researchers at Duke University have discovered that boomers are the most diverse of all current generations. Consequently, marketers must segment this market carefully to ensure that their marketing resonates with the correct boomer segment.

| EXHIBIT 4.1 | ISSUES TO BE CONSIDERED IN A SITUATION ANALYSIS |

The Internal Environment

Review of current objectives, strategy, and performance
Availability of resources
Organizational culture and structure

The Customer Environment

Who are our current and potential customers?
What do customers do with our products?
Where do customers purchase our products?
When do customers purchase our products?
Why (and how) do customers select our products?
Why do potential customers not purchase our products?

The External Environment

Competition
Economic growth and stability
Political trends
Legal and regulatory issues
Technological advancements
Sociocultural trends

Conducting a Situation Analysis

Before we move forward in our discussion, it is important to keep in mind four important issues regarding situation analysis. We hope our advice helps you overcome potential problems throughout the situation analysis.

Analysis Alone Is Not a Solution

Although it is true that a comprehensive situation analysis can lead to better planning and decision making, analysis itself is not enough. Put another way, situation analysis is a necessary, but insufficient, prerequisite for effective strategic planning. The analysis must be combined with intuition and judgment to make the results of the analysis useful for planning purposes. Situation analysis should not replace the manager in the decision-making process. Its purpose is to empower the manager with information for more effective decision making.

A thorough situation analysis empowers the marketing manager because it encourages both analysis and synthesis of information. From this perspective, situation analysis involves taking things apart: whether it's a customer segment (in order to study the heavy users), a product (in order to understand the relationship between its features and customers' needs), or competitors (in order to weigh their strengths and weaknesses against your own). The purpose of taking things apart is to understand why people, products, or organizations perform the way they do. After this dissection is complete, the manager can then synthesize the information to gain a big picture view of the complex decisions to be made.

Data Are Not the Same as Information

Throughout the planning process, managers regularly face the question: "How much data and information do I need?" The answer sounds simple, but in practice it is not. Today, there is no shortage of data. In fact, it is virtually impossible to know everything about a specific topic. Thankfully, the cost of collecting and storing vast amounts of data has dropped dramatically over the past decade. Computer-based marketing information systems are commonplace. Online data sources allow managers to retrieve data in a matter of seconds. The growth of wireless technology now gives managers access to vital data while in the field. The bottom line is that managers are more likely to be overwhelmed with data rather than face a shortage.

Although the vast amount of available data is an issue to be resolved, the real challenge is that good, useful information is not the same as data. Data are easy to collect and store, but good information is not. In simple terms, *data* are a collection of numbers or facts that have the potential to provide information. Data, however, do not become informative until a person or process transforms or combines them with other data in a manner that makes them useful to decision makers. For example, the fact that your firm's sales are up 20 percent is not informative until you compare it with the industry's growth rate of 40 percent. It is also important to remember that information is only as good as the data from which it comes. As the saying goes, Garbage in, garbage out. It is a good idea to be curious about, perhaps even suspicious of, the quality of data used for planning and decision making.

The Benefits of Analysis Must Outweigh the Costs

Situation analysis is valuable only to the extent that it improves the quality of the resulting marketing plan. For example, data that cost $4,000 to acquire, but improve the quality of the decision by only $3,999, should not be part of the analysis process. Although the costs of acquiring data are easy to determine, the benefits of improved decisions are quite difficult to estimate. Managers must constantly ask questions such as "Where do I have knowledge gaps?" "How can these gaps be filled?" "What are the costs of filling these gaps?" and "How much improvement in decision making will be gained by acquiring this information?" By asking these questions, managers can find a balance between jumping to conclusions and "paralysis by analysis," or constantly postponing a decision due to a perceived lack of information. Perpetually analyzing data without making any decisions is usually not worth the additional costs in terms of time or financial resources.

Conducting a Situation Analysis Is a Challenging Exercise

Situation analysis is one of the most difficult tasks in developing a marketing plan. Managers have the responsibility of assessing the quality, adequacy, and timeliness of the data and information used for analysis and synthesis. The dynamic nature of internal and external environments often creates breakdowns in the effort to develop effective information flows. This dynamism can be especially troubling when the firm attempts to collect and analyze data in international markets.

It is important that any effort at situation analysis be well organized, systematic, and supported by sufficient resources (e.g., people, equipment, information, budget). However, the most important aspect of the analysis is that it should be an ongoing effort. The analysis should not only take place in the days and weeks immediately preceding the formation of strategies and plans; the collection, creation, analysis, and dissemination of pertinent marketing data and information must be ingrained in the culture of the organization. Although this is not an easy task, if the organization is going to be successful it must have the ability to assess its current situation in real time. This type of live data is especially important when tracking customers and competitors.

A final challenge is the task of tracking all three environments (internal, customer, external) simultaneously. Although the rapid pace of change in today's economy is one cause of this difficulty, the relationship among all three environments creates challenges as well. As shown in Exhibit 4.2, the internal, customer, and external environments do not exist independently. Changes in one portion of the external environment can cause subsequent shifts in the customer environment or the internal environment. For example, after Mattel sued MGA Entertainment, Inc. for copyright infringement for its Bratz doll design, Mattel won a $100 million verdict against MGA. The company was ordered to transfer its Bratz line and all intellectual property

EXHIBIT 4.2

THE RELATIONSHIP AMONG THE INTERNAL, CUSTOMER, AND EXTERNAL ENVIRONMENTS

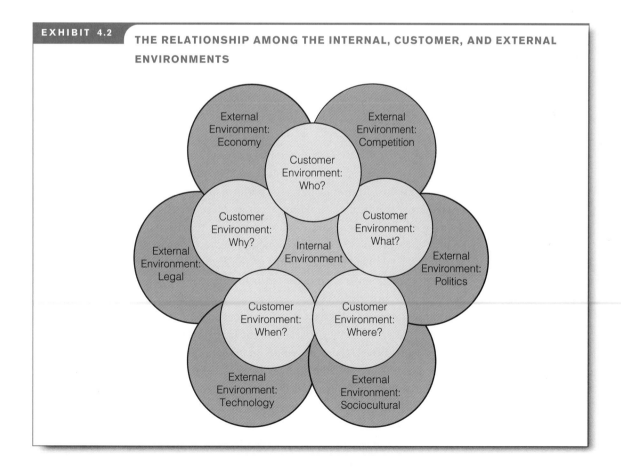

associated with the product to Mattel. This single dispute from its legal environment challenges the very existence of MGA.[2]

As we turn our attention to the three major components of the situation analysis, keep in mind that data and information about these environments will come from both internal and external sources. Even information about the firm's internal environment can be collected via external sources such as third-party analysis and ratings, financial commentaries, and customer opinion ratings. Finally, it is important to remember that the type of data and information source is not as important as having ready access to a wide variety of sources.

The Internal Environment

The first aspect of a situation analysis involves the critical evaluation of the firm's internal environment with respect to its objectives, strategy, performance, allocation of resources, structural characteristics, and political climate. In Exhibit 4.3, we provide a framework for analyzing the internal environment.

Review of Current Objectives, Strategy, and Performance

First, the marketing manager must assess the firm's current marketing objectives, strategy, and performance. A periodic assessment of marketing objectives is necessary to ensure that they remain consistent with the firm's mission and the changing customer and external environments. It may also be necessary to reassess the firm's marketing goals if the objectives prove to be out of date or ineffective. This analysis serves as an important input to later stages of the marketing planning process.

The marketing manager should also evaluate the performance of the current marketing strategy with respect to sales volume, market share, profitability, and other relevant measures. This analysis can take place at many levels: by brand, product line, market, business unit, division, and so on. It is also important to analyze the marketing strategy relative to overall industry performance. Poor or declining performance may be the result of (1) holding on to marketing goals or objectives inconsistent with the current realities of the customer or external environments, (2) a flawed marketing strategy, (3) poor implementation, or (4) changes in the customer or external environments beyond the control of the firm. The causes for poor or declining performance must be pinpointed before marketing strategies can be developed to correct the situation.

For example, in the mid-1990s Pepsi was locked in a seemingly endless market share battle with Coca-Cola. By all accounts, the battle was not going well for Pepsi: Its profits trailed Coke's by 47 percent, while its market value was less than half of its chief rival.[3] But losing out to Coke in the cola wars was just the kick that Pepsi needed to regroup. Forced to look outside of the soft-drink industry for new growth opportunities, PepsiCo, Inc. moved aggressively into noncarbonated and sports beverages, food, and snacks. Today, PepsiCo's Aquafina bottled water and Gatorade are dominant over Coke's Dasani bottled water and PowerAde in their respective markets.

> **EXHIBIT 4.3**   **A FRAMEWORK FOR ANALYZING THE INTERNAL ENVIRONMENT**
>
> *Review of Current Marketing Objectives, Strategy, and Performance*
>
> 1. What are the current marketing goals and objectives?
> 2. Are the marketing goals and objectives consistent with the corporate or business-unit mission, goals, and objectives? Are they consistent with recent changes in the customer or external environments? Why or why not?
> 3. How are current marketing strategies performing with respect to anticipated outcomes (for example, sales volume, market share, profitability, communication, brand awareness, customer preference, customer satisfaction)?
> 4. How does current performance compare to other organizations in the industry? Is the performance of the industry as a whole improving or declining? Why?
> 5. If performance is declining, what are the most likely causes? Are marketing objectives inconsistent? Is the strategy flawed? Was the strategy poorly implemented?
> 6. If performance is improving, what actions can be taken to ensure that performance continues to improve? Is the improvement in performance due to a better than anticipated environment or superior planning and implementation?
>
> *Review of Current and Anticipated Organizational Resources*
>
> 1. What is the state of current organizational resources (for example, financial, human, experience, relationships with key suppliers or customers)?
> 2. Are these resources likely to change for the better or worse in the near future? How?
> 3. If the changes are for the better, how can these added resources be used to better meet customers' needs?
> 4. If the changes are for the worse, what can be done to compensate for these new resource constraints?
>
> *Review of Current and Anticipated Cultural and Structural Issues*
>
> 1. What are the positive and negative aspects of the current and anticipated organizational culture?
> 2. What issues related to internal politics or management struggles might affect the organization's marketing activities?
> 3. What is the overall position and importance of the marketing function as seen by other functional areas? Are key executive positions expected to change in the future?
> 4. How will the overall market- or customer-orientation of the organization (or lack thereof) affect marketing activities?
> 5. Does the organization emphasize a long- or short-term planning horizon? How will this emphasis affect marketing activities?
> 6. Currently, are there positive or negative issues with respect to motivating employees, especially those in frontline positions (for example, sales and customer service)?

In addition, Pepsi's Frito-Lay division commands over 60 percent of the U.S. snack food market. PepsiCo also markets other leading brands including Quaker, Tropicana, Life Water, Ethos Water, Propel, Life Cereal, and Aunt Jemima. Since 2000, Pepsi's profits have climbed more than 100 percent.[4]

Availability of Resources

Second, the marketing manager must review the current and anticipated levels of organizational resources that can be used for marketing purposes. This review includes an analysis of financial, human, and experience resources, as well as any resources the firm might hold in key relationships with supply chain partners,

After losing the cola wars to rival Coca-Cola, Pepsi is dominant in bottled water, sports drinks, and snack foods.

strategic alliance partners, or customer groups. An important element of this analysis is to gauge whether the availability or level of these resources is likely to change in the near future. Additional resources might be used to create competitive advantages in meeting customer needs. If the marketing manager expects resource levels to decline, he or she must find ways to compensate when establishing marketing goals, objectives, and strategies for the next planning period.

In bad economic times, financial shortfalls get most of the attention. However, many experts predict that a shortage of skilled labor will be a major problem in the United States over the next few years. The problem is not the raw number of workers, but the skill set that each one brings to the job. After years of increasing technological innovation, workers must now possess the right set of skills to work with technology. Likewise, workers of today must possess knowledge-related skills such as abstract reasoning, problem solving, and communication. Firms are also trying to increase labor productivity by doing the same or more work with fewer employees. Companies in many industries—most notably services—have turned to offshoring jobs to other countries where highly educated, English-speaking employees will work for less pay than their U.S. counterparts. Of all white-collar jobs that have been offshored, a full 90 percent are now located in India. An interesting irony is that the same technology that demands increased skills from employees allows these jobs to be offshored to other countries.[5]

Organizational Culture and Structure

Finally, the marketing manager should review current and anticipated cultural and structural issues that could affect marketing activities. One of the most important issues in this review involves the internal culture of the firm. In some organizations, marketing does not hold a prominent position in the political hierarchy. This situation can create challenges for the marketing manager in acquiring resources and gaining approval of the marketing plan. The internal culture also includes any anticipated changes in key executive positions within the firm. The marketing manager, for example, could have difficulty in dealing with a new production manager who fails to see the benefits of marketing. Other structural issues to be considered include the overall customer orientation of the firm (or lack thereof), issues related to employee motivation and commitment to the organization (particularly among unionized employees), and the relative emphasis on long-term versus short-term planning. Top managers who concern themselves only with short-term profits are unlikely to see the importance of a marketing plan that attempts to create long-term customer relationships.

For most firms, culture and structure are relatively stable issues that do not change dramatically from one year to the next. In fact, changing or reorienting an organization's culture is a difficult and time-consuming process. In some cases, however, the culture and structure can change swiftly, causing political and power struggles within the organization. Consider the effects when two organizations combine their separate cultures and structures during a merger. For example, the largest merger in history took place in 2001 when Time Warner acquired AOL. At the time, the $111 billion merger was hailed as visionary in its combination of old media and the new online media. However, the massive size of the merger, the differences in corporate cultures, and intense competition in the Internet advertising business conspired to lessen the potential payoff from the merger. In fact, Time Warner's stock fell almost 80 percent after the merger. In 2009, Time Warner decided to begin the process of spinning off AOL as a separate company. The move, which came on the heels of Time Warner's spinoff of Time Warner Cable, was designed to refocus Time Warner's efforts on its core cable networks and magazines.[6]

The Customer Environment

In the second part of the situation analysis, the marketing manager must examine the current and future situation with respect to customers in the firm's target markets. During this analysis, information should be collected that identifies: (1) the firm's current and potential customers, (2) the prevailing needs of current and potential customers, (3) the basic features of the firm's and competitors' products perceived by customers as meeting their needs, and (4) anticipated changes in customers' needs.

In assessing the firm's target markets, the marketing manager must attempt to understand all relevant buyer behavior and product usage characteristics. One method that the manager can use to collect this information is the 5W Model: Who, What, Where, When, and Why. We have adapted and applied this model to customer analysis, as shown in Exhibit 4.4. Organizations that are truly market- or customer-oriented should know their customers well enough that they have easy access to the types of information that answer these questions. If not, the organization may need to conduct primary marketing research to fully understand its target markets.

Who Are Our Current and Potential Customers?

Answering the "who" question requires an examination of the relevant characteristics that define target markets. This includes demographic characteristics (gender, age, income, etc.), geographic characteristics (where customers live, density of the target market, etc.), and psychographic characteristics (attitudes, opinions, interests, etc.). Depending on the types of products sold by the firm, purchase influencers or users, rather than actual purchasers, may be important as well. For example, in consumer markets it is well known that the influence of children is critical for purchases such as cars, homes, meals, toys, and vacations. In business markets, the analysis typically focuses on the buying center. Is the buying decision made by an individual or by a committee? Who has the greatest influence on the purchase decision?

EXHIBIT 4.4   **THE EXPANDED 5W MODEL FOR CUSTOMER ANALYSIS**

Who Are Our Current and Potential Customers?

1. What are the demographic, geographic, and psychographic characteristics of our customers?
2. Who actually purchases our products?
3. How do these purchasers differ from the users of our products?
4. Who are the major influencers of the purchase decision?
5. Who is financially responsible for making the purchase?

What Do Customers Do with Our Products?

1. In what quantities and in what combinations are our products purchased?
2. How do heavy users of our products differ from light users?
3. Do purchasers use complementary products during the consumption of our products? If so, what is the nature of the demand for these products, and how does it affect the demand for our products?
4. What do our customers do with our products after consumption?
5. Are our customers recycling our products or packaging?

Where Do Customers Purchase Our Products?

1. From what types of vendors are our products purchased?
2. Does e-commerce have an effect on the purchase of our products?
3. Are our customers increasing their purchasing from nonstore outlets?

When Do Customers Purchase Our Products?

1. Are the purchase and consumption of our products seasonal?
2. To what extent do promotional events affect the purchase and consumption of our products?
3. Do the purchase and consumption of our products vary based on changes in physical/social surroundings, time perceptions, or the purchase task?

Why (and How) Do Customers Select Our Products?

1. What are the basic features provided by our products and our competitors' products? How do our products compare to those of competitors?
2. What are the customer needs fulfilled by our products and our competitors' products? How well do our products meet these needs? How well do our competitors' products meet these needs?
3. Are the needs of our customers expected to change in the future? If so, how?
4. What methods of payment do our customers use when making a purchase? Is the availability of credit or financing an issue with our customers?
5. Are our customers prone to developing close long-term relationships with us and our competitors, or do they buy in a transactional fashion (primarily based on price)?
6. How can we develop, maintain, or enhance the relationships we have with our customers?

Why Do Potential Customers Not Purchase Our Products?

1. What are the basic needs of noncustomers that our products do not meet?
2. What are the features, benefits, or advantages of competing products that cause noncustomers to choose them over our products?
3. Are there issues related to distribution, promotion, or pricing that prevent noncustomers from purchasing our products?
4. What is the potential for converting noncustomers into customers of our products?

Source: Adapted from Donald R. Lehmann and Russell S. Winer, *Analysis for Marketing Planning*, 6th edition (Boston: McGraw-Hill/Irwin, 2005). Copyright © 2005 The McGraw-Hill Companies, Inc.

The analysis must also assess the viability of potential customers or markets that may be acquired in the future. This involves looking ahead to situations that may increase the firm's ability to gain new customers. For example, firms around the world are particularly excited about the further opening of the Chinese market and its 1.4 billion potential consumers. Many firms, including Procter & Gamble, Walmart, Starbucks, and Pepsi have established a presence in China that they hope to leverage for future growth opportunities. The excitement about the Chinese market stems from its strong middle class of over 250 million consumers.[7]

What Do Customers Do with Our Products?

The "what" question entails an assessment of how customers consume and dispose of the firm's products. Here the marketing manager might be interested in identifying the rate of product consumption (sometimes called the usage rate), differences between heavy and light users of products, whether customers use complementary products during consumption, and what customers do with the firm's products after consumption. In business markets, customers typically use the firm's products in the creation of their own products. As a result, business customers tend to pay very close attention to product specifications and quality.

In some cases, marketers cannot fully understand how customers use their products without looking at the complementary products that go with them. In these cases of *derived demand*—where the demand for one product depends on (is derived from) the demand of another product—the marketer must also examine the consumption and usage of the complementary product. For example, tire manufacturers concern themselves with the demand for automobiles, and makers of computer accessories closely watch the demand for desktop and laptop computers. By following the demand for and consumption of complementary products, marketers are in a much better position to understand how customers use their own products.

Before customers and marketers became more concerned about the natural environment, many firms looked only at how their customers used products. Today, marketers have become increasingly interested in how customers dispose of products, such as whether customers recycle the product or its packaging. Another postconsumption issue deals with the need for reverse channels of distribution to handle product repairs. Car manufacturers, for example, must maintain an elaborate network of certified repair facilities (typically through dealers) to handle maintenance and repairs under warranty.

Sometimes recycling and repair issues come into conflict. The relatively low cost of today's home electronics leads many customers to buy new televisions, radios, computers, or cell phones rather than have old ones repaired. As discussed in *Beyond the Pages* 4.2 this causes a problem: What do consumers do with e-waste, or broken and obsolete electronic devices? Though e-waste makes up only 1 percent of our country's garbage volume, state governments and local communities have struggled for years with the e-waste that enters our nation's landfills.

Beyond the Pages 4.2

THE GROWING PROBLEM OF E-WASTE[8]

What do you do with an old computer, television, DVD player, cell phone, or any other consumer electronic device when it no longer works? Having the device repaired is typically not justifiable given the high repair cost relative to buying a new item. If you are like most people, you throw these devices into the trash or a drawer, or give them away. Therein lies the problem with electronic waste, or e-waste, which is now a major problem for electronics manufacturers, state and local governments, and the U.S. Environmental Protection Agency. Recent data show that over 86 percent of discarded electronics (2.2 million tons) ends up in our nation's landfills. Many of these discarded items contain toxins such as mercury, cadmium, and lead which can contaminate the soil and water if they are not disposed of properly.

Because of the growing problem of e-waste, many state and local governments have taken steps to solve the problem. In 2007, for example, Minnesota required manufacturers to collect and recycle 60 percent of discarded electronics they sold in the state. Oregon followed suit in 2009, with New York and Virginia looking to pass their own laws. California mandates 100 percent recycling of used electronics, but adds $6 to $10 to the price of new items to help offset the recycling costs. Now, the U.S. government is looking at ways to enhance recycling on a national scale. One such proposal adds recycling requirements for electronics retailers as well as manufacturers. Such actions put enormous pressure on these companies, many of which do not have reverse supply chain procedures in place to handle incoming e-waste. Television manufacturers face the biggest obstacles in recycling. Old televisions are big, heavy, and often very difficult for consumers to haul to recycling facilities. Further, the number of recycled televisions is growing rapidly as consumers switch from analog CRT televisions to flat-panel digital models.

To handle the growing demands for recycling, the industry established the Electronic Manufacturers Recycling Management Company, which is funded by its members—including Toshiba, Sharp, and Panasonic. Other companies use third-party recyclers, such as Waste Management, to handle recycling. Dell and Goodwill Industries developed one innovative strategy—the Reconnect Partnership—where Dell provides training and financial support to refurbish old computers. The effort saves over 2.7 million pounds of computer waste from going into landfills each year. The strategy is a huge win for Goodwill, which like other charities has been inundated with donations of unwanted electronics.

E-waste is now a lucrative business for recyclers. The industry generated over $3 billion in revenue in 2009. It also generated a fair amount of controversy when it was discovered that some recyclers were exporting e-waste to other countries (mostly Asia, Mexico, and Africa) for disposal. These countries have lax environmental laws that make the e-waste problem much more difficult in communities where the e-waste is stored. Such actions are a violation of the Basel Convention—an international agreement that restricts trade in hazardous waste. The United States has yet to ratify the agreement. However, the EPA does require approval before U.S. companies can export CRT displays (computer monitors and televisions with picture tubes), which are among the most dangerous types of e-waste. To bring more public scrutiny to the issue, Dell recently made public its formal policies and procedures that ban the export of e-waste to developing nations. Environmental groups hope that Dell's standards become the norm for the electronics industry.

Where Do Customers Purchase Our Products?

The "where" question is associated mainly with distribution and customer convenience. Until recently, most firms looked solely at traditional channels of distribution, such as brokers, wholesalers, and retailers. Thus, the marketing manager would have concerns about the intensity of the distribution effort and the types of retailers that the firm's customers patronized. Today, however, many other forms of distribution are available.

The fastest growing form of distribution today is nonstore retailing—which includes vending machines; direct marketing through catalogs, home sales, or infomercials; and electronic merchandising through the Internet, interactive television, and video kiosks. Business markets have also begun to capitalize on the lower costs of procurement via the Internet. Likewise, many manufacturers have bypassed traditional distribution channels in favor of selling through their own outlet stores or websites. For example, there are now so many different avenues for downloading or streaming movies, either online or via cable, that the traditional movie rental business is in jeopardy.

When Do Customers Purchase Our Products?

The "when" question refers to any situational influences that may cause customer purchasing activity to vary over time. This includes broad issues, such as the seasonality of the firm's products and the variability in purchasing activity caused by promotional events or budgetary constraints. Everyone knows that consumer purchasing activity increases just after payday. In business markets, budgetary constraints and the timing of a firm's fiscal year often dictate the "when" question. For example, many schools and universities buy large quantities of supplies just before the end of their fiscal years.

The "when" question also includes more subtle influences that can affect purchasing behavior, such as physical and social surroundings, time perceptions, and the purchase task. For example, a consumer may purchase a domestic brand of beer for regular home consumption, but purchase an import or microbrew when visiting a bar (physical surroundings), going out with friends (social surroundings), or hosting a party. Customers can also vary their purchasing behavior based on the time of day or how much time they have to search for alternatives. Variation by purchase task depends on what the customer intends to accomplish with the purchase. For example, a customer may purchase brand A for her own use, brand B for her children, and brand C for her coworker as a gift.

Why (and How) Do Customers Select Our Products?

The "why" question involves identifying the basic need-satisfying benefits provided by the firm's products. The potential benefits provided by the features of competing products should also be analyzed. This question is important because customers may purchase the firm's products to fulfill needs that the firm never considered. For example, most people think of vinegar as an ingredient in salad dressings. However, vinegar boasts many other uses, including cleaning floors, loosening rusted screws or nuts, tenderizing meat, and softening hard paint brushes.[9] The answer to the "why" question can also aid in identifying unsatisfied or undersatisfied customer needs. During the analysis, it is also important to identify potential changes in customers' current and future needs. Customers may purchase the firm's products for a reason that may be trumped by newly launched competitive products in the future.

The "how" part of this question refers to the means of payment that customers use when making a purchase. Although most people use cash (which also includes checks and debit cards) for most transactions, the availability of credit makes it possible for customers to take possession of high-priced products like cars and homes. The same is true in business markets, where credit is essential to the exchange of goods and services in both domestic and international transactions. Recently, a very old form of payment has reemerged in business markets—barter. Barter involves the exchange of goods and services for other goods or services; no money changes hands. Barter arrangements are very good for small businesses short on cash. According to the International Reciprocal Trade Association, over $10 billion of international trade in goods and services is conducted annually on a noncash basis—a number that represents 15 percent of the global economy. Barter has grown at the rate of roughly 8 percent each year, thanks in part to the advent of barter networks on the Internet. For example, consumers can trade books, textbooks, and audio books through PaperBackSwap.com. The service boasts over 4 million available book titles for trading—all with no transaction fees.[10]

Why Do Potential Customers Not Purchase Our Products?

An important part of customer analysis is the realization that many potential customers choose not to purchase the firm's products. Although there are many potential reasons why customers might not purchase a firm's products, some reasons include these:

- Noncustomers have a basic need that the firm's product does not fulfill.

- Noncustomers perceive that they have better or lower-priced alternatives, such as competing substitute products.

- Competing products actually have better features or benefits than the firm's product.

- The firm's product does not match noncustomers' budgets or lifestyles.

- Noncustomers have high switching costs.

- Noncustomers do not know that the firm's product exists.

- Noncustomers have misconceptions about the firm's product (weak or poor image).

- Poor distribution makes the firm's product difficult to find.

Once the manager identifies the reasons for nonpurchase, he or she should make a realistic assessment of the potential for converting noncustomers into customers. Although conversion is not always possible, in many cases converting noncustomers is as simple as taking a different approach. For example, Australian-based Casella Wines was able to convert noncustomers into wine drinkers by fundamentally changing their approach to the wine industry. Through its [yellow tail] brand, Casella converted nonwine drinkers by positioning itself as being easy to drink, easy to understand, easy to buy, and fun. [yellow tail] ignored long-held wine attributes such as prestige and complexity to make wine more approachable to the masses. The end result is that [yellow tail] is now the number one imported wine brand in the United States.[11]

Once the marketing manager has analyzed the firm's current and potential customers, the information can be used to identify and select specific target markets for the revised marketing strategy. The firm should target those customer segments where it can create and maintain a sustainable advantage over its competition.

The External Environment

The final and broadest issue in a situation analysis is an assessment of the external environment, which includes all the external factors—competitive, economic, political, legal/regulatory, technological, and sociocultural—that can exert considerable direct and indirect pressures on both domestic and international marketing activities. Exhibit 4.5 provides a framework for analyzing factors in the external environment. As this framework suggests, the issues involved in examining the external environment can be divided into separate categories (i.e., competitive, economic, legal, etc.). However, some environmental issues can fall into multiple categories.

One such example is the explosive growth in direct-to-consumer (DTC) advertising in the pharmaceutical industry. In 2007, the industry spent roughly $4.2 billion on DTC advertising through "ask your doctor" style ads aimed at encouraging consumers to request drugs by name from their physicians. This promotional strategy has been praised and criticized on a number of fronts. Some argue that DTC advertising plays an important role in educating the population about both disease and available treatments. Critics—including the U.S. Congress—argue that DTC advertising encourages consumers to self-diagnose and is often misleading about a drug's benefits and side effects. In response to these criticisms, the pharmaceutical industry developed a set of guiding principles for DTC advertising. However, most people expect Congress to eventually pass legislation curtailing or barring the practice.[12]

Issues in the external environment can often be quite complex. For example, a 1997 strike by UPS employees not only put them out of work, but also led to economic slowdowns in UPS hub cities. The strike also became a political issue for President Bill Clinton as he was continually pressured to invoke the Taft-Hartley Act to force striking UPS employees back to work. Although the effects of the UPS strike were short-lived, some changes have a lasting impact. The tragic events of September 11, 2001, led to many changes in the competitive, economic, political, legal, technological, and sociocultural environments that will be felt for decades to come. Thankfully, complex situations like these occur infrequently. As we examine each element of the external marketing environment, keep in mind that issues that arise in one aspect of the environment are usually reflected in other elements as well.

Competition

In most industries, customers have choices and preferences in terms of the goods and services they can purchase. Thus, when a firm defines the target markets it will serve, it simultaneously selects a set of competing firms. The current and future actions of these competitors must be constantly monitored, and hopefully even anticipated. One of the major problems in analyzing competition is the question of identification. That is, how does the manager answer the question "Who are our current and future competitors?" To arrive at an answer, the manager must look

---

EXHIBIT 4.5   **A FRAMEWORK FOR ANALYZING THE EXTERNAL ENVIRONMENT**

Competition

1. Who are our major brand, product, generic, and total budget competitors? What are their characteristics in terms of size, growth, profitability, strategies, and target markets?
2. What are our competitors' key strengths and weaknesses?
3. What are our competitors' key capabilities and vulnerabilities with respect to their marketing program (for example, products, distribution, promotion, and pricing)?
4. What response can we expect from our competitors if environmental conditions change or if we change our marketing strategy?
5. How is our set of competitors likely to change in the future? Who are our new competitors likely to be?

Economic Growth and Stability

1. What are the general economic conditions of the country, region, state, and local area in which our firm operates?
2. What are the economic conditions of our industry? Is our industry growing? Why or why not?
3. Overall, are customers optimistic or pessimistic about the economy? Why?
4. What are the buying power and spending patterns of customers in our industry? Are our industry's customers buying less or more of our products? Why?

Political Trends

1. Have recent elections changed the political landscape within our domestic or international markets? If so, how?
2. What type of industry regulations do elected officials favor?
3. What are we doing currently to maintain good relations with elected officials? Have these activities been effective? Why or why not?

Legal and Regulatory Issues

1. What proposed changes in international, federal, state, or local laws and regulations have the potential to affect our marketing activities?
2. Do recent court decisions suggest that we should modify our marketing activities?
3. Do the recent rulings of federal, state, local and self-regulatory agencies suggest that we should modify our marketing activities?
4. What effect will changes in global trade agreements or laws have on our international marketing opportunities?

Technological Advancements

1. What impact has changing technology had on our customers?
2. What technological changes will affect the way that we operate or manufacture our products?
3. What technological changes will affect the way that we conduct marketing activities such as distribution or promotion?
4. Are there any current technologies that we do not use to their fullest potential in making our marketing activities more effective and efficient?
5. Do any technological advances threaten to make our products obsolete? Does new technology have the potential to satisfy previously unmet or unknown customer needs?

Sociocultural Trends

1. How are society's demographics and values changing? What effect will these changes have on our customers, products, pricing, distribution, promotion, and our employees?
2. What challenges or opportunities have changes in the diversity of our customers and employees created?
3. What is the general attitude of society about our industry, company, and products? Could we take actions to improve these attitudes?
4. What social or ethical issues should we be addressing?

beyond the obvious examples of competition. Most firms face four basic types of competition:

1. **Brand competitors**, which market products with similar features and benefits to the same customers at similar prices.

2. **Product competitors**, which compete in the same product class, but with products that are different in features, benefits, and price.

3. **Generic competitors**, which market very different products that solve the same problem or satisfy the same basic customer need.

4. **Total budget competitors**, which compete for the limited financial resources of the same customers.

Exhibit 4.6 presents examples of each type of competition for selected product markets. In the compact SUV segment of the automotive industry, for example, the Chevrolet Equinox, Ford Escape, Honda CR-V, and Jeep Compass are brand competitors. However, each faces competition from other types of automotive products, such as midsize SUVs, trucks, minivans, and passenger cars. Some of this product competition comes from within each company's own product portfolio (e.g., Honda's Pilot SUV, Accord sedan, Odyssey minivan, and Ridgeline truck compete with the CR-V). Compact SUVs also face generic competition from motorcycles, bicycles, rental cars, and public transportation—all of which offer products that satisfy the same basic customer need for transportation. Finally, customers have many alternative uses for their money rather than purchasing a compact SUV: They can take a vacation, install a pool in the backyard, buy a boat, start an investment fund, or pay off debt.

All four types of competition are important, but brand competitors rightfully receive the greatest attention, as customers see different brands as direct substitutes for each other. For this reason, strategies aimed at getting customers to switch brands are a major focus in any effort to beat brand competitors. For example, Gatorade, far and

EXHIBIT 4.6	EXAMPLES OF MAJOR TYPES OF COMPETITION			
Product Category (Need Fulfilled)	Brand Competitors	Product Competitors	Generic Competitors	Total Budget Competitors
Compact SUVs (Transportation)	Chevrolet Equinox Ford Escape Honda CR-V Jeep Compass	Full-size SUVs Trucks Passenger cars Minivans	Rental cars Motorcycles Bicycles Public transportation	Vacation Debt reduction Home remodeling
Soft Drinks (Refreshment)	Coca-Cola Zero Diet Coke Pepsi Cola Diet Pepsi	Tea Orange juice Bottled water Energy drinks	Tap water	Candy Gum Potato chips
Movies (Entertainment)	*Harry Potter* *Twilight* *Star Trek*	Cable TV Pay-per-view Video rentals	Athletic events Arcades Concerts	Shopping Reading Fishing
Colleges (Education)	New Mexico Florida State Louisiana State	Trade school Community college Online programs	Books CD-ROMs Apprenticeship	New cars Vacations Investments

away the dominant sports drink, has lost market share in recent years to competitors such as Vitamin Water, Propel, and Powerade. To refresh the Gatorade brand, Pepsi repackaged and relabeled the line of well-known sports drinks, including Shine On (Gatorade AM), Bring It (Gatorade Fierce), Be Tough (Gatorade X-Factor), No Excuses (Gatorade Rain), Focus (Gatorade Tiger), and G2 (low-calorie Gatorade). These changes, along with the introduction of new bottles, multipacks, and refreshed labeling, have placed Gatorade squarely alongside other drink choices in supermarkets and convenience stores. Gatorade's bold moves into the mainstream make the brand a formidable product competitor among branded competition in the soft-drink market.[13]

Competitive analysis has received greater attention recently for several reasons: more intense competition from sophisticated competitors, increased competition from foreign firms, shorter product life cycles, and dynamic environments, particularly in the area of technological innovation. A growing number of companies have adopted formalized methods of identifying competitors, tracking their activities, and assessing their strengths and weaknesses—a process referred to as *competitive intelligence*. Competitive intelligence involves the legal and ethical observation, tracking, and analysis of the total range of competitive activity, including competitors' capabilities and vulnerabilities with respect to sources of supply, technology, marketing, financial strength, manufacturing capacities and qualities, and target markets. It also attempts to predict and anticipate competitive actions and reactions in the marketplace.[14] Competitive analysis should progress through the following stages:

1. **Identification**   Identify all current and potential brand, product, generic, and total budget competitors.

2. **Characteristics**   Focus on key competitors by assessing the size, growth, profitability, objectives, strategies, and target markets of each one.

3. **Assessment**   Assess each key competitor's strengths and weaknesses, including the major capabilities and vulnerabilities that each possesses within its functional areas (marketing, research and development, production, human resources, etc.).

4. **Capabilities**   Focus the analysis on each key competitor's marketing capabilities in terms of its products, distribution, promotion, and pricing.

5. **Response**   Estimate each key competitor's most likely strategies and responses under different environmental situations, as well as its reactions to the firm's own marketing efforts.

Many sources are available for gathering information on current or potential competitors. Company annual reports are useful for determining a firm's current performance and future direction. An examination of a competitor's mission statement can also provide information, particularly with respect to how the company defines itself. A thorough scan of a competitor's website can also uncover information—such as product specifications and prices—that can greatly improve the competitive analysis. Other, clever ways to collect competitive information include data mining techniques, patent tracking to reveal technological breakthroughs, creating psychological profiles of competitor's key executives, searching consumer review and blog websites, and attending trade shows and conferences.[15] Other valuable information sources include business periodicals and trade publications that provide newsworthy tidbits about companies. There are also numerous commercial databases, such as ABI/INFORM, InfoTrac, EBSCO, Hoover's, and Moody's, which provide a wealth of information on companies and their marketing activities. The information contained in these databases can be purchased in print form, on CD-ROM, or through an online connection with a data provider such as a school or public library.

Economic Growth and Stability

If there is one truism about any economy, it is that it will inevitably change. Therefore, current and expected conditions in the economy can have a profound impact on marketing strategy. A thorough examination of economic factors requires marketing managers to gauge and anticipate the general economic conditions of the nation, region, state, and local area in which they operate. These general economic conditions include inflation, employment and income levels, interest rates, taxes, trade restrictions, tariffs, and the current and future stages of the business cycle (prosperity, stagnation, recession, depression, and recovery). For example, the annual U.S. inflation rate trended downward for 16 years until it began to rise again in 2004. The upward trend ended in 2008 during the worldwide economic downturn. Inflation actually became negative (i.e., deflation) in 2009. This means that general price levels began to fall during the economic downturn, brought on by contractions in spending by the government and individuals. Deflation is also consistent with rising unemployment, which for the United States stood at 9.8 percent in late 2009 (up from roughly 4 percent in 2000).[16]

Equally important economic factors include consumers' overall impressions of the economy and their ability and willingness to spend. Consumer confidence (or lack thereof) can greatly affect what the firm can or cannot do in the marketplace. In times of low confidence, consumers may not be willing to pay higher prices for premium products, even if they have the ability to do so. In other cases, consumers may not have the ability to spend, regardless of the state of the economy. Another important factor is the current and anticipated spending patterns of consumers in the firm's target market. If consumers buy less (or more) of the firm's products, there could be important economic reasons for the change.

One of the most important economic realities in the United States over the last 50 years has been a steady shift away from a tangibles-dominant economy (goods, equipment, manufacturing) to one dominated by intangibles such as services and information. In fact, virtually everyone is aware that the U.S. economy is a knowledge-based economy. However, our methods of measuring and reporting on the economy have not kept pace with this change. Our methods are very good at capturing manufacturing output, capital expenditures, and investments in other tangible assets; but they cannot capture investments in intangibles such as innovation, employee training, brand equity, or product design. Consequently, the true nature of our economy is underreported by virtually all current statistics, such as the revered GDP. Innovation, creativity, and human assets—the main drivers behind the success of most U.S.

businesses—are not counted as a part of yearly GDP statistics. One of the major challenges moving forward is finding ways of capturing these intangibles in our regular reporting and economic analyses.[17]

Political Trends

Although the importance will vary from firm to firm, most organizations should track political trends and attempt to maintain good relations with elected officials. Organizations that do business with government entities, such as defense contractors, must be especially attuned to political trends. Elected officials who have negative attitudes toward a firm or its industry are more likely to create or enforce regulations unfavorable for the firm. For example, the anti-tobacco trend in the United States has been in full swing since the late 1990s. Today, many states and local communities have passed laws to prevent smoking in public places. One of the most hotly contested business-related political issues of late has been the status of illegal immigrants crossing the U.S. border, especially from Mexico. This single issue has potential ramifications for our economy (employment, healthcare, trade), our society (language, culture), and our political relations with other nations. As these examples show, political discussions can have serious, lasting consequences for an industry or firm.

Many organizations view political factors as beyond their control and do little more than adjust the firm's strategies to accommodate changes in those factors. Other firms, however, take a more proactive stance by seeking to influence elected officials. For example, some organizations publicly protest legislative actions, whereas others seek influence more discreetly by routing funds to political parties or lobbying groups. Whatever the approach, managers should always stay in touch with the political landscape.

Legal and Regulatory Issues

As you might suspect, legal and regulatory issues have close ties to events in the political environment. Numerous laws and regulations have the potential to influence marketing decisions and activities. The simple existence of these laws and regulations causes many firms to accept this influence as a predetermined aspect of market planning. For example, most firms comply with procompetitive legislation rather than face the penalties of noncompliance. In reality, most laws and regulations are fairly vague (for instance, the Americans with Disabilities Act), which often forces firms to test the limits of certain laws by operating in a legally questionable manner. The vagueness of laws is particularly troubling for e-commerce firms who face a number of ambiguous legal issues involving copyright, liability, taxation, and legal jurisdiction. For reasons such as these, the marketing manager should carefully examine recent court decisions to better understand the law or regulation in question. New court interpretations can point to future changes in existing laws and regulations. The marketing manager should also examine the recent rulings of federal, state, local and self-regulatory trade agencies to determine their effects on marketing activities.

One of the most profound legislative shifts in recent times occurred with President Bush's signing of the Sarbanes-Oxley Act on July 30, 2002. Sarbanes-Oxley was essentially the federal government's response to a string of corporate scandals—most notably Enron, Tyco, and WorldCom. The law introduced very stringent rules for financial practice and corporate governance designed to protect investors by increasing the accuracy and reliability of corporate disclosures of financial information. An interesting result of Sarbanes-Oxley is the intense media and public attention that it garnered. The accuracy of corporate disclosures is now such a closely watched issue that organizations are forced into compliance both legally and practically. It is estimated that compliance with the law—in the form of new information and reporting systems—has cost U.S. businesses more than $30 billion. Recently, many pro-business groups have claimed that the Sarbanes-Oxley act is unconstitutional and have petitioned the U.S. Supreme Court to look at it.[18]

Organizations that engage in international business should also be mindful of legal issues surrounding the trade agreements among nations. The implementation of the North American Free Trade Agreement (NAFTA), for example, created an open market of roughly 374 million consumers. Since NAFTA went into effect, many U.S. firms have begun, or expanded, operations in Canada and Mexico. Conversely, national governments sometimes use trade agreements to limit the distribution of certain products into member countries. Recurring disagreements between the United States, Canada, and Argentina and the European Union (EU) over genetically modified foods, for example, prompted the United States to file a complaint with the World Trade Organization in 2003. The EU has banned all genetically modified food and crops since 1998. The complaint argued that the ban lacked scientific support and amounted to an unfair trade barrier. The WTO ruled against the EU in 2006, opening the way for genetically modified foods to enter the EU. However, individual EU nations, such as Germany, have continued to ban the use of genetically modified seeds and food to this day. Even if the market eventually opens to U.S. producers, the going will be tough: Over 54 percent of European consumers believe that genetically modified foods are unsafe for consumption.[19]

Technological Advancements

When most people think about technology, they tend to think about new high-tech products such as wireless telephones, broadband Internet access, medical breakthroughs, GPS systems, or interactive television. However, technology actually refers to the way we accomplish specific tasks or the processes we use to create the "things" we consider as new. Of all the new technologies created in the past 30 years, none has had a greater impact on marketing than advances in computer and information technology. These technologies have changed the way consumers and employees live and the way that marketers operate in fulfilling their needs. In some cases, changes in technology can be so profound that they make a firm's products obsolete, such as with vinyl long-playing (LP) records, typewriters, cassette tapes, and pagers. Soon, we will add CDs, DVDs, and newspapers to that list.

Many changes in technology assume a frontstage presence in creating new marketing opportunities. By frontstage technology, we mean those advances that are most noticeable to customers. For example, products such as wireless phones, microwave ovens, and genetic engineering have spawned entirely new industries aimed at fulfilling previously unrecognized customer needs. Many frontstage technologies, such as smartphones and GPS satellite navigation systems, aim to increase customer convenience. Likewise, companies continue to push toward even more substantial changes in the ways that marketers reach customers through the use of interactive marketing via computers and digital television.

These and other technological changes can also assume a backstage presence when their advantages are not necessarily apparent to customers. Advances in backstage technology can affect marketing activities by making them more efficient and effective. For example, advances in computer technology have made warehouse storage and inventory control more efficient and less expensive. Similar changes in communication technology have made field sales representatives more efficient and effective in their dealings with managers and customers.

In some cases, technology can have both a frontstage and a backstage presence. One of the most promising breakthroughs is radio frequency identification (RFID), which involves the use of tiny radio-enabled chips that can be attached to a product or its packaging. The radio signals emitted or reflected from the chip can be used to track inventory levels, product spoilage, or prevent theft. They can also be used for the instantaneous checkout of an entire shopping cart of items. RFID is also used in other applications such as patient tracking in hospitals, real-time data analysis in Indy racecars, and EZ-Pass systems on the nation's toll roads. Many retailers and packaged goods manufacturers fund research to develop RFID, which is expected to replace bar code technology within 10 years.[20]

Sociocultural Trends

Sociocultural factors are those social and cultural influences that cause changes in attitudes, beliefs, norms, customs, and lifestyles. These forces profoundly affect the way people live and help determine what, where, how, and when customers buy a firm's products. The list of potentially important sociocultural trends is far too long to examine each one here. Exhibit 4.7 illustrates examples of some of these trends. Two of the more important trends, however, are changes in demographics and customer values.

There are many changes taking place in the demographic makeup of the U.S. population. For example, most of us know that the population as a whole has grown older as a result of advances in medicine and healthier lifestyles. Research suggests that the number of Americans age 65 and older will increase 147 percent by 2050—from 12.4 to 20 percent of the population.[21] Experts project that by 2050, the worldwide population of older people will be larger than the population of children ages 0 to 14 for the first time in human history.

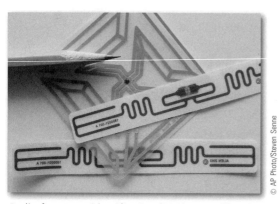

© AP Photo/Steven Senne

Radio frequency identification (RFID) tags will replace UPC bar codes in the not too distant future.

As a result, marketers of healthcare, recreation, tourism, and retirement housing can expect large increases in demand over the next several decades. Other important changes include a decline in the teenage population, an increasing number of singles and single-parent households, and still greater participation of women in the work-force. The increase in the number of two-income and single-parent families has, for example, led to a massive increase in demand and retail shelf space for convenient frozen entrees and meals. Our growing focus on health and nutrition has led many of the marketers of these meals to offer lower calorie and carbohydrate content in their products.

EXHIBIT 4.7   TRENDS IN THE SOCIOCULTURAL ENVIRONMENT

Demographic Trends

Aging of the American population
Decline in the teen population (as a percentage of the total population)
Population growth in Sun Belt states
Increasing number of single-member/individual households
Increasing participation of women in the workforce
Increasing number of single-parent families
Increasing population diversity, especially in the number of Hispanic Americans
Increasing immigration (legal and illegal)
Increasing number of wealthy Americans

Lifestyle Trends

Clothing becoming more casual, especially at work
Clothing becoming more revealing, especially for women
Growing participation in body modification (e.g., tattoos, piercings)
Americans having less time for leisure activities
Vacationing at home becoming more common
Less shopping in malls, more shopping from home
Continuing focus on health, nutrition, and exercise
Increasing importance of leisure time versus work time
Declining time spent watching television and reading newspapers
Increasing time spent using computers and talking/texting on wireless phones
Growing popularity of fuel-efficient hybrid vehicles
Growing ubiquity of digital entertainment

Value Trends

Shorter attention spans and less tolerance for waiting
Less focus on "me-oriented" values
More value-oriented consumption (good quality, good price)
Importance of maintaining close, personal relationships with others
Increasing importance of family and children
Increasing concerns about the natural environment
Greater focus on ethics and social responsibility
Increased interest in giving back to the community
Less tolerance of smoking in public places
More tolerance of individual lifestyle choices
Growing disconnect with government
Growing skepticism about business

One of the other most important demographic changes taking place is the increasing diversity of the U.S. population. The number of legal immigrants coming to the United States has risen steadily during the past 30 years. Between now and 2050, minority population growth will account for a full 90 percent of the growth of the total U.S. population. This trend is especially true among the Hispanic population, which will grow by 188 percent. By 2050, almost one-quarter of the U.S. population will be of Hispanic decent—up from 17 percent today.[22] These changes in diversity will create both threats and opportunities for most organizations. A diverse population means a diverse customer base. Firms must alter their marketing practices, including the way they recruit and select employees, to match these changing customer segments. For example, women of color, ignored by cosmetics companies for a long time, used to have a very difficult time finding makeup in shades appropriate for their skin tones. Now, virtually all cosmetics companies offer product lines designed specifically for these previously unserved markets. Furthermore, most well-known companies now specifically target Hispanic consumers. Not only is the Hispanic market growing, it also has a number of positive characteristics such as low household debt, two-income households, and an affinity for branded merchandise. General Mills alone has more than tripled its ad spending directed at the Hispanic market.[23]

Changes in our cultural values—the guiding principles of everyday life—can also create opportunities and challenges for marketers. Values influence our views of how to live, the decisions we make, the jobs we do, and the brands we buy. In a major study of American values, researchers found that the three most important values regardless of age, gender, race, income, or region are (1) having close relationships with other people, (2) being secure and stable, and (3) having fun. In fact, despite what we often see depicted on television and in advertising, few Americans actually concern themselves with "me-oriented" values like power, influence, or developing themselves personally.[24] Astute marketers can use this information to reflect our prevailing values in the products they design and the advertising they create.

As you can see, the external environment encompasses a wide array of important factors that must be analyzed carefully before developing the marketing plan. These issues are so important that most firms have specialists on staff to track emerging trends and develop strategies for dealing with external concerns. These specialists are typically housed in corporate affairs departments as outlined in *Beyond the Pages 4.3*. Although the external environment is the largest of the three environments we have discussed, it is not necessarily the most important. Depending on the firm, its industry, and the timing, the internal and/or customer environments can be much more important in developing marketing strategy. The important issue is that all three environments must be analyzed prior to developing a marketing strategy and marketing plan. Good analysis requires the collection of relevant data and information, our next topic.

Collecting Marketing Data and Information

To perform a complete situation analysis, the marketing manager must invest time and money to collect data and information pertinent to the development of the marketing

Beyond the Pages 4.3

A CORPORATE AFFAIRS PRIMER[25]

What is corporate affairs? In its broadest sense, corporate affairs is a collection of strategic activities aimed at marketing an organization, its issues, and its ideals to potential stakeholders (consumers, general public, shareholders, media, government, etc.). One way to think about corporate affairs is that it includes all of the organization's marketing activities not directed at the end users of its products. The activities that define corporate affairs vary; however, most organizations maintain departments that engage in the following strategic activities:

- **Corporate Communication**—activities aimed at telling the organization's story and promoting goodwill among a variety of stakeholders. It includes activities such as public relations, employee relations, corporate image advertising, public affairs, and media relations.

- **Government Relations**—activities aimed at educating and influencing elected officials, government officials, and regulatory agencies with respect to key issues that are pertinent to the firm. The most visible form of government relations is lobbying.

- **Investor Relations**—activities designed to promote investment in the organization through the sale of financial instruments such as stocks and bonds. It includes activities such as developing the annual report, planning shareholders' meetings, and other customer service activities directed at corporate shareholders.

- **Corporate Philanthropy**—activities aimed at serving the needs of the community at large (either domestically or globally) through product or cash donations, volunteerism, or support of humanitarian initiatives.

- **Corporate Sustainability**—activities aimed at reducing the organization's impact on the environment. It includes activities such as reducing the organization's carbon footprint, recycling of its products, and promoting environmental stewardship.

- **Policy Analysis**—activities designed to influence the national or international dialogue with respect to public or economic policy in an industry-related area. Policy analysis includes research and analysis designed to provide needed information for making policy decisions.

Perhaps the best way to understand corporate affairs is to see what several major organizations have to say about it. Here are a few examples:

Microsoft

We're a diverse team of professionals focused on a simply stated mission: To earn, day after day, the public's trust and build our company's enduring value. Delivering on our mission requires that we enact the following goals:

- Champion business integrity.
- Build mutually constructive relationships both inside and outside Microsoft.
- Pioneer innovative solutions.
- Protect and promote innovation.

In addition to paralegals and attorneys, the Legal and Corporate Affairs team includes professionals in areas such as government affairs, community affairs, intellectual property and licensing, corporate governance and compliance, and global citizenship. Together we're helping Microsoft to shape the future one relationship at a time.

Altria Group, Inc.

Altria and its operating companies engage with stakeholders in a number of ways. Our employees regularly meet with retailers, growers, suppliers, and adult consumers in the course of doing business. We interact with investors, media, elected officials, community leaders, public health professionals, scientists, and other members of the public who are interested in tobacco issues. We also monitor news reports, attend conferences, survey public opinion and use other means to stay informed about emerging trends and views of our businesses. These discussions have resulted in us taking action to address concerns raised by certain stakeholders.

Pfizer

Colleagues in the Worldwide Public Affairs and Policy division apply their expertise in the areas of government relations, public affairs, policy, philanthropy, stakeholder relations, corporate responsibility, and communications

(continued)

to help create the social and political conditions essential for Pfizer to sustain its industry leadership.

BlueScope Steel (Australia)

BlueScope Steel Corporate Affairs manages BlueScope Steel's corporate relationships with a number of key external stakeholders including media, governments, industry bodies, and other steelmakers. Corporate Affairs produces regular media releases and announcements, and is responsible for managing the production of corporate reports, including the Annual Report and the Community, Safety & Environment Report. Corporate Affairs is also responsible for the management of communications with the company's 21,000+ employees around the globe, including production of the company-wide employee newspaper, *Steel Connections.*

Given the complexity of the external environment in today's economy, strategic planning regarding corporate affairs is every bit as important as developing sound strategy for reaching the organization's customers. No organization exists in isolation. Consequently, all organizations must actively manage their relationships with potential stakeholders to ensure continued success.

plan. This effort will always involve the collection of secondary data, which must be compiled inside or outside the organization for some purpose other than the current analysis. However, if the required data or information are unavailable, primary data may have to be collected through marketing research. Accessing secondary data sources is usually preferable as a first option because these sources can be obtained more quickly and at less cost than collecting primary data. In this section, we will examine the different sources of environmental data and challenges in collecting these data.

Secondary Information Sources

There are four basic sources of secondary data and information: internal, government, periodicals/books, and commercial data sources. Most of these sources are available in both print and electronic formats. Let's look at the major strengths and weaknesses of these sources.

Internal Data Sources   The firm's own records are the best source of data on current objectives, strategy, performance, and available resources. Internal sources may also be a good source of data on customer needs, attitudes, and buying behavior. Internal data also have the advantage of being relevant and believable because the organization itself has responsibility for their collection and organization.

One of the biggest problems with internal data is that they are often not in a readily accessible form for planning purposes. Box after box of printed company records that sit in a warehouse are hardly useful for marketing planning. To overcome this problem, many organizations maintain virtual private networks (VPNs) that make data easily accessible and interactive. These systems enable employees to access internal data such as customer profiles and product inventory, and to share details of their activities and projects with other company employees across the hall or the world. VPNs provide an opportunity for company-wide marketing intelligence that permits coordination and integration of efforts to achieve a true market orientation.

Government Sources   If it exists, the U.S. government has collected data about it. The sheer volume of available information on the economy, our population, and business activities is the major strength of most government data sources. Government sources also have the added advantages of easy accessibility and low cost—most are even free. The major drawback to government data is timeliness. Although many government sources have annual updates, some are done much less frequently (e.g., the census every decade). As a result, some government sources may be out of date and not particularly useful for market planning purposes.

Still, the objectivity and low cost of government sources make them an attractive answer to the data need of many organizations. Some of the best government sources available on the Internet include the following:

- *Federal Trade Commission* (http://www.ftc.gov) provides reports, speeches, and other facts about competitive, antitrust, and consumer protection issues.

- *FedWorld* (http://www.fedworld.gov) offers links to various federal government sources of industry and market statistics.

- *Edgar Database* (http://www.sec.gov/edgarhp.htm) provides comprehensive financial data (10K reports) on public corporations in the United States.

- *U.S. Small Business Administration* (http://www.sba.gov) offers numerous resources for small businesses, including industry reports, maps, market analyses (national, regional, or local), library resources, and checklists.

Book and Periodical Sources   The articles and research reports available in books and periodicals provide a gamut of information about many organizations, industries, and nations. Forget any notion about books and periodicals appearing only in print. Today, many good sources exist only in electronic format. Timeliness is a major strength of these sources, as most are about current environmental trends and business practices. Some sources, such as academic journals, provide detailed results of research studies that may be pertinent to the manager's planning efforts. Others, such as trade publications, focus on specific industries and the issues that characterize them.

Many of these sources are freely available on the Internet. Most, however, require paid subscriptions. Some of the better examples include these:

- Subscription services such as *Moody's* (http://www.moodys.com), *Hoover's* (http://www.hoovers.com), *Standard and Poor's* (http://www.standardandpoors.com/), and *Dismal Scientist* (http://www.dismal.com) offer in-depth analyses and current statistics about major industries and corporations.

- Major trade associations such as the *American Marketing Association* (http://www.marketingpower.com) and *Sales and Marketing Executives* (http://www.smei.org) and trade publications such as *Adweek* (http://www.adweek.com) and *Chain Store Age* (http://www.chainstoreage.com) offer a wide range of news and information to their membership and readers.

- Academic journals, such as the *Harvard Business Review* (http://hbr.org) and the *Sloan Management Review* (http://sloanreview.mit.edu), are good sources of cutting-edge thinking on business and marketing.

- General business publications, such as the *Wall Street Journal* (http://www.wsj.com), *Fortune* (http://www.fortune.com), and *BusinessWeek* (http://www.businessweek.com), offer a wealth of information on a wide variety of industries and companies.

The two biggest drawbacks to book and periodical sources are information overload and relevance to the specific problem at hand. That is, despite the sheer volume of information that is available, finding data or information that pertains to the manager's specific and unique situation can feel like looking for that proverbial needle in a haystack.

Commercial Sources   Commercial sources are almost always relevant to a specific issue because they deal with the actual behaviors of customers in the marketplace. Firms such as Nielsen monitor a variety of behaviors from food purchases in grocery stores, to media usage characteristics. Commercial sources generally charge a fee for their services. However, their data and information are invaluable to many companies. Some commercial sources provide limited information on their websites:

- *The Nielsen Company* (http://www.nielsen.com) and *Information Resources, Inc.* (http://www.infores.com) supply data and reports on point-of-purchase sales.

- *Mediamark Research and Intelligence, Inc.* (http://www.mediamark.com) and *Arbitron* (http://www.arbitron.com) specialize in multimedia audience research by providing a wealth of customer demographic, lifestyle, and product usage data to major media and advertising companies.

- The *Audit Bureau of Circulations* (http://www.accessabc.com) provides independent, third party audits of print circulation, readership and website activity.

- *Surveys.com* (http://www.surveys.com) uses an online consumer panel to provide information to businesses about the products and services they provide.

The most obvious drawback to these and other commercial sources is cost. Although this is not a problem for large organizations, small companies often cannot afford the expense. However, many commercial sources provide limited, free access to some data and information. Additionally, companies often find "off-the-shelf" studies less costly than conducting primary research.

Primary Data Collection

The situation analysis should always begin with an examination of secondary data sources due to their availability and low cost. Because each secondary data source has its advantages and disadvantages, the best approach is one that blends data and information from a variety of sources. However, if the needed secondary data are not available or are out of date, inaccurate or unreliable, or irrelevant to the specific problem at hand, an organization may have little choice but to collect primary data through marketing research. Primary marketing research has the major advantages of being relevant to the specific problem, as well as trustworthy due to the control the manager has over data collection. However, primary research is extremely expensive and time-consuming. There are four major types of primary data collection:

- **Direct observation**, where the researcher records the overt behaviors of customers, competitors, or suppliers in natural settings. Historically, researchers have used direct observation to study the shopping and buying behaviors of customers. However, behavior can be observed today through the use of technology such as bar code scanners, RFID tags, and the analysis of clickstream data in online settings. The main advantage of observation research is that it accurately describes behavior without influencing the target under observation. However, the results of observation research are often overly descriptive and subject to a great deal of bias and researcher interpretation.

- **Focus groups**, where the researcher moderates a panel discussion among a gathering of 6 to 10 people who openly discuss a specific subject. Focus group research is an excellent means of obtaining in-depth information about a particular issue. Its flexibility also allows it to be used in a variety of settings and with different types of panel members (i.e., customers, suppliers, and employees). Focus groups are also very useful in designing a large-scale survey to ensure that questions have the appropriate wording. The main disadvantage is that focus groups require a highly skilled moderator to help limit the potential for moderator bias.

- **Surveys**, where the researcher asks respondents to answer a series of questions on a particular topic. Surveys can be administered using the paper-and-pencil method, either in person or through the mail; or they can be administered interactively via telephone, email, or the Internet. Although surveys are a very useful and time-efficient way to collect primary data, it has become increasingly difficult to convince people to participate. Potential respondents have become skeptical of survey methods due to overly long questionnaires and the unethical practices of many researchers. These concerns are one of the reasons behind the creation of the national Do Not Call Registry for telemarketers (http://www.donotcall.gov).

- **Experiments**, where the researcher selects matched subjects and exposes them to different treatments while controlling for extraneous variables. Because experiments are well suited to testing for cause-and-effect relationships, researchers use them quite often in test marketing programs. Marketers can experiment with different combinations of marketing mix variables to determine which combination has the strongest effect on sales or profitability. The major obstacles to effective experimentation in marketing are the expense and the difficulty of controlling for all extraneous variables in the test.

As with secondary data, often the best approach to primary data collection is to use a combination of data sources. Focus groups and direct observation can be used to gain a more complete understanding of a particular issue or marketing phenomenon. Surveys can then be used to further test for certain tendencies or effects before launching into a full-scale test-marketing program. At this point, the process comes full circle as observation and focus groups can be used to explore the outcomes of the test-marketing program.

Overcoming Problems in Data Collection

Despite the best intentions, problems usually arise in collecting data and information. One of the most common problems is an incomplete or inaccurate assessment of the situation that the gathering of data should address. After expending a great degree of effort in collecting data, the manager may be unsure of the usefulness or relevance of what has been collected. In some cases, the manager might even suffer from severe information overload. To prevent these problems from occurring, the marketing problem must be accurately and specifically defined before the collection of any data. Top managers who do not adequately explain their needs and expectations to marketing researchers often cause the problem.

Another common difficulty is the expense of collecting environmental data. Although there are always costs associated with data collection (even if the data are free), the process need not be prohibitively expensive. The key is to find alternative data collection methods or sources. For example, an excellent way for some businesses to collect data is to engage the cooperation of a local college or university. Many professors seek out marketing projects for their students as a part of course requirements. Likewise, to help overcome data collection costs, many researchers have turned to the Internet as a means of collecting both quantitative and qualitative data on customer opinions and behaviors.

A third issue is the time it takes to collect data and information. Although this is certainly true with respect to primary data collection, the collection of secondary data can be quite easy and fast. Online data sources are quite accessible. Even if the manager has no idea where to begin the search, the powerful search engines and indexes available on the Internet make it easy to find data. Online data sources have become so good at data retrieval that the real problem involves the time needed to sort through all of the available information to find something that is truly relevant.

Finally, it can be challenging to find a way to organize the vast amount of data and information collected during the situation analysis. Clearly defining the marketing problem and blending different data sources are among the first steps toward finding all of the pieces to the puzzle. A critical next step is to convert the data and information into a form that will facilitate strategy development. Although there are a variety of tools that can be used to analyze and organize environmental data and information, one of the most effective of these tools is SWOT analysis. As we will see in the next chapter, SWOT analysis—which involves classifying data and information into strengths, weaknesses, opportunities and threats—can be used to organize data and information and used as a catalyst for strategy formulation.

Lessons from Chapter 4

Collecting and analyzing marketing information through a situation analysis

- Is perhaps the most important task of the marketing manager because practically all decision making and planning depends on how well he or she conducts the analysis.

- Should be an ongoing effort that is well organized, systematic, and supported by sufficient resources.

- Involves analysis and synthesis to understand why people, products, and organizations perform the way they do.

- Is not intended to replace the marketing manager in the decision-making process, but to empower him or her with information for decision making.

- Recognizes that data and information are not the same. Data are not useful until converted into information.

- Forces managers to ask continually, "How much data and information do I need?"

- Is valuable only to the extent that it improves the quality of the resulting decisions. Marketing managers must avoid "paralysis by analysis."

- Should provide as complete a picture as possible about the organization's current and future situation with respect to the internal, customer, and external environments.

Analysis of the internal environment

- Includes an assessment of the firm's current goals, objectives, performance, and how well the current marketing strategy is working.

- Includes a review of the current and anticipated levels of organizational resources.

- Must include a review of current and anticipated cultural and structural issues that could affect marketing activities.

Analysis of the customer environment

- Examines the firm's current customers in its target markets, as well as potential customers that currently do not purchase the firm's product offering.

- Can be conducted by using the expanded 5W model:
  - Who are our current and potential customers?
  - What do customers do with our products?
  - Where do customers purchase our products?
  - When do customers purchase our products?
  - Why (and how) do customers select our products?
  - Why do potential customers not purchase our products?

Analysis of the external environment

- Examines the competitive, economic, political, legal and regulatory, technological, and sociocultural factors in the firm's external environment.
- Includes an examination of the four basic types of competitors faced by all businesses: brand competitors, product competitors, generic competitors, and total budget competitors.
- Is often handled by a team of specialists within an organization's corporate affairs department.

Marketing data and information

- Can be collected from a wide array of internal, government, periodical, book, and commercial sources, as well as through primary marketing research.
- Are often collected through four different types of primary research: direct observation, focus groups, surveys, and experiments.
- Must be blended from many different sources to be the most useful for planning purposes.

Problems that can occur during data collection include

- An incomplete or inaccurate definition of the marketing problem.
- Ambiguity about the usefulness or relevance of the collected data.
- Severe information overload.
- The expense and time associated with data collection.
- Finding ways to organize the vast amount of collected data and information.

Questions for Discussion

1. Of the three major environments in a situation analysis (internal, customer, external), which do you think is the most important in a general sense? Why? What are some situations that would make one environment more important than the others?

2. Understanding the motivations of a firm's noncustomers is often just as important as understanding its customers. Look again at the reasons why an individual would not purchase a firm's products. How can a firm reach out to noncustomers and successfully convert them into customers?

3. Do you think the Internet has made it easier or more difficult to collect marketing data and information? Why? How might the major data collection issues of today compare to the issues that occurred in the pre-Internet era?

Exercises

1. Choose a specific product that you use on a daily basis (such as food items, toiletries, or your car) and apply the 5W model in Exhibit 4.4 to yourself:

    a. Who are you (demographics, psychographics, etc.)?

    b. What do you do with the product (consumption, storage, disposal, etc.)?

    c. Where do you purchase the product? Why?

    d. When do you purchase the product? Why?

    e. Why and how do you select the product?

    f. Why do you not purchase competing products?

    Assume your responses are similar to millions of other consumers. Given this profile, how would you approach the marketing strategy for this particular product?

2. Consider the last purchase you made (maybe it was lunch or a soft drink). List all of the brand, product, generic, and total budget competitors for that product. In a general sense, what would it take for you to switch to another type of competitor? Are there situations that would encourage you to switch to a generic competitor? When would total budget competitors become more relevant to your decision making?

3. Review the sociocultural trends in Exhibit 4.7. What other trends could be added to the list? What trends are specific to your generation that cannot be universally applied to all Americans?

CHAPTER 5

Developing Competitive Advantage and Strategic Focus

Introduction

Situation analysis, as discussed in Chapter 4, can generate a great deal of data and information for marketing planning. But information, in and of itself, provides little direction to managers in preparing a marketing plan. If the analysis does not structure the information in a meaningful way that clarifies both present and anticipated situations, the manager will be unable to see how the pieces fit together. This synthesis of information is critical in developing competitive advantages and the strategic focus of the marketing plan. As illustrated in *Beyond the Pages 5.1*, this synthesis often comes from enhanced innovation, a stronger focus on customer needs, and tighter integration within the firm. Understanding the connectedness of the external environment is vital to enhanced innovation across a number of industries.

How should the marketing manager organize and use the information collected during the situation analysis? One widely used tool is SWOT analysis (strengths and weaknesses, opportunities and threats). A SWOT analysis encompasses both the internal and external environments of the firm. Internally, the framework addresses a firm's strengths and weaknesses on key dimensions such as financial performance and resources, human resources, production facilities and capacity, market share, customer perceptions, product quality, product availability, and organizational communication. The assessment of the external environment organizes information on the market (customers and competition), economic conditions, social trends, technology, and government regulations.

Many consider SWOT analysis to be one of the most effective tools in the analysis of marketing data and information. SWOT analysis is a simple, straightforward framework that provides direction and serves as a catalyst for the development of viable marketing plans. It fulfills this role by structuring the assessment of the fit between what a firm can and cannot do (strengths and weaknesses), and the environmental conditions working for and against the firm (opportunities and threats). When performed correctly, a SWOT analysis not only organizes data and information, it can be especially useful in uncovering competitive advantages that can be leveraged

Beyond the Pages 5.1

INNOVATION: THE KEY TO SUCCESS?[1]

Innovation is the buzzword of business in the twenty-first century. Of course, innovation has always been important, especially with respect to developing new products. What has changed, however, is the focus of innovation in most companies. The twentieth-century model of innovation was about quality control, cost cutting, and operational efficiency. Today, innovation is more about reinventing business processes, collaborating and integrating within the firm, and creating entirely new markets to meet untapped customer needs. Increasing globalization, the growth of the Internet, and more demanding customers are forcing marketers to find innovative ways of conducting business.

An important lesson that many companies have learned is that innovation is not always about technology or offering the latest gee-whiz product. Differences in innovation style are apparent in *BusinessWeek*'s most recent list of the World's Most Innovative Companies. The top 15 companies on the list include both cultural icons and manufacturing giants (U.S. companies except where noted):

Rank	Company	Revenue Growth 2005–2008	Stock Returns 2005–2008
1.	Apple	30.4%	5.9%
2.	Google	52.6%	-9.5%
3.	Toyota (Japan)	4.2%	-20.7%
4.	Microsoft	13.5%	-8.0%
5.	Nintendo (Japan)	61.1%	36.7%
6.	IBM	4.4%	2.3%
7.	Hewlett-Packard	10.9%	9.1%
8.	Research in Motion (Canada)	74.1%	24.6%
9.	Nokia (Finland)	14.0%	-8.3%
10.	Walmart	9.1%	8.0%
11.	Amazon	31.2%	2.8%
12.	Procter & Gamble	11.7%	4.5%
13.	Tata Group (India)	Private	Private
14.	Sony (Japan)	3.1%	-25.5%
15.	Reliance Industries (India)	28.5%	22.6%

Several types of innovation are evident in this list. For example, in launching the iPod, iPhone, and the App Store, Apple combined innovations in product design, branding, strategic alliances, and business model to create a cultural phenomenon. Innovation at Google is based on applications such as Google Voice and Google Docs that are not related to its ubiquitous search engine. Toyota makes the list due to relentless manufacturing expertise, tight integration within the firm, and advancements in hybrid technology with its Prius. At Nintendo, innovation is all about the gaming experience on the Wii and the DSi handheld system. At Research in Motion, it's about the Blackberry and its advances in wireless corporate email.

One thing that all innovative companies have in common is a laser-like focus on customer needs. Innovative companies find new ways of learning from customers in addition to traditional methods. For example, many companies closely watch blogs and online communities to learn what customers are thinking. Focusing on customers may not sound innovative, but increasing competition and shorter product cycles are forcing marketers to shift away from the price- and efficiency-driven approaches of the past. To escape from commodity hell, marketers must find innovation in unfamiliar places. For example, BMW (number 20 on the list) finds innovation in product design by relocating hundreds of employees from across the globe to a central design studio. Another example is the chewing gum industry. Wrigley has launched Airwaves (a wellness gum that contains vitamins and other ingredients that boost the immune system) and Orbit White (a tooth-whitening gum). Likewise, GumRunners has licensed the Jolt brand to launch a caffeinated gum to capitalize on the increasing popularity of energy drinks.

As reflected in the table, innovation is obviously good for the bottom line. Through increased growth, better collaboration, and a broader product mix, the most innovative companies are able to pull their products out of commodity status and increase their operating revenue. It is clear that innovation has become a key driver of competitive advantage and success in today's market.

in the firm's marketing strategy. These competitive advantages help establish the strategic focus and direction of the firm's marketing plan.

As a planning tool, SWOT analysis has many benefits, as outlined in Exhibit 5.1. In fact, SWOT analysis is so useful and logical that many underestimate its value in planning. However, this simplicity often leads to unfocused and poorly conducted analyses.[2] The most common criticisms leveled against SWOT analysis are that (1) it allows firms to create lists without serious consideration of the issues, and (2) it often becomes a sterile academic exercise of classifying data and information. It is important to remember that SWOT analysis, by itself, is not inherently productive or unproductive. Rather, the way that one uses SWOT analysis will determine whether it yields benefits for the firm.

Making SWOT Analysis Productive

Whether a firm receives the full benefits of SWOT analysis depends on the way the manager uses the framework. If done correctly and smartly, SWOT analysis can be a viable mechanism for the development of the marketing plan. If done haphazardly or

---

EXHIBIT 5.1   **MAJOR BENEFITS OF SWOT ANALYSIS**

Simplicity

SWOT analysis requires no extensive training or technical skills to be used successfully. The analyst needs only a comprehensive understanding of the nature of the company and the industry in which it competes.

Lower Costs

Because specialized training and skills are not necessary, the use of SWOT analysis can actually reduce the costs associated with strategic planning. As firms begin to recognize this benefit of SWOT analysis, many opt to downsize or eliminate their strategic planning departments.

Flexibility

SWOT analysis can enhance the quality of an organization's strategic planning even without extensive marketing information systems. However, when comprehensive systems are present, they can be structured to feed information directly into the SWOT framework. The presence of a comprehensive information system can make repeated SWOT analyses run more smoothly and efficiently.

Integration and Synthesis

SWOT analysis gives the analyst the ability to integrate and synthesize diverse information, both of a quantitative and a qualitative nature. It organizes information that is widely known, as well as information that has only recently been acquired or discovered. SWOT analysis can also deal with a wide diversity of information sources. In fact, SWOT analysis helps transform information diversity from a weakness of the planning process into one of its major strengths.

Collaboration

SWOT analysis fosters collaboration and open information exchange between different functional areas. By learning what their counterparts do, what they know, what they think, and how they feel, the marketing analyst can solve problems, fill voids in the analysis, and eliminate potential disagreements before the finalization of the marketing plan.

incorrectly, it can be a great waste of time and other valuable resources. To help ensure that the former, and not the latter, takes place, we offer the following directives to make SWOT analysis more productive and useful. Exhibit 5.2 outlines these directives.

Stay Focused

Marketing planners often make the mistake of conducting one generic SWOT analysis for the entire organization or business unit. Such an approach produces stale, meaningless generalizations that come from the tops of managers' heads or from press release files. Although this type of effort may make managers feel good and provide a quick sense of accomplishment, it does little to add to the creativity and vision of the planning process.

When we say SWOT analysis, we really mean SWOT *analyses*. In most firms, there should be a series of analyses, each focusing on a specific product/market combination. For example, a single SWOT analysis for the Chevrolet division of General Motors would not be focused enough to be meaningful. Instead, separate analyses for each product category (passenger cars, trucks, SUVs) or brand (Corvette, Impala, Avalanche, Tahoe) in the division would be more appropriate. Such a focus enables

---

EXHIBIT 5.2   DIRECTIVES FOR A PRODUCTIVE SWOT ANALYSIS

Stay Focused

A single, broad analysis leads to meaningless generalizations. Separate analyses for each product–market combination are recommended.

Search Extensively for Competitors

Although major brand competitors are the most important, the analyst must not overlook product, generic, and total budget competitors. Potential future competitors must also be considered.

Collaborate with Other Functional Areas

SWOT analysis promotes the sharing of information and perspective across departments. This cross-pollination of ideas allows for more creative and innovative solutions to marketing problems.

Examine Issues from the Customers' Perspective

Customers' beliefs about the firm, its products, and marketing activities are important considerations in SWOT analysis. The views of employees and other key stakeholders must also be considered.

Look for Causes, Not Characteristics

Rather than simply list characteristics of the firm's internal and external environments, the analyst must also explore the resources possessed by the firm and/or its competitors that are the true causes for the firm's strengths, weaknesses, opportunities, and threats.

Separate Internal Issues from External Issues

If an issue would exist even if the firm did not exist, the issue should be classified as external. In the SWOT framework, opportunities (and threats) exist independently of the firm and are associated with characteristics or situations present in the economic, customer, competitive, cultural, technological, political, or legal environments in which the firm resides. Marketing options, strategies, or tactics are not a part of the SWOT analysis.

SWOT analysis requires a careful investigation of many internal and external issues.

the marketing manager to look at the specific mix of competitors, customers, and external factors that are present in a given market. Chevrolet's Tahoe, for example, competes in the crowded SUV market where competitors release new models and competing crossover vehicles at a staggering pace. Consequently, market planning for the Tahoe should differ substantially from market planning for Chevrolet's Corvette. If needed, separate product/market analyses can be combined to examine the issues relevant for the entire strategic business unit, and business unit analyses can be combined to create a complete SWOT analysis for the entire organization. The only time a single SWOT analysis would be appropriate is when an organization has only one product/market combination.

Search Extensively for Competitors

Information on competitors and their activities is an important aspect of a well-focused SWOT analysis. The key is not to overlook any competitor, whether a current rival or one on the horizon. As we discussed in Chapter 4, the firm will focus most of its efforts on brand competition. During the SWOT analysis, however, the firm must watch for any current or potential direct substitutes for its products. Product, generic, and total budget competitors are important as well. Looking for all four types of competition is crucial because many firms and managers never look past brand competitors. Although it is important for the SWOT analysis to be focused, it must not be myopic.

Even industry giants can lose sight of their potential competitors by focusing exclusively on brand competition. Kodak, for example, had always taken steps to maintain its market dominance over rivals Fuji, Konica, and Polaroid in the film industry. However, the advent of digital photography added Sony, Nikon, and Canon to Kodak's set of competing firms. And as digital cameras have become integrated into wireless phones, Kodak must now add Motorola, LG, Samsung, Apple, and Nokia to its competitive set. A similar trend has occurred in financial services as deregulation has allowed brokers, banks, and insurance firms to compete in each other's traditional markets. State Farm, for example, offers mortgage loans, credit cards, mutual funds, and traditional banking services alongside its well-known insurance products. This shift has forced firms such as Charles Schwab and Wells Fargo to look at insurance companies in a different light.

Collaborate with Other Functional Areas

One of the major benefits of SWOT analysis is that it generates information and perspectives that can be shared across a variety of functional areas in the firm. The SWOT process should be a powerful stimulus for communication outside normal channels. The final outcome of a properly conducted SWOT analysis should be a fusion of information from many areas. Managers in sales, advertising, production, research and development, finance, customer service, inventory control, quality control, and other areas should learn what other managers see as the firm's strengths, weaknesses, opportunities, and threats. This allows the marketing manager to come to terms with multiple perspectives before actually creating the marketing plan.

When combining the SWOT analyses from individual areas, the marketing manager can identify opportunities for joint projects and cross selling of the firm's products. In a large firm, the first time a SWOT takes place may be the initial point at which managers from some areas have ever formally communicated with each other. Such cross-pollination can generate a very conducive environment for creativity and innovation. Moreover, research has shown that the success of introducing a new product, especially a radically new product, is extremely dependent on the ability of different functional areas to collaborate and integrate their differing perspectives. For example, every time BMW develops a new car, they relocate 200 to 300 engineering, design, production, marketing, and finance employees from their worldwide locations to the company's research and innovation center. For up to three years, these employees work alongside BMW's research and development team in a manner that speeds communication and car development.[3]

Examine Issues from the Customers' Perspective

In the initial stages of SWOT analysis, it is important to identify issues exhaustively. However, all issues are not equally important with respect to developing competitive advantages and strategic focus for the marketing plan. As the analysis progresses, the marketing manager should identify the most critical issues by looking at each one through the eyes of the firm's customers. To do this, the manager must constantly ask questions such as these:

- What do customers (and noncustomers) believe about us as a company?

- What do customers (and noncustomers) think of our product quality, customer service, price and overall value, convenience, and promotional messages in comparison to our competitors?

- Which of our weaknesses translate into a decreased ability to serve customers (and decreased ability to convert noncustomers)?

- How do trends in the external environment affect customers (and noncustomers)?

- What is the relative importance of these issues, not as we see them but as customers see them?

Marketing planners must also gauge the perceptions of each customer segment that the firm attempts to target. For example, older banking customers, due to their reluctance to use ATMs and online banking services, may have vastly different perceptions of a bank's convenience than younger customers. Each customer segment's perceptions of external issues, such as the economy or the environment, are also important. It matters little, for example, that managers think the economic outlook is positive if customers have curbed their spending because they think the economy is weak.

Examining issues from the customers' perspective also includes the firm's internal customers: its employees. The fact that management perceives the firm as offering competitive compensation and benefits is unimportant. The real issue is what the employees think. Employees are also a valuable source of information on strengths, weaknesses, opportunities, and threats that management may have never considered. Some employees, especially frontline employees, are closer to the customer and can offer a different perspective on what customers think and believe. Other key stakeholders, such as investors, the general public, and government officials, should also be considered. The key is to examine every issue from the most relevant perspective. Exhibit 5.3 illustrates how taking the customers' perspective can help managers interpret the clichés they might develop, and then break them down into meaningful customer-oriented strengths and weaknesses.

Taking the customers' perspective is a cornerstone of a well-done SWOT analysis. Managers have a natural tendency to see issues the way they think they are (e.g., "We offer a high quality product"). SWOT analysis forces managers to change their perceptions to the way customers and other important groups see things (e.g., "The product offers weak value given its price and features as compared to the strongest brand competitor"). The contrast between these two perspectives often leads to the identification of a gap between management's version of reality and customers' perceptions. As the planning process moves ahead, managers must reduce or eliminate this gap and determine whether their views of the firm are realistic.

EXHIBIT 5.3   **BREAKING DOWN MANAGERIAL CLICHÉS INTO CUSTOMER-ORIENTED STRENGTHS AND WEAKNESSES**

Cliché	Potential Strengths	Potential Weaknesses
"We are an established firm."	Stable after-sales service Experienced Trustworthy	Old-fashioned Inflexible Weak innovation
"We are a large supplier."	Comprehensive product line Technical expertise Longevity Strong reputation	Bureaucratic Focused only on large accounts Impersonal Weak customer service
"We have a comprehensive product line."	Wide variety and availability One-stop supplier Convenient Customized solutions	Shallow assortment Cannot offer hard-to-find products Limited in-depth product expertise
"We are the industry standard."	Wide product adoption High status and image Good marketing leverage Extensive third-party support	Vulnerable to technological changes Limited view of competition Higher prices (weaker value)

Source: Adapted from Nigel Piercy, *Market-Led Strategic Change* (Oxford, UK: Butterworth-Heineman, 2002).

Look for Causes, Not Characteristics

Although taking the customers' perspective is important, it often provides just enough information to get you into serious trouble. That is, it provides a level of detail that is often very descriptive, but not very constructive. The problem lies in listing strengths, weaknesses, opportunities, and threats as simple descriptions or characteristics of the firm's internal and external environments without going deeper to consider the causes for these characteristics. Although the customers' perspective is quite valuable, customers do not see behind the scenes to understand the reasons for a firm's characteristics. More often than not, the causes for each issue in a SWOT analysis can be found in the resources possessed by the firm and/or its competitors.

From a resource-based viewpoint, every organization can be considered as a unique bundle of tangible and intangible resources. Major types of these resources include the following:[4]

- **Financial Resources**—cash, access to financial markets, physical facilities, equipment, raw materials, systems and configurations

- **Intellectual Resources**—expertise, discoveries, creativity, innovation

- **Legal Resources**—patents, trademarks, contracts

- **Human Resources**—employee expertise and skills, leadership

- **Organizational Resources**—culture, customs, shared values, vision, routines, working relationships, processes and systems

- **Informational Resources**—customer intelligence, competitive intelligence, marketing information systems

- **Relational Resources**—strategic alliances, relations with customers, vendors, and other stakeholders, bargaining power, switching costs

- **Reputational Resources**—brand names, symbols, image, reputation

The availability or lack of these resources are the causes for the firm's strengths and weaknesses in meeting customers' needs, and determine which external conditions represent opportunities and threats. For example, Walmart's strength in low-cost distribution and logistics comes from its combined resources in terms of distribution, information, and communication infrastructure, as well as strong relationships with vendors. Likewise, 3M's strength in product innovation is the result of combined financial, intellectual, legal, organizational, and informational resources. These resources not only give Walmart and 3M strengths or advantages in serving customers, they also create imposing threats for their competitors.

Separate Internal Issues from External Issues

For the results of a SWOT analysis to be truly beneficial, we have seen that the analyst must go beyond simple descriptions of internal and external characteristics to explore the resources that are the foundation for these characteristics. It is equally important, however, for the analyst to maintain a separation between internal issues and external issues. Internal issues are the firm's strengths and weaknesses, whereas external issues refer to opportunities and threats in the firm's external environments. The key test to differentiate a strength or weakness from an opportunity or threat is to ask, "Would this issue exist if the firm did not exist?" If the answer is yes, the issue should be classified as external to the firm.

At first glance, the distinction between internal and external issues seems simplistic and immaterial. However, the failure to understand the difference between internal and external issues is one of the major reasons for a poorly conducted SWOT analysis. This happens because managers tend to get ahead of themselves and list their marketing options or strategies as opportunities. For example, a manager might state that the firm has "an opportunity to move into global markets." However, such a move is a strategy or action that the firm might take to expand market share. In the SWOT framework, opportunities (and threats) exist independently of the firm and are associated with characteristics or situations present in the economic, customer, competitive, cultural, technological, political, or legal environments in which the firm resides. For example, an opportunity in this case could be "increasing customer demand for U.S. products" or that "a competitor recently pulled out of the foreign market." Once the opportunities (and threats) are known, the manager's options, strategies, or tactics should be based on what the firm intends to do about its opportunities and threats relative to its own strengths and weaknesses. The development of these strategic options occurs at a later point within the marketing plan framework.

In summary, a SWOT analysis should be directed by Socrates' advice: "Know thyself." This knowledge should be realistic, based on how customers (external and internal) and other key stakeholders see the company, and viewed in terms of the firm's resources. If managers find it difficult to make an honest and realistic assessment of these issues, they should recognize the need to bring in outside experts or consultants to oversee the process.

SWOT-Driven Strategic Planning

As we discussed in Chapter 4, the collection of marketing information via a situation analysis identifies the key factors that should be tracked by the firm and organizes them within a system that will monitor and distribute information on these factors on an ongoing basis. This process feeds into and helps define the boundaries of a SWOT analysis that will be used as a catalyst for the development of the firm's marketing plan. The role of SWOT analysis then is to help the marketing manager make the transition from a broad understanding of the marketing environment to the development of a strategic focus for the firm's marketing efforts. The potential issues that can be considered in a SWOT analysis are numerous and will vary depending on the particular firm or industry being examined. To aid your search for relevant issues, we have provided a list of potential strengths, weaknesses, opportunities, and threats in Exhibit 5.4. This list is not exhaustive, as these items illustrate only a handful of potential issues that may arise in a SWOT analysis.

EXHIBIT 5.4   **POTENTIAL ISSUES TO CONSIDER IN A SWOT ANALYSIS**

Potential Internal Strengths

- Abundant financial resources
- Well-known brand name
- Number 1 ranking in the industry
- Economies of scale
- Proprietary technology
- Patented processes
- Lower costs (raw materials or processes)
- Respected company/product/brand image
- Superior management talent
- Better marketing skills
- Superior product quality
- Alliances with other firms
- Good distribution skills
- Committed employees

Potential Internal Weaknesses

- Lack of strategic direction
- Limited financial resources
- Weak spending on research and development
- Very narrow product line
- Limited distribution
- Higher costs (raw materials or processes)
- Out-of-date products or technology
- Internal operating problems
- Internal political problems
- Weak market image
- Poor marketing skills
- Alliances with weak firms
- Limited management skills
- Undertrained employees

Potential External Opportunities

- Rapid market growth
- Complacent rival firms
- Changing customer needs/tastes
- Opening of foreign markets
- Mishap of a rival firm
- New product discoveries
- Economic boom
- Government deregulation
- New technology
- Demographic shifts
- Other firms seeking alliances
- High brand switching
- Sales decline for a substitute product
- Changing distribution methods

Potential External Threats

- Entry of foreign competitors
- Introduction of new substitute products
- Product life cycle in decline
- Changing customer needs/tastes
- Declining consumer confidence
- Rival firms adopting new strategies
- Increased government regulation
- Economic downturn
- Change in Federal Reserve policy
- New technology
- Demographic shifts
- Foreign trade barriers
- Poor performance of ally firm
- International political turmoil
- Weakening currency exchange rates

Strengths and Weaknesses

Relative to market needs and competitors' characteristics, the marketing manager must begin to think in terms of what the firm can do well and where it may have deficiencies. Strengths and weaknesses exist either because of resources possessed (or not possessed) by the firm, or in the nature of the relationships between the firm and its customers, its employees, or outside organizations (e.g., supply chain partners, suppliers, lending institutions, government agencies, etc.). Given that SWOT analysis must be customer focused to gain maximum benefit, strengths are meaningful only when they serve to satisfy a customer need. When this is the case, that strength becomes a capability.[5] The marketing manager can then develop marketing strategies that leverage these capabilities in the form of strategic competitive advantages.

At the same time, the manager can develop strategies to overcome the firm's weaknesses or find ways to minimize the negative effects of these weaknesses.

A great example of strengths and weaknesses in action occurs in the U.S. airline industry. As a whole, the industry was in trouble even before September 11, 2001. Big carriers—such as American, Delta, Northwest, and US Airways—have strengths in terms of sheer size, passenger volume, and marketing muscle. However, they suffer from a number of weaknesses related to internal efficiency, labor relations, and business models that cannot compensate for changes in customer preferences. These weaknesses are especially dramatic when compared to low-cost airlines such as Southwest, Allegiant Air, AirTran, and JetBlue. Initially, these carriers offered low-cost service in routes ignored by the big carriers. Their strengths in terms of internal efficiency, flexible operations, and lower cost equipment gave low-cost carriers a major advantage with respect to cost economies. The differences in operating expenses per available seat mile (an industry benchmark) are eye opening: Allegiant (9.1¢), AirTran (10.0¢), JetBlue (10.2¢), Southwest (10.5¢), and Frontier (11.2¢) versus American (14.6¢), Delta (15.9¢), United (16.7¢), and US Airways (18.8¢). The ability of low-cost carriers to operate more efficiently and at reduced costs has changed the way customers look at air travel. Today, most customers see air travel as a commodity product, with price being the only real distinguishing feature among competing brands. As a result, many analysts predict that the internal operating weaknesses of the major air carriers will lead to additional mergers or their cessation of operations over the next five years.[6]

Opportunities and Threats

In leveraging strengths to create capabilities and competitive advantages, the marketing manager must be mindful of trends and situations in the external environment. Stressing internal strengths while ignoring external issues can lead to an organization that, although efficient, cannot adapt when external changes either enhance or impede the firm's ability to serve the needs of its customers. Opportunities and threats exist outside the firm, independently of internal strengths, weaknesses, or marketing options. Opportunities and threats typically occur within the competitive, customer, economic, political/legal, technological, and/or sociocultural environments. After identifying opportunities and threats, the manager can develop strategies to take advantage of opportunities and minimize or overcome the firm's threats.

Market opportunities can come from many sources. For example, when founder Howard Schultz first envisioned the idea of Starbucks in 1983, he never dreamed that his idea would create an entire industry. Schultz was on a trip to Milan, Italy, when he first conceived of a chain of American coffee bars. At that time, there was essentially no competition in coffee, as most consumers considered it a commodity. He knew that the demand for coffee was high, as it is only second to water in terms of consumption around the world. However, the U.S. coffee market was largely found on grocery store

Starbucks founder Howard Schultz seized an open market opportunity and forever changed the coffee industry.

shelves and in restaurants. In fact, only 200 coffeehouses existed in the United States when Starbucks began its expansion. This clear lack of competition gave Schultz the impetus to take Starbucks from its humble Seattle, Washington, beginnings to the rest of the world. Today there are almost 16,000 Starbucks coffeehouses around the world—71 percent of them are in the United States. Coffee is now a cultural phenomenon, as there are thousands of coffeehouses in the United States today, most being mom-and-pop businesses that piggyback on Starbucks' success. Starbucks customers eagerly spend $3 for a cup of coffee, but they get more than a mere drink. Starbucks is a place to meet friends, talk business, listen to music, or just relax. Starbucks' popularity has spread to grocery store shelves, where the brand is now a major threat to traditional in-store competitors. The combination of an obvious market opportunity and Schultz's idea has forever changed the worldwide coffee market.[7]

The SWOT Matrix

As we consider how a firm can use its strengths, weaknesses, opportunities, and threats to drive the development of its marketing plan, remember that SWOT analysis is designed to synthesize a wide array of information and aid the transition to the firm's strategic focus. To address these issues properly, the marketing manager should appraise every strength, weakness, opportunity, and threat to determine their total impact on the firm's marketing efforts. To utilize SWOT analysis successfully, the marketing manager must be cognizant of four issues:[8]

1. The assessment of strengths and weaknesses must look beyond the firm's resources and product offering(s) to examine processes that are key to meeting customers' needs. This often entails offering "solutions" to customers' problems, rather than specific products.

2. The achievement of the firm's goals and objectives depends on its ability to create capabilities by matching its strengths with market opportunities. Capabilities become competitive advantages if they provide better value to customers than competing offerings.

3. Firms can often convert weaknesses into strengths or even capabilities by investing strategically in key areas (e.g., customer support, research and development, supply chain efficiency, employee training). Likewise, threats can often be converted into opportunities if the right resources are available.

4. Weaknesses that cannot be converted into strengths become the firm's limitations. Limitations that are obvious and meaningful to customers or other stakeholders must be minimized through effective strategic choices.

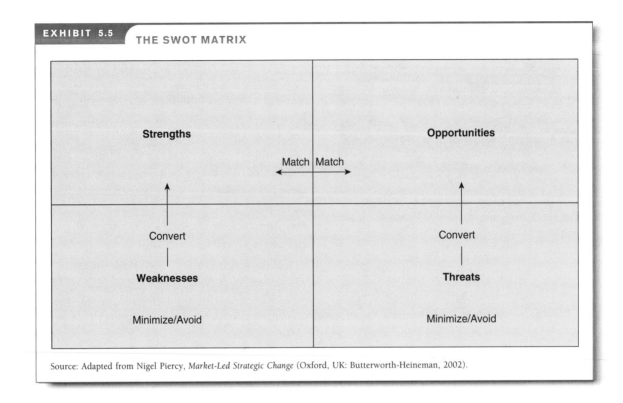

EXHIBIT 5.5   **THE SWOT MATRIX**

Source: Adapted from Nigel Piercy, *Market-Led Strategic Change* (Oxford, UK: Butterworth-Heineman, 2002).

One useful method of conducting this assessment is to visualize the analysis via a SWOT matrix. Exhibit 5.5 provides an example of this four-cell array that can be used to visually evaluate each element of a SWOT analysis. At this point, the manager must evaluate the issues within each cell of the matrix in terms of their magnitude and importance. As we have stated before, this evaluation should ideally be based on customers' perceptions. If customers' perceptions cannot be gathered, the manager should base the ratings on the input of employees, business partners, or his or her own intuition and expertise.

It is not mandatory that the SWOT matrix be assessed quantitatively, but it can be informative to do so. Exhibit 5.6 illustrates how this assessment might be conducted using information from the marketing plan example in Appendix B. The first step is to quantify the magnitude of each element within the matrix. Magnitude refers to how strongly each element affects the firm. A simple method is to use a scale of 1 (low magnitude), 2 (medium magnitude), or 3 (high magnitude) for each strength and opportunity, and –1 (low magnitude), –2 (medium magnitude), or –3 (high magnitude) for each weakness and threat. The second step is to rate the importance of each element using a scale of 1 (weak importance), 2 (average importance), or 3 (major importance) for all elements in the matrix. The final step is to multiply the magnitude ratings by the importance ratings to create a total rating for each element. Remember that the magnitude and importance ratings should be heavily influenced by customer perceptions, not just the perceptions of the manager.

EXHIBIT 5.6   **QUANTITATIVE ASSESSMENT OF THE SWOT MATRIX**

This analysis was conducted for the marketing plan example that appears in Appendix B. The ratings in each cell have their basis in a thorough analysis of the company and the industry.

Strengths	M	I	R	Opportunities	M	I	R
BOPREX approved to treat arthritis, migraine headache, and general pain	3	3	9	FDA has approved the transition of prescription NSAIDs into OTC market	3	3	9
Patent exclusivity for three years	3	3	9	Consumers will try new products as they become available	3	3	9
New product entry	3	2	6	NSAIDs can be used as general pain reliever and fever reducer	3	3	9
Prescription-strength pain relief available OTC	3	2	6	Potential market channels not currently exploited	3	3	9
Effective migraine treatment	3	2	6	Competing prescription pain relievers have been pulled from the market	3	2	6
Talented and motivated workforce	2	2	4	Weak product differentiation among OTC competitors	3	2	6
Lower cost of raw materials	3	1	3	U.S. population is increasingly seeking convenience of online shopping	2	3	6
Wide range of products	1	2	2	Increase in aging population	2	2	4
Weaknesses	**M**	**I**	**R**	**Threats**	**M**	**I**	**R**
Limited marketing budget	−3	3	−9	Competition from both prescription pain relievers and OTC pain relievers	−3	3	−9
Market position (number 6 in market)	−3	3	−9	Extremely crowded OTC market	−3	3	−9
Weak product differentiation	−3	3	−9	Consumer loyalty with existing competitors	−3	2	−6
Current brand name (new to market)	−3	2	−6	Negative publicity regarding NSAIDs	−2	3	−6
Mid-sized company	−2	2	−4	Declining physician recommendation of NSAIDs	−1	3	−3
BOPREX associated with gastrointestinal side effects	−1	3	−3	OTC NSAIDs not indicated for long-term use	−1	2	−2
Variability in offshore suppliers	−1	2	−2	Regulations on drug advertisements could intensify	−1	2	−2

M = magnitude of the element, I = importance of the element, R = total rating of the element.
Magnitude scale ranges from 1 (low magnitude) to 3 (high magnitude).
Importance scale ranges from 1 (low importance) to 3 (high importance).

Those elements with the highest total ratings (positive or negative) should have the greatest influence in developing the marketing strategy. A sizable strength in an important area must certainly be emphasized in order to convert it into a capability or competitive advantage. On the other hand, a fairly small and insignificant opportunity should not play a central role in the planning process. The magnitude and importance of opportunities and threats will vary depending on the particular product or market. For example, a dramatic increase in new housing starts would be very important for the lumber, mortgage, or real estate industries, but inconsequential for industries involving semiconductors or telecommunications. In this example, the magnitude of the opportunity would be the same for all industries; however, the importance ratings would differ across industries.

Developing and Leveraging Competitive Advantages

After the magnitude and importance of each element in the SWOT matrix have been assessed, the manager should focus on identifying competitive advantages by matching strengths to opportunities. The key strengths most likely to be converted into capabilities will be those that have a compatibility with important and sizable opportunities. Remember that capabilities that allow a firm to serve customers' needs better than the competition give it a competitive advantage. As outlined in Exhibit 5.7, competitive advantages can arise from many internal or external sources.

When we refer to competitive advantages, we usually speak in terms of real differences between competing firms. After all, competitive advantages stem from real strengths possessed by the firm or real weaknesses possessed by rival firms. However,

---

EXHIBIT 5.7   COMMON SOURCES OF COMPETITIVE ADVANTAGE

Relational Advantages

- Brand-loyal customers
- High customer-switching costs
- Long-term relationships with supply chain partners
- Strategic alliance agreements
- Comarketing or cobranding agreements
- Tight coordination and integration with supply chain partners
- Strong bargaining power

Legal Advantages

- Patents and trademarks
- Strong and beneficial contracts
- Tax advantages
- Zoning laws
- Global trade restrictions
- Government subsidies

Organizational Advantages

- Abundant financial resources
- Modern plant and equipment
- Effective competitor and customer intelligence systems
- Culture, vision, and shared goals
- Strong organizational goodwill

Human Resource Advantages

- Superior management talent
- Strong organizational culture
- Access to skilled labor
- Committed employees
- World-class employee training

Product Advantages

- Brand equity and brand name
- Exclusive products
- Superior quality or features
- Production expertise
- Guarantees and warranties
- Outstanding customer service
- Research and development
- Superior product image

Pricing Advantages

- Lower production costs
- Economies of scale
- Large-volume buying
- Low-cost distribution
- Bargaining power with vendors

Promotion Advantages

- Company image
- Large promotion budget
- Superior sales force
- Creativity
- Extensive marketing expertise

Distribution Advantages

- Efficient distribution system
- Real-time inventory control
- Extensive supply chain integration
- Superior information systems
- Exclusive distribution outlets
- Convenient locations
- Strong e-commerce capabilities

competitive advantages can also be based more on perception than reality. For example, Apple's iPod dominates the market for portable media players despite the fact that competing products from Toshiba, iRiver, Microsoft, and Creative typically match the iPod in terms of features and performance. Customers who are unaware of better players (or those that simply don't care) buy the iPod because of its slick image, integration with iTunes, and the availability of third-party accessories. Because consumers maintain the perception that the iPod is better than competing products, competing products have a difficult time breaking through.[9]

Effectively managing customers' perceptions has been a challenge for marketers for generations. The problem lies in developing and maintaining capabilities and competitive advantages that customers can easily understand and that solve their specific needs. Capabilities or competitive advantages that do not translate into specific benefits for customers are of little use to a firm. In recent years, many successful firms have developed capabilities and competitive advantages based on one of three basic strategies: operational excellence, product leadership, and customer intimacy:

- **Operational Excellence** Firms employing a strategy of operational excellence focus on efficiency of operations and processes. These firms operate at lower costs than their competitors, allowing them to deliver goods and services to their customers at lower prices or a better value. Low-cost airlines, like JetBlue and Southwest Airlines, are a prime example of operational excellence in action. Southwest's no-frills service and use of nearly identical Boeing 737 aircraft keep operating costs quite low compared to other air carriers. Other firms that employ operational excellence include Dell and Walmart.[10]

- **Product Leadership** Firms that focus on product leadership excel at technology and product development. As a result, these firms offer customers the most advanced, highest quality goods and services in the industry. For example, Microsoft, which dominates the market for personal computer operating systems and office productivity suites, continues to upgrade and stretch the technology underlying its software, while creating complementary products that solve customers' needs. Pfizer, Intel, and 3M are other examples of companies that pursue a product leadership strategy. *Beyond the Pages 5.2* explains some of the secrets to 3M's product leadership success.

- **Customer Intimacy** Working to know your customers and understand their needs better than the competition is the hallmark of customer intimacy. These firms attempt to develop long-term relationships with customers by seeking their input on how to make the firm's goods and services better or how to solve specific customer problems. Nordstrom, for example, organizes its store layout by fashion and lifestyle rather than by merchandise categories. The company offers high quality products with impeccable customer service. In fact, Nordstrom is consistently ranked tops in customer service among all retail chains.[11] Other firms that pursue customer intimacy include Amazon, DHL, and Ritz-Carlton.

Beyond the Pages 5.2

SUCCESSFUL PRODUCT LEADERSHIP AT 3M[12]

Most people know that 3M is the maker of everyday items such as Post-It Notes and Scotch Tape. Some might know that 3M makes other products such as O-Cel-O sponges, Clarity braces (for teeth), and Littmann stethoscopes. What most people don't know about 3M, however, is that the company has been developing innovative products like these for over 107 years. After all that time, what is most amazing about 3M is that the company's appetite for product innovation has never waned.

3M (Minnesota Mining and Manufacturing) began as an abrasives maker in 1902. However, the company didn't become well-known until the invention of masking tape in 1925. Even then, the company didn't become a household name until the invention of Post-It Notes in 1980. Today, the company sells an expansive line of Scotch tape products and has innovated Post-It into picture paper and index cards.

What is 3M's secret to successful product leadership? When Larry Wendling, former vice-president of 3M's corporate research labs was asked that question, he summed up the company's success based on a list of seven key factors:

1. **Commitment to Innovation**—Every employee, from the CEO down, is firmly committed to innovation. 3M backs up this commitment with massive spending on R&D: over $1 billion per year or 6 percent of its total revenue.

2. **Active Maintenance of the Corporate Culture**—Probably the main factor in 3M's success, the company's culture is based on hiring good people, giving them the freedom to do their work, and tolerating mistakes. A common characteristic of highly innovative companies is that they tolerate failure and try to learn from it.

3. **Broad Base of Underlying Technology**—Having a diverse expertise across many different technologies allows 3M to apply ideas from one area of the company to another. This is one of the secrets to why 3M never seems to run out of ideas.

4. **Active Networking**—3M actively promotes networking and internal conversations among its scientists and engineers. They host an annual Technical Forum where the roughly 10,000 members of the R&D staff talk and share ideas.

5. **Reward Employees for Outstanding Work**—3M maintains a dual-career track so experienced scientists and engineers can move up the career ladder without moving into corporate management. The company also honors its employees with scientific achievement awards each year.

6. **Measure Results**—A key benchmark for 3M is the percentage of revenue that comes from products introduced during the past four years. This prevents the company from resting on its laurels and allows management to determine whether R&D dollars are well spent.

7. **Listen to the Customer**—3M employees spend a great deal of time learning about customer needs and expectations. They take these ideas back to the lab, where innovative products are developed. For example, the idea for Post-It Photo Paper came directly from customers.

Wendling argues that innovation at 3M is not an accident. Throughout the company's history, these seven pillars of innovation have been developed, managed, and nurtured. It is no wonder that 3M regularly appears in the *BusinessWeek* rankings of the world's most innovative and most admired companies.

To be successful, firms should be able to execute all three strategies. However, the most successful firms choose one area at which to excel and then actively manage customer perceptions so that customers believe that the firm does indeed excel in that area. To implement any one of these strategies effectively, a firm must possess certain core competencies, as outlined in Exhibit 5.8. Firms that boast such competencies are more likely to create a competitive advantage than those that do not. However, before a competitive advantage can be translated into specific customer benefits, the firm's target markets must recognize that its competencies give it an advantage over the competition. Exhibit 5.8 includes a list of attributes that customers might use to describe a company that possesses each particular competitive advantage. The core competencies are internal (strength) issues, whereas specific attributes refer to activities that customers will notice as they interact with the firm.

Establishing a Strategic Focus

At the conclusion of the SWOT analysis, the marketing manager must turn his or her attention toward establishing the strategic focus of the firm's marketing program. By strategic focus, we mean the overall concept or model that guides the firm as it weaves various marketing elements together into a coherent strategy. A firm's strategic focus is typically tied to its competitive advantages. However, depending on the situation, the strategic focus can shift to compensate for the firm's weaknesses or to defend against its vulnerabilities. A firm's strategic focus can change over time to reflect the dynamic nature of the internal and external environments. The direction taken depends on how the firm's strengths and weaknesses match up with its external opportunities and threats. Using the results of the SWOT analysis as a guide, a firm might consider four general directions for its strategic efforts:[13]

- **Aggressive (many internal strengths/many external opportunities)**   Firms in this enviable position can develop marketing strategies to aggressively take on multiple opportunities. Expansion and growth, with new products and new markets, are the keys to an aggressive approach. These firms are often so dominant that they can actually reshape the industry or the competitive landscape to fit their agenda. Google offers a good example of this approach in its development of web-based applications that serve multiple needs and markets. Google Voice, Google Docs, Gmail, and YouTube are a few examples of Google's offerings.

- **Diversification (many internal strengths/many external threats)**   Firms in this position have a great deal to offer, but external factors weaken their ability to pursue aggressive strategies. To help offset these threats, firms can use marketing strategy to diversify their portfolio of products, markets, or even business units. A good example of this strategy in action is the Altria Group, whose divisions include Philip Morris USA, U.S. Smokeless Tobacco Company, John Middleton (cigars), Ste. Michelle Wine Estates, Philip Morris Capital Corporation (leasing), and partial ownership of SABMiller (the world's second-largest brewer). Although Altria owns many of the world's most recognizable brands (Marlboro, Virginia Slims, Skoal, Copenhagen, Prince Albert), the firm faces innumerable threats from low-cost competitors, taxes, and litigation. Until litigation against the company settles down, Altria plans to remain a diversified concern.[14]

EXHIBIT 5.8   **CORE COMPETENCIES NECESSARY FOR COMPETITIVE ADVANTAGE STRATEGIES**

Operational Excellence—Example Firms: Walmart, Southwest Airlines, Dell

Core Competencies
- Low-cost operations
- Totally dependable product supply
- Expedient customer service
- Effective demand management

Common Attributes of Operationally Excellent Firms
- Delivery of compelling value through the use of low prices, standardized product offerings, and convenient buying processes
- Targeting a broad, heterogeneous market of price-sensitive buyers
- Investing to achieve scale economies and efficiency-driven systems that translate into lower prices for buyers
- Developing information systems geared toward capturing and distributing information on inventories, shipments, customer transactions, and costs in real time
- Maintaining a system to avoid waste and highly reward efficiency improvement

Product Leadership—Example Firms: Pfizer, Intel, 3M

Core Competencies
- Basic research/rapid research interpretation
- Applied research geared toward product development
- Rapid exploitation of market opportunities
- Excellent marketing skills

Common Attributes of Product-Leading Firms
- Focusing their marketing plans on the rapid introduction of high-quality, technologically sophisticated products in order to create customer loyalty
- Constantly scanning the environment in search of new opportunities; often making their own products obsolete through continuous innovation
- Targeting narrow, homogeneous market segments
- Maintaining organizational cultures characterized by decentralization, adaptability, entrepreneurship, creativity, and the expectation of learning from failure
- Having an attitude of "How can we make this work?" rather than "Why can't we make this work?"

Customer Intimacy—Example Firms: Nordstrom, Amazon, Ritz-Carlton

Core Competencies
- Exceptional skills in discovering customer needs
- Problem-solving proficiency
- Flexible product/solution customization
- A customer relationship management mind-set
- A wide presence of collaborative (win–win) negotiation skills

Common Attributes of Customer-Intimate Firms
- Seeing customer loyalty as their greatest asset as they focus their efforts on developing and maintaining an intimate knowledge of customer requirements
- Consistently exceeding customer expectations by offering high-quality products and solutions without an apology for charging higher prices
- Decentralizing most decision-making authority to the customer-contact level
- Regularly forming strategic alliances with other companies to address customers' needs in a comprehensive fashion
- Assessing all relationships with customers or alliance partners on a long-term, even lifetime basis

Source: From 'Discipline of Market Leaders: Choose Your Customers' in "CSC Index" by Michael Treacy and Fred Wiersema (Addison-Wesley, 1995). Reprinted with permission from Helen Rees Literary Agency, Michael Treacy, and Fred Wiersema.

- **Turnaround (many internal weaknesses/many external opportunities)**   Firms often pursue turnaround strategies because they find themselves in the situation—often temporary—of having too many internal problems to consider strategies that will take advantage of external opportunities. In these cases, firms typically have to put their own house back in order before looking beyond their current products or markets. For example, GM was once the dominant carmaker in the world. However, a weak product portfolio, high pension costs, stiff competition, and the downturn in the world economy created a perfect storm that forced GM into bankruptcy in 2009. As a part of its turnaround strategy, GM took steps to eliminate its four noncore brands: Saturn, Hummer, Pontiac, and Saab.[15]

- **Defensive (many internal weaknesses/many external threats)**   Firms take a defensive posture when they become overwhelmed by internal and external problems simultaneously. For example, pharmaceutical giant Merck was dealt a serious blow in 2004 when it was announced that patients taking the company's pain reliever Vioxx were at an increased risk of heart attacks. Merck withdrew Vioxx from the market, which marked the beginning of a string of potentially damaging litigation against the firm. However, Merck won 10 out of 15 major lawsuits against them, and then eventually settled all remaining suits for $4.85 billion in 2007. Next, Merck began looking for ways to defend its market position given that many of its most popular drugs—including Zocor, Fosamax, and Singulair—would lose patent protection over the next several years. Merck announced its solution in 2009 with a $41 billion merger with Schering-Plough, which gave the company a strong development pipeline of 18 new drugs in Phase III trials.[16]

Although these four stances are quite common, other combinations of strengths, weaknesses, opportunities, and threats are possible. For example, a firm may have few internal strengths but many external opportunities. In this situation, the firm cannot take advantage of opportunities because it does not possess the needed resources to create capabilities or competitive advantages. To resolve this problem, the firm might focus all of its efforts toward small niche markets, or it might consider establishing alliances with firms that possess the necessary resources. It is also possible that a firm will possess many internal strengths but few external opportunities. In this situation, the firm might pursue a strategy of diversification by entering new markets or acquiring other companies. This strategy is dangerous, however, unless these new pursuits are consistent with the mission of the firm. Business history is replete with stories of firms that explored new opportunities that were outside of their core mission and values. Sears' expansion into real estate, financial services, and credit cards in the 1980s should remind us all that stepping beyond core strengths is often a bad idea.

Establishing a solid strategic focus is important at this stage of the planning process because it lays the groundwork for the development of marketing goals and objectives that follow. Unfortunately, many firms struggle with finding a focus that translates into a strategy that offers customers a compelling reason for purchasing the firm's products. Firms can use any number of tools and techniques for identifying a compelling strategic focus. We believe that one of the most useful tools is the strategy canvas, which was developed by professors W. Chan Kim and Renee Mauborgne in their book *Blue Ocean Strategy*.[17]

In essence, a strategy canvas is a tool for visualizing a firm's strategy relative to other firms in a given industry. As an example, consider the strategy canvas for Southwest Airlines depicted in Exhibit 5.9.[18] The horizontal axis of a strategy canvas identifies the key factors that the industry competes on with the products that are offered to customers. In the case of the airline industry, these factors include price, meals, seating choices, and service, among others. The vertical axis indicates the offering level that firms offer to buyers across these factors. The central portion of the strategy canvas is the value curve, or the graphic representation of the firm's relative performance across its industry's factors. The key to using the strategy canvas (and the key to developing a compelling strategic focus) lies in identifying a value curve that stands apart from the competition.

As illustrated in the exhibit, Southwest's strategic focus is based on downplaying the traditional competitive factors used in the airline industry (price, meals, etc.), stressing other factors (service, speed), and creating a new factor upon which to base its competitive advantage (frequent departures). In doing this, Southwest offers a compelling alternative to customers who dislike making the tradeoffs between air travel and car travel. Southwest's strategic focus, then, is offering fast, friendly, and frequent air travel at prices that appeal to customers who would have customarily opted to travel by car. As we have seen earlier in this chapter, Southwest is able to

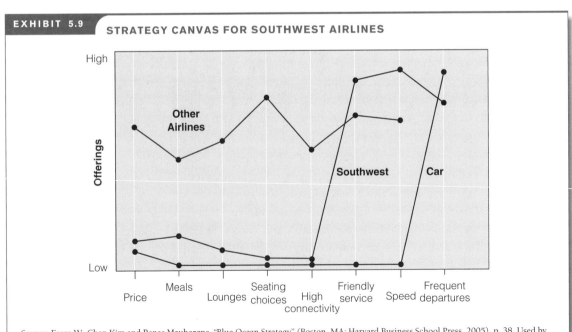

EXHIBIT 5.9   STRATEGY CANVAS FOR SOUTHWEST AIRLINES

Source: From W. Chan Kim and Renee Mauborgne, "Blue Ocean Strategy" (Boston, MA: Harvard Business School Press, 2005), p. 38. Used by permission of Harvard Business School Publishing.

support this focus through its competitive advantages based on operational excellence. It should be no surprise that Southwest has been one of the most successful and profitable carriers in the industry for quite some time.

To use the strategy canvas successfully, the marketing manager must identify a value curve with two major characteristics.[19] First, the value curve should clearly depict the firm's strategic focus. As shown in Exhibit 5.9, Southwest Airlines' focus on service, speed, and frequent departures is clear. All other competitive factors are downplayed in Southwest's strategy. Second, the value curve should be distinctively different from competitors. Again, this is the case for Southwest as its combination of competitive factors clearly separates the firm from the competition. More information on the blue ocean approach to developing a strategic focus can be found in *Beyond the Pages 5.3.*

The combination of the SWOT matrix and the strategy canvas offers a useful and powerful means of visualizing the firm's competitive advantage and strategic focus. Clearly articulating the firm's focus is crucial as the marketing manager moves ahead in developing the marketing plan. In the next phase of the planning process, the manager must identify the firm's marketing goals and objectives in order to connect the strategic focus to the outcomes that are desired and expected. These goals and objectives will also be crucial at the latter stages of planning as the manager identifies standards that will be used to assess the performance of the marketing strategy. In the next section, we look at the development of marketing goals and objectives in more detail.

Developing Marketing Goals and Objectives

After identifying a strategic focus, the marketing manager may have some ideas about potential marketing activities that can be used to leverage the firm's competitive advantages relative to the opportunities available in the market. At this stage, however, there are likely to be many different goals and objectives that coincide with the anticipated strategic direction. Because most firms have limited resources, it is typically difficult to accomplish everything in a single planning cycle. At this point, the manager must prioritize the firm's strategic intentions and develop specific goals and objectives for the marketing plan.

We reiterate that marketing goals and objectives must be consistent with the overall mission and vision of the firm. Once the firm has a mission statement that clearly delineates what it is, what it stands for, and what it does for others, the marketing manager can then begin to express what he or she hopes to achieve in the firm's marketing program. These statements of desired accomplishments are goals and objectives. Some use the terms *goals* and *objectives* interchangeably. However, failure to understand the key differences between them can severely limit the effectiveness of the marketing plan. Goals are general desired accomplishments, whereas objectives provide specific, quantitative benchmarks that can be used to gauge progress toward the achievement of the marketing goals.

A CLOSER LOOK AT BLUE OCEAN STRATEGY[20]

In addition to the strategy canvas discussed in the chapter, Professors Chan and Mauborgne developed a companion tool called the four actions framework. Where the strategy canvas graphically depicts the firm's strategic focus relative to competitors and the factors that define competition within an industry, the four actions framework is a tool for discovering how to shift the strategy canvas and reorient the firm's strategic focus. As shown in the diagram, the four actions framework is designed to challenge traditional assumptions about strategy by asking four questions about the firm's way of doing business.

As an example of how the four actions framework can be used, Chan and Mauborgne drew on the experiences of Casella Wine's successful launch of [yellow tail]. First, Casella *eliminated* traditional competitive factors such as impenetrable wine terminology, aging qualities, and heavy marketing expenditures. Casella reasoned that these factors made wine inaccessible to the mass of buyers who were unfamiliar with wine culture. Second, Casella *reduced* the importance of other factors such as wine complexity, range of wine selections, and prestige. At launch, for example, Casella introduced only two wines: Chardonnay and Shiraz. They also used a nontraditional label featuring an orange and yellow kangaroo on a black background to reduce the prestige or "snob appeal" common in most wines. Third, Casella *raised* the importance of competitive factors such as store involvement. Casella involved store employees by giving them Australian clothing to wear at work. This created a laid back approach to wine that made the employees eager to recommend [yellow tail] to their customers. Finally, Casella *created* easy to drink, easy to buy, and fun as new competitive factors. [yellow tail] has a soft fruity taste that makes it more approachable. Casella also put red and white wines in the same-shaped bottle—an industry first. This simple change greatly reduces manufacturing costs and makes point-of-sale displays simpler and more eye-catching.

In addition to Casella, the blue ocean approach is used successfully by Southwest Airlines, Cirque du Soleil, and Curves (a chain of women-only fitness centers), among others. Chan and Mauborgne argue that successfully reorienting a firm's strategic focus requires the firm to give up long-held assumptions about how business should be conducted. They caution firms to avoid benchmarking and extensive customer research because these approaches tend to create a typical "more for less" mentality that guides the strategic focus of most firms. Instead, the blue ocean approach requires firms to fundamentally alter their strategic logic. Therein lies the challenge of blue ocean thinking: It is very, very difficult for most businesses to change. Consequently, true blue ocean approaches tend to be a rare occurrence.

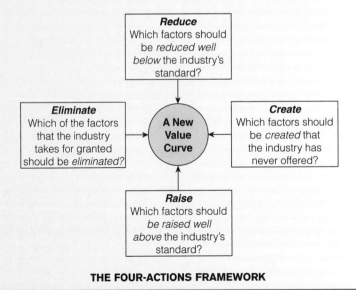

THE FOUR-ACTIONS FRAMEWORK

Developing Marketing Goals

As statements of broad, desired accomplishments, goals are expressed in general terms and do not contain specific information about where the organization presently stands or where it hopes to be in the future. Sears, for example, has a goal of having lower prices than the competition. This goal is not specific, however, because it does not specify a benchmark that defines what a lower price is. To achieve this goal, Sears offers a price guarantee that matches, then beats competitors' prices by 10 percent.[21] Goals like these are important because they indicate the direction in which the firm attempts to move, as well as the set of priorities it will use in evaluating alternatives and making decisions.

It is also important that all functional areas of the organization be considered in the goal-setting process. In developing goals for the marketing plan, it is important to keep in mind that marketing goals should be attainable, consistent, comprehensive, and involve some degree of intangibility. Failure to consider these issues will result in goals that are less effective, and perhaps even dysfunctional. Let's look more closely at these characteristics.

Attainability   Setting realistic goals is important because the key parties involved in reaching them must see each goal as reasonable. Determining whether a goal is realistic requires an assessment of both the internal and external environments. For example, it would not be unrealistic for a firm in second place in market share, trailing the leading brand by just 2 percent, to set a goal of becoming the industry leader. Other things being equal, such a goal could help motivate employees toward becoming "number one." In contrast, a firm in sixth place, trailing the fifth place firm by 5 percent and the leader by 30 percent, could set the same goal—but it would not be realistic. Unrealistic goals can be demotivational because they show employees that management is out of touch. Because one of the primary benefits of having goals is to motivate employees toward better performance, setting unrealistic goals can cause major problems.

Consistency   In addition to being realistic, management must work to set goals that are consistent with one another. Enhancing market share and working to have the highest profit margins in the industry are both reasonable goals by themselves, but together they are inconsistent. Goals to increase both sales and market share would be consistent, as would goals to enhance customer service and customer satisfaction. However, setting goals to reduce inventory levels and increase customer service are usually incompatible. Goals across and within functional areas should also mesh together. This is a major concern in large organizations, and it highlights the need for a great deal of information sharing during the goal-formulation process.

Comprehensiveness   The goal-setting process should also be comprehensive. This means that each functional area should be able to develop its own goals that relate to the organization's goals. For example, if goals are set only in terms of advancing the technology associated with a firm's products, members of the marketing department may wonder what role they will play in this accomplishment. The goal should be stated so that both marketing and research and development can work together to help advance the organizational goal of offering the most technologically advanced products. Marketing will need to work on the demand side of this effort (measuring customer needs and staying attuned to trends in the external environment), while research and development will focus on the supply side (conducting basic and applied research, as well as staying abreast of all major technological innovations). Goals should help clarify the roles of all parties in the organization. Functional areas that do not match any of the organization's goals should question their need for future resources and their ability to acquire them.

Intangibility   Finally, goals should involve some degree of intangibility. Some planners have been known to confuse strategies, and even tactics, with goals. A goal is not some action the firm can take; rather, it is an outcome the organization hopes to accomplish. Actions such as hiring 100 new salespeople or doubling the advertising budget are not goals, as any firm with adequate resources can accomplish both tasks. However, having "the best-trained sales force in the industry" or "the most creative and effective advertising campaign in the industry" are suitable goals. Note the intangibility associated with the use of terms such as *best trained*, *most creative*, and *most effective*. These terms are motivational because they promote comparisons with rival firms. They also continually push for excellence, as their open-ended nature always leaves room for improvement.

Developing Marketing Objectives

Objectives provide specific and quantitative benchmarks that can be used to gauge progress toward the achievement of the marketing goals. In some cases, a particular goal may require several objectives for its progress to be adequately monitored, usually across multiple business functions. For example, a goal of "creating a high-quality image for the firm" cannot be accomplished by better inventory control if accounts receivable makes mistakes and customer complaints about the firm's salespeople are on the rise. Similarly, the marketing department alone could not have accomplished Home Depot's phenomenal growth from a single Atlanta store in 1979 to over 2,200 stores worldwide in 2009.[22] Such an endeavor requires a carefully coordinated effort across many departments.

Goals without objectives are essentially meaningless because progress is impossible to measure. A typical marketing objective might be: "The sales division will decrease unfilled customer orders from 3 percent to 2 percent between January and June of this fiscal year." Note that this objective contains a high degree of specificity. It is this specificity that sets goals and objectives apart. Objectives involve measurable, quantitative outcomes, with specifically assigned responsibility for their accomplishment and a definite time period for their attainment. Let's look at the specific characteristics of marketing objectives.

Attainability   As with goals, marketing objectives should be realistic given the internal and external environments identified during the situation and SWOT analyses. A good objective is one that is attainable with a reasonable amount of effort. Easily attainable objectives will not motivate employees to achieve higher levels of performance. Likewise, good objectives do not come from false assumptions that everything will go as planned or that every employee will give 110 percent effort. In some cases, competitors will establish objectives that include taking customers and sales away from the firm. Setting objectives that assume inanimate or inept competitors, when history has proven otherwise, creates objectives that quickly lose their value as employees recognize them as being unreasonable.

Continuity   The need for realism brings up a second consideration, that of continuity. Marketing objectives can be either continuous or discontinuous. A firm uses continuous objectives when its current objectives are similar to objectives set in the previous planning period. For example, an objective "to increase market share from 20 to 22 percent in the next fiscal year" could be carried forward in a similar fashion to the next period: "to increase market share from 22 to 24 percent in the next fiscal year." This would be a continuous objective because the factor in question and the magnitude of change are similar, or even identical, from period to period.

An important caveat about continuous objectives: Objectives that are identical, or only slightly modified, from period to period often do not need new strategies, increased effort, or better implementation to be achieved. Marketing objectives should lead employees to perform at higher levels than would otherwise have been the case. Employees naturally tend to be objective oriented. Once they meet the objective, the level of creativity and effort tends to fall off. There are certainly circumstances where continuous objectives are appropriate, but they should not be set simply as a matter of habit.

Discontinuous objectives significantly elevate the level of performance on a given outcome factor or bring new factors into the set of objectives. If sales growth has been averaging 10 percent, and the SWOT analysis suggests that this is an easily obtainable level, an example of a discontinuous objective might be "to increase sales 18 percent during the next fiscal year." This would require new strategies to sell additional products to existing customers, expand the customer base, or at the very least develop new tactics and/or enhance the implementation of existing strategies. Discontinuous objectives require more analysis and linkage to strategic planning than continuous objectives.

Developing discontinuous objectives is one of the major benefits a company can gain from applying for the Malcolm Baldrige National Quality Award. Exhibit 5.10 identifies the performance criteria for the Baldrige Award. To demonstrate proficiency in these areas, a firm must first establish benchmarks, which typically are the quantitative performance levels of the leaders in an industry. The firm then develops

EXHIBIT 5.10   **MALCOLM BALDRIGE AWARD CRITERIA FOR PERFORMANCE EXCELLENCE**

Categories and Items	Point Values	
1 **Leadership**		**120**
1.1 Senior Leadership	70	
1.2 Governance and Social Responsibilities	50	
2 **Strategic Planning**		**85**
2.1 Strategy Development	40	
2.2 Strategy Deployment	45	
3 **Customer Focus**		**85**
3.1 Customer Engagement	40	
3.2 Voice of the Customer	45	
4 **Measurement, Analysis, and Knowledge Management**		**90**
4.1 Measurement, Analysis, and Improvement of Organizational Performance	45	
4.2 Management of Information, Knowledge, and Information Technology	45	
5 **Workforce Focus**		**85**
5.1 Workforce Engagement	45	
5.2 Workforce Environment	40	
6 **Process Management**		**85**
6.1 Work Systems	35	
6.2 Work Processes	50	
7 **Results**		**450**
7.1 Product Outcomes	100	
7.2 Customer-Focused Outcomes	70	
7.3 Financial and Market Outcomes	70	
7.4 Workforce-Focused Outcomes	70	
7.5 Process Effectiveness Outcomes	70	
7.6 Leadership Outcomes	70	
Total Points		**1,000**

Source: "2009–2010 Criteria for Performance Excellence," *Malcolm Baldrige National Quality Award Program* (Gaithersburg, MD: National Institute of Standards and Technology, U.S. Department of Commerce, 2009), p. 3.

objectives that center on improving performance in each area. Many companies feel that simply applying for the Baldrige Award has positive effects on performance, if for no other reason than the process forces the company to set challenging discontinuous objectives. This is also true for organizations that use the Baldrige guidelines as a planning aid.

Time Frame   Another key consideration in setting objectives is the time frame for their achievement. Although companies often establish marketing plans on an annual basis, marketing objectives may differ from this period in their time frame. Sales volume, market share, customer service, and gross margin objectives may be set for terms less than, equal to, or greater than one year. The time frame should be appropriate and allow for accomplishment with reasonable levels of effort. To set a target of doubling sales for a well-established company within six months would likely be unreasonable. On the other hand, objectives having an excessively long time frame may be attained without any increased effort or creativity. The combination of managerial expertise and experience, along with the information acquired during the situation and SWOT analyses, should lead to the establishment of an appropriate time frame.

For objectives with longer time frames, it is important to remind employees of the objective on a regular basis and to provide feedback on progress toward its achievement. For example, employees at FedEx's terminal in Memphis, Tennessee, can see a real-time accuracy gauge that displays the company's current performance in terms of getting packages to their rightful destinations. FedEx also uses a nightly countdown clock to remind employees of the speed needed to turn around packages and load them on outbound cargo planes. Whether a weekly announcement, a monthly newsletter, or a real-time gauge on the wall that charts progress toward the objective, feedback is a critical part of the objective-setting process, particularly for longer-term objectives.

Assignment of Responsibility   One final aspect of objectives that sets them apart from goals is that the marketing manager must identify the person, team, or unit responsible for achieving each objective. By explicitly assigning responsibility, the firm can limit the problems of stealing credit and avoiding responsibility. A bank might give the marketing department the responsibility of achieving an objective of "having 40 percent of its customers list the bank as their primary financial institution within one year." If by the end of the year, 42 percent of all customers list the bank as their primary financial institution, the marketing department gets credit for this outcome. If the figure is only 38 percent, the marketing department must provide an explanation.

Moving Beyond Goals and Objectives

Marketing goals and objectives identify the desired ends, both general and specific, that the organization hopes to achieve during the planning period. However, companies do not fulfill properly set goals and objectives automatically or through wishing and hoping. They set into motion a chain of decisions that serve as a catalyst for the subsequent stages in the planning process. Organizational goals and objectives must lead to the establishment of consistent goals and objectives for each functional area of the firm. Having recognized the desired ends, each area, including marketing, must next determine the means that will lead to these targeted results.

As we move forward, we focus our attention on the means issue as we address marketing strategy development. Although a firm might consider the steps of the market planning process sequentially, in reality the firm must move back and forth between steps. If marketing strategies that have the potential to achieve the marketing goals and objectives cannot be developed, the goals and objectives may not be reasonable and need to be reevaluated before the development of the marketing strategy. Given that the marketing plan must be a working document, the cycling among planning steps never truly ends.

Lessons from Chapter 5

SWOT analysis

- Is considered to be one of the most useful tools in analyzing marketing data and information.

- Links a company's ongoing situation analysis to the development of the marketing plan.

- Structures the information from the situation analysis into four categories: strengths, weaknesses, opportunities, and threats.

- Uses the structured information to uncover competitive advantages and guide the selection of the strategic focus for the firm's marketing strategy.

To make SWOT analysis as productive as possible, the marketing manager should

- Stay focused by using a series of SWOT analyses, each focusing on a specific product/market combination.

- Search extensively for competitors, whether they are a present competitor or one in the future.

- Collaborate with other functional areas by sharing information and perspectives.

- Examine issues from the customers' perspective by asking questions such as "What do customers (and noncustomers) believe about us as a company?" and "Which of our weaknesses translate into a decreased ability to serve customers (and a decreased ability to convert noncustomers)?" This includes examining the issues from the perspective of the firm's internal customers, its employees.

- Look for causes, not characteristics by considering the firm's resources that are the true causes for the firm's strengths, weaknesses, opportunities, and threats.

- Separate internal issues from external issues using this key test to differentiate: "Would this issue exist if the firm did not exist?" If the answer is yes, the issue should be classified as external to the firm.

Strengths and weaknesses

- Exist because of resources possessed (or not possessed) by the firm, or they exist due to the nature of key relationships between the firm and its customers, its employees, or outside organizations.

- Must be leveraged into capabilities (in the case of strengths) or overcome (in the case of weaknesses).

- Are meaningful only when they assist or hinder the firm in satisfying customer needs.

Opportunities and threats

- Are not potential marketing actions. Rather, they involve issues or situations that occur in the firm's external environments.

- Should not be ignored as the firm gets caught up in developing strengths and capabilities for fear of creating an efficient, but ineffective, organization.

- May stem from changes in the competitive, customer, economic, political/legal, technological, and/or sociocultural environments.

The SWOT matrix

- Allows the marketing manager to visualize the analysis.

- Should serve as a catalyst to facilitate and guide the creation of marketing strategies that will produce desired results.

- Allows the manager to see how strengths and opportunities might be connected to create capabilities that are key to meeting customer needs.

- Involves assessing the magnitude and importance of each strength, weakness, opportunity, and threat.

Competitive advantage

- Stems from the firm's capabilities in relation to those held by the competition.

- Can be based on both internal and external factors.

- Is based on both reality and customer perceptions.

- Is often based on the basic strategies of operational excellence, product leadership, and/or customer intimacy.

Establishing a strategic focus

- Is based on developing an overall concept or model that guides the firm as it weaves various marketing elements together into a coherent strategy.

- Is typically tied to the firm's competitive advantages.

- Involves using the results of the SWOT analysis as the firm considers four major directions for its strategic efforts: aggressiveness, diversification, turnaround, or defensiveness.

- Can help ensure that the firm does not step beyond its core strengths to consider opportunities that are outside its capabilities.

- Can be visualized through the use of a strategy canvas where the goal is to develop a value curve that is distinct from the competition.

- Is often done by downplaying traditional industry competitive factors in favor of new approaches.

- Is an important stage of the planning process because it lays the groundwork for the development of marketing goals and objectives and connects the outcomes of the SWOT analysis to the remainder of the marketing plan.

Marketing goals

- Are broad, desired accomplishments that are stated in general terms.

- Indicate the direction the firm attempts to move in, as well as the set of priorities it will use in evaluating alternatives and making decisions.

- Should be attainable, realistic, internally consistent, and comprehensive and help to clarify the roles of all parties in the organization.

- Should involve some degree of intangibility.

Marketing objectives

- Provide specific and quantitative benchmarks that can be used to gauge progress toward the achievement of the marketing goals.

- Should be attainable with a reasonable degree of effort.

- May be either continuous or discontinuous, depending on the degree to which they depart from present objectives.

- Should specify the time frame for their completion.

- Should be assigned to specific areas, departments, or individuals who have the responsibility to accomplish them.

Questions for Discussion

1. Strengths, weaknesses, opportunities, and threats: Which is the most important? Why? How might your response change if you were the CEO of a corporation? What if you were a customer of the firm? An employee? A supplier?

2. Support or contradict this statement: "Given the realities of today's economy and the rapid changes occurring in business technology, all competitive advantages are short-lived. There is no such thing as a *sustainable* competitive advantage that lasts over the long term." Defend your position.

3. Is it possible for an organization to be successful despite having a value curve that is not distinct from the competition's? In other words, can an organization be successful by selling a me-too product (a product that offers no compelling differences when compared to the competition)? Explain.

Exercises

1. Perform a SWOT analysis using yourself as the product. Be candid about your resources and the strengths and weaknesses you possess. Based on the opportunities and threats you see in the environment, where do you stand in terms of your ability to attend graduate school, get a job, begin a career, or change careers?

2. Choose two companies from the same industry: one that is quite successful and one that is struggling. For each company, list every strength and weakness you believe it possesses (both the company and its products). Compare your answers with those of your colleagues. What could these companies learn from your analysis?

3. Using the same companies from Exercise 2, draw a strategy canvas that depicts the value curve of both firms, as well as the "average" firm in the industry (i.e., draw three value curves). What does the successful firm offer that the struggling firm does not offer? What might a firm do to break away from the industry's traditional competitive factors?

Customers, Segmentation, and Target Marketing

Introduction

I n this chapter, we begin our discussion of marketing strategy by examining customers, segments, and target markets. In Chapter 1, we referred to a market as a collection of buyers and sellers. Now, we focus our attention on the buyers who collectively make up the major portion of most markets. From this perspective, we concern ourselves with markets as individuals, institutions, or groups of individuals or institutions that have similar needs that can be met by a particular product offering. As we shall see, firms can attempt to reach all buyers in a market, smaller groups or segments of the market, or even specific buyers on an individual level. Whether the firm aims for the entire market or smaller market segments, the goal of marketing strategy is to identify specific customer needs, then design a marketing program that can satisfy those needs. To do this effectively, the firm must have a comprehensive understanding of its current and potential customers, including their motivations, behaviors, needs, and wants.

The ability to determine in-depth information about customers is a fairly recent phenomenon in marketing. Fifty years ago, for example, technology and marketing know-how were less sophisticated. Marketers of the day were unable to fully understand customers' needs and wants, much less make fine distinctions among smaller segments of the total market. Marketers tended to offer products that came in only one variety, flavor, or style. Today, market segmentation is critical to the success of most firms. Segmentation allows marketers to more precisely define and understand customer needs, and gives them the ability to tailor products to better suit those needs. As discussed in *Beyond the Pages 6.1*, the level of detailed information available about customers today has changed the way firms do business. However, the use of such information raises concerns about consumer privacy. Still, without segmentation we would not enjoy the incredible variety of products available today. Consider the number of choices we have in categories such as soft drinks, cereals, packaged goods, automobiles, and clothing. In many respects, segmentation has improved our standard of living. Customers now expect firms to delve into their needs and wants, and to tailor products accordingly. This fact makes market segmentation a vital part of marketing

Beyond the Pages 6.1

TARGETING CUSTOMERS THROUGH DATA MINING[1]

Consider a world where what you eat, read, wear, listen to, watch, buy, and do can be reduced to a mathematical formula. Every move you make is tracked with such a level of specificity that your entire life can be captured in a computer model. Sound far-fetched? It's not. Today, the combination of computer science, mathematics, and business is changing our view of consumers and their behavior. The ability to track consumer behavior has never been more advanced than it is today. The new insights gained from the mathematical modeling of consumer behavior is creating new avenues for business, allowing marketers to develop one-to-one relationships with consumers, and causing a fair amount of anxiety. It is also causing a sharp increase in the hiring of math graduates from our nation's universities.

None of this is really new. Through advanced math, computer modeling, and data mining, businesses have been able to track consumer attitudes and behaviors for some time. The difference today is the unprecedented access to data made available via the Internet and other technologies. Over the past ten years, a sizable portion of the consuming public has moved its work, play, conversation, and shopping online. These integrated networks collect vast amounts of data and store our lives in databases that can be connected in ways that allow us to capture a more complete picture of consumer behavior. For example, researchers at companies like Yahoo!, Google, and Amazon are developing mathematical models of customers. These firms are also working with other companies and the government agencies to develop models that can predict voting behavior, how patients respond to disease intervention, or which employee is best suited for a job assignment. For example, the Democratic Party used data mining techniques during the 2008 presidential election. Their research indentified 10 key groups that were specifically targeted with political advertising messages in support of Barack Obama.

The advertising and media industries are perhaps the most affected by this shift. As mass audience advertising has declined, marketers have been looking for ways to target customers more directly. Google is a pioneer in this effort because the company has amassed an unfathomable amount of data on what customers do online. Other companies now provide data mining solutions. In research conducted with SPSS, for example, Italian carmaker Fiat was able to improve customer relations and increase customer retention by 6 to 7 percent. Microsoft uses its own analytical techniques to study the productivity of its workforce. Furthermore, Harrah's Entertainment (a major player in the casino industry) has increased their annual growth rate by using computer models to predict which customers will respond to the company's targeted advertising and promotional offers.

Of course, all of this sophistication comes at a price. The ability of companies to track customers and model their behavior raises a number of privacy concerns. Most companies take great pains to protect individual consumer identities and their private information. However, the continuing erosion of consumer privacy is likely to continue. A key question for marketers is, at what point will consumers say enough is enough? How far can firms push the boundaries of data collection and analysis before consumers mount a backlash? These issues will only become more prominent in the years ahead.

strategy. Until a firm has chosen and analyzed a target market, it cannot make effective decisions regarding other elements of the marketing strategy.

In this chapter, we examine issues associated with buyer behavior in both consumer and business markets. We also discuss traditional and individualized approaches to market segmentation, the criteria for successful market segmentation, and specific target marketing strategies. The potential combinations of target markets and marketing programs are essentially limitless. Choosing the right target market from among many possible alternatives is one of the key tests in developing a good marketing strategy.

Buyer Behavior in Consumer Markets

Trying to understand the buyer behavior of consumers is a very trying and challenging task. The behavior of consumers is often irrational and unpredictable. Consumers often say one thing but do another. Still, the effort spent trying to understand consumers is valuable because it can provide needed insight on how to design products and marketing programs that better meet consumer needs and wants. One of the most recent trends in learning about customers is the rising use of ethnography. Computer maker Lenovo, for example, has been using ethnographic research to learn more about how families in India use consumer electronics. One interesting finding is that the family social center in Indian homes is the parents' bedroom. The kitchen serves the same social function in American homes. Lenovo plans to use this type of information to develop consumer electronics that better fit differing family lifestyles in India and the United States. Similarly, Nokia uses ethnographic research to develop better ergonomics for its line of wireless phones.[2]

In this section, we look at key issues with respect to buyer behavior in consumer markets. Here, we examine the consumer buying process and the factors that alter the ways consumers buy goods and services. As we will see, successful marketing strategy depends on a clear understanding of customers with respect to who they are, what they need, what they prefer, and why they buy. Although this understanding clearly has relevance for designing the product offering, it also impacts the pricing, distribution, and promotion decisions in the marketing program.

The Consumer Buying Process

The consumer buying process shown in Exhibit 6.1 depicts five stages of activities that consumers may go through in buying goods and services. The process begins with the recognition of a need and then passes through the stages of information search, evaluation of alternatives, purchase decision, and postpurchase evaluation. A marketer's interest in the buying process can go well beyond these stages to include actual consumption behaviors, product uses, and product disposal after consumption. As we consider each stage of the buying process, it is important to keep a few key issues in mind.

First, the buying process depicts the possible range of activities that may occur in making purchase decisions. Consumers, however, do not always follow these stages in sequence and may even skip stages en route to making a purchase. For example, impulse purchases, such as buying a pack of chewing gum or a newspaper, do not involve lengthy search or evaluation activities. On the other hand, complex purchases like buying a home are often quite lengthy as they incorporate every stage of the buying process. Likewise, consumers who are loyal to a product or brand will skip some stages and are most likely to simply purchase the same product they bought last time. Consequently, marketers have a difficult time promoting brand switching because they must convince these customers to break tradition and take a look at what their products have to offer.

Second, the buying process often involves a parallel sequence of activities associated with finding the most suitable merchant of the product in question. That is,

---

EXHIBIT 6.1

THE CONSUMER BUYING PROCESS

Stages	Key Issues
Need Recognition	• Consumer needs and wants are not the same. • An understanding of consumer wants is essential for market segmentation and the development of the marketing program. • Marketers must create the appropriate stimuli to foster need recognition.
Information Search	• Consumers trust internal and personal sources of information more than external sources. • The amount of time, effort, and expense dedicated to the search for information depends on (1) the degree of risk involved in the purchase, (2) the amount of experience the consumer has with the product category, and (3) the actual cost of the search in terms of time and money. • Consumers narrow their potential choices to an evoked set of suitable alternatives that may meet their needs.
Evaluation of Alternatives	• Consumers translate their needs into wants for specific products or brands. • Consumers evaluate products as bundles of attributes that have varying abilities to satisfy their needs. • Marketers must ensure that their product is in the evoked set of potential alternatives. • Marketers must take steps to understand consumers' choice criteria and the importance they place on specific product attributes.
Purchase Decision	• A consumer's purchase intention and the actual act of buying are distinct concepts. Several factors may prevent the actual purchase from taking place. • Marketers must ensure that their product is available and offer solutions that increase possession utility.
Postpurchase Evaluation	• Postpurchase evaluation is the connection between the buying process and the development of long-term customer relationships. • Marketers must closely follow consumers' responses (delight, satisfaction, dissatisfaction, cognitive dissonance) to monitor the product's performance and its ability to meet customers' expectations.

while consumers consider which product to buy, they also consider where they might buy it. In the case of name brand products, this selection process may focus on the product's price and availability at different stores or online merchants. A specific model of Sony television, for example, is often available from many different retailers and may even be available at Sony's website (www.sonystyle.com). Conversely, in the case of private-label merchandise, the choice of product and merchant are made simultaneously. If a

© Susan Van Etten

When consumers purchase products like candy or gum on impulse, they rarely go through each stage of the buying process.

customer is interested only in Gap brand clothing, then that customer must purchase the clothing from a Gap store or the Gap website.

Third, the choice of a suitable merchant may actually take precedence over the choice of a specific product. In some cases, customers are so loyal to a particular merchant that they will not consider looking elsewhere. For example, many older consumers are fiercely loyal to American car manufacturers. These customers will limit their product selection to a single brand or dealership, greatly limiting their range of potential product choices. In other cases, customers might be loyal to a particular merchant because they hold that merchant's credit card or are a member of its frequent customer program. Finally, some merchants become so well-known for certain products that customers just naturally execute their buying process with that merchant. Sears, for example, is well-known for its selection of name-brand appliances and tools. For many customers, Sears is the natural place to go when they are in the market for a new refrigerator, washer, or wrenches.

Need Recognition   The buying process begins when consumers recognize that they have an unmet need. This occurs when consumers realize that there is a discrepancy between their existing situation and their desired situation (i.e., satisfaction or fulfillment). Consumers can recognize needs in a variety of settings and situations. Some needs have their basis in internal stimuli, such as hunger, thirst, and fatigue. Other needs have their basis in external stimuli, such as advertising, window shopping, interacting with salespeople, or talking with friends and family. External stimuli can also arouse internal responses, such as the hunger you might feel when watching an advertisement for Pizza Hut.

Typically, we think of needs as necessities, particularly with respect to the necessities of life (food, water, clothing, safety, shelter, health, or love). However, this definition is limited because everyone has a different perspective on what constitutes a need. For example, many people would argue that they need a car when their real need is for transportation. Their need for a car is really a "want" for a car. This is where we draw the distinction between needs and wants. A need occurs when an individual's current level of satisfaction does not equal their desired level of satisfaction. A want is a consumer's desire for a specific product that will satisfy the need. Hence, people need transportation, but they choose to fulfill that need with a car rather than with alternative products like motorcycles, bicycles, pubic transportation, a taxi, or a horse.

The distinction between needs and wants is not simply academic. In any marketing effort, the firm must always understand the basic needs fulfilled by its products. For example, people do not need drills; they need to make holes or drive screws. Similarly, they do not need lawnmowers; they need shorter, well-manicured grass. Understanding these basic needs allows the firm to segment markets and create marketing programs that can translate consumer needs into wants for their specific products. An important part of this effort involves creating the appropriate stimuli that will foster need recognition among consumers. The idea is to build on the basic need and convince potential consumers to want your product because it will fulfill their needs better than any competing product.

It is also important to understand that wants are not the same thing as demand. Demand occurs only when the consumer's ability and willingness to purchase a specific product backs up their want for the product. Many customers want a luxury yacht, for example, but only a few are able and willing to buy one. In some cases, consumers may actually need a product, but not want it. So-called "unsought products" like life insurance, cemetery plots, long-term health insurance, and continuing education are good examples. In these cases, the marketer must first educate consumers on the need for the product, and then convince consumers to want its products over competing products. For example, Allstate's "Are You in Good Hands?" campaign specifically questions whether potential customers are sure about their insurance coverage. Creating the seed of doubt in the consumer's mind is a good first step toward educating potential customers about the need for adequate insurance.

Understanding consumers' needs and wants is an important consideration in market segmentation. Some markets can be segmented on the basis of needs alone. College students, for example, have needs that are very different from senior citizens; and single consumers have very different needs than families with small children. However, the marketing of most products does not occur on the basis of need fulfillment alone. In the automobile market, for example, essentially no manufacturer promotes their products as being the best to get you from point A to point B (the basic need of transportation). Rather, they market their products on the basis of consumer wants such as luxury (Lexus), image (Mercedes), sportiness (Jaguar), durability (Ford trucks), fuel economy (Honda Civic), and value (Kia). These wants are the hot buttons for consumers, and the keys to promoting further activity in the buying process.

Information Search   When done correctly, marketing stimuli can prompt consumers to become interested in a product, leading to a desire to seek out additional information. This desire can be passive or active. In a passive information search, the consumer becomes more attentive and receptive to information, such as noticing and paying attention to automobile advertisements if the customer has a want for a specific car brand. A consumer engages in active information search when he or she purposely seeks additional information, such as by surfing the Internet, asking friends, or visiting dealer showrooms. Information can come from a variety of sources. Internal sources, including personal experiences and memories, are typically the first type of information that consumers search. Information can also come from personal sources, including word-of-mouth advice from friends, family, or coworkers. External sources of information include advertising, magazines, websites, packaging, displays, and salespeople. Although external sources are the most numerous, consumers typically trust these sources less than internal and personal sources of information.

The amount of time, effort, and expense dedicated to the search for information depends on a number of issues. First, and perhaps most important, is the degree of risk involved in the purchase. Consumers by nature are risk averse; they use their search for information to reduce risk and increase the odds of making the right choice. Buying risk comes in many forms, including financial risk (buying a home), social risk (buying the right clothing), emotional risk (selecting a wedding photographer), and personal risk (choosing the right surgeon). In buying a car, for example, consumers regularly turn to *Consumer Reports* magazine, friends, and government safety ratings to help reduce these types of risk. A second issue is the amount of expertise or experience the consumer has with the product category. A first-time buyer in the market for a notebook computer faces a bewildering array of choices and brands. This buyer is likely to engage in extensive information search to reduce risk and narrow the potential set of product choices. The same buyer, several purchases later, will not go through the same process. Finally, the actual cost of the search in terms of time and money will limit the degree to which consumers search for information. In some situations, such as time deadlines or emergencies, consumers have little time to consult all sources of information at their disposal.

Throughout the information search, consumers learn about different products or brands and begin to remove some from further consideration. They evaluate and reevaluate their initial set of products or brands until their list of potential product choices has been narrowed to only a few products or brands that can meet their needs. This list of suitable alternatives is called the evoked set, and it represents the outcome of the information search and the beginning of the next stage of the buying process.

Evaluation of Alternatives   In evaluating the alternative product or brand choices among the members of the evoked set, the consumer essentially translates his or her need into a want for a specific product or brand. The evaluation of alternatives is the black box of consumer behavior because it is typically the hardest for marketers to understand, measure, or influence. What we do know about this stage of the buying process is that consumers base their evaluation on a number of different criteria, which usually equate with a number of product attributes.

Consumers evaluate products as bundles of attributes that have varying abilities to satisfy their needs. In buying a car, for example, each potential choice represents a bundle of attributes, including brand attributes (e.g., image, reputation, reliability, safety), product features (e.g., power windows, automatic transmission, fuel economy), aesthetic attributes (e.g., styling, sportiness, roominess, color), and price. Each consumer has a different opinion as to the relative importance of these attributes—some put safety first, whereas others consider price the dominant factor. Another interesting feature of the evaluation stage is that the priority of each consumer's choice criteria can change during the process. Consumers may visit a dealership with price as their dominant criterion, only to leave the dealership with price dropping to third on their list of important attributes.

There are several important considerations for marketers during the evaluation stage. First and foremost, the marketer's products must be in the evoked set of potential alternatives. For this reason, marketers must constantly remind consumers of their company and its product offerings. Second, it is vital that marketers take steps to understand consumers' choice criteria and the importance they place on specific product attributes. As we will see later in this chapter, understanding the connection between customers' needs and product attributes is an important consideration in market segmentation and target marketing decisions. Finally, marketers must often design marketing programs that change the priority of choice criteria or change consumers' opinions about a product's image. Microsoft, for example, has moved aggressively to combat the slow erosion of its dominant share of the market for computer operating systems. The growing popularity of Apple's OS X operating system, along with the advent of cheap netbooks running Linux, prompted Microsoft to fight back with a flurry of advertisements touting the reliability and ease of use of Windows 7.[3]

Purchase Decision   After the consumer has evaluated each alternative in the evoked set, he or she forms an intention to purchase a particular product or brand. However, a purchase intention and the actual act of buying are distinct concepts. A consumer may have every intention of purchasing a new car, for example, but several factors may prevent the actual purchase from taking place. The customer may postpone the purchase due to unforeseen circumstances, such as an illness or job loss. The salesperson or the sales manager may anger the customer, leading him or her to walk away from the deal. The buyer may not be able to obtain financing for a purchase due to a mistake in his or her credit file. Or the buyer may simply change his or her mind. Marketers can often reduce or eliminate these problems by reducing the risk of purchase through warranties or guarantees, making the purchase stage as easy as possible, or by finding creative solutions to unexpected problems.

Assuming these potential intervening factors are not a concern, the key issues for marketers during the purchase stage are product availability and possession utility. Product availability is critical. Without it, buyers will not purchase from you, but from someone else who can deliver the product. The key to availability—which is closely related to the distribution component of the marketing program—is convenience. The goal is to put the product within the consumer's reach wherever that consumer happens to be. This task is closely related to possession utility (i.e., ease of taking possession). To increase possession utility, the marketer may have to offer financing or layaway for large dollar purchases, delivery and installation of products like appliances or furniture, home delivery of convenience items like pizza or newspapers, or the proper packaging and prompt shipment of items through the mail.

Postpurchase Evaluation   In the context of attracting and retaining buyers, postpurchase evaluation is the connection between the buying process and the development of long-term customer relationships. Marketers must closely follow consumers' responses during this stage to monitor the product's performance and its ability to meet consumers' expectations. In the postpurchase stage, buyers will experience one of these four outcomes:

- **Delight**   The product's performance greatly exceeds the buyer's expectations.
- **Satisfaction**   The product's performance matches the buyer's expectations.
- **Dissatisfaction**   The product's performance falls short of the buyer's expectations.
- **Cognitive Dissonance (Postpurchase Doubt)**   The buyer is unsure of the product's performance relative to his or her expectations.

Consumers are more likely to experience dissatisfaction or cognitive dissonance when the dollar value of the purchase increases, the opportunity costs of rejected alternatives are high, or the purchase decision is emotionally involving. Firms can manage these responses by offering liberal return policies, providing extensive post-sale support, or reinforcing the wisdom of the consumer's purchase decision. The firm's ability to manage dissatisfaction and dissonance is not only a key to creating customer satisfaction; it also has a major influence on the consumer's intentions to spread word-of-mouth information about the company and its products.

Factors That Affect the Consumer Buying Process

As we mentioned previously, the stages in the buying process depict a range of possible activities that may occur as consumers make purchase decisions. Consumers may spend relatively more or less time in certain stages, they may follow the stages in or out of sequence, or they may even skip stages entirely. This variation in the buying process occurs because consumers are different, the products that they buy are different, and the situations in which consumers make purchase decisions are different. There are a number of factors that affect the consumer buying process, including the complexity of the purchase and decision, individual influences, social influences, and situational influences. We will briefly examine each factor.

Decision-Making Complexity   The complexity of the purchase and decision-making process is the primary reason why the buying process will vary across consumers and with the same consumer in different situations. For example, highly complex decisions, like buying a first home, a first car, selecting the right college, or choosing elective surgery, are very involving for most consumers. These purchases are often characterized by high personal, social, or financial risk; strong emotional involvement; and the lack of experience with the product or purchase situation. In these instances, consumers will spend a great deal of time, effort, and even money to help ensure that they make the right decision. In contrast, purchase tasks that are low in complexity are relatively non-involving for most consumers. In some cases, these purchase tasks can become routine in nature. For example, many consumers buy groceries by selecting familiar items from the shelf and placing them in their carts without considering alternative products.

For marketers, managing decision-making complexity is an important consideration. Marketers of highly complex products must recognize that consumers are quite risk averse and need a great deal of information to help them make the right decision. In these situations, access to high-quality and useful information should be an important consideration in the firm's marketing program. Firms that sell less complex products do not have to provide as much information, but they do face the challenges of creating a brand image and ensuring that their products are easily recognizable. For these marketers, issues like branding, packaging, advertising, and point-of-purchase displays are key considerations in the marketing program.

Individual Influences   The range of individual influences that can affect the buying process is quite extensive. Some individual factors, such as age, life cycle, occupation, and socioeconomic status, are fairly easy to understand and incorporate into the marketing strategy. For the most part, these individual factors dictate preferences for certain types of products or brands. Married consumers with three children will clearly have different needs and preferences than young, single consumers. Likewise, more affluent consumers will have the same basic needs as less affluent consumers; however, their "wants" will be quite different. These individual factors are quite useful for marketers in target market selection, product development, and promotional strategy.

Other individual factors, such as perceptions, motives, interests, attitudes, opinions, or lifestyles, are much harder to understand because they do not clearly coincide with demographic characteristics like age, gender, or income levels. These individual factors are also very difficult to change. For that reason, many marketers adapt their products and promotional messages to fit existing attitudes, interests, or lifestyles. For example, Honda introduced the Fit subcompact car in the United States to appeal to a younger, nonconformist demographic that loves digital music, ringtones, video games, and graphic movies. The Fit's quirky style and flexible interior is appealing to this target market.[4]

Social Influences   Like individual influences, there is a wide range of social influences that can affect the buying process. Social influences such as culture, subculture, social class, reference groups, and family have a profound impact on what, why, and how consumers buy. Among these social influences, none is more important than the family. From birth, individuals become socialized with respect to the knowledge and skills needed to be effective consumers. As adults, consumers typically exhibit the brand and product preferences of their parents. The influence of children on the buying process has grown tremendously over the last 50 years.

Reference groups and opinion leaders also have an important impact on consumers' buying processes. Reference groups act as a point of comparison and source of product information. A consumer's purchase decisions tend to fall in line with the advice, beliefs, and actions of one or more reference groups. Opinion leaders can be part of a reference group or may be specific individuals that exist outside of a reference group. When consumers feel like they lack personal expertise, they seek the advice of opinion leaders, who they view as being well informed in a particular field of knowledge. In some cases, marketers will seek out opinion leaders before trying to reach more mainstream consumers. Software manufacturers, for example, release beta (test) versions of their products to opinion leaders before a full-scale launch. Not only does this practice work the bugs out of the product, it also starts a word-of-mouth buzz about the upcoming software release.

Situational Influences   There are a number of situational influences that can affect the consumer buying process. Exhibit 6.2 illustrates some of the most common situational influences, many of which affect the amount of time and effort that consumers devote to the purchase task. For example, hungry consumers who are in a hurry often grab the quickest lunch they can find—even if it comes from a vending machine. This fact accounts for the quick success of Pret a Manger, a chain of fast-food restaurants that offers prepackaged fare focusing on fresh, all-natural, and organic foods.[5] Consumers facing emergency situations have little time to reflect on their product choices and whether they will make the right decision. Consumers may also devote less time and effort to the buying process if they are uncomfortable. For this reason, sit-down restaurants should be inviting and relaxing to encourage longer visits and add-ons such as dessert or coffee after the meal.

EXHIBIT 6.2	COMMON SITUATIONAL INFLUENCES IN THE CONSUMER BUYING PROCESS

Situational Influences	Examples	Potential Influences on Buying Behavior
Physical and spatial influences	Retail atmospherics Retail crowding Store layout and design	A comfortable atmosphere or ambience promotes lingering, browsing, and buying. Crowded stores may cause customers to leave or buy less than planned.
Social and interpersonal influences	Shopping in groups Salespeople Other customers	Consumers are more susceptible to the influences of other consumers when shopping in groups. Rude salespeople can end the buying process. Obnoxious "other" customers may cause the consumer to leave or be dissatisfied.
Temporal (time) influences	Lack of time Emergencies Convenience	Consumers will pay more for products when they are in a hurry or face an emergency. Lack of time greatly reduces the search for information and the evaluation of alternatives. Consumers with ample time can seek information on many different product alternatives.
Purchase task or product usage influences	Special occasions Buying for others Buying a gift	Consumers may buy higher quality products for gifts or special occasions. The evoked set will differ when consumers are buying for others as opposed to themselves.
Consumer dispositional influences	Stress Anxiety Fear Fatigue Emotional involvement Good/bad mood	Consumers suffering from stress or fatigue may not buy at all or they may indulge in certain products to make themselves feel better. Consumers who are in a bad mood are exceptionally difficult to please. An increase in fear or anxiety over a purchase may cause consumers to seek additional information and take great pains to make the right decision.

Other situational influences can affect specific product choices. For example, if you have your boss over for dinner, your product choices would likely differ from those you make in everyday purchases of food and drink. Likewise, customers may purchase more expensive items for gifts or when they shop with friends. Product choices also change when customers make the purchase for someone else, such as buying clothing for children. In fact, many parents will purposely buy less expensive clothing for their children if they are growing rapidly or are exceptionally active. These parents want to save money on clothing that will quickly wear out or become too small.

Buyer Behavior in Business Markets

As we shift our attention to buyer behavior in business markets, keep in mind that business markets and consumer markets have many things in common. Both contain buyers and sellers who seek to make good purchases and satisfy their personal or organizational objectives. Both markets use similar buying processes that include stages associated with need identification, information search, and product evaluation. Finally, both processes focus on customer satisfaction as the desired outcome. However, business markets differ from consumer markets in important ways. One of the most important differences involves the consumption of the purchased products.

Consumers buy products for their personal use or consumption. In contrast, organizational buyers purchase products for use in their operations. These uses can be direct, as in acquiring raw materials to produce finished goods; or indirect, as in buying office supplies or leasing cars for salespeople. There are four types of business markets:

- **Commercial Markets**   These markets buy raw materials for use in producing finished goods, and they buy facilitating goods and services used in the production of finished goods. Commercial markets include a variety of industries, such as aerospace, agriculture, mining, construction, transportation, communication, and utilities.

- **Reseller Markets**   These markets consist of channel intermediaries such as wholesalers, retailers, or brokers that buy finished goods from the producer market and resell them at a profit. As we will see later in Chapter 9, channel intermediaries have the responsibility for creating the variety and assortment of products offered to consumers. Therefore, they wield a great deal of power in the supply chain.

- **Government Markets**   These markets include federal, state, county, city, and local governments. Governments buy a wide range of finished goods ranging from aircraft carriers to fire trucks to office equipment. However, most government purchases are for the services provided to citizens, such as education, fire and police protection, maintenance and repair of roads, and water and sewage treatment.

- **Institutional Markets**   These markets consist of a diverse group of noncommercial organizations such as churches, charities, schools, hospitals, or professional organizations. These organizations primarily buy finished goods that facilitate their ongoing operations.

Unique Characteristics of Business Markets

Business markets differ from consumer markets in at least four ways. These differences concern the nature of the decision-making unit, the role of hard and soft costs in making and evaluating purchase decisions, reciprocal buying relationships, and the dependence of the two parties on each other. As a general rule, these differences are more acute for firms attempting to build long-term client relationships. In business markets, buying needed products at the lowest possible price is not necessarily the most important objective. Many business transactions are based on long-term relationships, so trust, reliability, and overall goal attainment are often much more important than the price of the product.

The Buying Center   The first key difference relates to the role of the *buying center* — the group of people responsible for making purchase decisions. In consumer markets, the buying center is fairly straightforward: The adult head of household tends to make most major purchase decisions for the family, with input and assistance from children and other family members as applicable. In an organization, however, the buying center tends to be much more complex and difficult to identify, in part because it may include three distinct groups of people—economic buyers, technical buyers, and users—each of which may have its own agenda and unique needs that affect the buying decision.

Any effort to build a relationship between the selling and buying organization must include economic buyers—those senior managers with the overall responsibility of achieving the buying firm's objectives. In recent years, economic buyers have become increasingly influential as price has become less important in determining a product's true value to the buying firm. This has made economic buyers a greater target for promotional activities. Technical buyers—employees with the responsibility of buying products to meet needs on an ongoing basis—include purchasing agents and materials managers. These buyers have the responsibility of narrowing the number of product options and delivering buying recommendations to the economic buyer(s) that are within budget. Technical buyers are critical in the execution of purchase transactions and are also important to the day-to-day maintenance of long-term relationships. Users—managers and employees who have the responsibility of using a product purchased by the firm—comprise the last group of people in the buying center. The user is often not the ultimate decision maker, but frequently has a place in the decision process, particularly in the case of technologically advanced products. For example, the head of information technology often has a major role in computer and IT purchase decisions.

Hard and Soft Costs   The second difference between business and consumer markets involves the significance of hard and soft costs. Consumers and organizations both consider *hard costs*, which include monetary price and associated purchase costs such as shipping and installation. Organizations, however, must also consider *soft costs*, such as downtime, opportunity costs, and human resource costs associated with the compatibility of systems, in the buying decision. The purchase and implementation of a new payroll system, for example, will decrease productivity and increase training costs in the payroll department until the new system has been fully integrated.

Reciprocity   The third key difference involves the existence of reciprocal buying relationships. With consumer purchases, the opportunity for buying and selling is usually a one-way street: The marketer sells and the consumer buys. Business marketing, however, is more often a two-way street, with each firm marketing products that the other firm buys. For example, a company may buy office supplies from another company that in turn buys copiers from the first firm. In fact, such arrangements can be an upfront condition of purchase in purely transaction-based marketing. Reciprocal buying is less likely to occur within long-term relationships unless it helps both parties achieve their respective goals.

Mutual Dependence   Finally, in business markets, the buyer and seller are more likely to be dependent on one another. For consumer–marketer relationships, this level of dependence tends to be low. If a store is out of a product, or a firm goes out of business, customers simply switch to another source to meet their needs. Likewise, the loss of a particular customer through brand switching, relocation, or death is unfortunate for a company, but not in itself particularly damaging. The only real exception to this norm is when consumers are loyal to a brand or merchant. In these cases, consumers become dependent on a single brand or merchant, and the firm can become dependent on the sales volume generated by these brand-loyal consumers.

This is not the case in business markets where sole-source or limited-source buying may leave an organization's operations severely distressed when a supplier shuts down or cannot deliver. The same is true for the loss of a customer. The selling firm has invested significantly in the client relationship, often modifying products and altering information or other systems central to the organization. Each client relationship represents a significant portion of the firm's profit, and the loss of a single customer can take months or even years to replace. For example, after Rubbermaid's relationships with Walmart, Lowe's, and Home Depot soured in the mid-1990s, these retailers pulled Rubbermaid products from their shelves and turned to Sterilite, a small Massachusetts-based manufacturer, to supply plastic products (storage bins, containers, etc.) for their stores. Along with damaging Rubbermaid's reputation and profits, the considerable buying power of Walmart, Lowe's, and Home Depot turned Sterilite into a major competitor for Rubbermaid. Rubbermaid was able to recover somewhat by lavishing its buying partners with exceptional service.[6]

The Business Buying Process

Like consumers, businesses follow a buying process. However, given the complexity, risk, and expense of many business purchases, business buyers tend to follow these stages in sequence. Some buying situations can be quite routine, such as the daily or weekly purchase and delivery of raw materials or the purchase of office consumables like paper and toner cartridges. Nonetheless, business buyers often make even routine purchases from prequalified or single-source suppliers. Consequently, virtually all business purchases have gone through the following stages of the buying process at one time or another:

1. **Problem Recognition**   The recognition of needs can stem from a variety of internal and external sources, such as employees, members of the buying center, or outside salespeople. Business buyers often recognize needs due to special circumstances, such as when equipment or machinery breaks or malfunctions.

2. **Develop Product Specifications**   Detailed product specifications often define business purchases. This occurs because new purchases must be integrated with current technologies and processes. Developing product specifications is typically done by the buying center.

3. **Vendor Identification and Qualification**   Business buyers must ensure that potential vendors can deliver on needed product specifications, within a specified time frame, and in the needed quantities. Therefore, business buyers will conduct a thorough analysis of potential vendors to ensure they can meet their firm's needs. The buyers then qualify and approve the vendors that meet their criteria to supply goods and services to the firm.

4. **Solicitation of Proposals or Bids**   Depending on the purchase in question, the buying firm may request that qualified vendors submit proposals or bids. These

proposals or bids will detail how the vendor will meet the buying firm's needs and fulfill the purchase criteria established during the second stage of the process.

5. **Vendor Selection**   The buying firm will select the vendor or vendors that can best meet its needs. The best vendor is not necessarily the one offering the lowest price. Other issues such as reputation, timeliness of delivery, guarantees, or personal relationships with the members of the buying center are often more important.

6. **Order Processing**   Often a behind-the-scenes process, order processing involves the details of processing the order, negotiating credit terms, setting firm delivery dates, and any final technical assistance needed to complete the purchase.

7. **Vendor Performance Review**   The final stage of the buying process involves a review of the vendor's performance. In some cases, the product may flawlessly fulfill the needed specifications, but the vendor's performance is poor. In this stage, both product and vendor specifications can be reevaluated and changed if necessary. In the end, the result of these evaluations will affect future purchase decisions.

Like consumer markets, there are a number of factors that can influence the business buying process. Environmental conditions can have a major influence on buyer behavior by increasing the uncertainty, complexity, and risk associated with a purchase. In situations of rapid environmental change, business buyers may alter their buying plans, postpone purchases, or even cancel purchases until things settle down. Environmental conditions not only affect the purchase of products, they also affect decisions regarding the recruitment and hiring of employees.

Organizational factors can also influence business buying decisions. These factors include conditions within the firm's internal environment (resources, strategies, policies, objectives), as well as the condition of relationships with business or supply chain partners. A shift in the firm's resources can change buying decisions, such as a temporary delay in purchasing until favorable credit terms can be arranged. Likewise, if a supplier suddenly cannot provide needed quantities of products or cannot meet a needed delivery schedule, the buying firm will be forced to identify and qualify new suppliers. Internal changes in information technology can also affect the buying process, such as when technicians integrate electronic procurement systems with the legacy systems of the firm and its vendors. Finally, interpersonal relationships and individual factors can affect the buying process. A common example occurs when members of the buying center are at odds over purchase decisions. Power struggles are not uncommon in business buying, and they can bring the entire process to a halt if not handled properly. Individual factors, such as a manager's personal preferences or prejudices, can also affect business buying decisions. The importance of interpersonal and individual factors depends on the specific buying situation and its importance to the firm's goals and objectives. Major purchases typically create the most conflict among members of the buying center.

Market Segmentation

Understanding the processes that consumers and businesses use to make purchase decisions is critical to the development of long-term, mutually beneficial relationships with customers. It is also a necessary first step in uncovering similarities among groups of potential buyers that can be used in market segmentation and target marketing decisions. From a strategic perspective, we define *market segmentation* as the process of dividing the total market for a particular product or product category into relatively homogeneous segments or groups. To be effective, segmentation should create groups where the members within the group have similar likes, tastes, needs, wants, or preferences, but where the groups themselves are dissimilar from each other. As noted in *Beyond the Pages 6.2*, the increasing diversity of the U.S. population creates a number of opportunities and challenges when it comes to segmenting markets.

In reality, the most fundamental segmentation decision is really whether to segment at all. When a firm makes the decision to pursue the entire market, it must do so on the basis of universal needs that all customers possess. However, most firms opt to target one or more segments of the total market because they find that they can be more successful when they tailor products to fit unique needs or requirements. In today's economy, segmentation is often mandated by customers due to their search for unique products and their changing uses of communication media. The end result is that customer segments have become even more fragmented and more difficult to reach. Many firms today take segmentation to the extreme by targeting small niches of a market, or even the smallest of market segments: individuals.

Traditional Market Segmentation Approaches

Many segmentation approaches are traditional in the sense that firms have used them successfully for decades. It is not our intention to depict these approaches as old or out of date, especially when compared to individualized segmentation strategies that we discuss later. In fact, many of today's most successful firms use these tried-and-true approaches. Some organizations actually use more than one type of segmentation, depending on the brand, product, or market in question.

Mass Marketing   It seems odd to call mass marketing a segmentation approach, as it involves no segmentation whatsoever. Companies aim mass marketing campaigns at the total (whole) market for a particular product. Companies that adopt mass marketing take an undifferentiated approach that assumes that all customers in the market have similar needs and wants that can be reasonably satisfied with a single marketing program. This marketing program typically consists of a single product or brand (or, in the case of retailers, a homogeneous set of products), one price, one promotional program, and one distribution system. Duracell, for example, offers a collection of different battery sizes (D, C, A, AA, AAA, 9-volt), but they are all disposable batteries marketed to consumers for use in toys and small electronic devices. Likewise, the WD-40 Company offers an assortment of brands—including WD-40, 3-IN-ONE Oil, Lava Soap, 2000 Flushes, Carpet Fresh, and X14 Cleaner—used in a variety of household tasks.

The WD-40 Company uses mass marketing by offering an assortment of brands geared toward common household tasks.

© Susan Van Etten

Mass marketing works best when the needs of an entire market are relatively homogeneous. Good examples include commodities like oil and agricultural products. In reality, very few products or markets are ideal for mass marketing, if for no other reason than companies, wanting to reach new customers, often modify their product lines. For most of its existence, Vaseline manufactured and offered a single product. To reach new customers, Vaseline modified this strategy by launching its Intensive Care line of products and extending customers' perception of Vaseline's uses to various needs in the home, including in the garage/workshop. Furthermore, think of the many products that contain Arm & Hammer Baking Soda, a product that at one time was sold only as a baking ingredient.

Although mass marketing is advantageous in terms of production efficiency and lower marketing costs, it is inherently risky. By offering a standard product to all customers, the organization becomes vulnerable to competitors that offer specialized products that better match customers' needs. In industries where barriers to entry are low, mass marketing runs the risk of being seen as too generic. This situation is very inviting for competitors who use more targeted approaches. Mass marketing is also very risky in global markets, where even global brands like Coca-Cola must be adapted to match local tastes and customs.

Differentiated Marketing   Most firms use some form of market segmentation by (1) dividing the total market into groups of customers having relatively common or homogeneous needs, and (2) attempting to develop a marketing program that appeals to one or more of these groups. This approach may be necessary when customer needs are similar within a single group, but their needs differ across groups. Through well-designed and carefully conducted research, firms can identify the particular needs of each market segment to create marketing programs that best match those needs and expectations. Within the differentiated approach there are two options: the multisegment approach and the market concentration approach.

Firms using the *multisegment approach* seek to attract buyers in more than one market segment by offering a variety of products that appeal to different needs. Firms using this option can increase their share of the market by responding to the heterogeneous needs of different segments. If the segments have enough buying potential, and the product is successful, the resulting sales increases can more than offset the increased costs of offering multiple products and marketing programs. The multisegment approach is the most widely used segmentation strategy in medium- to large-sized firms. It is extremely common in packaged goods and grocery products. Maxwell House, for example, began by marketing one type of coffee and one brand. Today, this division of Kraft Foods offers 22 different brand varieties under the Maxwell House, Sanka, and Yuban labels, in addition to providing private label

Beyond the Pages 6.2

MULTICULTURAL MARKETING GOES MAINSTREAM[7]

Although there are obvious differences among the members of our population, many people are surprised to learn that the United States is more diverse than they would have realized. However, we should not be surprised. After all, the United States was founded as a melting pot of cultures. That pot of cultural differences creates many challenges and opportunities in finding and serving target markets. Consider the following statistics:

- Roughly one-third of the U.S. population is a minority. If these consumers were a separate country, they would be the 12th largest in the world.

- Ten percent of counties in the United States have a resident base that is greater than 50 percent minority.

- Minority populations have a large middle class with strong buying power. For instance, the buying power of Hispanics is currently over $860 billion and expected to grow to $1.2 trillion in five years. For African Americans, the number is expected to grow from $845 billion to $1.1 trillion. For Asian Americans, the current buying power of $459 billion will grow to $670 billion in five years.

- The defining characteristics of minority markets are not based on skin color or language. Instead, core values such as family, faith, nationalism, respect for the elderly and community leaders, and cultural institutions are the dominant features that define minority populations.

- Minority populations have stopped trying to "fit in" with traditional U.S. customs. Instead, these groups work hard to preserve their ethnic values and customs.

- Distinct minority populations have little in common with each other, other than their emotional connections to their own ethnic traditions.

Given these stark facts, it becomes clear that firms will have a hard time reaching a mass audience of U.S. consumers using a one-size-fits-all marketing approach. So, how can a firm reach across segments of society for maximum marketing effectiveness and efficiency? The truth is that most firms don't bother. Still, targeting specific minority groups has become more difficult. The tactics of yesterday—simple language translation, hiring diverse employees, or using photos of ethnic minorities in promotional images—won't work anymore.

One approach is digital communication. Despite our differences, marketers have learned that virtually all cultures have an affinity for gadgets and respond well to digital communication. For example, when Microsoft learned that Hispanic consumers are very interested in parental controls on their home computers, the company responded by changing its online advertising for Windows 7 to target these customers. Another approach is to promote ethnic individuality. When Toyota wanted to leverage the growing Asian-American film community, the company created a stand-alone website—called The Director's Chair—that offered interviews with Asian-American actors and directors, and Toyota advertisements. Other firms look to specialized advertising agencies for help. One example is Translation Advertising, a New York company that is co-owned by rapper Jay-Z. Rather than using traditional survey or focus group research, Translation helps firms connect with minorities on an emotional level via immersion research—an approach based on living and working inside the ethnic culture.

brands for retailers. A walk down the cereal aisle of your local supermarket offers additional examples. Firms such as Kellogg's and Nabisco offer seemingly hundreds of brands of breakfast cereals targeted at specific segments, including children (e.g., Fruity Pebbles, Apple Jacks), health-conscious adults (e.g., Shredded

Wheat, Total), parents looking for healthier foods for their children (e.g., Life, Kix), and so on.

Firms using the *market concentration* approach focus on a single market segment. These firms often find it most efficient to seek a maximum share in one segment of the market. For example, Armor All markets a well-known line of automotive cleaners, protectants, and polishes targeted primarily to young, driving-age males. The main advantage of market concentration is specialization, as it allows the firm to focus all of its resources toward understanding and serving a single segment. Specialization is also the major disadvantage of this approach. By "putting all of its eggs in one basket," the firm can be vulnerable to changes in its market segment, such as economic downturns and demographic shifts. Still, the market concentration approach can be highly successful. In the arts, where market concentration is almost universal, musical groups hone their talents and plan their performances to satisfy the tastes of one market segment, divided by genres of music such as country, rock, or jazz.

Niche Marketing   Some companies narrow the market concentration approach even more and focus their marketing efforts on one small, well-defined market segment or niche that has a unique, specific set of needs. Customers in niche markets will typically pay higher prices for products that match their specialized needs. One example of successful niche marketing is found in the gym industry. For example, Curves—a health club for women—now has 10,000 locations around the world. Other niche gyms for children and the over-55 age group are popping up around the United States. The goal of these gyms is to create highly customized workout experiences for niche markets that don't fit the profile of a typical health club member.[8] As the gym industry has learned, the key to successful niche marketing is to understand and meet the needs of target customers so completely that, despite the small size of the niche, the firm's substantial share makes the segment highly profitable. An attractive market niche is one that has growth and profit potential, but is not so appealing that it attracts competitors. The firm should also possess a specialization or provide a unique offering that customers find highly desirable.

Individualized Segmentation Approaches

Due to advances in communication and Internet technology, individualized segmentation approaches have emerged. These approaches are possible because organizations now have the ability to track customers with a high degree of specificity. By combining demographic data with past and current purchasing behavior, organizations can tweak their marketing programs in ways that allow them to precisely match customers' needs, wants, and preferences. Three types of individualized segmentation approaches are one-to-one marketing, mass customization, and permission marketing.

One-to-One Marketing   A company employs one-to-one marketing when it creates an entirely unique product or marketing program for each customer in the target segment. This approach is common in business markets where companies design unique programs and/or systems for each customer. For example, providers of enterprise software—such as Oracle, SAP, and Business Objects—create customized solutions that allow firms to track customers, business processes, and results in real time. Insurance companies or brokers, such as Britain's Sedgwick Group, design insurance and pension programs to meet a corporation's specific needs. The key to one-to-one marketing is personalization, where every element of the marketing program is customized to meet the specifics of a particular client's situation.

Historically, one-to-one marketing has been used less often in consumer markets, although Burger King was an early pioneer in this approach, with its "Have It Your Way" effort that continues today. One-to-one marketing is quite common in luxury and custom-made products, such as when a consumer buys a large sailboat, airplane, or a custom-built home. In such instances, the product has significant modifications made to it to meet unique customer needs and preferences. Many service firms—such as hairstylists, lawyers, doctors, and educational institutions—also customize their marketing programs to match individual consumer needs. One-to-one marketing has grown rapidly in electronic commerce where customers can be targeted very precisely. Amazon, for example, maintains complete profiles on customers who browse and buy from its site. These profiles assist Amazon with the customization of web pages in real time, product suggestions, and reminder e-mails sent to customers.

Mass Customization   An extension of one-to-one marketing, mass customization refers to providing unique products and solutions to individual customers on a mass scale. Along with the Internet, advances in supply chain management—including real-time inventory control—have allowed companies to customize products in ways that are both cost-effective and practical. For example, Dell builds thousands of custom-ordered computers every day. 1-800-Flowers.com can create custom flower arrangements, plants, or other gifts and deliver them to family and friends in the same day. Likewise, customers of the Build-A-Bear Workshop retail stores can select, stuff, wash, and dress a teddy bear or other animal of their choice. Customers can even include their own voice greeting with the stuffed animal.

Mass customization also occurs in business markets. Through a buying firm's electronic procurement system, employees can order products ranging from office supplies to travel services. The system allows employees to requisition goods and services via a customized catalog—unique to the firm—where the buying firm has negotiated the products and prices. E-procurement systems like these have become quite popular for good reason: They allow firms to save a great deal of money—not only on prices, but also on the costs of placing orders. Selling firms benefit as well by customizing their catalogs to specific buying firms, allowing them to sell more goods and services at a reduced cost.

Permission Marketing   Permission marketing, although similar to one-to-one marketing, is different in that customers choose to become part of a firm's market segment. In permission marketing, customers give companies permission to specifically target them in their marketing efforts. The most common tool used in permission marketing is the opt-in e-mail list, where customers permit a firm—or a third-party partner of the firm—to send periodic e-mail about goods and services that they have interest in purchasing. This scenario is ubiquitous in business-to-consumer e-commerce, so much so that many consumers fail to notice it. When customers order products online, they receive the option of receiving or not receiving future e-mail notifications about new products. In many cases, customers must deselect a box at the end of the order form or they will be added to the e-mail list.

Permission marketing has a major advantage over other individualized segmentation approaches: Customers who opt in have already shown interest in the goods and services offered by the firm. This allows the firm to precisely target only those individuals with an interest in their products, thereby eliminating wasted marketing effort and expense. For example, many airlines have the permission of their customers to send weekly e-mail notices of airfare and other travel-related specials. This system is in stark contrast to traditional mass media advertising, where only a portion of the viewing or reading audience has a real interest in the company's product.

One-to-one marketing, mass customization, and permission marketing will become even more important in the future because their focus on individual customers makes them critical to the development and maintenance of long-term relationships. The simple truth is that customers will maintain relationships with firms that best fulfill their needs or solve their problems. Unfortunately, individualized segmentation approaches can be prohibitively expensive. To make these approaches viable, firms must be mindful of two important issues. First, the delivery of the marketing program must be automated to a degree that makes it cost-efficient. The Internet makes this possible by allowing for individual customization in real time. Second, the marketing program must not become so automated that the offering lacks personalization. Today, personalization means much more than simply calling customers by name. We use the term to describe the idea of giving customers choices—not only in terms of product configuration, but also in terms of the entire marketing program. Firms like Dell and Amazon offer a great deal of personalization by effectively mining their customer databases. Customers can choose payment terms, shipping terms, delivery locations, gift wrapping, and whether to opt in to future e-mail promotions. Also, by monitoring clickstream data in real time, the best e-commerce firms can offer product suggestions on the fly—while customers visit their sites. This sort of customized point-of-sale information not only increases sales, it also better fulfills customers' needs and increases the likelihood of establishing long-term customer relationships.

Criteria for Successful Segmentation

It is important to remember that not all segmentation approaches or their resulting market segments are viable in a marketing sense. For example, it makes little sense to segment the soft drink market based on eye color or shoe size, as these characteristics have nothing to do with the purchase of soft drinks. Although markets can be segmented in limitless ways, the segmentation approach must make sense in terms of at least five related criteria:

- **Identifiable and Measurable**   The characteristics of the segment's members must be easily identifiable. This allows the firm to measure identifying characteristics, including the segment's size and purchasing power.

- **Substantial**   The segment must be large and profitable enough to make it worthwhile for the firm. The profit potential must be greater than the costs involved in creating a marketing program specifically for the segment.

- **Accessible**   The segment must be accessible in terms of communication (advertising, mail, telephone, etc.) and distribution (channels, merchants, retail outlets, etc.).

- **Responsive**   The segment must respond to the firm's marketing efforts, including changes to the marketing program over time. The segment must also respond differently than other segments.

- **Viable and Sustainable**   The segment must meet the basic criteria for exchange, including being ready, willing, and able to conduct business with the firm. The segment must also be sustainable over time to allow the firm to effectively develop a marketing strategy for serving the needs of the segment.

It is possible for a market segment to meet these criteria yet still not be viable in a business sense. Markets for many illegal products, such as illicit drugs or pornography, can easily meet these criteria. However, ethical and socially responsible firms would not pursue these markets. Other markets, like gaming or gambling, may not be illegal in geographical areas, but are often not in the best interests of the firm. More commonly, firms will identify perfectly viable market segments; however, these segments will rest outside of the firm's expertise or mission. Just because a market segment is viable or highly profitable does not mean the firm should pursue it.

Identifying Market Segments

A firm's segmentation strategy and its choice of one or more target markets depend on its ability to identify the characteristics of buyers within those markets. This involves selecting the most relevant variables to identify and define the target market or markets. Many of these variables, including demographics, lifestyles, product usage, or firm size, derive from the situation analysis section of the marketing plan. However, a new or revised marketing strategy often requires changes in target market definition to correct problems in the previous marketing strategy. Target markets also shift in response to required changes in specific elements of the marketing program, such as reducing price to enhance value, increasing price to connote higher quality, adding a new product feature to make the benefits more meaningful, or selling through retail stores instead of direct distribution, to add the convenience of immediate availability. In short, the target market and the marketing program are interdependent, and changes in one typically require changes in the other. *Beyond the Pages 6.3* outlines the challenges faced by companies as they attempt to target consumers in the lucrative Chinese market.

Segmenting Consumer Markets

The goal in segmenting consumer markets is to isolate individual characteristics that distinguish one or more segments from the total market. The key is to segment the

Beyond the Pages 6.3

THE LUCRATIVE AND CHALLENGING CHINESE MARKET[9]

It's hard to ignore a market that numbers 1.4 billion consumers in size. China is the world's most populous country and its second-largest economy. And though the size is appealing (China has 20 percent of the world's population compared to only 4.5 percent for the United States), it is China's growing middle class that gets U.S. firms excited about its market potential. Experts estimate that the number of middle-class households in China will nearly triple by 2020 and will account for over $800 billion in spending power.

Despite the enormous potential, China is a very challenging market for most firms. Some reasons are obvious: the sheer size of the country, its complicated language with multiple dialects, and its relatively low personal incomes compared to Western standards (a typical middle-class income in China equates to $9,000 U.S. per year). Despite these and other challenges, the market potential is so enticing that many U.S. firms are moving boldly into the Chinese market. Here, we examine the challenges faced by Coke, Walmart, and Starbucks in reaching the lucrative Chinese consumer.

Coke

Coke faces a number of challenges in the Chinese market. The first is demand, where Chinese citizens consume only 1/20th of the soft drinks per capita that their American counterparts do. One reason is that most Chinese prefer tea to soft drinks. A second challenge is competition. Although Coca-Cola controls 24 percent of the soft-drink market, China's Wahaha Future Cola is extremely popular in the rural areas of China. A third challenge is that the growth of the carbonated drink market is slowing due to increasing popularity of healthier drinks—especially juices. To leverage that trend, and expand on its 9.7% market share in juice, Coke acquired China Huiyuan Juice—the number one juice maker in China—for $2.4 billion. The move gives Coke a full 20 percent of the Chinese juice market.

Walmart

The retail market in China is attractive for many reasons. It is currently the seventh-largest retail market in the world, and will soon pass Italy and France to move into the number five position. Further, China's retail market is growing faster than the U.S. market. It is no surprise then that Walmart has moved aggressively into China. However, Walmart faces a number of challenges, including competition from European retailers. French retailer Carrefour operates more than 136 hypermarkets in China, while Tesco—a U.K. supermarket chain—operates 58 hypermarkets, with plans to open additional stores. Until recently, Walmart operated only 100 supercenters and Sam's Club stores, but that changed with their acquisition of Trust-Mart—China's top retailer. The move gave Walmart an additional 100 hypermarkets and the critical mass it needed to ensure profitability. Competition from local retailers, which account for 90 percent of retail sales in China, is also intense. These local merchants include traditional supermarkets as well as street markets (local vendors that sell everything from fresh produce to live animals). Chinese consumers favor local merchants because of their low prices and freshness of food. In addition to competition, Walmart also faces a unique problem in the structure of its workforce. Bowing to Chinese demands and an increasing shortage of qualified workers, Walmart reluctantly agreed to unionize its Chinese employees in 2008.

Starbucks

Starbucks quietly entered the Chinese market in 1999. In 2005, to raise its awareness among Chinese consumers, Starbucks donated a total of $5 million to charity projects within the country. The first was a $1.5 million donation to train 3,000 schoolteachers and provide books and computers to schools in China's poor Western provinces. Starbucks has made a strong commitment to China—the company's number one growth market outside the United States—despite the many challenges faced by the company. In addition to Chinese preferences for tea, Starbucks faces a daunting economic situation: Its coffee costs more than the average Chinese worker earns in one day. Despite this stark reality, Starbucks' 500-plus locations in Mainland China, Hong Kong, and Taiwan have been successful. The company has also developed its first China-sourced coffee, called South of the Clouds Blend. The company's success has bred a great deal of imitation by local competitors, many of which have pirated the Starbucks brand name and logo.

total market into groups with relatively homogeneous needs. As you may recall from our earlier discussion, consumers buy products because the benefits they provide can fulfill specific needs or wants. The difficulty in segmenting consumer markets lies in isolating one or more characteristics that closely align with these needs and wants. For example, marketers of soft drinks do not necessarily concern themselves with the age or gender of their customers, but rather with how age and gender relate to customers' needs, attitudes, preferences, and lifestyles.

In the discussion that follows, we look more closely at segmentation in consumer markets by examining the different factors that can be used to divide these markets into homogeneous groupings. As Exhibit 6.3 illustrates, these factors fall into one of four general categories: behavioral segmentation, demographic segmentation, psychographic segmentation, and geographic segmentation.

EXHIBIT 6.3

COMMON SEGMENTATION VARIABLES USED IN CONSUMER MARKETS

Category	Variables	Examples
Behavioral segmentation	Benefits sought	Quality, value, taste, image enhancement, beauty, sportiness, speed, excitement, entertainment, nutrition, convenience
	Product usage	Heavy, medium, and light users; nonusers; former users; first-time users
	Occasions or situations	Emergencies, celebrations, birthdays, anniversaries, weddings, births, funerals, graduation
	Price sensitivity	Price sensitive, value conscious, status conscious (not price sensitive)
Demographic segmentation	Age	Newborns, 0–5, 6–12, 13–17, 18–25, 26–34, 35–49, 50–64, 65+
	Gender	Male, female
	Income	Under $15,000, $15,000–$30,000, $30,000–$50,000, $50,000–$75,000, $75,000–$100,000, over $100,000
	Occupation	Blue collar, white collar, technical, professional, managers, laborers, retired, homemakers, unemployed
	Education	High school graduate, some college, college graduate, graduate degree
	Family life cycle	Single, married no children, married with young children, married with teenage children, married with grown children, divorced, widowed
	Generation	Generation Y, Generation X, baby boomers, seniors
	Ethnicity	Caucasian, African American, Hispanic, Asian
	Religion	Protestant, Catholic, Muslim, Hindu
	Nationality	American, European, Japanese, Australian, Korean
	Social class	Upper class, middle class, lower class, working class, poverty level
Psychographic segmentation	Personality	Outgoing, shy, compulsive, individualistic, materialistic, civic minded, anxious, controlled, venturesome
	Lifestyle	Outdoor enthusiast, sports-minded, homebody, couch potato, family-centered, workaholic
	Motives	Safety, status, relaxation, convenience
Geographic segmentation	Regional	Northeast, Southeast, Midwest, New England, Southern France, South Africa
	City/county size	Under 50,000; 50,000–100,000; 100,000–250,000; 250,000–500,000; 500,000–1,000,000; over 1,000,000
	Population density	Urban, suburban, rural

Behavioral Segmentation   Behavioral segmentation is the most powerful approach because it uses actual consumer behavior or product usage to make distinctions among market segments. Typically, these distinctions are tied to the reasons that customers buy and use products. Consequently, behavioral segmentation, unlike other types of consumer segmentation, is most closely associated with consumer needs. A common use of behavioral segmentation is to group consumers based on their extent of product usage—heavy, medium, and light users. Heavy users are a firm's bread-and-butter customers and they should always be served well. Marketers often use strategies to increase product usage among light users, as well as nonusers of the product or brand. One of the best uses of behavioral segmentation is to create market segments based on specific consumer benefits. Exhibit 6.4 illustrates how benefit segmentation might be applied in the snack food market. Once different benefit segments have been identified, marketers can conduct research to develop profiles of the consumers in each segment.

Behavioral segmentation is a powerful tool; however, it is also quite difficult to execute in practice. Conducting research to identify behavioral segments is quite expensive and time-consuming. Also, the personal characteristics associated with behavioral segments are not always clear. For example, although some consumers buy a new car solely for transportation, most buy specific makes and models for other reasons. Some consumers want cars that are sporty, fun to drive, and that enhance their image. The problem lies in identifying the characteristics of these consumers.

EXHIBIT 6.4   BENEFIT SEGMENTATION OF THE SNACK FOOD MARKET

	Nutritional Snackers	Weight Watchers	Guilty Snackers	Party Snackers	Indiscriminant Snackers	Economical Snackers
Benefits Sought	Nutritious, all-natural ingredients	Low calorie, quick energy	Low calorie, good tasting	Can be served to guests, goes well with beverages	Good tasting, satisfies hunger cravings	Low price, best value
Types of Snacks Eaten	Fruits, vegetables, cheeses	Yogurt, vegetables	Yogurt, cookies, crackers, candy	Potato chips, nuts, crackers, pretzels	Candy, ice cream, cookies, potato chips, pretzels, popcorn	No specific products
Snack Consumption Level	Light	Light	Heavy	Average	Heavy	Average
Percentage of Snackers	23%	15%	10%	16%	16%	19%
Demographic Characteristics	Better educated, have young children	Younger, single	Less educated, lower incomes	Middle aged, suburban	Teens	Better educated, larger families
Psychographic Characteristics	Self-assured, controlled	Outdoorsy, influential, venturesome	Anxious, isolated	Sociable, outgoing	Hedonistic, time deprived	Self-assured, price sensitive

Source: Adapted from Charles W. Lamb, Jr., Joseph F. Hair, Jr., and Carl McDaniel, *Marketing* 7th ed. (Mason, OH: South-Western, 2004), p. 224.

Are they older or younger, men or women, single or married, and do they live in urban or suburban areas? In some cases, consumer characteristics are easy to identify. Families purchase minivans because they want more room for their children and cargo. Older consumers tend to opt for comfortable and luxurious models. The key to successful behavioral segmentation is to clearly understand the basic needs and benefits sought by different consumer groups. Then this information can be combined with demographic, psychographic, and geographic segmentation to create complete consumer profiles.

Demographic Segmentation   Demographic segmentation divides markets into segments using demographic factors such as gender (e.g., Secret deodorant for women), age (e.g., Abercrombie & Fitch clothing for teens and young adults), income (e.g., Lexus automobiles for wealthy consumers), and education (e.g., online MBA programs for busy professionals). Demographic segmentation tends to be the most widely used basis for segmenting consumer markets because demographic information is widely available and relatively easy to measure. In fact, much of this information is easily obtainable during the situation analysis through secondary sources.

Some demographic characteristics are often associated with true differences in needs that can be used to segment markets. In these cases, the connection between demographics, needs, and desired product benefits can make demographic segmentation quite easy. For example, men and women have clearly different needs with respect to clothing and healthcare. Large families with children have a greater need for life insurance, laundry detergent, and food. Children prefer sweeter-tasting food and beverages than do adults. Unfortunately, demographic segmentation becomes less useful when the firm has a strong interest in understanding the motives or values that drive buying behavior. Often, the motives and values that drive actual purchases do not necessarily have anything to do with demographics. For example, how would you describe the demographic characteristics of a price-sensitive, value-conscious consumer? Before you answer, remember that Walmart customers come from all walks of life. Likewise, how would you describe the demographics of an adventuresome, outdoor-oriented consumer? When Honda first introduced its Element utility vehicle, the company targeted adventuresome, high school and college-age consumers. To its surprise, Honda quickly discovered that the Element was just as popular with 30- and 40-somethings who used it to haul kids and groceries. The problem in understanding consumer motives and values is that these variables depend more on what consumers *think and feel* rather than on who they are. Delving into consumer thoughts and feelings is the subject of psychographic segmentation.

Psychographic Segmentation   Psychographic segmentation deals with state-of-mind issues such as motives, attitudes, opinions, values, lifestyles, interests, and personality. These issues are more difficult to measure, and often require primary marketing research to properly determine the makeup and size of various market segments. Once the firm identifies one or more psychographic segments, they can be combined with demographic, geographic, or behavioral segmentation to create fully developed consumer profiles.

One of the most successful and well-known tools of psychographic segmentation is VALS, developed by SRI Consulting.[10] VALS, which stands for "values and life-styles," divides adult U.S. consumers into one of eight profiles based on their level of resources and one of three primary consumption motives: ideals (knowledge and principles), achievement (demonstrating success to others), or self-expression (social or physical activity, variety, and risk taking). Exhibit 6.5 describes the eight VALS profiles. Many companies use VALS in a variety of marketing activities, including new product development, product positioning, brand development, promotional strategy, and media placement. SRI has also developed a geographic version of VALS called GeoVALS, which links each consumer profile with geographic information such as zip codes. This tool is quite useful in direct marketing campaigns and retail site selection.

Psychographic segmentation is useful because it transcends purely descriptive characteristics to help explain personal motives, attitudes, emotions, and lifestyles directly connected to buying behavior. For example, companies such as Michelin and State Farm appeal to consumers motivated by issues such as safety, security, and protection when they are buying tires or insurance. Other firms, such as Subaru, Kia, and Hyundai, appeal to consumers whose values and opinions about transportation focus more on economy than status. Online degree programs appeal to consumers whose active lifestyles do not allow them to attend classes in the traditional sense.

Geographic Segmentation   Geographic characteristics often play a large part in developing market segments. For example, firms often find that their customers are geographically concentrated. Even ubiquitous products like Coke sell better in the southern United States than in other parts of the country. Consumer preferences for certain purchases based on geography are a primary consideration in developing trade areas for retailers such as grocery stores, gas stations, and dry cleaners. For example, geodemographic segmentation, or geoclustering, is an approach that looks at neighborhood profiles based on demographic, geographic, and lifestyle segmentation variables. One of the best-known geoclustering tools is Claritas' PRIZM NE segmentation system, which classifies every neighborhood in the United States into one of 66 different demographic and behavioral clusters. The "Kids and Cul-de-Sacs" cluster contains upscale, suburban, families living in recently built subdivisions. The adults in this cluster are typically 25- to 44-year-old, highly educated professionals working in administrative jobs that pay upper-middle-class incomes. They are prime targets for child-centered products, personal services, and travel. PRIZM is useful to marketers because it allows them to focus their marketing programs only in areas where their products are more likely to be accepted. Not only does this make their marketing activities more successful, it also greatly reduces marketing expenditures.[11]

Segmenting Business Markets

One of the most basic methods of segmenting business markets involves the four types of markets we discussed earlier in the chapter: commercial markets, reseller markets, government markets, and institutional markets. Marketers may focus on one or more

EXHIBIT 6.5   **VALS CONSUMER PROFILES**

Innovators

These consumers have abundant resources and high self-esteem. Innovators are successful, sophisticated consumers who have a taste for upscale, innovative, and specialized goods and services. Innovators are concerned about image as an expression of self, but not as an expression of status or power.

   Example products: fine wines, upscale home furnishings, lawn maintenance services, recent technology, luxury automobiles

Thinkers

Thinkers are well-educated consumers who value order, knowledge, and responsibility. These consumers like to be as well informed about the products they buy as they are about world and national events. Although Thinkers have resources that give them many choices or options, they tend to be conservative consumers who look for practicality, durability, functionality, and value.

   Example products: news and information services, low-emission vehicles, conservative homes and home furnishings

Achievers

The lifestyle of an Achiever is focused and structured around family, a place of worship, and career. Achievers are conventional, conservative, and respect authority and the status quo. These individuals are very active consumers who desire established, prestigious products and services that demonstrate their success. Achievers lead busy lives; hence, they value products that can save them time and effort.

   Example products: SUVs, family vacations, products that promote career enhancement, online shopping, swimming pools

Experiencers

Experiencers are young, enthusiastic, and impulsive consumers who are motivated by self-expression. These consumers emphasize variety, excitement, the offbeat, and the risky. Experiencers enjoy looking good and buying "cool" products.

   Example products: fashion, entertainment, sports/exercise, outdoor recreation and social activities

Believers

Believers are conservative, conventional consumers who hold steadfast beliefs based on traditional values related to family, religion, community, and patriotism. These consumers are predictable in that they follow established routines centered on family, community, or organizational membership. Believers prefer familiar and well-known American brands and tend to be very loyal customers.

   Example products: membership in social, religious, or fraternal organizations; American made products; charitable organizations

Strivers

Strivers are motivated by achievement, yet they lack the resources to meet all their desires. As a group, Strivers are trendy, fun loving, and concerned with the opinions and approval of others. These consumers see shopping as a social activity and an opportunity to demonstrate their purchasing power up to the limits imposed by their financial situations. Most Strivers think of themselves as having jobs rather than careers.

   Example products: stylish products, impulse items, credit cards, designer "knock-offs," shopping as entertainment

(continued)

Makers

Makers, like Experiencers, are motivated by self-expression. However, these consumers experience the world by engaging in many do-it-yourself activities such as repairing their own cars, building houses, or growing and canning their own vegetables. Makers are practical consumers who value self-sufficiency and have the skills to back it up. Makers are also unimpressed by material possessions, new ideas, or big business. They live traditional lives and prefer to buy basic items.

   Example products: Auto parts, home-improvement supplies, gardening supplies, sewing supplies, discount retailers

Survivors

Survivors live narrowly focused lives and have few resources with which to cope. They are primarily concerned with safety, security, and meeting needs rather than fulfilling wants. As a group, Survivors are cautious consumers who represent a fairly small market for most products. They are loyal to favorite brands, especially if they can buy them on sale.

   Example products: Basic necessities and staples; old, established brands

Source: Strategic Business Insights, http://www.strategicbusinessinsights.com/vals/ustypes.shtml.

of these markets, as each has different requirements. However, even within one type of market, marketers will discover that buying firms have unique and varying characteristics. In these cases, further segmentation using additional variables might be needed to further refine the needs and characteristics of business customers. For example, Canon sells a line of wide format printers aimed at CAD and architectural design users, as well as other segments such as fine art, photography, office, and signage. Each segment has different uses for wide format printing, as well as different requirements with respect to the types of inks used in the printers. In addition to the types of business markets, firms can also segment business buyers with respect to the following:

- **Type of Organization**   Different types of organizations may require different and specific marketing programs, such as product modifications, different distribution and delivery structures, or different selling strategies. A glass manufacturer, for example, might segment customers into several groups, such as car manufacturers, furniture makers, window manufacturers, or repair and maintenance contractors.

- **Organizational Characteristics**   The needs of business buyers often vary based on their size, geographic location, or product usage. Large buyers often command price discounts and structural relationships that are appropriate for their volume of purchases. Likewise, buyers in different parts of the country, as well as in different nations, may have varying product requirements, specifications, or distribution arrangements. Product usage is also important. Computer manufacturers often segment markets based on how their products will be used. For example, K–12 educational institutions have different requirements for computers and software than do major research universities.

- **Benefits Sought or Buying Processes**   Organizations differ with respect to the benefits they seek and the buying processes they use to acquire products. Some business buyers seek only the lowest cost provider, whereas others require extensive product support and service. Additionally, some businesses buy using highly structured processes, most likely through their buying center. Others may use online auctions or even highly informal processes.

- **Personal and Psychological Characteristics**   The personal characteristics of the buyers themselves often play a role in segmentation decisions. Buyers will vary according to risk tolerance, buying influence, job responsibilities, and decision styles.

- **Relationship Intensity**   Business markets can also be segmented based on the strength and longevity of the relationship with the firm. Many organizations structure their selling organization using this approach, with one person or team dedicated to the most critical relationships. Other members of the selling organization may be involved in business development strategies to seek out new customers.

As we have seen, segmentation in business markets addresses many of the same issues found in consumer markets. Despite some differences and additional considerations that must be addressed, the foundation remains the same. Marketers must understand the needs of their potential customers and how these needs differ across segments within the total market.

Target Marketing Strategies

Once the firm has completed segmenting a market, it must then evaluate each segment to determine its attractiveness and whether it offers opportunities that match the firm's capabilities and resources. Remember that just because a market segment meets all criteria for viability does not mean the firm should pursue it. Attractive segments might be dropped for several reasons, including a lack of resources, no synergy with the firm's mission, overwhelming competition in the segment, an impending technology shift, or ethical and legal concerns over targeting a particular segment. Based on its analysis of each segment, the firm's current and anticipated situation, and a comprehensive SWOT analysis, a firm might consider five basic strategies for target market selection. Exhibit 6.6 depicts the following strategies.[12]

- **Single Segment Targeting**   Firms use single segment targeting when their capabilities are intrinsically tied to the needs of a specific market segment. Many consider the firms using this targeting strategy to be true specialists in a particular product category. Good examples include New Belgium Brewing (craft beer), Porsche, and Ray-Ban. These and other firms using single segment targeting are successful because they fully understand their customers' needs, preferences, and lifestyles. These firms also constantly strive to improve quality and customer satisfaction by continuously refining their products to meet changing customer preferences.

EXHIBIT 6.6   BASIC STRATEGIES FOR TARGET MARKET SELECTION

Single Segment Targeting

	M_1	M_2	M_3
P_1		•	
P_2			
P_3			

Selective Targeting

	M_1	M_2	M_3
P_1	•		
P_2			•
P_3		•	

Mass Market Targeting

	M_1	M_2	M_3
P_1	•	•	•
P_2	•	•	•
P_3	•	•	•

Product Specialization

	M_1	M_2	M_3
P_1	•	•	•
P_2			
P_3			

Market Specialization

	M_1	M_2	M_3
P_1		•	
P_2		•	
P_3		•	

P = Product Category; M = Market

- **Selective Targeting**   Firms that have multiple capabilities in many different product categories use selective targeting successfully. This strategy has several advantages, including diversification of the firm's risk and the ability to cherry pick only the most attractive market segment opportunities. Procter & Gamble uses selective targeting to offer customers many different products in the family care, household care, and personal care markets. Besides the familiar deodorants, laundry detergents, and hair care products, P&G also sells products in the cosmetics, snack food and beverages, cologne, and prescription drug markets. One of the keys to P&G's success is that the company does not try to be all things to all customers. The company carefully selects product/market combinations where its capabilities match customers' needs.

- **Mass Market Targeting**   Only the largest firms have the capability to execute mass market targeting, which involves the development of multiple marketing programs to serve all customer segments simultaneously. For example, Coca-Cola offers roughly 400 branded beverages across many segments that fulfill different consumer needs in over 200 countries around the world. Likewise, Frito-Lay sells hundreds of different varieties of snack foods around the world.

- **Product Specialization**   Firms engage in product specialization when their expertise in a product category can be leveraged across many different market segments. These firms can adapt product specifications to match the different needs of individual customer groups. For example, many consider Littmann Stethoscopes, a division of 3M, as the worldwide leader in auscultation technology. Littmann offers high-performance electronic stethoscopes for cardiologists, specially designed stethoscopes for pediatric/infant use, lightweight stethoscopes for simple physical assessment, and a line of stethoscopes for nursing and medical students. The company also offers a line of veterinary stethoscopes.[13]

- **Market Specialization**   Firms engage in market specialization when their intimate knowledge and expertise in one market allows them to offer customized marketing programs that not only deliver needed products but also provide needed solutions to customers' problems. The Follett Corporation is a prime example. Follett specializes in the education market by serving over 760 schools, colleges, and universities in the United States and Canada. The company's slogan "Powering education. Worldwide." is based on the firm's goal to be the leading provider of educational solutions, services, and products to schools, libraries, colleges, students, and lifelong learners.[14]

In addition to targeting a subset of current customers within the product/market, firms can also take steps to target noncustomers. As we discussed in Chapter 4, there are many reasons why noncustomers do not purchase a firm's products. These reasons can include unique customer needs, better competing alternatives, high switching costs, lack of product awareness, or the existence of long-held assumptions about a product. For example, products associated with tooth whitening were at one time associated only with dentists. Consequently, consumers were hesitant to use these products due to the expense, effort, and anxiety involved. Oral care companies were able to break this tradition and reach out to noncustomers by developing high-quality, low-price, over-the-counter alternatives that were much easier to purchase. Today, these at-home tooth-whitening products—such as Procter & Gamble's Crest Whitestrips—are a $300 million market in the United States.[15]

As this example illustrates, the key to targeting noncustomers lies in understanding the reasons why they do not buy and then finding ways to remove these obstacles. Removing obstacles to purchase, whether they exist in product design, affordability, distribution convenience, or product awareness, is a major strategic issue in developing an effective marketing program. Over the next four chapters, we turn our attention to the important strategic issues involved in creating this marketing program by examining product, pricing, distribution/supply chain, and integrated marketing communications strategies.

Lessons from Chapter 6

Buyer behavior in consumer markets

- Is often irrational and unpredictable as consumers often say one thing but do another.

- Can progress through five stages: need recognition, information search, evaluation of alternatives, the purchase decision, and postpurchase evaluation.

- Does not always follow these stages in sequence and may even skip stages en route to the purchase.

- May be characterized by loyalty where consumers simply purchase the same product that they bought last time.

- Often involves a parallel sequence of activities associated with finding the most suitable merchant. That is, while consumers consider which product to buy, they also consider where they might buy it.

- May occur with only one merchant for a particular product category if the consumer is fiercely loyal to that merchant.

Keys to understanding consumer needs and wants:

- Defining needs as "necessities" has limitations because everyone has a different perspective on what constitutes a need.

- Needs occur when a consumer's current level of satisfaction does not equal the desired level of satisfaction.

- Wants are a consumer's desire for a specific product that will satisfy a need.

- The firm must always understand the basic needs fulfilled by its products. This understanding allows the firm to segment markets and create marketing programs that can translate consumer needs into wants for their specific products.

- Although some products and markets can be segmented on the basis of needs alone, most product categories are marketed on the basis of wants, not need fulfillment.

- Wants are not the same thing as demand, as demand occurs only when the consumer's ability and willingness to pay backs up a want for a specific product.

The information search stage of the consumer buying process

- Can be passive—where the consumer becomes more attentive and receptive to information—or active—where the consumer engages in a more aggressive information search by seeking additional information.

- Depends on a number of issues, including the degree of risk involved in the purchase, the amount of expertise or experience the consumer has with the product category, and the actual cost of the search in terms of time and money.

- Culminates in an evoked set of suitable buying alternatives.

During the evaluation of alternatives

- Consumers essentially translate their needs into wants for specific products or brands.

- Consumers evaluate products as bundles of attributes that have varying abilities to satisfy their needs.

- The priority of each consumer's choice criteria can change.

- Marketers must ensure that their product is in the evoked set of potential alternatives by constantly reminding consumers of their company and its product offerings.

During the purchase stage of the buying process

- It is important to remember that the intention to purchase and the actual act of buying are distinct concepts.

- The key issues for marketers are product availability and possession utility.

During postpurchase evaluation

- The outcome of the buying process is linked to the development of long-term customer relationships. Marketers must closely follow customers' responses to monitor the product's performance and its ability to meet customers' expectations.

- Consumers will experience one of four potential outcomes: delight, satisfaction, dissatisfaction, or cognitive dissonance.

Overall, the consumer buying process can be affected by

- The complexity of the purchase and decision-making process.

- Individual factors, such as age, life cycle, occupation, socioeconomic status, perceptions, motives, interests, attitudes, opinions, and lifestyles.

- Social influences such as culture, subculture, social class, family, reference groups, and opinion leaders.

- Situational influences, such as physical and spatial influences, social and interpersonal influences, time, purchase task or usage, and the consumer's disposition.

Business markets

- Purchase products for use in their operations, such as acquiring raw materials to produce finished goods or buying office supplies or leasing cars.

- Consist of four types of buyers: commercial markets, reseller markets, government markets, and institutional markets.

- Possess four unique characteristics not typically found in consumer markets:

  - The buying center: economic buyers, technical buyers, and users.

  - Hard and soft costs: Soft costs (downtime, opportunity costs, human resource costs) are just as important as hard costs (monetary price or purchase costs).

  - Reciprocity: Business buyers and sellers often buy products from each other.

  - Mutual dependence: Sole-source or limited-source buying makes both buying and selling firms mutually dependent.

The business buying process

- Follows a well-defined sequence of stages, including (1) problem recognition, (2) development of product specifications, (3) vendor identification and qualification, (4) solicitation of proposals or bids, (5) vendor selection, (6) order processing, and (7) vendor performance review.

- Can be affected by a number of factors, including environmental conditions, organizational factors, and interpersonal and individual factors.

Market segmentation

- Is the process of dividing the total market for a particular product or product category into relatively homogeneous segments or groups.

- Should create groups where the members are similar to each other but where the groups are dissimilar from each other.

- Involves a fundamental decision of whether to segment at all.

- Typically allows firms to be more successful due to the fact that they can tailor products to meet the needs or requirements of a particular market segment.

Traditional market segmentation approaches

- Have been used successfully for decades, are not out of date, and are used by many of today's most successful firms.

- Are sometimes used in combination with newer approaches by the same firm, depending on the brand/product or market in question.

Mass marketing

- Involves no segmentation whatsoever as it is aimed at the total (whole) market for a particular product.

- Is an undifferentiated approach that assumes that all customers in the market have similar needs and wants that can be reasonably satisfied with a single marketing program.

- Works best when the needs of an entire market are relatively homogeneous.

- Is advantageous in terms of production efficiency and lower marketing costs.

- Is inherently risky because a standardized product is vulnerable to competitors that offer specialized products that better match customers' needs.

Differentiated marketing

- Involves dividing the total market into groups of customers having relatively common or homogeneous needs, and attempting to develop a marketing program that appeals to one or more of these groups.

- May be necessary when customer needs are similar within a single group, but their needs differ across groups.

- Involves two options: the multisegment approach and the market concentration approach.

Niche marketing

- Involves focusing marketing efforts on one small, well-defined market segment or niche that has a unique, specific set of needs.
- Requires that firms understand and meet the needs of target customers so completely that, despite the small size of the niche, the firm's substantial share makes the segment highly profitable.

Individualized segmentation approaches

- Have become viable due to advances in technology, particularly communication technology and the Internet.
- Are possible because organizations now have the ability to track customers with a high degree of specificity.
- Allow firms to combine demographic data with past and current purchasing behavior so they can tweak their marketing programs in ways that allow them to precisely match customers' needs, wants, and preferences.
- Will become even more important in the future because their focus on individual customers makes them critical to the development and maintenance of long-term relationships.
- Can be prohibitively expensive to deliver.
- Depend on two important considerations: automated delivery of the marketing program and personalization.

One-to-one marketing

- Involves the creation of an entirely unique product or marketing program for each customer in the target segment.
- Is common in business markets where unique programs and/or systems are designed for each customer.
- Is growing rapidly in consumer markets, particularly in luxury and custom-made products, as well as in services and electronic commerce.

Mass customization

- Refers to providing unique products and solutions to individual customers on a mass scale.
- Is now cost-effective and practical due to advances in supply chain management, including real-time inventory control.
- Is used quite often in business markets, especially in electronic procurement systems.

Permission marketing

- Is different from one-to-one marketing because customers choose to become a member of the firm's target market.

- Is commonly executed via the opt-in e-mail list, where customers permit a firm to send periodic e-mail about goods and services that they have an interest in purchasing.

- Has a major advantage in that customers who opt in are already interested in the goods and services offered by the firm.

- Allows a firm to precisely target individuals, thereby eliminating the problem of wasted marketing effort and expense.

Successful segmentation

- Requires that market segments fulfill five related criteria: segments must be identifiable and measurable, substantial, accessible, responsive, and viable and sustainable.

- Involves avoiding ethically and legally sensitive segments that are profitable but not viable in a business sense.

- Involves avoiding potentially viable segments that do not match the firm's expertise or mission.

Identifying market segments

- Involves selecting the most relevant variables to identify and define the target market, many of which come from the situation analysis section of the marketing plan.

- Involves the isolation of individual characteristics that distinguish one or more segments from the total market. These segments must have relatively homogeneous needs.

- In consumer markets involves the examination of factors that fall into one of four general categories:

  - Behavioral segmentation, the most powerful approach because it uses actual consumer behavior or product usage helps to make distinctions among market segments

  - Demographic segmentation, which divides markets using factors such as gender, age, income, and education

  - Psychographic segmentation, which deals with state-of-mind issues such as motives, attitudes, opinions, values, lifestyles, interests, and personality

- Geographic segmentation, which is often most useful when combined with other segmentation variables. One of the best examples is geodemographic segmentation, or geoclustering.

- In business markets is often based on type of market (commercial, reseller, government, or institutional) or on other characteristics such as type of organization, organizational characteristics, benefits sought or buying processes, personal or psychological characteristics, or relationship intensity.

Target marketing strategies

- Are based on an evaluation of the attractiveness of each segment and whether each offers opportunities that match the firm's capabilities and resources.

- Include single segment targeting, selective targeting, mass market targeting, product specialization, and market specialization.

- Should also consider issues related to noncustomers, such as reasons why they do not buy and finding ways to remove obstacles to purchase.

Questions for Discussion

1. Many people criticize marketing as being manipulative based on the argument that marketing activities create needs where none previously existed. Marketers of SUVs, tobacco products, diet programs, exercise equipment, and luxury products are typically the most criticized. Given what you now know about the differences between needs and wants, do you agree with these critics? Explain.

2. Many consumers and consumer advocates are critical of individualized segmentation approaches due to personal privacy concerns. They argue that technology has made it far too easy to track buyer behavior and personal information. Marketers counter that individualized segmentation can lead to privacy abuses, but that the benefits to both consumers and marketers far outweigh the risks. Where do you stand on this issue? What are the benefits and risks associated with individualized segmentation?

3. As we have seen thus far, the size of the consuming population over the age of 50 continues to grow. What are some of the current ethical issues involved in targeting this age group? As this group gets older, will these issues become more or less important? Explain.

Exercises

1. Consider the last purchase you made in these categories: personal electronics, clothing, and vacation destination. To what extent was your purchase decision

influenced by decision-making complexity, individual influences, social influences, and situational influences? What specific issues were the most influential in making the decision? How could a marketer have swayed your decision in each case?

2.   One of the most exciting advances in market segmentation is the increasing use of geographic information systems (GIS) to map target markets. Go to http://www.gis.com and get a feel for the use of GIS in business and other fields. Then, enter your zip code into "Community Profile Report" to learn more about where you live. What are the advantages of using GIS in market segmentation?

3.   As discussed in the chapter, VALS is one of the most popular proprietary segmentation tools used in marketing segmentation. Go to the SRI Consulting website http://www.strategicbusinessinsights.com/vals/presurvey.shtml and take the free VALS survey. Do you agree with the survey results? Why or why not?

7

Product Strategy

Introduction

O
f all the strategic decisions to be made in the marketing plan, the design, development, branding, and positioning of the product are perhaps the most critical. At the heart of every organization lie one or more products that define what the organization does and why it exists. As we stated in Chapter 1, the term *product* refers to something that buyers can acquire via exchange to satisfy a need or a want. This is a very broad definition that allows us to classify many different things as products: food, entertainment, information, people, places, ideas, etc. An important strategic fact about products is that they are not created and sold as individual elements; rather, products are developed and sold as offerings. An organization's product offering is typically composed of many different elements—usually some combination of tangible goods, services, ideas, images, or even people. As *Beyond the Pages 7.1* illustrates, individuals who purchase a Steinway piano buy much more than a musical instrument. They also get exceptional craftsmanship, unparalleled customer service, a highly prestigious brand name, and over 156 years of technical innovation.

Given the complex makeup of most products, we prefer to discuss products as offerings, or the bundle of physical (tangible), service (intangible), and symbolic (perceptual) attributes designed to satisfy customers' needs and wants. Good product strategy focuses on all elements of the product offering rather than on only a single element. We have noted throughout this text how most firms today compete in rather mature markets characterized by commoditization. In these cases, the core product (the element that satisfies the basic customer need) typically becomes incapable of differentiating the product offering from those of the competition. Consequently, most organizations strive to enhance the service and symbolic elements of their product offerings. Note that this means focusing primarily on the intangible aspects of a product, not on its tangible or physical elements. This makes product strategy even more challenging for the firm. It also requires product strategy to be fully integrated with pricing, distribution, and promotion, as these components of the marketing program add value to the product offering.

Beyond the Pages 7.1

STEINWAY: MORE THAN A PIANO[1]

One of the most dominant strengths any firm can possess occurs when the firm enjoys an image of superior quality that is backed by patent protection. Such is the case for Steinway and Sons, makers of the world's finest pianos. For over 156 years, Steinway's art and craftsmanship have made it the world's most renowned brand for high-end, "concert hall–quality" pianos. In fact, virtually every top pianist in the world performs on a Steinway.

The company holds 120 technical patents and innovations that distinguish its pianos from all others. Each piano made in the Long Island City (Queens), New York factory takes 9 to 12 months to complete and is hand assembled from 12,000 parts—most of them also made by hand. Despite its reputation, Steinway is not a large company. It sells roughly $235 million in pianos each year—a number dwarfed by other firms in the industry. Steinway, however, does not define success in terms of numbers, but in its reputation. Steinway is the piano of choice for concert halls, composers, professional musicians, and wealthy customers. Although the company accounts for only 2 percent of piano sales in the United States, it earns 35 percent of the industry's profit. Customers enjoy the quality, beauty, and reputation of a Steinway piano, and don't mind paying the $40,000 to $100,000 price tag. In fact, many argue that a Steinway is more akin to a work of art than a musical instrument. The advantages earned from this type of reputation and customer loyalty are hard to beat.

However, Steinway's stellar image and reputation presented a problem for the company at one point in its history. Although Steinway dominated the upper end of the piano market, the company did not compete in the rapidly growing and much larger entry-level and mid-level piano markets. These markets were dominated by Asian brands such as Yamaha and Kawai—good names in their own right, but not in the same league as Steinway. Piano dealers were forced to stock these brands alongside Steinways in order to meet the needs of other customer segments. The challenge for Steinway was to find a way to compete in these markets without damaging the brand equity in the Steinway name.

The company's solution involved the launch of two new brands: "Boston, designed by Steinway" for the mid-level market and "Essex, designed by Steinway" for the entry-level market. Both the Boston and the Essex are manufactured in Japan and sold through exclusive channels. The decision to launch these new brands was agonizing for Steinway's management. The company's top management once said, "There is no such thing as a cheaper Steinway." With that in mind, the launch of the Boston and Essex represented a real risk for the company.

Steinway argues that the only way to maintain brand equity, especially with a name like Steinway, is to take a long-term view and move very slowly. This is the company's strategy with its most recent move into Asian markets—the home turf of Steinway's less expensive rivals. The company has expanded distribution in Japan and China to the point where it now earns 31 percent of its business from outside the United States. Steinway also raises its prices 3 to 4 percent each year—another long-term strategy aimed at maintaining brand equity. The company argues that you cannot put a discounted price on the passion associated with a worldwide icon like Steinway.

As we consider product decisions in this chapter, it is important to remember that product offerings in and of themselves have little value to customers. Rather, an offering's real value comes from its ability to deliver benefits that enhance a customer's situation or solve a customer's problems. For example, customers don't buy pest control; they buy a bug-free environment. Lexus customers don't buy a car; they buy luxury, status, comfort, and social appeal. Students who frequent a local nightclub are not thirsty; they want to fulfill their need for social interaction. Likewise, companies do not need computers; they need to store, retrieve, distribute, network, and analyze data and information. Marketers who keep their sights set on developing product offerings that truly meet the needs of the target market are more likely to be successful.

The Product Portfolio

Products fall into two general categories. Products purchased for personal use and enjoyment are called consumer products, whereas those purchased for resale, to make other products, or for use in a firm's operations are called business products. Exhibit 7.1 illustrates examples of each type of product category. Although the distinction may seem simplistic, it is important in a strategic sense because the type of product in question can influence its pricing, distribution, or promotion. For example, marketing strategy for consumer convenience products must maximize availability and ease of purchase—both important distribution considerations. The strategy associated with consumer shopping products often focuses more on differentiation through image and symbolic attributes—both important branding and promotion issues. Marketing strategies for raw materials are especially challenging because these products are commodities by definition. Here, conformance to exacting product specifications and low acquisition costs are the keys to effective strategy. Many business products are also characterized by derived demand, where the demand for the product is derived from, or dependent upon, the demand for other business or consumer products. For example, the demand for business products such as glass, steel, rubber, chrome, leather, and carpeting is dependent upon the demand for automobiles.

It is very rare for a company to sell only one product. Most firms sell a variety of products to fulfill a variety of different needs. In general terms, the products sold by a firm can be described with respect to product lines and product mixes. A *product line* consists of a group of closely related product items. As shown in Exhibit 7.2, Procter & Gamble sells a number of famous brands in its line of house and home products, including Tide, Bounty, Pringles, and Duracell. Most companies sell a variety of different product lines. The different product lines at General Motors carry well-known brand names like Corvette, Chevrolet, Cadillac, and Buick. Likewise, FedEx offers a number of logistics and supply chain services in its family of brands, such as FedEx Express, FedEx Ground, and FedEx Freight. A firm's *product mix* or *portfolio* is the total group of products offered by the company. For example, Procter & Gamble's entire product portfolio consists of personal and beauty products, health and wellness products, baby and family products, and pet nutrition and care products in addition to the products in its house and home line.

© Marjan Murat/dpa/Landov

This symbol, recognizable around the world, embodies a number of important symbolic product attributes.

EXHIBIT 7.1   TYPES OF CONSUMER AND BUSINESS PRODUCTS

	Type of Product	Examples
Consumer Products	**Convenience Products** Inexpensive, routinely purchased products that consumers spend little time and effort in acquiring.	Soft drinks Candy and gum Gasoline
	Shopping Products Products that consumers will spend time and effort to obtain. Consumers shop different options to compare prices, features, and service.	Dry cleaning Appliances Furniture Clothing Vacations
	Specialty Products Unique, one-of-a-kind products that consumers will spend considerable time, effort, and money to acquire.	Sports memorabilia Antiques Plastic surgery Luxury items
	Unsought Products Products that consumers are unaware of or a product that consumers do not consider purchasing until a need arises.	True innovations Repair services Emergency medicine Insurance
Business Products	**Raw Materials** Basic natural materials that become part of a finished product. They are purchased in very large quantities based on specifications or grades.	Iron ore Chemicals Agricultural products Wood pulp
	Component Parts Finished items that become part of a larger finished product. They are purchased based on specifications or industry standards.	Spark plugs Computer chips Pane glass Hard drives
	Process Materials Finished products that become unidentifiable upon their inclusion in the finished product.	Food additives Wood sealants Paint colorings
	Maintenance, Repair, and Operating Products Products that are used in business processes or operations but do not become part of the finished product.	Office supplies Janitorial services Building security Bathroom supplies
	Accessory Equipment Products that help facilitate production or operations but do not become part of the finished product.	Tools Office equipment Computers Furniture
	Installations Major purchases, typically of a physical nature, that are based on customized solutions including installation/construction, training, financing, maintenance, and repair.	Enterprise software Buildings Heat and air systems
	Business Services Intangible products that support business operations. These purchases often occur as a part of outsourcing decisions.	Legal services Accounting services Consulting Research services

Source: This material is adapted from William M. Pride and O.C. Ferrell, Marketing: 2010 Edition (Mason, OH: Cengage Learning, 2010), pp. 285–289.

EXHIBIT 7.2

PROCTER & GAMBLE'S PORTFOLIO OF HOUSE AND HOME PRODUCTS

| | Product Mix Width (Variety) | | | | | |
	Dish Washing	Household Cleaners	Batteries	Laundry and Fabric Care	Paper Products	Snacks
Product Mix Depth (Assortment)	Dawn	Swiffer	Duracell	Tide	Charmin	Pringles
	Joy	Mr. Clean		Cheer	Bounty	
	Cascade	Mr. Clean Autodry		Bounce	Puffs	
	Ivory	Carwash		Gain		
		Bountry		Downy		
		Febreze		Dreft		
				Era		
				Febreze		
				Ivory		

Source: Taken from the Procter & Gamble website (http://www.pg.com/en_US/products/all_products/index.shtml).

Decisions regarding product lines and product mixes are important strategic considerations for most firms. One of these important decisions is the number of product lines to offer, referred to as the width or variety of the product mix. By offering a wide variety of product lines, the firm can diversify its risk across a portfolio of product offerings. Also, a wide product mix can be used to capitalize on the strength and reputation of the firm. Sony, for example, enjoys this advantage as it uses its name to stake out a strong position in electronics, music, and movies. The second important decision involves the depth of each product line. Sometimes called *assortment*, product line depth is an important marketing tool. Firms can attract a wide range of customers and market segments by offering a deep assortment of products in a specific line. Each brand or product in the assortment can be used to fulfill different customer needs. For example, Hilton, Inc., offers 10 different lodging brands—including Hilton, Hilton Garden Inn, Hampton Inn, Conrad, and Embassy Suites—that cater to different segments of the hospitality market.

Although offering a large portfolio of products can make the coordination of marketing activities more challenging and expensive, it also creates a number of important benefits:

- **Economies of Scale** Offering many different product lines can create economies of scale in production, bulk buying, and promotion. Many firms advertise using an umbrella theme for all products in the line. Nike's "Just Do It" and Maxwell House's "Good to the Last Drop" are examples of this. The single theme covering the entire product line saves considerably on promotional expenses.

- **Package Uniformity** When all packages in a product line have the same look and feel, customers can locate the firm's products more quickly. It also becomes easier for the firm to coordinate and integrate promotion and distribution. For example, Duracell batteries all have the same copper look with black and copper packaging.

- **Standardization**   Product lines often use the same component parts. For example, Toyota's Camry and Highlander use many of the same chassis and engine components. This greatly reduces Toyota's manufacturing and inventory handling costs.

- **Sales and Distribution Efficiency**   When a firm offers many different product lines, sales personnel can offer a full range of choices and options to customers. For the same reason, channel intermediaries are more accepting of a product line than they are of individual products.

- **Equivalent Quality Beliefs**   Customers typically expect and believe that all products in a product line are about equal in terms of quality and performance. This is a major advantage for a firm that offers a well-known and respected line of products. For example, Crest's portfolio of oral care products all enjoy the same reputation for high quality.

A firm's product portfolio must be carefully managed to reflect changes in customers' preferences and the introduction of competitive products. Product offerings may be modified to change one or more characteristics that enhance quality and/or style, or lower the product's price. Firms may introduce product line extensions that allow it to compete more broadly in an industry. The recent trend of flavored soft drinks, such as Vanilla Coke, Diet Pepsi Vanilla, Sprite Zero, and Dr. Pepper Cherry Vanilla, is a good example of this. Sometimes, a firm may decide that a product or product line has become obsolete or is just not competitive against other products. When this happens, the firm can decide to contract the product line, as GM did when it dropped its Pontiac, Saturn, and Hummer divisions.

The Challenges of Service Products

It is important to remember that products can be intangible services and ideas as well as tangible goods. Service firms such as airlines, hospitals, movie theaters, and hair stylists, as well as nonprofit organizations, charitable causes, and government agencies, all develop and implement marketing strategies designed to match their portfolio of intangible products to the needs of target markets. In this section, we look at some of the key issues in developing product strategy for services.

Products lie on a continuum ranging from tangible-dominant goods (salt, soap) to intangible-dominant services (education, consulting). Firms lying closer to the intangible end of this spectrum face unique challenges in developing marketing strategy. These challenges are the direct result of the unique characteristics of services, as shown in Exhibit 7.3. Obviously, the primary difference between a good and a service is that a service is intangible. Some services, such as business consulting and education, are almost completely intangible, whereas others have elements that are more tangible. The services provided by UPS and FedEx, for example, include tangible airplanes, trucks, boxes, and air bills. Another challenging characteristic of services is that they cannot be stored for future use. This lack of inventory means that service firms experience major problems in balancing service supply (capacity) and service

EXHIBIT 7.3	UNIQUE CHARACTERISTICS OF SERVICES AND RESULTING MARKETING CHALLENGES

Service Characteristics	Marketing Challenges
Intangibility	It is difficult for customers to evaluate quality, especially before purchase and consumption.
	It is difficult to convey service characteristics and benefits in promotion. As a result, the firm is forced to sell a promise.
	Many services have few standardized units of measurement. Therefore, service prices are difficult to set and justify.
	Customers cannot take possession of a service.
Simultaneous Production and Consumption	Customers or their possessions must be present during service delivery.
	Other customers can affect service outcomes including service quality and customer satisfaction.
	Service employees are critical because they must interact with customers to deliver service.
	Converting high-contact services to low-contact services will lower costs but may reduce service quality.
	Services are often difficult to distribute.
Perishability	Services cannot be inventoried for later use. Therefore, unused service capacity is lost forever.
	Service demand is very time-and-place sensitive. As a result, it is difficult to balance supply and demand, especially during periods of peak demand.
	Service facilities and equipment sit idle during periods of off-peak demand.
Heterogeneity	Service quality varies across people, time, and place, making it very difficult to deliver good service consistently.
	There are limited opportunities to standardize service delivery.
	Many services are customizable by nature. However, customization can dramatically increase the costs of providing the service.
Client-Based Relationships	Most services live or die by maintaining a satisfied clientele over the long term.
	Generating repeat business is crucial for the service firm's success.

demand. Likewise, the demand for services is extremely time-and-place dependent because customers must typically be present for service to be delivered. Consider the issues faced by popular restaurants every Friday and Saturday night. The increased demand forces restaurant managers to preschedule the right amount of food ingredients and employees to accommodate the increase in guests. And, given that the restaurant's capacity is fixed, the manager and employees must serve guests efficiently and effectively in a crowded, noisy atmosphere. This precarious balance is quite common across most industries in the services sector of our economy.

Because of the intangibility of service, it is quite difficult for customers to evaluate a service before they actually purchase and consume it. Third-party evaluations and recommendations for services are not as prevalent as they are with respect to tangible goods. Of course, customers can ask friends and family for recommendations, but in many cases a good assessment of quality is hard to obtain. This forces customers to place some degree of trust in the service provider to perform the service correctly and in the time frame promised or anticipated. One way companies can address this issue is by providing satisfaction guarantees to customers. For example, Hampton Inn, a national chain of mid-priced hotels, offers guests a free night if they are not

100 percent satisfied with their stay.[2] Similar guarantees are offered by Midas, H&R Block, and FedEx.

Moreover, because most services are dependent upon people (employees, customers) for their delivery, they are susceptible to variations in quality and inconsistency. Such variations can occur from one organization to another, from one outlet to another within the same organization, from one service to another within the same outlet, and even from one employee to another within the same outlet. Service quality can further vary from week to week, day to day, or even hour to hour. Also, because service quality is a subjective phenomenon, it can also vary from customer to customer, and for the same customer from one visit to the next. As a result, standardization and service quality are very difficult to control. The lack of standardization, however, actually gives service firms one advantage: Services can be customized to match the specific needs of any customer. Such customized services are frequently very expensive for both the firm and its customers. This creates a dilemma: How does a service firm provide efficient, standardized service at an acceptable level of quality while simultaneously treating every customer as a unique person? This dilemma is especially prevalent in the health care industry today, where care is managed to carefully control both access and cost.

Another major challenge for service marketers is to tie services directly to customers' needs. Although customers typically have few problems in expressing needs for tangible goods, they often have difficulty in expressing or explaining needs for services. In some cases, the need is vague. For example, you may decide that you need a relaxing vacation, but how do you know which services will best meet your need? Which is best for relaxation: a trip to the beach, a cruise, or a stay at a bed-and-breakfast? The answer depends on how you personally define "relaxing." Because different customers have different definitions, vacation providers have a more difficult job in connecting their service offerings to customers' needs. In other cases, customers may not understand the need for a specific service. For example, business consultants, insurance agents, financial planners, and wedding consultants often have to educate customers on why their services are needed. This is a necessary first hurdle to overcome before these service providers can offer their products as the solution that will best fulfill the need.

New Product Development

One of the key issues in product strategy deals with the introduction of new products. The development and commercialization of new products is a vital part of a firm's efforts to sustain growth and profits over time. The success of new products depends on the product's fit with the firm's strengths and a defined market opportunity. Market characteristics and the competitive situation will also affect the sales potential of new products. For example, new GPS devices are consistently being developed by manufacturers such as Garmin, TomTom, and Magellan. However, the future of stand-alone GPS devices is unclear given that GPS functionality is now an option on most new cars and is fully integrated into many wireless phones. As these GPS-enabled devices add more features, consumers are going to be much less likely to purchase stand-alone

GPS units. This is why many GPS units can now sync with telephones or serve as music players. Some manufacturers, such as Garmin, are looking to enter the wireless phone business as a way to remain competitive.[3]

Many firms base their new product introductions on key themes such as product or technological superiority. New product introductions in the electronics, computer, and automotive industries often take this approach. In other firms and industries, new product introductions may stem from only minor tweaking of current products. This approach is common in packaged goods and household items. Truthfully, what is considered to be a new product depends on the point of view of both the firm and its customers. Although some product introductions are actually new, others may only be *perceived* as being new. There are six strategic options related to the newness of products. These options follow, in decreasing degrees of product change:

- **New-to-the-World Products (Discontinuous Innovations)**   These products involve a pioneering effort by a firm that eventually leads to the creation of an entirely new market. New-to-the-world products are typically the result of radical thinking by individual inventors or entrepreneurs. For example, Fred Smith's idea for an overnight package delivery service gave us FedEx.

- **New Product Lines**   These products represent new offerings by the firm, but the firm introduces them into established markets. Dell's move to offer flat-panel televisions and small consumer electronics is an example. Procter & Gamble's launch of a national chain of car washes is a new product line for the company. New product lines are not as risky as true innovation, and they allow the firm to diversify into closely related product categories.

- **Product Line Extensions**   These products supplement an existing product line with new styles, models, features, or flavors. Anheuser-Busch's introduction of Budweiser Select and Honda's launch of the Civic Hybrid are good examples. Product line extensions allow the firm to keep its products fresh and exciting with minimal development costs and risk of market failure.

- **Improvements or Revisions of Existing Products**   These products offer customers improved performance or greater perceived value. The common "new and improved" strategy used in packaged goods and the yearly design changes in the automobile industry are good examples. Clorox, for example, now offers "splashless" and "anti-allergen" bleach in addition to its perennial "regular" bleach product. The common "shampoo plus conditioner" formulas of many shampoos are another example.

- **Repositioning**   This strategy involves targeting existing products at new markets or segments. Repositioning can involve real or perceived changes to a product. An example is Carnival Cruise Line's effort to attract senior citizens to supplement its younger crowd. Likewise, many design schools have repositioned themselves toward a growing business need for employees who are well versed in the art of innovation. As such, these design schools are now competing with top MBA programs around the country.

- **Cost Reductions** This strategy involves modifying products to offer performance similar to that of competing products, but at a lower price. Book publishers use this strategy when they convert hardcover books to paperbacks or e-books. Similarly, a firm may be able to lower a product's price due to improved manufacturing efficiency or a drop in the price of raw materials. For example, many computer manufacturers offer lower-priced products that use standard or slightly dated technology.

The first two options are the most effective and profitable when the firm wants to significantly differentiate its product offering from competitors' offerings. The consulting firm of Booz Allen Hamilton found that 30 percent of the product introductions they studied were innovations or new product lines, and 60 percent of the profitable product changes were of this type.[4] Despite this, there are often good reasons to pursue one of the remaining four options, particularly if resource constraints are an issue or if the firm's management does not want to expose the firm to increased market risk.

A firm's ability to develop new products successfully will hinge on many internal and external factors. However, despite any favorable or unfavorable conditions, the key to new product success is to create a differential advantage for the new product. What unique benefit does the new product offer to customers? Although this benefit can be based on real differences or based entirely on image, it is the customers' *perception* of differentiation that is critical. For example, the razor wars have turned into a game of one-upmanship between Procter & Gamble's Fusion and Schick's Quattro. At issue is whether the Fusion's five-blade design is truly better than Quattro's four blades (or Procter & Gamble's own Mach 3 razor) and whether the battery-powered version of each razor really produces better results. Despite *Consumer Reports* tests that battery-powered razors do not provide a closer shave, many consumers believe that they do. In the battle for supremacy in the razor market, customer perceptions are often all that matter.

Customer perceptions are also critical in the process of developing new products. Although the new product development process varies across firms, most firms will go through the following stages:

- **Idea Generation** New product ideas can be obtained from a number of sources, including customers, employees, basic research, competitors, and supply chain partners.

- **Screening and Evaluation** New product ideas are screened for their match with the firm's capabilities and the degree to which they meet customers' needs and wants. In some cases, prototype products are developed to further test the commercial viability of a product concept. New product concepts are also evaluated with respect to projected costs, revenues, and profit potential.

- **Development** At this stage, product specifications are set, the product design is finalized, and initial production begins. In addition, the full marketing plan is developed in order to acquire the resources and collaboration needed for a full-scale launch.

- **Test Marketing**   As a final test before launch, the new product is test marketed in either real or simulated situations to determine its performance relative to customer needs and competing products.

- **Commercialization**   In this final stage, the product is launched with a complete marketing program designed to stimulate customer awareness and acceptance of the new product.

Many firms try to think outside the box in designing new products. Kia, for example, turned to Peter Schreyer, a German automotive designer, to reinvigorate the South Korean company's brand image. When he was hired away from Volkswagen, Schreyer's first task was to design two new vehicles—the Kia Forte and the Kia Soul—to compete against new designs from Nissan and Scion. He then redesigned Kia's popular Sorento SUV. The results have been impressive: Kia's sales increased 6.7 percent, while the company's market share increased 29 percent in the United States and 26 percent in South Korea.[5] Kia's success highlights the importance of maintaining proactive product innovation even in a down economy. As we noted in Chapter 5, many of the world's most powerful brands—like Apple, Microsoft, Walmart, and Nokia—are well-known for their continuous efforts at product innovation.

Branding Strategy.

One of the most important product decisions that marketers must make relates to branding. A *brand* is a combination of name, symbol, term, and/or design that identifies a specific product. Brands have two parts: the brand name and the brand mark. The brand name is the part of a brand that can be spoken, including words, letters, and numbers (Honda, 7-Eleven, WD-40, GMC, Citi). The brand mark—which includes symbols, figures, or a design—is the part of a brand that cannot be spoken. Good brand marks, like McDonald's golden arches, Nike's swoosh, and Prudential's rock, effectively communicate the brand and its image without using spoken words. Brand marks are also useful in advertising and product placement, such as when college football broadcasts clearly depict the Nike logo on the clothing and uniforms of both coaches and players.

Although these technical aspects of branding are important, branding strategy involves much more than developing a clever brand name or unique brand mark. To be truly effective, a brand should succinctly capture the product offering in a way that answers a question in the customer's mind.[6] Good brands are those that immediately come to mind when a customer has a problem to be solved or a need to be fulfilled. Consider these questions that might be asked by a customer:

- Where can I find information quickly?

- Where can I get a quick meal and make my kids happy?

- Where can I buy everything I need, all at decent prices?

- Where can I get the best deal on car insurance?

- How do I find a value-priced hotel in midtown Manhattan?

How do you answer these questions? How many customers do you think would give the following answers: Google, McDonald's, Walmart, GEICO, and Expedia? To successfully develop a brand, the firm should position the product offering (which includes all tangible, intangible, and symbolic elements) as the answer to questions like these. Customers tend to buy products whose combination of attributes is the best solution to their problems. As shown in Exhibit 7.4, brands may have many different attributes that make up the way customers think about them. For example, the iPhone possesses many different attributes that make up customers' overall knowledge about the brand: alliances (AT&T, Google), company (Apple), extensions (iTunes, accessories), employees (Steve Jobs), endorsers (Justin Long, the "Mac guy"), events (Macworld Expo, Apple keynote speeches), and channels (the Apple store). Other

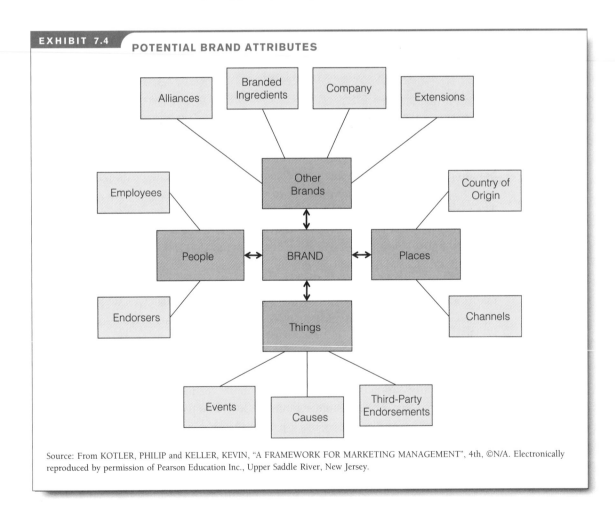

EXHIBIT 7.4   **POTENTIAL BRAND ATTRIBUTES**

Source: From KOTLER, PHILIP and KELLER, KEVIN, "A FRAMEWORK FOR MARKETING MANAGEMENT", 4th, ©N/A. Electronically reproduced by permission of Pearson Education Inc., Upper Saddle River, New Jersey.

brands are enhanced via strong country-of-origin (Guinness, IKEA), branded ingredients (Dell computers use Microsoft and Intel components), causes (Ben and Jerry's), and endorser (Nike) effects.

Strategic Issues in Branding Strategy

The key advantages associated with branding, as shown in Exhibit 7.5, make branding decisions one of the most important pieces in the development of marketing strategy. Branding offers advantages to both firms and customers. For one, branding makes the customer buying process much more efficient because customers can locate and purchase products more easily than without branding. In this section, we examine some of the key strategic issues to be considered in branding strategy.

Manufacturer Versus Private-Label Brands   The distinction between manufacturer brands and private-label brands (brands owned by the merchants that sell them) is an important issue in distribution and supply chain decisions related to branding. Private-label brands, sometimes called store brands, range from well-known products like Gap clothing and Craftsman tools, to other products such as Walmart's Ol' Roy

---

EXHIBIT 7.5   ADVANTAGES OF BRANDING

Overall Advantages of Branding

Product Identification	Customers can easily identify the brands they like.
Comparison Shopping	Branding assists customers in comparing and evaluating competing products.
Shopping Efficiency	Branding speeds up the buying process and makes repeat purchases easier by reducing search time and effort.
Risk Reduction	Branding allows customers to buy a known quantity, thereby reducing the risk of purchase.
Product Acceptance	New products under a known brand name are accepted and adopted more easily.
Enhanced Self-Image	Brands convey status, image, or prestige.
Enhanced Product Loyalty	Branding increases psychosocial identification with the product.

Unique Advantages of Selling Manufacturer (Name) Brands

Reduced Costs	Heavy promotion by the manufacturer reduces the marketing costs of the merchant that carries the brand.
Built-In Loyalty	Manufacturer brands come with their own cadre of loyal customers.
Enhanced Image	The image and prestige of the merchant are enhanced.
Lower Inventory	Manufacturers are capable of time-certain delivery, which allows the merchant to carry less inventory and reduce inventory costs.
Less Risk	Poor quality or product failures become attributed to the manufacturer rather than the merchant.

Unique Advantages of Selling Private-Label (Store) Brands

Increased Profit	The merchant maintains a higher margin on its own brands and faces less pressure to cut prices to match the competition.
Less Competition	Where manufacturer brands are carried by many different merchants, private-label brands are exclusive to the merchant that sells them.
Total Control	The merchant has total control over the development, pricing, distribution, and promotion of the brand.
Merchant Loyalty	Customers who are loyal to a private-label brand are automatically loyal to the merchant.

dog food, Equate aspirin, or Sam's Choice soft drinks. Strategically, the choices to sell, carry, or distribute manufacturer brands or private-label brands are not either–or decisions. As Exhibit 7.5 illustrates, both types of brands have key advantages. For that reason, many distributors, wholesalers, and retailers carry both types of brands. For example, department stores carry manufacturer brands—such as Nike, Polo, and Hilfiger—because customers expect to find them. Hence, manufacturer brands are important in driving customer traffic. They also give customers confidence that they are buying a widely known brand from a respected company. Department stores also carry a number of private label brands because of the increased profit margins associated with them. JCPenney, for example, is well-known for its popular private label brands. Over 40 percent of Penney's sales come from private-label brands, seven of which—including Arizona, Worthington, and St. John's Bay—individually sell over $1 billion each year. Penney's has also added a private brand of clothing and home furnishings called American Living, which is manufactured by Polo Ralph Lauren.[7]

Brand Loyalty   *Brand loyalty* is a positive attitude toward a brand that causes customers to have a consistent preference for that brand over all other competing brands in a product category. There are three degrees of brand loyalty: brand recognition, brand preference, and brand insistence. Brand recognition exists when a customer knows about the brand and is considering it as one of several alternatives in the evoked set. This is the lowest form of brand loyalty and exists mainly due to the awareness of the brand rather than a strong desire to buy the brand. Brand preference is a stronger degree of brand loyalty where a customer prefers one brand to competitive brands and will usually purchase this brand if it is available. For example, a customer may hold a brand preference for Diet Coke. However, if this brand is not available, the customer will usually accept a substitute such as Diet Pepsi or Coke Zero rather than expending extra effort to find and purchase Diet Coke. Brand insistence, the strongest degree of brand loyalty, occurs when customers will go out of their way to find the brand and will accept no substitute. Customers who are brand insistent will expend a great deal of time and effort to locate and purchase their favorite brand. For example, there is not a Mercedes dealer in the state of Wyoming. Consequently, a loyal Mercedes customer will have to drive to Colorado, Idaho, or Utah to obtain service or purchase a vehicle. Brand loyalty is quite high in many different product categories, including cigarettes, mayonnaise, toothpaste, coffee, photographic film, bath soap, medicines, body lotion, makeup, soft drinks, ketchup, and diapers. Note that most of these examples include products that customers put in their mouths or on their bodies—a common trait of products that enjoy the highest brand loyalty.

Brand Equity   The value of a brand is often referred to as brand equity. Another way of looking at brand equity is the marketing and financial value associated with a brand's position in the marketplace. Brand equity usually has ties to brand name awareness, brand loyalty, brand quality, and other attributes shown in Exhibit 7.4. Although brand equity is hard to measure, it represents a key asset for any firm and an important part of marketing strategy. Exhibit 7.6 lists the world's 25 most valuable

EXHIBIT 7.6	THE WORLD'S TWENTY-FIVE MOST VALUABLE BRANDS				
2005 Brand Rank	Brand Name	2008 Brand Value ($Mil)	2004 Brand Value ($Mil)	Change in Brand Value (%)	Country of Ownership
1	Coca-Cola	66,667	65,324	2	United States
2	IBM	59,031	57,091	3	United States
3	Microsoft	59,007	58,709	1	United States
4	GE	53,086	51,569	3	United States
5	Nokia	35,942	33,696	7	Finland
6	Toyota	34,050	32,070	6	Japan
7	Intel	31,261	30,954	1	United States
8	McDonald's	31,049	29,398	6	United States
9	Disney	29,251	29,210	0	United States
10	Google	25,590	17,837	43	United States
11	Mercedes-Benz	25,577	23,568	9	Germany
12	Hewlett-Packard	23,509	22,197	6	United States
13	BMW	23,298	21,612	8	Germany
14	Gillette	22,069	20,415	8	United States
15	American Express	21,940	20,827	5	United States
16	Louis Vuitton	21,602	20,321	6	France
17	Cisco	21,306	19,099	12	United States
18	Marlboro	21,300	21,283	0	United States
19	Citi	20,174	23,443	−14	United States
20	Honda	19,079	17,998	6	Japan
21	Samsung	17,689	16,853	5	South Korea
22	H&M	13,840	New	New	Sweden
23	Oracle	13,831	12,448	11	United States
24	Apple	13,724	11,037	24	United States
25	Sony	13,583	12,907	5	Japan

Source: *BusinessWeek*, September 29, 2008 (http://bwnt.businessweek.com/interactive_reports/global_brand_2008/), based on data from Interbrand Corporation.

brands. Brands like these take years to develop and nurture into the valuable assets that they have come to represent. This reality makes it easier and less expensive for firms to buy established brands than to develop new brands from scratch. For example, Johnson & Johnson's acquisition of Pfizer's consumer products unit allowed the company to add several powerful brands to its portfolio—Listerine, Sudafed, Visine, Neosporin, and Nicorette. The equity associated with these brands would have taken Johnson & Johnson decades to develop on its own.[8]

Brand equity stems from four elements: brand awareness, brand loyalty, brand quality, and brand associations.[9] Brand awareness and brand loyalty increase customer familiarity with a brand. Customers familiar or comfortable with a specific brand are more likely to consider the brand when making a purchase. When this familiarity is combined with a high degree of brand quality, the inherent risk in purchasing the brand decreases dramatically. Brand associations include the brand's image, attributes, or benefits that either directly or indirectly give the brand a certain personality. For example, customers associate 7-Up with "uncola," Charmin tissue with "squeezably soft," Michelin tires with family safety, Allstate insurance with "the good hands," and Honeycomb cereal with a "big, big bite." Associations like these are every bit as important as quality and loyalty, and they also take many years to develop. Unfortunately, it is also possible for brand associations (and brand equity) to be negative. Earlier in the chapter, we described how Kia has enjoyed recent success through new product development. Unfortunately for Kia, however, the South Korean carmaker has struggled with a weak quality image associated with its brands. To counteract this negative brand association, Kia backs its products with a 10-year, 100,000-mile powertrain warranty.[10]

Brand Alliances   As we have stated in previous chapters, relationships with other firms are among the most important competitive advantages that can be held by an organization. Many of these relationships are based on joint branding strategies. For

example, *co-branding* is the use of two or more brands on one product. Co-branding leverages the brand equity of multiple brands to create distinctive products with distinctive differentiation. Co-branding is quite common in processed foods and credit cards. For example, General Mills partners with Hershey's on its Betty Crocker chocolate cake mixes with Hershey's cocoa. This brand alliance gives Betty Crocker a distinct advantage over competitors like Duncan Hines. Likewise, credit card companies like Visa and MasterCard offer co-branded versions of their cards emblazoned with the logos of sports teams, universities, professions, or other firms like American Airlines and Disney World. Co-branding is quite successful because the complementary nature of the brands used on a single product increases perceived quality and customer familiarity.

Co-branding with other well-known brands is a very popular strategy in the credit card industry.

Brand licensing is another type of branding alliance. *Brand licensing* involves a contractual agreement where a company permits an organization to use its brand on noncompeting products in exchange for a licensing fee. Although this royalty can be quite expensive, the instant brand recognition that comes with the licensed brand is often worth the expense. Fashion brands such as Calvin Klein, Ralph Lauren, Bill Blass, and Tommy Hilfiger appear on numerous products in a variety of product categories. Licensing is also quite common in toys, where manufacturers will license the characters and images from popular movies like *Cars* or *Harry Potter* to create a variety of products. Even Jack Daniels and Jim Beam whiskeys have licensed barbeque sauces that bear their famous brands.

As you can see, branding can be a very challenging and complicated part of marketing strategy. However, the value of a good brand to product identification and differentiation is without question. So important are these fundamental roles of branding that marketers go to great lengths to protect their brand names and brand marks. For example, the Beatles' record label Apple Corps has tried several times to stop Apple from using its famous logo, most recently in connection with the iTunes music store. The courts have always upheld Apple's use of its logo, arguing that consumers do not confuse the branding of the separate companies.[11] Companies like Apple expend significant money and effort to monitor potential brand abuses. Although the U.S. legal system provides many laws to protect brands, most of the responsibility for enforcing this protection falls on the company to find and police abuses. Due to the differing and often lax legal systems in other nations, brand abuse is quite common in foreign markets. It is not surprising that patent, copyright, and intellectual property law has become a growth industry both in the United States and around the world.

In addition to brand misidentification, firms protect their brands if there is any danger that the brand can become synonymous with an entire product category. Examples of brands that constantly fight this battle include Scotch tape, Xerox copiers, Band-Aid adhesive bandages, Coca-Cola, FedEx, and Kleenex. To protect their brands, firms obtain trademarks to legally designate that the brand owner has exclusive use of the brand and to prohibit others from using the brand in any way. Former brand names that their parent companies did not protect sufficiently include aspirin, escalator, nylon, linoleum, kerosene, and shredded wheat.

Packaging and Labeling

At first glance, the issues of packaging and labeling might not seem like important considerations in branding strategy. Although packaging and labeling strategy does involve different goals than branding, the two often go hand in hand in developing a product, its benefits, its differentiation, and its image. Consider, for instance, the number of products that use distinctive packaging as part of their branding strategy. Obvious examples include the brand names and brand marks that appear on all product packaging. The color used on a product's package or label is also a vital part of branding, such as Tide's consistent use of bright orange on its line of laundry detergents. The size and shape of the label is sometimes a key to brand identification. For example, Heinz uses a unique crown-shaped label on its ketchup bottles. The physical characteristics of the package itself sometimes become part of the brand. Coca-Cola's unique 10-ounce glass bottle, Pringles' potato chip canister, and the bottles used by Absolut vodka and Crown Royal whiskey are good examples. Finally, products that use recyclable packaging are gaining favor. For example, NatureWorks (a joint venture between Cargill and Teijin of Japan) has developed polylactic acid (or PLA)—a fully compostable bio-plastic made from corn. PLA is used by BIOTA Spring water, whose bottles degrade in 75 to 80 days in commercial composting. Not to be outdone, Coca-Cola introduced the PlantBottle, a recyclable bottle made from 70 percent petroleum and 30 percent sugar and molasses, which reduces carbon emissions by 25 percent over standard plastic bottles. Unlike PLA, the PlantBottle can be recycled.[12]

Packaging serves a number of important functions in marketing strategy. Customers take some functions—like protection, storage, and convenience—for granted until the package fails to keep the product fresh or they discover that the package will not conveniently fit in the refrigerator, medicine cabinet, or backpack. Packaging can also play a role in product modifications and repositioning. An improved cap or closure, an "easy open" package, a more durable box or container, or the introduction of a more conveniently sized package can create instant market recognition and a competitive advantage. Sometimes, a change in package design can create major problems for a brand, as explained in *Beyond the Pages 7.2*. Packaging can also be used as a part of a co-branding strategy. Hillshire Farms, for example, formed an alliance with The Glad Products Company to package its Deli Select line of lunchmeats in GladWare reusable plastic containers. The package is easy to seal and completely reusable once the lunchmeat has been consumed.[13]

Labeling, in and of itself, is an important consideration in marketing strategy. Product labels not only aid in product identification and promotion; they also contain a great deal of information to help customers make proper product selections. Labeling is also an important legal issue as several federal laws and regulations specify the information that must be included on a product's packaging. The Nutritional Labeling and Education Act of 1990 was one of the most sweeping changes in federal labeling law in history. The law mandated that packaged food manufacturers must include detailed nutritional information on their packaging. The law also set standards for health claims such as "low fat," "light," "low calorie," and "reduced cholesterol."

Beyond the Pages 7.2

TROPICANA'S PACKAGING DEBACLE[14]

In January 2009 as a part of a major overhaul of brands in the PepsiCo family, Tropicana dropped the long-familiar labeling of its popular Pure Premium brand of orange juice. That labeling, which contained the familiar logo of a straw sticking out of an orange, was replaced with a more modern, streamlined look with a glass of juice and the "Tropicana" brand written vertically on the packaging. The move was a part of a $35 million "Squeeze: It's a Natural" campaign that promoted fresh taste and family imagery.

Unfortunately for Tropicana, the redesigned packaging met with instant criticism and complaints from loyal consumers. Many consumers argued that the packaging was "ugly" and that it looked like "a generic or store brand." Others complained that the new packaging made it harder for consumers to recognize Tropicana on supermarket shelves. In fact, many consumers complained that they had bought the wrong orange juice. After less than two months in its redesigned packaging, Tropicana Pure Premium sales fell 20 percent, or roughly $33 million. At the same time, competing brands—such as Minute Maid, Florida's Natural, and Tree Ripe—enjoyed

double-digit sales growth. Sales of private-label brands also increased.

After the rapid drop in sales and thousands of consumer letters, emails, and telephone calls, PepsiCo announced that it would scrap the new packaging and return to the old packaging. Industry critics lauded the move and compared it with Coke's "New Coke" fiasco from 1985. Pepsi, like Coke at the time, had failed to see the deep bond that loyal consumers had with Tropicana's packaging. Once the old packaging had returned, Tropicana's sales returned to normal.

Although the Tropicana story is an important lesson against meddling with an iconic brand, it also points out the clout that consumers have today. It is easier to connect with, and harder to avoid, customers who can easily and effectively interact with companies and each other through social technologies. Just 10 years ago, it would have taken Tropicana months to determine that there was a backlash against its packaging. Now, through email, Facebook, and Twitter, companies can discover customer reactions in almost real time.

Recently, the U.S. Supreme Court ruled that manufacturers bear full responsibility for the content of the labeling and warnings on its packaging. This ruling also applies to manufacturers of products that are inspected and certified by the government, such as foods and pharmaceuticals.[15]

Differentiating and Positioning the Product Offering

Though we have focused solely on product issues to this point in the chapter, it is vital to remember that product strategy is intricately tied to the other elements of the marketing program. This integration with other strategic elements comes to the forefront when the firm attempts to differentiate and position its product offering relative to competing offerings. People sometimes confuse differentiation and positioning with market segmentation and target marketing. *Product differentiation* involves creating differences in the firm's product offering that set it apart from competing offerings. Differentiation typically has its basis in distinct product features, additional services, or other characteristics. *Positioning* refers to creating a mental image of the product offering and its differentiating features in the minds of the target market. This mental image can be based on real or perceived differences among competing offerings. Whereas differentiation is about the product itself, positioning is about customers' perceptions of the real or imaginary benefits that the product possesses.

Although differentiation and positioning can be based on actual product features or characteristics, the principal task for the firm is to develop and maintain a *relative position* for the product in the minds of the target market. The process of creating a favorable relative position involves several steps:

1. Identify the characteristics, needs, wants, preferences, and benefits desired by the target market.

2. Examine the differentiating characteristics and relative position of all current and potential competitors in the market.

3. Compare the position of your product offering with the positions of the competition for each key need, want, preference, or benefit desired by the target market.

4. Identify a unique position that focuses on customer benefits that the competition does not currently offer.

5. Develop a marketing program to leverage the firm's position and persuade customers that the firm's product offering will best meet their needs.

6. Continually reassess the target market, the firm's position, and the position of competing offerings to ensure that the marketing program stays on track and also to identify emerging positioning opportunities.[16]

The concept of relative position is typically addressed using a tool called perceptual mapping. A *perceptual map* represents customer perceptions and preferences spatially by means of a visual display. A hypothetical perceptual map for automotive brands is shown in Exhibit 7.7. The axes represent underlying dimensions that customers might use to form perceptions and preferences of brands. Any number of dimensions can be represented using computer algorithms such as multidimensional scaling or cluster analysis. However, simple two-dimensional maps are the most common form because a limited number of dimensions are typically the most salient for consumers.

Perceptual maps illustrate two basic issues. First, they indicate products/brands that are similar in terms of relative mental position. In the example perceptual map, customers are likely to see the offerings of Toyota and Honda as being very similar. Positioning a brand to coincide with competing brands becomes more difficult when many brands occupy the same relative space. Second, perceptual maps illustrate voids in the current mindscape for a product category. In the map, note the empty space in the extreme bottom-left corner. This indicates that consumers do not perceive any current products to be both conservative and affordable. This lack of competition within the mindspace might occur because (1) customers have unmet needs or preferences, or (2) customers have no desire for a product offering with this combination of dimensions. Obviously, additional research would be needed to determine

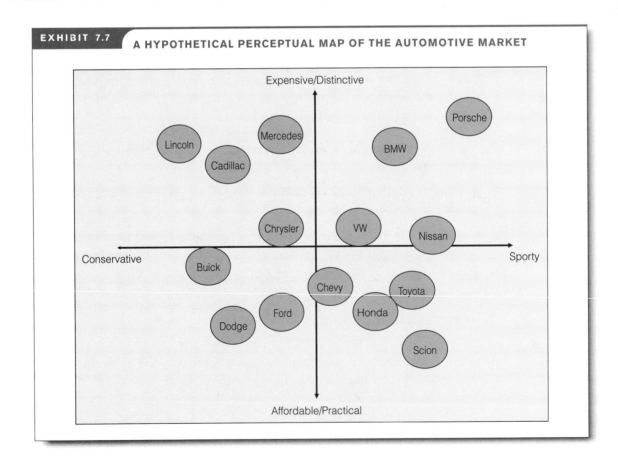

EXHIBIT 7.7   **A HYPOTHETICAL PERCEPTUAL MAP OF THE AUTOMOTIVE MARKET**

whether this lack of perceived competition indicates a viable unmet segment of the market.

Differentiation Strategies

Generally, the most important tool of product differentiation is the brand. Customer perceptions of a brand are of utmost importance in product differentiation because differences among competing brands can be based on real qualities (e.g., product characteristics, features, or style) or psychological qualities (e.g., perception and image). In addition to the brand, other important bases for differentiation include product descriptors, customer support services, and image.

Product Descriptors   Firms generally provide information about their products in one of three contexts, as shown in Exhibit 7.8. The first context is *product features*, which are factual descriptors of the product and its characteristics. For example, Apple's 13-inch MacBook Pro includes key features such as an Intel Core 2 Duo processor and aluminum unibody construction. However, features—although they tell something about the nature of the product—are not generally the pieces of information that lead customers to buy. Features must be translated into the second context, advantages. *Advantages* are performance characteristics that communicate how the features make the product behave, hopefully in a fashion that is distinctive and appealing to customers. The advantages of the MacBook Pro include a lightweight, compact design, fast performance, and long battery life. However, as we have said before, the real reason customers buy products is to gain *benefits*—the positive outcomes or need satisfaction they acquire from purchased products. Thus, the benefits of the MacBook Pro include ultimate mobility and rugged entertainment on the road. Other benefits, like increased productivity and connectivity, might also be implied in Apple's promotional program.

Increasingly, one aspect of a product's description that customers value highly is quality. Product characteristics that customers associate with quality include reliability, durability, ease of maintenance, ease of use, and a trusted brand name. In business markets, other characteristics, such as technical suitability, ease of repair, and company reputation, become included in this list of quality indicators. In general, higher product quality—real or imagined—means that a company can charge a higher price for their product and simultaneously build customer loyalty. In the case of Apple and the MacBook Pro, this is certainly true. The relationship between quality and price (inherent in the concept of value) forces the firm to consider product quality carefully when making decisions regarding differentiation, positioning, and the overall marketing program.

Customer Support Services   A firm may have difficulty differentiating its products when all products in a market have essentially the same quality, features, or benefits. In such cases, providing good customer support services—both before and after the sale—may be the only way to differentiate the firm's products and move them away from a price-driven commodity status. For example, over the past 10 years, small,

EXHIBIT 7.8   USING PRODUCT DESCRIPTORS IN PRODUCT DIFFERENTIATION

Product	Features	Advantages	Benefits
Apple MacBook Pro 13-inch laptop	Intel Core 2 Duo processor	Very lightweight and compact	Ultimate mobility
	Mac OS X operating system with iLife	Blazingly fast multi-media performance	Rugged entertainment on the road
	Precision aluminum unibody construction	Out-of-the-box photo, video, and audio editing	No need to purchase separate photo-, video-, or audio-editing software
	Less than 1″ thick and only 4.5 lbs	Long-lasting battery	Stay connected wherever you are
	High performance NVIDIA graphics	Hassle-free connectivity	
	7-hour, 58-watt lithium-polymer battery		
	Integrated Wi-Fi and Bluetooth		
Chevrolet Camaro	6.2L, 426-horsepower LS3 V8	0 to 60 in 5 seconds	Enhanced self-image
	Variable-ratio power steering	Superb handling	Fun to drive
	Low, wide, aggressive stance and 52/48 front/rear weight distribution	Better road grip	Easy to drive
		24 mpg highway	Fuel-efficient muscle
	Stabilitrack electronic stability control		Safety
Bounty Select-a-Size paper towels	Sheets can be torn in varying sizes	Great for any size cleaning job	More control over cleaning
	More sheets per roll	Less waste	Reduces cost of buying paper towels
	Increased wet strength	Superior absorbency	Can be sized for use as placemats
		Won't run out as often	

locally owned bookstores have disappeared at an alarming rate as competition from Barnes and Noble, Books-A-Million, and Amazon has taken its toll. The local stores that have remained in business thrive because of the exceptional, personalized service they provide to their customers. Many local bookstores create customer loyalty by being actively involved in the community, including contributing to local schools, churches, and charities. Many customers value this level of personalization so highly that they will pay slightly higher prices and remain loyal to *their* bookstore.

Support services include anything the firm can provide in addition to the main product that adds value to that product for the customer. Examples include assistance in identifying and defining customer needs, delivery and installation, technical support for high-tech systems and software, financing arrangements, training, extended warranties and guarantees, repair, layaway plans, convenient hours of operation, affinity programs (e.g., frequent flier/buyer programs), and adequate parking. If you buy a Kenmore refrigerator, for example, you can expect Sears to provide financing, delivery and installation, and warranty repair service, if necessary. Through research, the firm can discover the types of support services that customers value most. In some cases, customers may want lower prices rather than an array of support services. Low-cost airlines—such as JetBlue and Allegiant Air—and budget hotels—such as Motel 6 and La Quinta—are good examples. The importance of having the proper mix of support services has increased in recent years, causing many firms to design their customer services as carefully as they design their products.

Image   The image of a product or organization is the overall impression, positive or negative, that customers have of it. This impression includes what the organization has done in the past, what it presently offers, and projections about what it will do in the future. All aspects of the firm's marketing program, as perceived by customers, will affect this impression. Consider the car rental industry. In the industry's early years, Hertz not only stood in first place, the company also maintained a vast lead over second-place Avis. The management of Avis, intent on capturing a larger portion of Hertz's customers, asked its advertising agency to develop an effective positioning strategy relative to Hertz. After searching for any advantage that Avis held over Hertz, the agency concluded that the only difference was that Avis was number two. Avis management decided to claim this fact as an advantage, using the theme "We're number two. We try harder!" Avis rentals soared, putting the company in a much stronger number-two position.

In the case of product differentiation, reality is often not as important as perception. Firms that enjoy a solid image or reputation can differentiate their product offerings based solely on the company or brand name alone. Examples of firms that have this ability include BMW, Mercedes, Michelin, Budweiser, Campbell's, Ritz-Carlton Hotels, Disney World, and Princess Cruises. A good image is not only one of the best means of product differentiation; it is also a major sustainable competitive advantage. However, a good image can also be lost over time—or shattered in an instant.

Positioning Strategies

Firms can design their marketing programs to position and enhance the image of a product offering in the minds of target customers. To create a positive image for a product, a firm can choose from among several positioning strategies, including strengthening the current position, repositioning, or attempting to reposition the competition.

Strengthen the Current Position   The key to strengthening a product's current position is to monitor constantly what target customers want and the extent to which customers perceive the product as satisfying those wants. Any complacency in today's dynamic marketplace is likely to result in lost customers and sales. For example, a firm known for excellent customer service must continue to invest time, money, talent, and attention to its product position to protect its market share and sales from competitive activity. This is especially true for firms such as Ritz-Carlton and Nordstrom that pursue competitive advantage based on customer intimacy.

Strengthening a current position is all about continually raising the bar of customer expectations. For example, Honda has always been known for quality and reliability. Recently, however, Honda has shifted its positioning focus to wrap quality and value in the context of long-term value. The company's promotional campaigns explain how its cars have a lower cost of ownership when factors such as insurance, fuel, and maintenance are taken into consideration.[17] Honda's positioning is different from the strategies pursued by Toyota (fuel economy), Kia (quality), and Volkswagen (engineering). By tweaking its positioning strategy, Honda understands that it must constantly raise expectations about value if it is to hold its position and remain competitive.

Repositioning   At times, declining sales or market share may signal that customers have lost faith in a product's ability to satisfy their needs. In such cases, a new position may be the best response, as strengthening the current position may well accelerate the downturn in performance. Repositioning may involve a fundamental change in any of the marketing mix elements, or perhaps even all of them. J. Crew, for example, dropped its preppy style of clothing in favor of more "urban and hip" merchandise. The traditional catalog-based retailer also expanded its number of retail stores. As its traditional baby boom customers age, J. Crew has tried to attract younger shoppers who have traditionally favored stores like Hollister and Abercrombie & Fitch. J. Crew is among a group of brands (including Amazon, Apple, Bed Bath & Beyond, Nike, and Safeway) that have benefited from the slowdown in the U.S. economy, due to their image for good value and excellent service. J. Crew is also a favorite brand of first lady Michelle Obama—a fact that has led to a renaissance of J. Crew's brand caché.[18]

Some of the most memorable marketing programs involve attempts to move to new positions. The "Not Just for Breakfast Anymore" campaign for orange juice and the "Pork: The Other White Meat" campaign are good examples. A continuing example is Cadillac's attempt to reposition the brand because of the aging of its traditional target. The erosion of Cadillac's share of the luxury car market has forced the company to focus on and attract younger audiences to the brand. Cadillac's recent marketing programs have been headlined by the "Fusion of Design and Technology," "Heritage Reborn," "Break Through," and "It's a Lifestyle" campaigns. In some cases, repositioning requires a focus on new products. For example, Sony, the third-largest camera manufacturer in the world (behind Canon and Nikon), was not taken seriously as a camera brand until it launched the Alpha—a digital SLR (single-lens reflex) camera aimed at the high end of the market. Before the Alpha, Sony offered only point-and-shoot models.[19]

Reposition the Competition   In many cases, it is better to attempt to reposition the competition rather than change your own position. A direct attack on a competitor's strength may put its products in a less favorable light or even force the competitor to change its positioning strategy. We are all familiar with the dueling campaigns of Microsoft and Apple, Coke and Pepsi, and Pizza Hut and Papa John's. Napster uses a similar strategy when it compares its Napster To Go service to Apple's iTunes. The company describes Napster To Go as a "buffet style" assortment of music, where users can access all 7 million songs on Napster for $14.95 per month. Napster compares this to iTunes' "à la carte" style where songs must be purchased for $0.69 to $1.29 each.[20] Microsoft uses a similar tactic against iTunes in ads for its Zune music player. Microsoft's ads argue that it would cost $30,000 to completely fill an iPod with music, whereas the company's ZunePass service costs $14.99 per month.[21]

Managing Products and Brands Over Time

Decisions related to products, product lines, branding, differentiation, and positioning are ongoing strategic issues. So is managing the entire portfolio of products and brands over time. To address this issue, we use the traditional product life cycle—shown in Exhibit 7.9—to discuss product strategy from a product's conception, through its growth and maturity, and to its ultimate death. Our use of the product life cycle is based on its ability to describe the strategic issues and key objectives that should be considered during each phase of a product's life. We note, however, that the product life cycle has many limitations. For one, most new products never get past development and most successful products never die. Second, the product life cycle really refers to the life of a product/market, industry, sector, or product category—not to specific brands or firms. Hence, if we trace the life cycle of the bricks-and-mortar DVD rental business, we deal with market characteristics for this sector and not single firms like Blockbuster or Movie Gallery. Further, the length of each stage and the time involved in the overall cycle depend heavily on the actions of the firms within the

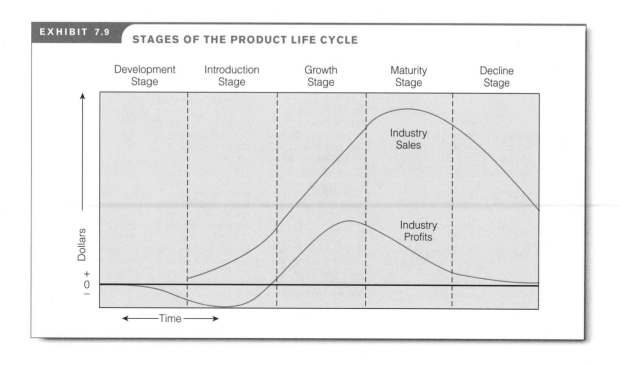

EXHIBIT 7.9   STAGES OF THE PRODUCT LIFE CYCLE

industry. Firms and industries constantly reinvent themselves, which can cause the life cycle to speed up, slow down, or even recycle.

Despite these issues, the product life cycle offers a useful framework for discussing product strategy over time. Exhibit 7.10 summarizes these strategic considerations for each stage of the life cycle. It is important for product managers to consider the stage of their market's life cycle with respect to planning in the current period as well as planning for the future. Using the product life cycle as a framework has the distinct advantage of forcing managers to consider the future of their industry and their brand. For example, many experts believe that the traditional DVD rental industry is heading rapidly into its decline phase. The advent of DVD distribution via the mail and technological innovations such as video on demand and IPTV (Internet Protocol Television) offer a dramatic increase in convenience for consumers. Given this fact, it is not surprising that traditional rental houses Blockbuster and Movie Gallery have suffered. Conversely, Netflix, the pioneer in through-the-mail DVD rentals, currently boasts 10.3 million members and enjoys 21 percent annual revenue increases. Despite this success, Netflix is looking to the future by investing in online movie distribution, movie production, and the acquisition of distribution rights of independent films. Netflix's strategy is a hedge against Hulu and YouTube, as well as the future of fully digital transmission of movies via ever improving technology.[22]

EXHIBIT 7.10   STRATEGIC CONSIDERATIONS DURING THE PRODUCT LIFE CYCLE

	Life Cycle Stages			
	Introduction	Growth	Maturity	Decline
Overall Marketing Goals	Stimulate product awareness and trial	Increase market share by acquiring new customers; discover new needs and market segments	Maximize profit by defending market share or stealing it from competitors	Reduce expenses and marketing efforts to maximize the last opportunity for profit
Product Strategy	Introduce limited models with limited features; frequent product changes	Introduce new models with new features; pursue continuous innovation	Full model line; increase supplemental product offerings to aid in product differentiation	Eliminate unprofitable models and brands
Pricing Strategy	Penetration pricing to establish a market presence or price skimming to recoup development costs	Prices fall due to competition; price to match or beat the competition	Prices continue to fall; price to beat the competition	Prices stabilize at a lower level
Distribution Strategy	Gradually roll out product to expand availability; get channel intermediaries on board	Intensify efforts to expand product reach and availability	Extensive product availability; retain shelf space; phase out unprofitable outlets or channels	Maintain a level necessary to keep brand loyal customers; continue phasing out unprofitable channels
Promotion Strategy	Advertising and personal selling to build awareness; heavy sales promotion to stimulate product trial	Aggressive brand advertising, selling, and sales promotion to encourage brand switching and continued trial	Stress brand differences and benefits; encourage brand switching; keep the brand/product fresh	Reduce to a minimal level or phase out entirely

Source: Adapted from William M. Pride and O.C. Ferrell, *Marketing: 2010 Edition.* (Mason, OH: Cengage Learning, 2010), pp. 290–295.

Development Stage

As Exhibit 7.9 indicates, a firm has no sales revenue during the product development stage. In fact, the firm experiences a net cash outflow due to the expenses involved in product innovation and development. For most innovations, a substantial investment of financial resources and time are necessary for product development. In addition, the firm assumes a great deal of financial, market, and opportunity risk due to the uncertainty involved in developing new products. For example, the pharmaceutical industry understands the challenges of new product development like no other industry. Firms such as Merck, Pfizer, and AstraZeneca spend millions each year developing new drugs. Upon identifying a new drug, it takes years of testing before earning FDA approval. Then, once the new drug is on the market, the firm has only a few years to recoup its investment before patent protection expires and the market opens to generic competition. In this highly competitive industry, pharmaceutical firms live or die based on the number and quality of drugs they have in their development pipelines.

The development stage usually begins with a product concept, which has several components: (1) an understanding of the specific uses and benefits that target customers seek in a new product; (2) a description of the product, including its potential uses and benefits; (3) the potential for creating a complete product line that can create synergy in sales, distribution, and promotion; and (4) an analysis of the feasibility of the product concept, including such issues as anticipated sales, required return on investment, time of market introduction, and length of time to recoup the investment. Given the odds stacked against most new products, it is not surprising that over 80 percent of all new products fail. This unfortunate fact of life underscores the need to correctly identify target customer needs *before* developing the product strategy. Through effective test marketing, the firm can gauge customer response to a new product before the full-scale launch. New products that closely match customers' needs and have strong advantages over competing products are much easier to market as the new product enters the introduction stage of its life cycle.

Introduction Stage

The introduction stage begins when development is complete and ends when sales indicate that target customers widely accept the product. The marketing strategy devised during the development stage is fully implemented during the introduction stage and should be tightly integrated with the firm's competitive advantages and strategic focus. Marketing strategy goals common to the introduction stage include the following:

- Attracting customers by raising awareness of, and interest in, the product offering through advertising, public relations, and publicity efforts that connect key product benefits to customers' needs and wants.

- Inducing customers to try and buy the product through the use of various sales tools and pricing activities. Common examples include free samples of the product and the use of price incentives.

- Engaging in customer education activities that teach members of the target market how to use the new product.

- Strengthening or expanding channel and supply chain relationships to gain sufficient product distribution to make the product easily accessible by target customers.

- Building on the availability and visibility of the product through trade promotion activities that encourage channel intermediaries to stock and support the product.

- Setting pricing objectives that will balance the firm's need to recoup investment with the competitive realities of the market.

Mozilla was able to rapidly introduce its Firefox web browser through a creative viral word-of-mouth campaign.

Although all elements of the marketing program are important during the introduction stage, good promotion and distribution are essential to make customers aware that the new product is available, teach them how to use it correctly, and tell them where to purchase it. Although this is typically a very expensive undertaking, it doesn't have to be. For example, when Mozilla released its open-source Firefox web browser, it garnered 150 million downloads and 10 million permanent users in only 18 months, without any marketing staff. The secret to Mozilla's success was a word-of-mouth buzz campaign that centered on its SpreadFirefox.com website. Today, Firefox users can still post ideas on how to market Firefox or volunteer to put other ideas into action.[23]

The length of the introduction stage can vary. In business markets, new products often have long introduction periods while buyers become convinced to adopt them. In consumer markets, many products experience an immediate upsurge in sales as consumers and retailers take advantage of special introductory offers. After the introduction, the firm must continually track market share, revenues, store placement, channel support, costs, and product usage rates to assess whether the new product pays back the firm's investment. Even when the firm has patent protection or hard-to-copy technology, it must carefully track competitors' reactions. Tracking this information is critical if the product is to make the grade, continue along the gradually rising sales curve, and enter the profitable growth stage. Unfortunately, most new product introductions start off very slowly and never enjoy rising demand or profits. Failures during introduction are even more expensive than in the development stage, as marketing and distribution costs accrue to the total expenses involved in the product's launch.

Growth Stage

The firm should be ready for the growth stage, as sustained sales increases may begin quickly. The product's upward sales curve may be steep, and profits should rapidly increase, then decline toward the end of the growth stage. The length of the growth stage varies according to the nature of the product and competitive reactions. For example, disposable diapers had a long growth stage as they experienced over 30 percent yearly growth for a decade. A short growth stage is typical for new technologies such as the iPhone, YouTube, or the Nintendo Wii.

Regardless of the length of the growth stage, the firm has two main priorities: (1) establishing a strong, defensible market position, and (2) achieving financial objectives that repay investment and earn enough profit to justify a long-term commitment to the product. Within these two priorities, there are a number of pertinent marketing strategy goals:

- Leverage the product's *perceived* differential advantages in terms of branding, quality, price, value, and so on, to secure a strong market position.

- Establish a clear product and brand identity through coordinated promotional campaigns aimed at both customers and the trade.

- Create unique positioning through the use of advertising that stresses the product's benefits for target customers relative to other available solutions or products.

- Maintain control over product quality to assure customer satisfaction.

- Maximize availability of the product through extensive distribution and promotion activities that capitalize on the product's popularity.

- Maintain or enhance the product's ability to deliver profits to key channel and supply chain partners, especially retailers that control shelf space and product placement.

- Find the ideal balance between price and demand as price elasticity becomes more important as the product moves toward the maturity stage.

- Always keep an eye focused on the competition.

During the growth stage, the overall strategy shifts from acquisition to retention, from stimulating product trial to generating repeat purchases and building brand loyalty. This is not only true for customers but also for wholesalers, retailers, and other supply chain members. The key is to develop long-term relationships with customers and partners in order to prepare for the maturity stage. As the market matures, the firm will need loyal customers and good friends in the supply chain in order to remain competitive. Maintaining key relationships is a challenging and expensive proposition. For this reason, the growth stage is the most expensive stage for marketing.

Pricing also becomes more challenging during the growth stage. As more competitors enter the market, the firm must balance its need for cash flow with its need to be competitive. The relationship between price and perceived quality is a complicating factor, as is the increasing price sensitivity of customers. It is not surprising during the growth stage to see competitors stake out market positions based on premium or value-based pricing strategies. Other firms solve the pricing dilemma by offering different products at different price points. You can see this strategy in action in the wireless phone market, where each service provider offers tiered service offerings (i.e., minutes and features) at different pricing levels. FedEx implements the same strategy with its tiered service offerings (overnight by 8:30 AM, overnight by 10:30 AM, etc.).

Another major challenge during the growth stage is the increasing number of competitors entering the market. There is a tendency for many firms to pay less attention to competitors during the growth stage. After all, the market has grown rapidly and there is enough business for everyone to have a piece. Why not worry about competitors later? Because growth will eventually end and the market will become mature. To protect itself, the firm must build a defensible market position as it prepares for market maturity. This position may be based on image, price, quality, or perhaps some technological standard. Eventually, the market will go through a shakeout period and the dominant firms will emerge. This process is already underway in the wireless telephone market, where U.S. companies such as Nextel and Alltel have been acquired by their rivals. Similarly, Europe's Vodafone has been looking to acquire another company in its effort to gain market dominance over O2, its biggest competitor. A similar shakeout has been underway for some time in the digital photography market. Today, two firms—Nikon and Canon—control 80 percent of the market, whereas other firms have gone out of business (Minolta, Konica, Kyocera, Contax). As these markets enter the maturity phase, the fate of the remaining firms will depend on their ability to create defensible market positions.

Maturity Stage

After the shakeout occurs at the end of the growth stage, the strategic window of opportunity will all but close for the market. No more firms will enter the market unless they have found some product innovation significant enough to attract large numbers of customers. The window of opportunity often remains open, however, for new product features and variations. A good example is the introduction of light, dry, ice, microbrew, low-alcohol, and low-carb products in the beer industry. These variations can be quite important as firms attempt to gain market share. In the face of limited or no growth within the market, one of the few ways for a firm to gain market share is to steal it from a competitor. Such theft often comes only with significant promotional investments or cuts in gross margin because of the lowering of prices. The stakes in this chess match are often very high. For example, just a fractional change in market share in the soft-drink industry means millions in additional revenue and profit for the lucky firm.

In the typical product life cycle, we expect maturity to be the longest stage. For the firm that has survived the growth stage, maturity can be a relatively status quo period of time. As long as one maintains sales volume to keep market share constant, a longer-term perspective can be taken due to decreasing market uncertainty. Typically, a firm has four general goals that can be pursued during the maturity stage:

- **Generate Cash Flow**   By the time a market reaches maturity, the firm's products should be yielding a very positive cash flow. This is essential to recoup the initial investment and to generate the excess cash necessary for the firm to grow and develop new products.

- **Hold Market Share**   Marketing strategy should stress holding market share among the dominant brands in the market. Firms having marginal market share must decide whether they have a reasonable chance of improving their position. If not, they should consider pulling out of the market.

- **Steal Market Share**   Any firm in a mature market can pursue this goal; however, it is more likely to be used by firms holding weaker market positions. The key to this strategy is to create incentives that encourage brand switching, even if only temporarily. Even small gains in market share can lead to large increases in profits.

- **Increase Share of Customer**   Share of customer refers to the percentage of each customer's needs in a particular area met by the firm. This strategy is quite common in financial services. Likewise, many large grocery chains increase share of customer by adding features ranging from restaurants to video rentals to dry cleaning services in an effort to create one-stop shopping for family needs.

To achieve these goals, the firm has at least four general options for strategy selection throughout the maturity stage: (1) develop a new product image; (2) find and attract new users to the product; (3) discover new applications and uses for the product; or (4) apply new technology to the product. Kraft Foods, for example, launched a massive promotional campaign to create a new product image for Jell-O after a long decline in sales. Today, Jell-O has once again achieved gourmet status with America's children. Similarly, Whirlpool used product innovation to shake itself free from the "sea of white," a phrase that is often used to describe the bland range of offerings in household appliances. Whirlpool's Duet washers and dryers—industry leaders in design, ease of use, and energy efficiency—now command 40 percent of the front-loading market.[24] Finally, as described in *Beyond the Pages* 7.3, Nintendo used a rebranding strategy to attract casual gamers to its handheld and home gaming systems.

Stealing customers away from the competition involves creating incentives for noncustomers to try the firm's product. This may entail heavy expenditures in sales promotion activities such as product sampling, couponing, or trade promotion to encourage prominent display of the product on the store's shelves. In some cases, once the brand switch has been accomplished, customers can be locked in through the use of contractual agreements. This is common among wireless phone providers, health clubs, and satellite television providers. A more common approach is to simply match competitive prices, as is the case among many competing retail firms. For example, most pizza chains will accept competitor's coupons and match their promotional incentives to gain business.

Beyond the Pages 7.3

NINTENDO'S REBRANDING STRATEGY[25]

Admit it. You've always thought of Nintendo's line of game systems as being strictly for kids. You're not alone. Most people associate the Nintendo 64, Gamecube, Wii, GameBoy, and DSi with famous characters such as Mario, Luigi, and Princess Peach. However, several years ago, Nintendo set out to change everyone's opinions about video games and the gamers that enjoy them.

Nintendo's first step toward rebranding occurred in early 2006 with the redesign of its original DS handheld game system. Dubbed the DS Lite, the handheld was a smaller, lighter, brighter-screened, and distinctly iPod-looking version of the original DS system. It boasted a touch-sensitive screen, a stylus, long battery life, and the ability to play all DS and GameBoy Advance games. To coincide with the launch, Nintendo rebranded many of its popular puzzle and skill-building games under the Touch Generations brand. Titles in the series—including *Brain Age*, *Big Brain Academy*, *Tetris DS*, *Nintendogs*, *Magnetica*, *Electroplankton*, *Sudoku Gridmaster*, and *True Swing Golf*—had been available for a while; however, they had not been collectively branded and targeted toward a particular audience. That audience included 40- and 50-something men and women in the so-called casual gamer market. Unlike younger gamers that enjoy playing for long periods of time, casual gamers prefer to play games for shorter periods: while waiting for the kids to finish dance class or riding in mass transit, or as a fun way to fill 10 minutes before a meeting. At that time, Nintendo's website for Touch Generations stated this market's needs perfectly:

> Not a hard-core gamer? That's OK. We've made games for you in mind. Nintendo's Touch Generations series, exclusive to the Nintendo DS handheld game system, allows you simple, engaging interaction with games that promote production over destruction, contemplation over domination. No complex instructions. No steep learning curve. Play a little. Play a lot. It's up to you.

Nintendo's second step toward rebranding occurred in late 2006 with the launch of the Wii home gaming console. The defining characteristic of the Wii is its wireless controller—the Wii Remote. It allows gamers to play games interactively by moving their arms and body in distinct game-like motions (such as playing tennis, baseball, or driving a car). Nintendo also expanded the Touch Generations brand to include Wii games such as *Wii Fit*, *Wii Music*, and *Big Brain Academy*. After launch, both the DS Lite and the Wii quickly became the best selling gaming platforms in the world.

In 2009, Nintendo further refined its strategy with the launch of the DSi handheld gaming system. Although the system looks very much like the DS Lite, it incorporates larger screens, front- and rear-facing cameras, an online game store, removable storage, and picture-editing software. Together, these changes make the DSi much more of a social tool than the original system. In fact, Nintendo's goal was to create a system that does more than play games. The company wanted to create a system that enriches people's lives. This shift necessitated a change in Nintendo's marketing about Touch Generations:

> No matter what your age, gender, or background, fun is a universal idea. The Touch Generations family of software lets people from all walks of life connect with each other through engaging and fulfilling interactive experiences. Titles like *Wii Music* and *Personal Trainer: Walking* can bring your family together in new and exciting ways.

Nintendo's Touch Generations strategy takes advantage of recent trends in the gaming market. The average age of frequent game purchasers is 40, with a full 25 percent of all gamers being over the age of 50. In addition, women account for 47 percent of all gamers who are parents. Nintendo believes that there is large segment of "dormant" gamers in the market who enjoyed playing *Pac-Man* and *Pong* as children or young adults. Many experts agree and point to the huge success of *The Sims* as an example of a game that appeals to this market.

Decline Stage

A product's sales plateau will not last forever, and eventually a persistent decline in revenue begins. A firm has two basic options during the decline stage: (1) attempt to postpone the decline, or (2) accept its inevitability. Should the firm attempt to postpone the decline, the product's demand must be renewed through repositioning, developing new uses or features for the product, or applying new technology. For example, despite the decline in sales of muscle cars over the past two decades, Ford, Chrysler, and GM have successfully launched redesigned versions of their famous brands. The Ford Mustang Shelby GT 500 was introduced in 2007 to eager buyers willing to pay $20,000 over sticker price (which was around $40,000) to get the first Shelbys produced. Chrysler's Dodge Challenger debuted in 2008, with GM's Chevy Camaro launching in 2009.[26] Postponing a product's decline in this manner takes a great deal of time and a substantial investment of resources. Many firms, however, do not have the resources or opportunity to renew a product's demand and must accept the inevitability of decline. In such instances, the firm can either harvest profits from the product while demand declines or divest the product, taking steps to abandon it or sell it to another firm.

The *harvesting* approach calls for a gradual reduction in marketing expenditures and uses a less resource-intensive marketing mix. A harvesting strategy also allows the firm to funnel its increased cash flow into the development of new products. For example, GM phased out the Oldsmobile brand over several years by offering discounts and other special incentives, such as longer product warranties, to allay customer fears of limited product support. A company using the *divesting* option withdraws all marketing support from the product. It may continue to sell the product until it sustains losses, or arrange for the product to be acquired by another firm. For example, Procter & Gamble dropped its Oxydol laundry detergent and sold it to Redox Brands (now known as CR Brands) for $7 million. Though P&G had sold Oxydol for 73 years, the company decided to delete the brand after its sales fell from a high of $64 million in 1950 to only $5.5 million just before the sale. CR Brands now markets the brand as Oxydol Extreme Clean and targets Generation X consumers with liquid versions and vibrant packaging.[27]

There are several factors that the firm should take into consideration before deciding on an appropriate marketing strategy during the decline stage:

- **Market Segment Potential** The firm might have loyal customer segments that will continue to buy the product. If these segments are viable and profitable, the firm should postpone the decline or slowly harvest the product.

- **The Market Position of the Product** A product in a leading market position with a solid image may be profitable and generate excess cash by attracting customers from competitors' abandoned products.

- **The Firm's Price and Cost Structure** If the firm is a low-cost producer in the industry and can maintain its selling price, the product can remain viable even in a declining market. The firm's cost structure could also be enhanced by no longer having to invest in the product's marketing program.

- **The Rate of Market Deterioration**   The faster the rate of market deterioration, the sooner the firm should divest the product.

Although the firm should carefully consider these factors, it should not be sentimental about dropping a failing product. On the other hand, the firm should not quickly dismiss a renewal attempt, particularly if the firm does not have a better alternative use for its resources.

Throughout the product life cycle, it is imperative that the firm stay focused on changes in the market, not on the firm's products. Products have life cycles only because markets and customers change. By focusing on changing markets, the firm can attempt to create new and better quality products to match customers' needs. Only in this way can a firm grow, prosper, remain competitive, and continue to be seen as a source of solutions by the target market.

Lessons from Chapter 7

Product strategy

- Lies at the heart of every organization in that it defines what the organization does and why it exists.

- Involves creating a product offering that is a bundle of physical (tangible), service (intangible), and symbolic (perceptual) attributes designed to satisfy customers' needs and wants.

- Strives to overcome commoditization by differentiating product offerings via the service and symbolic elements of the offering.

The product portfolio

- Is used in both consumer (convenience, shopping, specialty, and unsought products) and business (raw materials, component parts, process materials, MRO supplies, accessory equipment, installations, and business services) markets.

- Is used in most firms due to the advantages of selling a variety of products rather than a single product.

- Consists of a group of closely related product items (product lines) and the total group of products offered by the firm (product mix).

- Involves strategic decisions such as the number of product lines to offer (variety), as well as the depth of each product line (assortment).

- Can create a number of important benefits for firms, including economies of scale, package uniformity, standardization, sales and distribution efficiency, and equivalent quality beliefs.

The challenges of service products

- Stem mainly from the fact that services are intangible. Other challenging characteristics of services include simultaneous production and consumption, perishability, heterogeneity, and client-based relationships.

- Include the following issues:

  - Service firms experience problems in balancing supply (capacity) with demand.

  - Service demand is time-and-place dependent because customers or their possessions must be present for delivery.

  - Customers have a difficult time evaluating the quality of a service before it is purchased and consumed.

  - Service quality is often inconsistent and very difficult to standardize across many customers.

  - The need for some services is not always apparent to customers. Consequently, service marketers often have trouble tying their offerings directly to customers' needs.

New product development

- Is a vital part of a firm's efforts to sustain growth and profits.

- Considers six strategic options related to the newness of products:

  - New-to-the-world products (discontinuous innovations)—which involve a pioneering effort by a firm that leads to the creation of an entirely new market

  - New product lines—which represent new offerings by the firm, but they become introduced into established markets

  - Product line extensions—which supplement an existing product line with new styles, models, features, or flavors

  - Improvements or revisions of existing products—which offer customers improved performance or greater perceived value

  - Repositioning—which involves targeting existing products at new markets or segments

  - Cost reductions—which involves modifying products to offer performance similar to competing products at a lower price

- Depends on the ability of the firm to create a differential advantage for the new product.

- Typically proceeds through five stages: idea generation, screening and evaluation, development, test marketing, and commercialization.

Branding strategy

- Involves selecting the right combination of name, symbol, term, and/or design that identifies a specific product.

- Has two parts: the brand name (words, letters, and numbers) and the brand mark (symbols, figures, or a design).

- Is not only critical to product identification; it is also the key factor used by marketers to differentiate a product from its competition.

- To be truly successful, should develop a brand that succinctly captures the product offering in a way that answers a question in the customer's mind.

- Involves the many different attributes that make up the way customers think about brands: people (employees and endorsers), places (country of origin and chan-nels), things (events, causes, and third-party endorsements), and other brands (alliances, branded ingredients, the company, and extensions).

- Has many advantages, including making it easier for customers to find and buy products.

- Involves having a solid understanding of four key issues:

    ○ Manufacturer versus private-label brands—private-label brands are more profitable than manufacturer brands for the retailers that carry them. How-ever, manufacturer brands have built-in demand, recognition, and product loyalty.

    ○ Brand loyalty—a positive attitude toward a brand that causes customers to have a consistent preference for that brand over all other competing brands in a product category. Three levels of loyalty include brand recognition, brand preference, and brand insistence.

    ○ Brand equity—the value of a brand or the marketing and financial value associated with a brand's position in the marketplace.

    ○ Brand alliances—branding strategies, such as co-branding or brand licensing, that involve developing close relationships with other firms.

- Also involves taking steps to protect brand names and brand marks from trade-mark infringement by other firms.

Packaging and labeling

- Are important considerations in branding strategy because packaging often goes hand in hand in developing a product, its benefits, its differentiation, and its image.

- Includes issues such as color, shape, size, and convenience of the package or the product's container.

- Are often used in product modifications or co-branding to reposition the product or give it new and improved features.

- Are vital in helping customers make proper product selections.

- Can have important environmental and legal consequences.

Differentiation and positioning

- Involve creating differences in the firm's product offering that set it apart from competing offerings (product differentiation), as well as the development and maintenance of a relative position for a product in the minds of the target market (product positioning).

- Can be monitored through the use of perceptual mapping—a visual, spatial display of customer perceptions on two or more key dimensions.

- Is fundamentally based on the brand, but is often based on product descriptors, customer support services, and image.

- Includes the positioning strategies of strengthen the current position, reposition, or reposition the competition.

Managing products and brands over time

- Can be addressed via the traditional product life cycle, which traces the evolution of a product's development and birth, growth and maturity, and decline and death over five stages:

  ○ Development—a time of no sales revenue, negative cash flow, and high risk

  ○ Introduction—a time of rising customer awareness, extensive marketing expenditures, and rapidly increasing sales revenue

  ○ Growth—a time of rapidly increasing sales revenue, rising profits, market expansion, and increasing numbers of competitors

  ○ Maturity—a time of sales and profit plateaus, a shift from customer acquisition to customer retention, and strategies aimed at holding or stealing market share

  ○ Decline—a time of persistent sales and profit decreases, attempts to postpone the decline, or strategies aimed at harvesting or divesting the product

- Can be influenced by shifts in the market, or by the actions of the firms within the industry as they constantly reinvent themselves.

Questions for Discussion

1. Consider the number of product choices available in the U.S. consumer market. In virtually every product category, consumers have many options to fulfill their needs. Are all of these options really necessary? Is having this many choices a good thing for consumers? Why or why not? Is it a good thing for marketers and retailers that have to support and carry all of these product choices? Why or why not?

2. Given the unique characteristics of services, what potential ethical issues could arise in service marketing and delivery? How can a service marketer prevent ethical challenges and convey a sense of trust to customers?

3. Consider the notion that a truly effective brand is one that succinctly captures the product offering in a way that answers a question in the customer's mind. Now, consider these brands (or choose your own): Coca-Cola, Disney, Marlboro, American Express, and Ford. What questions do these brands answer? Why are these effective brands?

Exercises

1. Look back at the list of the Top 25 Brands in Exhibit 7.6. What key attributes do these brands have in common? Which brands seem out of place on the list? Why? Which brands should be on this list but are missing? Why? How do you think this list will look in 5 to 10 years?

2. Do some background research in the following markets: wireless phone service, DVD players, and pizza. Which stage of the product life cycle is each of these markets in currently? What market characteristics lead you to feel this way? Is there evidence that any of these markets are on the verge of moving into the next stage of the life cycle? Explain.

3. Think about the last purchase you made in each of the following product categories. What were the features, advantages, and benefits of the specific product or brand that you selected? After completing the table, consider the positioning of the product or brand in the market. Does its positioning match your responses in the table? Explain.

	Features	Advantages	Benefits
Shoes Brand _____			
Sit-down Restaurant Name or Franchise_____			
Airline Brand _____			

Pricing Strategy

Introduction

There is no other component of the marketing program that firms become more infatuated with than pricing: "Is our price too high? Is that why our sales are not stronger?" Conversely, managers might ask, "Is our price too low? Our sales are up, but are we leaving money on the table?" These are common concerns that run through the minds of decision makers in all firms. There are at least four reasons for the attention given to pricing. First, the revenue equation is pretty simple: Revenue equals the price times quantity sold. There are only two ways for a firm to grow revenue: Increase prices or increase the volume of product sold. Rarely can a firm do both simultaneously. Although there are literally hundreds of ways to increase profit by controlling costs and operating expenses, the revenue side has only two variables—one being price and the other being heavily influenced by price.

A second reason that firms become enamored with pricing is that it is the easiest of all marketing variables to change. Although changing the product and its distribution or promotion can take months or even years, changes in pricing can be executed immediately in real time. Likewise, product, distribution, or promotion changes can also be quite expensive, especially if R&D or production must be rescheduled. Conversely, changing prices is a very low-cost option. For example, Walmart can decide that Green Giant whole kernel corn should be $1.29 per can rather than $1.42, and immediately enter this change into the store's point-of-sale system. Similar real-time price changes occur in many other industries, including air travel, hotels, and electronic commerce. As illustrated in *Beyond the Pages 8.1*, prices for the same product vary around the world to account for differences in currencies, taxes/tariffs, and consumer demand.

The third reason for the importance of pricing is that firms take considerable pains to discover and anticipate the pricing strategies and tactics of other firms. Salespeople learn to read a competitor's price sheet upside down at a buyer's desk. Retailers send "secret shoppers" into competitors' stores to learn what they charge for the same merchandise. In this age of e-commerce, tracking what competitors charge

Beyond the Pages 8.1

PRICING AROUND THE WORLD[1]

If you do much traveling around the world, you'll quickly learn that products are not priced the same in different countries. In fact, despite widespread American sentiment to the contrary, the prices we pay in the United States are among the lowest in the world. In the latest annual survey done by Mercer Consulting, New York—the most expensive U.S. city—ranked 8th on the list of the most expensive cities in the world. Other U.S. cities in the top 50 include Los Angeles (23rd), White Plains, NY (31st), San Francisco (34th), Honolulu (41st), Miami (45th), and Chicago (50th). The top 10 cities on the list, shown below, are dominated by Asian and European cities due to their strong currencies, high consumer confidence, and low interest rates. Cities at the bottom of the list are mostly from Latin America, the Middle East, and Africa. For example, Johannesburg, South Africa, is the least expensive city in the survey, with an index of 49.6.

Differences in pricing across national boundaries are also true with respect to typical purchases. In most cases, the products sold around the world under the same brand name are virtually identical. They are even sold using similar promotional campaigns to the same types of target markets who consume these products in roughly the same manner. Yet, the prices set in different markets can vary dramatically. Consider the examples in the table shown below.

In some cases, there are logical differences in pricing, such as higher costs of transportation or other extra costs associated with bringing a product to market. Other differences are associated with currency valuation. The U.S. dollar is relatively weak compared to other currencies, so it buys less in some cases. Other differences are based on the tax and tariff structures in each country. The United States and Britain, for example, impose very high taxes on tobacco sales. Firms have a great deal of latitude in setting prices and will often raise prices in some countries simply because consumers are willing to pay the cost to acquire a popular product with few substitutes.

Generally speaking, average prices will be lower in poorer countries than in developed countries. This is especially true in services, which are less expensive to deliver due to lower wage rates. The lower cost of labor in developing countries has spawned a groundswell of activity in outsourcing of services to other countries.

Rank	City	Index
1	Tokyo	143.7
2	Osaka	119.2
3	Moscow	115.4
4	Geneva	109.2
5	Hong Kong	108.7
6	Zurich	105.2
7	Copenhagen	105
8	New York	100
9	Beijing	99.6
10	Singapore	98

SOURCE: Index is based on New York at 100.

	Tokyo	Moscow	Geneva	Hong Kong	New York	Beijing
Movie Ticket	$19	$9	$14	$10	$12	$10
Lunch	$16	$18	$28	$15	$19	$18
Washing machine	$887	$630	$1,214	$701	$1,112	$920
Soft drink (can)	$1.75	$0.97	$1.02	$0.88	$1.49	$0.75

All prices shown in U.S. dollars.

for their goods and services has become so daunting that an entire price-tracking industry has emerged. For example, RivalWatch uses a proprietary software program to track the prices, assortment, and promotions of merchants, and then sells competitive intelligence reports to subscribing firms.[2]

Finally, pricing is given a great deal of attention because it is considered to be the only real means of differentiation in mature markets plagued by commoditization. When customers see all competing products as offering the same features and benefits, their buying decisions are primarily driven by price. This chapter addresses this and other key issues involved in developing pricing strategy. Having a solid understanding of these issues is important because far too many firms and their managers use a seat-of-the-pants approach to pricing by guessing the best price for their goods and services. Guessing is never a good strategy in marketing; it can be downright deadly when it comes to setting prices.

The Role of Pricing in Marketing Strategy

The fact that prices are easy to change should not be taken to mean that most firms do a good job of setting prices. Many manufacturers, wholesalers, and retailers readily admit that they spend more time worrying about price than they do actually managing pricing strategy. In this section, the role of pricing in marketing strategy will be discussed. First, we look at both the seller's and the buyer's perspectives on pricing. Pricing is often a major source of confrontation between sellers and buyers. Sellers obviously want to sell a product for as much as possible, whereas buyers would love to get the products they want for free. Somewhere between these two extremes, sellers and buyers must find a way to meet. We will also look at the relationship between pricing and revenue, which is an important consideration in pricing strategy.

The Seller's Perspective on Pricing

By their nature, sellers have a tendency to inflate prices because they want to receive as much as possible in an exchange with a buyer. Consider the housing market. Homeowners who list their houses for sale have typically invested a great deal of time, energy, and memories into their homes. So, when they decide to sell, their initial feelings of their home's worth are exaggerated. Because of this emotional attachment, a homeowner may think his or her house is worth $250,000. However, the home is only worth that amount if a buyer can be found who will pay that much for the house. If a buyer cannot be found, then the homeowner is guilty of letting sentiment cloud his or her perception of market reality.

This example illustrates that for homeowners or any other seller, price is often more about what the seller will accept in exchange for a product, rather than market reality. Sound pricing strategy should ignore sentimental feelings of worth and instead focus on the market factors that affect the exchange process. From the seller's perspective, four key issues become important in pricing strategy: (1) cost, (2) demand, (3) customer value, and (4) competitors' prices.

Cost is an important consideration in any pricing strategy. A firm that fails to cover both its direct costs (e.g., finished goods/components, materials, supplies, sales commission, transportation) and its indirect costs (e.g., administrative expenses, utilities, rent) will not make a profit. Firms make money either through profit margin, high sales volume, or both. Still, some measure of profit margin, even if rather small, is vital to the viability of the firm. Most smart pricing strategies build in a target profit margin as if it were a cost. Firms that use this approach recognize that a dollar reduction in price is a dollar off the bottom line, whether it comes from a high- or low-margin product.

When the availability of a product is limited, firms must also consider opportunity costs in their pricing strategy. This is particularly appropriate for service firms. For example, if an airline sells a seat from Atlanta to Chicago for $250, then that seat disappears from the inventory. If a different customer would be willing to pay $300 for the same seat and would not want to travel at a different time, then the airline lost $50 in revenue. Manufacturers of tangible goods who do not sell a product today can sell that same product tomorrow. This is not true for service firms, which is why airlines use complex pricing systems in an attempt to squeeze every dollar out of every seat on every plane. U.S. Airways, for example, offers deep discounts on remaining seats for flights departing on Saturday and returning on Tuesday. U.S. Airways offers these "e-Savers" to customers because they realize that an empty seat generates no revenue and that the incremental cost of adding these passengers is negligible.[3]

Market demand is also a key issue in a seller's pricing strategy. The fact that a firm covers its costs does not mean that customers will pay their prices. In this vein, more efficient firms—like low-cost airlines or discount retailers—are able to cover their costs while simultaneously offering lower prices to customers. Customer expectations also play a role in market demand. For example, business travelers who will be reimbursed by their firm will pay more for an airline seat or a hotel room than pleasure travelers. Similarly, moviegoers will pay high prices for popcorn and soft drinks because they are a captive audience with few choices. To fully understand the relationship between price and demand, firms must have a good knowledge of the price elasticity associated with their product offering. We will address this topic in greater depth later in the chapter.

In certain cases, pricing strategy should encompass more than the product and its price. The bottom-line impact or value delivered to the customer is often an issue in setting viable prices. This is particularly true in business markets. For example, if an insurance broker can offer a solution that reduces a client's risk costs by $10 million, what is the solution worth to the client? The same question can be asked about a new piece of production machinery that can increase capacity by 25 percent while utilizing 50 percent less labor. Setting a price for this product may have little to do with costs, but instead focuses on the value associated with the innovation and intellectual capital of the selling firm. Firms in sectors such as marketing research, consulting, information technology, and other professional services increasingly chart the bottom-line impact or value that their services provide to clients.

Finally, a selling organization should be very much aware of what its competitors charge for the same or comparable products. All firms, however, should resist the temptation to blindly meet or beat competitors. Unless the company promotes itself as always having the lowest price, it should think in terms of pricing within an acceptable range of its competitors. Mercedes, for example, does not have to match BMW's pricing. In the case of highly commoditized markets, pricing lower than competitors can be the only viable means of differentiation. Still, rather than beating competitors' prices, a better strategy may be to create real or perceived differentiation for the product offering. This would allow the firm to charge different prices for the same or comparable products.

The Buyer's Perspective on Pricing

In many ways, the buyer's perspective on pricing is the opposite of the seller's perspective. Where sellers tend to bid prices up, buyers often see prices as being lower than market reality dictates. In our housing market example, the buyer does not hold an appreciation for the time, energy, and emotion invested into the home by the homeowner. The buyer only sees a house and whether its features will fulfill his or her needs and preferences. Despite the seller's $250,000 asking price, a prospective buyer may think the house is worth only $200,000, given its features, condition, and the prices of other homes in the area.

For buyers, price is about what the buyer will give up in exchange for a product. The key for the selling firm, and for the development of pricing strategy, is to determine just how much the buyer will give up. Firms must also recognize that buyers give up much more than their money when they buy goods and services. From the buyer's perspective, two key issues determine pricing strategy for most firms: (1) perceived value and (2) price sensitivity.

What buyers will give up in exchange for a product depends to a great extent on their perceived value of the product. Value is a difficult term to define because it means different things to different people.[4] Some customers equate good value with high product quality, whereas others see value as nothing more than a low price. The most common definition of value relates customer benefits to costs; or to use a more colloquial expression, good value gives "more bang for the buck." For our purposes, we define *value* as a customer's subjective evaluation of benefits relative to costs to determine the worth of a firm's product offering relative to other product offerings. A simple formula for value might look like this:

$$\text{Perceived Value} = \frac{\text{Customer Benefits}}{\text{Customer Costs}}$$

Customer benefits include everything the customer obtains from the product offering such as quality, satisfaction, prestige/image, and the solution to a problem. Customer costs include everything the customer must give up such as money, time, effort, and all nonselected alternatives (opportunity costs). Although value is a key component in setting a viable pricing strategy, good value depends on much more than pricing. In fact, value is intricately tied to every element in the marketing program. We will discuss the strategic implications of value more fully in Chapter 12.

Good pricing strategy is also based on a thorough understanding of the price elasticity associated with a firm's goods and services. On the buyer's side, price elasticity translates into the unique and varying buying situations that cause buyers to be more or less sensitive to price changes. Not only must firms know what customers will pay for a product, they must understand their buying behavior in specific situations that lead to price sensitivity. We will discuss these buying situations in greater depth later in the chapter.

A Shift in the Balance of Power

Phrases such as "It's a buyer's market" and "It's a seller's market" refer to who holds the power in the exchange relationship. Buyers have increased power over sellers when there is a large number of sellers in the market or when there are many substitutes for the product. Buyers also have power when the economy is weak and fewer customers will part with their money. During a seller's market, prices go up, and terms and services become less favorable. Sellers have increased power over buyers when certain products are in short supply or in high demand. Sellers also have increased power during good economic times when customers will spend more money.

A seller's market exists when products are wildly popular or in short supply. Antiques are a good example.

For most products and markets, a buyer's market prevails. Of course, there are exceptions, such as new automotive designs (such as the 2010 Chevy Camaro) and virtually all of Apple's products. A buyer's market exists in most markets due to the large number of product choices that are available, increased commoditization among competing products and brands, and a general decline in brand loyalty among customers. This state of affairs is tempered somewhat by sluggish consumer spending and guarded consumer confidence. However, both business and consumer markets have become much more savvy and sophisticated in their buying behavior.

For these reasons, firms must carefully manage price in relation to the entire marketing program. Firms that get greedy in their pricing strategy may find no one standing in line to buy their products.

The Relationship Between Price and Revenue

All marketers understand the relationship between price and revenue. However, firms cannot charge high prices without good reason. In fact, virtually all firms face intense price competition from their rivals, which tends to hold prices down. In the face of this competition, it is natural for firms to see price cutting as a viable means of increasing sales. Price cutting can also move excess inventory and generate short-term cash flow. However, all price cuts affect the firm's bottom line. When setting prices, many firms hold fast to these two general pricing myths:[5]

Myth No. 1: When business is good, a price cut will capture greater market share.
Myth No. 2: When business is bad, a price cut will stimulate sales.

Unfortunately, the relationship between price and revenue challenges these assumptions and makes them a risky proposition for most firms. The reality is that any price cut must be offset by an increase in sales volume just to maintain the same level of revenue. Let's look at an example. Assume that a consumer electronics manufacturer sells 1,000 high-end stereo receivers per month at $1,000 per system. The firm's total cost is $500 per system, which leaves a gross margin of $500. When the sales of this high-end system decline, the firm decides to cut the price to increase sales. The firm's strategy is to offer a $100 rebate to anyone who buys a system over the next three months. The rebate is consistent with a 10 percent price cut, but it is in reality a 20 percent reduction in gross margin (from $500 to $400). To compensate for the loss in gross margin, the firm must increase the volume of receivers sold. The question is by how much. We can find the answer using this formula:

$$\text{Percent Change in Unit Volume} = \frac{\text{Gross Margin \%}}{\text{Gross Margin \%} \pm \text{Price Change \%}} - 1$$

$$0.25 = \frac{0.50}{0.50 - 0.10} - 1$$

As the calculation indicates, the firm would have to increase sales volume by 25 percent to 1,250 units sold in order to maintain the same level of total gross margin. How likely is it that a $100 rebate will increase sales volume by 25 percent? This question is critical to the success of the firm's rebate strategy. In many instances, the needed increase in sales volume is too high. Consequently, the firm's gross margin may actually be lower after the price cut.

Rather than blindly use price cutting to stimulate sales and revenue, it is often better for a firm to find ways to build value into the product and justify the current price, or even a higher price, rather than cutting the product's price in search of higher sales volume. In the case of the stereo manufacturer, giving customers $100 worth of CDs or DVDs for each purchase is a much better option than a $100 rebate. Video game manufacturers, such as Microsoft (Xbox) and Sony (PlayStation 3), often bundle games and accessories with their system consoles to increase value. The cost of giving customers these free add-ons is low because the marketer buys them in bulk quantities. This added expense is almost always less costly than a price cut. And the increase in value may allow the marketer to charge higher prices for the product bundle.

Key Issues in Pricing Strategy

Given the importance of pricing in marketing strategy, pricing decisions are among the most complex decisions to be made in developing a marketing plan. Decisions regarding price require a tightly integrated balance among a number of important issues. Many of these issues possess some degree of uncertainty regarding the reactions to pricing among customers, competitors, and supply chain partners. Some issues like the firm's pricing objectives, supply and demand, and the firm's cost structure, are critically important in establishing initial prices. Other issues become important after the initial price has been set, especially with respect to modifying the pricing strategy over time.

As we review these issues, keep in mind that they are interrelated and must be considered in the context of the firm's entire marketing program. For example, increases in product quality or the addition of new product features often come with an increase in price. This is especially true when the product contains the latest technology, such as video recording and messaging on wireless telephones. Pricing is also influenced by distribution, especially the image and reputation of the outlets where the good or service is sold. Finally, companies often use price as a tool of promotion. Coupons, for example, represent a combination of price and promotion that can stimulate increased sales in many different product categories. In services, price changes are often used to fill unused capacity (e.g., empty airline or theater seats) during nonpeak demand.

Pricing Objectives

Setting specific pricing objectives that are realistic, measurable, and attainable is an important part of pricing strategy. As shown in Exhibit 8.1, there are a number of pricing objectives that firms may pursue. Remember that firms make money on profit margin, volume, or some combination of the two. A firm's pricing objectives will always reflect this market reality.

Pricing objectives are not always about tweaking price to increase profit or volume. Sometimes, firms simply want to maintain their prices in an effort to retain their position relative to the competition. This pricing objective is called status quo pricing. Although status quo pricing sounds like it involves little or no planning, the decision to maintain prices must be done after a careful analysis of all factors that affect pricing strategy.

Supply and Demand

The basic laws of supply and demand have an obvious influence on pricing strategy. Although the inverse relationship between price and demand is well-known and

EXHIBIT 8.1	DESCRIPTION OF COMMON PRICING OBJECTIVES	
Pricing Objectives	**Description**	
Profit-Oriented	Designed to maximize price relative to competitors' prices, the product's perceived value, the firm's cost structure, and production efficiency. Profit objectives are typically based on a target return, rather than simple profit maximization.	
Volume-Oriented	Sets prices in order to maximize dollar or unit sales volume. This objective sacrifices profit margin in favor of high product turnover.	
Market Demand	Sets prices in accordance with customer expectations and specific buying situations. This objective is often known as "charging what the market will bear."	
Market Share	Designed to increase or maintain market share regardless of fluctuations in industry sales. Market share objectives are often used in the maturity stage of the product life cycle.	
Cash Flow	Designed to maximize the recovery of cash as quickly as possible. This objective is useful when a firm has a cash emergency or when the product life cycle is expected to be quite short.	
Competitive Matching	Designed to match or beat competitors' prices. The goal is to maintain the perception of good value relative to the competition.	
Prestige	Sets high prices that are consistent with a prestige or high status product. Prices are set with little regard for the firm's cost structure or the competition.	
Status Quo	Maintains current prices in an effort to sustain a position relative to the competition.	

understood (as price goes up, demand goes down), it is essentially a supply-side perspective. That is, the relationship between price and demand is most often seen from the marketer's point of view. However, the demand-side perspective is often quite different. Consider what happens when customer demand increases for a particular product. Does the inverse relationship hold? Do prices fall? Hardly. In fact, during periods of heavy customer demand, prices tend to stay the same or even increase. Gasoline prices over the summer are a good example, as is a new high-tech product in high demand.

Another important supply-and-demand issue is customer expectations regarding pricing. Customers always hold expectations about price when they purchase products. However, in some situations, customer expectations about price can be the driving force in pricing strategy. For example, moviegoers expect to pay $3 to $4 for a small soft drink or popcorn. Summer vacationers expect to pay more for gasoline. And college students expect to get roughly half price when they resell their textbooks. Situations such as these allow marketers to set prices in accordance with what the market will pay with little or no regard for their costs, the competition, or other factors that typically affect pricing strategy. However, the flip side is also true. If customers expect to pay five cents or less for one minute of long distance telephone service, then that is all the firm can charge for the product.

The Firm's Cost Structure

The firm's costs in producing and marketing a product are an important factor in setting prices. After all, costs must be factored out of the revenue equation in order to determine profits, and ultimately the survival of the firm. Perhaps the most popular way to associate costs and prices is through breakeven pricing, where the firm's fixed and variable costs are considered:

$$\text{Breakeven in Units} = \frac{\text{Total Fixed Costs}}{\text{Unit Price} - \text{Unit Variable Costs}}$$

To use breakeven analysis in setting prices, the firm must look at the feasibility of selling more than the breakeven level in order to make a profit. The breakeven number is only a point of reference in setting prices, as market conditions and customer demand must also be considered.

Another way to use the firm's cost structure in setting prices is to use cost-plus pricing—a strategy that is quite common in retailing. Here, the firm sets prices based on average unit costs and its planned markup percentage:

$$\text{Selling Price} = \frac{\text{Average Unit Cost}}{1 - \text{Markup Percent (decimal)}}$$

Cost-plus pricing is not only intuitive; it is also very easy to use. Its weakness, however, lies in determining the correct markup percentage. Industry norms often come into play at this point. For example, average markups in grocery retailing are typically in the 20 percent range, whereas markups can be several hundred percent or more in furniture or jewelry stores. Customer expectations are also an important consideration in determining the correct markup percentage.

Although breakeven analysis and cost-plus pricing are important tools, they should not be the driving force behind pricing strategy. The reason is often ignored: Different firms have different cost structures. By setting prices solely on the basis of costs, firms run a major risk in setting their prices too high or too low. If one firm's costs are relatively higher than other firms, it will have to accept lower margins in order to compete effectively. Conversely, just because a product costs very little to produce and market does not mean that the firm should sell it at a low price (remember the movie theater popcorn example). Cost is best understood as an absolute floor below which prices cannot be set for an extended period of time.

Competition and Industry Structure

Firms that use competitive matching pricing objectives face a constant struggle to monitor and respond to competitors' price changes. This struggle is a way of life in the travel and tourism industry. However, a firm does not always have to match competitors' prices to compete effectively. The competitive market structure of the industry in which a firm operates affects its flexibility in raising or lowering prices. Industry structure also affects how competitors will respond to changes in price. There are four basic competitive market structures:

- **Perfect Competition**   A market containing an unlimited number of sellers and buyers who exchange for homogeneous products. Market entry is easy and no single participant can influence price or supply significantly. For the most part, perfect competition does not exist, although some agricultural and commodity markets come reasonably close.

- **Monopolistic Competition**   A market containing many sellers and buyers who exchange for relatively heterogeneous products. Marketing strategy involves product differentiation and/or niche marketing to overcome the threats imposed by the wide availability of substitute products. The heterogeneous nature of the products gives firms some control over prices. Most markets fall into this category.

- **Oligopoly**   A market containing relatively few sellers who control the supply of a dominant portion of the industry's product. However, no one seller controls the market. One firm's prices affect the sales of competing firms, and all firms typically match the price changes of competitors. These firms often turn to nonprice strategies to differentiate their product offerings. Examples of U.S. oligopolies include the automobile, tobacco, oil, steel, aerospace, and music recording industries.

- **Monopoly**   A market dominated by a single seller who sells a product with no close substitutes. The single seller is the sole source of supply. Essentially, the only monopolies operating in the United States today are regulated utilities.

Monopolies obviously have the most pricing flexibility, unless regulated by federal, state, or local governments. Firms operating in oligopolies gain little advantage in pricing due to quick reaction by competitors. The heavy discounting in the automobile industry over the past several years is a good example. Firms facing monopolistic competition must be able to create real or perceived differentiation in order to justify higher prices relative to competitors. Firms also face significant pricing challenges when their industry shifts to a different structure. In the telecommunications industry, for example, decreased regulation and increased merger activity has shifted the industry away from monopolistic competition to an oligopolistic structure.

Stage of the Product Life Cycle

As we noted in Chapter 7, marketing strategy shifts as a product moves through the stages of its life cycle. Pricing changes, like changes in the other elements of the marketing program, occur as demand, competition, customer expectations, and the product itself change over time. Exhibit 8.2 illustrates how pricing changes might occur over the product life cycle.

Pricing strategy in the introduction stage is critical because it sets the standard for pricing changes over time. As price changes over the life cycle, the initial price set during a product's introduction determines whether the firm will make a profit or lose money as time goes on. By the time a product enters the maturity stage, competitive dynamics have established an acceptable and expected range of prices that firms must fall within to remain competitive. As a result, firms must look inward to find ways to cut costs and maintain profits later in the life cycle. Also, very few firms enjoy the luxury of raising prices during the decline stage. Vintage items like antique cars, vinyl records, and collectables are among the few to command higher prices at the end of their life cycles.

Pricing Service Products

When it comes to buying services, customers have a difficult time determining quality prior to purchase. Consequently, service pricing is critical because it may be the only quality cue that is available in advance of the purchase experience. If the service provider sets prices too low, customers will have inaccurate perceptions and

EXHIBIT 8.2	PRICING STRATEGY OVER THE PRODUCT LIFE CYCLE
Introduction	The price sensitivity of the market determines the initial pricing strategy. When the market is relatively insensitive to price, prices are set high to recoup investment and generate high profits to fuel growth (a price skimming strategy). If the market is sensitive to price, prices are set at, or lower than, the competition to gain a foothold in the market (a price penetration strategy).
Growth	A gradual lowering of prices occurs due to increasing competition and growing economies of scale that reduce production and marketing costs. The product also begins to appeal to a broader base of customers, many of whom are quite price sensitive.
Maturity	Prices continue to decrease as competition intensifies and ineffective firms are eliminated from the market. Most firms focus heavily on cost savings; economies of scale; or synergies in production, promotion, and distribution to maintain profit margins. Specific pricing tactics encourage brand switching in an attempt to steal business away from the competition.
Decline	Prices continue to fall until only one or a few firms remain. At that point, prices begin to stabilize or even increase somewhat as firms squeeze the last bit of profit from a product. Some products can experience sharp increases in price if their popularity and unique appeal remain high.

expectations about quality. If prices are too high, customers may not give the firm a chance. In general, services pricing becomes more important—and more difficult—when

- Service quality is hard to detect prior to purchase.
- The costs associated with providing the service are difficult to determine.
- Customers are unfamiliar with the service process.
- Brand names are not well established.
- Customers can perform the service themselves.
- The service has poorly defined units of consumption.
- Advertising within a service category is limited.
- The total price of the service experience is difficult to state beforehand.

Most services suffer from the challenges associated with determining costs because intangible expenses such as labor, insurance, and overhead must be taken into account. Poorly defined units of consumption characterize some services. For example, what is the unit of measure for hairstyling services? Is it time, hair length, type of style, or gender of the customer? Many female customers complain that they have to pay more for a cut and style than men, even when a man's hair is longer. When the firm offers services that customers can do for themselves—such as lawn maintenance, oil changes, or house painting—it must be especially mindful of setting the correct price. In these instances, the firm is competing with the customer's evaluation of his or her time and ability, in addition to other competing service providers.

Setting prices for professional services (lawyers, accountants, consultants, doctors, and mechanics) is especially difficult as they suffer from a number of the conditions in the list above. Customers often balk at the high prices of these service providers because they have a limited ability to evaluate the quality or total cost until the service process has been completed. The heterogeneous nature of these services limits standardization; therefore, customer knowledge about pricing is limited. Heterogeneity also limits price comparison among competing providers. The key for these firms is to be up-front about the expected quality and costs of the service. This is often done through the use of binding estimates and contractual guarantees of quality.

Due to the limited capacity associated with most services, service pricing is also a key issue with respect to balancing supply and demand during peak and off-peak demand times. In these situations, many service firms use yield management systems to balance pricing and revenue considerations with their need to fill unfilled capacity. Exhibit 8.3 depicts an example of yield management for a hotel.

Yield management allows the service firm to simultaneously control capacity and demand in order to maximize revenue and capacity utilization.[6] This is accomplished in two ways. First, the service firm controls capacity by limiting the available capacity at certain price points. In the hotel example in Exhibit 8.3, limited rooms are available to different market segments at different times of the year. In the off-season, many

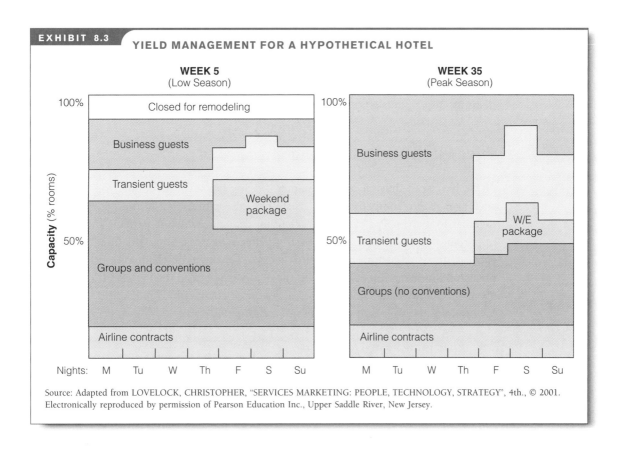

EXHIBIT 8.3 — YIELD MANAGEMENT FOR A HYPOTHETICAL HOTEL

Source: Adapted from LOVELOCK, CHRISTOPHER, "SERVICES MARKETING: PEOPLE, TECHNOLOGY, STRATEGY", 4th., © 2001. Electronically reproduced by permission of Pearson Education Inc., Upper Saddle River, New Jersey.

hotels schedule routine maintenance and remodeling, and reduce rates for conventions in order to fill unused capacity. Airlines do this by selling a limited number of seats at discount prices three or more weeks prior to a flight's departure. Southwest Airlines, for example, sells limited seats in three categories: Wanna Get Away (the lowest priced seats), Anytime, and Business Select (the highest priced seats).[7]

Second, the service firm controls demand through price changes over time and by overbooking capacity. These activities ensure that service demand will be consistent and that any unused capacity will be minimized. These practices are common in services characterized by high fixed costs and low variable costs, such as airlines, hotels, rental cars, cruises, transportation firms, and hospitals. Because variable costs in these services are quite low, the profit for these firms directly relates to sales and capacity utilization. Consequently, these firms will sell some capacity at reduced prices in order to maximize utilization.

Yield management systems are also useful in their ability to segment markets based on price elasticity. That is, yield management allows a firm to offer the same basic service to different market segments at different price points. Customers who are very price sensitive with respect to travel services—vacation travelers and families with children—can get a good deal on a hotel if they book it early. Conversely, consultants are less price sensitive because their clients reimburse them for expenses. Likewise, business travelers book flights on the spur of the moment, so they are more forgiving of the higher prices just prior to departure. Other firms can reach different market segments with attractive off-peak pricing. Many customers take advantage of the lower prices at theme parks and beach resorts by traveling during the off-season. Similar situations occur in lower-priced movie matinees and lower prices for lunch items at most restaurants.

Price Elasticity of Demand

As we have seen thus far in this chapter, pricing has intricate connections to issues such as demand, competition, and customer expectations. All of these issues come together in the concept of price elasticity of demand, which is perhaps the most important overall consideration in setting effective prices. Simply defined, *price elasticity* refers to customers' responsiveness or sensitivity to changes in price. A more precise definition defines elasticity as the relative impact on the demand for a product, given specific increases or decreases in the price charged for that product. The following formula is used to calculate price elasticity:

$$\text{Price Elasticity of Demand} = \frac{\text{Percentage Change in Quantity Demanded}}{\text{Percentage Change in Price}}$$

For products where this calculation produces a number less than 1, the product has *inelastic* demand. In this case, an increase or decrease in price does not significantly affect the quantity demanded. When the calculation produces a number greater than 1, the product has *elastic* demand. Here, the quantity demanded is sensitive to price fluctuations, so a change in price will produce a change in demand and total revenue. If the calculation produces a number that equals 1 or is very close to 1, the product has *unitary* demand. In this situation, the changes in price and demand offset, so total revenue remains the same. Exhibit 8.4 displays a graphical illustration of price elasticity.

Firms cannot base prices solely on price elasticity calculations because they will rarely know the elasticity for any product with great precision over time. Further, price elasticity is not uniform over time and place because demand is not uniform over time and place. As a result, the same product can have different elasticities in different times, places, and situations. Because the actual price elasticity calculation is difficult to pinpoint precisely, firms often consider price elasticity in regard to differing customer behavior patterns or purchase situations. Understanding when, where, and how customers are more or less sensitive to price is crucial in setting fair and profitable prices. In the sections that follow, we examine many of these behavior patterns and purchase situations that can affect customers' sensitivity to pricing and price changes.

Situations That Increase Price Sensitivity

Generally speaking, customers become much more sensitive to price when they have many different choices or options for fulfilling their needs and wants. Price elasticity is higher (more elastic) in the following situations:

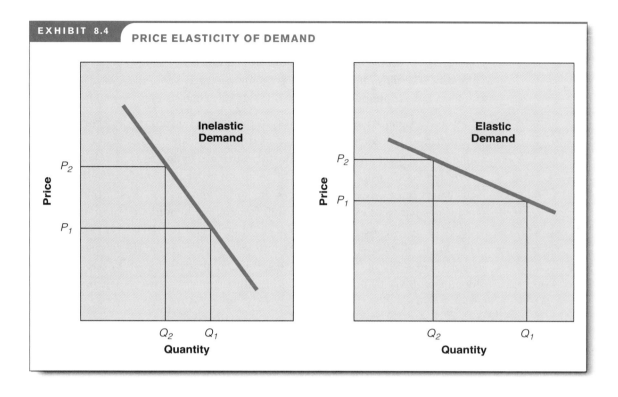

EXHIBIT 8.4   **PRICE ELASTICITY OF DEMAND**

- **Availability of Product Substitutes**   When customers can choose among a number of different product substitutes, they will be much more sensitive to price differences. This situation occurs very frequently among name-brand products and in markets where product offerings have become commoditized. For example, when AirTran began flying out of Atlanta in the 1990s, travelers saw the carrier as an acceptable alternative to Delta and other existing carriers. As a result, the fare for a flight between Atlanta and other destinations suddenly became more elastic. If Delta had not matched AirTran's lower fare on these routes, their planes would have had more empty seats.

- **Higher Total Expenditure**   As a general rule, the higher the total expense, the more elastic the demand for that product will be. This effect is actually easier to see if we look at a low-priced product. A 20 percent increase in the price of Q-Tips, for example, would not have a large impact on demand. If the price of a 100-count box increased from $1.00 to $1.20, most customers would not notice the change. However, if the price of a $20,000 car increases by 20 percent, then the impact is a much more noticeable $4,000. At that rate of change, some customers will look for a different car or pull out of buying all together.

- **Noticeable Differences**   Products having heavily promoted prices tend to experience more elastic demand. Gasoline is a classic example. An increase of three cents per gallon is only 45 cents more on a 15-gallon fill-up. However, many customers will drive several miles out of their way to find a lower price (often spending more in gas consumption than they save). Noticeable price differences sometimes occur at specific pricing thresholds. Using the gasoline example, many customers will not notice price increases until gas reaches $3.00 per gallon. At this price, these customers suddenly move from an inelastic mindset to an elastic mindset. The move from $2.80 to $2.90 may not have an impact on these customers, but the jump from $2.90 to $3.00 totally changes their mental framework.

- **Easy Price Comparisons**   Regardless of the product or product category, customers will become more price sensitive if they can easily compare prices among competing products. In industries such as retailing, supermarkets, travel, toys, and books, price has become a dominant purchase consideration because customers can easily compare prices. It should come as no surprise that these industries have also experienced a shift from offline to online sales. Consider how easy it is to compare prices for air travel, hotels, and rental cars on Expedia or Travelocity. Likewise, at Fetchbook.info, customers can find the lowest prices on books across 145 different bookstores. Price comparison has also become a dominant driver behind the success of online retailers such as Amazon.

Situations That Decrease Price Sensitivity

In general, customers become much less sensitive to price when they have few choices or options for fulfilling their needs and wants. Price elasticity is lower (more inelastic) in these situations:

- **Lack of Substitutes**   When customers have few choices in terms of product substitutes, they will be much less sensitive to price. This situation is common in some categories, including baking/cooking ingredients, add-on or replacement parts, one-of-a-kind antiques, collectables or memorabilia, unique sporting events, and specialized vacation destinations. The more unique or specialized the product, the more customers will pay for it. For example, Super Bowl tickets often sell for thousands of dollars, just for one ticket in a bad location. Recently, a wealthy collector paid $11.5 million for a painting of a swordsman by Picasso.[8] The lack of substitutes also makes customers less sensitive to the time and effort required to obtain products. For example, avid antique collectors often devote every free moment to traveling in search of hidden treasures.

- **Real or Perceived Necessities**   Many products, such as food, water, medical care, cigarettes, and prescription drugs, have extremely inelastic demand because customers have real or perceived needs for them. If the price of food doubles overnight, we might make some adjustments, but we would still have to eat. Some product categories are price inelastic because customers perceive those products as true necessities. It matters little whether a customer truly has a need for a specific product. If that customer perceives the product as a necessity, then that customer becomes much less sensitive to price increases for that product.

- **Complementary Products**   Complementary products have an effect on the price sensitivity of related products. If the price of one product falls, customers will become less sensitive to the price of complementary products. For example, when the price of a cruise goes down, the price of shore excursions becomes more inelastic. With more travelers on board, and each having more money to spend, excursion operators realize that travelers are less sensitive to the prices they charge. The same is true for strawberries and shortcake, computers and software, or any other set of complementary goods or services.

- **Perceived Product Benefits**   For some customers, certain products are just worth the price. For these purchases, the phrase "expensive but worth it" comes to mind. All of us have certain products that we indulge in from time to time, such as fine wines, gourmet chocolates, imported coffee, or trips to a day spa. Because these products do not comprise the bulk of our purchasing activities, customers rarely notice, or simply ignore, price increases. Other customers, however, base their entire purchasing patterns on buying the best products in all categories. From Rolex watches to Monte Blanc pens, many customers see high-quality and high-priced products as just being worth it. Customers who embrace this purchasing mentality do not concern themselves with the price of a product or any price increase.

- **Situational Influences**   The circumstances surrounding a purchase situation can vastly alter the elasticity of demand for a product. Many of these situational influences occur because time pressures or purchase risk increase to the point that an immediate purchase must be made or the availability of product substitutes falls dramatically. For example, there is a dramatic difference between leisurely shopping for a new set of tires and finding yourself stranded on the highway with a blown tire. The same inelastic demand situation occurs in other emergency situations, such as when you need a plumber in the middle of the night or on the weekend. Other common situational influences revolve around purchase risk, typically the social risk involved in making a bad decision. In a general sense, customers tend to be much less price sensitive when they purchase items for others or for gift giving.

- **Product Differentiation**   The inherent goal of differentiation is to make the demand curve for a product more inelastic. Differentiation reduces the number of perceived substitutes for a product. For example, Coke's differentiation strategy has worked so well that Coke drinkers will buy the soft drink at $2.49 or $3.49 per six-pack. Product differentiation does not have to be based on real differences in order to make customers less price sensitive. Many times the differences are perceptual. Blindfolded, a person may not know the difference between Coke and Pepsi, but consumers do not buy or consume soft drinks blindfolded. The look of the can, the advertising, and prior experiences all come together to differentiate the product.

In a strategic sense, product differentiation is the best way to ensure that customers are not sensitive to price changes. The ultimate goal of this effort is to differentiate the product so well that customers perceive that no competing product can take its place. When this happens, customers will become brand loyal and the demand for the product will become very inelastic. Nike, for example, commands extreme brand loyalty because the firm has successfully differentiated its products through technological innovation, effective advertising, and the ubiquitous swoosh. Likewise, Intel has done a great job using real and perceived differentiation to become the dominant supplier of processor chips in the computer industry. Customers who demand a computer with "Intel inside" do not know the technological differences between a Core 2, Xeon, or Centrino processor; or competing processors such as AMD's Phenom, Athlon, and Sempron. These customers want an Intel chip because they trust it to be fast, reliable, and compatible with other products.

Pricing Strategies

Although prices for individual products are made on a case-by-case basis, most firms have developed a general and consistent approach—or general pricing strategy—to be used in establishing prices. The relationship between price and other elements of the marketing program dictates that pricing decisions cannot be made in isolation. In fact, price changes may result in minor modifications to the product, distribution, or promotion strategies. As we have discussed, it is not so much the actual price being charged that influences buying decisions as the way that members of the target market perceive the price. This reality reminds us that many of the strategic issues involved in pricing have close ties with customer psychology and information processing: What customers think about prices is what those prices are to them.

Base Pricing Strategies

A firm's base pricing strategy establishes the initial price and sets the range of possible price movements throughout the product's life cycle. The initial price is critical, not only for initial success, but also for maintaining the potential for profit over the long term. There are several different approaches to base pricing, including market introduction pricing, prestige pricing, value-based pricing (EDLP), competitive matching, and nonprice strategies. We have briefly touched on some of these strategies in earlier portions of the chapter. Let's look more closely at these approaches.

Market Introduction Pricing   Firms often use different pricing strategies when their products are first launched into the market. The two most common introduction approaches are called price skimming and penetration pricing. The idea behind *price skimming* is to intentionally set a high price relative to the competition, thereby skimming the profits off the top of the market. Price skimming is designed to recover the high R&D and marketing expenses associated with developing a new product. It may also be used to initially segment the market based on price, or to control the initial demand for the product. Virtually all new high-tech products, new computer technology, and new prescription drugs use a price-skimming approach.

    For price skimming to work, the product must be perceived as having unique advantages over competing products. When the high price brings unique or new benefits, customers do not mind paying for the product. For example, the $80 per month price for Pfizer's cholesterol-lowering drug Lipitor is worth it to patients who suffer from high cholesterol. The high prices associated with prescription medications like Lipitor are designed to recoup the expenses associated with developing and marketing new drugs. However, in the case of pharmaceuticals, price skimming only works as long as the drug is protected by patent. In Pfizer's case, the patent on Lipitor expires in 2011. However, the patent on Merck's Zocor, a major competitor, expired in 2006, opening the way for generic pricing. Despite its patent protection, Lipitor sales have declined as managed care companies have forced patients to switch to lower-priced Zocor clones. Eventually, the price support for Lipitor will collapse once its patent expires and generic competition enters the market.[9]

The goal of *penetration pricing* is to maximize sales, gain widespread market acceptance, and capture a large market share quickly by setting a relatively low initial price. This approach works best when customers are price sensitive for the product or product category; when research and development and marketing expenses are relatively low; or when new competitors will quickly enter the market. Because of its flexibility, penetration pricing can be used to launch a new product or to introduce new product lines to an established product portfolio. For example, when Palm introduced its Pre smartphone, it did so exclusively through Sprint at a penetration price of $199 after rebate. This relatively low price not only encouraged customers to switch to the Pre, it also established a presence in the market in a strong number two position behind Apple's iPhone. Unfortunately for Palm, Apple countered the move by dropping the price on its 8GB iPhone 3G to $99 without the hassle of a rebate.[10]

The benefits of penetration pricing—rapid market acceptance and maximum sales—also have the benefit of discouraging competition from entering the market. This is a powerful advantage that makes a penetration approach quite appealing. However, the strategy is not for all firms. To use penetration pricing successfully, the firm must have a cost structure and scale economies that can withstand narrow profit margins. As illustrated in *Beyond the Pages 8.2,* some firms adopt a penetration pricing strategy by selling their products at a loss, hoping to make up the lost revenue via the sale of accessories, add-ons, or subscription services. Although price penetration does not necessarily mean low profit per unit sold, it does require a higher volume of sales to achieve the same total profit that would be achieved using a price-skimming approach. For these reasons, price penetration occurs primarily in situations where the firm has a reasonable expectation of achieving the necessary sales volume to make the product financially viable.

Prestige Pricing   Firms using prestige pricing set their prices at the top end of all competing products in a category. This is done to promote an image of exclusivity and superior quality. Ritz-Carlton Hotels, for example, never wants to compete with other hotels on price. Instead, the company competes only on service and the value of the unique, high-quality experience that they deliver to hotel guests. Prestige pricing is a viable approach in situations where it is hard to objectively judge the true value of a product. In these instances, a higher price may indicate a higher-quality product. Inexperienced wine consumers, for example, might assume that a $40 bottle of wine is better than a $15 bottle. Only a true connoisseur would actually know, but the average

Beyond the Pages 8.2

SELLING AT A LOSS[11]

Sometimes the best pricing strategy involves giving away the product, especially if the firm is looking for rapid adoption among customers. This has long been the case in computer software, where manufacturers give away restricted "trial" versions of their software to encourage use and, hopefully, purchase. Adobe, for example, gives away its popular Reader to help maintain branding of its other software products. McAfee and Norton freely package their antivirus programs with new computer purchases in hopes that buyers will subscribe to their continuous update services (priced between $40 and $200 per year based on features). The strategy is also used in consumer products. Procter & Gamble gives away (or sells below cost) its razors in the anticipation that it will sell more blades in the future.

The free or below-cost pricing strategy is common among products that are sold as platforms. A platform product is one that consists of a base product with numerous add-ons or supplemental products. Video gaming systems are a good example. When Microsoft originally launched the Xbox 360, it did so using a "neutral gross margin" strategy that sold each console at a loss. When the cost of parts, cables, and controllers are factored in, Microsoft loses less than $100 per console. Similarly, when rival platform maker Sony first introduced the PlayStation 3, the

company lost an estimated $240 for every console it sold. Today, after reducing manufacturing costs, Sony loses roughly $50 per console. Both Microsoft and Sony make up for the losses with higher profit margins on games and accessories, as well as brand licensing.

Many experts believe that Apple employs a neutral profit strategy in its operation of the iTunes store. It is estimated that for each 99-cent song sold on iTunes, Apple earns only 10 cents after paying royalties, micropayment fees, and infrastructure fees. Apple must then use that revenue to cover its operating and marketing costs. Furthermore, after discounting the price of movie rentals and purchases on the iTunes store, Apple loses roughly $1 on each movie. However, Apple more than makes up for these losses via the high profit margins of its iPod, iPhone, Apple TV, and portable computers.

There are many other examples of products sold at a loss to stimulate sales of other products. Inkjet printers are typically sold at or below cost because they stimulate future sales of ink and toner. Wireless phones are sold at a loss, or are subsidized at lower prices, in exchange for a one- or two-year service agreement. In grocery retailing, this practice is referred to as a loss-leader strategy. Common grocery loss leaders include milk, eggs, cereal, and soft drinks.

wine-buying public would see the $40 bottle as more appropriate for a special occasion or celebration. Consulting and research services are often sold in this fashion as well. Former U.S. presidents and corporate CEOs can command up to $100,000 for a one-hour speech to a company's employees. The presumption held by the firm is that a notable speaker's message will have a stronger impact than a local professional speaker who earns $5,000 for the same amount of time.

Value-Based Pricing (EDLP)   Firms that use a value-based pricing approach set reasonably low prices but still offer high-quality products and adequate customer services. Many different types of firms use value-based pricing; however, retailing has widely embraced this approach, where it is known as everyday low pricing or EDLP. The goal of value-based pricing is to set a reasonable price for the level of quality offered. Prices are not the highest in the market, nor are they the lowest. Instead, value-based pricing sets prices so they are consistent with the benefits and costs associated with acquiring the product.

Many well-known firms use value-based pricing, including Walmart, Lowe's, Home Depot, IKEA, and Southwest Airlines. Each of these firms exhibits the two major characteristics of the value-based pricing approach. First, these firms have the capacity to offer reasonable prices because they have engineered themselves to be a low-cost provider in their industry. Value-based pricing requires that the firm be highly efficient in operations and marketing in order to keep costs, and prices, low. Second, firms adopting value-based pricing maintain consistent prices over time; they use sales, discounts, and other pricing tactics infrequently. Value-based pricing naturally draws customers because they have confidence in the value of the products they buy. Customers also like the approach because it requires less effort to find good prices on the products they want and need.

Competitive Matching   In many industries, particularly oligopolies, pricing strategy focuses on matching competitors' prices and price changes. Although some firms may charge slightly more or slightly less, these firms set prices at what most consider to be the "going rate" for the industry. Two competitive factors largely drive this strategy. First, firms that offer commodity-type products (e.g., airlines, oil, steel) have a very difficult time finding any real or perceived basis for product differentiation. So, when customers see all products as being about the same, the prices have to be about the same as well. Second, some industries are so highly competitive that competitive price matching becomes a means of survival. The automobile industry and its long-running zero-percent financing and generous rebate offers are a good example.

Nonprice Strategies   It may seem odd to discuss nonprice strategies in this chapter, but building a marketing program around factors other than price is an important strategic pricing decision. By downplaying price in the marketing program, the firm must be able to emphasize the product's quality, benefits, and unique features, as well as customer service, promotion, or packaging in order to make the product stand out against competitors, many of whom will offer similar products at lower prices. Nonprice strategies are most effective when (1) the product can be successfully differentiated; (2) customers see the differentiating characteristics as being important; (3) competitors cannot emulate the differentiating characteristics; and (4) the market is generally not sensitive to price. For example, theme parks like Disney World, Sea World, and Universal Studios compete on excellent service, unique benefits, and one-of-a-kind experiences rather than price. Customers willingly pay for these experiences because they cannot be found in any other setting.

Adjusting Prices in Consumer Markets

In addition to a base pricing strategy, firms also use other techniques to adjust or fine-tune prices. These techniques can involve permanent adjustments to a product's price, or temporary adjustments used to stimulate sales during a particular time or situation. Although the list of potentially viable pricing techniques is quite long, we look at four of the most common techniques: promotional discounting, reference pricing, odd–even pricing, and price bundling.

Promotional Discounting   The hallmark of promotional discounting is a sale. All customers love a sale and that is precisely the main benefit of promotional discounting. Virtually all firms, even those using value-based pricing, will occasionally run special promotions or sales to attract customers and create excitement. Many retailers, particularly department stores, use a type of promotional discounting called high–low pricing. This strategy involves charging higher prices on an everyday basis, then using frequent promotions and sales to increase store traffic. Dillard's, for example, will hold a quick sale early in a selling season, and then return prices to their normal levels. Near the end of the season, Dillard's will begin to make these sale prices (or markdowns) permanent as time draws closer to the end-of-season clearance sale. It is interesting to note that the main benefit of promotional discounting is also its main drawback. Customers become so accustomed to sales and promotions that they will postpone purchases until retailers discount prices. Many vacation travelers and car buyers wait until special promotions are offered before making a purchase.

Reference Pricing   Firms use reference pricing when they compare the actual selling price to an internal or external reference price. All customers use internal reference prices, or the internal expectation for what a product should cost. As consumers, our experiences have given us a reasonable expectation of how much to pay for a combo meal at McDonald's, a gallon of gas, or a T-bone steak at a nice restaurant. For these and other common purchases, internal reference prices are critically important. However, customers often have little experience with certain products or product categories. This is especially true in services where the intangibility and heterogeneity of most services makes it difficult for customers to judge prices prior to purchase. In these instances, external reference prices become more important.

Typically the manufacturer or retailer of the good or service in question will provide the external reference price. A common use of reference pricing occurs when sale prices are compared to regular prices. You see this on television when marketers promote their goods as "A $50 value for only $19.99" or in stores such as when Best Buy promotes a television as "Regularly $399, Now $349." To be effective, the reference price—$399 in the case of Best Buy—must be seen as a legitimate, regular price. In other words, the retailer would not be able to inflate the reference price in order to make the sale price more attractive. Further, the sale price of $349 must be available for a limited time; otherwise, customers will come to see the sale price as the regular price. This is an important legal issue with reference pricing: The reference price must truly be the regular price. Retailers that offer nothing but sale prices essentially mislead customers by comparing the sale price to a higher, but never used, reference price.

Reference pricing also occurs when firms set prices slightly below most competing products, even the firm's other product offerings. In these cases, the prices of other competing products become the reference price. One natural truth in customer behavior is that there is always a segment of customers who will choose the lowest priced product. Firms use this to their advantage by creating lines of products that are quite similar in appearance and functionality, but are offered with slightly different features and at different price points. This technique is called price lining. For example, Sony can cut a few features off its top-of-the-line Model A1 digital camcorder and Model B2 can be on the shelf at $799 rather than the original $999. Cut a few more features and the price can drop to $599 for Model C3. Here, each model in the Sony line establishes reference prices for the other models in the line. The same is true for all competing camcorders from other manufacturers.

Odd–Even Pricing   Everyone knows that prices are rarely set at whole, round numbers. Concert tickets are $49.95, the breakfast special is $3.95, and a gallon of gas is $2.599. A couple of factors drive the prevalence of odd prices over even pricing. The first is that demand curves are not straight lines. As we noted earlier, the elasticity of a product's demand will change significantly at various price points. The move from $45.95 to $49.95 may result in very little drop in demand. When the price hits $50.00, just 5 cents more, the drop in demand may be sizable. Many concertgoers see $49.95 as $40, even though with taxes the price would be well over $50. They will tell a friend or a parent that they spent about $40, or that it certainly was not $50 for the ticket. Another reason that odd–even pricing works is that customers perceive that the seller did everything possible to get the price as fine (and thus as low) as he or she possibly could. To say you will cut my grass for $47 sounds like you put a lot more thought into it than if you just said, "Oh, I will do it for about $40," even though the first figure is $7 higher.

Price Bundling   Price bundling is sometimes called solution-based pricing, or all-inclusive pricing. This approach brings together two or more complementary products for a single price. At its best, the bundled price is less than if a company sold the products separately. Slow-moving items can be bundled with hot sellers to expand the scope of the product offering, build value, and manage inventory. Some resorts, including Sandals and Club Med, use price bundling because many customers want to simplify their vacations and add budget predictability. The room, food, beverages, and entertainment are all included in a per-person price for a class of room. This allows guests to leave their credit cards and money in their safe and just enjoy themselves. Some packages even include the airfare, purchased in large quantities of seats by the resorts from major departure points. Bundling is an attractive strategy in the banking, travel, insurance, communication, computer, and automobile markets because these customers desire convenience and fewer hassles. Still, many customers dislike bundling because they believe they can do a better job of creating their own solution and getting better value.

The all-inclusive pricing used by the Club Med Resort is an example of a price-bundling strategy.

© Jacky Naegelen/Reuters/Landov

Adjusting Prices in Business Markets

Many of the techniques just discussed are also used in business markets to adjust or fine-tune base prices. However, there are a number of pricing techniques unique to business markets, including these:

- **Trade Discounts** Manufacturers will reduce prices for certain intermediaries in the supply chain based on the functions that the intermediary performs. In general, discounts are greater for wholesalers than for retailers because the manufacturer wants to compensate wholesalers for the extra functions they perform, such as selling, storage, transportation, and risk taking. Trade discounts vary widely and have become more complicated due to the growth of large retailers who now perform their own wholesaling functions.

- **Discounts and Allowances** Business buyers can take advantage of sales just like consumers. However, business buyers also receive other price breaks, including discounts for cash, quantity or bulk discounts, seasonal discounts, or trade allowances for participation in advertising or sales support programs.

- **Geographic Pricing** Selling firms often quote prices in terms of reductions or increases based on transportation costs or the actual physical distance between the seller and the buyer. The most common examples of geographic pricing are uniform delivered pricing (same price for all buyers regardless of transportation expenses) and zone pricing (different prices based on transportation to predefined geographic zones).

- **Transfer Pricing** Transfer pricing occurs when one unit in an organization sells products to another unit.

- **Barter and Countertrade** In business exchanges across national boundaries, companies sometimes use products, rather than cash, for payments. Barter involves the direct exchange of goods or services between two firms or nations. Countertrade refers to agreements based on partial payments in both cash and products, or to agreements between firms or nations to buy goods and services from each other.

Another important pricing technique used in business markets is price discrimination, which occurs when firms charge different customers different prices. When this situation occurs, firms set different prices based on actual cost differences in selling products to one customer relative to the costs involved in selling to other customers. Price discrimination is a viable technique because the costs of selling to one firm are often much higher than selling to others. However, price discrimination also has major legal implications, which we will discuss later in the chapter.

Fixed Versus Dynamic Pricing

Up to this point in our discussion, we have assumed that once a price is set, all buyers will pay the same price. Historically, this has been the case for almost all products in the United States except automobiles, where we expect to haggle and bargain to get the best deal. Sticker prices are only a starting point and usually represent the highest price anyone would have to pay. Interestingly, as cars have moved toward fixed pricing, it seems that almost everything else has become negotiable.

The Internet has played a large role in fostering the dynamic pricing approach to buying everything, including airline tickets, hotel rooms, and cars. Firms such as Priceline, eBay, and Hotels.com have been major trendsetters in this area. Their approach is simple: Use an online auction strategy to bring buyers and sellers together in a competitive bidding process. Auction strategies, like the ones illustrated in Exhibit 8.5, allow firms to lower marketing and transaction costs, find new buyers or markets, and reduce unwanted inventory. Critics of online auctions contend that they are inconvenient (haggling takes time and you may end up with an unattractive option), are unfair (the person in the next room may have paid 20 percent less than you did), and promote disloyalty to a company or brand (price is the only thing that matters). Others argue that the online auction process only capitalizes on the underlying nature and structure of these markets. Whatever your opinion, online auction firms have been wildly successful. In fact, eBay Motors is now the world's largest car dealer, doing over $14 billion in online vehicle sales per year.[12]

Although relatively new to consumer markets, dynamic pricing has long been a staple of business markets. Salespeople have a great deal of flexibility in terms of the prices they charge to business buyers, offering big discounts for large-volume purchases. Business buyers go through comprehensive training programs to learn how to squeeze every dime out of every deal. In a dynamic pricing situation, there are three pricing levels that both the buyer and the seller must understand and plan for. The first is the *opening position*. This is the figure that each side will put on the table as a starting point. For example, in a deal for 500 cases of 20-pound paper, a salesperson

EXHIBIT 8.5   MAJOR ONLINE AUCTION STRATEGIES

Auction Type	Description	Examples
Traditional English Auction	This auction system allows individuals and businesses to sell products online using a competitive bidding process where prices increase until the close of the auction. Sellers sometimes use "reserve prices" to ensure that a minimum price is achieved.	eBay, uBid
Reverse Auction	In this auction system, sellers bid down prices until a lowest price is reached. Business buyers typically use reverse auctions to force suppliers to compete for their business.	Many large firms use reverse auctions to cut their procurement costs.
Dutch Auction	In this format, a seller has multiple, identical items to sell. The seller specifies the opening bid price and potential buyers bid at or above that price. At the close of the auction, the highest bidders purchase the items at the lowest successful bid.	eBay; OpenIPO uses Dutch auctions to attract individual and institutional investors to an initial stock offering.
Buyer-Driven Commerce	This system allows customers to specify how much they will pay for a good or service. Different providers then determine whether they will sell at the stated price.	Priceline.com owns the patent on this buyer-driven bidding process.

Source: Adapted from Brad Alan Kleindl, *Strategic Electronic Marketing*, 2nd ed. (Mason, OH: South-Western, 2003), p. 155.

might open with a price of $23.50 per case. The buyer might counter with his or her opening position of $17.50 per case. It is important to note that neither side expects to get the number it initially proposes. Rather, these two opening positions establish the negotiation range. If there is to be a deal, it will take place somewhere between $23.50 and $17.50 per case.

Alongside these opening positions, buyers and sellers must know their *aspiration price*, or the number that each side will use to distinguish between a successful negotiation and an unsuccessful negotiation. For the salesperson, this price might be $20.25 per case, whereas for the buyer it might be $20.00 per case. If the two reach an agreement at a price higher than $20.25, the salesperson will be happy. If they reach an agreement at a price below $20.00, the buyer will be happy. Throughout the negotiation process, both sides move via concessions from their opening position toward their aspiration price in an effort to find common ground. A *concession* is a reduction in the asking price or an increase in the buying price. Some important guidelines for making concessions include these:

- Avoid being the first side to make a concession.

- Avoid making concessions early in the negotiation. Instead, the opening position should be supported by additional facts about the exchange. For a salesperson, high quality and good service can support an opening position. For a buyer, high volume and the potential for additional business can back up an opening offer.

- Start with modest concessions and make them smaller as you proceed. For the salesperson, a pricing sequence might be $23.50 to $22.50, to $22.10, to $21.85.

- Do not give up anything without getting something in return. For example, a salesperson might drop the price by 5 percent if the buyer will commit to a longer-term commitment or a larger-volume order.

The third important pricing level is the *limit*, or the least favorable price either side will agree to during the negotiation. For example, the salesperson's limit might be $18.50, whereas the buyer's limit might be $20.50. In this example, because the two limits overlap, we know that the two parties will eventually come to an agreement if they continue to negotiate. Unless something changes to alter the conditions of the negotiation, their agreed-upon price will lie somewhere between $18.50 and $20.50. Whether the buyer or the seller feels good about the deal depends on the relationship of the final price to each side's aspiration price.

Dynamically negotiating prices can be a long and frustrating process, but it is the most logical and systematic way for two parties who do not initially agree to reach an agreement. Some firms give their salespeople and buyers total authority to negotiate prices within a broad range. Others require management involvement, and some decide they will not negotiate off their published list prices. Increasingly in today's challenging marketplace, the development of good negotiation skills is a prerequisite for survival.

Legal and Ethical Issues in Pricing

Pricing is one of the most heavily watched and regulated of all marketing activities. Given that a difference in price can create such a significant competitive advantage, any effort to artificially give one company an edge over another is subject to legal or regulatory intervention. We conclude our chapter on pricing by examining four of the most common legal and ethical issues in pricing: price discrimination, price fixing, predatory pricing, and deceptive pricing.

Price Discrimination

As we mentioned previously, price discrimination occurs when firms charge different prices to different customers. This is fairly common in consumer markets, such as when cable and satellite companies offer lower prices to new customers or when fast-food restaurants offer lower-priced meals for children. Price discrimination is very common in business markets where it typically occurs among different intermediaries in the supply chain. In general, price discrimination is illegal unless the price differential has a basis in actual cost differences in selling products to one customer relative to another. The overriding question in cases of price discrimination is whether the price differential injures competition. The Robinson-Patman Act and the Clayton Act both regulate discriminatory pricing. The intent of these regulations is to provide a level playing field for all competitors.

Essentially, there are two ways to defend price discrimination. One is to base the difference on the lower costs of doing business with one customer compared to another. For example, large-volume orders are generally less expensive per item to deliver than small-volume orders. These cost savings must be documented, and the price reduction cannot exceed the amount of the savings. In the book retailing industry, large players such as Barnes and Noble, Books-A-Million, Borders, and Amazon can obtain lower prices than smaller book retailers due to their bulk-buying practices. The second defense of price discrimination occurs when one customer receives a lower price offer in order to meet the price of a competitor. Again, this lower price must be documented, and the selling organization can only match—but not beat—the lower price.

Price Fixing

Although managers within a firm need to talk about pricing strategies and pricing decisions on a regular basis, they should never discuss pricing with a competitor or in the presence of a competitor. Such collaboration is known as price fixing, which is illegal under the Sherman Antitrust Act. Sizable fines and prison terms for those convicted are the norm. Usually one firm in an industry will be a price leader and others will be the price followers. The Justice Department has determined that, although following a competitor's lead in an upward or downward trend is acceptable, there can be no signaling of prices for particular products in this process. One of the most famous cases of price fixing occurred in the late 1990s when Archer Daniels Midland—a major agribusiness firm—was found guilty of fixing prices in the international lysine (a feed additive) and citric acid markets. ADM was fined $100 million for its role in the price-fixing conspiracy, in addition to the millions of dollars it paid in different civil and antitrust lawsuits filed by many companies. More recently, the Federal Trade Commission issued rules to monitor prices in the crude oil, petroleum, and gasoline markets. Violators who distort market prices through false or misleading statements about stockpiles, prices, or output can be fined up to $1 million per day.[13] *Beyond the Pages 8.3* discusses pricing issues in the oil and gasoline markets.

Predatory Pricing

Predatory pricing occurs when a firm charges very low prices for a product with the intent of driving competition out of business or out of a specific market. Prices then return to normal once the competitors have been eliminated. Predatory pricing is

---

Beyond the Pages 8.3

WHAT'S BEHIND FLUCTUATING GAS PRICES?[14]

Have you wondered why gasoline prices change as often as they do? Although the basic principles of competition and supply/demand are alive and well in the gasoline market, most consumers believe that gasoline prices are tied directly to the price of oil, and to the profit motives of oil and gas companies. The truth, however, is that the connection between oil and gas prices is only indirect and not clearly predictable.

To understand gasoline prices, one first has to understand that the price of oil—gasoline's raw material—varies based on its origin. The U.S. benchmark for oil, West Texas Intermediate (WTI), is less expensive than other types of oil because it is recovered and refined in the United States. In other words, the supply chain for WTI is shorter; therefore, it is less expensive than oil obtained from foreign sources. In addition to differences based on origin, oil prices also vary based on futures contracts. Oil refineries (or speculators as we will see in a moment) purchase these contracts to guarantee delivery of crude oil anywhere from the next month to years in the future. This action helps to ensure a stable supply of oil at predictable prices well into the future.

The price of oil futures contracts varies based on a number of factors. One of the most important is oil production (i.e., supply). When oil companies cut back on production, the price of oil rises on the futures market. This is what happens, for example, when OPEC cuts production. Oil futures can also vary based on the actions of

speculators. Speculators—typically pension funds, mutual funds, hedge funds, or private investors—invest in oil futures contracts to profit off of their price fluctuations. Most experts agree that the actions of speculators caused the price of oil to soar above $147 per barrel during the summer of 2008.

Despite fluctuations in the oil market, the real reason that gasoline prices do not closely follow oil prices is that the gasoline futures market is not the same as the oil futures market. Just like oil, gasoline can be purchased using futures contracts that guarantee delivery of gasoline at predetermined prices. However, different buyers dominate the gasoline futures market: gas station owners, gasoline chains, and wholesalers. Further, gasoline futures contracts have much shorter delivery times—days or weeks rather than months or years. Gasoline prices are also affected by the actions of refiners, who often cut gasoline production to reduce retail supply and raise prices. Other factors, such as supply and demand in local markets, time of year (demand typically increases during the summer), and supply chain interruptions (such as hurricanes along the Gulf), also affect gasoline prices.

The bottom line is that the price of gas that you purchase today may or may not be related to the past, present, or future price of crude oil. The oil and gasoline markets are separate. They have different buyers and sellers, different delivery times, and different demand characteristics.

illegal; however, it is extremely difficult to prove in court. The challenge in predatory pricing cases is to prove that the predatory firm had the willful intent to ruin the competition. The court must also be convinced that the low price charged by the predator is below their average variable cost. The variable cost definition of predatory pricing is a major reason why very few lawsuits for predatory pricing are successful. The reality is that large firms with lean, efficient cost structures dominate today's competitive landscape. These firms have lower variable costs that allow them to legitimately charge lower prices than the competition in many cases. This is the reason that large retailers such as Walmart, Home Depot, Lowe's, and Barnes and Noble have been slowly and methodically putting smaller retailers out of business. These large firms are not guilty of predatory pricing—they are only guilty of being more efficient and competitive than other firms.

Deceptive Pricing

Intentionally misleading customers with price promotions is another area that has seen significant court action in recent years. This pricing tactic, known as deceptive pricing, is illegal under the Federal Trade Commission Act and the Wheeler-Lea Act. One carefully watched form of deceptive pricing is superficial discounting. This form of deception has ties to reference pricing and occurs when a firm advertises a sale price as a reduction below the normal price when it is not the case. Typically, the firm does not sell the product at the regular price in any meaningful quantities, or the sale price period is excessively long. To avoid this legal violation, a firm should offer a product at the original price, discount the price in a specified dollar amount for a specified period, and then revert to the original price at the end of that period. If the product is a discontinued item, that fact should be noted in the advertisement. Most of the legal activity regarding superficial discounting has taken place at the state attorney general level.

Lessons from Chapter 8

Pricing

- Is a key factor in producing revenue for a firm.

- Is the easiest of all marketing variables to change.

- Is an important consideration in competitive intelligence.

- Is considered to be the only real means of differentiation in mature markets plagued by commoditization.

- Is among the most complex decisions to be made in developing a marketing plan.

With respect to pricing, sellers

- Tend to inflate prices because they want to receive as much as possible in an exchange.

- Must consider four key issues in pricing strategy: (1) costs, (2) demand, (3) customer value, and (4) competitors' prices.
- Have increased power over buyers when certain products are in short supply, in high demand, or during good economic times.

With respect to pricing, buyers

- Often see prices as being lower than market reality dictates.
- Must consider two key issues: (1) perceived value and (2) price sensitivity.
- Consider value to be the ratio of benefits to costs, expressed colloquially as "more bang for the buck."
- Have increased power over sellers when there are a large number of sellers in the market, when the economy is weak, when product information is easy to obtain, or when price comparisons between competing firms or products are easy to make.

In terms of pricing strategy, cutting prices

- Can be a viable means of increasing sales, moving excess inventory, or generating short-term cash flow.
- Is usually based on two general pricing myths: (1) when business is good, a price cut will capture greater market share, and (2) when business is bad, a price cut will stimulate sales.
- Can be a risky proposition for most firms because any price cut must be offset by an increase in sales volume to maintain the same level of gross margin.
- Is not always the best strategy. Instead, firms are often better off if they can find ways to build value into the product and justify the current, or a higher, price.

The key issues in pricing strategy include

- The firm's pricing objectives.
- The nature of supply and demand in the industry or market.
- The firm's cost structure.
- The nature of competition and the structure of the industry.
- The stage of the product life cycle.

The firm's cost structure

- Is typically associated with pricing through the use of breakeven analysis or cost-plus pricing.

- Should not be the driving force behind pricing strategy because different firms have different cost structures.
- Should be used to establish a floor below which prices cannot be set for an extended period of time.

Pricing strategy in services

- Is critical because price may be the only cue to quality that is available in advance of the purchase experience.
- Becomes more important—and more difficult—when
    - Service quality is hard to detect prior to purchase.
    - The costs associated with providing the service are difficult to determine.
    - Customers are unfamiliar with the service process.
    - Brand names are not well established.
    - Customers can perform the service themselves.
    - The service has poorly defined units of consumption.
    - Advertising within a service category is limited.
    - The total price of the service experience is difficult to state beforehand.
- Is often based on yield management systems that allow a firm to simultaneously control capacity and demand in order to maximize revenue and capacity utilization.

Yield management

- Involves knowing when and where to raise prices to increase revenue, or to lower prices to increase sales volume.
- Is implemented by limiting the available capacity at certain price points, controlling demand through price changes over time, and overbooking capacity.
- Is common in services characterized by high fixed costs and low variable costs, such as airlines, hotels, rental cars, cruises, transportation firms, and hospitals.
- Allows a firm to offer the same basic product to different market segments at different prices.

Price elasticity of demand

- Refers to customers' responsiveness or sensitivity to changes in price.
- Can be inelastic, where the quantity demanded does not respond to price changes.
- Can be elastic, where the quantity demanded is sensitive to price changes.
- Can be unitary, where the changes in price and demand offset, keeping total revenue the same.

- Is not uniform over time and place because demand is not uniform over time and place.

Situations that increase price sensitivity include

- When substitute products are widely available.
- When the total expenditure is high.
- When changes in price are noticeable to customers.
- When price comparison among competing products is easy.

Situations that decrease price sensitivity include those when

- Substitute products are not available
- Products are highly differentiated from the competition.
- Customers perceive products as being necessities.
- The prices of complementary products go down.
- Customers believe that the product is just worth the price.
- Customers are in certain situations associated with time pressures or purchase risk.

Major base pricing strategies include

- Market introduction pricing—the use of price skimming or penetration pricing when products are first launched into the market
- Prestige pricing—intentionally setting prices at the top end of all competing products in order to promote an image of exclusivity and superior quality.
- Value-based pricing (EDLP)—setting reasonably low prices, but still offering high quality products and adequate customer services.
- Competitive matching—charging what is considered to be the "going rate" for the industry.
- Nonprice strategies—building a marketing program around factors other than price.

Strategies for adjusting or fine-tuning prices in consumer markets include

- Promotional discounting—putting products on sale.
- Reference pricing—comparing the actual selling price to an internal or external reference price.
- Odd–even pricing—setting prices in odd numbers, rather than in whole, round numbers.

- Price bundling—bringing together two or more complementary products for a single price.

Strategies for adjusting or fine-tuning prices in business markets include

- Trade discounts—reducing prices for certain intermediaries in the supply chain based on the functions that the intermediary performs.
- Discounts and allowances—giving buyers price breaks, including discounts for cash, quantity or bulk discounts, seasonal discounts, or trade allowances for participation in advertising or sales support programs.
- Geographic pricing—quoting prices based on transportation costs or the distance between the seller and the buyer.
- Transfer pricing—pricing that occurs when one unit in an organization sells products to another unit.
- Barter and countertrade—making full or partial payments in goods, services, or buying agreements rather than in cash.
- Price discrimination—charging different prices to different customers.

Dynamic pricing

- Has started to replace fixed pricing in many different product categories.
- Has been growing in importance and popularity due to the growth of online auction firms.
- Involves three distinct pricing levels: (1) the opening position, (2) the aspiration price, and (3) the price limit.
- Can be a long and frustrating process, but it is the most logical and systematic way for two parties who do not initially agree to reach an agreement.

Major legal and ethical issues in pricing include

- Price discrimination—occurs when firms charge different prices to different customers. The practice is illegal unless the price differential has its basis in the actual cost differences in selling products to one customer relative to another.
- Price fixing—occurs when two or more competitors collaborate to set prices at an artificial level.
- Predatory pricing—occurs when a firm sets prices for a product below the firm's variable cost with the intent of driving competition out of business or out of a specific market.
- Deceptive pricing—occurs when firms intentionally mislead customers with price promotions.

Questions for Discussion

1. One of the key themes stressed throughout this text is the challenge of marketing goods and services in mature markets that are plagued by commoditization. In what ways is pricing strategy related to commoditization? How can a firm offer good value in a mature market where price is the only visible means of differentiation? Are most firms too concerned about their costs to really deliver value in other ways? Explain.

2. Pricing strategy associated with services is typically more complex than the pricing of tangible goods. As a consumer, what pricing issues do you consider when purchasing services? How difficult is it to compare prices among competing services or to determine the complete price of the service before purchase? What could service providers do to solve these issues?

3. Price elasticity often varies for the same product based on the situation. What situational factors might affect the price elasticity of these products: (a) sporting event or concert tickets; (b) staple goods such as milk, eggs, or bread; (c) an electric razor; and (d) eye surgery to correct vision?

Exercises

1. You are in the process of planning a hypothetical airline flight from New York to St. Louis. Visit the websites of three different airlines and compare prices for this trip. Try travel dates that include a Saturday night layover and those that do not. Try dates less than 7 days away, and compare those prices with flights that are more than 21 days out. How do you explain the similarities and differences you see in these prices?

2. Visit eBay (http://www.ebay.com), choose a product category, and look at some of the current auctions. With respect to everything you have learned in this chapter, answer these questions:

   A. How might sellers determine the prices they set for opening bids and reserve prices (the minimum price they will accept for an item)?

   B. For any particular item, how might potential buyers determine internal and external reference prices?

   C. Why do so many sellers use odd pricing?

   D. Does price elasticity play a role in determining the final bid price? If so, how?

3. Visit PriceFarmer (http://www.pricefarmer.com) and search for any book. How do you explain the differences in pricing for that book across different retailers? If you were purchasing this book, which retailer would you select? Why? Is price the most important factor, or are other issues like retailer reputation, product availability, and discount level more important? Explain.

CHAPTER 9

Distribution and Supply Chain Management

Introduction

Distribution and supply chain relationships are among the most important strategic decisions for many marketers. Walmart, Best Buy, and even Starbucks depend on effective and highly efficient supply chains to provide competitive advantage. Throughout most of the twentieth century, distribution was the forgotten element of marketing strategy. After all, most considered marketing to consist of the four "Ps": product, price, promotion, and something most people had a hard time remembering. The fourth "P" really didn't fit. Marketing textbook authors passed it off as "place," but it was really a "D" for distribution. Distribution and supply chain management have remained essentially invisible to customers because the process occurs behind the scenes. Customers rarely appreciate how manufacturers connect to their supply lines, how goods move from manufacturers to retailers, or how retailers' shelves become filled. For example, consider the fact that over 60 percent of products sold in Walmart stores are manufactured in China. Customers take this and other supply chain issues for granted and only notice when supply lines are interrupted. Although the nature of today's economy has forced customers to notice and appreciate distribution to a much greater extent, most remain naïve about distribution activities and the complex nature of supply chain relationships.

The picture of distribution is drastically different from the firm's perspective. Beginning in the late 1980s and into today, firms have learned the extreme importance of distribution and supply chain management. As described in *Beyond the Pages 9.1*, these concerns now rank at the top of the list for achieving a sustainable advantage and true differentiation in the marketplace. Prices can be copied easily, even if only for the short term. Products can become obsolete almost overnight. Good promotion and advertising in September can easily be passè when the prime selling season in November and December comes around. The lesson is clear: Distribution is vital to the success and survival of every firm. In fact, firms that neglect the distribution component of marketing strategy face a different kind of "D"—death.

Beyond the Pages 9.1

SUPPLY CHAIN MANAGEMENT AT BARNES & NOBLE[1]

In the course of operating more than 778 bookstores across the United States, a popular website that features over 1 million titles available for immediate delivery, and 624 college bookstores serving over 4 million students, Barnes & Noble has become an expert at supply chain management. The largest U.S. bookstore chain made retailing history when it opened the first category-killer bookstore in the late 1980s. At that time, the store was five times the size of a typical bookstore. Today, Barnes & Noble routinely opens massive 100,000-square-foot stores while managing hundreds of smaller mall-based stores, a fast-growing Internet business, and a network of gigantic warehouses. This multipronged distribution strategy has helped the chain boost annual sales to over $5 billion.

For years, Barnes & Noble managed inventory by having suppliers and wholesalers send orders directly to individual stores. However, as the company opened larger stores, each stocked with up to 200,000 books, it needed a new system to ensure that the right items would be available in the right quantities at the right time and in the right place. To accomplish this, Barnes & Noble built three warehouses totaling 1 million square feet to receive and store products until they were shipped to the stores. When the website became operational, even this massive amount of warehouse space proved too small to accommodate the amount of merchandise needed to keep up with the surge in sales. Today, the warehouses can hold an inventory of 20 million items, ready to go out to Barnes & Noble stores and to online customers in more than 200 countries.

To manage all the intricate details of store and Internet sales, orders, and shipments, Barnes & Noble has forged close relationships with publishers, wholesalers, and other supply chain partners. Sophisticated Internet-based systems help the retailer capture and communicate customer demand data to improve sales forecasting and help suppliers plan ahead for production. The system also gathers and communicates supplier information about product availability to help Barnes & Noble's buyers plan ahead for ordering. Finally, the system analyzes location-by-location inventory levels to help managers time shipments to stores and customers.

Recently, Barnes & Noble launched the world's largest e-bookstore in a move that eschews traditional supply chain management in favor of immediate electronic delivery of books. The Barnes & Noble eBookstore offers over 1 million titles that can be read on a number of devices, including personal computers, the iPhone or iPod touch, and Blackberry smartphones. However, the company's launch of its own e-book reader—the Nook—is gathering the most attention. The combination of Barnes & Noble's large e-book assortment and the Nook is expected to give Amazon and its Kindle e-reader a run for its money.

Distribution and supply chain issues are among the most important strategic decisions for any marketer.

Although costly in both money and time to construct, a solid distribution system will generate profits for years or decades. With great distribution, a firm can overcome some weaknesses in pricing, products, and promotion. However, a poor distribution strategy will certainly kill a firm's efforts to market a superior product, at a good price, using effective marketing communication. Top managers of North American manufacturing firms realize the importance of this; they nearly unanimously rank supply chain management as critical or very important to their firms' successes.

Distribution and Supply Chain Concepts

Distribution and supply chain management are important for many different reasons. Ultimately, however, these reasons all come down to providing time, place, and possession utility for consumer and business buyers. Without good distribution, buyers would not be able to acquire goods and services when and where they need them. However, the expense of distribution requires that firms balance customers' needs with their own need to minimize total costs. Exhibit 9.1 provides a breakdown of total distribution costs across key activities. Note that 42 percent of these expenses are associated with storing and carrying inventory—key factors in ensuring product availability for customers. To manage these costs efficiently, distribution strategy must balance the needs of customers with the needs of the firm.

When we think of distribution and supply chain management, we tend to think of two interrelated components:

- **Marketing Channels**   An organized system of marketing institutions through which products, resources, information, funds, and/or product ownership flow from the point of production to the final user. Some channel members or intermediaries physically take possession or title of products (e.g., wholesalers, distributors, retailers), whereas others simply facilitate the process (e.g., agents, brokers, financial institutions).

- **Physical Distribution**   Coordinating the flow of information and products among members of the channel to ensure the availability of products in the right places, in the right quantities, at the right times, and in a cost-efficient manner. Physical distribution (or logistics) includes activities such as customer service/order entry, administration, transportation, warehousing (storage and materials handling), inventory carrying, and the systems and equipment necessary for these activities.

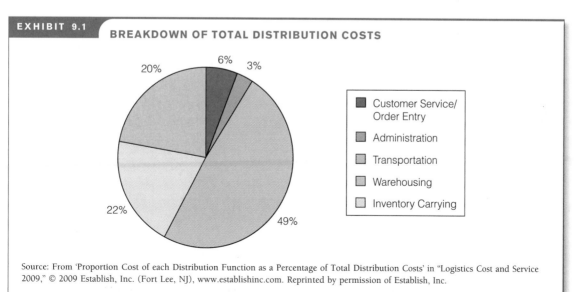

EXHIBIT 9.1

BREAKDOWN OF TOTAL DISTRIBUTION COSTS

Source: From 'Proportion Cost of each Distribution Function as a Percentage of Total Distribution Costs' in "Logistics Cost and Service 2009," © 2009 Establish, Inc. (Fort Lee, NJ), www.establishinc.com. Reprinted by permission of Establish, Inc.

The term *supply chain* expresses the connection and integration of all members of the marketing channel. As depicted in Exhibit 9.2, a supply chain integrates firms such as raw material suppliers, manufacturers, resellers, and final customers into a seamless flow of information, products, and funds. Supply chains also include flows that occur forward toward end users, and reverse channels where returns and repairs flow away from end users. Velocity or the need to speed inventory to and from channel members requires collaborating with technology, transportation, and other outside logistics experts. This supply chain process is designed to increase inventory turns and get the right products to the right place at the right time, maintaining the appropriate service and quality standards.[2] As we will discuss throughout this chapter, the keys to this effective flow through the supply chain are integration and collaboration.

Marketing Channel Functions

Marketing channels make our lives much easier because of the variety of functions performed by channel members. Likewise, channel members, particularly manufacturers, can cut costs by working through channel intermediaries. The most basic benefit of marketing channels is contact efficiency, where channels reduce the number of contacts necessary to exchange products. Without contact efficiency, consumers would have to visit a bakery, poultry farm, slaughterhouse, and dairy just to assemble the products necessary for breakfast. Likewise, contact efficiency allows companies such as Del Monte Foods to maximize product distribution by selling to select intermediaries. For Del Monte, Walmart stores account for over 31 percent of the company's sales volume. Del Monte's next nine largest customers

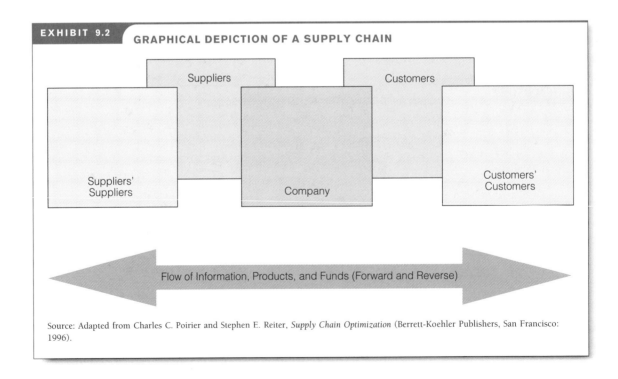

EXHIBIT 9.2   GRAPHICAL DEPICTION OF A SUPPLY CHAIN

Suppliers

Customers

Suppliers' Suppliers

Company

Customers' Customers

Flow of Information, Products, and Funds (Forward and Reverse)

Source: Adapted from Charles C. Poirier and Stephen E. Reiter, *Supply Chain Optimization* (Berrett-Koehler Publishers, San Francisco: 1996).

account for another 30 percent of the company's sales. These percentages will increase if additional consolidation among food retailers and growth of mass merchandisers continues.[3]

Throughout a marketing channel, some firms are good at manufacturing, some are good at transportation or storage, and others are better at selling to consumers. Given the costs involved, it is virtually impossible for a single firm to perform all channel functions well. As a result, channel intermediaries typically attain a level of specialization in one or more of the following functions:

- **Sorting**   Manufacturers make one or a few products, whereas customers need a wide variety and deep assortment of different products. By sorting products in the channel, intermediaries overcome this discrepancy of assortment.

- **Breaking Bulk**   Manufacturers produce large quantities of a product to gain the benefits of economies of scale. However, customers typically want only one of a particular item. By breaking bulk in the channel, intermediaries—particularly retailers—overcome this discrepancy of quantity.

- **Maintaining Inventories**   Because manufacturers cannot make products on demand, the channel must provide for the storage of products for future purchase and use. By maintaining inventories, intermediaries overcome this temporal (time) discrepancy. Note that this does not apply to services—such as haircuts or airline flights—where the product is produced and consumed simultaneously.

- **Maintaining Convenient Locations**   Because manufacturers and customers are separated geographically, the channel must overcome this spatial discrepancy by making products available in convenient locations.

- **Provide Services**   Channels add value to products by offering facilitating services (e.g., insurance, storage, financing) and standardizing the exchange process (e.g., payment processing, delivery, pricing).

With the exception of highly intangible services like consulting, education, or counseling, the fulfillment of these functions occurs in every marketing channel. Also, these functions must be fulfilled in order for the channel to operate effectively. It does not matter which intermediary performs these functions; the fact remains that they must be performed. For example, Sam's Club does not break bulk in the traditional sense. Sam's customers buy in large quantities and actually break bulk after purchase. Further, many emerging trends in distribution and supply chain management have blurred the responsibilities of different intermediaries. Today, large retailers are essentially a one-stop channel of distribution. Due to their immense size and bulk-buying ability, these firms now fulfill virtually all traditional channel functions.

Channel Effectiveness and Efficiency

Increasingly, distribution decisions are being evaluated using two criteria: (1) Is the channel effective? and (2) Is the channel efficient? For a firm to be competitive, the answer to both questions must be "yes." Effectiveness involves meeting the goals and objectives of both the firm and its customers. Today, the key effectiveness issue is whether the channel provides exceptional time, place, and possession utility. With respect to time utility, the new standard is 24/7/365. Business buyers and consumers both want the ability to access information and purchase products every hour of the day, every day of the week, and every day of the year (including holidays). This requires utilizing a system of technologies and processes that senses and reacts to real-time demand signals across the network of marketing channel members.

Although firms have gotten better in terms of time utility, exceptional place utility remains elusive for many firms. The primary reason is expense. In the past, buyers would often travel great distances to purchase a product. Today, they do not want to leave their home or office. The increasing place demands of customers forces firms to build a distribution infrastructure that puts products in convenient locations. Although the Internet has certainly helped in many industries (movies, music, software, pizza, consumer electronics, etc.), many firms cannot leverage the Internet for distribution effectiveness. For these firms, the expense of building multiple outlets in convenient locations is a major challenge.

With respect to possession utility, a key issue in channel effectiveness is the ease of the actual purchase process. Customers want to buy products only in the amounts they need, using the means of payment they most prefer. These desires increase the need for facilitating services in the channel. For example, the phenomenal growth of PayPal is the result of the increased need to conduct online payments. PayPal facilitates both online and offline transactions by handling online payments for over 75 million members in 190 markets and 19 currencies around the world.[4] Ease of use is also an issue in reverse channels, especially when tied to recycling and product recalls. For example, when Dell recalled over 4.1 million defective laptop batteries in 2006, it immediately created a website and call center to make the recall process run more efficiently. In the first day alone, Dell received more than 100,000 phone calls, 23 million hits to its website, and roughly 77,000 replacement orders. Many customers received replacement batteries in only one or two days.[5]

To increase channel efficiency, firms must be able to cut costs by eliminating redundancies and waste. Increasing logistical efficiency alone can significantly reduce inventory, transportation, warehousing, and packing costs. For example, General Mills' 10-year plan to cut $1 billion out of the firm's supply chain uses a holistic margin management approach to eliminate costs that do not add value for customers. General Mills was able to improve teamwork skills at one plant and cut cereal production costs by 25 percent. General Mills then takes such savings and reinvests them into worldwide consumer marketing programs.[6] Packaged goods firms like General Mills can easily reduce costs from 4 to 5 percent by adopting a coordinated supply chain strategy. This may not sound like a lot, but given the large sales volume involved, a small reduction in costs can easily result in a $25 to $30 million cost advantage over a less efficient competitor.

Strategic Issues in Distribution and Supply Chain Management

Although the terms often become used interchangeably, there is a key distinction that separates a traditional marketing channel from a true supply chain. With the traditional channel, each channel member has as its main concern how much profit it makes, or the size of its piece of the pie. In a supply chain, the primary concern is the share of the market the entire channel captures. In this case, there is a clear understanding that the channel is competing against other channels. In order for firms in the supply chain to achieve their objectives, the entire supply chain must meet its objectives by winning customers' business. In a supply chain, the focus shifts from the size of each individual piece of the pie to the size of the whole pie.

As Exhibit 9.3 shows, any single firm can demand a larger portion of the profit made from the channel's activities, but if the channel's share of the market shrinks, then that firm will earn less profit (outcome #1 in the exhibit). On the other hand, if the channel's share increases, a firm may get a smaller share (outcome #2) or maintain a constant share (outcome #3), yet still earn more profit. Results show clearly that

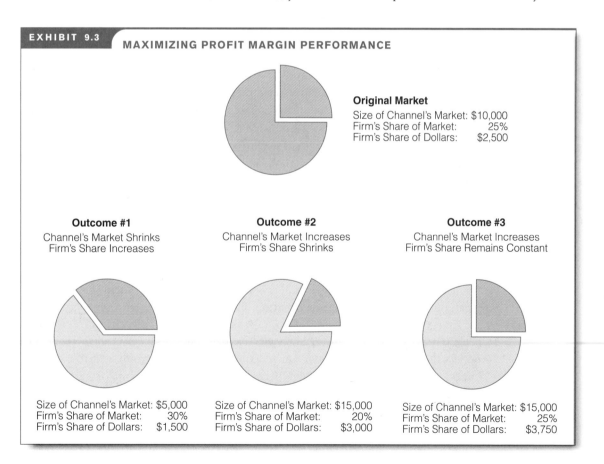

EXHIBIT 9.3

MAXIMIZING PROFIT MARGIN PERFORMANCE

Original Market
Size of Channel's Market: $10,000
Firm's Share of Market: 25%
Firm's Share of Dollars: $2,500

Outcome #1
Channel's Market Shrinks
Firm's Share Increases

Size of Channel's Market: $5,000
Firm's Share of Market: 30%
Firm's Share of Dollars: $1,500

Outcome #2
Channel's Market Increases
Firm's Share Shrinks

Size of Channel's Market: $15,000
Firm's Share of Market: 20%
Firm's Share of Dollars: $3,000

Outcome #3
Channel's Market Increases
Firm's Share Remains Constant

Size of Channel's Market: $15,000
Firm's Share of Market: 25%
Firm's Share of Dollars: $3,750

firms involved in supply chains outperform those in traditional marketing channels by a wide margin. Thus, focusing on the size of the channel's market share is not only good for the viability of the channel; it is good for each individual channel member involved.

This section will consider three key strategic aspects of any supply chain: the structure of the channel, channel integration, and the means to build value in the supply chain. Each of these combines to determine the extent to which the firms involved can advance their relationship from a loosely configured marketing channel to a truly integrated supply chain.

Marketing Channel Structure

There are many strategic options for the structure of a marketing channel; these strategies are often complex and very costly to implement. However, a good distribution strategy is essential for success because once a firm selects a channel and makes commitments to it, distribution often becomes highly inflexible due to long-term contracts, sizable investments, and commitments among channel members. There are three basic structural options for distribution in terms of the amount of market coverage and level of exclusivity between vendor and retailer: exclusive distribution, selective distribution, and intensive distribution.

Exclusive Distribution   Exclusive distribution is the most restrictive type of market coverage. Firms using this strategy give one merchant or outlet the sole right to sell a product within a defined geographic region. This channel structure is most commonly associated with prestige products, major industrial equipment, or with firms that attempt to give their products an exclusive or prestige image. For example, BMW, Jaguar, and Mercedes typically grant exclusive distribution to only one dealer in any given area. Companies sometimes use exclusive distribution for specialty products and occasionally for shopping goods like furniture or clothing.

Firms that pursue exclusive distribution usually target a single, well-defined market segment. Buyers in this segment must be willing and able to search or travel to buy the product, and will typically do so given the prestige or exclusivity of the product or brand. Exclusive distribution is a necessity in cases where the manufacturer demands a significant amount of input regarding the presentation of its products to buyers. This added control also allows the firm to influence pricing to a much greater degree than the other distribution options.

Selective Distribution   Firms using selective distribution give several merchants or outlets the right to sell a product in a defined geographic region. Selective distribution is desirable when customers need the opportunity to comparison shop, and after-sale services are important. For example, Kodak digital cameras are available at Best Buy, Office Depot, Walmart, Target, and many online merchants. This broad distribution coverage allows shoppers to collect information on Kodak and competitive products, compare prices, shop at their favorite store, use a variety of means of payment, and get the model they want, even when one location is out of stock on a model. Kodak does not make the cameras available in convenience stores or grocery stores due to their relatively high prices, the customer's need for information, and the company's desire to maintain some control over prices and the point-of-sale displays for the cameras.

Clinique's line of upscale cosmetics is an example of a product made available through selective distribution.

Companies widely use selective distribution across many product categories, including clothing (Tommy Hilfiger), cosmetics (Clinique), electronics (Bose), and premium pet food (Science Diet). McDonald's and most other franchisers also utilize selective distribution in the allocation of franchises. Such selectivity may be based on population and demographics (e.g., one franchise per 250,000 people), dollar volume (e.g., when sales reach $5 million in an area, the franchiser awards another franchise), or some other factor. In each case, selective distribution allows the manufacturer to have more control over prices, product display, and selling techniques. Companies carefully screen the image and selling practices of merchants and outlets to ensure that they match those of the manufacturer and its products.

Intensive Distribution   Intensive distribution makes a product available at the maximum number of merchants or outlets in each area to gain as much exposure and as many sales opportunities as possible. This distribution strategy is the option of choice for most consumer convenience goods, such as candy, soft drinks, over-the-counter drugs, or cigarettes; and for business office supplies like paper and toner cartridges. To gain this visibility and sales volume, the manufacturer must give up a good degree of control over pricing and product display. Given the sheer number of intensively distributed products, manufacturers often have difficulty convincing channel members, particularly retailers, to handle and stock another product that is distributed in the same manner.

Consider the J.M. Smucker Company, the leading manufacturer of fruit spreads and peanut butter in North America. The company's strategy is to own and market leading icon food brands found in the center of the supermarket. Smucker distributes its brands—such as Jif, Smucker's, Crisco, Hungry Jack, Pillsbury, and Martha White—through grocery and other retail outlets, foodservice establishments, schools, specialty and gourmet shops, health and natural food stores, and consumer direct vehicles such as the Internet and a showcase store in Orrville, Ohio.[7]

Firms that employ a mass marketing approach to segmentation often opt for an intensive distribution strategy. If customers cannot find one firm's products in a given location, they will simply substitute another brand to fill the need. As products age over the life cycle, they often move toward more intensive distribution.

Channel Integration

The linchpin of effective supply chain management in today's economy is channel integration. Through informational, technological, social, and structural linkages, the goal of channel integration is to create a seamless network of collaborating suppliers, vendors, buyers, and customers. When done correctly, this level of integration results in an extended enterprise that manages value by coordinating the flow of information, goods, and services both upstream and downstream in the supply chain. Creating an extended enterprise requires investments in and commitment to three key factors:[8]

- **Connectivity**   The informational and technological linkages among firms in the supply chain network. Connectivity ensures that firms can access real-time information about the flow in the supply chain network.

- **Community**   The sense of compatible goals and objectives among firms in the supply chain network. All firms must be willing to work together to achieve a common mission and vision.

- **Collaboration**   The recognition of mutual interdependence among members of the supply chain network. Collaboration goes beyond contractual obligations to establish principles, processes, and structures that promote a level of shared understanding. Firms learn to put the needs of the supply chain ahead of their own, because they understand that the success of each firm separately has a strong connection to the success of other firms, as well as the entire supply chain.

Channel integration and creating an extended enterprise are extremely challenging goals. In the most seamlessly integrated supply chains, the boundaries among channel members blur to the point where it is difficult to tell where one firm ends and another firm begins. This level of integration creates a tenuous balance of competition and collaboration, as well as teamwork and self-serving behaviors.[9] We will explore these topics more fully later in the chapter when we discuss power, conflict, and collaboration in the supply chain.

Creating and Enhancing Value in the Supply Chain

Another key consideration in making strategic supply chain decisions is to have a firm grasp on the value components that target customers find attractive. Synergy (the idea that the whole is greater than the sum of the parts) is the driving force behind value creation in the supply chain. By combining and integrating their unique capabilities, channel members can create synergies that enhance communication and sales, improve after-sale service, increase the efficiency of product delivery, add product enhancements, or offer solutions rather than individual products. By combining complementary products, a supply chain can offer solutions to customers' problems that increase overall value. For example, Dell customers can create their own solutions by combining products from a number of different vendors. Likewise, combining wine, cheese, crackers, other snacks, plates, flatware, napkins, and a tablecloth all inside a picnic basket results in a combined value much greater that the sum of the individual products in the mix.

Creating value also takes the focus off the price of individual items, as both consumers and business buyers tend to put less downward pressure on prices and profit margin when the solution offered meets a genuine need or problem. For example, the value of a Canon printer will be perceived differently depending upon whether it is a stand-alone item or part of a system, and whether it is packaged as part of a solution for the college student, a home office, or for business use. This type of value building can be done at any level of the supply chain. However, the need for rapid delivery, service, or training in close proximity to the customer will tend to push value building downstream in the supply chain to local distributors, merchants, or retailers. Large grocery retailers, for example, are quite good at building value and solutions by offering full-course meal replacements that can be purchased on the way home from work. Separate food manufacturers and distributors could never offer these types of solutions to consumers.

Conflict and Collaboration in the Supply Chain

True supply chain integration requires a fundamental change in how channel members work together. Among these changes is a move from a "win–lose" competitive attitude to a "win–win" collaborative approach in which there is a common realization that all firms in the supply chain must prosper. This change shifts the participants from short-term to long-term assessments in evaluating decisions affecting the relationship. The focus has been modified from one of selling to the next level in the channel, to one of selling products through the channel to a satisfied, ultimate customer. Information flows move from guarded secrecy to open, honest, and frequent communications. Perhaps most importantly, the points of contact in the relationship expand from one-on-one at the salesperson–buyer level, to multiple interfaces at all levels and in all functional areas of each firm. The goal of this shift is to create supply chains where all members work together to reduce costs, waste, and unnecessary movement in the entire marketing channel in order to satisfy ultimate customers.

The Basis of Conflict in the Supply Chain

As we mentioned, achieving a high degree of channel integration is a challenging task. The reasons are easy to see. First, each firm in a supply chain has its own mission, goals, objectives, and strategies. Consider the Toro Company that sells turf maintenance equipment, irrigation systems, landscaping equipment, and yard products to both professional and residential markets. This requires many different distributors and dealers (many of which are quite small), as well as supplying products to large national retailers such as Home Depot. Because each firm knows that its survival ultimately depends on its ability to achieve its goals, it is not surprising that firms often assess their own interests before considering others in the supply chain. For example, if one of Toro's products is made available in Home Depot, it is likely to have a lower retail price (due to bulk buying) than the same or similar product at a local tractor supply company. This situation is clearly not in the best interests of the local firm, so it will strive to put its interests ahead of others in the supply chain. Self-interest-seeking behavior is natural in both business and everyday life.

Second, the recognition and acceptance of mutual interdependence within the supply chain goes against our natural self-interest-seeking tendencies. To work toward mutual interdependence means that each firm must give up some measure of control over its goals, its activities, and even its own destiny. In our Toro example, local tractor supply companies understand that they must service Toro equipment—no matter where it was purchased—if they are to remain a certified service facility. For these local firms, putting the needs of the supply chain ahead of their own needs is likely to create tension and conflict as firms collaborate and move toward the creation of the extended enterprise.

Conflict also arises in a supply chain because each firm possesses different resources, skills, and advantages. Thus, each firm will exhibit a different degree of authority or power in managing or controlling the activities within the supply chain. Power can be defined as the influence one channel member has over others in the supply chain. Powerful channel members have the ability to get other firms to do things they otherwise would not do. Depending on how the channel member uses its influence, power can create considerable conflict, or it can make the entire supply chain operate more smoothly and effectively. There are five basic sources of power in a supply chain:[10]

- **Legitimate Power**   This power source is based on the firm's position in the supply chain. Historically, manufacturers have held most of the legitimate power, but this power balance shifted to retailers in the 1990s. In today's economy, retailers still wield a great deal of power. However, the only channel member that can now claim legitimate power with any consistency is the final customer.

- **Reward Power**   The ability to help other parties reach their goals and objectives is the crux of reward power. Rewards may come in terms of higher volume sales, sales with more favorable margins, or both. Individual salespeople at the buyer end of the channel may be rewarded with cash payments, merchandise, or vacations to gain more favorable presentation of a manufacturer's or wholesaler's products. Consumers can be rewarded with free goods or services based upon their purchases of a company's products.

- **Coercive Power**   In contrast to reward power, coercive power is the ability to take positive outcomes away from other channel members, or the ability to inflict punishment on other channel members. Legislative and judicial actions have limited coercive power, but it does occur in subtle forms. For example, a manufacturer may slow down deliveries or postpone the availability of some portions of a product line to a wholesaler or retailer (see *Beyond the Pages 9.3* for an example). Likewise, a retailer can decide not to carry a product, not to promote a product, or to give a product unfavorable placement on its shelves.

- **Information Power**   Having and sharing knowledge is the root of information power. Such knowledge makes channel members more effective and efficient.

Information power may stem from knowledge concerning sales forecasts, market trends, competitive intelligence, product uses and usage rates, or other critical pieces of information. In many supply chains, retailers hold the most information power because their close proximity to customers gives them access to data and information that is difficult to obtain from other sources.

- **Referent Power**   Referent power has its basis in personal relationships and the fact that one party likes another party. It has long been said that buyers like to do business with salespeople they enjoy being around. This is still true, but increasingly, referent power has its roots in firms wanting to associate with other firms, as opposed to individual one-on-one relationships. Similar cultures, values, and even information systems can lead to the development of referent power.

The sources of power or influence change as a supply chain moves toward integration and collaboration. Traditional marketing channels have made heavy use of legitimate, reward, and coercive power sources. The use of these types of power is consistent with the high level of conflict that exists in such channels. Firms want to sell a product for as much as possible, provide as few additional services as it can get away with, obtain payment in advance, and deliver the product at its own convenience. By contrast, buyers want to purchase a product for as little as possible, get a large number of additional services both now and in the future, pay months or even years later with no interest, and get immediate delivery. Collaborative supply chains focus on win–win outcomes and work to get past these natural sources of confrontation. Here, reward and referent power become used most frequently, with the most important source of influence being information. Successfully confronting the problems that naturally materialize in a supply chain depends on the effective development, communication, and utilization of information.

Collaborative Supply Chains

Exhibit 9.4 depicts the key factors to successful collaboration in a supply chain. Trust appears at the center of this diagram; it is the glue that holds supply chain relationships together.[11] Without trust, firms will be unwilling to give up control over supply chain activities, unable to put the needs of the supply chain ahead of their own, and prompted to engage in selfish behaviors that will lead to increased conflict and frustration. The presence of trust, however, allows firms to fully cooperate to develop interdependencies that will lead to mutual benefits over the long term. Other keys to supply chain collaboration include top management commitment and investment, clearly stated goals and objectives, complete sharing of data and information, and increased quantity and quality of communication among firms. Finally, firms must also be willing to share in the cost savings realized from collaboration and tighter integration of supply chain activities.[12]

One of the best and most widespread collaborative supply chain initiatives is category management, an ongoing and highly successful initiative by innovative members of food product distribution channels. Category management came into being because a group of consumer food product manufacturers and leading

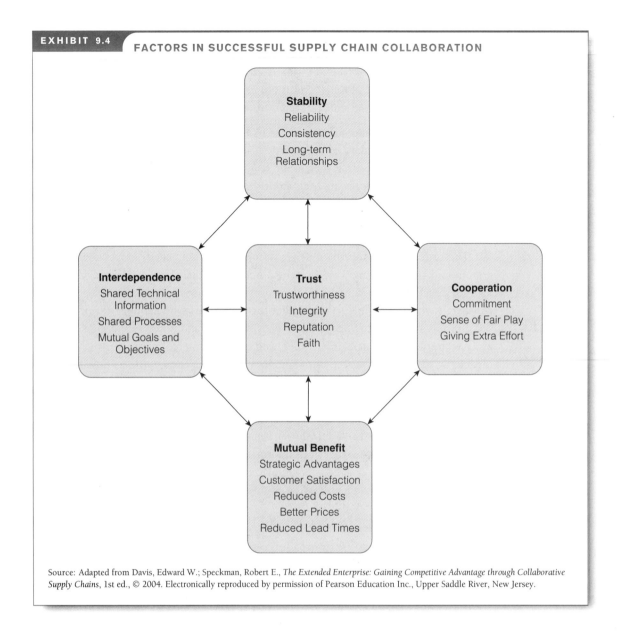

EXHIBIT 9.4   FACTORS IN SUCCESSFUL SUPPLY CHAIN COLLABORATION

Stability
Reliability
Consistency
Long-term
Relationships

Interdependence
Shared Technical
Information
Shared Processes
Mutual Goals and
Objectives

Trust
Trustworthiness
Integrity
Reputation
Faith

Cooperation
Commitment
Sense of Fair Play
Giving Extra Effort

Mutual Benefit
Strategic Advantages
Customer Satisfaction
Reduced Costs
Better Prices
Reduced Lead Times

Source: Adapted from Davis, Edward W.; Speckman, Robert E., *The Extended Enterprise: Gaining Competitive Advantage through Collaborative Supply Chains*, 1st ed., © 2004. Electronically reproduced by permission of Pearson Education Inc., Upper Saddle River, New Jersey.

supermarket chains were dissatisfied with the traditional, highly competitive channel relationships that existed among their firms. Through their Joint Industry Project on Efficient Consumer Response (ECR), the group developed the concept of category management and defined it as "a supplier process of managing categories (of products) as strategic business units, producing enhanced business results by focusing on delivering continuously enhanced consumer value."[13] Through their combined efforts, the industry task force determined that category management must be[14]

- **Customer Driven**   Manufacturers and wholesalers should make all decisions with a concern for the challenges faced by retailers in the channel.

- **Strategically Driven**   The relationship between the parties should be driven by a strategic plan to advance the relationship, and through this, advance the outcomes for the parties involved.

- **Multifunctional**   Contact points should go beyond marketing and buying to include areas such as finance, logistics, quality control, and facilities management, in addition to the senior management teams of all firms.

- **Financially Based**   Solid financial targets should be set and met in terms of profitability and the management of both hard and soft costs.

- **Systems Dependent**   Systems (operational and technical) should be designed and put in place to support the activities of the relationship.

- **Focused on Immediate Consumer Response**   Successful channel members implementing category management should be able to give consumers what they want more rapidly than firms operating within traditional marketing channels.

Exhibit 9.5 outlines six components of an ongoing category management process that must be jointly managed by the category manager (retail buyer or merchandising manager) and the channel consultant (manufacturer's or wholesaler's account manager). Each of the components in the process depends on the quality, planning, and performance of the other five components. Retailers such as Barnes & Noble, Costco, and Walmart are leaders in establishing and coordinating category management with their suppliers. In recent years, firms outside the consumer products industries have

EXHIBIT 9.5	MAJOR COMPONENTS OF CATEGORY MANAGEMENT
Component	**Description**
Strategy	This step involves an informed choice by the retailer to move from managing brands or SKUs (stockkeeping units) to managing groups of products that satisfy similar consumer needs. Such groups are known as categories (e.g., deli meats, fresh cut flowers, appearance chemicals, home cleaning products).
The Business Process	An eight-step process that includes: (1) defining categories and subcategories, (2) determining each category's role in meeting retailer goals and objectives, (3) assessing the present performance of each category, (4) setting scorecard targets for measuring performance, (5) jointly developing strategies for achieving scorecard targets, (6) selecting specific tactics to implement selected strategies, (7) implementing plans with calendars and assigned responsibilities, and (8) appraising categories and refining plans.
Scorecard	An ongoing process of setting targets and establishing the means to monitor and improve performance in targeted areas (e.g., profit per square foot of category space, or average dollars purchased per consumer in each category).
Organization Capabilities	Changes in the design and structure of organizations; the required skill bases of the parties to the relationship; and the employee performance measurement, reward, and recognition systems.
Information Technology	Addresses the acquisition, analysis, and movement of information within and between the organizations involved. It must involve the supplier's marketing information system (MIS), the retailer's MIS, and external syndicated data suppliers (e.g., Nielsen).
Collaborative Trading Partners	The methods used to structure and conduct interactions between members of both the supplier and retailer organizations in a win-win fashion with the open and honest exchange of information for the purpose of identifying and solving problems.

Source: *Category Management Report* © 1995 by the Joint Industry Project on Efficient Consumer Response.

begun to adopt components of the ECR category management process to enhance their own supply chain relationships.

Trends in Marketing Channels

In addition to the trends associated with channel integration discussed to this point in the chapter, a number of other trends have shaped the structure of marketing channels and the ways that supply chains function. In this section, we examine a number of these trends.

The Growth of Electronic Commerce

Significant advancements in information processing and digital communication have created new methods for placing and filling orders for both business buyers and consumers. The growth of the Internet and electronic commerce is the most obvious sign of these changes. As business buyers and consumers more fully embrace these technologies, the growth of e-commerce is expected to flourish. For example, e-commerce accounted for fewer than 20 percent of transactions in the manufacturing sector in 2002. Today, that number is over 35 percent. In the wholesaling sector, e-commerce accounts for roughly 21 percent of all transactions. Conversely, e-commerce accounts for only 3.2 percent of all retail transactions, and only 1.8 percent of transactions in service-based industries. Still, e-commerce in these consumer markets is growing at roughly 12 to 14 percent per year. These statistics show that electronic commerce still has a great deal of room to grow, especially in consumer markets.[15]

Another promising technology is radio frequency identification (RFID), which involves the use of tiny computer chips with radio transmission capability that can be attached to a product or its packaging. The radio signals reflected from the chip can be used to track inventory levels and product spoilage, or prevent theft. They can also be used for instantaneous checkout of an entire shopping cart of items. As addressed in *Beyond the Pages 9.2*, large retailers and packaged goods manufacturers have funded research to develop RFID, which will eventually replace bar codes as a means to manage inventory.[16] Innovations in web-based communication technologies, such as global positioning, are also taking rail and truck equipment to a new level of service in supply chain integration.

Consumer demands for convenience, as well as increased pressures on channel members to cut distribution expenses, have been the primary sparks for the growth in technologies like e-commerce and RFID. Faster, better, *and* cheaper is the demand coming from both business buyers and consumers, with a thunderous voice. As the ownership of personal computers and Internet access has literally exploded, the Internet has become a critical channel component for both manufacturers and retailers to consider. Even when the purchase is not made online, the Internet is increasingly viewed as an important source of information in the decision-making process for both consumers and business buyers.

WALMART'S DISTRIBUTION TECHNOLOGY[17]

Walmart Stores Inc.—the world's largest corporation—is possibly the most controversial business in America. With sales over $374.5 billion in 2008 and approximately 2 million employees worldwide (of these, 1.4 million are U.S. employees) managing stakeholder relationships is a major challenge. The Walmart that saves the average family an estimated $2,300 per year has its critics. Walmart claims that it is committed to improving the standard of living for its customers throughout the world. Their key strategy is a broad assortment of quality merchandise and services at everyday low prices (EDLP) while fostering a culture that claims to reward and embrace mutual respect, integrity, and diversity. Walmart uses the data it collects about customers as well as radio frequency identification (RFID) technology throughout its distribution system to maintain its competitive advantage and low costs.

Walmart is not only the world's largest retailer, it also operates the world's largest data warehouse, an organization-wide data collection and storage system that gathers data from all of the firm's critical operating systems as well as from selected external data sources. Walmart's data warehouse contains more than 1,000 terabytes (or 1 petabyte) of data with sales information on every item it sells (roughly 800 million transactions across 30 million customers every day).

Walmart collects reams of data about products and customers primarily from checkout scanners at its Walmart discount and Sam's Club membership stores. Clerks and managers may also use wireless handheld units to gather additional inventory data. The company stores the detailed data and classifies them into categories such as product, individual store, or region. The system also serves as a basis for the Retail Link decision-support system between Walmart and its suppliers. Retail Link permits some vendors, like Kraft, to access data about how well their products are selling at Walmart stores.

The mountain of data Walmart collects helps boost efficiency dramatically by matching product supplies to demand. This information, for example, helped the firm determine to stock not only flashlights but also extra strawberry Pop-Tarts prior to a hurricane strike on the coast. (It seems that Pop-Tart sales increase as much as seven times their normal rate ahead of a hurricane.) The data may also help the company track supplier performance, set ideal prices, and even determine how many cashiers to schedule at a certain store on a certain day. Most importantly, it helps the retailer avoid carrying too much inventory or not having enough to satisfy demand.

Technology is a driving force in operational efficiency that lowers costs for Walmart. The merchandise-tracking system uses RFID to ensure that a product can be tracked from the time it leaves the supplier's warehouse to the time it enters and leaves a Walmart store. Walmart began the move to RFID in 2004 by insisting that its top 100 suppliers adopt RFID technology. The cost to suppliers was much larger than the cost to Walmart because suppliers needed to continually buy the RFID tags, whereas Walmart only needed a system to read the tags. The cost to adopt and implement RFID technology has been estimated to be roughly $9 million per supplier. To ensure compliance, Walmart threatened to impose penalties of $2 to $3 per pallet for goods arriving at distribution centers without RFID tags (the company later reduced the fines to $0.12 per pallet). Smaller Walmart suppliers also have to adopt RFID, but they have a longer lead time to comply.

RFID helps Walmart keep its shelves stocked and curbs the loss of retail products as they travel through the supply chain. RFID at Walmart has directly resulted in a 16 percent reduction in stockouts and a 67 percent drop in replenishment times. As customers go through checkout, the RFID system swiftly combines point-of-sale data on their purchases, with RFID-generated data on what is available in the stockroom to produce pick lists that are automatically created in real time. It also ensures that suppliers are notified when products are sold and can ensure that enough of a product is always at a particular store. This strategy also results in time and labor savings because Walmart associates no longer need to scan shelves to determine what is out of stock; nor do they have to scan cartons and cases arriving at the stockroom. The scanners tag incoming pallets and translate the data into supply chain management database forecasting models to address out-of-stock items and reduce stocking/restocking mix-ups.

Shifting Power in the Channel

In days gone by, manufacturers had all the power in the channel of distribution. The scarcity and popularity of many products allowed manufacturers to dictate strategy throughout the supply chain. Further, manufacturers were the best source of information about sales, product trends, and customer preferences. Wholesalers and retailers, who lacked sophisticated inventory management systems at the time, had to rely upon manufacturers for this information. These conditions still exist in many business markets where manufacturers are the chief supply chain strategists. In consumer markets, however, the power of manufacturers eroded as UPC barcode technology, point-of-sale systems, and inventory management systems converged to give retailers control over information at the point of sale.

Today, discount mass merchandise retailers—like Walmart, Costco, and Target—and category-focused retailers (also known as category killers)—such as Best Buy, Barnes & Noble, Office Depot, and AutoZone—hold the power in most consumer channels. These large retailers have gained power in their respective channels for several reasons. First, the sheer size and buying power of these firms allows them to demand price concessions from manufacturers. Second, these firms perform their own wholesaling functions; therefore, they receive trade discounts traditionally reserved for true wholesalers. Third, their control over retail shelf space allows them to dictate when and where new products will be introduced. Manufacturers typically must pay hefty fees, called *slotting allowances*, just to get a single product placed on store shelves. Finally, their closeness to millions of customers allows these large retailers to gather valuable information at the point of sale. As mentioned previously, control over information is a valuable commodity and a source of power in virtually all supply chains.

Outsourcing Channel Functions

Outsourcing—shifting work activities to businesses outside the firm—is a rapidly growing trend across many different industries and supply chains.[18] In the past, outsourcing was used primarily as a way of cutting expenses associated with labor, transportation, or other overhead costs. Today, though cutting expenses is still a main factor, the desire of many firms to focus on core competencies drives outsourcing. By outsourcing noncore activities, firms can improve their focus on what they do best, free resources for other purposes, and enhance product differentiation—all of which lead to greater opportunities to develop and maintain competitive advantages. The hourly labor costs in countries such as China, India, and Mexico are far less than in the United States or Europe. These developing countries have improved their manufacturing capabilities, infrastructure, and technical and business skills, making them more attractive regions for global sourcing.

On the other hand, the costs and risks of outsourcing halfway around the world must be taken into consideration. Firms that outsource give up a measure of control over key factors such as data security and the quality of service delivered to customers. To combat these issues, many firms have shifted from outsourcing to offshoring of their own activities. These companies set up their own offshore operations (called captives) to handle tasks such as IT, business processing, or customer service in foreign countries where wage rates are lower. Barclays Bank, for example, uses captives to ensure better control and security over sensitive data and information.[19]

As illustrated in Exhibit 9.6, information technology is the primary activity outsourced today. Currently, however, firms are shifting supporting processes to outside businesses. These supporting processes include administrative activities, distribution, human resources, financial analysis, call centers, and even sales and marketing. When a firm has significant needs and insufficient in-house expertise, the importance of outsourcing will increase. For example, an entire industry known as 3PLs (third-party logistics providers) has emerged in the United States and Europe as retailers look toward outside expertise as a way to reduce costs and make their products more readily available. In fact, roughly 77 percent of Fortune 500 firms use 3PLs to manage inventories and handle the physical movement of products in the supply chain to ensure that items are in the right amounts and in the right places when needed.[20] The next-day delivery services offered by FedEx, UPS, and DHL have been a boon to companies practicing just-in-time inventory methods, but some companies are looking

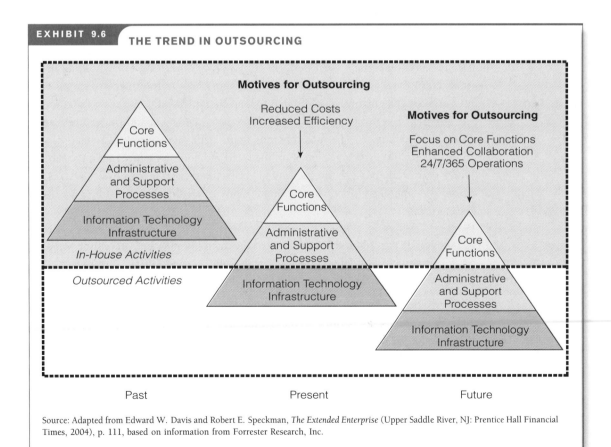

EXHIBIT 9.6 **THE TREND IN OUTSOURCING**

Source: Adapted from Edward W. Davis and Robert E. Speckman, *The Extended Enterprise* (Upper Saddle River, NJ: Prentice Hall Financial Times, 2004), p. 111, based on information from Forrester Research, Inc.

for even faster delivery for an extra edge. San Francisco-based Ensenda has designed a same-day delivery system that is attracting the attention of shippers who are looking for new ways to cut costs and streamline their delivery fleets. Many of these firms outsource the production of some component parts and need to obtain these supplies just in time for production. To give them what they need, Ensenda developed a business model based on a system of local delivery networks: The company contracts with small, regionally based couriers to provide same-day delivery in markets where there is sufficient demand for such services. Some of its largest customers are Home Depot, Best Buy, Sony, and Crate and Barrel.[21]

The Growth of Direct Distribution and Nonstore Retailing

Used to distribute a wide range of products, the traditional marketing channel of manufacturer to wholesaler to retailer is alive and well today. However, customers' demands for lower prices and greater convenience have put pressure on all channel intermediaries to justify their existence. Every time a different intermediary handles a product, the cost to the final customer increases. This places a great deal of downward pressure on profit margins as firms struggle to balance their need for profit with the need to offer customers good value and fair prices. When margins get squeezed, there just may not be enough to go around for everyone in a channel. Under such circumstances, the channel must evolve into a more direct form or risk its very survival. Keep in mind, however, that channel evolution does not replace or alter the basic functions that all channels must perform (e.g., sorting, breaking bulk, holding inventory, etc.). Even after the elimination of certain channel intermediaries, other firms—or even the customer—will have to step in and fulfill these basic functions.

A number of nontraditional channels have emerged to expand opportunities for more direct distribution. The most obvious is the explosive growth of nonstore retailing. The fastest growing segment of the retail industry, nonstore retailing refers to activities that occur outside the traditional "bricks-and-mortar" of physical stores. In addition to e-commerce channels, there are many other types of nonstore channels, including these:

- **Catalog and Direct Marketing**   Some of the most popular and successful nonstore merchants, including Lands' End, J. Crew, Cabela's, and GEICO Insurance, are catalog and direct marketers.

- **Direct Selling**   These merchants sell through face-to-face contact with sales associates. Examples include Avon, Tupperware, Discovery Toys, and Pampered Chef. Avon is far and away the largest, with over $10 billion in sales each year.

- **Home Shopping Networks**   Networks like QVC and the Home Shopping Network serve millions of satisfied customers every week.

- **Vending**   The advantage of vending is 24/7/365 product availability in virtually any location. Though soft drinks account for over 50 percent of vending sales, products such as flowers, toothpaste, movies, and fishing bait can now be purchased via vending machines.

- **Direct Response Advertising**   Many companies sell music, toy, and book products via television commercials and 1-800 phone numbers. One of the largest is Time Life, which sells millions of books, CDs, and DVDs each year. Infomercials, a cross between an advertisement, a news program, and a documentary, are also popular programs for products such as exercise equipment and kitchen appliances.

An example of these nontraditional distribution approaches is described in *Beyond the Pages 9.3*, where Redbox uses vending machines to challenge its competitors in the movie distribution industry. Distribution activities have also changed as manufacturers expand their direct offerings to customers. In some cases, manufacturers have increased direct distribution by opening their own retail outlets. Firms that have done this for some time include Nike (Nike Town stores), Dell, Apple, and Bass Pro Shops; as well as a host of manufacturers that operate stores in factory outlet centers (e.g., Mikasa, Carter's, Black and Decker, Bose, Zales).

The Growth of Dual Distribution

Supply chain strategy often requires multiple channels to reach various markets. The use of multiple channels may arise out of necessity in order to meet customer needs or by design. Multiple channels enable a manufacturer to offer two or more lines of the same merchandise through two or more means, thus increasing sales coverage. For example, Hallmark makes extensive use of dual distribution. The company sells its highly respected Hallmark line of greeting cards primarily through selective distribution at Hallmark stores. They make their Ambassador and Shoebox Greetings card lines available on an intensive basis through supermarkets, drugstores, and discount retailers. In addition, Hallmark offers both cards and e-cards online.

The use of dual distribution is a strategic decision that manufacturers must consider very carefully. Dual distribution requires considerable resources to implement as it spreads time, effort, and money across two or more channels. Dual distribution also increases the risk of disintermediation, where customers deal directly with manufacturers and bypass traditional channel intermediaries. Consequently, the use of dual channels can create conflict between the manufacturer and its supply chain members. This is particularly true when target market segments do not have clear definitions or distinctions for each channel. For example, the wall covering industry has seen great conflict between traditional decorating centers, 1-800 telephone resellers, and online merchants. Traditional decorating centers resent doing all of the presale service to help a customer select the appropriate wall covering, only to have that customer buy from a distributor or online vendor who does not have overhead costs associated with sales associates or a physical store. As a result, many decorating centers boycott the products of manufacturers engaged in aggressive dual distribution.

Legal and Ethical Issues in the Supply Chain

Like every other aspect of marketing strategy, distribution and supply chain decisions must be made with an eye toward ethical and legal considerations. Exhibit 9.7

Beyond the Pages 9.3

REDBOX'S MOVIE VENDING SUCCESS STORY[22]

One buck for one night. That's the promise of Redbox, a fledgling DVD rental company that distributes movies from roughly 18,000 kiosks in supermarkets, drugstores, Walmart stores, 7-Eleven stores, and McDonald's around the country. The idea is simple: With the push of a button and the swipe of a credit card, customers can rent a movie from a bright red machine about the size of a refrigerator. Each kiosk holds 700 DVDs with about 150 different movie titles, virtually all of which are six months old or less. Customers pay $1 per day and can return movies to any Redbox kiosk anywhere in the country. Customers can even reserve movies online before visiting a kiosk. Customers can also buy older movies for $7, or can simply keep the newer, rented releases; after 25 days, a customer has paid $25 and the movie is his or hers to keep.

Surprisingly, the idea for Redbox began as a new business venture for McDonald's in 2002. At that time, McDonald's was experimenting with vending machines to sell a variety of different items. The concept was based on research that indicated customers prefer dealing with machines, rather than people, for some transactions (think banking, choosing airline seats, movie tickets at theaters, etc.). After the concept proved to be a success, Redbox was sold to Coinstar—a Bellevue, Washington, company that also operates coin-counting machines and gift card dispensers. Soon after, Coinstar inked deals with Walmart, Kroger, Winn-Dixie, Walgreens, Kangaroo (gas stations), and other national outlets to place Redbox kiosks in high-traffic locations. As it turned out, the timing couldn't have been better. As the recession of 2008 lingered into 2009 and 2010, customers who began to reconsider their $15 per month Netflix plans or $5 DVD rentals from Blockbuster suddenly saw the $1 Redbox rentals as a bargain.

Redbox's sales in 2008 were only $400 million—a figure dwarfed by the $14.5 billion spent on DVD sales in the same year. Nonetheless, Redbox has achieved phenomenal sales growth in a very short time: up 110 percent in the first quarter of 2009 (after achieving 180 percent growth in 2008). This number is startling when compared to the 9

percent decline in DVD sales during 2008 and the 13.5 percent decline in the first quarter of 2009. Despite this success, Redbox's growth has been greeted with trepidation by Hollywood movie studios. Universal Studios and 20th Century Fox, for example, asked distributors to stop supplying Redbox with DVDs until six weeks after their release dates. Redbox, in return, filed suit, claiming abuse of copyright and a violation of antitrust law. For movie studios, the issue boils down to money. When a customer buys a DVD from Walmart, the studio collects $17 per disc. That number drops to $1.50 for a Blockbuster rental, and to $0.60 for a Redbox rental. Needless to say, movie executives are afraid that Redbox will erode demand for higher-priced DVD purchases.

While the issue is being resolved, Redbox has turned to buying DVDs from Walmart and Best Buy in order to stock their kiosks. Although movie studios are powerless to stop Redbox in this action, paying the higher retail cost for DVDs significantly cuts into Redbox's revenue (estimated at $25 per disc). Although some studios fight Redbox, others have decided to work with the company or take a wait-and-see approach. Sony Pictures, for example, signed a five-year deal to supply Redbox with DVDs at reduced prices. However, the agreement requires Redbox to destroy DVDs at the end of their useful rental lives instead of selling them for $7 per copy. Walt Disney Co. has a similar arrangement with Redbox. For the studios, reducing or eliminating the number of previously viewed DVDs in the market is a key issue.

In deciding the fate of Redbox, the movie studios have a fundamental question to answer: Should they supply Redbox with DVDs and promote the company's incredible growth, or should they try to kill it? Redbox contends that customers are more likely to buy DVDs after renting them—not unlike what happens in the music industry. However, instead of waiting on the movie studios to act, Redbox plans to increase the number of kiosks to 27,000 by 2010. In spite of this, Redbox needs a deal with movie studios to reduce the prices it must pay for DVDs and ensure continued profitability.

EXHIBIT 9.7   COMMON EXAMPLES OF SUPPLY CHAIN MISCONDUCT

Source: KPMG Forensic's Integrity Survey 2008–2009 (http://us.kpmg.com/RutUS_prod/Documents/8/IntegritySuvey08_09.pdf)

provides examples of the most common types of misconduct in supply chains. Other examples of ethical issues in supply chain management are discussed in the remaining sections of this chapter.

Dual Distribution

Dual distribution is not necessarily unethical or illegal. However, concerns do arise when a manufacturer uses its own physical or online stores to dominate independent retailers or to drive them out of business. To avoid these issues, manufacturers should not undercut the prices that independent retailers can charge with a reasonable margin. For example, Nike is very careful to protect the retailers who sell its products. Although its Nike Town stores do sell Nike products, the stores are more about brand building than driving sales volume. It is obviously in any firm's best interests to pursue dual distribution in an ethical and legal manner. Those who abuse the strategy may find that they are the only ones who want to retail their products. Because most manufacturers do not want to run a complex retail system, their relationships with retail intermediaries are critical to success.

Exclusive Channel Arrangements

Exclusive channel arrangements benefit a manufacturer by limiting the distribution of its products in one of two ways. First, manufacturers can limit distribution by allowing intermediaries to sell their products in restricted geographic territories. Second, manufacturers can require that wholesalers, brokers, agents, or retailers not carry or represent products from any competing manufacturer. Violations of these exclusive arrangements can cause a manufacturer to cut off supply to the intermediary in question.

Exclusive arrangements give manufacturers control over pricing, distribution, and sales activities. Such arrangements are useful when brand image or quality control are critical to the manufacturer's success. However, not all exclusive channel agreements are legal. There are three tests that determine their validity. First, the arrangement cannot block competitors from 10 percent or more of the overall market. Second, the sales revenue involved must not be so sizable that competition could be disrupted. Finally, the manufacturer cannot be much larger (and therefore more intimidating) than the intermediary. Regulators view exclusive arrangements most favorably when consumers and business buyers have access to similar products from other channels or when the exclusivity of a relationship strengthens the otherwise weak market position of the manufacturer.[23]

Tying Arrangements

These arrangements occur when a firm conditions the availability of one product (the "tying" product) on the purchase of a different product (the "tied" product). In other words, if a firm wants to buy product A, it will have to also buy product B to get it. Tying arrangements, which are considered to be illegal in certain circumstances, can occur at any level in a marketing channel. The legality of tying arrangements depends on several factors. First, the arrangement is more likely to be legal if the tying and tied products are in close relation to each other, required for the proper functioning of the other product, or part of a total package or solution. Franchisors can often successfully argue for tying arrangements when raw materials or components are required for brand image or quality control reasons. Second, the legality of tying depends on the market power of the firm requiring the arrangement. Powerful firms are less likely to be successful in tying because it gives them an unfair advantage. For example, the U.S. Supreme Court found Kodak guilty of an illegal tying arrangement when the firm would only sell replacement copier parts to customers if they agreed not to use independent service and repair firms.[24] Finally, tying arrangements are illegal if they restrain trade or competition in a meaningful way.

Counterfeit Products

Buyers and sellers alike must make reasonable efforts to be aware of a product's origin. Counterfeit products abound today, particularly in the areas of clothing, audio and video products, and computer software. Any product that can be easily copied is vulnerable to counterfeit activities. Some people argue that only manufacturers become injured when consumers purchase counterfeit products. This is clearly mistaken reasoning. For example, the loss of tax revenues has a huge impact on governments, as they can't collect both direct and indirect taxes on the sale of counterfeit products. Likewise, counterfeits leech profits necessary for ongoing product development away from the channel, as well as thousands of jobs at legitimate companies. Customers also feel the impact of counterfeit products, as their quality almost never lives up to the quality of the original. For example, faced with increasing risks associated with counterfeit drugs, the FDA has strongly endorsed the use of RFID to combat the growing problem and to protect American consumers. The FDA's action was prompted by their 2003 discovery of over 150,000 bottles of counterfeit Lipitor (a popular cholesterol drug). The FDA is monitoring the use of RFID but has yet to mandate its use throughout the U.S. pharmaceutical supply chain.[25]

Lessons from Chapter 9

Distribution and supply chain management

- Are among the most important strategic decisions for many marketers.

- Were the forgotten elements of marketing strategy throughout most of the twentieth century.

- Have remained essentially invisible to customers because the processes occur behind the scenes.

- Now rank at the top of the list in achieving a sustainable advantage and true differentiation in the marketplace.

- Can overcome some weaknesses in pricing, products, and promotion. However, a poor distribution strategy will kill a firm's efforts to market a product.

- Are important to providing time, place, and possession utility for consumer and business buyers.

- Are expensive; therefore, distribution strategy must balance the needs of customers with the needs of the firm.

- Consist of two interrelated components: marketing channels and physical distribution.

Marketing channels

- Are organized systems of marketing institutions through which products, resources, information, funds, and/or product ownership flow from the point of production to the final user.

- Depend on logistics strategies to coordinate the flow of information and products among members of the channel to ensure that products are available in the right places, in the right quantities, at the right times, and in a cost-efficient manner.

- Can be considered as supply chains when all members of the channel are connected and integrated.

- Greatly increase contact efficiency by reducing the number of contacts necessary to exchange products.

- Perform a variety of functions: sorting, breaking bulk, maintaining inventories, maintaining convenient locations, and providing services.

- Are increasingly evaluated using two criteria: effectiveness and efficiency.

- Are distinct from supply chains, where the primary concern is the share of the market the entire channel captures.

Marketing channel structures include

- Exclusive distribution, where a firm gives one merchant or outlet the sole right to sell a product within a defined geographic region.

- Selective distribution, where a firm gives several merchants or outlets the right to sell a product in a defined geographic region.

- Intensive distribution, which makes a product available in the maximum number of merchants or outlets in each area to gain as much exposure and as many sales opportunities as possible.

Marketing channel integration

- Is the linchpin of effective supply chain management in today's economy.

- Has as its goal the creation of a seamless network of collaborating suppliers, vendors, buyers, and customers.

- Focuses on connectivity, community, and collaboration to create an extended enterprise that manages value by coordinating the flow of information, goods, and services both upstream and downstream in the supply chain.

- Creates a tenuous balance of competition and collaboration, and teamwork and self-serving behaviors.

- Strives to create value in the supply chain by developing synergies that enhance communication and sales, improve after-sale service, increase the efficiency of product delivery, add product enhancements, or offer solutions rather than individual products.

Conflict in the supply chain

- Stems from each firm attempting to fulfill its mission, goals, objectives, and strategies by putting its own interests ahead of other firms.

- Is natural because the notion of mutual interdependence goes against a firm's natural self-interest-seeking tendencies.

- Can arise because each firm possesses different resources, skills, and advantages.

- Can result as each firm exhibits one of the five different sources of power in the supply chain: legitimate power, reward power, coercive power, information power, and referent power.

Collaborative supply chains

- Are characterized by reward and referent power, with the most important source of influence being information.

- Depend on trust to hold relationships together.

- Can work only if firms will give up some control over supply chain activities, allowing them to fully cooperate to develop interdependencies that will lead to mutual benefits over the long term.

- Share in the cost savings realized from collaboration and tighter integration of supply chain activities.
- Are exemplified by category management, a highly successful initiative by members of food-product distribution channels.

Trends in marketing channels include

- The growth of electronic commerce and the increasing use of radio frequency identification (RFID).
- Shifting power in the channel, where retailers hold most of the power in consumer channels.
- Outsourcing and offshoring of work activities, particularly information technology operations and supporting functions.
- The growth of direct distribution and nonstore retailing. In addition to e-commerce activities, other examples of these nontraditional channels include catalog and direct marketing, direct selling, home shopping networks, vending, and direct response advertising.
- The growth of dual distribution, as firms use multiple channels to reach various markets.

Legal and ethical issues in supply chain management include

- Dual distribution, if a manufacturer uses its own physical or online stores to dominate independent retailers or to drive them out of business.
- Exclusive channel arrangements, if (1) a manufacturer's restrictions block competitors from 10 percent or more of the overall market; (2) the sales revenue involved is sizable enough to disrupt competition; and (3) the manufacturer is much larger and more intimidating than the channel intermediary.
- Tying arrangements, which occur when a firm conditions the availability of one product (the "tying" product) on the purchase of a different product (the "tied" product).
- Counterfeit products, which result in lost profits for legitimate firms, lost tax revenue for governments, and inferior products for customers.

Questions for Discussion

1. What are the major differences you have experienced in buying a product through a traditional retail store, a manufacturer's store, a catalog, and an online merchant? What have some retailers in your area done to justify their ongoing presence in the channel?

2. Describe the characteristics of a product that represents something you would go to great lengths to acquire, thus supporting a manufacturer's use of an exclusive distribution strategy. Why is the service better and the salespeople more knowledgeable at an exclusive distribution location versus an intensive distribution location?

3. Some manufacturers and retailers advertise that customers should buy from them because they "eliminate the middleman." Evaluate this comment in light of the functions that must be performed in a marketing channel. Does a channel with fewer members always deliver products to customers at lower prices? Defend your position.

Exercises

1. Locate a product offered by a manufacturer using a dual distribution approach. Are there differences between the customers targeted by each channel? How do the purchase experiences differ? In the end, why would a customer buy directly from a manufacturer if the prices are higher?

2. Spend some time looking at what is offered for sale on QVC or the Home Shopping Network. Why do you believe these direct marketers are so popular? If you have purchased an item from these merchants, why did you do so? If you haven't made a purchase, why not?

3. Visit RFID Journal (http://www.rfidjournal.com) to learn as much as possible about the growth of radio frequency identification (RFID) as a logistics and supply chain tool. What are the current obstacles to widespread adoption of the technology?

CHAPTER 10

Integrated Marketing Communications

Introduction

Without a doubt, promotion and marketing communications are the most ubiquitous elements of any firm's marketing strategy. This is not surprising because promotional activities are necessary to communicate the features and benefits of a product to the firm's intended target markets. Marketing communications includes conveying and sharing meaning between buyers and sellers, either as individuals and firms, or between individuals and firms. Integrated marketing communications (IMC) refers to the strategic, coordinated use of promotion to create one consistent message across multiple channels to ensure maximum persuasive impact on the firm's current and potential customers. IMC takes a 360-degree view of the customer that considers each and every contact that a customer or potential customer may have in his or her relationship with the firm. The key to IMC is consistency and uniformity of message across all elements of promotion as shown in Exhibit 10.1.

Due to the many advantages associated with IMC, most marketers have adopted integrated marketing as the basis for their communication and promotion strategies.[1] By coordinating all communication "touch points," firms using IMC convey an image of truly knowing and caring about their customers that can translate into long-term customer relationships. Likewise, IMC reduces costs and increases efficiency because it can reduce or eliminate redundancies and waste in the overall promotional program. Many firms have embraced IMC because mass-media advertising has become more expensive and less predictable than in the past. As discussed in *Beyond the Pages 10.1*, marketers are being forced to adopt new marketing strategies as advancing technology and customer preferences are threatening to make traditional forms of promotion obsolete. Many firms are also embracing technology in order to target customers directly through product placement and online promotion. This increased focus on individual customers requires that the overall promotional program be integrated and focused as well.

In this chapter, we examine the role of IMC in marketing strategy. We discuss the strategic use of IMC in informing, persuading, and reminding customers about the firm's products. We also explore the strategic decisions to be made with respect to advertising, public relations, personal selling and sales management, and sales promotion.

Beyond the Pages 10.1

FRAGMENTATION THREATENS TRADITIONAL TV ADVERTISING[2]

The traditional media business is hanging on for the ride of its life. That ride is called fragmentation and it's going to forever change the way both media and advertisers do business. The problem is that consumers' attention is being spread across an increasing array of media and entertainment choices. Those choices include the Internet, targeted cable programming, video-on-demand, TiVo (or digital video recorders), iPods, DVDs, video games, and wireless phones. Today, mass audiences are dwindling fast as consumers spend less time with traditional media such as television, magazines, and newspapers. Consumers now expect to use media whenever and wherever they want, and on any device. They are no longer wed to full-length television programming or to leisurely reading the newspaper. For advertisers, the trend is alarming because it is their traditional bread-and-butter demographic that is fragmenting the most. For example, the number of 18- to 34-year-old men who watch primetime television has been declining steadily since 2000. Those who watch television increasingly use TiVo or other DVR devices to skip advertising. Today, approximately 25 percent of TV households use these devices to skip commercials, a trend likely to double by 2014.

These changes are forcing marketers to adapt by finding newer, more effective ways to reach their target audiences. One way marketers are countering the trend is by linking sales promotion to target markets through strategic integration into related television programming. Company sponsorship of programming can allow a close connection between brand and target market. For example, Bravo's Top Chef has successfully partnered with Toyota, Clorox, Food & Wine magazine, Campbell Soup, Diet Dr. Pepper, Glad, and Quaker. Sponsorship opportunities like these work better than traditional advertising, especially with respect to brand recall. For Toyota, brand recall from the Top Chef sponsorship was 67 percent versus 49 percent for regular cable TV advertising. Other sponsors posted similar results: Glad had a 77 percent brand recall (vs. 73 percent for cable), while Food & Wine also enjoyed 77 percent brand recall (vs. 70 percent for cable).

In addition to outright sponsorship of popular programs, marketers are also making deals with television and cable networks to place their products into actual programs. In-program product placements have been successful in reaching consumers as they are being entertained rather than during the competitive commercial breaks. For example, the NBC hit comedy show 30 Rock has included numerous product placements, including rather obvious placements for Verizon's wireless services and Snapple's beverages. Reality programming in particular has been a natural fit for product placement because of the close interchange between the participants and the products (e.g. Sears and Extreme Makeover: Home Edition; Levi's, Burger King, Marquis Jet, and Dove in The Apprentice; Coca Cola and America Idol).

Media companies themselves have also been forced to adapt, most notably by fragmenting their content and business models to match their fragmented audiences. One way that companies have addressed the problem is by making their content available on multiple platforms. CBS, for example, first experimented with its broadcast of the 2008 NCAA Basketball Tournament by broadcasting live action on the Internet. The service, called March Madness on Demand, attracted roughly 5 million different viewers (via computers and wireless phones) and over $30 million in advertising revenue during the 2009 tournament. CBS and other major networks also distribute their most popular programming on television, online, and via DVD at the completion of a season of episodes. NBC also partners with Hulu to make its programming available via its web-based service.

As these and other examples illustrate, the key to meeting the demands of fragmented audiences is to disaggregate content and make it available á la carte style. Consumers can purchase individual songs via iTunes, Rhapsody, or Amazon. They can access digital RSS (really simple syndication) feeds of newspaper and magazine content to read only parts of a publication. Episodes of popular television shows, such as ABC's Desperate Housewives, are available in high definition on iTunes for $2.99 per episode. Cable giant Comcast now offers more than 4,000 on-demand features. Netflix allows its subscribers to watch select programming on demand via the Roku box and other Netflix-enabled televisions and Blu-ray players.

Despite the challenges of reaching fragmented audiences, the trend actually has a big side benefit. The science behind traditional broadcast television ratings and audience measurement has always been uncertain. With on-demand services, advertisers are able to precisely measure audience characteristics whether the content is delivered via the Internet, cable, or wireless devices. This one-two punch of profits and precise measurement may mark the death of the traditional 30-second primetime television spot.

EXHIBIT 10.1   **COMPONENTS OF IMC STRATEGY**

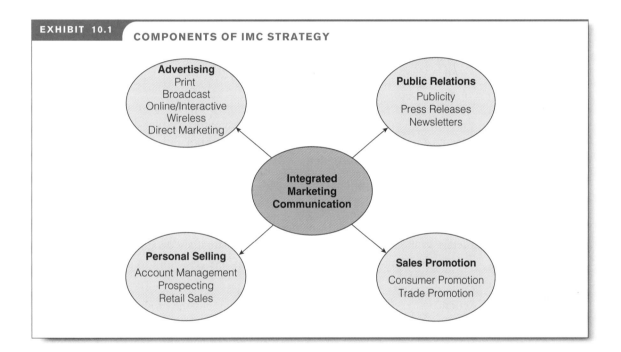

Strategic Issues in Integrated Marketing Communications

When selecting elements to include in the IMC program, it is important to take a holistic perspective that coordinates not only all promotional elements but also the IMC program with the rest of the marketing program (product, price, and supply chain strategy). Taking this approach allows a firm to communicate a consistent message to target customers from every possible angle, thereby maximizing the total impact on those customers. For example, if the advertising campaign stresses quality, the sales force talks about low price, the supply chain pushes intensive distribution, and the website stresses product innovation, then what is the customer to believe? Not readily seeing that a product can deliver all these benefits, the customer is likely to become confused and go to a competitor with a more consistent message.

All too frequently, firms rush to launch an intensive IMC campaign that has no clear promotional objectives. The vast majority of promotion activities do not create

Target customers are spending more time online and less time with traditional media such as television, radio, and newspapers.

results in the short term, so firms must focus on long-term promotional objectives and have the patience to continue the program long enough to gauge true success. It takes a great deal of time, effort, and resources to build a solid market position. Promotion based on creativity alone, unlinked to the rest of the marketing strategy, can waste limited and valuable marketing resources.

Ultimately, the goals and objectives of any promotional campaign culminate in the purchase of goods or services by the target market. The classic model for outlining promotional goals and achieving this ultimate outcome is the AIDA model—attention, interest, desire, and action:

- **Attention**   Firms cannot sell products if the members of the target market do not know they exist. As a result, the first major goal of any promotional campaign is to attract the attention of potential customers.

- **Interest**   Attracting attention seldom sells products. Therefore, the firm must spark interest in the product by demonstrating its features, uses, and benefits.

- **Desire**   To be successful, firms must move potential customers beyond mere interest in the product. Good promotion will stimulate desire by convincing potential customers of the product's superiority and its ability to satisfy specific needs.

- **Action**   After convincing potential customers to buy the product, promotion must then push them toward the actual purchase.

The role and importance of specific promotional elements vary across the steps in the AIDA model. Mass-communication elements, such as advertising and public relations, tend to be used more heavily to stimulate awareness and interest due to their efficiency in reaching large numbers of potential customers. For example, a mix of Super Bowl ads, social and digital media, and event marketing were utilized to launch Gatorade's G2, a low-calorie version of the popular Gatorade sports drink. Pulling in sales of approximately $160 million in its first year, G2 succeeded, whereas 75 percent of new products fail to earn even $7.5 million in their first year.[3]

Along with advertising, sales promotion activities, such as product samples or demonstrations, are vital to stimulating interest in the product. The enhanced communication effectiveness of personal selling makes it ideally suited to moving potential customers through internal desire and into action. Other sales promotion activities, such as product displays, coupons, and trial-size packaging, are well suited to pushing customers toward the final act of making a purchase.

Alongside the issue of promotional goals and objectives, the firm must also consider its promotional goals with respect to the supply chain. In essence, the firm must decide whether it will use a pull strategy, a push strategy, or some combination of the two. When firms use a pull strategy, they focus their promotional efforts toward stimulating demand among final customers, who then exert pressure on the supply chain to carry the product. The coordinated use of heavy advertising, public relations, and consumer sales promotion has the effect of pulling products through the supply chain, hence its name. In a push strategy, promotional efforts focus on members of the supply chain, such as wholesalers and retailers, to motivate them to spend extra time and effort on selling the product. This strategy relies heavily on personal selling and trade sales promotion to push products through the supply chain toward final customers.

The role and importance of specific promotional elements also vary depending on the nature of the product. Industrial products, such as heavy equipment, rely more heavily on personal selling; consumer products require greater use of advertising, sales promotion, and public relations. This variability also occurs across stages in a product's life cycle, as shown in Exhibit 10.2. Early in a product's life cycle, even before its introduction, the heavy expenditures on promotional activities are often a significant drain on the firm's resources. At this stage, it is important to consider these expenditures as investments for the long term because the true impact of the promotional program may not be felt for some time. By the time a product has moved into the maturity phase of its life cycle, the firm can reduce promotional expenditures somewhat, thereby enjoying lower costs and higher profits.

Coordinating promotional elements within the context of the entire marketing program requires a complete understanding of the role, function, and benefits of each element. The advantages and disadvantages of each element must be carefully balanced against the promotional budget and the firm's IMC goals and objectives. To ensure a constant and synergistic message to targeted customers, the firm must ultimately decide how to weigh each promotional element in the overall IMC strategy. In the remainder of this chapter, we discuss the important issues associated with advertising, public relations, personal selling, and sales promotion.

EXHIBIT 10.2	PROMOTIONAL STRATEGY OVER THE PRODUCT LIFE CYCLE
Introduction	Promotion depends on heavy advertising and public relations to build brand awareness and educate customers on the product's benefits. Personal selling ensures distribution coverage and supply chain cooperation. Consumer sales promotion stimulates product trial, while trade sales promotion facilitates or expedites distribution activities, especially in obtaining favorable shelf space or product display.
Growth	To sustain growth, firms spend heavily on advertising and public relations to build and maintain brand loyalty. Personal selling maintains distribution and supply chain cooperation. Sales promotion activities decline in importance.
Maturity	A firm's use of advertising shifts to emphasize reminding customers of the firm's products. Sales promotion efforts strongly encourage brand switching for both consumers and the trade. Personal selling remains important to ensure supply chain support and distribution coverage.
Decline	Firms begin to drastically reduce their advertising and public relations efforts in an attempt to reduce expenses. Sales promotion and personal selling drop to levels that are just sufficient enough to maintain product support.

Advertising

Advertising is a key component of promotion and is usually one of the most visible elements of an integrated marketing communications program. Advertising is paid, nonpersonal communication transmitted through media such as television, radio, magazines, newspapers, direct mail, outdoor displays, the Internet, and mobile devices. Exhibit 10.3 outlines the changing trends in national media advertising. Note that Internet advertising is the fastest-growing medium, while traditional media such as newspapers, radio, and magazines are struggling with meaningful declines in ad revenues. This spending pattern follows trends in media usage, as consumers are spending more time online and less time with traditional media. For example, from 1993 to today, the percentage of people stating that they listened to the radio yesterday has declined from 47 to 35 percent. For newspapers, the decline is a more dramatic 58 percent in 1993 to 34 percent today. Similarly, the number of people watching nightly network news has dropped from 60 to 29 percent.[4]

Because advertising is so flexible, it can be used to reach an extremely large target audience or a very small, precisely defined market segment. For example, websites and magazines often focus on narrow market segments such as organic gardening, snow skiing, or women's health. One such website is MensHealth.com, which provides information and sells products aimed at men's issues and men's lives. Advertising targeted to market segments such as African Americans, gays, Hispanics, and Asian Americans has been an accelerating trend among advertisers over the last decade as the buying power of minorities continues to rise. For example, Hispanics wield nearly $951 billion in buying power—a number expected to increase to $1.4 trillion by 2013.[5]

Regardless of the medium used, targeting potential customers by coordinating the message with their lifestyles is an important strategic consideration. A recent example

EXHIBIT 10.3 SPENDING ON NATIONAL ADVERTISING		
Advertising Media	2008 National Ad Spending (in billions)	Percent Change
Four TV Networks	$17.2	+ 3.5
Spot TV	9.8	− 3.0
Cable TV	21.4	+ 4.0
Syndication TV	3.6	+ 7.0
Radio	3.8	− 10.0
Magazines	12.7	− 6.0
Newspapers	5.9	− 10.0
Direct Mail	59.6	− 1.0
Yellow Pages	2.1	− 2.0
Internet	11.4	+ 8.0
Other Media	37.1	+ 0.4

Source: *Bob Coen's Insider's Report*, Universal McCann (http://www.mccann.com/news/pdfs/Insiders12_2008.pdf), December 2008.

© Courtesy of Univision.

Spanish-language network Univision is one of the fastest-growing media companies in the United States.

of this trend is the increased effort of marketers to reach out to the growing Hispanic community by using the Spanish language in marketing campaigns. The California Milk Processor Board, for example, has been targeting Latinos with Spanish-language campaigns designed to resonate among the diverse Hispanic market, which includes Mexican-Americans, Cuban-Americans, Puerto Ricans, Dominicans, Salvadorans, and more Hispanic subcultures. The industry group recently moved away from its long-running campaign, "Familia, Amor y Leche" ("Family, Love, and Milk") to a more dynamic campaign themed "Toma Leche" ("Drink Milk") to promote the health benefits to younger Latinos.[6]

Advertising can be a cost-efficient element of an IMC program when used to reach a large number of people via television, magazines, outdoor displays, or online ads. For example, *Time* magazine has a guaranteed audience of 19.5 million, making the cost to reach 1,000 subscribers (or CPM—an industry cost benchmark) about $83 for a four-color, full-page ad.[7] The cost of a 30-second slot during the 2009 Super Bowl was $3 million or a CPM of over $30—the highest ever and a 600 percent increase over the 1967 Super Bowl.[8] Prices like these do not mean that advertisers must always spend a fortune on advertisements to be effective. Although newer advertisers may find it hard to compete with large corporations that can afford to spend millions on promotional campaigns, there is a definite niche for innovative advertising regardless of budget constraints. This fact was emphasized during the 2009 Super Bowl when the winners of the Ad Meter Award were two amateur ad-making brothers who filmed their ad for a mere $2,000. Their ad upstaged 50 advertisements by the nation's top advertising agencies, breaking the winning streak of Anheuser-Busch.[9]

Despite the new opportunities for amateur ad makers, the initial expense for advertising is generally quite high, which is a major drawback of advertising in general. However, online advertising provides an opportunity to reach highly specialized markets at a relatively low cost. The most recent estimates point to continued growth in online ad spending, which amounted to 2009 revenues of $23.4 billion in the United States. As shown in Exhibit 10.4, most online ad revenue comes from search advertising, followed by classifieds and banner ads. Nearly one-fourth of these advertisements were from the retail industry. The use of rich media advertising, including animations and audio/video combinations, will continue to grow as broadband Internet access becomes more widely available both in the home and via mobile connections. As shown in Exhibit 10.5, most of the top Internet advertisers

EXHIBIT 10.4

INTERNET AD REVENUES BY ADVERTISING FORMAT

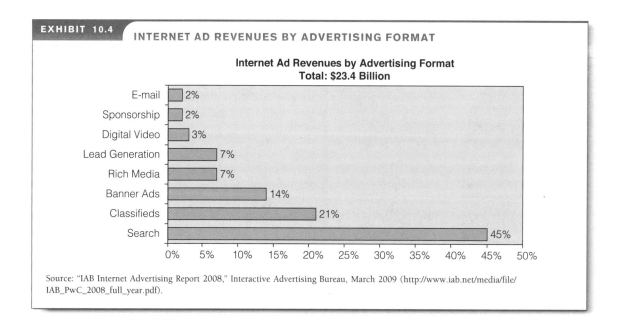

Source: "IAB Internet Advertising Report 2008," Interactive Advertising Bureau, March 2009 (http://www.iab.net/media/file/IAB_PwC_2008_full_year.pdf).

EXHIBIT 10.5

TOP 20 INTERNET ADVERTISERS

Rank	Advertiser	Media Value($000)	Sector
1.	Sprint	54,787.0	Technology
2.	Weight Watchers Online	53,555.2	Health/Fitness
3.	Scottrade (Online)	45,826.1	Financial
4.	FreeScore.com	44,877.6	Financial
5.	Verizon Wireless	38,362.2	Technology
6.	FRS	29,948.3	Health/Fitness
7.	Ad Council	27,588.7	Media
8.	SnorgTees	26,726.6	Retail
9.	US Airways	24,528.5	Travel/Hospitality
10.	AT&T	23,529.6	Technology
11.	Scottrade (Brokerage)	21,367.7	Financial
12.	E-Trade Financial (Consumer)	20,930.0	Financial
13.	StubHub	18,227.6	Retail
14.	TD Ameritrade	17,922.9	Financial
15.	Travelocity	17,722.0	Travel/Hospitality
16.	RadioShack	16,842.5	Retail
17.	Military.com	16,709.4	Media
18.	Dairy Farmers of America	15,159.0	Consumer Packaged Goods
19.	E-Trade Financial (Online)	15,014.2	Financial
20.	Chevrolet Malibu	14,408.5	Automotive

Source: TNS Media Intelligence, "Top 50 Advertisers by Media Value in May 2009," ClickZ, July 7, 2009 (http://www.clickz.com/3634265).

come from the technology and financial services sectors. Although these and other companies enjoy the large number of impressions that can be generated via online advertising, their efforts suffer from the fleeting nature of most online ads. Getting a potential customer to click on a banner ad or look at a message for more than a few seconds can be quite challenging.

Types of Advertising

Advertising promotes all types of products, including goods, services, ideas, issues, people, and anything else that marketers want to communicate to potential customers. Because the total expenditures for advertising may be great, larger firms with greater market shares tend to advertise the most. Whether used in consumer or business markets, there are two basic types of advertising: institutional and product advertising.

Institutional Advertising   Institutional advertising promotes a firm's image, ideas, and culture, with the goal of creating or maintaining an overall corporate image. For example, IBM advertises that it provides infrastructure and solutions for e-business. Although the company offers a wide array of products for e-business, many of IBM's advertisements do not name these products or explain how their infrastructure and solutions actually work. Instead, the purpose of the advertisements is to give potential customers the impression that IBM is a company that understands e-business and that has the ability to solve problems.

Aimed at various stakeholders, including shareholders, consumer advocacy groups, government regulators, or the public at large, institutional advertising can create a positive view of the organization. When a firm promotes a position on a public issue, such as tax policy, international trade regulations, or social issues, it uses a type of institutional advertising called advocacy advertising. This type of advertising often promotes socially approved behavior such as recycling, the responsible use of alcoholic beverages, support for the arts, or the firm's support for cultural diversity. Some firms are well known for their use of advocacy advertising and their long-standing positions on social issues. Ben & Jerry's Ice Cream, for example, is an ardent participant in many social causes such as global warming and social injustice.

Product Advertising   Product advertising promotes the image, features, uses, benefits, and attributes of products. Product advertising comes in many different forms. For example, pioneer advertising stimulates demand for a product category rather than any one specific brand. The goal is to increase customer interest and awareness in the product category in order to increase the size of the entire market—an outcome that benefits all firms in the market. The Dairy Board's famous "Got Milk?" campaign is a good example. Another type of product advertising, competitive advertising, attempts to stimulate demand for a specific brand by promoting the brand's image, features, uses, and benefits. This is the type of advertising that we see most often in the media. Exhibit 10.6 describes the top 25 ad slogans, voted on by 100 marketing, branding, and advertising professionals. As can be seen, some popular slogans are a sentence long, whereas others are just as effective with as little as two words. Typically, the

EXHIBIT 10.6   **TOP 25 BRAND SLOGANS**

1.	Got milk?	California Milk Processor Board	1993
2.	Don't leave home without it.	American Express	1975
3.	Just do it.	Nike	1988
4.	Where's the beef?	Wendy's	1984
5.	You're in good hands with Allstate.	Allstate Insurance	1956
6.	Think different.	Apple	1998
7.	We try harder.	Avis	1962
8.	Tastes great, less filling.	Miller Lite	1974
9.	Melts in your mouth, not in your hands.	M&Ms	1954
10.	Takes a licking and keeps on ticking.	Timex	1956
11.	When it absolutely, positively has to be there overnight.	FedEx	1982
12.	Reach out and touch someone.	AT&T	1979
13.	A diamond is forever.	DeBeers	1948
14.	Finger-lickin' good!	KFC	1952
15.	The uncola.	7-Up	1973
16.	Let your fingers do the walking.	Yellow Pages	1964
17.	There are some things that money can't buy. For everything else there's MasterCard.	MasterCard	1997
18.	What happens here, stays here.	Las Vegas Visitors Bureau	2002
19.	You've come a long way, baby.	Virginia Slims	1968
20.	We bring good things to life.	General Electric	1981
21.	Please don't squeeze the Charmin.	Charmin	1964
22.	Does she or doesn't she?	Clairol	1964
23.	Have it your way.	Burger King	1973
24.	I can't believe I ate the whole thing.	Alka-Seltzer	1966
25.	Come alive! You're in the Pepsi generation.	Pepsi	1964

Source: Derrick Daye and Brad Van Aucken, "The 100 Most Influential U.S. Taglines Since 1948," *Branding Strategy Insider*, November 24, 2007 (http://www.brandingstrategyinsider.com/2007/11/the-100-most-in.html).

most successful slogans and ad campaigns are those that are combined with other promotional elements in an integrated marketing effort. Other types of product advertising include reminder advertising to let customers know that a brand is available and reinforcement advertising to assure current customers that they made the right choice in buying and consuming a certain product. Sam Adams Boston Lager and its "Always a Good Decision" campaign is a good example of reinforcement advertising.

Perhaps the most controversial type of advertising is comparative advertising, which occurs when one firm compares its product with one or more competing products on specific features or benefits. Comparative advertising is common in product categories such as soft drinks, automobiles, computers, and over-the-counter medications. In some cases, this comparison is direct, as in Burger King's "Whopper Virgin" taste test, where the company had people who had never tasted a hamburger before compare a McDonald's Big Mac with the Burger King Whopper. In other cases, the comparison used in the advertisement is indirect or implied. Procter & Gamble uses this tactic when promoting its Mach10 razors as "The Best a Man Can Get." The implied comparison in this case involves all competing razors on the market. Under the provisions of the Trademark Law Revision Act, marketers using comparative advertising must ensure they do not misrepresent the characteristics of competing products. A visit to the Federal Trade Commission website (http://www.ftc.gov) usually provides examples of companies who have crossed the line by misrepresenting their competitors or their products.

Determining the Advertising Budget

The advertising budget, or the total amount of money a firm allocates to advertising activities for a specific time period, is difficult to determine because the effects of advertising are difficult to measure. There are many factors that can determine a firm's decision about the appropriate level to fund advertising activities, including the geographic size of the market, the distribution or density of customers, the types of products advertised, sales volume relative to the competition, and the firm's own historical advertising budget. Usually, the advertising budget for business products is small compared to consumer convenience products such as cigarettes, soft drinks, detergents, and cosmetics. There are several different ways to determine an appropriate advertising budget:

- **Percentage of Sales Approach**   This approach is the most widely used method for determining the advertising budget. The approach is simple, straightforward, and based on what the firm traditionally spends on advertising. The obvious flaw of this approach is its implied assumption that sales create advertising. Also, during periods of declining sales, setting the budget as a percentage of sales may be a mistake because reduced advertising is often not the best strategy.

- **Objectives and Task Approach**   This approach requires that the firm lay out its goals for the advertising campaign and then list the tasks required to accomplish specific advertising objectives. The firm calculates and sums the costs of each task to determine the total budget. The major drawback of this approach is that the level of effort needed to accomplish advertising objectives is difficult to know with certainty.

- **Competitive Matching Approach**   This approach involves firms attempting to match major competitor's advertising expenditures in absolute dollars. Many firms review competitive advertising and compare competitor's expenditures across various media in relation to their own spending levels. This competitive tracking can occur at the national and regional levels and at least can provide a benchmark for comparing advertising resources to market share movements. The problem with competitive matching is that all firms are different, so competitors are likely to have different advertising objectives and different resources to devote to advertising.

- **Arbitrary Approach**   Intuition and personal experience set the advertising budget under this approach. The arbitrary approach can lead to mistakes in budgeting because it is not necessarily scientific, objective, or logical. On the other hand, deciding how much to spend on advertising is not an exact science.

Determining the appropriate advertising budget is an important part of any marketing strategy. Setting the budget too high will obviously result in overspending, waste, and lower profits. However, setting the budget too low may be even worse. Firms that do not spend enough on advertising find it very difficult to stand out in an extremely crowded market for customer attention.

Evaluating Advertising Effectiveness

Evaluating the effectiveness of advertising is one of the most challenging tasks facing marketers. Many of the effects and outcomes of advertising take a long time to develop, especially regarding important outcomes such as enhanced brand image, corporate reputation, and positive product attitudes. The effect of advertising on sales lags in some cases, with the effect occurring long after the campaign has ended. The seemingly unending methods that can be used to evaluate advertising effectiveness further complicate the task of measuring advertising results. Some methods include evaluating the achievement of advertising objectives; assessing the effectiveness of advertising copy, illustrations, and layouts; and evaluating the effectiveness of various media. Effectiveness measures can also look at different market segments and their responses to advertising—including brand image; attitudes toward the advertising, the brand, or the firm; and actual customer purchasing behavior. As discussed in *Beyond the Pages 10.2*, one of the issues facing social media as an advertising medium is the difficulty associated with tracking the effectiveness of social media advertisements and "fan" sites.

Advertising effectiveness can be evaluated before, during, or after the campaign. A pretest attempts to evaluate the potential effectiveness of one or more elements of the advertising program. To pretest advertisements, firms often use a panel of actual or potential buyers who judge one or more aspects of an advertisement. Pretests are founded on the belief that customers are more likely to know what type of advertising will influence them. During an ad campaign, the company typically measures effectiveness by looking at actual customer behavior patterns, such as purchases, responses to toll-free telephone numbers, rate of coupon redemption, page visits to the firm's website, or even personal communications. The firm may record the number of inquiries or communication contacts, and judge advertising effectiveness based on industry norms or the firm's own internal benchmarks. Firms may even peruse blogs for evidence of the effectiveness of their promotional campaigns.

The evaluation of advertising effectiveness after a campaign is a posttest. The nature of the firm's advertising objectives will determine what kind of posttest is most appropriate. For example, if a campaign's objective is to increase brand awareness or create a more favorable attitude toward the firm, then the posttest will measure changes in these variables. Customer surveys, panels, or experiments may be used to evaluate a campaign based on communication objectives. Firms will also use performance outcomes such as sales or market share changes to determine campaign effectiveness.

Unfortunately, the connection between advertising and these types of outcomes is not always clear. The difficulty in linking advertising to sales becomes compounded by

Beyond the Pages 10.2

SOCIAL MEDIA OFFERS BOTH MARKETING OPPORTUNITIES AND CHALLENGES[10]

Many companies are taking advantage of the social media craze by using sites like Facebook and Twitter to market products and collect information on potential customers. Social media provides technology that links and networks consumers as well as friends and family. These websites allow for the exchange of personal information, professional information, and connections related to products and common interests. New forums are emerging that allow consumers to track ordinary aspects of their lives, from a person's daily calorie intake to infant feeding times, and share them with online communities. Consumers hope to use these services to improve their own lives, but some companies are using this information to improve sales. Netflix and Amazon, for example, use personal information to profile customers and recommend new products for them. Because two-thirds of all online users visit social media websites or blogs, marketing on social media websites offers a lucrative opportunity to target a large audience and use consumer information to better profile potential customers.

This fact is not lost on the owners of social media companies. Web services such as Facebook, LinkedIn, YouTube, Twitter, and others allow marketers to make information available to interested groups. Online communities are also becoming powerful tools for promoting products and gathering information. Some companies, like Johnson & Johnson, are even creating their own social networks for customers. One new tool marketers are using is rewarding consumers who pass company advertising messages onto other consumers in their online communities.

However, social media does have some disadvantages. On the consumers' side, the amount of personal information consumers are providing online could have unintended negative consequences. "All this stuff is creating a huge digital paper trail that could come back and haunt you," says Christopher Soghoian from Harvard's Berkman Center for Internet and Society. Future conflicts over privacy may arise over how much personal information marketers or companies can use from these websites.

Another challenge is due to the relative newness of social media. Marketers have yet to determine the most effective use of social media. Of 400 executives surveyed, 56 percent said they have no programs for tracking positive word of mouth through social networks. Only 16 percent of those responding indicated systems that monitor consumer comments on their brands. Some companies create Facebook pages for their products, where consumers who like the product can become "fans" with a click of the mouse. However, the loyalty of these "fans" is questionable; many people who sign up as fans of a product leave the fan club later. Procter & Gamble has developed a Social Media Lab to better understand the impact of social media on brands. Other companies should also create programs to track the effectiveness of social media advertisements in generating interest in a product or company. Such knowledge will enable marketers to use social media to better tailor their advertisements to consumer needs.

the fact that many factors can affect sales. Furthermore, most of these factors are beyond the control of the firm. For instance, competitors' actions, regulatory decisions, changes in economic conditions, and even the weather might influence or diminish a firm's sales or market share during a specific time period when advertising effectiveness is under scrutiny.

Public Relations

Corporate affairs is a collection of strategic activities aimed at marketing an organization, its issues, and its ideals to potential stakeholders (consumers, general public, shareholders, media, government, and so on). Public relations is one component of a firm's corporate affairs activities. The goal of public relations is to track public attitudes, identify issues that may elicit public concern, and develop programs to create and maintain positive relationships between a firm and its stakeholders. A firm uses public relations to communicate with its stakeholders for the same reasons that it develops advertisements. Public relations can be used to promote the firm, its people, its ideas, and its image and can even create an internal shared understanding among employees. Because various stakeholders' attitudes toward the firm affect their decisions relative to the firm, it is very important to maintain positive public opinion.

Public relations can improve the public's general awareness of a company and can create specific images such as quality, innovativeness, value, or concern for social issues. For example, New Belgium Brewery in Fort Collins, Colorado, has a strong reputation for its stance on environmental efficiency and conservation. The brewery takes an aggressive stance toward recycling and uses windmills to generate electricity.[11] Likewise, Starbucks has gained international awareness through its fair treatment of employees. The company was also the first coffee retailer to establish a global code of conduct for fair treatment of agricultural suppliers—the small farmers who supply the coffee beans for its products. Additionally, True North, a division of Frito-Lay, used public relations to announce an essay contest for inspirational stories that could potentially be the subject of an upcoming ad. Lisa Nigro the founder of the Inspiration Café in Chicago, which delivers food to the homeless, won. The advertisement received significant positive publicity for the homeless and helped to achieve the goal of treating them with "dignity and respect" and providing them with training and resources to improve their situation.[12]

Public Relations Methods

Firms use a number of public relations methods to convey messages and to create the right attitudes, images, and opinions. An in-house staff often executes the public relations program; however, many firms use public relations professionals to prepare materials such as brochures, newsletters, annual reports, and news releases that reach and influence desired stakeholders. Public relations is sometimes confused with publicity. Although publicity is one part of public relations, it is more narrowly defined to include the firm's activities designed to gain media attention through articles, editorials, or news stories. By encouraging the media to report on a firm's accomplishments, publicity helps maintain positive public awareness, visibility, and a desired image. Publicity can be used for a single purpose, such as to launch a new product or diminish the public's opinion regarding a negative event, or it can be used for multiple purposes to enhance many aspects of the firm's activities. Having a good publicity strategy is important because publicity can have the same effect as advertising, though typically with greater credibility. There are a number of different methods used in public relations and publicity efforts:

- **News (or Press) Releases** A news release is a few pages of typewritten copy— typically fewer than 300 words—used to draw attention to a company event, product, or person affiliated with the firm. News releases can be submitted to newspapers, magazines, television contacts, suppliers, key customers, or even the firm's employees.

- **Feature Articles**   A feature article is a full-length story prepared for a specific purpose or target audience. For example, a firm building a new production facility in northeast Georgia might supply a feature article to regional and local media outlets, chambers of commerce, local governments, and major firms in the area. Feature articles typically focus on the implications or economic impact of a firm's actions. They are also very useful when responding to negative events or publicity.

- **White Papers**   White papers are similar to feature articles; however, they are more technical and focus on very specific topics of interest to the firm's stakeholders. White papers promote a firm's stance on important product or market issues and can be used to promote the firm's own products and solutions. White papers have been used extensively in the information technology field, where firms continually work to establish standards and keep up with technological innovation.

- **Press Conferences**   A press conference is a meeting with news media called to announce or respond to major events. Media personnel receive invitations to a specific location, with written materials, photographs, exhibits, and even products given to them. Multimedia materials may be distributed to broadcast stations in hopes that they will air some of the activities that occurred at the press conference. Firms typically hold press conferences when announcing new products, patents, mergers or acquisitions, philanthropic efforts, or internal administrative changes.

- **Event Sponsorship**   Corporate sponsorship of major events has become an entire industry in itself. Sponsorships can range from local events, such as high school athletics and local charities, to international events such as the Tour de France or NASCAR. Another popular sponsorship strategy involves the naming of sports stadiums and venues.

- **Product Placement**   As *Beyond the Pages 10.1* demonstrated, product placement in movies and television programs is a rapidly growing practice, especially among highly identifiable brands like beverages, computers, clothing, and automobiles. These firms have a strong interest in placing their products in the hands of movie and television characters that consumers see as enjoying the product or using the product as a part of the action.

- **Employee Relations**   Employee relations are every bit as important as public and investor relations. Employee relations activities provide organizational support for employees with respect to their jobs and lives. Employee relations can encompass many different activities, including internal newsletters, training programs, employee assistance programs, and human resource programs.

When these methods generate publicity in the media, the public perceives the message as having more credibility due to the implied endorsement of the media that carries the story. The public will typically consider news coverage more truthful and credible than advertising because the firm has not paid for the media time. One major drawback of public relations activities is that the firm has much less control over how the message will be delivered. For example, many media personnel have a reputation for inserting their own opinions and biases when communicating a news story. Another drawback involves the risk of spending a great deal of time and effort in developing public relations messages that fail to attract media attention.

Negative Public Relations

One of the most important aspects of public relations deals with the unexpected and often unfavorable public reactions resulting from an ethical or legal inquiry, unsafe products, accidents, or the controversial actions of employees and executives. For example, all airlines have carefully planned procedures and personnel in place to respond to an aviation accident; however, they always face a very difficult and distressing situation when these accidents occur. Likewise, the news has been filled with ethical and legal scandals involving many firms. For example, Microsoft (anti-competitive activities) and AIG (executive compensation after receiving government bailout monies) have had to deal with negative publicity in recent years.

Sometimes public relations campaigns themselves cause problems, leading to unintended consequences on the parts of the campaign's creators. For example, the city of Boston underwent a bomb scare after Ted Turner and Turner Broadcasting attached wired devices to bridges and buildings around the city. The devices were a guerilla marketing stunt and consisted of battery-powered lights in the shape of a cartoon character from the Cartoon Network's "Aqua Teen Hunger Force." The scare effectively crippled the city as bomb squads and police were called in. What started out as a clever and harmless PR stunt ended up costing Ted Turner and Turner Broadcasting $2 million to pay for the time and cost associated with the police and other city personnel engaged in the response.[13] This emphasizes the importance for public relations practitioners to examine all the potential consequences of a public relations campaign.

Negative coverage of a company's problems can have quick, dramatic, and long-lasting effects. Negative publicity is critically important when its effects reduce the degree of trust that customers have in a specific industry or firm. Exhibit 10.7 lists U.S. firms having some of the strongest and weakest public reputations. Note that firms with lower reputation scores, such as Halliburton, have experienced a number of scandals and legal problems in recent years. For the first time, major financial corporations are also listed as companies with the worst reputations because of the financial scandals that recently plagued the industry. Faith in the financial sector is at an all-time low, and it may take years for these companies to rebuild their reputations.

The range of reputation scores in Exhibit 10.7 is also quite telling of the effects that negative publicity can have on a firm. Exxon's response to the Valdez accident in 1989 is one of the classic examples of how not to respond to negative publicity. When faced with the massive oil spill in Alaska, Exxon failed to communicate effectively with the press and various stakeholders. It took several days before top executives communicated clearly how Exxon was going to deal with the environmental disaster.

EXHIBIT 10.7	THE STRONGEST AND WEAKEST U.S. CORPORATE REPUTATIONS	
Rank	Company	Reputation Quotient^{SM}
The Strongest Reputations		
1.	Johnson & Johnson	82.39
2.	Google	81.89
3.	Sony Corporation	81.71
4.	The Coca-Cola Company	80.63
5.	Kraft Foods, Inc.	80.54
6.	Amazon	80.13
7.	Microsoft Corporation	79.77
8.	General Mills	79.65
9.	3M Company	79.63
10.	Toyota Motor Corporation	78.82
11.	Berkshire Hathaway, Inc.	78.79
12.	The Procter & Gamble Company	78.69
13.	The Walt Disney Company	78.44
14.	Apple	77.75
15.	Unilever	77.12
The Weakest Reputations		
46.	Sprint Corporation	63.63
47.	Bank of America Corporation	62.64
48.	Comcast Corporation	60.50
49.	JPMorgan Chase	60.01
50.	Wachovia	59.47
51.	Ford Motor Company	58.49
52.	ExxonMobil Corporation	57.84
53.	Merrill Lynch	54.86
54.	Citgo Oil	54.83
55.	Citigroup	54.77
56.	Washington Mutual	53.57
57.	Chrysler	53.27
58.	General Motors Corporation	52.43
59.	Halliburton Company	51.19
60.	AIG	43.78

Source: From Harris Interactive, "The Annual RQ 2008: The Reputations of the Most Visible Companies". Copyright © 2008 Harris Interactive, (http://www.harrisinteractive.com/services/pubs/HI_BSC_REPORT_AnnualRQ2008_Rankings.pdf), accessed July 31, 2009.

As shown in the exhibit, Exxon still struggles with a relatively weak corporate reputation more than 20 years after the incident. Conversely, Johnson & Johnson's response to the Tylenol cyanide-tampering scare in 1982 is the classic example of effective crisis management. When faced with tremendous negative publicity, Johnson & Johnson immediately recalled all Tylenol products that were on store shelves. The company's quick action and honesty in dealing with the situation was a tremendous boost to the company's image and Tylenol's market share. Today, Johnson & Johnson and Tylenol continue to enjoy a high degree of customer trust. Contrast this to AIG, which scored the lowest ratings. Not only was AIG implicated in financial scandals and required government bailout money, but AIG executives rewarded top officials with bonuses and hosted conferences in luxurious resorts after receiving the money. AIG's actions worsened its reputation in the eyes of the public, and, together with companies like ExxonMobil, are good examples of what not to do during a crisis.

A single negative event, especially one that is potentially dangerous to customers, can wipe out a company's image and negate the goodwill generated over decades. Today, the media, and individual consumers, can report incidents through television and the Internet faster than ever before. As a result, negative stories receive more attention now than in the past. To avoid negative publicity, it is vital to avoid negative incidents and events that can create problems. Firms can achieve this goal through effective ethical and legal compliance programs, safety programs, quality-control procedures, and programs designed to enhance employee integrity. However, no matter how hard a firm tries to avoid negative events, the potential for negative incidents and publicity is always present. Therefore, all firms should have plans and procedures in place to respond to negative events when they occur. In particular, specific policies and procedures for handling the media and their coverage of the event are absolutely necessary. One of the great public relations lessons learned over time is that firms must expedite news coverage of negative events rather than try to block the news or cover up facts about the incident.

Personal Selling and Sales Management

Personal selling is paid personal communication that attempts to inform customers about products and persuade them to purchase those products. Personal selling takes place in many forms. For example, a Best Buy salesperson who describes the benefits of a Hewlett-Packard laptop to a customer engages in personal selling. So is the salesperson who attempts to convince a large industrial organization to purchase photocopy machines. Some types of personal selling are highly complex and relational in nature. The complexity of these types of contracts requires a long-term, personal relationship between salespeople and companies.

Compared to other types of promotion, personal selling is the most precise form of communication because it assures companies that they are in direct contact with an excellent prospect. Though one-on-one contact is highly advantageous, it does not come without disadvantages. The most serious drawback of personal selling is the cost per contact. In business markets, a single sales presentation can take many months and thousands of dollars to prepare. For instance, to give government officials a real feel for the design and scope of a bridge construction project, Parsons, Inc. (a large engineering and construction firm) must invest thousands of dollars in detailed scale models of several different bridge designs. Personal selling is also expensive due to the costs associated with recruiting, selecting, training, and motivating salespeople. Despite the high costs, personal selling plays an increasingly important role in IMC and overall marketing strategy.

The goals of personal selling vary tremendously based on its role in a long-run approach to integrated communications. These goals typically involve finding prospects, informing prospects, persuading prospects to buy, and keeping customers satisfied through follow-up service after the sale. To effectively deliver on these goals, salespeople have to be not only competent in selling skills but also thoroughly trained in technical product characteristics. For example, pharmaceutical salespeople (drug reps) who sell to physicians and hospitals must have detailed training in the technical medical applications of the drugs and medical devices that they sell. In fact, it is not unusual for salespeople who sell medical implants such as knee or hip replacements to have as much technical training about the product as the physicians who actually implant these devices during surgery. Obviously, when the products and buyers are less sophisticated, salespeople will require much less training.

Very few businesses can survive on the profits generated from purely transactional marketing (one-time purchases). For long-term survival, most firms depend on repeat sales and the development of ongoing relationships with customers. For this reason, personal selling has evolved to take on elements of customer service and marketing research. More than any other part of the firm, salespeople are closer to the customers and have many more opportunities for communication with them. Every contact with a customer gives the sales force a chance to deliver exceptional service and learn more about the customer's needs. Salespeople also have the opportunity to learn about competing products and the customer's reaction toward them. These relational aspects are important—whether the salesperson makes a sale or not. *Beyond the Pages 10.3* underscores the importance of building relationships during the sales process. In today's highly competitive markets, the frontline knowledge held by the sales force is one of the most important assets of the firm. In fact, the knowledge held by the sales force is often an important strength that can be leveraged in developing marketing strategy.

The Sales Management Process

Because the sales force has a direct bearing on sales revenue and customer satisfaction, the effective management of the sales force is vital to a firm's marketing strategy. In addition to generating performance outcomes, the sales force often creates the firm's reputation, and the conduct of individual salespeople determines the perceived ethicalness of the entire firm. The strategic implementation of effective sales management requires a number of activities, discussed in the following sections.

Developing Sales Force Objectives   Sales force objectives are vital to the overall IMC strategy and must be fully integrated with the objectives and activities of other promotional elements. Sales objectives will determine the type of salespeople that the firm needs to hire. For example, salespeople may be needed to find new customers through prospecting—the identification of potential customers most likely to buy the firm's products. The selling skills required for prospecting differ from those associated with generating repeat sales from current customers. Furthermore, a different skill set must be developed to provide product support, educate customers, and provide service after the sale. The connection between selling skills and sales force objectives reinforces the importance of having a fully integrated sales management process.

Beyond the Pages 10.3

IBM'S CELEBRITY SALESMAN[14]

In Vivek Gupta's opinion, making a sale is similar to a courtship. Based in India, Gupta is technology giant IBM's top wireless salesperson in the world. This means that he is the top salesperson in the company's fastest growing-industry in the fastest-growing part of the world. Gupta has elevated the courtship of large, high profile clients to an art form. It did not take Gupta long to rise to the top of IBM's salesperson pack. He did it in less than five years by relying on his 17 years in the telecom industry to give him the expertise to form relationships with some of India's biggest telecom companies. Among his many sales victories, Gupta secured a five-year contract with Vodafone, India's fourth-largest cellular phone company. Gupta has also secured contracts with India's number one telecom account, Bharti Airtel, and sixth-ranked Idea Cellular. Gupta, like many salespeople who obtain large business accounts, had to invest significant time and resources into winning these contracts.

At first, the prospects of a contract with Vodafone were not promising. Vodafone explicitly told Gupta that the company intended never to do business with IBM. However, Gupta managed to convince Vodafone to transfer much of its information technology-related responsibilities to IBM. The secret to Gupta's sales success is his strategy. He works on studying customers to discover their underlying needs, or what he terms the customer's "pain points." During this study period, Gupta familiarizes himself with the company so well that he often knows more about it than its employees do. Once he understands what his customers want, he finds the best way for IBM to meet those needs. He has also become adept at recognizing key signals that his prospects give off.

When first meeting with Vodafone, Gupta could tell when his prospects were losing interest. This is where his courtship analogy came in. "Look, this customer is not prepared for marriage; he is prepared for courtship, so let's spend some time on courtship," he told his sales team. Eventually, Gupta was able to sell Vodafone on a $600-million contract. With millions of dollars of sales under his belt and opportunities to expand his sales globally, Gupta is the epitome of a super salesperson. He is prepared to make these long-term relationships by anticipating needs, resolving problems, and providing superior service.

The technical aspects of establishing sales force objectives involve desired sales dollars, sales volume, or market share. These sales objectives can be translated into sales quotas for individual salespeople. Further, individual sales objectives might be based on order size, the number of sales calls, or the ratio of orders to calls. Ultimately, sales objectives help evaluate and control sales force activities, as well as compensate individual salespeople.

Determining Sales Force Size   The size of the sales force is a function of many variables, including the type of salespeople used, specific sales objectives, and the importance of personal selling within the overall IMC program. The size of the sales force is important because the firm must find a balance between sales expenses and revenue generation. Having a sales force that is too large or too small can lead to inflated expenses, lost sales, and lost profit. Achieving this balance in practice is challenging because the sales force is one of the first targets for cost cutting when a firm must find ways to reduce expenses. Although trimming the sales force is a quick and easy way to cut costs, doing so often gives competitors an opportunity to improve their market position with valued customers. Perhaps for this reason, when the

Container Store experienced a downturn in sales for the first time in 30 years, it took an alternative route to laying off sales staff. The Container Store froze salaries for everyone in the company and introduced sales contests as a way to motivate staff. It also refused to halt store expansion plans. Partially due to this bold business strategy in a period of cost cutting, the Container Store ranked 32 on *Fortune's* 100 Best Companies to Work For in 2009.[15]

Although there is no exact analytical method for determining the optimum size of the sales force, there are several general approaches. Determining the specific objectives and tasks that are required to fulfill sales and IMC goals is one approach. For example, this method might focus on the number of sales calls per year necessary to effectively serve a market. This number can be divided by the average number of sales calls that a salesperson can make in one year to derive an estimate of sales force size. Another method involves marginal analysis, where additional salespeople join the sales force until the cost of adding an additional salesperson equals the potential sales that can be generated by that salesperson. Though firms can develop sophisticated, quantifiable models to determine the size of the sales force, most companies make these decisions subjectively based on the experience of sales managers.

Recruiting and Training Salespeople   Recruiting the right types of salespeople should be closely tied to the personal selling and IMC strategies. Firms usually recruit potential salespeople from a number of sources including within the firm, competing firms, employment agencies, educational institutions, and direct-response advertisements placed on the Internet, in magazines, or in newspapers. Salesperson recruitment should be a continuous activity because firms must ensure that new salespeople are consistently available to sustain the sales program. Contrary to popular belief, the best applicant these days may be male or female. In a study of gender differences in sales organizations, results indicated that there are few differences among men and women salespeople in areas such as expectations, job satisfaction, compensation, or performance.[16]

The cost of hiring and training a salesperson can be expensive. Lockheed Martin, for example, has a total training budget of roughly $389 million.[17] In recent years, successful salespeople have had many opportunities to leave their current firms and earn higher salaries at competing firms. This situation creates a serious problem with sales force turnover, a considerable cost of doing business in highly technical fields. In an effort to reduce turnover, many firms have instituted very restrictive recruitment and selection procedures. For example, State Farm Insurance strives for low sales force turnover by forcing applicants for agent positions to undergo a yearlong series of interviews, tests, and visits with agents before finding out whether they will be hired.

Sales training has moved toward formal programs in recent years, although some companies still depend on less formal methods like on-the-job training. Formal training methods have moved toward self-directed, online training modules and away from classroom training. Although the majority of training continues to be in the classroom, projections indicate that within a few years the majority of sales training will be done online or via wireless delivery to handheld devices. As of 2007, 10 percent of training hours were completed through virtual classrooms, and 20 percent through online self-study. Among companies with over 10,000 employees, 25 percent received training via online self-study and another 12 percent through virtual classrooms.[18] The worldwide online sales training market is growing mainly because it is much more cost-effective than traditional training.

Controlling and Evaluating the Sales Force   Controlling and evaluating the sales force require a comparison of sales objectives with actual sales performance. This analysis can be made at the individual salesperson level or for the entire sales force. To effectively evaluate a salesperson, predetermined performance standards must be in place. These standards also determine the compensation plan for the sales force. Exhibit 10.8 provides a comparison of various sales force compensation systems. Systems using a combination of salary and commission are the most commonly used because they offer the best balance of the benefits offered by salary- and commission-only programs.

Without a formal evaluation and control system, the firm will not be able to determine whether its performance targets have been met. Well-designed evaluation and control systems have built-in mechanisms for corrective action when personnel do not achieve sales targets. To improve sales performance, the firm can increase incentives to better motivate the sales force, provide additional training to salespeople, or perhaps even change the performance standards if they are inconsistent with market realities. It is also possible that the entire IMC program will require corrective action if the sales strategy is inconsistent with the overall promotional program.

EXHIBIT 10.8   COMPARISON OF SALES FORCE COMPENSATION METHODS

Method	Most Useful When:	Advantages	Disadvantages
Straight Salary	• Salespeople are new • Salespeople move into new territories • Products require intense presale and postsale service	• Easy to administer • Gives salespeople more security • Greater control over salespeople • More predictable selling expenses	• Little or no incentive for salespeople • Salespeople require close supervision
Straight Commission	• Aggressive selling is required • Nonselling tasks can be minimized • The firm outsources some selling functions	• Gives salespeople maximum incentive • Ties selling expenses to sales volume • Can use differential commissions for different products to boost sales	• Less security for salespeople • Managers have less control over salespeople • Small accounts may receive less service
Combination	• Sales territories have similar sales potential • The firm wants to provide incentive and still have some control	• Good balance of incentive and security for salespeople	• Selling expenses are less predictable • May be difficult to administer

Source: Adapted from William M. Pride and O.C. Ferrell, *Marketing* (Mason, OH: South-Western - Cengage Learning, 2010), p. 530.

The Impact of Technology on Personal Selling

Across many industries, sales forces have shrunk due to advances in communications technology and mobile computing. The development of integrated supply chains and the procurement of standardized products over the Internet have reduced the need for salespeople in many industries. Although these developments reduce selling costs, they create a major management challenge for most firms: How can firms use new technology to reduce costs and increase productivity while maintaining personalized, one-to-one client relationships?

One of the keys to using sales technology effectively is to seamlessly integrate it with customer relationship management systems, competitive intelligence activities, and internal customer databases. By automating many repetitive selling tasks, like filling repeat orders, sales technology can actually increase sales, productivity, and one-to-one client relationships at the same time. Although many firms develop and maintain their own sales automation systems, others who lack the resources to do so can turn to third-party providers like Salesforce.com—an on-demand, web-based provider of integrated CRM and sales automation solutions. Whether in-house or third party, the key to these solutions is integration. By pushing integrated customer, competitive, and product information toward the salesperson, technology can increase salesperson productivity and sales revenue by allowing the sales force to serve customers' needs more effectively.

Sales Promotion

Despite the attention paid to advertising, sales promotion activities account for the bulk of promotional spending in many firms. This is especially true for firms selling consumer products in grocery stores and mass-merchandise retailers, where sales promotion can account for up to 70 percent of the firm's promotional budget.[19] Sales promotion involves activities that create buyer incentives to purchase a product or that add value for the buyer or the trade. Sales promotion can be targeted toward consumers, channel intermediaries, or the sales force. Exhibit 10.9 breaks down total spending for various sales promotion activities. As can be seen in the exhibit, sales promotion includes a broad assortment of promotional elements because it encompasses activities other than advertising, public relations, and personal selling. Regardless of the activity and toward whom it is directed, sales promotion has one universal goal: to induce product trial and purchase.

Most firms use sales promotion in support of advertising, public relations, or personal selling activities rather than as a stand-alone promotional element. Advertising is frequently coordinated with sales promotion activities to provide free product samples, premiums, or value-added incentives. For example, a manufacturer might offer free merchandise to channel intermediaries who purchase a stated quantity of product within a specified time frame. A 7-Up bottler, for example, might offer a free case of 7-Up for every 10 cases purchased by a retailer. On the consumer side,

EXHIBIT 10.9

BREAKDOWN OF SPENDING ON VARIOUS SALES PROMOTION ACTIVITIES

Promotional Activity	Percent of Total Promotional Spending
Trade promotion	31.8%
Direct mail	16.4%
Business-to-business promotions	13.2%
Premiums	9.1%
Trade shows	7.2%
POP displays	5.2%
Ad specialties	5.1%
Sponsorships	3.2%
Couponing	2.9%
Specialty print	1.9%
Promotional licensing	1.8%
Interactive	1.0%
Contests and sweepstakes	0.5%
Sampling	0.5%
In-store promotions	0.3%

Source: From Promotional Marketing Association, "State of the Promotion Industry Report," © 2005 Promotional Marketing Association, (http://www.pmalink.org/resources/pma2005report.pdf), accessed September 19, 2009.

Coca-Cola's innovative "Don't Dew it" promotion took steps to increase market share of the company's Vault brand over Pepsi's Mountain Dew. In a bold move, Coca-Cola offered free samples of Vault by giving away 16-, 20-, or 24-ounce Vaults to consumers who purchased a 20-ounce Mountain Dew.[20]

Sales Promotion in Consumer Markets

Any member of the supply chain can initiate consumer sales promotions, but manufacturers and retailers typically offer them. For manufacturers, sales promotion activities represent an effective way to introduce new products or promote established brands. Coupons and product sampling are frequently used during new product launches to stimulate interest and trial. Retailers typically offer sales promotions to stimulate customer traffic or increase sales at specific locations. Coupons and free products are common examples, as are in-store product demonstrations. Many retailers are known for their sales promotions such as the free toys that come with kid's meals at McDonald's, Burger King, and other fast-food establishments.

A potentially limitless variety of sales promotion methods can be used in consumer markets. Truthfully, developing and using these methods is limited

The toy prizes inside of a McDonald's Happy Meal may be the best-known consumer sales promotion of all time.

© PR NewsFoto/McDonald's

only by the creativity of the firm offering the promotion. For example, to promote its three value sandwiches, Wendy's held an online auction in which high-end items like an Xbox 360 console were auctioned to bidders for 99 cents each.[21] However, firms will typically offer one or more of the following types of sales promotions to consumers:

- **Coupons**   Coupons reduce the price of a product and encourage customers to try new or established brands. Coupons can be used to increase sales volume quickly, to attract repeat purchasers, or even to introduce new product sizes or models. To be most effective, coupons need to be accessible, easy to recognize, and easy to use. For the most part, this requires that coupons be distributed on packages (the highest redemption rates), through inserts in print advertising, through direct mail, or through in-store displays. Although coupon cutting (cutting coupons from newspapers or direct mail) was once quite common, the practice declined over the years. This mentality changed with the latest economic recession as many consumers returned to using coupons, especially electronic coupons. For example, overall coupon use increased 23 percent in 2009, and online coupon use more than doubled during the same time frame.[22] Marketers perceive a bright future for electronic coupons because redemption rates are higher, and because printing and processing costs are lower. Electronic coupons are quite popular among younger consumers, as shown in Exhibit 10.10.

- **Rebates**   Rebates are very similar to coupons except that they require much more effort on the consumer's part to obtain the price reduction. Although consumers prefer coupons because of the ease of use, most firms prefer rebates for several

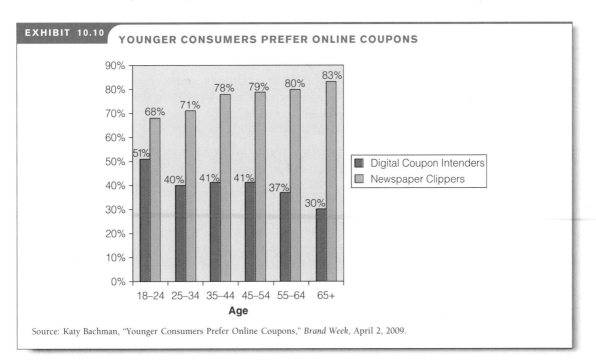

EXHIBIT 10.10   **YOUNGER CONSUMERS PREFER ONLINE COUPONS**

Source: Katy Bachman, "Younger Consumers Prefer Online Coupons," *Brand Week*, April 2, 2009.

reasons. First, firms have more control over rebates because they can be launched and ended very quickly. Second, a rebate program allows the firm to collect important consumer information that can be used to build customer databases. The best reason is that most consumers never bother to redeem rebate offers. This allows a firm to entice customers to purchase a product with only a minimal loss of profit.

- **Samples**   Free samples are one of the most widely used consumer sales promotion methods. Samples stimulate trial of a product, increase volume in the early stages of the product's life cycle, and encourage consumers to actively search for a product. Samples can be distributed through the mail, attached to other products, and given out through personal selling efforts or in-store displays. Samples can also be distributed via less direct methods. For example, free samples of soap, shampoo, coffee, or sunscreen might be placed in hotel rooms to create consumer awareness of new products.

- **Loyalty Programs**   Loyalty programs, or frequent-buyer programs, reward loyal customers who engage in repeat purchases. These programs are popular in many industries due to their potential to dramatically increase profits over the long term. We are all familiar with the frequent-flier programs offered by major airlines. Other companies, such as hotels, auto rental agencies, and credit card companies, offer free goods or services for repeat purchases. For instance, the Discover Card provides a 1 percent cash-back bonus to each cardholder at the end of the year, and Hallmark rewards loyal customers with the Hallmark Gold Crown Card, which allows frequent buyers to accrue points that are redeemable for merchandise and discounts. There are over 1.8 billion memberships in U.S. loyalty programs.[23]

- **Point-of-Purchase Promotion**   Point-of-purchase (POP) promotion includes displays, counter pieces, display racks, or self-service cartons that are designed to build traffic, advertise a product, or induce impulse purchases. POP promotions are highly effective because they are used in a store where consumers make roughly 70 to 80 percent of all purchase decisions. Another type of POP promotion is an in-store product demonstration. Examples of these demonstrations include fashion shows, food preparation demonstrations in grocery stores like Whole Foods, and free makeovers in the cosmetics departments of department stores and specialty stores. Clinique, for instance, offers potential customers free makeovers to demonstrate the features of their cosmetics and to teach customers proper application techniques.

- **Premiums**   Premiums are items offered free or at a minimum cost as a bonus for purchasing a product. Examples of premiums include a free car wash with a gasoline fill-up, a free toothbrush with a purchase of a tube of toothpaste, and the toys offered inside a McDonald's Happy Meal. Premiums are good at increasing consumption and persuading consumers to switch brands.

- **Contests and Sweepstakes**   Consumer contests, games, and sweepstakes encourage potential consumers to compete for prizes or try their luck by submitting their names in a drawing for prizes. In addition to being valuable information collection tools, contests and sweepstakes are good at attracting a large number of participants and generating widespread interest in a product. Because they require no skill to enter, sweepstakes are an effective way to increase sales or market share in the short term.

- **Direct Mail**   Direct mail, which includes catalog marketing and other printed material mailed to individual consumers, is a unique category because it incorporates elements of advertising, sales promotion, and distribution into a coordinated effort to induce customers to buy. The use of direct mail has grown tremendously in recent years due to consumer time constraints, relatively low cost, and the advent of sophisticated database management tools.

Firms can use any one or all of these consumer promotion methods in their overall IMC program. However, the choice of one or more methods must be made in consideration of the firm's IMC objectives. Furthermore, the choice must also consider the use of sales promotions by competitors and whether a particular method involves ethical or legal dimensions. Consumer sweepstakes, in particular, have specific legal requirements to ensure that each entrant has an equally likely chance of winning.

Sales Promotion in Business Markets

Sales promotion in business markets is also known as trade promotion. By targeting channel intermediaries with promotional activities, manufacturers hope to push their products through the channel by increasing sales and encouraging increased effort among their channel partners. Manufacturers use many of the same promotional methods that target consumers; however, a number of sales promotion methods are unique to business markets:

- **Trade Allowances**   Manufacturers offer a number of different trade allowances, or price reductions, to their channel intermediaries. Buying allowances are price reductions for purchasing specified quantities of a product at a single time (the equivalent of a bulk discount). Related to this is a buy-back allowance where the reduction is proportional to the total amount of product purchased during the time frame of the promotional offer. Finally, a merchandise allowance is a manufacturer's agreement to pay intermediaries a specific sum of money in exchange for specific promotional efforts such as special displays or advertising. In each case, the goal of the allowance is to induce intermediaries to perform specific actions.

- **Free Merchandise**   Manufacturers sometimes offer free merchandise to intermediaries instead of quantity discounts. Typically, they provide the free merchandise to reduce invoice costs as a way of compensating the intermediary for other activities that assist the manufacturer.

- **Training Assistance**   In some cases, a manufacturer can offer free training to an intermediary's employees. This typically occurs when the products involved are rather complex.

- **Cooperative Advertising**   Cooperative advertising is an arrangement whereby a manufacturer agrees to pay a certain amount of an intermediary's media cost for advertising the manufacturer's products. This is a very popular sales promotion method among retailers.

- **Selling Incentives**   Selling incentives come in two general forms: push money and sales contests. Intermediaries, particularly their salespeople, receive push money in the form of additional compensation to encourage a more aggressive selling effort for a particular product. Push money is appropriate when personal selling is an important part of the marketing effort and it is necessary to gain commitment from an intermediary's sale force. This method is expensive and should be used carefully to avoid any ethical or legal issues. Sales contests encourage outstanding performance within an intermediary's sales force. Sales personnel can be recognized for outstanding achievements by receiving money, vacations, computers, or even cars for meeting or exceeding certain sales targets.

Trade sales promotion encompasses a wide variety of activities and is often one of the largest expenditures in the overall promotional budget. Trade promotion is vital when a manufacturer needs the cooperation and support of the channel to fulfill its own sales and marketing objectives. This is particularly true when a manufacturer must obtain support for a new product launch or a new consumer sales promotion. Given the importance of integrated supply chains that we discussed in Chapter 9, it should not be surprising that effective trade promotion is also vital to fulfilling a firm's distribution strategy.

Lessons from Chapter 10

Integrated marketing communications

- Includes conveying and sharing meaning between buyers and sellers, either as individuals or firms, or between individuals and firms.

- Includes the traditional elements of the promotion mix: advertising, public relations, personal selling, and sales promotion.

- Refers to the strategic, coordinated use of promotion to create one consistent message across multiple channels to ensure maximum persuasive impact on the firm's current and potential customers.

- Takes a 360-degree view of the customer that considers every contact that a customer or potential customer may have in his relationship with the firm.

- Can reduce or eliminate redundancies and waste in the overall promotional program.

- Has become widely embraced as firms struggle to adapt to fragmented audiences across a wide variety of traditional media outlets.

- Typically sets goals and objectives for the promotional campaign using the AIDA model—attention, interest, desire, and action.
- Can change depending on whether the firm uses a pull or push strategy with respect to its supply chain.
- Varies in its emphasis on specific promotional elements, depending on the nature of the product and its stage in the product life cycle.

Advertising

- Is one of the most visible and key components of promotion.
- Is identified as paid, nonpersonal communication transmitted through media such as television, radio, magazines, newspapers, direct mail, outdoor displays, the Internet, and mobile devices.
- Is rapidly expanding online as consumers spend less time with traditional media.
- Offers many benefits because it is extremely cost-efficient when it reaches a large number of people. On the other hand, the initial outlay for advertising can be expensive.
- Is hard to measure in terms of its effectiveness in increasing sales.
- Comes in two general forms: institutional advertising—used to promote a firm's image, ideas, and culture; or product advertising—used to promote the image, features, uses, benefits, and attributes of products.
- Budgets can be set using one of several approaches, including the objectives and task approach, the percentage of sales approach, the competitive matching approach, and the arbitrary approach.
- Effectiveness can be measured before, during, or after the campaign has been executed. Consumer panels, surveys, or experimental designs may be used to evaluate a campaign based on communication objectives.

Public relations

- Is one component of a firm's corporate affairs activities.
- Is the element of an IMC program that tracks public attitudes, identifies issues that may elicit public concern, and develops programs to create and maintain positive relationships between a firm and its stakeholders.
- Can be used to promote the firm, its people, its ideas, and its image and even to create an internal shared understanding among employees.
- Can improve the public's general awareness of a company and can create specific images such as quality, innovativeness, value, or concern for social issues.

- Is often confused with publicity; however, publicity is more narrowly defined to include the firm's activities designed to gain media attention through articles, editorials, or news stories.

- Can involve the use of a wide variety of methods, including news or press releases, feature articles, white papers, press conferences, event sponsorship, product placement, and employee relations.

- Includes the management of unexpected and unfavorable public relations resulting from an ethical or legal inquiry, unsafe products, accidents, or the controversial actions of employees and executives.

Personal selling

- Is paid, personal communication that attempts to inform customers about products and persuade them to purchase those products.

- Is the most precise form of communication because it assures companies that they are in direct contact with an excellent prospect.

- Does not come without disadvantages. The most serious drawback of personal selling is the cost per contact.

- Has goals that are typically associated with finding prospects, informing prospects, persuading prospects to buy, and keeping customers satisfied through follow-up service after the sale.

- Has evolved to take on elements of customer service and marketing research in order to generate repeat sales and develop ongoing relationships with customers.

- And sales management activities include the development of sales force objectives, determining the size of the sales force, recruiting and training salespeople, and controlling and evaluating the sales force.

- Has been greatly impacted by technological advances, especially online sales training and sales automation systems that push integrated customer, competitive, and product information toward the salesperson.

Sales promotion

- Involves activities that create buyer incentives to purchase a product or that add value for the buyer or the trade.

- Can be targeted toward consumers, channel intermediaries, or the sales force.

- Has one universal goal: to induce product trial and purchase.

- Is typically used in support of advertising, public relations, or personal selling activities rather than as a stand-alone promotional element.

- Directed toward consumers

  - Can be initiated by any member of the supply chain, but manufacturers or retailers typically offer them.
  - Represents an effective way to introduce new products or promote established brands.
  - Can include such activities as coupons, rebates, samples, loyalty programs, point-of-purchase promotion, premiums, contests and sweepstakes, and direct mail.

- Directed toward the trade (business markets)

  - Is undertaken to push products through the channel by increasing sales and encouraging increased effort among channel partners.
  - Uses many of the same promotional methods that are targeted toward consumers; however, it involves a number of unique methods including trade allowances, free merchandise, training assistance, cooperative advertising, and selling incentives offered to an intermediary's sales force.

Questions for Discussion

1. Review the steps in the AIDA model. In what ways has promotion affected you in various stages of this model? Does promotion affect you differently based on the type of product in question? Does the price of the product (low versus high) make a difference in how promotion can affect your choices? Explain.

2. What does the future hold for traditional mass-media advertising? If you were the CEO of a major television network, magazine publisher, or newspaper company, what would you be doing now to ensure the livelihood of your company in 10 to 20 years?

3. What would happen if a company suddenly stopped using sales promotion activities after having used them for a long period of time? Is it possible for a company to become dependent on the use of sales promotion activities? Explain.

Exercises

1. Go to *BusinessWeek*'s cover story podcasts (http://www.businessweek.com/mediacenter/podcasts/cover_stories/current.html) and listen to one or more of the podcasts that are available. What advertising is inserted into each podcast? Do you believe that podcast advertising has a mainstream future, or will advertising be limited to products that match tech- and Internet-oriented audiences?

2. Shadow a salesperson for a day and talk about how his or her activities integrate with other promotional elements used by their firm. How does the

salesperson set objectives? How is he or she made aware of the firm's overall IMC strategy? Does the sales force participate in planning marketing or promotional activities?

3.   Visit the Cents Off website (http://www.centsoff.com) and browse the available coupons and read the FAQs. What are the benefits of the Cents Off service for advertisers and consumers? If you were a manufacturer that issues coupons, what factors would make you favor using the Cents Off website for distribution rather than the traditional Sunday newspaper insert?

CHAPTER 11

Marketing Implementation and Control

Introduction

Throughout the history of business, many firms and their top executives have emphasized strategic planning at the expense of strategic implementation. Historically, and even today, this emphasis on planning occurs because many executives believe that strategic planning, by itself, is the key to marketing success. This belief is logical because a firm must have a plan before it can determine where it is going. Many firms are quite good at devising strategic marketing plans; however, they are often unprepared to cope with the realities of implementation.

Marketing implementation is the process of executing the marketing strategy by creating and performing specific actions that will ensure the achievement of the firm's marketing objectives. Strategic planning without effective implementation can produce unintended consequences that result in customer dissatisfaction and feelings of frustration within the firm. Likewise, poor implementation will most likely result in the firm's failure to reach its organizational and marketing objectives. Unfortunately, many firms repeatedly experience failures in marketing implementation. Out-of-stock items, overly aggressive salespeople, long checkout lines, and unfriendly or inattentive employees are examples of implementation failure that occur all too frequently today. These and other examples illustrate that even the best-planned marketing strategies are a waste of time without effective implementation to ensure their success.

To track the implementation process, firms must have ways of evaluating and controlling marketing activities, as well as monitoring performance to determine whether marketing goals and objectives have been achieved. As illustrated in *Beyond the Pages 11.1*, implementation, evaluation, and control go hand in hand in determining the success or failure of the marketing strategy, and ultimately the entire firm. One of the most important considerations in implementing and controlling marketing activities involves gaining the support of employees. Because a marketing strategy cannot implement itself, all firms depend on employees to carry out marketing activities. As a result, the firm must devise a plan for implementation, just as it devises a plan for marketing strategy.

Beyond the Pages 11.1

GREEN MOUNTAIN COFFEE GETS IT DONE[1]

Green Mountain Coffee Roasters, Inc., is a leader in the specialty coffee industry. The Waterbury, Vermont, company uses a coordinated multi-channel distribution network that is designed to maximize brand recognition and product availability. Green Mountain roasts high-quality Arabica beans and offers over 100 coffee selections including single-origins, estates, certified organics, Fair Trade Certified, proprietary blends, and flavored coffees sold under the Green Mountain Coffee Roasters and Newman's Own Organics brands. Its products come in a variety of packages, including whole bean, fractional packages, premium one-cup coffee pods, and Keurig K-Cup single-serving coffee cartridges. The company also operates an active e-commerce business at www.GreenMountainCoffee.com.

Most of Green Mountain's revenue is derived from over 8,000 wholesale customer accounts located primarily in the Eastern United States. Green Mountain's customers include supermarkets, specialty food stores, convenience stores, food service companies, hotels, restaurants, universities, and office coffee services. One of the company's signature accounts is McDonald's, which sells Green Mountain's organic coffee under the Newman's Own label at 658 restaurants across the Northeast. Roughly 30 percent of Green Mountain's business comes from the convenience store sector, where the company counts ExxonMobil and its 1,000 stores as one of its largest customers.

Green Mountain has an ambitious goal to increase sales at an annual rate of 20 to 25 percent. To achieve this goal, the company pursues three key strategies: boosting market share, expanding into new markets, and making key acquisitions. To increase market share and expand, the company relies on direct relationships with farms, coffee estates, cooperatives, and other parties to ensure a consistent supply and price of 75 different varieties of high-quality coffee beans. This, combined with a custom roasting process, allows Green Mountain to differentiate its coffee offerings. One of Green Mountain's key acquisitions was Keurig—the company that makes its K-Cup coffee cartridges. While Keurig had been a dominant player in the office coffee service segment, its expansion into the home market under Green Mountain has been extraordinary. Sales of Keurig brewers increased 187 percent in the first half of 2009. Not bad for a $100 coffee maker in a down economy. Green Mountain is also doing well. The company has delivered a compound annual revenue growth rate of 18.7 percent over the past five years. Green Mountain recently acquired Tully's—a Seattle-based coffee company. That acquisition greatly expands Green Mountain's national footprint in manufacturing and distribution.

One of the major reasons for Green Mountain's success is its overall focus on implementation. The company employs roughly 1,200 people but has a very flat organizational structure. This promotes open communication, passion, and commitment among employees, who have open access to all levels of the organization including the CEO Bob Stiller. As a part of the company's evaluation and control system, Green Mountain uses a process called the after-action review—a process adapted from the U.S. Army. The goal of the review is to answer four key questions: What did we set out to do? What happened? Why did it happen? What are we going to do about it? Most of the effort is spent on this last question to ensure that the company learns from both its successes and failures. Employees are empowered to apply these lessons and encouraged to share their views in a "constellation of communication" that ensures a collaborative style of getting things done.

Green Mountain Coffee has consistently appeared on *Forbes'* list of the "200 Best Small Companies in America" and *Fortune*'s list of the "100 Fastest-Growing Small Companies in America." The company was also ranked as number one on *Business Ethics* magazine's list of the "100 Best Corporate Citizens." In addition, the Society of Human Resource Management has recognized Green Mountain for its socially responsible business practices, including a strong focus on sustainability.

In this chapter, we examine the critical role of marketing implementation and control in the strategic planning process. First, we discuss a number of important strategic issues involved in implementation, including the major components of implementation that must work together in order for a strategy to be executed successfully. Then we examine the advantages and disadvantages of major marketing implementation approaches. This discussion also describes how internal marketing can be used to motivate employees to implement marketing strategy. Finally, we look at the marketing evaluation and control process.

Long waiting lines are a common symptom that can be tied to problems in strategy, implementation, or both.

© Xinhua/Landov

Strategic Issues in Marketing Implementation

Marketing implementation is critical to the success of any firm because it is responsible for putting the marketing strategy into action. Simply put, implementation refers to the "how" part of the marketing plan. Marketing implementation is a very broad concept, and for that reason it is often misunderstood. Some of this misunderstanding stems from the fact that marketing strategies almost always turn out differently than expected. In fact, all firms have two strategies: their intended strategy and a realized strategy.[2] Intended marketing strategy is what the firm wants to happen—it is the firm's planned strategic choices that appear in the marketing plan itself. The realized marketing strategy, on the other hand, is the strategy that actually takes place. More often than not, the difference between the intended and the realized strategies is a matter of the implementation of the intended strategy. This is not to say that a firm's realized marketing strategy is necessarily better or worse than the intended marketing strategy, just that it is different in execution and results. Such differences are often the result of internal or external environmental factors that change during implementation.

In the sections that follow, we discuss a number of important strategic issues in planning for the implementation phase of the marketing plan. First, we examine the relationship between implementation and strategic planning. As we will see, planning and implementation are really two sides of the same coin that must be integrated to achieve maximum effectiveness in the marketing plan. Then we will explore the major elements of marketing implementation and discuss how these elements must work together to fully execute the marketing plan.

The Link Between Planning and Implementation

One of the most interesting aspects of marketing implementation is its relationship to the strategic planning process. Many firms assume that planning and implementation are interdependent but separate issues. In reality, planning and implementation intertwine within the marketing planning process. Many of the problems of marketing implementation occur because of its relationship to strategic planning. The three most common issues in this relationship are interdependency, evolution, and separation.

Interdependency   Many firms assume that the planning and implementation process is a one-way street. That is, strategic planning comes first, followed by implementation. Although it is true that the content of the marketing plan determines how it will be implemented, it is also true that how the marketing strategy is to be implemented determines the content of the marketing plan. Exhibit 11.1 depicts this symbiotic relationship between marketing strategy and marketing implementation.

Certain marketing strategies will define their implementation by default. For example, a firm such as Southwest Airlines with a strategy of improving customer service may turn to employee training programs as an important part of that strategy's implementation. Through profit sharing, many Southwest employees are also stockholders with a vested interest in the firm's success. Employee training and profit-sharing programs are common in firms that depend on their employees' commitment and enthusiasm to ensure quality customer service. However, employee training, as a tool of implementation, can also dictate the content of the firm's strategy. Perhaps a competitor of Southwest, who is in the process of implementing its own customer service strategy, realizes that it does not possess adequate resources to offer profit sharing and extensive training to its employees. Maybe the company simply lacks the financial resources or the staff required to implement these activities. Consequently, the company will be forced to go back to the planning stage and adjust its customer

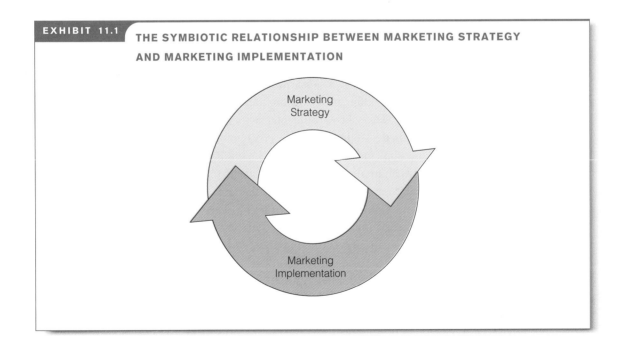

EXHIBIT 11.1   **THE SYMBIOTIC RELATIONSHIP BETWEEN MARKETING STRATEGY AND MARKETING IMPLEMENTATION**

Marketing Strategy

Marketing Implementation

service strategy. These continual changes in marketing strategy make implementation more difficult. Clearly, a SWOT analysis and strategic thrust conducted with an eye toward what the company can reasonably implement can reduce, but not completely eliminate, this problem.

Evolution   All firms face a simple truth in planning and implementation: Important environmental factors constantly change. As the needs and wants of customers change, as competitors devise new marketing strategies, and as the firm's own internal environment changes, the firm must constantly adapt. In some cases, these changes occur so rapidly that once the firm decides on a marketing strategy, it quickly becomes out of date. Because planning and implementation are intertwined, each must constantly evolve to fit the other. The process is never static because environmental changes require shifts in strategy, which require changes in implementation, which require shifts in strategy, and so on.

A related problem is that executives often assume there is only one correct way to implement a given strategy. This is simply not true. Just as strategy often results from trial and error, so does marketing implementation. Firms that are truly customer-oriented must be flexible enough to alter their implementation on the fly to fully embrace customer intimacy and respond to changes in customers' preferences. Firms that operate in oligopolistic markets face the evolution of strategy and implementation every day. In the airline industry, for example, competitors quickly alter their pricing strategies when one firm announces a reduction in fares on certain routes. These rapid changes require that firms be flexible in both marketing strategy and implementation.

Separation   The ineffective implementation of marketing strategy is often a self-generated problem that stems from the way that planning and implementation are carried out in most firms. As shown in Exhibit 11.2, middle- or upper-level managers often do strategic planning; however, the responsibility for implementation almost always falls on lower-level managers and frontline employees. Top executives often fall into a trap of believing that a good marketing strategy will implement itself. Because there is distance between executives and the day-to-day activities at the front line of the firm, they often do not understand the unique problems associated with implementing marketing strategy. Conversely, frontline employees—who do understand the challenges and hurdles of implementation—usually have a limited voice in planning the strategy.

Another trap that top executives often fall into is believing that frontline managers and employees will be excited about the marketing strategy and motivated to implement it. However, because they are separated from the planning process, these managers and employees often fail to identify with the firm's goals and objectives, and thus fail to fully understand the marketing strategy.[3] It is unrealistic for top executives to expect frontline managers and employees to be committed to a strategy they had no voice in developing, or to a strategy that they do not understand or they feel is inappropriate.[4]

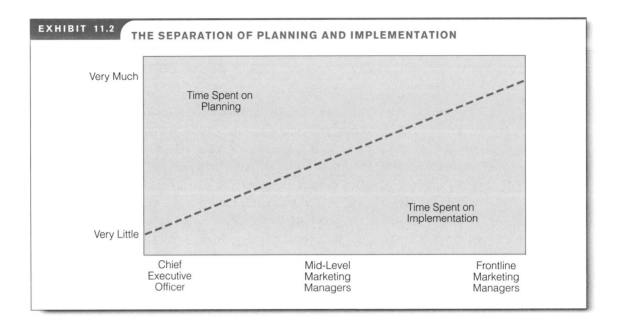

EXHIBIT 11.2   THE SEPARATION OF PLANNING AND IMPLEMENTATION

The Elements of Marketing Implementation

Marketing implementation involves a number of interrelated elements and activities, as shown in Exhibit 11.3. These elements must work together for strategy to be implemented effectively. Because we examined marketing strategy issues in previous chapters, we now look briefly at the remaining elements of marketing implementation.

Shared Goals and Values   Shared goals and values among all employees within the firm are the "glue" of successful implementation because they bind the entire organization together as a single, functioning unit. When all employees share the firm's goals and values, all actions will be more closely aligned and directed toward the betterment of the organization. Without a common direction to hold the organization together, different areas of the firm may work toward different outcomes, thus limiting the success of the entire organization. For example, one of the reasons for the tremendous success of the New Belgium Brewery is the fact that all employees have a commitment to make excellent craft beer in ways that conserve environmental resources.[5] Other firms, such as FedEx, Google, and ESPN, are well-known for their efforts to ensure that employees share and are committed to corporate goals and values.

Institutionalizing shared goals and values within a firm's culture is a long-term process. The primary means of creating shared goals and values is through employee training and socialization programs.[6] Although creating shared goals and values is a difficult process, the rewards are worth the effort. Some experts have argued that creating shared goals and values is the single most important element of implementation because it stimulates organizational commitment so that employees become more motivated to implement the marketing strategy, achieve the firm's goals and objectives, and serve more fully the needs of the firm's customers.[7]

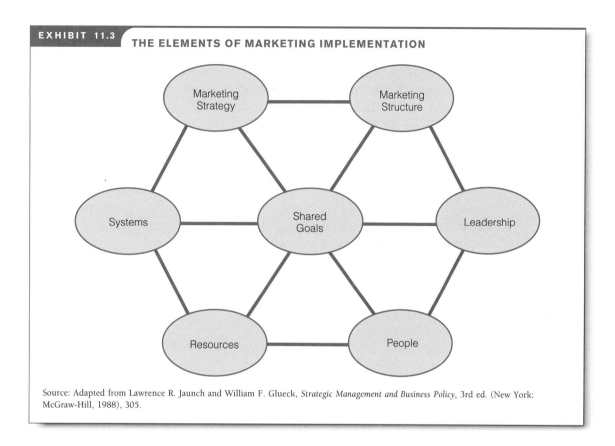

EXHIBIT 11.3 **THE ELEMENTS OF MARKETING IMPLEMENTATION**

Source: Adapted from Lawrence R. Jaunch and William F. Glueck, *Strategic Management and Business Policy*, 3rd ed. (New York: McGraw-Hill, 1988), 305.

Marketing Structure   Marketing structure refers to the methods of organizing a firm's marketing activities. Marketing structure establishes formal lines of authority, as well as the division of labor within the marketing function. One of the most important decisions that firms make is how to divide and integrate marketing responsibilities. This decision typically comes down to the question of centralization versus decentralization. In a centralized marketing structure, the top of the marketing hierarchy coordinates and manages all marketing activities and decisions. Conversely, in a decentralized marketing structure, the front line of the firm coordinates and manages marketing activities and decisions. Typically, decentralization means that frontline marketing managers have the responsibility of making day-to-day marketing decisions.

Both centralized and decentralized marketing structures have advantages. Centralized structures are very cost-efficient and effective in ensuring standardization within the marketing program. These advantages can be particularly critical to firms whose competitiveness depends upon maintaining a tight control over marketing activities and expenses.[8] For example, firms employing a strategy of operational excellence, such as Walmart or Dell, may find a centralized structure beneficial to ensuring operational efficiency and consistency. Decentralized marketing structures have the important advantage of placing marketing decisions closer to the front line, where serving customers is the number one priority. By decentralizing marketing decisions, frontline managers can be creative and flexible, allowing them to adapt to changing market conditions.[9] For this reason, firms that employ a strategy of customer intimacy, such as Ritz-Carlton or Nordstrom, may decentralize to ensure that they can respond to customers' needs in a timely manner. The decision to centralize or decentralize marketing activities is a trade-off between reduced costs and enhanced flexibility. However, there is no one correct way to organize the marketing function. The right marketing structure will depend on the specific firm, the nature of its internal and external environments, and its chosen marketing strategy.[10]

Systems and Processes   Organizational systems and processes are collections of work activities that absorb a variety of inputs to create information and communication outputs that ensure the consistent day-to-day operation of the firm.[11] Examples include information systems, strategic planning, capital budgeting, procurement, order fulfillment, manufacturing, quality control, and performance measurement. At IBM, for example, research engineers are evaluated on one- and three-year time frames. Employees receive bonuses based on the one-year evaluation, but are awarded rank and salary based on the three-year time frame. This unique system is designed to encourage innovation by minimizing the risk of failure in any single yearly evaluation.[12]

Resources   A firm's resources can include a wide variety of assets that can be brought together during marketing implementation. These assets may be tangible or intangible. Tangible resources include financial resources, manufacturing capacity, facilities, and equipment. Although not quite as obvious, intangible resources such as marketing expertise, customer loyalty, brand equity, corporate goodwill, and external relationships/strategic alliances are equally important.

Regardless of the type of resource, the amount of resources available can make or break a marketing strategy. However, a critical and honest evaluation of available resources during the planning phase can help ensure that the marketing strategy and marketing implementation are within the realm of possibility. Upon completion of the marketing plan, the analyst or planner must seek the approval of needed resources from top executives. This makes the communication aspects of the actual marketing plan document critical to the success of the strategy. Top executives allocate scarce resources based on the ability of the plan to help the firm reach its goals and objectives.

People (Human Resources)   The quality, diversity, and skill of a firm's human resources can also make or break the implementation of the marketing strategy. Consequently, human resource issues have become more important to the marketing function, especially in the areas of employee selection and training, evaluation and compensation policies, and employee motivation, satisfaction, and commitment. In fact, the marketing departments of many firms have taken over the human resources function to ensure that employees have a correct match to required marketing activities.[13] A number of human resource activities are vitally important to marketing implementation:

- **Employee Selection and Training**   One of the most critical aspects of marketing implementation is matching employees' skills and abilities to the marketing tasks to be performed.[14] It is no secret that some people are better at some jobs than others. We all know individuals who are natural salespeople. Some individuals are better at working with people, while others are better at working with tools or computers. The key is to match these employee skills to marketing tasks. A weakening economy and tightening job markets in recent years have forced firms to become more demanding in finding the right employee skills to match their required marketing activities.

Employee diversity is an increasingly important aspect of selection and training practices. As the U.S. population becomes more ethnically diverse, many firms take steps to ensure that the diversity of their employees matches the diversity of their customers. Many firms also face challenges with generational diversity in that most middle and upper managers are baby boomers (born 1946–1964), whereas most entry-level positions consist of members of Generation X (born 1965–1976) or Generation Y (born after 1976). In many cases, these younger employees have better training, more technological sophistication, and fewer political inclinations than their baby-boomer bosses. Managers must recognize these issues and adapt selection and training practices accordingly.

- **Employee Evaluation and Compensation**   Employee evaluation and compensation are also important to successful marketing implementation. An important decision to be made in this area is the choice between outcome- and behavior-based systems.[15] An outcome-based system evaluates and compensates employees based on measurable, quantitative standards such as sales volume or gross margin. This type of system is fairly easy to use, requires less supervision, and works well when market demand is fairly constant, the selling cycle is relatively short, and all efforts directly affect sales or profits. Conversely, behavior-based systems evaluate and compensate employees based on subjective, qualitative standards such as effort, motivation, teamwork, and friendliness toward customers. This type of system ties directly to customer satisfaction and rewards employees for factors they can control. However, behavior-based systems are expensive and difficult to manage because of their subjective nature and the amount of supervision required. The choice between outcome- and behavior-based systems depends on the firm and its products, markets, and customers' needs. The important point is to match the employee evaluation and compensation system to the activities that employees must perform in order to implement the marketing strategy.

- **Employee Motivation, Satisfaction, and Commitment**   Other important factors in the implementation of marketing strategy are the extent to which employees have the motivation to implement the strategy, their overall feelings of job satisfaction, and the commitment they feel toward the organization and its goals.[16] For example, one of the major contributors to Google's success is the strong social culture fostered by the company's leaders. Google provides its employees with things such as paid childcare, onsite laundry service, free transportation, gourmet food, onsite haircuts, and time off for personal activities. In return, Google's employees reward the company with exceptionally strong motivation and commitment.[17]

Though factors such as employee motivation, satisfaction, and commitment are critical to successful implementation, they are highly dependent on other elements of implementation, especially training, evaluation/compensation systems, and leadership. Marketing structure and processes can also have an impact on employee behaviors and attitudes. The key is to recognize the importance of these factors to successful marketing implementation and to manage them accordingly.

Leadership   The leadership provided by a firm's managers and the behaviors of employees go hand in hand in the implementation process. Leadership—often called the art of managing people—includes how managers communicate with employees, as well as how they motivate their people to implement the marketing strategy. As discussed in *Beyond the Pages 11.2*, today's business leaders must be courageous enough to take a long-term view of corporate success—one that often sacrifices short-term gains for the sake of the future.

Leaders have responsibility for establishing the corporate culture necessary for implementation success.[19] A good deal of research has shown that marketing

---

Beyond the Pages 11.2

THE NEW RULES OF CEO LEADERSHIP[18]

As we have discussed throughout this text, the rules of the road in marketing have changed in today's economy. Customers now hold most of the power due to increasing access to information, massive product selection and its associated competition, and increasingly mature markets characterized by commoditization. The dynamic nature of today's marketplace has touched all sectors of the global economy. Nowhere is this truer than in the executive suite of today's corporations. Many CEOs struggle with managing their monolithic organizations in an increasingly fast-paced environment.

According to *Fortune* magazine, there is a good reason for the challenges facing today's CEOs: Many of them operate using a set of rules developed in the 1980s and 1990s glory days of corporate expansion and global domination. Many of those rules were developed by the celebrity CEOs of the day such as Jack Welch (GE), Lou Gerstner (IBM), Al Dunlap (Sunbeam), and Roberto Goizueta (Coca-Cola). Of these, Jack Welch was the iconic leader. Most major corporations adopted his rules for business during the 1980s and 1990s. Welch's rules focused on corporate growth, maximizing market share, and the preeminence of quarterly earnings. However,

Fortune argues that Welch's corporate playbook is ill suited for today's market because the rapid pace of change and increasingly relentless competition force CEOs to take a long-term view of competitiveness. That view is less about market share and stock price and more about making decisions that ensure the viability and long-term survival of the corporation. Today's problems are different from those of 10 to 25 years ago. Consequently, old solutions no longer work.

As a way to provoke discussion of the issue, *Fortune* published a set of seven new rules for business that contradict virtually all of the old-school rules advocated by CEOs both past and present. These new rules argue for a dramatic shift away from short-term results in favor of long-term survival.

Of these new rules, the sixth (hiring a courageous CEO) may be the most critical. CEOs who adopt *Fortune*'s new rules for business must be willing to make investments that will not pay off for years—when that CEO is no longer in charge. The old ways of doing business—such as driving down costs through efficiency, growth through mergers and acquisitions, and careful manipulation of financial and accounting decisions—are solutions

(continued)

that simply do not work any longer. Anne Mulcahy, former CEO of Xerox, puts it this way: "You have to change when you're at the top of your game in terms of profit. If you're not nimble, there's no advantage to size. It's like a rock."

Unfortunately, Wall Street gives today's CEOs little incentive to change. A study by Booz Allen found that CEOs become vulnerable to being fired if their company's stock price falls below the S&P 500 by an average of 2 percent. To be courageous in the face of this obstacle, today's CEOs must be willing to take risks and stand up for what they believe is in the long-term interest of their firm. "You have to have the courage of your convictions," argues John Chambers, CEO of Cisco Systems.

Old Rules	New Rules	Examples
Big dogs own the street	Agile is best; being big can bite you	Big pharmaceutical companies are losing to smaller biotech firms; the decline of major U.S. automakers such as General Motors; Samsung's rise above Sony
Be No. 1 or No. 2 in the market	Find a niche, create something new	Energy drinks are more profitable than traditional soft drinks; the growth of Starbucks from a niche player to a coffee powerhouse
Shareholders rule	The customer is king	Businesses are better at managing earnings than the goods and services that produce those earnings; major scandals at firms like Enron and WorldCom
Be lean and mean	Look outside, not inside	Innovation drives today's success (i.e., Apple's iPod); the drive for quality and efficiency only improves *current* processes—it does not promote innovation
Rank your players; go with the A's	Hire passionate people	Employees want purpose and meaning in their work; the growth in hiring employees with passion (Apple, ESPN, Genentech)
Hire a charismatic CEO	Hire a courageous CEO	Today's CEOs must have the fortitude to make decisions that have long-term payoffs, not the quick fixes that are rewarded by Wall Street investors
Admire my might	Admire my soul	Powerful corporations are increasingly targeted by activists on a number of fronts; it is better to be company with a long-term vision that legitimizes its role in society

implementation is more successful when leaders create an organizational culture characterized by open communication between employees and managers. In this way, employees are free to discuss their opinions and ideas about the marketing strategy and implementation activities. This type of leadership also creates a climate where managers and employees have full confidence and trust in each other.

Approaches to Marketing Implementation

Whether good or bad, all leaders possess a leadership style, or way of approaching a given task. Managers can use a variety of approaches in implementing marketing strategies and motivating employees to perform implementation activities. In this section, we examine four of these approaches: implementation by command, implementation through change, implementation through consensus, and implementation as organizational cultural.[20]

Implementation by Command

Under this approach, the firm's top executives develop and select the marketing strategies, which are transmitted to lower levels where frontline managers and employees implement them. Implementation by command has two advantages: (1) It makes decision making much easier, and (2) it reduces uncertainty as to what is to be done to implement the marketing strategy. Unfortunately, this approach suffers from several disadvantages. The approach places less emphasis on the feasibility of implementing the marketing strategy. It also divides the firm into strategists and implementers: Executives who develop the marketing strategy are often far removed from the targeted customers it is intended to attract. For these reasons, implementation by command often creates employee motivation problems. Many employees do not have motivation to implement strategies in which they have little confidence.

Implementation by command is quite common in franchise systems. For example, the use of this approach by McDonald's creates a great deal of ongoing tension between the corporate office and its franchisees around the globe. In some cases, the tensions have become so hostile that franchisees have flatly refused to implement some corporate strategies, including service guarantees and some specific promotions. The latest battle is over the company's dollar menu promotion. Faced with rising food costs and an increase in the minimum wage, many McDonald's franchisees have stopped offering the dollar menu because the items have become unprofitable. The McDonald's corporate office, however, continues to expand the geographic scope of the dollar menu promotion. Franchisees are worried because the promotions are working a little too well: Dollar menu items now comprise 15 percent of McDonald's U.S. sales. As customers trade down to the dollar menu items, franchisees see their bottom line getting smaller.[21]

Implementation by command is common in franchise systems such as McDonald's.

Implementation Through Change

Implementation through change is similar to the command approach except that it focuses explicitly on implementation. The basic goal of implementation through change is to modify the firm in ways that will ensure the successful implementation of the chosen marketing strategy. For example, the firm's structure can be altered; employees can be transferred, hired, or fired; new technology can be adopted; the employee compensation plan can be changed; or the firm can merge with another firm. Mergers and acquisitions are common today in many industries, particularly in pharmaceuticals. Given the enormous expense of developing new drugs, many pharmaceutical firms have decided that it is easier and less expensive to offer new products or enter new markets by acquiring firms that already possess those capabilities.

The manager who implements through change is more of an architect and politician, skillfully crafting the organization to fit the requirements of the marketing strategy. There are many good historical examples of implementation through change: Lee Iacocca (Chrysler), Fred Smith (FedEx), and Steve Jobs (Apple) come to mind. A recent success story is Samsung and CEO Yun Jong Yong's passion for marketing. Once recognized as a cheap, high-volume supplier of computer chips, circuit boards, and electronic components, Samsung has emerged as a serious threat in the consumer electronics market. Samsung changed by dropping its 50-plus low-budget brands in favor of a single master Samsung brand. The shift has been so successful that Interbrand, a brand consulting firm, has ranked Samsung as one of the world's fastest growing brands since 2000. By shifting Samsung's operational focus from production to marketing, Yong has guided the company past Sony and Nokia in many product categories. In fact, Samsung is now the worldwide leader in the television market.[22]

Because many business executives are reluctant to give up even a small portion of their control (as is the case with the next two implementation approaches), they often favor implementation through change. The approach achieves a good balance between command and consensus, and its successes are quite evident in business today. However, despite these advantages, implementation through change still suffers from the separation of planning and implementation. By clinging to this power-at-the-top philosophy, employee motivation often remains an issue. Likewise, the changes called for in this approach often take a great deal of time to design and implement. This can create a situation where the firm becomes stagnant while waiting on the strategy to take hold. As a result, the firm can become vulnerable to changes in the marketing environment.

Implementation Through Consensus

Upper- and lower-level managers work together to evaluate and develop marketing strategies in the consensus approach to implementation. The underlying premise of this approach is that managers from different areas and levels in the firm come together as a team to "brainstorm" and develop the strategy. Each participant has different opinions as well as different perceptions of the marketing environment. The role of the top manager is that of a coordinator, pulling different opinions together to ensure the development of the best overall marketing strategy. Through this collective decision-making process, the firm agrees upon marketing strategy and reaches a consensus as to the overall direction of the firm.

Implementation through consensus is more advantageous than the first two approaches in that it moves some of the decision-making authority closer to the front line of the firm. Lower-level managers who participate in the strategy-formulation process have a unique perspective on the marketing activities necessary to implement the strategy. These managers are also more sensitive to the needs and wants of the firm's customers. In addition, because they have more involvement in developing the marketing strategy, lower-level managers often have a stronger motivation and commitment to the strategy to see that it is properly implemented. The inclusion of managers from other functional areas within the firm also ensures the coordination of the strategy across the entire firm. This too helps make the implementation process run more smoothly.

Implementation through consensus tends to work best in complex, uncertain, and highly unstable environments. The collective strategy-making approach works well in this environment because it brings multiple viewpoints to the table. However, implementation through consensus often retains the barrier between strategists and implementers. The end result of this barrier is that the full potential of the firm's human resources is not realized. Thus, for implementation through consensus to be truly effective, managers at all levels must communicate openly about strategy on an ongoing, rather than an occasional, basis.

Implementation as Organizational Culture

Under this approach, marketing strategy and its implementation become extensions of the firm's mission, vision, and organizational culture. In some ways, this approach is similar to implementation through consensus, except that the barrier between strategists and implementers completely dissolves. When personnel see implementation as an extension of the firm's culture, employees at all levels have permission to participate in making decisions that help the firm reach its mission, goals, and objectives.

With a strong organizational culture and an overriding corporate vision, the task of implementing marketing strategy is about 90 percent complete.[23] This occurs because all employees adopt the firm's culture so completely that they instinctively know what their role is in implementing the marketing strategy. Employees can design their own work procedures, as long as they are consistent with the organizational mission, goals, and objectives. This extreme form of decentralization is often called empowerment. Empowering employees means allowing them to make decisions on how to best perform their jobs. The strong organizational culture and a shared corporate vision ensure that empowered employees make the right decisions.

Although creating a strong culture does not happen overnight, it is absolutely necessary before employees can be empowered to make decisions. Employees must be trained and socialized to accept the firm's mission and to become a part of the firm's culture.[24] Despite the enormous amount of time involved in developing and using this approach to implementation, its rewards of increased effectiveness, efficiency, and increased employee commitment and morale are often well worth the investment. Notable firms that incorporate implementation within their cultures include ESPN, Google, and General Electric.

To summarize, firms and their managers can use any one of these four approaches to implement marketing strategy. Each approach has advantages and disadvantages as outlined in Exhibit 11.4. The choice of an approach will depend heavily on the firm's resources, its current culture, and the manager's own personal preferences. Many managers don't want to give up control over decision making. For these managers, connecting implementation and culture may be out of the question. Regardless of the approach taken, one of the most important issues that a manager must face is how to deal with the people who have responsibility for implementing the marketing strategy.

EXHIBIT 11.4 **ADVANTAGES AND DISADVANTAGES OF IMPLEMENTATION APPROACHES**

Implementation by Command

Basic Premise:	Marketing strategies are developed at the top of the organizational hierarchy and then passed to lower levels where frontline managers and employees are expected to implement them.
Advantages:	Reduces uncertainty and makes decision making easier Good when a powerful leader heads the firm Good when the strategy is simple to implement
Disadvantages:	Does not consider the feasibility of implementing the strategy Divides the firm into strategists and implementers Can create employee motivation problems

Implementation through Change

Basic Premise:	The firm is modified in ways that will ensure the successful implementation of the chosen marketing strategy.
Advantages:	Specifically considers how the strategy will be implemented Considers how strategy and implementation affect each other Used successfully by a large number of firms
Disadvantages:	Clings to a "power-at-the-top" mentality Requires a skilled, persuasive leader Changes can take time to design and implement, leaving the firm vulnerable to changes in the marketing environment

Implementation through Consensus

Basic Premise:	Different areas of the firm come together to "brainstorm" and develop the marketing strategy. Through collective agreement, a consensus is reached as to the overall direction of the firm.
Advantages:	Considers multiple opinions and viewpoints Increases firm-wide commitment to the strategy Moves some decision making closer to the front line of the firm Useful in complex, uncertain, and unstable environments
Disadvantages:	Some managers will not give up their authority Can lead to groupthink Slows down the strategy development and implementation process Requires open horizontal and vertical communication

Implementation as Organizational Cultural

Basic Premise:	Marketing strategy is a part of the overall mission and vision of the firm; therefore, the strategy is embedded in the firm's culture. Top executives manage the firm's culture to ensure that all employees are well versed in the firm's strategy.
Advantages:	Eliminates the barrier between strategists and implementers Increases employee commitment to organizational goals Allows for the empowerment of employees Can make marketing implementation much easier to accomplish
Disadvantages:	Must spend more money on employee selection and training Creating the necessary culture can be painful and time-consuming Quickly shifting to this approach can cause many internal problems

To examine this issue, we now turn our attention to internal marketing—an increasingly popular approach to marketing implementation.

Internal Marketing and Marketing Implementation

As more firms come to appreciate the importance of employees to marketing implementation, they have become disenchanted with traditional implementation approaches.

Several factors have caused these forces for change: U.S. businesses losing out to foreign competitors, high rates of employee turnover and its associated costs, and continuing problems in the implementation of marketing strategy. These problems have led many firms to adopt an internal marketing approach to marketing implementation.

The practice of internal marketing comes from service industries, where it was first used as a means of making all employees aware of the need for customer satisfaction. Internal marketing refers to the use of a marketing-like approach to motivate, coordinate, and integrate employees toward the implementation of the firm's marketing strategy. The goals of internal marketing are to (1) help all employees understand and accept their roles in implementing the marketing strategy, (2) create motivated and customer-oriented employees, and (3) deliver external customer satisfaction.[25] Note that internal marketing explicitly recognizes that external customer satisfaction depends on the actions of the firm's internal customers—its employees.

The Internal Marketing Approach

In the internal marketing approach, every employee has two customers: external and internal. For retail store managers, for example, the people who shop at the store are external customers, whereas the employees who work in the store are the manager's internal customers. In order for implementation to be successful, the store manager must serve the needs of both customer groups. If the internal customers do not receive proper information and training about the strategy and are not motivated to implement it, then it is unlikely that the external customers will be satisfied completely.

This same pattern of internal and external customers takes place throughout all levels of the firm. Even the CEO is responsible for serving the needs of his or her internal and external customers. Thus, unlike traditional implementation approaches where the responsibility for implementation rests with the front line of the firm, the internal marketing approach places this responsibility on all employees regardless of their level within the firm. In the end, successful marketing implementation comes from an accumulation of individual actions where all employees have responsibility for implementing the marketing strategy. Walmart founder Sam Walton was keenly aware of the importance of internal marketing. He visited Walmart stores on a regular basis, talking with customers and employees about how he could better serve their needs. He felt so strongly about the importance of his associates (his term for store personnel), that he always allowed them the opportunity to voice their concerns about changes in marketing activities. Sam had strong convictions that if he took good care of his associates, they would take good care of Walmart's customers.

The Internal Marketing Process

The process of internal marketing is straightforward and rests on many of the same principles used in traditional external marketing. As shown in Exhibit 11.5, internal marketing is an output of and input to both marketing implementation and the external marketing program. That is, neither the marketing strategy nor its implementation can be designed without a consideration for the internal marketing program.

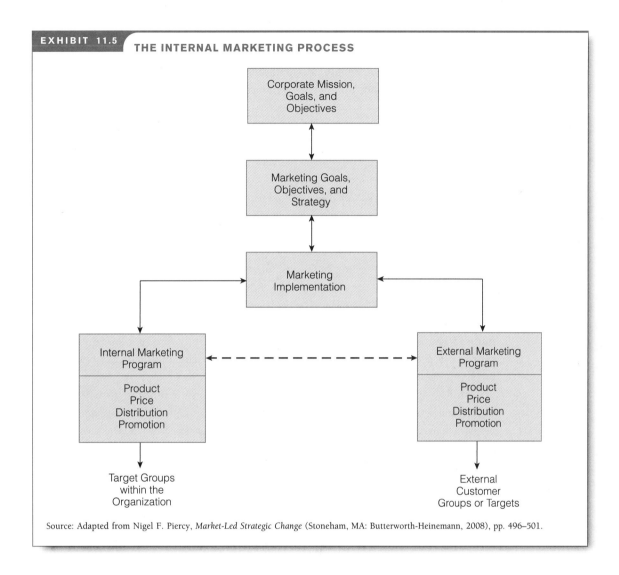

EXHIBIT 11.5   **THE INTERNAL MARKETING PROCESS**

Source: Adapted from Nigel F. Piercy, *Market-Led Strategic Change* (Stoneham, MA: Butterworth-Heinemann, 2008), pp. 496–501.

The product, price, distribution, and promotion elements of the internal marketing program are similar to the elements in the external marketing program. Internal products refer generally to marketing strategies that must be "sold" internally. More specifically, however, internal products refer to any employee tasks, behaviors, attitudes, or values necessary to ensure implementation of the marketing strategy.[26] Implementation of a marketing strategy, particularly a new strategy, typically requires changes on the part of employees. They may have to work harder, change job assignments, or even change their attitudes and expand their abilities. The increased effort and changes that employees must exhibit in implementing the strategy are equivalent to internal prices. Employees pay these prices through what they must do, change, or give up when implementing the marketing strategy.

Internal distribution refers to the internal communication of the marketing strategy. Planning sessions, workshops, formal reports, and personal conversations are all examples of internal distribution. Internal distribution also includes employee education, training, and socialization programs designed to assist in the transition to a new marketing strategy. Finally, all communication aimed at informing and persuading employees about the merits of the marketing strategy comprise internal promotion. Internal promotion can take the form of speeches, video presentations, audiotapes, and/or internal company newsletters. Given the growing diversity of today's employees, it is unlikely that any one medium will communicate with all employees successfully. Firms must realize that telling employees important information once in a single format is not good communication. Until the employees "get the strategy," communication has not taken place.

Successfully using an internal marketing approach requires an integration of many factors already discussed in this chapter. First, the recruitment, selection, and training of employees must be considered an important element of marketing implementation, with marketing having input to these human resource and personnel activities as necessary.[27] This ensures that employees will be matched to the marketing tasks to be performed. Second, top executives must be completely committed to the strategy and the overall marketing plan. It is naïve to expect employees to be committed when top executives are not. Simply put, the best planned strategy in the world cannot succeed if the employees responsible for its implementation do not believe in it or have a commitment to it.[28]

Third, employee compensation programs must be linked to the implementation of the marketing strategy. This means that employees should be rewarded on the basis of behaviors consistent with the marketing strategy. Fourth, the firm should be characterized by open communication among all employees, regardless of their level in the firm. Through open, interactive communication, employees come to understand the support and commitment of top executives, and how their jobs fit into the overall marketing implementation process. Finally, the firm's structure, policies, and processes should match the marketing strategy to ensure that the strategy can be implemented in the first place. On some occasions, the firm's structure and policies constrain the ability of employees to implement the strategy effectively. Although eliminating these constraints may mean that employees should be empowered to creatively fine-tune the strategy or its implementation, empowerment should be used only if the firm's culture can support it. However, if a company uses empowerment correctly as a part of the internal marketing approach, the firm can experience more motivated, satisfied, and committed employees, as well as enhanced customer satisfaction and improved marketing performance.[29]

Evaluating and Controlling Marketing Activities

A marketing strategy can achieve its desired results only if implemented properly. *Properly* is the key word. It is important to remember that a firm's intended marketing strategy often differs from the realized strategy (the one that actually takes place). This also means that actual performance is often different from expectations. Typically, there are four possible causes for this difference:

1. The marketing strategy was inappropriate or unrealistic.

2. The implementation was inappropriate for the strategy.

3. The implementation process was mismanaged.

4. The internal and/or external environments changed substantially between the development of the marketing strategy and its implementation.

To reduce the difference between what actually happened and what the company expected—and to correct any of these four problems—marketing activities must be evaluated and controlled on an ongoing basis. Although the best way to handle implementation problems is to recognize them in advance, no manager can successfully recognize all of the subtle and unpredictable warning signs of implementation failure.

With that in mind, it is important that the potential for implementation failures be managed strategically by having a system of marketing controls in place that allows the firm to spot potential problems before they cause real trouble. Exhibit 11.6 outlines a framework for marketing control that includes two major types of control: formal controls and informal controls.[30] Although we discuss each type of marketing control separately, most firms use combinations of these control types to monitor strategy implementation.

Formal Marketing Controls

Formal marketing controls are activities, mechanisms, or processes designed by the firm to help ensure the successful implementation of the marketing strategy. The elements of formal control influence the behaviors of employees before and during implementation, and are used to assess performance outcomes at the completion of the implementation process. These elements are referred to as input, process, and output controls, respectively.

Input Controls   Actions taken prior to the implementation of the marketing strategy are input controls. The premise of input control is that the marketing strategy cannot be implemented correctly unless the proper tools and resources are in place for it to succeed. Among the most important input controls are recruiting, selecting, and training employees. Another critical input control deals with financial resources. These control activities include resource allocation decisions (manpower and financial), capital outlays for needed facilities and equipment, and increased expenditures on research and development. Financial resources can make or break a marketing strategy or its implementation. For example, General Motors was quite slow to infuse additional capital into its Saturn division after it was first launched. For years, Saturn was unable to compete effectively due to constrained resources that limited its ability to develop and market new vehicles. A case in point: Saturn did not enter the highly profitable SUV market until 2002—long after its competitors. By the time GM did give Saturn additional

---

EXHIBIT 11.6   **A FRAMEWORK FOR MARKETING CONTROL**

Formal Controls: Control Activities Initiated by Management

Input controls—actions taken prior to implementation of the strategy

- Employee recruitment, selection, and training processes
- Human resource allocations
- Allocation of financial resources
- Capital outlays
- Research and development expenditures

Process controls—actions taken during implementation of the strategy

- Employee evaluation and compensation systems
- Employee authority and empowerment
- Internal communication programs
- Lines of authority/structure (organizational chart)
- Management commitment to the marketing plan
- Management commitment to employees

Output controls—evaluated after implementation of the strategy

- Formal performance standards (for example, sales, market share, and profitability)
- Marketing audits

Informal Controls: Unwritten Control Activities Initiated by Employees

Employee self-control—control based on personal expectations and goals

- Job satisfaction
- Organizational commitment
- Employee effort
- Commitment to the marketing plan

Social control—small-group control based on group norms and expectations

- Shared organizational values
- Social and behavioral norms in work groups

Cultural control—cultural control based on organizational norms and expectations

- Organizational culture
- Organizational stories, rituals, and legends
- Cultural change

Source: Adapted from Bernard J. Jaworski, "Toward a Theory of Marketing Control: Environmental Context, Control Types, and Consequences," *Journal of Marketing*, 52 (July 1988), pp. 23–39.

---

resources, it was too late to repair the brand's tarnished image. General Motors later dropped the Saturn division as a part of its corporate restructuring.[31]

Process Controls   Process controls include activities that occur during implementation, designed to influence the behavior of employees so they will support the strategy and its objectives. Although the number of process controls is potentially limitless and will vary from one firm to the next, Exhibit 11.6 provides some examples of universal process controls that all firms must employ and manage well.

The process control that stands out above all others is management commitment to the strategy. Several research studies have confirmed that management commitment to the marketing strategy is the single most important determinant of whether the strategy will succeed or fail.[32] This commitment is critical because employees learn to model the behavior of their managers. If management is committed to the marketing strategy, it is more likely that employees will be committed to it as well. Commitment to the marketing strategy also means that managers must be committed to employees and support them in their efforts to implement the strategy.

Another important process control is the system used to evaluate and compensate employees. In general, employees should be evaluated and compensated based on criteria relevant to the marketing strategy.[33] For example, if the strategy requires that salespeople increase their efforts at customer service, they should be rewarded on the basis of this effort, not on other criteria such as sales volume or the number of new accounts created. Further, the degree of authority and empowerment granted to employees is another important process control. Although some degree of empowerment can lead to increased performance, employees given too much authority often become confused and dissatisfied with their jobs.[34] Having good internal communication programs—another type of process control—can help to alleviate these problems.

Output Controls   Output controls ensure that marketing outcomes are in line with anticipated results. The primary means of output control involves setting performance standards against which actual performance can be compared. To ensure an accurate assessment of marketing activities, all performance standards should be based on the firm's marketing objectives. Some performance standards are broad, such as those based on sales, profits, or expenses. We say these are broad standards because many different marketing activities can affect them. Other performance standards are quite specific, such as many customer service standards (e.g., number of customer complaints, repair service within 24 hours, overnight delivery by 10:00 AM, on-time airline arrivals). In most cases, how the firm performs relative to these specific standards will determine how well it performs relative to broader standards.

But how specific should performance standards be? Standards should reflect the uniqueness of the firm and its resources, as well as the critical activities needed to implement the marketing strategy. In setting performance standards, it is important to remember that employees are always responsible for implementing marketing activities, and ultimately the marketing strategy. For example, if an important part of increasing customer service requires that employees answer the telephone by the second ring, then a performance standard should be set for this activity. Standards for the performance of marketing personnel are typically the most difficult to establish and enforce.

One of the best methods of evaluating whether performance standards have been achieved is to use a marketing audit to examine systematically the firm's marketing objectives, strategy, and performance.[35] The primary purpose of a marketing audit is to identify problems in ongoing marketing activities and to plan the necessary steps to correct these problems. A marketing audit can be long and elaborate, or it can be short and simple. Exhibit 11.7 displays a sample marketing audit. In practice, the elements of the audit must match the elements of the marketing strategy. The marketing audit should also be used to gauge the success of ongoing implementation activities—not just when problems arise.

Regardless of the organization of the marketing audit, it should aid the firm in evaluating marketing activities by

1. Describing current marketing activities and their performance outcomes.

2. Gathering information about changes in the external or internal environments that may affect ongoing marketing activities.

3. Exploring different alternatives for improving the ongoing implementation of marketing activities.

4. Providing a framework to evaluate the attainment of performance standards, as well as marketing goals and objectives.

EXHIBIT 11.7   A SAMPLE MARKETING AUDIT

Marketing Activities

1. In what specific marketing activities is the company currently engaged?
   - Product activities: research, concept testing, test marketing, quality control, etc.
   - Customer service activities: installation, training, maintenance, technical support, complaint handling, etc.
   - Pricing activities: financing, billing, cost control, discounting, etc.
   - Distribution activities: availability, channels used, customer convenience, etc.
   - Promotion activities: media, sales promotion, personal selling, public relations, etc.
2. Are these activities conducted solely by the company, or are some provided by outside contractors (either domestically or offshore)? If outside contractors are used, how are they performing? Should any of these outside activities be brought in-house?
3. What marketing activities do our competitors conduct that we do not offer? What additional marketing activities do customers want, need, or expect?

Standard Procedures for Each Marketing Activity

1. Do written procedures (manuals) exist for each marketing activity? If so, are these procedures (manuals) up to date? Do employees fully understand and follow these procedures (manuals)?
2. What oral or unwritten procedures exist for each marketing activity? Should these procedures be formally included in the written procedures or should they be eliminated?
3. Do marketing personnel regularly interact with other functional areas to establish standard procedures for each activity?

Performance Standards for Each Marketing Activity

1. What specific quantitative standards exist for each activity?
2. What qualitative standards exist for each activity?
3. How does each activity contribute to customer satisfaction within each marketing program element (i.e., product, pricing, distribution, promotion)?
4. How does each activity contribute to marketing goals and objectives?
5. How does each activity contribute to the goals and objectives of the company?

(continued)

Performance Metrics for Each Marketing Activity

1. What are the internal, profit-based measures for each marketing activity?
2. What are the internal, time-based measures for each marketing activity?
3. How is performance monitored and evaluated internally by management?
4. How is performance monitored and evaluated externally by customers?

Evaluation of Marketing Personnel

1. Are the company's current recruiting, selection, and retention efforts consistent (matched) with the requirements of the marketing activities?
2. What are the nature and content of employee training activities? Are these activities consistent with the requirements of the marketing activities?
3. How are customer-contact personnel supervised, evaluated, and rewarded? Are these procedures consistent with customer requirements?
4. What effect do employee evaluation and reward policies have on employee attitudes, satisfaction, and motivation?
5. Are current levels of employee attitudes, satisfaction, and motivation adequate?

Evaluation of Customer Support Systems

1. Are the quality and accuracy of customer service materials (e.g., instruction manuals, brochures, letters, etc.) consistent with the image of the company and its products?
2. Are the quality and appearance of physical facilities (e.g., offices, furnishings, layout, store decor, etc.) consistent with the image of the company and its products?
3. Are the quality and appearance of customer service equipment (e.g., repair tools, telephones, computers, delivery vehicles, etc.) consistent with the image of the company and its products?
4. Is the record keeping system accurate? Is the information always readily available when it is needed? What technology could be acquired to enhance record keeping abilities (e.g., bar code scanners, RFID, notebook computers, wireless telephones or smartphones)?

The information in a marketing audit is often obtained through a series of questionnaires that are given to employees, managers, customers, and/or suppliers. In some cases, outside consultants perform this ongoing evaluation. Using outside auditors has the advantages of being more objective and less time-consuming for the firm. However, outside auditors are typically quite expensive. A marketing audit can also be very disruptive, especially if employees are fearful of the scrutiny.

Despite their drawbacks, marketing audits are usually quite beneficial for the firms that use them. They are flexible in that the scope of the audit can be broad (to evaluate the entire marketing strategy) or narrow (to evaluate only a specific element of the marketing program). The results of the audit can be used to reallocate marketing efforts, correct implementation problems, or even to identify new opportunities. The end results of a well-executed marketing audit are usually better marketing performance and increased customer satisfaction.

Informal Marketing Controls

Formal marketing controls are overt in their attempt to influence employee behavior and marketing performance. Informal controls, on the other hand, are more subtle.

Informal marketing controls are unwritten, employee-based mechanisms that subtly affect the behaviors of employees, both as individuals and in groups.[36] Here, we deal with personal objectives and behaviors, as well as group-based norms and expectations. There are three types of informal control: employee self-control, social control, and cultural control.

Employee Self-Control   Through employee self-control, employees manage their own behaviors (and thus the implementation of the marketing strategy) by establishing personal objectives and monitoring their results. The type of personal objectives that employees set depends on how they feel about their jobs. If they have high job satisfaction and a strong commitment to the firm, they are more likely to establish personal objectives that are consistent with the aims of the firm, the marketing strategy, and the firm's goals and objectives. Employee self-control also depends on the rewards employees receive. Some employees prefer the intrinsic rewards of doing a good job rather than the extrinsic rewards of pay and recognition. Intrinsically rewarded employees are likely to exhibit more self-control by managing their behaviors in ways that are consistent with the marketing strategy.

Social Control   Social, or small group, control deals with the standards, norms, and ethics found in work groups within the firm.[37] The social interaction that occurs within these work groups can be a powerful motivator of employee behavior. The social and behavioral norms of work groups provide the "peer pressure" that causes employees to conform to expected standards of performance. If employees fall short of these standards, the group will pressure them to align with group norms. This pressure can be both positive and negative. Positive group influence can encourage employees to increase their effort and performance in ways consistent with the firm's goals and objectives. However, the opposite is also true. If the work group's norms encourage slacking or shirking of job responsibilities, employees will feel pressured to conform, or risk being ostracized for good work.

Cultural Control   Cultural control is very similar to social control, only on a much broader scale. Here, we concern ourselves with the behavioral and social norms of the entire firm. One of the most important outcomes of cultural control is the establishment of shared values among all members of the firm. Marketing implementation is most effective and efficient when every employee, guided by the same organizational values or beliefs, has a commitment to the same organizational goals.[38] Companies such as Lockheed Martin and Lexmark have strong organizational cultures that guide employee behavior. Unfortunately, cultural control is very difficult to master, in that it takes a great deal of time to create the appropriate organizational culture to ensure implementation success.

It is important to note that the formal controls employed by the firm affect, to a great extent, the informal controls that occur within an organization. However, the premise of informal control is that some aspects of employee behavior cannot be influenced by formal mechanisms, and therefore must be controlled informally through individual and group actions. *Beyond the Pages 11.3* describes how formal and

Beyond the Pages 11.3

MANAGING RISK THROUGH CULTURE[39]

Given the many examples of corporate misconduct and lapses in managerial judgment over the past 5 to 10 years, top executives have become keenly aware of the importance of managing corporate risk. The risks that today's organizations face come in many forms: financial risk, insurance risk, operational risk, product liability risk, strategic risks, reputational risks, and so on. As top executives try to better understand the stakes in enterprise risk management, they are beginning to realize that managing risk involves more than making the right decisions in the boardroom. True risk management involves assessing the risk culture of the entire firm.

Experts define risk culture as a system of values and behaviors within an organization that shape risk decisions. An organization's risk culture influences all employees, whether they are aware of it or not. It is this lack of awareness that creates potential problems. Even seemingly small decisions can have implications for corporate risk. The key is to ensure that all employees have a common understanding of risk, and how it is potentially connected to their day-to-day activities.

Sadly, the evidence suggests that most organizations do a poor job of nurturing their risk cultures. In a recent study, 58 percent of top executives stated that their employees had little to no understanding of their company's risk exposure. One-third said that even top managers had no formal risk training. Without training and an open dialogue about risk, organizations cannot ensure that well-informed and consistent decisions about risk occur throughout the firm.

How can an organization inspire a risk culture? Here are some suggested guidelines:

- **Set the tone at the top and the middle.** A key axiom of management is that leaders communicate their priorities through what they measure, discuss, praise, and criticize. These aspects of "setting the tone" are important because they provide examples for other employees to follow. However, this tone must emanate from all managers, not just those in the boardroom. The organization and its leaders must have a clearly articulated risk policy, as well as clear penalties for noncompliant behavior.

- **Understand the difference between good and bad risk.** Risk management has the potential to stifle an organization's creativity. Thus, it is critical that all employees understand the difference between acceptable risk based on innovation, and reckless behavior that jeopardizes the organization. The firm must also encourage and be willing to tolerate mistakes, and then learn from them.

- **Promote open communication about ethics and risk.** Creating the proper risk culture requires consistent messages to employees about risk and the importance of managing risk as a part of daily operations. This means that collaboration is essential in order to mitigate the ambiguity and competitiveness that typically lead to overly risky decisions.

- **Give employees incentives to manage risk.** Giving proper incentives to manage risk is important. However, it is often more important to eliminate any incentives that reward reckless behavior. This applies to everyone in the organization—from the boardroom to the mailroom.

- **Consider the risk cultures of potential partners.** To manage risk fully, an organization must ensure that its vendors, suppliers, and strategic partners share its risk tolerances. Risk should always be a consideration in choosing new partners or suppliers. Note that this also applies to the company's most important partners—its employees. Risk should always be a consideration in the hiring process.

Having a strong risk culture means that everyone knows the principles and boundaries within which the organization operates. It means that risk is openly discussed and weighed in all decisions. It ensures that everyone stays on the right path. However, creating this type of culture takes a great deal of patience and time. But then again, the crises that result from poor risk management are often far more costly in terms of time, money, and corporate reputation.

informal controls overlap to promote risk management principles in today's astute organizations.

Scheduling Marketing Activities

Through good planning and organization, marketing managers can provide purpose, direction, and structure to all marketing activities. However, the manager must understand the problems associated with implementation, understand the coordination of the various components of implementation, and select an overall approach to implementation before actually executing marketing activities. Upon taking these steps, the marketing manager with the responsibility for executing the plan must establish a timetable for the completion of each marketing activity.

Successful implementation requires that employees know the specific activities for which they are responsible and the timetable for completing each activity. Creating a master schedule of marketing activities can be a challenging task because of the wide variety of activities required to execute the plan, the sequential nature of many activities (some take precedence over others and must be performed first), and the fact that time is of the essence in implementing the plan.[40] The basic steps involved in creating a schedule and timeline for implementation include the following:

1. **Identify the specific activities to be performed.** These activities include all product, pricing, distribution, and promotion activities contained within the marketing plan. Specific implementation activities, such as employee training, structural changes, or the acquisition of financial resources, should be included as well.

2. **Determine the time required to complete each activity.** Some activities require planning and time before they can come to fruition. Others can occur rather quickly after the initiation of the plan.

3. **Determine which activities must precede others.** Many marketing activities must be performed in a predetermined sequence (such as creating an advertising campaign from copywriting, to production, to delivery). These activities must be identified and separated from any activities that can be performed concurrently with other activities.

4. **Arrange the proper sequence and timing of all activities.** In this step, the manager plans the master schedule by sequencing all activities and determining when each activity must occur.

5. **Assign responsibility.** The manager must assign one or more employees, teams, managers, or departments to each activity and charge them with the responsibility of executing the activity.

A simple, but effective way to create a master implementation schedule is to incorporate all marketing activities into a spreadsheet, like the one shown in Exhibit 11.8. A master schedule such as this can be simple or complex, depending on the level of detail included within each activity. The master schedule will also be unique to the

EXHIBIT 11.8

A HYPOTHETICAL THREE-MONTH MARKETING IMPLEMENTATION SCHEDULE

Activities	March 1	2	3	4	April 1	2	3	4	May 1	2	3	4
Product Activities												
Finalize package changes	•											
Production runs	•	•			•	•			•	•		
Pricing Activities												
Hold 10% off sale at retail						•						
Hold 25% off sale at retail											•	
Distribution Activities												
Shipments to warehouses	•		•		•		•		•		•	
Shipments to retail stores		•		•		•		•		•		•
10% quantity discount to the trade	•	•	•	•	•	•	•	•	•	•	•	•
Promotion Activities												
Informational website operational	•											
Television advertising		•	•		•	•				•	•	
Newspaper advertising		•		•	•	•		•	•	•		•
Online advertising	•		•			•		•	•		•	
Coupon in newspaper insert				•					•			
In-store POP displays		•	•	•	•							
In-store signage			•	•	•		•				•	•
Product placements	•	•	•	•	•	•	•	•	•	•	•	•

specific marketing plan tied to it. As a result, a universal template for creating a master schedule does not truly exist.

Although some activities must be performed before others, some activities can be performed concurrently with other activities or later in the implementation process. This requires tight coordination between departments—marketing, production, advertising, sales, and so on—to ensure the completion of all marketing activities on schedule. Pinpointing those activities that can be performed concurrently can greatly reduce the total amount of time needed to execute a given marketing plan. Because scheduling can be a complicated task, most firms use sophisticated project management techniques, such as PERT (program evaluation and review technique), CPM (critical path method), or computerized planning programs, to schedule the timing of marketing activities.

Lessons from Chapter 11

Marketing implementation

- Is critical to the success of any firm because it is responsible for putting the marketing strategy into action.

- Has been somewhat ignored throughout the history of business as most firms have emphasized strategic planning rather than strategic implementation.

- Is the process of executing the marketing strategy by creating and performing specific actions that will ensure the achievement of the firm's marketing objectives.

- Goes hand in hand with evaluation and control in determining the success or failure of the marketing strategy, and ultimately for the entire firm.

- Is usually the cause for the difference between intended marketing strategy—what the firm wants to happen—and realized marketing strategy—the strategy that actually takes place.

- Maintains a relationship with strategic planning that causes three major problems: interdependency, evolution, and separation.

The elements of marketing implementation include

- Marketing strategy—the firm's planned product, pricing, distribution, and promotion activities.

- Shared goals and values—the glue of implementation that holds the entire firm together as a single, functioning unit.

- Marketing structure—how the firm's marketing activities are organized.

- Systems and processes—collections of work activities that absorb a variety of inputs to create information and communication outputs that ensure the consistent day-to-day operation of the firm.

- Resources—include a wide variety of tangible and intangible assets that can be brought together during marketing implementation.

- People—the quality, diversity, and skill of a firm's human resources. The people element also includes employee selection and training, evaluation and compensation, motivation, satisfaction, and commitment.

- Leadership—how managers communicate with employees, as well as how they motivate their employees to implement the marketing strategy.

Approaches to implementing marketing strategy include

- Implementation by command—marketing strategies are developed and selected by the firm's top executives, then transmitted to lower levels where frontline managers and employees are expected to implement them.

- Implementation through change—focuses explicitly on implementation by modifying the firm in ways that will ensure the successful implementation of the chosen marketing strategy.

- Implementation through consensus—upper- and lower-level managers from different areas of the firm work together to evaluate and develop marketing strategies.

- Implementation as organizational culture—marketing strategy and implementation are seen as extensions of the firm's mission, vision, and organizational culture. Employees at all levels can participate in making decisions that help the firm reach its mission, goals, and objectives.

Internal marketing

- Refers to the use of a marketing-like approach to motivate, coordinate, and integrate employees toward the implementation of the firm's marketing strategy.

- Explicitly recognizes that external customer satisfaction depends on the actions of the firm's internal customers—its employees. If the internal customers are not properly educated about the strategy and motivated to implement it, then it is unlikely that the external customers will be satisfied completely.

- Places the responsibility for implementation on all employees regardless of their level within the firm.

- Is based on many of the same principles used in traditional external marketing. The product, price, distribution, and promotion elements of the internal marketing program are similar to the elements in the external marketing program.

In evaluating and controlling marketing activities

- The firm's intended marketing strategy often differs from the realized strategy for four potential reasons: (1) the marketing strategy was inappropriate or unrealistic; (2) the implementation was inappropriate for the strategy; (3) the implementation process was mismanaged; or (4) the internal and/or external environments changed substantially between the development of the marketing strategy and its implementation.

- It is important that the potential for implementation failures be managed strategically by having a system of marketing controls in place.

- Firms design and use formal input, process, and output controls to help ensure the successful implementation of the marketing strategy.

- Firms use output controls, or performance standards, extensively to ensure that marketing outcomes are in line with anticipated results.

- Employees individually (self-control), in workgroups (social control), and throughout the firm (cultural control) use personal objectives and group-based norms and expectations to informally control their behaviors.

Scheduling marketing activities

- Requires that employees know the specific activities for which they are responsible and the timetable for completing each activity.

- Can be a challenging task because of the wide variety of activities required to execute the plan, the sequential nature of many marketing activities, and the fact that time is of the essence in implementing the plan.

- Involves five basic steps: (1) identifying the specific activities to be performed, (2) determining the time required to complete each activity, (3) determining which activities must precede others, (4) arranging the proper sequence and timing of all activities, and (5) assigning responsibility to employees, managers, teams, or departments.

Questions for Discussion

1. Forget for a moment that planning the marketing strategy is equally as important as implementing the marketing strategy. What arguments can you make for one being more important than the other? Explain your answers.

2. If you were personally responsible for implementing a particular marketing strategy, which implementation approach would you be most comfortable using, given your personality and personal preferences? Why? Would your chosen approach be universally applicable to any given situation? If not, what would cause you to change or adapt your approach? Remember, adapting your basic approach means stepping out of your personal comfort zone to match the situation at hand.

3. What do you see as the major stumbling blocks to the successful use of the internal marketing approach? Given the hierarchical structure of employees in most organizations (e.g., CEO, middle management, staff employees), is internal marketing a viable approach for most organizations? Why or why not?

Exercises

1. Find a recent news article about an organization that changed its marketing strategy. What were the reasons for the change? How did the organization approach the development and implementation of the new strategy?

2. One of the best sources for shared goals and values to guide implementation is the firm's own mission or values statement. Find the mission or values statement for the organization you identified in Exercise 1. Do you see evidence of the mission or values in the way the organization handled its change in marketing strategy? Explain.

3. Think about the unwritten, informal controls in your life. Develop a list of the controls that exist at work, at home, or at school (or substitute another context

such as church, social gatherings, or public activities). Are these controls similar or different? Why?

	Controls at Work	Controls at Home	Controls at School
Self-Control (personal norms and expectations for behavior)			
Social Control (norms and expectations in small groups)			
Cultural Control (norms and expectations in the entire organization)			

CHAPTER 12

Developing and Maintaining Long-Term Customer Relationships

Introduction

Up until now, we have examined the process of strategic planning from its initial stages through the implementation of the marketing plan. At this point, however, we take the opportunity to step back from the process to look at it holistically. Firms often lose sight of the big picture as they rush to complete product development and test marketing, or put the finishing touches on a media campaign. All of the activities involved in developing and implementing the marketing program have one key purpose: to develop and maintain long-term customer relationships. However, as we have seen, implementing a marketing strategy that can effectively satisfy customers' needs and wants has proven difficult in today's rapidly changing business environment. The simple fact is that thorough research, strong competitive advantages, and a well-implemented marketing program are often not enough to guarantee success.

In times past, developing and implementing the "right" marketing strategy was all about creating a large number of transactions with customers in order to maximize the firm's market share. Companies paid scant attention to discovering customers' needs and finding better ways to solve customers' problems. In today's economy, however, that emphasis has shifted to developing strategies that attract and retain customers over the long term. As illustrated in *Beyond the Pages 12.1*, 1-800-Flowers.com does this effectively through a comprehensive understanding of its customers, including their expectations, motivations, and behaviors. With this knowledge in hand, firms like 1-800-Flowers.com can then offer the right marketing program to increase customer satisfaction and retain customers over the long term.

In this chapter, we examine how the marketing program can be leveraged as a whole to deliver quality, value, and satisfaction to customers. We begin by reviewing the strategic issues associated with the customer relationship management process. Developing long-term customer relationships is one of the best ways to insulate the firm against competitive inroads and the rapid pace of environmental change and product commoditization. Next, we address the critical topics of quality and value as we concern ourselves with how the entire marketing program is tied to these issues.

Beyond the Pages 12.1

1-800-FLOWERS.COM FOCUSES ON CUSTOMERS[1]

Customer service. Trust. One-to-one customer interactions. Customer loyalty. These are the foundations of the steady growth of 1-800-Flowers.com over the past 20 years. Since the company went online in 1991, CEO Jim McCann has used a laser-like focus on customers to make 1-800-Flowers the number one floral retailer in the United States. McCann's company earned $919 million in 2008 and adds roughly 3 million new customers every year.

1-800-Flowers uses the Internet to connect to customers and puts a lot of effort into creating a 360-degree, holistic view of each customer. The company collects customer information at every point where it contacts a customer—sales, loyalty programs, surveys, direct mail advertising, sales promotions (contests and sweepstakes), and affiliate programs (with florists, credit card companies, and airlines)—and uses it to create customized communications and product offerings for each of the roughly 30 million customers in its database. 1-800-Flowers uses a sophisticated segmentation system that analyzes transactional behaviors (recency, frequency, monetary) and combines it with gift-buying behaviors. This information is then tied to each customer's psychographic profile to create targeted messages for each customer segment. The company then uses a variety of different metrics—financial, customer retention and acquisition, brand awareness, purchase intentions, and customer recommendations—to measure performance.

To increase customer loyalty, 1-800-Flowers launched Fresh Rewards, a point-based loyalty program. Customers earn one point for every dollar they spend, and then receive a Fresh Reward pass via email when they have accumulated 200 points. There are also higher tiered programs for customers who spend $400 or $800 per year. The program is somewhat unique in that it offers only 1-800-Flowers merchandise as rewards. In addition to increasing customer loyalty, the Fresh Rewards program also allows the company to collect more in-depth information from customers.

To further develop customer relationships, 1-800-Flowers recently expanded its product mix well beyond floral products. The company now sells traditional gifts such as gift baskets, popcorn, cupcakes, and monogrammed bath towels—through both 1-800-Flowers and its new 1-800-Baskets venture. Today, 50 percent of the company's sales come from nonfloral products. To develop even stronger social links with customers, the company has launched applications for the Blackberry and the iPhone, and plans to open an online store through Facebook.

For 1-800-Flowers, the key to success has been its ability to integrate and leverage the massive amount of data that it collects from its customers. However, CEO McCann also favors the old-school approach to understanding customers. McCann states that his training as a social worker helps him to understand the importance of solid relationships. True to his background, McCann regularly goes into the field to talk with customers. On key occasions such as Mother's Day and Valentine's Day, McCann and other executives answer the phones, deliver products, and work in the company's retail stores. McCann puts it this way: "Our competitors are all about the sales, we're about relationships. We are helping our customers connect with the important people in their lives through flowers and gifts created and designed for specific relationships, occasions, and sentiments. That's the difference."

Finally, we explore key issues with respect to customer satisfaction, including customer expectations and metrics for tracking customer satisfaction over time.

Managing Customer Relationships

As we briefly mentioned in Chapter 1, creating and maintaining long-term customer relationships requires that organizations see beyond the transactions that occur today to look at the long-term potential of a customer. To do this, the organization must strive to develop a relationship with each customer rather than generate a large number of discrete transactions. Before a relationship can be mutually beneficial to both the firm and the customer, it must provide value to both parties. This is one of the basic requirements of exchange noted in Chapter 1. Creating this value is the goal of *customer relationship management* (CRM), which is defined as a business philosophy aimed at defining and increasing customer value in ways that motivate customers to remain loyal.[2] In essence, CRM is about retaining the right customers. It is important to note that CRM does not focus solely on end customers. Rather, CRM involves a number of different groups:[3]

- **Customers**   They are the end users of a product, whether they are businesses or individual consumers.

- **Employees**   Firms must manage relationships with their employees if they are to have any hope of fully serving customers' needs. This is especially true in service firms where employees *are* the service in the eyes of customers. Retaining key employees is a vital part of CRM.

- **Supply Chain Partners**   Virtually all firms buy and sell products upstream and/or downstream in the supply chain. This involves the procurement of materials from, or the sale of finished products to, other firms. Either way, maintaining relationships with key supply chain partners is critical to satisfying customers.

- **External Stakeholders**   Relationships with key stakeholders must also be managed effectively. These include government agencies, nonprofit organizations, or facilitating firms that provide goods or services that help a firm achieve its goals.

Delivering good value to customers requires that firms use CRM strategies to effectively manage relationships with each of these groups. This effort includes finding ways to integrate all of these relationships toward the ultimate goal of customer satisfaction.

To fully appreciate the concepts behind customer relationship management, organizations must develop a new perspective on the customer—one that shifts the emphasis from "acquiring customers" to "maintaining clients," as shown in Exhibit 12.1. Although this strategic shift has been underway for some time in business markets, technological advancements allow CRM to be fully embraced in consumer markets as well. Firms that are exceptionally good at developing customer relationships possess "relationship capital" that stems from the value generated by the trust, commitment, cooperation, and interdependence among relationship partners. With respect to competitive advantages, many see relationship capital as the most important resource or asset that an organization can possess, as it represents a powerful advantage that can be leveraged to make the most of marketing opportunities.[4]

Developing Relationships in Consumer Markets

Developing long-term customer relationships can be an arduous process. Over the life of the relationship, the firm's goal is to move the customer through a progression of

---

EXHIBIT 12.1

STRATEGIC SHIFT FROM ACQUIRING CUSTOMERS TO MAINTAINING CLIENTS

Acquiring Customers	Maintaining Clients
Customers are "customers"	Customers are "clients"
Mass marketing	One-to-one marketing
Acquire new customers	Build relationships with current customers
Discrete transactions	Continuous transactions
Increase market share	Increase share of customer
Differentiation based on groups	Differentiation based on individual customers
Segmentation based on homogeneous needs	Segmentation based on heterogeneous needs
Short-term strategic focus	Long-term strategic focus
Standardized products	Mass customization
Lowest-cost provider	Value-based pricing strategy
One-way mass communication	Two-way individualized communication
Competition	Collaboration

---

stages, as shown in Exhibit 12.2. The objective of CRM is to move customers from having a simple awareness of the firm and its product offering, through levels of increasing relationship intensity, to the point where the customer becomes a true advocate for the firm and/or its products. Note that true CRM attempts to go beyond the creation of satisfied and loyal customers. Ultimately, the firm will possess the highest level of relationship capital when its customers become true believers or sponsors for the company and its products. For example, Harley-Davidson, which is now over 100 years old, is a great example of a firm that enjoys the highest levels of customer advocacy. Harley owners exhibit a cult-like love for the brand that most other companies do not possess. Other firms, such as Apple, Coca-Cola, and Nike also enjoy a high degree of customer advocacy.

© Susan Van Etten

Harley-Davidson enjoys one of the highest levels of customer advocacy around the world.

In consumer markets, one of the most viable strategies to build customer relationships is to increase the firm's *share of customer* rather than its market share. This strategy involves abandoning the old notions of acquiring new customers and increasing transactions to focus on more fully serving the needs of current customers. Financial services are a great example of this strategy in action. Most consumers purchase financial services from different firms. They bank at one institution, purchase insurance from a different institution, and handle their investments through another. To counter this fact of life, many companies now offer all of these services under one

EXHIBIT 12.2   STAGES OF CUSTOMER RELATIONSHIP DEVELOPMENT

Relationship Stage	CRM Goals	Examples
Awareness	Promote customer knowledge and education about the product or company. Prospect for new customers.	Product advertising Personal selling (cold calls) Word of mouth
Initial purchase	Get product or company into customers' evoked set of alternatives. Stimulate interest in the product. Stimulate product trial.	Advertising Product sampling Personal selling
Repeat customer	Fully satisfy customers' needs and wants. Completely meet or exceed customers' expectations or product specifications. Offer incentives to encourage repeat purchase.	Good product quality and value-based pricing Good service before, during, and after the sale Frequent reminders and incentives
Client	Create financial bonds that limit the customer's ability to switch products or suppliers. Acquire more of each individual customer's business. Personalize products to meet evolving customer needs and wants.	Frequent customer cards Frequent-flier programs Broad product offering
Community	Create social bonds that prevent product or supplier switching. Create opportunities for customers to interact with each other in a sense of community.	Membership programs Affinity programs Ongoing personal communication
Advocacy	Create customization or structural bonds that encourage the highest degree of loyalty. Become such a part of the customer's life that he or she is not willing to end the relationship. Think of customers as partners.	Customer events and reunions Long-term contracts Brand-related memorabilia

roof. For example, Regions Financial Corporation offers retail and commercial banking, trust, securities brokerage, mortgage, and insurance products to customers in a network of over 1,900 offices in 16 states across the South, Midwest, and Texas. Regions' commitment to relationships is evident in its product offerings such as "personal banking" and "relationship money market accounts."[5] Rather than focus exclusively on the acquisition of new customers, Regions tries to more fully serve the financial needs of its current customers, thereby acquiring a larger share of each customer's financial business. By creating these types of relationships, customers have little incentive to seek out competitive firms to fulfill their financial services needs. This relationship capital gives Regions an important strategic asset that can be leveraged as it competes with rival banks and financial institutions, both locally and online.

Focusing on share of customer requires an understanding that all customers have different needs; therefore, not all customers have equal value to a firm. The most basic application of this idea is the 80/20 rule: 20 percent of customers provide 80 percent of business profits. Although this idea is not new, advances in technology and data collection techniques now allow firms to profile customers in real time. In fact, the ability to track customers in detail can allow the firm to increase sales and loyalty among the bottom 80 percent of customers. The goal is to rank the profitability of individual customers to express their lifetime value (LTV) to the firm. Some customers—those who require considerable handholding or who frequently return products—are simply too expensive to keep given the low level of profits they generate. These bottom-tier customers can be "fired" or required to pay very high fees for additional service. Banks and brokerages, for example, slap hefty maintenance fees on small accounts. This allows the firm to spend its resources to more fully develop relationships with its profitable customers.

The firm's top-tier customers (those that fall into the top 20 percent) are the most obvious candidates for retention strategies. These customers are the most loyal and the most profitable, so the firm should take the necessary steps to ensure their continuing satisfaction. Customers that fall just outside of this tier, or second-tier customers, can be encouraged to be better customers or even loyal customers with the right incentives. Exhibit 12.3 outlines strategies that can be used to enhance and maintain customer relationships. The most basic of these strategies is based on financial incentives that encourage increased sales and loyalty. However, financial incentives are easily copied by competitors and are not typically good for retaining customers in the long run. To achieve this ultimate goal, the firm must turn to strategies aimed at closely tying the customer to the firm. These structural connections are the most resilient to competitive action and the most important for maintaining long-term customer relationships.

Developing Relationships in Business Markets

Relationship management in business markets is much like that in consumer markets. The goal is to move business buyers through a sequence of stages, where each stage represents an increasing level of relationship intensity. Although business relationships may not approach the cult-like, emotional involvement found in some consumer markets, businesses can nonetheless become structurally bound to their supply chain partners. These relationships can give both parties an advantage with respect to relationship capital: One firm maintains a loyal and committed customer; the other maintains a loyal and committed supplier. Both parties may also consider each other to be strong partners or advocates within the entire supply chain.

Although our discussion certainly involves generalizations (e.g., some consumer marketers are better at building relationships than many business marketers), relationship development in business markets can be more involving, more complex, and much riskier than relationships in consumer markets. This occurs because business buyers typically have fewer options to choose from; and the financial risks are typically higher. For example, when computer processor maker AMD purchased ATI (a respected maker of graphics chips), the buying and partnering options for AMD, Intel, and other firms in the computer industry changed overnight. Intel, not wanting to support its closest competitor, began working with Nvidia (ATI's major competitor) in producing compatible chipsets for computers. Later, Apple's partnership with Intel meant that they also had to turn to Nvidia for graphics chips.[6] The tight integration of firms in the business market is due to the nature of business buying, the presence of long-term contractual obligations, and the sheer dollars involved in many business purchases. Further, business relationships are built on win–win strategies that focus on cooperation and improving the value of the exchange for both parties, not on strict negotiation strategies where one side "wins" and the other side "loses."

EXHIBIT 12.3   STRATEGIES FOR ENHANCING AND MAINTAINING CUSTOMER RELATIONSHIPS

Increasing Relationship Intensity →

	Financial Incentives	Social Bonding	Enhanced Customization	Structural Bonding
Strategy	Using financial incentives to increase customer loyalty	Using social and psychological bonds to maintain a clientele	Using intimate customer knowledge to provide one-to-one solutions or mass customization	Creating customized product offerings that create a unique delivery system for each client
Examples	• Volume discounts • Coupons • Frequent-customer programs	• Membership programs • Customer-only events • Community outreach programs	• Customer reminder notifications • Personal recommendations • Personal shopping programs	• Structured, lock-step programs • Automated electronic transactions • Contractual relationships
Used by	• Airlines • Grocery retailers • Music clubs	• Health clubs • Churches • Credit cards	• Auto service centers • Electronic retailers • Department stores • Professional services	• Colleges and universities • Banks • Bundled telecom services
Advantages	• Effective in the short term • Easy to use	• Difficult for competitors to copy • Reduces brand switching	• Promotes strong loyalty and greatly reduces brand switching • Very difficult for competitors to copy customer knowledge	• Ultimate reduction in brand switching • Products become intertwined in customers' lifestyles
Disadvantages	• Easily imitated • Hard to end incentives once started • Can promote continual brand switching	• Social bonds take time to develop • Customer trust is critical and must be maintained at all times	• Can be quite expensive to deliver • Takes time to develop	• Customer resistance • Time-consuming and costly to develop

Business relationships have become increasingly complex, as decisions must be made with an eye toward the entire supply chain, not just the two parties involved. In these cases, the relationships that are developed enhance the ability of the entire supply chain to better meet the needs of final customers. Over the past several years, a number of changes have occurred in business relationships, including these:

- **A Change in Buyers' and Sellers' Roles** To build stronger relationships, buyers and sellers have shifted away from competitive negotiation (trying to drive prices up or down) to focus on true collaboration. This represents a major change for many companies.

- **An Increase in Sole Sourcing** Supplier firms will continue to sell directly to large customers or move to selling through systems suppliers that put together a set of products from various suppliers to deliver a comprehensive solution. The continuing growth in online e-procurement systems is one result of this trend.

- **An Increase in Global Sourcing** More than ever, buyers and sellers scan the globe in search of suppliers or buyers that represent the best match with their specific needs and requirements. The relationship building process is so costly and complex that only the best potential partners will be pursued.

- **An Increase in Team-Based Buying Decisions** Increasingly, teams from both buying and supplying firms make purchase decisions. These teams consist of employees from different areas of expertise that are central to the success of both firms. Increasingly, senior management of both firms will be represented on these teams as economic buyers, for both sides play a major role in setting goals and objectives.

- **An Increase in Productivity Through Better Integration** Firms that closely align their buying and selling operations have the capacity to identify and remove any inefficiency in the process. This increased productivity leads to a reduction in both hard and soft costs, thereby enhancing the profitability of both firms. This integration can be extended throughout the supply chain. In the future, only the most efficient supply chains will survive, particularly as more procurement moves into the electronic arena.

These fundamental changes in the structure of most business relationships will lead to dramatic changes in the way that organizations work together. Only those firms willing to make strategic, as opposed to cosmetic, changes in the way they deal with their customers or suppliers are likely to prosper as we move forward in this century.

Quality and Value: The Keys to Developing Customer Relationships

To build relationship capital, a firm must be able to fulfill the needs of its customers better than its competitors. It must also be able to fulfill those needs by offering high-quality goods and services that are a good value relative to the sacrifices customers must make to acquire them. When it comes to developing and maintaining customer relationships, quality is a double-edged sword. If the quality of a good or service is poor, the organization obviously has little chance of satisfying customers or maintaining relationships with them. The adage of "trying something at least once" applies here. A firm may be successful in generating first-time transactions with customers, but poor quality guarantees that repeat purchases will not occur. On the other hand, good quality is not an automatic guarantee of success. Think of it as a necessary but insufficient condition of successful customer relationship management. It is at this point that value becomes critical to maintaining long-term customer relationships.

Understanding the Role of Quality

Quality is a relative term that refers to the degree of superiority of a firm's goods or services. We say that quality is relative because it can only be judged in comparison to competing products or when compared to an internal standard of excellence. The concept of quality also applies to many different aspects of a firm's product offering. The total product offering of any firm consists of at least three interdependent components, as illustrated in Exhibit 12.4: the core product, supplemental products, and symbolic and experiential attributes.

The Core Product   The heart of the offering, the core product, is the firm's *raison d'tre*, or justification for existence. As shown in Exhibit 12.4, the core can be a tangible good—such as a Chevy Silverado—or an intangible service—such as the Verizon Wireless communication network. Virtually every element of the marketing program

EXHIBIT 12.4 COMPONENTS OF THE TOTAL PRODUCT OFFERING			
	Core Product	Supplemental Products	Symbolic and Experiential Attributes
Chevrolet Silverado 1500	Transportation Hauling/towing	Accessories GMAC financing Replacement parts Service department	"The most dependable, longest-lasting full-size pickup on the road"
Verizon Wireless communication network	Communication	Phone options Rate plan options Free long distance VCAST music and video	"America's largest and most reliable network"
John Deere lawn tractor	Lawn and garden maintenance	Accessories Financing Delivery	John Deere "Green" "Nothing Runs Like a Deere"
Michelin Tires	Tires Safety	Broad availability Installation Financing	Security—"Because a lot is riding on your tires" "A Better Way Forward" The Michelin Man
Waldorf Astoria New York City	Lodging	Mid-Manhattan location Restaurants Room service Executive lounge	Extraordinary hospitality The first "Grand Hotel" Art Deco styling

has an effect on the quality (or perceived quality) of the core product; however, the firm's product and branding strategies are of utmost importance. Because the core product is the part of the offering that delivers the benefits desired by customers, the form utility offered by the core product is vital to maintaining its quality. For example, the quality of an entrée in a restaurant depends on the form utility created through the combination of quality raw ingredients and expert preparation. In service offerings, the core product is typically composed of three interrelated dimensions:[7]

- **People** The interaction among the customer, the firm's employees, and other customers present during service delivery.

- **Processes** The operational flow of activities or steps in the service delivery process. Processes can be done through technology or face-to-face interaction.

- **Physical Evidence** Any tangible evidence of the service, including written materials, the service facility, people, or equipment; includes the environment in which the service is delivered.

As a whole, service firms struggle daily with maintaining the quality of their core service offerings. Because services are so people intensive, effective implementation of the marketing strategy (i.e., shared goals, employee motivation, and employee skills) is a major factor that helps to ensure consistency and quality. The quality of service also depends more on issues such as responsiveness to customer requests, consistent and reliable service over time, and the friendliness and helpfulness of the firm's employees. The quality of tangible goods depends more on issues such as durability, style, ease of use, comfort, or suitability for a specific need.

Whether a good or a service, the firm has little chance of success if its core product is of inferior quality. However, even providing a high-quality core product is not enough to ensure customer satisfaction and long-term customer relationships. This occurs because customers expect the core product to be of high quality or at least at a level necessary to meet their needs. When the core product meets this level of expected quality, the customer begins to take it for granted. For example, customers take their telephone service for granted because they expect it to work every time. They only take notice when clarity becomes an issue or when the service is unavailable. The same thing can be said for a grocery retailer who consistently delivers high-quality food and service. Over time, the core product no longer stands out at a level that can maintain the customer relationship in the long term. It is at this point that supplemental products become critical.

Supplemental Products Supplemental products are goods or services that add value to the core product, thereby differentiating the core product from competing product offerings. In most cases, supplemental products are extra features or benefits that enhance the total product experience; however, they are not necessary for the core product to function correctly. In many product categories, the true difference between competing products or brands lies in the supplemental products provided by the firm. For example, every hotel is capable of delivering the core product—a room with a bed in which to spend the night. Although the quality of the core product varies among hotels, the important differences lie in the supplemental products. Upscale hotels such as Hyatt or Hilton offer many amenities—such as spas, restaurants, health clubs, valet parking, and room service—that budget hotels like Motel 6 or Econolodge do not. Wireless phone service is another example. All wireless firms can fulfill their customers' communication needs; however, customers use supplemental products such as different phone options; rate plans; and freebies like rollover minutes, free roaming, and free long distance to differentiate one product offering from another. In business markets, supplemental services are often the most important factor in developing long-term relationships. Services such as financing, training, installation, and maintenance must be of top quality to ensure that business customers will continue to maintain a relationship with the supplier firm.

It is interesting to note that companies do not market many products with the core product in mind. When was the last time an automaker touted a car or truck on its ability to fulfill your transportation needs (i.e., getting you from point A to point B)? Rather, they focus on supplemental product attributes such as special financing, roadside assistance, and warranties. Supplemental products such as these depend heavily on the product, pricing, and distribution elements of the marketing program. For example, in addition to selling a wide range of name-brand products, Amazon also offers its own credit card and free "super saver" shipping on many orders of $25 or more. These supplemental services, along with 24/7 access and competitive pricing, make Amazon a formidable competitor in many different product categories.

Symbolic and Experiential Attributes   Marketers also use symbolic and experiential differences—such as image, prestige, and brand—to differentiate their products. These features are created primarily through the product and promotional elements of the marketing program. Without a doubt, the most powerful symbolic and experiential attributes are based on branding. In fact, many brands—like Mercedes, iPod, Ritz-Carlton, Coca-Cola, Rolex, Disney World, and Ruth's Chris Steak House—only need their names to get the message across. These brands have immense power in differentiating their products because they can project the entire product offering (core, supplemental, and symbolic/experiential) with one word or phrase. Other types of products don't necessarily rely upon branding, but on their uniqueness to convey their symbolic and experiential nature. Major sporting events, such as the Super Bowl, the NCAA Final Four, or the Tour de France are certainly good examples of this. Even local athletic events, such as high school football games, can have symbolic and experiential qualities if the rivalry is intense.

Delivering Superior Quality

Delivering superior quality day in and day out is one of the most difficult things that any organization can do with regularity. In essence, it is difficult to get everything right—even most of the time. During the 1980s and 1990s, strategic initiatives such as total quality management, ISO 9000, and the advent of the Baldrige Award were quite successful in changing the way businesses thought about quality. As a result, virtually every industry saw dramatic improvements in quality during that time.

Today, however, most businesses struggle with improving the quality of their products, whether they are the core product or supplemental products. As we discussed in Chapter 1, this has happened because (1) customers have very high expectations about quality; (2) most products today compete in mature markets; and (3) many businesses compete in markets with very little real differentiation among product offerings. As products become further commoditized, it becomes very difficult for marketers to make their products stand out among a crowd of competitors. A great deal of research has been conducted to determine how businesses can improve the quality of their products. These four issues stand out:[8]

- **Understand customers' expectations.** It is not surprising that the basis of improving quality is also the starting point for effective customer relationship management. The delivery of superior quality begins with a solid understanding of customers' expectations. This means that marketers must stay in touch with customers by conducting research to better identify their needs and wants. Although this research can include large-scale efforts such as surveys or focus groups, it can also include simple and inexpensive efforts such as customer comment cards or having managers interact in a positive fashion with customers. Advances in technology have greatly improved our ability to collect and analyze information from individual customers. New tools such as data warehousing and data mining hold great promise in enabling firms to better understand customers' expectations and needs.

- **Translate expectations into quality standards.** Firms that can successfully convert customer information into quality standards ensure that they hear the voice of the customer. If customers want better ingredients, friendlier employees, or faster delivery, then standards should be set to match these desires. It is often the case, however, that managers set standards that meet organizational objectives with no consideration for customer expectations. As discussed in *Beyond the Pages 12.2*, this commonly occurs when managers set standards based on productivity, efficiency, or cost reductions rather than quality or customer service. In these cases, the temptation is to focus on internal benchmarks such as cost control or speed rather than customer benchmarks such as quality and satisfaction.

- **Uphold quality standards.** The best quality standards are of little use if they are not delivered accurately and consistently. At issue is the ability of managers and employees to deliver quality that is consistent with established standards. Greeting customers by name, answering the phone on the second ring, and delivering a hot pizza within 30 minutes are all examples of quality standards that may, or may not, be achieved. Successfully achieving these standards depends mostly on how well the strategy is implemented. However, it also depends on the ability of the firm to fully fund the quality effort. For example, many retailers—including Walmart—at one time had standards for opening additional checkout lanes when there were more than three people in line. However, these retailers failed to deliver on this

Beyond the Pages 12.2

CUSTOMER SERVICE VERSUS EFFICIENCY[9]

As consumers, we are supposed to be living the good life. After all, we have access to an unprecedented variety and assortment of goods and services from around the globe. Everything we need is practically at arm's length and available 24/7. If things are so great, then why do we still suffer from poor service, long wait times, ignored complaints, and the feeling that we are just another number to most firms? In other words, why is customer service so bad? Are we just spoiled or do companies not care anymore?

Although we may be spoiled and some companies might not care about service, the truth is that our own demands for convenient, fast, and low-priced products are at odds with our demands for better customer service. As firms look to drive down costs and increase speed, they focus more on internal efficiency benchmarks based on costs and time-based measures of performance. This means they focus less on customer-driven benchmarks like customer service performance. This tendency is also driven by human nature: It is much easier to measure costs and time than something as subjective as customer satisfaction. As a result, more and more firms must continuously walk a fine line between service and operational efficiency.

Some companies successful walk this line (Southwest Airlines is a good example). Others, however, have damaged customer relationships in their attempt to reduce costs. This has been especially true with the recent downturn in the economy. In some cases, firms have been forced to reduce customer service to maintain or improve profitability. Three recent examples include the car rental industry, Home Depot, and Dell.

Hertz and Avis

After Hertz laid off 4,000 employees in early 2009, customers were faced with a shortage of customer service personnel. The company reduced its "instant return" hours at smaller airports, along with reducing the number of personnel at all locations. Avis took a similar route to reduce expenses during the economic downturn. The company cut service, reduced staff, and moved most of their instant return staff to airport counters. The result for

customers: longer lines, increased wait time, and declining customer satisfaction. The result wasn't what Hertz and Avis had hoped for either. Both companies saw many of their most loyal customers move to competing rental companies. In time, both Hertz and Avis reversed their policies and increased the number of agents for their instant return customers.

Home Depot

After years of record growth and profits, Home Depot shifted its strategy to focus on expanding its contractor supply business and increasing efficiency through cost cutting and streamlined operations. Along the way, customer service slipped on the company's list of priorities. Full-time employees were replaced by part-timers, employee incentives for good service were cut, and the employee profit-sharing pool declined from $90 million to $44 million in one year. The end result: Home Depot slipped to dead last in customer satisfaction among major U.S. retailers. More importantly, the company finds itself 6 percentage points behind Lowe's, which has pursued a strategy that promotes more customer-friendly stores. Home Depot argues that delivering perfect service is impossible because it processes 1.3 billion transactions per year. However, the company has launched a major customer service program that provides millions of dollars in employee incentives to deliver top-quality service. Home Depot has also abandoned many of its command-and-control practices that significantly reduced employee morale.

Dell

Dell's strategy and its success have long been tied to internal efficiency. Its business model of selling via phone and Internet is a textbook example of supply chain integration and operational excellence. In recent years, however, Dell has pursued cost cutting with a vengeance. The reason is competition. Virtually all of Dell's competitors now match the company on pricing and product availability. Unfortunately, Dell's moves have alienated its customers, especially in the company's call center

(continued)

operations, which Dell outsourced to firms in foreign countries. Not surprising, Dell's customer satisfaction ratings, along with its market share, fell dramatically.

To turn things around, Dell initiated a $100 million program to improve customer service. The company began by appointing a new director of customer service, who immediately expanded the size of Dell's call centers to 1,000 to 3,000 reps and began an aggressive cross-training program. Before the training, 45 percent of customer service calls required at least one transfer to an appropriate specialist. By

cross-training reps to handle more issues, Dell plans to buck that trend.

If business can learn anything from these examples, it's that they can never win the fight between customer service and efficiency. Cost cutting that reduces customer service almost always has to be reinstated once customers start demanding better quality, more attention, and increased value for their money. Customer expectations are simply too high—and competitors too plentiful—for businesses to ignore.

standard due to the expense of staffing additional employees to operate the registers.

- **Don't overpromise.** It goes without saying that customers will be disappointed if an organization fails to deliver on its promises. The key is to create realistic customer expectations for what can and cannot be delivered. All communication to customers must be honest and realistic with respect to the degree of quality that can be delivered. Intentionally misleading customers by making promises that cannot be kept is a guaranteed recipe for disaster.

Of these four issues, having a thorough understanding of customer expectations is the most critical because it sets the stage for the entire quality improvement effort. Customer expectations are also vital to ensuring customer satisfaction. We will look more closely at customer expectations later in this chapter.

Understanding the Role of Value

Earlier, we stated that quality is a necessary, but insufficient, condition of effective customer relationship management. By this, we mean that exceptionally high product quality is of little use to the firm or its customers if the customers cannot afford to pay for it or if the product is too difficult to obtain. In the context of utility (want satisfaction), sacrificing time, place, possession, and psychological utility for the sake of form utility may win product design awards, but it will not always win customers.

Value is critical to maintaining long-term customer relationships because it allows for the necessary balance among the five types of utility and the elements of the marketing program. As a guiding principle of marketing strategy, value is quite useful because it includes the concept of quality, but is broader in scope. It takes into account every marketing program element and can be used to consider explicitly customer perceptions of the marketing program in the strategy development process. Value can also be used as a means of organizing the internal aspects of marketing strategy development.

In Chapter 8, we defined value as a customer's subjective evaluation of benefits relative to costs to determine the worth of a firm's product offering relative to other product offerings. To see how each marketing program element is related to value, we need to break down customer benefits and costs into their component parts, as shown below and in Exhibit 12.5:

$$\text{Perceived Value} = \frac{(\text{Core Product Quality} + \text{Supplemental Product Quality} + \text{Experiential Quality})}{(\text{Monetary Costs} + \text{Nonmonetary Costs})}$$

Different buyers and target markets have varying perspectives on value. Although monetary cost is certainly a key issue, some buyers place greater importance on other elements of the value equation. To some, good value is about product quality. To these customers, the product element of the marketing program is the most crucial to achieving good value. To others, value hinges on the availability and quality of supplemental products. Here, the firm's product, customer service, pricing, and

EXHIBIT 12.5   CONNECTIONS BETWEEN VALUE AND THE MARKETING PROGRAM

Value Components	Marketing Program Elements			
	Product Strategy	Pricing Strategy	Distribution Strategy	IMC Strategy
Core Product Quality	Product features Brand name Product design Quality Ease of use Warranties Guarantees	Image Prestige	Availability Exclusivity	Image Prestige Reputation Personal selling

Supplemental Product Quality	Value-added features
	Accessories
	Replacement parts
	Repair services
	Training
	Customer service
	Friendliness of
	    employees
		Financing
		Layaway
		Image
		Prestige
			Availability
			Exclusivity
			Delivery
			Installation
			On-site training
				Friendliness of
				    employees
				Personal selling

Experiential Quality	Entertainment Uniqueness Psychological benefits	Image Prestige	Convenience Retail atmosphere Retail décor 24/7 availability Overnight delivery	Image Prestige Reputation Personal selling
Monetary Transactional Costs	Quality Exclusive features	Selling price Delivery charges Installation charges Taxes Licensing fees Registration fees	Delivery charges Installation charges Taxes	Image Prestige Reputation Personal selling

Monetary Life Cycle Costs	Durability
	Reliability
	Product design
		Maintenance costs
		Cost of consumables
		Repair costs
		Costs of replacement
		    parts
			Availability of
			    consumables
			Availability of
			    replacement parts
			Speed of repairs
				Reputation
				Personal selling

Nonmonetary Costs	Durability
	Reliability
	Minimize
	    opportunity costs
		Guarantees
		Return policy
			Convenience
			Wide availability
			24/7 access
				Reputation
				Reinforce purchase
				    decision

distribution strategies come together to create value. For other buyers, good value is all about convenience. These customers place greater emphasis on distribution issues such as wide product availability, multiple locations, 24/7 access, or even home delivery to achieve good value. The relationships among marketing program elements must constantly be managed to deliver good value to customers. It is important for managers to remember that any change in one program element will have repercussions for value throughout the entire marketing program.

Core Product, Supplemental Product, and Experiential Quality   The relationship between quality and value is most apparent in the quality of the customer benefits depicted in the top portion of the value equation. Here, good value depends on a holistic assessment of the quality of the core product, supplemental products, and experiential attributes. Although each can be judged independently, most customers look at the collective benefits provided by the firm in their assessments of value. Consequently, firms are able to create unique combinations of core, supplemental, and experiential benefits that help drive value perceptions. Consider a hotel stay at the Hyatt versus Motel 6. Despite their obvious differences, both can deliver the same value to different customers at different points in time. The Hyatt may offer better form utility and caché, but Motel 6 may be less expensive and closer to attractions. The overall perception of value is driven by customer needs, expectations, and the sacrifices required in obtaining the benefits provided by each firm.

Monetary and Nonmonetary Costs   Customer costs include anything that the customer must give up to obtain the benefits provided by the firm. The most obvious cost is the monetary cost of the product, which comes in two forms: transactional costs and life-cycle costs. *Transactional costs* include the immediate financial outlay or commitment that must be made to purchase the product. Other than the purchase price of the product, examples of these costs include sales taxes, usage taxes, licensing fees, registration fees, and delivery or installation charges. For example, appliance or furniture retailers can increase value by offering free delivery or installation when their competitors charge for these services. *Life-cycle costs* include any additional costs that customers will incur over the life of the product, such as the costs of consumable supplies, maintenance, and repairs. Hyundai and Kia, for example, offer long-term warranties on their cars, vans, and SUVs that significantly reduce life cycle costs for their customers. Product quality, warranties, and the availability of repair services all play into the equation when customers judge monetary costs. Firms that have the capability to reduce transactional or life-cycle costs can often provide a better value than their competitors.

Nonmonetary costs are not quite as obvious as monetary costs, and customers sometimes ignore them. Two such costs include the time and effort customers expend to find and purchase goods and services. These costs are closely related to a firm's distribution activities. To reduce time and effort, the firm must increase product availability, thereby making it more convenient for customers to purchase the firm's products. The growth in nonstore and electronic retailing is a direct result of firms taking steps to reduce the time and effort required to purchase their products, thereby reducing customers' nonmonetary costs. The sheer number of products that customers can have delivered directly to their homes is a testament to the growing importance of customers' time.

Offering good basic warranties or extended warranties for an additional charge can reduce risk, another nonmonetary cost. Retailers reduce risk by maintaining liberal return and exchange policies. Personal safety and security risks come into play when customers purchase products that are potentially dangerous. Common examples include tobacco products, alcohol, firearms, and exotic products such as skydiving, bungee jumping, and dangerous pets. The final nonmonetary cost, opportunity costs, is harder for the firm to control. Customers incur opportunity costs because they forgo alternative products in making a purchase. Some firms attempt to reduce opportunity costs by promoting their products as being the best or by promising good service after the sale. To anticipate opportunity costs, marketers must consider all potential competitors, including total budget competitors that offer customers alternatives for spending their money.

Competing on Value

After breaking down value into its component parts, we can better understand how a firm's marketing strategy can be designed to optimize customer value. By altering each element of the marketing program, the firm can enhance value by increasing core, supplemental, or experiential quality and/or reducing monetary or non-monetary costs. This effort must be based on a thorough understanding of customers' needs and wants, as well as an appreciation for how the firm's customers define value.

In consumer markets, retailers offer good examples of how value can be delivered by altering one or more parts of the value equation. Convenience stores offer value to customers by reducing nonmonetary costs (time and effort) and increasing monetary prices. These high-priced (in dollars) stores stay in business because customers value their time and effort more than money in many situations. Online retailers offer a similar mix of value by reducing time and effort costs, and in some cases by reducing monetary costs through free shipping or by not collecting sales taxes. Customers who want the best quality may be willing to spend large sums of money and/or spend more time searching because they consider their non-monetary costs to be less important. These consumers are likely to shop at retailers such as Macy's, Nordstrom, or Saks rather than discount chains. Finally, specialty stores, like Victoria's Secret or Banana Republic, offer an attractive mix of value in terms of quality clothing, fashionable styling, excellent service, and attractive décor, albeit at higher monetary prices.

Those in business markets often define value in terms of product specifications, availability, and conformity to a delivery schedule rather than in terms of price or convenience. Business customers must ensure that the products purchased will work right the first time, with minimal disruption to ongoing operations. In some cases, products have value not only because of their features or quality, but because the buying firm has a long-standing relationship with the supplying firm. Business buyers tend to become loyal to suppliers that consistently meet their expectations, solve their problems, and cause them no headaches. All of this is not to say that monetary considerations are not important. In fact, unlike most consumers, business buyers are keenly aware of total transactional and life-cycle costs as they seek to reduce the total lifetime expenditure associated with a particular purchase. Business customers will quite often pay more in up-front costs if the total lifetime cost can be reduced.

Obviously, different market segments will have different perceptions of good value. The key is for the marketer to understand the different value requirements of each segment and adapt the marketing program accordingly. From a strategic perspective, it is important to remember that each marketing program element is vital to delivering value. Strategic decisions about one element alone can change perceived value for better or worse. If a decision lowers overall value, the firm should consider modifying other marketing program elements to offset this decrease. For example, an increase in price may have to be offset by an increase in customer benefits to maintain the value ratio.

Customer Satisfaction: The Key to Customer Retention

In the final part of this chapter, we look at customer satisfaction and the role it plays in maintaining long-term customer relationships. To maintain and manage customer satisfaction from a strategic point of view, managers must understand customer expectations and the differences between satisfaction, quality, and value. They must also make customer satisfaction measurement a long-term, continuous commitment of the entire organization.

Understanding Customer Expectations

Although customer satisfaction can be conceived in a number of ways, it is typically defined as the degree to which a product meets or exceeds the customer's expectations about that product. Obviously, the key to this definition lies in understanding customer expectations and how they are formed. Marketing researchers have discovered that customers can hold many different types of expectations, as shown in Exhibit 12.6. Customer expectations can vary based on the situation. For example, expectations are likely to be very high (i.e., closer to the ideal end of the range) in situations where personal needs are very high. In highly involving situations such as weddings, birthdays, or funerals, customers will demand a great deal from the firm. Expectations also tend to be higher when customers have many alternatives for meeting their needs. This connection between expectations and alternatives is one reason that serving customers in highly commoditized markets is so challenging. Other situations can cause customer expectations to be lower (i.e., closer to the tolerable end of the range), such as when the purchase is not involving, or when the monetary or nonmonetary prices are low. Customers can also become more tolerant of weak or poor performance when they have fewer product alternatives or when the poor performance is beyond the control of the firm (e.g., bad weather, excessively high demand, natural disasters).

EXHIBIT 12.6   RANGE OF CUSTOMER EXPECTATIONS

Type of Expectation	Descriptive Example	Typical Situations	Expectation Range
Ideal Expectations	"Everyone says this is the best MP3 player on the market. I want to get my sister something special for her birthday."	Highly involving purchases Special occasions Unique events	High (Desired)
Normative Expectations	"As expensive as this MP3 player is, it ought to hold a lot of music and come with several included accessories."	Shopping comparisons Value judgments	
Experience-Based Expectations	"I bought this brand of MP3 player last time and it served me very well."	Frequent purchase situations Brand loyalty	
Minimum Tolerable Expectations	"I know it's not the best MP3 player out there. I only bought it because it was inexpensive."	Price-driven purchases Low-involvement purchases	Low (Adequate)

Source: Adapted from James H. Myers, *Measuring Customer Satisfaction* (Chicago: American Marketing Association, 1999); and Valarie A. Zeithaml, Leonard L. Berry, and A. Parasuraman, "The Nature and Determinants of Customer Expectations of Service," *Journal of the Academy of Marketing Science*, 21 (January 1993), pp. 1–12.

The Zone of Tolerance   The difference between the upper and lower end of the range of possible customer expectations is an important strategic consideration in managing customer satisfaction. Marketers often refer to the upper end of expectations as desired performance expectations (what customers want) and the lower end of the range as adequate performance expectations (what customers are willing to accept). As shown in Exhibit 12.7, the extent of the difference between desired and adequate performance is called the zone of tolerance.[10] The width of the zone of tolerance represents the degree to which customers recognize and are willing to accept variability in performance (i.e., quality, value, or some other measurable aspect of the marketing program). Performance can fall above the zone of tolerance, within the zone of tolerance, or below it:

- **Customer Delight** occurs when actual performance exceeds the desired performance expectation. This level of performance is rare and quite surprising when it occurs. Therefore, customers find it to be memorable.

- **Customer Satisfaction** occurs when actual performance falls within the zone of tolerance. Satisfaction levels vary based on where performance falls within the zone (high or low).

- **Customer Dissatisfaction** occurs when actual performance falls below the adequate performance expectation. Depending upon the severity of the performance level, customers may go beyond dissatisfaction to become frustrated or even angry. This too can be very memorable for customers.

We addressed these three issues in Chapter 6 as being a consequence of the buying process. Now, with the marketing plan developed and implemented, we can think of

EXHIBIT 12.7   **THE ZONE OF TOLERANCE**

Customer Delight	Customer Satisfaction	Customer Dissatisfaction
(Performance Exceeds Desired Expectations)	(Performance Within Zone of Tolerance)	(Performance Falls Below Adequate Expectations)
Marketing Performance Desired Expectations Adequate Expectations	Desired Expectations Marketing Performance Adequate Expectations	Desired Expectations Adequate Expectations Marketing Performance
Typical Zone of Tolerance (Performance Factors of Average Importance)	Wide Zone of Tolerance (Performance Factors of Less Importance)	Narrow Zone of Tolerance (Performance Factors of Highest Importance)

these issues in a strategic sense by considering the zone of tolerance as a moving target. If the zone is narrow, the difference between what customers want and what they are willing to accept is also narrow. This means that the marketer will have a relatively more difficult time matching performance to customer expectations. Hence, customer satisfaction is harder to achieve when the zone of tolerance is narrow. Conversely, customer satisfaction is relatively easier to achieve when the zone of tolerance is wide. In these instances, the marketer's hurdle is lower and the satisfaction targets are easier to hit. Delighting the customer by exceeding desired expectations is an exceedingly difficult task for any marketer. And causing customer dissatisfaction by failing to meet even adequate expectations is a situation that should be avoided at all times.

Customers will typically hold different expectation levels and zones of tolerance for different factors of performance. In a restaurant, for example, customers might have a narrow zone of tolerance for food quality, an even narrower zone of tolerance for service quality, an average zone of tolerance for wait time, and a relatively wide zone of tolerance for cleanliness. From the marketer's point of view, two issues are important. First, the firm must clearly understand the relevant performance factors about which customers will hold performance expectations. Customers can have expectations for just about anything, though there are typically only a few factors that are critical for most customers. Many firms look first at factors dealing with product strategy; however, critical performance factors can cut across the entire marketing program. Second, the firm must track expectations and performance over time. Tracking performance levels vis-á-vis expectations and the zone of tolerance is a useful diagnostic tool for both strategic planning and the management of customer satisfaction. The approach is also useful for tracking the effectiveness of performance improvements and in assessing the performance of new goods or services. In the end, tracking both expectations and performance is an important way to ensure that customer satisfaction remains stable or improves over time. Declining customer satisfaction suggests a need for immediate corrective action.

Managing Customer Expectations   Many marketers ask two key questions as they work toward managing customer expectations: (1) Why are customer expectations unrealistic? and (2) Should we strive to delight our customers by consistently exceeding their desired expectations? Although it is true that customers are more demanding today than ever (especially American consumers), their expectations are typically not very unrealistic. Most customers are looking for the basics of performance—things that a firm is supposed to do or has promised to do.[11] For example, flights should take off and land on time, meals in a restaurant should taste good and be prepared as ordered, new cars should be hassle-free throughout the warranty period, and your soft drink should be cold and fresh. On these and other basic factors of performance, it is essentially impossible for the firm to exceed customer expectations. These basic factors represent the bare minimum: If the firm wants to exceed expectations, it has to go above and beyond the call of duty. *Beyond the Pages 12.3* explains how exceeding customer expectations is an important component of customer loyalty.

The second question about delighting the customer is a bit more controversial. Firms should always strive to exceed adequate expectations. After all, this is the basic delineation between satisfaction and dissatisfaction. The tougher question is whether the firm should try to exceed desired expectations. The answer depends on several issues. One is the time and expense involved in delighting customers. If delighting a customer does not translate into stronger customer loyalty or long-term customer retention, then it is not likely to be worth the effort. It may also not be a good investment if delighting one customer lowers performance for other customers. Another issue is whether continually delighting customers raises their expectations over time. To be effective, customer delight should be both surprising and rare, not a daily event. Firms should look for small ways to delight customers without elevating expectations beyond what can reasonably be delivered. Finally, the firm must be aware of whether its initiatives to delight the customer can be copied by competitors. If customer delight is easily copied, it ceases to be a key means of differentiation for the firm.

Beyond the Pages 12.3

SATISFIED, BUT NOT LOYAL[12]

Generally speaking, American consumers are a satisfied lot. At least that's what survey after survey reveals. Sure there are ups and downs, and some industries or firms fare better than others, but the general tendency is a positive one. Despite this good news, however, a recent survey indicated that roughly 30 percent of satisfied customers would switch to a new company if given a good reason to do so. This begs the question: Why will satisfied customers leave a firm for a competitor? The answer is that customer satisfaction is not the same thing as customer loyalty.

Customer satisfaction by itself tells a firm very little about where it stands with customers. There are two issues at work: relative satisfaction and customer expectations. Relative satisfaction tells a firm where it ranks against the competition. For example, Coca-Cola's satisfaction rating of 85 says little about the firm and its products until that scored is compared with Dr. Pepper (87) and Pepsi (84). Similarly, Apple might consider its most recent satisfaction score of 84 to be somewhat low until that score is compared to Dell (75) and HP (74). Comparisons like these are important because customers make similar comparisons when making purchase decisions. Customers may be satisfied with a specific product or company but will switch if they believe they will be better satisfied (via higher quality, a better user experience, or a better value) by another firm. For this reason, satisfied customers are not necessarily loyal customers.

To increase loyalty, firms must look at the second issue: customer expectations. Customer expectations are key because they serve as the anchor points for customer satisfaction. Research suggests that firms that simply meet customer expectations do little to create loyalty. Thus, although customers may have no complaints, the firm's products probably do not stand out in any meaningful way. In other words, loyalty comes from providing products that exceed customer expectations. Loyalty can be especially strong in situations where customers believe the firm's performance is better than can be expected from a competitor. In this situation, the customer has little incentive to switch.

Most firms do a good job of tracking customer satisfaction over time. However, many do a rather poor job in tracking customer expectations.

A recent survey found that 47 percent of customers believe that company executives do not understand their expectations or what they experience in day-to-day contact with their firms. Another 41 percent don't believe that companies take their complaints seriously. Further, half of customers who do complain will leave the firm if their complaints are not resolved. The other half may stay, but they spread negative word of mouth either in person or via online forums. Across all industries, 17 percent of customer interactions result in a lost customer.

As we have seen, to promote genuine loyalty to the firm, executives must have a full understanding of their customers' expectations. Then, the firm must set out to deliver on those expectations and create value beyond the norm for the industry. Presented here are some tips on how to make this happen:

- **Seek out negative feedback.** In addition to carefully considering customer complaints, firms must look outside to gather information from dissatisfied customers who do not complain. This can be done via websites, blogs, message boards, and third-party rating services.

- **Manage from the outside in.** This involves leveraging customer information (both positive and negative) to improve business practices. Firms must take what customers tell them and use it to improve the customer experience.

- **Recognize that one size does not fit all.** Different customers have different preferred avenues to meeting their expectations. For example, some customers prefer high automation, or even self-service, with respect to the customer experience. Young customers are a good example. Others prefer a personal, customized experience. Older customers, for instance, prefer to bank with live tellers than use automation.

- **Put service over personalization.** The majority of customers—78 percent—place more importance on good service than personalized service. This means that firms must be able to address customers' needs on the first try. Simply knowing the customer's name is not enough.

(continued)

Research shows that about 33 percent of a firm's customers feel loyal to the firm and show their loyalty by making most of their purchases in a category with the firm. Unfortunately, the same research shows that only 20 percent of the firm's customers are profitable, and that most of the company's profitable customers are not loyal. To get past this enigma, executives must ask three questions about their customers: (1) Which loyal customers are good for our business? (2) How do we retain these customers? and (3) How do we get more customers like them? Customers who do not meet this profile are simply not worth having as customers. In the end, most executives will discover that even some of their most satisfied and loyal customers are not worth the effort.

Satisfaction Versus Quality Versus Value

Now that we better understand customer expectations, let's look at how satisfaction differs from quality and value. The answer is not so obvious because the concepts overlap to some extent. Because customer satisfaction is defined relative to customer expectations, it becomes difficult to separate satisfaction from quality and value because customers can hold expectations about quality or value or both. In fact, customers can hold expectations about any part of the product offering, including seemingly minor issues such as parking availability, crowding, or room temperature in addition to major issues like quality and value.

To solve this dilemma, think of each concept not in terms of what it is, but in terms of its size. The most narrowly defined concept is quality, which customers judge on an attribute-by-attribute basis. Consider a meal at a restaurant. The quality of that meal stems from specific attributes: the quality of the food, the drink, the atmosphere, and the service are each important. We could even go so far as to judge the quality of the ingredients in the food. In fact, many restaurants, like Ruth's Chris Steakhouse, promote themselves based on the quality of their ingredients. When customers consider the broader issue of value, they begin to include things other than quality: the price of the meal, the time and effort required getting to the restaurant, parking availability, and opportunity costs. In this case, even the best meal in a great restaurant can be viewed as a poor value if the price is too high in terms of monetary or nonmonetary costs.

When a customer considers satisfaction, he or she will typically respond based on his or her expectations of the item in question. If the quality of the food is not what the customer expected, then the customer will be dissatisfied with the food. Similarly, if the value of the meal is not what the customer expected, the customer will be dissatisfied with the value. Note that these are independent judgments. It is entirely possible for a customer to be satisfied with the quality of the meal, but dissatisfied with its value. The opposite is also true.

However, most customers do not make independent judgments about satisfaction. Instead, customers think of

© AP Photo/Charles Rex Arbogast

Toyota typically scores well in both customer and third-party ratings of customer satisfaction.

satisfaction based on the totality of their experience without overtly considering issues like quality or value. We are not saying that customers do not judge quality or value. Rather, we are saying that customers think of satisfaction in more abstract terms than they do quality or value. This happens because customers' expectations—hence their satisfaction—can be based on any number of factors, *even factors that have nothing to do with quality or value.* Continuing with our restaurant example, it is entirely possible for a customer to receive the absolute best quality and value, yet still be dissatisfied with the experience. The weather, other customers, a bad date, and a bad mood are just a few examples of nonquality and nonvalue factors that can affect customers' expectations and cloud their satisfaction judgments.

Customer Satisfaction and Customer Retention

Customer satisfaction is the key to customer retention. Fully satisfied customers are more likely to become loyal customers, or even advocates for the firm and its products. Satisfied customers are less likely to explore alternative suppliers and they are less price sensitive. Therefore, satisfied customers are less likely to switch to competitors. Satisfied customers are also more likely to spread positive word of mouth about the firm and its products. However, the way that customers think about satisfaction creates some interesting challenges for marketers. It is one thing to strive for the best in terms of quality and value, but how can a firm control the uncontrollable factors that affect customer satisfaction? Certainly, marketers cannot control the weather or the fact that their customers are in a bad mood. However, there are several things that marketers can do manage customer satisfaction and leverage it in their marketing efforts:

- **Understand what can go wrong.** Managers, particularly those on the front line, must understand that an endless number of things can and will go wrong in meeting customers' expectations. Even the best strategies will not work in the face of customers who are in a bad mood. Although some factors are simply uncontrollable, managers should be aware of these factors and be ready to respond if possible.

- **Focus on controllable issues.** The key is to keep an eye on the uncontrollable factors but focus more on things that can be controlled. Core product quality, customer service, atmosphere, experiences, pricing, convenience, distribution, and promotion must all be managed in an effort to increase share of customer and maintain loyal relationships. It is especially important that the core product be of high quality. Without that, the firm stands little chance of creating customer satisfaction or long-term customer relationships.

- **Manage customer expectations.** As we have seen already, managing customer expectations is more than promising only what you can deliver. To manage expectations well, the marketer must educate customers on how to be satisfied by the firm and its products. These efforts can include in-depth product training, educating customers on how to get the best service from the company, telling customers about product availability and delivery schedules, and giving customers tips and hints for improving quality and service. For example, the U.S. Postal Service routinely reminds customers to mail early during the busy holiday season in November and December. This simple reminder is valuable in managing customers' expectations regarding mail delivery times.

- **Offer satisfaction guarantees.**   Companies that care about customer satisfaction back up their offerings by guaranteeing customer satisfaction or product quality. Exhibit 12.8 provides several examples of customer satisfaction guarantees. Guarantees offer a number of benefits. For the firm, a guarantee can serve as a corporate vision, creed, or goal that all employees can strive to meet. A good guarantee is also a viable marketing tool that can be used to differentiate the firm's product offering. For customers, guarantees reduce the risk of buying from the firm and give the customer a point of leverage if they have a complaint.

- **Make it easy for customers to complain.**   Over 90 percent of dissatisfied customers never complain—they just go elsewhere to meet their needs. To counter this customer defection, marketers must make it easy for customers to complain. Whether by mail, phone, e-mail, or in person, firms that care about customer satisfaction will make customer complaints an important part of their ongoing research efforts. However, tracking complaints is not enough. The firm must also be willing to listen and act to rectify customers' problems. Complaining customers are much more likely to buy again if the firm handles their complaints effectively and swiftly.

- **Create relationship programs.**   As we discussed earlier in the chapter, firms can use relationship strategies to increase customer loyalty. Today, loyalty or membership programs are everywhere: banks, restaurants, supermarkets, and even bookstores. The idea behind all of these programs is to create financial, social, customization, and/or structural bonds that link customers to the firm.

- **Make customer satisfaction measurement an ongoing priority.**   If you don't know what customers want, need, or expect, everything else is a waste of time. A permanent, ongoing program to measure customer satisfaction is one of the most important foundations of customer relationship management.

Customer Satisfaction Measurement

There are a number of different methods for measuring customer satisfaction. The simplest method involves the direct measurement of performance across various factors, using simple rating scales. For example, a customer might be asked to rate the quality of housekeeping services in a hotel using a 10-point scale ranging from poor to excellent. Although this method is simple and allows the firm to track satisfaction, it is not diagnostic in the sense that it permits the firm to determine *how* satisfaction varies over time. To do this, the firm can measure both expectations and performance at the same time. Exhibit 12.9 illustrates how this might be done for a hypothetical health club.

EXHIBIT 12.8 **EXAMPLES OF CUSTOMER SATISFACTION GUARANTEES**

Hampton Inn

Our friendly service and complimentary amenities are all backed by our 100% Hampton Guarantee™. If you're not 100% satisfied, we don't expect you to pay. That's our promise and your guarantee. That's 100% Hampton™.

L.L.Bean

Our products are guaranteed to give 100% satisfaction in every way. Return anything purchased from us at any time if it proves otherwise. We do not want you to have anything from L.L.Bean that is not completely satisfactory.

FedEx Express

FedEx offers a money-back guarantee for every U.S. shipment. You may request a refund or credit of your shipping charges if we miss our published (or quoted, as in the case of FedEx SameDay®) delivery time by even 60 seconds. This guarantee applies to all U.S. shipments, commercial and residential, to all 50 states.

Xerox

If you are not totally satisfied with any Xerox equipment ordered under this Agreement, Xerox will, at your request, replace it without charge with an identical model or, at the option of Xerox, with a machine with comparable features and capabilities.

   This guarantee will be effective for 3 years following initial Equipment delivery, unless the equipment is financed by Xerox for more than 3 years, in which event it will be effective during the entire term of Xerox financing (except for certain previously-installed models which receive coverage for one year). This guarantee applies only to equipment which has been continuously maintained by Xerox or its authorized representatives under a Xerox express warranty or Xerox Maintenance agreement.

Midas

We believe that auto care should be a hassle-free experience. For almost 50 years, we have built trusted customer relationships based on Midas reliability and professional service. And because we know that quality parts and services are important to you, we stand behind them with our guarantees. In fact, we guarantee *all* our work. And, we're known for our lifetime-guaranteed brake pads, shoes, mufflers and shocks and struts. Our lifetime guarantee is valid for as long as you own your car.

Eddie Bauer

Every item we sell will give you complete satisfaction or you may return it for a full refund.

Publix Supermarkets

The philosophy of pleasing our customers was established from the beginning by our founder, George W. Jenkins. The purpose of his guarantee remains to satisfy the customer: "We will never knowingly disappoint you. If for any reason your purchase does not give you complete satisfaction, the full purchase price will be cheerfully refunded immediately upon request."

The ongoing measurement of customer satisfaction has changed dramatically over the last decade. Although most firms track their customer satisfaction ratings over time, firms that are serious about customer relationship management have adopted more robust means of tracking satisfaction based on actual customer behavior. Advances in technology, which allow firms to track the behaviors of individual

EXHIBIT 12.9	MEASURING EXPECTATIONS AND PERFORMANCE FOR A HYPOTHETICAL HEALTH CLUB					
	The Lowest Adequate Level of Service I Expect is:		The Highest Desired Level of Service I Expect is:		The Actual Performance of this Health Club is:	
When it comes to….	Low	High	Low	High	Low	High
The quality and variety of exercise equipment provided	1 2 3 4 5		1 2 3 4 5		1 2 3 4 5	
The amount of time I have to wait for a specific piece of exercise equipment	1 2 3 4 5		1 2 3 4 5		1 2 3 4 5	
The quality and variety of exercise classes offered	1 2 3 4 5		1 2 3 4 5		1 2 3 4 5	
The availability of specific exercise classes	1 2 3 4 5		1 2 3 4 5		1 2 3 4 5	
The availability of facilities, such as racquetball or basketball courts, the running track, or the pool	1 2 3 4 5		1 2 3 4 5		1 2 3 4 5	
Having a clean, attractive, and inviting facility	1 2 3 4 5		1 2 3 4 5		1 2 3 4 5	
Having a comfortable atmosphere (temperature, lighting, music)	1 2 3 4 5		1 2 3 4 5		1 2 3 4 5	
The overall helpfulness and friendliness of the staff	1 2 3 4 5		1 2 3 4 5		1 2 3 4 5	
Having convenient hours of operation	1 2 3 4 5		1 2 3 4 5		1 2 3 4 5	
Having plenty of available parking	1 2 3 4 5		1 2 3 4 5		1 2 3 4 5	

customers over time, provide the basis for these new metrics. Some of these new metrics include the ones listed here:[13]

- **Lifetime Value of a Customer (LTV)**   The net present value of the revenue stream generated by a specific customer over a period of time. LTV recognizes that some customers are worth more than others. Companies can better leverage their customer satisfaction programs by focusing on valuable customers and giving poor service or charging hefty fees to customers with low LTV profiles to encourage them to leave.

- **Average Order Value (AOV)**   A customer's purchase dollars divided by the number of orders over a period of time. The AOV will increase over time as customer satisfaction increases and customers become more loyal. E-commerce companies use AOV quite often to pinpoint customers that need extra incentives or reminders to stimulate purchases.

- **Customer Acquisition/Retention Costs**   It is typically less expensive to retain current customers than to acquire new customers. As long as this holds true, a company is better off keeping its current customers satisfied.

- **Customer Conversion Rate**   The percentage of visitors or potential customers that actually buy. Low conversion rates are not necessarily a cause for concern if the number of prospects is high.

- **Customer Retention Rate**   The percentage of customers who are repeat purchasers. This number should remain stable or increase over time. A declining retention rate is a cause for immediate concern.

- **Customer Attrition Rate**   The percentage of customers who do not repurchase (sometimes called the churn rate). This number should remain stable or decline over time. An increasing attrition rate is a cause for immediate concern.

- **Customer Recovery Rate**   The percentage of customers who leave the firm (through attrition) that can be lured back using various offers or incentives. Companies that sell products via subscriptions (e.g., record and movie clubs, magazines, satellite radio, or television) frequently offer special incentives to lure back former customers.

- **Referrals**   Dollars generated from customers referred to the firm by current customers. A declining referral rate is a cause for concern.

- **Social Communication**   Companies can track satisfaction by monitoring customers' online commentary. The number of blogs, newsgroups, chat rooms, and general websites where customers praise and complain about companies is staggering.

Firms also have another research method at their disposal: the focus group. Long used as a means of understanding customer requirements during product development, companies use focus groups more often to measure customer satisfaction. Focus groups allow firms to more fully explore the subtleties of satisfaction, including its emotional and psychological underpinnings. By better understanding the roots of customer satisfaction, marketers should be better able to develop marketing strategies that can meet customers' needs.

Lessons from Chapter 12

Developing and implementing the marketing program

- Must be looked at holistically to avoid getting caught up in the details.

- Has one key purpose: to develop and maintain long-term customer relationships.

- Is often not enough to guarantee success in today's rapidly changing economy.

The "right" marketing strategy

- Is not necessarily about creating a large number of customer transactions in order to maximize market share.

- Is one that attracts and retains customers over the long term.

- Considers customers' needs, wants, and expectations in order to ensure customer satisfaction and customer retention.

- Develops long-term relationships with customers in order to insulate the firm against competitive inroads and the rapid pace of environmental change.

Customer relationship management

- Requires that firms look beyond current transactions to examine the long-term potential of a customer.
- Is based on creating mutually beneficial relationships where each party provides value to the other party.
- Is a business philosophy aimed at defining and increasing customer value in ways that motivate customers to remain loyal to the firm.
- At its core is about retaining the right customers.
- Involves a number of stakeholders in addition to customers, including employees, supply chain partners, and external stakeholders such as government agencies, nonprofits, and facilitating firms.
- Shifts the firm's marketing emphasis from "acquiring customers" to "maintaining clients."
- Involves the creation of relationship capital—the ability to build and maintain relationships with customers, suppliers, and partners based on trust, commitment, cooperation, and interdependence.

CRM in consumer markets

- Is a long-term process with the goal of moving consumers through a series of stages ranging from simple awareness, through levels of increasing relationship intensity, to the point where consumers become true advocates for the firm and its products.
- Attempts to go beyond the creation of satisfied and loyal customers to create true believers and sponsors for the company.
- Is usually based on strategies that increase share of customer rather than market share.
- Abandons old notions of acquiring new customers and increasing transactions to focus more on fully serving the needs of current customers.
- Is based on the precept that all customers have different needs; therefore, not all customers have equal value to the firm.
- Involves estimating the worth of individual customers to express their lifetime value (LTV) to the firm. Some customers are simply too expensive to keep given the low level of profits they generate.
- Not only involves strategies to retain top-tier customers; it also involves finding ways to encourage second-tier customers to be even better customers.

- Involves the use of four types of relationship strategies: financial incentives, social bonding, enhanced customization, and structural bonding.

CRM in business markets

- Also involves moving buyers through a sequence of stages, where each stage represents an increasing level of relationship intensity.

- Is based more on creating structural bonds with customers or supply-chain partners.

- Creates win–win scenarios where both parties build relationship capital: one firm maintains a loyal and committed customer; the other maintains a loyal and committed supplier.

- Is typically more involving, more complex, and much riskier due to the nature of business buying, the presence of long-term contractual obligations, and the sheer dollars involved in many business purchases.

- Leads to many changes in the way that companies conduct business, including a change in buyers' and sellers' roles; as well as increases in sole sourcing, global sourcing, team-based buying decisions, and productivity through better integration of operations.

As one of the keys to customer relationship management, quality

- Is a relative term that refers to the degree of superiority of a firm's goods or services.

- Is a double-edged sword: Good quality can successfully generate first-time transactions, but poor quality guarantees that repeat purchases will not occur.

- Is not an automatic guarantee of success—it is a necessary but insufficient condition of customer relationship management.

- Is affected by every element in the marketing program. However, the firm's product and branding strategies are of utmost importance.

- Depends heavily on the form utility offered by the core product. In service offerings, the core product is typically based on a combination of people, processes, and physical evidence.

- Is often taken for granted in the core product because customers expect the core product to be of high quality, or at least at a level necessary to meet their needs.

- Is critical in supplemental products that add value to the core product. In most cases, these supplemental products, not the core product, are responsible for product differentiation.

- Is often found in the symbolic and experiential attributes of a product. Characteristics such as image, prestige, or brand have immense power in differentiating product offerings.

- Is hard to maintain with regularity because (1) customers have very high expectations about quality; (2) most products today compete in mature markets; and (3) many businesses compete in markets with very little real differentiation among product offerings.

- Is difficult to continuously improve over time. Delivering superior quality involves understanding customers' expectations, translating expectations into quality standards, upholding quality standards, and avoiding the tendency to overpromise.

As one of the keys to customer relationship management, value

- Is critical to maintaining long-term customer relationships because it allows for the necessary balance among the five types of utility and the elements of the marketing program.

- Is a useful guiding principle of marketing strategy because it takes into account every marketing program element and can be used to consider explicitly customer perceptions of the marketing program in the strategy development process.

- Is defined as a customer's subjective evaluation of benefits relative to costs to determine the worth of a firm's product offering relative to other product offerings.

- Breaks down into customer benefits (e.g., core product quality, supplemental product quality, experiential quality) and customer costs (monetary and non-monetary costs).

- Can vary across different situations or points in time, depending on a customer's expectations and needs.

- Depends on much more than the selling price of a product. Value perceptions are also affected by transaction costs (taxes, fees, other charges), life-cycle costs (maintenance, repairs, consumables), and nonmonetary costs (time, effort, risk, opportunity costs).

- Can be altered by changing one or more parts of the marketing program. If a change lowers overall value, the firm should consider modifying other marketing program elements to offset this decrease.

Customer expectations

- Are at the core of customer satisfaction.

- Can be described as ideal (essentially perfect performance), normative ("should be" or "ought to be" performance), experience-based (based on past experiences), or minimum tolerable (lowest acceptable performance).

- Can be examined strategically by considering the zone of tolerance between desired performance expectations and adequate performance expectations. The zone of tolerance represents the degree to which customers recognize and are willing to accept variability in performance.

- As measured against the zone of tolerance can lead to three outcomes:

    - Customer delight—Actual performance exceeds desired expectations.
    - Customer satisfaction—Actual performance falls within the zone of tolerance.
    - Customer dissatisfaction—Actual performance falls below adequate expectations.

- Are typically not unrealistic. Customers are looking for the basics of performance—things that the firm is supposed to do or has promised to do.

- Can be increased over time if the firm is not mindful of its initiatives aimed at delighting customers on a continuous basis.

Customer satisfaction

- Is defined as the degree to which a product meets or exceeds the customer's expectations about that product.

- Is typically judged by customers within the context of the total experience, not just with respect to quality and value. Customer satisfaction can also include any number of factors that have nothing to do with quality or value.

- Is the key to customer retention. Fully satisfied customers are

    - More likely to become loyal customers or even advocates for the firm.
    - Less likely to explore alternative suppliers.
    - Less price sensitive.
    - Less likely to switch to competitors.
    - More likely to spread good word of mouth about the firm and its products.

- Creates some interesting challenges for marketers. Some of the steps that marketers can take to manage customer satisfaction include

    - Understanding what can go wrong.
    - Focusing on controllable issues.
    - Managing customer expectations.
    - Offering satisfaction guarantees.
    - Making it easy for customers to complain.
    - Creating relationship programs.
    - Making customer satisfaction measurement an ongoing priority.

- Can be measured using simple rating scales to directly measure performance across various factors in the marketing program.

- Can be tracked diagnostically by measuring both expectations and performance at the same time.

- Is now tracked using a number of new metrics based on actual customer behavior, including lifetime value of a customer; average order value; customer acquisition/retention costs; customer conversion, retention, attrition, and recovery rates; referrals; and social communication.

Questions for Discussion

1. One of the common uses of customer relationship management (CRM) in consumer markets is to rank customers on profitability or lifetime value measures. Highly profitable customers get special attention, whereas unprofitable customers get poor service or are often "fired." What are the ethical and social issues involved in these practices? Could CRM be misused? How and why?

2. Given the commoditized nature of many markets today, does customer relationship management—and its associated focus on quality, value, and satisfaction—make sense? If price is the only true means of differentiation in a commoditized market, why should a firm care about quality? Explain.

3. Of the two types of customer expectations, adequate performance expectations fluctuate the most. Describe situations that might cause adequate expectations to increase, thereby narrowing the width of the zone of tolerance. What might a firm do in these situations to achieve its satisfaction targets?

Exercises

1. Visit *1to1* magazine (http://www.1to1media.com) to learn more about customer relationship management. You can register for free access to useful tools, articles, discussions, and webinars about CRM and its use in a number of different industries.

2. Think about all of the organizations with which you maintain an ongoing relationship (banks, doctors, schools, accountants, mechanics, etc.). Would you consider yourself to be unprofitable for any of these organizations? Why? How might each of these organizations fire you as a customer? What would you do if they did?

3. J.D. Power and Associates (http://www.jdpower.com) is a well-known research company specializing in the measurement of product quality and customer satisfaction. Explore their website to look at their customer satisfaction ratings for a number of industries. What role will third-party firms like J.D. Power play in the future given the increasing use of internal customer satisfaction metrics?

Gillette: Product and Marketing Innovation

Synopsis: *Gillette has long been known for innovation in both product development and marketing strategy. In the highly competitive, but mature, razor and blade market, Gillette holds a commanding worldwide market share. The peak of its innovation occurred in 2006 with the introduction of the Fusion 5-bladed razor. Today, innovation in razors and blades is thwarted by a lack of new technology and increasing consumer reluctance to pay for the "latest and greatest" in shaving technology. Gillette must decide how to put the razor wars behind them and maintain or increase its share of the global razor market.*

Themes: *Product leadership, product innovation, pricing strategy, integrated marketing communication, segmentation, sports marketing, global marketing, SWOT analysis, strategic focus*

Since its inception in 1901, Gillette has always prided itself on providing the best shaving care products for men and women. In fact, the company was so visionary that it didn't have any serious competition until 1962, when Wilkinson Sword introduced its stainless steel blade. Since that time, the Wilkinson Sword–Schick Company has evolved into Gillette's primary competitor. Through the years, Gillette has strived to stay on the cutting edge of shaving technology in a market that thrives on innovation. This focus has led to a game of one-upmanship with Schick as each company introduced 3-bladed (Gillette's Mach3), 4-bladed (Schick's Quattro), and 5-bladed (Gillette's Fusion) razors in rapid succession. Now, under the ownership and guidance of Procter & Gamble, Gillette faces a saturated U.S. market that fluctuates only when newer, more innovative products are introduced. However, many analysts believe that Gillette and Schick have reached the end of meaningful product innovation. Given this, Gillette faces the challenge of further expanding its already dominant market share around the world. And in a market that thrives on innovation, Gillette must determine how to balance the continued investment of resources in research and development, searching for "the next big thing" in the global shaving market, with capturing more of

Leanne Davis, Florida State University MBA Class of 2010, prepared this case for classroom discussion rather than to illustrate effective or ineffective handling of an administrative situation. This is a revised version of the case developed by Don Roy, Middle Tennessee State University, and Michael D. Hartline, Florida State University.

their loyal consumers through product-line expansions and inspiring marketing campaigns.

The History of Innovation at Gillette

Born in Fond du Lac, Wisconsin in 1855, King Camp Gillette learned from an early age the importance of self-sufficiency, innovation, and invention. After his family's home was destroyed in the Chicago Fire of 1871, Gillette left home at 16 years of age to become a traveling salesman. His experiences in his position led him to William Painter, the inventor of the disposable Crown Cork bottle cap, who assured him that a successful invention was one that was purchased over and over again by a satisfied customer. In 1895, after several years of considering and rejecting possible inventions, Gillette suddenly had a brilliant idea while shaving one morning. It was an entirely new razor and blade that flashed in his mind—a razor with a safe, inexpensive, and disposable blade. According to reports, Gillette's idea wasn't immediately successful, as technical experts said it would be impossible to produce steel that was hard, thin, and inexpensive enough for commercial development of the disposable razor blade. However, in 1901, with the technical partnership of MIT graduate William Nickerson, Gillette produced the original Gillette safety razor and blade, establishing the foundation for the Gillette Safety Razor Company.

Since 1901, the Gillette Company has led the personal care and grooming industry through manufacturing efficiency and exceptional marketing. By offering "consumers high-quality shaving products that would satisfy basic grooming needs at a fair price," Gillette effectively captured more than half of the entire razor and blades market across the globe. In fact, in the 1920s Gillette said the following of his razor product: "There is no other article for individual use so universally known or widely distributed. In my travels, I have found it in the most northern town in Norway and in the heart of the Sahara Desert."

Gillette's success in this market carried the company through economic droughts in the 1920s and 1930s, as well as allowed it to weather the storm brought on by World War II. In 1948, Gillette set its all-time performance record with profits per share of $6.80. Encouraged by the successful development of his razor products, Gillette felt inclined to challenge his entrepreneurial spirit with the acquisition of two unrelated ventures: the Toni Company, maker of do-it-yourself home permanent-wave kits, and the Paper Mate Pen company, producer of retractable, refillable ballpoint pens. Although seemingly profitable at first, both acquisitions proved to be unsuccessful as sales and revenue waned due to declining demand and innovative competitors, such as Bic's low-priced disposable (nonrefillable) pens from France. As a result, Gillette's unblemished track record for success became tarnished as net profits slumped to $1.33 per share in 1964.

Despite this fact, Gillette reigned as a visionary monopoly in the personal shaving market until 1962, when English firm Wilkinson Sword introduced its stainless-steel blade. Distracted by its experimental ventures with the Toni Company and Paper Mate, Gillette neglected to foresee the impact this small company could have on its core business of razors and blades and began to lose a substantial portion of market share. Although Gillette retained 70 percent, the arrival of Wilkinson Sword's stainless-steel blade initiated a transition in niche markets. For the first time, Gillette executives were unsure how to respond. Should they introduce their own stainless-steel blade or ignore the rival and hope that its market niche would remain small? Fortunately for Gillette, Wilkinson Sword lacked the resources necessary to exploit the niche markets it had penetrated and where it competed with Gillette. Eventually, Wilkinson Sword sold much of its blade business to Gillette. Unfortunately, by this time Gillette had already begun to feel the impact of competition as its market share had dipped to an all-time low of 49 percent.

To revive Gillette's market share and bounce back from unsuccessful product ventures into do-it-yourself permanent-wave kits and refillable ballpoint pens, Gillette's new CEO Vincent Ziegler spearheaded an acquisition and product development campaign. Ziegler was often described as aggressive, marketing oriented, and ambitious for the company, believing in diversification through the acquisition of companies in other business segments. Under Ziegler's leadership, Gillette purchased the following companies: Braun AG (German manufacturer of small appliances), S.T. Dupont (French maker of luxury lighters), Eve of Roma (high-fashion perfume), Buxton Leather goods, Welcome Wagon, Inc., Sterilon hospital razors, and Jafra Cosmetics (home sales). Unfortunately, four of these acquisitions proved to be unprofitable or unsuitable and were divested, and the other three yielded low profits by Gillette's standards. These ill ventures exposed the company to competitive pressures, especially in the form of Bic's disposable razors and lighters. In addition, Bic's 19-cent disposable stick pens particularly affected the Paper Mate line of refillable pens and drove Paper Mate's share of the retail ballpoint pen market from more than 50 percent down to 13 percent. In 1975, Gillette retaliated with the introduction of its new Write Brothers line of disposable pens and salvaged a good portion of the lost market share with heavy price promotions.

Despite these pressures, Gillette experienced moderate successes under the leadership of Ziegler with the introduction of Cricket disposable lighters and Soft & Dri antiperspirant (until the industry experienced a sharp decline in sales of the spray product due to the belief that aerosols destroy the ozone layer). Furthermore, the introduction of the Trac II razor was deemed a "great success" and thus continued Gillette's dominance in this market. Other successful product developments came under the leadership of Colman Mockler, Gillette's next CEO, whose strategy was to "cut costs dramatically and pour the money saved into ad and product development budgets." Under Mockler, Gillette experienced some of its greatest successes including memorable innovations such as the Atra razor, the Good News! disposable razor, and the Daisy razor for women. After these product additions, Gillette held roughly 75 percent of the global market in razors and blades, including a majority of the U.S. shaving market (razors, blades, and the leading shaving cream). By the end of 1980, Gillette's sales rose above $2 billion for the first time in the company's history.

The foundation of this success was the introduction of new products for the razor and blade market developed in Gillette's home laboratories. As previously mentioned,

Gillette's Atra-Plus shaving system, which featured a refillable Atra cartridge with a lubricating strip, overtook the Trac II as the number one selling razor. In addition, to directly compete with Bic and other razor companies, Gillette updated its Good News! line to include a disposable razor with a lubricating strip. Furthermore, in the personal care segment, Gillette made several introductions, including Aapri facial care products, Dry Idea deodorant, Bare Elegance body lotion, Mink Difference hair spray, White Rain hair care products, and Silkience shampoo and moisturizers. These additions had mixed results and left Gillette still searching for the keys to success in this business segment. In the writing instruments segment, Gillette achieved moderate success with the development of Eraser Mate erasable, disposable pens. Also, the steady sales of Paper Mate pens and Liquid Paper correction fluids helped to maintain company performance.

The Razor Wars Begin

By 1990, Gillette found itself in the interesting position of cannibalizing its own successful products with the launch of the Sensor razor. The Sensor soared in sales globally and quickly dominated the market, only to be succeeded by the Sensor Excel in 1993. This was not the first competing product produced by Gillette; however, it represented the first product that was able to effectively shift consumer demand and sales away from the Atra and Trac II—Gillette's leading products. A similar effect occurred in the women's razor market with the development of the Sensor for Women in 1992 and the Sensor Excel for Women in 1996. As to be expected, the continued success of the Sensor family of shaving systems led to the gradual decline of the Atra and Trac II twin-blade shaving systems. However, despite this decline, the Atra and Trac II razors continued to hold decent market share positions worldwide. In addition, holding steady since 1976, Gillette's Good News! brand maintained its position as the best-selling disposable razor in its product category worldwide.

Gillette's internal competition heated up with the introduction of the Mach3 razor in 1998. Touting three thin blades designed to provide a closer shave with fewer strokes and less irritation, the Mach3 became Gillette's most successful new product ever as sales rose to $1 billion in the first 18 months. Recognized for its innovative design (blades on tiny springs), the Mach3 was named winner of the American Marketing Association's Grand Edison Award for the best new product of 1998. Similar to the marketing strategy employed for the Sensor and Sensor Excel products, Gillette sequentially produced the Mach3 Turbo for men and the Venus system for women in an attempt to further expand the reach of Mach3 technology and market share.

In 2003, the razor wars got ugly as Gillette faced a new, more threatening competitor: Schick and the Quattro—the world's first four-bladed razor. Before Schick introduced the Quattro to the market, Gillette sued Energizer holdings and its Schick division, arguing that the Quattro illegally used the same "progressive geometry" technology as the Mach3. However, despite the lawsuit, Schick was allowed to launch the Quattro. To combat the suit, Schick countersued Gillette, claiming that Gillette's advertisements stating "the world's best shave" and "the best a man can get" were misleading. While Gillette and Schick engaged in a legal ping-pong match, consumer preferences and purchases were changing. In addition to Schick's Quattro for men, its Intuition for women began to encroach upon Gillette's hold of the women's shaving market. Schick's total share of the U.S. market had risen 2.9 percent to 17 percent, while Gillette's total share of the razor and blades market had fallen 4.3 percent to 63 percent.

To fight back, Gillette aggressively established a twofold plan of attack for recapturing market share. This strategy included converting consumers to higher-priced razors and blades, such as the Sensor, Sensor Excel, and Mach3 lines, from the single- and twin-blade razors, and geographically expanding into the areas of Romania and the former Yugoslavia, the Soviet Union, and the Czech Republic. At the forefront of Gillette's strategy sat its secret weapon: the Fusion—the world's first 5 (+1) blade razor, introduced in 2006. Using a unique five-blade design with a single blade on the back of the cartridge for use in trimming mustaches and sideburns, the Fusion exploded off the shelves and sold more than 4 billion razors within the first two months. Furthermore, the Fusion razor represented the first product introduction since Proctor & Gamble finalized its purchase of The Gillette Company and its subsidiaries, including Braun, Duracell, and Oral-B.

Although the Fusion represented a victory for Gillette and P&G, the hype surrounding its initial success was quickly fleeting. Other than being more expensive than the Mach3 (each cartridge costing 75 cents to $1 more than the Mach3 cartridge), critics questioned why five blades were needed to get the best shave when Gillette had touted its three-bladed Mach3 as "the best a man can get" since the late 1990s. In addition, *Consumer Reports* concluded that there were no additional performance benefits provided by the five-bladed Fusion, especially when compared to the Mach3. However, what was the most concerning for Gillette was the fact that sales reports indicated that the razors were outselling the cartridge refills. This translated to a consumer perception akin to a "novelty" product with a lack of staying power and product loyalty. Further, from a financial standpoint, Gillette feared not reaching the sales potential for the product combination, because it is well-known that razor manufacturers earn most of their profits from refills, not the initial razor purchase. Despite these concerns, the Fusion line continues to be a successful revenue generator for Gillette and its top-selling razor to date.

Gillette's Recent Marketing Strategies

Rather than continue the razor wars by producing a six- or seven-blade razor, Gillette focused on releasing complementary products, enhancing its existing product lines and expanding its intensely successful marketing strategy. To complement its already successful razor and blades division, Gillette sought to expand its product portfolio inside the shower doors to create the full "shower experience." For example, the launch of Gillette Hair Care and Body Wash for men, as well as its Clinical Strength deodorant, represented the most significant Gillette brand extensions outside of the razor and blades division, and aimed to reinforce the brand's standing as the world's leading male-grooming authority. "We've earned the trust of the more than 600 million men who start their day with a Gillette razor," said Chip Bergh, group president, Global Personal Care, Procter & Gamble. "By offering superior deodorant, body washes, and shampoos, we are able to reward that trust by giving guys what they want and need in other areas of their grooming routines."

Because Gillette is in the maturity stage of its product life cycle, focusing on these complementary products allows the company to increase its share of customer. Defined, share of customer refers to the percentage of each customer's needs in a particular area met by the firm and is exploited when a company with brand loyalty effectively capitalizes on that preference to market other products. Gillette's ability to increase its share of customer is greatly enhanced due to the resources available at Proctor & Gamble. According to Clayton C. Daley, Jr., vice chairman and chief financial officer of P&G, "One of the objectives of the Gillette integration has been to leverage the strengths and technologies of both companies to develop new products. We're generating revenue synergies by combining our superior science and male-grooming expertise to introduce these adjacent Gillette-branded products."

In addition to complementary products, Gillette's primary focus has been on the extension of its core business and the marketing programs that support it. Going beyond simple brand advertising, many of the initiatives and activities introduced by Gillette created a synergy between product development and marketing strategy. For example, building off the success of the Fusion and Fusion Power razor and blades, Gillette released the Fusion Power Phantom (Stealth in the United Kingdom) in February 2007. The Phantom razor featured a redesigned handle and a darker color scheme than the original Fusion Power. In addition, in February 2008, Gillette released another revision, the Fusion Power Phenom, redesigned with a metallic blue and silver satin chrome handles color scheme. Most recently, Gillette launched the gaming-inspired Fusion Power Gamer razor at the EA SPORTS Champions of Gaming Tournament in early 2009.

Sports Marketing Activities

Gillette's lethal combination of marketing and product development stemmed from the fact that when it came to blades and razors, Gillette was not content with merely having an innovative product. The company virtually turned its marketing into a quantitative science, pouring time and resources into marketing plans that were almost military in their precision and implementation. Gillette's stellar marketing strategies date back to the Sensor and Senor Excel products and can be attributed, in large part, to the success of its current market position and yearly sales volume. Focused heavily on male-dominated sports marketing activities, Gillette's marketing atlas included the following elements:

- On a grand scale, the company's most visible promotion was and still is Gillette Stadium – home to the NFL's New England Patriots and soccer's New England Revolution. The facility, which seats nearly 70,000 fans, hosted the 2002 MLS Cup, 2003 AFC Championship game, and four games of the 2003 FIFA Women's World

Cup. By sponsoring these types of athletic activities, Gillette is able to reach a worldwide audience, as soccer is tremendously popular in Latin America and European countries. It is particularly important to note that 60 percent of Gillette's sales are generated outside the United States, so worldwide appeal is critical in its marketing strategies. Case in point: The company's image and reputation more than doubled in popularity after it signed soccer superstar David Beckham as its worldwide spokesman in 2004.

- Launched in February 2007, Gillette heavily marketed the Gillette Champions program centered on the athletic and personal accomplishments of three of the world's greatest athletes—Tiger Woods, Roger Federer, and Thierry Henry. According to Gillette, each of these athletes personifies the essence of Gillette's brand: on and off the field, and "the best a man can get." As a group, the Gillette Champions blurred the lines of ethnicity, nationality, and language, making them attractive in the global arena. As part of the Champions program, Gillette featured numerous multimarket, targeted promotions based on the type of sport played by each of its champions. For example, as part of the "Look Like a Champion Sweepstakes," customers were offered a "once in a lifetime opportunity to learn how to look and play like a like real champion with a private training session from legendary golf coach, Hank Haney."

- Other sports-themed marketing programs include the heavily invested NASCAR marketing program and the Gillette Young Guns program. Aimed at racing fans with the purpose of driving sales for Gillette's premium razors and shave care products, NASCAR and Gillette promoted the fast and furious life of men though television, print, online, public relations, and event marketing tactics. Example promotions included Gillette's consumer program coordinated with NASCAR's Chase for the Sprint Cup, and the Daytona 500 Flip Card Stunt. In the Case for the Sprint Cup promotion, 10 lucky sweepstakes finalists from all over the country had the opportunity to experience "a race fan's dream" as they zipped up their fire suits and raced actual stockcars in a five-lap race. In addition to winning trophies, each finalist was coached by one of the six Gillette Young Guns, NASCAR's top drivers (Kurt Busch, Dale Earnhardt, Jr., Carl Edwards, Jimmie Johnson, Jamie McMurray, and Ryan Newman). Other NASCAR/Gillette marketing partnerships included the largest ever-attempted Daytona 500 Flip Card Stunt. Prior to the start of the race, more than 118,000 fans seated along the front stretch and backstretch of the racetrack participated in the stunt, which promoted the Fusion and Fusion Power shaving line. During the National Anthem, the fans held up the front of the cards, which displayed a patriotic design. Following the Anthem, participants flipped the cards over and revealed the Gillette Fusion logo. These and other promotions earned Gillette the 2008 NASCAR Marketing Achievement Award, racing's top sponsor award.

- Gillette continues to foster its relationship with Major League Baseball, a partnership that dates back to 1910, when Gillette featured baseball greats like Honus Wagner in ads for the original Gillette Safety Razor. In 2008, Gillette and MLB created the "MLB Rookie of the Month Award presented by Gillette" that encouraged fans to go online to the Gillette website and vote for their favorite player. This proved to be mutually beneficial for Gillette and MLB as it drove Internet traffic to Gillette's website as well as encouraged fans to become more engaged and involved in the sport of baseball. "Major League Baseball and Gillette have a long standing and successful business relationship, so it is a great pleasure to announce this new program that allows fans greater access to Major League Baseball," said John Brody, Senior Vice President, Corporate Sales & Marketing, Major League Baseball. "The 'MLB Rookie of the Month Award presented by Gillette' will honor the finest young talent in the game, and our fans will play an integral role in selecting the top performing rookie in both the American and National League each month."

- Capitalizing on one of the most fanatic audiences available, Gillette also partnered with the NCAA to promote a clean, shaven "game face" with the Gillette "Game Face" college football promotion. "This is a truly a one-of-a-kind contest for the ultimate college football fan," said Michelle Potorski, Associate Marketing Director, Gillette Male Blades and Razors. "We're looking to find the college football fan who can best display their favorite school's pride in the most unique way. We are looking to college football fans to prove their pride." Winners received the opportunity to be on a Gillette television commercial, take home an Xbox 360, and be crowned the 2008 National "Game Face" Champion.

- Gaming has also become a Gillette-sponsored pastime. Reaching out to this previously untargeted market group opened up a whole new ocean of customers who may not have been as attracted to Gillette's prior sports-heavy marketing strategy. By partnering with EA Sports and launching the Fusion Power Gamer razor, Gillette was able to tap into this market by launching the world's largest multisport gaming competition. Giving gamers the attention they frequently lack in worldwide marketing schemes has been beneficial to both Gillette's image and their market share. According to Gillette Champion Tiger Woods, "This program will give guys the chance to play games at the highest level possible, which is always exciting. To be the best at anything is an amazing feat."

- Audience marketing strategies include targeting alternative audience groups such as young adults, the gay and lesbian market, and WWE wrestling fans. For example, current promotions include shipping a promotional Fusion razor to males in the United States around the time of their 18th birthday, as well as providing free razors to college campuses and national gym franchises. In Europe, Gillette has also attempted to reach the gay and lesbian market by placing ads in media such as the United Kingdom's *Gay Times*.

Furthermore, in light of the depressed economy and decline in consumer spending, Gillette added an additional layer to its traditional sports-themed marketing concerning pricing strategy. At the end of 2008, Gillette launched an advertising campaign reminding consumers of the value of Gillette's blade technology. The new

Gillette Fusion television ad, featuring NASCAR star and Gillette Young Gun Carl Edwards, focused on the performance of the Gillette Fusion through sleek shots of the razor and the sounds of revving engines. The ad asked, "In the world of high performance, what machine can you run for as low as $1 a week?" Edwards noted that, for as low as $1 a week, Gillette Fusion blades, are "money well spent." The purpose of the campaign was to put into perspective the cost per week of the system and downplay the concerns that Gillette's razors and blades were too expensive in times of economic distress.

Also in late 2008, Gillette debuted a new global brand campaign, the first in five years, building upon the recent introduction of men's hair styling and personal care products. With the purpose of expanding the brand and strengthening the emotional bond among men, Gillette introduced "The Moment" campaign, a modernization of Gillette's "The Best a Man Can Get." According to P&G, Gillette "conducted extensive global research among thousands of men, which revealed that even the most confident guys have doubts at many moments throughout their lives. Also revealed was that men are looking for products that give them the confidence they want and need to step up, perform and look, feel and be their best." "The Moment" campaign features everyday guys, as well as the Gillette Champions (Tiger Woods, Roger Federer, and Derek Jeter), experiencing moments of doubt faced by every guy, whether it is the moment he steps on the doorstep before a date, just before he delivers a presentation, or the seconds before sinking a crucial putt, and the role Gillette's high-performance products play in helping him gain the confidence to succeed in that moment.

Price vs. Innovation

Since 2007, Gillette has acknowledged that product quality and efficient marketing are the core value propositions that set the pace for the success of Gillette's product lines. "If you have a significantly and demonstrably superior product or service, it really is quite meaningful," said Benson P. Shapiro, a marketing consultant in Concord, Massachusetts. However, "If you don't put it into language that gives a promise of something better, people won't try it." But, according to William J. Flynn, the business director of blades and razors at Gillette, "If you can create an appeal that gets them to try the product, the product will sell itself."

Unfortunately, despite its stellar marketing efforts, U.S. unit sales of Gillette's blade cartridges fell roughly 10 percent every month during the economic recession of 2008–2009. When combined with the fact that Gillette consistently raised prices to offset higher production costs, it becomes clear that consumers have slowed their purchases of Gillette's razor products. This is especially evident when compared to the sales of private-label disposable razors, which increased 19 percent over the same time frame. "Sticker shock is happening now," says Burt Flickinger III, a managing director at consultancy Strategic Resource Group. "As we get deeper into the economic slowdown, there will be some really pronounced growth of private-label blades."

P&G, however, does not expect Fusion sales to slow and in fact asserts that the Fusion shaving system continues to gain market share, which now stands at 36 percent of the U.S. shaving-systems market (up 4 percentage points from 2007). Instead of private-label blades, the company blames declines in Gillette's older shaving systems for taking away from Fusion's gains. "P&G says that, although sales of blades and razors have slowed in North America and Western Europe by about 1 percentage point, that has been offset by robust sales in emerging markets, which are growing at double-digit rates. According to P&G, Gillette holds 71 percent of the global shaving market.

Looking Toward the Future

To succeed in the future and effectively "win" the razor wars and beyond, Gillette must find new ways to innovatively out-produce or out-market the competition. In essence, the challenge for Gillette is to push the envelope without creating innovations that are seen as trivial. In order to do so, they must consider several key factors.

Pricing Strategy

Approximately 1.3 billion men worldwide shave with a razor blade. Within the United States, 94 million men ages 15 years and older remove hair in some fashion. Of these, 85 percent prefer to wet shave with a razor blade. The average American male begins to shave between the ages of 14 and 16 and continues to shave for the majority of his life. In addition, 100 million women in the United States, ages 13 years and older, remove hair in some fashion. Of these women, 94 percent prefer to shave with a razor blade.

On average, men in the United States shave 5.33 times per week, or 24 times a month, and spend approximately $22 a month for razors, blades, and shave preparations. The retail price of a Fusion Power razor for men and a four-pack of replacement cartridges is $26.28—a full $4 higher than what the average man pays per month. The retail price of a Fusion Power razor and an 8-pack of replacement cartridges is $40.98, almost doubling what the average man spends in a month. Similarly, U.S. women shave an average of 11 times per month and spend approximately $11 a month for razors, blades, and shave preparations. Gillette's Venus Vibrance razor sells for $8.29 and its replacement cartridges cost $8.49 for a 4-pack. The total purchase price of $16.78 is almost $6 higher than the monthly average. The price of an 8-pack of Venus Vibrance replacement cartridges increases the total to $28.28, approximately $17 higher than the average amount spent per month. A price comparison of various brands in the men's and women's wet-shaving market is shown in Case Exhibit 1.1.

Global Target Markets

When considering possible increased global expansion, Gillette must consider the roles that culture, religion, and Western influences play in shaving behavior. For example, internationally, 15 percent of the world's male population does not shave due to discomfort from shaving; 7 percent does not shave for religious reasons; and 3 percent

CASE EXHIBIT 1.1	WET-SHAVING PRODUCTS AND PRICES		
	Brand	Initial Price of Razor	Price of Replacement Cartridges
Men's Products			
Gillette	Mach3	$8.79	12 for $25.19
	Mach3 Turbo	$9.79	8 for $21.29
	Fusion (includes Phenom)	$9.99	4 for $14.49
			8 for $27.49
	Fusion Power (includes Power Phenom)	$11.99	4 for $14.49
			8 for $27.49
Schick	Quattro	$9.99	4 for $10.49
			8 for $19.99
	Quattro Titanium	$9.99	4 for $10.99
			8 for $20.99
Bic	Comfort 3	4 for $4.99	
	Comfort 3 Advanced	4 for $6.99	
Women's Products			
Gillette	Venus	$5.99	4 for $10.49
			8 for $19.29
	Venus Divine	$9.79	8 for $21.29
	Venus Breeze	$9.99	4 for $11.99
	Venus Vibrance	$11.99	4 for $11.99
	Venus Embrace	$12.99	4 for $15.49
			8 for $28.49
Schick	Quattro for Women	$9.99	4 for $10.99
			8 for $21.39
	Silk Effects	$5.99	5 for $8.99
	Intuition Plus Refreshing Moisture	$9.99	6 for $19.99
	Intuition Plus Sensitive Care	$9.99	6 for $19.99
Bic	Soleil Triple Blade	4 for $6.99	
	Soleil Twilight	4 for $6.99	

Source: Drugstore.com (http://www.drugstore.com) and CVS.com (http://www.cvs.com), accessed September 24, 2009.

simply does not care to shave. Being aware of these behavioral and cultural characteristics will allow Gillette to effectively segment and target those they will be most successful in transforming into customers. Similarly, although some women in European countries choose not to shave for cultural reasons, others now prefer to engage in the activity as they increasingly embrace Western lifestyles. For example, younger generations of European women are being influenced by American movies and television that depict women with sleek underarms and legs. By fostering adoption of the shaving lifestyle, Gillette can effectively capitalize on this trend. In fact, if European women embraced hair elimination at the same pace as American women, total blade sales would increase by hundreds of millions each year.

Technological Advances vs. Development Costs

In the past, razor manufacturers experimented with numerous technological advancements to provide the perfect shave, including increasing the number of blades contained in the cartridge, adding tiny electric motors for a powered shave, and improving supplemental shaving products such as gels and lotions. In various patent infringement suits attempting to defend its technology, Gillette lost in both the United States and in Europe. This proves that any innovation must be unique enough to warrant patent protection and not be categorized as a "trivial" enhancement. However, to develop truly unique products, firms like Gillette must spend millions in research and development. When Gillette introduced the Mach3 in 1998, it spent $680 million on research and product testing. The company spent slightly less than that amount to develop the Fusion. In both cases, Gillette more than recouped its research investment. However, as Gillette looks to future technological innovations, the company must be concerned about broad consumer acceptance and whether its research investment can be recovered in a reasonable time frame.

Conclusion

In many ways, Gillette and Procter & Gamble are in an enviable position. Gillette's products dominate the global wet-shaving market. The company continues to grow, although slowly, in every worldwide market. Still, many industry analysts wonder if Gillette has reached the end of its historical innovation in wet-shaving technology. Thus far, Schick has not responded to the Fusion with a breakthrough innovation of its own. Given that the wet-shaving market is mature, Gillette must depend on innovation to perpetuate its dominance (whether in product design or marketing), as well as create an appeal that entices customers to try and purchase its products. By aligning that appeal with what customers value, Gillette has the potential to establish a position of long-term product maturity and market dominance. In that position, it won't matter how many blades a competitor puts on a razor.

Questions for Discussion

1. Evaluate product innovation at Gillette throughout its history. Has Gillette been a victim of its own success? Has product innovation in the wet-shaving market come to an end? Explain.

2. What do you make of the battle between Gillette and Schick? Is the battle of one-upmanship good for either company?

3. What actions would you recommend over the next five years that would help Gillette maintain its worldwide dominance in the shaving market? What specific marketing program decisions would you recommend? Should Gillette be worried about Schick? Explain.

Sources

The facts of this case are from Gen Abelson, "Gillette Sharpens Its Focus on Women," *The Boston Globe*, January 4, 2009 (http://www.boston.com/business/articles/2009/01/04/gillette_sharpens_its_focus_on_women/?page=3); Afrooz Family, "Vibrating Gillette Razors," MadPhysics.com, April 2, 2006; "Anti-RFID Campaigners Launch Gillette," *Frontline Solutions* (Pan-European edition), 12(7), September 2003, p. 8; Julia Boorstin, "Can Fusion Become a Billion-Dollar Razor?" *MSN Money*, July 7, 2006 (http://articles.moneycentral.msn.com/Investing/CNBC/TVReports/AfterHypedStartFusionHitsLull.aspx); Ellen Byron, "Gillette Sharpens Its Pitch for Expensive Razor," *The Wall Street Journal*, October 6, 2008 (http://online.wsj.com/article/SB122325275682206367.html); Mercedes M. Cardona, "Gillette's Mach3 Captures Top Prize at Edison Awards," *Advertising Age*, March 22, 1999, p. 54; Catherine Colbert, "Global Gillette," Hoovers.com, July 6, 2006; "Shaving Stats for Men," Razor-gator.com (http://www.razor-gator.com/ShavingFacts/shaving_facts_for_men.htm); Wes Conard, "3-blade Razor a Cut Above, Gillette says," *The Commercial Appeal*, April 15, 1998; "Cutting Edge: Moore's Law for Razor Blades," *The Economist*, March 16, 2006, p. 8; CVS website, Consumer Products, Shaving (http://www.cvs.com/CVSApp/catalog/shop_sub_category.jsp?itemId=cat2120&filterBy=&navCount=20&navAction=push), accessed September 24, 2009; "Gillette Launches New Global Marketing Campaign," Gillette website, July 1, 2009 (http://www.gillette.com/erresourcesite/pressRelease.aspx?id=75); "Gillette Reaches Agreement to Sell White Rain Brand, St. Paul Manufacturing Center," Gillette News Release, March 23, 2000; "Gillette Reaches Definitive Agreement to Sell Stationery Products Business," Gillette News Release, August 22, 2000; "Gillette Rings in New Era as World's Leading Male Grooming Brand," *Reuters*, July 11, 2008 (http://www.reuters.com/article/pressRelease/idUS119120+11-Jul-2008+BW20080711), accessed September 24, 2009; "Gillette's Edge," *BusinessWeek*, January 19, 1998, pp. 70–77; "Gillette Sues Schick over Razor Launch," *Promo*, November 20, 2003 (http://www.promomagazine.com/ar/marketing_gillette_sues_schick/); "Gillette Unveils Newest Members of Its Gillette Young Guns Lineup," Procter & Gamble website (http://www.pginvestor.com/phoenix.zhtml?c=104574&p=irol-newsArticle&ID=1106705&highlight=), accessed September 24, 2009; "History of Gillette Razors," The Executive Shaving Company (http://www.executive-shaving.co.uk/gillette-history.php), accessed September 24, 2009; "How Gillette Is Honing Its Edge," *BusinessWeek*, Sept. 28, 1992, p. 60; Lawrence Ingrassia, "Gillette Ties New Toiletries to Hot Razor," *The Wall Street Journal*, September 18, 1992, pp. B1, B6; Lawrence Ingrassia, "Keeping Sharp," *The Wall Street Journal*, December 10, 1992, pp. A1, A6; Jeremy Kahn, "Gillette Loses Face," *Fortune*, November 8, 1999, pp. 147–152; W. Chan Kim and Renee Mauborgne, *Blue Ocean Strategy* (Cambridge, MA: Harvard Business School Publishing, 2005); Mark Maremont, "Gillette to Shut 14 of Its Plants, Lay Off 4,700," *The Wall Street Journal*, September 29, 1998, p. A3; Mark Maremount, "Gillette to Unveil Women's Version of Mach3 Razor," *The Wall Street Journal*, December 2, 1999, p. B14;

Mark Maremount, "Gillette's New Strategy Is to Sharpen Pitch to Women," *The Wall Street Journal*, May 11, 1998, p. B1; Slaven Marinovich, "A Competitive Edge in a Cutthroat Market" brandchannel.com, November 21, 2005; Molly Prior, "Fighting for the Edge in Shaving—Blade Wars: Shaving Report," March 8, 2004 (http://www.findarticles.com/p/articles/mi_m0FNP/is_5_43/ai_114404714); Seema Nayyar, "Gillette Jumps into Men's Toiletries," *Brandweek*, July 20, 1992, p. 6; Proctor & Gamble website, News Releases 2007–2009 (http://www.pginvestor.com), accessed September 24, 2009; Glenn Rifkin, "Mach3: Anatomy of Gillette's Latest Launch," (http://www.strategy-business.com/press/16635507/16651), accessed September 24, 2009; Elayne Saltzberg and Joan C. Chrisler, "Beauty Is the Beast: Psychological Effects of the Pursuit of the Perfect Female Body," in Jo Freeman (ed.), *Women: A Feminist Perspective* (Mountain View, CA: Mayfield, 1995), pp. 306–315; William Symonds, "Gillette's Five-Blade Wonder," *BusinessWeek Online*, September 15, 2005 (http://www.businessweek.com/bwdaily/dnflash/sep2005/nf20050915_1654_db035.htm); "The Power of Fusion?" *Consumer Reports* (online—subscription required for access), July 2006 (http://www.consumerreports.org); Steve Ulfelder, "Raising an RFID Ruckus," *Network World*, September 29, 2003, p. 73; and Michael Wilke, "L'Oreal, Gillette and SC Johnson Crowd onto Gay Shelves," *The Commercial Closet*, March 17, 2005.

Monsanto Balances the Needs and Concerns of Multiple Stakeholders

Synopsis: This case focuses on Monsanto's desire to balance the many significant benefits that its products bring to society (and the company's resulting profits) with the concerns of a variety of stakeholders. The case examines Monsanto's history as it shifted from a chemical company to one focused on biotechnology. Monsanto's development of genetically modified seeds and bovine growth hormone are discussed, along with the safety and environmental concerns expressed by a number of Monsanto's stakeholders around the world. Some of Monsanto's ethical and patent-enforcement issues are addressed, along with the company's major corporate responsibility initiatives. The case concludes by examining the challenges and opportunities that Monsanto may face in the future.

Themes: Ethics and social responsibility, sustainability, product strategy, product liability, corporate affairs, stakeholder relationships, product labeling, government regulation, legal environment, global marketing

Think Monsanto, and you probably do not think about small farms. Rather, the phrase *genetically modified* likely comes to mind. The Monsanto Company is the world's largest seed company, with sales over $8.6 billion. It specializes in biotechnology, or the genetic manipulation of organisms. Monsanto scientists have spent the last few decades modifying crops, often by inserting new genes or adapting existing genes within plant seeds, to better meet certain aims such as higher yield or insect resistance. Monsanto produces plants that can survive weeks of drought, ward off weeds, and kill invasive insects. Monsanto's genetically modified seeds have increased the quantity and availability of crops, helping farmers worldwide increase food production and revenues.

Today, 90 percent of the world's genetically modified seeds are sold by Monsanto or by companies that use Monsanto genes. Monsanto also holds a 70 to 100 percent market share on certain crops. Yet Monsanto has met with criticism from sources as

---

Jennifer Sawayda—under the direction of O.C. Ferrell and Jennifer Jackson, University of New Mexico—prepared this case for classroom discussion rather than to illustrate effective or ineffective handling of an administrative situation.

diverse as governments, farmers, activists, and advocacy groups. Monsanto supporters say the company is creating solutions to world hunger by generating higher crop yields and hardier plants. Critics accuse the multinational giant of trying to take over the world's food supply and destroying biodiversity. Because biotechnology is relatively new, the critics also express concerns about the possibility of negative health and environmental effects from biotech food. However, such criticisms have not deterred Monsanto from becoming one of the world's most successful companies.

Monsanto's History: From Chemicals to Food

The original Monsanto was very different from the current company. It was started by John F. Queeny in 1901 in St. Louis and was named after his wife, Olga Monsanto Queeny. The company began by making artificial food additives. Its first product was the artificial sweetener saccharine, which it sold to Coca-Cola. Monsanto followed by selling Coca-Cola caffeine extract and vanillin, an artificial vanilla flavoring. At the start of WWI, company leaders realized the growth opportunities in the industrial chemicals industry and renamed the company The Monsanto Chemical Company. The company began specializing in plastics, its own agricultural chemicals, and synthetic rubber. Due to its expanding product lines, Monsanto was renamed again as the "Monsanto Company" in 1964. By this time, Monsanto was producing such diverse products as petroleum, fibers, and packaging. A few years later, Monsanto created its first Roundup herbicide, a successful product that would propel the company even more into the public's consciousness.

However, during the 1970s, Monsanto hit a major legal snare. The company had produced a chemical known as Agent Orange that was used during the Vietnam War to quickly deforest the thick Vietnamese jungle. Agent Orange contained dioxin, a chemical that caused a legal nightmare for Monsanto. Dioxin was found to be extremely carcinogenic, and in 1979 a lawsuit was filed against Monsanto on behalf of hundreds of veterans who claimed they were harmed by the chemical. Monsanto and several other manufacturers agreed to settle for $180 million. The repercussions of dioxin would continue to plague the company for decades.

In 1981, Monsanto leaders determined that biotechnology would be the company's new strategic focus. Monsanto's quest for biotechnology continued for over a decade, and in 1994 Monsanto introduced the first biotechnology product to win regulatory approval. Soon the company was selling soybean, cotton, and canola seeds that were engineered to be tolerant to Monsanto's Roundup Ready herbicide. Many other herbicides killed the good plants as well as the bad ones. Roundup Ready seeds allowed farmers to use the herbicide to eliminate weeds while sparing the crop.

In 1997, Monsanto spun off its chemical business as Solutia, and in 2000 the company entered into a merger and changed its name to the Pharmacia Corporation. Two years later, a new Monsanto, focused entirely on agriculture, broke off from Pharmacia, and the companies became two separate legal entities. The company before 2000 is often referred to as "old Monsanto," while today's company is known as "new Monsanto."

The emergence of new Monsanto was tainted by some disturbing news about the company's conduct. It was revealed that Monsanto had been covering up decades of environmental pollution. For nearly 40 years, the Monsanto Company had released toxic waste into a creek in Anniston, Alabama. It had also disposed of polychlorinated biphenyls (PCBs), a highly toxic chemical, in open-pit landfills in the area. The results were catastrophic. Fish from the creek were deformed, and the population had elevated PCB levels that astounded environmental health experts. A paper trail showed that Monsanto leaders had known about the pollution since the 1960s but had not stopped production. Once the cover-up was discovered, thousands of plaintiffs from the area filed a lawsuit against the company. In 2003, Monsanto and Solutia agreed to pay $700 million to more than 20,000 Anniston-area residents.

When current CEO Hugh Grant took over in 2003, scandals and stakeholder uncertainty had tarnished the company's reputation. The price of Monsanto's stock had fallen almost 50 percent, down to $8 a share. The company had lost $1.7 billion the previous year. Grant knew the company was fragile; yet through a strategic focus on genetically modified foods, the company has recovered and is now prospering. Monsanto became so successful with its genetically modified seeds that it acquired Seminis, Inc., a leader in the fruit and vegetable seed industry. The acquisition transformed Monsanto into a global leader in the seed industry. Today, Monsanto employs nearly 20,000 people in 160 countries. It has been recognized as the top employer in Argentina, Mexico, India, and, for eight years in a row, Brazil.

The Seeds of Change: Monsanto's Emphasis on Biotechnology

Although the original Monsanto made a name for itself by manufacturing chemicals, the new Monsanto took quite a different turn. After switching its emphasis from chemicals to food, today's Monsanto owes its $8.6 billion in sales to biotechnology, specifically to the sale of genetically modified plant seeds. These seeds have revolutionized the agriculture industry.

Throughout history, weeds, insects, and drought have been the banes of the farmer's existence. In the past century, herbicides and pesticides were invented to ward off pests. Yet applying these chemicals to an entire crop was both costly and time-consuming. Monsanto scientists, through their work in biotechnology, were able to implant seeds with genes to make the plants themselves kill bugs. They also created seeds containing the Roundup Ready herbicide, an herbicide that kills weeds but spares the crops. In spite of their controversial nature, genetically modified foods have become popular both in developed and developing countries.

The broad introduction of these genetically modified seeds in the 1990s unleashed a stream of criticism. Monsanto was nicknamed "Mutanto," and genetically modified produce was called "Frankenfood." Critics believed that influencing the genes of edible plants could result in negative health consequences, a fear that remains to this day. Others worried about the health effects on beneficial insects and plants. Could pollinating genetically modified plants have an effect on nearby insects and non-genetically modified plants? CEO Hugh Grant decided to curtail the tide of criticism by focusing biotechnology on products that would not be directly placed on the dinner plate, but instead on seeds that produce products like animal feed and corn syrup. In this way, Grant was able to reduce some of the opposition. Today, the company invests largely in four crops: corn, cotton, soybeans, and canola.

Thus far, the dire predictions of critics have not occurred. Monsanto owes approximately 60 percent of its revenue to its work in genetically modified seeds, and today, more than half of U.S. crops, including most soybeans and 70 percent of corn, are genetically modified. Approximately 282 million acres worldwide are now devoted to biotech crops, and the fastest growth is in developing countries. However, critics are wary that long-term effects still might be discovered.

Farmers who purchase genetically modified seeds can now grow more crops on less land and with less left to chance. Genetically modified crops have saved farmers billions by preventing loss and increasing crop yields. For example, in 1970 the average corn harvest yielded approximately 70 bushels per acre. With the introduction of biotech crops, the average corn harvest has increased to roughly 150 bushels per acre. Monsanto predicts even higher yields in the future, possibly up to 300 bushels per acre by 2030. "As agricultural productivity increases, farmers are able to produce more food, feed, fuel, and fiber on the same amount of land, helping to ensure that agriculture can meet humanity's needs in the future," said Monsanto CEO Hugh Grant, concerning Monsanto technology.

As a result of higher yields, the revenues of farmers in developing countries have increased dramatically. According to company statistics, the cotton yield of Indian farmers rose by 50 percent, doubling their income in one year. Additionally, the company claims that its insect-protected corn has raised the income level in the Philippines to above poverty level. Critics argue that these numbers are inflated; they say the cost of genetically modified seeds is dramatically higher than that of traditional seeds, and therefore they actually reduce farmers' take-home profits.

Monsanto's genetically modified seeds have not been accepted everywhere. Attempts to introduce them into Europe have been met with extreme consumer backlash. Consumers have gone so far as to destroy fields of genetically modified crops and arrange sit-ins. Greenpeace has fought Monsanto for years, especially the company's efforts to promote genetically modified crops in developing countries. This animosity toward Monsanto's products is generated by two main concerns: worries about the safety of genetically modified food and concerns about potential environmental effects.

Safety Concerns About Genetically Modified Food

Of great concern for many stakeholders are the moral and safety implications of genetically modified food. Many skeptics see biotech crops as unnatural, with Monsanto scientists essentially "playing God" by controlling what goes into the seed. Also, because genetically modified crops are relatively new, critics maintain that the health implications of biotech food may not be known for years to come. They also contend that effective standards have not been created to determine the safety of biotech crops. Some geneticists believe the splicing of these genes into seeds could create small changes that might negatively impact the health of humans and animals that eat them. Although the FDA has declared biotech crops safe, critics say they have not been around long enough to gauge their long-term effects.

One major health concern is the potential allergenic effects of genetically modified products. Critics fear that a lack of appropriate regulation could allow allergens to creep into the products. Another concern is toxicity, particularly considering that many Monsanto seeds are equipped with a gene to allow them to produce their own Roundup Ready herbicide. Could ingesting this herbicide, even in small amounts, cause detrimental effects on consumers? Some stakeholders say yes and point to statistics on glyphosate, Roundup's chief ingredient, for support. According to an ecology center fact sheet, glyphosate exposure is the third most commonly reported illness among California agriculture workers, and glyphosate residues can last for a year. Yet the EPA lists glyphosate as having a low skin and oral toxicity, and a study from the New York Medical College states that Roundup does not create a health risk for humans.

Despite consumer concerns, the FDA has proclaimed that genetically modified food is safe to consume. As a result, it also has determined that Americans do not need to know when they are consuming genetically modified products. Thus, this information is not placed on labels in the United States, although other countries, most notably Great Britain and the European Union, do require genetically modified food products to state this fact in their labeling.

Safety Concerns About Bovine Growth Hormone

Monsanto has also come under scrutiny for its synthetic hormone Posilac, the brand name of a Monsanto drug that contains recombinant bovine growth hormone (rBST). This hormone is a supplement to the naturally occurring hormone BST in cows. Posilac causes cows to produce more milk, a boon to dairy farmers but a cause of concern to many stakeholders who fear that Posilac may cause health problems in cows and in the humans who drink their milk. After numerous tests, the FDA has found that milk from Posilac-treated cows is no different in terms of safety than milk from rBST-free cows. Yet these assurances have done little to alleviate stakeholder fears, especially because some studies maintain that rBST increases health problems in cows.

Public outcry from concerned consumers has become so loud that many grocery stores and restaurants have stopped purchasing rBST-treated milk. Starbucks, Kroger, Ben & Jerry's, and even Walmart have responded to consumer demand by only using or selling rBST-free milk, which has put a damper on Monsanto's Posilac profits.

In the past few years, certain groups, including Monsanto, have fought back against the popularity of rBST-free milk. They maintain that consumers are being misled by implications that rBST-free milk is safer than rBST-treated milk. The grassroots organization AFACT, short for American Farmers for the Advancement and Conservation of Technology, has pressured the government to pass laws forbidding the use of labels that state that milk is free of rBST. Their efforts have been met with some support from legislators. In 2006, Pennsylvania senator and agriculture secretary Dennis Wolff tried to ban milk that was labeled as rBST-free, but stakeholder outrage prevented the law from being enforced. Instead, tighter restrictions on labels have been initiated. All rBST-free milk must now contain the following FDA claim: "No significant difference has been shown between milk derived from rBST-treated and non-rBST-treated cows."

Although Monsanto denies influencing AFACT in any way, many have accused the company of secretly governing the organization. Lori Hoag, spokeswoman for the dairy unit of Monsanto, admitted that the company did provide funds to AFACT but says that the company has nothing to do with the governing decisions AFACT makes. In fact, on its website Monsanto stresses that it has no problem with milk labels listed as rBST-free as long as the label contains the claim of the FDA. However, critics are still accusing Monsanto of being behind AFACT in what they say is an attempt to curtail the unpopularity of Posilac.

Concerns About The Environmental Effects of Monsanto's Products

Studies have supported the premise that Roundup herbicide, which is used in conjunction with the Roundup Ready seeds, can be harmful to birds, insects, and particularly amphibians. Such studies have revealed that small concentrations of Roundup may be deadly to tadpoles, which is a major concern, as frog and toad species are rapidly disappearing around the globe. A test using Roundup, performed at the University of Pittsburgh, killed 71 percent of tadpoles in outdoor tanks at one-third the maximum concentrations found in nature. The study also found that contact with the soil does not lessen the herbicide's negative effects. Roundup was never approved for water use; however, scientists fear that runoff may carry Roundup into water sources.

Another concern with genetically modified seeds in general is the threat of environmental contamination. Bumblebees, insects, and wind can carry a crop's seeds to other areas, sometimes to fields containing non-genetically modified crops. Many organic farmers have complained that genetically modified seeds from nearby farms have "contaminated" their crops. This environmental contamination could pose a serious threat. Some scientists fear that genetically modified seeds that are spread to native plants may cause those plants to adopt the genetically modified trait, thus creating new genetic variations of those plants that could negatively influence (through genetic advantages) the surrounding ecosystem. Andrew Kimbrell, director of the Centre for Technology Assessment in Washington, predicts "biological pollution will be the environmental nightmare of the twenty-first century."

Monsanto has not been silent on these issues and has acted to address some of these concerns. The company maintains that the environmental impact of everything it creates has been studied by the EPA and approved. Monsanto officials claim that the glyphosate in Roundup Ready does not usually end up in groundwater and cites a study which revealed that less than 1 percent of glyphosate contaminates groundwater through runoff. The company also claims that when it does contaminate groundwater, it is soluble and will not have much effect on aquatic species. This conflicts with the University of Pittsburgh study, leaving stakeholders unsure about what to believe.

Crop Resistance to Pesticides and Herbicides

Another environmental problem that has emerged is the possibility of weed and insect resistance to the herbicides and pesticides on Monsanto crops. Critics fear that continual use of the chemicals could result in "super weeds" and "super bugs," much like the overuse of antibiotics in humans has resulted in drug-resistant bacteria. The company's Roundup Ready line, in particular, has come under attack. Monsanto points out, and rightly so, that Roundup herbicide has been used for 30 years, largely without resistance issues. However, genetically modified plants labeled "Roundup Ready" are genetically engineered to withstand large doses of the herbicide. As Roundup has been used more frequently and exclusively, significant numbers of Roundup-resistant weeds have been found in the United States and Australia.

To combat "super bugs," the government requires farmers using Monsanto's products to create "refuges" in which they plant 20 percent of their fields with a non-genetically modified crop. The theory is that this allows nonresistant bugs to mate with those that are resistant, preventing a new race of super bugs. To prevent resistance to the Roundup herbicide, farmers are supposed to vary herbicide use and practice crop rotation. However, because Roundup is so easy to use, particularly in conjunction with Roundup Ready seeds, many farmers do not take the time to take these preventative measures. When they do rotate their crops, some will rotate one Roundup Ready crop with another type of Roundup Ready crop, which does little to solve the problem. This is of particular concern in Latin America, Africa, and Asia, where farmers may not be as informed of the risks of herbicide and pesticide overuse.

Monsanto has taken action to deter weed herbicide resistance. In 2009, the company agreed to offer rebates, up to $12/acre, to farmers in 13 states who use combinations of herbicides on their crops. Monsanto is offering rebates on six of the products, only one of which is a Monsanto product. The company is taking a proactive stance to show that it cares about preventing resistance; however, this does little to stem what many fear will become a global problem.

Monsanto Addresses Organizational Ethics

In addition to concerns over the safety of genetically modified seeds and environmental issues, Monsanto has had to deal with concerns about organizational conduct. Organizations face significant risks from strategies and also from employees striving for high performance standards. Such pressure sometimes encourages employees to engage in illegal or unethical conduct. All firms have these concerns, and in the case of Monsanto, bribes and patents have resulted in legal, ethical, and reputational consequences.

Bribery Issues

Bribery presents a dilemma to multinational corporations because different countries have different perspectives on it. Although it is illegal in the United States, other countries allow it. Monsanto faced such a problem with Indonesia, and its actions resulted in the company being fined a large sum.

In 2002, a senior manager at Monsanto instructed an Indonesian consulting firm to pay a bribe of $50,000 to a high-level official in the country's environment ministry. The bribe apparently was for the company to disguise an invoice, which showed that Monsanto was facing opposition from farmers and activists in regard to the introduction of genetically modified cotton in Indonesia. It was later revealed that such bribery was not an isolated event; the company had paid off many officials between 1997 and 2002. Monsanto first became aware of the problem after discovering some irregularities at their Indonesian subsidiary in 2001. As a result, the company launched an internal investigation and reported the bribery to the U.S. Department of Justice and the Securities and Exchange Commission (SEC).

Monsanto accepted full responsibility for its employees' behavior and agreed to pay $1 million to the Department of Justice and $500,000 to the SEC. It also agreed to three years of close monitoring of its activities by American authorities. The incident showed that although Monsanto has not been immune to scandals, it has been willing to work with authorities to correct them.

Patent Issues

Like most businesses, Monsanto wants to patent its products. A problem arises, however, when it comes to patenting seeds. As bioengineered creations of the Monsanto Company, Monsanto's seeds are protected under patent law. Under the terms of the patent, farmers using Monsanto seeds are not allowed to harvest seeds from the plants for use in upcoming seasons. Instead, they must purchase new Monsanto seeds each season. By issuing new seeds each year, Monsanto ensures it will secure a profit as well as maintain control over its intellectual property.

Unfortunately, this is a new concept for most farmers. Throughout agricultural history, farmers have collected and saved seeds from previous harvests to plant the following year's crops. Critics argue that requiring farmers to suddenly purchase new seeds year after year puts an undue financial burden on them and gives Monsanto too much power. However, the law protects Monsanto's right to have exclusive control over its creations, and farmers must abide by these laws. When they are found guilty of using Monsanto seeds from previous seasons, either deliberately or out of ignorance, the farmers are often fined.

Because it is fairly easy for farmers to violate the patent, Monsanto has found it necessary to employ investigators to look into suspected violations. The resulting investigations are a source of contention between Monsanto and accused farmers. According to Monsanto, investigators approach the farmers suspected of patent infringement and ask them questions. The investigators must practice transparency with the farmers and tell them why they are there and who they represent. If suspicions still exist after the initial interview, investigators may pull the farmer's records (after assuring the farmer they will do so in a respectful manner). Sometimes they bring in a sampling team, with the farmer's permission, to test the farmer's fields. If found guilty, the farmer often has to pay Monsanto. According to Monsanto, the company has only filed suit against farmers 120 times in the past 10 years, and only eight of those suits have proceeded to trial. Each time the ruling was in Monsanto's favor.

Some farmers, on the other hand, tell a different story about Monsanto and its seed investigators, calling the investigators the "seed police" and even referring to them with such harsh words as "Gestapo" or "mafia." One controversial suit was a case involving storeowner Gary Rinehart from Missouri. According to Rinehart, a Monsanto seed investigator entered his store and accused him of saving seeds from previous seasons. The investigator then threatened him with a suit if he did not settle. The company filed suit but eventually found it had the wrong man. Monsanto dropped the suit against him but never apologized. Rinehart also claims the investigators were inspecting other farmers in the area. Other complaints against investigators include similar acts of intimidation, with some farmers even going so far as to accuse investigators of following them and secretly videotaping them.

Such accusations are disturbing, but Monsanto has countered them with its own stories. It claims that Rinehart refused to cooperate and became irate, finally throwing the investigators out of his store. Monsanto filed suit but eventually found that it was Rinehart's nephew who was transporting the saved seed. The company dropped the suit against Rinehart, and the nephew eventually agreed to settle. According to their website, the nephew still has not paid the settlement.

In order to prevent so many instances of patent infringement, some have suggested that Monsanto make use of GURT, or gene use restriction technology. This technology would let Monsanto create "sterile" seeds. Dubbed by stakeholders as "Terminator seeds," these seeds have several risks and have spurred much controversy among the public, including a concern that these sterile seeds might somehow get transported to other plants, which could create sterile plants that would reduce genetic diversity. In 1999, Monsanto pledged not to commercialize sterile seed technology in food crops. The company has promised that it will only do so in the future after consulting with experts, stakeholders, and relevant nongovernmental organizations.

Corporate Responsibility at Monsanto

It is a common expectation today for multinational companies to take actions to advance the interests and well-being of the people in the countries in which they do business. Monsanto is no exception. The company has given millions of dollars in programs to help improve the communities in developing countries. In fact, *Corporate Responsibility Magazine* ranked Monsanto number 20 on its 100 Best Corporate Citizens list of 2009, a jump from number 88 the previous year.

In addition, as an agricultural company, Monsanto must address the grim reality facing the world in the future: The world's population is increasing at a fast rate, and the amount of available land and water for agriculture is decreasing. Some experts believe that our planet will have to produce more food in the next 50 years to feed the world's population than it has grown in the past 10,000 years, requiring us to double our food output. As a multinational corporation dedicated to agriculture, Monsanto is expected to address these problems. In fiscal year 2008, the company expended $980 million for research into new farming techniques. The company has also developed a three-tiered commitment policy: (1) Produce more yield in crops, (2) conserve more resources, and (3) improve the lives of farmers. The company hopes to achieve these goals by taking initiatives in sustainable agriculture.

Sustainable Agriculture

Agriculture intersects the toughest challenges we all face on the planet. Together, we must meet the needs for increased food, fiber and energy while protecting the environment. In short, the world needs to produce more and conserve smarter.

This quote by Monsanto CEO Hugh Grant demonstrates the challenges agriculture is facing today, along with Monsanto's goals to meet these challenges. For instance, Monsanto is quick to point out that its biotech products added more than 100 million tons to worldwide agriculture production between 1996 and 2006, which they estimate has increased farmer's incomes by $33.8 billion. Monsanto has also created partnerships between nonprofit organizations across the world to enrich the lives of farmers in developing countries. Two regions on which Monsanto is focusing are India and Africa.

The need for better agriculture is apparent in India, where the population is expected to reach 1.3 billion by 2017. Biotech crops have helped to improve the size of yields in India, allowing some biotech farmers to increase their yields by 50 percent. Monsanto estimates that cotton farmers in India using biotech crops earn approximately $176 more in revenues per acre than their non-biotech contemporaries. In February 2009, Monsanto announced that it would launch Project SHARE, a sustainable yield initiative done in conjunction with the nonprofit Indian Society of Agribusiness, to try and improve the lives of 10,000 cotton farmers in 1,100 villages.

In Africa, Monsanto has helped many farmers prosper and thrive through difficult periods. For example, in 2007 the government of Malawi provided farmers with vouchers worth about $3 each, which farmers could exchange for Monsanto seeds. Some of the farmers using these seeds saw their crop yields increase from a few bags to hundreds. Monsanto has also provided help to Project Malawi, a program to improve food security and health care to thousands of Malawians. Monsanto has provided the program with hybrid maize seed and has sent experts from the company to provide training for farmers in how to use the seed. Additionally, Monsanto has agreed to donate 240 tons of hybrid corn seed through 2010 to villages in Malawi, Tanzania, and Kenya. Monsanto's goal is to improve farmers' lives in a way that will help them become self-sufficient.

Not all view Monsanto's presence in Africa as an outreach in corporate responsibility. Some see it as another way for Monsanto to improve the bottom line. Critics see the company as trying to take control of African agriculture and destroy African agricultural practices that have lasted for thousands of years. Yet, despite this criticism, there is no denying that Monsanto has positively affected African farmers' lives, along with increasing the company's profits for its shareholders. As CEO Hugh Grant writes, "This initiative isn't simply altruistic; we see it as a unique business proposition that rewards farmers and shareowners."

Charitable Giving

In 1964, the Monsanto Company established the Monsanto Fund, which today funds many of the company's projects in Africa. In 2006, the Fund awarded a $15 million gift to the Donald Danforth Plant Science Center, which supported crop research in Africa. Other projects of the Fund include the "Healthy Children, Healthy Future" program, which seeks to reduce diseases in Brazilian children through education on good health and basic hygiene, and the funding of the Monsanto Insectarium at the St. Louis Zoo.

The Monsanto Company also supports youth programs. In the first decade of the twenty-first century, the company donated nearly $1.5 million in scholarships to students who want to pursue agriculture-related degrees. The company also supports Future Farmers of America, the 4-H program, and the program Farm Safety 4 Just Kids, a program which helps teach rural children about safety while working on farms.

The Future of Monsanto

Monsanto faces some challenges that it needs to address, including lingering concerns over the safety and environmental impact of its products. The company needs to enforce its code of ethics effectively to avoid organizational misconduct (like bribery) in the future. Monsanto also may be facing increased competition from other companies. The seed company Pioneer Hi-Bred International, Inc., is using pricing strategies and seed sampling to attract price-conscious customers. Additionally, lower grain prices may convince farmers to switch from Monsanto to less expensive brands.

Yet, despite the onslaught of criticism from Monsanto detractors and the challenge of increased competition from other companies, Monsanto has numerous opportunities to thrive in the future. The company is currently working on new innovations that could increase its competitive edge as well as provide enormous benefits to farmers worldwide. In 2009, the company announced that it had finished regulatory submissions for the planet's first biotech drought-tolerant corn. This corn could be a major boon to farmers in areas where drought is prevalent. Monsanto is also working with the African Agriculture Technology Foundation to bring drought-resistant technology to Africa (without having them pay royalties).

Although Monsanto has made some mistakes in the past, it is trying to portray itself as a socially responsible company dedicated to improving agriculture. As noted, the company still has some problems. The predictions from Monsanto critics about biotech food have not yet come true, but that has not totally eradicated the fears of stakeholders. With the increasing popularity of organic food and staunch criticism from opponents, Monsanto will need to continue working with stakeholders to promote its technological innovations and to eliminate fears concerning its industry.

Questions for Discussion

1. If you were Monsanto's CEO, how would you best balance the conflicting needs of the variety of stakeholder groups that Monsanto must successfully engage?

2. Companies like Monsanto that can offer technology to improve human lives are often said to have a moral obligation to society. How can Monsanto best fulfill this moral obligation while also protecting society and the environment from the potential negative consequences of its products?

3. What can Monsanto do to alleviate stakeholder concerns? How could these actions be woven into the marketing strategy for the company's products?

Sources

The facts of this case are from "Agriculture Scholarships," Monsanto website (http://www.monsanto.com/responsibility/youth/scholarship.asp), accessed April 1, 2009; "Backgrounder: Glyphosate and Environmental Fate Studies," Monsanto website (http://www.monsanto.com/monsanto/content/products/productivity/roundup/gly_efate_bkg.pdf), accessed April 1, 2009; Donald L. Barlett and James B. Steele, "Monsanto's Harvest of Fear," *Vanity Fair*, May 5, 2008 (http://www.vanityfair.com/politics/features/2008/05/monsanto200805); "Biotech Cotton Improving Lives of Farmers, Villages in India," Monsanto website (http://www.monsanto.com/responsibility/sustainable-ag/biotech_cotton_india.asp), accessed March 31, 2009; "Corporate Profile," Monsanto website (http://www.monsanto.com/investors/corporate_profile.asp), accessed March 15, 2009; Environmental Protection Agency, "R.E.D. Facts," September 1993 (http://www.epa.gov/oppsrrd1/REDs/factsheets/0178fact.pdf); "Even Small Doses of Popular Weed Killer Fatal to Frogs, Scientist Finds," *Science Daily,* August 5, 2005 (http://www.sciencedaily.com/releases/2005/08/050804053212.htm); "Farm Safety 4 Just Kids," Monsanto website (http://www.monsanto.com/responsibility/youth/fs4jk.asp), accessed April 1, 2009; "Follow-Up to Monsanto Lawsuits," Monsanto website (http://www.monsanto.com/monsanto_today/for_the_record/monsanto_farmer_lawsuits_followup.asp), accessed March 30, 2009; Ellen Gibson, "Monsanto," *BusinessWeek,* December 22, 2008, p. 51; "GMOs Under a Microscope," Science & Technology in Congress, October 1999 (http://www.aaas.org/spp/cstc/pne/pubs/stc/bulletin/articles/10-99/GMOs.htm), accessed March 25, 2009; "Great Place to Work," Monsanto website (http://www.monsanto.com/careers/culture/great_place.asp), accessed April 2009; "Growing Hope in Africa," Monsanto website (http://www.monsanto.com/responsibility/our_pledge/stronger_society/growing_self_sufficiency.asp), accessed March 31, 2009; Michael Grunwald, "Monsanto Hid Decades of Pollution," *Washington Post,* January 1, 2002, p. A1; "Healthy Children, Healthy Future Project—Brazil," Monsanto Fund (http://www.monsantofund.org/asp/pop_ups/BRAZIL_HealthyChildren_Project.asp), accessed April 1, 2009; "Is Monsanto Going to Develop or Sell 'Terminator' Seeds?" Monsanto website (http://www.monsanto.com/monsanto_today/for_the_record/monsanto_terminator_seeds.asp), accessed March 28,

2009; Andrew Martin, "Fighting on a Battlefield the Size of a Milk Label," *The New York Times,*March 9, 2008 (http://www.nytimes.com/2008/03/09/business/09feed.html?ex=1362805200&en=56197f6ee92b4643&ei=5124&partner=permalink&exprod=permalink); "Milk Labeling—Is Monsanto Opposed to Truth in Labeling?" Monsanto website (http://www.monsanto.com/monsanto_today/for_the_record/rbst_milk_labeling.asp), accessed March 2, 2009; "Monsanto & NGO ISAP Launch Project Share—Sustainable Yield Initiative to Improve Farmer Lives," Monsanto website (http://monsanto.mediaroom.com/index.php?s=43&item=693), accessed March 31, 2009; "Monsanto Company—Company Profile, Information, Business Description, History, Background Information on Monsanto Company," Reference for Business: Encyclopedia of Small Business website (http://www.referenceforbusiness.com/history2/92/Monsanto-Company.html), accessed March 20, 2009; "Monsanto Completes Regulatory Submissions in U.S. and Canada for World's First Biotech Drought-Tolerant Corn Product," Monsanto website (http://monsanto.mediaroom.com/index.php?s=43&item=695\), accessed April 1, 2009; "Monsanto Expanding Residual Herbicide Rebates," *Delta Farm Press,* January 12, 2009 (http://deltafarmpress.com/cotton/herbicide-rebates-0112/); "Monsanto Fined $1.5M for Bribery," *BBC News,*January 7, 2005 (http://news.bbc.co.uk/2/hi/business/4153635.stm); "Monsanto Fund," Monsanto Fund (http://www.monsantofund.org/asp/About_the_Fund/Main_Menu.asp), accessed April 1, 2009; "Monsanto Mania: The Seed of Profits," *iStockAnalyst* (http://www.istockanalyst.com/article/viewarticle.aspx?articleid=1235584&zoneid=Home), accessed April 12, 2009; Claire Oxborrow, Becky Price, and Peter Riley, "Breaking Free," *Ecologist,* 38(9) (November 2008), pp. 35–36; "Phinizy Swamp Nature Park," Monsanto Fund (http://www.monsantofund.org/asp/Priorities/pop_ups/science.asp), accessed April 1, 2009; Andrew Pollack, "So What's the Problem with Roundup?" Ecology Center, January 14, 2003 (http://www.ecologycenter.org/factsheets/roundup.html); Michael Pollan, "Playing God in the Garden," *The New York Times Magazine,* October 25, 1998 (http://www.michaelpollan.com/article.php?id=73); "Produce More," Monsanto website (http://www.monsanto.com/responsibility/sustainable-ag/produce_more.asp), accessed April 1, 2009; "Report on Animal Welfare Aspects of the Use of Bovine Sematotrophin," Report of the Scientific Committee on Animal Health and Animal Welfare, March 10, 1999 (http://ec.europa.eu/food/fs/sc/scah/out21_en.pdf); "Seed Police?" Monsanto website (http://www.monsanto.com/seedpatentprotection/monsanto_seed_police.asp), accessed March 30, 2009; "$700 Million Settlement in Alabama PCB Lawsuit," *The New York Times,* August 21, 2001 (http://www.nytimes.com/2003/08/21/business/700-million-settlement-in-alabama-pcb-lawsuit.html); Arlene Weintraub, "The Outcry over 'Terminator' Genes in Food," *BusinessWeek,* July 14, 2003 (http://www.businessweek.com/magazine/content/03_28/b3841091.htm); "Widely Used Crop Herbicide Is Losing Weed Resistance," *The New York Times,* January 14, 2003 (http://www.nytimes.com/2003/01/14/business/widely-used-crop-herbicide-is-losing-weed-resistance.html); and G. M. Williams, R. Kroes, and I. C. Monro, "Safety Evaluation and Risk Assessment of the Herbicide Roundup and Its Active Ingredient, Glyphosate, for Humans," NCBI, April 2000 (http://www.ncbi.nlm.nih.gov/pubmed/10854122).

NASCAR: A Branding Success

Synopsis: This case highlights NASCAR's successful branding strategy and how it became one of the top sports in America. The history of NASCAR is reviewed, followed by a discussion of the challenges NASCAR has encountered and will continue to encounter, including how the troubling circumstances of the Big Three automakers may impact the sport. An extensive overview of NASCAR's marketing efforts and branding strategies are discussed to show how NASCAR has used branding effectively to achieve its current success. The case concludes with a brief look toward NASCAR's future and reemphasizes some of the problems NASCAR will have to overcome to retain its top spot in the sporting arena.

Themes: Branding strategy, branding alliances, brand image, pricing strategy, integrated marketing communication, sports marketing, differentiation

In the past 60 years, the National Association for Stock Car Auto Racing, better known as NASCAR, has become the top auto-racing series in the United States and the number one spectator sport in America. It has also become well-known for its branding alliances, with drivers sporting everything from coffee to deodorant logos. The sport is currently made up of three national series, the NASCAR Sprint Cup Series, the NASCAR Camping World Cup Series, and the NASCAR Nationwide Series, along with some regional and international series. Although primarily a U.S. sport, NASCAR has held races in Mexico, Canada, Australia, and Japan. It currently sanctions over 1,200 races on 100 tracks.

NASCAR's popularity has soared in recent years, partially due to its extensive media coverage. Drivers like Jeff Gordon and Dale Earnhardt, Jr., have become heroes of the auto racing industry, and many NASCAR drivers have made appearances in movies and television. NASCAR's growth has been so dramatic that it is now second only to the NFL in popularity. Despite its immense success, the sport has had to overcome challenges in its 60-year history and will likely have to face many more

Timothy Aurand, Northern Illinois University, prepared this case for classroom discussion rather than to illustrate effective or ineffective handling of an administrative situation. A student team including Kimberly Judson, Nick Gerovac, David Keding, Dawn Keding, Kristan Mattson, Kurt Paquin, Loenette Rizzi, and Charles Sellers contributed to the development of this case. Jennifer Sawayda, The University of New Mexico, provided editorial assistance.

because of declining attendance and other difficulties from the most recent economic recession. Still, its strong brand image and brand alliances with other companies will likely keep the sport afloat through these tough times.

NASCAR'S History

NASCAR began with the vision of one man, a worker at an automobile dealership named William Henry France. France was already in love with auto racing when he moved to Daytona Beach, Florida, during the 1930s. Daytona Beach was the perfect place for auto racing enthusiasts like France, as the beach's open expanses and flat ground offered a perfect area for races. In fact, by the time of NASCAR's founding over a decade later, automobile racing had become popular in places like Florida, Alabama, and North Carolina. Many sources give bootleggers the credit for promoting auto racing during the '20s and '30s, as moonshine cars had to be built to go fast in order to evade the law. The popular idea of bootleggers racing from the law is etched in racing mythology as one of the precursors of stock car racing, although in reality its influence on stock car racing is likely overemphasized. Auto racing continued to increase in popularity in the early decades of the twentieth century.

France recognized the potential popularity and profitability that auto racing offered. Yet at the time, this lucrative movement lacked what it needed to become a professional sport, including promoters, racetracks, rules, or respectability on the part of the racers. Therefore, in 1947 France met with owners, drivers, and mechanics at the Streamline Hotel to launch his idea of creating a professional sport out of stock car racing. Over the next few days, they worked on the details for the organization. The first race of the newly formed organization—held on February 15, 1948—was won by stock car racer Red Byron. A few days later, on February 21, NASCAR was officially incorporated, with France serving as president and CEO. What is today known as the NASCAR Sprint Cup Series was created in 1949.

Racing fans flocked to the tracks, and soon NASCAR names like Lee Petty, the Flock brothers, and Fireball Roberts became household names among NASCAR enthusiasts. Originally, many of the races were held on simple makeshift tracks, but in 1959 France opened Daytona International Speedway, which offered a paved racetrack. The 2.5 mile racetrack provided an enclosure and more accommodations for spectators. Ten years later, France opened the Talladega Superspeedway in Alabama, a 2.7 mile racetrack that is the largest oval track in the world. France would serve as NASCAR president and CEO until 1972, when his son William France, Jr., took over. NASCAR continues to remain largely under the control of the France family to this day, a source of some contention among NASCAR fans and critics.

In the late 1960s and 1970s, NASCAR tracks began to emerge outside of the Southeast. Tracks were built in Delaware and Pennsylvania. Since then, NASCAR has tried to become more of a national sport, building racetracks in Chicago, California, and Texas.

Early Corporate Sponsors of NASCAR

NASCAR's growth really took off when it partnered with automakers Ford, General Motors (GM), and Chrysler in the 1950s. The automakers hoped their support of NASCAR would boost their own sales. The marketing phrase "Win on Sunday, Sell on Monday" became popular with the automakers as it was believed that success in the races meant greater success for their companies. In 1971, the R.J. Reynolds Tobacco Company's Winston brand became a sponsor of NASCAR. During that time period, NASCAR also formed limited sponsorships with Union 76, Goodyear Tires, and Pepsi. Anheuser-Busch began to sponsor NASCAR's Budweiser Late Model Sportsman Series in 1984. NASCAR would soon become famous for its branding partnerships, and the support of major sponsors and brands has contributed to NASCAR's well-known image.

NASCAR's Jump in Attendance

NASCAR began to experience unprecedented growth in the 1990s, coming a long way from its 1.4 million attendees in 1976. To help with this growth, it launched its first website in 1995, which offers up-to-date news on NASCAR activities and even has a NASCAR community where members can chat online and post opinions and videos. In five years, NASCAR attendance increased by 57 percent to over 6.3 million. Its television viewership grew 48 percent between 1993 and 2002, and by 2006 about 6 percent of U.S. households watched NASCAR races on television, compared to less than 2 percent for its competitor, the Indy Racing League. New, younger NASCAR stars such as Ryan Newman, Dale Earnhardt, Jr., and Kurt Busch began emerging, which helped attract the youth market to the sport. Women also began racing for NASCAR, including drivers Tina Gordon, Deborah Renshaw, and Kelly Sutton, the only NASCAR driver with multiple sclerosis. Consequently, female NASCAR fans grew to roughly 40 percent of its fan base.

Today NASCAR has approximately 75 million fans and has the second-highest television ratings for regular season sports. NASCAR fans are believed to be the most brand-loyal of any sport, and one estimate claims that fans spend over $2 billion in licensed product sales. For this reason, NASCAR has attracted the attention of numerous Fortune 500 companies. NASCAR has done especially well over the past decade, with attendance jumping 19 percent. Currently, NASCAR is broadcast in over 150 countries in over 30 languages.

NASCAR's Challenges

Despite NASCAR's immense success, the road to stardom has not always been an easy one. As with all major companies, the organization has had its share of criticism. One major criticism involves the control the France family has over NASCAR. A descendent of William France has been CEO of NASCAR ever since the sport was founded in 1948. In 1972, William France's son Bill France, Jr., took over as CEO of the company, and in 2003 his grandson followed suit. The family continues to be the majority stockholder of the company, allowing them to call many of the shots. Indeed, even those within NASCAR refer to the sport as a "benevolent dictatorship." Some argue that this gives the France family too much power. For instance, William France was known for replacing drivers that would try to unionize. So far, business decisions made by the France family have seemed to work out well for the sport. Many of the marketing ploys and changes the France CEOs have implemented have served to effectively promote NASCAR and attract an increased fan base. Still, some view the dictatorial style of the France family with concern because it depends largely upon the leadership abilities and business savvy of a few.

Another major issue involves vehicle safety. Critics claim that NASCAR often does not implement safety precautions until after a disaster has happened, even if those safety features have been around for years. Its own drivers have expressed concerns over the lack of appropriate medical care received after a crash. NASCAR drivers who have died in crashes include Adam Petty, Tony Roper, Kenny Irwin, and perhaps most publicized, Dale Earnhardt. Earnhardt's death in 2001 was perhaps the most influential in convincing NASCAR to implement more safety features.

After Earnhardt's death, NASCAR made it mandatory for drivers to wear a head-and-neck support system, known as HANS, with a seat-belt restraint system. Cars are now equipped with a fire-suppressant system and equipment that will measure the forces placed on drivers' heads in a crash. NASCAR has also installed SAFER barriers on the concrete walls of the racetrack, which are made of foam and steel tubing that will lessen the impact of a crash. A more controversial safety measure is the use of restrictor plates, a piece of equipment used on superspeedways like the Daytona and Talladega racetracks to reduce speeds of the cars. Drivers have accused NASCAR of trying to manipulate the races with these, but NASCAR insists they are a necessary safety measure. Finally, NASCAR integrated a car with additional safety features, called the Car of Tomorrow, into the 2008 Nextel Cup Series Season. Through these measures, NASCAR hopes to position itself as a safer sport.

Environmentalists have also cited NASCAR for its lack of environmental responsibility. NASCAR estimates that it uses 6,000 gallons of fuel during a race weekend, which comes out to about 216,000 gallons for one season. It also used leaded gasoline for years after the Environmental Protection Agency (EPA) asked it to quit. Because a law makes NASCAR exempt from the EPA's regulation on gasoline, NASCAR is under no obligation to comply. Yet the pressures to go green have caught up with NASCAR, and in the past few years it has instituted many changes to improve its environmental footprint. NASCAR eventually partnered with the EPA and its fuel supplier Sunoco to phase in unleaded gasoline in 2006 and switch to unleaded gasoline in 2007. In an attempt to carry its green efforts further, NASCAR hired Mike Lynch in 2008 to head the company's new green initiative. NASCAR plans to build some of its new buildings with LEED certification and in the long-term work with Sunoco to come up with an alternative fuel. NASCAR is also now using tracks with recyclable parts and introduced its first green car, the Ford Fusion Hybrid, during a race in 2008. Becoming more eco-friendly will benefit NASCAR by attracting more environmentally conscious consumers to the sport as well as helping to effectively address environmentalists' concerns.

NASCAR has also been criticized for its lack of driver diversity. The majority of NASCAR drivers are white males, which has caused concern among some minority fans. There are still few women in the NASCAR driver populace, even though 40 percent of NASCAR fans are women. Sexual discrimination allegations have also been a problem. In 2008, NASCAR official Mauricia Grant filed a $225 million lawsuit for racial discrimination (Grant is African-American), sexual discrimination, and wrongful termination. Additionally, NASCAR has not had many African-American drivers. In 2006, Bill Lester became the first African-American driver in almost 20 years to qualify for a race in NASCAR's top series. According to Lester, many African-Americans are secret NASCAR fans, but are not comfortable coming to the races because they cannot identify with the drivers. Indeed, only a few African-American drivers have participated in the Cup series in 60 years.

To enhance participant and driver diversity, NASCAR has worked to attract more minorities to the sport. In addition to its Drive for Diversity program, NASCAR gained two African-American drivers in 2009. Chase Austin and Marc Davis raced in the Camping World Truck Series and Nationwide Series. Austin drove a car owned by African-American businessman Art Shelton, owner of the Trail Motorsport team and the largest African-American investor in NASCAR's history. NASCAR also promotes supplier diversity and vendor programs, performs NASCAR college tours at ethnically diverse colleges, participates in civil rights conferences, and provides scholarship funding to historically black colleges and Hispanic institutions.

The onset of the most recent recession introduced new challenges for NASCAR. One major problem is the financial situation of NASCAR's sponsors and partners. The Big Three automakers, GM (through Chevrolet), Ford, and Chrysler, experienced extreme financial setbacks. Traditionally, these automakers have lent enormous support to NASCAR, with estimates spanning from $120 million to $140 million. In the 2008 premier Cup Circuit, 75 percent of the NASCAR cars in the races consisted of cars from the Big Three. With GM filing for bankruptcy in 2009 and the other two automakers struggling as well, NASCAR will have to deal with a loss of financial support from these automakers. Additionally, other NASCAR sponsors feeling the crunch may not renew their NASCAR contracts, some of which total $15 million. Domino's Pizza Inc. and Eastman Kodak Co. have already pulled out. As it is estimated that funds from corporate sponsors comprise 80 percent of the NASCAR teams' budgets, a huge pullout will negatively impact NASCAR. This may be one instance where branding alliances, a major contributor to NASCAR's success, may actually do more harm than good.

Despite these potential setbacks, CEO Brian France is confident the sport can adapt and get through the situation. NASCAR survived the pullout of manufacturers before, and NASCAR champion Richard Petty believes the fans will still be there with or without the manufacturers. At the same time, NASCAR is working to lessen the costs for sponsors who are running teams, including trying to reduce testing costs. Also, NASCAR's situation is not unique; other racing circuits like Formula One are also suffering from manufacturer pullout. Even sports like the National Football League and the National Basketball Association have had to reduce jobs. Additionally, Toyota, another major sponsor of NASCAR, announced it will maintain its sponsorship with NASCAR despite its lowered budget, believing that its partnership with NASCAR is critical to coming out of the recession. However, it too will have to reduce NASCAR spending as a result of the recession. Yet other sponsors, such as AFLAC Inc. and Camping World, are even increasing their spending on NASCAR.

NASCAR is also experiencing a decrease in attendance due to the recent recession, though it is only in the single-digit percentage range. Still, the downturn in attendance during the NASCAR race at the Atlanta Motor Speedway in 2009 shocked some racers, as the stands were only two-thirds full. NASCAR is also experiencing a significant drop in its television ratings, which dropped 13 percent from the previous year. Consequently, NASCAR has had to lay off some workers in order to cut costs.

NASCAR is hoping that lower ticket prices will help give fans a greater incentive to attend. In January 2009, NASCAR reduced its 20,000 Sprint Cup tickets to $40. It is also working with communities to lower hotel prices so that fans can more easily travel to the cities in which the races are held. It is uncertain how well these deals will boost NASCAR attendance, but many are optimistic. NASCAR spokesman Ramsey Poston pointed out that average NASCAR attendance is still 100,000 and its TV ratings remain high. NASCAR officials are confident that NASCAR will successfully weather the storm of the recession.

NASCAR's Branding Strategy

Early on, NASCAR worked hard to promote its brand name. It has been largely successful in its endeavors by integrating multiple marketing initiatives into a well-organized branding strategy. Part of this strategy dealt with partnering and co-branding with other companies. Driver jumpsuits and racecars are filled with the logos of various companies that NASCAR has formed brand alliances with. At the same time, NASCAR has successfully differentiated its own brand and, through the launch of campaigns, has effectively marketed its brand throughout the world.

Television Broadens NASCAR's Reach

Before the mid-1970s, the only way to watch a NASCAR racing event was to attend a race in person. During the mid- to late 1970s, NASCAR began to receive sporadic television coverage, and in 1979 the Daytona 500 was the first NASCAR event televised in its entirety. NASCAR started to rely on television as a branding medium, and by 1989 all races on the Winston Cup schedule were televised (later changed to the NASCAR NEXTEL Cup and then the Sprint Cup). This did not mean that television did not introduce some problems for NASCAR. Each track negotiated its own television contract, which meant that each race could potentially be shown on a different network. This hindered NASCAR's exposure and presented a problem that NASCAR was not able to overcome until the turn of the century.

In 2001, NASCAR took a proactive stance by signing a comprehensive television contract with FOX and NBC that was worth $2.4 billion and enabled the televising of all the NASCAR races that season. Just four years later, another contract was signed for $4.48 billion, providing broadcasts in a total of 167 countries including Thailand, Pakistan, New Zealand, and Venezuela. Such media coverage has, in part, accounted for a fan base of over 75 million, 40 percent of which are women.

Co-Branding Enhances Profits and Brand Image

NASCAR also recognizes the benefits of co-branding relationships. It realizes that a successful branding alliance can give the companies involved a greater competitive advantage. In the early 1970s, NASCAR was primarily sponsored by R. J. Reynolds Tobacco Company. Today, NASCAR has marketing and sponsorship deals with a wide range of Fortune 500 companies such as Sunoco, Coca-Cola, Allstate, DuPont, Gillette, and UPS. In 2004, Sprint Nextel replaced R. J. Reynolds as the series' sponsor, with Nextel paying NASCAR $70 million annually for the title rights. In 2006, Toyota announced that it would start supporting NASCAR's three series.

NASCAR takes its sponsorship deals very seriously. A sponsor may spend several million dollars for a race team and then spend just as much on promotional events. It is not a task to be taken lightly. Brian France even has a team that runs seminars to help sponsors get the greatest advantage out of their sponsorships. Of course, the relationship between NASCAR and its sponsors may change somewhat due to the recession as NASCAR tries to retain sponsors who are tempted to pull out. Yet although NASCAR has already lost sponsors due to the financial crisis, numerous manufacturers still consider NASCAR to be a profitable investment. The awareness people have of NASCAR is unmatched by any other sport.

One potential weakness of NASCAR co-branding is that some experts feel that the sport is becoming flooded with sponsorships. It has about 50 league sponsors and numerous team sponsors. This creates a cluttered environment of signage at the racetracks. Sponsorship has also increased in price within the last few decades, which means sponsors are now expecting more from drivers. Drivers are now expected not only to race well but also to show up for marketing functions and appear early on the morning of the race to sign autographs and answer questions. The pressure is on to win races, not only for the glory of the driver and for NASCAR but to retain the sponsor as well. New teams, even when they are owned by legendary racecar drivers, also have a hard time attracting sponsors, despite the teams' talent. NASCAR driver Jeff Gordon, for example, had a difficult time finding sponsors for his new team featuring novice driver Jim Johnson despite Gordon's legendary status.

Sponsors find that co-branding with NASCAR is extremely profitable, saving them from having to promote themselves through traditional media. And, because NASCAR fans are some of the most brand-loyal consumers to be had, NASCAR-sponsored products have benefited from sizable sales and market share increases. As a result of its co-branding alliances, NASCAR itself offers a plethora of consumer products either as brand extensions or through a direct relationship with other firms. Currently, NASCAR has licensing and merchandising rights for watches, clothes, chairs, tables, grills, hats, clocks, flags, doormats, blankets, auto accessories, sunglasses, and even food products.

Differentiation Seeks New Audiences

In spite of its various brand partnerships, NASCAR has worked hard to differentiate its brand from other companies, particularly from competitor racing circuits. This often takes place in the form of well-coordinated marketing campaigns, such as the lavish campaign NASCAR launched to celebrate its 50th anniversary. One of the strongest differentiating factors for NASCAR is the experience of the race. NASCAR fans like the constant, unpredictable, and even dangerous action. Crashes, live entertainment, and danger all make up the NASCAR experience.

With only a single driver per racecar, NASCAR also offers a human touch in the bargain. The driver provides a face and personality to fans, allowing them to strongly identify with NASCAR. Additionally, NASCAR lets several drivers share the spotlight throughout the race. From an owner's perspective, it is more efficient to manage the public relations opportunities of one driver as opposed to an entire team of athletes.

A similar dynamic can be observed in advertising and sponsorship during the competition. Within the NASCAR culture, a large amount of sponsorship signage around the track and on the drivers' cars has historically been acceptable and is perceived to be part of the NASCAR experience. Although clutter is an issue that sponsoring organizations must consider, it does not appear to be viewed as negatively by the NASCAR fan base as it is viewed in professional golf and tennis, which are more conservative and traditional sports.

NASCAR also differentiates its sport through connections cultivated within the media and Hollywood. Brian France, CEO of NASCAR, realizes that to remain successful, NASCAR must continuously attract new fans. He understands that to attract and retain a young fan base year after year, the promotional strategy requires the support of Hollywood and films such as *Talladega Nights*. The film features strategic brand placement that includes the official NASCAR Nextel Cup logo and corporate sponsors such as Nextel and Bass Pro Shops. NASCAR plans to continue its relationship with Hollywood by having one film created each year with a stock-car-related theme.

NASCAR has also attempted to further differentiate itself in order to attract other, more diverse market segments. In recent years, NASCAR has made it a priority to create awareness among diverse ethnic groups and among women. Called the "Drive for Diversity," this program has been in place since 1999. In 2009, NASCAR announced that 12 drivers would participate in its Drive for Diversity program, an increase of four from the year before.

NASCAR is also pursuing the Hispanic market in both the United States and Mexico through a joint venture with the entertainment subsidiary OCESCA. The venture oversees NASCAR licensing and marketing in Mexico. As of 2009, the program will be in its third year under NASCAR. Racetracks have been built in Mexico for these events. NASCAR also held the 2006 NEXTEL Cup Series in southern California, home to a large Hispanic community. It created numerous Hispanic promotions leading up to the California race to show respect for Hispanic culture. Additionally, Columbian NASCAR racer Juan Pablo Montoya is also garnering attention from different segments of the population. Montoya is a Sprint Cup racer and won the Busch race in Mexico City in 2008. NASCAR hopes Montoya's success will portray it as a diversified sports venue as well as attract more Hispanic fans. This integration of racers, sponsors, and fans from the United States, Latin America, and South America seeks to expand NASCAR's popularity and audience over different countries, which separates it from other sports mainly geared toward American audiences.

Due to lower TV ratings and competition from other sports venues, NASCAR attempted to generate greater fan interest by implementing the Chase for the Cup Series in 2004. Chase for the Cup involves the last 10 races of NASCAR's 36-race season. The top 12 drivers from the season are eligible to participate in Chase for the Cup. Chase for the Cup is a playoff format for NASCAR; the top 12 racers play off each other to see who will win the Chase for the Cup championship. Other racers are allowed to compete in the last 10 events as well, but it is uncommon for racers to win the Cup if they are not in the top 12. Each of the top 12 racers begins with a score of 5,000 points, and whoever gains the most points in the following races becomes the Cup Series Champion. With this event, NASCAR differentiated itself from previous NASCAR seasons and is effectively competing with other American sports. NASCAR's Chase for the Cup was such a popular strategy, in fact, that the Professional Golfers' Association adopted a similar format.

Innovative co-branding relationships have also helped differentiate the NASCAR brand and catapult it into new markets. The partnership between NASCAR and Harlequin (romance novels) launched in 2006 created awareness among women who may not have even been otherwise exposed to the sport. It also provided a way for NASCAR to tap into emotional branding strategies. Another effort to attract women and younger people to NASCAR includes a joint venture between the rock band Three Doors Down and Dale Earnhardt, Jr., in which he participated in a music video and the band members drove his car in a race. Additionally, the partnership between The Cartoon Network and NASCAR emphasizes sponsorship diversification directed at the younger consumer.

NASCAR's Brand Equity and Brand Loyalty

NASCAR's brand equity is the value that is added to a product or service by having the NASCAR brand attached to the offering. As a result, many companies choose to sport the NASCAR logo on their products. A 2005 study by James Madison University revealed that fans appreciate the sponsorship associated with NASCAR. Approximately 93 percent feel that corporate sponsors are "very important" to NASCAR, and 51 percent said that when they buy a NASCAR product, they feel as if they are supporting the sport. This would account for the $2 billion fans spend on NASCAR-licensed products. A whopping 47 percent of fans claimed they appreciate a sponsor's brand more because it sponsors NASCAR, giving companies a major incentive to sponsor NASCAR. Finally, unlike some sports figures who are seen as endorsing products just for the money, 56 percent of fans believe that NASCAR drivers use the products they endorse, which further increases the respectability of the drivers in their fans' eyes.

Despite all the efforts made by NASCAR to engage the customer, fan interest has begun to decline in the past few years. This situation is likely to be exacerbated by the recession. The median income of NASCAR fans is below that of the national average, making it harder for fans to afford to attend the races. It is also expected that concession stand sales will decrease for those that actually do attend NASCAR events. In addition to lowering the cost of tickets, NASCAR is also cutting the costs of food at its events. To show that it cares about its fans, NASCAR reimbursed the difference to fans at Daytona who had bought tickets before NASCAR began offering lower ticket offerings. NASCAR is clearly making significant efforts to maintain its brand equity and its loyal fan base.

NASCAR fans are loyal for several reasons. One reason is the sense of community NASCAR fans feel when engaged in the sport. NASCAR's brand is embodied in its drivers. When fans feel connected to the drivers, a bond is created that promotes the sport's brand image. NASCAR recognizes the sense of community that fans experience as a competitive advantage. Thus, a major link on NASCAR's website is "Community," where fans can become members of an online community devoted to NASCAR. The area allows fans to meet, discuss, and establish emotional bonds. Thus, a strong sense of community is a driving force behind NASCAR. NASCAR also cashes in on brand loyalty by using loyal fans as brand ambassadors and by establishing an emotional component with the brand.

Customers as Brand Ambassadors   Numerous studies have shown that word-of-mouth advertising is the most successful and trusted form of advertising for a company. Highly attached fans like those of NASCAR tend to serve as brand ambassadors by spreading positive word of mouth to other people and brand communities. Their loyalty makes them more likely to overlook weaknesses in the NASCAR brand and less likely to switch brands themselves when faced with competing brands. Even rival racetracks can be strong ambassadors for the NASCAR brand. The Rockford Speedway (located in Rockford, Illinois) hosts NASCAR-sponsored events. Rather than view NASCAR tracks as competition, this speedway embraces the benefits from a NASCAR connection. The Rockford Speedway carries the NASCAR message to the community through television and radio advertisements and through the actual racing events it sponsors.

NASCAR and Emotional Branding   Fans that have a strong interest in NASCAR and follow the sport diligently do so because of their emotional connection to the brand. NASCAR is able to achieve a high level of emotional branding because the fans connect with the drivers and experience the rush of the races. Studies reveal that 72 percent of NASCAR fans are strongly loyal to NASCAR sponsors, which is particularly helpful to today's automakers like General Motors who are facing bankruptcy. According to a Nielson People's Meter Sample and the Survey for the American Consumer, NASCAR fans give drivers of Chevrolet cars 70 percent higher ratings than other cars, Dodge 59 percent higher ratings, and Ford 64 percent higher ratings. The emotional connection consumers feel for these automakers contributes to their loyalty even in the face of financial woes.

NASCAR events and the "Community" link on the NASCAR website also allow fans to connect with one another. Additionally, NASCAR works hard to portray its drivers as accessible men and women who care about their sponsors and fans. It recognizes that NASCAR drivers help elicit emotions in fans through their personalities and individual attributes. The sport is so committed to portraying its drivers as positive role models that driver Dale Earnhardt, Jr., was fined and docked points after uttering an expletive on television. This shows that NASCAR's attempts to be customer-oriented and build emotional ties are essential toward constructing an effective, customer-friendly brand image.

The NASCAR Experience   For many NASCAR enthusiasts, the sport does more than simply offer entertainment. NASCAR also offers an experience—the chance to experience the thrills of auto racing without actually going through the dangers. The action of NASCAR races keeps many fans on the edge of their seats, waiting to see what will happen next. They are able to connect with the drivers, who they tend to view as down-to-earth, respectable role models. NASCAR also tries to capitalize on the fact that the act of driving is a daily experience for most people. This allows fans to envision themselves as the driver, thus increasing their relationship to the sport. Increased connection increases attachment, which in turn strengthens the emotional connections between fans and NASCAR. Experiencing the brand in this way helps to increase the loyalty of NASCAR fans.

Conclusion

Branding has evolved to represent the personality of a company, and NASCAR is a shining example of an organization that successfully embraces the branding mantra. Throughout its 60 years of existence, NASCAR has developed and implemented a branding strategy that encompasses a wide range of marketing initiatives. Brands are built on powerful emotional connections through an extremely wide variety of touch points. NASCAR delivers these connections through event marketing, emotional branding, brand communities, customer understanding, brand drivers, differentiation, co-branding, and the understanding that once a brand has been created, it must be monitored and allowed to continuously evolve.

However, in spite of NASCAR's highly successful branding strategy, the future of NASCAR is uncertain. The most recent economic recession has hit NASCAR hard. The majority of sports are suffering as sponsors pull their endorsements. Yet for NASCAR, which depends so much on its brand alliances and partnerships with other companies, the pullout of sponsors will have an even greater impact. Automaker support has been a crucial component to NASCAR's success, and as the financial situation of key automakers deteriorates, their funding of NASCAR events is likely to decrease. Still, experts foresee that manufacturers will continue to play a major part in NASCAR.

The lower attendance at NASCAR events is also born of the recession. As consumers strive to save money, discretionary spending on entertainment is one of the first budget items to be cut. NASCAR has taken a proactive stance toward the issue by lowering ticket and concession prices, and working with communities to offer incentives to get fans to travel to the events. Whether these actions will be successful remains to be seen, but the intense brand loyalty of fans certainly lies in NASCAR's favor.

Questions for Discussion

1. Evaluate NASCAR's branding strategy in relation to its overall marketing strategy. Could NASCAR have done anything differently to insulate itself against the economic downturn?

2. Conduct a strategic SWOT analysis for NASCAR at this point in its history. What opportunities are available for NASCAR to take advantage of given its many significant strengths?

3. What strategies do you recommend to counter the criticisms leveled against NASCAR? Should the company become more involved in sustainability initiatives? If so, how might that be tied in with NASCAR's branding strategies?

4. What strategies can you offer to move NASCAR to the next level in its evolution? How can the company maintain, or even increase, its sponsor and fan base?

Sources

The facts of this case are from "2009 NASCAR Mexico Series Announced," *NASCAR*, March 18, 2009 (http://localracing.nascar.com/node/2282), accessed July 10, 2009; "10-race Chase for the Cup Crowns Series Champion," *NASCAR.com*, July 17, 2008 (http://www.nascar.com/news/features/chase.format/index.html), accessed July 10, 2009; "About NASCAR," *NASCAR.com* (http://www.nascar.com/guides/about/nascar/), accessed June 3, 2009; Allen Adamson, *Brand Simple* (Palgrave MacMillan Press, 2006), pp. 221–222; J. Agarwal and N. K. Malhotra (2005), "An Integrated Model of Attitude and Affect: Theoretical Foundation and Empirical Investigation," *Journal of Business Research*, 58, pp. 483–493; "Bootlegging Roots," *All About Racin'* (http://nascarfans.wetpaint.com/page/Bootlegging+Roots), accessed June 3, 2009; Liz Clarke, "NASCAR Looks for Some Fast Buzz," *The Washington Post*, May 31, 2009 (http://www.washingtonpost.com/wp-dyn/content/article/2009/05/30/AR2009053001696.html), accessed November 17, 2009; Mark Davies and Melvin Prince (2002); "Co-branding Partners: What Do They See in Each Other?" *Business Horizons*, 45(5), pp. 51–55; Larry DeGaris, "NASCAR Fans Have Unparalleled Awareness of Sport's Sponsors, New Study Finds," James Madison University, February 7, 2005 (www.jmu.edu/kinesiology/pdfs/NASCAR.pdf), accessed June 1, 2009; Bill Elliot, "Safety Worst," *Fox Sports*, October 12, 2006 (http://msn.foxsports.com/nascar/story/6045306), accessed June 4, 2009; "EPA Asked NASCAR to Switch Six Years Ago," *ESPN*, March 1, 2005 (http://sports.espn.go.com/rpm/news/story?id=2002571), accessed June 5, 2009; "Fan Loyalty to NASCAR Sponsors," *Marketing at 200 MPH* (http://it.darden.virginia.edu/itpreview/Nascar/128/html/fanloyal.htm), accessed July 10, 2009; Marky Finney (2006), "Like the Cars, Fuel Goes Fast in NASCAR," *azcentral.com* (http://www.azcentral.com/sports/speed/articles/0602nascargas-ON.html), accessed June 5, 2009; "Former NASCAR Official Files $225 Million Lawsuit," *NASCAR.com*, June 11, 2008 (http://www.nascar.com/2008/news/headlines/cup/06/10/former.official.lawsuit/index.html), accessed July 10, 2009; Jenna Fryer, "NASCAR to Begin Phasing in Unleaded Fuel," *USA Today*, June 19, 2006 (http://www.usatoday.com/sports/motor/nascar/2006-06-19-unleaded-fuel_x.htm), accessed June 5, 2009; Sean Gregory and Steve Goldberg, "Daytona Race: NASCAR Tries To Outrace the Recession," *Time*, February 12, 2009 (http://www.time.com/time/business/article/0,8599,1879136-2,00.html); "Growth of the Sport," *All About Racin'* (http://nascarfans.wetpaint.com/page/The+Growth+of+the+Sport), accessed June 3, 2009; Ed Hinton, "Drive for Diversity Shifts Out of Neutral," *ESPN*, January 21, 2009 (http://sports.espn.go.com/rpm/nascar/cup/columns/story?columnist=hinton_ed&id=3850027); "History of NASCAR," *NASCAR.com* (http://www.nascar.com/news/features/history/), accessed June 3, 2009); IEG Sponsorship Report (1994), "Performance Research Quantifies NASCAR Impact," 13, pp. 3–6; "It's Official: COT Will Be Used Full Time in '08 Season," *NASCAR.com* May 23, 2007 (http://www.nascar.com/2007/news/headlines/cup/05/22/cot.full.time/index.html); Chris Jenkins, "Sponsors Make NASCAR's Wheels Go 'Round," *USA Today*, July 12, 2002 (http://usatoday.com/sports/motor/nascar/2002-07-12-acov-sponsors.htm); Tom Jensen, "CUP: Win on Sunday, Sell on Monday," *Speed TV.com*, March 18, 2009 (http://nascar.speedtv.com/article/cup-win-on-sunday-sell-on-monday/); "Juan Pablo Montoya," *All About Racing,* November 29, 2008 (http://www.nascarfans.wetpaint.com/page/Juan+Pablo+Montoya), accessed July 10, 2009; Goodwin Kelly, "How NASCAR, ISC Prospered with France Jr. at the Helm," *News-journalonline.com*, June 5, 2007 (http://www.news-journalonline.com/special/billfrancejr/newHEAD08060507.htm), accessed June 8, 2009; Ben Klayman, "NASCAR Expects Lower Attendance in 2009," *Reuters,* February 11, 2009 (http://www.reuters.com/article/reutersEdge/idUSTRE51B03J20090212), accessed June 8, 2009; Tim Lemke, "Future Starts Now for NASCAR; Tweaks Designed to Halt Decline in Attendance and Ratings," *The Washington Times*, February 8, 2007; "Lester Hopes He Inspires More Blacks into NASCAR," *ESPN*, March 18, 2008 (http://sports.espn.go.com/rpm/news/story?seriesId=2&id=2373984), accessed July 10, 2009; "NASCAR and California Speedway Launch NASCAR 'Te Lleva a Las Carreras,'" *Hispanic Business.com*, August 10, 2006 (http://www.hispanicbusiness.com/news/news_print.asp?id=43677); "NASCAR's Commitment to Diversity," *NDIP* (http://www.diversityinternships.com/about_diversity.htm), accessed July 10, 2009; "NASCAR Drive for Diversity Initiative Moves Forward in 2009 with an Expanded Driver Lineup," *Auto Racing Daily,* January 23, 2009 (http://www.autoracingdaily.com/news/nascar/nascar-drive-for-diversity-initiative-moves-forward-in-2009-with-an-expande/); "NASCAR Extends to Mexico,"

Sport Business International, June 8, 2004 (http://www.sportbusiness.com/news/ 155357/nascar-extends-to-mexico); "NASCAR Fans Embrace Patriotic Brand Loyalty," *Brandweek*, July 6, 2009 (http://www.brandweek.com/bw/content_display/news-and-features/digital/e3iba9a089c3eafb2f59088ad986aa0bf1d); "NASCAR Hires Lynch to Head 'Green' Initiative," *NASCAR.com*, November 14, 2008 (http://www.nascar.com/ 2008/news/headlines/official/11/11/mlynch.q.a/); "NASCAR History," *All About Racin'* (http://nascarfans.wetpaint.com/page/NASCAR+History), accessed June 3, 2009; "NASCAR Racing Series," *NASCAR.com* (http://www.nascar.com/news/features/ nascar.series/index.html), accessed June 3, 2009; "New NASCAR Playoff Structure Announced," *NASCAR.com*, July 20, 2004 (http://www.nascar.com/2004/news/ headlines/cup/01/20/points_revision/index.html); "Notes: Good Weather Can't Save Atlanta Attendance," *NASCAR.com*, May 9, 2009 (http://www.bigwestracing.com/ forums/showthread.php?t=21514); "Official Sponsors: 2009 NASCAR Season," *NASCAR.com* (http://www.nascar.com/guides/sponsors/), accessed July 10, 2009; Brian O'Keefe, "America's Fastest Growing Sport," *Fortune*, September 5, 2005 (http:// money.cnn.com/magazines/fortune/fortune_archive/2005/09/05/8271412/index.htm); David Poole, "Poole's Best: Dale Earnhardt's Last Gift 5 Years After the Crash," *THATSRACIN.COM*, February 19, 2006 (http://www.thatsracin.com/158/story/ 7999.html); George Pyne, "In His Own Words: NASCAR Sharpens Winning Strategy," *Advertising Age*, October 28, 2002, 73(43), p. S6; David Rodman, "Still More to Learn About New Car After First Year," *NASCAR.com*, December 12, 2008 (http:// www.nascar.com/2008/news/features/12/12/enterprise.new.car.after.year.one/in-dex.html); Don Roy, "Champ Car World Series," in O. C. Ferrell and Michael D. Hartline, eds., *Marketing Strategy*, 4th ed. (Mason, OH: Cengage, Thomson/ South-Western Publishing, 2008), pp. 416–426; Nate Ryan, "Pinch on Automakers Could Leave NASCAR 'Truly Hurting,'" *USA Today*, December 21, 2008 (http:// www.usatoday.com/sports/motor/nascar/2008-12-21-cover-automakers_N.htm]); Rong-An Shang, Yu-Chen Chen, and Hsueh-Jung Liao (2006), "The Value of Participation in Virtual Consumer Communities on Brand Loyalty," *Internet Research*, 16(4), pp. 398–418; Eric Spanberg, "Business in Racing: Tough Economic Times Expected in 2009 for NASCAR," *Scenedaily.com*, October 30, 2008 (http://www. scenedaily.com/news/articles/sprintcupseries/Erik_Spanberg_Business_in_racing_. html); "Talladega Reduces Ticket Prices for Cup Series Races," *NASCAR.com*, January 8, 2009 (http://www.nascar.com/2009/news/headlines/cup/01/08/talladega.reduces. ticket.prices/index.html); "The Birth of NASCAR," *All About Racin'* (http:// www.nascarfans.wetpaint.com/page/The+Birth+of+NASCAR), accessed June 8, 2009; "Toyota Racing President Expects NASCAR Cutbacks," *NASCAR.com*, January 14, 2009 (http://www.nascar.com/2009/news/headlines/cup/01/14/toyota.expected. cutbacks/index.html?eref=/rss/news/headlines/cup); and Nolan Weidner, "NASCAR Thriving with Some Variety; Five Years Later, the Organization's Drive for Diversity Is Bearing Fruit," *The Post-Standard* (NY: Syracuse), August 13, 2005, p. D1.

The Indy Racing League (IRL): Driving for First Place

Synopsis: Auto racing is the fastest growing spectator sport in the United States. Unfortunately, the IRL and open-wheel racing in general have experienced a period of decline while other forms of auto racing—most notably NASCAR— have grown. The IRL is a distant second to NASCAR in terms of popularity in the motorsports market. After years of damaging competition, the IRL and Champ Car (CART) have finally reunified. The new IRL must strengthen its standing in the American motorsports market, begin the task of reconnecting with former fans, and build connections with new fans. New sponsors and a new television contract are positive signs for the IRL, but many questions remain about its future.

Themes: Competition, market segmentation, product and branding strategy, sports and event marketing, sponsorship, global marketing, corporate governance, marketing implementation

The origins of the Indy Racing League (IRL) can be traced back to the formation of Championship Auto Racing Teams (CART) in 1978. Several automobile racing team owners created CART as a sanctioning body for open-wheel racing in the United States. Open-wheel racing refers to cars having wheels located outside the body of the car rather than underneath the body or fenders as found on street cars. Also, they have an open cockpit, also called a pod, with the engine housed at the rear of the vehicle. The United States Auto Club (USAC) had sanctioned the sport since the mid-1950s, but many racing teams were dissatisfied with USAC's administration and promotion of open-wheel racing. Consequently, CART was founded when 18 of the 21 team owners left USAC to form the new league.

Don Roy, Middle Tennessee State University, prepared this case, with the editorial assistance of Jennifer Sawayda, The University of New Mexico, for classroom discussion rather than to illustrate effective or ineffective handling of an administrative situation.

Growth and Division of Open-Wheel Racing in the United States

For the first 17 years of its existence, CART dominated auto racing in the United States, and open-wheel racing enjoyed greater success than other forms of racing, including stock car racing. However, not everyone associated with open-wheel racing in the United States welcomed the success enjoyed by CART. One person with major concerns about the direction of CART was Anton H. "Tony" George, President of the Indianapolis Motor Speedway. George's family had founded the Indianapolis 500 and developed it into the premier American auto race and an event of worldwide significance. George was concerned that CART was beginning to lose sight of the interests of American open-wheel racing by holding events in foreign countries, putting too much emphasis on racing at road courses instead of oval tracks, and focusing too much on promoting top foreign drivers as CART stars.

In 1994, George announced that he was creating a new open-wheel league that would compete with CART beginning in 1996. The Indy Racing League (IRL) was divisive to open-wheel racing in the United States, as team owners were forced to decide whether to remain with CART or move to the new IRL. Only IRL members would be allowed to race in the Indianapolis 500. CART teams responded by planning their own event on the same day as the Indianapolis 500. CART held the U.S. 500 at the Michigan International Speedway on Memorial Day weekend, 1996, and drew over 100,000 spectators to the event. The rift between CART and the IRL moved to the courts when lawsuits were filed over use of the terms "IndyCar" and "Indy car," which CART had licensed from the Indianapolis Motor Speedway for several years. The result of the lawsuit was that neither party could use the terms until December 31, 2002.

The IRL-CART feud distracted both leagues, and stock car racing solidified its standing as the favorite motorsport in the United States. A 2001 ESPN Sports Poll found that 56 percent of American auto racing fans said stock car racing was their favorite type of racing, with open-wheel racing third at 9 percent (drag racing was second at 12 percent). The diminished appeal of open-wheel racing contributed to additional problems with sponsor relationships. Three major partners left CART, including two partners (Honda and Toyota) that provided engines and technical support to CART and its teams. In addition, FedEx discontinued its title-sponsor relationship with CART after the 2002 season. During the same time, the IRL struggled to find corporate partners as a weakened economy and a fragmented market for open-wheel racing made both the IRL and CART less attractive to sponsors.

The IRL experienced ups and downs in the years following the split. Interest in IRL as measured by television ratings took a noticeable dip between 2002 and 2004, with 25 percent fewer viewers tuning in during 2004 than just two years earlier. The declining television audience was a factor in the IRL's inability to sell naming rights for its series. The IRL last had a title sponsor for the series in 2001, Internet search engine Northern Light. In contrast, the National Association for Stock Car Auto Racing

(NASCAR) signed a blockbuster deal with Nextel that called for more $700 million over 10 years beginning in 2004. Industry experts believe that the most the IRL could command for its title sponsorship as long as it competed with CART was about $50 million over 10 years.

In response to declining interest in the IRL, marketing initiatives were taken to reverse the trend. The IRL beefed up its marketing staff. The league did not even have a dedicated marketing staff until 2001. In 2005, the IRL launched a new ad campaign that targeted 18- to 34-year-old males. The focus of the ads was different too. Instead of focusing on the cutting-edge technology found in IRL cars, as had been done in previous ad campaigns, the focus shifted to drivers and the drama created on the track. The campaign was part of a broader strategy to expand the association of the IRL beyond a sport for middle-aged, Midwestern males. The idea was to position the brand as hip and young.

In support of this effort, two developments can be noted. First, the IRL followed a trend observed in NASCAR and got several celebrities involved in the sport through team ownership. Among the celebrities involved with the IRL are talk show host David Letterman, NBA star Carmelo Anthony, former NFL quarterback Jim Harbaugh, and actor Patrick Dempsey. Another celebrity involved with the IRL is rock star Gene Simmons. He is a partner in Simmons Abramson Marketing, who was hired to help the IRL devise new marketing strategies. The firm's entertainment marketing savvy is being tapped to help the IRL connect with fans on an emotional level through its drivers, whom Simmons referred to as "rock stars in rocket ships."

Second, driver personalities began to give the IRL some visibility. The emergence of Danica Patrick as a star in the IRL has broadened appeal of the league and assists the efforts to reach young males. In 2005, Patrick was a 23-year-old IRL rookie, who finished fourth in the Indianapolis 500. The combination of the novelty of a female driver and her captivating looks and personality made her the darling of American sports that year. Patrick's effect on the IRL was very noticeable; the IRL reported gains in event attendance, merchandise sales, website traffic, and television ratings during Patrick's rookie season. Patrick has drawn the interest of many companies that have hired her as a product endorser, including Motorola, Go Daddy, Boost Mobile, and XM Radio. In addition, she has appeared in photo shoots in *FHM* and the 2008 and 2009 *Sports Illustrated* swimsuit issues. Another driver who has gained fame is Helio Castroneves, a Brazilian driver who won the Indianapolis 500 in 2001, 2002, and 2009. He enhanced his celebrity status by appearing on the popular television show *Dancing with the Stars* in 2007, winning the competition.

The Motorsports Market

Although many forms of motorsports exist, competition for the IRL can be narrowed to two major racing series: Formula One and NASCAR. Formula One is an open-wheel series that has the greatest global reach in terms of race venues and races exclusively on road courses. Formula One's 17-race 2009 schedule included nine races in Europe as well as races in Australia, Bahrain, Brazil, China, Japan, Malaysia, Singapore, and the United Arab Emirates. A Formula One race is known as a Grand Prix, with each race taking on the name of the country hosting a particular race (e.g., Grand Prix of Spain). Formula One was the first racing league in the Western hemisphere to stage an event in the lucrative Chinese market. Formula One drivers have an international flavor. Most hail from European countries, although there are also drivers from Canada, Columbia, and Japan. The winner of the Formula One season series is referred to as the "World F1 Driving Champion," further reinforcing Formula One as a global racing league.

The clear leader in the U.S. motorsports market is NASCAR, founded in the early 1950s, approximately the same time period when USAC was founded. NASCAR fields three racing circuits in the United States: The Sprint Cup Series, the Nationwide Series, and the Camping World Truck Series. The Sprint Cup Series is NASCAR's premier circuit. Its 36 races are held primarily on oval tracks and exclusively in U.S. markets. Like the IRL, NASCAR has a strong regional following, with the Southeast being a long-time hotbed for the league. NASCAR was predominantly a southern United States sport until the 1990s, as exposure provided by cable television and the emergence of strong driver personalities such as Dale Earnhardt and Jeff Gordon led to an explosion in NASCAR's popularity. The league has become even more popular as it has focused on marketing drivers, especially young drivers often referred to as NAS-CAR's "Young Guns." League and sponsor promotion of drivers such as Dale Earn-hardt, Jr., Jimmie Johnson, Ryan Newman, and Kasey Kahne has vaulted NASCAR to a level of popularity in the United States second only to the National Football League.

Today, NASCAR towers over the IRL in the United States in terms of sponsor support and audiences. NASCAR has sought to expand to become a truly national sport, adding races in Chicago, southern California, and Texas, while eliminating races in smaller markets such as Rockingham, North Carolina. Future expansion plans include adding events in the Pacific Northwest and the New York City area. The average television audience for NASCAR races in 2008 averaged approximately 5 percent of U.S. households, compared to less than 2 percent for the IRL. As a result of NASCAR's popularity growth, it was able to negotiate a lucrative, multi-billion dollar contract with Fox and ESPN, while the IRL has struggled to secure a favorable television deal.

Reunification of U.S. Open-Wheel Racing

Many racing observers believe that open-wheel racing could have been as popular as NASCAR is today. In the 1980s and early 1990s, CART enjoyed greater popularity and television ratings. The split in open-wheel racing that led to the formation of the IRL was a setback to open-wheel racing in general. The split resulted in a dilution of competition quality, sponsor dollars, and fan support. Many experts believed that a reunification of open-wheel racing was the only way to compete against NASCAR.

That long awaited reunification occurred before the beginning of the 2008 season. Champ Car's operations (CART had changed ownership and its name in 2007) were on the verge of ceasing following the cancellation of its final event in 2007 and uncertainty whether a 2008 schedule would be run. Tony George's IRL bought the assets of Champ Car for a mere $10 million and provided a $30 million capital investment for equipment and incentives to bring Champ Car teams into the IRL fold. The IRL's reunified open-wheel racing circuit was branded the IndyCar Series. Decisions had to be made about the markets and racing courses that the IndyCar Series would target following the merger of Champ Car and the IRL. The 2010 schedule included 17 races—about one-half the number of NASCAR's Sprint Cup Series. The 2010 IndyCar Series schedule is shown in Case Exhibit 4.1. One change has been an increase in the number of street and road course races. The IndyCar Series added street races in markets that had been very successful for CART/Champ Car: Long Beach, California, and Toronto. A total of 10 of the 17 races on the 2010 schedule were held in former CART/Champ Car markets. Road/street races make up 9 of the 17 races on the IndyCar Series schedule. In contrast, only 2 of NASCAR Sprint Cup's 36 races are held on road courses.

In addition to the influence of Champ Car's strategy of more street/road courses, another feature of Champ Car that the IRL could leverage is the positioning of races as entertainment events. The race itself is only one piece of the product. Champ Car used the term "Festival of Speed" to position its events. In addition to the race, fans can often partake in such activities as kids' zones, beach volleyball, wine tasting, or live concerts. One description of this approach is "We throw a party and a race breaks out. We don't want people to come out and sit in metal grandstands for three hours and get sweaty and get sunburned and go home. We want stuff going on everywhere." The festival concept appeared to be a success. The 2006 Champ Car street race at Long Beach, California attracted an estimated 200,000 people during the three-day event, including more than 80,000 people on race day.

CASE EXHIBIT 4.1   2010 INDYCAR SERIES SCHEDULE

DATE	RACE
March 14	Streets of Sao Paulo 300 (Sao Paulo, Brazil)
March 28	Honda Indy Grand Prix of St. Petersburg (FL)
April 11	Indy Grand Prix of Alabama (Birmingham)
April 18	Long Beach (CA) Grand Prix
May 1	Road Runner Turbo Indy 300 (Kansas City, KS)
May 30	Indianapolis 500
June 5	Bombardier Learjet 550K (Fort Worth, TX)
June 20	Iowa Corn Indy 250 (Newton, IA)
July 4	Watkins Glen (NY) Indy Grand Prix
July 18	Grand Prix of Toronto
July 25	Rexall Edmonton Indy Grand Prix
Aug. 8	Honda Indy 200 at Mid-Ohio (Lexington/Cleveland, OH)
Aug. 22	Indy Grand Prix of Sonoma County (San Francisco, CA)
Aug. 28	PEAK Antifreeze and Motor Oil Indy 300 (Joliet/Chicago, IL)
Sept. 4	Kentucky Indy 300 (Sparta, KY / Cincinnati, OH)
Sept. 19	Indy 300 (Motegi, Japan)
Oct. 2	Homestead-Miami Indy 300 (Homestead/Miami, FL)

Another development for the IndyCar Series is a new television broadcast partner. ABC has televised the Indianapolis 500 for 45 years, and the IRL will continue that relationship. Most of the other races on the IndyCar Series schedule (at least 13 per season) will be televised by VERSUS, a cable channel that replaces ESPN as the IRL's broadcast partner. Although VERSUS has a smaller audience than ESPN, it covers fewer sports and plans to give IndyCar Series more coverage than ESPN did when it owned the broadcast rights. VERSUS is committed to carrying 7 hours of IndyCar programming each week during the season. The depth of coverage will give the IRL and its drivers greater exposure and potentially allow more fans to identify with the league's personalities. Also, VERSUS made a long-term commitment by signing a 10-year, $67 million contract with the IRL.

Moving Forward

Both optimism and uncertainty exist as the Indy Racing League moves beyond re-unification. Optimism exists in growing business opportunities coming the IRL's way. New marketing agreements are in place with Coca-Cola, Orbitz, National Guard, and Izod. A partnership with Mattel will bring Hot Wheels-branded IndyCars to retail stores and IndyCar Series events, promoting drivers and the series schedule by including it on product packaging. Michael Andretti, a former IRL driver and now team owner, believes the cost advantage of attending IndyCar races compared to NASCAR gives the league an upper hand in a difficult economic environment. Market expansion could be a possibility too. Cities such as Baltimore, Dallas, Houston, Las Vegas, and Los Angeles have all been discussed as possible locations for IndyCar races, although there appears to be little interest in expanding beyond the current 17-race season.

Despite the positive developments for the IRL, the long-term future is unclear. A primary concern is top leadership. Tony George resigned his top positions with the IRL and the Indianapolis Motor Speedway (IMS) in July 2009. He was a proponent of using profits from IMS to prop up operations of the IRL, funneling an estimated hundreds of millions of dollars over the years to sustain the IRL. It is uncertain whether the IMS board, controlled primarily by Tony George's siblings and step-mother, will continue with the strategy.

Other concerns deal with the mix of racetracks and markets targeted. The 2010 schedule now has more road/street races than oval track races, a characteristic of the former CART/Champ Car circuits. The IRL touts the mix of races as challenging to drivers, forcing them to master a variety of tracks in order to win the IRL season championship. Critics fear fewer oval tracks will take the IndyCar Series away from its roots. The trend toward scheduling more races outside the United States is another concern. Although only 4 of the 17 races will be held outside the United States (2 in Canada and 1 each in Brazil and Japan), some observers feel the IRL is neither doing enough to market itself in the United States nor adequately promoting American drivers. The IRL driver roster has a more global flavor to it than NASCAR, with drivers hailing from Brazil, England, Spain, New Zealand, and Japan, in addition to American drivers. The strong Midwestern U.S. influence of IndyCars seems to be at odds with the globalization of auto racing in general and the IndyCar Series in particular.

Finally, there is a possibility that top IndyCar drivers could leave to pursue more lucrative opportunities in NASCAR or Formula One. If popular drivers like Danica Patrick, Helio Castroneves, or Marco Andretti leave to drive in another league, it would certainly be a negative for the IRL. It is a concern because it has happened before, with drivers such as Tony Stewart, Sam Hornish, Jr., and Robby Gordon leaving the IRL for NASCAR in recent years.

Questions for Discussion

1. Identify the external factors that have impacted and continue to impact the Indy Racing League and its marketing efforts. Which factors appear to be the IRL's greatest threats?

2. What are the IRL's greatest strengths? Which weaknesses would you recommend that the IRL attempt to convert into strengths? How might these weaknesses be converted?

3. What advantages does the IRL possess over NASCAR? How should these advantages be used by the IRL to compete with NASCAR?

4. How should the IRL be positioned to differentiate it from other racing leagues, both in the United States and abroad?

5. What can the IRL learn from NASCAR's success? Are there elements of NASCAR's marketing strategy that the IRL could adopt?

Sources

The facts of this case are from "Andretti Has Eye on Regaining Market Share," *Street & Smith's Sports Business Journal*, May 18, 2009, p. 19; Debbie Arrington, "Racing Factions Talking Merger: Champ Car and the IRL Could Be on the Verge of Mending a Decade-Old Rift," *Knight Ridder Tribune Business News*, April 14, 2006, p. 1; Debbie Arrington, "IRL Preview: IRL Tweaks Tune, Vies for New Dance Partners," *Knight Ridder Tribune Business News*, March 24, 2006, p. 1; Steve Ballard, "Championship Auto Racing Teams' Board Votes to Accept Buyout," *Knight Ridder Tribune Business News*, December 16, 2003, p. 1; Terry Blount, "Reuniting IRL, Champ Car Is an Uphill Climb," *Knight Ridder Tribune Business News*, June 4, 2006, p. 1; Theresa Bradley, "Racing League Gears Hip Events at Youth," *Knight Ridder Tribune Business News*, March 23, 2006, p. 1; "Celebrities Who Are Revved Up over Racing," *Street & Smith's Sports Business Journal*, May 22, 2006, p. 27; Tony Fabrizio, "Racer Danica Patrick Embraces Celebrity Exposure," *Tampa Tribune*, February 27, 2009; Shawn Fenner, "IRL Sees Significance of Selling Product to U.S. Market," *Richmond Times-Dispatch*, June 23, 2009; Reggie Hayes, "What's Next for IndyCar?"

Fort Wayne News-Sentinel, July 1, 2009; "Hot Wheels Announces Partnership with the IndyCar Series, Indianapolis 500," *Entertainment Newsweekly*, April 24, 2009, p. 140; John Korobanik, "Toronto, Edmonton on IRL 2010 Schedule," *National Post*, July 31, 2009; Terry Lefton, "Ad Sales Encouraging as IRL Launches Season," *Street & Smith's Sports Business Journal*, March 30, 2009, p. 8; Robin Miller, "A Brief History of CART," SpeedTV.com, April 16, 2008 (http://auto-racing.speedtv.com/article/miller-a-brief-history-of-cart/); Marty O'Brien, "Helio Castroneves is Happier Making Headlines on the Race Track," *Daily Press*, June 27, 2009; John Oreovicz, "Brazil, Bama on 2010 IndyCar Schedule (http://sports.espn.go.com/espn/blog/index?entryID=4370121& name=oreovicz_john), July 31, 2009;" John Ourand, "Early IRL Numbers Small, but Please Versus," *Street & Smith's Sports Business Journal*, May 18, 2009, 18; John Ourand, "IRL to Get at Least 7 Hours Weekly on Versus," *Street & Smith's Sports Business Journal*, February 23, 2009, p. 7; Jennifer Pendleton, "Danica Patrick," *Advertising Age*, November 7, 2005, p. S4; "Say It's So: Champ Car and IRL to End War?" *Autoweek*, February 27, 2006, pp. 37–38; Anthony Schoettle, "Merger Talks Near Finish?" *Indianapolis Business Journal*, May 8, 2006, p. 1; Anthony Schoettle, "IRL Ratings Continue Their Skid," *Indianapolis Business Journal*, November 1, 2004, p. 3; Anthony Schoettle, "IRL Shops for Title Sponsor," *Indianapolis Business Journal*, August 18, 2003, p. 3; Michael Smith, "United Series Begins Long Trek of Rebuilding," *Street & Smith's Sports Business Journal*, March 3, 2008, p. 5; Alan Snel, "Kiss Rocker Lends Voice to Indy Races," *Knight Ridder Tribune Business News*, April 1, 2006, p. 1; "Turnkey Sports Poll," *Street & Smith's Sports Business Journal*, May 22, 2006, p. 24; J. K. Wall, "Indy Racing League Sets Sights on Marketing Dollars," *Knight Ridder Tribune Business News*, May 27, 2004, p. 1; Scott Warfield, "IRL Marketing Chief Aims for Consistency," *Street & Smith's Sports Business Journal*, February 20, 2006, p. 9; Scott Warfield, "Danica Patrick Provides Sizzle to IRL," *Street & Smith's Sports Business Journal*, May 23, 2005, p. 1; Scott Warfield, "IRL in Line to Court Young Males," *Street & Smith's Sports Business Journal*, November 29, 2004, p. 4; Jeff Wolf, "George's Ouster Clouds IRL's Future," *Las Vegas Review-Journal*, July 3, 2009.

Blockbuster Fights for Survival Against Intense Competition

Synopsis: *Blockbuster has consistently faced competitive challenges throughout its history. However, changing technology and shifting customer preferences with respect to movie distribution have become Blockbuster's biggest challenges to date. Today, the company finds itself trapped in its bricks-and-mortar business model of the past, while strong competitors have emerged to dominate movie distribution via the mail (Netflix), kiosks (Redbox), and online (Apple, Amazon, Hulu, and others). Looking to the future, Blockbuster's very survival depends on its ability to adapt to and adopt new technology and marketing practices—issues the company has struggled with in the past because of its reactive, rather than proactive, stance toward a rapidly changing market.*

Themes: *Changing technology, changing consumer preferences, competition, competitive advantage, product strategy, services marketing, pricing strategy, distribution strategy, nonstore retailing, customer relationships, value, implementation*

Blockbuster has recently been described as a dinosaur—some say a dinosaur on life support. What a dramatic change from the company's peak only a few years ago. In 2005, Blockbuster, Inc. sat at the top of the global home video rental industry. However, that dominant position has quickly eroded in the face of stiff competition on a number of fronts. Until recently, Blockbuster dealt with a change in competition fueled by changes in technology and consumer preferences. Whether it involves movies delivered via mail, cable on-demand, or online, Blockbuster has struggled to figure out the best way to compete against Netflix, Apple, Amazon, cable providers, and a host of online services. Most recently, Blockbuster has faced a different form of competition from Redbox and its vending-based solution to movie distribution. Blockbuster now finds itself in the unenviable position of having to compete on both price and convenience. As more and more consumers move to these and other types of movie distribution services, Blockbuster has become trapped in its bricks-and-mortar business model of the past.

Keith C. Jones, North Carolina A&T State University, prepared this case for classroom discussion rather than to illustrate effective or ineffective handling of an administrative situation.

Blockbuster's History

Blockbuster started in 1985 as a small entrepreneurial venture. David Cook sold his computing services business and started a handful of computerized video rental stores. Then in 1986, he transformed his company into Blockbuster Entertainment. As the company showed strong growth and potential, investors eyed the company as a potential investment opportunity. One of these investors was Wayne Huizenga, who in 1987 brought the company a large financial boost ($18 million) and a vision to expand the company into the largest video rental company in the United States. By the end of 1987, Huizenga bought full interest in the company. In three years Huizenga took the company from 130 stores to 1,500 stores. The growth included the acquisition of Major Video (175 stores) and Erol's, which was the third-largest U.S. video rental chain at the time.

Early Expansion

In the 1990s, the company maintained a very aggressive expansion and acquisition program. Blockbuster expanded into the music industry when it acquired Sound Warehouse and Music Plus in 1992. These acquisitions allowed the company to develop the Blockbuster Music component of its overall business. While this was taking place, the company also expanded internationally. One of its largest international moves was the purchase of Cityvision, which provided Blockbuster with 875 stores throughout the United Kingdom. Then in 1993, Blockbuster made its next expansion move with the acquisition of the Spelling Entertainment group. This provided Blockbuster with key industry access. Huizenga's final visionary action before moving on to other entrepreneurial ventures was the handing off of Blockbuster to Viacom, which created the Blockbuster Entertainment Group.

The mid-1990s were a tumultuous era for Blockbuster. From 1994 to 1997, Blockbuster experienced frequent turnover in upper management and a repositioning—changes that almost proved fatal to the company. When Huizenga stepped down as CEO, Steven Berrard filled the vacancy. Berrard stayed on as CEO until 1996 when he left the company and joined forces with Huizenga. Then Bill Fields stepped in from an executive position at Walmart. Fields brought with him the Walmart persona and immediately started repositioning Blockbuster from a rental format to a retail sales format. During this repositioning, Fields closed 50 of the music stores and moved the corporate headquarters from Florida to Dallas, Texas. Some members of the upper management group opted not to follow the company to Texas, creating critical vacancies in the company. Fields resigned from his position in 1997.

Back to Basics

In a lifesaving move, Blockbuster's board brought in John Antioco as the next CEO. After a review of the company, Antioco immediately repositioned the company back to its traditional competitive advantage in home entertainment rentals. In doing so, Antioco reformatted the stores as rental facilities for movies and games. He retained a minimal retail sales component but focused all promotional efforts on the rental industry. To improve the competitive advantage of the company, Antioco renegotiated contracts with movie studios. Traditionally, movie rental companies were required to pay large sums of money per copy of a movie (as much as $120). Antioco developed a revenue-sharing approach that allowed Blockbuster to obtain more copies of a movie (paying a smaller fee) but sharing with the movie studio a royalty per rental. This provided Blockbuster with the ability to develop an availability guarantee for new releases through a larger inventory holding.

The next major strategic change Antioco instituted was the harvesting of the Blockbuster Music component of the company in 1998. This finalized the transformation of Blockbuster back to a focus on the movie and game rental industry. When Viacom spun off a partial interest in Blockbuster in 1999, Antioco restructured the company into three operating units: retail, e-commerce, and database and brand marketing. This new operating structure allowed Blockbuster to be on the forefront of innovation as DVDs had solidly replaced VHS tape in 2001.

Not all of Antioco's changes during this time were successful. In 2001, Blockbuster attempted to partner with Radio Shack by providing store space to sell necessary equipment to renters. This was a short-lived relationship as Radio Shack pulled out in 2002 and accused Blockbuster of limiting access to customer information. This was a mutual dissolution as Blockbuster accused Radio Shack of selling unnecessary items to customers and thus negatively impacting the image of Blockbuster in the eyes of the consumer.

Blockbuster Evolves

By 2002, customers' demands for home entertainment had evolved beyond traditional movie rentals. In a letter to Blockbuster shareholders, Antioco stated, "In 2002, we again began to change the way we do business to capitalize on the changes in the home entertainment marketplace brought about by DVD and introduction of the next-generation game platforms." The mission for Blockbuster was to become the complete source for movies and games. This led to the purchase of Game Station (a retail format specializing in electronic games) and an expansion of the gaming section of the stores to include equipment sales and rentals. To stay competitive, Blockbuster also purchased a chain of movie trading stores and an online company called Film Caddy. Antioco also recognized the threat posed by the growing popularity of rent-by-mail formats such as Netflix. And, not forgetting the international component of the company, Blockbuster began testing a nonsubscription online rental with a postal delivery approach in the United Kingdom.

By 2003, Blockbuster had launched its rental subscription program, which allowed subscribers to rent an unlimited number of movies during the subscription period (there were limitations within the program). Through this program, subscribers no longer had to worry about the extended viewing fees to which renters were subject. The company also continued to expand and improve on its in-store concepts, especially in the DVD and electronic game sections. Finally, Antioco continued to emphasize the importance of the e-commerce component and the Blockbuster.com website. During this time, the main function of the website was to provide potential renters with movie, promotion, and feedback information. Although contemplating entering the online rental market in the United States, Blockbuster did not make the jump during 2003.

Blockbuster was able to capitalize on the home entertainment growth trends during this time. Game software sales in the United States grew from $5.8 billion to $6.2 billion. The movie rental sector was growing at 7 percent annually and was expected to be a $1.1 billion industry by 2008. While Blockbuster continued to improve its rental subscription programs and the movie and game trading components, the company's critical move was the launch of its online movie rental program in 2004. This strategic move was a reaction to the burgeoning level of competition in alternative movie rental options. However, Blockbuster did not want to abandon its flagship in-store offerings, so the company gave online subscribers two free in-store rentals (movies or games) each month. This program was designed to overcome customer complaints about having to wait for online movies to arrive. It was also seen as a competitive advantage against Netflix.

Another Change in Command

Antioco's term as CEO came to an abrupt end in July 2007 after he clashed with the board of directors over his compensation package. In a swift and decisive move, the board of directors enlisted James Keyes to replace Antioco. Keyes was the turn-around artist for 7-Eleven (CEO from 2000–2005) and had entered "retirement" after the sale of 7-Eleven in 2005. Keyes came on board with two clear initiatives. First, he wanted to use technology to transform Blockbuster into a dominant force in both the in-store and online formats, thus making content more readily available. Second, he wanted to change the image of the company from being a rental shop to a content shop.

The environment Keyes stepped into was not a comfortable one. In 2006, Blockbuster closed 290 stores and planned to close another 280 in 2007. Financially, Blockbuster and Keyes were under the gun: The company's stock price had fallen from a high of just over $26 in 2002 to $4.30 when Keyes took over. Under Keyes, store closings continued. After closing 217 stores in 2007 (less than projected), the company planned to shutter another 167 stores in 2008.

Changing Movie Distribution Technology

Since the creation of home entertainment systems, technology has played a leading role in the evolution of the movie industry. For example, the growth of home theaters created a change in the competitive environment. A study by the Pew Research Center reported that 75 percent of adults prefer to watch movies at home rather than go to a theater. The study also reported that half of adults watch at least one movie per week via DVD rental or pay-per-view. This increase in home movie watching was largely a result of vastly improved and less expensive home theater electronics and the readily available access to movies through movie rental chains or pay-per-view cable and satellite services. The result has been challenging for the traditional movie theater business, where ticket sales have declined dramatically in recent years.

Now, evidence is mounting that a similar fate is awaiting the traditional movie rental industry. Several of the major movie production companies have now opted to bypass the theater experience and instead promote a selection of their movies directly to the home viewing audience. Consequently, movie distribution is slowly moving more toward a direct model where customers can access movies via on-demand services or via broadband downloads. This trend creates an interesting relationship between the movie studios and the movie distribution channel. Through increasing disintermediation (bypassing theaters and rental chains), movie studios stand to increase profit margins dramatically. Of the various movie distribution methods, many experts believe that broadband distribution stands to gain the most traction with customers. Broadband technology did not really gain steam until 2000 with the widespread access to high-speed Internet services in millions of U.S. households. Now, as broadband speeds have improved, customers have the ability to quickly download full-length feature films. The same is now true of handheld devices such as iPods and smartphones.

The increasing capabilities of ever-improving broadband technology caught the attention of the movie industry. In 2002, five major Hollywood studios (MGM, Paramount, Sony Pictures, Universal, and Warner Bros.) created Movielink, LLC—an online service that offered both sales and rentals of movies from their vast libraries, plus movies from Disney, Miramax, Artisan, and others. Movielink customers could rent movies by downloading them to their computers. Movies remained on the hard drive for 30 days or until they were activated (rented movies could not be burned to a DVD). Once activated, a movie could be watched as many times as possible within 24 hours. Rental prices started at 99 cents, but most new releases rented for $4.99. Recognizing the importance of the online market, Blockbuster acquired Movielink in 2007 after the studios realized they lacked the expertise needed in the retail business. By December 2008, Movielink had been fully incorporated into Blockbuster's product offerings.

Competition Forces Blockbuster's Hand

Many companies have danced in and out of the movie rental industry since the 1980s. When Blockbuster was first formed, the competitive market consisted of many small local and regional entrepreneurial businesses. Major players such as Walmart dabbled in the industry but didn't stay long. From 2005 to 2007, Blockbuster faced increasing competition, primarily from Movie Gallery and Netflix. To remain competitive, Blockbuster fine-tuned its rental program and introduced a "no late fee" policy. This strategy became a legal nightmare for Blockbuster when a barrage of lawsuits followed over the language and the fine print of the rental contract.

To further promote its online service and create a more efficient service, Blockbuster began online rental order fulfillment through 1,000 of its local stores. This change in fulfillment process allowed the company to get to customers in remote locations in an expedited nature. By the end of 2005, Blockbuster had approximately 1.2 million online subscribers, with a goal of reaching 2 million subscribers within the next year. To further entice new subscribers, Blockbuster changed its tactics by giving new subscribers a free movie or game rental each week (rather than two per month). Through these changes, Blockbuster was attempting to integrate click-and-brick to create an image and level of service that Netflix was unable to duplicate.

Today there are at least 21 major competitors in the sales and rental industry that compete with Blockbuster. These include major retail firms such as Walmart, Target, Best Buy, Amazon, and Time Warner. In the rental sector, Blockbuster continues to face intense competition from Movie Gallery, Netflix, Redbox, Hastings Entertainment, and a variety of online-only services such as Apple, Amazon, and Hulu.

Movie Gallery

It is ironic that Movie Gallery—the number two company in the movie rental industry—was also founded in 1985 in a manner similar to Blockbuster. Through the acquisition of Hollywood Video, Video Update, and Game Crazy, Movie Gallery peaked in 2005 with 4,800 stores (owned or franchised) in the United States, Canada, and Mexico (all stores in Mexico were closed in 2008). Before its international expansion, Movie Gallery focused on small communities with little or no competition. However, Movie Gallery's growth forced the company into very intense competition with Blockbuster. This rivalry came to a head in 2004 when Movie Gallery successfully outbid Blockbuster in its $1.2 billion acquisition of Hollywood Entertainment (i.e., Hollywood Video). Unfortunately for Movie Gallery, the Hollywood Entertainment purchase was the root cause for its bankruptcy filing in 2008. Movie Gallery moved into online rentals via its acquisition of VHQ Entertainment of Canada in 2005. Today, Movie Gallery owns or franchises 3,300 stores located throughout the United States and Canada. The company has experienced a decrease in revenues and recorded losses for the previous four years of operation. Their current focus is on expanding the gaming component of the company rather than their movie rental business.

Netflix

Intense competition from Netflix was a main reason that Blockbuster dropped its late-fee program in 2005 (a shift that led to a $400 million loss in revenue for Blockbuster). Netflix, with over 10 million subscribers, touts itself as the largest online entertainment subscription service. CEO Reed Hastings set a goal of reaching 20 million subscribers by 2012—a number that would equate to roughly 20 percent of all U.S. households. This goal far exceeds analysts' growth projections of 13 million subscribers. In addition to its subscriber base, Netflix also enjoys increasing sales. Quarterly sales topped $320 million in late 2008, followed by $394 million during the first quarter of 2009. Even more impressive, Netflix managed to increase sales at a time when the entire movie rental industry experienced an 8 percent sales decline.

Netflix built its success around the online rental of movies with next day delivery (in most cases). Netflix subscribers can rent as many movies as they want within a month for one flat fee. Once they return a movie, the next movie on their list is shipped to their home. Shipping is free in both directions. Netflix achieves this fast turnaround time because it ships over 2 million DVDs per day from 58 different locations around the United States.

Netflix's strategy differs somewhat from those of Blockbuster and Movie Gallery. Within its catalog of 100,000 movie titles, only 30 percent of Netflix rentals are new releases. This compares to 70 percent for Blockbuster. Netflix makes over 17,000 of these titles available via its Watch Instantly service. Customers can watch movies instantly using a computer, or they can use third-party devices—such as the Roku Digital Player, the Xbox 360, TiVo, and Internet-enabled Blu-Ray players and televisions—to stream movies wirelessly to their televisions.

Looking forward, CEO Hastings is cognizant of the new technology entering the home entertainment industry. The company is confident that the traditional DVD format will be the mainstay of the rental industry for at least the next decade. With that said, however, Netflix has explored the viability of online movie downloads. The company has also explored moving away from the mainstay movie studios into investment in small film production products. This strategy of content creation and ownership is similar to HBO's strategy of releasing its own content for distribution via DVD.

Hastings Entertainment

Compared to Blockbuster, Movie Gallery, and Netflix, Hastings Entertainment is a small player in the industry. Founded in 1968 as a part of Western Merchandisers, Hastings is primarily a regional company with more than 150 stores in 20 western and midwestern states. Its stores, which are rarely larger than 20,000 square feet, are located in small communities with a population base ranging between 33,000 and 150,0000 people. Some of Hastings' larger stores offer unique amenities including coffee bars, reading chairs, listening stations, and play areas for children. Roughly 50 percent of the company's sales are generated through the sale and rental of movies and video games. Another 15 percent comes from sales of new and used CDs; the remainder is generated by books, magazines, and related electronics. Hastings' growth is slow and methodical, with only one or two store openings per year. The company has felt the impact of mail-order rental houses and video-on-demand competitors, and has experienced a drop in the movie rental component of its business.

Redbox

Whether you are ordering a hamburger at McDonald's, getting gas at 7-Eleven, buying groceries at Walmart, or waiting on a flight at the airport, your favorite movie may be available for a low rental fee of $1.00 per day at a Redbox kiosk. Each kiosk holds 700 DVDs, with about 150 different movie titles, virtually all of which are six months old or less. Customers pay $1 per day and can return movies to any Redbox kiosk anywhere in the country. Customers can even reserve movies online before visiting a kiosk. The advantage of Redbox over Blockbuster, in addition to the price, is that renting a movie doesn't require a special trip. Since its initial launch with just 12 kiosks, Redbox has grown to roughly 18,000 kiosks located in all 48 continental states. That level of penetration maximizes convenience for customers, who now rent movies while they are out doing other things.

Surprisingly, the idea for Redbox began as a new business venture for McDonald's in 2002. At that time, McDonald's was experimenting with vending machines to sell a variety of different items. After the concept proved to be a success, Redbox was sold to Coinstar—a Bellevue, Washington, company that also operates coin-counting machines and gift card dispensers. Soon after, Coinstar inked deals with Walmart, Kroger, Winn-Dixie, Walgreens, Kangaroo (gas stations), and other national outlets to place Redbox kiosks in high-traffic locations. As it turned out, the timing couldn't have been better. As a consequence of the most recent economic recession, customers who began to reconsider their $15 per month Netflix plans or $5 DVD rentals from Blockbuster suddenly saw the $1 Redbox rentals as a bargain.

Redbox's sales in 2008 were only $400 million—a figure dwarfed by the $14.5 billion spent on DVD sales in the same year. Nonetheless, Redbox has achieved phenomenal sales growth in a very short time: up 110 percent in the first quarter of 2009 (after achieving 180% growth in 2008). This number is startling when compared to the 9 percent decline in DVD sales during 2008 and the 13.5 percent decline in the first quarter of 2009.

Fully Digital Competitors

In addition to firms that rent traditional DVDs, Blockbuster faces increasing competition from digital-only competitors. Although digital movie rentals are an emerging business, at some point in the future digital downloads will replace DVDs as the de facto standard for movie rentals. Still, DVDs are likely to remain dominant for some time due to their ubiquity, low cost, and compatibility with older televisions and home theater systems.

A number of firms offer downloadable movie rentals. Apple, for example, offers thousands of titles in both standard and high-definition formats via its iTunes store. Apple's key advantage is that iTunes works seamlessly with the millions of iPods and iPhones that have sold in recent years. What Apple is missing, however, is an easy way to connect its handheld devices to older televisions—many of which do not have wireless connectivity or even HDMI ports. Amazon offers over 14,000 titles for rent via its Video on Demand service. Amazon's key advantage is its partnership with Roku's Digital Video player that allows consumers to wirelessly stream Amazon's movies to their televisions. The "Roku Box," as it is called, costs only $99 and allows users to watch both Netflix and Amazon titles, in addition to the recent addition of Major League Baseball broadcasts.

In 2008, NBC and Fox joined forces on a new venture called Hulu (www.hulu.com) which has experienced a steady growth since its inception. Hulu is a web-based service that provides access to movies and traditional broadcast shows such as *Lost*, *Grey's Anatomy*, *Miami Vice*, and *Desperate Housewives*. Hulu offers a video menu exceeding 100 providers, including such names as ABC, NBC, FOX, MGM, and Sony. These companies provide access to over 900 television series and full-length movies streamed on demand. Although Hulu is ad-supported, its biggest advantage is that the service does not charge a fee for viewing shows or movies.

Other competitors are expected to enter the digital rental market soon. Microsoft has already ventured into movie rentals via its Xbox 360 gaming platform. Most recently, YouTube announced that it is in negotiations with Sony Pictures, Lions Gate Entertainment Corp., and Warner Bros. Studios to offer movie rentals via its popular website. YouTube already offers ad-supported films from Sony and MGM.

Blockbuster's Uncertain Future

As Blockbuster looks toward the future, one key challenge on the horizon is that the traditional DVD rental industry is clearly heading into its decline phase. The continued growth of Netflix, Redbox, video on-demand, digital downloads, as well as the coming move to IPTV (Internet Protocol Television), offer dramatic increases in moving-renting convenience for consumers. Given this level of increasing competition, it is not surprising that Blockbuster lost $36.9 million in the second quarter of 2009. As the company looks for ways to compete with advancing technology—especially electronic distribution—Blockbuster has recently unveiled several new strategic initiatives:

- Close approximately 960 unprofitable stores (22% of current stores).

- Expand access to standalone Blockbuster kiosks (up to 10,000).

- Offer movie rentals on Motorola phones.

- Offer streaming movie rentals on TiVo systems and Samsung televisions.

- Reconfigure 250 stores to a smaller format.

Although these decisions are likely to help in the short-term, Blockbuster still finds itself reacting to the competitive environment rather than proactively searching for newer, better alternatives. The heart of this challenge is simple in concept but difficult to execute in practice: How can Blockbuster increase the value-added components of its product offering in order to offset the inconveniences associated with its traditional brick-and-mortar movie rental business?

Questions for Discussion

1. What role has Netflix played in the development of Blockbuster's strategic planning? How important is Netflix to Blockbuster's future strategic plans?

2. How will new competition from Redbox and digital content providers force Blockbuster to alter its strategy?

3. As an adviser to Keyes, what strategic options would you recommend for Blockbuster as the company moves forward? In particular, how would you approach the technology issues facing the company?

4. What value-added components could Blockbuster offer to the movie studios that might entice them to more closely align with Blockbuster as a distribution channel?

5. In the long term, how can Blockbuster increase the value-added components of its product offering in order to offset the inconveniences associated with its traditional brick-and-mortar movie rental business? Will Blockbuster survive as we know it today? Explain.

Sources

The facts of this case are from "Airport Check-In: Nashville Installs 2 Redbox DVD-Rental Machines," *USA Today* (http://www.usatoday.com/travel/flights/item.aspx?type=blog&ak=54796906.blog), accessed September 29, 2009; Thomas K. Arnold, "Economic Downturn May Be Behind a Rise in DVD Rentals," *USA Today*, May 4, 2009 (http://www.usatoday.com/life/movies/dvd/2009-05-04-rentals-recession_N.htm); Claire Atkinson, "Disney-Hulu Puts Focus on CBS," *Broadcasting and Cable*, May 4, 2009, p. 3; Lauren Barack, "Blockbuster Pushes Fast Forward: CEO James Keyes has a Vision for His Company—and It's Not Going Back to the Videotape," *On Wall Street*, September 1, 2007, p. 1; Eric Berte, "Blockbuster Cuts Losses Despite Lower Revenue," *Fox Business*, August 13, 2009 (http://www.foxbusiness.com/story/markets/industries/retail/blockbuster-cuts-losses-despite-lower-revenue/); Alexandra Biesada, *Netflix, Inc.*, Hoovers Company Capsules (http://hoovers.com/netflix/--ID__100752--/free-co-factsheet.xhtml), accessed November 17, 2009; Alexandra Biesada, *Movie Gallery, Inc.*, Hoovers Company Capsules (http://hoovers.com/movie-gallery/--ID__42198--/free-co-factsheet.xhtml), accessed November 17, 2009; Blockbuster, Inc. Annual Reports for 2008, 2007, 2006, 2005, 2004, 2003, and 2002 (http://investor.blockbuster.com/phoenix.zhtml?c=99383&p=irol-reportsannual); "Blockbuster Selects 7-Eleven Veteran," *The Wall Street Journal*, July 3, 2007, p. A13; Alexandra Biesada, *Blockbuster, Inc.*, Hoover's Company Capsules (http://hoovers.com/blockbuster-inc./--ID__10218--/free-co-factsheet.xhtml), accessed November 17, 2009; Jefferson Graham, "Netflix Looks to Future But Still Going Strong with DVD Rentals," *USA Today*, July 1, 2009 (http://www.usatoday.com/tech/products/2009-06-30-netflix-future_N.htm); Peter Grant, "Telecommunications; Outside the Box: As Broadband Connections Proliferate, So Do the Opportunities for Niche Video-Content Providers," *The Wall Street Journal*, December 19, 2005, p. R11; Ronald Grover, "Will *Bubble* Burst a Hollywood Dogma?" *Business Week Online*, January 24, 2006 (http://www.businessweek.com/bwdaily/dnflash/jan2006/nf20060124_4959_db011.htm); Bruce Horovitz, "McDonald's Wades Deeper into DVDs," *USA Today*, May 23, 2004 (http://www.usatoday.com/money/industries/retail/2004-05-23-mcdvd_x.htm); Richard Hull, "Content Goes Hollywood: How the Film Industry Is Struggling with

Digital Content," *EContent*, October 2004, p. 22; Unmesh Kher, "A Bid for Bigger," *Time*, December 6, 2004, p. A3; David Lieberman, "DVD Kiosks Like Redbox Have Rivals Seeing Red", *USA Today*, August 13, 2009 (http://www.usatoday.com/money/media/2009-08-11-rental-dvd-redbox_N.htm); Michael Liedtke, "Blockbuster to Stream Video Rentals on Samsung TVs," *USA Today*, July 14, 2009, (http://www.usatoday.com/tech/news/2009-07-14-blockbuster-samsung_N.htm); Anna Wilde Mathews, "E-Commerce (A Special Report): Selling Strategies—Stop, Thief! Movie Studios Hope to Slow Widespread Online Piracy Before It Takes Off; They're Convinced They Can," *The Wall Street Journal*, April 28, 2003, p. R6; Jessica Mintz, "Redbox's Machines Take on Netflix's Red Envelopes," *USA Today*, June 22, 2009 (http://www.usatoday.com/tech/news/2009-06-22-redbox_N.htm); Timothy J. Mullaney, "Netflix," *BusinessWeek Online*, May 25, 2006 (http://www.businessweek.com/smallbiz/content/may2006/sb20060525_268860.htm); Timothy J. Mullaney, "The Mail-Order Movie House That Clobbered Blockbuster," *BusinessWeek*, June 5, 2006, pp. 56–57; Netflix, Inc., Annual Reports for 2002 and 2005 (http://ir.netflix.com/annuals.cfm); Netflix, Inc., Overview (http://ir.netflix.com); Rachel Pierce, *Hastings Entertainment, Inc.*, Hoover's Company Capsules (http://hoovers.com/hastings-entertainment/--ID__42256--/free-co-factsheet.xhtml), accessed November 17, 2009; Redbox website, http://www.redbox.com; Greg Sandoval, "YouTube Wants to Offer Film Rentals," *CNET News*, September 2, 2009 (http://news.cnet.com/8301-1023_3-10337004-93.html); and Amy Schien, *Hulu, LLC*, Hoovers Company Capsules (http://cobrands.hoovers.com/global/cobrands/proquest/factsheet.xhtml?ID=159434).

Sigma Marketing: Innovation in a Changing Environment

Synopsis: *This case reviews the growth of a small, family-owned business, from a regional provider of generic printing services to a global provider of specialty advertising products. Throughout its history, Sigma Marketing has exhibited the uncanny ability to understand market opportunities and to adapt its strategic focus accordingly. As its marketing environment changes, Sigma Marketing gathers information from existing and potential customers to develop the most effective marketing strategy possible. Even in the face of changing technology, communication, and advertising methods, Sigma Marketing has managed to reinvent its mindset and strategies in order to remain successful.*

Themes: *Changing marketing environments, market opportunities, strategic focus, product strategy, direct marketing, promotion, personal selling, implementation, customer relationships, family-owned business*

I n 1967, Don Sapit purchased a small printing company as a hands-off personal investment that would later grow into what is today a successful specialty advertising business located in Orange Park (Jacksonville), Florida. Sigma Marketing has a unique identity that has evolved over the past 40 years from a small-town printing company to a marketing services company with diverse, multinational clientele. As firms learn more about their market, they often switch from a production orientation to a marketing orientation. Sigma is an excellent example of this type of strategic shift.

Don Sapit was president of Weston Laboratories, a small research facility in Ottawa, 80 miles southwest of Chicago, when he had an opportunity to acquire Dayne Printing Company of Streator, Illinois. Sapit had been a Dayne client for several years. When Dayne was on the verge of bankruptcy, Don was able to buy the company as an investment while still focusing most of his day-to-day efforts on Weston Labs. The managers of Dayne at the time were willing to stay on and handle the operations with

Mike Sapit, President, Sigma Marketing (http://www.sigmamktg.com), with assistance from O. C. Ferrell, University of New Mexico, prepared this case for classroom discussion rather than to illustrate effective or ineffective handling of an administrative situation. Jennifer Sawayda, University of New Mexico, provided editorial assistance.

little outside help. Don felt that with the increased volume that Weston would provide, the operation could become profitable within a 12-month period. To enhance the corporate image, the name was changed to Sigma Press, Inc. A new sales manager was hired to focus on the sales aspect of the business, while Sapit took the position of absentee owner. Over the next few years, sales efforts provided only minimal increases in volume. The business held its own but made little progress—typical results for an absentee-owned business. In addition, Sigma mainly focused on the production process and selling generic printing services.

In spite of the slow progress, Sapit continued to see the potential for making Sigma into a quality-oriented printing business that could make substantial gains against its local competition. The area served by the shop covered a radius of approximately 30 miles around the city of Streator and had a number of major manufacturing plants that were potential users of substantial quantities of printing. Unfortunately, most of these plants were headquartered in other cities and did not have authority for local purchasing of anything beyond the basic necessities required for daily plant operations. Although Sigma could do custom printing, the small firm did not have a unique niche other than its quality and service.

The Desk Calendar: A Strategic Opportunity

In seeking alternatives to improve sales, Sapit and Sigma's staff developed an advertising desk pad calendar for distribution as a customer gift. Its purpose was to keep the Sigma name, phone number, and list of services in front of the customer as a constant reminder of its existence. It was freely offered to any customer thought to have sufficient volume potential to justify the expense of the calendar and its distribution costs. At the time, Sigma thought of the calendar as a promotional tool for its own business and did not consider the calendar as a product that could potentially differentiate the company and give it a competitive edge.

One of the customers that received the calendar, Oak State Products, an Archway Cookie Bakery, asked whether Sigma could produce similar calendars for them with the Archway advertisement printed at the top. Sigma filled this initial order, and it proved popular with Archway's customers. The next year, Archway asked whether the calendars could be produced with a color photo of the plant in the ad space. This version was so well received that Oak State recommended the use of the calendar as a marketing tool to other Archway Bakeries around the country. Sigma recognized that the opportunity for a new marketing strategy was developing. The small printer with a generic product identified an opportunity to expand its market beyond its small geographic service area.

The sales volume realized from the calendar was not substantial, but Sapit saw in it a good possibility for a totally new marketing strategy, divorced from the limitations imposed by Sigma's present sales territory. Furthermore, he conceived a direct marketing effort that would permit sales penetration into a much larger geographical area than was practical to serve with Sigma's limited sales staff.

It was at this time that Weston Laboratories was sold, and Sapit was forced to make a decision to leave the company due to philosophical differences with the new owners. Although Sigma was starting to show potential for very modest profitability and good growth, it was still just barely able to support itself. After a family council meeting in 1971, the decision was made to "tough it out." Sapit chose to enter the Sigma operation on a full-time basis and to prove that it really could become a first-class operation based on a new marketing strategy.

The New Marketing Strategy

After coming aboard full time, Sapit assumed all marketing and management responsibilities himself. Previously, sales representatives had been making calls on a hit-or-miss basis with no real continuity. Sapit developed a general marketing strategy, which included defining specific sales territories, and developing target markets and sales prospect databases. He also implemented a scheduled mailing program as part of the strategy. On the commercial printing side, a sample "job of the month" was sent to customers and prospects at regular intervals. On the calendar side, direct mail materials promoting the desk calendar to specific target markets were utilized. At that time, direct mail promotion of printing services was relatively unheard of in the printing industry. Most of Sigma's competitors performed custom printing based on the needs and projects that the customer desired, and did not promote specific products.

The advertising desk calendar was marketed on the theme of "constant exposure advertising." It was given the product name "Salesbuilder," which moved Sigma into the specialty advertising business. Each customer was offered a standard calendar format with an individual ad imprint customized to fit the needs of the company's business. The imprint could contain line drawings, photos, product lists, or any special information necessary to convey the company's message to customers. Sigma's willingness to encourage attractive and creative designs received immediate attention and acceptance by customers. It set the company apart from the competition, which would allow "four lines of block type, not to exceed 32 letters." In effect, Sigma was at the forefront of a new specialty advertising product.

Within a year of Sapit's entry into the business, total volume was up 50 percent; even more important, the response to the calendar marketing effort was starting to show real promise. As a result, Sigma was experiencing the need for additional capital to finance the growth. Capital was obtained through the private sale of one-third of the company stock to Sapit's friend and colleague, who was a local attorney. The new investor was not involved in the daily operations of the business, but served as corporate secretary, legal counsel, board member, and adviser. The cash raised from the stock was used to help fund the day-to-day operations and expand accounts receivable resulting from the increased volume.

By late 1972, Sigma's commercial printing sales were gaining at a modest rate of increase, but calendar sales were increasing at a rate of 40 percent per year. It was becoming apparent that larger manufacturing facilities would be required in the immediate future or the sales efforts would have to be scaled back. The company purchased a more visible and accessible 5-acre site in Ottawa, Illinois, and constructed a new facility with a focus on improved production as well as image. Sapit decided to capitalize on the new visibility and image by changing the strategic emphasis of the business.

Sigma Expands the Strategy

Over the next few years, Sigma's strategy was oriented toward building a reputation for producing the most creative and highest quality printing in its service area, which had a 35- to 40-mile radius around Ottawa. Sapit anticipated that this new direction would give his firm a solid reputation as a quality printer, one that fully justified the higher prices it charged. Several of the larger local companies obtained permission from their corporate offices to procure their printing locally. The downstate division of Carson Pirie Scott & Company, a large department store chain, chose Sigma for the production of its catalogs. The new marketing strategy paid off, and total sales volume had increased 220 percent by 1976.

Calendar sales increased slowly but steadily. Management wanted growth, but in an orderly and controlled manner. Management also wanted its growth to be more profitable than the industry average of approximately 5 percent on sales. It was becoming obvious that to be successful in the printing business, Sigma needed to specialize. After long and deliberate discussion during 1976, company management wrote a three-year corporate plan.

The corporate plan emphasized marketing, which at this time was considered unique for a small commercial printer. The marketing plan focused a major share of the sales and marketing effort on building a market for the "Salesbuilder" desk calendar. The target market consisted primarily of smaller corporate accounts, while the marketing mix emphasized a quality product and advertising with an internal sales staff, direct marketing distribution, and a superior price point. Space advertising in sales and marketing-oriented publications created substantial numbers of inquiries, but sales levels did not follow. Direct mail, primarily to manufacturers, produced a much higher response and return on investment. Sigma had created a unique product that was very flexible in terms of unique designs, advertising messages, photographic techniques, and other special requirements. In short, "Salesbuilder" became a highly effective marketing tool.

Within the next few calendar seasons, solid accounts such as Serta Mattress, Domino Sugar, and Borden, Inc., were added to the list of satisfied customers. Reorder rates were very high, usually in the 88 to 90 percent range. Quantities ordered by individual companies tended to increase annually for three or four years and then level off. Total calendar sales had increased at a rate of approximately 40 percent per year during the 1976–1980 period, during which time commercial printing sales increased at a rate of about 15 percent annually.

Implementing the New Strategy

Because of the success of the new strategy, production capacity was being taxed. In 1979–1980, major capital commitments were made to add a new high-speed two-color press and to purchase, redesign, and rebuild a specialized collating machine to further automate calendar assembly, previously assembled by hand. This opened the way to mass marketing of the "Salesbuilder" calendar line. Direct mail techniques were improved to allow selection of prospects by SIC number and sales volume. A toll-free 1-800 number encouraged direct response by interested parties. Whenever possible, Sigma responded to inquiries by sending a sample calendar that contained advertising ideas related to the respondent's line of business. The sample would be followed up with a personal phone call within two to three weeks. Calendar sales continued to improve until, by 1983, they represented 50 percent of total sales and approximately 75 percent of net profit.

In spite of the success of the calendar marketing programs and attractive profit levels, Sapit was disturbed by trends in the printing industry that pointed toward a diminishing market and increased competition for the commercial segment, particularly in Sigma's local Rust Belt area. Rapid development of new technology and high-speed equipment had caused industry-wide investments in new equipment well beyond immediate need, creating excess capacity. The result was cost cutting and reduced margins.

Sigma's management had for some time been considering selling the commercial portion of its business in favor of becoming an exclusive marketer of calendar products. Through its membership in the Printing Industry of Illinois, a buyer was found for the plant, equipment, and the goodwill of the commercial portion of the business. The buyer agreed to enter into a long-term contract to handle the majority of calendar production for Sigma, using the same plant and staff that had been handling the production for the previous 10 years. The sale was completed in June 1983. This signaled the strategic move from a company based on production to one based on marketing.

Sigma's management now found itself free of the daily problems of production and plant management and able to commit all its efforts to creating and marketing new calendar products. Sapit had a long-standing personal desire to move the business to the Sun Belt for the better weather and, more importantly, for the better business climate. In May 1985, Sigma's corporate offices were moved to Orange Park, Florida. Concurrently, Sapit's son, Mike, a graduate of Illinois State University in graphic arts management, joined the business.

Adapting the Marketing Strategy Again

To take advantage of Sigma's marketing expertise, Sigma took actions to expand its product line to include several additional calendar items, all designed to be personalized. The new items included a year-at-a-glance wall planning calendar, desk diary, pocket diary, and a smaller version of the original desk calendar.

Sigma had built its calendar business on products that were basically "off-the-shelf" formats that could be imprinted with the customer's advertising message. In the late 1980s and into the 1990s, Sigma began to see a growing demand for products that were totally customized not only in graphic design but in product specifications as well. Sigma's management perceived the market for their new line of "super customized" calendars to be the medium-to-large corporation with a substantial customer base. These companies were service oriented with large advertising budgets, thus providing the potential for orders of larger magnitudes. The market being studied was relatively small in terms of number of companies, but very large with respect to total sales potential. It would require a totally different marketing approach than previously utilized.

Test advertisements for custom-designed calendars were run in *Advertising Age* and in several marketing trade journals. These advertisements appealed to larger corporate accounts. In addition, the Sigma sales staff became much more aggressive in searching out individual accounts that appeared to have high potential as customized calendar customers. Prospects were researched, and contacted by phone and mail, to determine the individual with the responsibility to specify and authorize this type of purchase. Unsolicited samples of several different customized products were sent via FedEx in order to attract attention. Each prospect was followed up by a phone call within a few days to confirm interest and provide additional information.

The goal was to establish Sigma as a publisher of high-quality, creatively designed custom calendars. Initial response to the new marketing strategy was good, with indications that the blue chip companies could, in fact, be reached through this approach. To reach its growth goals, Sigma felt it had to be successful in this marketing strategy. This type of highly customized product design was very demanding on the creative staff. Because only 10 to 15 new accounts of this type could be handled each year, it was important that creative time be spent on high-potential accounts. The new strategy was successful in landing substantial orders from Nabisco, Fidelity Investments, and FedEx. Realizing that these blue chip companies were consumers, Sigma focused the entire organization on meeting five customer needs: (1) flexibility, (2) production of a quality product consistent with the client's image and marketing goals, (3) personal service and attention from beginning to end, (4) fair pricing, and (5) timely, efficient fulfillment.

The Total Service Package

With the blue chip accounts, Sigma realized that it had to be able to offer its products on a turnkey, or concept-through-fulfillment, basis. Many of these corporations wanted to use a calendar program, but were not able to devote staff, time, or expertise to such a project. Sigma offered the solution—handling the entire calendar promotion, including conception, design, production, and delivery—so that customers could devote their time to more productive efforts, confident that their calendar program was running smoothly and efficiently. They dubbed this the "Total Service Package."

In order to provide total service effectively, Sigma installed new computer equipment and programs to enable comprehensive order fulfillment for a variety of programs. Special shipping manifest programs were developed to simplify the handling of large quantities of drop shipments. From established customer lists or those generated through Sigma's direct order programs, calendars could be shipped to as many as 20,000 locations for a single account. This was particularly helpful to accounts that had dealers or customers scattered across the country.

The business grew rapidly from 1985 to 1990, and by 1991, Don and Mike Sapit saw a new opportunity to expand the business again. After carefully analyzing the characteristics of its buyers and their buying decisions, Sigma found new market opportunities. During its first 15 years in the promotional calendar business, Sigma focused on large companies that usually distributed their promotional calendars through their sales forces to customers. These companies usually supplied Sigma with the basic idea for their calendar promotion, including an imprint or art design for the firm's individualized calendar.

With its own computer order-tracking and manifest system in place, Sigma was able to offer its customers and prospects an efficient and cost-saving order and distribution system. With a customer-supplied list, Sigma began marketing the calendars directly to the customer's distributors. Flyers and samples were produced and mailed by Sigma. Orders were then returned directly to Sigma. This process allowed individual distributors or a single branch to include its own imprint on the calendar. A customer list may have over 10,000 names, and a single order may consist of over 1,000 different imprints. Because each customer has its own requirements, a staff member dedicated to personalized service is assigned to each customer. Sigma learned how its customers made decisions about specialty advertising purchases such as promotional calendars and then developed a program to satisfy the needs of purchasing agents and buyers in large organizations. The strategy was very successful, and during the 1990s, the company added prime accounts such as Milwaukee Electric Tool Corporation, Hoffman LaRoche, Inc., International Paper Company, and Nabisco Brands, Inc.

Emphasis on Implementation: The Key to Service

After focusing on the "Total Service Package" approach as its primary marketing strategy, Sigma experienced a large increase in corporate clientele with very specialized product and service requirements. The "Salesbuilder" orders that were the foundation of the business became secondary to "programs"—larger corporate accounts with networks of dealers, franchises, or sales representatives to place orders—as well as multiple products and services offered as part of their calendar promotion. Sigma's reputation was bolstered by strong clientele references and testimonials. Companies were drawn to the custom calendar vendor known for high-quality products and a staff with tremendous flexibility and creativity. In an effort to distance itself from competitors, Sigma improved on the "Total Service Package," which had become an important part of its marketing strategy. Customers were surveyed before and after they received the product, and large corporate account contacts received a visit from their account representative early in the year to review the previous year's program and begin laying groundwork on the upcoming promotion. In addition, international promotions and shipping became important aspects of several large accounts. Account representatives began developing large corporate accounts by promoting multiple products, while some promotional items beyond calendars were produced in an effort to maintain exclusivity with a client.

The company continued to add to its list of satisfied customers such prime accounts as Unisource, xpedx, Volvo Cars, Volvo Trucks, Ditch Witch, and Enterprise Leasing. Mega-accounts also came on board, such as Yellow Freight Systems (including all of its subsidiaries) and CNH, the parent company who brought along the business of its multiple operating divisions including Case IH/Case Construction and New Holland Agricultural/New Holland Construction.

After many instances of being asked by corporate clients to include additional advertising products as companion pieces to their calendar program, management began to consider the viability of becoming an ASI (Advertising Specialty Institute) dealer. The annual cost was acceptable, considering the cost savings to be realized in purchasing specialty items and specialized printing products wholesale through ASI vendors. Sigma became an ASI distributor in March of 2000, providing new and useful resources to enhance the calendar programs and meet specific needs of established customers. The ASI resources opened up new markets for additional business from many of their existing customers, without the need to aggressively sell the specialty promotions segment of business and without diluting the focus on calendar programs.

Customer demand has obviously led to changes and the expansion of the sales and administrative areas, as well as the graphics department. A stronger focus on the service aspect of the business was a strategic move for the sales and administrative areas, resulting in the creation of a dedicated customer service department. Sigma has also seen tremendous growth in its graphics capabilities—a response to the major technical changes in the printing industry itself, as well as the needs of its customers.

Despite the additional staff and resources, the demand from program accounts is so great that the company is in danger of overselling its production capabilities to its vendors. Recognizing that possibility, Sigma has become more selective in its marketing efforts for program accounts. In recent years, the company has begun to reevaluate the potential of smaller, easy-to-produce and profitable "Salesbuilder" calendar orders as a product to be marketed on their corporate e-commerce website, suitable for smaller companies who can't support a completely customized program.

Linking Technology to the Marketing Program

In the late 1980s and early 1990s, Sigma offered limited in-house design/layout services. Prior to desktop publishing, type was set, paste-ups were created, and film was shot manually on a camera. Graphic needs beyond the company's capabilities were outsourced to service bureaus. Even though Sigma's capabilities were limited, very few of its customers had complex needs or technologically capable marketing departments. That has completely changed with the onset of the digital age.

Sigma's pre-press capabilities were transformed over a 10-year period, and the company continues to welcome changes and new technology to remain competitive. Graphics workstations became an integral part of the business, with increasing storage capacity and applications to handle larger and more complex files. In the mid-1990s, a digital image setter replaced the old camera and film technology. That evolved in less than 10 years to a direct-to-plate workflow with color management, digital color proofing, and multiplatform capability. Photos are now almost completely digital—scanning is becoming a thing of the past—and many customers have their own in-house design and graphics staff that work closely with Sigma's graphics department. The sophisticated technology created the need for advanced training and continued education and upgrades. Sigma's management has maintained a commitment to stay in the forefront of graphics technology through strong staffing and investment in equipment and software applications.

The mid-1990s also ushered in the company's Internet presence and online capabilities. A corporate identity on the Internet is absolutely essential in today's marketplace, and Sigma has taken the additional steps to utilize the Internet for e-commerce: product promotion and ordering capabilities. Many of the company's larger clients demand online ordering and communications with their networks in order to maintain their accounts.

Upgrading technology on the administrative side has allowed the company to better serve its customers. A centralized file and information system has integrated many previously separate functions and increased flexibility among the staff. Sigma is now online with several transportation companies, making package tracking an easy task. The company has added many features with the improved technology, such as direct invoicing, credit card sales, digital faxing, and proofing online or via email.

Sigma's Future

During the expansion period, Don began to turn over the daily operations of the business to his son Mike. In early 1996, the transition was complete, with Mike in full charge of the business. Don has retired but remains chairman of the board, acting in an advisory capacity. Stock was purchased back from Don's attorney/colleague who had invested in the company many years ago, and Sigma issued stock to key employees, creating a greater sense of ownership and commitment to the business. A major concern was to develop personnel strategies and a succession plan in the event of Mike's death or disability. Key employees with long tenure will soon be considering retirement, and the skills held by management and key employees would need to be taught and transferred to newer employees. In 2007, a succession plan was developed for the company to ensure its continuation.

Annual marketing meetings have been scheduled each year since 1991 for staff members to meet and review the past year, addressing and solving both internal and external problems. The meetings encourage teamwork, foster company loyalty, and increase employee's knowledge about Sigma's status in the marketplace. In addition to the business meetings, the company has also conducted a number of pleasure trips for employees (sometimes with their spouses and/or families) to promote stronger personal relationships and interaction. The employees have visited a number of resort complexes and major cities, and even sailed together on a cruise ship to the Caribbean. These events have contributed to a strong sense of community and teamwork among the employees. Sigma has constructed a diverse team of people with a wide range of skills, each playing a key role in the overall success of the company. Within that core of employees, top management selects two people with the strongest potential. One of these people focuses on sales and marketing, while the other takes over management of IT, personnel, finance, and operations. Mike believes that the knowledge and skills of these key managers are an important part of what gives Sigma its edge.

One of Sigma's many strengths is the ability to understand market opportunities and to develop and continue to adapt its strategic focus. As the environment changes, Sigma gathers information from existing and potential customers to develop the most effective marketing strategy. For example, as more companies become concerned about sustainability issues, particularly renewable resources, Sigma has responded. In 2008, Sigma became a Chain-of-Custody (CoC) certified company—a designation that ensures the integrity of the paper supply chain (forest to mill) by certifying that the paper used by Sigma comes from responsibly managed forests. The company is also working on becoming certified with the Sustainable Forestry Initiative and the Program for the Endorsement of Forest Certification. Chain-of-Custody certification is a response to the demands of Sigma's customers and the company's own desires to reduce their environmental impact.

In the future, there will be new challenges, including the changing environment related to technology, communication, and methods of advertising. So far, the desktop calendar has not been replaced by potential competitors like Google or other specialty advertising methods. However, Sigma's team is aware that the industry is constantly changing, and that to survive, the company must adapt. Above all, Sigma holds a philosophy of always being prepared. In the words of Mike Sapit, "The future is bright."

Questions for Discussion

1. Discuss potential key changes in technology, communications, and competition that Sigma will face in the future. Which will have the most impact on Sigma's future marketing strategies?

2. Prepare a SWOT analysis for long-term strategic planning at Sigma Marketing.

3. Suggest some possible strategic initiatives that Sigma could pursue to continue its growth.

Sources

The facts of this case are from the personal knowledge of the author; "Chain-of-Custody Certification," Sigma Marketing (http://www.sigmamktg.com/coc.html), accessed October 2, 2009; and "Up Close with Mike Sapit, President of Sigma Marketing," *HPxpressions*, pp. 14–15.

Mattel: Overcoming Marketing and Manufacturing Challenges

Synopsis: *As a global leader in toy manufacturing and marketing, Mattel faces a number of potential threats to its ongoing operations. Like most firms that market products for children, Mattel is ever mindful of its social and ethical obligations and the target on its corporate back. This case summarizes many of the challenges that Mattel has faced over the past decade, including tough competition, changing consumer preferences and lifestyles, lawsuits, product liability issues, global sourcing, and declining sales. Mattel's social responsibility imperative is discussed along with the company's reactions to its challenges and its prospects for the future.*

Themes: *Environmental threats, competition, social responsibility, marketing ethics, product/branding strategy, intellectual property, global marketing, product liability, global manufacturing/sourcing, marketing control*

It all started in a California garage workshop when Ruth and Elliot Handler and Matt Matson founded Mattel in 1945. The company started out making picture frames, but the founders soon recognized the profitability of the toy industry and switched their emphasis. Mattel became a publicly owned company in 1960, with sales exceeding $100 million by 1965. Over the next 40 years, Mattel went on to become the world's largest toy company in terms of revenue. Today, Mattel, Inc. is a world leader in the design, manufacture, and marketing of family products. Well-known for toy brands such as Barbie, Fisher-Price, Disney, Hot Wheels, Matchbox, Tyco, Cabbage Patch Kids, and board games such as Scrabble, the company boasts nearly $6 billion in annual revenue. Headquartered in El Segundo, California, with offices in 36 countries, Mattel markets its products in more than 150 nations.

In spite of its overall success, Mattel has had its share of losses over its history. During the mid to late 1990s, Mattel lost millions due to declining sales and bad

Debbie Thorne, Texas State University–San Marcos, John Fraedrich, Southern Illinois University–Carbondale, O. C. Ferrell, University of New Mexico, and Jennifer Jackson, University of New Mexico, developed this case for classroom discussion rather than to illustrate effective or ineffective handling of an administrative situation. Jennifer Sawayda provided editorial assistance.

business acquisitions. In January 1997, Jill Barad took over as Mattel's CEO. Barad's management style was characterized as strict, and her tenure at the helm proved challenging for many employees. Although Barad had been successful in building the Barbie brand to $2 billion near the end of the twentieth century, growth slowed rapidly after that time. Declining sales at outlets such as Toys "R" Us and the mismanaged acquisition of The Learning Company marked the start of some difficulties for the toy maker, including a dramatic 60 percent drop in stock price under Barad's three-year stint as CEO. Barad accepted responsibility for these problems and resigned in 2000.

The company soon installed Robert Eckert, a 23-year Kraft veteran, as chairman and CEO. During Eckert's first three years on the job, the company's stock price increased to over $20 per share, and Mattel was ranked fortieth on *Business Week's* list of top-performing companies. Implementing techniques used by consumer-product companies, Eckert adopted a mission to bring stability and predictability to Mattel. He sold unprofitable units, streamlined work processes, and improved relations with retailers. Under Eckert, Mattel was granted the highly sought-after licensing agreement for products related to the *Harry Potter* series of books and movies. The company continued to flourish and build its reputation, even earning the Corporate Responsibility Award from UNICEF in 2003. By 2008, Mattel had fully realized a turnaround and was recognized as one of *Fortune* magazine's "100 Best Companies to Work For" and *Forbes* magazine's "100 Most Trustworthy U.S. Companies."

Mattel's Core Products

Barbie

Among its many lines of popular toy products, Mattel is famous for owning top girls' brands. In 1959, Mattel made the move that would establish them at the forefront of the toy industry. After seeing her daughter's fascination with cutout paper dolls, Ruth suggested that a three-dimensional doll should be produced so that young girls could live out their dreams and fantasies. This doll was named "Barbie," the nickname of Ruth and Elliot Handler's daughter. The first Barbie doll sported open-toed shoes, a ponytail, sunglasses, earrings, and a zebra-striped bathing suit. Fashions and accessories were also available for the doll. Although buyers at the annual Toy Fair in New York took no interest in the Barbie doll, little girls of the time certainly did. The intense demand seen at the retail stores was insufficiently met for several years. Mattel just could not produce the Barbie dolls fast enough. Today, Barbie is Mattel's flagship brand and its number one seller—routinely accounting for approximately half of Mattel's sales revenue. This makes Barbie the best-selling fashion doll in most global markets. The Barbie line today includes dolls, accessories, Barbie software, and a broad assortment of licensed products such as books, apparel, food, home furnishings, home electronics, and movies.

Although Barbie was introduced as a teenage fashion model, she has taken on almost every possible profession. She has also acquired numerous male and female friends and family over the years. Ken, Midge, Skipper, Christie, and others were introduced from the mid-1960s on. The Barbie line has even seen a disabled friend in a wheelchair: Share a Smile Becky. Barbie's popularity has even broken stereotypes. Retrofitted versions of Barbie dolls, on sale in select San Francisco stores, feature "Hooker" Barbie, "Trailer Trash" Barbie, and "Drag Queen" Barbie. There are also numerous "alternative" Barbies, such as "Big Dyke" Barbie, but Mattel does not want the Barbie name to be used in these sales. Redressed and accessorized Barbies are okay with Mattel as long as no one practices trademark infringement.

Barbie's Popularity Slips   Although Barbie remains a blockbuster by any standard, Barbie's popularity has slipped over the past decade. There are two major reasons for Barbie's slump. First, the changing lifestyles of today's young girls are a concern for Mattel. Many young girls prefer to spend time with music, movies, or the Internet than play with traditional toys like dolls. Second, Barbie has suffered at the hands of new and innovative competition, including the Bratz doll line that gained significant market share during the early 2000s. The dolls, which featured contemporary, ethnic designs and skimpy clothes, were a stark contrast to Barbie and an immediate hit with young girls. In an attempt to recover, Mattel introduced the new line of My Scene dolls aimed at "tweens." These dolls are trendier, look younger, and are considered to be more hip for this age group who is on the cusp of outgrowing playing with dolls. A website (http://www.myscene.com) engages girls in a variety of fun, engaging, and promotional activities.

Barbie's Legal Battle with MGA Entertainment   Since 2004, Mattel has been embroiled in a bitter intellectual property battle with former employee Carter Bryant and MGA Entertainment, Inc., over rights to MGA's popular Bratz dolls. Carter Bryant, an on-again/off-again Mattel employee, designed the Bratz dolls and pitched them to MGA. A few months after the pitch, Bryant left Mattel to work at MGA, which began producing Bratz in 2001. In 2002, Mattel launched an investigation into whether Bryant had designed the Bratz dolls while employed with Mattel. After two years of investigation, Mattel sued Bryant. A year later MGA fired off a suit of its own, claiming that Mattel's My Scene dolls were an attempt to copy the Bratz line. Mattel answered by expanding its own lawsuit to include MGA and its CEO, Isaac Larian.

For decades, Barbie had reigned supreme in the doll market. However, Bratz dolls gave Barbie a run for her money. In 2005, four years after the brand's debut, Bratz sales were at $2 billion. By 2009, Barbie's worldwide sales had fallen by 15 percent, although Bratz was not immune to sluggish sales either once consumers began to cut back on spending during the 2008–2009 recession.

Much evidence points toward Bryant having conceived of Bratz dolls while at Mattel. Four years after the initial suit was filed, Bryant settled with Mattel under an undisclosed set of terms. However, although some decisions were made, the battle between Mattel and MGA has continued. In July 2008, a jury deemed MGA and its CEO liable for what it termed "intentional interference" regarding Bryant's contract with Mattel. In August 2008, Mattel received damages of $100 million. Although

Mattel first requested damages of $1.8 billion, the company was pleased with the principle behind the victory. MGA is appealing the decision.

In December 2008, Mattel appeared to win another victory when a California judge banned MGA from making or selling Bratz dolls. The decision was devastating to the Bratz line, as retailers have avoided the brand in anticipation of Mattel's take-over. Many industry analysts, however, expect Mattel to work out a deal with MGA in which MGA can continue to sell Bratz dolls as long as Mattel shares in the profits. MGA plans to appeal the court ruling. Whatever the outcome, Mattel has managed to gain some control over Barbie's toughest competition.

American Girl

In 1998, Mattel acquired Pleasant Company, maker of the American Girl collection—a well-known line of historical dolls, books, and accessories. Originally, American Girl products were sold exclusively through catalogs. Mattel extended that base by selling American Girl accessories (not the dolls) in major chain stores like Walmart and Target. More recent efforts to increase brand awareness include the opening of American Girl Place shops in New York, Chicago, Los Angeles, Atlanta, Dallas, Boston, and Minneapolis. The New York store features three floors of dolls, accessories, and books in the heart of the 5th Avenue shopping district. The store also offers a café where girls can dine with their dolls and a stage production where young actresses bring American Girl stories to life.

The American Girl collection is wildly popular with girls in the 7- to 12-year-old demographic. The dolls have a wholesome and educational image—the antithesis to Barbie. This move by Mattel represented a long-term strategy to reduce reliance on traditional products and to take away the stigma surrounding the "perfect image" of Barbie. Each American Girl doll lives during a specific time in American history, and all have stories that describe the hardships they face while maturing into young adults. For example, Felicity's stories describe life in 1774 just prior to the Revolutionary War. Likewise, Josephina lives in New Mexico in 1824 during the rapid growth of the American West. Other dolls include Kaya (a Native American girl growing up in 1764), Elizabeth (Colonial Virginia), Kirsten (pioneer life in 1854), Addy (1864 during the Civil War), Samantha and Nellie (1904 New York), Kit (1934 during the Great Depression), Molly (1944 during World War II), and Emily (a British girl who comes to America during World War II). The American Girl brand includes several book series, accessories, clothing for dolls and girls, and a magazine that ranks in the top 10 American children's magazines.

Hot Wheels

Hot Wheels roared into the toy world in 1968. More than 40 years later, the brand is hotter than ever and includes high-end collectibles, NASCAR (National Association for Stock Car Auto Racing) and Formula One models for adults, high-performance cars, track sets, and play sets for children of all ages. The brand is connected with racing circuits worldwide. More than 15 million boys ages 5 to 15 are avid collectors, each owning an average of 41 cars. Two Hot Wheels cars are sold every second of every day. The brand began with cars designed to run on a track and has evolved into a "lifestyle" brand with licensed Hot Wheels shirts, caps, lunch boxes, backpacks, and more. Together, Hot Wheels and Barbie generate about 65 percent of Mattel's profits.

Fisher-Price

Acquired in 1993 as a wholly owned subsidiary, Fisher-Price is the umbrella brand for all of Mattel's infant and preschool lines. The brand is trusted by parents around the world and appears on everything from children's software to eyewear, and books to bicycles. Some of the more classic products include the Rock-a-Stack, Power Wheels vehicles, and Little People play sets. Through licensing agreements, the brand also develops character-based toys such as *Sesame Street*'s Elmo, Disney's Winnie the Pooh, and Nickelodeon's Dora the Explorer.

Fisher-Price has built a trust with parents by creating products that are educational, safe, and useful. For example, during recent years, the brand has earned high regard for innovative car seats and nursery monitors. Fisher-Price keeps pace with the interests of today's families through innovative learning toys and award-winning products. One example is the Computer Cool School, a kid-friendly keyboard with a tablet and stylus, which turns a standard Windows-based computer into an interactive classroom for kids ages 3 to 6. The product was awarded the "Best Toy of 2008" by both *Parents Magazine* and *Family Fun Magazine*.

Mattel's Global Manufacturing

As a U.S.-based multinational company owning and operating facilities and contracting worldwide, Mattel's Global Manufacturing Principles reflects the company's needs to both conduct manufacturing responsibly and respect the cultural, ethical, and philosophical differences of the countries in which it operates. These principles set uniform standards, across Mattel manufacturers, that attempt to benefit both employees and consumers.

Mattel's principles cover issues such as wages, work hours, child labor, forced labor, discrimination, freedom of association, and working conditions. Workers must be paid at least minimum wage or a wage that meets local industry standards (whichever is greater). No one under the age of 16 or the local age limit (whichever is higher) may be allowed to work for Mattel facilities. Mattel refuses to work with facilities that use forced or prison labor, or to use these types of labor itself. Additionally, Mattel does not tolerate discrimination. The company states that an individual should be hired and employed based on his or her ability—not on individual characteristics or beliefs. Mattel recognizes all employees' rights to choose to affiliate with organizations or associations without interference. Regarding working conditions, all Mattel facilities and its business partners must provide safe working environments for their employees.

Manufacturing Issues Lead to Product Recalls

Despite Mattel's best efforts, not all overseas manufacturers have faithfully adhered to its high standards. In 2007, Mattel came under scrutiny over its sale of unsafe products as it announced recalls of toys containing lead paint. The problem surfaced when a European retailer discovered lead paint on a toy. An estimated 10 million individual toys produced in China were affected. Mattel quickly stopped production at Lee Der, the company officially producing the recalled toys, after it was discovered that Lee Der had purchased lead-tainted paint to be used on the toys. Mattel blamed the fiasco on the manufacturers' desire to save money in the face of increasing prices. "In the last three or five years, you've seen labor prices more than double, raw material prices double or triple," CEO Eckert said in an interview, "and I think that there's a lot of pressure on guys that are working at the margin to try to save money."

The situation began when Early Light Industrial Co., a subcontractor for Mattel owned by Hong Kong toy tycoon Choi Chee Ming, subcontracted the painting of parts of *Cars* toys to another China-based vendor. The vendor, named Hong Li Da, decided to source paint from a nonauthorized third-party supplier: a violation of Mattel's requirement to use paint supplied directly by Early Light. The products were found to contain "impermissible levels of lead." When it was announced that another of Early Light's subcontractors, Lee Der Industrial Company, used the same lead paint found on *Cars* products, China immediately suspended the company's export license. Afterward, Mattel pinpointed three paint suppliers working for Lee Der: Dongxin, Zhongxin, and Mingdai. This paint was used by Lee Der to produce Mattel's line of Fisher-Price products. It is said that Lee Der purchased the paint from Mingdai due to an intimate friendship between the two company's owners. In the latter part of 2007, Zhang Shuhong, operator of Lee Der, hung himself after paying his 5,000 staff members.

That same year, Mattel was forced to recall several more toys because of powerful magnets in the toys that could come loose and pose a choking hazard for young children. If more than one magnet is swallowed, the magnets can attract each other inside the child's stomach, causing potentially fatal complications. Over 21 million Mattel toys were recalled in all, and parents filed several lawsuits claiming that these Mattel products harmed their children.

At first, Mattel blamed Chinese subcontractors for the huge toys recalls; but the company later accepted a portion of the blame for the trouble, while maintaining that Chinese manufacturers were largely at fault. The Chinese viewed the situation quite differently. As reported by the state-run Xinhua news agency, the spokesperson for China's state Administration of Quality Supervision and Inspection and Quarantine (AQSIQ) said, "Mattel should improve its product design and supervision over product quality. Chinese original equipment manufacturers were doing the job just as importers requested, and the toys conformed to the U.S. regulations and standards at the time of the production." Mattel also faced criticism from many of its consumers, who believed Mattel was denying culpability by placing much of the blame on China. Mattel was later awarded the 2007 "Bad Product" Award by Consumers International.

How did this crisis occur under the watch of a company praised for its ethics and high safety standards? Although Mattel had investigated its contractors, it did not audit the entire supply chain, including subcontractors. This oversight left room for these violations to occur. Mattel has moved to enforce a rule that subcontractors cannot hire suppliers two or three tiers down the supply chain. In a statement, Mattel claimed to have spent more than 50,000 hours investigating its vendors and testing its toys. Mattel also announced a three-point plan designed to tighten Mattel's control of production, discover and prevent the unauthorized use of subcontractors, and test the products itself rather than depending on contractors.

The Chinese Government's Reaction

Chinese officials eventually did admit the government's failure to properly protect the public. The Chinese government is now promising to tighten supervision of exported products, but effective supervision is challenging in such a large country that is so burdened with corruption. In 2008, the Chinese government launched a four-month nationwide product quality campaign, offering intensive training courses to domestic toy manufacturers to help them brush up on their knowledge of international product standards and safety awareness. As a result of the crackdown, the state AQSIQ announced that it had revoked the licenses of more than 600 Chinese toy makers. Also in 2008, the State Administration for Commerce and Industry (SACI) released a report claiming that 87.5 percent of China's newly manufactured toys met quality requirements. Although this represents an improvement, the temptation to cut corners remains strong in a country that uses price, not quality, as its main competitive advantage.

Mattel's Social Responsibility Imperative

Because Mattel's core products are designed primarily for children, the company must be sensitive to social concerns about children's rights. It must also be aware that the international environment often complicates business transactions. Different legal systems and cultural expectations about business can create many complex issues. Finally, the use of technology may present many dilemmas, especially regarding consumer privacy. Mattel has recognized these potential issues and taken steps to strengthen its commitment to business ethics. The company also purports to take a stand on social responsibility, encouraging its employees and consumers to do the same.

Privacy and Marketing Technology

One issue Mattel has tried to address repeatedly is that of privacy and online technology. Advances in technology have created special marketing issues for Mattel. The company recognizes that, because it markets to children, it must communicate with parents regarding its corporate marketing strategy. Mattel has taken steps to inform both children and adults about its philosophy regarding Internet-based marketing tools, such as the Hot Wheels website. This website contains a lengthy online privacy policy, part of which reads as follows:

> *Mattel, Inc. and its family of companies ("Mattel") are committed to protecting your online privacy when visiting a website operated by us. We do not collect and keep any personal information online from you unless you volunteer it and you are 13 or older. We also do not collect and keep personal information online from children under the age of 13 without consent of a parent or legal guardian, except in limited circumstances authorized by law and described in this policy.*

By assuring parents that their children's privacy will be respected, Mattel demonstrates that it takes its responsibility of marketing to children seriously.

Expectations of Mattel's Business Partners

Mattel also makes a serious commitment to business ethics in its dealings with other industries. In late 1997, the company completed its first full ethics audit of each of its manufacturing sites as well as the facilities of its primary contractors. The audit revealed that the company was not using any child labor or forced labor, a problem plaguing other overseas manufacturers. However, several contractors were found to be in violation of Mattel's safety and human rights standards and were asked to change their operations or risk losing Mattel's business. The company now conducts an independent monitoring council audit in manufacturing facilities every three years.

In an effort to continue its strong record on human rights and related ethical standards, Mattel instituted a code of conduct entitled Global Manufacturing Principles in 1997. One of these principles requires all Mattel-owned and contracted manufacturing facilities to favor business partners committed to ethical standards comparable with those of Mattel. Other principles relate to safety, wages, and adherence to local laws. Mattel's audits and subsequent code of conduct were designed as preventative, not punitive, measures. The company is dedicated to creating and encouraging responsible business practices throughout the world.

Mattel also claims to be committed to its workforce. As one company consultant noted, "Mattel is committed to improving the skill level of workers … [so that they] will experience increased opportunities and productivity." This statement reflects Mattel's concern for relationships between and with employees and business partners. The company's code is a signal to potential partners, customers, and other stakeholders that Mattel has made a commitment to fostering and upholding ethical values.

Legal and Ethical Business Practices

Mattel prefers to partner with businesses similarly committed to high ethical standards. At a minimum, partners must comply with the local and national laws of the countries in which they operate. In addition, all partners must respect the intellectual property of the company, and support Mattel in the protection of assets such as patents, trademarks, or copyrights. They are also responsible for product safety and quality, protecting the environment, customs, evaluation and monitoring, and compliance.

Mattel's business partners must have high standards for product safety and quality, adhering to practices that meet Mattel's safety and quality standards. As noted earlier in the case, safety standards have been seriously violated in the past. Also, because of the global nature of Mattel's business and its history of leadership in this area, the company insists that business partners strictly adhere to local and international customs laws. Partners must comply with all import and export regulations. To assist in compliance with standards, Mattel insists that all manufacturing facilities provide the following:

- Full access for onsite inspections by Mattel or parties designated by Mattel

- Full access to those records that will enable Mattel to determine compliance with its principles

- An annual statement of compliance with Mattel's Global Manufacturing Principles, signed by an officer of the manufacturer or manufacturing facility

With the creation of the Mattel Independent Monitoring Council (MIMCO), Mattel became the first global consumer products company to apply such a system to facilities and core contractors worldwide. The company seeks to maintain an independent monitoring system that provides checks and balances to help ensure that standards are met.

If certain aspects of Mattel's manufacturing principles are not met, Mattel will try to work with contractors to help them fix their problems. New partners will not be hired unless they meet Mattel's standards. If corrective action is advised but not taken, Mattel will terminate its relationship with the partner in question. Overall, Mattel is committed to both business success and ethical standards, and it recognizes that it is part of a continuous improvement process.

Mattel Children's Foundation

Through the Mattel Children's Foundation, the company promotes philanthropy and community involvement among its employees and makes charitable investments to better the lives of children in need. Funding priorities have included building a new Mattel Children's Hospital at the University of California, Los Angeles (UCLA), sustaining the Mattel Family Learning Program, and promoting giving among Mattel employees.

In November 1998, Mattel donated a multiyear, $25 million gift to the UCLA Children's Hospital. The gift was meant to support the existing hospital and provide for a new state-of-the-art facility. In honor of Mattel's donation, the hospital was renamed Mattel Children's Hospital at UCLA.

The Mattel Family Learning Program utilizes computer-learning labs as a way to advance children's basic skills. Now numbering more than eighty throughout the United States, Hong Kong, Canada, and Mexico, the labs offer software and technology designed to help children with special needs or limited English proficiency.

Mattel employees are also encouraged to participate in a wide range of volunteer activities, including Team Mattel, a program that allows Mattel employees to partner with local Special Olympics programs. Employees serving on boards of local nonprofit organizations or helping with ongoing nonprofit programs are eligible to apply for volunteer grants supporting their organizations. Mattel employees contributing to higher education or to nonprofit organizations serving children in need are eligible to have their personal donations matched dollar for dollar up to $5,000 annually.

Mattel Looks Toward the Future

Like all major companies, Mattel has weathered its share of storms. In recent years, the company has faced a series of difficult and potentially crippling challenges. During the wave of toy recalls, some analysts suggested that the company's reputation was battered beyond repair. Mattel, however, has refused to go quietly. Although the company admits to poorly handling recent affairs, it is attempting to rectify its mistakes and to prevent future mistakes as well. The company appears to be dedicated to shoring up its ethical defenses to protect both itself and its customers. Mattel's experiences should teach all companies that threats could materialize within the marketing environment in spite of the best-laid plans to prevent such issues from occurring.

With slowing demand for toys and the most recent economic recession, Mattel may be in for slow growth for some time to come. Today, Mattel faces many market opportunities and threats including the rate at which children are growing up and leaving toys, the role of technology in consumer products, and purchasing power and consumer needs in global markets. The continuing lifestyle shift of American youth is of particular concern for Mattel. The phenomenal success of gaming systems, portable music players, text messaging, and social networking sites among today's youth is a testament to this shift. Children and teens are also more active in extracurricular activities (for example, sports, music, and volunteerism) than ever before. Consequently, these young consumers have less time to spend with traditional toys.

Despite these concerns, Mattel has a lot to offer both children and investors. Barbie remains the number one doll in the United States and worldwide. And Barbie.com, the number one website for girls, routinely gets over 50 million visits per month. Furthermore, all of Mattel's core brands are instantly recognizable around the world. Hence, the ability to leverage one or all of these brands is high. A few remaining issues include Mattel's reliance on Walmart and Target (which lessens Mattel's pricing power), volatile oil prices (oil is used to make plastics), and increasing competition on a global scale. However, analysts believe Mattel has a great growth potential with technology-based toys, especially in international markets, in spite of changing demographic and socioeconomic trends. For a company that began with two friends making picture frames, Mattel has demonstrated marketing dexterity and longevity. The next few years, however, will test the firm's resolve and strategy within the highly competitive yet lucrative toy market.

Questions for Discussion

1. Do manufacturers of children's products have special obligations to consumers and society? If so, what are these responsibilities?

2. Comment on the strengths and weaknesses of Mattel's core brands. In looking at Barbie specifically, what actions would you recommend to stem Barbie's sales decline? Should Mattel accept the fact that the brand will never regain its former sales status? Explain.

3. To what extent was Mattel responsible for issues related to its production of toys in China? How might Mattel have avoided these issues?

4. What opportunities and threats does Mattel face as it looks toward its future?

Sources

The facts of this case are from "About Us: Philanthropy," *Mattel* (http://www.mattel.com/about-us/philanthropy/), accessed October 6, 2009; American Girl website, http://www.americangirl.com, accessed October 6, 2009; Bannon, Lisa and CarltaVitzhum, "One-Toy-Fits-All: How Industry Learned to Love the Global Kid," *The Wall Street Journal*, April 29, 2003 (http://online.wsj.com/article/SB105156578439799000.html?mod=googlewsj), accessed October 6, 2009; Barboza, David, "Scandal and Suicide in China: A Dark Side of Toys," Iht.com, August 23, 2007 (http://www.iht.com/articles/2007/08/23/business/23suicide.php?page=1), accessed September 8, 2009; Barboza, David, and Louise Story, "Toymaking in China, Mattel's Way," *The New York Times*, July 26, 2007 (http://www.nytimes.com/2007/07/26/business/26toy.html?pagewanted=1&_r=3&hp), accessed September 8, 2009; "Bratz Loses Battle of the Dolls," *BBC News*, December 5, 2008 (http://news.bbc.co.uk/2/hi/business/7767270.stm), accessed October 6, 2009; Adam Bryant, "Mattel CEO Jill Barad and a Toyshop That Doesn't Forget to Play," *The New York Times*, October 11, 1998; Nicholas Casey, "Mattel Prevails Over MGA in Bratz-Doll Trial," *The Wall Street Journal*, July 18, 2008, pp. B-18, B-19; Nicholas Casey, "Mattel to Get Up to $100 Million in Bratz Case," *The Wall Street Journal*, August 27, 2008 (http://online.wsj.com/article/SB121978263398273857-email.html), accessed October 6, 2009; Shu-Ching Chen, "A Blow to Hong Kong's Toy King," *Forbes*, August 15, 2007 (http://www.forbes.com/2007/08/15/mattel-china-choi-face-markets-cx_jc_0815auto-facescan01.html), accessed October 6, 2009; "Children's Foundation," *Mattel* (http://corporate.mattel.com/about-us/philanthropy/childrenfoundation.aspx), accessed October 6, 2009; Bill Duryea, "Barbie-holics: They're Devoted to the Doll," *St. Petersburg Times*, August 7, 1998; Miranda Hitti, "9 Million Mattel Toys Recalled," WebMD, August 14, 2007 (http://children.webmd.com/news/20070814/9_million_mattel_toys_recalled), accessed September 8, 2009; "Independent Monitoring Council Completes Audits of Mattel Manufacturing Facilities in Indonesia, Malaysia and Thailand," Mattel press release, November 15, 2002 (http://

children.webmd.com/news/20070814/9_million_mattel_toys_recalled), accessed September 8, 2009; "International Bad Product Awards 2007," Consumers International (http://www.consumersinternational.org/Shared_ASP_Files/ UploadedFiles/527739D3-1D7B-47AF-B85C-6FD25779149B_InternationalBadProd-uctsAwards-pressbriefing.pdf), accessed September 8, 2009; "Investors and Media," *Mattel* (http://investor.shareholder.com/mattel), accessed October 6, 2009; Gina Keating, "MGA 'Still Assessing' Impact of Bratz Ruling: CEO," *Reuters*, December 4, 2008 (http://www.reuters.com/article/ousivMolt/idUSTRE4B405820081205), accessed September 8, 2009; "Learning from Mattel," Tuck School of Business at Dartmouth (http://mba.tuck.dartmouth.edu/pdf/2002-1-0072.pdf), accessed September 8, 2009; "Mattel and U.S. Consumer Product Safety Commission Announce Voluntary Refund Program for Cabbage Patch Kids Snacktime Kids Dolls," U.S. Consumer Product Safety Commission, Office of Information and Public Affairs, Release No. 97-055, January 6, 1997; "Mattel Annual Report 2008," Shareholder.com (http:// www.shareholder.com/mattel/downloads/2007AR.pdf), accessed September 8, 2009; "Mattel Awarded $100M in Doll Lawsuit," *USA Today*, August 27, 2008, p. B-1; "Mattel Children's Foundation Rewards Second Round of Domestic Grants to 34 Nonprofit Organizations," *Mattel*, December 7, 2005 (http://investor.shareholder.com/ mattel/releasedetail.cfm?ReleaseID=181309), accessed September 8, 2009; "Mattel's Commitment to Ethics," *eBusiness Ethics* (http://www.e-businessethics.com/ mattel9.htm), accessed October 6, 2009; "Mattel Continues to Lead the Toy Industry with Release of Its First Corporate Social Responsibility Report," Shareholder.com, October 12, 2004 (http://www.shareholder.com/mattel/news/20041012-145079.cfm), accessed September 8, 2009; "Mattel History," *Mattel* (http://corporate.mattel.com/ about-us/history/default.aspx), accessed October 6, 2009; Mattel, Inc., Hot Wheels website (http://www.hotwheels.com), accessed October 6, 2009; "Mattel, Inc., Launches Global Code of Conduct Intended to Improve Workplace, Workers' Standard of Living," *Canada NewsWire*, November 21, 1997; "Mattel, Inc., Online Privacy Policy," *Mattel* (http://www.hotwheels.com/PrivacyPolicy/ index.aspx?site=hw&lang=), accessed October 6, 2009; "Mattel Magnetic Toy Set Recall: Company Has History of Ignoring Product Safety Disclosure Laws. Did It Do So Again?" *Parker Waichman Alonso LLP*, September 4, 2007 (http:// www.yourlawyer.com/articles/read/13072), accessed September 8, 2009; "Mattel Recalls Batman™ and One Piece™ Magnetic Action Figure Sets," U.S. Consumer Product Safety Commission, August 14, 2007 (http://service.mattel.com/us/recall/ J1944CPSC.pdf), accessed September 8, 2009; "Mattel to Sell Learning Co.," *Direct*, October 2, 2000 (http://directmag.com/news/marketing_mattel_sell_learning), accessed September 8, 2009; Marla Matzer, "Deals on Hot Wheels," *Los Angeles Times*, July 22, 1998; Benjamin B. Olshin, "China, Culture, and Product Recalls," *Specialized Research + Reports*, August 20, 2007, p. S2R (http://www.s2r.biz/s2rpapers/papers-Chinese_Product.pdf), accessed September 8, 2009; "Our Toys," Mattel Inc. (http:// corporate.mattel.com/our-toys), accessed October 6, 2009; Christopher Palmeri, "Could Mattel End Up with Bratz?" *BusinessWeek Online*, July 18, 2008 (http:// www.businessweek.com/bwdaily/dnflash/content/jul2008/db20080718_684426.htm);

Christopher Palmeri, "The Bratz Designer Counterpunches Mattel," *BusinessWeek Online*, October 2, 2009 (http://www.businessweek.com/bwdaily/dnflash/content/oct2009/db2009102_823460.htm); "Product Recalls," Mattel Consumer Relations Answer Center (http://service.mattel.com/us/recall.asp), accessed September 8, 2009; Jack A. Raisner, "Using the 'Ethical Environment' Paradigm to Teach Business Ethics: The Case of the Maquiladoras," *Journal of Business Ethics*, 1997 (http://www.springerlink.com/content/nv62636101163v07/fulltext.pdf), accessed October 6, 2009; Patricia Sellers, "The 50 Most Powerful Women in American Business," *Fortune*, October 12, 1998, pp. 76, 95; Laura S. Spark, "Chinese Product Scares Prompt US Fears," *BBC News*, July 10 2007 (http://news.bbc.co.uk/2/hi/americas/6275758.stm), accessed September 8, 2009; "The United States Has Not Restricted Imports Under the China Safeguard," U.S. Government Accountability Office, September 2005 (http://www.gao.gov/new.items/d051056.pdf), accessed September 8, 2009; "Third Toy Recall by Mattel in Five Weeks," *Business Standard*, September 6, 2006 (http://www.business-standard.com/india/storypage.php?autono=297057), accessed September 8, 2009; "Toymaker Mattel Bans Child Labor," *Denver Post*, November 21, 1998, p. A8; "UCLA Children's Hospital Receives $25 Million Pledge from Mattel Inc., November 12, 1998 (http://investor.shareholder.com/mattel/releasedetail.cfm?ReleaseID=141937), accessed September 8, 2009; and Michael White, "Barbie Will Lose Some Curves When Mattel Modernizes Icon," *Detroit News*, November 18, 1997, p. E32.

New Belgium Brewing (A): Social Responsibility as a Competitive Advantage

Synopsis: *From its roots in a Fort Collins, Colorado, basement, New Belgium Brewing has always aimed for business goals loftier than profitability. The company's tremendous growth to become the nation's third-largest craft brewery and ninth-largest overall has been guided by a steadfast branding strategy based on customer intimacy, social responsibility, and whimsy. The company's products, especially Fat Tire Amber Ale, have always appealed to beer connoisseurs who appreciate New Belgium's focus on sustainability as much as the company's world-class brews. Despite its growth and success, New Belgium has managed to stay true to its core values and brand authenticity—the keys to its marketing advantage in the highly competitive craft brewing industry.*

Themes: *Customer intimacy, competitive advantage, social responsibility, sustainability, branding strategy, product strategy, distribution strategy, marketing implementation, customer relationships*

Many companies frequently cited as examples of ethical and socially responsible businesses are large corporations. However, the social responsibility initiatives of small businesses often have the greatest impact on local communities and neighborhoods. These businesses create jobs and provide goods and services for customers in smaller markets that larger corporations are often are not interested in serving. Moreover, they also contribute money, resources, and volunteer time to local causes. Their owners often serve as community and neighborhood leaders, and many choose to apply their skills and some of the fruits of their success to tackling local problems and issues that benefit everyone in the community. Managers and employees become role models for ethical and socially responsible actions. One such small business is the New Belgium Brewing Company, Inc., based in Fort Collins, Colorado. In fact, New Belgium's business model has been so successful that it is increasingly easy to find its beers around the country as more consumers embrace what the company stands for.

O.C. Ferrell, University of New Mexico, prepared this case for classroom discussion rather than to illustrate effective or ineffective handling of an administrative situation. Jennifer Jackson and Jennifer Sawayda, University of New Mexico, provided editorial assistance. Nikole Haiar and Melanie Drever provided assistance on earlier editions of this case.

History of the New Belgium Brewing Company

The idea for the New Belgium Brewing Company began with a bicycling trip through Belgium—home to some of the world's finest ales, many of which have been brewed for centuries in that country's monasteries. As Jeff Lebesch, an American electrical engineer, cruised around that country on his fat-tired mountain bike, he wondered whether he could produce such high-quality beers back home in Colorado. After acquiring the special strain of yeast used to brew Belgian-style ales, Lebesch returned home and began to experiment in his Colorado basement. When his beers earned thumbs up from friends, Lebesch decided to market them.

The New Belgium Brewing Company (NBB) opened for business in 1991 as a tiny basement operation in Lebesch's home in Fort Collins. Lebesch's wife, Kim Jordan, became the firm's marketing director. They named their first brew Fat Tire Amber Ale in honor of Lebesch's bike ride through Belgium. New Belgium beers quickly developed a small but devoted customer base, first in Fort Collins and then throughout Colorado. The brewery soon outgrew the couple's basement and moved into an old railroad depot before settling into its present custom-built facility in 1995. The brewery includes an automated brew house, two quality assurance labs, and numerous technological innovations for which New Belgium has become nationally recognized as a "paradigm of environmental efficiencies."

Today, New Belgium Brewing Company offers a variety of permanent and seasonal ales and pilsners. The company's standard line includes Sunshine Wheat, Blue Paddle, Abbey, Mothership Wit, 1554, Trippel, and the original Fat Tire Amber Ale, still the firm's bestseller. Some customers even refer to the company as the Fat Tire Brewery. The brewery also markets four types of specialty beers on a seasonal basis. Seasonal ales include Frambozen, released at Thanksgiving, Skinny Dip, released during the summer, 2° for winter, and Mighty Arrow for spring. The firm has also started a Lips of Faith program, where small batch brews like La Folie, Biere de Mars, and Abbey Grand Cru are created for internal celebrations or landmark events. New Belgium is also working in collaboration (or collabeeration) with Elysian Brewing Company, in which each company will be able to use the other's brew houses, though they remain independent businesses. Through this, they hope to create better efficiency and experimentation along with taking collaborative strides toward the future of American craft beer making. One collabeeration resulting from this partnership is Trippel IPA.

NBB's most effective form of advertising has always been its customers' word of mouth, especially in the early days. Indeed, before New Belgium beers were widely distributed throughout Colorado, one liquor-store owner in Telluride is purported to have offered people gas money if they would stop by and pick up New Belgium beer on their way through Fort Collins. Although New Belgium has expanded distribution to a good portion of the U.S. market, the brewery receives numerous e-mails and phone calls every day inquiring when its beers will be available in other parts of the country.

Although still a small brewery when compared to many beer companies, like fellow Coloradan Coors, NBB has consistently experienced strong growth and has become the ninth-largest brewery in the nation (and the third-largest "craft" brewery), with 2007 sales of roughly $96 million (because New Belgium is a private firm, detailed sales and revenue numbers are not available). It now has its own blog, as well as MySpace and Facebook pages. The plant is currently capable of producing 700 bottles of beer a minute, and it is developing a capacity for canned beer of 50 to 60 per minute. Currently, New Belgium's products are distributed in 26 states from the Pacific Coast, throughout the Midwest, and most recently into the Southeastern United States. (See Case Exhibit 8.1.) Beer connoisseurs that appreciate the high quality of NBB's products, as well as the company's environmental and ethical business practices, have driven this growth. For example, when the company began distribution in Minnesota, the beers were so popular that a liquor store had to open early and make other accommodations for the large amount of customers. The store sold 400 cases of Fat Tire in the first hour it was open.

With expanding distribution, however, the brewery recognized a need to increase its opportunities for reaching its far-flung customers. It consulted with Dr. Douglas Holt, an Oxford professor and cultural branding expert. After studying the company, Holt, together with Marketing Director Greg Owsley, drafted a 70-page

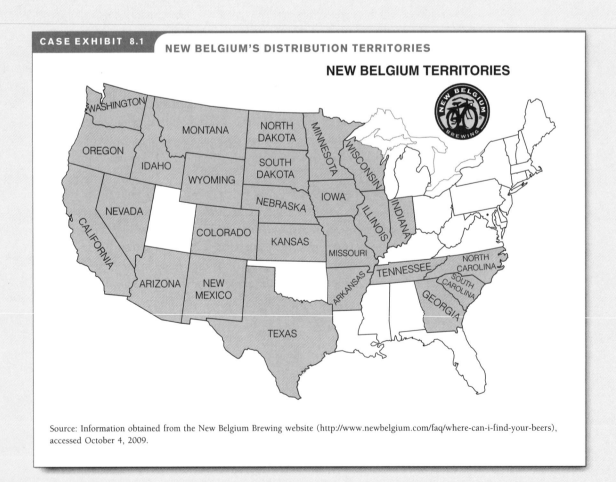

CASE EXHIBIT 8.1 NEW BELGIUM'S DISTRIBUTION TERRITORIES

NEW BELGIUM TERRITORIES

Source: Information obtained from the New Belgium Brewing website (http://www.newbelgium.com/faq/where-can-i-find-your-beers), accessed October 4, 2009.

"manifesto" describing the brand's attributes, character, cultural relevancy, and promise. In particular, Holt identified in New Belgium an ethos of pursuing creative activities simply for the joy of doing them well and in harmony with the natural environment.

With the brand thus defined, New Belgium went in search of an advertising agency to help communicate that brand identity; it soon found Amalgamated, an equally young, independent New York advertising agency. Amalgamated created a $10 million advertising campaign for New Belgium that targeted high-end beer drinkers, men ages 25 to 44, and highlighted the brewery's down-to-earth image. The grainy ads focused on a man, Charles the Tinkerer, rebuilding a cruiser bike out of used parts and then riding it along pastoral country roads. Shot around Hotchkiss and Paonia, Colorado, the producers were going for a spontaneous, easygoing vibe. The product appeared in just five seconds of each ad between the tag lines, "Follow Your Folly . . . Ours Is Beer." At first, New Belgium thought that "Folly" carried too much of a negative connotation, but department support encouraged the company to keep the line. With nostalgic music playing in the background, the ads helped position the growing brand as whimsical, thoughtful, and reflective. In addition to the ad campaign, the company maintained its strategy of promotion through event sponsorships.

New Belgium Embraces Social Responsibility

According to Greg Owsley, New Belgium's Director of Marketing, the company maintains a fundamental focus on the ethical culture of the brand. Although consumer suspicion of business is at an all-time high, those in good standing—as opposed to those trading on hype—are eyed with icon-like adoration. Today, businesses that fully embrace citizenship in the communities they serve can forge enduring bonds with customers. At New Belgium, the synergy between branding and corporate citizenship occurred naturally as the firm's ethical culture (in the form of core values and beliefs) and was in place long before NBB had a marketing department.

Back in early 1991, when New Belgium was just a fledgling home-brewed business, Jeff and Kim took a hike into Rocky Mountain National Park. Armed with a pen and a notebook, they took their first stab at what the company's core purpose would be. If they were going forward with this venture, what were their aspirations beyond profitability? What was at the heart of their dream? What they wrote down that spring day, give or take a little editing, was the core values and beliefs you can read on the NBB website today. More importantly, ask just about any New Belgium employee and he or she can list for you many, if not all, of these shared values and can inform you which are the most personally poignant. For NBB, branding strategies are as rooted in its company values as in its other business practices. New Belgium's dedication to quality, the environment, and its employees and customers is expressed in its mission statement and core values:

Mission Statement:

To operate a profitable brewery which makes our love and talent manifest.

Company Core Values and Beliefs:

1. Remembering that we are incredibly lucky to create something fine that enhances people's lives while surpassing our consumers' expectations

2. Producing world-class beers

3. Promoting beer culture and the responsible enjoyment of beer

4. Kindling social, environmental, and cultural change as a business role model

5. Environmental stewardship: Honoring nature at every turn of the business

6. Cultivating potential through learning, high involvement culture, and the pursuit of opportunities

7. Balancing the myriad needs of the company, our coworkers, and their families

8. Trusting each other and committing to authentic relationships and communications

9. Continuous, innovative quality and efficiency improvements

10. Having Fun

Employees believe that these statements help communicate to customers and other stakeholders what New Belgium, as a company, is about. These simple values developed roughly 20 years ago are just as meaningful to the company and its customers today, even though there has been much growth.

Responsibilities to the Environment

New Belgium's marketing strategy involves linking the quality of its products, as well as its brand, with the company's philosophy of environmental friendliness. From leading-edge environmental gadgets and high-tech industry advancements to employee-ownership programs and a strong belief in giving back to the community, New Belgium demonstrates its desire to create a living, learning community.

NBB strives for cost-efficient energy-saving alternatives for conducting its business and reducing its impact on the environment. In staying true to the company's core values and beliefs, the brewery's employee-owners unanimously agreed to invest in a wind turbine, making New Belgium the first fully wind-powered brewery in the United States. Since the switch from coal power, New Belgium has been able to reduce its CO_2 emissions by 1,800 metric tons per year. The company further reduces its energy use by employing a steam condenser that captures and reuses the hot water that boils the barley and hops in the production process to start the next brew. The steam is redirected to heat the floor tiles and de-ice the loading docks in cold weather. NBB also purchased an energy efficient brew kettle, the second of its kind installed in the nation. This novel kettle heating method conserves energy more than standard kettles do. Another way that NBB conserves energy is by using "sun tubes," which provide natural daytime lighting throughout the brew house all year long. Finally, the brewery uses a complex system to capture its wastewater and extract methane from it. This can contribute up to 15 percent of the brewery's power needs while reducing the strain on the local municipal water treatment facility.

New Belgium also takes pride in reducing waste through recycling and creative reuse strategies. The company strives to recycle as many supplies as possible, including cardboard boxes, keg caps, office materials, and the amber glass used in bottling. The brewery also stores spent barley and hop grains in an on-premise silo and invites local farmers to pick up the grains, free of charge, to feed their pigs. Going further down the road to producing products for the food chain, NBB is working with partners to take the same bacteria that create methane from NBB wastewater and convert them into a harvestable, high-protein fish food. NBB also buys recycled products when it can, and even encourages its employees to reduce air pollution by using alternative transportation. Reduce, Reuse, Recycle—the three R's of environmental stewardship—are taken seriously at NBB. Case Exhibit 8.2 depicts New Belgium's 2008 recycling efforts.

Additionally, New Belgium has been a long-time participant in green building techniques. With each expansion of the facility, it has incorporated new technologies and learned a few lessons along the way. In 2002, NBB agreed to participate in the United States Green Building Council's Leadership in Energy and Environment Design for Existing Buildings (LEED-EB) pilot program. From sun tubes and day lighting throughout the facility to reusing heat in the brew house, NBB continues to search for new ways to close loops and conserve resources.

New Belgium has made significant achievements in sustainability, particularly compared to other companies in the industry. For one, New Belgium uses only

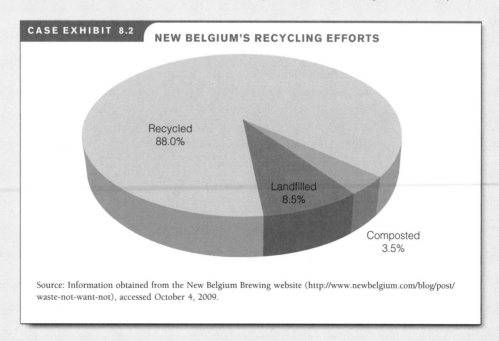

CASE EXHIBIT 8.2   **NEW BELGIUM'S RECYCLING EFFORTS**

Recycled 88.0%

Landfilled 8.5%

Composted 3.5%

Source: Information obtained from the New Belgium Brewing website (http://www.newbelgium.com/blog/post/waste-not-want-not), accessed October 4, 2009.

4 gallons of water to make 1 gallon of beer, which is 20 percent less than most other companies. New Belgium was able to recycle 88 percent of its waste in 2008, and today 100 percent of its electricity comes from renewable sources. Despite these achievements, New Belgium has no intention of halting its sustainability efforts. By 2015, the company hopes to reduce the amount of water used to make beer by 10 percent through better production processes and decrease its carbon footprint by 25 percent per barrel.

Responsibilities to Society

Beyond its use of environmentally friendly technologies and innovations, New Belgium also strives to improve communities and enhance people's lives through corporate giving, event sponsorship, and philanthropic involvement. Since its inception, NBB has donated more than $2.9 million to philanthropic causes. For every barrel of beer sold the prior year, NBB donates $1 to philanthropic causes within their distribution territories. The donations are divided between states in proportion to their percentage of overall sales. This is the company's way of staying local and giving back to the communities who support and purchase NBB products. In 2008, NBB donated $490,000 for philanthropic causes. NBB also participates in 1 percent for the Planet, a philanthropic network to which the company donates 1 percent of its profits.

Funding decisions are made by New Belgium's Philanthropy Committee, which is comprised of employees throughout the brewery, including owners, employee owners, area leaders, and production workers. New Belgium looks for nonprofit organizations that demonstrate creativity, diversity, and an innovative approach to their mission and objectives. The Philanthropy Committee also looks for groups that involve the community to reach their goals.

Additionally, NBB maintains a community bulletin board in its facility, where it posts an array of community involvement activities and proposals. This community board allows tourists and employees to see the different ways they can help out the community, and it gives nonprofit organizations a chance to make their needs known. Organizations can even apply for grants through the NBB website, which has a link designated for this purpose. In 2009, the company hopes to award grants in the areas of water stewardship, sensible transportation and bike advocacy, sustainable agriculture, and youth environmental education.

NBB also sponsors a number of events, with a special focus on those that involve "human-powered" sports that cause minimal damage to the natural environment. Through event sponsorships, such as the Tour de Fat, NBB supports various environmental, social, and cycling nonprofit organizations. In the Tour de Fat, one participant hands over his or her car keys and vehicle title in exchange for an NBB commuter bike and trailer. The participant is then filmed for the world to see as he or she promotes sustainable transportation over driving. In addition, New Belgium sponsors the MS 150 "Best Damn Bike Tour," a two-day, fully catered bike tour, from which all proceeds go to benefit more than 5,000 local people with multiple sclerosis. NBB also sponsors the Ride the Rockies bike tour, which donates proceeds from beer sales to local nonprofit groups. The money raised from this annual event funds local projects, such as improving parks and bike trails. In the course of one year, New Belgium can be found at anywhere from 150 to 200 festivals and events across 15 western and Midwestern states.

Responsibilities to Employees

Recognizing employees' role in the company's success, New Belgium provides many generous benefits for its 320 employees. In addition to the usual paid health and dental insurance and retirement plans, employees get a free lunch every other week as well as a free massage once a year, and they can bring their children and dogs to work. Employees who stay with the company for five years earn an all-expenses paid trip to Belgium to "study beer culture." Perhaps most importantly, employees can also earn stock in the privately held corporation, which grants them a vote in company decisions. Employees currently own about 32 percent of company stock. Open book management also allows employees to see the financial costs and performance of the company.

New Belgium also wishes to get its employees involved not only in the company but in its sustainability efforts as well. To help their own sustainability efforts, employees are given a fat-tired cruiser bike after one year's employment so they can bike to work instead of drive. The NBB sales force drives Toyota Prius hybrids provided by the company. An onsite recycling center is also provided for employees. Additionally, each summer New Belgium hosts the Tour de Fat, where employees can dress in costumes and lead locals on a bike tour. Other company perks include inexpensive yoga classes, free beer at quitting time, and a climbing wall. *Outside* magazine voted New Belgium the Best Place to Work in 2008.

Responsibility Breeds Success

New Belgium Brewing's efforts to live up to its own high standards have paid off with numerous awards and a very loyal following. It was one of three winners of Business Ethics Magazine's Business Ethics Awards for its "dedication to environmental excellence in every part of its innovative brewing process." Kim Jordan and Jeff Lebesch were named the recipients of the Rocky Mountain Region Entrepreneur of the Year Award for manufacturing, and NBB was listed in *The Wall Street Journal* as one of the 15 best small workplaces. The company also captured the award for "best mid-sized brewing company of the year" and "best mid-sized brewmaster" at the Great American Beer Festival. New Belgium took home medals for three different brews: Abbey Belgian Style Ale, Blue Paddle Pilsner, and La Folie specialty ale. Additionally, the exemplary leadership of CEO Kim Lebesch was recognized as she won *ColoradoBiz* magazine's 2008 CEO of the year and was invited to meet President Barack Obama.

According to David Edgar, director of the Institute for Brewing Studies, "They've created a very positive image for their company in the beer-consuming public with smart decision-making." Although some members of society do not believe that a company whose major product is alcohol can be socially responsible, New Belgium has set out to prove that for those who make a choice to drink responsibly, the company can do everything possible to contribute to society. Its efforts to promote beer culture and the connoisseurship of beer have even led it to design a special "Worthy Glass," the shape of which is intended to retain foam, show off color, enhance visual presentation, and release aroma. New Belgium also promotes the responsible appreciation of beer through its participation in and support of the culinary arts. For instance, it frequently hosts New Belgium Beer Dinners, in which every course of the meal is served with a complementary culinary treat.

According to Greg Owsley, Director of Marketing, although the Fat Tire brand has a bloodline straight from the enterprise's ethical beliefs and practices, the firm's work is not done. New Belgium must continually reexamine its ethical, social, and environmental responsibilities. In 2004, New Belgium received the Environmental Protection Agency's regional Environmental Achievement Award. It was both an honor and a motivator for the company to continue its socially responsible goals. After all, there are still many ways for NBB to improve as a corporate citizen. For example, the manufacturing process is a fair distance from being zero waste or emission free. Although all electric power comes from renewable sources, the plant is still heated in part by using natural gas. Additionally, there will always be a need for more public dialogue on avoiding alcohol abuse. Practically speaking, the company has a never-ending to-do list.

NBB executives acknowledge that as its annual sales increase, so do the challenges to remain on a human scale and to continue to be culturally authentic. How to boldly grow the brand while maintaining its humble feel has always been a challenge. Additionally, reducing waste to an even greater extent will take lots of work on behalf of both managers and employees, creating the need for a collaborative process that will require the dedication of both parties toward sustainability.

Every six-pack of New Belgium Beer displays the phrase "In this box is our labor of love. We feel incredibly lucky to be creating something fine that enhances people's lives." Although Jeff Lebesch has "semiretired" from the company to focus on other interests, the founders of New Belgium hope this statement captures the spirit of the company. According to employee Dave Kemp, NBB's social responsibilities give the company a competitive advantage because consumers want to believe in and feel good about the products they purchase. NBB's most important asset is its image—a corporate brand that stands for quality, responsibility, and concern for society. Defining itself as more than a beer company, the brewer also sees itself as a caring organization that is concerned for all stakeholders.

Questions for Discussion

1. What environmental issues does the New Belgium Brewing Company work to address? How has NBB taken a strategic approach to addressing these issues? Why do you think the company has taken such a strong stance toward sustainability?

2. Do you agree that New Belgium's focus on social responsibility provides a key competitive advantage for the company? Why or why not?

3. What are the challenges associated with combining the need for growth with the need to maintain customer intimacy and social responsibility? Does NBB risk losing focus on its core beliefs if it grows too quickly? Explain.

4. Some segments of society contend that companies that sell alcoholic beverages and tobacco products cannot be socially responsible organizations because of the nature of their primary products. Do you believe that New Belgium's actions and initiatives are indicative of a socially responsible corporation? Why or why not?

Sources

The facts of this case are from Peter Asmus, "Goodbye Coal, Hello Wind," *Business Ethics*, 13 (July/August 1999), pp. 10–11; "A Tour of the New Belgium Brewery—Act One," LiveGreen blog, April 9, 2007 (http://www.livegreensd.com/2007/04/tour-of-new-belgium-brewery-act-one.html), accessed October 4, 2009; Robert Baun, "What's in a Name? Ask the Makers of Fat Tire," [Fort Collins] *Coloradoan.com*, October 8, 2000, pp. E1, E3; "Collabeeration," New Belgium website (http://www.newbelgium .com/beerline/collabeeration), accessed October 4, 2009; "Colorado Rides on Fat Tire to Beer Heights," *Rocky Mountain News*, November 24, 2007; Robert F. Dwyer and John F. Tanner, Jr., *Business Marketing* (Irwin McGraw-Hill, 1999), p. 104; "Four Businesses Honored with Prestigious International Award for Outstanding Marketplace Ethics," Better Business Bureau, press release, September 23, 2002 (http:// www.bbb.org/alerts/2002torchwinners.asp); Julie Gordon, "Lebesch Balances Interests in Business, Community," *Coloradoan.com*, February 26, 2003; Del I. Hawkins, Roger J. Best, and Kenneth A. Coney, *Consumer Behavior: Building Marketing Strategy*, 8th ed. (Irwin McGraw-Hill, 2001); David Kemp, Tour Connoisseur, New Belgium Brewing Company, personal interview by Nikole Haiar, November 21, 2000; "Lips of Faith," New Belgium website (http://www.newbelgium.com/beerline/lips-of-faith), accessed October 4, 2009; New Belgium Brewing Company 2007 Sustainability Report (http://www.newbelgium.com/files/shared/07SustainabilityReportlow.pdf), accessed October 4, 2009; "New Belgium Brewing," MySpace (http://www.myspace.com/ follyyourfolly), accessed October 4, 2009; New Belgium Brewing Blog, New Belgium website (http://www.newbelgium.com/blog/post/2008-sustainability-nonreport), accessed October 4, 2009; "New Belgium Brewing to Cut CO_2 Emissions by 25% Per Barrel," *Environmental Leader*, January 20, 2009 (http://www.environmentalleader. com/2009/01/20/new-belgium-brewing-to-cut-co2-emissions-by-25-per-barrel), accessed October 4, 2009; "New Belgium Brewing Wins Ethics Award," *Denver Business Journal*, January 2, 2003 (http://denver.bizjournals.com/denver/stories/2002/12/30/ daily21.html), accessed October 4, 2009; New Belgium website, http://www .newbelgium.com/sustainability and http://www.newbelgium.com/sponsorship, accessed November 17, 2009; Greg Owsley, "The Necessity for Aligning Brand with

Corporate Ethics," in Sheb L. True, Linda Ferrell, O. C. Ferrell, *Fulfilling Our Obligation, Perspectives on Teaching Business Ethics* (Atlanta, GA: Kennesaw State University Press, 2005), pp. 128–132; "Philanthropy," New Belgium website (http://www.newbelgium.com/sponsorship), accessed October 4, 2009; Steve Raabe, "New Belgium Brewing Turns to Cans," *Denver Post*, May 15, 2008 (http://www.denverpost.com/breakingnews/ci_9262005), accessed November 17, 2009; Bryan Simpson, "New Belgium Brewing: Brand Building Through Advertising and Public Relations," *eBusiness Ethics* (http://e-businessethics.com/NewBelgiumCases/newbelgiumbrewing.pdf), accessed May 13, 2009; Kelly K. Spors, "Top Small Workplaces 2008," *The Wall Street Journal*, February 22, 2009 (http://online.wsj.com/article/SB122347733961315417.html); "Sustainability," New Belgium website (http://www.newbelgium.com/sustainability), accessed October 4, 2009; "The Carbon Footprint of a 6-Pack of Fat Tire Amber Ale," New Belgium Brewing Blog, August 18, 2008 (http://www.newbelgium.com/blog/post/carbon-footprint-6-pack-fat-tire-amber-ale), accessed October 4, 2009; and "Trade Your Car for a Bike," New Belgium website (http://www.newbelgium.com/trade), accessed October 4, 2009.

New Belgium Brewing (B): Developing a Brand Personality

Synopsis: This case, a follow-up to New Belgium A, discusses how New Belgium Brewing expanded its branding and communication strategy from a focus on word of mouth and event sponsorship to include television advertising, web-based communication, and social media. The development of New Belgium's "Brand Manifesto" is reviewed, along with the company's decisions regarding media selection, messaging components, and advertising production. Despite the company's continued growth in terms of both distribution and promotional complexity, New Belgium has remained focused on its core values of customer intimacy, sustainability, whimsy, and fun.

Themes: Integrated marketing communication, branding strategy, positioning, advertising, customer intimacy, distribution strategy, sustainability, marketing implementation, customer relationships

The idea for the New Belgium Brewing Company began with a bicycling trip through Belgium. Belgium is arguably home to many of the world's finest ales, some of which have been brewed for centuries in that country's monasteries and small artisan breweries. As Jeff Lebesch, an American electrical engineer by trade and a home brewer by hobby, cruised around that country on his fat-tired mountain bike, he wondered whether he could produce such high-quality beers back home in Colorado. After acquiring the special strain of yeast used to brew Belgian-style ales, Lebesch returned home and began to experiment in his Colorado basement. When his beers earned thumbs up from friends, Lebesch decided to market them.

The New Belgium Brewing Company (NBB) opened for business in 1991 as a tiny basement operation in Lebesch's home in Fort Collins. Lebesch's wife, Kim Jordan, handled all the marketing, sales, and deliveries from her station wagon. NBB beers quickly developed a small but devoted customer base, first in Fort Collins and then

Bryan Simpson, New Belgium Brewing, 500 Linden Street, Fort Collins, CO 80524. All rights reserved. This case was prepared for classroom discussion rather than to illustrate effective or ineffective handling of an administrative situation. Jennifer Sawayda, University of New Mexico, provided editorial assistance.

throughout Colorado. The brewery soon outgrew the couple's basement and moved into an old railroad depot before settling into its present custom-built facility in 1995. The company's standard product line has grown to include Sunshine Wheat, Blue Paddle Pilsner, Abbey Ale, Trippel Ale, 1554 Black Ale, and the original Fat Tire Amber Ale, still the firm's bestseller. Today, NBB is America's third-largest craft brewer; with Sam Adams number one and Sierra Nevada number two. The craft beer market accounts for just over 4 percent of the total U.S. beer market. However, it is the fastest-growing segment of the U.S. alcoholic beverage market. Case Exhibit 9.1 illustrates that craft beer's overall market share has increased over 66 percent in the decade between 1999 and 2008, with market share rising rapidly since 2005.

New Belgium's Initial Marketing Strategy

When a company grows as rapidly as NBB, the tendency is not to mess with a good thing. This applies to the beer portfolio, the culture, and the marketing process. For many years, the brewer, best known for Fat Tire Amber Ale, thrived on word-of-mouth communication to sell the brand. In fact, for the first four years of its existence, NBB's marketing consisted of traveling to beer festivals and handing out free samples. Relational marketing, done barstool to barstool, launched the advent of its Ranger Team—a sales staff who acts as brand stewards throughout the U.S. distribution network.

When Greg Owsley was hired as marketing director in 1996, NBB became more focused and proactive in its marketing efforts. Festivals and sponsorships, coupled

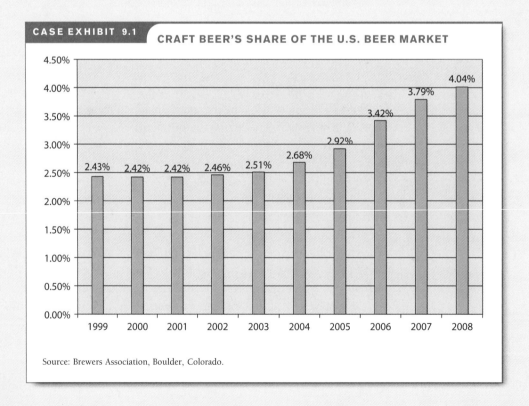

CASE EXHIBIT 9.1

CRAFT BEER'S SHARE OF THE U.S. BEER MARKET

Source: Brewers Association, Boulder, Colorado.

with print media in alternative weeklies, increased brand sales to over 100,000 barrels annually by 1998 (In 2008, NBB sold almost 500,000 barrels). Owsley and his team introduced such signature NBB events as the multicity philanthropic bike festival, Tour de Fat. They launched an educational "Beerstream" in the form of a traveling slide show and beer tasting in an old Airstream trailer. NBB developed engaging contests like "What's Your Folly?" which invites consumers to pitch their Beerdream (an adventure enhanced by NBB beers) to win immortal fame on an NBB postcoaster (mailable postcard and coaster). "The Worthy Endeavor" is a web-based contest in which applicants can win a trip to the Crested Butte Al Johnson Uphill Downhill. All events, sponsorships, and interactive games have been bolstered by strategic purchase of print media advertising.

In 2003, as NBB expanded into northern California, it became evident that new avenues would have to be considered to effectively reach the increasingly far-flung consumer base. For the first time, NBB looked to a more formalized and systematic approach to analyzing its audience. A consulting firm conducted research in Colorado and in other markets and suggested a mind-share approach to branding. However, Owsley rejected the consulting firm's suggestion and continued researching branding's foremost progressive thinkers, eventually coming across the works of Douglas Holt.

Developing a Brand Manifesto

Holt, then of Harvard Business School and currently with Oxford, is the leading proponent of "cultural branding"—a philosophy of branding that tries to speak to tensions within society. Owsley contacted Holt after reading some of his published work online. The two agreed to meet, and Holt was hired as a consultant in September 2003. Holt came to NBB on several occasions to study the brand and immerse himself in the brewery's unique culture. This process led to the creation of a brand manifesto—a 70-page document, coauthored over many months by Owsley and Holt, describing the brand's attributes, character, cultural relevancy, and potential. This opened the door to a relationship with Amalgamated Inc., a young upstart advertising agency in New York. In discussing the brand with the agency, NBB's creative team collaborated with Amalgamated to flesh out the brand's cultural contributions and messaging components.

Media Selection

Working with the manifesto as a guide, Amalgamated explored a wide array of possibilities within a somewhat restrictive budget. Underwriting of National Public Radio, production of radio shorts, television, and theatrical screenings were all thrown into the mix. Television, with its low cost per viewer and wide reach, quickly rose as the preferred option. It also seemed more authentic to embrace the medium where consumers expected to see advertising interwoven with entertainment.

Creating a television campaign for a craft brewer provided a litany of challenges and opportunities. The "Big Three" brewers—Anheuser-Bush, Coors, and Miller— have long dominated mainstream televised beer advertising in the United States. Boston Brewing's foray into television several years back presented an interesting case study. The makers of Sam Adams started a campaign with founder Jim Koch delivering a folksy voice-over that positioned Sam Adams as a beer of the highest quality. Over time, this morphed into televised spots that looked more and more like the positioning of America's Big Three brewers.

Message Development

NBB understood at the inception that the power of television could work to bolster or undermine the brand with equal efficacy. If the spots did not ring true to the NBB character, there was a potential to alienate the core consumers who had helped build the company to this point. Within the ethos of NBB, Holt unearthed a mindset where a highly creative activity or avocation is pursued for the intrinsic value of doing it, as well as performed in a balanced manner with nature. It is the cultural counterpoint to the "urban professional." The mindset personified is the mountain local who eschews a high-dollar job in Denver to pursue a simpler existence. It is the unsigned musician who writes songs just to entertain her friends. It is the amateur bread maker who bakes experimental breads and then hand delivers them on his bike. It is the juxtaposition of traditional American values that compels people to compromise their true selves in order to exist within a modern technopoly, with the values of people who live in a way that emphasizes experience for the sake of experience rather than for the sake of profit.

With these shared attributes in mind, the audience for NBB's commercials would likely be the professional who follows the traditional route of existing within a capitalist economy but still has artistic leanings and desires. These are the executives, lawyers, and accountants who live in Kansas or Missouri but come to Colorado for a ski week every year to indulge in the mountain lifestyle. These are folks who look at the mountain local and envy his dedication but could never fathom making that career sacrifice. The cultural tension then can be seen as the compromise between living the life one wants with balancing the economic needs of existing within a technopoly. NBB beers could be positioned as a manifestation of that lifestyle. It would be possible to pop a cap off a Fat Tire in Springfield, Missouri, and travel metaphorically to the Colorado mountains and the mountain local's life.

With this understanding, Amalgamated developed a series of storyboards for the commercials featuring the "Tinkerer," a character who discovers an old cruiser bike that has been customized, modernized, and ultimately left for scrap. The Tinkerer then proceeds to strip the cruiser bike back down to its bare elements. The original boards featured three complete narratives with a potential fourth when Amalgamated flew to NBB to present its material at the company's monthly staff meeting. True to a culture based on employee ownership and ownership mentality, every NBB employee was offered the opportunity to weigh in on the storyboards.

The NBB team reacted positively to the presentation with the exception of Amalgamated's suggested tagline: "Follow Your Folly ... Ours Is Beer." Several people suggested that folly had too negative a connotation or undermined the science and technology it took to produce such consistently high-quality beers. The debate built steam over several weeks, with the creative team suggesting that a word like *folly* had fallen so far from the vernacular that it was ripe for reinterpretation and a fresh new definition. Following one's folly also aptly alluded to the ideal of offbeat endeavors versus the traditional "follow the money" thinking that created the social tensions inherent to potential consumers' lives. After a healthy volley of emails from nearly every NBB department, the creative team won out and "Follow Your Folly" became the campaign's tagline.

Advertising Production

At this stage in the process, a search for the right director for the commercials ensued. Amalgamated reviewed dozens of highlight reels and passed the most likely fits along to NBB. Much of the work represented had great visual power with big budget, 70-millimeter sheen. The look and feel of such glossy and cinematic work was tempting, but in the end NBB went with Jake Scott, who suggested shooting the spots on grittier 16-millimeter film stock and giving the work a timeless feel influenced by the photography of the 1960s documentarian William Eggelston. Scott flew to the brewery to learn about NBB and then jumped into a car and scouted locations throughout Colorado. He sent still photos from a variety of locales, and ultimately the group committed to shooting in and around Hotchkiss and Paonia. After reviewing a tape of locals for potential casting shot outside bike shops in Fort Collins and Boulder, Scott decided on Boulder craftsman Charles Srbecky to play the Tinkerer. Srbecky, formerly of the Czech Republic, was an atypical choice with tousled hair, weathered features, and a maturity not seen in contemporary U.S. beer advertising.

In September 2004, members of NBB, Amalgamated, and the production company RSA out of Los Angeles met in Hotchkiss and commenced shooting over a three-day period. Much of the talent and crew came from surrounding Colorado communities. The production quickly took on a collaborative and improvisational feel reflective of NBB's culture. Although great attention was paid to fulfilling the promise of Amalgamated's storyboards, spontaneous opportunities were embraced as they arose. This led to no fewer than nine potential spots coming out of the three-day shoot.

Amalgamated returned to New York to begin postproduction of the spots with NBB's input. Choosing a musical bed quickly developed into the next creative challenge. Editors at Whitehouse Post in New York tried a variety of genres, from progressive to country alternative, and landed on an artist in the category of "Freak Folk" by the name of Devendra Banhart. Banhart's tunes added a haunting sense of cheerful nostalgia to the works. With the 16-millimeter film stock giving a mid-1970s feel buoyed by Banhart's acoustic tunes, the campaign took a far more muted and poignant tone than the ubiquitous mainstream beer advertising seen elsewhere. The NBB product appeared only in the final five seconds of film between the tag lines, "Follow Your Folly ... Ours Is Beer." Quick to embrace the latent talents of their own crew, NBB allowed brewery employees to compose a reggae-like score for one of the 15-second spots—a playful little film called *Joust*.

Maintaining a Local Touch

Even as NBB decided to speak to a wider audience through television, the roots-style marketing that launched the company could not be abandoned. It became even more important to speak to the insiders who helped build the brand in the same authentic and personal tone they had come to know and embrace. Rather than redirect energies from event sponsorship to media, events became an even greater opportunity to maintain that vital dialogue. Rather than test the spots on focus groups, NBB turned to insiders in the bike community and friends of the brewery with some personal history and knowledge of the brand. The theory was that television would reach those faraway outposts where Ranger sales staff penetration was difficult and not cost-effective. In mature markets, the personal touch would be redoubled.

The spots first aired in Arizona in January 2005, with a summer campaign to follow throughout the rest of the Western United States. After viewing the NBB spots at a brewing industry conference in March 2005, Miller SAB vice president of marketing, Bob Mikulay, had this to say:

> *At its heart, the basic proposition of beer has to be about fun. The small brewers have always done this well ... often with great irreverence, quirkiness or just plain silliness ... but always with a strong, instinctive understanding of the unique personality of their brands. And we need them to keep it coming ... and even step it up a bit. In fact, I was encouraged to see New Belgium actually taking their brand of fun into a television spot.*
>
> *Now humility will probably prevent Kim [Kim Jordan, CEO of New Belgium] from saying this later ... but I believe that's a truly great piece of advertising. Is there anybody who doesn't now have a very good idea about what Fat Tire is all about? So the specialty and other small brewers are showing every sign that they are ready to fulfill their role in the industry better than ever.*

In the end, NBB's first television-based advertising campaign—approached with a great deal of inner reflection—mirrored well the craft brewer's personality. In a sea of loud, flashy beer advertising aimed seemingly at a youthful demographic, NBB positioned itself as whimsical, thoughtful, and reflective. The bicycling imagery shot in Colorado gave a palpable sense of place to the brand among viewers on the coasts and in the plains. The iconic cruiser bike itself harkened the idea of creative play. The act of rescuing the bike from bad technology and neglect can be read as metaphor for NBB's efforts to recycle and reuse materials to the point of 98 percent diversion of their waste stream. The Tinkerer himself pays homage to the bicycle tour that NBB's founder Jeff Lebesch took through Belgium that inspired his home-brewing shift toward Belgian-based beers. Even the texture of the film and the musical tone capture the ideals of whimsy and joy inherent to NBB's philosophy of brewing and quality of life. At a time when marketers were seeking ever-more insidious means to cut through the clutter, NBB chose to redefine a category in a very traditional medium where ads are acceptable and the rare good ones can still be groundbreaking, thoughtful, and effective. To see New Belgium's television spots, go to http://www.newbelgium.com/videos/tv.

New Media, but Consistent Brand Messaging

Over the years, New Belgium has used a variety of different media to advertise its products and establish brand recognition. Although the type of media may change, New Belgium's principles and brand image have remained the same. To reach audiences more efficiently and effectively, NBB launched a series of web and print campaigns in 2007 to promote NBB's sustainability practices. According to Greg Owsley, NBB particularly wanted to emphasize that consumers do not have to practice abstinence to be sustainable. They can still indulge and be green, with New Belgium beers being a case in point. Keeping the company's "Follow Your Folly" focus, the new campaign featured people outside the brewery who came up with whimsical ideas for sustainability. NBB created an interactive website (www.followyourfolly.com) to showcase people and organizations in NBB's marketing campaign. The website presents New Belgium's sustainability goals along with stories and "folly videos" from participants.

Today, New Belgium is using new forms of media to promote its brand while still maintaining its overall branding philosophy. In 2008, NBB announced a partnership with Backbone Media LLC of Carbondale, Colorado, to help manage NBB's media planning and buying. Although the company has not ruled out new television advertisements, NBB has focused on other forms of "new media" such as social networking sites in order to attract new consumers to the brand. (As of early 2010, NBB has roughly 63,000 fans on its Facebook site.) NBB abandoned its newsletter in exchange for a blog, to which viewers can subscribe and receive news articles and feeds. NBB has also begun to use Twitter. Called "beer tweets," consumers can post their comments and thoughts about New Belgium on Twitter. The Twitter team, consisting of four employees, responds to the beer tweets in what web developer Kurt Herrman calls "a two-way street" of communication. (As of early 2010, the NBB Twitter site has roughly 12,000 followers and continues to grow.)

Although New Belgium may vary the types of media it utilizes, the company's goals to be a truly sustainable brand have remained the same. Its message is, and always has been, that consumers can be environmentally conscious and still have fun. Some people scoff at the idea that a company that sells alcohol can be a socially responsible brand, but with each new social and environmental initiative, New Belgium seeks to prove its critics wrong.

Conclusion

NBB has always remained committed to its initial mission of being a fun, socially and environmentally responsible company. More recently, the company has renewed its efforts to appeal to the environmentally conscious consumer. In order to learn more about the consumption habits and desires of its consumers, NBB developed and distributed a survey to 612 beer drinkers. The results indicate that 39 percent of beer consumers will make extra efforts to buy from and support sustainable companies.

Larger studies outside NBB suggest that as many as 60 million consumers frequently support businesses that broadcast their sustainable practices.

Studies also reveal that environmentally conscious consumers are on the lookout for deceptive business practices, such as greenwashing and spin doctoring, or as NBB's Greg Owsley put it, "casual dating between core values and brand [that] leaves both short of their optimal potential." Because NBB has focused on sustainable business practices since the company's inception, the authenticity of NBB's environmentally conscious actions and messaging is solid. However, the challenge for NBB, and for other sustainable companies as well, is to convince the public of the genuineness of these claims, particularly because the public is often inundated with deceptive claims from businesses that want to appear green. To help businesses take a genuine approach to sustainability and communicate this approach to the public, NBB has adopted five principles that it calls its Sustainable Branding Strategy:

- **Walk before talk.** This principle is perhaps the most apparent, but certainly no less challenging, as it requires the business to live up to its sustainable claims. The business must practice sustainability before promoting its environmentally friendly practices.

- **Admit the flaws.** Even NBB admits that its sustainable business practices are far from perfect. Instead of covering up flaws in their sustainability plans, businesses should own up to them. Intelligent green consumers are likely to investigate a company's green claims, and they will undoubtedly find areas that need improving. Preparing responses about how to address these flaws will convince consumers that the company recognizes the problems in their plan and will take a proactive stance to address them.

- **Provide the smile.** Green businesses should be optimistic, seeking to make their customers feel good about making a positive difference by being green rather than causing them to feel pessimistic and guilty about their actions.

- **Go slow to go fast.** Be empathetic to the customer by not bogging them down with all the company's core values at once. The purpose is communication: Make sure the customer clearly understands these values, which requires the company to go slow rather than throwing everything at the consumer.

- **Make ripples.** Starting out as a small company, NBB could not immediately expect its marketing efforts to take hold all at once. Companies must have a clear purpose and show commitment to the cause. Cause-based marketing is particularly useful because it convinces the company's public that its advertisements are not just to promote its brand, but to create a positive difference as well. Of course, the public must be able to trust that a company's cause-based marketing is sincere, which requires the previous steps to convince consumers of the company's sustainable authenticity.

Although New Belgium is a much larger company than it was when it started nearly two decades ago, its mission and core values have remained the same. Although employee numbers have increased, product offerings are more diverse, and marketing media are ever-changing, New Belgium remains an example of a company that continues to have a strong, stable brand image—one that consumers continue to trust.

Questions for Discussion

1. Rather than use focus groups to test its branding and messaging, New Belgium used insiders in the bike community and brewery friends who had a personal history and knowledge of the brand. Evaluate this decision. Should New Belgium have used the more traditional approach to ensure the widest possible input to its marketing strategy?

2. NBB seemed to agonize over the use of the word "folly" in its advertising campaign. What do you make of the company's struggle with this decision? Also, how do you personally feel about their use of the word?

3. New Belgium's focus on sustainability, whimsy, and fun is clearly rooted in its Colorado-based culture and the ethos of its founders and employees. As New Belgium's distribution continues to expand away from that locale, how can the company make its branding and messaging resonate with consumers in different parts of the country?

4. The case mentions how the branding and communication strategy of Boston Brewing Company (makers of Sam Adams) shifted as the company grew. The positioning for Sam Adams changed from a folksy tone to one that looked to position Sam Adams in relation to Budweiser, Miller, and Coors. Does New Belgium face this same risk, or will the company be able to maintain its whimsical and personal touch with consumers? Explain.

Sources

The facts of this case are from Janet Forgrieve, "Sales of Craft Beer Make Biggest Jump in Decade," *Rocky Mountain News*, August 22, 2006 (http://www.rockymountainnews.com/drmn/other_business/article/0,2777,DRMN_23916_4936608,00.html); Mike Hooker, "More Colorado Businesses Turn to Social Networks," CBS 4 Denver, March 26, 2009 (http://cbs4denver.com/technology/kcnc.twitter.new.2.968540.html), accessed August 14, 2009; Jeremy Mullman, "Craft Beer Steps into Wine Country," *Advertising Age*, June 19, 2006; New Belgium Brewing Company website (http://www.newbelgium.com/story.php), accessed August 21, 2009; "New Belgium Brewing Launches Follow Your Folly Campaign Integrating Web And Print," PRWeb, February 20, 2007 (http://www.prweb.com/releases/2007/02/prweb506247.htm), accessed August 14, 2009; "New Belgium Brewing Selects Backbone to Handle Media," New Belgium Brewing Social Media Release, September 10, 2008 (http://www.pitchengine.com/free-release.php?id=443), accessed August 14, 2009; "New Belgium Expansion on

Tap," *Rocky Mountain News*, May 25, 2006 (http://www.rockymountainnews.com/drmn/other_business/article/0,2777,DRMN_23916_ 4725068,00.html); "New Belgium FAQ," New Belgium website (http://www.newbelgium.com/faq), accessed August 14, 2009; "New Belgium New Expansion," Probrewer.com, May 30, 2006 (http://www.probrewer.com/news/news-002935.php); Greg Owsley, "Sustainable Branding: Five Steps to Gaining the Approval of the Environmentally-Conscious Consumer," *Advertising Age*, June 25, 2007; and Greg Owsley, "The Necessity for Aligning Brand with Corporate Ethics," in Sheb True, Linda Ferrell, and O. C. Ferrell, eds., *Fulfilling Our Obligation* (Kennesaw, GA: Kennesaw State University Press, 2005).

IKEA Looks to Further Penetrate the U.S. Market

Synopsis: IKEA is known around the world for its stylish, quality, and low-cost furniture and home furnishings. The company's success is based on a strategy of operational excellence in production, supply chain operations, and marketing. IKEA—wildly popular in Europe—has leveraged its brand reputation to penetrate markets in other countries. However, its penetration of the U.S. market has been hampered by a weakened economy and the inconsistency between the traditional U.S furniture market and IKEA's low-cost operating philosophy. IKEA must find a balance between its operational excellence strategy and U.S. consumers' demands for customization, good service, convenience, and quality.

Themes: Operational excellence, target marketing, product design, branding strategy, positioning, global marketing, pricing strategy, supply chain strategy, retailing, implementation, customer relationships, SWOT analysis, strategic focus

When 17-year-old Ingvar Kamprad founded IKEA in 1943, he could not have imagined that his company would become one of the world's most popular and iconic brands or the world's largest home furnishings retailer. The IKEA name is a combination of Kamprad's initials (IK) and the first letters of the farm (Elmtaryd) and village (Agunnaryd) in southern Sweden where he grew up. From the beginning, IKEA was founded on different principles—namely, frugality and low cost. Most furniture companies offer personalized service and advice in lavish showrooms where salespeople compete for sales commissions. Kamprad, however, recognized that customers were willing to trade off typical amenities to save money. Today, the no-frills frugality is the cornerstone of the IKEA caché and one of the reasons for its immense popularity.

IKEA operates under a unique corporate structure. When Kamprad founded the company, he wanted to create an independent organization that would be sustainable for the long term. Since 1982, the Stichting INGKA Foundation, a Netherlands-based

Christin Copeland, Florida State University MBA Class of 2006, and Michael D. Hartline, Florida State University, prepared this case for classroom discussion rather than to illustrate effective or ineffective handling of an administrative situation. Kimberly Gaskin, Amy Minkewicz, and Mandy Walz, Florida State University MBA Class of 2010, provided research support during the case revision.

charitable foundation, has owned the IKEA Group. Many estimates peg the foundation as one of the world's wealthiest charities—worth an estimated $36 billion. INGKA Holding B.V., also based in the Netherlands, is the parent company for all IKEA Group companies. The IKEA Group includes IKEA of Sweden (which designs and develops all IKEA products), Swedwood (which makes all IKEA furniture), the sales companies that operate IKEA stores, and all purchasing and supply chain functions. This type of ownership is unique in that the foundation is a nonprofit organization designed to promote innovation in architectural and interior design. Some criticize IKEA's ownership as an arrangement that leverages the uniqueness of Dutch law to avoid taxes and prevent a hostile takeover attempt.

Today, IKEA is Sweden's best-known export. The company had 2009 worldwide sales totaling $32 billion and an annual growth rate of 7 percent (down from 14 percent in 2008)—the company's slowest growth rate in more than 10 years. Roughly 80 percent of IKEA's sales come from operations in Europe, with North America and Asia/Australia contributing 15 percent and 5 percent, respectively. The company has 123,000 employees (down more than 5,000 since 2008) and more than 301 IKEA stores in 25 countries, with 267 of these stores belonging to the IKEA Group. The remaining stores are owned and operated by franchisees. There are currently 36 U.S. stores, with plans to open two more. IKEA had originally planned to have 50 stores operating in the United States by 2010, but the recent worldwide economic recession slowed IKEA's plans. Worldwide, the company plans to open 26 additional stores within the next year.

The IKEA Concept

The backbone of IKEA's success is "The IKEA Concept." IKEA's vision statement reflects this core operating philosophy:

> Our vision is to create a better everyday life for the many people. Our business idea is to offer a wide range of well-designed, functional, home furnishing products at prices so low that as many people as possible can afford them.

To fulfill its vision, IKEA provides stylish, functional, low-cost home furnishings that customers must assemble themselves. Furniture products are shipped in flat packs to save money on manufacturing and distribution, which IKEA then passes on to customers in the form of lower prices at retail. To compensate for the customer having to "do it yourself," IKEA offers other services that make this proposition a little more attractive. These extra services include in-store child-care and play areas, restaurants, and longer store hours. To help visitors prepare for this experience, IKEA provides its customers with pencils, paper, tape measures, store guides, catalogs, strollers, and shopping bags. IKEA even offers delivery for the bulky items that customers cannot carry themselves. For those who want to carry their own bulky furniture home, IKEA rents car racks for convenience. IKEA stores are designed as a circle so that everything can be seen no matter in what direction the customer is headed. The aisles are wide to reduce traffic congestion that could occur when customers stop to look at different showrooms and displays.

Production

IKEA's key objective regarding production is to establish and maintain long-term supplier relationships. When designing new products, IKEA actually begins with a target retail price in mind, and then works with roughly 1,400 suppliers in fifty-four countries to find the lowest cost way to manufacture that product. Its oldest suppliers are Swedish; however, other major suppliers are located in China (21 percent), Poland (17 percent), Italy (8 percent), and Germany (6 percent). IKEA accounts for up to 10 percent of the furniture market in each country where its products are manufactured.

One strategy that IKEA has implemented is to place 41 trading offices in 30 countries around the world to localize its operations. This gives IKEA leverage to increase production capacity (that is, labor hours and purchasing materials) when needed. The strategy also allows IKEA to closely monitor manufacturing performance. Producing high-quality products at the lowest possible cost drives IKEA's production mentality. In addition to local trading offices, IKEA also manages production through long-term contractual relationships based on bulk buying. Committing to high-volume purchases over a longer time frame allows IKEA to dramatically cut costs. Additionally, IKEA is in a position to offer its suppliers financial assistance if necessary. This optimization is key to achieving the low-cost business model that IKEA wants to maintain.

Cost consciousness dominates all aspects of IKEA's operations. In land acquisition, IKEA locates stores on property just outside of target cities. In production, the remnants of fabric and wood used for products are used to create more products. IKEA uses natural colors to cut production costs and increase social responsibility to the environment through the manufacturing process. Across its 27 distribution centers in 16 countries, flat packages are used to efficiently transport the large bulk of products from suppliers to IKEA stores. The use of flat packages lowers warehousing and distribution costs and the environmental impact throughout the supply chain.

Marketing

IKEA's marketing program has four focal areas: product design, catalogs, advertising, and public relations/promotions. IKEA's product designs are arguably the most important part of its brand image. Customers love the clean lines, frugal styling, and caché that ownership affords. IKEA admits that creating stylish and inexpensive products is a challenging task. To fulfill its vision, the company's full-time and free-lance designers work closely with in-house production teams to pair the appropriate materials with the least costly suppliers. Though the work is tedious, IKEA is well-known for its product innovation.

IKEA's main marketing focus is its printed catalog, where the company spends the majority of its annual marketing budget. The 376-page catalog is produced in 52 different editions in 27 languages. In 2008, 200 million copies were put into circulation. The online catalog and website feature product information and free downloadable programs to help redesign kitchens, bathrooms, and bedrooms. The website also provides information about each store's local events and promotions, services, and product specials. Because the website offers little online purchasing capabilities, customers are often forced to visit the stores to buy products.

In addition to the catalog, IKEA also uses television, radio, and Internet-based communication to reach its target customers. The company's advertising is intended to increase both brand awareness and store traffic. Some of the company's advertising is controversial, especially ads that portray gay customers or sexually suggestive story-lines. Advertising, however, is not a major focus of IKEA's promotional efforts. The company prefers to rely on word-of-mouth communication. This is reflected in its use of social media. For example, IKEA's Facebook page (87,000 fans strong and growing) provides up-to-date information on company activities, sales, and local store events.

Local store events are another key marketing focus for IKEA. The San Diego, California, store offers birthday parties for children on the first Tuesday of every month. The Atlanta, Georgia, store features activities such as culinary tasting events, Tree Hugger celebrations, face painting, and fundraising events for local charities. In a unique promotion prior to the grand opening of the Atlanta store, IKEA managers invited locals to apply for the post of Ambassador of Kul (Swedish for "fun"). The five winners of an essay contest received $2,000 in vouchers, had to live in the store for three days, sleep in the bedding department, and participate in contests. Finally, the entire IKEA family holds "Antibureaucracy Weeks" on a regular basis. These are times when executives work on the shop floor or stockroom, operate cash registers, and even load trucks and cars for IKEA customers. This simple step goes a long way in upholding the IKEA culture and maintaining employee morale.

IKEA's marketing program is designed to be thrifty but still effective. In fact, all of IKEA's marketing activities are designed to maintain a downward pressure on operating expenses. For example, in most stores, IKEA does not accept checks—only cash or credit cards, including its own "IKEA Card." This helps to reduce IKEA's accounts receivable and eliminates the need to maintain an expensive collections operation. With policies like these, it is not surprising the company's operating margin of 10 percent is among the best in the home furnishings industry. And, despite its low cost and price model, IKEA aims to cut prices by an average of 2 to 3 percent every year.

The Future of IKEA's U.S. Expansion

IKEA considers the United States an important part of its plans for global expansion. The U.S. standard of living is higher than most countries'; however, most American consumers actively buy into the cost-conscious mentality. The value of the U.S. dollar is stable and not prone to wide exchange rate fluctuations. The United States is number one in the world for Internet usage, and IKEA's sustainability efforts are welcomed by a wide margin of the consuming public. Another factor that makes the United States favorable to IKEA is its melting pot of cultures. The IKEA Concept can appeal to the different lifestyles and ways of life found in the United States.

Despite these advantages, IKEA must address two key issues regarding U.S. expansion. The first is the overwhelming individuality of U.S. consumers. American consumers are very demanding and tend to reward marketers that go out of their way to address individual tastes and needs. Further expansion into the U.S. market will require IKEA to adapt its offerings and stores to local tastes—a marketing strategy that is much more expensive to deliver and contrary to IKEA's cost-conscious operating philosophy. IKEA's franchised structure is well suited to this task. This allows IKEA to get closer to customers by hiring local employees that represent the same values, cultures, and lifestyles of the local area. Another adaptation issue involves IKEA's promotional strategy, which must be tailored to U.S. standards. For example, most of IKEA's television commercials are considered too "edgy" for American viewers.

The second key issue is quality. Although American consumers are increasingly value-driven, they also demand quality products. In this regard, IKEA's low-cost, do-it-yourself concept misses the mark for many potential furniture consumers. Many Americans view self-assembled furniture as being lower in quality, and similar to the types of furniture one might buy at Walmart or Target.

Facing these challenges, IKEA's U.S. expansion is expected to move fairly slowly. The company does not have the financial resources and marketing experience to roll out a large number of products and stores simultaneously. The most recent economic conditions have not helped either. As the company looks toward further expansion into the U.S. market, it must consider a number of relevant issues in both its internal and external environments.

IKEA's Strengths

Low Cost Structure   IKEA's low cost structure has been the very essence of its success. Being that low cost measures are ingrained into IKEA's corporate DNA, the company does not have a hard time tailoring its operations around this business model. This model also pairs nicely with customers who appreciate IKEA's operating style. Furthermore, IKEA's low cost structure has kept the company profitable while competitors, such as Pier 1 in the United States, are struggling. Despite the state of the economy, IKEA has continued to see positive revenue growth, though President and CEO Anders Dahlvig has admitted that the economy has caused sales to increase more slowly than in recent years. Dahlvig also explains that in reaction to the constricting economy, IKEA has continued to use every possible avenue to maintain its low cost structure and competitiveness without compromising customer value.

Corporate Culture   IKEA values antibureaucracy in its operations, and strongly follows worker and environmental protection rules. These tenets are codified in the company's code of conduct known as "The IKEA Way." The company's culture is based on the core values of togetherness, cost consciousness, respect, and simplicity. Kamprad once said, "Work should always be fun for all colleagues. We all only have one life; a third of life is work. Without desire and fun, work becomes hell." To ensure the company culture is upheld, the company looks for very specific traits in potential employees. IKEA's managers look for people who "display a desire to learn, motivation to do things better, common sense, and the ability to lead by example." The company believes in keeping employees happy by engaging in activities throughout the year that promote well-being and job satisfaction. These are all reasons that IKEA has been ranked in *Fortune* magazine's annual list of "100 Best Companies to Work For" three years in a row.

Do-It-Yourself Approach   IKEA maintains its low-cost business model by creating a different furniture shopping experience. IKEA supplies customers with all possible materials needed to complete their shopping when they enter the store (that is, measuring tape, paper, and pencils). The floor has showrooms displaying IKEA furniture with multiple accessories that will accentuate the style. With this approach, customers do not have to be bothered with salespeople who work on commission. Customers can pick and choose among the different options of accessories that they would like to use with furniture. Many customers appreciate the feeling of accomplishment that comes from doing things for themselves. For those customers who do not like the DIY approach, IKEA offers assembly services and home delivery options.

Added Amenities   Although IKEA is not set up as a traditional furniture store, the company does provide several added amenities. IKEA rents car racks that customers can use to get bulky items to their homes. IKEA also provides child-care services to give parents time to shop. Once their children are in a safe place, parents will delegate more time to browsing and purchasing IKEA furniture and accessories. The company also provides restaurants in some of its stores to encourage customers to stay a little longer. Offering breakfast, lunch, and dinner, the restaurants also generate strong profits for the company each year. Customers can also schedule consultations with professional designers. In sum, the IKEA experience is designed to make the stores destinations in themselves. IKEA wants the customer to feel as if there is not a rush to leave the store and customers can do more than just shop for furniture.

Brand Image   There is no denying that brand image is a key strength for IKEA. Even if they have not been in a store, most people around the globe recognize the blue and yellow logo as a symbolic representation of trendy, modern, and fashionable furniture. Customers flock to the furniture giant to experience what *Business Week* has referred to as "IKEA world, a state of mind which revolves around contemporary design, low prices, wacky promotions, and an enthusiasm that few institutions can muster."

Part of IKEA's brand strength comes from its wide array of products that exude a high-quality, low-cost focus. The company offers home furnishings and appliances for the bedroom, bathroom, and kitchen, as well as furniture for business offices. In addition to home furnishings, the company sells accent pieces and everyday products such as rugs, linens, and kitchen utensils. Some of the company's newest ventures include home building materials. Customers can build an IKEA home with reasonably priced, environmentally friendly materials.

Strong Focus on Sustainability   IKEA considers the environmental impact of every step in its business processes by making products that are environmentally conscientious and cost-effective. Suppliers are required to comply with strict environmental standards and to use renewable, reusable, and recycled materials as much as possible. With wood as a primary source of material, IKEA also employs field specialists to ensure the wood obtained comes from responsibly managed forests. The company has even paired with the World Wildlife Fund to train cotton farmers in Pakistan and India to use more sustainable cotton practices. From product design to disposal, the organization truly practices what it preaches in terms of its environmental responsibilities.

IKEA's Weaknesses

Do-It-Yourself Approach   Some customers may not appreciate IKEA's do-it-yourself approach. IKEA targets young, cost-conscious customers who want stylish furniture. However, these same consumers also like convenience and usually have the money to pay for it. For them, the time and effort involved in shopping for furniture, bringing it home, and assembling it may not be worth it. Furthermore, some customers enjoy having a conversation with a salesperson and getting individual ideas and advice from employees. These customers may continue to buy furniture from traditional retailers.

Limited Customization   To ensure alignment with its low cost structure and easy-assembly promise, IKEA's products are very basic and simple in terms of both structure and design. The ability for individualized customization is limited. Many American consumers prefer items with more style, accent, and color options.

Limited Promotional Expenditures   IKEA does not spend an enormous amount of money on promotion. Instead, the company depends on word of mouth and catalogs to generate a buzz among customers. Sadly, most U.S. consumers are not highly responsive to catalog marketing, making IKEA's bread-and-butter promotion less efficient and cost-effective for the U.S. market. American consumers also watch television and use the Internet more often than consumers in other countries. However, most of IKEA's television commercials are unknown outside of the United Kingdom. Further, many of the company's ads are controversial and not suitable for a U.S. audience. As a result of these issues, IKEA may be missing out on a larger potential customer base.

Weak Online Support   Many aspects of the company's website leave much to be desired. Although product descriptions are available, the majority of the items shown cannot be ordered online. IKEA basically forces consumers to shop at their nearest brick-and-mortar locations. Because IKEA's physical presence in the U.S. market is small, the company is losing valuable sales due to its lack of online buying options.

IKEA's Market Opportunities

Economic Conditions   IKEA's low-cost, high-quality strategy fits with the current state of the economy. As many consumers look for ways to cut personal spending, IKEA is well positioned to be a logical choice for home furnishings for the cost-conscious customer. Most American consumers still subscribe to a value-dominant logic when it comes to purchasing goods and services. However, these customers want not only high quality at a good price but also convenient access and time-saving services. IKEA can play into this buying logic but may have to expand its service offerings to increase customer convenience.

Demand for Convenience   The number of consumers shopping online continues to rise. With the average schedule getting busier, technically savvy consumers increasingly enjoy the convenience and ease of online shopping. Comparison shopping is also a convenience afforded by the Internet that could allow IKEA to dominate the low-cost, quality furnishing sector. Offering convenient online shopping experiences would fit well with IKEA's low cost structure because it would allow them to sell items using a distribution network instead of a complete reliance on physical stores and their higher overhead costs. Convenience factors within IKEA's stores, such as restaurants and daycare, are already well suited to customer needs.

Popularity of Stylish, but Sustainable, Products   Swedish design—the simple, futuristic, edgy, and fashionable designs offered by IKEA—is becoming more popular among consumers overall. For example, Target Stores offers a line of products from Swedish designer Todd Oldham. In addition to style, consumers are also interested in "green" products that enhance the sustainability of natural resources. The recent corporate movement toward "green" practices is becoming more prevalent, and consumers are becoming more aware of a company's carbon footprint. IKEA is well positioned to take advantage of this trend.

IKEA's Market Threats

Competition   Several other large retailers are vying for the do-it-yourself furniture segment. As consumers become more cost conscious in today's economy, the offerings of traditional bricks-and-mortar stores such as Home Depot, Target, and Walmart become more acceptable. IKEA also faces online competitors such as BluDot.com and Furniture.com. BluDot is a direct brand competitor that also claims to offer quality, unassembled furniture at low prices. It too offers simply designed and modern furniture. Furniture.com is a product competitor that uses the traditional furniture store concept but offers the ease and convenience of online price and product comparison.

Changing Customer Needs/Tastes   Customers' needs and tastes constantly change. At some point, customer interest in Swedish design and do-it-yourself furniture will wane. This is especially true as the U.S. population continues to age. The typical baby-boomer consumer demands quality, values his or her time, and appreciates convenience more than saving a few dollars. Overall, there are relatively fewer younger customers—IKEA's main target market—as compared to baby boomers. The end result is a likely decline in demand for trendy, low-cost furniture. IKEA's low-cost and high-quality designs might appeal to some baby boomers, but the inconveniences associated with the company's DIY approach would probably send them looking elsewhere.

Mature Market Preferences   Most American consumers have preconceived notions of what the "best of the best" is when it comes to specialty furniture and furnishings purchases. For example, the average consumer may not purchase a mattress from IKEA because it is not a Select Comfort, Sealy, or Simmons mattress. Although IKEA focuses strongly on high-quality products, in the U.S. market the company must compete with well-established companies that have earned significant brand awareness.

Questions for Discussion

1. Given the SWOT analysis presented in the case, what are IKEA's key competitive advantages? What strategic focus should the company take as it looks to further expand into the U.S. market?

2. What factor is the biggest reason for IKEA's growth and popularity: value or image? What can IKEA do to sustain growth after it loses some caché?

3. What strategic alternatives would you suggest IKEA employ to further penetrate the U.S. market?

4. Speculate on what will happen at IKEA stores as they are adapted to fit local tastes. Is the company's trade-off of service for low cost sustainable in the long term?

Sources

The facts of this case are from "25 Innovators, 6 Industries," *BusinessWeek Online*, April 13, 2006 (http://www.businessweek.com/print/innovate/content/apr2006/id20060413_268232.htm), accessed October 9, 2009; Meera Bhatia and Armorel Kenna, "IKEA Has Slowest Sales Growth in More Than a Decade," *Bloomberg*, September 17, 2009 (http://www.bloomberg.com/apps/news?pid=20601085&sid=aSvPmp60dCL8), accessed October 9, 2009; "Business: Flat-Pack Accounting; IKEA," *The Economist*, May 13, 2006, p. 76; Kerry Capell, "IKEA: How the Swedish Retailer Became a Global Cult Brand," *BusinessWeek Online*, November 14, 2005 (http://www.businessweek.com/magazine/content/05_46/b3959001.htm?campaign_id=nws_insdr_nov4&link_position=link1), accessed October 9, 2009; Kerry Capell, "Online Extra: Sweden's Answer to Sam Walton," *BusinessWeek Online*, November 14, 2005 (http://www.businessweek.com/print/magazine/content/05_46/b3959011.htm), accessed October 9, 2009; Cora Daniels, "Create IKEA, Make Billions, Take Bus," *Fortune*, via CNNMoney.com, May 3, 2004 (http://money.cnn.com/magazines/ fortune/fortune_archive/2004/05/03/368549/index.htm), accessed October 9, 2009; IKEA website (http://www.ikea.com), accessed October 9, 2009; Philip Reynolds, "IKEA Cleans House," *Forbes*, June 25, 2009 (http://www.forbes.com/2009/06/25/ikea-redudancies-furniture-markets-equities-retail.html), accessed October 9, 2009; "Sweden's IKEA Posts Record Earnings, Growth Slows, *Bay Ledger News Zone*, September 16, 2009 (http://www.blnz.com/news/2009/09/17/Swedens_Ikea_posts_ record_earnings_8604.html), accessed November 18, 2009; and Gianfranco Zaccai, "What IKEA Could Teach Alitalia," *BusinessWeek Online*, January 19, 2006 (http:// www.businessweek.com/print/innovate/content/jan2006/id20060119_361779.htm), accessed October 9, 2009.

USA Today: Innovation and Evolution in a Troubled Industry

Synopsis: *As the entire newspaper industry sits on the brink of collapse, Gannett and* USA Today *are working to avoid disaster and transform the nation's most read newspaper into tomorrow's best resource for news and information. This case reviews the history of* USA Today, *including its continued use of innovation to stay on top of the technological and sociocultural shifts that are rapidly changing the newspaper industry. In the face of continual competition across a variety of media sources, the future of* USA Today *depends on its ability to continually push the envelope of innovation and offer value-added, proprietary content to ensure continued differentiation and the future of the* USA Today *brand.*

Themes: *Product strategy, innovation, target marketing, distribution strategy, changing technology, changing sociocultural patterns, customer relationships, competition, differentiation, strategic focus, SWOT analysis*

*U*SA Today, subtitled "The Nation's Newspaper," debuted in 1982 as America's first national general-interest daily newspaper. The paper was the brainchild of Allen H. Neuharth, who until 1989 was Chairman of Gannett Co., Inc., a diversified international $6.8 billion news, information, and communications company. Gannett is a global information juggernaut that publishes 85 daily and 1,000 nondaily newspapers, operates 23 broadcast television stations reaching 20 percent of the U.S. population, and is engaged in marketing, commercial printing, newswire services, data services, and news programming. Gannett is currently the largest U.S. newspaper group in terms of circulation. Its daily newspapers, including *USA Today*, have a combined circulation of 14 million readers every weekday and 12.6 million readers every Sunday. Gannett's total online audience in the United States is roughly 27.1 million unique visitors per month—an astounding 16.1 percent of the total U.S. Internet audience.

When *USA Today* debuted in 1982, it achieved rapid success due to its innovative format. No other media source had considered a national newspaper written in shorter

Geoffrey Lantos, Stonehill College, prepared this case for classroom discussion rather than to illustrate effective or ineffective handling of an administrative situation. Leanne Davis, Florida State University MBA Class of 2010, provided significant editorial and research assistance during the case revision.

pieces than a traditional paper and sprinkled with eye-catching, colorful photos, graphs, and charts. Designed to address the needs of a sound-byte generation, readers found *USA Today's* content refreshing and more engaging than other papers. Circulation grew rapidly from roughly 350,000 in 1982 to approximately 2.1 million today (Monday through Friday). This compares to approximately 2 million for second-place *The Wall Street Journal* and 1 million for *The New York Times*. *USA Today's* website, www.usatoday.com, is one of the Internet's top sites for news and information.

The History and Growth of *USA Today*

In February 1980, Allen Neuharth met with "Project NN" task force members to discuss his vision for producing and marketing a unique nationally distributed daily newspaper. Satellite technology had recently solved the problem of limited geographical distribution, so Neuharth was ready to take advantage of two trends in the reading public: (1) an increasingly short attention span among a generation nurtured on television, and (2) a growing hunger for more information. Neuharth believed that readers faced a time crunch in a world where so much information is available, but there is so little time to absorb it. His vision for *USA Today* positioned the paper as an information source that would provide more news about more subjects in less time.

Research suggested that *USA Today* should target achievement-oriented men in professional and managerial positions who were heavy newspaper readers and frequent travelers. Where *The New York Times* targeted the nation's intellectual elite, thinkers and policy makers, and *The Wall Street Journal* targeted business leaders, *USA Today* was to be targeted at Middle America—young, well-educated Americans who were on the move and cared about current events.

By early 1982, a team of news, advertising, and production personnel from the staffs of Gannett's daily newspapers developed, edited, published, and tested several different prototypes. Gannett sent three different 40-page prototype versions of *USA Today* to almost 5,000 professional people. Along with each prototype, they sent readers a response card that asked what they liked best and least about the proposed paper, and whether they would buy it. Although the content of each prototype was similar, the layout and graphics presentations differed. For example, one prototype included a section called "Agenda" that included comics and a calendar of meetings to be held by various professional organizations. According to marketplace feedback, readers liked the prototypes. The Gannett Board of Directors unanimously approved the paper's launch. On April 20, 1982, Gannett announced that the first copies of *USA Today* would be available in the Washington and Baltimore areas.

USA Today Launches

On September 15, 1982, 155,000 copies of the newspaper's first edition hit the newsstands. On page one, founder Neuharth wrote a short summary of *USA Today's* mission statement, explaining that he wanted to make *USA Today* enlightening and enjoyable to the public, informative to national leaders, and attractive to advertisers.

The first issue sold out. A little over a month following its debut, *USA Today*'s circulation hit 362,879—double the original year-end projection. In April 1983, just seven months after its introduction, the newspaper's circulation topped the 1 million mark. Case Exhibit 11.1 illustrates *USA Today*'s growth in circulation over time. The typical reader turned out to be a professional, usually a manager, about 40 years old, well educated, with an income of about $60,000 a year. The typical reader was also a news or sports junkie.

For a newspaper, *USA Today* was truly unique. Designed for the TV generation, the paper was laid out for easy access and quick comprehension by time-pressed readers. Examples of this formatting included extensive use of briefs, columns, secondary headlines, subheads, breakouts, at-a-glance boxes, and informational graphics. These techniques captured the most salient points of a story and presented them in a format that readers appreciated. Gannett's research had shown that readers got most of their information from such snippets and that they were just as interested in sports, movie reviews, and health information as they were in traditional news. Each issue presented four sections: News, Money, Life, and Sports. The paper's motto fit its design: "An economy of words. A wealth of information."

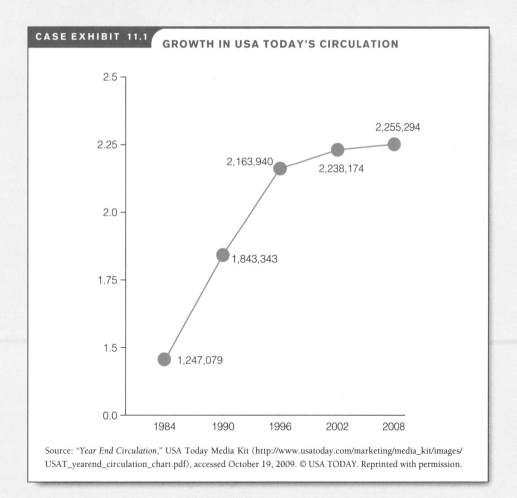

CASE EXHIBIT 11.1   **GROWTH IN USA TODAY'S CIRCULATION**

Source: "*Year End Circulation*," USA Today Media Kit (http://www.usatoday.com/marketing/media_kit/images/ USAT_yearend_circulation_chart.pdf), accessed October 19, 2009. © USA TODAY. Reprinted with permission.

Because *USA Today* was nontraditional, the critics were numerous and fierce. In their view, the paper was loaded with gimmicks—tight, short stories; no jumps from page to page, except for the cover story (stories that jump to another page are one of newspaper readers' major complaints); splashy, colorful graphics everywhere; a distinctive, casual writing style; a colorful national weather map; a roundup of news items from each state, one paragraph each; summary boxes; little charts and statistics-laden sports coverage; and a focus on celebrities and sports, with more detailed sports stories than almost any other paper in the nation. There was no foreign staff and little interest in the world outside the United States. It was quickly derided for its shallowness by journalists and labeled "McPaper"—junk-food journalism or the fast food of the newspaper business—due to its terse, brash writing style and its short coverage of complex issues. Even within Gannett, Neuharth met with bitter resistance from some senior executives. Nevertheless, readers admired the paper for its focus on brevity and clarity, short sentences, and short words.

Clearly, the paper filled a gap in the market, satisfying several unmet needs and wants. *USA Today*'s success has come from listening to its readers and giving them what they want. The paper communicates with readers on a personal level very quickly (many of the short, fact-filled stories are under 250 words), clearly, and directly, in an upbeat and positive way. The color is riveting and gives the paper a contemporary look, and so is the space-defying number of stories, factoids, larger than usual pictures, bar graphs, and charts, all squeezed onto each page without seeming too crowded. Instead of confusion, readers get neatness and order. The paper's dependably consistent organization enables readers to go directly to any one of *USA Today*'s major sections. As a result, it takes an average of only 25 minutes for a reader to peruse the paper.

Marketing Program Innovation

In spite of its critics, *USA Today*'s circulation surpassed 1.4 million by late 1985 as the paper expanded to 56 pages in length. The cover price had also increased to 50 cents, double its original price of 25 cents per issue. By this time, *USA Today* had become the second-largest paper in the country, with a circulation topped only by *The Wall Street Journal*. Although Neuharth had predicted that *USA Today* would quickly turn a profit, it took about five years to move into profitability, with *USA Today* losing an estimated $600 million during its first decade. By 1993, however, profits were approximately $5 million. One year later profits doubled to about $10 million.

During its early growth, the paper unearthed a class of newspaper reader few others had stumbled upon: the business traveler. Airline deregulation had led to a large general price decline for airline tickets, inducing a swell in business travel. On-the-road business travelers wished to keep abreast of both world and national news as well as what was going on in their home state and how their local sports teams were doing. *USA Today* rushed in to fill the void; but in doing so quickly entered direct competition with *The Wall Street Journal*. By this time, hard-line newspapers, including *The New York Times*, began adding color; shorter, more tightly written stories; and beefed-up circulation campaigns to compete with "The Nation's Newspaper." *The Wall Street Journal* followed suit by introducing two new sections—Money & Investing and

Marketplace—to broaden the paper's coverage of media, marketing, technology, and personal investing. In the face of this competition, as well as an awareness of changing reader needs, *USA Today* responded through innovation of its own.

Product Innovation   To stay ahead of the imitative competition, *USA Today* decided to become a more serious newspaper with improved journalism. The shift from primarily soft news to hard news began with the space shuttle Challenger disaster in 1986. By 1991, editors began focusing much more sharply on hard news rather than soft features, and by 1994 under president and publisher Tom Curley, there was a massive drive to upgrade the paper to be a more serious, more responsible news-oriented product.

Gannett also incorporated less traditional value-added features to keep readers interested. The paper added 1-800 and 1-900 "hot-line" numbers that readers could call for expert information on financial planning, college admissions, minority business development, taxes, and other subjects. Thousands of readers responded to reader-opinion polls and write-in surveys on political and current event issues. Editorial pages were also redesigned to provide more room for guest columnists and to encourage debate. Gannett also initiated a high school "Academic All Star" program that was later expanded to include colleges and universities. The increasing ubiquity of the Internet in the late 1990s also resulted in some changes in content. For instance, the Money section began to focus more on technology issues and to look at business through an ecommerce perspective.

The first major redesign in *USA Today*'s history occurred in 2000 as the paper moved from a 54-inch to a 50-inch width. The goal of the redesign was to make the paper easier to read and cleaner in design. The pages were slimmer and hence easier to handle, especially in tight spaces like airplanes, trains, buses, and subways, and the paper fit more readily into briefcases as Gannett had learned from focus groups.

Promotional Innovation   *USA Today* also innovated in its promotional activities. Historically, the paper had limited its promotion to outdoor advertising and television. However, in the late 1980s Neuharth undertook a "BusCapade" promotion tour, traveling to all 50 states to talk with people about *USA Today*. Neuharth succeeded in raising public awareness of his paper, which was credited for *USA Today*'s move into profitability. Encouraged by his success, Neuharth forged ahead with a "JetCapade" campaign where he and a small news team traveled to 30 countries in seven months, stimulating global demand for the paper. During a visit to the troops of Operation Desert Storm in the Persian Gulf in 1991, General Norman Schwarzkopf expressed a need for news from home. *USA Today* arranged for delivery of 18,000 copies per day. The overseas success of *USA Today* led to the publication of *USA Today International*, which is now available in more than 60 countries in Western Europe, the Middle East, North Africa, and Asia.

Early on, *USA Today* faced a challenge in selling ad space to advertisers because they were not convinced that it would pay to advertise in the paper. Gannett's first strategy for enlisting advertisers was the Partnership Plan, which provided six months of free space to those who purchased six months of paid advertising. *USA Today* also began to accept regional advertising across a wide variety of categories such as travel, retail, tourism, and economic development. Color advertisements could arrive as late as 6:00 PM the day before publication, giving local advertisers increased flexibility. The paper also moved aggressively into "blue-chip circulation," where bulk quantities of *USA Today* are sold at discounted prices to hotels, airlines, and restaurants, and are provided free of charge to customers. Today, over 500,000 copies of *USA Today* are distributed through blue-chip circulation every day.

USA Today pulled off another promotional first in 1999 when it broke one of the most sacred practices of daily newspapers and began offering advertising space on the front page (one-inch strips across the entire width of the bottom of the page). This highly sought after front-page position was sold through one-year contracts for $1 to $1.2 million each, with each advertiser taking one day a week. As *USA Today* continued to prosper, advertisers became quite attracted to the paper's large volume of readers. To help cope with advertiser demand, the paper implemented the necessary technology to allow advertisers to transmit copy electronically 24 hours per day.

Distribution Innovation   Fast delivery has always been important to *USA Today*. By the late-1990s, the paper was earning kudos for its ability to deliver timely news, thanks to its late deadlines. For instance, in many parts of the country *USA Today* could print later sports scores than local or regional papers. In hard news, *USA Today* was able to offer more up-to-date coverage by rolling the presses over four hours earlier than *The Wall Street Journal* and almost three hours later than *The New York Times*. The paper added print sites around the world in a move to further speed up distribution. An innovative readership program was also added that brought *USA Today* to more than 160 college campuses around the nation. Likewise, technological advances allowed the paper's production to become totally digital. A new computer-to-plate technology was implemented to give newsrooms later deadlines and readers earlier delivery times.

USA Today Moves Online

A decade after *USA Today*'s launch, Gannett found itself in the enviable position of owning one of America's most successful newspapers. *USA Today* was the most widely read newspaper in the country, with daily readership of over 3.7 million (readership numbers are higher than paid circulation numbers due to the passing of copies to other readers). In an era when nearly all major national media were suffering declines in readership or viewing audience, *USA Today* continued to grow. Rising distribution and promotion costs, however, were beginning to make the newspaper slightly un-profitable. To reverse this trend, *USA Today* created several spin-offs, including its first special interest publication, *Baseball Weekly*. During its first month of operation, *Baseball Weekly*'s circulation reached 250,000 copies. *Baseball Weekly* was eventually expanded to include a variety of sports coverage and was renamed *Sports Weekly*. At the end of 2007, *Sports Weekly* was ranked the highest sports magazine in newsstand sales. Due to the success of the *Sports Weekly* format, *USA Today* launched a similar magazine in March 2009. *USA Today*'s *Open Air* magazine was geared toward the "busy, well-informed, affluent customer" and designed to inspire "millions of readers to find adventure and its rewards in their everyday lives." According to *USA Today*, "*Open Air* offers a compelling new look at the possibilities for adventure that surround us each day—from regular activities like improving your golf game with a stretch the pros use, or finding the best gear for your next softball tournament, to once-in-a-lifetime opportunities like a six-day hike into the spectacular Rio Grande Gorge in New Mexico." However, rather than marketing the publication as a stand-alone product, *Open Air* was used to increase demand in the print sector and made available four times a year in Friday editions of *USA Today*. Also, venturing into news media, *USA Today* joined with CNN to produce a football TV program and launched Sky-Radio to provide live radio on commercial airline flights.

The major spin-off, in terms of current success and future potential, was *USA Today Online*, which the company introduced on April 17, 1995. The online version was seen as a natural companion to the print version of *USA Today*, given the paper's worldwide distribution. The first version was available through CompuServe's Mosaic browser and required special software, a CompuServe Network connection, and a monthly subscription of $14.95 plus $3.95 per hour. By June of 1995, *USA Today Online* converted to a free service that worked with any web browser and Internet service provider. The "online" was later dropped in favor of *USAToday*.com.

Like its print sister, *USAToday*.com is bright, upbeat, and full of nugget-sized news stories. The online version allows readers to receive up-to-the-moment news that incorporates colorful visuals and crisp audio. It provides one of the most extensive sites on the Internet, featuring thousands of pages of up-to-the-minute news, sports, business and technology news, four-day weather forecasts, and travel information available 24 hours a day, seven days a week.

Another revenue generator, launched in 1998 in response to frequent reader requests for archived material, was the pay-per-view archives service (http://archives.usatoday.com). The *USA Today* Archives section allows readers to do a free, unlimited search of the paper's articles that have appeared since April 1987. Articles may be downloaded for $3.95 per story or as a part of the site's monthly and yearly service plans.

Because *USA Today* is not an operation that rests on its laurels, the website has been updated several times. A number of partnerships have been added to the site in the areas of online classifieds and a marketplace where users can purchase a variety of goods and services. The company added a companion travel site in 2002.

USA Today Moves to On-Demand News and Information

As part of the Internet explosion that began in the early 2000s, *USAToday*.com has evolved from an online news media source to an on-demand, information-rich community. This movement toward online media was a result of rising newsprint costs, which, in fact, forced virtually all newspaper firms to add online news as a means to increase readership and cut distribution expenses. In addition, to align with the advancing pace of communication and technology, new CEO Craig Dubow announced his commitment to "getting news and information into the hands of consumers faster than ever before." To aid the company in this initiative, *USAToday*.com added blogs,

RSS (really simple syndication), and podcasting to ensure that its news stayed relevant to busy and mobile readers. Gannett also purchased interest in a company with unique technology that aggregated news on the Internet and categorized the information into 300,000 topics. This technology also had the ability to sort information by zip code. Other acquisitions included PointRoll, a service that allowed Internet advertisers to expand their online space. One innovative way Gannett leveraged this service was to provide local advertisers with a means to direct consumers to local merchants. As a web user rolled the cursor over an ad, the ad expanded, revealing information about the closest retailer.

Also, in an effort to become the one-stop shop for all types of information, *USAToday*.com began providing readers and site visitors with the opportunity to search for their unique interests and connect with other like-minded individuals. For instance, in the first quarter of 2008, *USAToday*.com introduced "Network Journalism," a site that combines professionally created content from *USA Today* writers with consumer-generated content, comments, and recommendations, as well as instant message news alerts and advanced search functions. In addition, the website launched nearly 200,000 unique online topics pages available via links threaded in the story pages or through a stand-alone topics section. According to Jeff Webber, publisher of *USAToday*.com, "*USA Today* has always focused on what America is talking about and provides the content that fuels the nation's conversation. Our new topics pages go in-depth into subjects ranging from Sarah Palin to Starbucks; Barack Obama to Bono; and American Idol to the iPhone, all the things that make America tick." The topics page categories include Brands; Culture; Events and Awards; Health and Wellness; Legislation and Acts; Natural and Physical Sciences; Organizations; People; Places, Geography; and Religion and beliefs.

To literally execute Dubow's vision of "getting news and information into the hands of consumers faster than ever before," *USAToday*.com capitalized on the emerging trend of portable technology and information by launching multiple applications through Apple's App Store. Available via a free download from Apple's iTunes Store, the *USA Today* for iPhone application provides readers access to the latest news stories, weather, photos and interactive polls. News, Money, Sports, Life, Tech, and Travel articles can be shared via e-mail, text message, Facebook, or Twitter, and are automatically saved for later reading. In addition, *USA Today* also partnered with Hampton Hotels to offer the AutoPilot application, targeting its business and travel consumer groups. The AutoPilot app offers users the ability to easily track trip and flight itineraries, utilize GPS capabilities in real time, get "up to the minute delay information for more that 16,000 airports, 1,400 airlines and 100,000 daily flights," monitor departing and arriving flight information, access a comprehensive directory and obtain current and future weather conditions. For the business traveler community, an online community was also made available with discussion forums, polls, and other interactive content. Even now, *USAToday*.com's online community groups are continuously expanding, with forums targeting individuals interested in MMA (Mixed Martial Arts), automotives ("Open Road"), and video gaming. Other strategies to expand its image as an all-encompassing portable information source included expansion into downloadable media via the Amazon Kindle. The Kindle is a portable e-reader that wirelessly downloads books, blogs, magazines, and newspapers to a crisp, high-resolution electronic paper display that looks and reads like real paper. For a monthly subscription cost of $11.99, Kindle users can have *USA Today* content delivered each weekday.

Brand Extensions

In 2008, *USA Today* began to look beyond the scope of daily news media and ventured into brand extensions by way of retail locations and television. As an attempt to capture more share of customer (rather than market share), *USA Today* opened three *USA Today* Travel Zone retail locations in airport terminals in late 2008. These retail shops carry all products travelers expect to find, including reading materials, sundries, travel accessories, and other convenience items. To align with the current look and feel of the paper its customers recognize, sections of the store are clearly identified and utilize colors representing *USA Today's* signature sections: News (blue), Money (green), Sports (red), and Life (purple).

Also in 2008, the company launched *USA Today Live*—a television service designed to extend the company's reach beyond current concentrated efforts and target business professionals and travelers. By partnering with Fuse, the national music television network, Versus, and MOJO HD on a variety of series-based programming, *USA Today Live* has introduced new audiences to the *USA Today* brand. The programming partnerships included: "City Limits Fishing," a six-part weekly series on Versus that highlighted places where anglers regularly catch limits of fish in not so far-off, exotic destinations; "10 Great Reasons," an eight-part weekly series on Fuse designed to "pay tribute to acts, genres, rumors and stories about our musical guilty pleasures and why we love them so, but may be just a tad embarrassed to admit;" as well as "Gotta Get Gold," a 10-part series on MOJO HD that focused on what it takes to train and to compete at the highest levels in athletics.

USA Today—Today and Tomorrow

In looking at the total national newspaper market, *USA Today* has been quite successful. It has seen more than 25 years of continuous growth and is the most widely read newspaper in the United States. The paper's total network audience, comprised of *USA Today* print readers and visitors to *USA Today*.com, is nearly 10 million adults. According to David Hunke, president and publisher of *USA Today*, "The most recent numbers ... show that more people are choosing to read *USA Today* more than any other newspaper in the country, with 414,000 more print readers per day than our nearest competitor *The Wall Street Journal*, and 817,000 more print readers than *The New York Times*." On the online front, *USA Today*.com reported more than 11.9 million unique visitors in April 2009, a 12 percent year-over-year increase. According to *USA Today*, internal data reveal page view increases to *USA Today*.com were driven by an increase in users sharing and consuming content via social media tools like Twitter, Facebook, MySpace, and Yahoo Buzz.

Despite positive reports on the online front, this success has occurred during a time when overall newspaper sales, advertising revenue, and readership are declining. *USA Today* has recently faced a reported 14.3 percent decline in publishing advertising revenues, a 20 percent drop in classified advertising revenues, and, even more damaging, an 18.4 percent decrease in paid ad pages. Operationally, combining these declines with sharp increases in newsprint costs, which caused *USA Today* to increase its single-copy price to $1.00 from 75 cents, results in a slippery slope for "The Nation's Newspaper." In fact, in late 2009, the Audit Bureau of Circulations reported declines in circulation for 24 of the top 25 newspapers in the United States. *The Wall Street Journal*, which managed a 0.6 percent gain, was the only exception. *USA Today* reported a 17 percent drop in circulation, partly due to the slump in tourism during the economic recession, and cutbacks by several hotels no longer offering free newspapers to guests. Consequently, when the final circulation figures were released in late 2009, *The Wall Street Journal* had eclipsed *USA Today* as the country's largest newspaper by weekday circulation.

In addition to declines in print media, *USA Today* also faces fierce competition in online information distribution through television and magazine sites, blogs, and podcasts. And, Internet-based companies, like Yahoo! and Google, have now moved into the advertising market. The multitude of choices for both consumers and advertisers means that *USA Today* will have to work harder at innovation, finding a way to differentiate its products from the sea of competition. This will be a challenging task given the continuing decline in newspaper readership and the growing consumer demand for free online news.

As *USA Today* looks ahead, a number of issues must be considered. The following sections describe some of the key issues that the company must face as it plans for its future.

USA Today's Customers

The overwhelming majority of *USA Today*'s circulation is within the United States. The readers of the print version are 70 percent male and 30 percent female, with an average age of 47 and an average income of $76,073. The readers of the online site are 54 percent male and 46 percent female, and are more educated than its print readers. Most *USA Today* readers work in middle-to upper-management positions and are often purchasing decision makers for their offices and households, as well as technological junkies and sports fans. They also participate in a wide range of leisure activities. Eighty-six percent of print and online readers combined own a computer, and most of those have Internet access. Seventy-five percent of readers participate in sports and are active sports fans. Three-fourths of *USA Today* readers have active lives that include attending movies and domestic and foreign travel.

Important players in the purchase process are subscribers, single-copy buyers, and third-party sponsors, often referred to as blue-chip buyers. Eighty percent of *USA Today*'s purchasers are also users and they bear the financial responsibility for the product. These consumers also share their papers with family and friends, which increases readership. Twenty percent of paid copies are purchased by third parties, which distribute complimentary copies to the end user to add value to their own goods or services. For example, hotels, restaurants, banks, and other service organizations offer customers the opportunity to enjoy a copy of *USA Today* during breakfast or while waiting in the lobby. Newspapers purchased at coin-operated vending machines do not always have associated complementary products.

Paid editions of *USA Today* are currently distributed via newsstand retailers, large grocery store chains, bookstores, coin-operated vending machines, and directly to the consumer through home delivery. Home delivery customers are the newspaper's most loyal customers and are most likely to buy daily delivery at 13- to 52-week intervals. Single copy buyers tend to purchase the paper out of daily routine (heavy users) or on occasion based on specific newsworthy events (light users). Complimentary distribution of *USA Today* occurs primarily in hotels, airport terminals, restaurants, and at college campuses across the U.S. *USA Today* content is also available in electronic formats from *USAToday*.com, mobile phone access, and e-mail updates. The availability of *USA Today* via electronic distribution is a deterrent for some consumers to purchasing the print product. Currently, however, customers are unable to receive updated news in real time unless they have access to an RSS-enabled mobile device.

Competition

Gannett has competitors from several fields, including other national newspapers, such as *The Wall Street Journal* and *The New York Times*, cable networks, nationally syndicated terrestrial and satellite radio, such as Sirius/XM, and Internet sites such as Yahoo!, Google, and AOL.

The Wall Street Journal   One of *USA Today*'s biggest newspaper competitors is *The Wall Street Journal*, owned by Dow Jones & Co. Inc. The company's product lines include newspapers, newswires, magazines, websites, indexes, television, and radio. The *Journal's* website, www.wsj.com, adds over 1,000 news stories per day and includes price information on over 30,000 stocks and funds worldwide. *The Wall Street Journal* has strategic alliances with other information companies, including CNBC, Reuters, and SmartMoney.

Circulation for *The Wall Street Journal* print version is 2 million, whereas wsj.com receives 175,000 unique visitors per day and has 768,000 paid subscriptions. It is interesting to note that *The Wall Street Journal* is the only newspaper to require a subscription to view its online content. *The Wall Street Journal* targets influential business readers as its primary audience. Sixty percent of the print newspaper's readers and 54 percent of its online readers are employed as top management. The average household income is $191,000 and net worth is $2.1 million. Net worth for online readers is $1.6 million. The company charges a subscription fee of $119 per year for the print version and $103 per year for its online content. This paper also offers a bundled package with both print and online content for $140 per year. Single copies of the weekday print version cost $1 and the weekend print version costs $1.50.

Dow Jones has made several improvements to the *Journal* in an attempt to make it more competitive. It added a Weekend Edition in 2005, designed to help advertisers reach the paper's audience at home on the weekends. Some new plans for improvement include reformatting the paper to a 48-inch width and changing the navigational format and content of the print version. The change is expected to reduce operating expenses by $18 million per year. *The Wall Street Journal* has already launched changes in their international version. The international print edition has become more compact and includes stronger links to the website. They expect these changes to improve profits by $17 million per year. *The Wall Street Journal* is also planning to add advertisements to its front page. *USA Today* was criticized for doing this in the past, but this practice is becoming more common as newspapers look for ways to increase revenue. As stated previously, *The Wall Street Journal* was the only top-25 newspaper to see a positive gain in circulation for 2009.

The New York Times   In addition to *The New York Times*, the New York Times Co. owns other newspapers and related websites, two New York City radio stations, nine television stations serving seven states, and search engine About.com, which they acquired in 2005 for $410 million. *The New York Times* is available at 60,000 newsstands and retailers and 4,000 Starbucks coffee shops.

Circulation for *The New York Times* is 1 million, while the website, www.nytimes.com, enjoys 1.3 million unique visitors per day and 10.8 million registered users. The newspaper's target market is the intellectual elite. As explained in their press kit, "*The New York Times*—Influential people read it because influential people read it." The average household income is $88,523. For circulation within New York, *The New York Times* costs $304.20 per year for the seven-day paper, $161.20 per year for the weekday paper, or $197.60 the weekend paper. Outside of New York, the paper costs $384.80 per year for the seven-day paper, $192.40 per year for the weekday paper, or $270.40 per year for the weekend paper. *The New York Times'* online content is free although it requires a registration. Online users can also acquire extra content, including access to the archives, through its electronic version, which is $87.95 per year Monday through Friday, or $174.95 per year for seven-day access. The price of a single copy of the print version is $1.

The company has recently made changes in an attempt to be more profitable. *The New York Times* raised its home-delivery rates by 4 percent and reduced the number of pages in its stock section, a combination that is expected to boost the bottom line by roughly $10 million per year. Additionally, the paper has also begun to implement cost-saving policies, including staff reductions, which is expected to reduce costs by $45 million per year. And, they have decided to follow the examples of other newspapers by making plans to reduce the width of its print version.

Other Media Competitors   *USA Today* also faces competition for audience attention and advertising dollars from companies outside its industry, including television, radio, and Internet providers. As shown in Case Exhibit 11.2, newspapers fare poorly in terms of daily media consumption when compared to other media options.

Internet information providers are another source of competition for *USA Today*. A billion people globally have access to the Internet either at home or at work. Most Internet information providers make their money through subscriptions, advertising,

CASE EXHIBIT 11.2

U.S. ADULT MEDIA USAGE BY AGE

	Echo Boomers (ages 18–27)	Gen X (ages 28–39)	Baby Boomers (ages 40–58)	Matures (ages 59+)
Watch local broadcast news	52	69	83	88
Watch network broadcast or cable news	51	57	74	88
Read a local daily newspaper	43	49	66	80
Go online to get news	53	68	70	57
Listen to radio news broadcasts	26	49	64	58
Listen to talk radio stations	24	35	40	41
Read a national newspaper (*The Wall Street Journal, USA Today, The New York Times,* etc.)	15	23	19	17
Listen to satellite radio programming	21	23	19	16

Numbers reflect the percentage of adults saying that they use a particular medium "daily" or "several times a week."

Source: "Seven in 10 U.S. Adults Say They Watch Broadcast News at Least Several Times a Week," Harris Interactive, February 24, 2006 (http://www.harrisinteractive.com/harris_poll/index.asp?PID=644), accessed October 18, 2009.

or both. It is important to note that the Internet as a communications and advertising medium is no longer tied to desktop computers. Virtually all major Internet providers and content developers now make their content available via handheld devices, including *USA Today*.

Economic Woes

Higher newsprint costs, a shaky advertising environment, and declining circulation have been plaguing the newspaper industry. The high cost of newsprint is a constant problem for newspapers; however, the industry has been able to cut costs through the increased use of recycled fiber. With respect to advertising, newspapers have been struggling in the midst of an economic recession that has triggered a soft ad market, particularly in the automotive, retail, and employment sectors. In fact, 2008 was the worst year ever for the U.S. newspaper industry. Total ad revenues were down 16.6 percent or $7.5 billion. Classified advertising, down 29.7 percent, took the brunt of the decline. Print advertising was down 17.7 percent, while online advertising was down 1.8 percent. To make matters worse, the pace of the decline in newspaper advertising is accelerating: from a decline of 7.4 percent in late 2007 to a decline of 19.7 percent by late 2009. In response, many newspapers have been forced to close, while others have cut staff.

Changing Technology

Technology is central to the future of the newspaper industry because of the changes it has brought in the way consumers are able to seek out timely and relevant news and information. Technological advancements offer interested consumers more options than ever to access news and news coverage, and this has led to a marked decline in newspaper circulation as people use the Internet and other means to get timely news and information. Not only has technology given consumers more options, but it has also provided consumers the ability to customize the news they receive at a level they were never able to do before.

Delivering news via the latest wireless devices is perhaps the most threatening alternative to newsprint. However, these devices are also an opportunity for *USA Today* to maintain its readership. Wireless handheld devices, such as the Blackberry, iPhone, and a growing list of smartphones, are increasingly being used to deliver news coverage in specific content areas, such as stock reports and sports scores. For example, *USA Today* and Gannett have developed partnerships with such companies as MobileVoiceControl, Inc., to allow those who have Blackberries to enjoy natural voice access to *USA Today*'s news content. The partnership allows *USA Today* to give Blackberry users the ability to search and receive continuously updated and customizable coverage in news, finances, sports, and even weather by merely pressing a button and speaking a command. The company's iPhone apps—*USA Today* and AutoPilot—are other ways that *USA Today* has reached out to mobile consumers. *USA Today* clearly recognizes the need to transition from print to wireless, and Gannett has begun to do just that in partnering with companies on the leading edge of wireless technology.

Other information distribution technologies are on the horizon. One of the most promising is electronic paper or e-paper. E-papers are flexible digital screens that are similar to newsprint with respect to thickness, rolling/curling ability, and portability. Unlike newspapers, however, e-papers are reusable in that users can download up-to-date information to them via wireless technology. The technology is already being used for electronic poster advertisements in stores. One example of this type of technology is the Amazon Kindle, which *USA Today* has already recognized. Smaller, lighter and more portable devices with advances in readability and reduced costs are expected to evolve from this innovation.

Overall, advancing technology may have initiated the decline of the newspaper industry. However, technology is also likely to be the industry's savior. Technology allows *USA Today* and other newspapers to deliver news in more cost-efficient, customizable, and useful ways than will ever be possible using newsprint.

Cultural Shifts

As many in the industry are aware, newspaper readership stands to lose a great deal due to changing demographics. The Newspaper Association of America notes that newspaper readership is strongest among adults ages 59 and older as 70 percent of this group reads a newspaper daily. Within other mature age groups, specifically those constituting Baby Boomers such as adults ages 40 to 58, only 50 to 60 percent read a newspaper daily. These figures support the contention that newspapers will lose readers at an alarming rate as this segment of the population ages over the next 10 to 30 years. To offset this trend, newspapers are attempting to attract and cater to new and younger readers. The transition is a difficult one, however, as there is a significant difference between the interests of current newspaper readers and the younger demographic newspapers hope to gain. Baby Boomers are most interested in major news stories and local news coverage. Younger readers, however, are more interested in sports (mainly males) and entertainment coverage along with comics.

Addressing this concern and hoping to boost readership among younger generations, *USA Today* now includes in its online version a blog entitled "Pop Candy" where readers can exchange information and opinions about aspects of pop culture such as music and celebrities. Also, *USA Today* plans to include excerpts from its "On Deadline" blog in the print edition. One part of the blog, "Looking Ahead," will serve in print as a guide to upcoming events, while another will round up other outlets' news coverage in true blog fashion.

Evolving to Meet the Future

Although increasing digital options for news and information have some industry observers bemoaning the death of newspapers, some feel that newspapers do have a bright future and will thrive if they develop a healthy online presence and adapt to evolving media consumption patterns. On the other side, rising costs and declining readership have caused several newspapers to adapt to an online-only news format and forego the printed edition completely. In fact, an article in the print edition of *USA Today* titled "Newspaper closings raise fears about industry" states that during 2009, numerous newspapers have closed shop or reduced publication days, cut thousands of employee positions, and reduced salaries of those who remained. In the face of continual competition in both offline and online markets, the future of *USA Today* depends on its ability to continually push the envelope of innovation and marketing strategy. To remain successful, *USA Today* must continue to use a value-added strategy that can further enhance distribution of its proprietary content and ensure continued differentiation with respect to the competition.

Questions for Discussion

1. What opportunities in the marketing environment did Gannett seize in launching *USA Today*? How did the company learn about and respond to these opportunities? Answer these same questions for *USAToday*.com.

2. How has a continuous strategy of marketing innovation proved successful for *USA Today* and *USAToday*.com? Do you believe that *USA Today* is well positioned for the future? Explain.

3. What are the SWOT implications for *USA Today* as it looks toward its future? What strengths and opportunities can *USA Today* leverage as it looks for a competitive advantage in the distribution of news and information?

4. Based on *USA Today*'s experiences with print and online news, evaluate the long-term potential of printed news and the newspaper publishing industry. Do you believe printed newspapers will continue to survive despite digital competition?

Sources

The facts of this case are from Tim Arango, "Drop in Newspaper Circulation Accelerates," NYTimes.com. April 27, 2009 (http://www.nytimes.com/2009/04/28/business/media/28paper.html?_r=2); Steven Anderson, Director of Communications, *USA Today*, personal interview, August 5, 2003; *Bob Coen's Insider's Report*, Universal McCann, June 2006 (http://www.mccann.com/news/pdfs/Insiders6_06.pdf); R. Curtis, "Introducing Your New *USA Today*," *USA Today*, April 3, 2000, 27A; "Deadline," *Fortune*, July 8, 2002, pp. 78–86; Dow Jones, Inc. Fact Sheet (http://www.dj.com/djcom/FactSheets/DowJones.htm), accessed October 19, 2009; "Electronic Paper," *Wikipedia* (http://en.wikipedia.org/wiki/Electronic_paper), accessed October 19, 2009; Gannett Company, Inc., 2008 Annual Report (http://media.corporate-ir.net/media_files/irol/84/84662/08GCIAnnualReport.pdf), accessed October 19, 2009; "Gannett Hits Heights in Print but Falls Short of TV Stardom," *Campaign*, January 17, 1997, 24; Peter Johnson, "Internet News Supplements Papers, TV," *USA Today*, July 31, 2006, p. 5D; K. Jurgensen, "Quick Response; Paper Chase: *USA Today* Editor Sees Shifts in How Information is Generated and Delivered to Readers," *Advertising Age*, February 14, 2000, p. S6; K. Jurgensen, "*USA Today's* New Look Designed for Readers," *USA Today*, April 3, 2000, p. 1A; Kenneth Li, "E-newspapers Just Around the Corner. Really," *Newswatch India*, June 12, 2006 (http://www.newswatch.in/?p=5032); P. Long, "After Long Career, *USA Today* Founder Al Neuharth Is Ready for More," *Knight-Ridder/Tribune Business News*, April 28, 1999; "Media Trends Track," Television Bureau of Advertising (http://www.tvb.org/mediacomparisons/02_A_Consumers_Continue.asp?mod=R), accessed September 1, 2006; J. McCartney, "*USA Today* Grows Up," *American Journalism Review*, September 1997, 19; Douglas McIntyre, "*USA Today* Ad Revenue in Free Fall, a Nightmare for the Future of Print," BloggingStocks.com, June 18, 2008 (http://www.bloggingstocks.com/2008/06/18/usa-today-ad-revenue-in-free-fall-a-nightmare-for-the-future-of); B. Miller, "*USA Today*, Gannett to Launch *USA Today Live*," *Television & Cable*, February 8, 2000; "Newspaper Closings Raise Fears About Industry," USAToday.com, March 19, 2009 (http://www.usatoday.com/money/media/2009-03-17-newspapers-downturn_N.htm); New York Times Revenue and Circulation Data, New York Times, Inc. (http://www.nytco.com/excel/1208adrev/ad-circ-other-rev.xls), accessed October 19, 2009; Shira Ovide, "USA Today Likely to Fall To No. 2 in Circulation," Wall Street Journal.com, October 10, 2009 (http://online.wsj.com/article/SB125513318195777441.html); Eric Sass, "Newspaper Revenues Plunge 28% in Q1, Online Falling Too," MediaDaily News.com. May 28, 2009 (http://www.mediapost.com/publications/?fa=Articles.showArticle&art_aid=106948); Erick Schonfeld, "The Wounded U.S. Newspaper Industry Lost $7.5 Billion in Advertising Revenues Last Year," *TechCrunch*, March 29, 2009 (http://www.techcrunch.com/2009/03/29/the-wounded-us-newspaper-industry-lost-75-billion-in-advertising-revenues-last-year/), accessed October 18, 2009; M. L. Stein, "Don't Sweat the Internet Says *USA Today's* Curley," *Editor & Publisher*, August 22, 1998, p. 40; M. Stone, "*USA Today Online* Listens to Its Logs," *Editor & Publisher*, August 7, 1999, p. 66; J. Strupp, "*USA Today* Ads Go Page

One," *Editor & Publisher*, May 8, 1999, p. 40; "*USA Today* and Gannett Partner with MobileVoiceControl to Bring Voice-Driven Mobile Search to Blackberry," TMCnet, May 23, 2006 (http://www.tmcnet.com/usubmit/2006/05/23/1658295.htm); "*USA Today* Launches New Life Section Friday Format," *PR Newswire*, March 16, 1998, p. 316; "*USA Today* Launches Online Classifieds Area and 17 New Marketplace Partnerships," *Business Wire*, April 15, 1997; "*USA Today* Launches Pay-per-View Archives Service," *Business Wire*, January 5, 1998; "*USA Today* No Longer a Newspaper," *Advertising Age*, September 9, 2002, p. 18; "*USA Today Online* Launches Real Time Survey System," *Business Wire*, February 18, 1998; USA Today Press Kit: Audience (http://www.usatoday.com/marketing/media_kit/pressroom/audience.html), accessed October 19, 2009; USA Today Press Kit: USA Today (http://www.usatoday .com/marketing/media_kit/pressroom/press_kit_usat.html), accessed October 19, 2009; USA Today Press Kit: USAToday.com (http://www.usatoday.com/marketing/ media_kit/pressroom/press_kit_usatcom.html), accessed October 19, 2009; "*USA Today* Sells Page One Advertising Space," *PR Newswire*, May 5, 1999, p. 351; *USA Today*, "Snapshot," August 22, 2006, p. 1; I. Wada, "*USA Today* Marketplace Signs Up Six for On-line Services," *Travel Weekly*, April 28, 1997, p. 44; and Andrew Vanacore, "USA Today to Post 17 Percent Drop in Circulation," *BusinessWeek Online*, October 9, 2009 (http://www.businessweek.com/ap/financialnews/D9B7OR2O0.htm), accessed October 18, 2009.

Hottie Hawg's Smokin' BBQ Embraces its Future

Synopsis: Hottie Hawg's BBQ faces an interesting challenge. After initial success and recognition as a BBQ caterer in the Southeast, including becoming a NASCAR sponsor, the company is presented with an opportunity to be the official BBQ vendor at the Pepsi Center in Denver, Colorado. The Pepsi Center easily hosts over 100 events per year, including the NBA, NHL, concerts, and monster truck rallies. In addition to the opportunity to feed an average crowd of 16,000 per event, Hottie Hawg's also stands to gain tremendous exposure that could lead to additional licensing agreements and potentially the opening of Hottie Hawg's restaurants. Although most fledgling companies would jump at such an opportunity, the Atlanta-based company is hesitant given its current cash flow, the required up-front investment costs, and its limited experience. CEO Kyle Vaughn must make a decision that will affect the current and future operations of the company he founded less than one year ago.

Themes: Entrepreneurship, partnerships, brand licensing, product strategy, brand strategy, target marketing, positioning, strategic focus, customer relationships

The Creation of Hottie Hawg's

Hottie Hawg's Smokin' BBQ, Inc., began in 2008 as the brainchild of long-time friends Eric Rybka and Kyle Vaughn. Rybka had been in the catering business for over 25 years and was already operating a successful organization. Vaughn, a charismatic entrepreneur, had been a successful businessman for more than 20 years with Auto Claim Technology (ACT), a paint overspray removal company. Although Rybka was the food service professional, he was very impressed with Vaughn's grilling techniques and the creativity he incorporated with his meat preparation—a skill Vaughn picked up in Dallas, Texas, where he was raised. Also, very aware of the weak state of the U.S. economy, Rybka was looking to invest in a more basic catering concept with simpler food versus the cuisine his current business offered.

Jessie Lee, Hottie Hawg's Smokin' BBQ, Inc., prepared this case for classroom discussion rather than to illustrate effective or ineffective handling of an administrative situation.

When Rybka initially approached Vaughn about a partnership, there were no numbers or facts given—just a casual suggestion that the two should become partners in a new catering business. When Vaughn later asked Rybka about the suggestion, Rybka explained his idea of a barbecue catering service using Vaughn's Texas-style barbecuing talents. Vaughn concurred with the idea, trusting Rybka's experience and success within the industry. Shortly after, Rybka told Vaughn about a kitchen and smoker on wheels made by Viking that would outfit the operation perfectly. In late August 2008, much to Vaughn's surprise and only one week after their conversation, the open-air kitchen on wheels appeared being pulled by a new Ford F-250. Their partnership agreement was simple: Rybka would provide the technical knowledge and support of the operation, while Vaughn would use his recipes and essentially create the brand image. Vaughn was literally given a clean slate of a white trailer and truck to create a brand for a company that did not yet have a name.

The one thing Rybka and Vaughn knew immediately was that they wanted to incorporate women into the brand concept and do for BBQ what Hooter's had done for wings. They decided that attractive waitresses would serve barbecue at events and parties from the outdoor kitchen on wheels. The concept also resonated with Rybka's concerns over the dismal economy and the basic idea that the company needed an aggressive approach to be successful. Rybka's initial vision was to be extreme and offensive to purposely alienate a large portion of the population. His idea was to create enough negative publicity to make the brand infamous, and then slowly morph the brand to be politically correct enough to be mainstream. Hopefully, by the time this would happen, everyone would know of the new BBQ company.

Names were bounced around, and Vaughn even created a contest among his friends and family to name the company; however, nothing clicked. Finally, one night when Vaughn could not sleep, it hit him—Hottie Hawg's Smokin' BBQ. Once he had the name, Vaughn immediately went to his sister and brother-in-law, who work in marketing and web design, respectively, to create a logo. After an intense brainstorming session, Vaughn's brother-in-law came back with a seductive blonde pig in a strapless red dress and a come hither look. It fit perfectly. The rig, now affectionately named the "The 18 Squeeler," and the truck, "Boss Hawg," were wrapped with graphics of the sexy pig logo and flames. With that, the brand image of Hottie Hawg's was born. Instead of the rustic-wood look of virtually every other barbecue company on the market, Hottie Hawg's was modern and sexy—a unique look for its menu.

Vaughn began testing recipes in his home kitchen immediately. With over 20 years of traveling the United States tasting different regional barbecue and reading multiple books on the topic, Vaughn was thoroughly educated in the craft of barbecue sauce. Rybka, being the highly accredited gourmet chef, had created his own ginger spice sauce. Inspired by this unique combination, Vaughn began looking for a distinctive flavor combination of his own. One fateful night in his kitchen, after combining various recipes found on the Internet and substituting random ingredients, Vaughn created Maple Habanero—Hottie Hawg's first sauce. Vaughn invited neighbors and friends over to test the new sauce and slowly perfected it. Shortly afterward, Hot Bastard, a mustard-based sauce was created.

An Unexpected Loss

Everything was progressing smoothly until tragedy struck in February 2009 when Rybka faced an untimely death, leaving Vaughn to run the business by himself. Before Rybka passed, he had become increasingly obsessed with the band Journey and their wildly successful hit "Don't Stop Believin'." After his death, Vaughn adopted the song for himself as a personal inspirational message and incorporated the band and song into every part of the business. Using the Squeeler's flat-screen TVs, Vaughn would play Journey concert footage at events and parties. Vaughn also developed a rub named DSB (Don't Stop Believin') in honor of the band that Rybka loved. Ironically, the song experienced a comeback around this time period and began getting more radio airtime. Vaughn took this as his sign and personal message from Rybka not to give up on the vision the two had shared.

Although Vaughn was experienced in running a business, his primary job had nothing to do with the food or the catering industry. Now he was left with new equipment, the minimal information he had absorbed about the catering business through Rybka, and a determination to make Hottie Hawg's a success—if for no other reason than for his late friend and business partner. He knew he had a great concept, fantastic brand image, and most of all a great product. Now the issue was running an organization where he had no experience and no longer any guidance.

A Tried and True Concept

The concept of utilizing young, attractive women in the food industry is hardly an original business idea. Hooters pioneered the business model of a restaurant being known more for its waitresses than the quality of its food. Like Hottie Hawg's, Hooters is also Atlanta-based, yet started operations in Florida in 1983. The original concept was based around the "Hooters Girl" and ever since the first restaurant in Clearwater, Florida, the uniform and menu have hardly changed. Calendars and pageants have contributed to creating an iconic standing for the Hooters Girl, as she is expected to be on par with legitimate beauty queens. Hooters Girls appear at community events, perform charity work, and are, of course, camera ready at all times. The company promotes a very specific image, which is broken down to recommended shades of lipstick and what highlights are acceptable. This attention to detail has no doubt contributed to the company's success with 450 locations in 43 U.S. states and 26 countries.

Although the idea of selling through sex appeal may not seem family friendly, Hooters considers itself a neighborhood place, not a typical family restaurant. Hooters defends its business concept this way:

> *The element of female sex appeal is prevalent in the restaurants, and the company believes the Hooters Girl is as socially acceptable as a Dallas Cowboy cheerleader, Sports Illustrated swimsuit model, or a Radio City Rockette. Claims that Hooters exploits attractive women are as ridiculous as saying the NFL exploits men who are big and fast. Hooters Girls have the same right to use their*

natural female sex appeal to earn a living as do super models Cindy Crawford and Naomi Campbell. To Hooters, the women's rights movement is important because it guarantees women have the right to choose their own careers, be it a Supreme Court Justice or Hooters Girl.

Hooters does not market to families but acknowledges that families with children comprise 10 percent of the parties that it serves. The company strives to provide the best possible service to any potential customer, but notes that its main demographic includes men between the ages of 25 and 54. Sixty-eight percent of its customers are male. Hooters also enjoys strong merchandising sales, which account for 3 percent of the company's total revenue.

Although Hooters and Hottie Hawg's share the concept of promoting their company image through female sex appeal, Hottie Hawg's chose from the beginning not to start a restaurant through a traditional storefront. The dismal economy during 2008–2010 did not inspire Rybka or Vaughn to be stuck in one location with heavy upfront investment costs. The appeal of the Squeeler was being able to go to the crowds as opposed to waiting for the crowds to come to them. Plus, this way the company would be well-known and have built-in demand if physical restaurants were to be opened at a later time.

Besides Hooters, Hottie Hawg's faces little to no competition. Of course, there are other BBQ companies, but none with Hottie Hawg's sexy, modern image. By all indications, the company has found a niche combining sex appeal and BBQ catering.

The Squeeler Hits the Road

Still mourning the death of his close friend, Vaughn nonetheless proceeded with promoting Hottie Hawg's as planned. The 18 Squeeler's first trip was to Panama City, Florida, for Spring Break. He may not have had any Hotties (i.e., waitresses) yet, but Vaughn played to the Spring Break crowd and created a presence next to the local Coyote Ugly Saloon. He decided not to sell any food on this trip, but instead ran a sampling campaign to create interest and demand for the next event he planned to attend. After the crowds evaporated, Vaughn went back to Atlanta to see to his primary business and start planning the next trip to Panama City.

In late April 2009, he returned to the same spot for the semi-annual Thunder Beach motorcycle rally—this time with Hotties. The rig and girls attracted much attention, and the event most likely would have been profitable had it not been for massive overstaffing and cash mishandling from fly-by-night workers. However, without the crowds it was simply too expensive to keep the Squeeler in Panama City full-time in an attempt to create a semi-permanent location.

Early Growing Pains

The next big event was in May 2009 at Monteagle, Tennessee, for Thunder on the Rock, another biker rally. This time, the Squeeler was set up within a fairground setting instead of the parking lot of a storefront as in Panama City. The event was projected to draw more than 10,000 people and the rig was given a prime location away from other vendors and next to a beer serving station. Learning from his mistakes in Panama City, Vaughn cut staff for the event to only two Pit Masters (cooks) and one returning Hottie from Panama City, Jessie Lee, who was responsible for finding other local girls to work the weekend.

Although the event looked to be an immensely profitable opportunity, it was a flop. Only 3,000–4,000 people actually attended the event, and most of those camped out and prepared their own food in an effort to save money. Hottie Hawg's was left with an enormous amount of wasted food and hardly any revenue. Because having extra food after the event was not anticipated, no measures had been taken to preserve the leftovers, and as a result, hundreds of pounds of meat and other inventory were lost.

In addition, the Hottie image was less than desirable. Lee had relied on Craigslist to hire the additional local girls in an attempt to save on transportation and lodging costs. Because there was no time to meet any of the girls in person, Lee was left to phone interviews, pictures the girls had submitted, and research on social networking sites. The results were far different from what Lee had anticipated. Because of this, the company lost virtually all photo opportunities and did little to promote its "Hottie" image. At this point, Vaughn was beginning to doubt the profitability of big events where he could not guarantee to sell a specific amount of food as he had done in smaller catering events. In addition, the overhead costs of transporting the 18 Squeeler and lodging for employees negated a sizable portion of his profit margin.

Although the Atlanta market was always intended to be a focal point for local catering parties and events, Vaughn now had even more incentive to readdress opportunities in Atlanta. His biggest constraint was the time he spent with his other company, ACT, which was soon to demand more of his attention as it entered into a busy season.

Good Luck and Marketing Genius

At the end of June 2009, one of Vaughn's friends landed the ultimate free advertising spot for Hottie Hawg's: a 7½-minute segment on FOX Atlanta that focused exclusively on Hottie Hawg's the Friday before the Fourth of July Weekend—one of the busiest BBQ holidays throughout the year. The segment was a tremendous opportunity to showcase the rig and focus on the quality of the food. Shortly after the segment aired, NASCAR called Vaughn to ask Hottie Hawg's to sponsor the Terry Labonte/Carter Simo 08 Toyota. Much to Vaughn's surprise and excitement, NASCAR liked the brand image so much that they gave the company a free spot on the rear quarter panel of the 08 car for the upcoming race at Bristol. The company logo in red and black combined with the flames that decorated both the Squeeler and matching truck fit right into NASCAR's image. Later in August at the Atlanta Speedway Race, Hottie Hawg's dominated both sides of the 08 car's quarter panels. Once again, because the brand image was so appealing, Vaughn got a great rate for a spot worth tens of thousands of dollars—less than the cost of an inexpensive television commercial.

Luck was not the only thing Vaughn had going for him. Rybka's initial investment in the flashy wrapped truck and Squeeler gave an impression that Hottie Hawg's was already a big-time success. This image was solidified with professionally produced video segments documenting all of HHBBQ's adventures. These videos were posted on YouTube, while the company's first photo shoot took place with a professional photographer. All of these visual elements—video, photo, the Squeeler, and the Hotties—gave the impression that Hottie Hawg's was not only an established company but also a successful company in great demand. The challenge now was to actually make the profits that the company looked like it was making.

The Billfish Tournament – Success At Last

In July 2009, the 18 Squeeler headed back to Panama City for the Bay Point Invitational Billfish Tournament. Unlike Thunder on the Rock, this event was proven to draw consistent crowds in the range of 5,000 to 6,000 per day over three days. Still reeling from the loss in Monteagle however, Hottie Hawg's had a different goal for Billfish: to sell completely out of product for the first time. Vaughn brought enough food to serve only one-third of the anticipated crowd, and prices were discounted steadily throughout the event until all food had been sold. Despite the discounts, Hottie Hawg's turned a profit for the first time.

Although slightly overstaffed with three Pit Masters, an additional joint-vendor, and two local Hotties, the extra help gave Vaughn time to network and promote the brand further. Hottie Hawg's received even more publicity when Jessie Lee, a Hottie Hawg's Hottie, was awarded the title of "Miss Billfish" at the event. With this, the Hottie image had risen to the pageant level, on par with the traditional Hooters girl. It was also becoming apparent that the Hottie Hawg's brand was growing much more quickly in Panama City than in Atlanta. Although growth in any location would be considered beneficial for a new company, Hottie Hawg's had inadvertently set itself up for regular commutes and high overhead expenses by focusing on a market outside of the local Atlanta area.

Hottie Hawg's Grows Through Brand Licensing

Although the idea of licensing or franchising the Hottie Hawg's concept had always been in the back of Vaughn's mind, he would have never guessed an opportunity would present itself as quickly as it did. On a whim, Vaughn sent a rack of ribs to Todd Seymour, an old high school friend with whom he had recently reconnected. Seymour was an entrepreneur himself, and upon learning of Vaughn's company, knew a great opportunity and product when he saw one. He and Vaughn immediately began discussing licensing options after Seymour fell in love with Hottie Hawg's ribs.

With the company still less than one year old and not yet fully developed, Vaughn was hesitant to relinquish too much control by entering into a typical franchise agreement. Instead, he agreed to a licensing agreement where Seymour purchased the use of the name and all the food already prepared from Hottie Hawg's. Vaughn maintained final approval on use of the brand and marketing materials to preserve the company's image. This agreement guaranteed that HHBBQ would turn a profit regardless of actual sales, as the cost of labor, food, packaging, shipping, and a guaranteed 6 percent profit were factored in the prices that Seymour paid. Even if the Colorado division never grew to be successful, Hottie Hawg's would benefit from the built-in profit and the $50,000 licensing fee that Seymour paid for the five-year agreement. The agreement benefited Seymour because he would not have to invest in a location to prepare food or the staff to perform the labor. Instead, Seymour was only responsible for coordinating events, hiring a few Hotties, and showing up with the barbecue.

Although the agreement allowed HHBBQ to maintain the most control over the brand and product, it also strained resources. With no commissary or kitchen, all food preparation was performed out of the 18 Squeeler and stored in freezers at the Atlanta headquarters—space that also doubled as the office for Vaughn's Auto Claim Technology. If Seymour needed food for an event, the Squeeler was for all intents and purposes booked in preparation for his event. This meant that resources were further distracted from the Atlanta market for a venture that demanded high overhead costs. Though these costs were being recouped through sales to Seymour, there was still an opportunity cost in the form of lost potential revenue in the Atlanta market.

Within a short amount of time, Seymour began booking events and placing food orders. It quickly became apparent that a full-time staff was needed to support the Colorado market. Vaughn was traveling the majority of the time operating ACT and had less time to devote to HHBBQ's operations. Vaughn had one consistent Pit Master, Chris Doolin, who spent the majority of his time in Atlanta even though he was based out of Orlando. Other than Vaughn and Doolin, Hottie Hawg's only maintained a few part-time freelance event coordinators and friends willing to help if needed.

Jessie Lee, the reigning Miss Billfish and HHBBQ's event coordinator based in Panama City, was the closest person Vaughn had in an administrative position. In addition to her role as event coordinator in Panama City, Lee also served as the company's "Head Hottie" and was responsible for hiring Hotties for all events. Lee had been with the company since the first bike rally in Panama City, and had coordinated the Billfish Tournament event while pursuing her MBA. Given her business knowledge and background with the company, Vaughn asked Lee to become the Office Manager/Controller for HHBBQ in September 2009. After Lee relocated to Atlanta, Vaughn had a full-time employee with a vested interest and experience with Hottie Hawg's to help manage operations and the Colorado venture.

The Aramark/Pepsi Center Opportunity

Within Lee's first week in Atlanta, news came from Colorado about a potential deal with Aramark to become a vendor at the Pepsi Center in Denver. The one-year contract would include at least 100 events and make Hottie Hawg's the exclusive BBQ vendor for the arena. Without a doubt, there was tremendous excitement about the opportunity and its unbelievable upside potential. In addition to solid revenues and profits, the deal would give HHBBQ incredible exposure that could potentially lead to other catering or restaurant opportunities. Vaughn and Lee, however, were also quite hesitant about the deal. There was no possible way the sole 18 Squeeler could feed a projected 16,000 people per event multiple times per week.

Given the licensing contract with Seymour, HHBBQ could not let Seymour establish his own commissary in Denver as other franchisees might have done. Because Hottie Hawg's maintained all rights to food preparation, the company would have to establish its own commissary capable of providing the quantities of food required to meet the needs of the Pepsi Center. In short, HHBBQ would have to invest its own capital in setup costs that would benefit a licensee who had not yet been with the company for six months. With virtually no regular cash flow and Auto Claim Technology paying the majority of Hottie Hawg's bills, the idea of any upfront investment made Vaughn hesitant. However, the opportunity to finally have a steady cash flow was undeniably appealing.

Seymour created a spreadsheet with three forecast scenarios. The least profitable forecast was generated using figures from the previous BBQ vendor at the Pepsi Center. Even using ultra-conservative estimates, Seymour was still able to realistically show a profit on his end—not one to necessarily make the effort worthwhile, but profit nonetheless. The middle- and high-profit scenarios projected revenues that clearly made the effort worthwhile. Seymour believed that these latter scenarios were more likely as the previous BBQ vendor had no marketable brand image and a significantly less sophisticated product.

After analyzing the spreadsheets and filling in fine details, Vaughn and Lee were both convinced that the contract would benefit Seymour but were not sure it would benefit HHBBQ. After filling Seymour's first few orders, Vaughn was starting to think there was not enough markup in the product he was shipping. Even though having a Denver commissary would widen profit margins by eliminating freight and packaging costs, the issue of recouping the setup costs remained. Raising Seymour's prices was not an option, as it would reduce his profitability to the point of demotivation. In the end, Hottie Hawg's wanted to encourage Seymour's breakneck pace and did not want to turn down such an immense opportunity for either party.

Hottie Hawg's Considers Its Options

Because a Denver commissary was inevitable, Lee began researching locations. Vaughn estimated $25,000 to $30,000 in initial setup fees for the commissary, including labor, equipment, the rental space, and the cost of licensing. For most businesses, a line of credit or short-term loan would have enabled this process. However, because HHBBQ had no measurable cash flow or credit, the company was once again going to have to rely on ACT to pay its expenses. The theory, though, was that once Seymour was supplied with the tools necessary to truly expand, cash flow would begin and Hottie Hawg's would be able to stand on its own. This cash flow would not just be for the minimum year the Aramark contract provided, but also from the potential catering events and demand Hottie Hawg's would receive off the exposure of being in such a high-visibility arena. Even if the markup on the product supplied to Seymour were not ideal, other supplemental events would theoretically bridge the gap. Another benefit to such high visibility would be the potential for additional licensing agreements with other venues or firms.

The Aramark contract was clearly the type of opportunity that Vaughn aspired to at some point in the future. However, that future came very quickly for HHBBQ, and Vaughn wondered if the timing, up-front costs, and cash flow considerations made the venture too risky at this point in his company's history. Vaughn estimated total setup time for a commissary, if rushed, would take at least 30 days. In the meantime, he feared that the high food demand would put a tremendous strain on the Squeeler—one that it might not be able to withstand.

As an option to buy time until a commissary could be established, Vaughn considered partnering with a local Denver kitchen to begin producing food immediately. This would allow Hottie Hawg's to begin collecting revenue from the Aramark contract and invest that into an independent commissary. Lee opposed this idea, as she believed the legal costs and profit lost due to a partnership agreement with a local kitchen were not worth the time it bought for the company. In addition, Lee argued that partnering allowed entirely too many opportunities for the company's food quality and brand image to be compromised. Maintaining control of the Hottie Hawg's brand image was her primary concern as it was the cornerstone of the company's success thus far.

The Pepsi Center deal was beginning to become more complicated than it looked at first glance. To accept the Aramark contract, Hottie Hawg's could find a kitchen partner in Denver or put the Squeeler through a grueling schedule—all while establishing its own local commissary. Partnering could mean potential lost profits and less control over brand image during the critical startup period at Pepsi Center. However, using the Squeeler as the sole food source for the first 30 days was also problematic in that Vaughn might not be able to produce sufficient quantities of food to serve its customers. Of course, another option was to simply pass on the deal; but that would mean passing up an opportunity for exposure that might not come again. Vaughn also had to consider the financial strain that Hottie Hawg's was now putting on ACT. In any case, Vaughn had to make a decision on the Pepsi Center opportunity—and he had to do it soon.

Questions for Discussion

1. If you were in Kyle Vaughn's position, which strategic option would you take? Explain your reasoning.

2. Comment on the decision to license the Hottie Hawg's brand rather than enter into a franchise agreement with Seymour. In the company's situation, is it better to promote easier expansion through franchising or maintain tight control over brand image through licensing? Explain.

3. Assume that Hottie Hawg's is successful with the Aramark/Pepsi Center opportunity. What should Vaughn's next move be to continue that growth and success?

4. If the Aramark/Pepsi Center opportunity turns out to be unsuccessful, what should Vaughn do to ensure the ongoing viability of Hottie Hawg's?

Sources

The facts of this case are from "About Hooters," Hooters, Inc. website (http://www.hooters.com/About.aspx), accessed October 21, 2009; "Did You Know: Hooters Facts," Hooters, Inc. website (http://www.hooters.com/Didyouknow.aspx), accessed October 21, 2009; internal company records, Hottie Hawg's Smokin' BBQ, Inc.; Hottie Hawg's website (http://www.hottiehawgsbbq.com/), accessed October 21, 2009; and Kyle Vaughn personal interview, October 18, 2009.

FedEx: Building a Global Distribution Powerhouse

Synopsis: *This case reviews the history of FedEx's growth from a domestic express carrier to a global distribution and supply chain powerhouse. FedEx's growth strategy is based primarily on the acquisition of firms offering the individual pieces needed to create a full-scale, global distribution infrastructure. Through the collective, but independent, operation of eleven companies, FedEx provides one-stop shopping for businesses and individuals looking to fulfill their office and/or shipping needs. Although FedEx's growth has been remarkable, the company is faced with several issues that threaten its once unstoppable success.*

Themes: *Global marketing, mergers and acquisitions, competitive advantage, service strategy, distribution strategy, marketing implementation, employee relations, legal environment*

Frederick W. Smith founded the Federal Express Corporation in 1971 with part of an $8 million inheritance. At the time, the U.S. Postal Service and United Parcel Service (UPS) provided the only means of delivering letters and packages, and they often took several days or more to get packages to their destinations. While a student at Yale in 1965, Smith wrote a term paper proposing an independent, overnight delivery service. His arguments were based on the inadequate routes used by most airfreight companies at the time and stressed the need for a system that would support time-sensitive shipments such as medicines, computer parts, and electronics. Although Smith received a C on the paper, his vision and belief that businesses would pay more to get letters, documents, and packages delivered overnight was right on the mark.

The specific idea for Federal Express came to Smith after he purchased controlling interest in Arkansas Aviation Sales, located in Little Rock. Smith designed a highly efficient distribution system to overcome the inherent difficulties in moving packages and airfreight to their destinations within one or two days. Being ex-military, the

---

Michael D. Hartline, Florida State University, prepared this case for classroom discussion rather than to illustrate effective or ineffective handling of an administrative situation.

choice of "Federal" for the company's name was a natural for Smith. He felt that the patriotic meaning associated with the word, in combination with "Express," would attract attention and promote strong name recognition.

The fledgling Federal Express began operations on April 17, 1973, when it shipped 186 packages to 25 U.S. cities using 14 small aircraft flown out of Memphis International Airport. Today, FedEx Corporation, as the company is now called, employs more than 275,000 people and handles over 7.5 million shipments per day around the world. Though most people are familiar with FedEx's overnight delivery services, the company is actually divided into four segments and 11 operating companies, as shown in Case Exhibit 13.1.

CASE EXHIBIT 13.1

FEDEX CORPORATION OPERATING SEGMENTS AND COMPANIES

FedEx Express Segment

- **FedEx Express**   The world's largest express transportation company, serving over 220 countries and territories and every address in the United States.
- **FedEx Trade Networks**   Offers flexible end-to-end international shipping services, including global cargo distribution, customs brokerage, and trade facilitation.

FedEx Ground Segment

- **FedEx Ground**   Specializes in cost-effective, small-package delivery from business to business or to residential addresses.
- **FedEx SmartPost**   Consolidates and delivers high volumes of low-weight, less time-sensitive business-to-consumer packages (e-commerce and catalog companies) using the U.S. Postal Service for final delivery to residential addresses.

FedEx Freight Segment

- **FedEx Freight**   The leading U.S. regional less-than-truckload (LTL) freight company, provides next-day and second-day delivery of heavyweight freight in both the United States and international markets.
- **FedEx Custom Critical**   Provides 24/7 nonstop, door-to-door delivery of urgent freight, valuable shipments, and hazardous materials throughout the world.
- **Caribbean Transportation Services**   Provides airfreight forwarding throughout the Caribbean.

FedEx Services Segment

- **FedEx Services**   Coordinates sales, marketing, and information technology support for all FedEx brands.
- **FedEx Office**   (Formerly FedEx Kinko's) Offers a wide range of printing and shipping services, including copying, professional printing, direct mail, signs/graphics, and more.
- **FedEx Customer Information Services**   Provides FedEx customers with a convenient, single point of access to the entire FedEx family of services.
- **FedEx Global Supply Chain Services**   Orchestrates a modular and scalable portfolio of transportation and information solutions to firms wanting to outsource their supply chain operations.

Source: FedEx Corporation 2009 Annual Report, FedEx website (http://ir.fedex.com/annuals.cfm), accessed October 13, 2009.

The FedEx Express and FedEx Ground segments account for the bulk of the company's business, offering valuable services to anyone who needs to deliver letters, documents, and packages. FedEx is the clear leader in express shipping, controlling more than 49 percent of the market in the United States. In the ground delivery market, FedEx runs second place to UPS and its sector-leading 54 percent of the market. In 2009, FedEx registered over $747 million in operating income and an astounding $35.5 billion in total revenue (see Case Exhibit 13.2). However, operating revenue was down significantly from 2008.

According to the company, FedEx is not in the package and document transport business; rather, it delivers "certainty" by connecting the global economy with a wide range of transportation, information, and supply chain services. Whether dropped off at one of over 44,000 drop boxes (roughly 5,000 of which can be found at U.S. Postal Service locations), over 700 world service centers, over 1,800 FedEx Office locations, over 6,500 FedEx Authorized ShipCenters, or picked up by FedEx courier, packages are taken to a local FedEx office where they are trucked to the nearest airport. The package is flown to one of the company's distribution hubs for sorting and then flown to the airport nearest its destination. The package is then trucked to another FedEx office where a courier picks it up and hand delivers it to the correct recipient. Much of this takes place overnight, with many packages being delivered before 8:00 AM the next day. FedEx confirms that roughly 99 percent of its deliveries are made on time.

CASE EXHIBIT 13.2

FEDEX FINANCIAL INFORMATION BY BUSINESS SEGMENT

	FedEx Express ($ Millions)	FedEx Ground ($ Millions)	FedEx Freight ($ Millions)	Total ($ Millions)
2009				
Total Revenue	22,364	7,047	4,415	35,497
Operating Income	794	807	(44)	747
Operating Margin	3.6%	11.5%	(1.0%)	2.1%
2008				
Total Revenue	24,421	6,751	4,934	37,953
Operating Income	1,901	736	329	2,075
Operating Margin	7.8%	10.9%	6.7%	5.5%
2007				
Total Revenue	22,681	6,043	4,586	35,214
Operating Income	1,991	822	463	3,276
Operating Margin	8.8%	13.6%	10.1%	9.3%

Note: Revenues from the FedEx Services segment are allocated to FedEx Express and FedEx Ground.

Source: FedEx Corporation 2009 and 2008 Annual Reports, FedEx website (http://ir.fedex.com/annuals.cfm), accessed October 13, 2009.

To accomplish this amazingly high delivery rate, FedEx maintains an impressive infrastructure of equipment and processes. The company owns over 80,000 vehicles and its 658 aircraft fly to more than 375 airports worldwide. FedEx operates its own weather-forecasting service, ensuring that most of its flights arrive within 15 minutes of schedule. Most packages shipped within the United States are sorted at the Memphis super hub, where FedEx takes over control of the Memphis International Airport at roughly 11 PM each night. FedEx planes land side-by-side on parallel runways every minute or so for well over one hour each night. After the sorting of packages, all FedEx planes take off in time to reach their destinations. Not all packages are shipped via air. When possible, FedEx uses ground transportation to save on expenses. For international deliveries, FedEx uses a combination of direct services and independent contractors.

FedEx services are priced using a zone system where the distance a package must travel to reach its final destination determines the price. Case Exhibit 13.3 illustrates typical rates for a 1-pound package shipped within the contiguous United States using various FedEx Express services. The company also offers FedEx SameDay Delivery for $173 for packages up to 25 pounds. FedEx Ground rates vary widely by package weight and shipping zone. For an extra $4, customers can have a courier pick up their packages rather than dropping them off at a drop box. Saturday or Sunday pickup and delivery is also available for an additional $15.00 per package. Prices vary for larger packages and international shipments.

FedEx Express garnered a major coup in January 2001 when it announced two 7-year service agreements with the U.S. Postal Service. In the first agreement, FedEx Express provided air transportation for certain postal services, including Priority Mail. The second agreement gave FedEx Express the option to place a drop box in every U.S. post office. These domestic agreements were renewed in 2006 and extended until 2013. A similar international agreement was forged in 2004 and later renewed in 2009. The international agreement created the Postal Service's Global Express Guaranteed service, which offers date-certain international delivery to over 190 countries. All together, these agreements with the USPS have produced billions in revenue for FedEx over time.

CASE EXHIBIT 13.3

EXPRESS 1-POUND PACKAGE RATES (CONTIGUOUS UNITED STATES)

FedEx Express Services	Delivered By	Zone Rates ($)
First Overnight	8:00 or 8:30 AM next day	45.25 to 70.00
Priority Overnight	10:30 AM next day	20.25 to 45.00
Standard Overnight	3:00 PM next day	16.90 to 39.90
2-Day Delivery	4:30 PM second day	10.95 to 17.20
Express Saver	4:30 PM third day	9.75 to 13.65

Source: FedEx Express Standard List Rates, FedEx website (http://images.fedex.com/us/services/pdf/2010_FedEx_Express_Rates_Preview.pdf), accessed October 13, 2009.

The Growth of FedEx into a Global Distribution Powerhouse

Despite its tremendous successes, FedEx has faced some difficult times in its efforts to grow and compete against strong rival firms. The overnight delivery market matured very rapidly as intense competition from the U.S. Postal Service, UPS, Emery, DHL, RPS, and electronic-document delivery (that is, fax machines and e-mail) forced FedEx to search for a viable means of expansion. In 1984, facing a growing threat from e-document delivery, FedEx introduced its ZapMail service for customers who could not afford expensive fax machines. For $35, FedEx would fax up to 10 pages of text to any FedEx site around the world. The document was then hand delivered to its recipient. Soon after the service was introduced, the price of fax machines plummeted, ultimately forcing FedEx to drop ZapMail after losing over $190 million. Many analysts still argue that the overnight delivery market could eventually lose as much as 30 percent of its letter business to e-document delivery, especially e-mail.

After its experience with ZapMail, FedEx began to focus its resources on expanding its overseas operations, the most rapidly growing area of the overnight market. In an increasingly global economy, businesses must be able to communicate quickly with employees around the world, with partners in other nations, with other businesses, and with customers. Though FedEx had been shipping packages from the United States to Canada since 1975, its acquisition of Gelco International in 1984 enabled FedEx to expand its operations to Europe and the Far East. Political changes in foreign markets—such as the establishment of the European Union and the dismantling of once-closed Eastern European markets—allowed FedEx to gain entry into large, untapped markets.

Global Expansion

FedEx's most important strategic move into international markets was its 1988 purchase of Tiger International, Inc., owner of the Flying Tiger Line airfreight service. The $880 million purchase gave FedEx valuable routes, airport facilities, and expertise in European and Asian markets that it had been struggling to enter. Such valuable assets would have taken the company years to develop alone. The purchase also gave the company valuable landing slots in Sydney, Singapore, Bangkok, Hong Kong, Seoul, Paris, Brussels, and Tokyo. However, the purchase of Flying Tiger created some problems for FedEx. The purchase left the company with a debt of $2.1 billion. It also thrust FedEx into the heavy-freight distribution market, which was more cyclical and capital intensive than small-package distribution. In addition, many of Tiger's key customers, including UPS, were competitors of FedEx. Finally, FedEx had trouble integrating Tiger's 6,500 union employees into its own nonunion workforce. Despite the difficulties in merging the two companies, the merger was a key ingredient in making FedEx a powerful global delivery service.

By 1991, the company had taken advantage of its opportunities and was offering international service to more than 100 countries. By 1992, next-morning service was available to and from major markets including Paris, London, Frankfurt, Milan, Brussels, Geneva, Zurich, Antwerp, Amsterdam, Hong Kong, Tokyo, Singapore, and Seoul. FedEx's Canadian operations remained strong, and the company's operations in Latin America were growing. Despite this success, however, FedEx's international operations were troublesome. This was particularly true in Europe, where the total volume of express shipments between European countries was only 150,000 packages per day. Deciding that the intra-European market lacked potential, FedEx abandoned it and closed some domestic businesses in Italy, Germany, France, and the United Kingdom. The company took a $254 million restructuring charge in the third quarter of its 1992 fiscal year to cover the closures. FedEx then restricted its European focus to shipments to and from Europe, rather than within Europe. By the end of 1992, FedEx experienced a total loss of $113 million and negative earnings per share of $2.11. Company officials pointed to several reasons for the losses. First, the company was still recovering from its purchase of Flying Tiger, which increased its fixed costs in international operations. Second, FedEx had difficulty building a global infrastructure to support its operations. Negotiating for landing rights, dealing with foreign customs regulations, and establishing information networks all proved to be very costly.

Despite the problems in Europe, FedEx was doing very well in Asia. The Asian economy was growing rapidly—seven of the top-10 growth economies at the time were in Asia. Additionally, Asia's manufactured product exports were increasing at a rate of 28 percent per year. To capitalize on this growth, FedEx introduced its AsiaOne network in 1995 and began offering effective "late-day" pickups and "next-day" deliveries not only across Asia but also between Asia and North America. AsiaOne grew quickly, in part due to FedEx's unparalleled capability to gain Asian air-route authority. For instance, FedEx was the only U.S. all-cargo airline with aviation rights to the Chinese trade centers of Shenzhen, Shanghai, and Beijing. FedEx was also the first to offer express services in India with direct international air routes—connecting 4,348 Indian cities and towns with the rest of the world. The company started the first overnight express flight from India to China and doubled its capacity from Europe to Asia through an eastbound around-the-world flight. The AsiaOne network provided quick, reliable package delivery to, from, and within Asia—all backed up by a money-back guarantee.

In 1997, FedEx became the only cargo carrier allowed to fly its own aircraft and use its own warehousing facilities in Moscow. This was a breakthrough for FedEx because the Moscow and overall Russian market was growing rapidly. This exclusive capability allowed FedEx customers to receive reliable next-business-day service (by 10:30 AM) from Moscow to North America and Western Europe. Likewise, FedEx offered two- to three-day service between Moscow and many Asian cities. At the same time, FedEx instituted a similar service from the United States to Argentina, as projections indicated that the South American market would also grow substantially. To maintain its impressive growth, FedEx introduced several new international services during this time. FedEx introduced International First service offering one- to two-day, 8:00 AM delivery to and from 20 European countries. They also introduced

International Priority service (one- to three-day, 10:30 AM delivery to 210 countries) and International Economy service (four- to five-day delivery to 29 countries).

Recent acquisitions have only strengthened FedEx's position in international markets. In 2006, FedEx acquired ANC Holdings, a UK-based express transportation firm. The company was rebranded as FedEx UK shortly thereafter. In 2007, FedEx bought out its Chinese delivery partner, Tianjin Datian Group, which gave FedEx complete control over Datian's fleet and hubs. This later led to the creation of an Asian super hub in Guangzhou, China. Also in 2007, FedEx acquired Prakash Air Freight (an Indian express company) and Flying Cargo (a Hungarian express company). In sum, FedEx's global acquisition strategy has given it unprecedented access to global express markets—one of the company's key competitive advantages over rival firms.

Emergence of the FedEx Family of Services

Despite its growth and success in the global express market, FedEx did not become a complete transportation delivery network until its 1998 acquisition of Caliber System, a trucking company whose RPS subsidiary was second only to UPS in ground shipments. The $2.7 billion merger created a new holding company, called FDX Corporation, which owned both Federal Express and Caliber System. Caliber's subsidiaries included RPS (a ground service), Roberts Express (an expedited delivery service), Viking Freight (a regional, LTL freight carrier), Caribbean Transportation Services (airfreight forwarding between the United States and Caribbean nations), and Caliber Logistics and Caliber Technology (integrated logistics services).

Though Caliber had many attractive assets, RPS was the crown jewel in the deal. RPS's fleet of delivery trucks and its customer base helped FedEx grow and compete more effectively with UPS in the nonexpress, ground-delivery business. The acquisition of RPS, along with the 1997 UPS strike, allowed FedEx to steal business from UPS and increase its market share. The purchase of RPS made FedEx not only more profitable but also more attractive to current and potential customers. Suddenly, FedEx had the ability to fulfill any customer's needs by providing one-stop shopping for express and nonexpress shipping and delivery.

To better leverage and integrate the Caliber assets, Federal Express made a number of internal structural changes between 1998 and 2001. First, the FDX Corporation was renamed FedEx Corporation in order to better leverage the FedEx brand. In a similar fashion, Federal Express was renamed FedEx Express, RPS was renamed FedEx Ground, and Roberts Express was renamed FedEx Custom Critical. FedEx also combined Caliber Logistics and Caliber Technology to establish FedEx Global Logistics as a world leader in transportation management and integrated logistics. A new subsidiary, FedEx Services, was also created to centralize all sales, marketing, customer service, and information technology (IT) operations.

Also during this time, FedEx acquired Tower Group International—a firm specializing in international logistics and trade information—and WorldTariff—a customs duty and tax information firm. These firms were combined with Caribbean Transportation Services and FedEx Global Logistics to create FedEx Trade Networks. FedEx also acquired American Freightways, a leading LTL freight carrier, and merged the company with Viking Freight to create FedEx Freight. Caribbean Transportation Services was moved from FedEx Trade Networks and aligned with FedEx Freight at this time. Rounding out its freight business, FedEx acquired Watkins Motor Lines and merged it into the FedEx Freight segment.

FedEx's transformation was extended when it acquired Kinko's in February 2004. Shortly thereafter, Kinko's was rebranded as FedEx Kinko's Office and Print Services. With over 1,500 locations in over 11 countries, Kinko's was a natural addition to the FedEx family. FedEx could now offer office and print services alongside its many shipping options. In 2008, the service was rebranded again as FedEx Office.

Today, FedEx has successfully transformed into a global distribution and logistics powerhouse that offers virtually any transportation, supply chain, or business service or solution that any customer might need. FedEx summarizes the FedEx family this way:

> *FedEx provides customers and businesses worldwide with a broad portfolio of transportation, e-commerce and business services. We offer integrated business applications through operating companies competing collectively and managed collaboratively, under the respected FedEx brand. Consistently ranked among the world's most admired and trusted employers, FedEx inspires its more than 290,000 employees and contractors to remain absolutely, positively focused on safety, the highest ethical and professional standards, and the needs of their customers and communities.*
>
> *The unique FedEx operating strategy works seamlessly—and simultaneously—on three levels.*
>
> - *Compete collectively by standing as one brand worldwide and speaking with one voice.*
>
> - *Operate independently by focusing on our independent networks to meet distinct customer needs.*
>
> - *Manage collaboratively by working together to sustain loyal relationships with our workforce, customers, and investors.*

FedEx's Current Challenges

Although FedEx continues to expand and succeed, the company currently faces some difficult challenges. One key issue involves the rising costs associated with employee salaries and fuel. The nature of the delivery business dictates that FedEx, along with competing firms, must rely on labor and fuel to get work done. FedEx's single largest expense involves labor, which accounts for over 37 percent of revenues. Rising salaries and the cost of health care benefits are one reason for the increase in labor costs. Rising fuel costs—up roughly 30 percent in the past three years—are another concern for FedEx. Although the company offset most of this increase with fuel surcharges, the decline in the worldwide economy in 2008–2009 slowed business enough that FedEx's operating income suffered dramatically. One complication is that FedEx is more vulnerable to rising fuel prices than UPS because a greater percentage of FedEx's business is based on express deliveries (and the higher costs for jet fuel). For the FedEx segment, fuel accounts for 14 percent of revenues. In the FedEx ground segment, that percentage drops to 9 percent.

Another issue involves the organization of FedEx's employees. Since the creation of the FedEx family of services, each FedEx segment has operated independently—a key reason that the vast majority of FedEx employees are not unionized (FedEx Express pilots are unionized and employed under a four-year agreement ratified in 2007). This structure is very different from UPS, where the majority of employees are unionized. As of late 2009, Congress was considering a bill that would move FedEx Express drivers from the jurisdiction of the Railway Labor Act to the jurisdiction of the National Labor Relations Act. If the bill passes, FedEx Express drivers would be allowed to organize by location, rather than the current requirement to organize at a national level. This would make it much easier for the drivers to unionize. FedEx is fiercely opposed to the bill, arguing that it amounts to a bailout for UPS (see www.brownbailout.com for FedEx's arguments). FedEx also argues that passage of the bill into law would increase customer costs by as much as 30 percent.

FedEx's most publicized issue has been a number of lawsuits filed by its FedEx Ground/Home Delivery drivers over the past few years. FedEx considers these drivers to be independent owners/operators rather than employees of the company. The plaintiffs argue that given the demands placed on them by FedEx, they should be classified as employees and entitled to company benefits. According to the drivers, FedEx strictly dictates working hours and routes, requires them to wear FedEx uniforms and purchase company scanners, and enforces all company rules upon them. The drivers also claim they are prohibited from working for other companies. Although FedEx claims that these contractors have the potential to earn $80,000 to $120,000 annually before paying for trucks and gasoline (an earning potential that FedEx says should equal roughly $50,000 per year), the drivers cite low wages as another issue. In June 2006, a federal judge rejected FedEx's request to dismiss the claims.

In late 2008, FedEx settled one of the longest running suits (i.e., the Estrada case) for $27 million, including $14.5 million to 203 California drivers and $12.5 million in legal fees. According to a website devoted to the lawsuits (www.fedexdriverslawsuit .com), this action opened the floodgates for additional lawsuits and state investigations into FedEx's labor practices. However, FedEx won a stand-alone class action case (i.e., the Anfinson case) in 2009 when a Washington jury found that all 320 class members were independent contractors rather than FedEx employees. As of late 2009, FedEx Ground was involved in roughly 50 class action lawsuits across 40 states; however, the bulk of them have been consolidated in Indiana. FedEx Ground is also under investigation by the IRS for the potential misclassification of employees. The IRS had imposed a $319 million (plus interest) assessment against FedEx Ground for lost payroll taxes associated with the alleged misclassification. The IRS later withdrew the assessment but continued its audit. In its 2009 Annual Report, FedEx addressed these issues by saying that the company strongly believes its drivers to be correctly classified as independent contractors and that the company intends to prevail. It does acknowledge that, should it have to convert its FedEx Ground/Home Delivery drivers to employee status, it will dramatically increase the company's costs.

Looking Ahead

FedEx continuously strives to improve its services by enhancing its distribution networks, transportation infrastructure, IT, and employee performance. FedEx also continues to invest heavily in IT by installing computer terminals at customers' offices and giving away its proprietary tracking software—FedEx Ship Manager. Today, over 19 million packages per month are shipped via FedEx Ship Manager as customers electronically generate their own pickup and delivery requests. The company's website, FedEx.com, receives over 20 million unique visitors each month and handles more than 5.5 million package tracking requests daily. FedEx has also moved more aggressively into e-commerce with respect to order fulfillment for business-to-business and business-to-consumer merchants. For example, FedEx's Home Delivery network has grown rapidly and now reaches virtually every U.S. residential address.

An interesting competitive development occurred in 2009 when DHL pulled out of the domestic U.S. express market. German-based DHL had become a key competitor in 2003 when it acquired U.S.-based Airborne Express. Although Airborne was the third-largest overnight service in the United States at the time, DHL led the market for international express services in all countries outside of the U.S. market. DHL pulled out of the U.S. domestic market, citing its inability to compete with both FedEx and UPS. DHL still provides services from the United States to international markets, where it is a fierce competitor for both FedEx and UPS. For example, DHL has been delivering packages in the Korean market since 1977, whereas FedEx has only been fully operational in Korea since 2000. In all of Asia, FedEx's market share of 22 percent is second to DHL's leading 32 percent share. However, FedEx does have an advantage internationally in that it provides better coverage to the world's emerging markets than either DHL or UPS.

As FedEx moves ahead, the company has a lot going for it. No other carrier can match FedEx's global capabilities or one-stop shopping. To increase its competitiveness, FedEx is focusing on increasing revenue and reducing costs through tighter integration and consolidation, improved productivity, and reduced capital expenditures. Six themes frame FedEx's efforts to fully leverage the strong franchise of the FedEx brand:

- *People—We value our people and promote diversity in our workplace and in our thinking.*

- *Service—Our absolutely, positively spirit puts our customers at the heart of everything we do.*

- *Innovation—We invent and inspire the services and technologies that improve the way we work and live.*

- *Integrity*—We manage our operations, finances, and services with honesty, efficiency, and reliability.

- *Responsibility*—We champion safe and healthy environments for the communities in which we live and work.

- *Loyalty*—We earn the respect and confidence of our FedEx people, customers, and investors every day, in everything we do.

Why has FedEx been so successful? A major reason is the company's enviable corporate culture and workforce. Because employees are critical to the company's success, FedEx strives to hire the best people and offers them the best training and compensation in the industry. FedEx employees are loyal, highly efficient, and extremely effective in delivering good service. In fact, FedEx employees claim to have "purple blood" to match the company's official color. It is not surprising that *Fortune* has named FedEx as one of the "100 Best Companies to Work For" and one of the "World's Most Admired Corporations" many times over. Furthermore, Harris Interactive has ranked FedEx number one in customer service, while the University of Michigan's American Customer Satisfaction Index has ranked the company number one in customer satisfaction among express delivery companies.

Another reason for FedEx's success is well-planned expansion through strategic acquisitions. The company's focus on "delivering certainty" has allowed it to hone in on opportunities that give FedEx added capabilities in virtually all transportation and logistics services. A final reason for success is good marketing: FedEx is a master at recognizing untapped customer needs and filling them well. FedEx is also never content to sit on its laurels, as it constantly strives to improve service and offer more options to its customers. After almost 40 years of success, there is little doubt that Fred Smith's "C" paper has become an indispensable part of the business world.

Questions for Discussion

1. Evaluate the methods used by FedEx to grow domestically and internationally. Why do you think that the company initially had problems in its global operations?

2. What are the major SWOT considerations in FedEx's attempt to continue its growth and dominance in the domestic and global express delivery markets?

3. Comment on the competitive landscape among FedEx, UPS, and DHL. How can FedEx make inroads into UPS's dominance in the ground delivery market or DHL's dominance in international express delivery?

Sources

The facts of this case are from Peter Bradley, "Express Service," DCVelocity.com, April 2005 (http://dcvelocity.com/articles/20050401/enroute.cfm), accessed August 29,

2006; "DHL/Airborne Deal Could Shake Up U.S. Express Market," *Logistics Management,* April 1, 2003 (http://www.allbusiness.com/transportation/freight-package-postal-shipping-shipping/6289722-1.html), accessed November 18, 2009; "DHL's American Adventure," *BusinessWeek Online,* November 29, 2004 (http://www.businessweek.com/magazine/content/04_48/b3910115_mz017.htm), accessed August 29, 2006; "DHL Pulls Plug on Domestic Service," *Multichannel Merchant,* November 10, 2008 (http://multichannelmerchant.com/opsandfulfillment/news/1010-dhl-ends-domestic-service/), accessed October 13, 2009; "FedEx (FDX)," Wikiinvest (http://www.wikinvest.com/stock/FedEx_%28FDX%29), accessed October 13, 2009; FedEx Corporation 2004, 2005, 2006, 2007, 2008, and 2009 Annual Reports, FedEx website (http://ir.fedex.com/annuals.cfm), accessed October 13, 2009; "FedEx Drivers Lawsuit," Background (http://www.zimmreed.com/FedEx_Drivers_Lawsuit.htm), accessed August 29, 2006; "FedEx Facts: FedEx Corporation," FedEx website (http://about.fedex.designcdt.com/our_company/company_information/fedex_corporation), accessed October 13, 2009; "FedEx Facts: FedEx History," FedEx website (http://about.fedex.designcdt.com/our_company/company_information/fedex_history), accessed October 13, 2009; "FedEx Facts: Mission, Strategy, Values," FedEx website (http://about.fedex.designcdt.com/our_company/company_information/mission_statement), accessed October 13, 2009; "FedEx Ground Opens 'Super Hub,'" *Transportation & Distribution,* November 2000, pp. 12–13; "FedEx Loses Ruling over Contractor Status," *Pittsburgh Tribune-Review Online,* August 22, 2006 (http://www.pittsburghlive.com/x/pittsburghtrib/search/print_467079.html), accessed August 29, 2006; "FedEx Pilots Reach a Tentative Contract, *The New York Times,* August 28, 2006 (http://www.nytimes.com/2006/08/28/business/28fedex.html?_r=1&oref=slogin), accessed August 29, 2006; "FedEx Profit Drops 75%, More than Estimated," *The New York Times*, March 19, 2009 (http://www.nytimes.com/2009/03/20/business/20fedex.html), accessed October 13, 2009; "FedEx Shows Gains in Market Share," *Logistics Today Online,* March 21, 2005 (http://www.logisticstoday.com/sNO/7030/LT/displayStory.asp), accessed September 10, 2006; "FedEx: Taking Off Like 'a Rocket Ship,'" *Business Week Online,* April 3, 2006 (http://www.businessweek.com/magazine/content/06_14/b3978412.htm), accessed August 29, 2006; "FedEx to Create China Hub Office in Shanghai," *Memphis Business Journal,* October 24, 2003 (http://memphis.bizjournals.com/memphis/stories/2003/10/20/daily26.html), accessed November 18, 2009; Thomas L. Gallagher, "USPS, FedEx Renew Global Express Guaranteed," *The Journal of Commerce*, August 19, 2009 (http://www.joc.com/node/412981), accessed October 13, 2009; Linda Grant, "Why FedEx Is Flying High," *Fortune,* November 10, 1997, p. 155; "The Ground War at FedEx," *BusinessWeek Online,* November 28, 2005 (http://www.buinessweek.com/magazine/content/05_48/b3961086.htm), accessed August 29, 2006; Nicole Harris, "Flying into a Rage?" *Business Week,* April 27, 1998, p. 119; "Jury Awards $61 Million to Two FedEx Drivers," MSNBC, June 4, 2006 (http://www.msnbc.msn.com/id/13132754), accessed August 29, 2006; Michele Kayal, "FedEx Launches Sunday Service amid Skepticism," *Journal of Commerce and Commercial,* March 11, 1998, p. 1A; Kristin S. Krause, "Handling the Holiday Crush," *Traffic World,* December 4, 2000, p. 33; Park

Kyong-ki, "FedEx, DHL Set Up Battle in Korea," *Korea Times Online* (http://times.hankooki.com/lpage/200608/kt2006081717530510220.htm), accessed August 29, 2006; "Major Victory in Pre-Trial Stage of FedEx Ground/Home Delivery Drivers Lawsuit," FedEx News Release (http://www.fedexdriverslawsuit.com), accessed August 29, 2006; Theo Mullen, "Delivery Wars Go High-Tech—FedEx Ground Sends Message with $80M Investment to Improve Package Tracking," *Internetweek,* October 23, 2000, p. 18; Jayne O'Donnell, "FedEx-Postal Service Alliance Delivers Goods," *USA Today Online,* January 11, 2001 (http://www.usatoday.com/money/mds2.htm), accessed September 10, 2006; Deborah Orr, "Delivering America," *Forbes,* September 20, 2004 (http://www.forbes.com/global/2004/0920/064_print.html), accessed August 29, 2006; Monica Roman, "FedEx Hitches Up a New Trucker," *Business Week,* November 27, 2000, p. 66; Bob Sechler, "FedEx Begins Campaign Against Labor Bill," *The Wall Street Journal,* June 9, 2009 (http://online.wsj.com/article/SB124450587313396177.html), accessed October 13, 2009; Marc L. Songini, "FedEx Expects CRM System to Deliver," *Computerworld,* November 6, 2000, p. 10; "Stand Your Ground: The Official Website of the FedEx Ground/Home Delivery Drivers Nationwide Class-Action Lawsuit," (http://www.fedexdriverslawsuit.com/CaseOverview/welcome.html), accessed October 13, 2009; Richard Tomkins, "The Bear and the Alligator Enter into a Race to Deliver," *Financial Times,* March 13, 1998, p. 30; "UPS Wants Fed Probe into DHL-Airborne Deal," *San Francisco Business Times,* March 27, 2003 (http://www.bizjournals.com/sanfrancisco/stories/2003/03/24/daily40.html); and Michael Weingarten and Bart Stuck, "No Substitutions?" *Telephony,* February 2, 1998, p. 26.

Mistine: Direct Selling in the Thai Cosmetics Market

Synopsis: This case summarizes the growth of Better Way (Thailand) and its highly successful Mistine brand of cosmetics. From its meager beginnings in 1991, Mistine has risen to become the dominant brand in Thailand's direct selling cosmetics market. The brand's value-based positioning (high quality at affordable prices), along with successful target marketing and a tightly integrated marketing program, has kept the company at the top of the market despite strong competition. Mistine's success has allowed Better Way to expand its efforts into other countries, most notably in Asia, Europe, the Middle East, and Africa. Better Way is now looking to further expand its operations, perhaps into Western countries and China.

Themes: Direct selling, global marketing, branding strategy, value, positioning, distribution strategy, integrated marketing communication, marketing implementation

Under the principle to "create a better way of life" for Thai people, Dr. Amornthep Deerojanawong, Thailand's king of direct selling, in partnership with Boonyakiat Chokwatana, founded Better Way (Thailand) in 1988. In 1991, the company launched its "Mistine" brand and began its rapid ascent as a key player in Thailand's direct selling cosmetics industry. Mistine started with fewer than 10 employees and less than 100 products at a time when the Thai people were not familiar with the direct selling model for cosmetics. Based on Mistine's success, direct selling now accounts for well over 50 percent of the market and is the preferred method of selling and distributing cosmetics in Thailand. Mistine and Better Way quickly became the leader in the Thai direct selling cosmetics market—a position it has held since 1997. The company's distribution warehouses, among the largest in Asia, handle more than 6,000 products under the Mistine umbrella. These warehouses distribute products to more than 860,000 Mistine sales representatives around the globe.

Ekachai Wangprapa, Nuntiya Ittiwattanakorn, Rawadee Mekwichai, and Supishsha Sajjamanochai (Thammasat University, Thailand) prepared this case under the direction of O. C. Ferrell and Linda Ferrell (University of New Mexico) for classroom discussion rather than to illustrate effective or ineffective handling of an administrative situation.

Mistine's Marketing Operations

Cosmetics under the Mistine brand are divided into five categories and target markets: Body Care, Personal Care, Make Up, Fragrance, and Skin Care. All of Mistine's cosmetics are produced by manufacturers who are certified by ISO 9001, 9002, and Good Manufacturing Principles espoused by the U.S. Food and Drug Administration. These international standards ensure customers of the quality of Mistine's products. An experienced production team develops hundreds of new and unique products each year. At least two to three new products are launched each month. Every Mistine product is thoroughly inspected and tested before being delivered to the warehouse. Customers can be assured that they will receive only the highest quality, "value-for-money" products. In addition, every Mistine product comes with a satisfaction guarantee that if for any reason a customer is unsatisfied with his or her purchase, Mistine will replace the product or offer a full refund without condition.

Mistine's core target market, which accounts for 70 to 80 percent of sales, includes housewives with a high school diploma, an occupational certificate level or high occupational certificate level of education, and a monthly household income of about $125 to $200 (U.S.). The company also targets professional women who earn $200 to $300 (U.S.) per month. Mistine targets these markets using sales representatives and catalogs. In addition to the cosmetics portfolio, Mistine also offers its "Friday" collection of clothes, home décor, electronics, appliances, ladies' and men's accessories, sports gear, stationery, toys, gifts, and souvenirs.

The most recent worldwide economic recession has been very good for the direct selling sector, and Mistine in particular. All told, Better Way increased sales by 15 percent in 2009 to over $258 million (U.S.). The increase is due mainly to a tremendous growth in exports as financially strapped consumers turned to the direct selling model to purchase cosmetics and other items. In addition to Thailand, Mistine products are sold in many Asian, European, Middle Eastern, and African markets, including such countries as Ghana, Iran, and the Democratic Republic of the Congo. Additionally, to better prepare the company to analyze costs, Mistine spent approximately $3 million (U.S.) to upgrade its information technology systems. With all these measures, Better Way executives expect sales to grow by 12 to 16 percent and exports to grow by 25 percent, for the foreseeable future.

Key Thai Competitors

Cosmetics are the number one product sold through direct selling channels in Thailand. The total direct selling market is roughly $1 billion (U.S.) per year and growing at a rate of 10 to 15 percent annually. Of that amount, the cosmetics market accounts for roughly 60 percent of all products sold via direct selling channels. In terms of direct selling market share, the top four cosmetics companies are Mistine, Avon, Giffarine, and Amway. Prospects for continued growth in the industry are excellent: Only 24 percent of Thailand's population has bought products via direct selling channels. Price, quality, and attractive packages are the three most important criteria for Thai consumers when buying cosmetics.

Avon   Founded in 1978, AVON Cosmetics (Thailand) Co., Ltd., is the 22nd branch of AVON Products Inc, USA. It was the first company in Thailand at that time to use a single-level marketing direct selling approach for Thai consumers. With the company's motto—*The Company for Women*—Avon targets teenagers and working women. Avon cosmetics are truly high-quality products for which the brand is recognized throughout the world. As such, it is not difficult for Avon Thailand to sell its products and gain the confidence of consumers. Customer service is offered through distributors called Avon Members. The company has a team of representatives from the headquarters in Bangkok that go out and visit all the customers in their areas of responsibility. Not only do they sell products, but these Avon Members also provide beauty tips for customers and ensure that they are all satisfied with the products.

Giffarine   Giffarine Skyline Unity Co., Ltd., was founded in 1966 by a team of Thai doctors and pharmacists. The company's medical roots translate into its positioning today: Giffarine's products are developed and tested with the highest standards of quality. However, like Mistine, the company also focuses on affordable pricing. Giffarine's portfolio includes a wide range of cosmetics, body treatments, household items, diet supplements, and health food products. Giffarine's success can be attributed to several factors. In addition to product quality, the company places a great deal of emphasis on social responsibility and ethics in the treatment of both customers and employees. Giffarine is also a master of multilevel marketing, which is how it structures its sales force.

Amway   Established in May 1988, Amway (Thailand) Co., Ltd., sells various consumer products in addition to cosmetics, using a multilevel marketing approach. The company's catalog offers more than 100 different products and 500 SKUs. Its most popular products include health products, herbal products, air purifiers, and water purifiers. Amway offers nutritional supplements under the Nutrilite brand and cosmetics products under the Artistry brand. Amway Thailand's sales amount to approximately $344 million (U.S). The company has received ISO 14001 certification for environmental management systems and ISO 9001 certification for quality service standards. The company has also received awards for promoting social and environmental causes along with outstanding industrial relations and employee welfare.

Mistine's Competitive Positioning   To combat its key competitors, Mistine positions itself as an Asian company that produces products that are developed and formulated especially for Asian woman. Mistine products are created to blend well with Asian complexions and skin tones. They are also made to better suit the warmer and more humid climate of the Asian region, so that the product stays on longer and looks fresher throughout the day.

Furthermore, Mistine is looking to fully leverage its product quality, popularity, and market-leading position. To increase revenue, the company has started to increase prices as the worldwide economic recession begins to soften. Historically, 80 percent of Mistine's sales were for products that cost an average of $3 (U.S.) each. By boosting the average price to $6 (U.S.), Mistine expects the average order to increase from $27 (U.S.) to $45 (U.S.). Along with price increases, Mistine plans to increase its marketing budget by 10 percent. Company executives believe that Mistine's double-digit growth will continue over the next few years. Their main concerns are primarily related to political situations in the countries where it does business, and to the worldwide volatility of oil prices (oil is a key ingredient in many cosmetics).

Mistine's Direct Selling Operations

In the direct selling business, the length of a selling period is critical and shapes the operation of the business. A selling period starts when the product catalog is sent to the sales force. The selling period ends when the sales force submits purchase orders to the company. Normally, direct selling companies use a three-week selling period, totaling 18 periods within a year. Although Mistine used this approach, the company found that most salespeople did not begin selling products to customers until the last week of the selling period. As such, most of the customers' purchase orders were generated from sales during the third week of the selling period. Accordingly, Mistine's management decided to reduce the selling period to two weeks, resulting in 26 selling periods per year.

The change was a challenge for Mistine's operations. Because as many as 20,000 purchase orders were submitted to the company each day, the company was forced to implement an efficient mail traffic management plan to control and balance the workload. Within a two-week selling period, personnel had only 10 days to work. If order processing were not completed each day, sales personnel would not be able to deliver the products as promised. After some time, the new operating plan worked smoothly and was a resounding success. Sales increased by 80 percent compared to the previous year and salespeople became more active in selling products. Impressive sales were not only a result of reducing the distribution cycle but were also due to the positive attitude created throughout the company. The company's pledge–*"We will make Mistine No. 1"*–was successful in motivating salespeople and office personnel to adapt to the changes and cooperate with the company's direction.

Mistine's single-level marketing approach to its direct sales operations is simple and efficient. It is also suitable to the Thai culture and lifestyle. The company recruits district managers who in turn recruit as many salespeople as he/she can handle. Each day the new recruits make their rounds to meet customers and prospective customers. Once a sale is confirmed, the salesperson submits a purchase order. Each salesperson earns a full 25 to 30 percent commission without having to share his or her earnings with others. The more sales a salesperson makes, the more income he or she receives. Each district manager earns a fixed salary plus commission based on sales generated by the salespersons under his or her responsibility. In addition, as a means to increase morale, mobility, and efficiency, the company provides a car to each of its district managers. The district manager's fuel expenses are borne by the company.

In terms of recruiting, the company welcomes anyone, male or female, with free time who would like to earn money, make new friends, and develop self-confidence. Salespeople can plan their own schedule and movement in order to reach target sales and obtain rewards. Mistine's turnover rate for salespeople had averaged 200 percent per year because most salespeople sell Mistine as a second job. Recently, the company reduced turnover by 30 percent through simple improvements in order processing and fulfillment that streamlined many of the mundane, time-consuming tasks for salespeople. One example is the "Mistine Corporate Solution," a strategic alliance with DTAC, a major Thai telecommunications provider. The system greatly increases efficiency and productivity by enabling salespeople to call the 24-hour Mistine Call Center for free when using the DTAC network. This innovative alliance not only made Mistine sales reps happier, it also cut Better Way's phone expenses by $25,000 (U.S.) per month.

With the belief that the salespeople can live without Mistine, but Mistine cannot live without its salespeople, Mistine has launched several programs to maximize employee loyalty. Internal relationship programs such as the "Mistine Thank You Concert" were organized in nine Thai provinces to gather Mistine salespeople together as a family and demonstrate the company's concern for its employees. The company also provides life insurance with coverage of $50,000 (U.S.) to each salesperson. Nonmonetary rewards and recognition incentives for salespeople include crystal trophies and photos in the Hall of Fame.

Mistine's Advertising

Direct selling companies normally depend on word of mouth to develop brand awareness, recruit salespeople, and encourage product purchases. Better Way decided to do things differently by being the first direct selling company in Thailand to use mass media advertising. Continuous advertising campaigns have been executed to build brand image and positioning in the customers' minds. Many advertising campaigns have been developed to recruit additional salespeople.

When the company first started, Dr. Deerojanawong used his credibility to advertise Mistine during interviews with the media and at seminars with educational institutions. People applied as district managers with the company mainly because of his reputation. He was certain that the district managers would be able to establish a large network of salespeople. To increase knowledge about the company, however, Mistine wanted to reach greater audiences. This eventually led them to move into television advertising.

"Mistine is here!" was launched as the company's very first television campaign with the objectives to communicate to the public that Mistine is a direct selling cosmetics business and to create a brand character of beauty for Mistine's products. Using the message "Mistine is here!" was an effective way for the public to envision a salesperson coming to visit them with Mistine products. After only two months, the campaign generated an incredible buzz as it increased brand awareness from 10 percent to roughly 70 percent.

Mistine's second campaign was designed to assist district managers in their efforts to recruit new salespeople. This campaign consisted of two advertisements. The message of the first ad was that it was possible to buy a car by becoming a Mistine salesperson. Within three months, a total of 30,000 people applied and were recruited. Sales rose by 100 percent. The message of the second ad was that it was possible to buy a house by becoming a Mistine salesperson. Again, the company succeeded in creating stronger brand awareness through this campaign.

Based on this success, the company decided that it needed to increase its customers' confidence in Mistine products, as well as generate more product trial. As such, *"If you're not satisfied, we will give you your money back."* was the concept for the third campaign. This campaign was not only successful in stimulating product trial, but it also created a great deal of brand switching from competitors' products to Mistine products. In the end, there were very few cases of product dissatisfaction or customers requesting their money back.

The company's fourth campaign was a series of six 30-second television spots—each spot was shown for two to three weeks over a four-month run for the campaign. The spots were like short scenes of a mini soap opera. The campaign, the most expensive in the history of the Thai cosmetics direct selling industry and the longest commercial in that country to date, firmly cemented Mistine in the number one position. The campaign, which was produced by a small agency called Fameline, also proved that good advertising need not be created by a well-known advertising agency. Together the two companies succeeded in positioning Mistine products and in creating a unique selling proposition for Better Way.

Additionally, Mistine has remained a first mover in the direct selling market by launching advertising campaigns featuring popular actresses, actors, and music bands that match with Mistine's brand personality. Such advertising campaigns have had much impact and have been designed to capture specific target groups:

- One advertisement, targeting housewives, used a very popular Thai actress as the presenter for Mistine's *Neo Bright* products. As a result of this advertisement, Better Way was able to successfully expand its network of salespeople to cover upcountry provinces.

- Another advertisement, using another very popular Thai actress who was voted by the public as the sexiest girl in Thailand, targeted working women. This advertisement imparted a sexier, more modern and confident image to Mistine's products.

- Another advertisement, targeting teenagers, used a very popular boy band called D2B to promote Mistine's *Pink Magic* lipstick. As a result of this advertisement, Mistine increased its share of the teen market by 10 percent. The total breakdown of Mistine's sales also shifted to a point where teens generated 30 percent of the company's sales.

- To acquire new salespeople, Mistine launched an ad using a very popular Thai actor as the presenter. Mistine was also interested in building brand image among men.

Due to competitive pressures and growing consumer interest, Mistine's recent advertising campaigns have focused on corporate social responsibility. For example, the company spent $2.1 million (U.S.) on its "Beauty Mind" campaign. The ads, featuring popular movie actress Petchara Chaowarat, promoted the donation of a portion of the sales revenue of Mistine's Diamond Lipstick to Thailand's Foundation for the Blind.

Looking Ahead

Mistine successfully conquered Thailand's direct selling cosmetics market within a very short period of time. The company's success is based on Dr. Deerojanawong's clear vision and determination. Since his death in 2000, his son Danai has been at the helm of Better Way. Danai's contribution to the Better Way vision has been to take the Mistine brand into the modern era via an aggressive strategy of expansion into foreign markets. Considering the relationship of Thailand to its neighboring countries, its geographic proximity, and Thailand's position in Asia, foreign markets are an extremely interesting prospect for Mistine. The company opened manufacturing sites in the Philippines and Vietnam, and has successfully offered products for sale in Cambodia, Laos, Myanmar, as well as several Middle Eastern and African countries. These successes are due to Mistine's affordable prices that match the income of the people in these countries. Moreover, Mistine's advertising campaigns use popular actresses who are also well-known to people in these countries.

Danai knows that there will be many bumps on the road ahead, with strong competitors at Mistine's doorstep. In looking ahead to the next 10 years, Danai is considering the best way to take Mistine further into the global arena. How can Better Way and Mistine leverage its current strengths to take advantage of global opportunities? How can Mistine maintain its number one position in Thailand while it simultaneously looks outside its borders, particularly in China, Russia, and even Western nations? As Danai considers these issues, his father's words–*Face what you fear!*–echo in his mind.

Questions for Discussion

1. What are the major SWOT considerations in Mistine's attempt to continue its growth and dominance in the Thai market?

2. How can Better Way stay on top in Thailand while it looks to expand internationally?

3.   What specific marketing initiatives would you recommend over the next five years?

Sources

The facts of this case are from the Better Way (Thailand) Company website (http://www.mistine.co.th), accessed October 12, 2009; "Big Five Direct Sellers," *Business Thailand*, October 12, 2001 (http://www.businessthai.in.th); "Branding for Direct Selling," *Business Thailand*, December 12, 2003 (http://www.businessthai.in.th); "Cosmetics and Toiletries in Thailand," *Euromonitor International*, July 2009 (http://www.euromonitor.com/Cosmetics_And_Toiletries_in_Thailand), accessed October 16, 2009; Anuwat Dharamadhaj, "How Direct Selling is Regulated and Managed in Different Markets in Thailand," Asian Symposium on Direct Selling, 2003; "Direct Selling," *Marketeer*, 43 (September 2003), p. 62; "Direct Selling War," *Bangkok Business News*, March 24, 2003 (http://www.bangkokbiznews.com); "Global Networks, 'Dream Big' Danai D. Robert and Family," Bangkokbiznews.com, January 21, 2009; Sujintana Hemtasilpa, "Mobile Phones, Appliances Join Growing Mistine Cosmetics Lineup in Thailand," *Bangkok Post*, October 2004 (http://findarticles.com/p/articles/mi_hb5553/is_200410/ai_n22251558/), accessed October 16, 2009; "History," *Amber Way, Thailand*, 2008 (https://www.amwayshopping.com/amwayshopping-frontend/shopping/contentPage?id=177), accessed October 19, 2009; Jaturong Kobkaew, *King of Direct Sales* (Bangkok: Thai Public Relations and Publishing, 2002); "Mistine Distributor Lifts Sales Target to B8.6bn," *Bangkok Post*, September 29, 2009 (http://www.bangkokpost.com/business/economics/24719/mistine-distributor-lifts-sales-target-to-b8-6bn), accessed October 16, 2009; Kwanchai Rungfapaisarn, "Better Way Hikes 2009 Sales Target," *The Nation (Thailand)*, September 29, 2009 (http://www.nationmultimedia.com/2009/09/29/business/business_30113357.php), accessed October 16, 2009; Thomas Schmid, "Article: Cosmetics Firm Debuts Thailand's Longest TV Commercial," *HighBeam Research*, September 1, 2002, (http://www.highbeam.com/doc/1G1-106646831.html), accessed October 16, 2009; "Successful and Prestigious Award," *Amber Way, Thailand*, 2008 (https://www.amwayshopping.com/amwayshopping-frontend/shopping/contentPage?id=178), accessed October 19, 2009; "Thailand Direct Selling," Competitive Strategies in Marketing, Thammasat University, Thailand, 2004; "'Together as One'—A New Joint Venture Between Mistine and DTAC," Newswit.com, November 23, 2003 (http://www.newswit.com/enews/2003-11-24/1700-together-as-one—a-new-joint-venture-between/), accessed October 17, 2009; Nalin Viboonchart, "Better Way Shifts Focus to Boost Revenue," *The Nation (Thailand)*, August 22, 2009 (http://www.nationmultimedia.com/2009/08/22/business/business_30110418.php), accessed October 16, 2009; and; Ara Wilson, "The Empire of Direct Sales and the Making of Thai Entrepreneurs," *Critiques of Anthropology*, 19 (1999), pp. 402–22.

BP Focuses on Sustainability to Repair Its Reputation

Synopsis: This case provides an opportunity to observe the efforts of BP as it improves its reputation and manages decisions related to ethics and social responsibility. Although BP has sought to establish itself as an ethically responsible company, environmental and ethical mistakes resulting from BP's negligence are reviewed to show that the company has often failed at this goal in the past. In recent years, BP has realized the need to become more environmentally responsible and was the first energy company to recognize the presence of global warming and launch initiatives to produce cleaner forms of energy. In so doing, the company also hopes to educate others about how they can personally reduce their impact on the environment in the hopes of repairing its reputation and repositioning itself as an environmentally responsible company.

Themes: Ethics and social responsibility, sustainability, corporate branding and positioning, corporate affairs, stakeholder engagement, strategic thrust

BP, formerly British Petroleum and the Anglo-Persian Oil Company, has experienced many ups and downs over its hundred-year history—from nearly bankrupting its founder William D'Arcy to becoming one of the world's largest energy companies. BP has also experienced its fair share of controversies regarding its business practices, environmental damage, and hazards to workers. All large energy companies, including BP, have come under fire for the release of vast amounts of greenhouse gases into the atmosphere. BP, however, has attempted to turn a page in its history book toward a more environmentally friendly future. The company has invested heavily in renewable energy sources and become a strong supporter of ethics and compliance initiatives, even writing an expansive code of conduct for its 92,000 employees.

O. C. Ferrell and Jennifer Jackson, University of New Mexico, with the editorial assistance of Jennifer Sawayda, developed this case for classroom discussion rather than to illustrate effective or ineffective handling of an administrative situation. This case was adapted from an earlier version by Eve Sieber and Lameck Lukanga, University of New Mexico.

The 100-Year History of BP

BP was founded more than a century ago by William D'Arcy, a wealthy British gentleman who had invested his life savings in the quest for oil in the Middle East. Although experts and scientists had encouraged D'Arcy to pursue the venture, both his patience and finances were running low after more than six years of drilling. Finally, in 1908 the drilling effort reached almost 1,200 feet and a fountain of oil spewed out. After long years filled with disappointment and despair, the Anglo-Persian Oil Company—what would later become BP—was born. The company quickly began trading on the stock market, and D'Arcy, who had lost nearly his entire net worth, became rich.

The Anglo-Persian Oil Company established its first refinery in a naphtha field in Iran—formerly known as Persia—roughly 130 miles from the mouth of the Persian Gulf. (Naphtha is a Greek word that refers to any petroleum product, but in this case the Anglo-Persian Oil Company was pumping crude oil.) George Reynolds, D'Arcy's head manager in Persia, quickly discovered that navigating this rugged land was not going to be an easy task. Simply moving equipment to the site had been a monumental task that took months to accomplish. To facilitate transportation of the oil, BP started building a pipeline through the area, and many of the necessary supplies had to be shipped from the United States. Because there were no paved roads at the time, everything had to be hauled through the sand using manpower and mules. Because of the difficult mountainous terrain, the pipeline project took over two years to complete. The huge scope of the undertaking drew workers not only from nearby Arab countries but also from India and China—all of whom were seeking work helping to build the largest refinery in the world. The medical director for the project eventually founded a hospital in Abadan to serve BP employees. That hospital would go on to become one of the two most important medical centers in the entire region.

By 1914, BP was on the verge of bankruptcy. The company had a great deal of oil but nowhere to sell it. The automobile had not become a mass-market product at the time, and companies in North America and Europe had first-mover advantages in the industrial oil markets. BP also had another serious disadvantage: The strong smell of Persian oil eliminated it from the heating and kerosene lamp markets.

Winston Churchill, who was at the time the British's First Lord of the Admiralty, changed all that. He felt that the British navy, which was the envy of the world, needed a reliable and dedicated source of oil. Oil executives had been courting the British navy for some years, but until Churchill, commanders had been reluctant to abandon coal. Churchill was adamant that only Anglo-Persian, because it was a British-owned company, could adequately protect British interests. Parliament overwhelmingly agreed and soon was a major shareholder in the oil company. Thus began the debate over the repercussions of involving politics in the oil industry, a debate that only became louder throughout World War II, the Persian Gulf War, and the Iraq War.

The remainder of the twentieth century saw enormous growth in the oil industry, along with massive power shifts in the Middle East. In 1969, Muammar al-Gaddafi led a coup in Libya and promptly demanded a tax increase on all oil exports. Gaddafi eventually nationalized BP's share of an oil operation in Libya. This move led other oil-rich countries in the Middle East, including Iran, Saudi Arabia, Abu Dhabi, and Qatar, to eventually nationalize oil operations. The effect on BP was massive: Between 1975 and 1983, oil production in the Middle East fell from 140 million barrels to only 500,000 barrels.

To survive, BP had to find new sources for oil. The Forties Field off the coast of Scotland, capable of producing 400,000 barrels of crude oil a day, and Prudhoe Bay in Alaska, where BP had tapped its largest oil field yet in 1969, were the two great hopes for BP's future at the time. However, transporting the oil was again a problem. The remoteness of BP's best sites would challenge not only BP's engineering capabilities, but more importantly its commitment to the environment. The Forties Field pipeline would eventually become the largest deepwater pipeline ever constructed, a project that required special attention due to the harsh weather. The Trans-Alaska pipeline system, measuring nearly 746 miles, would become the largest civil engineering project in North America. The company performed extensive research to identify potential environmental risks, making sure the pipeline included long aboveground stretches to ensure that the warm oil moving through it would not melt the permafrost. BP also took steps to ensure that habitat disruption would be minimal. The company tried to assuage stakeholders' concerns and promised to address environmental issues with an intense level of focus and commitment.

Questions About BP's Ethics

Unfortunately, BP's actions have not always coincided with its words. The company's promises to act as a responsible environmental steward have been marred by numerous instances of questionable behavior. As the company's operating environment became more complex and chaotic, BP often lost sight of its responsibilities to the environment, employees, society, and shareholders.

In March 2005, an explosion at a BP-owned oil refinery in Texas killed 15 employees and injured another 170 people. The explosion was the result of a leak of hydrocarbon liquid and vapor. BP admitted that it had ignored several procedures required by the Clean Air Act for ensuring mechanical integrity and safe startup between 1999 until the explosion in 2005. BP was later fined $50 million after it was found guilty of violating the Clean Air Act. The BP case was the first prosecution under a section of the Clean Air Act, which was created to help prevent injuries from such accidental leaks of explosive substances.

BP was also charged with violating the Clean Water Act when Alaskan oil pipelines leaked crude oil into the tundra and a frozen lake. The leaks occurred in March and August of 2006 after BP failed to respond to numerous red flags—one being a dangerous corrosion of the pipes that went unchecked for more than a decade. The first leak, discovered in March 2006 by a contract worker, resulted in more than 200,000 gallons of crude oil spilling onto the fragile tundra and was the largest spill to ever occur on the North Slope. A second, 1,000-gallon leak occurred in August 2006. Although small, the second leak led to the shutdown of oil production in the east side of Prudhoe Bay until BP could guarantee that the pipelines were fit for use. After these incidents, BP was fined $20 million, including $12 million in criminal fines, $4 million in payments to the National Fish and Wildlife Foundation, and $4 million in criminal restitution to the state of Alaska. Yet another leak occurred in October 2007 near Prudhoe Bay. This time, 2,000 gallons of toxic methanol, a deicing agent, spilled onto the tundra and killed many plants and animals.

In the Northern District of Illinois, BP was charged with conspiring to violate the Commodity Exchange Act and also to commit mail and wire fraud. The fraud involved purchasing more than the available supply of TET propane and then selling it to other market participants at a price inflated well above market value. Because this sort of market manipulation is not tolerated in the United States, the violation resulted in a 20-count indictment by a federal grand jury in Chicago. BP was later forced to pay $100 million in criminal penalties, $25 million to the U.S. Postal Inspection Consumer Fraud Fund, and a restitution of $53 million to consumers who overpaid for propane. Additionally, BP had to pay a civil penalty of $125 million to the Commodity Futures Trading Commission. Furthermore, four former employees were indicted for conspiring to manipulate the propane market at an artificially high price.

BP Repairs Its Reputation

BP's environmental, legal, and ethical transgressions demonstrate that the company has a history of disregarding the well-being of stakeholders. The mistakes of BP and similar companies have caused many types of stakeholders to become more wary, especially after decades of repeated violations and misconduct across many different industries. Being an energy company, however, BP also finds itself in the midst of a key debate over the future of the world's energy supply and such key issues as global warming and greenhouse gas emissions. In this regard, BP has taken major steps toward repairing its tattered image.

The company's first step was to change its name from British Petroleum to simply BP—shorthand for Beyond Petroleum. John Browne, BP group chief executive stated, "We are all citizens of one world, and we must take shared responsibility for its future and for its sustainable development." The key difference in the name change for BP was removing "petroleum" from its name, thus allowing the company to focus on a full spectrum of energy sources. The new BP was the first global energy firm to publicly announce its recognition of the problem of climate change. Browne has publicly discussed BP's involvement in finding new energy sources and has stated that he believes in balancing the needs of development and environmental protection. Although its primary product is still petroleum, BP accepts that global warming is human-made, and has begun to seek diversified revenue streams in alternative energy offerings and other low-emission sources. The company now invests around $1.4 billion annually in renewable energy sources such as wind, solar, and biofuels.

BP also has worked hard to overcome its image by focusing renewed efforts on areas such as Alaska, where the company has received a lot of bad press. Every winter, when the Alaskan tundra is icy and frozen, a team of BP specialists heads for the remote areas of the Alaska North slope oilfields. The specialists' purpose is to excavate gravel from the pads on which drilling rigs once stood. They also remove drill cuttings and other waste left behind by the original exploration teams. Most of the excavated gravel can be reused immediately or treated on-site. The remainder of the gravel is either processed for future use or is ground down before it is injected back into the ground. The specialists aim to do as much as possible to return the sites to their original state. This includes selective replanting and reseeding of the area. The specialists are guided by scientists and engineers from BP's remediation management team. They have already completed approximately 40 percent of a cleanup and restoration exercise agreed upon by BP and the state of Alaska. The Sag Delta 1 site on the Beaufort Sea Coast and the Kuparuk 24-12-12 site by the Kuparuk River are two examples of the 16 sites already sanitized. The specialists will return on a regular basis until their job is complete. The estimated cost of BP's future restoration efforts will be close to $250 million. Even with all that effort, ultimately, the final restoration is best left to nature, with native tundra species soon returning to cover any remaining evidence of human presence.

BP Works to Improve Sustainability

To adapt to changing world energy demands, BP launched its Alternative Energy business in 2005. Although still a small part of its overall company, at $1.4 billion in investments, BP sees "going green" as an increasingly important part of its business, which it will expand as it becomes more profitable to do so.

Wind   BP has over 500 megawatts (MW) of installed capacity, with 432 MW in operation. Starting in 2008, BP began full-scale commercial operation in conjunction with wind farms across the country, including Cedar Creek in Colorado—a 274-unit wind farm. BP's installed wind capacity has the potential to supply power to 6 million homes.

Solar   In order to affordably expand its solar capacity, BP signed agreements with numerous solar panel producers in Asia. BP has installed only four MW of solar panels in the United States, those going to Walmart stores in California. BP does 70 percent of its solar business in Europe, where demand is higher. BP has also developed two of the largest solar power plants in the world in Spain, projects that will supply energy to up to a million homes. BP also supports the Solar Cities concept, which has brought more access to solar power to seven cities across Australia.

As BP has continued its worldwide efforts to reduce greenhouse gas emissions, it has introduced a new solar-driven pump system at the Moxa Gas Field site in Wyoming. Two kinds of pumps are located at each of the 460 wells: one type pumps methanol, while the other circulates heated glycol to prevent the freezing of equipment. BP has installed 230 solar-driven methanol pumps to help reduce the amount of natural gas needed to run the site. BP estimates that by using these solar pumps, it has reduced Moxa's annual natural gas needs by over 48 million cubic feet, which amounts to around $200,000 in savings. The new pumps also create a safer work environment, as they reduce the risk of gas cloud–related hazards for the employees. BP plans to install an additional 460 solar-driven glycol pumps. By replacing all of the pumps, BP has the potential to completely eliminate the use of natural gas at the Moxa site, making the pumping system virtually greenhouse gas free.

Biofuels   Biofuels have received a lot of negative press for their contributions to diminished food supplies and increasing food prices, and for causing deforestation in places like the Philippines and Brazil, where it has become increasingly profitable to plant biofuel stock like sugarcane and palm. However, BP sees biofuels as a significant part of its energy portfolio for the next two decades, until better alternative energy sources are perfected.

BP became the single largest foreign stockholder in a Brazilian bioethanol company when it purchased a 50 percent stake in Tropical Energia S.A. The company's facility in Goias state, Brazil, has a capacity of 115 million gallons of sugarcane bioethanol. BP has also been working with DuPont to develop biobutanol, a biofuel with higher energy content than bioethanol.

BP's push in the alternative energy sector prompted the creation of a special purpose entity (SPE) with Verenium Corporation, a leader in the development of cellulosic ethanol, a fuel that is still in its infancy but that many hope will be the future of biofuels. Both partners hope to speed the development of cellulosic ethanol and to one day make it commercially viable. Cellulosic ethanol is a renewable fuel produced from grasses and nonedible plant parts, such as sugarcane waste (called bagasse), rice straw, switchgrass, and wood chips. Although at this point it is much more difficult and energy intensive to produce cellulosic ethanol than corn or sugarcane ethanol, many believe that as the technology improves, cellulosic ethanol will provide such benefits as greater per-acre yields and lower environmental impact. Cellulosic ethanol also has the added benefit of not affecting commodity or food prices, because it uses only waste products. If all goes as planned, BP and Verenium's strategic partnership will stimulate the development, production, and consumption of cellulosic ethanol over other types of liquid fuels.

Carbon Sequestration and Storage   Although it is a tremendously expensive undertaking, many experts believe that one of the best ways to control greenhouse gas emissions is through carbon sequestration and storage (CSS). CSS involves capturing greenhouse gas emissions from smokestacks and other sources of the pollutant and pumping the gases deep underground to empty oil or gas fields or aquifers. BP has been researching CSS since 2000 and opened the Salah Gas Field in Algeria for experimentation in 2004. BP captures and stores up to 1 million tons of carbon dioxide per year at Salah, which is equivalent to removing 250,000 cars from the road. BP hopes to do the same thing at Hydrogen Energy, its joint venture with Rio Tinto to develop low-carbon emissions power plants for Abu Dhabi and California. Although questions remain about the long-term effectiveness of CSS (no one knows for sure whether the CO_2 stays underground or whether it eventually leaks out), many energy companies such as BP see it as a promising technology.

Other Energy-Saving Measures

Beyond alternative energy sources, BP is also looking to save energy through better planning and implementation of its many operations around the world. The BP Zhuhai (BPZ) purified terephthalic acid (PTA) plant is setting an example by using more efficient forms of energy. (PTA is a raw material used to manufacture polymers for use in the production of textiles, bottles, and packaging and film products.) This development of more efficient, cleaner energy and the reduction of CO_2 emissions is an increasing priority in China. Many companies in China still use heavy oil and coal for fuel. For the past four years, BPZ has worked to set new standards and make a greater contribution in this area. A sequence of heat recovery projects has allowed the plant to optimize the use of steam as a way to reduce liquefied petroleum gas (LPG) consumption significantly. Since 2005, BPZ has reduced its CO_2 emissions by 35 percent and has reduced the use of LPG by 48 percent. Additionally, by reducing fuel consumption, BPZ also has reduced the road safety and operational risks associated with delivery and unloading of LPG. BPZ is recognized locally and regionally for its promotion of environmental values, and it has set an environmental standard for other companies to follow. The company also is a prime example of how being green can be cost-efficient. It has achieved annual net savings for BP worth approximately $7.6 million.

BP is also working in Algeria to help sustainability. The Algerian business unit of BP is striving to lessen groundwater and soil impacts from its operations. The company is doing this by incorporating liability prevention processes early in the process, even into the planning stages of operations. However, in a desert area, where sandstorms and other disastrous weather patterns are common, planning ahead and anticipating problems is not easy to do. The BP Algeria team, working in conjunction with the state oil company Sonatrach and Norway's Statoil, has established two primary environmental objectives: (1) to impact the environment as minimally as possible, and (2) to take action swiftly to correct for any potential liabilities from earlier operations. BP's Remediation Management Liability Prevention team supports the Algeria team and Sonatrach in identifying potential causes of soil and groundwater problems incurred at any point during BP's operations. Together, they have been able to identify problems by conducting a series of site visits, doing risk-analysis work, administering prevention assessment tool surveys, and identifying improvement opportunities in the area of operations. All parties involved have been able to synthesize their findings into a long-term plan for the management and prevention of environmental liabilities in Algeria.

Stakeholder Education

In addition to its Alternative Energy program, BP also has implemented environmental awareness programs in Britain to help stakeholders understand the impact of global warming and the importance of sustainability issues. BP is trying to help the environment by making people more aware of their carbon footprint. For example, BP Educational Service (BPES) initiated the distribution of the Carbon Footprint Toolkit—an award-winning program designed to help high school students understand the effects of climate change and their own carbon footprint. Developed in conjunction with teachers and BP's experts, the toolkit enables students to examine their school's carbon footprint and to help develop carbon reduction plans for their schools. The Carbon Footprint Toolkit was originally developed as a response to teachers' demands that came out of a series of BP-sponsored "green" workshops. Available online and free of charge to all high school students and their teachers, the Carbon Footprint Toolkit has been a successful initiative for BP. The kit is used in 80 percent of all British high schools.

The toolkit received a prestigious award for e-learning at the 2007 International Visual Communications Association (IVCA) Awards. Follow-up research has shown that the toolkit has greatly helped to increase the profile of BPES and also has raised the level of trust and recognition for BP's education initiatives. In addition, the proportion of teachers surveyed who judged their students to be environmentally aware increased from 62 percent to 89 percent after using BPES resources.

The BP Code of Conduct

To help deal with BP's growing reputation for ethical misconduct, BP's Ethics and Compliance team organized the creation, publication, and distribution of a company code of conduct in 2005. The code was distributed to BP employees around the globe and made publicly available at the BP website. Given the multinational nature of BP's business, the code seeks to unite its diverse employees behind a set of universal standards of behavior. The cross-functional team that drafted the code of conduct faced many major challenges, like how to agree upon and communicate consistent standards for all BP employees regardless of location, culture, and language. They had to devise a plan to make the code a one-stop reference and guide to individual behavior at BP. It would have to cover everything from health and safety to financial integrity. The code of conduct was the largest mass communications exercise ever attempted in BP's history.

Work began in 2004 with a large-scale benchmarking exercise. The ethics and compliance team, with the help of many external specialists, studied in great detail the codes of 52 other companies. Using the information collected from preliminary research, a team of senior regional, functional, and business segment leaders worked to develop the content of the BP code. A preliminary version of the code was tested in global workshops involving more than 450 BP employees from all levels of the company. The final version, called "Our Commitment to Integrity," provides clear guidelines for individuals covering five key areas: (1) health, safety, security, and the environment; (2) employees; (3) business partners; (4) government and communities; and (5) company assets and financial integrity. The opening statement of the code reads this way:

> As one of the world's leading companies, we have a responsibility to set high standards: to be, and be seen to be, a business which is committed to integrity. In a complex global business environment like ours, that's not always easy. Our code of conduct is designed to help us achieve this.
>
> Our code of conduct is the cornerstone of our commitment to integrity. As Tony Hayward, the group chief executive, affirms: "Our reputation, and therefore our future as a business, depends on each of us, everywhere, every day, taking personal responsibility for the conduct of BP's business". The BP code of conduct is an essential tool to help our people meet this aspiration.

All BP employees are expected to read and follow the code of conduct. To facilitate understanding, it is translated into languages as diverse as Mandarin, German, Azeri, and Arabic. The company also holds awareness meetings to help employees understand the contents of the code. Perhaps the most important role of the code is that it put into writing, for the first time, BP's ethical and legal expectations.

Conclusion

From the beginning, BP proved that it was able to overcome significant obstacles. It went from near bankruptcy to being one of the largest energy companies worldwide. BP has experienced a range of ethical issues, the most well-known stemming from the company's own negligence and misconduct. Yet, although BP has had a spotty past when it comes to integrity, the company has worked hard to overcome its negative reputation. It is not only investing in cleaner energy but also is trying to repair its image by reducing its environmental impact and cleaning up areas after it has used them. Some question whether BP's new socially responsible initiatives are a public relations ploy or a genuine attempt toward change. However, there is no question that BP's emphasis on environmental responsibility is having a positive impact around the world. From publishing a thorough code of conduct, to investing in more renewable energy, to being the first major oil company to admit that global warming is a threat to our future, BP has sought to establish itself at the forefront of ethical and socially responsible energy companies. The company realizes that being environmentally sustainable and ethically responsible not only is the right thing to do but also can be profitable. Good publicity and stakeholder goodwill can be powerful forces in helping companies maintain a competitive edge and thrive.

Questions for Discussion

1. Based on the history of the company, why did BP get involved in so much questionable conduct?

2. Analyze BP's efforts to improve sustainability and its reputation. Do you think they are sufficient, or does the company need to do more?

3. Do you believe the BP code of conduct will prevent future misconduct? Why or why not?

4. How can BP prove to its stakeholders that it is serious about social responsibility, sustainability, and ethics, and that its efforts are not just a public relations ploy?

Sources

The facts of this case are from BP Sustainability Review 2008 (http://www.bp.com/liveassets/bp_internet/globalbp/STAGING/global_assets/e_s_assets/e_s_assets_2008/downloads/bp_sustainability_review_2008.pdf), accessed October 10, 2009; "British Petroleum to Pay More Than $370 Million in Environmental Crimes, Fraud Cases," *PR Newswire* (http://www.prnewswire.com/cgi-bin/stories.pl?ACCT=104&STORY=/www/story/10-25-2007/0004690834&EDATE), accessed October 10, 2009; John Browne, "Breaking Ranks," *Stanford Business* (http://www.gsb.stanford.edu/community/bmag/sbsm0997/feature_ranks.html), accessed October 10, 2009; Darcey Frey, "How Green Is BP?" *The New York Times*, December 8, 2002 (http://www.nytimes.com/2002/12/08/magazine/08BP.html?scp=3&sq=how%20green%20is%20BP&st=cse), accessed October 14, 2009; Russell Gold, "BP Jumps into Next-Generation Biofuels with Plans to Build Florida Refinery," *The Wall Street Journal*, February 19, 2009, p. B1; "The History of BP," BP International website, (http://www.bp.com/sectiongenericarticle.do?categoryId=2010123&contentId=7027817), accessed October 10, 2009; Amy Judd, "British Petroleum Ordered to Pay $180 Million in Settlement Case," *Now Public*, February 19, 2009 (http://www.nowpublic.com/environment/british-petroleum-ordered-pay-180-million-settlement-case), accessed October 14, 2009; Jack Kaskey, "BP, Dow Chemical Post Losses as Recession Cuts Demand (Update 2)," *Bloomberg*, February 3, 2009 (http://www.bloomberg.com/apps/news?pid=20601102&sid=a2e75bA8i47k&refer=uk), accessed October 14, 2009; Jad Mouawad, "Oil Giants Loath to Follow Obama's Green Lead," *The New York Times*, April 7, 2009 (http://www.nytimes.com/2009/04/08/business/energy-environment/08greenoil.html?fta=y), accessed October 14, 2009; "Our Commitment to Integrity," BP Code of Conduct (http://www.bp.com/sectiongenericarticle.do?categoryId=9003494&contentId=7006600), accessed October 14, 2009; and Greg Palast, "British Petroleum's 'Smart Pig,'" Greg Palast: *Journalism and Film*, August 9, 2006 (http://www.gregpalast.com/british-petroleums-smart-pig/), accessed October 10, 2009.

MIKOŁAJ JAN PISKORSKI
HANNA HAŁABURDA
TROY SMITH

eHarmony

Greg Waldorf, the CEO of eHarmony, was in his car driving down the Interstate 10 Freeway after a day-long meeting with eHarmony's senior leadership team. The sole purpose of this October 2007 meeting was to decide how the company should address recent competitor actions. After many deliberations, Waldorf's executive team was able to identify four strategic options. Now, Waldorf and Greg Steiner, the President and COO, who was sitting next to him, were debating which option the company should pursue.

As the two whizzed down the car pool lane, passing cars stuck in traffic, they reflected on eHarmony's success. This online personals site targeted marriage-minded individuals and offered a unique product which combined an extensive relationship questionnaire, a patented matching system and a guided communication system. Despite charging a premium for its services, eHarmony had experienced phenomenal membership growth while its competitors stalled. As a consequence, it was able to increase its paying membership base to slightly less than a half of its largest competitor, even though it entered the market six years after they did.

The success of eHarmony did not go unnoticed. From the beginning, competitors had been copying some of the company's product features and closing the price gap. More recently, Match, eHarmony's biggest competitor, had increased its advertising expenditures by 80 percent. Some of the increase was aimed at reviving Match's sagging growth. However, most of it was spent on supporting the growth of Match's new dating site, called Chemistry, which like eHarmony was a match-making service. It utilized different matching criteria and methodology, and was priced roughly 10% below eHarmony. To make matters worse, free personals sites and online social networks were exploding in popularity, challenging the business model of paid online personals.

As the two approached downtown Los Angeles, the carpool lane came to an abrupt end, leading them into a dense traffic jam. They could not help but wonder—was this also eHarmony's future, or would one of these four options provide them with a new on-ramp to fuel growth and profitability?

Marriage Markets

Although the institution of marriage had differed substantially through time and across cultures, at the beginning of the 21st century, it remained one of the most central social institutions throughout the world. Created by a contract between two people, usually one man and one woman, marriage conferred special state, social, or religious privileges. It allowed a couple to share wealth; it regulated inheritance arrangements; and it legitimized sexual relationships and reproduction. It also regulated

Professors Mikołaj Jan Piskorski and Hanna Hałaburda and Research Associate Troy Smith prepared this case. HBS cases are developed solely as the basis for class discussion. Cases are not intended to serve as endorsements, sources of primary data, or illustrations of effective or ineffective management.

Harvard Business School

political and commercial ties among families from which the couple descended. Spouses were expected to remain exclusive to each other and, traditionally, couples followed a strict division of labor, with women responsible for childbearing and men engaged in outside labor. Although this arrangement often led to significant power inequalities in the relationship, couples were expected to stay married until one partner died, with divorce being rare. Some cultures even regulated patterns of re-marriage, expecting, for example, a widow to marry the brother of her late husband.

In some cultures, couples were betrothed to each other by their families even before they became teenagers. Other cultures allowed the process to take place later, but still with significant assistance from family, close friends, elders, or even astrologers. In some instances, third-party matchmakers were employed to find advantageous mates. Even as modernity progressed, people were expected to choose their spouses through an elaborate process, often overseen by parents. In the U.S., the concept of a potential couple meeting privately at specified times and places to get to know each other started among middle-class teenagers in the 1920s.[1] However, such encounters remained relatively formal through the 1950s. Cultural changes brought more freedom in the 1960s, with the first TV show focused on dating appearing in 1965.[2] By this time, most individuals found spouses through friends, colleagues, or family members, or at work, church, or school.[3] By the early 1980s, the concept of marriage had evolved from a functional partnership to an institution based on "love, sexual passion, or even close friendship."[4] Indeed, Americans no longer believed that the purpose of marriage was to have children. Now, 70% wanted "their spouse to make them happy."[5] This shift in expectations made potential spouses less of "search goods," with clearly identifiable characteristics, and more of "experience goods," which could only be "judged by the feelings they evoked rather than the functions they performed."[6]

Modern Marriage Markets

These cultural changes, coupled with several economic factors, had a substantial effect on the marriage market in the 21st century (see **Exhibit 1**). First, only about 16% of U.S. singles (about 7% of the adult population) reported currently looking for a romantic partner. Men were less active than women in going on dates, but men and women were equally likely to report that it was difficult to meet people.[7]

Second, the marriage rate had reached its lowest point in recorded history. In 1890, men married at a median age of 26, while women typically married at 22. By 2004 the age had increased to 27 for men and 26 for women (see **Exhibit 2**). The later marriage age was partly attributable to cohabitation before marriage. Only 25% of those who cohabited got married within five years of first moving in together, but almost 60% of those who married in the early 2000s had lived with their future spouse for two years before getting married.[8] Between March 1995 and March 2005, cohabitation rates had risen from 2.9% of adults to 4.7%.[9] Although the cause was uncertain, couples who lived together before marriage were 50% more likely to get divorced than non-cohabiting couples.[10]

Third, divorce rates had changed substantially. Starting from a low rate in the 1950s, the divorce rate rose rapidly in the mid-1960s, reached its peak in 1981, and had been declining since.[11] The divorce rate was lower for people who were well-educated, wealthy, and religious, and for those who married someone of the same race after the age of 25, came from an intact family, and did not have a child before marriage (see **Exhibit 3**). A general increase in the age at first marriage and the educational attainment of married couples were often used as explanations for the overall decline in the divorce rate.[12] Despite the trend, the American marriage market experienced more "churning" than most developed nations (see **Exhibits 4**). Whether this was caused by financial disagreements, infidelity, communication problems, sexual problems, mid-life crises, addictions, career strains, and/or emotional or physical abuse, divorce put an end to about 45% of marriages, with most divorces occurring in the fourth year of marriage.[13] Americans were also more likely to re-marry, with a median time between divorce and second marriage of 3.5 years, and with men more likely to get re-married. 12% of men and 13% of women had married twice, but only 3% of either group married three or more times (see **Exhibit 5**).[14]

Personals Industry

The oldest surviving record of a personal ad was published in the *Collection for the Improvement of Husbandry Trade* in 1695. It read: "A Gentleman about 30 years of age, that says he has a Very Good Estate, would willingly Match Himself to some young Gentlewoman that has a fortune of 3,000, or thereabouts." As time went on, personal ads became more common, particularly where men faced a shortage of women. An ad for "any gal that got a bed, calico dress, coffee pot and skillet, knows how to cut out britches and can make a hunting shirt, knows how to take care of children can have my services till death do us part" would not be unusual on the American frontier.[15] Women, however, were often not allowed the same social rights. Helen Morrison, for example, a lonely English spinster, placed a personal ad in 1727 in the Manchester Weekly Journal; the ad caused so much stir in the community that she was committed to an insane asylum for four weeks.[16]

As dating became more popular in the twentieth century, individuals began to advertise for potential partners more frequently. Initially people took out personal ads in newspapers and magazines. These ads usually gave a short blurb about themselves and the type of partner they sought. Increasingly sophisticated communication and recording technology led to the creation of telephone personals. The advent of video tapes in the 1980s brought images to personal ads, which could be cataloged by dating services and exchanged among spouse seekers. These services were complemented by professional matchmakers, who charged up to 100 times more for their services, but who used individual interviews and background checks to personally select dates for clients.

Internet personals

The advent of the Internet expanded partner seeking opportunities. The first online personals firms, started in 1992, met with lukewarm response. Internet savvy people were the most likely to try the new services, but these individuals preferred to meet future spouses through AOL chat rooms or free bulletin boards. By doing so they could avoid the social stigma of being on an online personals site, which at the time was considered appropriate only for the truly desperate. The use of the Internet for quick hookups made the stigma even worse. Even as paid online personals sites became more acceptable, the level of customer dissatisfaction remained high. Frustration and disillusionment affected the serious relationship segment the most. Successful customers got married and left the site; few would publicly admit to having met online. Those who could not find a match remained in the market, vociferously complaining about the problems with online dating. As a consequence, the online personals market was growing very slowly, reaching only $40 million in 2001.[17]

By 2005 the situation had changed dramatically, with 16 million people claiming to have visited an online personals site at least once.[18] Growth was attributed to changes in attitudes toward online dating; social acceptability grew as more people knew someone who had met their spouse online. This change in attitude was so extensive that it even benefitted offline matchmakers, whose number increased by 25%, despite charging $1,500 to $10,000 for their services.[19] Initially, online daters were younger than the general population, but quickly the 40– and 50–year-olds became the fastest-growing segment of the market (see **Exhibit 6**). Significant growth also came from people who signed up at the request of their families. This category could comprise as much as 20% of paying members, although this number varied depending on the target market of the site. Of those who had ever used personals websites, 45% had never been married; 31% were divorced, separated, or widowed; and

23% were married.[20] Seven million people had gone on dates with people they had met through an online personals site, with 40% entering some type of a long-term relationship. Of the 2.2 million marriages that took place every year in the U.S., reportedly 120,000 occurred between people who had met on an online personals site.[21] Industry insiders claimed a much higher rate, believing that nearly one-fifth of marriages were initiated through an online encounter.

After 2005 the percentage of Internet users who visited online personals sites fell from 20% to 10%, but the decline in visitors did not translate into a decline in paying subscribers, allowing the industry to grow to $900 million in 2007. Many believed there was still substantial room for growth in the market (see **Exhibit 7**). Only 37% of people who declared themselves as looking for a relationship and with access to the Internet had actually been to a personals website. However, once someone subscribed to a service they tended to be repeat customers of online personals sites. Consequently, observers believed that the industry could double in size by 2012.[22]

eHarmony

eHarmony was founded by Dr. Neil Clark Warren and his son-in-law, Greg Forgatch, in 1998. The company officially launched in August 2000, six months after receiving $3 million from a Houston investment firm, Fayez Sarofim & Company.[23] After earning his Ph.D. from the University of Chicago, Dr. Warren spent 35 years as a practicing psychologist focused on marriage and family relationships. During that time, Dr. Warren had also written nine books on love, marriage, and emotional health and made numerous appearances as a speaker at conferences and seminars as a relationship expert. Warren had also been dean of the graduate school at Fuller Theological Seminary. With decades of professional counseling experience, Dr. Warren saw the opportunity to help people with mate selection. He focused eHarmony on singles seeking a serious relationship—a segment of the market that had not been well served until then. Unlike other websites, eHarmony also introduced matching on the basis of long-term compatibility.

In the early years of eHarmony, Dr. Warren worked very hard to spread the word on eHarmony's unique offering. He appeared on a wide range of TV and radio programs including local news programs, two appearances on *Politically Incorrect* with Bill Maher, and *Good Morning America*. A major breakthrough occurred in August 2001, after the company was featured on a Christian radio program affiliated with Focus on the Family, an evangelical organization, which had published some of Warren's books. eHarmony's focus on serious relationships resonated well with faith communities—a market segment also untapped by traditional dating sites—resulting in over 100,000 registrations in just a few weeks. By early 2002 registrations had grown to over 300,000, allowing the firm to break even that year and become cash-flow positive the next.[24]

Subsequently, the company expanded its TV and radio advertising campaigns to appeal to a broader audience.[25] As a result, by early spring 2004, eHarmony hit three million registrations, at least 40% of which were considered active users. The company was famous for being able to convert these active members to paying members three times more effectively than the industry average.[26] Later that year, Technology Crossover Ventures and Sequoia Capital invested in the company. In 2005, Greg Forgatch stepped down as CEO, while continuing to serve on the board of directors. Greg Steiner, previously the Vice President of Operations, stepped into the President and COO role. The Board led a search for the CEO position, with Greg Waldorf, the founding investor and Board member, taking the role temporarily and leading the search process. Ultimately, the Board asked Greg Waldorf to remain on as CEO permanently.[27] Under Steiner and Waldorf's leadership the company grew to 230 employees, approximately a half of whom were in customer service.

Product

eHarmony distinguished itself from other personals sites by offering a tightly integrated system that encompassed a Personality Profile, which fed into a matching algorithm, which then led to a Guided Communication system.

The Personality Profile initially contained 436 questions, which the company pared down to 258 (see **Exhibit 8**). The questions covered 29 basic measures of compatibility, including personal lifestyle preferences, communication style, values, beliefs, attitudes, personality traits, family background, birth order, energy level, intelligence, spirituality, special interests, and future aspirations. eHarmony developed the Personality Profile internally. "We went through the whole process of establishing content validity and developing a voluminous set of items to assess the domain. We then had different people look at the items and pare them down and give them to focus groups, and then to larger groups to get some initial estimates of reliability. We were quite rigorous in every step of developing the questionnaires of personality, values, and interests, which were the three primary constructs" recalled Dr. Galen Buckwalter, Chief Scientist at eHarmony. Having developed the instrument, Warren and his team surveyed over 2,000 couples before the website was launched.

The Personality Profile formed the central part of the Relationship Questionnaire, which was required of anyone who wanted to become an eHarmony customer. The questionnaire was free, but the original version with over 450 questions required at least 1.5 to 2 hours to complete.[28] More recently, the questionnaire has been abbreviated to about 250 questions, which takes about 45 minutes to complete. Men were less likely to complete the questionnaire once they started. Waldorf explained: "Since it is hard to sign-up, the eHarmony person self-selects. There is a shared sense of investment to be part of eHarmony. It says, 'I'm serious.'" Despite the length of the questionnaire, more than 14 million people completed it in the first seven years of eHarmony's existence.

The completion of the Relationship Questionnaire did not automatically guarantee access to the service. The company declined to sell memberships to as many as 20% of its potential customers. The majority of the time, the company declined to sell memberships because people were already married, followed by those who were underage, or had been divorced more than three times. This policy was challenged in a lawsuit, Claassen v. eHarmony, filed by a married man under California's Unruh Civil Rights Act accusing eHarmony of discriminating against him because he was not offered a membership due to his marital status. When the Plaintiff registered for the site, he was married and living with his wife , which was inconsistent with the company's policy that all of its members be "free of relationship commitments."

Since its inception, the company has declined to sell memberships to at least one million people who sought to become paying customers, costing the company an estimated $10 million per year. Waldorf believed this was a sound business decision: "We leave a lot of short-term value on the table, but the idea is to keep the quality of our pool really healthy."[29] The final distribution of members reflected the geographic distribution of the U.S. quite well, with a slight skew toward less populous areas. Approximately 60% of eHarmony users were women, who generated slightly more than two-thirds of visits to the website.[30] In 2007, people 45 years and older constituted the fastest-growing segment of users for the company.

The company also did not offer its singles matching service to women seeking women or men seeking men. This choice has attracted considerable positive and negative attention. Given eHarmony's limited resources and the relatively small size of the same-sex market, the Company did not believe it made sense to enter that marketplace. eHarmony did not exclude the possibility that it would engage in the research needed to establish statistically valid and reliable matching models for the same-sex market in the future. The company also faced a second lawsuit, which it believed was baseless, also under California's Unruh Act, Carlson v. eHarmony, filed by a lesbian woman accusing it of discrimination because it does not offer services for people who want same-sex matches. Other companies that specialize in same-sex matching that do not offer opposite-sex matching have not been targets of similar litigation.

Matching Algorithm   After an applicant had completed the Personality Profile, the answers were fed into the matching algorithm. If the applicant had the potential to be successfully matched, then she or he would be able to purchase a subscription. The matching algorithm had been developed by a team that included Warren and Buckwalter, among others. Although most psychological literature on the topic suggested that "opposites attract," Buckwalter recalled that the team was "convinced that successful relationships were almost universally characterized by a high degree of similarity, particularly in areas like intellectual ability and emotional stability. We considered similarity to be more important for personality characteristics, then values, then interests. We also thought that agreeableness and emotional stability were very important." Having identified the algorithm, the team set out to conduct a set of studies of married couples to test and refine it. Buckwalter believed that "the ideal design would have been a longitudinal study, but we could not do that within the constraints of the business model. So the decision was made early on to study married couples, and to make the assumption that if we got really good at predicting satisfied and happy marriages, that we could apply that to singles." Between 2000 and 2004, eHarmony did numerous rounds of matching algorithm validation with over 4,000 couples. The results were very encouraging: the algorithm could predict to a high degree of accuracy whether couples would end up in the top quartile of the Dyadic Adjustment Scale, a tool used by researchers to measure long-term relationship happiness.[31] The company secured a patent for the algorithm in May 2004. Although critics believed the patent amounted to little more than a marketing gimmick, further company research revealed that successful couples who had met on eHarmony were significantly happier than couples who had met "in the wild" or through other online means.[32]

When eHarmony made a match between two people, both sides were informed and could review basic demographic characteristics about the other, along with answers to some of the "about me" questions (cf **Exhibit 8**). Each party could then decide whether to start communicating. If one of them decided not to pursue the match, both sides were informed and the match was considered "closed." Although the matching system took full advantage of the initial Personality Profile, it did not use information from the matches a customer decided not to pursue. "You don't like that this person has a pet, or you're a vegetarian but you keep being matched with hunters" reflected one eHarmony team member. Improving the ability of members to set screening preferences was a next generation feature in the works.

In order to communicate with one's matches, a member had to buy a subscription, for which eHarmony charged almost twice as much as other online personals sites (see **Exhibits 9** and **10**). "Subscription is driven by how users like their matches. It's almost like everyone has an implicit dollar amount they are willing to pay for a match. We can predict re-subscription rates based on the number of hypothetical pairings—how many matches are available for a person—so people who are easier to match are more likely to re-subscribe," commented Waldorf. He continued: "People see the value of a good match when they see an attractive profile, of which an important piece is the photo. Philosophically, we are trying to help people get to know each other more deeply and at a more fundamental level. But we had to face facts that members who have photos are between 9 and 15 times more likely to receive a message. Now, 80% of paying subscribers have a photo posted."

The distinction between paying and non-paying members created some problems for the company. Non-paying members were still matched to others, meaning that a paying member could initiate an interaction, leading to the conversion of non-paying members to subscribers. However, some paying subscribers felt frustrated by this system. "If I am a paying user and you are not, I can send you a message and you might never respond because you don't want to pay. And then I don't know—did you not like me? Did you even see me? I want some kind of feedback. Otherwise, it feels like I am investing all this time to start communication but after all this investment, I never hear back," reflected an eHarmony user. To address this concern, eHarmony was considering adding a feature to allow users to see which messages had been read.

Guided Communication   Unlike the matching algorithm which was the result of intense study, Warren came up with the initial design for Guided Communication, which led potential couples through a set of questions before allowing them to communicate directly. Based on his years as a clinical psychologist, Warren believed that people, when left on their own, would "gravitate to the most superficial questions, like sports or activities, not to what really matters in relationships." Waldorf echoed the sentiment: "you need to give people a way to talk about deep issues such as children and ideal locations. Guided Communication allows for such information-seeking without the social stigma."

Guided Communication comprised three distinct activities. First, each member in the pair was asked to choose five easy-to-answer questions from a list provided by eHarmony, and send them to their match. Questions such as, "If you were taken by your date to a party where you knew no one, how would you respond?" would be followed by multiple-choice answers, such as "(a) Stay close to my date, letting him/her introduce me, (b) Find a quiet spot and relax alone, (c) Strike out on my own and make friends, or (d) Ask my date if I could skip the event." Once both parties answered, they moved to the next stage where they were asked to exchange their personal list of "must haves" and "can't stands." In the final stage they were asked to exchange three open-ended questions to allow for more detailed description of both parties' values. eHarmony provided some sample questions, such as "What person in your life has been most inspirational, and why?" or "Tell me about your closest friend. How long have you known them, and what do you like best about them?" But members could also write in their own questions. Once this exchange was completed, and a message from Warren was displayed, the two parties could move into Open Communication. During Open Communication the pair could send emails to each other, exchange photos, and prepare for their first meeting. A potential couple could then decide when, where, and how to meet in the offline world if they wanted to pursue a relationship. Buckwalter commented, "When people meet in person, they have all this collective history and discussion, and it's almost like they know each other right off the bat." The company estimated that on average a successful subscriber took four to six months to get matched to someone they would eventually marry.

At any point in the process, either party could "close" the match and cease any further communication. Given the number of opportunities to drop out, only 20% to 30% of matches ended up in open communication. Upon mutual agreement, the pair could also elect to Fast Track their interaction directly to Open Communication, without going through Guided Communication. Only 10% of eHarmony members used Fast Track. Though men had most frequently requested the Fast Track feature before its introduction, they were less likely to use it, because within the standards of eHarmony it could be seen as intrusive. The company recently allowed users to state their preferred communication method, leading to a tripling of Fast Track requests. Members who used Fast Track communicated with more potential matches and renewed their subscriptions more often, leading to higher lifetime value. "These people come to us because they want to meet somebody, and they want to interact to determine whether they would like to get to know their matches better. The first step is emailing back and forth, then talking on the phone, or meeting in person. Our members who are able to do this more quickly have a higher satisfaction rate and stay on the service a lot longer" commented a senior Product team member.

The results of this integrated system were astounding. eHarmony commissioned a study, conducted by Harris Interactive between August 2004 and August 2005. The study found that on average, 90 eHarmony members married every day in the United States as a result of being matched on eHarmony.[33] A follow-up study in 2007 found that on average, 236 eHarmony members marry every day in the United States as a result of being matched on eHarmony, representing a stunning 2% of marriages in America.[34]

Marketing

To support growth in its membership base, eHarmony invested substantial resources into marketing. The company aired its first radio commercials in 2002, with TV spots following in June 2003. Soon thereafter eHarmony stumbled on a very successful campaign, which paid for itself in increased subscriptions within a week! It featured testimonials from happy couples who had found love through eHarmony, in short upbeat segments. A senior marketing team member believed that the commercials clearly communicated that "eHarmony is about serious relationships and helping people find lasting love. Nothing could convey this more authentically than the couples. A lot of our early growth came from bringing people into the category who previously wouldn't have considered online dating, because it seemed too sleazy, too casual." Although there were at least 100 different executions of the campaign, the couple was always placed against a white background and accompanied by Natalie Cole's "This Will Be" song. The spots often mentioned the Personality Profile, the 29 dimensions of compatibility, and automatic matching. Warren, a "wise, experienced doctor," was also featured prominently in the ads, although it was never explained that he was a psychologist.

In 2007, the company was considering adjusting its four year old signature campaign to appeal to those interested who have so far shied away from eHarmony's service. The new campaign featured spots focused on one couple, shot in their real environment in a documentary style, highlighting that couples love story. Any changes to eHarmony's successful marketing formula had to be introduced with care; the company had earlier experimented with telling the story of lonely individuals who were afraid that they would never meet anyone, followed by a happy conclusion. These commercials backfired, because "the initial ten seconds spent recounting the 'problem' just flared up anxiety in people and dampened our response rates... so we went back to focusing on the end benefit," explained a team member.

The successful advertising formula made eHarmony one of the few online companies that made offline marketing work and pay for itself. But with marketing expenses reaching as much as $80 million per year, firm profitability depended on efficient customer acquisition. eHarmony was extremely judicious in its use of advertising dollars, avoiding any pure brand-building activities and focusing on direct-response marketing. The marketing team worked only with advertising and media buying agencies, "who really understood direct-response advertising...   This means they are incredibly diligent about buying media at lower rates – both by locking in good 'upfront' deals and searching for last-minute remnant inventory." As a result, eHarmony advertised only on national cable networks and avoided broadcast television, where prices where higher because local stations allowed for greater targetability than national cable. Match, eHarmony's close competitor, used broadcast TV and aired its commercials during primetime shows, paying $20 to $30 per thousand impressions—at least four times more than cable TV prices.

With three-quarters of the marketing budget spent on TV and radio, eHarmony spent the remainder on online marketing, including paid Internet search and banner ads. The latter had high visibility and got decent click-through rates, but the conversion rates were low, which made banner search more expensive than paid search in terms of customer acquisition.

Research & Development

Since its inception the company had made significant investments in R&D, culminating in the opening of eHarmony Labs in 2007. Staffed with five research scientists, the Labs were tasked with studying the biological, sociological, and neurological underpinnings of love. The Labs boasted over 2,000 square feet of clinical space, including several rooms set up with chairs and couches. In this setting, couples were observed as they interacted to examine relationship dynamics.

eHarmony was also pursuing research on physical attraction. Buckwalter noted that "physical attraction plays a large role in the initial meeting but is a very poor predictor of long-term success. After the initial meeting, people find themselves attracted to others with whom they share common values. But if we can give people matches with whom they're also going to feel this 'click' factor, they're more likely get to the point of actually developing a relationship."

Finally, the company has invested substantial resources into a five year study of 400 couples. Couples were enrolled during their engagement and followed through their marriage and subsequent life stage transitions, such as pregnancy and childbirth. Early results already suggested that "the biggest adjustment of every marriage is the birth of the first child." Now, the study sought to identify what characteristics and behaviors in couples predicted successful transitions. The company believed that its team of research psychologists was uniquely positioned to identify specific insights and turn them into products and services that could become new businesses for eHarmony.

Competitors

Competitor Types

Paid Do-It-Yourself sites were the most common type of online personals site. Some of eHarmony's direct competitors, such as Yahoo! Personals and Match, were in this category. In contrast to eHarmony, these sites put up very few barriers to joining. Individuals were required to provide basic information about themselves, such as their age, location, gender identification, and sexual orientation. Optionally, they could provide a short blurb about themselves and provide a set of pictures. For most heterosexual sites, men were more likely to sign up than women. As soon as the short registration process was complete, individuals could specify the criteria for their partner search. The website instantaneously provided them with a set of profiles and pictures of individuals who matched their search criteria. Members could then browse profiles to identify their own choices for a match. Some sites allowed unlimited browsing, and all required a subscription to communicate with other members. On average, 5% of those who signed up became paying subscribers, with men more likely than women to sign up. Paying members had little loyalty and, on average, belonged to at least three other personals sites, either as visitors or paying members.[35] Sites tried to develop some differentiation by offering compatibility tests, or by conducting background screenings to weed out sex offenders, felons, and married people, but most of these features were ineffective or easy to replicate. Perhaps the only meaningful distinction was the advertising spend.[36] One firm, True, spent $90 million on advertising in a single year—an amount that exceeded its revenues numerous times, without much long-term impact.

The process of looking for a match was fairly time consuming. By some estimates, online daters spent nearly seven times as long searching for potential partners as interacting with them. Heterosexual sites reported fairly skewed patterns of interactions, with a select group of women being inundated by messages from men. Patterns of interactions between the two genders could be easily predicted by basic characteristics. A study of speed-dating found, for example, that "men avoided women whom they perceived to be smarter than themselves. When women were the ones choosing, the more intelligence and ambition the men had, the better....Women also exhibit a preference for men who grew up in affluent neighborhoods....Women also put greater weight on the intelligence and the race of the partner, while men responded more to physical attractiveness."[37]

Online interaction was designed to lead to offline meetings. However, researchers found that online daters typically "ended up going out with fewer than 1% of the people whose profiles they studied, and....those dates often ended up being huge letdowns."[38] Acknowledging the difficulties of dating in general, researchers found that "most participants were so dissatisfied with both online and offline dating that they would have preferred to stay home and watch a movie."[39]

Free Do-It-Yourself sites had been rapidly growing in membership base. The growth defied the common industry wisdom which claimed that requiring people to pay to join a dating site served as an important barrier separating lurkers and casual daters from serious ones. Being free, these sites could attract members quickly, leaving it to the members to interact with the vast number of others to identify their own match. In addition to SinglesNet, the fastest growing among these was Plenty of Fish, founded by a 29-year old entrepreneur in Canada, Marcus Frind. Despite a terrible user interface, Plenty of Fish had become the most frequently visited dating site in the U.K. and Canada and had reached No. 4 in the U.S. by the end of 2007. Although Plenty of Fish only had half as many visitors as eHarmony, the website received 20% more visits than eHarmony did. Such user engagement on the site resulted in 900 million page views per month, allowing this one-person company to become one of Google's AdSense top earners, with revenues close to $500,000 per month. A significant portion of this revenue came from referring people who were dissatisfied with the quality of matches on Plenty of Fish to more selective paid sites, such as Match or eHarmony. Not all free personals sites were equally successful, however. OKCupid, started by the founders of eDonkey (a free file-sharing service), was only beginning to catch up, despite having a more appealing interface and much better functionality. Some sites, such as Craigslist, did not even care about making profit, even though they possessed a significant market share of personals, particularly those targeted at casual hookups. Few doubted that the existence of these sites put a cap on how much the paid sites could charge for their services (see **Exhibit 11**).

Niche sites were also in competition with eHarmony. Waldorf referred to the niche sites as "community of interest sites," which he said were "characterized by low customer acquisition costs. For the generalists, it is basically a customer acquisition story." The gay and lesbian market was the largest niche market, attracting about a tenth of the internet traffic of the heterosexual personals sites.[40] Some sites catered exclusively to this market, while others added it on top of heterosexual matching. Sites targeted at African Americans, such as BlackPeopleMeet or Black Singles, were a close second, followed by faith-based personals site, which included sites such as JDate.com, ChristianSingles.com, Hindu-Dating.com, Muslima.com, and LDSsingles.com. Of these, JDate, targeted at a Jewish audience, was considered the most successful, with almost 10% of Jewish singles enrolled on the site. Other sites covered just about every conceivable demographic—some targeted at graduates of elite colleges, such as TheSquare, others focused on people with health conditions, such as HIV, Crohn's disease, cancer, or diabetes. Internet users could also sign up on RichorBeautiful, HotEnough, or HotorNot, as well as SingleParentLoveLife, SweetOnGeeks, FarmersOnly, SugarDaddyForMe, VeggieFishing, and GothScene, not to mention MarriedButPlaying. Overall there were at least 850 different personals sites on the Internet. About the same number entered the industry every year, with most failing quickly without making a penny of profit.[41]

Online social networks provided an important substitution threat to the online personals industry. Large online social networks, such as MySpace or Facebook, did not have to incur the vast advertising expenses required to attract customers, instead relying on a "viral" process through which friends encouraged their friends to join. Such networks also held a significant advantage over personals websites in the veracity of information they provided about potential matches. The online dating industry was plagued by people misrepresenting personal information—ranging from subtracting a year or two from their real age or increasing their height by a couple of inches, through posting 10-year-old pictures or losing 50 lbs. overnight, to outright fraud, by failing to disclose that they were married. Because people were connected to their friends in online social networks, however, they would find it hard to post a 10-year-old picture or forget to mention a spouse, without eliciting comments from friends. Online social networks were also attractive to people who were currently in long-term relationships and could not easily join a dating site without jeopardizing their current relationship. Under the guise of interacting with their friends on an online social network, they could scan the market for new partners. Indeed, some industry experts estimated that the most traffic was generated by men in relationships looking at women they did not know. Whether such actions translated into offline liaisons was still unknown. Finally, online social networks held a significant advantage over dating sites for gay men and women. Due to inherent search difficulties in this market segment, and the importance of compatibility between one's partner and one's friends, online social networks provided a valuable search tool.

Despite these apparent advantages, online social networks presented a number of limitations compared with online personals sites. First, online social networks did not make it easy to send a clear signal about whether one was interested in forming a relationship. Even though online social networks allowed people to indicate whether they had joined only to interact with friends or to establish a new romantic relationship, at least 40% did not indicate their marital status at all, making it hard to figure out whom to approach. Second, with more people concerned about the privacy of their information, an increasing number of profiles were becoming private, with access available only to one's direct friends. This shift severely curtailed the usefulness of online social networks for meeting or finding out detailed information about people one did not know. Finally, online social networks were used less often than personals sites by people in their 40s and 50s, making them less useful for that segment of the population. Weighing the advantages and disadvantages, experts at Jupiter Research saw "no signs that the eruption of social networks has burned the paid online personals market."[42] Waldorf shared this view: "I don't believe that social networking will hit us in ways that everyone expects….I think it will have less to do with pricing and more to do with user expectations and the user experience. We have a new cohort of users from MySpace and Facebook coming every day. Will they find the guided process to be a breath of fresh air or too constraining?" Others within the industry concurred, believing that social networks played in a different space and that among all the people meeting online, only about 5% had met through a social network site.

Direct Competitor Profiles

Match eHarmony considered Match its biggest competitor. Match was owned by InterActiveCorp (IAC) and contributed roughly 5% of IAC's revenue. IAC owned other online and offline businesses, including Home Shopping Network (HSN), Ticketmaster, Interval Timeshare, Lending Tree, Citysearch, ShoeBuy, ReserveAmerica, and Ask. In 2006, IAC boasted $5.9 billion in revenue, but it earned margins of only 4%. Its biggest division, the Home Shopping Network, made up 50% of revenue and more than 85% of the total margin. In 2007, IAC lost $150 million on $6.3 billion in sales.

IAC acquired Match in 1999, four years after it had been founded by Gary Kremen and Peng Ong. Two years after the acquisition, the company boasted 382,000 paying customers, each of whom contributed roughly $10 in revenue and $2 in operating profit per month. By 2003, the company had signed extensive co-marketing agreements with AOL and MSN, which increased the number of paying customers to 930,000 and revenues to $185 million. Match also made significant investments in overseas expansion. In 2005, Match was present in 30 countries and boasted revenues of approximately $250 million on 1.2 million paying customers, with equal membership from men and women. Most of the membership growth had come from overseas, accounting for 30% of the firm's revenues. To boost US growth, Match invested in new features that made Match more similar to eHarmony. For example, it started to offer dating advice from a doctor, Dr. Phil McGraw, a popular daytime TV personality who had gained celebrity status following his appearances on *The Oprah Winfrey Show*. Match featured Dr. Phil prominently on its website, advertising his "Mind, Find, Bind" method for finding "enduring romance," while carefully avoiding references to marriage. The campaign did not boost the membership base, as the number of paying customers had increased only to 1.3 million despite the company's presence in 7 new countries. [43] Unsurprisingly, by early 2007 Dr. Phil had faded into the background, while Match focused on its campaigns of "It's OK to look" and "Find someone special in 6 months, or we'll give you the next 6 months free," designed to attract new members who would hopefully convert to paying customers.

However, despite the slow growth, margins were predicted to remain at 20%–22% on projected revenues of $349 million and an asset base of $333 million.[44] Maintaining margins would be a major achievement for the company, as it has just increased its advertising spend from $80 million to an estimated $145 million, matching eHarmony's advertising spend as a percentage of sales.[45] Among other online personals companies, only Match had any kind of TV presence to rival eHarmony. Given the fact that Match's website traffic in 2007 was only 20% of 2004 levels, many expected the company's advertising expenditures to increase in the future.

In early 2006, Match also launched a new brand, called Chemistry to challenge eHarmony in the serious relationship segment. "At some point Match realized that was a lot of money to be made in the serious relationship market. Those consumers are often much more willing to pay for memberships," recalled a Marketing team member. Chemistry shared many similarities with eHarmony, with a few important points of difference. Like eHarmony, Chemistry required that prospective members fill out a questionnaire before joining the site (see **Exhibit 12**). However, unlike eHarmony, Chemistry sold memberships to anyone who wished to sign-up, giving them a major and minor personality designation, from the menu of Explorer, Builder, Director, and Negotiator. Chemistry was also similar to eHarmony in that it delivered a pre-set number of matches to its members using an algorithm developed by another doctor—Dr. Helen Fisher, a visiting research professor of anthropology at Rutgers, and author of four major books and numerous publications. Unlike eHarmony, Chemistry claimed that its algorithm focused on interpersonal chemistry rather than psychosocial compatibility. To appraise such attraction, Chemistry asked its members to compare the length of their ring finger to the pointing finger of their right hand—a characteristic apparently determined by the amount of testosterone present in the womb during fetal development. This, in turn, was thought to determine certain personality characteristics. Chemistry applied for patents, claiming a system to determine early-stage attraction between prospective mates.

Finally, like eHarmony, Chemistry required that members go through a three step guided communication process. The first step required that both people rank criteria, such as neatness, feelings on family life, sense of humor, and pets and send their answers to their match. The second step entailed sending two questions for the match to answer. Chemistry provided questions asking about proudest moments, greatest regrets, and lessons learned from previous relationships, but members could also write in their own questions. If the matched members decided to pursue their relationship further, they could proceed to email contact. Chemistry did not offer the equivalent of eHarmony's Fast Track. However, it did allow people to come back to the site and report how their offline dates went. This feedback was reportedly used to deliver better matches.

In its first year of operation, Chemistry spent $10 million on advertising and claimed 2 million registered users, even as some users reported a fairly low "successful first meeting" rate.[46] In 2007

Chemistry tried a "rejected by eHarmony" advertising campaign, with the tagline, "Who knows why eHarmony has rejected over a million people looking for love? But at Chemistry.com, you can come as you are."[47] eHarmony did not react to the advertisements.

Yahoo! Personals eHarmony also competed with Yahoo! Personals which attracted seven million unique visitors and 5% of all visits to dating sites. Personals was a business line of the Search division of Yahoo!, which also included Yellow Pages, Maps, and Shopping. In addition to Search, Yahoo! had the following divisions: Front Page, Mail and Messenger, Media, and Co-Branded Internet. In 2007, Yahoo! attracted a total of 107 million unique visitors, and earned $695 million on $6.9 billion of revenues, $12 billion of assets, and $9 billion of equity. Yahoo!'s overall profitability was at least 5 percentage points lower than it was in 2006, as operating expenses increased faster than revenues. Sales and marketing accounted for one-half of Yahoo's! overall operating expenses, while product development contributed one-quarter.

Yahoo! developed the Personals line internally in 1997 and relatively quickly rolled out the service to 15 different countries. The service was not differentiated from a typical paid dating website—users could browse a few personals for free, but to continue browsing or to communicate with others they had to buy a subscription. The service did not change much over the first 10 years of operation, except for the introduction of Yahoo! Personals Premier in November 2004. Launched in response to eHarmony's success, the new service used results from relationship and personality tests to search and match individuals. It cost $34.95 a month, $15 more than Yahoo!'s regular service. The service was not very successful, largely because Yahoo! did not put significant resources behind the business. The company did not advertise on television, but spent a total of $17 million in 2007 on Internet advertising through diverse Yahoo! properties and other search engines. Despite the lack of advertising support, Personals contributed approximately 2.5% to Yahoo!'s revenue, with estimated average revenue per customer of $16 per month.[48]

Options

With the competitors in full attack mode, Waldorf knew that eHarmony needed to respond very soon. Together with Steiner, the COO, they continued to debate four different options.

The first option was targeted at defending eHarmony's position as the leading matchmaking company in the long term relationship segment of the market. Central to this option was a rapid increase in the number of paying members to deny Chemistry a chance to grow. Reflecting on this option, Waldorf commented "Two years ago, I believed that we had diminishing returns to subscribers in the network. I no longer believe this at all. There is still a massive user satisfaction effect to having more users." Few at the company believed that increased advertising alone would be sufficient to drive customer growth; some favored reduction of barriers to joining the site and encouraging the use of Fast Track communication. Selling memberships to anyone who wanted to purchase a subscription could also be considered, but then the company could not be as confident in recommending matches that resulted in high levels of marital satisfaction.

The second option entailed broadening the customer base to include more casual daters. Waldorf believed that the company could only expand as far as medium-term relationships without seriously undermining its credibility with marriage-minded individuals. Although this option would expose eHarmony to more intense competition with Yahoo! Personals and Match, the introduction of the matching algorithm to this segment could provide a strong point of differentiation. Given that no more than 5% of the 94 million U.S. singles were paying members of an online personals site, Waldorf reasoned there were many people interested in medium-term relationships who could benefit from eHarmony's matching algorithm.

The third option called for growing a new business based on eHarmony's own research and development efforts – particularly the long term research project aimed at understanding successful life stage transitions. If chosen, this option would entail building a network of eHarmony-branded sites, each focused on key life stages such as weddings, pregnancy-fertility, parenting, and elder care. The sites would offer expert advice from eHarmony as well as support and community from other website users who are considering similar life decisions. The sites would be free to use with most of the revenue coming from advertising.

The final option called for rapid geographic expansion, starting with English speaking countries and then rolling out the services to European Union nations where online dating was already very popular. Match was present in many of these countries, suggesting that Chemistry could be rolled out globally, too. If eHarmony did not expand to new geographies soon, it could find that its target segments were already taken by competitors. However, some questioned whether U.S.-based research could credibly predict matching patterns in other countries.

Despite its profitability, resources were always scarce, preventing eHarmony from making sweeping changes. It was clear to Waldorf that the company could afford to invest in only one or two of the options he was considering. It was less clear, however, which of them would address the short-term competitive threats and position the company for long-term success.

Exhibit 1   Characteristics of People 15 Years and Over with Marital Event Within the Last Year: 2001

Characteristic at time of interview	Men				Women			
	Married	**Separated**	**Divorced**	**Widowed**	**Married**	**Separated**	**Divorced**	**Widowed**
Total (in thousands)	2,476	1,031	1,038	484	2,442	1,201	1,181	1,222
Race and Ethnicity								
White Non-Hispanic (%)	64	70	76	77	64	68	76	73
Hispanic of any race (%)	21	11	9	5	19	16	11	7
African American (%)	10	17	11	14	10	11	11	16
Asian American and Pacific Islander (%)	6	1	4	7	8	4	2	3
Age								
15 to 24 years (%)	23	9	4	1	33	19	9	2
25 to 34 years (%)	45	32	28	1	42	29	35	2
35 to 44 years (%)	18	36	40	3	14	32	36	4
45 to 54 years (%)	7	17	20	8	9	13	14	12
55 to 64 years (%)	4	5	6	14	2	6	5	20
65 years and over (%)	2	3	2	74	1	1	1	62
Median age (in years)	30	37	39	74	28	36	37	71
Educational Attainment								
Less than high school (%)	16	17	13	40	17	18	12	32
High school graduate (%)	31	36	30	28	25	34	29	32
Some college (%)	28	30	37	14	30	32	35	23
Bachelor's degree or more (%)	25	18	20	19	28	15	23	13
Employment Status[1]								
Worked full-time last month (%)	82	73	83	12	55	57	66	20
Worked part-time last month (%)	8	8	4	9	12	15	13	8
Did not work last month (%)	10	19	14	80	33	29	21	72
Poverty Level								
Below poverty level (%)	12	13	8	14	11	23	23	17
100-199 percent of poverty level (%)	17	21	17	28	17	22	21	31
200+ percent of poverty level (%)	71	64	73	58	71	51	52	51
Income not reported (%)	0	3	3	1	1	4	4	1

Source: Rose M. Kreider, "Number, Timing, and Duration of Marriages and Divorces: 2001: Household Economic Studies," U.S. Census Bureau, February 2005, pp. 70–97, http://www.census.gov/prod/2005pubs/p70-97.pdf, accessed November 2007.

[1] Full-time includes those who usually work 35 or more hours per week; part-time includes those who usually work 1-34 hours per week; those who did not work last month include individuals who were unemployed or were not in the labor force.

Exhibit 2   Percent Married by Age, 1880–2000

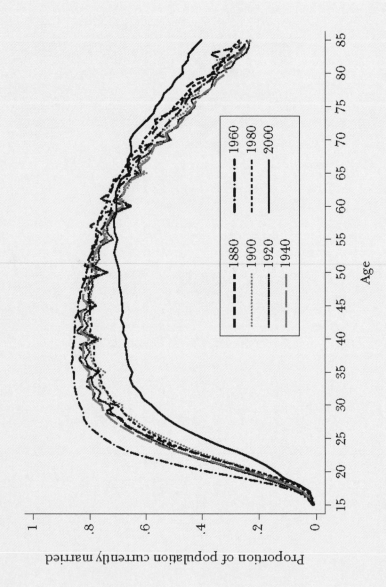

Source: Betsey Stevenson and Justin Wolfers, "Marriage and Divorce: Changes and their Driving Forces," Journal of Economic Perspectives, 21, 2 (Spring 2007): 32, via ProQuest, ABI/Inform, www.proquest.com, accessed November 2007.

Exhibit 3   Factors Affecting the Risk of Divorce

Factors	Percent Decrease in Risk of Divorce
Annual income over $50,000 vs. under $25,000	-30
Having a baby seven months or more after marriage vs. before marriage	-24
Marrying over 25 years of age vs. under 18	-24
Own family of origin intact vs. divorced parents	-14
Religious affiliation vs. none	-14
Some college vs. high-school dropout	-13

Source: David Popenoe, "The State of Our Unions: The Social Health of Marriage in America," published by The National Marriage Project, Rutgers State University of New Jersey, 2007, http://marriage.rutgers.edu/Publications/SOOU/ TEXTSOOU2007.htm, accessed October 2007.

Exhibit 4   Marriage Markets across the World

	U.S.	Canada	U.K.	France	Germany	Italy	Sweden
Marriage							
Annual marriages per 1,000 unmarried adults	18	13	11	9	12	11	9
% of adult population currently married	60	63	55	54	60	60	45
% of adult population ever married	77	76	72	70	76	73	64
% of marriages where bride previously married	28		29	17	28	6	24
% of marriages where bride was older than 34	31	28	30	28	NA	15	33
Divorce							
Divorces per 1,000 married people / year	9	5	7	5	6	1	7
% of adult population currently divorced	10	5	8	7	6	10	11
Cohabitation							
% of nonmarital cohabitation	5	11	12	11	7	4	12
Fertility							
Annual births per thousand people	14	10	12	13	9	10	11
Mean age at childbirth	27	29	29	30	29	30	30
Non-marital births (% of all births)	35	36	42	45	28	15	55
Attitudes: % Agree that...							
Marriage is an out-dated institution	10	22	26	36	18	17	20
People who want children ought to get married	65	50	52	41	53	61	31
Divorce is the best solution when a couple can't seem to work out their problems (%)	43	78	61	61	75	65	55

Source: Adapted from Betsey Stevenson and Justin Wolfers, "Marriage and Divorce: Changes and their Driving Forces," Journal of Economic Perspectives," 21, 2 (Spring 2007): 40, via ProQuest, accessed November 2007.

Exhibit 5   Percent Reaching Stated Anniversary, by Marriage Cohort and Gender: 2001

Sex and year of marriage	Number of marriages (In thousands)	Anniversary[1]							
		5th	10th	15th	20th	25th	30th	35th	40th
First Marriages									
Men									
1955 to 1959	4,100	96	90	82	76	72	69	66	64
1960 to 1964	5,033	94	82	71	66	62	60	58	
1965 to 1969	6,357	93	78	68	62	58	55		
1970 to 1974	7,436	90	73	61	56	53			
1975 to 1979	7,109	89	72	63	58				
1980 to 1984	7,606	90	75	66					
1985 to 1989	8,048	88	75						
1990 to 1994	7,718	90							
Women									
1955 to 1959	5,162	94	87	79	73	67	64	59	54
1960 to 1964	5,714	94	84	73	67	61	57	53	
1965 to 1969	7,138	91	78	66	59	56	52		
1970 to 1974	8,176	88	70	60	54	49			
1975 to 1979	7,852	85	68	59	53				
1980 to 1984	8,448	87	72	64					
1985 to 1989	8,299	87	75						
1990 to 1994	7,967	87							
Second Marriages									
Men									
1975 to 1979	1,985	91	81	58	49				
1980 to 1984	2,544	91	72	55					
1985 to 1989	2,881	90	72						
1990 to 1994	2,834	89							
Women									
1975 to 1979	2,187	86	76	56	47				
1980 to 1984	2,703	89	71	55					
1985 to 1989	3,008	87	68						
1990 to 1994	3,126	87							

Source: Rose M. Kreider, "Number, Timing, and Duration of Marriages and Divorces: 2001: Household Economic Studies," U.S. Census Bureau, February 2005, pp. 70–97, http://www.census.gov/prod/2005pubs/p70-97.pdf, accessed November 2007.

[1] People reaching stated anniversary for the specified marital order.

Note: Limited to spouses surviving the interview date.

Exhibit 6   Percent of web users within a demographic group who have gone to a personals website

Category	Percentage	Category	Percentage	Category	Percentage
All Internet Users	11[a]				
Gender		**Home Internet Speed**			
Men	12	Broadband	12		
Women	9	Dialup	9		
Race/Ethnicity		**Location**			
White	10	Urban	13		
Black	13	Suburban	10		
Hispanic	14	Rural	9		
Age		**Household Income**		**Education Level**	
18-29	18	Less than $30,000	14	Less than High School	14
30-49	11	$30,000 to $49,999	13	High School Grad	10
50-64	6	$50,000 to $74,999	10	Some College	11
65+	3	$75,000+	9	College+	10

Source: Adapted from Mary Madden and Amanda Lenhart, "Online Dating: Americans who are seeking romance use the Internet to help them in their search, but there is still widespread public concern about the safety of online dating," Pew Internet & American Life Project, March 5, 2006, p. 10.

Exhibit 7   How Internet Users in Committed Relationships Met Their Partners

Mode of Meeting	Percent	Mode of Meeting	Percent
Met at work or school	38	Met at church	2
Met through family or friends	34	Met by chance, such as on the street	2
Met at a club, bar, café, or social gathering	13	Met at a recreational facility like a gym	1
Met through the Internet	4	Other	6

Source: Adapted from Mary Madden and Amanda Lenhart, "Online Dating: Americans who are seeking romance use the Internet to help them in their search, but there is still widespread public concern about the safety of online dating," Pew Internet & American Life Project, March 5, 2006, p. 6.

Exhibit 8　eHarmony Personality Profile

	No of questions	Theme	Sample Questions
Section 1	26	My general Information	What is your height? What ethnicity are you? Which ethnicities are you willing to be matched with? How many times have you been married? How many children do you have who are 18 years old or younger and living full time in your home?
Section 2	6	My personal beliefs	Which religion do you affiliate yourself with?
Section 3	19	About me	On the scale of 1 to 7 rate yourself on items such as "I do things according to a plan" and "I often leave a mess in my room."
Section 4	58	My self-descriptions	On the scale of 1 to 7 rate yourself on self descriptions such as "agreeable," "spiritual," "cold," "quarrelsome," "attractive," and "liberal."
Section 5	36	My personal characteristics	On the scale of 1 to 7 rate yourself on the following statements "I enjoy mingling with people on social occasions" or "I ask questions in search of information."
Section 6	20	About my feelings	On the scale of 1 to 7 rate how often you felt the following way during the past month. Feelings include "Happy", "Fearful about future", "Misunderstood" and "Fortunate."
Section 7	30	Important qualities in a partner	On the scale of 1 to 7 rate how important the following characteristics are in your potential partner. Characteristics include "my partner's energy level" and "my partner's ability to communicate." This section also asks for three things for which the applicant is most grateful.
Section 8	19	My personality	True or False? "If a store-clerk gave me too much change, I might keep it without telling them" or "I sometimes wish that certain other people would fail."
Section 9	30	My personal interests	On the scale of 1 to 7 rate how interested you are in the following activities. Choices include "board games," "church involvement," "movies," and "shopping." These choices were followed by open ended questions such as "What are you most passionate about?" and "Please describe two or three things that you most enjoy doing with your leisure time."
Section 10	1	My living skills	Choose three living skills that you do best out of a list of 34. Choices include "Using humor to make friends laugh," "Helping those who are less fortunate or in need," and "Car maintenance and repair"
Section 11	13	My matching preferences	How much do you smoke? Would you accept being matched to a smoker? How much do you drink? Indicate the most you would accept your ideal match to drink? How far are you willing to relocate if you met the right person?
Picture Upload		Optional	

Source:　Compiled by the case writers from http://www.eharmony.com/.

Exhibit 9   Subscription List Prices in 2002 (monthly equivalents in 2008 dollars)

Membership Length	eHarmony	Match	Yahoo! Personals
1 month	59.86	23.91	23.91
3 months	39.92	15.96	15.96
6 months	31.95	11.97	8.98
12 months	24.95	11.97	8.98

Source: Compiled from http://www.onlinedatingmagazine.com/datingservicereviews/matchcomreview.html, accessed February 2008. CPI was used to convert 2002 to 2008 dollars (http://www.greatdepressionbook.com/research/data/us/calc/).

Exhibit 10   Subscription List Prices in 2008

Membership Length	eHarmony	Chemistry	Match	Yahoo! Personals
1 month	59.95	49.95	39.99	29.99
3 months	39.95	33.32	22.99	19.99
6 months	29.95	26.65	19.99	15.99
12 months	19.95	26.65	19.99	13.99

Source: Compiled from company websites, https://www.eharmony.com/singles/servlet/subscription?PURCHASE_REASON=10, http://www.match.com/subscribe/subscribe.aspx?lid=1, http://personals.yahoo.com/us/reg/billingsplash, https://www.chemistry.com/subscribe/subscribe.asp, accessed February 2008.

Exhibit 11   Monthly List Prices in 2008 dollars (based on 12-month commitment)

Name	Service	Price
Offline subscriptions		
Boston Sports Club	Gym access in Boston	74.99
AT&T	900 cell phone minutes	59.99
Verizon	3.0 Mbps Internet Access	29.99
One-time online payments		
Carfax	Second-hand car history	24.99
Equifax	Personal credit rating	12.95
Online subscriptions		
eHarmony	On-line dating	19.95
Ancestry	Search for ancestors	12.95
Gmail	40 GB extra storage space	6.25

Source: Compiled from https://www.google.com/accounts/PurchaseStorage,http://www.ancestry.com/subscribe/signup.aspx, https://www.eharmony.com/singles/servlet/subscription, http://www22.verizon.com/ForHomeDSL/Channels/DSL/olo_landing_new.asp, http://www.mysportsclubs.com/member/, http://www.equifax.com/home/ https://secure.carfax.com/cfm/CCard_Options.cfm.

Exhibit 12   Chemistry Personality Test

	No of questions	Theme	Sample Questions
Section 1	1	Right hand image	Which of the following four pictures most closely resembles your right hand?
Section 2	4	Interpersonal	What kind of relationship are you looking for? Is your sock drawer ready for public inspection?
Section 3	8*	Self perception	Do you enjoy the challenge of managing people? Do you have children? How often do you drink?
Section 4	19	Communication dynamics	How important is it for you to share very personal matters with your partner? When you see two people madly kissing in public, would you rather not look? Do you get restless if you have to stay home for any length of time?
Section 5	50*	Personal traits and preferences	Would you buy a used car from this person (pictures of four people appear)? If you're stuck in a boring meeting, or waiting in the airport, what would your doodles typically look like (pictures of 8 doodles appear)? On the scale of 1 to 4, rate the following statements: "I consider every option thoroughly before making a plan", "I would rather have loyal friends than interesting friends", "Sex is an essential part of a successful relationship", "I am more analytical and logical than most people".
Section 6	2	Aspects of identity	On the scale of 1 to 4, rate the following statement: "There is something on the other side of the wall" (picture of a young man looking over a concrete wall is displayed).
Section 7	14	About me	How tall are you? What color are your eyes? What is the highest level of education you have completed? What is your relationship history? Where would you most like to live? Tell us about yourself and who you're looking for (2000 characters essay).
Section 8	12*	About my match	Is it OK if your future partner drinks? What body types do you find attractive? Which ethnic backgrounds are you willing to consider?
Picture Upload		Optional	

Source: Compiled by the case writers from http://www.chemistry.com/lovemap/lovemap.aspx?rm=1.

Note: * denotes one of the questions entails a visual game

ZEYNEP TON

CATHERINE ROSS

The Home Depot, Inc.

The year 2007 started with a bang at the Atlanta, Georgia-based do-it-yourself home improvement chain the Home Depot, Inc. ("Home Depot"). With 364,400 employees, Home Depot was the largest specialty retailer in the U.S., and the second largest American retailer after Wal-Mart.[1] On January 3, 2007, Frank Blake took over as chairman and CEO, one day after former chairman and CEO Robert Nardelli's surprise resignation. A January 2 Board of Directors meeting had addressed the board's simmering discontent with the company's depressed share price despite improved revenues and profits under Nardelli. During the company's May 2006 annual meeting, the board had suggested that Nardelli's generous compensation package be tied to the company's share price, a proposal Nardelli had flatly rejected.[2] On January 2, 2007, Home Depot and Nardelli announced they had "mutually agreed" on Nardelli's immediate resignation.

Formerly a top executive of General Electric (GE) in charge of its Power Systems Division, Nardelli had arrived at Home Depot to considerable fanfare in December 2000 to take over for retiring founders Bernard Marcus and Arthur Blank. After years of rapid growth, Home Depot in 2000 was a $45.7 billion, 1,134 store home improvement retail chain.[3] (See **Exhibits 1** and **2** for Home Depot's financial data.) Nardelli set out to bring greater discipline to the sprawling retailer's operations, including merchandising and store management. He introduced cost-cutting measures at various levels, including centralizing purchasing and shifting from mostly full-time store staffing to depend on more flexible part-time contracts. By 2006 sales had shot up to $90.8 billion. Profits had more than doubled from 2000 to 2005 to $5.8 billion.[4] (See **Exhibit 2**.) Yet Home Depot's stagnant share price throughout Nardelli's tenure compared poorly with close competitor Lowe's, which saw soaring gains in its share price over the same period.[5] Furthermore, Nardelli's centralization had been criticized by employees, managers and customers as negatively affecting the quality of service and company morale and identity.[6]

As successor to Nardelli, Blake faced significant challenges. Share price remained low, although it rose 2.3% the day after the announced change in leadership.[7] (See **Exhibit 3**.) In 2007, Home Depot was facing a downturn in the housing market, a principal driver of the home improvement retail industry.[8] Home Depot's chief competitor, Lowe's, was adding stores and directly challenging Home Depot in its previously uncontested turf of urban markets.

Blake also faced skepticism on Wall Street. Like Nardelli, Blake lacked experience in retail. He was also a former GE man, having served as general counsel and head of business development in Nardelli's GE Power Systems division.[9] A lawyer by training, he had worked for the U.S. government after leaving GE and before following Nardelli to Home Depot in 2002 to become his deputy.[10] However, in contrast to the abrasive Nardelli, Blake had a reputation for being a listener and for

Harvard Business School

Professor Zeynep Ton and Research Associate Catherine Ross, Global Research Group, prepared this case. This case was developed from published sources. HBS cases are developed solely as the basis for class discussion. Cases are not intended to serve as endorsements, sources of primary data, or illustrations of effective or ineffective management.

Copyright © 2008, 2009 President and Fellows of Harvard College. To order copies or request permission to reproduce materials, call 1-800-545- 7685, write Harvard Business School Publishing, Boston, MA 02163, or go to www.hbsp.harvard.edu/educators. This publication may not be digitized, photocopied, or otherwise reproduced, posted, or transmitted, without the permission of Harvard Business School.

seeking consensus.[11] Some analysts expressed surprise that he had not been named merely an interim leader while Home Depot looked for a top retail executive for the post.[12] An analyst at Goldman Sachs commented to *Business Week*: "This is the second-largest retailer in the nation, and [Blake] has never run a company, or one of Home Depot's major operating businesses."[13] To reassure Wall Street and all of the firm's stakeholders, Blake would have to decide rapidly which of Nardelli's strategies to maintain and strengthen, which ones to modify, and which ones to dismantle.

The Home Depot Story

Home Depot was founded in 1978 in Atlanta, Georgia by Bernie Marcus and Arthur Blank. The founders had both been fired from their executive posts at the Handy Dan Home Improvement Centers in California. Rather than seeking employment elsewhere, they sought start-up capital to fund their vision of "one-stop shopping for the do-it-yourselfer"[14]—vast home improvement stores akin to warehouses that would offer a broad selection of tools and products and would be staffed by knowledgeable experts in home improvement and customer service.[15] The new company's first two 60,000 square-foot stores opened in 1979 in Atlanta with 25,000 stock keeping units (SKUs), far more than offered at that time under any one roof.[16]

The company popularized the concept of "do-it-yourself" (DIY), in which homeowners and other individuals purchased products and tools and then built, repaired and improved homes on their own. Home Depot facilitated the DIY concept not only by prioritizing customer service, but also by providing customers with training workshops and clinics to teach them how to go about "laying tile, changing a fill valve, or handling a power tool."[17] Sales associates underwent rigorous training in product use before attending to customers. From the outset, Home Depot was characterized by a close focus on the customer: Bernie and Arthur, as Marcus and Blank were known to employees, championed the customer service philosophy of "whatever it takes," encouraging sales associates to develop relationships with customers rather than seeing sales as a transaction.[18]

The company grew quickly, achieving $22 million in sales in four stores by 1980, and $3.8 billion with 145 stores by 1990, as it became the top U.S. retailer in the home improvement industry.[19] It was the youngest retailer ever to reach $30 billion in revenues, a feat that would be repeated as it attained $40 billion, $50 billion, $60 billion and $70 billion in sales faster than any other retail company worldwide.[20] By January 2007, Home Depot had 1,800 stores in the U.S.,[21] had expanded into Canada, Mexico, Puerto Rico and Chile, and had just entered China.[22] (See **Exhibit 1** for Home Depot performance data.) An average Home Depot store was 105,000 square feet in size and carried 40,000 SKUs[23].

The Home Improvement Industry and Competitive Landscape

Throughout the 1980s, the home improvement industry was fragmented, with sales divided among niche players such as hardware, lawn and garden, and paint and wallpaper stores as well as big box home center stores such as Home Depot and Lowe's. Beginning in the early 1990s, independent stores began losing market share to the growing big box giants, a trend that continued throughout the 1990s.

When the ABC television program *Home Improvement* debuted in 1991, Home Depot's annual sales were about $3.8 billion and the company employed 21,500 people. Throughout the 1990s and into the new millennium, weekend "DIY-ing" became so popular that two cable networks—Home & Garden Television and the Do It Yourself Network—were devoted to the pastime. Fueled by a housing boom—a bubble that since burst—home improvement outperformed most U.S. retail sectors, reaching an estimated $291.3 billion in 2005.[24]

In 2006, the deteriorating housing market negatively impacted the home improvement retail market; the industry reported $200 billion in sales in the U.S. that year.[25] Analysts reported indications of market saturation as well. However, analyst reports were not entirely pessimistic about the strength of the home improvement industry, citing continued population growth and the need for new homes as well as for repair and renovation of existing ones.[26] Providing services such as tool rental, and increasingly, installation was a new trend in the home improvement retail industry—one that became known as "do-it-for-me" or DIFM.[27]

Retailers in the home improvement business carried products such as building supplies and lumber, plumbing and electrical items, tools, hardware, paint and wallpaper, floor tile, upholstery, glass and window fixtures, blinds, lawn and garden supplies and even home appliances.[28] Home Depot was the biggest player in the home improvement market, followed by Lowe's. These two companies were each other's most significant competitors, and held approximately 60% of the U.S. market share between them in 2006.[29] Wal-Mart, America's largest retailer also competed with Lowe's and Home Depot. Hardware stores such as True Value Hardware and Ace Hardware, which maintained cooperatives among independent retailers, followed at some distance, along with hardware store Menard's.[30] (See **Exhibits 4** and **5**.) In 2006, the average size of a transaction for hardware stores was reported to be $15, compared to an average transaction of $41 for home centers.[31]

Big box stores purchased from a wide array of vendors. In 2006, Lowe's received supplies from approximately 7,000 distinct vendors. Efficient management of information and of the supply chain was crucial. The home improvement industry was cyclical. The period from 2001-2006 demonstrated variable growth. See **Exhibits 6**, **7**, and **8** for trends in expenditures for residential improvements and repairs, housing built, and housing sales.

Lowe's

Founded in 1921, Lowe's business had focused primarily on selling materials to contractors, but the housing decline in 1980 resulted in a decrease in profits, prompting the company to rethink its target market. Over a two-year period Lowe's redesigned half of its 229 stores to serve the needs of DIY consumers, creating a friendlier and more accessible setting with softer lighting and full room displays. The design overhaul was a success, and in 1982 over half of Lowe's customers were non-homebuilding professionals.[32]

Lowe's maintained its small store format through the 1980s, a move that potentially cost it the #1 position among U.S. home retail chains, which Home Depot took over in 1989.[33] It was not until the 1990s that Lowe's pursued a warehouse-style layout for its stores. In 1991 Lowe's began to phase out smaller stores and by 1993 it opened 57 warehouse stores, nearly doubling its overall floor space.[34] Lowe's opened more than 140 stores during the 1990s, and in 1998 announced a $1.5 billion expansion plan that would grow the company by 100 stores across the U.S. over several years.[35] Three years later in 2001, Lowe's allocated $2.4 billion for further store expansion and the building of new distribution centers.[36] Between 2001-2002 Lowe's opened over 200 new stores, a trend that continued through 2007, bringing Lowe's total stores close to 1,500.[37] (See **Exhibit 9** and **10** for Lowe's performance data.)

Lowe's rapid growth between 2000 and 2007 reflected the company's growing customer base. The introduction of upscale product lines, home appliances, and installation services, all offered against a welcoming backdrop, helped Lowe's attract new consumers, specifically wealthy baby boomers and women shoppers.[38] The decision to sell home appliances in Lowe's stores resulted in Lowe's ranking second to Sears in U.S. home appliance sales.[39] These successes translated into monetary gain: Lowe's shoppers spent an average of $10 more per trip than Home Depot customers.[40]

Home Depot's First Decades

For its first 20 years, Home Depot was widely known for its entrepreneurial spirit and focus on customer service and sales growth. Stores were run largely informally. Store managers had almost complete autonomy in their own store operations.[41] They were not only allowed but even encouraged by senior management to ignore or send back directives from headquarters that they felt to be intrusive to their own stores.[42] Because it was commonly believed that managers should spend their time on the sales floor with customers, company paperwork often ended up buried under piles on someone's desk, tossed in a wastebasket, or even marked with a company-supplied "B.S." stamp and sent back to the head office. "The idea was to challenge senior managers to think about whether what they were sending out to the stores was worth store managers' time," said Tom Taylor, who started at Home Depot in 1983 as a parking lot attendant and in 2006 was executive vice president for merchandising and marketing.[43]

Merchandising, Store Operations, and Vendor Management

Local autonomy was intended to encourage innovation and responsiveness to the needs and preferences of the local market. "Whether it was an aisle, department or store, you were truly in charge of it," explained a former Home Depot store manager.[44] Store managers decided on merchandizing, displays and promotions and set employee wages. Merchandising was based on each store manager's local market intuition and not on particular metrics, tools or data for quantitative analysis. Nine regional purchasing offices negotiated separately with suppliers. Agreements would vary from region to region. Blank believed that decentralization helped boost sales 15% to 20% because Home Depot buyers understood local needs.[45]

Decentralized purchasing meant that "the retailer was acting as if it were nine $5 billion companies rather than a single $45 billion company, thus squandering the chance to drive down costs and boost gross margins," wrote one industry observer.[46] Promoting autonomy and responsiveness also implied difficulty in delivering on agreements with vendors. In one case, a purchasing center made a deal for garden furniture that included a 10% discount for Home Depot in return for prominent displays in the stores in that region. But many store managers simply ignored the deal, deciding the display was not what their store needed.[47] Home Depot's decentralization also meant there was little communication among managers, and limited ability to negotiate national deals.[48] While the company could generate nationwide store displays from its headquarters, it could not easily coordinate them with nationwide purchasing.[49]

Most Home Depot stores depended principally on full-time personnel who were knowledgeable about home improvement. One analyst in early 2000 praised this strategy as one that kept productivity high and turnover low. "Home Depot traditionally shies away from minimum wage labor and believes that paying the best people will drive higher store sales and productivity."[50]

In 2000, a company executive cited the high level of customer service—a central tenet of Home Depot's management philosophy under Marcus and Blank[51]—as one of two major reasons for Home Depot's success.[52] The company's 2000 annual report referenced a "recent study" in which "Home Depot associates ranked 40% higher than the competition in customer service and product knowledge."[53]

Need for Change

Despite Home Depot's astounding success, Marcus and Blank stated that further growth would require new ways of thinking and doing. The founders pointed out the need to apply new technologies, build efficiencies and reallocate resources, while still listening and responding to customers.[54] To bring more operational discipline to the company, the founders recruited Robert Nardelli from GE.

The Nardelli Era

In his first week as CEO Nardelli asked how to email all 1,134 stores and was told it was not possible.[55] The Atlanta headquarters generally communicated with store managers by fax.[56] In 2000, the company employed 227,000 associates, yet had no head Human Resources officer.[57] Despite its rapid growth and innovative store format, Nardelli said the company had been "in start-up mode for 20 years,"[58] and that the company's decisions were generally "based on emotion rather than data."[59] The retailer was years behind other retailers like Wal-Mart in technology. For example, bills and invoices were largely processed by hand[60] and for those items that did not have barcodes, employees had to manually go to a book to look up the code. There was no general counsel, no chief marketing function, and no CFO. Nardelli quipped, "Call me old-fashioned, but I kind of like the CFO reporting to the chairman."[61]

To respond to falling sales, rising costs and stiffening competition, Nardelli devised a three-part strategy: extending the business into new lines; expanding the market both geographically and with new types of customers; and making existing operations more sound and profitable.[62]

In 2001, Home Depot began providing "specialized products and services to smaller professional customers" and announced the intention of growing the professional business.[63] By 2003, Nardelli had expanded its wholesale business, Home Depot Supply, which provided products and services to a wide range of professionals including real estate developers, plumbers, electricians, construction crews and industrial contractors rather than to the ordinary do-it-yourselfer.[64] HD Supply grew largely through acquisitions,[65] and was a $12 billion business by 2006.[66] Nardelli also expanded Home Depot's market by announcing steps to move into other countries. Previous leadership had already taken the company into Canada, and Nardelli brought it to Mexico. In 2001, 2002, and 2004, Home Depot bought three separate home improvement chains based there. "We went from zero to number one in Mexico," said Nardelli.[67] To him, international expansion and diversification into the wholesale business were strategic responses to the declining U.S. housing market.[68]

Nardelli referred to the central strategy of improving existing operations as "enhancing the core."[69] Several initiatives fit under this banner, including major changes to fundamental retail functions such as merchandising, vendor management, and store operations. In keeping with this focus, Home Depot prominently displayed the new slogan "Improve Everything We Touch."[70]

Changes Introduced in Merchandising

Nardelli centralized Home Depot's merchandising and purchasing. By July 2001, he had reassigned these functions to 12 merchandising vice presidents who would work out of the Atlanta headquarters. Stripped of purchasing power, the former regional purchasing offices' efforts were redirected toward sales, service and supporting stores for the presentation of merchandise procured through the new centralized system.[71] The centralization was aimed at realizing gains in purchasing power and addressing inefficiencies in operations.[72]

In September 2001, Nardelli used his keynote address at the National Hardware Show in Chicago to promote Home Depot's new policy of consolidated purchasing, saying the reorganization would give the regional managers of the chain "more time to convert merchandise into sales."[73] An executive for merchandising and marketing in a Canadian home improvement store commented, "I think what they are doing is absolutely right. When you buy regionally, you find you're losing too much control of your inventory. And when stores don't pay attention to inventory management, you find your customer service goes down because there's too much product on the [sales] floor."[74]

Detractors feared the centralization would lead to stores offering exactly the same product mix, disregarding local variation.[75] But Nardelli maintained that centralized purchasing was necessary for Home Depot to have greater control of over the mix of products available in stores, to ensure greater consistency in merchandising, and to better manage vendors and inventory.[76] By 2003, the company had eliminated almost 20,000 SKUs from its overall inventory and added others—mostly higher-priced, higher-end items aimed at increasing revenue—as part of centralization of merchandising.[77]

Greater purchasing power allowed Nardelli to broker exclusive deals with certain vendors including John Deere, Mill's Pride Cabinets and furniture-maker Thomasville. He placed emphasis on driving relationships with loyal vendors and developing more business with fewer entities.[78] "Two years ago we never could have done [a deal with] John Deere," Nardelli said in 2003. "Every business, every store was their own sourcing center. Now we can negotiate an exclusive arrangement with the strongest national brand in the country."[79] Home Depot used its beefed-up purchasing power to negotiate better deals, extending payment terms to 45 or 50 days up from the typical 30 days.[80]

To support centralized merchandising Home Depot spent over $1 billion to modernize the retailer's technological infrastructure and IT systems, including a new system for inventory management.[81] By 2004, Home Depot implemented assortment planning, markdown management, and store space planning software.[82] By 2005, 11% of sales were replenished automatically.[83]

Six Sigma Approach to Store Operations

Nardelli was a firm believer in the power of process discipline and operational execution. Drawing on his GE training, he was steeped in the culture of Six Sigma, a management methodology that used rigorous analysis to improve quality, and was eager to implement this methodology at Home Depot. With approximately 1.3 billion customer transactions a year, a slight improvement in these key metrics could boost financial performance, he wrote to his shareholders in the 2004 Annual Report.[84]

The Six Sigma method had been pioneered (and trademarked) by Motorola in the 1980s and was later adopted by GE and others.[85] Motorola estimated that it saved at least $15 billion by using Six Sigma from the time of its development through 1999.[86] Former GE CEO Jack Welch, an enthusiastic proponent of the methodology, believed that Six Sigma techniques led to $600 million in savings in 1998 alone.[87]

In its initial use at Motorola and elsewhere, Six Sigma aimed at eliminating defects in manufacturing processes through reducing variation. A defect was defined as nonconformance of a product or service to its specifications and *sigma* referred to a measure of variation. A process with six sigma quality produced less than 3.4 defects per (one) million opportunities whereas a process with three sigma quality produced less than 2.7 defects per thousand opportunities.

The Six Sigma methodology filtered out of the manufacturing world into other business segments, including the management of sales and human resources. A former statistical methods department manager at Motorola said projects that can be "broken down into discrete, manageable activities"[88] are "the right projects for Six Sigma."[89] In the context of retail store operations, processes associated with the flow and storage of products (i.e. in-store logistics activities) were good candidates for Six Sigma process improvement.

The Six Sigma approach was embodied in a four-step process to achieve improved quality: measure, analyze, improve, and control. Measurement was the crucial first step which allowed a company to quantify its quality and accuracy in business processes. Anything and everything could be measured, from the number of high quality parts produced to the time it took to process orders from customers or the number of daily sales made per sales representative. Measurements and variables were then subjected to a process of analysis to determine optimal outcomes and objectives for the performance of certain business processes. Improvement came from changing processes and methods to better achieve the performance goals that had been set. Finally, once new processes were implemented, they were monitored with an eye to controlling and maintaining quality levels.[90]

Changes Made in Store Operations

Consistent with Six Sigma methodology, Nardelli focused on precision, measurement and quantitative analysis to bring to the fore a focus on efficiencies in operational processes. "When I came here, I was told, 'If you get 50 percent compliance, that's a good day,'" Nardelli recalled. "And I said, 'Well, that's not a good day because customers' expectation is to have consistency of delivery not only in the store they shop, but as they go from Home Depot to Home Depot. "We can't live with 50 percent compliance. You have to have 100 percent compliance."[91]

Changes to improve productivity   Nardelli's method for improving store productivity included simplification of each store associate's job function with an eye toward more specialization.[92] For example, with the Service Performance Improvement initiative, Home Depot began to stock new inventory at night, so that sales associates could spend more time during the day with customers.[93] Sales associates were still responsible for replenishing products from storage areas during the day. Nardelli also worked on standardizing in-store logistics activities, from the moment freight arrived at the backdoor of the store to its eventual sale or return to the vendor. Productivity metrics were introduced around each step of the freight flow process (e.g. pallets per hour).[94] Stores also had to track "inventory velocity," the length of time it took for products to flow through stores.[95]

To improve labor productivity, Nardelli also invested heavily in technology. Through the Front End Accuracy and Service Transformation (FAST) initiative,[96] all stores were equipped with new point-of-sales terminals with touch screens. These terminals made looking up unbarcoded items simpler and faster for cashiers. Self checkout registers were installed in 800 of the company's highest volume stores.[97] Cordless scan guns were introduced at a number of cash registers after a Six Sigma study found that cashiers were faster and more accurate when they used them.[98] By 2004, cordless scan guns had been installed in all stores, and over 1,000 self-checkout aisles were in operation.[99] By mid-2005, Home Depot had also installed a computerized process to scan incoming inventory.

Changes to increase data accuracy   The FAST and back-end scanning and receiving process initiatives were intended to improve accuracy of point-of-sales data and inventory data, respectively. In addition, ordering carts were introduced to facilitate restocking of shelves from storage locations. Home Depot stores received more stock of products to the store than they could present on the display shelves. The extra stock was typically stored on the selling floor in the overheads—the upper shelves that were 8, 12, or 16 feet above. Large products were sometimes stored in the backrooms.

Many products were placed in overheads in areas away from their display locations[i]. Previously, an associate would walk down the aisle and manually write down out-of-stocks from the shelves, take that list to the computer room, generate a report with a "pick list," and then pick those products from the storage locations. With the new ordering cart, associates could walk down the aisles and scan any shelf with an empty space in order to electronically create a pick list. If additional stock of the missing product was present in the store, it was included in the pick list so that associates would know the product was in a storage location and would look for it. In the case of a discrepancy between what the system said the store had in stock and what actually was in stock, associates could make inventory adjustments.[100] That is, associates could change the inventory levels in the computer system to reflect the physical quantities at the stores.

Changes to improve labor scheduling   Nardelli invested in tools for Home Depot's store managers to better forecast staffing needs and to schedule labor. The new computerized workload management system allowed store managers to see what activities were scheduled to take place at the store and historical and future trends to inform decision-making about hiring, staffing and training.[101]

Seeking flexibility for scheduling labor at stores, Home Depot announced it would extend benefits to part-time staff. The company tried to increase the number of part-time employees, from 15% of personnel to 50%.[103] Although a negative reaction to this caused top management to backpedal on the number of part-timers hired, the net increase of part-timers was still significant.[104]

Personnel Changes

Nardelli's arrival resulted in significant changes for employees at the corporate and store level. Within two years of Nardelli's arrival, 22 of the company's top 29 managers left.[106] Between 2001 and 2006, 98% of Home Depot's 170 top executive positions changed hands, and over half of the new hires were from outside the company.[107]

In an effort to recruit new managers and train them in the new management approach, Nardelli and Dennis Donovan—a former GE executive whom Nardelli recruited to join Home Depot as his chief human resources officer—developed a two-year intensive program to fast-track new store managers.[108] The program carefully selected participants and aimed to train newcomers in company practices, analytics methodologies and culture.

In 2002, 528 of 1,142 future managers hired from outside the company had military experience.[109] Donovan explained that the company was seeking "people who deliver results, act strategically, and drive excellence," in contrast to traditional store managers who were frequently experts in hardware. "Leaders excel in customer service," he said. "They inspire achievement, they live [with] integrity, they build strong relationships, and they create an environment of inclusion. Junior military officers have these essentials."[110] A former Navy Lieutenant who in 2005 was Home Depot's director of implementation--a position created to standardize processes at Home Depot—agreed. "Military structure is very similar to how our stores are structured," he said. "A store manager is basically the equivalent of a ship captain. You've got a leadership team under you, and I think the relationships you need to build between your hourly and management associates are a natural fit for military leaders."[111] "Bob Nardelli and I have hired military through a big part of our careers, so we know this model works."[112]

---

[i] Information on storage locations is based on case writer's store observations.

Analyzing Metrics and Making Plan

Nardelli also introduced discipline through data analysis and performance evaluation. Store managers were required to "make plan" by achieving weekly and monthly sales or other performance targets. All personnel were ranked according to four "performance metrics:" financial, operational, customer, and people skills.[113] Nardelli and Donovan placed Human Resource managers in every store to track these metrics.[114] One market analyst gave the new discipline a positive review, saying Home Depot was becoming "much more disciplined, more numbers-oriented and more accountable for everything."[115] To reinforce the new discipline and to better communicate with employees and store managers, Nardelli established an internal TV Channel (Home Depot TV, or "HDTV") that piped in messages to stores.[116] Every Monday night, EVPs for marketing and merchandising delivered the store staff's "marching orders for the week" through a 25-minute live program named "The Same Page."[117] At other times, HDTV ran segments reminding staff of key messages and policies.

Under Nardelli, Home Depot developed personnel incentive plans with the aim of better tying incentives to employee performance. In 2002, the "Success Sharing" program debuted, specifically targeting hourly workers.[118] The program linked employee performance on the new metrics used for evaluation with bonus payments. In 2004, payouts from the program totaled nearly $90 million.[119]

The whole cloth culture change that Nardelli introduced, symbolized by the focus on analytics, did not always lead to the desired results. Managers had to monitor their store numbers, reducing the time they spent on the floor. Former Chief Information Officer Ron Griffin expressed his frustration at having to demonstrate a "return on every nickel."[120] Several stores responded to the "inventory velocity" metric requirement by reducing the amount of inventory coming in, leading to stockouts.[121] A former Home Depot merchandising executive explained, "On paper, all these changes make sense. Unfortunately, they don't work on the floor of the stores."[122] And employees resented the sensation that Big Brother was watching, generated by Home Depot TV. They surreptitiously dubbed it "Bobaganda."[123]

Reactions from Wall Street

Wall Street's initial reaction to the changes introduced by Nardelli was mostly positive. There was widespread agreement with Nardelli's assessment that what had made Home Depot successful in its first 20 years was unlikely to continue to work as the company aimed for $100 billion in revenues.[124] Although some analysts noted that Home Depot under Nardelli opted for a more centralized structure at a time when retailers were devolving more autonomy to stores, many agreed that in Home Depot's case, centralization was a necessary move.[125] Analysts approved of Nardelli's investment in information systems infrastructure, improved supply chain logistics, the strengthened opportunities for economies of scale through the centralization of merchandising, and Nardelli's introduction of greater analytics as a basis for decision-making.[126] Home Depot's strategic alliances with John Deere and others were also cited as strengths.[127] While analysts noted the disgruntlement of present and former employees with the changing culture at Home Depot, it seemed par for the course. Many felt there was bound to be a reaction against cultural change in a company that had previously been famous for and proud of having little corporate discipline.[128]

In 2005, some analysts reflected some reservations. Many doubted Nardelli's strategy to move away from consumer retail and place emphasis on selling to professional contractors through HD Supply. Some analysts asked whether Home Depot was pursuing too many strategic initiatives at once and gave the company a less enthusiastic rating.[129] Other reports fretted about the languishing stock, the housing market and the "disconnect between Nardelli's pay and Home Depot's performance."[130] Nardelli had received $200 million over the previous five years while shareholders saw "cumulative total shareholder returns of approximately -13%." Still, other analysts were bullish enough about Home Depot in late 2005 to place it above Lowe's as their top home center equity because of its positioning for future growth and its relatively low valuation.[131]

Performance Under Nardelli

In addition to the doubling of revenue under Nardelli's leadership, his relentless focus on cost-cutting had been successful in pushing gross margins from 30% in 2000 to 33.8% in 2005. Between 2000 and 2005 Home Depot had a 12% average annual growth rate in sales. Riding the same housing boom, Lowe's had managed to increase its sales by an annual average of 19% over the same time period.[132]

But while Nardelli successfully slashed costs and improved Home Depot's financial management, he did little for the share price. In December 2000, when Nardelli took the reins as CEO, Home Depot's stock price was trading slightly under $37 per share. Six years later when Nardelli left Home Depot the stock was only slightly better off (refer to **Exhibit 3**). By mid-2006 total return to shareholders was down 6%. During the same six-year period, Home Depot's rival Lowe's saw its split-adjusted stock price rise more than 200%.[133] (See **Exhibit 10** for a comparison of share price performance between Home Depot and Lowe's.) Analysts explained the poor share performance as a result of Nardelli's approach to management; one analyst noted that the "numbers were quite good [but] the fact is that this retail organization never really embraced his leadership style."[134]

Customer Service

Research suggested that the slide in customer service was likely related to Home Depot's declining stock price.[135] "He's made Home Depot much more profitable and more streamlined, but messed up everything that has to do with serving the customer," said one analyst. "They've got people in there working for less money and are less knowledgeable and less experienced. It's all about profitability, at the cost of serving the customer."[136] Increased use of part-timers was a source of concern for many. While part-time employees were generally cast in the role of cashiers or shelf-stockers,[137] part-timers undercut a fundamental customer service premise—that of giving the do-it-yourselfer the confidence that prepared staff in orange aprons were available to help. "We built the entire company around the idea that a customer could come in and ask us how to do anything—fix a toilet, build a deck, whatever—and we'd tell them how to do it," said a supervisor at a Florida store. "Now we've got kids who don't even know what the products look like."[138]

Nardelli rejected the notion that an emphasis on part-time staff was inconsistent with excellent customer service. He defended the shift as a positive move for customers who would have more salespeople to attend to them at peak hours. Like the self check-out machines, Nardelli saw increasing the number of part-time employees as a way to ensure better coverage on the floor, and more attention to customers.[139] Investments in store processes and technologies meant that two to three additional associates could be redeployed to the selling floor per store per week to assist customers.[140] Investments in store modernization made stores more attractive.[ii] The centralized merchandising system resulted in higher in-stock levels.[141] One industry expert noted "Nardelli is very acutely aware of the personnel cost of providing personalized service and I think they've done a

---

[ii] In 2004, the company reported having spent $1 billion on store remodeling and refurbishing.

fairly good job at making the stores as self-serviceable as possible. It's easier to find product than it was before and stores are cleaner and easier to shop."[142]

Yet, many employees who had grown up in the Marcus and Blank era felt the new focus and strategies prevented them from delivering excellent service. Some insiders began referring to the chain as "Home GEpot" or "Home Despot," monikers that leaked out to the business press.

Business Week reported that Nardelli had "alienated customers just as thoroughly as he did employees. Staffing cuts led to persistent complaints that there weren't enough workers in Home Depot's cavernous stores to help do-it-yourself customers."[143] In the summer of 2002, the Better Business Bureau's Atlanta chapter—in Home Depot's hometown—suspended the retailer's membership in response to the skyrocketing number of customer complaints that had remained unresolved.[144] The University of Michigan's annual American Customer Satisfaction Index in 2005 ranked Home Depot at the bottom of the heap of major U.S. retailers in customer service (**Exhibit 11**).[145] The retailer received a score of 67 that year, down from 73 in 2004. The ranking put Home Depot 11 points behind Lowe's and 3 points behind Kmart. (See **Exhibit 12** for readers' comments to *BusinessWeek*'s story.)

By 2006, the CEO and his top executives had realized they had a customer service problem, and elevated the issue to one of their top priorities. Various initiatives were announced to support better merchandising and customer service.[146] Nardelli announced an employee bonus program, called "orange juiced"[147] that would award up to $10,000 bonuses to sales associates for outstanding customer service;[148] Nardelli said, "We open every board meeting with customer service data."[149]

The Road Ahead

Nardelli's departure had been prompted by the quarrel over executive compensation and share price, and not by any rejection of the changes he had introduced to Home Depot. There was widespread agreement that Nardelli had ushered in a technological revolution that had brought the company out of the IT dark ages, and established a series of useful business functions and processes that had not existed under the prior leadership. Yet questions lingered regarding the impact the command and control approach might have had on what had previously been the prized centerpiece of Home Depot's brand: its customer service.

Blake had to decide which of his predecessor's strategies to consolidate, which to alter, and how to go about strengthening a culture of customer service at Home Depot. These decisions would inevitably take place within the pressure of a declining housing market and growing competition in Home Depot's urban markets from the ever more confident Lowe's.

Exhibit 1   Home Depot Performance Data, 1997–2006 ($ amounts in millions, except average customer ticket, number of customer transactions also in millions)

Home Depot	1997	1998	1999	2000	2001	2002	2003	2004	2005	2006
Gross Margin as a % of sales	28.1%	28.5%	29.7%	29.9%	30.2%	31.1%	31.8%	33.4%	33.5%	32.8%
Amount of inventory	$3,602	$4,293	$5,489	$6,556	$6,725	$8,338	$9,076	$10,076	$11,401	$12,822
Inventory per store	$5.8	$5.6	$5.9	$5.8	$5.0	$5.4	$5.3	$5.3	$5.6	$6.0
Number of stores	624	761	930	1,134	1,333	1,532	1,707	1,890	2,042	2,147
Number of employees	124,400	156,700	201,400	227,300	256,300	280,900	298,800	323,149	344,800	364,400
Number of customer transactions	550	665	797	936	1,091	1,161	1,246	1,295	1,330	1,330
Average customer ticket	$43.63	$45.05	$47.87	$48.65	$48.64	$49.43	$51.15	$54.89	$57.98	$58.90
Same-store (comp store) sales growth	7%	7%	10%	4.0%	--	(0.5)%	3.7%	5.1%	3.1%	(2.8)%

Source: Adapted from Home Depot Annual Report data for 2000–2006, accessed February 21, 2008.

Exhibit 2   Home Depot Income Statement Data, 1997–2006 (in $ millions)

Home Depot	1997	1998	1999	2000	2001	2002	2003	2004	2005	2006
Sales	24,156	30,219	38,434	45,738	53,553	58,247	64,816	73,094	81,511	90,837
Cost of Goods Sold	17,375	21,614	27,023	32,057	37,406	40,139	44,236	48,664	54,191	61,054
Gross Margin	6,781	8,605	11,411	13,681	16,147	18,108	20,580	24,430	27,320	29,783
Operating expenses										
Selling and Store Operating	4,303	5,341	6,832	8,513	10,163	11,180	12,502	15,105	16,485	18,348
Pre-opening	65	88	113	142	117	96	86	--	--	--
General and Administrative	413	515	671	835	935	1,002	1,146	1,399	1,472	1,762
Non-recurring Charge	104	--	--	--	--	--	--	--	--	--
Total	4,885	5,944	7,616	9,490	11,215	12,278	13,734	16,504	17,957	20,110
Operating Income	1,896	2,661	3,795	4,191	4,932	5,830	6,846	7,926	9,363	9,673
Interest income (expense)										
Interest and investment income	44	30	37	47	53	79	59	56	62	27
Interest expense	-42	-37	-28	-21	-28	-37	-62	-70	-143	-392
Net Interest	2	-7	9	26	25	42	-3	-14	-81	-365
EBIT	1,898	2,654	3,804	4,217	4,957	5,872	6,843	7,912	9,282	9,308
Income taxes	738	1,040	1,484	1,636	1,913	2,208	2,539	2,911	3,444	3,547
Net Earnings	1,160	1,614	2,320	2,581	3,044	3,664	4,304	5,001	5,838	5,761

Source: Home Depot annual reports.
Notes: Fiscal years ending: February 1, 1998; January 31, 1999 and January 30, 2000; January 28, 2001; February 3, 2002; February 2, 2003; February 1, 2004, January 30, 2005; January 29, 2006; and January 28, 2007.

Exhibit 3   Home Depot Share Price, 1984–2006 in $USD

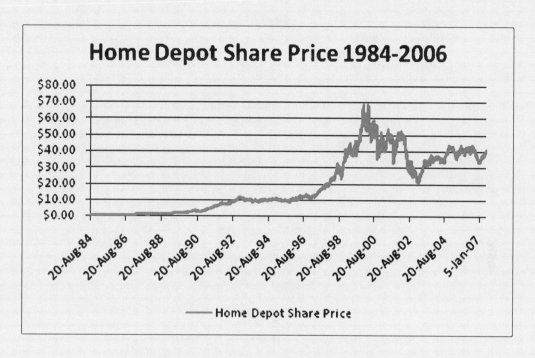

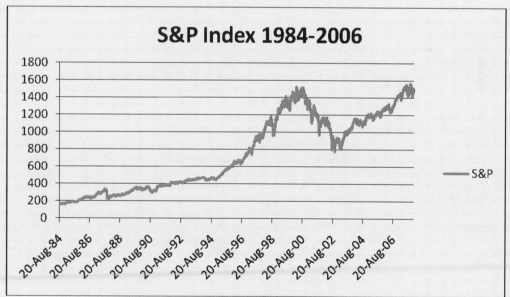

Source: Adapted from Google Finance data for August 20, 1984 through August 20, 2006, accessed February 21, 2008.

Exhibit 4   Home Channel Sales, by Retailer, 2004 and 2006

| Store Name | 2004 | | 2006 | | 2004–06 | 2004–06 |
	Sales ($ million)	Share (%)	Sales ($ million)	Share (%)	% Sales Change	% Point Share Change
Home Depot	73,094	19.9	90,837	21.5	24.3	1.6
Lowe's	36,460	9.9	46,900	11.1	28.6	1.2
Wal-Mart	19,200	5.2	23,300	5.5	21.4	0.3
Sears	11,400	3.1	11,500	2.7	0.9	-0.4
CCA Global Partners	8,700	2.4	9,600	2.3	10.3	-0.1
Menards	7,000	1.9	8,000	1.9	14.3	0.0
Pro-Build	4,050	1.1	5,800	1.4	43.2	0.3
Stock Bldg. Supply	3,580	1.0	5,305	1.3	48.2	0.3
Sherwin-Williams	3,977	1.1	5,260	1.3	32.3	0.2
84 Lumber	3,490	1.0	3,920	1.0	12.3	0.0
Total of Top 10	170,951	46.6	210,422	50.0	23.1	3.4
All other	195,548	53.4	211,578	50.0	8.2	-3.4
Total	366,499	100.0	422,000	100.0	15.1	N/A

Source: Home Channel News/Mintel.

Exhibit 5   Top Home Improvement Centers' Operating Statistics, Latest Fiscal Year-end, 2006

Company (end fiscal year 2006)	Annual Sales ($ billion)	Outlets (#)	Total Sales Area ('000 sq. ft.)	Employees (#)
Home Depot (1/2006)	90.8	2,147	224,000	364,400
Lowe's (1/2006)	46.9	1,385	157,000	210,142
Menards (1/2006)	8	210	27,000	38,000

Source: Home Channel News/Mintel.

Exhibit 6   New Privately Owned Housing Units Started in the United States (Thousands of Units)

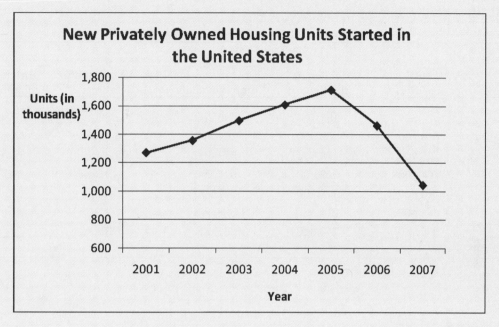

Source: U.S. Census.

Exhibit 7   New Houses Sold in the United States

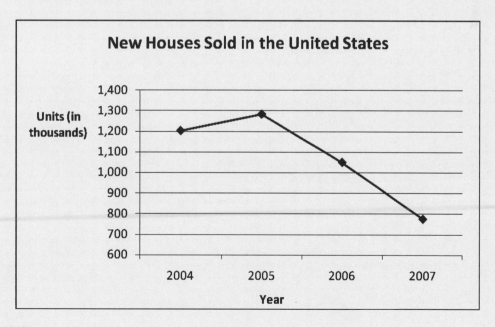

Source: U.S. Census.

Exhibit 8   Expenditures for Residential Improvements and Repairs

Seasonally Adjusted Annual Rate in Millions of Dollars

| | | | | Improvements | |
Year	Total Expenditures	Maintenance and Repairs	Improvements	Additions and Alterations	Major Replacements
2001	627,300	191,100	436,200	308,300	127,900
2002	689,700	188,300	501,200	353,600	147,500
2003	707,000	179,600	527,400	372,300	155,100
2004	794,100	202,200	591,900	(X)	(X)
2005	860,800	212,900	647,900	(X)	(X)
2006	914,400	214,400	699,900	(X)	(X)
2007	908,400	219,800	688,600	(X)	(X)

Source: U.S. Census.

Exhibit 9 Lowe's Performance Data, 2000–2006 ($ amounts in millions, except average customer ticket, number of customer transactions also in millions)

Lowe's	1997	1998	1999	2000	2001	2002	2003	2004	2005	2006
Gross Margin as a % of sales	27%	27%	28%	28%	29%	30%	31%	34%	34%	35%
Amount of inventory	$1,985	$2,385	$2,812	$3,285	$3,611	$3,968	$4,584	$5,982	$6,706	$7,144
Inventory per store	$ 4.16	$ 4.59	$ 4.88	$ 5.05	$ 4.85	$ 4.65	$ 4.82	$ 5.50	$ 5.43	$ 5.16
Number of Stores	477	520	576	650	744	854	952	1,087	1,234	1,385
Number of Employees	64,070	72,715	86,160	94,601	108,317	121,600	147,052	161,964	185,314	210,142
Number of customer transactions	231	268	298	342	394	460	521	575	639	680
Average customer ticket	$48.09	$49.70	$53.42	$54.88	$55.96	$57.55	$59.21	$63.43	$67.67	$68.98
Same-store (Comp store) sales growth	4.00%	6.00%	6.00%	1.00%	2.50%	5.80%	6.70%	6.60%	6.10%	--

Source: Adapted from Lowe's Annual Report data for 2000–2006, accessed February 21, 2008.

Exhibit 10 Lowe's Income Statement Data, 1997–2006 (in $ millions)

Lowe's	1997	1998	1999	2000	2001	2002	2003	2004	2005	2006
Sales	$11,108	$13,331	$15,906	$18,779	$22,111	$26,491	$30,838	$36,464	$43,243	$46,927
Cost of Goods Sold	$8,155	$9,757	$11,525	$13,488	$15,743	$18,465	$21,231	$24,165	$28,443	$30,729
Gross Margin	$2,953	$3,574	$4,381	$5,291	$6,368	$8,026	$9,607	$12,299	$14,800	$16,198
Expenses										
Selling, General and Administrative	1,954	2,341	2,772	3,348	3,913	4,730	5,543	7,562	9,014	9,738
Store Opening Costs	73	76	98	132	140	129	128	123	142	146
Nonrecurring Merger Costs	--	--	24	--	--	--	--	--	--	--
Total	2,027	2,417	2,894	3,480	4,053	4,859	5,671	7,685	9,156	9,884
Operating Income	$ 926	$ 1,156	$ 1,486	$ 1,811	$ 2,314	$ 3,167	$ 3,936	$ 4,614	$ 5,644	$ 6,314
Depreciation, Interest Income (expense)										
Depreciation	256	289	337	409	517	626	758	902	980	1,162
Interest	72	81	85	121	174	182	180	176	158	154
EBIT	$ 598	$ 786	$ 1,064	$ 1,281	$ 1,623	$ 2,359	$ 2,998	$ 3,536	$ 4,506	$ 4,998
Income Tax Provision	216	287	390	472	601	888	1,136	1,360	1,731	1,893
Net Earnings	383	500	673	810	1,023	1,471	1,877	2,176	2,765	3,105

Source: Adapted from Lowe's Annual Report data for 2000–2006, accessed February 21, 2008.

Note: Fiscal years ending: January 30, 1998; January 29, 1999; January 28, 2000; February 2, 2001; February 1, 2002; January 31, 2003; January 30, 2004; January 28, 2005; February 3, 2006; and February 2, 2007.

Exhibit 11   Comparison of Share Price of Home Depot and Lowe's, 2000–2006 in $USD

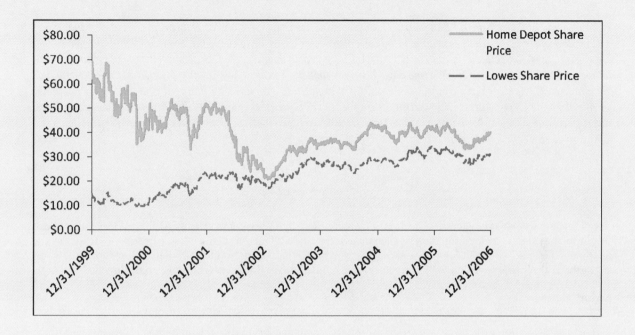

Source: Adapted from Google Finance data for December 31, 1999 through December 31, 2006, accessed February 21, 2008.

Exhibit 12   University of Michigan American Customer Satisfaction Index Scores, 2000–2006

Category: Specialty Retail Stores

Company	2000	2001	2002	2003	2004	2005	2006
Costco Wholesale Corporation	77	76	79	80	79	79	81
SAM'S CLUB (Wal- Mart Stores, Inc.)	74	78	77	77	75	76	78
All Others	NM	72	73	73	75	73	75
Lowe's Companies, Inc.	NM	75	76	77	76	78	74
Specialty Retail Stores Average	**76**	**73**	**74**	**74**	**75**	**74**	**75**
Best Buy Co., Inc.	NM	NM	NM	72	72	71	76
Circuit City Stores, Inc.	NM	NM	NM	73	72	70	69
Home Depot, Inc., The	NM	75	71	73	73	67	70

Source: http://www.theacsi.org/, accessed February 21, 2008.

Exhibit 13   Comments to *BusinessWeek* Cover Story: "Renovating Home Depot," March 27, 2006

Our Mar. 6 Cover Story, "Renovating Home Depot," took a close look at the corporate culture that Chief Executive Robert L. Nardelli is trying to build—one that's based in part on military concepts and personnel. We argued that the command-and-control discipline Nardelli has imposed is getting financial results. But a deluge of letters, online posts, and message board responses—nearly 300 in all—indicates the overhaul has come at a cost. Many readers connected the military-style ethic promoted by Nardelli to a decline in customer service at Home Depot stores. In a startlingly similar refrain, they complained of indifferent workers, long lines, and unpleasant stores. Only two correspondents praised America's largest home supply store. What follows is a sampling of reader reaction, with a reply from Home Depot

CUSTOMER VIEWS

As a submarine Navy veteran, as well as a General Electric (GE) veteran (Heavy Military Electronics), I can only applaud Home Depot's military-style management and Robert Nardelli. What's missing is focus on the customers. I'm also a veteran home improver. I've watched Home Depot under Nardelli follow in the footsteps of Northern Virginia's now-defunct Hechinger stores, while Lowe's (LOW) eats Home Depot's lunch.

Anonymous

Gross sales at Home Depot may be soaring, but the customer service is, well, just gross. For example, Home Depot stores have lots of checkout lanes, but often most of them are closed, and they attempt to push customers to the awful self-checkout area. I wrote a letter to Home Depot corporate and told them I did not wish to become their unpaid employee, even for five minutes.

Jeffrey E. Schmidt
Kissimmee, Fla.

I searched "Renovating Home Depot (HD)" in vain for some reference to military veterans' value as employees—besides their maturity, discipline, and a willingness to relocate to unsavory locales.

The veteran employee's ability to "think on his feet" was praised, but the critical plans are now being made by Home Depot central management. I read no reference to how the plans are developed—for example, how those target sales numbers (nervously tracked by store managers on their BlackBerrys) are defined. What thinking is the veteran employee empowered to do?

Similarly, Home Depot has responded to its "strategic" needs by replacing its seasoned, well-compensated professional staff with a vast crew of business personnel who will be willing to accept more demands and question authority less. It seems that decisions are being made strictly on the basis of numbers, often without a sense of their root cause or interconnected nature.

Jennifer Kirley
(Formerly HT1 Hull Maintenance Technician First Class, U.S. Navy), Greene, Me.

The first problem at Home Depot after Nardelli's arrival was extensive violation of Carl Liebert's "Customers cannot buy what we do not have" slogan. When Home Depot first appeared on the scene, before Nardelli, it corrected two flagrant problems that were Hechinger's undoing: out-of-stock items, poor display of existing stock, and floor employees' lack of responsiveness to customers. Home Depot, before Nardelli, was fully stocked and hired people in the trade who were available in force on the floor. They understood the stock and could help customers use it.

Many of us now find broader and more complete stock, along with better staff availability and knowledge, at Lowe's. I go more than an extra mile to shop accordingly. Home Depot would do well to change its focus from command-and-control to customers.

George F. Steeg
Potomac Falls, Va.

I applaud CEO Bob Nardelli's efforts to make the shopping experience consistent throughout each store. He has brought order to what was at times an experience in futility trying to find a particular item. Unfortunately, it provides me the speed and efficiency I crave for all the wrong reasons—to get in and out of the place as quickly as I can so that I don't have to hear the workers gripe about yet another change being implemented by senior management.

Scott Haines
Foster City, Calif.

I recently visited Home Depot to buy a simple polyvinyl chloride (PVC) elbow for my sprinkler system, something that probably would cost less than a dollar. After spending an inordinate amount of time just looking for the item, I went to the front of the store only to be greeted by one clerk and two checkout lines, 10 to 12 people deep. It wasn't worth the wait. Shop again at Home Depot? Never.

Larry Paquette
Fresno, Calif.

After reading the Cover Story, I have to say I am a Nardelli supporter. Having experience in the Marine Corps during Vietnam and also as a manager of 1,000 people in business, I see great parallels for success. Most successful businesses require balanced performance—financial, operational (or process improvement), customer focus, and developing people. To deem this militaristic when it is just good business is a bit naive. In today's all-volunteer military, there is much more focus on balanced performance and people skills, as opposed to the blood-and-guts perception created by Hollywood. To keep the volunteers, the military has actually improved more quickly than some U.S. businesses. To hire people who are well-trained is an excellent strategic advantage for which I commend Mr. Nardelli.

Richard Jozwiakowski
Round Rock, Tex.

* * * * *

HOME DEPOT RESPONDS

With 1.3 billion transactions a year, we're bound to make mistakes, but nothing disappoints us more than letting down a customer. We're making continuous improvements in our customer service levels and are working harder than ever to make sure that our service delivery meets the high expectations our customers have of Home Depot.

Jose Lopez
Senior Vice President Chief Customer Officer, Home Depot Atlanta

Source: BusinessWeek.

MOLSON CANADA: SOCIAL MEDIA MARKETING[1]

On November 23, 2007, the Molson brewing company pulled its promotion on Facebook, after numerous complaints that it promoted binge drinking. The promotion in question involved a photo contest targeting 19- to 24-year-old college and university students. The failure of this promotion on a social networking site forced Molson to think hard about its strategy vis-à-vis social media. What should be Molson's next move? How should it handle one of the fast emerging marketing channels? Should Molson use the social media for any commercial activities?

MOLSON COMPANY

The Molson Company was founded by John Molson in 1786, in Montreal. It was the second oldest company in Canada, preceded only by the Hudson's Bay Company. Molson Canada was part of the Molson Coors Brewing Company. At 41 per cent market share by volume in 2006, Molson was Canada's most preferred brand, slightly ahead of Labatt beer. Worldwide, Molson had 3.8 per cent market share, placing it fourth behind InBev NV, Anheuser-Busch and SABMiller. Molson offered a range of brands in Canada, including Molson Canadian, Coors Light, Rickard's Red and Pilsner. Molson Canada also partnered with other leading brewers to offer such brands as Heineken and Miller Genuine Draft. Molson employed 3,000 Canadians and operated six breweries, including the boutique brewery in Creemore, Ontario.

Molson Canada invested in communities from coast to coast through its various charitable initiatives and through sports and entertainment sponsorships. It was proud to be a socially responsible company, which was reflected in its code of conduct:

> As a manufacturer of alcohol beverages, Molson Coors is committed to promoting legal and responsible decisions about drinking our products. In our sales and marketing practices, Molson Coors promotes the responsible use of our products by adults of legal drinking age. The Company makes every effort to avoid even the appearance of condoning

---

underage drinking, drunk driving or other irresponsible activity involving consumption. When pursuing your work responsibilities or representing the Company, you should be aware that any inappropriate behaviour reflects negatively upon the Company's reputation and the equity of its brands. If you choose to consume alcohol beverages, you are expected to set a positive example of responsible alcohol consumption.[2]

Following what it espoused in its code of conduct, Molson organized annual awareness programs to encourage responsible drinking. In December 2007, Molson spent more than $100,000 to raise awareness and support communities across Canada in their efforts to encourage responsible drinking during the holiday season. Molson's sponsorship included complimentary New Year's Eve transit service in Ottawa and supporting Operation Red Nose in western and eastern Canada.

Elaborating on the company's efforts, Ferg Devins, vice-president Government and Public Affairs, Molson, explained:

> Community involvement is a major part of Molson heritage. Molson has long promoted responsible choices and this year's local initiatives across the country are consistent with how Molson has built its business in communities from coast to coast. This is our way of celebrating those who choose to make sure all their holiday memories are good ones.[3]

Over the years, the company had focused its efforts on brewing quality beers and taking social and community obligations seriously. The responsible drinking program was an example of Molson's commitment to consumers making responsible choices (see Exhibit 1). Because it was producer of alcohol, Molson directed its community investment donations to programs that encouraged adult audiences to make responsible decisions regarding drinking. Historically, Molson had focused most of its efforts on traditional marketing channels. However, since the beginning of 2007, Molson had started experimenting with social media and social marketing tools as means of targeting its potential young customers.

Social Media

Molson had already experimented with blogs and had tried having a static web presence at social networking sites. However, both these attempts had been at very early stages. Molson did not fully engage the social media (i.e. online technologies and practices used by people to share their experiences, opinions and perspectives others).

Like many other companies, Molson was still trying to make sense of how best to integrate its marketing efforts with various online activities that used technology for social interaction by integrating words, pictures and videos. Some examples were web content, such as blogs and wikis, created by individuals or a collaboration of individuals. Molson's executives found it intuitive that social media was a way of using the Internet to instantly collaborate, share information or have a conversation on anything — or everything. However, how to use these features to promote Molson products was a bit of intellectual exercise.

---

[2] *Molson Coors Brewing Company, Company, Living Our Values, p. 4, available online at http://www.molsoncoors.com/templates/molson_coors/pdf/Code_of_Business_Conduct.pdf, accessed May 10, 2008.*
[3] *Molson Coors Brewing Company, "Molson Celebrates Responsible Choices across Canada This Holiday Season," press release, December 19, 2007, available online at http://www.molsoncoors.com/newsroom/press-releases/2007, accessed February 17, 2008.*

To make the matter more complex, in social media, anyone can be an expert, a poet, a musician, a photographer, a publisher or a reporter. Thus, how a potential community member would respond to content created by Molson and how much credence Molson should give to that response was very difficult to ascertain. This quandary was one of the primary reasons why many organizations had hesitated to enter the social media realm. In addition, in social media, the contents of one service could be mashed up with data from other services:

> Mashup is a web application that combines data from more than one source into a single integrated tool. An example is the use of cartographic data from Google Maps to add location information to real-estate data from Craigslist, thereby creating a new and distinct web service that was not originally provided by either source.[4]

Mashups led to issues of control and ownership. Content in social media could not be controlled by the individual who created it, especially in terms of how content could be used by others and the sorts of evolutionary trajectories they could take. Thus, nobody had complete control over social media content, which had great implications on how businesses could to use social media for promotion of their image and products.

Social media was characterized by such features as connectivity, community and inclusiveness that made it fundamentally different from traditional media, such as newspapers, television, books and radio. Exhibit 2 provides a partial list of social media characteristics. Primarily, these characteristics were related to interactions between people that were facilitated by the technology and design aspects of the social media websites. Companies tried to leverage one or more of these features of social media for building awareness and creating communities around their products.

For creating awareness about its product, Molson could choose from a variety of social media, such as blogs, forums, microblogging and news aggregation. To create communities, Molson could resort to sites that offered photo sharing, video sharing, social bookmarking and social networking. Some of the common categories of social media are described in the Exhibit 3. Based on the primary objectives of the social media sites, they could be classified into various communities that organized and shared particular kinds of content. Some of the most popular content communities tended to form around friendship (Facebook), photos (Flickr), bookmarked links (del.icio.us) and videos (YouTube). Similar to other media, the type of social media and the features that were leveraged were determined by the target customers, the type of product and the marketing strategy.

Social Media Marketing

> Social networking sites like MySpace.com and Facebook attract large numbers of mostly young users who are eager to engage with their favorite brands. But most marketers use traditional marketing tactics like run-of-site advertising[5] and static microsites[6] to push messages into these networks. Instead, to realize the full value of marketing on social

---

[4]Wikipedia, available online at http://en.wikipedia.org/wiki/Mashup_(web_application_hybrid), accessed September 16, 2008.

[5] Run-of-site advertising is an advertisement buying option, in which advertisements can be placed on any pages of the target site. This option is usually inexpensive and hence advertisers generally give up their say over placement. Advertisements may be placed in the unsold, less valuable portions of the target site randomly.

[6] Static microsites are related pages on a website that have their own URL, which is not a derivative of home page. These websites are used for contextual advertisements or pay-per-click advertisements and are created with topic-specific, keyword-rich contents to attract web traffic; however, they are not dynamic and have very low customizability.

networking sites, marketers should be prepared to engage in a personal relationship with users by providing something of value. Promotions are good in this context, but even better are information or brand elements that users can pass on to their friends.[7]

Social Media Marketing (SMM) is a form of Internet marketing that utilizes social media to achieve branding and marketing communication goals. Social media sites, such as MySpace, Facebook, Bebo, YouTube, Digg, Flickr and Twitter, are used to communicate information about a company and its brand and products. Which social medium is most effective and how it can best be targeted depends in part on the goals of SMM campaign and the product offered by the company. In general, most campaigns involved propagating an idea, creating brand awareness, increasing visibility, encouraging brand feedback and dialogue and, in some cases, selling a product or service.

Social media marketers took advantage of the fact that average users of social networking sites were young. In a Forrester survey conducted in 2006, only 20 per cent of adults reported using social networking sites. In contrast, almost 47 per cent of teenagers and 69 per cent of young adults (ages 18 to 21) had a profile and had interacted with other users on social networking sites, such as MySpace and Facebook. Among the users of social networking sites, young adults' (18- to 21–year-olds) usage rate was higher compared with other groups, using social networking sites much more frequently (68 per cent reported making a daily visit) than 12- to 17-year-olds (60 per cent reported daily visits) or adult users (42 per cent reported daily visits).[8]

Another interesting aspect, from a social media marketer's perspective, was that social networking site users wanted to engage with their favorite brands. A Forrester survey found that the most common approach to marketing on social networking sites was to set up a profile for the brand, which members could then join, or "friend," as some social networking sites preferred to call it. For example, Molson's Facebook profile, Molson Canadian Nation, had more than 19,000 members (other Facebook users) as friends.[9] The Forrester survey also found that many social networking site users welcomed interactions with the brands that they loved: more than one-third of 18- to 26-year-old social networking users admitted that they would be interested in seeing a marketer's profile (see Exhibit 4).

Cold Shots Campus Challenge

In mid-October, on behalf of Molson Canada, Toronto-based ad agency Henderson Bas announced the launch of a campaign targeted at the 19- to 24-year-old demographic. The goal of this campaign was to use Facebook, a social networking site, to increase brand awareness of Molson products in Canada to reach Molson's "target demographics in most efficient manner."[10] The plan was to use the Molson Canadian Nation group profile on Facebook, which then had more than 17,500 members, to spread the word about Molson's products.

---

[7] Charlene Li, "Marketing on Social Networking Sites," Forrester Research Inc., Cambridge, MA, 2007.
[8] For more details on consumer usage of social networking sites, refer to Charlene Li, "How Consumers User Social Networks," Forrester Research Inc., Cambridge, MA, 2007.
[9] Molson Canadian Nation Facebook group had 19,063 members as of March 29. 2008.
[10]Marina Strauss, "Molson Photo Contest Brews up Anger," Globe and Mail, available at http://www.theglobeandmail.com/servlet/story/RTGAM.20071122.wmolsonface1122/BNStory/Technology, accessed January 6, 2008

"Utilizing Facebook for this program made strategic sense," stated Heather Clark, creative strategy director at Henderson Bas, at the launch of the campaign.[11] The demographics present on most social network websites, including Facebook, were "ideal" for marketers such as Molson. Facebook, primarily created for college and university students, had a very young membership base. Moreover, these websites provided an environment where friends interacted in a trusted and open setting. Thus, social network websites presented opportunities to marketers to build their brands and promote their products through viral marketing as word of "mouse" spread among friends. These websites were a virtual space "where they hang out and it's a great opportunity to engage them in a dialogue. If you do it right, you can find yourself with a whole nation of brand ambassadors," claimed Heather Clark.[12] The campaign was planned to run from the end of October to the end of November, 2007.[13]

The *modus operandi* of the campaign was to have a virtual "dorm room" in the name of each university or college, where students from those institutions could post photos of themselves and their friends in full party mode. The school with the most photos would be awarded the title of number-one party school in Canada. The best photo, as determined by a panel of Molson judges, would win the Spring Break Trip Give Away Contest — a trip for the winner and three friends to Cancun, Mexico, for Spring Break 2008, sponsored by Breakaway Tours.[14] In addition, the Molson Canadian Nation group on Facebook would provide some features to attract members, including the Cold Shots Amped Up game, screen savers, wallpaper and MSN icons, the "Party Finder" section and customized searches for pictures and polls.

The students who were the target of this campaign grew up in the age of Internet and felt comfortable sharing their personal details in an online environment. They routinely upload their personal photos, shared their videos and spent more time on the social networking website than in a physical social space. Social networking sites such as Facebook were a common "hanging around place" for them. For these reasons, the contest became popular among students, particularly those from Memorial University of Newfoundland (MUN). By November 23, students from MUN had uploaded 67 photos, much ahead of University of Victoria, which was in second place with 26 photos. However, not all the students were proud of having their university "leading" this competition. Some argued that students in skimpy costumes who had consumed excess quantities of alcohol hardly matched their image of a wonderful time at university.

Criticism of the Contest

Many students and administrators across the Canadian universities felt that Molson's "Cold Shot" was giving their school's image a bad reputation. They felt that the contest encouraged irresponsible behavior by inciting students to post their photos in outrageous situations. To get noticed, students who were posing for photos may have felt the need to present themselves in an extraordinary condition, which typically meant wearing skimpy costumes, behaving unusually and drinking more than what could be considered safe and responsible amounts of alcohol.

The non-participating students at the front-runner MUN felt this contest was giving their university image a "hangover." *The Muse*, a student-run newspaper at MUN, published an editorial bashing the competition.

[11] Kara Nicholson, "Molson Using Facebook to Engage Canadian Students," available at http://www.mediaincanada.com/articles/mic/20071122/molson.html, accessed January 6, 2008.
[12] Ibid.
[13] Karen Rouse, "Molson Ends Facebook 'Party School' Contest," Denver Post, November 26, 2007, available at http://www.denverpost.com/business/ci_7562948, accessed January 12, 2008.
[14] Kara Nicholson, "Molson Using Facebook to Engage Canadian Students," available at http://www.mediaincanada.com/articles/mic/20071122/molson.html, accessed January 12, 2008.

Editor Kerri Breen labeled the contest "really kind of lame." She criticized Molson's approach as inappropriate and stated "beer bongs and letterman's jackets, it's really not something MUN should strive to be associated with."[15] Another student at MUN found the contest frustrating because it gave an impression of the school that wasn't fair to students who attended MUN to study and achieved good grades. In her view, it was unfair "to have other people coming in, looking at the school as a whole and saying that we're a group of people who don't care about the academics, that we're just here to party."[16] Many students at MUN agreed that Molson's contest presented the wrong view about having a good experience at the university.

The University of Western Ontario (Western), which prided itself in providing best student experience wasn't amused with its eighth overall ranking (only 10 entries had been received by November 22) of "best party" school, which, according to Cynthea Galbraith, a Molson spokesperson, meant "the context of celebrating good times with friends after the academics are over for the day."[17] Students and officials at Western argued that if this was what "best party" school meant then Western should be at the top of the list and not at the eighth place:

> Party school is a very narrow definition of what we believe to be the best student experience in the country. When we talk to students, alumni and the public we emphasize [Western] has both an in-class component but also a great social experience . . . social experience means many different things. It means having great student government and opportunities to involve yourself in that, along with clubs, organizations, and the opportunity to involve yourself in varsity sport. It's the opportunity to build great networks because so many of our students live on campus. There are more important things to the student experience than just partying and drinking[18]

Responses from other universities also followed the same lines. Jason Laker, associate vice-principal and dean of Student Affairs at Queen's University, felt disgusted:

> Such an apparent and dangerous disregard . . . promotes an abusive use of alcohol . . . . In order for the photos to be eligible, to be notable, would require outrageous behaviour or profoundly dangerous levels of drinking, and of course the kind of decision making and behaviour that follow that. [Molson] are either unaware of it or simply placing profits above ethics.[19]

Similar sentiments were expressed by Joe MacDonald, dean of Students Affairs at St. Francis Xavier University:

> These kinds of programs put added stress on our ability to ensure that students have a very positive, successful academic and non-academic development . . . . This is not something that is welcome within our campus community. It's cheap marketing, I'm concerned about Molson's lack of contrition[20].

---

[15] "Molson's Facebook Contest Leaves Some MUN Students Frothing," CBC News, November 20, 2007.
[16] Ibid.
[17] Ken Meaney, "Anger Brews over Molson Contest," Calgary Herald, November 21, 2007, p. 5.
[18] Ted Garrard, vice-president external at Western, quoted in Mike Hayes, "Memorial Is the Number One Party School? Really?" The Gazette, November 15, 2007, pp. 1-2.
[19] Sarah Miller, "Molson Promo Challenged by Universities," The Gazette, November 28, 2007, p. 3.
[20] Marina Strauss, "Molson Photo Contest Brews up Anger," Globe and Mail, available at http://www.theglobeandmail.com/servlet/story/RTGAM.20071122.wmolsonface1122/BNStory/Technology, accessed January 6, 2008.

Phil Wood, associate vice-president of student affairs at McMaster University agreed, "It is hard to believe that a leading corporation like Molson would stoop to such a . . . way of doing business."[21] He expressed his dismay especially because Molson Coors Brewing Co. was targeting students in residence even though many of them were too young to legally consume alcohol. Zach Churchill, national director of the Canadian Alliance of Student Associations, termed the Molson campaign as unfortunate because it stereotyped university students as being interested only in partying.[22]

However, the best articulation of universities' opposition to Molson contest came in the letter sent by Brenda Whiteside, chair of Ontario Committee on Student Affairs, the University of Guelph. In her letter to Molson she wrote:

> As professionals dealing with the transition of young students to university, we are continuously combating the stereotype of universities being places to party . . . . One of the risks of a "party university" culture is the increased potential for over consumption of alcohol by students with no previous experience. Each year we send a small but concerning number of students to hospital with alcohol poisoning. Some of us have had to deal with a student death due to over consumption. In addition, we continually struggle with the by-products of over consumption — vandalism, assault, sexual assault, and academic failure . . . we devote endless energy, resources and programming towards responsible drinking campaigns . . . . Imagine our dismay when we learned of this campaign — a competition for a party environment in residence. This campaign not only dismantles university efforts to create a culture of academics in residences, it also helps to establish an environment that could encourage irresponsible drinking. Our second concern with this campaign is the use of Facebook . . . . Facebook has the potential to be dangerous for students . . . . Of particular concern is students posting pictures of themselves in behaviour that could impact negatively on future careers or opportunities. There are numerous examples of students who have regretted the posting of such pictures. Thus, please understand again our dismay with a program that encourages students to potentially place such damaging photos on the internet . . . . This present campaign runs counter to Molson's commitment to responsible drinking. We hope that your company will be more thoughtful about possible risks of advertising campaigns prior to future launches[23]

Her letter raised two critical aspects: 1) this contest was run against the often cited Molson virtue that it encourages responsible drinking and 2) this contest overlooked the privacy risk of sharing objectionable photos on a public website such as Facebook. Most of the objections from students and university administrators were around the first issue; however, some objections were raised about the second issue as well.

Administrators were of the view that Molson's Facebook initiative could jeopardize students' future career, especially those seeking jobs in near future, if potential employers stumble upon their not-so-graceful photos on Facebook. Phil Wood was concerned that some students' pictures may have been viewed by prospective employers or graduate schools, and these students could face biased treatment that could compromise their chances of landing a job or gaining admission to graduate school. He felt that encouraging students to post pictures of themselves engaging in excessive drinking or dangerous behavior

---

[21] *Ibid.*
[22] *Ibid.*
[23] *Brenda Whiteside "A Cold Shot to Responsible Drinking," available at www.macdrphil.wordpress.com/2007/11/27/a-cold-shot, accessed on January 27, 2008.*

was not a good idea in itself because students "don't understand the danger of the public-ness of Facebook. You're not anonymous."[24]

Because Facebook was a public virtual space, these photos were accessible to potential future employers, administrators and society at large. This exposure created a potential risk of students not being hired, being pre-judged if hired and being monitored in prejudiced way. Moreover, some students had become unconsenting participants. Not everyone who was partying and happened to be in photo wanted to be part of the contest, which had privacy implications. It was not clear whether Molson had any guidelines in place to ensure the consent of all those who appeared in the photographs was obtained before photo was uploaded for the contest. Many similar issues were raised regarding privacy and future implications of compromising this privacy.

One blogger's comment about Molson contest summed it up humorously:

> Capturing these young heavy drinkers in Facebook is a great idea. We will have a vibrant montage of "before" pictures to mix with the "after" pictures of:
> - people killed by drunk drivers
> - students choking on their vomit
> - students sexually assaulted or robbed while incapacitated (by heavy drinking)
> - students later running for public office or other positions of trust etc.
>
> Then as the years go by, and Molson tracks their "best customers," we can see whether they reach their potential from a university degree, or struggle with alcoholism and its social and physical effects. Without using Facebook, we would never have such a well-organized audit trail, with poignant photographs, on which to base lawsuits for those who drink to tragic ends.[25]

The final proverbial straw in the coffin of Molson's photo contest came when administrators from four universities wrote letters to Molson and also expressed their opinions in the *Globe and Mail*, squarely criticizing the contest. They slammed Molson's contest saying it promoted irresponsible drinking and demanded immediate withdrawal of the contest. They argued that Molson should pull the campaign because it was inconsistent with the company's own promotion of safe and responsible drinking.

Molson's Response

Sensing the probable outrage from the academic community, Molson pulled its contest on November 23, almost a week before its scheduled end. Molson, however, argued that the contest was simply an effort to engage its target market with socially oriented advertising and should not be interpreted as any attempt to encourage irresponsible drinking. The company also initiated damage control by issuing public statements through various officials. Molson issued a public note on its Facebook page explaining why it withdrew the contest: "we promote responsible choices and wanted to be pro-active in responding to concerns expressed from a number of different audiences."

---

[24] Mary Jane Credeur, "Molson Coors Ends Facebook Contest after Complaints," available at http://www.bloomberg.com/apps/news?pid=newsarchive&sid=aFC76olDqrJQ, accessed January 9, 2008.
[25] Ziad Fazel, comments on the article "Molson Photo Contest Brews up Anger," available at http://www.theglobeandmail.com/servlet/story/RTGAM.20071122.wmolsonface1122/CommentStory/Technology, accessed January 11, 2008.

However, Molson executives felt that the company's initiative had been misunderstood and misinterpreted as promoting irresponsible drinking. Ferg Devins, Molson's vice president, Government and Public Affairs, agreed that Molson had learned a lot from the contest:

> The whole realm of social media — there's lots to learn. It's really a new area. We're probably groundbreaking and leading in a lot of things we've been doing.[26]

Similar sentiments were expressed by Cynthea Galbraith, a spokeswoman for Molson: "Our take is that this whole social media realm is new. There's going to be some experimentation, there's going to be some learning." In spite of this failure, Galbraith was very positive about the future possibility of social media. She expressed cautious optimism:

> I don't know if surprised is the word, but we learn from these things. Our intention is to become a leader in that area and we'll go back and develop some new innovations in communications for next time.[27]

Like many others at Molson, Galbraith identified social media as one of the most important channels to communicate with the 19- to 24-year-old demographic. She observed "Social interaction is key with that [demographic], it seems to be all the rage right now." Ferg Devins was in total agreement: "We need to be communicating with our consumers because that's where our consumers are communicating among themselves . . . . We need to make sure we're in that relevant channel." Despite the setback to its contest, Molson planned to expand its social media marketing, and Devins highlighted the efforts Molson had initiated in terms of blogs and other social technologies.

With its marketing vision firmly rooted in the exploitation of social media, some Molson executives wondered whether they had really done the right thing by calling off the photo contest a week ahead of its scheduled conclusion. Had they given into unreasonable pressure or had they acted responsibly? Did they forgo the opportunity of using social media in its true sense by not taking the view of the participants of the contest into account? Should they continue to try to use social media as part of their marketing, and if so how? How would they combat the challenges they had encountered with the Facebook promotion, and what other challenges should they foresee?

Whether future attempts of Molson with social media would bear fruit would depend on how the company applied the lessons learned from the failure of the photo contest. How should Molson address the privacy issues? Should Molson include all the relevant stakeholders in the loop? And how could Molson best put the potential of social media to use?

---

[26] "A Cold Shot to Responsible Drinking," available at www.macdrphil.wordpress.com/ 2007/11/27/a-cold-shot, accessed January 27, 2008.
[27] Sarah Miller, "Molson Promo Challenged by Universities," The Gazette, November 28, 2007, p. 3.

Exhibit 1

RESPONSIBLE CHOICES CAMPAIGN

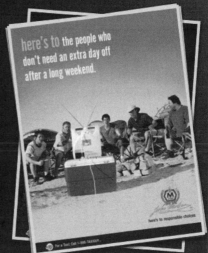

here's to responsible choices

Responsible Choices Campaign

In our new Here's to Responsible Choices campaign, we are speaking directly to consumers and we are doing so in a positive way. We are not only encouraging responsible drinking, we are celebrating it.

Responsible choices are as different and as individual as our consumers. Many factors affect how much alcohol, if any, one chooses to drink. At Molson, we believe beer can be part of a healthy, balanced lifestyle but we also recognize a person's individual choice. What is important to us is that our products are consumed in a responsible way by all those who enjoy them.

What does it take to make a responsible choice?

The courage to make the choice between being popular, and doing what's right. Enough character to decide not to go overboard at night, so one can enjoy the morning after.

Sometimes it takes sacrifice - the decision to be the designated driver for instance. The retailer who chooses to check ID's and not sell to minors displays integrity. These are all choices consumers are faced with every day.

Let's celebrate them.

here's to responsible choices

Making Responsible Choices

Responsible choices are as different and as individual as our consumers. Many factors affect how much alcohol, if any, one chooses to drink. At Molson, we believe beer can be part of a healthy, balanced lifestyle but we also recognize a person's individual choice. What is important to us is that our products are consumed in a responsible way by all those who enjoy them.

Here are the ways some of our consumers are making responsible choices everyday…

Plan ahead - Whether that means arranging to stay at a friend's house, having a designated driver or putting aside money for a cab, have a plan to get home safely. Never drink and drive.

No man (or woman) left behind - When out with friends, keep an eye out for each other and make sure everyone gets home safely.

Eat before you drink and get merry - Make sure you eat before drinking as having food in your stomach delays the absorption of alcohol.

Don't fear the mornings - Have a good time and drink in moderation so you can enjoy the morning after and still remember the night before.

Enough is enough - Know your limits and avoid binge drinking.

Source: Molson Canada, "Here's to Responsible Choices," http://www.responsiblechoices.ca/, accessed January 29, 2008.

Exhibit 2

CHARACTERISTICS OF SOCIAL MEDIA

Archival and retrieval	In social media, all the events are automatically archived and normally available for retrieval to anyone who may have interest in looking them at later date. Retrieval of information in traditional media is not that easy
Community	Social media facilitates community building. It allows communities to form around a common interest, such as a favorite celebrity, a political issue, a sport, a hobby, etc.
Connectedness	Social media is also characterized by the endless possibility of connectedness, which may manifest itself in the form of links to other individuals, groups, forums or web resources.
Democratic	Most social media services are open to feedback and participation, which are actively encouraged. They also encourage discussion, voting, comments and at times some sort of ranking about shared information.
Dialogue	Traditional media, such as newspaper, radio and television, work on the principles of broadcast where readers, listeners and viewers are passive receivers. Social media is seen as a two-way conversation in which roles of "broadcasters" and "receivers" are continuously changed back and forth.
Dynamic	Traditional print media cannot be changed once it is off the press. Similarly, radio and TV programs once delivered are in the public domain without any possibility of revision. However, social media can be modified or corrected instantaneously. Moreover social media continuously evolves due to regular feedback and comments.
Inclusive	Contributions and feedback are encouraged from anyone who may be interested. No entry barriers exist. Digital divide issues may limit some people, but otherwise it is absolutely open.
Lack of control	In social media, the content of one service can be mashed up with data from other services. Thus, nobody has complete control over any content.
Real-time evaluation	It is very easy to evaluate the popularity of a social media service in real time, based on a site visit, comments left, growth of membership and number of links that the service solicits. Sites such as Wordpress (http://wordpress.org/) can identify how much traffic each blog receives. Visitors to Digg (http://digg.com/) can see voting on someone's blog items. In addition, sites such as TechMeme (http://www.techmeme.com/), provide statistics on which blog items received the most links in the past few hours. Traditional media provide some statistics on popularity but they are very coarse and available at the best in annual intervals and generally with the lag of one or two years.

Source: Compiled from various sources and authors own experiences. Sources include: What is Social Media? An e-book from iCrossing – available at www.icrossing.co.uk/ebooks, accessed January 15, 2008. What is Social Media? available at http://scobleizer.com/2007/02/16/what-is-social-media/, accessed on January 16, 2008. Social Media Sociology, available at http://social-media-sociology.com/, accessed on January 15, 2008.

Exhibit 3

SOME EXAMPLES OF SOCIAL MEDIA

Blogs	Blogs are the most common form of social media. Blogs are online journals, with the most recent entries appearing first. These journal entries are available for other to read and comment on.
Forums	Forums are websites for online discussion, often around specific topics and interests. These online spaces provide an outlet for debates, arguments and counter-arguments.
Microblogging (Presence apps)	Microblogging is combination of social networking with bite-sized blogging, where micro blog-like posts, such as an announcement of what you are currently doing, are distributed online and through the mobile phone network. Twitter (http://twitter.com/) is a well-known example of microblogging website.
News aggregation	News aggregator websites provide a list of the latest news stories published by users from a range of different websites. Digg (http://digg.com) is one of the web's largest news aggregators.
Online gaming	Online gaming is often based around communities. World of Warcraft (http://www.worldofwarcraft.com/index.xml) is one of the popular examples of online gaming. Some aspects of Second Life (http://secondlife.com/) may also be included in online gaming.
Photo sharing	Photo-sharing sites facilitate uploading of pictures and images to a personal account, which can then be shared or viewed by web users the world over. A well-known example of a photo-sharing website is Flickr (http://www.flickr.com).
Social bookmarking	Social bookmarking sites allow users to publicly bookmark web pages they find valuable in order to share them with other Internet users. One famous example is del.icio.us (http://del.icio.us).
Social Networking sites	Social networking websites provide opportunities for individuals who either want to build online social networks to share their interests and activities or are interested in exploring the interests and activities of others. These sites allow people to build personal web pages and then connect with friends to communicate or share content. Some of the common social networking sites are Linkedin, MySpace, Facebook and Orkut.
Video sharing	Video-sharing sites facilitate the uploading and sharing of personal videos with the rest of the web community. A common example of a video-sharing website is YouTube (www.youtube.com).
Wikis	These websites allow people to add, edit, challenge or debate their content. The contents are collectively owned and act as a communal document or database. The best-known wiki is Wikipedia, the online encyclopedia, which has more than 2.3 million English language articles and more than 6.5 million articles in all the available languages (information as of March 29, 2008 on http://www.wikipedia.org)

Source: Compiled from various sources and authors own experiences. Sources include: What is Social Media? An e-book from iCrossing – available at www.icrossing.co.uk/ebooks, accessed January 15, 2008. What is Social Media? available at http://scobleizer.com/2007/02/16/what-is-social-media/, accessed on January 16, 2008. Social Media Sociology, available at http://social-media-sociology.com/, accessed on January 15, 2008.

Exhibit 4

AGE AND FREQUENCY OF USAGE
(INDICATORS OF WILLINGNESS TO ENGAGE WITH FAVORITE BANDS)

4.1 By age

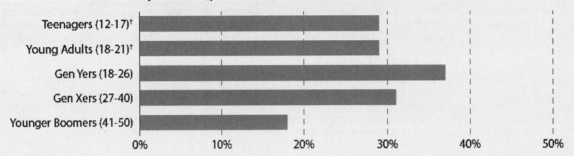

"How interested are you in social network profiles from a favorite marketer, retailer, or service provider?" [percent who answered 4 or 5 on a scale of 1 to 5]*

4.2 By usage

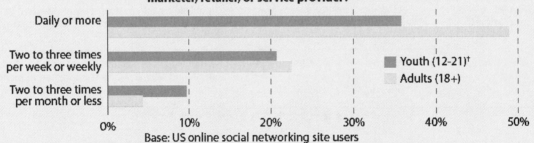

"How interested are you in social network profiles from a favorite marketer, retailer, or service provider?"

Base: US online social networking site users

Source: Forrester's NACTAS Q3 2006 Media & Marketing Online Survey
†Source: Forrester's NACTAS Q4 2006 Youth Media & Marketing And Finance Online Survey
*Note: Bases for Older Boomers (51-61) and Seniors (62+) were too small to report values

Source: Charlene Li, "Marketing on Social Networking Sites," Forrester Research Inc., Cambridge, MA, 2007.

IMAX: LARGER THAN LIFE[1]

Anil Nair wrote this case solely to provide material for class discussion. The author does not intend to illustrate either effective or ineffective handling of a managerial situation. The author may have disguised certain names and other identifying information to protect confidentiality.

Version: (A) 2009-05-15

FLASHBACK 2004

In Daytona, Florida, John watched a racecar going at more than 100 miles per hour crash into a concrete barrier. John ducked to escape the debris that appeared to be flying straight at him. A few moments later John was virtually within a racecar, next to the driver, zooming at more than 120 miles per hour around the racetrack. For the next half an hour, John experienced in three dimensions and on a larger-than-life scale crashing cars, dizzying turns, efficient pit crews, shining metal, burning rubber, swirling gas fumes and screaming fans. Finally, as the overhead lights at the theater gradually lit up, the audience sitting around John started applauding. John had just witnessed a screening of the IMAX movie *NASCAR*.

NASCAR set a box-office record as an original IMAX 3D film with the highest grossing opening weekend and the highest per-screen average. At $21,579, *NASCAR's* per-screen average was higher than that of the weekend's top 10 films.[2] Reports of *NASCAR's* box-office success would have surely pleased Richard Gelfond and Bradley Wechsler, the co-CEOs of IMAX Corporation.

INTRODUCTION

Gelfond and Wechsler had bought IMAX along with Wasserstein Perella Partners from the original owners in 1994 for $80 million. They took it public the same year to raise capital to fund IMAX's growth. For investors in IMAX, the years since then had been like a ride on a rollercoaster in the IMAX film *Thrill Ride*: exciting peaks when movies achieved commercial and critical acclaim, and scary drops when analysts questioned whether a niche player such as IMAX would be able to achieve consistent growth or even survive.

---

[1] This case has been written on the basis of published sources only. Consequently, the interpretation and perspectives presented in this case are not necessarily those of IMAX or any of its employees.
[2] IMAX press release, March 14, 2004.

NASCAR's success at the box office was evidence that the co-CEOs' efforts to reach a new audience — distinct from those typically attracted to IMAX's educational documentaries — might work. Another movie that was indicative of IMAX's emerging strategy was *The Polar Express*. *The Polar Express* was the first time a Hollywood movie would be released simultaneously in commercial multiplexes and IMAX theaters. *NASCAR* and *The Polar Express* were symbolic of the direction in which Gelfond and Wechsler had pushed the company to achieve faster growth and higher margins. The two-pronged strategy involved expanding the reach of IMAX by (a) going beyond its cloistered museum environments into multiplexes and (b) presenting Hollywood films in IMAX format.

Despite the success of *NASCAR* and *The Polar Express*, IMAX faced several questions about its future:

- Could IMAX thrive as a niche player that made large format films and systems?
- Would increasing the number of Hollywood movies released in IMAX format save the firm or dilute the IMAX brand?
- Should Hollywood movies be released simultaneously in regular and large format?

THE BACKGROUND SCORE

Since the first moving images flickered in a dark theater, movies have captivated audiences around the world. About the time that people were getting familiar with programming their VCRs and learning to enjoy movies on the small television screen, a small group of people was developing a technology to project movies on giant screens. The idea for IMAX originated in 1967 when the success of a multi-screen theater system at the Montreal Expo led filmmakers Graeme Ferguson, Robert Kerr and Roman Kroitor to create a large format movie system. IMAX was founded as the only company in the world that was involved in all aspects of large format films. The first IMAX film premiered in 1970 at the Fuji Pavilion in Osaka, Japan.

IMAX was listed in the NASDAQ exchange in 1994 and achieved a market capitalization of $196 million in the first year itself.[3] As of December 12, 2008, market capitalization was down to $125 million. There were about 295 theaters showing IMAX movies in 40 countries, with almost 60 per cent of the theaters in North America.[4] Almost 50 per cent of the theaters were located in museums, aquariums, zoos and other institutions, and about the same percentage had the IMAX 3D technology. The IMAX movie library at the end of 2007 stood at 226 films; some produced by IMAX, many others produced by independent filmmakers or studios such as Time-Warner. In 2007/2008, some of the well-known films to be released in IMAX included *Harry Potter and the Order of the Phoenix*, *Shine a Light* — a film about the Rolling Stones by the famous film director Martin Scorcese — and *The Spiderwick Chronicles*.

THE IMAX STORY

Scope of IMAX

The company's main sources of revenues were long-term theater system lease and maintenance agreements, film production and distribution, and theater operations. Given its scope of operations, IMAX could be considered a part of three different industries: Photographic Equipment and Supplies (SIC code

---

[3] S. N. Chakravarty, "A really big show," <u>Institutional Investor</u>, 35:10, October 2002, p. 20.
[4] Hoover's, www.Hoovers.com.

3861), Motion Picture and Video Tape Production (SIC code 7812), and Motion Picture and Video Distribution (SIC code 7822). IMAX was a relatively small firm compared to a rival studio such as Disney/Pixar or a theater chain such as Regal Entertainment.

In 2007, it generated $59.12 million (51.04 per cent of total revenue) from IMAX systems sales, $36.57 million (31.57 per cent of total revenue) from films and $16.58 million (14.31 per cent of total revenue) from theater operations.[5] Order trends suggested that newer agreements were for 3D systems. The theater leases were generally for 10 to 20 years and renewable by the customer. As part of the lease, IMAX advised customers on theater design, supervised the installation of the system, trained theater staff and maintained the system.[6]

Inside IMAX

Hardware: The Film Technology

IMAX films were printed on films that were 10 times larger than the 35 mm films that were used in traditional multiplexes and were projected on screens that were (on average) eight stories high (approximately 88 feet) and 120-feet-wide, or in domes that were 81 feet in diameter. Please see Exhibit 1 for a comparison of 35 mm and IMAX film sizes.

IMAX theaters were designed so that projected images stretched up to the peripheral vision of the viewer, thus the viewer was completely immersed in the scene. Each frame of an IMAX film had 15 sprocket holes to guide it through projectors (compared to four in each frame of a 35 mm film). The films were projected to screens by IMAX-designed projectors that had special features — a higher shutter speed, rolling loop motion and vacuum to hold the film to the lens.[7] IMAX projectors used 15,000-watt bulbs, whereas the regular 35 mm projectors used bulbs between 3,000-4,000 watts. The projectors were cooled by circulating more than 50,000 cubic feet of air and nine gallons of distilled water per minute. These features of the IMAX projection system produced images on-screen that were brighter and sharper than those found in conventional movie theaters.

IMAX had developed the skills, knowledge and capabilities to design and assemble the critical elements involved in its projector and camera systems, though most of the components were purchased from vendors with whom it maintained long-term relationships. Strict quality control of components and end products had ensured an average service time of 99.9 per cent for its equipments installed in theaters. Company personnel visited each theater for servicing the systems; the projection systems were serviced every three months and the audio systems were serviced once a year.

In 2007, IMAX spent almost five per cent of its sales revenue on Research and Development, and 50 of its 318 employees were involved in it. The company had spent about $12.6 million in R & D in the past three years.[8] It had also received grants from Ontario Technology Fund for its R & D, and held 46 patents and had seven patents pending in the United States.[9] IMAX had successfully developed 3D cameras and projection systems to produce realistic 3D images. The audience used polarized or electronic glasses that split the images for the left and right eye by using liquid crystal shutter lenses that were controlled by an

---

[5] *Annual Report, 2007.*
[6] *Annual Reports.*
[7] *Computer-Aided Engineering*, 15:8, 1996, pp. 8-9.
[8] *Annual Report, 2007.*
[9] *Annual Report, 2007.*

infrared signal and opened and shut 48 times per second in coordination with the projector to create a 3D effect.   Another example of the firm's technological capabilities was a lightweight 3D camera that it had developed to shoot a movie about the International Space Station in space.   IMAX worked with MSM Design, a small firm owned by Marty and Barbara Mueller, and developed a camera that weighed only 90 pounds, compared to the traditional IMAX 3D cameras that weighed 228 pounds.[10]   IMAX 3D projectors were also capable of projecting 2D images.   The visuals were supported by six-channel digital audio that typically produced 12,000 watts of realistic, distortion-free sound.   The sound systems were developed by Sonics Associates Inc., a subsidiary in which IMAX had 51 per cent ownership.   The company had even developed a 3D directional sound technology that offered location and depth to the audio.   A testament to IMAX's technological prowess was the 1997 Oscar Award it received for Scientific and Technical Achievement.[11]

Because of its larger size, printing and distributing IMAX films was costlier than 35 mm films.   IMAX had developed digital cameras and projectors that it planned to install in theaters starting in 2008 so that it could produce and distribute its movies in digital format.   While the conversion to digital format required substantial upfront investment, it was expected that this shift would allow IMAX to lower its operational costs (of film production and distribution) significantly.

Software: IMAX Films

The motion picture industry produced several types of movies: horror, adventure, comedy, romantic comedy, family, drama and documentaries.   Of these, the documentary segment was considered so significant that the Motion Picture Association of America (MPAA) in its annual Oscar Award ceremony gave out separate awards for these films.   While the large format film itself was a unique feature of IMAX, it had also differentiated itself by its library of films and locations.   IMAX films were often educational and entertaining, and involved documentaries of natural and scientific wonders such as the Grand Canyon, space stations, etc.   An IMAX film, *Fires of Kuwait*, was nominated for an Academy Award in 1993.

By locating itself in prestigious venues such as the Smithsonian Institution in Washington, Liberty Science Center in New Jersey, Museum of Science and Industry in Chicago, and Port Vell in Barcelona, Spain, the firm had created a unique brand image.   In an interview with CNN, co-CEO Gelfond noted IMAX's advantage: "IMAX is also a brand, so we don't have to pay the same kind of talent that Hollywood has to pay, which is really a huge percentage of the costs.   Once you take those costs down and you look at just making the film with the world around you as the talent, you get into much more manageable budget ranges. A typical two-dimensional film at IMAX is about $5 million; a typical 3D film at IMAX is about $10 million."[12]   Hollywood studios would have to pay a major star (such as Tom Cruise or Eddie Murphy) more than $10 million for a movie.   While top movie stars were celebrities and drew huge compensation, many others involved in the production, distribution and marketing of a film were neither well known nor highly paid.   In 2007, according to the Bureau of Labor Statistics (BLS), the median salary for an actor in the motion picture and video industry was about $17 per hour.[13]   Some of these talents had formed unions, such as the Screen Artists Guild, to negotiate higher wages for their labor.   The disruption of TV

[10] "*Cam programming helps design 3d IMAX movie camera for NASA,*" Computer Aided Engineering, 19:3, March 2000, p. 10.

[11] W. C. Symonds, "*Now showing in IMAX: Money!; The giant-screen technology will even bag an Oscar,*" Business Week, 3520, March 31, 1997, p. 80.

[12] D. Michael, "*Bigger is better: IMAX knocking competition down to size,*" CNN, November 6, 1998, www.cnn.com/SHOWBIZ/Movies/9811/06/imax/index.html?iref=newssearch, accessed March 23, 2008.

[13] www.bls.gov/oes/current/naics4_711500.htm, accessed December 23, 2008.

programming in spring 2008 caused by the brief Writers Guild strike was suggestive of the power such groups had on studios.

Besides stars, the other major cost of movie-making was the marketing. It was estimated that a studio spent almost 30-50 per cent of the total cost of production and distribution of a movie in its marketing. According to the Motion Picture Association of America (MPAA), the average cost of making and marketing a movie rose to more than $106 million in 2007, with marketing budgets averaging $36 million.[14] The marketing of the movie was done through several channels such as TV, the press, theaters, websites and promotions with retailers. Please see Exhibit 2 for average spending in each media. For example, most kids' movies released by studios such as Disney and SKG Dreamworks were promoted through tie-ups with restaurants such as McDonald's and Burger King, and also toy manufactures and other retailers. The Hollywood business model used the awareness created by the presence of stars and substantial marketing budgets to draw large audiences into theaters in the opening weekend itself.[15] To achieve high ticket sales on opening weekends, large numbers of prints of the movie were distributed. In contrast, traditionally, IMAX had not marketed its films aggressively. The company did have a sales force and marketing staff at its offices in Canada, the United States, Europe, Japan and China to market its theater systems. The movies were sold to theaters separately; as such, there was no national marketing or advertising.[16] Unlike Hollywood movies that had short lifespans in the theater circuit and were then withdrawn for release on DVD and pay-per-view format, IMAX films were often shown in theaters for years after their release. In recent years, IMAX films had received some marketing support. For example, for IMAX movie *Everest*, producer Greg MacGillivray spent $2 million in marketing and reportedly saw a 20-45 per cent increase in box-office revenues at each theater. Moreover, IMAX's alliances were helping in cross-promoting its movies. For example, for its *T-Rex: Back to the Cretaceous* 3-D movie, it had a month-long promo on Showtime that was also shown in Imaginarium stores in malls across the United States.[17] The increasing number of Hollywood movies that were released in IMAX format allowed IMAX to ride on the coat-tails of marketing campaigns launched by the studios.

IMAX films were often produced by the firm or partially or fully financed by other parties. The firm hired the talent for the film on a project-by-project basis. Most of the post-production work was performed at David Keighley Production, a wholly-owned subsidiary of IMAX.   IMAX (and any investors or sponsors) shared the ownership rights for a film, while usually IMAX controlled the distribution rights. As a result, IMAX had the distribution rights to the largest number of large format films. The distributor received a percentage of the theater box office revenues. IMAX films often remained in distribution for four or five years. (Please see Exhibit 3 for box office revenues for IMAX films.)

Generating Growth

IMAX used a two-pronged strategy to maintain its growth. First, it had sought to expand beyond its institutional environment by opening IMAX theaters within multiplexes or converting existing multiplexes' screens to IMAX format. Second, it had launched Hollywood films in IMAX format.

---

[14] M. Marr, "Now playing: Expensive movies; Average cost of a film tops $100 million for first time; Valenti set to leave MPAA," The Wall Street Journal, March 24, 2004, p. B. 4, www.mpaa.org/researchStatistics.asp, accessed December 23, 2008.

[15] Adam Leipzig, "How to Sell a Movie (or Fail) in Four Hours," The New York Times, November 13, 2005.

[16] D. Oestricher, "IMAX hopes for big run with Matrix," The Wall Street Journal, June 18, 2003, p. b5c.

[17] T. L. Stanley, "IMAX lands showtime, GTE for 1st X-Promo," Brandweek, July 13, 1998, 39:28, p. 5.

An IMAX Near You

While early IMAX theaters were mostly located in institutional settings such as museums and aquariums, to reach a wider audience IMAX had engaged in alliances with commercial movie theater owners.[18] It grew rapidly during the late 1990s as theater owners such as AMC, Cinemark and Regal went on a building spree and bought IMAX systems to install in their multiplexes. According to Wechsler, this strategy backfired when IMAX could not escape the crisis that hit the theater industry in the late 1990s because of the overbuilding during that decade. As many theater-owners filed for bankruptcy, IMAX had to engage in belt-tightening of its own because of its receivable problems. Moody's downgraded IMAX's debt of $200 million senior notes from Ba2 to B2 and a $100 million note from B1 to Caa1 because of the risk of default by customers. In response, IMAX cut $14 million in overhead, laid off 200 employees and bought back $90 million of its debt.[19] Debt remained a critical problem for IMAX (please see Exhibits 4, 5 and 6 for IMAX financials).

In recent years, IMAX entered into partnerships with AMC and Regal Cinemas to screen IMAX films in multiplexes using its MPX technology. MPX technology allowed IMAX and theater-owners to convert traditional theaters to IMAX format.[20] It was estimated that it now cost only $175,000 to retrofit a multiplex and another $500,000 to install the IMAX system.[21] Regal Cinemas had built IMAX theaters in several markets and waited to see how they performed before adding more.[22] In March 2008, it signed another agreement with IMAX for 38 more theaters, bringing the total number of Regal IMAX theaters to 52 by 2010. Regal theaters would charge $2.50-5.00 more than their regular feature admission for IMAX films.[23] In December 2007, IMAX signed a deal with AMC to install 100 IMAX digital theaters systems in 33 markets, thereby substantially increasing its presence in the U.S. market. IMAX had identified 655 multiplexes without an IMAX nearby.[24] However, IMAX co-CEO Wechsler had stated that he did not expect IMAX theaters to be ubiquitous but exclusive, like flying first-class; while co-CEO Gelfond had suggested that the IMAX experience would be so unique that it could not be replicated at home. Consistent with this vision, the theater agreement that it recently signed gave AMC territorial exclusivity.[25] Unlike past agreements where theaters chains bought the system from IMAX, the newer agreements required the partner theater chain to make the investment for retrofitting the theater, while IMAX paid for the system installation in return for revenue-sharing on future ticket sales. Analysts expected that such agreements (and digital conversion) would lower IMAX's capital requirements and help it pay off its debt.[26]

---

[18] L. Gubernick, Hollywood Journal: Hollywood think bigger — your favorites, only taller: Can re-released movies breathe life into IMAX," The Wall Street Journal, February 15, 2002, p. W. 5.

[19] Z. Olijnyk, "One giant leap," Canadian Business, 75:17, September 16, 2002, pp. 46-48.

[20] D. Oestricher, "IMAX hopes for big run with Matrix," The Wall Street Journal, June 18, 2003, p. b5c.

[21] Katy Marquardt, "Imax Parlays a Huge Screen and 3-D Tech into an Experience You Can't Duplicate at Home. Coming soon to a multiplex near you," US News and World Report, Feb. 6, 2008, www.usnews.com/articles/business/2008/02/06/imax-parlays-3-d-tech-into-an-experience-you-cant-duplicate-at-home.html, accessed December 23, 2008.

[22] The Wall Street Journal, 2000.

[23] B. Pulley, "The really big screen," Forbes, 172:13, December 22, 2003, p. 222.; The Wall Street Journal, 2003.

[24] D. Oestricher, "IMAX hopes for big run with Matrix," The Wall Street Journal, June 18, 2003, p. b5c.

[25] Katy Marquardt, "Imax Parlays a Huge Screen and 3-D Tech Into an Experience You Can't Duplicate at Home. Coming soon to a multiplex near you," US News and World Report, February 6, 2008, www.usnews.com/articles/business/2008/02/06/imax-parlays-3-d-tech-into-an-experience-you-cant-duplicate-at-home.html, accessed December 23, 2008.

[26] Ibid.

Go West IMAX!

Another strategic move by IMAX to ensure its growth was the conversion of Hollywood movies into IMAX format. IMAX had developed a patented digital re-mastering (DMR) technology that allowed it to convert traditional 35 mm films such as *Harry Potter, Spiderman, Antz* and *The Simpsons* into the large-screen format and even develop 3D versions of such movies. The development of this technology was critical because merely projecting a 35 mm film on the large IMAX screen would have produced a grainy picture. According to co-CEO Gelfond, the firm invested millions of dollars to sharpen the resolution of the converted pictures and it took more than five years to develop the technology.[27] The re-mastering of *Apollo 13* took 16 weeks, while *The Matrix Revolutions* was re-mastered as it was being produced, allowing for near-simultaneous theater and IMAX releases. As IMAX had worked out the teething problems with this technology, the costs of conversion had come down. For each print, it now cost $22,500 to convert a standard two-dimensional film and $45,000 to convert a 3-D film. It was expected that moving to a digital format would further lower the conversion costs. If the conversion succeeded at the box office, more studios might be willing to spend the extra money to convert their standard 35 mm films to IMAX format.[28] This would also attract theater chains to open new IMAX screens. Though IMAX made only seven per cent of the box office revenue from reformatted films by other studios, compared to the nearly 30 per cent that it made on its own movies,[29] the conversion of Hollywood movies might allow IMAX to survive, according to co-CEO Gelfond.[30] An announcement to launch the *Harry Potter* movie on IMAX resulted in an almost 11 per cent surge in its stock price that day. Gelfond noted that IMAX could continue making educational films that could be screened in theaters during daytime for families, students and tourists, while its reformatted Hollywood movies could be screened in the evening. In an interview with Amusement Business, co-CEO Wechsler noted that the IMAX strategy of moving into the commercial movie business would hopefully expand the core audience.[31] "Our research tells us that a lot of people will pay that extra $3 to $5," Gelfond said in an interview with USA Today.[32]

The first full-length Hollywood movie released on IMAX was *Fantasia* 2000 in January 2000.[33] The classic *Beauty and the Beast*, which had a 20-week show on 67 IMAX screens in 2002, generated $32 million in revenue.[34] The first live action commercial movie to be launched in IMAX format was *Apollo 13*, which generated an additional $2 million in revenue. Later, *Star Wars* was released on IMAX followed by *The Matrix Reloaded*, which generated $11.7 million.[35] These movies were released in IMAX after their theatrical release.[36]

As more Hollywood movies were converted to IMAX format, the studios had to decide whether these should be released simultaneously in theaters and IMAX format. Could the expansion into IMAX theaters cannibalize the traditional theatrical revenues? It was found that almost 90 per cent of *The Matrix Reloaded* IMAX viewers had seen the movie in theaters earlier. *The Polar Express*, which was released

---

[27] S. N. Chakravarty, "A really big show," *Institutional Investor*, 35:10, October 2002, p. 20.

[28] *The Wall Street Journal*, 2000; *Institutional Investor*, 2002.

[29] D. Lieberman, "IMAX supersizes its plans for future flicks," *US Today*, December 16, 2002, www.usatoday.com/tech/news/techinnovations/2002-12-16-IMAX_x.htm, accessed December 23, 2008.

[30] Z. Olijnyk, "One giant leap," *Canadian Business*, 75:17, September 16, 2002, pp. 46-48.

[31] N. Emmons, "IMAX may turn toward mainstream," *Amusement Business*, 112:49, December 4, 2000, p. 1, pp. 20-21.

[32] D. Lieberman, "IMAX supersizes its plans for future flicks," *US Today*, December 16, 2002, www.usatoday.com/tech/news/techinnovations/2002-12-16-IMAX_x.htm, accessed December 23, 2008.

[33] R. Ricklefs, "IMAX hopes to take cast screen into mainstream — a new 'fantasia' tests film strategy of Canadian firm," *The Wall Street Journal*, December 10, 1999, p. 1.

[34] D. Oestricher, "IMAX hopes for big run with Matrix," *The Wall Street Journal*, June 18, 2003, p. b5c.

[35] T. Lowry, "Now playing at IMAX: Hit movies" *Business Week*, 3807, November 11, 2002, p. 46.; N. Sperling, "IMAX executives hoping Warner's 'The Matrix' is 'the one'," *Amusement Business*, 115:46, 2003, pp. 24-25.

[36] T. King, "Hollywood Journal: When a 'Sure thing' Isn't — Even the $20 million stars can't guarantee a hit; trying to ignore 'Pluto'," *The Wall Street Journal.* October 11, 2002, p. w11.

simultaneously in IMAX and traditional theaters during the 2004 Christmas season, was a big hit with $45 million in revenues in the IMAX format.[37] On December 12, 2008, the movie *The Day the Earth Stood Still* was released simultaneously on IMAX and multiplex screens. At $31 million, the movie had the highest box office gross over a weekend. More than $3.8 million (about 12 per cent) of the total revenue came from IMAX theaters. Notably, the average revenue per IMAX theater was $30,800, compared to the national average theater revenues of $8,100.[38] Such track records should give more studios the confidence to release their movies simultaneously in commercial and IMAX theaters.

INDUSTRY DYNAMICS

Motion picture production and distribution was part of the service sector of the economy and included firms such as Disney/Pixar, MGM, Regal Entertainment, Lions Gate and Carmike. Many of the production and distribution companies were now part of other, larger, diversified firms. For example, Columbia Pictures was now part of Sony, Warner Brothers was a subsidiary of Time-Warner, Paramount Studios was part of Viacom and Pixar and Miramax were part of Disney. Over the years, media firms had sought to vertically integrate their operations by owning not only the production facilities but also distribution networks.

Film production remained a risky business. Only one in 10 films ever recovered its investment from domestic theater release; and only six out of 10 movies ever recouped the original investment. Competition among movies within the same genre was so high that studios scheduled releases carefully to avoid direct competition.   Thus, release dates were announced several years in advance and production was designed around preferred holiday release dates such as Thanksgiving, July 4th, Memorial Day weekends or the first weekend of May.

IMAX films faced competition from other films produced by studios such as Pixar/Disney that were targeted for families or children. Within the large format film segment, Iwerks was the only rival to IMAX.[39] Iwerks was founded in 1986 and continued to be involved in all aspects of large format films and simulation rides. It produced films in the 15/70 and 8/70 formats; however, the focus of the firm was more on ride simulation packages located in theme parks, zoos, museums and other destinations. Iwerks had received two Academy Awards for Scientific and Technical Achievement. In 2002, Iwerks merged with SimEx (a firm founded in 1991), which was involved in ride simulation and animation production. Another firm, Megasystems, which was involved in the development of large format projection systems, production and consulting in marketing, operations and technical services, had discontinued its projection system production and was renamed Pollavision. Pollavision was now only involved in consulting (and maintenance) services for large format film theaters.[40]

Technology Trends

Potential IMAX viewers could consume many alternative sources of entertainment such as live plays, sport events, TV programs, the Internet, etc. Please see Exhibits 7 and 8 for admissions, prices and time spent

[37] W. D. Crotty, "IMAX's screen gets bigger," The Motley Fool, September 15. 2005,
www.fool.com/investing/general/2005/09/15/imaxs-screen-gets-
bigger.aspx?terms=Imax+screen+gets+bigger&vstest=search_042607_linkdefault, accessed December 23, 2008.
[38] "Imax rises as consumers embrace large screens," Associated Press, December 16, 2008,
http://biz.yahoo.com/ap/081216/imax_mover.html?.v=1, accessed December 23, 2008.
[39] C. Booth, "IMAX gets bigger (by getting smaller)," Time, June 29, 1998, 151:25, pp. 48-49.
[40] www.pollavision.com, accessed December 23, 2008.

on alternative entertainment sources. Viewers might choose to watch a movie on DVD, pay-per-view or video on demand rather than at the theater. The development of high-definition DVD recording, big-screen TVs and cheaper home theater projection and sound systems posed an even bigger threat to box office ticket sales. Please see Exhibit 9 for DVD sales trends in the United States. According to one estimate, almost 85 per cent of a film's revenue now came from home viewing through various channels such as DVD/VHS, cable and TV.[41] Yet, it had been found that the success of secondary sources such as DVD sales and rentals was a function of the movie's box office success.[42] According to Jack Valenti, former president of MPAA, 50 per cent of DVD viewers and almost 38 per cent of VCR movie-users were frequent moviegoers. He said, "People who love movies are eager to watch them again in different environments."[43]

The development of new technologies, such as cheaper high definition camcorders, as well as the proliferation of new distribution channels such as cable, satellite and the Internet, had also created opportunities for new independent firms to enter the industry. One such firm that leveraged its knowledge of computer technology to develop blockbuster animated films was Pixar. New firms might enter one or more parts of the film industry value chain — talent management, production, post-production, distribution, etc. Specialists in post-production processes had emerged who were responsible for editing, special effects, media transfers, subtitling, etc. However, entry into all aspects of the value chain simultaneously had been rare. A recent example of such an entry was SKG Dreamworks, a studio that was started by film industry veterans Spielberg, Katzenberg and Geffen.

Such technological changes had also increased the potential for piracy. According to the Motion Picture Association of America, the U.S. film industry lost more than $3 billion annually because of piracy. Section 8, Article 1 of the U.S. Constitution offers Congress the power to offer copyright protection. The Copyright Act of 1976 that was amended in 1982 offers strong penalties for copyright violations. Please see www.copyright.gov/title17 for recent development in copyright law. Violations were considered felonies and were subject to federal criminal charges and civil lawsuits. The Motion Picture Association was working closely with the U.S. Congress to enforce sentencing guidelines and improve copyright protection as newer technologies emerged and posed fresher challenges. According to Karen Randall of Vivendi, whose production *The Hulk* was released on the Internet by pirates before its theatrical release, the FBI was very cooperative and aggressive in pursuing the case.[44]

Other Trends

IMAX had to cease screening its movie *Volcanoes of the Deep Sea* in some parts of the United States, as certain religious groups were offended by its position on, and depiction of, evolution.[45] Concerns about violence and sex in movies had generated considerable efforts to organize and lobby political action to regulate the industry. For example, Tipper Gore and Lynn Cheney (spouses of former vice-presidents Al Gore and Dick Cheney, respectively) had worked hard to curtail the levels of violence, sex and vulgar language found in popular media.[46]

---

[41] E. J. Epstein, "Hollywood's death spiral," Slate, July 25, 2005.

[42] Bruce Orwall, "A Dud at Theaters Will Be a Dud DVD," The Wall Street Journal, November 26, 2005, p. A2.

[43] J. Valenti, MPAA Press Release, 2002.

[44] S. McBride and B. Orwall, "Movie industry steps up drive against pirates," The Wall Street Journal, January 27, 2004, p. B1.

[45] Cornelia Dean, "A new test for IMAX: The Bible vs. the volcano," March. 19, 2005.

[46] Richard Goldstein, "Scary Move: When Both Parties Team Up to Target Hollywood, Be Afraid. Be Very Afraid!" Village Voice, October 3, 2000 p.20.

Another trend that might help firms such as IMAX was the increased consumption of educational entertainment. Ever since Sesame Street succeeded in educating and entertaining kids simultaneously, the "edutainment" market had grown as parents increasingly sought out play activities for their children that were educational. This trend had been attributed to increasing belief among parents that in a knowledge economy, their kids' success might depend on education. The widespread popularity among parents of the concept of the "Mozart effect" — a finding that babies that listened to Mozart recordings in the womb or at early stages of birth had richer cognitive development — was seen as evidence of their desire to produce smart kids.[47] Other trends that were driving this growth could include higher education levels of parents and overscheduled kids and parents.[48] As a result, zoos, museums, software, TV shows and toys were all redesigning their products to entertain and educate.

According to IMAX, more than 20 per cent of IMAX audiences were school groups. About 70 per cent of IMAX viewers were between 19 and 65 years of age, and the majority were college- or university-educated, with an average household income of more than $70,000, and with 33 per cent earning more than $100,000.[49] MPAA offered a more fine-grained analysis of demographic data on movie attendance. It reported that 12-24 year olds (38 per cent of admissions) had the largest attendance for feature films in theaters in 2007, followed by the 25- to 39-year-olds group (29 per cent of admissions).[50] The 12-24-year-olds were also frequent moviegoers (at least one movie per month), representing 41 per cent of frequent moviegoers. IMAX needed to figure out a way to attract this demographic.

U.S. and Global Market

In 2007, 603 movies were released in the United States and collected revenues of $9.6 billion.[51] According to the MPAA, there were 1.4 billion movie theater attendances in the United States in 2007.[52] Jack Valenti, former president of the MPAA, noted that Americans had the highest per capita movie attendance in the world at 5.3 films a year. By excluding those who did not see at least one movie a year, the per capita attendance rose to 8.6 films per year.[53] Exhibit 10 displays theater revenues, average U.S. ticket prices, attendance annual growth rate, consumer price index (CPI) and growth of the U.S. economy. Theater-owners realized that ticket prices could not go up forever, as this might drive away more viewers; so they tried to generate revenue by screening more commercials before showing the feature film. According to some experts, release of big budget franchise movies or sequels of popular movies attenuated the adverse impact of the economy on theater attendance.

Movies were now increasingly becoming a global industry. More than 5000 films were released worldwide in 2007, with seven billion attendances and annual global box office revenues estimated at $26.7 billion.[54] The Asia-Pacific region had the largest share of the global market. While Hollywood movies had always enjoyed an international audience, with globalization and the increased movement of people across national borders movies from other regions such as Hong Kong and India were also finding an international audience. For Hollywood movies, a significant part of the revenues now came from

[47] Jeffrey Kluger and Alice Park, "The Quest For A Superkid," _Time,_ April 22, 2001 www.time.com/time/nation/article/0,8599,107265-1,00.html, accessed December 23, 2008.
[48] R. White, "That's Edutainment," White Hutchinson Leisure & Learning Group, 2003.
[49] www.IMAX.com.
[50] J. Valenti, MPAA Press Release, 2002.
[51] US Entertainment Industry: 2007 MPAA statistics. See also, M. Marr, "Now playing: Expensive movies; Average cost of a film tops $100 million for first time; Valenti set to leave MPAA," _The Wall Street Journal_, March 24, 2004, p. B. 4.
[52] James Jaeger, The Movie Industry, www.mecfilms.com/moviepubs/memos/moviein.htm, accessed December 23, 2008.
[53] 2007 movie attendance study, MPAA.
[54] 2007 International Theatrical Snapshot, MPAA;www.mpaa.org/International%20Theatrical%20Snapshot.pdf, accessed March 4, 2009.

outside the United States. Please see Exhibit 11 on domestic and foreign sources for the top 10 films in 2007.

THE LARGER ISSUES

At this point in its evolution, IMAX faced two critical questions. Would IMAX lose its differentiation if it exhibited too many Hollywood movies? Greg MacGillvray, who had made several films in the IMAX format, including the highly successful *Everest*, argued that IMAX ran the risk of losing its brand identity as it moved into non-educational entertainment films. He said: "There's also been a slight brand erosion given that these films have not been really educational experiences, but more entertainment experiences." According to MacGillvray, IMAX's own research showed that the brand's trustworthiness was rooted in the fact that IMAX grew up in institutional settings.[55]

Another question that the present co-CEOs had faced for several years was: Should IMAX be sold to a larger studio such as Sony, Disney or Time-Warner? That is, was it too small to survive on its own? Some analysts had speculated that IMAX was ripe for acquisition. Co-CEO Gelfond had once stated, "Someday it will make sense for IMAX to be part of a studio."[56]

The author would like to thank Professors Barbara Bartkus, Alan Eisner, Jim Key, participants at a case writing workshop organized by the Society for Case Research, and students at Old Dominion University for comments on earlier versions of the case. Thanks also to Lee-Hsien Pan for his research assistance.

---

[55] P. Waal, "Call in the barbarians," <u>Canadian Business</u>, 73:17, September 18, 2000, pp. 85-87.
[56] P. Waal, "The plot quickens," <u>Canadian Business</u>, 71:11, June 26-July 10, 1998, pp. 51-57.

Exhibit 1

IMAX FILM SIZE

15/70mm

Standard 70mm

Standard 35mm

Source: IMAX, with permission.

Exhibit 2

AVERAGE MARKETING SPENDING ON VARIOUS MEDIA, 2007

Newspapers	12.9 %
Network TV	16.1 %
Spot TV	13.7 %
Internet	5.3 %
Trailers	4.9 %
Other Media (cable TV, radio, magazines, billboards)	24.5 %
Other Non-media (production/creative services, exhibitor services, promotion & publicity, market research)	22.6 %

Source: www.mpaa.com.

Exhibit 3

BOX OFFICE REVENUES FOR IMAX MOVIES (IN MILLIONS OF $)

Rank	Title	Studio	Gross-to-date	Year
1	Everest	MFF	$87.18	1998
2	Space Station 3-D	IMAX	$77.10	2002
3	T-Rex: Back to the Cretaceous	IMAX	$53.14	1998
4	Fantasia 2000	BV	$52.26	2000
5	Mysteries of Egypt	IMAX	$40.59	1998
6	Deep Sea 3-D	WB	$37.09	2006
7	Magnificent Desolation	IMAX	$26.67	2005
8	Beauty and the Beast	BV	$25.49	2002
9	NASCAR 3D: The IMAX Experience	WB	$21.58	2004
10	Sea Monsters: A Prehistoric Adventure	NGC	$20.05	2007

Source: www.boxofficemojo.com. IMAX box office receipts have only recently started being tracked.

628   CASE 19   IMAX: Larger than Life

Exhibit 4

IMAX CORPORATION ANNUAL BALANCE SHEET
(in thousands of dollars)

Period Ending	31-Dec-07	31-Dec-06	31-Dec-05	31-Dec-04
Assets				
Current Assets				
Cash and Cash Equivalents	16,901	25,123	24,324	28,964
Short-Term Investments	-	2,115	8,171	-
Net Receivables	25,505	26,017	89,171	19,899
Inventory	22,050	26,913	28,294	29,001
Other Current Assets	2,187	3,432	3,825	2,279
Total Current Assets	**66,643**	**83,600**	**153,785**	**80,143**
Long-Term Investments	59,092	65,878	-	59,492
Property Plant and Equipment	23,708	24,639	26,780	28,712
Goodwill	39,027	39,027	39,027	39,027
Intangible Assets	4,419	3,782	6,030	3,931
Accumulated Amortization	-	-	-	-
Other Assets	10,928	6,646	9,756	7,532
Deferred Long-Term Asset Charges	4,165	3,719	10,806	12,016
Total Assets	**207,982**	**227,291**	**246,184**	**230,853**
Liabilities				
Current Liabilities				
Accounts Payable	74,267	69,720	62,057	62,724
Short/Current Long-Term Debt	-	-	-	-
Other Current Liabilities	-	-	-	-
Total Current Liabilities	**74,267**	**69,720**	**62,057**	**62,724**
Long-Term Debt	160,000	160,000	160,000	160,000
Other Liabilities	-	-	-	-
Deferred Long-Term Liability Charges	59,085	55,803	44,397	50,505
Minority Interest	-	-	-	-
Negative Goodwill	-	-	-	-
Total Liabilities	**293,352**	**285,523**	**266,454**	**273,229**
Stockholders' Equity				
Common Stock	122,455	122,024	121,674	116,281
Retained Earnings	(213,407)	(184,375)	(144,347)	(160,945)
Other Stockholder Equity	5,582	4,119	2,403	2,288
Total Stockholder Equity	**(85,370)**	**(58,232)**	**(20,270)**	**(42,376)**

Source: Annual Reports.

Exhibit 5

IMAX CORPORATION ANNUAL INCOME STATEMENT
(in thousands of dollars)

Period Ending	31-Dec-07	31-Dec-06	31-Dec-05	31-Dec-04
Total Revenue	115,832	129,452	144,930	135,980
Cost of Revenue	74,673	76,902	73,005	70,062
Gross Profit	41,159	52,550	71,925	65,918
Operating Expenses				
Research & Development	5,789	3,615	3,264	3,995
Selling General and Administrative	44,705	42,527	39,503	36,066
Non-recurring	562	1,073	-859	-639
Others	547	1,668	911	719
Total Operating Expenses	51,603	48,883	42,819	40,141
Operating Income or Loss	(10,444)	3,667	29,106	25,777
Income from Continuing Operations				
Total Other Income/Expenses Net	(933)	1,036	1,004	265
Earnings Before Interest and Taxes	(11,377)	4,703	30,110	26,042
Interest Expense	17,093	16,759	16,773	16,853
Income Before Taxes	(28,470)	(12,056)	13,337	9,189
Income Tax Expense	472	6,218	934	(255)
Minority Interest	0	0	0	0
Net Income from Continuing Ops	(28,942)	(18,274)	12,403	9,444
Non-recurring Events				
Discontinued Operations	2,002	1,425	1,979	800
Extraordinary Items	0	0	0	0
Effect of Accounting Changes	0	0	0	0
Other Items	0	0	0	0
Net Income	(26,940)	(16,849)	14,382	10,244

Source: Annual Reports.

Exhibit 6

IMAX CORPORATION CASH FLOW STATEMENT
(in thousands of dollars)

Period Ending	31-Dec-07	31-Dec-06	31-Dec-05	31-Dec-04
Net Income	(26,940)	(16,849)	14,382	10,244
Cash Flows Provided By or Used In Operating Activities				
Depreciation	17,738	16,872	15,867	14,947
Adjustments to Net Income	(3,520)	10,349	(8,678)	(4,577)
Changes in Accounts Receivables	675	(11,106)	(8,324)	(6,673)
Changes in Liabilities	4,781	4,399	(11,749)	(6,830)
Changes in Inventories	(1,603)	57	(383)	(283)
Changes in Other Operating Activities	2,648	(9,659)	(1,545)	4,583
Total Cash Flow from Operating Activities	(6,221)	(5,937)	1,786	11,411
Cash Flows Provided By or Used In Investing Activities				
Capital Expenditures	(2,150)	(1,985)	(1,597)	(320)
Investments	2,115	6,396	(7,818)	393
Other Cashflows from Investing Activities	(702)	2,105	(1,301)	(1,435)
Total Cash Flows from Investing Activities	(737)	6,516	(10,716)	(1,362)
Cash Flows Provided By or Used In Financing Activities				
Dividends Paid	-	-	-	-
Sale Purchase of Stock	420	286	3,633	558
Net Borrowings	(1,714)	-	-	(29,769)
Other Cash Flows from Financing Activities	-	-	786	800
Total Cash Flows from Financing Activities	(1,294)	286	4,419	(28,411)
Effect of Exchange Rate Changes	30	(66)	(129)	44
Change in Cash and Cash Equivalents	($8,222)	$799	($4,640)	($18,318)

Source: Annual Reports.

Exhibit 7

SUBSTITUTE ACTIVITIES TO MOVIES IN 2007

	Activity	Attendance (in millions)	Average Ticket Price (in $)
1	Movies	1400	6.88
2	Theme Parks	341	35.30
3	Ice Hockey/NHL	21	44.60
4	Basketball/NBA	22	46.75
5	Football/NFL	17	65.25
6	Baseball/MLB	77	23.50

Source: MPAA, www.mpaa.com.

Exhibit 8

MEDIA CONSUMPTION BASED ON HOURS PER PERSON PER YEAR

Filmed Entertainment	2003	2004	2005	2006	2007
Cable & Satellite TV	886	909	980	997	1,010
Broadcast TV	729	711	679	676	676
Consumer Internet	153	164	169	177	181
Home Video (DVD & VHS)	60	67	63	62	64
Box Office	13	13	12	12	13
In-flight Entertainment & Mobile Content	5	8	10	13	18
Subtotal	1,846	1,872	1,913	1,937	1,962
Other Entertainment					
Broadcast & Satellite Radio	831	821	805	778	769
Recorded Music	187	196	195	186	171
Newspapers	195	192	188	178	172
Consumer Magazines	122	125	124	121	119
Consumer Books	108	108	107	108	108
Video Games	76	78	73	76	82
Subtotal	1,522	1,520	1,492	1,447	1,421

Source: MPAA, www.mpaa.com.

Exhibit 9

DVD CONSUMPTION IN THE UNITED STATES
(in millions of units)

	Rental DVDs	Sell-through DVDs	Total DVDs	Avg. Price of DVD
2007	171.2	1,084.6	1,255.8	22.11
2006	180.2	1,129.0	1,309.2	22.29
2005	179.0	1,114.5	1,293.6	21.20
2004	149.3	1,063.3	1,212.6	20.32
2003	105.4	768.3	873.6	20.15

Source: MPAA, www.mpaa.com.

Exhibit 10

THEATER BOX OFFICE REVENUES, AVERAGE U.S. ATTENDANCE, PRICE AND ECONOMY

Year	Revenue (in billions $)	Ticket price (in $)	Attendance (in billions)	GDP Growth (in %)	CPI Inflation (in %)
1990	5.02	4.22	1.19	1.9	5.4
1991	4.8	4.21	1.14	-0.2	4.2
1992	4.56	4.15	1.1	3.3	3.0
1993	4.89	4.14	1.18	2.7	3.0
1994	5.18	4.08	1.24	4.0	2.6
1995	5.27	4.35	1.21	2.5	2.8
1996	5.81	4.42	1.32	3.7	3.0
1997	6.21	4.59	1.35	4.5	2.3
1998	6.76	4.69	1.44	4.2	1.6
1999	7.31	5.06	1.44	4.5	2.2
2000	7.46	5.39	1.38	3.7	3.4
2001	8.12	5.65	1.44	0.8	2.8
2002	9.27	5.8	1.60	1.6	1.6
2003	9.16	6.03	1.52	2.5	2.3
2004	9.21	6.21	1.48	3.6	2.7
2005	8.83	6.41	1.38	2.9	3.4
2006	9.14	6.55	1.39	2.8	3.2
2007	9.63	6.88	1.40	2.0	2.8

Source: National Association of Theater Owners (NATO), www.natoonline.org; Bureau of Economic Analysis, www.bea.gov; and Bureau of Labor Statistics, www.bls.gov.

Exhibit 11

DOMESTIC AND OVERSEAS REVENUES FOR 2007
(in millions of dollars)

Rank	Title	Domestic	Overseas	World
1	Pirates of the Caribbean: At World's End	309.4	649.0	958.4
2	Harry Potter and the Order of the Phoenix	292.0	645.0	937.0
3	Spider-Man 3	336.5	548.9	885.4
4	Shrek the Third	321.0	470.4	791.4
5	Transformers	319.1	382.0	701.1
6	Ratatouille	206.4	409.5	615.9
7	I Am Legend	256.4	327.6	584.0
8	Simpsons Movie, The	183.1	342.4	525.5
9	300	210.6	246.0	456.6
10	National Treasure: Book of Secrets	220.0	234.0	454.0

Source: www.worldwideboxoffice.com.

BEST BUY INC.– DUAL BRANDING IN CHINA

R. Chandrasekhar wrote this case under the supervision of Professor Niraj Dawar solely to provide material for class discussion. The authors do not intend to illustrate either effective or ineffective handling of a managerial situation. The authors may have disguised certain names and other identifying information to protect confidentiality.

Ivey Management Services prohibits any form of reproduction, storage or transmittal without its written permission. Reproduction of this material is not covered under authorization by any reproduction rights organization. To order copies or request permission to reproduce materials, contact Ivey Publishing, Ivey Management Services, c/o Richard Ivey School of Business, The University of Western Ontario, London, Ontario, Canada, N6A 3K7; phone (519) 661-3208; fax (519) 661-3882; e-mail cases@ivey.uwo.ca.

In June 2006, John Noble, senior vice president at Best Buy International, a division of Best Buy Inc. (Best Buy), the largest retailer of consumer electronics (CE) in the United States, faced a major strategic branding decision. Earlier that month, the company had acquired a majority stake in Jiangsu Five Star Appliances (Five Star), the third-largest retailer of appliances and consumer electronics in China. Noble had been assigned to the international division just a month earlier from the company's Canadian operations, where he had held a similar position since 2002. In his new role, Noble was tasked to decide and plan how Best Buy should implement a dual-brand strategy in China. The dual-brand strategy adopted in Canada four years earlier seemed to have worked well. "Will the dual-brand strategy work in China?" he wondered. "How should I make it work?"

While negotiating for a majority stake in Five Star, which had 135 stores in China, Best Buy announced plans to open its first Best Buy store in China in December 2006, to be followed by two more stores in the next 12 to 18 months. Five Star also announced its own agenda of opening 25 additional stores in China, under the Five Star banner, during approximately the same period.

CONTEXT

When Best Buy decided to go beyond the domestic market in the United States in December 2000, the company had found neighboring Canada to be a logical first step. The Canadian CE market was fragmented, with only one dominant player, Future Shop. Best Buy's original objective was to set up its own stores in various Canadian cities to compete directly with Future Shop stores. It had planned to open the first of several stores in the Toronto area in 2003, and then embark on a three-year expansion program that would see the launch of 15 stores in major Canadian cities. Best Buy had a target of setting up 60 to 65 stores across Canada, competing with the 95 stores of Future Shop, which itself was planning to increase its stores to 120 over four years. As part of a defense strategy, Future Shop was also finalizing plans to relocate or renovate at least half of its existing stores by 2005.

In August 2001, the founders of the two companies met and decided, over the course of three weeks, that "together we could accomplish infinitely more than if we were to go our own ways and compete with each other."[1] By January 2002, Best Buy had acquired 100 per cent ownership in Future Shop. Then, when the time came to finalize integration, the management of Best Buy took a surprising decision: to retain the Future Shop brand and let it compete with Best Buy as an independent brand, a strategy that had no precedent within the company. The dual-brand strategy — wherein two brands, both part of a common corporate entity, vied for market share — was an initiative being tested for the first time at Best Buy (see Exhibit 1).

In reference to whether the dual brand strategy could be implemented, Richard Schulze, the founder of Best Buy, was famously quoted for saying, at the time of the acquisition, "I'm not saying it can't be done, I'm saying it's never been done before . . . ."

BEST BUY

Headquartered in Minneapolis in the United States, Best Buy was driven by a vision of "meeting consumers at the intersection of technology and life."[2] The company saw its core strategy as "bringing technology and consumers together in a retail environment that focuses on educating consumers on the features and benefits of technology and entertainment while maximizing overall profitability."[3] Best Buy was positioned to deliver new technologies at the retail level in the three segments of devices, connections and content, enabling the company to capitalize on the progressive digitization of analog products and the accelerating digital product cycles to mobilize consumer demand. The company was selling its products at moderate to upper moderate price points.

Growing at a rate of between 15 per cent and 20 per cent every year, Best Buy had attained sales revenues of US$30.9 billion for the year ending March 2006 (see Exhibit 2). The company had more than 20 per cent share of the retail American consumer electronics market, which was valued at US$152 billion in 2006.[4] Globally, the CE market was averaging a growth rate of 10 per cent and was expected, according to CEA/GfK Worldwide Consumer Electronics Sales & Forecast, to reach revenues of US$700 billion by 2009.[5] In planning to maintain double-digit growth rate year after year, Best Buy saw, in its international expansion, a window of opportunity.

History

Best Buy was founded in 1966, by Richard Schulze, an American entrepreneur from the mid-west. The chain, which was known at the time as Sound of Music, was retailing audio components sourced from vendors. The company struggled through the recession years of the 1970s, and with the arrival of the video cassette recorder in the early 1980s, the music chain expanded into retailing video components. In 1983, Sound of Music moved into mass merchandising by switching to a superstore format (characterized by a wide range of products and boxes of merchandise in a warehouse atmosphere) under the new, distinctive yellow Best Buy banner. Six years later, Best Buy refined its retailing techniques in three ways: the introduction of self-service, the placement of its salespersons (referred to as "Blue Shirts") on fixed pay instead of on commission and reconfiguration of stores' formats to a discount style. The changes were

---

[1] "Best Buy Snaps up Future Shop for $580 Million," CBCNews.ca, August 14, 2001, http://www.cbc.ca/money/story/2001/08/14/futureshop140801.html, accessed September 12, 2008.

[2] Best Buy 10-K filings 2001 p 5.

[3] Ibid.

[4] www.ce.org/research/US.CE industry growth 2004-2009(e), referenced March 31, 2009.

[5] Consumer Electronics Association, "Global Consumer Electronics Industry Will Grow to $700 Million by 2009, CEA/GfK Study Finds," press release, July 9, 2008, http://www.ce.org/Press/CurrentNews/press_release_detail.asp?id=11535, accessed March 31, 2009.

made in recognition of both a trend in customers of being knowledgeable enough to choose products on their own and their preference of shopping in a consumer-friendly environment.

Innovations

The company's decision to stop paying commissions to salespersons and put them on salary did not go well initially with vendors such as Toshiba and Hitachi. These manufacturers had long felt that a high-pressure, incentives-oriented and results-driven approach at the store was necessary to move products. But Best Buy soon realized that its customers were comfortable in the new, informal ambience at its stores.

After entering new domestic markets, such as Chicago, Philadelphia and Boston, Best Buy became the biggest seller of home personal computers (PCs) in 1995, in time for the Internet boom. In 1996, Best Buy surpassed Circuit City to become the top CE retailer in the United States, a position that Best Buy had since held.

Best Buy had spotted another trend. Digital devices and home networks were growing in complexity, opening up a prospect for marketing the necessary technical services to homes and small businesses. This opportunity was pegged at being worth more than US$20 billion a year in the United States. Best Buy had acquired, in October 2002, a Minneapolis-based startup specializing in repairing and installing PCs, called Geek Squad. Within a year, Best Buy had Geek Squad precincts, staffed by newly recruited techies, in more than 20 stores. By 2005, the geeks had set up shop in all Best Buy stores. The move was an advantage over competitors, such as Wal-Mart, which did not provide service back-up for their CE sales.

Centricity

Best Buy had identified the technology enthusiast as its core customer. This target group was characterized by the following attributes: aged 15 to 39, male, highly educated, above-average income and eager for products and services that would render personal time both productive and enjoyable, and resonate with being fun, honest, young and techno-savvy. Best Buy was building its brand promise on those very lines: "being fun, honest, young and techno-savvy."

In the late 1990s, Best Buy established a standard operating platform (SOP) for replication across the chain, which included procedures for inventory management, transaction processing, customer relations, store administration, products sales and merchandising. SOP had a harmonizing effect on the company, helping ensure consistency and enforcing discipline across the network of stores. Best Buy was now a process-driven organization with systems and procedures firmly in place. By early 2000, however, Best Buy was evolving from being an organization thriving on standardization to one offering, within a standard format, different value propositions appealing to different groups of customers. Thus, the company began in 2001 to test and implement a concept it called centricity.

The concept was based on four elements:

1. Identifying customers generating the most revenue
2. Segmenting these customers
3. Realigning the stores to meet the needs of these customers
4. Empowering the store sales staff, known as Blue Shirts, to steer these customers toward products and services that would encourage them to visit more often and spend more on each visit

The company's market researchers combed through reams of sales and demographic data to determine whether a particular location should be tailored to, say, empty nesters or small business owners. A store located in a geographical area characterized by a higher density of homemakers would, for example, include features such as personal shopping assistants (PSAs) who were chosen from among Blue Shirts to help a shopper with such tasks as selecting the right digital camera for her family. Blue Shirts were schooled in financial metrics, such as return on capital, so that they could ascertain for themselves the effectiveness of merchandising.

Centricity was a big investment in terms of enhancing end user experience. The company examined, in detail, everything from store fixtures and layout to the product–employee mix and staff training. Recasting a store toward affluent tech-enthusiasts would cost approximately US$600,000 alone for lighting and fixtures. The concept of centricity, which was built essentially on customer insights, was also meant to encourage employee innovations in support of a better customer experience, not just at a single moment in time but on a continuous basis. The goal was to drive customer engagement and foster repeat visits.

Store Operations

At headquarters in Minneapolis, Best Buy store operations were organized into three divisions. Each division was divided into regions under the supervision of a senior vice president overseeing store performance through regional managers who were with responsibility for a number of districts within the region. The district managers monitored store operations closely. Each district also had a loss prevention manager, and product security personnel employed at each store controlled inventory shrinkage. Best Buy controlled advertising, pricing and inventory policies from corporate headquarters.

Competitors

The CE retail market in the United States was competitive at four levels. The major competitors were mass merchandisers (e.g. Wal-Mart and Costco). These competitors were regularly increasing their portfolio of CE products, particularly of those products less complex to sell, install and operate. Contemporary channels of distribution (such as Internet shopping, facilitated by e-commerce platforms set up by some manufacturers themselves) were the second source of competition. Also competing in the CE market and gaining market share were factory-direct shopping services (e.g. Dell Computers). Finally, home improvement retailers (e.g. Home Depot and Lowe's) were also entering into the consumer electronic product market. Lines were blurring as retailers of all kinds were widening their product assortments in pursuit of revenues and margins.

DUAL BRANDING IN CANADA

Best Buy paid Cdn$560.71 million (US$363.95 million) to acquire Future Shop, based on the offering price of Cdn$17 per share, a 47.8 per cent premium over the market price of Cdn$11.50 per share. However, a little over a year after deciding to expand internationally, Best Buy experimented with a concept that was novel in the CE market worldwide. Said Noble:

> There were four reasons why Best Buy veered towards a dual-branding strategy in Canada. First, the Canadian CE market was fragmented with the leader, Future Shop, having only about 15 per cent share. We felt there was room for a second brand. Given that most retail sectors in the US had at least two major players — for example, Home Depot/Lowe's and Staples/Office Depot — we felt that a second major retailer in CE in Canada would be in order. Second, Best Buy had already signed, before perceiving Future Shop as a potential target for acquisition, about eight real estate leases as part of its original greenfield approach. Some of these leased spaces (as in the Heartland location at Mississauga, a suburb of Toronto) were situated right next to Future Shop stores for

planned head-to-head competition. We were committed to those locations. Third, there were operational factors. Conversion of Future Shop stores into Best Buy stores would take a while, particularly in terms of store redesigns and staff transition. Not all the elements of Best Buy's SOP could simply be set up "as is" in Canada. There would be a period of time when the two brands had to be managed independently. As it turned out, it gave us a window through which to look at issues differently. But, the most important reason was the recognition that Future Shop was a well established brand, with over 95 per cent unaided brand awareness among Canadians. Replacing such a hugely successful brand with Best Buy, which was unknown in Canada, seemed counter-intuitive.

Best Buy also had other reasons for pursuing a dual-brand strategy. If the senior staff at Future Shop were focused on setting up the Best Buy operation, their activities risked affecting negatively on the existing sales of Future Shop stores. Putting together a separate team at Best Buy, fully dedicated to opening the greenfield stores of Best Buy, as originally planned, would speed up the process of the company's market entry.

But the dual-brand strategy also had some downsides. Said Noble:

> We had four concerns about the dual-branding strategy. Cannibalization was, of course, a major issue. It was likely that each Best Buy store would eat into the earnings of a Future Shop store and vice versa, particularly when the two were in close proximity. Since the company would have to manage two different brands, the marketing dollars in Canada would be split in half, minimizing the impact of ad-spend. Also imminent was the possibility of a blurring of brand identity in the eyes of the consumer. Finally, there would be duplication of roles at the corporate headquarters at Minneapolis, with the two brands requiring separate staff inputs.

The two brands were each headed by a vice president based in Vancouver, the location of Best Buy Canada Ltd. (BBYC), the newly formed subsidiary that maintained the two brands. BBYC took several steps to reinforce the operations of both brands at ground level: opening an automated 450,000-square-foot distribution center in Ontario and, eventually, another 500,000-square-foot distribution center in British Columbia, to support store growth for both brands; outsourcing a call center to provide 24-hour service, seven days a week; and retaining a premier insurance company to underwrite product warranties. Stores of both brands were open 60 to 75 hours per week, seven days a week. All stores used the parent company's SOP.

An average Future Shop store was staffed by a general manager, an operations manager, one to four department managers and 48 to 95 sales associates, as well as part-time sales associates. An average Canada Best Buy store was staffed by a general manager; assistant managers for operations, merchandising, inventory and sales; and 80 to 110 sales associates, including full-time and part-time sales associates.

Although Best Buy and Future Shop effectively competed for market share, the positioning for each company was different. Best Buy, with its yellow-price-tag logo continued to offer the "grab and go" option by providing an open floor plan that allowed customers to shop on their own or with the help of a no-pressure (i.e. non-commissioned) Blue Shirt product specialist if desired. Future Shop focused on offering the trusted, personalized customer service for which it was already well known in Canadian cities.

By the end of the first year of operations, there were indications that the dual-branding strategy was working in Canada. For example, the Future Shop store at Mississauga had sales revenues of $40 million in 2001/02. In 2002/03, post-acquisition, revenues were $38 million. Cannibalization was minimal because the Best Buy store, located across the street, had delivered an additional $30 million in sales for the same period. Overall, Best Buy had achieved a combined market share in Canada of 34 per cent. In some places, the proximity of the two banners had created a shopping destination. The company's research also pointed out that the customer bases of Best Buy and Future Shop were different. Canadian customers viewed the two brands as distinct, not interchangeable. One indication was that only 18 per cent of customers applying for a Best Buy credit card in fiscal 2004 already held a Future Shop credit card (see Exhibit 3).

The board of Best Buy was now willing to support the dual-brand strategy in Canada as long as Best Buy entered new markets in Canada and delivered on sales targets, while Future Shop continued to deliver on its own sales targets. In negotiating with Five Star in China, the board was willing to support a similar strategy on similar expectations (see Exhibit 4).

ENTERING CHINA

A country of 1.3 billion consumers, China had been attracting the attention of overseas investors since it began liberalizing the economy in 1985. Over the next two decades, its manufacturing side boomed, with the growth in gross domestic product (GDP) averaging 10 per cent per annum. The consumption side, however, was growing at a pace slower than output and not catching up. Consumption as a percentage of GDP had in fact dropped from 47 per cent in 1995 to 37 per cent in 2005.[6] A process of adjustment was under way, and because the Chinese economy was moving from the historical investment-led growth model to a consumption-led growth model, many multinational marketers were beginning to see an opportunity. McKinsey Global Institute had predicted that China would become the third-largest consumer market in the world by 2025 (see Exhibit 5).

Best Buy's original interest in China had been flagged by China's manufacturing base. Since the 1990s, the China had become a major hub in the Asian region for the manufacture of CE components. In a little more than a decade, China was playing host to a number of manufacturers from the United States and Europe. Attracted by the country's low labor costs, these manufacturers had started relocating their domestic manufacturing operations to China. A fast-growing home market was also spurring China's CE manufacturing industry. According to Instat, an American high-tech market research firm with an office in China, the manufacturing end of the CE industry in China, which was estimated at $71.5 billion in 2006, was expected to more than double by 2010.[7]

In September 2003, Best Buy opened a 25-person sourcing office in Shanghai, China. This move complemented the company's plans to expand its existing 450 stores in the United States and 127 stores in Canada to at least 1,200 stores in North America over the long haul. The Shanghai office was seen as a means of both lowering the cost of goods sold and driving gross profit rates on individual products. This office was also meant to fill the gaps in the company's product assortment with private labels from the Asian region. Said Noble:

> China was chosen as the second international expansion market primarily due to the overall market opportunity, consumer fundamentals and macro-economic factors. We did look at other markets such as Europe, especially France and Germany, but, they were mature, competitive and offered less quality retail real estate at a high cost.[8]

---

[6] Diana Farrell et al., *From "Made in China" to "Sold in China": The Rise of the Chinese Urban Consumer*,' McKinsey Global Institute, November 2006.

[7] Instat, "China's Consumer Electronics Manufacturing Will More Than Double by 2010," press release, October 11, 2006, http://www.instat.com/press.asp?ID=1768&sku=IN0602785CSM, accessed November 28, 2008.

[8] In May 2008, Best Buy and Carphone Warehouse announced the creation a new joint venture company, in which Best Buy acquired 50% of The Carphone Warehouse's European and U.S. retail interests for a cash consideration of £1.1 billion, or US$2.1 billion.

The Chinese CE retail market was fragmented. The top five players together held less than 20 per cent of the market share. However, the Chinese market was expected to account for 25 per cent of the global CE market by 2010. Taking a slice of the new growth opportunity ranked high on the agendas of multinational corporations. Best Buy was the first, and so far the only, multinational to have entered the retail end of Chinese CE market.

China's CE retail market was, however, a complex terrain to navigate for a new entrant. Price wars were rampant. In categories such as TVs and white goods, excess capacity had squeezed profit margins to less than three per cent, the lowest in the world. Although consolidation among electronics retailers had been ongoing, a new wave of mergers and acquisitions (M&As) was evident within a space of a few months in early 2006. Gome Electrical Appliances Holdings Ltd. (Gome), China's leading electronics specialty chain, had already mounted a bid on China Paradise Electronics Retail Ltd. (China Paradise), which itself had struck — and then put on hold — an alliance with the privately owned Dazhong Electrical Appliance Co. Ltd., the fifth-largest CE retailer in China The formalities pertaining to acquisition of China Paradise by Gome were to reach closure in late July 2006. Best Buy had already acquired Jiangsu Five Star in April 2006.

The Chinese CE market had some unique characteristics. For example, approximately two-thirds of the sales staff in a retail store were on the payroll of suppliers. Also, the rate of growth of "other income" was often higher than the rate of growth in sales. The gross margin of Chinese retailers was understated without taking into account "other income," which included rebates and listing fees, often the equivalent of a retailer's gross profit. Instead of a mark-up on the cost of goods sold, the retailers received rebates.[9]

Buyer Behavior

In 2004, approximately 36 million urban Chinese households had a disposable income of at least RMB25,000 (approximately US$3,000) a year, which was considered, by local standards, a reasonable threshold for entering the consumer class. By 2009, the number was expected to almost triple, to 105 million urban households. A massive influx of new consumers was now reaching the retail cash registers. Every year, approximately 20 million Chinese (the population of Australia) turned 18 years of age. Prosperity was lifting the incomes of tens of millions more.[10]

Chinese consumers were not prone to opening their wallets freely. The savings rate in China in 2006 was 28 per cent of monthly household income, compared with three per cent in the United Kingdom and two per cent in Canada. Chinese consumers were also not accustomed to the concept of credit. The credit card penetration rate in urban households was less than four per cent, compared with 75 per cent in the United States, 78 per cent in Japan and 91 per cent in Germany. Less than six per cent of credit card holders in China carried forward their ongoing balances.[11]

Observers had found that Chinese consumers responded better to messages focusing on functional features than those focusing on brand imagery. At one level, Chinese consumers were attracted to brand names but, on another level, they were wary of premium prices. Brand preferences of customers did not always translate into revenues in the form of increased market share for companies. Salespersons held sway over the buying decisions of consumers who were also influenced by point-of-sale promotions to make last-minute switches. Because Chinese consumers had a sense of national pride, a multinational corporation, by seeming foreign, could lose potential customer segments.[12]

---

[9] Jean Zhou, Deutsche Bank equity research report on Suning Appliances, dated April 7, 2006.
[10] Andrew Grant, "The New Chinese Consumer," The McKinsey Quarterly, Special Edition, June 2006 p 1.
[11] Claudia Suessmeth-Dykerhoff et al., "Marketing to China's New Traditionalists," Far Eastern Economic Review, April 2008. p 29.
[12] Kevin P. Lane et al., "Building Brands in China," The McKinsey Quarterly, Special Edition, June 2006. p 39.

Growth Centers

In markets such as the United States and Canada, consumers exhibited few differences between regions, which required companies to make choices only between products and segments. In China, the trade-offs had an additional dimension, requiring product-segment-region choices. Marketers had to factor in regional differences because as one moved across tiers of cities in China, a steep drop-off was experienced in infrastructure, channels and disposable income. When a mass merchandiser entered China, it evaluated the country's cities, giving each locale a tier designation on the basis of size, sophistication, purchasing habits, attitudes and disposable income of its population and its own product offerings.[13] A typical classification is shown in Exhibit 6.

A massive increase in retail space was evidence of increasing competition in China's tier-one cities in particular. Major players were eyeing growth opportunities in tier-two and tier-three cities. The attendant risk was the longer breakeven point because, given the much lower income levels in those cities, sales would be slower. However, the costs of retail space would be lower, and given less competition, margins were likely to be higher.

China also had other limitations. Land acquisition in cities was often difficult; procedural delays meant that a new entrant would take at least six months to open a store; relationships between vendors and retailers were so close and guarded by local customs and preferences, that an outsider did not have an easy time getting a foot in the door. Manufacturers of CE were not likely to cut a new entrant such as Best Buy much slack on pricing, particularly because personal relationships (referred to as "guanxi" in local terminology) influenced the conduct of business among Chinese who were more comfortable dealing with people they knew. China was also experiencing a crunch of quality human resources because retailing, as an industry, had not yet developed in the country.

MAJOR COMPETITORS

Before being acquired by Best Buy, Five Star had two major competitors, Gome Electrical Appliances Holdings Ltd. (Gome) and Suning, both publicly held (see Exhibit 7). Together, the two companies had saturated many of the country's largest cities over the past few years. Although the total market shares in 2005 of the top five in 2005 (comprising Gome, Suning, Five Star and two others) accounted for less than 20 per cent of market share, Gome and Suning held a combined market share of 70 per cent in some appliance product categories, such as air conditioners.

Gome Group

The Gome Group had two companies: Gome Electrical Appliances Holdings Ltd. and Beijing Gome (an unlisted company). In 1993, Gome opened its first store in Beijing, and soon expanded into other major cities in China, gaining widespread consumer acceptance. By mid-2005, the group had 437 stores (of which 263 belonged to the listed company) in 132 cities in China, with the most extensive distribution network of all the home appliance retailers in China. It was leading in all regional markets (Northeast China, North China, Northwest China, South West China and South China) with the exception of East China, the home market of Suning, where Gome was ranked number three.[14] Gome was the largest CE retailer in China with six per cent market share, prior to its acquisition of China Paradise. The company

---

[13] Normandy Madden, "Tier Tale: How Marketers Classify Cities in China," <u>Advertising Age</u>, March 19, 2007 p 21.
[14] Sandy Chen, Citigroup equity research report on Gome, dated October 12, 2005.

was mounting a bid on China Paradise, likely to come through in a few weeks, for a record sum of $677 million.[15]

At the beginning of 2005, Gome had announced its four-year growth initiative aimed at enlarging its geographical coverage and raising its national market share to 10 to 15 per cent by the end of 2008. Although Gome had set itself apart, to start with, on a super-store format offering the lowest prices, the differentiation had been subsequently commoditized in by its competitors. Gome had then cracked the traditional business model (of selling through intermediaries to various retail formats) by dealing directly with mega brands. In introducing category killers, the company had set a new trend in CE retailing in China. The company had also begun to focus on pre-sales service, as opposed to the industry practice of after-sales service, by advising customers on which brands to choose. Because this service was not easy to implement at the store level, where brands had their own commission-based sales staff, Gome was examining a new store format it called Eagle (Gome had been known earlier as China Eagle). Gome opened its first Eagle store in December 2005, in Shenyang. This mega-store, which occupied 15,000 square meters differed in two ways: all sales staff at Eagle were on the payroll of Gome; and the display format was based on categories not brands. The company was planning to open six to nine Eagle stores in the next three years, depending upon how the performance of the first two.

The group was planning to expand rapidly into tier-two cities in particular, not only because of improvements in economies of scale and customer acquisition but also because, as a first mover, it could secure preferential tax treatments from local governments welcoming jobs creation opportunities. It was unlikely that the second or third movers would be entitled to the benefits offered to the first mover.[16]

Suning

Suning had grown from a regional air-conditioning retailer to a leading CE retail chain in China in less than a decade. It was in the process of converting its stores into a customer-oriented format it called 3C (computers, communications and consumer electronics). The company was on an expansion spree, increasing its stores five fold in the last three years to 224, with more than half of them opening in 2005 alone, covering 61 cities. It was now planning to double the number of stores in two years. By the end of 2006, only 25 per cent of Suning's retail space would have been opened for two years or more. In common with Gome, which also had a high proportion of new retail space, rapid store expansion and entry into less affluent tier-two cities had led to lower productivity of retail space at Suning.[17]

Suning operated three types of stores that shared the same format: flagship, central and community. The stores differed in size and product assortment. Flagship stores were found in large cities or regional headquarters. These stores were the largest in size and sold a wide variety of products. The central stores were most common. All the stores were CE retail stores targeting the mass market.

Suning sought differentiation in two ways. It was aligning its product assortment to address the needs of what it called "3C"customer groups (computers, communications and consumer electronics). It was also using service as its key competitive advantage. The company had set up 15 regional distribution centers, 30 customer service centers and 500 service stations of its own to reinforce the message that service was its main product.

---

[15] Russell Flannery, "Best Buy's Art of War," Forbes.com. http://www.forbes.com/services/forbes/2007/1015/066.html, accessed November 27, 2008.
[16] Sandy Chen, Citigroup equity research report on Gome, dated October 12, 2005.
[17] Jean Zhou, "Suning Appliance," Deutsche Bank Equity Research Report dated April 7, 2006.

FIVE STAR

Five Star was China's third-largest electronics and appliances chain. It had 135 stores located mostly in the fast-growing, second-tier cities, in eight of China's 34 provinces. Founded in 1998 and headquartered in Nanjing in Jiangsu province, it had revenues of US$700 million in 2005, a 50 per cent increase over 2004. The company's founder Wang Jianguo wanted to expand internationally but was constrained by delays in official permissions for listing his company abroad. "Our scale was becoming a bottleneck to development," he said.[18] When Best Buy sounded the idea of making an investment in the company, he decided to cash out and offload 75 per cent stake in the company to Best Buy for $180 million. Five Star employed more than 12,000 of its own employees (see Exhibit 8).

ISSUES IN JUNE 2006

In examining the prospects of dual-branding strategy in China, Noble had to make a call on whether it would serve as well in China as it did in Canada. He had to define the road map for implementing the strategy in China. In a broader context, he also had to explore the possibility of developing dual branding into Best Buy's main competence over time. Best Buy was now at a stage at which the learning it had gained from international expansion, initiated in 2002, could be used to accelerate the company's transformation in the U.S. domestic market, which it considered its core market. In his new role at Best Buy International, Noble was regularly tracking and evaluating global opportunities, looking for growing economies with buoyant consumer demand. Turkey and Mexico were potential targets for international expansion.

Customer centricity was a home-grown competence that Best Buy had deployed in Canada, and that seemed to have a universal appeal, applicable to any new market. SOP, which the company owned, was another. Geek Squad, a company innovation, seemed to be equally pervasive. Noble wondered whether a dual-branding strategy, which had been executed in Canada, could be as readily implemented in the international markets of the future. Was there a template of dual-branding that could be deployed, with a minor tweaking where necessary, to any new market, he wondered. What would that template be?

---

[18] Russell Flannery, "Best Buy's Art of War," Forbes.com, http://www.forbes.com/services/forbes/2007/1015/066.html, accessed November 28, 2008.

Exhibit 1

BEST BUY AND FUTURE SHOP IN 2002

	Best Buy	**Future Shop**
Typical store size	35,000 square feet	26,000 square feet
Store associates	Blue Shirts	Product Experts
Staff mandate	Technology is fun. We make it easy for the customer	Providing Trusted Personalized Service
Customers	Tech enthusiasts who enjoy the interactive shopping experience and grab-and-go convenience	Tech savvy; a notch higher than the Best Buy customer; at the cutting edge of developments in technology
Aisles	Wide aisles to provide for grab-and-go shopping	Highlights key technologies first
Service	Upon request	Attentive
Sales	Customer led No high-pressure salesmanship	Sales-person led Commission-based sales
Target group	Higher success rate with female customers	Male-oriented
Customer profile	15 to 39 years	25 to 44 years
Brand identity	"Turn on the fun"	"The place to get it first"
In-store experience	Relaxed	Guided
Product mix	Although by category the two store brands were very similar, each was able to offer a unique selection of products and brands. Product brands and depth of selection differed within product categories. On average, 45 per cent overlap of the product assortment (excluding entertainment software) between the two store brands.	
Areas of distinction	Higher propensity towards self-service; non-commissioned sales staff; greater assortment of ready-made electronics packages; wider aisles and more interactive displays; higher ratio of female customers, seeking to integrate products into their lifestyles; customers with higher incomes and higher levels of education	Commissioned sales staff guiding the customer by providing customized, trusted and personalized approach; tech savvy, early adopters looking for the best deal; customer base more diverse

Source: Company files

Exhibit 2

BEST BUY INC – INCOME STATEMENT

Year ending March (in US$million)	2006	2005	2004	2003	2002	2001	2000	1999
Revenue								
Domestic	27,380	24,616	22,225	20,946	17,711	15,326	12,494	10,064
International	3,468	2,817	2,323	–	–	–	–	–
Total	**30,848**	**27,433**	**24,548**	20,946	**17,711**	15,326	**12,494**	**10,064**
Less: Cost of goods sold	23,122	20,938	18,677	15,710	13,941	12,267	10,100	8,250
Gross profit	7,726	6,495	5,871	5,236	3,770	3,059	2,394	1,814
Less: S&G expenses	6,082	5,053	4,567	4,226	2,862	2,455	1,854	1,463
Operating income	1,644	1,442	1,304	1,010	908	604	539	351
Net interest income	77	1	(8)	4	18	37	23	1
Earnings before tax	1,721	1,443	1,296	1,014	926	641	562	352
Income tax	581	509	496	392	356	245	215	136
Other (Loss)/Gain	–	50	(95)	(523)	–	–	–	–
Net earnings	1,140	984	705	99	570	396	347	216
Category wise revenue								
Domestic								
- Home Office	8,762	8,380	7,556	–	–			
-Video & Audio	11,773	9,609	8,445	–	–			
- Ent. Software	5,202	5,169	4,889	–	–			
- Appliances	1,643	1,476	1,335	–	–			
International								
- Home Office	1,526	1,127	929	–	–			
- Video & Audio	1,318	1,155	930	–	–			
- Ent. Software	487	422	348	–	–			
- Appliances	139	113	116	–	–			
Number of employees (in 000s)	128							
Cash and equivalents (in US$million)	681	354	245					

Source: Best Buy annual report.

Exhibit 3

BEST BUY AND FUTURE SHOP — PERFORMANCE METRICS 2000 AND 2006

Metric		2000		2006	
		Best Buy (in US)	Future Shop	Best Buy (in Canada)	Future Shop
Sales growth		21.4%	17.0%	34.3%	14.2%
Gross margin		20.2%	22.7%	24.2%	24.8%
SG&A expense ratio		16.2%	20.1%	17.8%	16.7%
Operating margin		4.0%	2.6%	6.4%	8.1%
Sales per square foot		$870	$746	$1,010	$1,069
Inventory turn		7.5	7.4	6.4	6.4
Operating ROA		18.7%	12.77%	n/a	n/a

Note: SG&A = selling, general and administrative; ROA = return on assets; n/a = not applicable
Source: Deutsche Banc Alex. Brown estimates for 2000 data, Company records for 2006 data.

Exhibit 4

BEST BUY —NUMBER OF INTERNATIONAL STORES 2006

Province/State	Canada		China	
	Best Buy stores	Future Shop stores	Best Buy stores	Five Star stores
Alberta	7	15		
British Columbia	7	21		
Manitoba	2	5		
New Brunswick	–	3		
Newfoundland	–	1		
Nova Scotia	1	3		
Ontario	25	55		
Prince Edward	–	1		
Quebec	8	24		
Saskatchewan	1	3		
Anhui			–	12
Henan			–	9
Jiangsu			–	99
Shandong			–	9
Shanghai			1	–
Sichuan			–	6
Yunnan			–	4
Zhejiang			–	21
Total	51	131	1	160

Source: Best Buy 2008 annual report.

Exhibit 5

CHINA'S ECONOMY, 2003–2005

	Unit	2005	2004	2003
Gross National Income	100 million Yuan	183,956.1	159,586.7	135,174.0
Gross Domestic Product	100 million Yuan	183,084.8	159,878.3	135,822.8
Per capita Gross Domestic Product	Yuan per person	14,040.0	12,336.0	10,542.0
Population	Million	1,307.56	1,299.88	1,292.27
- Male		673.75	669.76	665.56
- Female		633.81	630.12	626.71
- Urban		562.12	542.83	523.76
- Rural		745.54	757.05	768.51
Economically active persons	Million	778.77	768.23	767.05
Number of employed persons	Million	758.25	752.00	744.32
Annual Per Capita Income	Yuan			
- Urban households		10,493	9,422	5,160
- Rural households		3,255	2,936	2,090
Annual Per Capita Consumption	Yuan			
Expenditure-Urban households		7,943	7,182	4,186
- Rural households		2,955	2,185	1,617

Source: National Bureau of Statistics of China, Chinese Statistical Yearbook, 2006, http://www.stats.gov.cn/tjsj/ndsj/2006/indexeh.htm, accessed December 10, 2008.

Exhibit 6

CHINA'S TIERED CITIES

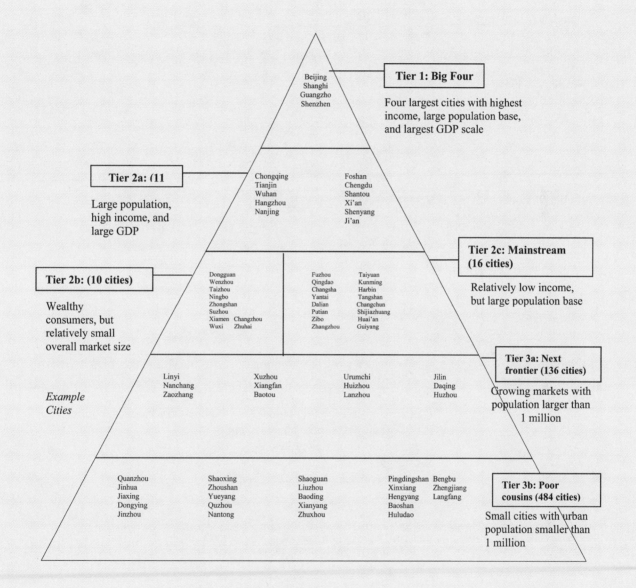

Source Diana Farrell et al., <u>From "Made in China" to "Sold in China": The Rise of the Chinese Urban Consumer</u>, McKinsey Global Institute, November 2006.

Exhibit 7

MAJOR COMPETITORS IN CHINA

	Gome		Suning	
Financials (in RMB million)	2004	2005	2004	2005
Revenue	12,647	17,959	9,107	15,936
Net profit	486	496		
Revenue by geography (%)				
- Northeast China		5		3
- North China		33		15
- East China		9		59
- West China		23		5
- South China		26		15
- Central China		4		3
Sales per square meter	25,940		32,141	23,929
Number of stores	442		94	224
Revenue by category (%)				
- Air conditioners		16		
- Audiovisual		28		
- Refrigerators/Washing machines		18		
		16		
- Telecom		10		
- Small electrical appliances		12		
- Digital/IT products		–		
- Service				
Mission	"Competitive pricing from high volume"		"Service is the sole product of Suning"	
Store formats, positioning	a. Traditional (3,500 square meters): price-conscious mass market b. Digital (260 square meters): high-end customer in downtown c. Eagle (15,000 square meters): service-conscious, mid to high-end customers		Flagship: in large cities Central: the most common	

Sources: Gome Electrical Appliances Holdings Limited website, http://www.gome.com.hk/eng, accessed December 5, 2008; Suning website, www.cnsuning.com/include/english, accessed December 5, 2008; Jean Zhou, Deutsche Bank equity research Report, dated April 7, 2006; Sandy Chen, Citigroup equity research report on Gome, dated October 12, 2005

Exhibit 8

BEST BUY AND FIVE STAR – JULY 2006

Metric		Best Buy[1]	Five Star
Store size		86,000 square feet	35,000 square feet
Customers		Middle-to upper-income young singles and couples	Middle-income families Somewhat price sensitive
Service		Mixed-brand packaged solutions displayed by lifestyle requirements	Personal shopping assistants guiding customers through vendor booths; Attentive
Sales		Led by non-commissioned staff on Best Buy's payroll	Led by staff on the payroll of manufacturer
Customer profile		18–42 years old	20–50 years old
Brand identity		Premium full service	Good price with good services
In-store experience		Grab and go	Guided
Product mix (%)			White goods: 16% Air conditioning: 23% Home Entertainment: 25% Digital Products: 7% Cell phones: 13% Kitchen utensils: 9% Small appliances: 5%
Store associates		100% employed by Best Buy and non-commissioned	30% employed by Five Star on non-commission; 70% employed by vendors on commission
Sales growth Gross margin SG&A expense ratio Operating margin Sales per square foot Inventory turn Operating ROA			44% 13.5% 11.5% 2.0% $230 7 5%

Note: SG&A = selling, general and administrative; ROA = return on assets
Source: Company files

---

[1] Best Buy was yet to open its store in China as of June 2006.

Exhibit 8

BEST BUY AND FIVE STAR – JULY 2006

Metric		Best Buy[1]	Five Star
Store size		86,000 square feet	35,000 square feet
Customers		Middle-to upper-income young singles and couples	Middle-income families Somewhat price sensitive
Service		Mixed-brand packaged solutions displayed by lifestyle requirements	Personal shopping assistants guiding customers through vendor booths; Attentive
Sales		Led by non-commissioned staff on Best Buy's payroll	Led by staff on the payroll of manufacturer
Customer profile		18–42 years old	20–50 years old
Brand identity		Premium full service	Good price with good services
In-store experience		Grab and go	Guided
Product mix (%)			White goods: 16% Air conditioning: 23% Home Entertainment: 25% Digital Products: 7% Cell phones: 13% Kitchen utensils: 9% Small appliances: 5%
Store associates		100% employed by Best Buy and non-commissioned	30% employed by Five Star on non-commission; 70% employed by vendors on commission
Sales growth			44%
Gross margin			13.5%
SG&A expense ratio			11.5%
Operating margin			2.0%
Sales per square foot			$230
Inventory turn			7
Operating ROA			5%

Note: SG&A = selling, general and administrative; ROA = return on assets
Source: Company files

---

[1] Best Buy was yet to open its store in China as of June 2006.

Appendix A

Marketing Plan Worksheets

These worksheets will assist you in writing a formal marketing plan. Worksheets are a useful planning tool because they help to ensure that important information is not omitted from the marketing plan. Answering the questions on these worksheets will enable you to:

1. Organize and structure the data and information you collect during the situation analysis.

2. Use this information to better understand a firm's strengths and weaknesses, and to recognize the opportunities and threats that exist in the marketing environment.

3. Develop goals and objectives that capitalize on strengths.

4. Develop a marketing strategy that creates competitive advantages.

5. Outline a plan for implementing the marketing strategy.

These worksheets are available in electronic format on our text's website at www.cengage.com/marketing/ferrell. By downloading these worksheets, you will be able to change the outline or add additional information that is relevant to your situation. Remember that there is no one best way to organize a marketing plan. We designed our outline to serve as a starting point and to be flexible enough to accommodate the unique characteristics of your situation.

As you complete the worksheets, it might be useful to refer back to the text of the chapters. In completing the situation analysis section, be sure to be as comprehensive as possible. The viability of your SWOT analysis depends on how well you have identified all of the relevant environmental issues. Likewise, as you complete the SWOT analysis, you should be honest about the firm's characteristics. Do not depend on strengths that the firm really does not possess. Honesty is also important for your listing of weaknesses.

  I. **Executive Summary**

    The executive summary is a synopsis of the overall marketing plan. It should provide an overview of the entire plan including goals/objectives, strategy elements, implementation issues, and expected outcomes. The executive summary should be the last part of the marketing plan that you write.

  II. **Situation Analysis**

    A. **The Internal Environment (refer to Exhibit 4.3)**

Review of marketing goals and objectives

Identify the firm's current marketing goals and objectives.

Explain how these goals and objectives are being achieved.

Explain how these goals and objectives are consistent or inconsistent with the firm's mission, recent trends in the external environment, and recent trends in the customer environment.

Review of current marketing strategy and performance

Describe the firm's current marketing strategy with respect to products, pricing, distribution, and promotion. Which elements of the strategy are working well? Which elements are not?

Describe the firm's current performance (sales volume, market share, profitability, awareness, brand preference) compared to other firms in the industry. Is the performance of the industry as a whole improving or declining? Why?

If the firm's performance is declining, what is the most likely cause (e.g., environmental changes, flawed strategy, poor implementation)?

Review of current and anticipated organizational resources

Describe the current state of the firm's organizational resources (e.g., financial, capital, human, experience, relationships with key suppliers or customers). How are the levels of these resources likely to change in the future?

If resource levels are expected to change, how can the firm leverage additional resources to meet customer needs better than competitors?

If additional resources are not available, how can the firm compensate for future resource constraints (lack of resources)?

Review of current and anticipated cultural and structural issues

In terms of marketing strategy development and implementation, describe the positive and negative aspects of the current and anticipated culture of the firm. Examples could include

The firm's overall customer orientation (or lack thereof)

The firm's emphasis on short-term versus long-term planning

Willingness of the firm's culture to embrace change

Internal politics and power struggles

The overall position and importance of the marketing function

Changes in key executive positions

General employee satisfaction and morale

Explain whether the firm's structure is supportive of the current marketing strategy.

B. **The Customer Environment (refer to Exhibit 4.4)**

Who are the firm's current and potential customers?

Describe the important identifying characteristics of the firm's current and potential customers with respect to demographics, geographic location, psychographic profiles, values/lifestyles, and product usage characteristics (heavy vs. light users).

Identify the important players in the purchase process for the firm's products. These might include purchasers (actual act of purchase), users (actual product user), purchase influencers (influence the decision, make recommendations), and the bearer of financial responsibility (who pays the bill?).

What do customers do with the firm's products?

How are the firm's products connected to customer needs? What are the basic benefits provided by the firm's products?

How are the firm's products purchased (quantities and combinations)? Is the product purchased as a part of a solution or alongside complementary products?

How are the firm's products consumed or used? Are there special consumption situations that influence purchase behavior?

Are there issues related to disposition of the firm's products, such as waste (garbage) or recycling, which must be addressed by the firm?

Where do customers purchase the firm's products?

Identify the merchants (intermediaries) where the firm's products are purchased (e.g., store-based retailers, ecommerce, catalog retailers, vending, wholesale outlets, direct from the firm).

Identify any trends in purchase patterns across these outlets (e.g., how has e-commerce changed the way the firm's products are purchased?).

When do customers purchase the firm's products?

How does purchase behavior vary based on different promotional events (communication and price changes) or customer services (hours of operation, delivery)?

How does purchase behavior vary based on uncontrollable influences such as seasonal demand patterns, time-based demand patterns, physical/social surroundings, or competitive activities?

Why (and how) do customers select the firm's products?

Describe the advantages of the firm's products relative to competing products. How well do the firm's products fulfill customers' needs relative to competing products?

Describe how issues such as brand loyalty, value, commoditization, and relational exchange processes affect customers' purchase behaviors.

Describe how credit or financing is used in purchasing the firm's products. Also, do customers seek long-term relationships with the firm, or do they buy in a transactional fashion (based primarily on price)?

Why do potential customers not purchase the firm's products?

Identify the needs, preferences, and requirements of noncustomers that are not being met by the firm's products.

What are the features, benefits, and advantages of competing products that cause noncustomers to choose them over the firm's products?

Explain how the firm's pricing, distribution, and/or promotion are out of sync with noncustomers. Outside of the product, what causes noncustomers to look elsewhere?

Describe the potential for converting noncustomers into customers.

C. **The External Environment (refer to Exhibit 4.5)**

Competition

Identify the firm's major competitors (brand, product, generic, and total budget).

Identify the characteristics of the firm's major competitors with respect to size, growth, profitability, target markets, products, and marketing capabilities (production, distribution, promotion, pricing).

What other major strengths and weaknesses do these competitors possess?

List any potential future competitors not identified above.

Economic Growth and Stability

Identify the general economic conditions of the country, region, state, or local area where the firm's target customers are located. How are these economic conditions related to customers' ability to purchase the firm's products?

Describe the economics of the industry within which the firm operates. These issues might include the cost of raw materials, patents, merger/acquisition trends, sales trends, supply/demand issues, marketing challenges, and industry growth/decline.

Political Trends

Identify any political activities affecting the firm or the industry with respect to changes in elected officials (domestic or foreign), potential regulations favored by elected officials, industry (lobbying) groups or political action committees, and consumer advocacy groups.

What are the current and potential hot button political or policy issues at the national, regional, and local levels that may affect the firm's marketing activities?

Legal and Regulatory Issues

Identify any changes in international, federal, state, or local laws and regulations affecting the firm's or industry's marketing activities with respect to recent court decisions; recent rulings of federal, state, or local government entities; recent decisions by regulatory and self-regulatory agencies; and changes in global trade agreements or trade law.

Technological Advancements

How have recent technological advances affected the firm's customers with respect to needs/wants/preferences, access to information, the timing and location of purchase decisions, the ability to compare competing product offerings, or the ability to conduct transactions more effectively and efficiently?

Have customers embraced or rejected these technological advances? How is this issue related to customers' concerns over privacy and security?

How have recent technological advances affected the firm or the industry with respect to manufacturing, process efficiency, distribution, supply chain effectiveness, promotion, cost reduction, or customer relationship management?

What future technologies offer important opportunities for the firm? Identify any future technologies that may threaten the firm's viability or its marketing efforts.

Sociocultural Trends

With respect to the firm's target customers, identify changes in society's demographics, values, and lifestyles that affect the firm or the industry.

Explain how these changes are affecting (or may affect) the firm's products (features, benefits, branding), pricing (value), distribution and supply chain (convenience, efficiency), promotion (message content, delivery, feedback), and people (human resource issues).

Identify the ethical and social responsibility issues that the firm or industry faces. How do these issues affect the firm's customers? How are these issues expected to change in the future?

III. **SWOT Analysis**

A. **Strengths**

Strength 1: _____

Strength 2: _____

(Repeat as needed to develop a complete list of strengths.)

How do these strengths enable the firm to meet customers' needs?

How do these strengths differentiate the firm from its competitors?

B. **Weaknesses**

Weakness 1: _____

Weakness 2: _____
(Repeat as needed to develop a complete list of weaknesses.)

How do these weaknesses prevent the firm from meeting customers' needs?
How do these weaknesses negatively differentiate the firm from its competitors?

C. **Opportunities (external situations independent of the firm—not strategic options)**

Opportunity 1: _____

Opportunity 2: _____
(Repeat as needed to develop a complete list of opportunities.)

How are these opportunities related to serving customers' needs?

What is the time horizon of each opportunity?

D. **Threats (external situations independent of the firm)**

Threat 1: _____

Threat 2: _____
(Repeat as needed to develop a complete list of threats.)

How are these threats related to serving customers' needs?

What is the time horizon of each threat?

E. **The SWOT Matrix**

Strengths:	Opportunities:
•	•
•	•
•	•
•	•
Weaknesses:	Threats:
•	•
•	•
•	•
•	•

F. **Developing Competitive Advantages**

Describe ways that the firm can match its strengths to its opportunities to create capabilities in serving customers' needs.

Are these capabilities and competitive advantages grounded in the basic principles of operational excellence, product leadership, and/or customer intimacy? If so, how are these capabilities and advantages made apparent to customers?

Can the firm convert its weaknesses into strengths or its threats into opportunities? If not, how can the firm minimize or avoid its weaknesses and threats?

Does the firm possess any major liabilities (unconverted weaknesses that match unconverted threats) or limitations (unconverted weaknesses or threats that match opportunities)? If so, are these liabilities and limitations apparent to customers?

Can the firm do anything about its liabilities or limitations, especially those that impact the firm's ability to serve customers' needs?

G. **Developing a Strategic Focus**

What is the overall strategic focus of the marketing plan? Does the strategic focus follow any particular direction, such as aggressiveness, diversification, turnaround, defensiveness, or niche marketing?

Describe the firm's strategic focus in terms of a strategy canvas. How does the firm's strategic thrust provide sufficient focus and divergence from other firms in the industry?

IV. **Marketing Goals and Objectives**

A. **Marketing Goal A:** _____
   (should be broad, motivational, and somewhat vague)

   Objective A1: _____
   (must contain a specific and measurable outcome and a time frame for completion, and must identify the person/unit responsible for achieving the objective)

   Objective A2: _____
   (must contain a specific and measurable outcome and a time frame for completion, and must identify the person/unit responsible for achieving the objective)

B. **Marketing Goal B:** _____
   (should be broad, motivational, and somewhat vague)

   Objective B1: _____
   (must contain a specific and measurable outcome and a time frame for completion, and must identify the person/unit responsible for achieving the objective)

Objective B2: _____

(must contain a specific and measurable outcome and a time frame for completion, and must identify the person/unit responsible for achieving the objective)

(can be repeated as needed to develop a complete list of goals and objectives; however, having one goal and two or three objectives is advisable to greatly reduce the complexity of the marketing strategy)

V. Marketing Strategy

A. Primary (and Secondary) Target Market

Primary target market

Identifying characteristics (demographics, geography, values, psychographics):

Basic needs, wants, preferences, or requirements:

Buying habits and preferences:

Consumption/disposition characteristics:

Secondary target market (optional)

Identifying characteristics (demographics, geography, values, psychographics):

Basic needs, wants, preferences, or requirements:

Buying habits and preferences:

Consumption/disposition characteristics:

B. Product Strategy

Brand name, packaging, and logo design:

Major features and benefits:

Differentiation/positioning strategy:

Supplemental products (including customer service strategy):

Connection to value (core, supplemental, experiential/symbolic attributes):

C. Pricing Strategy

Overall pricing strategy and pricing objectives:

Price comparison to competition:

Connection to differentiation/positioning strategy:

Connection to value (monetary costs):

Profit margin and breakeven:

Specific pricing tactics (discounts, incentives, financing, etc.):

D. **Distribution/Supply Chain Strategy**

Overall supply chain strategy (including distribution intensity):

Channels and intermediaries to be used:

Connection to differentiation/positioning strategy:

Connection to value (nonmonetary costs):

Strategies to ensure channel support (slotting fees, guarantees, etc.):

Tactics designed to increase time, place, and possession utility:

E. **Integrated Marketing Communication (Promotion) Strategy**

Overall IMC strategy, IMC objectives, and budget:

Consumer promotion elements

Advertising strategy:

Public relations/publicity strategy:

Personal selling strategy:

Consumer sales promotion (pull) strategy:

Trade (channel) promotion elements

Advertising strategy:

Public relations/publicity strategy:

Personal selling strategy:

Trade sales promotion (push) strategy:

VI. **Marketing Implementation**

A. **Structural Issues**

Describe the overall approach to implementing the marketing strategy.

Describe any changes to the firm's structure needed to implement the marketing strategy (e.g., add/delete positions, change lines of authority, change reporting relationships).

Describe any necessary internal marketing activities in the following areas: employee training, employee buy-in and motivation to implement the marketing strategy, overcoming resistance to change, internal communication and promotion of the marketing strategy, and coordination with other functional areas.

B. **Tactical Marketing Activities**

Be *very* specific—this lays out the details of the marketing strategy and how it will be executed.

Specific Tactical Activities	Person/Department Responsible	Required Budget	Completion Date
Product Activities 1. 2. 3.			
Pricing Activities 1. 2. 3.			
Distribution/Supply Chain Activities 1. 2. 3.			
IMC (Promotion) Activities 1. 2. 3.			

VII. **Evaluation and Control**

A. **Formal Controls**

Describe the types of **input controls** that must be in place *before* the marketing plan can be implemented. Examples include financial resources, capital expenditures, additional research and development, and additional human resources.

Describe the types of **process controls** that will be needed *during* the execution of the marketing plan. Examples include management training, management commitment to the plan and to employees, revised employee evaluation/compensation systems, enhanced employee authority, and internal communication activities.

Describe the types of **output controls** that will be used to measure marketing performance and compare it to stated marketing objectives *during and after* the execution of the marketing plan.

Overall performance standards (these will vary based on the goals and objectives of the marketing plan). Examples include dollar sales, sales volume, market share, share of customers, profitability, customer satisfaction, customer retention, or other customer-related metrics.

Product performance standards (these are optional and will vary based on the product strategy). Examples include product specifications, core product quality, supplemental product quality, experiential quality, new product innovation, branding, and positioning.

Price performance standards (these are optional and will vary based on the pricing strategy). Examples include revenue targets, supply/demand balance, price elasticity, yield management, or metrics based on specific price adjustments.

Distribution performance standards (these are optional and will vary based on the distribution strategy). Examples include distribution effectiveness/efficiency, supply chain integration, value (time, place, and possession utility), relationship maintenance (collaboration, conflict), outsourcing, and direct distribution performance.

IMC (promotion) performance standards (these are optional and will vary based on the IMC strategy). Examples include communication objectives; brand awareness, recognition, or recall; campaign reach, frequency, and impressions; purchase intentions; and public relations, sales, and sales promotion effectiveness.

B. **Informal Controls**

Describe issues related to **employee self-control** that can influence the implementation of the marketing strategy. Examples include employee satisfaction, employee commitment (to the firm and the marketing plan), and employee confidence in their skills. If any of these controls are lacking, how can they be enhanced to support the implementation of the marketing plan?

Describe issues related to **employee social control** that can influence the implementation of the marketing strategy. Examples include shared organizational values, work group relationships, and social or behavioral norms. If any of these controls are lacking, how can they be enhanced to support the implementation of the marketing plan?

Describe issues related to **cultural control** that can influence the implementation of the marketing strategy. Examples include organizational culture and organizational rituals. If any of these controls are lacking, how can they be enhanced to support the implementation of the marketing plan?

C. Implementation Schedule and Timeline

Activities Week	Month											
	1	2	3	4	1	2	3	4	1	2	3	4
Product Activities												
Pricing Activities												
Distribution Activities												
IMC Activities												

D. Marketing Audits

Explain how marketing activities will be monitored. What are the specific profit- and time-based measures that will be used to monitor marketing activities?

Describe the marketing audit to be performed, including the person(s) responsible for conducting the audit.

If it is determined that the marketing strategy does not meet expectations, what corrective actions might be taken to improve performance (overall or within any element of the marketing program)?

If the marketing plan, as currently designed, shows little likelihood of meeting the marketing objectives, which elements of the plan should be reconsidered and revised?

Appendix B

Example Marketing Plan

This marketing plan was written using the worksheets in Appendix A. As a result, this plan is consistent with the outline of the textbook. Florida State University MBA students wrote this plan as a part of their course requirements. The text's authors edited the plan prior to its inclusion here. Furthermore, this plan is meant to be an example and nothing more. We do not suggest that this plan is ideal, feasible, or capable of generating desired goals and objectives. This plan is intended for classroom discussion and to demonstrate how a finished marketing plan might look and read. You should consult with your instructor regarding the format, layout, and other specific requirements that are needed in your particular situation.

Background on the Assignment

Students were assigned the task of developing a marketing plan for the launch of a new over-the-counter (OTC) pain medication. The fictitious client is VirPharm, Inc., a mid-sized Florida-based pharmaceutical company that specializes in quality-of-life prescription and OTC medications for the consumer market. VirPharm has been quite successful with a range of products in recent years. However, the big push at VirPharm has been to transition its prescription medications to the OTC market as patents expire and generic competition enters the market.

The task is to continue VirPharm's past successes by developing a plan to move BOPREX from the prescription market to the OTC market. As a prescription medication, butoprofen (the active ingredient in BOPREX) has been prescribed by doctors to treat rheumatoid arthritis, osteoarthritis, and migraine headache. However, as a nonsteroidal anti-inflammatory drug (NSAID), butoprofen is also suitable to treat general pain and fever. The use of BOPREX by doctors has been declining steadily over the years as more powerful treatments for arthritis and migraine have come into favor. VirPharm recently received FDA approval to market BOPREX as an OTC treatment for rheumatoid arthritis, osteoarthritis, and migraine headache, as well as a general-purpose analgesic (pain reliever) and antipyretic (fever reducer).

In planning for the launch of BOPREX to the OTC market, students were given three positioning options:

1. Launch as a treatment for rheumatoid arthritis and osteoarthritis. Here, the key issues are

   - Strong competition from more effective prescription medications and well-known OTC drugs claiming similar benefits.

- Age- and lifestyle-related target market issues.
- Potential for higher profit margin, but with a smaller target market (lower volume).

2. Launch as a treatment for migraine headache. Here, the key issues are

- Strong competition from more effective prescription medications and well-known OTC drugs claiming similar benefits.
- Consumer education regarding migraines versus headaches, as well as the need for immediate pain relief availability.
- Potential for higher profit margin, but with a smaller target market (lower volume).

3. Launch as a general-purpose pain reliever and fever reducer. Here, the key issues are

- Intense competition from very strong OTC drugs such as aspirin, acetaminophen, ibuprofen, and naproxen sodium.
- Overcoming fairly strong consumer loyalty to branded pain medications.
- Potential for very high volume due to wide target market applicability, but with a lower profit margin.

Students were assigned the task of choosing one of these options after conducting extensive research on the industry, the market, and the competition. This comprised the first half of the marketing plan (situation analysis, SWOT analysis, goals and objectives). The next task was to develop a marketing program to launch BOPREX in a manner consistent with the chosen positioning option. Students were required to make decisions regarding the entire marketing program.

Marketing Plan for the Over-the-Counter Launch of BOPREX[1]

Executive Summary

VirPharm, Inc., is a mid-size pharmaceutical company that manufactures several quality-of-life, over-the-counter (OTC), and prescription drugs. Their primary objective is to grow their market share for several of their products. They have realized success through Hapizine, an antidepressant; however, the patent for this drug will soon expire, exposing its market share to generic competition. VirPharm, Inc., recently received approval to sell BOPREX in the OTC market to treat general pain and migraines as well as to act as an anti-inflammatory.

---

[1]Florida State University MBA students developed this marketing plan under the supervision of Dr. Michael Hartline as a part of their course requirements. This marketing plan is intended for classroom discussion rather than to illustrate effective or ineffective strategic planning.

Currently, BOPREX ranks sixth in its market for sales, and this strategic marketing plan aims to increase the market share that the drug holds through its introduction into the OTC market. VirPharm, Inc., intends to leverage its strengths in a highly saturated and competitive market to accomplish this goal. Its primary competitors are other OTC nonsteroidal anti-inflammatory drugs (NSAIDs), aspirin, and acetaminophen. Among other weaknesses, there is weak product differentiation in the market as a whole. Currently there are two primary outlets for OTC pain relief: drugstores and grocery stores.

There are several challenges in the NSAID marketplace. NSAIDs are currently under attack in the media due to negative heart-related side effects. In addition, there are many competitors already in this market, and brand loyalty is difficult to overcome. However, VirPharm, Inc., has several strengths that they intend to leverage to overcome these challenges. They have a market-leading sales force and a highly motivated workforce. Cost of production is comparatively low for their products.

VirPharm, Inc., will explore new markets not currently exploited by their competitors. The name of the product will be changed to "RELEVEN." This newly packaged product will be priced competitively in the marketplace, higher than generic competition but slightly lower than many of their name-brand competitors. The primary target market will be young executives, ages 21 to 40, with a predominant focus on pain relief associated with day-to-day overexertion rather than just headache relief. Another target market will be the older generation that is increasing in population. VirPharm will focus its efforts to market RELEVEN to the age range of 50 to 75, for particularly active seniors. RELEVEN will be differentiated from other products through its use of new distribution channels, specifically office supply websites/stores and online distribution. VirPharm expects to capture 20 percent of the OTC pain reliever's market share within two years of the product launch. This represents $438 million in revenue in 2010.

Situation Analysis

The Internal Environment

Marketing Goals and Objectives VirPharm has specific marketing goals and objectives that have brought historical success, which will provide the foundation for future successes. The primary objective set forth for VirPharm involves the focus on efforts to grow the sales and market share of each product that it manufactures. VirPharm engages in the manufacturing of a number of quality-of-life prescription and over-the-counter (OTC) drugs for the consumer market, which has brought brand-preference and leading market share positions with several of their offerings.

As with any publicly traded company, one of the underlying missions of the organization must include the maximization of shareholder wealth. VirPharm's leading marketing objective is clearly aligned with its mission, particularly as it relates to the subsequent impact on shareholder value. In addition, the marketing objective to grow sales and market share allows the organization the flexibility to respond to external environment changes as well as consumer needs and wants. VirPharm is somewhat uniquely structured by engaging in both the prescription and the OTC market, which allows the organization additional flexibility in market preferences and requirements.

Current Marketing Strategy and Performance   The main objective for VirPharm, Inc., is focused on the marketing efforts used to grow sales and market share position through the products that the company produces. The objective is primarily fostered through a strategy in which profits resulting from their successes are funneled back through research and development to create new and improved products for the markets they choose to serve. In addition, VirPharm, Inc., has also followed a transitional approach into the OTC market from their respective prescription product line as patents expire, such as the recently expired patent of the antidepressant Hapizine, which is the most successful in the marketplace. In combination with drug performance, the prescription drug market depends heavily on the medical profession's endorsement for success, whereas the OTC market depends heavily on relationships with trade, wholesalers, mass retailers, and drugstores.

Recent performance by VirPharm has been fairly successful, with a sales growth rate of 23.4 percent and a net income growth of just over 19 percent. This recent performance has translated into a 2009 revenue level of $8.6 billion and net income of $474.2 million. One of the drivers for the increased growth by VirPharm has been their strong brand preference, which has pushed them to being one of the top pharmaceutical providers in both the prescription and OTC drug markets. For the six different product lines that VirPharm offers in the prescription drug market, which account for 75 percent of the business, they are approximately the second- or third-largest player overall and appear to be maintaining that position, without much concern for a recently expired patent on Hapizine, which is number one in the market. The primary concern involves BOPREX, which has been in decline the last few years and currently finds itself as the sixth-preferred drug in its market. In regard to the macro position of the over-the-counter market, VirPharm holds approximately the third-largest position.

VirPharm, Inc., has experienced aggressive growth in sales and has established itself in the top tier of the various product categories they service, which can be largely attributed to their "best in the industry" sales force. However, VirPharm has come to the recent realization that they will need to address the periodic decline in the market position of one of their prescription drugs, BOPREX. This respective decline in BOPREX has been primarily the result of more powerful nonsteroidal anti-inflammatory drugs (NSAIDs), from competitors that provide Vioxx, Celebrex, and Bextra. Currently only Celebrex remains on the market.

Current and Anticipated Organizational Resources   The overall resources for VirPharm are described as good; the company is led by a highly motivated sales force that has been recognized as a leader in the pharmaceutical industry and has good working relationships with both suppliers and customers. As a midsize company competing with a large number of major firms, VirPharm has been able to develop a strong reputation for employee integrity, customer satisfaction, and commitment. Conversely, as a midsize player in the industry, VirPharm has realized some limitation on consumer and trade budgets, which operate at nearly half the rate of the major competitors.

Although the resource levels and relationships are expected to be virtually unchanged in the future, VirPharm must be cautious in some of the variability they have experienced with their offshore suppliers, particularly those in China. The use of suppliers in this region has allowed VirPharm to leverage their market position through lower costs of raw materials. Current alternatives to these resources will lead VirPharm to source supplies and materials from more-expensive vendors located in Europe and Puerto Rico.

Any potential threats related to offshore suppliers that sustain competitive leverages might need to be combated through a potential merger with a larger player in the pharmaceutical industry. VirPharm has entertained these very possibilities and has engaged in discussions with leading firms such as GlaxoSmithKline, Aventis, Pfizer, and Proctor & Gamble. Results from a merger with any of these respective firms would allow VirPharm greater access to resources, specific expertise to be leveraged, supplier leverage, and the ability to focus on the core of what they have established.

Current and Anticipated Cultural and Structural Issues   The current organizational culture and structure at VirPharm are depicted as very customer driven, with a foundation that is particularly employee oriented. This culture is best depicted by a sales force that is nearly half of the entire organization's population and by the embracing of an ethical means of doing business through their Code of Integrity. The organization's philosophy recognizes that they operate in a customer and market-driven industry, and that success will not be realized if they do not have the internal motivation and commitment to the firm by their most valued asset: the employees.

The Customer Environment

Current and Potential Customers   A study published by *ABC News*, *USA Today*, and Stanford University Medical Center found that more than half of Americans live with chronic or recurrent pain. Nearly 6 in 10 said their last pain experience was moderate or worse, and 2 in 10 rated their pain as severe. Fifty-seven percent of seniors ages 55 and older experience pain often, compared to 43 percent of people ages 31 to 55 and 17 percent of adults 30 and under. Back and knee pain account for 37 percent of pain locations, followed by headaches/migraines at 9 percent, and leg and shoulder at 7 percent each. Together, these account for 60 percent of all pain by location. To eliminate this pain, 84 percent of respondents said they use OTC drugs and 81 percent use home remedies such as heating pads, ice packs, and hot baths or showers.

The use of OTC pain relievers is increasing. *American Demographics* concluded that the four major uses for OTC pain relievers are headaches, sore muscles, arthritis, and heart-attack prevention. In 1996, an estimated 177 million Americans used an OTC pain reliever for one problem or another. This number is expected to grow to 205 million by 2010. Exhibit B.1 indicates how American consumers use OTC pain relievers.

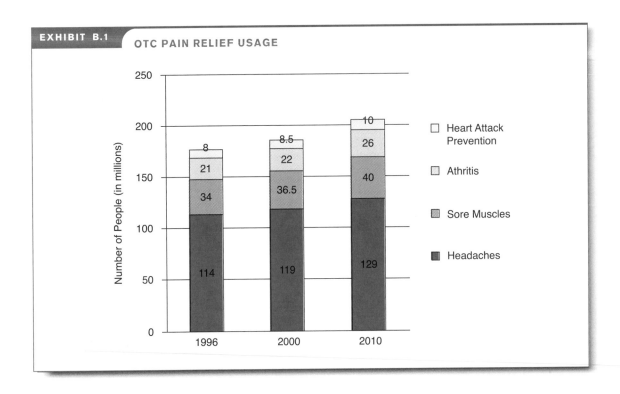

EXHIBIT B.1 **OTC PAIN RELIEF USAGE**

Customer's Need for Pain Relievers   Headaches and migraines are the number one reason people take OTC pain relievers. Migraines affect 13 percent of the U.S. population, or 29.5 million people, and are most prevalent in people between 20 to 40 years old. This results in one in every four households having a migraine sufferer. Approximately 60 percent of adults have taken an OTC pain reliever for a headache in the past six months. This number has been declining over the past few years due to the acceptance of headaches as a legitimate and sometimes serious medical problem. Individuals have begun seeing doctors for prescription medications that are more effective than typical analgesics for specific types of headaches.

The second most popular reason for taking pain relievers is sore muscles. This is also the fastest-growing reason for the use of OTC pain relievers, specifically NSAIDs. In the early '90s, this reason grew by 17 percent in the young-adult age segment, from ages 18 to 24. This was initially believed to be due to their more active lifestyle, but the market segment of ages 65 and up has grown by 17 percent as well. The aggressive marketing of ibuprofen as an antidote for sore muscles can be credited for this increase. Prior to this marketing campaign, individuals believed that not much could be done for their achy muscles and that it was something they would have to live with. The aging baby-boomer generation could also help this segment along, with the arthritis segment expected to grow rapidly in the future.

Arthritis sufferers have also found relief from OTC pain relievers. Almost 43 million people have been diagnosed as having some form of arthritis, and an estimated 23.2 million live with chronic joint symptoms but have not been diagnosed by a doctor. This is equivalent to one in three adults. Some types of arthritis include osteoarthritis, a degenerative joint disease; rheumatoid arthritis, which attacks the joint lining causing it to become inflamed; and juvenile arthritis that affects children. Arthritis affects people of all ages, including over 300,000 children, and is the most prevalent chronic health problem and the leading cause of disability among Americans over the age of 15. Arthritis also affects women more than men, with 25.9 million women being doctor diagnosed compared with 16.8 million men.

Customer Purchase Patterns   Customers typically purchase pain relievers at supermarkets, pharmacies, and mass merchandise retailers. Individuals may buy OTC pain relievers after surgery or to help eliminate pain after they have used all their prescription painkillers. Purchases typically occur no more than one or two times per month, as indicated in Exhibit B.2.

A number of issues play a role in the consumers' selection of which OTC pain reliever to use. Some consumers look for the lowest price, in which case most generic forms of pain relievers, such as Walmart's Equate brand, cost considerably less than name-brand Tylenol or aspirin. Other consumers look for the absence of certain side effects such as gastrointestinal bleeding or effects on one's liver. Few OTC pain relievers can be taken during pregnancy, whereas others cannot be used in conjunction with certain prescription drugs. When consumers have multiple symptoms, such as a headache with a stuffy head or congestion, they often choose a medication that will solve all of their problems. Products such as Tylenol Sinus serve to eliminate headaches and clear congestion. As an added benefit, the user does not need to be concerned with possible side effects of mixing medications. Once consumers find a pain reliever that works well, they tend to buy only this brand in the future.

Rationale of Noncustomers   Aspirin and ibuprofen should not be taken if you are taking blood pressure medications like ACE inhibitors and/or beta-blockers. Some people have allergic reactions to aspirin, which can cause wheezing, hives, facial swelling, and/or shock. Other individuals have a holistic approach to medicine and

---

EXHIBIT B.2   **FREQUENCY OF PURCHASE OF OTC PAIN RELIEVERS**

How often have you purchased an over-the-counter pain reliever in the past six months?

	Frequency	Percent	Cumulative Percent
0 times	370	30.8	30.8
1–2 times	520	43.3	74
3–4 times	175	14.6	88.6
5–6 times	79	6.6	95.2
7+ times	56	4.7	99.8
Don't know	2	0.2	100
Total	1,202	100	

prefer not to take any sort of medication. Because of these reasons, many individuals experiment with alternative means of pain relief. Sports creams like Bengay and Icy Hot, along with ice packs, can be used to eliminate achy muscles and reduce swelling. Electric heat pads are commonly used to reduce lower back pain, and acupuncture has grown in popularity in recent years as an alternative to medications as well.

Competition

VirPharm's likely competition for BOPREX can be categorized into three groups, organized by the common ailment they are intended to remedy. The groups are (1) the treatment of rheumatoid arthritis and osteoarthritis, (2) the treatment of migraines, and (3) the general treatment of fever and pain.

For the treatment of arthritis, competition exists in both the prescription market and the OTC market. The only true prescription competitor is Celebrex, as Vioxx and Bextra have been pulled from the market due to concerns about side effects. Major OTC competitors are Aleve, Excedrin, and aspirin. New competitors on the prescription front, although not publicly well-known, are Enbrel, Remicade, and Avara. For the treatment of migraines, competition exists in both the prescription and OTC markets. Common prescription competitive medications for the treatment of migraines are Imitrex, Axert, and Midrin. The OTC counterparts are Excedrin Migraine and Advil Migraine. Next, there is strong competition in the OTC market for a general fever/pain reliever from many well-known brand names and generics. Aspirin makers Bayer and Excedrin are the major brand players for an otherwise generic product. Acetaminophen is a competing product, most often associated with the Tylenol brand. Next, there is ibuprofen with common brand names of Motrin and Advil. Finally, there is Aleve, which employs naproxen sodium as its active ingredient. Finally, VirPharm could look at a different market for the product, such as offering the product as a multisymptom treatment. In this arena, competition comes from many of the same organizations, which supply multisymptom products such as Tylenol Cold, Advil Cold & Sinus, and Nyquil.

Analysis of Major Competitors   As BOPREX will compete for shelf space and market share against drugs promoting various types of symptom relief, it will compete against several different drug types, specifically aspirin, ibuprofen, naproxen sodium, and acetaminophen. Each of these drugs carries unique qualities to provide symptom relief, with uniquely corresponding side effects. Exhibit B.3 summarizes these symptom-relief and side-effect combinations.

Competing Nondrug Therapies   In response to the high cost of prescription and nonprescription drugs, and in conjunction with these drugs' side effects, the use of nondrug therapies for the treatment of pain and other ailments is thriving. Nondrug therapies are also the first option by choice for some, as they choose not to introduce drugs into their bodies. Examples of these therapies include exercise, weight control, the use of hot and cold packs, attitude, education, and assistive devices. Advantages to these methods can take the form of improved health, lower cost, and the ability to maintain the treatment indefinitely, unlike many drugs. Some disadvantages may

EXHIBIT B.3   STRENGTHS AND WEAKNESSES OF COMPETING DRUGS

Drug Type (Common Brands)	Strengths/Major Symptoms Relieved	Weaknesses/Side Effects
Aspirin (Bayer) (Excedrin) (St. Joseph's)	• Preventive care for cardiovascular issues • Reduces inflammation • Trusted pain reliever	• Can cause stomach irritation • Not suitable for infants or use during the last three months of pregnancy
Ibuprofen (Motrin) (Advil)	• Effective pain reliever and fever reducer • Reduces inflammation • Trusted, with strong brand names • Formulas available for adults, children, and infants	• Like all NSAIDs, can cause stomach irritation • May have cardiovascular side effects • Not recommended for prolonged use
Naproxen Sodium (Aleve) (Naprosyn)	• Long-lasting pain and fever relief from minimal dosage • Excellent at reducing inflammation	• Like all NSAIDs, can cause stomach irritation • May have cardiovascular side effects • Not recommended for prolonged use • Not as well known as other NSAIDs
Acetaminophen (Tylenol)	• Excellent pain and fever reducer • Very high brand loyalty • Does not cause stomach irritation • Formulas available for adults, children, and infants • Can be used during all stages of pregnancy	• Does not reduce inflammation • Dosage must be repeated every 4 hours • Long term use may cause liver damage
COX-2 Inhibitors (Celebrex) (Vioxx) (Bextra)	• Highly effective at reducing inflammation • Significant arthritis pain relief • Does not cause stomach irritation	• Documented cardiovascular health issues (especially Vioxx) • Only Celebrex is currently on the market

include the continuance of pain or discomfort during the healing process that could be avoided with the use of medication.

Economic Growth and Stability

The U.S. economy has deteriorated dramatically since 2008, with the weakest housing market and highest unemployment rate in decades. Overall, economic activity in the United States fell 2.7 percent in the third quarter of 2008, followed by quarterly declines of 5.4 percent, 6.4 percent, and 0.7 percent in the second quarter of 2009. The current U.S. unemployment rate stands at 9.8 percent, while the rate in Florida is higher at 10.7 percent. Although the U.S. economy remains quite soft, the worst appears to be over for now. The recession is expected to last well into 2010.

Despite the weak economy, consumers still need to purchase medicines and other necessities. In this sense, drugs and other medications are somewhat recession proof. However, the prescription market has suffered during the most recent economic decline as consumers have shifted to the OTC market in search of less expensive alternatives. U.S. prescription drug sales topped $291 billion in 2008 (an increase of

1.3 percent, down from 9 percent growth the previous year), while the OTC market totaled $16.8 billion (an increase of 4.3 percent). The United States accounts for 46 percent of the world's pharmaceutical market. Taking a broader look across the industry, no fewer than 19 blockbuster prescription drugs saw their patents expire in 2008. Analysis suggests that 150 new drug compounds are needed now to plug this gap in the drug innovation pipeline.

The OTC market has also been growing as more consumers turn to self-diagnosis and treatment. There are currently more than 100,000 OTC products that consumers can choose from. The trend to use OTC medications has also been supported by physicians, who have been prescribing them more frequently than in the past. Some drugs that move from prescription to OTC enjoy greater attention from doctors. For example, after Claritin moved from prescription to OTC, 42 percent of purchasers in the first six months were advised to buy it by their physicians. There are currently more than 600 OTC drugs that were once available only by prescription. When drugs move to the OTC market, their prices typically drop. However, these drugs also enjoy a dramatic increase in demand, whereas demand for comparable OTC and prescription drugs sharply declines.

Political Trends

A great deal of political attention has centered on COX-2 inhibitors, sold via prescription under the Vioxx, Bextra, and Celebrex brands. After Vioxx was found to double the rate of heart attacks among its users, Merck voluntarily withdrew the product from the market. Similarly, Pfizer withdrew Bextra when its use was associated with life-threatening skin reactions. Celebrex continues to be sold legally in the United States. The fallout of the COX-2 controversy has placed a great deal of scrutiny on the entire pain relief market, particularly with OTC NSAIDs.

Price controls and advertising regulations are also hot-button political issues. The United States and New Zealand are the only current nations where direct-to-consumer (DTC) drug advertising is permitted by the government. Some politicians are very clear regarding their stance on advertising by drug manufacturers. They argue that drug advertisements increase America's skyrocketing drug costs and should not be allowed until two years after a drug is released. A secondary objective of such a probationary period on advertising would be to prevent unnecessary prescriptions of drugs, where drug awareness created by advertising is inflating the number of prescriptions being written.

Drug manufacturers marshal a great deal of resources to lobby Congress to extend their patents and block generic competition. In the seven years leading up to 2005, pharmaceutical companies spent $800 million in federal lobbying and campaign contributions. These efforts helped to fend off the importation of drugs from countries that place caps on drug prices. In 2004, lobbying efforts helped pass the Medicare Modernization Act of 2003, which set up a government-based reliable purchaser for pharmaceutical companies.

Drug importation is also a hotly contested political debate in the industry. Although technically illegal and forbidden by the FDA, the practice of acquiring prescription and nonprescription drugs from nondomestic markets is very popular in the United States. Politicians have stated their positions regarding the importation of nondomestic drugs into the United States. President Obama, for example, supports the importation of drugs from other countries as long as they are safe and the practice will lower drug prices for American consumers. The most recent health care reform plan, however, is basically silent on this issue. Although the importation of foreign drugs seems to have the President's support, the FDA has yet to clear the way for the process to become legal. The FDA claims foreign drug providers may import drugs that are either counterfeit or untested. Those not in support of importing foreign drugs, especially U.S. pharmaceutical companies, side with the FDA and restate the safety concerns with foreign drugs. Those in support of foreign drug importation denounce this stance, as they suspect the pharmaceutical companies are only taking this position to maintain artificially high profit margins.

Legal and Regulatory Issues

Pharmaceutical firms have faced a number of challenges relating to regulation as well as to consumer perception. As a result of the COX-2 controversy, the FDA distributed letters to promoters of NSAIDs that called for changes in the labeling of such products. This new labeling was intended to inform consumers of the potential for increased risk of cardiovascular events and potentially life-threatening gastrointestinal (GI) bleeding associated with COX-2 and other NSAIDs. In addition, the FDA warned that NSAIDs should not be used in conjunction with aspirin due to the increased risk of bleeding and reduced kidney function. Though these warnings have scared many consumers, the FDA has reaffirmed the safety of OTC NSAIDs for short-term use of low doses. In addition to not being recommended for long-term use, OTC NSAIDs are also recommended at lower starting and maintenance doses than prescription NSAIDs. However, OTC medicines do not require a doctor's visit or prescription, and therefore offer an additional level of convenience.

Additional regulations have been passed to enhance patient safety. The Prescription Drug Marketing Act of 1987 aids in the reduction of counterfeiting prescription drugs. Furthermore, in 2004 the FDA announced a ruling requiring hospitals to use bar codes on prescription medications that they distribute. The purpose of this is to minimize the chance of error within drug dispensing. Recently, the FDA went one step further to begin trials of radio frequency identification (RFID) as a stronger means of tracking and controlling the nation's drug supply. Concerns are looming, however, regarding potential radio interference with life-saving equipment within hospitals.

The impending reform of the U.S. health care system by President Obama and Congress leaves many question marks about the prescription drug market. The new insurance exchanges created under the plan would likely lead to prescription drug coverage for more Americans. The prices that consumers will pay for drug coverage will depend on the level of insurance coverage they choose. One outcome that seems likely is the reduction or elimination of the gap in drug coverage under Medicare Part D, which affects roughly 4 million seniors. It is expected that drugs falling within that gap would see price reductions of at least 50 percent. A major unresolved issue is the effect that health care reform will have on the OTC market. Even though patients may find comparable or improved relief from over-the-counter medications, the new legislation may in fact encourage the use of prescription drugs. In the meantime, over-the-counter medications still qualify as reimbursable expenses through pretax dollars. The ability of consumers to pay for BOPREX with pretax dollars offers them greater choice in their health while providing greater opportunity to VirPharm.

Technological Advancements

As in most industries, technological advancements have affected consumer activity in a number of ways. The Internet has created an abundance of information, not all of which is reliable. Consumers have easy access to information, much of which is promotional material presented in a manner to appear unbiased. Internet sources, however, can also offer educational and potentially useful information. For instance, sites such as www.rxlist.com and www.webmd.com provide useful information on uses and side effects of virtually all prescription and OTC pain relievers.

In addition to the impact on customers, technological advances also offer a number of opportunities and challenges pertaining to manufacturing, distribution, and promotional activities. Technology generates more-extensive research, greater accuracy in manufacturing, more-effective methods for tracking issues, and faster processes for development. With regard to distribution, technology has provided opportunities for environmentally friendly packaging while increasing safety mechanisms to prevent tampering. The most promising of these technologies is radio frequency identification, or RFID. Potential benefits include inventory control, counterfeit deterrence, patient protection, and prompt communications relating to recalls. The cost to implement such technology, however, is significant and has prevented widespread implementation thus far. The FDA has developed a timeline in which drugs that are more likely to be duplicated by counterfeiters will be serialized sooner than others. The adoption of RFID technology affects drug manufacturers such as VirPharm and must be considered when developing packaging.

Technology influences not only marketing and distribution techniques but also the type of pain relief that is available and the delivery mechanism. In addition to traditional pain management, there are a number of technological advances now available to patients seeking relief of acute and chronic pain. For example, neuro-muscular stimulators run electrical currents through the body to generate healthy tissue and repair tissues that cause pain. Facet rhizotomy, a procedure that uses an electrode to deaden the nerves that are causing pain in specific areas, is another specialized method of relief for joint pain. Nerve blockers, magnetic therapies, in-frared technology, and energy waves also represent technological advances for relief of localized pain.

In addition to new methods of pain relief, there are also new mechanisms for delivering medications. Beyond the traditional oral medications that include tablets, caplets, capsules, powders, and liquid forms, transdermal patch systems are gaining popularity. These systems have already been implemented in areas such as motion sickness, smoking cessation, and birth control. Furthermore, drug delivery may also be in the form of injections, inhalers, magnets, or lighting systems. Recognizing the effectiveness and convenience offered in alternative drug delivery systems creates future opportunities for makers of pain relief medications.

Sociocultural Trends

The changing values and demographics of today's society offer both opportunities and challenges to pharmaceutical firms. For instance, the increased size of an elderly population creates a large customer base for manufacturers of pharmaceutical products. In addition, this elderly population does not maintain the same lifestyles as those of past decades. Elderly people are remaining employed well into their 60s and 70s and are maintaining active lifestyles. Those in the workforce are increasingly using computers and keyboards, requiring manual dexterity and the ability to remain seated for hours at a time. Today's elderly population is not content to remain inactive. Active lifestyles create a market of on-the-go Americans who require effective pain relief to maintain the quality of life they demand.

More active populations and dual-income households also result in consumers' placing an increased value on their time. The convenience of purchasing items and the convenience of dosing are both significant. Many want to purchase their pain relievers at the same place they purchase milk, on the way home from work. This may be their local supermarket, a large supercenter, or the convenience store down the road. Shopping online is becoming increasingly common, due to convenience, as well. Busy schedules result in convenience being a critical aspect for today's shoppers.

Furthermore, patients are increasingly vocal about their health care, and they are active in seeking solutions to health issues. Television advertising of pharmaceuticals has risen, creating a new level of competition for drug manufacturers. A challenge for manufacturers of OTC medications is that, in recent years, there has been a significant increase in direct-to-consumer advertising of prescription drugs. "Ask your doctor if product X is right for you," suggests one commercial. With prescription medications promoting directly to consumers, manufacturers of OTC drugs are faced with increased competition from makers of similar products of prescription strength.

However, OTC drug manufactures are able to take advantage of the growing trend of self-diagnosis and self-medication. With the diverse selection of vitamins, natural supplements, and OTC products that are available, consumers often self-diagnose their ailments and purchase products targeted to treat their symptoms. The inconveniences of visiting the doctor's office, coupled with increasing medical costs, have resulted in consumers' increasingly looking toward alternative solutions outside of conventional healthcare. The drawback to VirPharm, however, is that self-medication may result in a lack of compliance with recommended dosing. This presents a potential risk to consumers in that over-the-counter NSAIDs are not intended for long-term use.

SWOT Analysis

Strengths	M	× I	= R	Opportunities	M	× I	= R
BOPREX approved to treat arthritis, migraine headache, and general pain	3	3	9	FDA has approved the transition of prescription NSAIDs into OTC market	3	3	9
Patent exclusivity for three years	3	3	9	Consumers will try new products as they become available	3	3	9
New product entry	3	2	6	NSAIDs can be used as general pain reliever and fever reducer	3	3	9
Prescription-strength pain relief available over the counter	3	2	6	Potential market channels not currently exploited	3	3	9
Effective migraine treatment	3	2	6	Competing prescription pain relievers have been pulled from the market	3	2	6
Talented and motivated workforce	2	2	4	Weak product differentiation among OTC competitors	3	2	6
Lower cost of raw materials	3	1	3	U.S. population is increasingly seeking convenience of online shopping	2	3	6
Wide range of products	1	2	2	Increase in aging population	2	2	4
Weaknesses	M	× I	= R	**Threats**	M	× I	= R
Limited marketing budget	−3	3	−9	Competition from both prescription pain relievers and OTC pain relievers	−3	3	−9
Market position (#6 in market)	−3	3	−9	Extremely crowded OTC market	−3	3	−9
Weak product differentiation	−3	3	−9	Consumer loyalty with existing competitors	−3	2	−6
Current brand name (new to market)	−3	2	−6	Negative publicity regarding NSAIDs	−2	3	−6
Midsize company	−2	2	−4	Declining doctor recommendation of NSAIDs	−1	3	−3
BOPREX associated with gastrointestinal side effects	−1	3	−3	OTC NSAIDs not indicated for long-term use	−1	2	−2
Variability in offshore suppliers	−1	2	−2	Regulations on drug advertisements could intensify	−1	2	−2

Developing Competitive Advantages

Shifting BOPREX to the over-the-counter medication is a huge opportunity for Vir-Pharm. By moving OTC, VirPharm can take maximum advantage of its past R&D spending and use its remaining patent exclusivity to capture OTC dominance in the butoprofen pain relief category. VirPharm will be able to tout BOPREX as prescription-strength butoprofen at an OTC price. VirPharm has previous success in moving its prescription products to the OTC market, and that experience will be invaluable as VirPharm attempts this transition with BOPREX. VirPharm's low manufacturing costs are also critical, as the OTC market is very price competitive.

In moving OTC, VirPharm will be able to leverage its strength and newness in a market that consistently looks for the newest, most effective pain relief on the market. In addition, VirPharm can take advantage of the relatively weak differentiation among OTC competitors, as well as the relative softness in the market for COX-2 inhibitors. Furthermore, VirPharm can take advantage of marketing channels that are relatively underutilized by competing OTC firms.

Despite the tremendous opportunities, VirPharm must also be cognizant of its weaknesses in the crowded OTC market. Although being a midsize company does not allow for significant financial backing, it does allow VirPharm to react quickly to changing markets and customer requests. To compensate for its relatively small marketing budget, VirPharm's industry-leading sales force will work with doctors and pharmacists to emphasize the effectiveness and lower cost of BOPREX. Likewise, VirPharm's promotional campaign will need to be lean, efficient, and cost-effective.

Developing a Strategic Focus

The overall strategy of this marketing plan incorporates key opportunities in the industry into VirPharm's focus. The ability to transition VirPharm's prescription medication into an over-the-counter medication offers an opportunity for market launch within the general pain relief market. VirPharm will benefit from a large adult population, many whom work beyond the age of 65. As a part of this launch, BOPREX will be renamed RELEVEN (pronounced ree-lee-ven)—a name that plays on the relief offered by prescription-strength butoprofen. The strategic focus is to position RELEVEN as a medication that is stronger and more effective than traditional pain relievers and one that is easier to access than by obtaining a prescription.

In terms of distribution and access, RELEVEN will be offered for sale through traditional grocery, mass merchandise, and drugstore channels. However, VirPharm will also aggressively pursue nontraditional venues, such as office supply merchants and online stores. VirPharm will develop partnerships with companies such as Staples, Office Max, and Office Depot to offer RELEVEN as an add-on item through online purchases. This partnership will assist corporate office supply buyers to satisfy multiple office needs with a "one-stop" shop concept. RELEVEN will gain an online presence and develop an "e-drug" status, as well evolve as the preferred pain relief product in the office environment. Realizing the weaknesses of VirPharm's limited marketing budget and its unrecognizable brand name, this approach to marketing and selling RELEVEN will minimize marketing costs.

Marketing Goals and Objectives

Based on careful consideration of the situational and SWOT analysis, the following goal and objectives have been identified to provide the blueprint for an opportunity to transition RELEVEN to the over-the-counter market.

> **Goal**   To launch and position RELEVEN as the convenient, prescription-strength, over-the-counter pain reliever.

Convenience is the driving theme of this marketing plan. One of the underlying demands of consumers for products in the OTC market involves convenience, whether it is off the shelf or the convenience of online ordering. In addition, RELEVEN has the unique characteristic of its move to the over-the-counter market. This will give consumers the confidence, satisfaction, and convenience of acquiring a prescription-strength medication without the need of doctor direction.

> **Objective 1**   Obtain a 20 percent share of the multipurpose pain relief market within two years of launch.

Whereas most competing products are positioned as relief for specific ailments, RELEVEN will be positioned as a broad-spectrum pain reliever for a number of different ailments (headaches, migraines, general aches, pains, and fever). This positioning will be focused on the adult population who suffers from overexertion at work—whether it be from tension, stress, computer strain, or noise—or at home from the physical exertion of exercise or household demands.

Objective 2   Garner 20 percent of sales from online ordering within one year of launch.

As strength continues to build in RELEVEN's market share, the availability of nontraditional procurement options (online ordering and availability from office supply retailers) will position RELEVEN as a leader in the office environment. Online buyers will be able to meet their needs without leaving the office.

Marketing Strategy

A summary of our marketing strategy based on the product life cycle is shown in Exhibit B.4. The elements of this strategy will be discussed in the following sections.

EXHIBIT B.4   SUMMARY OF RELEVEN MARKETING STRATEGY

	Introduction	Growth	Maturity	Decline
Overall Marketing Goals	Transition RELEVEN to the OTC market; position as a prescription-strength product for general pain relief.	Increase product awareness and market share through sales to users of prescription medications and other pain relievers.	Continually increase market share through increased office and online presence.	Having gained brand awareness, maximize profit through reduced promotional efforts.
Product Strategy	RELEVEN will be offered in one form (capsule) and in one dosage strength (50mg).	As patent expires, RELEVEN will be offered in other forms; single-dose packaging will be offered.	The product will sustain an "e-drug" reputation and be perceived as *the* solution for general aches and pains.	The most popular forms of RELEVEN will remain on the market; other forms will be dropped.
Pricing Strategy	RELEVEN will be priced higher than generics and aspirin, but lower than prescription medications and specialty products.	As patent expires, prices will be reduced to maintain market position.	Prices will remain consistent with the growth phase.	Lower costs through reduced promotional efforts will allow further price reductions.
Distribution Strategy	Obtain shelf space from traditional outlets such as drugstores and large retailers; primary focus will be on office supply retailers and online merchants; trial packs will be distributed with office supplies.	Further penetration into nontraditional vendors such as shipping and photocopy centers; single-dose packs will be available through vending machines.	Maximum availability through traditional and nontraditional merchants.	Only most profitable channels and merchants will be retained; significant online presence will continue.
Promotion Strategy	Heavy use of in-store promotions; trial-size packs will be available with office-related items.	Continued in-store promotions; online promotion via office supply websites; promotion via vending services and providers of water cooler suppliers; TV advertising to attract older adults.	Heavy advertising on online news sites.	To further reduce costs, online promotion will be reduced.

Primary Target Market

VirPharm's primary target market consists of men and women, ages 21 to 40, who work in an office environment. Their ethnic background is increasingly diverse. These individuals are found in both urban and suburban locations. Most have some college, and many possess Bachelor's and Master's degrees. They typically remain single well into their 20s and often do not have children until their 30s. Once married, they maintain dual-income households and therefore have larger incomes but less free time. This segment represents an easily identifiable and measurable group. This is a substantial consumer group that is accessible through many diverse communication channels.

Although the primary focus is on young professionals, a second focus within the growth phase will include a target market of active, older adults. This target, which includes both men and women, ranges in age from 50 to 74. The population of this segment continues to grow, and this group will be the largest consumer of pharmaceutical products in the future.

Identifying Characteristics   Most of the young professionals in our target market have web access through multiple locations including home and work. Many also maintain a home office or a laptop for working from home. The target maintains an on-the-go lifestyle where they work extended hours and are motivated to succeed in their career. They also sustain active social lives that include frequenting sports events, social gatherings, and restaurants and bars. Because of the lifestyle they lead, the target is seeking convenient access to medications, as they have little time for doctor's visits or for filling prescriptions, and they expect quick relief for their pain. The younger portion of this target was brought up with pagers, cell phones, and the Internet. They often have short attention spans and are accustomed to having information at their fingertips. To break into this market, it is essential to allow quick and easy access to RELEVEN. Many in this segment have become accustomed to periodic headaches and muscle aches, and they choose to endure the pain rather than to address it.

The older target now leads an active lifestyle well beyond the typical retirement age. The nation's baby boomers represent a large percentage of the population and therefore a large consumer segment. Those in their 50s have yet to peak in their career. Many others remain employed well beyond the age of 65 and have no intentions of retiring. These individuals also lead active lives including maintaining primary and sometimes secondary careers, participating in social activities such as bowling and sports events, and beautifying their homes through landscaping and gardening.

Basic Needs and Requirements   In terms of pain relief, the primary market seeks effective pain relief for general symptoms including headaches, eyestrain from the computer, and a miracle cure for hangovers. Because of the time constraints for this active generation, they are seeking prescription-strength medications that are available over the counter. Others need relief but have failed to seek resolution due to lack of convenience. The younger group is more impressionable and more easily influenced by products that are perceived as popular and trendy. The older segment, on the other hand, simply has a need for effective treatment at a reasonable price. In terms of pain relief, the primary market is seeking effective pain relief for sporadic pain such as aching muscles and occasional arthritic pain.

Purchasing/Shopping Habits and Preferences   The younger generation increasingly purchases items online. They seek quick and convenient access for all of their shopping needs. In addition to shopping online, many frequent a local convenience store. They are also willing to pay a little more to save time. Furthermore, younger professionals are of a generation that demonstrates items are affordable as long as one can pay the minimum payment. Financing is common, and price is often less a factor than status. The reverse is more likely to be true with the older market. Given the increased cost of healthcare coverage and of prescription medications, these older people are seeking a low-cost alternative for pain relief.

As mentioned previously, price is less of a factor for the primary target. They seek the best solution regardless of price. If a product costs a little more but is easily accessible or can be taken less frequently, that added convenience adds greater utility. Also within this group is a subsegment that tends to endure their pain rather than treat it. A focus of the marketing strategy is to sway nonusers of pain relief medication by offering an effective alternative to relief, one that can be used conveniently, on a short-term basis, and with minimal side effects. The consumers that comprise the older segment are more price sensitive and more likely to be loyal to well-known medications that have maintained a long-term existence in the OTC market. They are exposed to media through TV and newspapers and are typically aware of publicity related to drug recalls and issues relating to products being pulled from the market.

Product Strategy

One primary feature of RELEVEN that will be emphasized repeatedly is its prescription-strength formula. In addition, it has been approved to treat osteoarthritis and migraine headaches as well as to provide general pain relief. At the outset, RELEVEN will be offered in capsule form and in one dosage strength. In order to simplify the initial product offering, there will not be an "extra strength" formula or a formula positioned specifically for migraines or headaches. Instead, RELEVEN will be offered for general relief of pain symptoms that arise from headaches, migraines, arthritis, and other aches and pains. Future offerings will include alternate product forms, including tablets in varying dosages.

A key advantage for VirPharm is RELEVEN's patent protection for three years after launch. This patent will help to prevent imitations and generic substitutions in the immediate future. Our patent will also support our initial pricing structure for three full years after launch.

Brand Name and Packaging   The product previously referred to as BOPREX will be designated as RELEVEN in its over-the-counter form. The name was selected to subtly communicate its purpose of providing relief. The capsule—which is white with red "RELEVEN" on it—will initially be packaged in three different sizes: a "Trial Pack" with 10 capsules, a "Personal Relief" pack with 100 capsules, and an "Office Pack" with 250 capsules. Although most competitors offer larger packages as "Family" packs, our "Office" pack is designed to maximize positioning in the office/work environment. Future packaging will include a single-dose (two capsules) that will be made available in vending machines throughout the United States.

Differentiation and Positioning   There are several features that differentiate RELE-VEN. First, it will be developed with an "office presence" that is positioned as the best solution for general pain relief among office workers. The focus will be upon pain relief for many ailments related to an office environment including eyestrain, head-aches, and migraines. The office presence is further enhanced through distribution in office supply stores and websites. Moreover, based on the distribution focus, RELE-VEN will be differentiated as an "e-drug" solution that is easily accessible through online shopping. It will be positioned as a solution for active, young professionals and will gain brand loyalty through the newness, prestige, and coolness factors.

RELEVEN itself will not be sold with accompanying supplemental products. However, RELEVEN is unique in that it will be sold as a supplemental product within office supply stores. In addition to partnering with retailers such as Staples, Office Max, and Office Depot, VirPharm will partner with manufacturers of specific product lines to include free trial packages of RELEVEN with their product offerings.

Pricing Strategy

RELEVEN is positioned toward young professionals who, in their consumption habits, have demonstrated that price is not the number one factor in selecting products. Convenience is critical to this market, and status is also desirable. By positioning RELEVEN as the best solution for pain relief, and by securing a significant office presence, the affordability of RELEVEN will not be the primary focus of its appeal.

Though price is not the most critical factor in marketing RELEVEN, VirPharm can nonetheless capitalize on its access to cheaper raw materials and therefore lower its cost of production. The pricing strategy, while primarily dependent upon retailers, will position RELEVEN as an affordable solution to pain relief. Revenues will be gained through both volume and substantial profit margins. With a list price of $5.63 for the 100-count "Personal Relief" pack, we expect RELEVEN to sell at an average retail price of $8.99. This price is comparable with Advil and Aleve and less expensive than migraine-specific medications. The 10-capsule trial pack will have a list price of $0.83 and the 250-count "Office Pack" will list for $8.77.

Distribution Strategy

The overall distribution strategy contains multiple approaches. In the introduction phase, shelf space will be sought through traditional venues such as drugstores and other retailers such as grocery stores and mass merchandise retailers. The primary focus, however, will be through office supply retailers and websites. During the growth phase, access will be extended through less traditional venues such as shipping and photocopy centers. These venues attract the specific target market of young professionals.

Furthermore, RELEVEN will be offered through online office retailers such as Staples.com, OfficeMax.com, and OfficeDepot.com. Company buyers of office supplies and/or technological equipment and supplies will be exposed to RELEVEN through their regular buying activities. A third strategy will present single-dose packages through vending machines in offices, shopping centers, health clubs, golf courses, and bowling alleys. Given the primary venue of online retailers, the focus will be upon national distribution.

Integrated Marketing Strategy

The overall integrated marketing communications directed specifically toward the consumer include advertising primarily through Internet advertising, outdoor advertising such as billboards, through add-on sales via online venues, and through in-store promotions at office suppliers. Additional TV advertising will allow RELEVEN to enhance its initial brand name recognition. Advertising efforts will include 50 percent to Internet advertising, 20 percent to outdoor advertising, and 30 percent to television advertising. VirPharm's advertising budget includes $125 million for consumer advertising, and an equivalent amount has been dedicated to trade marketing activities.

The advertising strategy will be specific to the product, images of the target market, types of pain that it treats, and the relief it provides. The strategy will focus upon general-purpose pain relief on the days (and nights) that adults have exerted themselves. Exertions include stress from work, eyestrain from the computer, headaches caused by screaming children, and general aches and pains resulting from a late night. Images of a young professional working on a laptop or of a young man waking up after a rough night will be demonstrated to illustrate the uses for RELEVEN.

Sales promotions will include free trial packages that are offered with office supplies in retail stores and online. Further indirect advertising will be presented in the form of office-related items to increase brand awareness. Items will include pens, paperweights, mouse pads, and office calendars. These inexpensive items will be shared through the vending services and through contact with office managers.

Secondary Target Market and Marketing Program

Secondary Target Market   Although VirPharm's secondary market will include numerous retailers, the primary focus will be on obtaining shelf space in office supply stores as well as in the warehouses of online suppliers. Other businesses such as shipping and photocopy centers will also be targeted. Finally, vending machine services will be targeted as an opportunity for more direct access to customers. The primary need of these merchants is to increase sales through increased use and visitation of their product offerings. With regard to the vending services, the goal is to increase sales, as profitability is directly related to sales quantities.

Product Strategy   The general-purpose relief offered by RELEVEN aligns well with the needs of office supply customers. For online retailers, offering RELEVEN as an add-on sales item is an easy way to increase sales. Because RELEVEN will be positioned with a strong office presence, office suppliers will benefit from their affiliation with RELEVEN.

Pricing Strategy   The primary pricing objective is to blend midsize profit margins with substantial sales volumes for profitability. RELEVEN will be offered to retailers at a price higher than generics and aspirin, but at a price that is lower than most specialized arthritis and migraine products. As mentioned previously, the list price to retailers and wholesalers is $5.63 for the 100-count "Personal Relief" pack, $0.83 for the 10-count trial pack and $8.77 for the 250-count "Office Pack."

Distribution Strategy   The overall distribution strategy contains multiple approaches. VirPharm will initially gain shelf space in major retailer stores through the use of slotting fees and discounts on other VirPharm OTC products. These incentives will be phased out by the end of the first year when RELEVEN is established in the market. Freestanding display packs will also be offered to major retailers. Point-of-sale displays will be offered to office supply stores, shipping and copy centers, and convenience stores to capture customers at the checkout. Distribution via vending machines will be outsourced to a third-party vending supply company. After the initial launch through both traditional and nontraditional venues, the primary distribution strategy will be online availability. Online intensity is expected to increase beyond 50 percent once initial distribution has created brand name recognition.

Integrated Marketing Strategy   Given the utilization of the organization's sales staff and consulting firm, communications with the supply chain will be primarily through site visits and sales negotiations. The budget of $125 million dedicated to the trade marketing activities will be consumed through consulting services, travel expenses of the sales staff, and through trial packages that will be offered to a substantial number of retail locations.

Marketing Implementation

Given the specific focus and direction of the marketing plan, VirPharm will follow an initial structural approach that is somewhat centralized in nature. This choice is based on the specific strategy that has been derived, with new and somewhat unfamiliar channels, and will provide efficient and effective use of limited human and financial resources. The charge of implementing this marketing plan will fall to the Senior Vice President of the Over-the-Counter Division. This sponsor will have responsibility for the overall plan and project, and will be utilized as a "sounding board" to obtain feedback on issues and to help alleviate any discrepancies or conflicts that could jeopardize the plan and/or the organization's goals and values. Second, a key account manager from the Consumer Group will be assigned role of Implementation Leader. This person will be responsible for ensuring timelines are met, recruiting internal talent, ensuring resources are adequate, and overseeing the completion of the endeavor.

In addition to internal resources, VirPharm will also solicit the expertise of a consulting firm that is well versed on web-based selling, promotion, advertising, and procurement. Because the thrust of the marketing strategy is focused on end-user sales from the use of the Internet, this creates an unfamiliar strategy that has not been previously employed by VirPharm. Therefore, an experienced and skilled resource should be used to ensure pitfalls are avoided and to provide general direction/feedback to the effort. One of the essential deliverables that the consultant will provide will be a scientific study on the buying habits of corporate buyers and the venues and retailers that are most prevalent and preferred. A detailed listing of implementation activities is provided in Exhibit B.5.

Evaluation and Control

Output Controls

To ensure the proper implementation of VirPharm's marketing strategy for RELEVEN, procedures must be in place to evaluate outcomes relative to the plan's stated

---

EXHIBIT B.5   **TACTICAL IMPLEMENTATION ACTIVITIES**

Specific Activities	Assigned Responsibility	Required Budget $250M/100%	Estimated Completion Time
Product Activities	**Implementation Leader**	**$37.5M / 15%**	
1 Launch RELEVEN capsule, 50mg dosing, trial pack of 10 capsules.	Marketing and R&D	$12.5M	Month 1
2 Develop 100-count "Personal Relief" and 250-count "Office" packaging.	Marketing and R&D	$8M	Month 2
3 Offer product in single-dose packages containing two pills.	Marketing and R&D	$17M	Month 3
Pricing Activities		**$25M / 10%**	
1 Offer initial trial packs free for the first two months.	Wholesale Group	$25M	Month 1
Distribution Activities		**$62.5M / 25%**	
1 Obtain contracts with traditional venues such as drugstores and large retailers.	Consultant and Wholesale Group	$17M	Month 1
2 Obtain contracts with mass office supply retailers and gain initial entrance through trial packs.	Wholesale Group and Marketing	$8M	Month 1
3 Gain entrance to vending sales by outsourcing vending to a third party; develop single-dose package for vending machines.	Wholesale Group and Marketing	$17M	Month 3
4 Work with office supply retailers to provide product through their respective online ordering systems.	Consultant, Marketing, Wholesale Group, and Consumer Group	$20.5M	Month 6
IMC Activities		**$125M / $50%**	
1 Set up in-store promotions through trial packs.	Wholesale Group and Marketing	$8M	Month 1
2 Use television advertising to enhance awareness utility for the office professional, the active person, and the older adult; targeted time slots include sporting events, morning news, and afternoon daytime programming.	Wholesale Group and Marketing	$37.5M	Month 1
3 Make use of online advertising through Internet search engines and news portals, such as Google, Bing, CNN, and Bloomberg.	Consultant, Marketing, Wholesale Group, and Consumer Group	$31.25M	Month 2
4 Work with office supply retailers to advertise add-on sales through online ordering system.	Consultant, Marketing, Wholesale Group, and Consumer Group	$31.25M	Month 6
5 Sponsor major television and sporting events.	Marketing	$17M	Month 12

objectives. Recapping the objectives to be measured, VirPharm has established the following objectives for the launch of RELEVEN into the OTC market:

Objective 1   Obtain a 20 percent share of the multipurpose pain relief market within two years of launch.

This objective will be assessed via a combination of internal and third-party research reports. Specifically, VirPharm will use the results of Nielsen's point-of-sale measurement reports to track sales and market share by region and type of merchant.

Objective 2   Garner 20 percent of sales from online ordering within one year of launch.

This objective will be assessed via internal company sales records, along with support from members of the supply chain. We anticipate that 8 to 10 percent of sales will come from purely online vendors such as Drugstore.com and Amazon.com. The remaining 10 to 12 percent will come from online ordering at traditional brick-and-mortar stores such as Staples, Office Max, Office Depot, Walmart, CVS, and Walgreens.

Implementation Timeline

Exhibit B.6 outlines a three-month schedule for the launch of RELEVEN. Because a number of activities such as product artwork need to be finalized and a test run of the website conducted, and production runs and distribution of the medication need to occur, the product will not be sold until the first week of June. During this initial week of sales, most of our promotional activities will kick off simultaneously. These include television ads, online banners, and promotional giveaways associated with office supply stores.

Final production of RELEVEN will begin during the first week of May. This will provide sufficient supply to warehouses and retail shelf space prior to launch. After launch, we anticipate production will run continuously, though not in the high quantities necessary prior to launch.

This is only a three-month schedule because most of these activities revolve around the product launch. Marketing activities will continue in the future and will be adjusted based on effectiveness and product demand.

EXHIBIT B.6   THREE-MONTH IMPLEMENTATION SCHEDULE FOR RELEVEN LAUNCH

Month	May				June				July			
Week	1	2	3	4	1	2	3	4	1	2	3	4
Product Activities												
Finalize artwork, packaging, and label design	X	X	X									
Begin employee training and education on new strategy	X	X										
Produce packaging materials	X	X	X	X	X	X	X	X				
Start production runs	X	X	X	X				X		X	X	X
Distribution Activities												
Finalize distribution issues with retailers and vending services firm	X	X	X									
Send shipments to warehouses and distribution centers			X	X			X	X	X		X	X
Send shipments to retailers				X	X				X	X	X	X
Pricing Activities												
Give a 5% discount on 100-count packs to retailers selling RELEVEN online					X	X	X	X	X	X	X	X
Give a 10% discount on 250-count packs to retailers selling RELEVEN online					X	X	X	X	X	X	X	X
IMC Activities												
Finalize website design			X									
Start website testing				X								
Launch website					X							
Kick off television advertising					X	X	X	X				
Launch online advertising					X	X	X	X	X			
Commence in-store promotions at office supply centers					X	X	X	X	X	X	X	X
Offer free trial packs with online purchase (>$50) at office supply retailers					X	X	X	X				
Offer free 250-count pack with online purchase (>$200) at office supply retailers					X	X	X	X	X	X	X	X

Endnotes

Chapter 1

1. These facts are from "Best Buy: How to Break Out of Commodity Hell," *BusinessWeek Online*, March 27, 2006 (http://www.businessweek.com/magazine/content/06_13/b3977007.htm); "The 50 Most Innovative Companies," *BusinessWeek Online* (http://bwnt.businessweek.com/interactive_reports/innovative_50_2009/?chan=magazine+channel_in%3A+inside+innovation), accessed April 20, 2009; James V. Cammisa, "*Midyear Industry Review and Outlook*," Association of Travel Marketing Executives, July 28, 2005; Robert D. Hof, "*Building an Idea Factory*," *BusinessWeek Online,* October 11, 2004 (http://www.businessweek.com/magazine/content/04_41/b3903462.htm); David Koenig, "Southwest Airlines Posts 1Q Loss," *ABC News* (via AP), April 16, 2009 (http://abcnews.go.com/Business/wireStory?id=7350499), Dan Mitchell, "The State of Starbucks," *Slate: The Big Money*, March 19, 2009, (http://www.thebigmoney.com/articles/saga/2009/03/19/state-starbucks).

2. Rick Wartzman, "Out with the Dead Wood for Newspapers," *BusinessWeek Online*, March 10, 2009 (http://www.businessweek.com/managing/content/mar2009/ca20090310_251590.htm).

3. Ronald Grover, "Hollywood Is Worried as DVD Sales Slow," *BusinessWeek Online*, February 19, 2009 (http://www.businessweek.com/magazine/content/09_09/b4121056770437.htm), and Ronald Grover, "Icahn's Blockbuster Move: So Far, a Bust," *BusinessWeek Online*, April 17, 2009 (http://www.businessweek.com/technology/content/apr2009/tc20090416_957369.htm).

4. William B. Baker, "Sony Pays Record Civil Penalty to Settle COPPA Violations," *Privacy in Focus*, January 2009 (http://www.wileyrein.com/publication.cfm?publication_id=14098), and "Mrs. Fields Cookies and Hershey's Foods Assessed Largest Penalties to Date for COPPA Violations," *Computer and Internet Lawyer*, 20 (May 2003), pp. 30–31.

5. "Google, Internet Portals Targeted by Chinese Crackdown Apologize," *ABS-CBN News*, January 8, 2009 (http://www.abs-cbnnews.com/technology/01/08/09/google-internet-portals-targeted-chinese-crackdown-apologize), and Laura Sydell, "Google Unveils Censored Search Engine in China," *All Things Considered*, January 25, 2006 (http://www.npr.org/templates/story/story.php?storyId=5172204).

6. Wenran Jiang, "Watchful and Wary: China's Hu Visits Bush," *BusinessWeek Online*, April 13, 2006 (http://www.businessweek.com/globalbiz/content/apr2006/gb20060413_186631.htm).

7. Bruce Einhorn, "Microsoft Has Hope in Asian Piracy Fight," *BusinessWeek Online*, February 27, 2009 (http://www.businessweek.com/globalbiz/content/feb2009/gb20090227_551561.htm).

8. Eric Chabrow, "Retailers Agree to Online Tax," *InformationWeek*, February 10, 2003, 16.

9. "Internet Sales Tax Fairness," *New Rules Project* (http://www.newrules.org/retail/node/2196); accessed April 19, 2009.

10. American Marketing Association (http://www.marketingpower.com).

11. Ibid.

12. Jeffrey F. Rayport and Bernard J. Jaworski, *e-Commerce* (Boston: McGraw-Hill/Irwin, 2001), p. 3.

13. Mohanbir Sawhney, "Making New Markets," *Business 2.0*, May 1999, pp. 116–121.

14. http://www.amazon.com.

15. This list is adapted from Philip Kotler, *A Framework for Marketing Management*, 2nd ed. (Upper Saddle River, NJ: Prentice Hall, 2003), pp. 4–5.

16. http://www.americanlegacy.org.

17. Alabama Development Office, "Teamwork Drives Hyundai to Alabama!" *Developing Alabama*, Spring 2002.

18. These facts are from Ellen Byron, "Mr. Clean Takes Car-Wash Gig," *Wall Street Journal Online*, February 5, 2009 (http://online.wsj.com/article/SB123379252641549893.html); Andria Cheng, "Retailers Try New Tricks Amid Global Downturn," *MarketWatch*, March 23, 2009 (http://www.marketwatch.com/news/story/wal-marts-great-value-signals-coming/story.aspx?guid={81136A47-8D95-4FB9-92A4-F98A8F7B1E6A}); Reena Jana, "P&G's Trickle-Up Success: Sweet as Honey," *BusinessWeek Online*, March 31, 2009 (http://www.businessweek.com/innovate/content/mar2009/id20090331_127029.htm?chan=innovation_innovation+%2B+design_innovation+strategy); Tom Lowry, "NBC and New Corp.'s Hulu Is Off to a Strong Start," *BusinessWeek Online*, September 25, 2008 (http://www.businessweek.com/magazine/content/08_40/b4102052685561.htm); and Jeneanne Rae, "Innovative Ways to Grow During the Downturn," *BusinessWeek Online*, April 15, 2009 (http://www.businessweek.com/innovate/content/apr2009/id20090415_238678.htm).

19. These facts are from http://www.joinred.com, accessed April 20, 2009.

20. The Society of Competitive Intelligence Professionals (http://www.scip.org).

21. These facts are from Arik Hesseldahl, "Mac vs. PC: What you Don't Get for $699," *BusinessWeek Online*, April 15, 2009 (http://www.businessweek.com/technology/content/apr2009/tc20090415_602968.htm?chan=rss_topStories_ssi_5).

22. Hampton Inn's Satisfaction Guarantee (http://hamptoninn.hilton.com/en/hp/brand/about.jhtml), accessed April 20, 2009.

23. These facts are from Alex Halperin, "No Space for MySpace," *BusinessWeek Online*, May 12, 2006 (http://www.businessweek.com/technology/content/may2006/tc20060512_299340.htm); Jesse Hempel, "The MySpace Generation," *BusinessWeek*, December 12, 2005; Ryan Nakashima, "MySpace Hopes to Turn Free Songs into Needed Cash," *BusinessWeek Online*, April 19, 2009 (http://www.businessweek.com/ap/tech/D97LHCMG0.htm); Jeffrey F. Rayport, "Social Networks Are the New Web Portals," *BusinessWeek Online*, January 21, 2009 (http://www.businessweek.com/technology/content/jan2009/tc20090121_557202.htm); Steve Rosenbush and Timothy Mullaney, "Social Networking's Gold Rush," *BusinessWeek Online*, April 19, 2006 (http://www.businessweek.com/technology/content/apr2006/tc20060419_514268.htm); "From MySpace to Safer Space?" *BusinessWeek Online*, April 11, 2006 (http://www.businessweek.com/technology/content/apr2006/tc20060411_341338.htm).

24. Michael Grigsby, "Getting Personal," *Marketing Research*, 14 (Fall 2002), pp. 18–22.

25. Grant Gross, "RFID and Privacy: Debate Heating Up in Washington," *InfoWorld* (IDG News Service), May 28, 2004 (http://www.infoworld.com/article/04/05/28/HNrfidprivacy_1.html).

26. These facts are from Mark Kassof & Company, "McDonald's Arch McFlop," *Research Insights: Lessons from Marketing Flops*, Summer 1997.

27. These facts are from the AFLAC corporate website (http://www.aflac.com) and "The 100 Best Companies to Work For 2009," *Fortune* (http://money.cnn.com/magazines/fortune/bestcompanies/2009/), accessed April 20, 2009.

28. These facts are from Parija Bhatnagar, "Wal-Mart's Challenge in China," CNNMoney.com, January 12, 2006 (http://money.cnn.com/2006/01/12/news/companies/walmart_china/index.htm) and Kerry Capell, "Tesco: 'Wal-Mart's Worst Nightmare,'" *BusinessWeek Online*, December 28, 2008 (http://www.businessweek.com/globalbiz/content/dec2008/gb20081229_497909.htm).

Chapter 2

1. These facts are from Frederik Balfour, "China's Geely Eyes GM's Saab, Ford's Volvo," *BusinessWeek Online*, May 7, 2009 (http://www.businessweek.com/globalbiz/content/may2009/gb2009057_

609995.htm); David Kiley, "Commentary: Mulally Led Ford Seems Like a Good Risk for Taxpayers," *BusinessWeek Online*, March 5, 2009 (http://www.businessweek.com/autos/autobeat/archives/2009/03/commentary_mula.html); Joann Muller, "Ford: Irrational Exuberance," *Forbes Online*, April 23, 2009 (http://www.forbes.com/2009/04/22/ford-alan-mulally-earnings-business-autos-ford.html); Alex Taylor, "Ford Stands Alone," *Fortune Online*, October 22, 2008 (http://money.cnn.com/2008/10/22/news/companies/taylor_ford.fortune/index.htm); and Alex Taylor, "Fixing up Ford," *Fortune Online*, May 12, 2009 (http://money.cnn.com/2009/05/11/news/companies/mulally_ford.fortune/index.htm).

2. The authors thank Dr. Elaine S. Potoker, Maine Maritime Academy, for her insight and suggestions on the concept of strategic planning as a funnel.

3. The Texas Instruments mission and vision statements are from http://www.ti.com/corp/docs/company/factsheet.shtml.

4. The Southwest Airlines mission statement is from http://www.southwest.com/about_swa/mission.html.

5. The Ben & Jerry's mission statement is from http://www.benjerry.com/activism/mission-statement/.

6. "Johnson & Johnson Reincarnates a Brand," *Sales and Marketing Management*, January 16, 1984, p. 63; and Elyse Tanouye, "Johnson & Johnson Stays Fit by Shuffling Its Mix of Businesses," *The Wall Street Journal*, December 22, 1992, pp. A1, A4.

7. These facts are taken from "Turning Compassion into Action—Donor Dollars at Work: Hurricanes Katrina, Rita and Wilma," http://www.redcross.org/news/ds/hurricanes/support05/report.html.

8. This information is from http://www.sony.com.

9. This information is from http://www.3m.com.

10. These facts are from Kevin Allison, "More Than Price behind Dell's Fall," *Financial Times* (London: UK), May 10, 2006, 30; Louise Lee, "Dell: Burned by a Fire Sale," *BusinessWeek Online*, May 9, 2006 (http://www.businessweek.com/technology/content/may2006/tc20060509_664617.htm); Louise Lee, "Dell Goes High-end and Hip,"

BusinessWeek Online, March 23, 2006 (http://www.businessweek.com/technology/content/mar2006/tc20060323_034268.htm); Louise Lee, "From Servers to Service: Dell's Makeover," *BusinessWeek Online*, May 19, 2006 (http://www.businessweek.com/technology/content/may2006/tc20060519_475997.htm); Aaron Ricadela, "Has Dell's Comeback Hit a Roadblock?" *BusinessWeek Online*, August 29, 2008 (http://www.businessweek.com/technology/content/aug2008/tc20080828_973195.htm); and Aaron Ricadela, "Will This Bold Shakeup Save Dell?" *BusinessWeek Online*, January 1, 2009 (http://www.businessweek.com/technology/content/dec2008/tc20081231_749138.htm).

11. Howard Sutton, *The Marketing Plan in the 1990s* (New York: The Conference Board, Inc., 1990).

12. Ibid., p. 9.

13. Cindy Claycomb, Richard Germain, and Cornelia Droge, "The Effects of Formal Strategic Marketing Planning on the Industrial Firm's Configuration, Structure, Exchange Patterns, and Performance," *Industrial Marketing Management*, 29 (May 2000), pp. 219–234.

14. "Marketing Plan Help," *ABA Banking Journal*, 95 (October 2003), p. 18.

15. Sutton, *The Marketing Plan in the 1990s*, p. 16.

16. Ibid., p. 17.

17. These facts are from "Amazon Unwraps the New Kindle," *BusinessWeek Online*, February 9, 2009 (http://www.businessweek.com/bwdaily/dnflash/content/feb2009/db2009029_964407.htm); Philip Elmer-DeWitt, "Amazon re-Kindles the iPhone," *Fortune Online*, May 11, 2009 (http://apple20.blogs.fortune.cnn.com/2009/05/11/amazon-re-kindles-the-iphone/); Douglass MacMillan, "Amazon's Kindle Is Off to College," *BusinessWeek Online*, May 4, 2009 (http://www.businessweek.com/technology/content/may2009/tc2009054_280910.htm); and Jeffrey M. O'Brien, "Amazon's Next Revolution," *Fortune Online*, May 26, 2009 (http://money.cnn.com/2009/05/26/technology/obrien_kindle.fortune/index.htm?postversion=2009052605).

18. Bernard J. Jaworski and Ajay K. Kohli, "Market Orientation: Antecedents and Consequences," *Journal of Marketing*, 57 (July 1993), pp. 53–70.

19. Ibid; and Stanley F. Slater and John C. Narver, "Market Orientation and the Learning Organization," *Journal of Marketing*, 59 (July 1995), pp. 63–74.

20. These facts are from the "Nissan Altima Hybrid: A Better Toyota," The Car Family Blog, July 15, 2008 (http://carfamily.wordpress.com/2008/07/15/nissan-altima-hybrid-a-better-toyota/); and "GM Seeks to Replace Vibe at Toyota Joint Venture," The CarTech Blog, May 6, 2009 (http://reviews.cnet.com/8301-13746_7-10232762-48.html).

21. The material in this section is adapted from Robert S. Kaplan and David P. Norton, *The Strategy-Focused Organization* (Boston, MA: Harvard Business School Press, 2001).

22. Descriptions of each perspective are adapted from "What Is the Balanced Scorecard?" The Balanced Scorecard Institute (http://www.balancedscorecard.org/basics/bsc1.html).

23. Kaplan and Norton, *The Strategy-Focused Organization*, pp. 8–17.

Chapter 3

1. These facts are from Stuart Elliot, "Trumpeting a Move to Put the Sun in Sun Chips," *New York Times*, March 27, 2008 (http://www.nytimes.com/2008/03/27/business/media/27adco.html?_r=2&scp=2&sq=&st=nyt&oref=slogin), accessed September 8, 2009; Melissa Lee, "Market for Wind Power Picks Up Speed," *MSNBC.com*, March 31, 2006 (http://today.msnbc.msn.com/id/12053296/ns/business-cnbc_tv/), accessed September 10, 2009; "Whole Foods Market Announces Alternative Energy Investment, Energy Savings with New Store Designs, Existing Store Retrofits," Grocery Retail Online (http://www.groceryretailonline.com/article.mvc/Whole-Foods-Market-Announces-Alternative-0001), accessed September 8, 2009; and Ryan H. Wiser, *Wind Power Development in the United States: Current Progress, Future Trends* (Berkeley, CA: Lawrence Berkeley National Laboratory, 2009).

2. "WHO Experts Raise Antiquated Nutrition Standards," Doctors Without Borders, October 10, 2007 (http://doctorswithoutborders.org/news/issue.cfm?id=2396), accessed September 8, 2009; and "Plumpy'nut in the Field," Nutriset (http://www.nutriset.fr/index.php?option=com_content&task=view&id=41&Itemid=33), accessed September 8, 2009.

3. Nike Inc. Responsibility (http://www.nikebiz.com/responsibility), accessed September 8, 2009.

4. Archie Carroll, "The Pyramid of Corporate Social Responsibility: Toward the Moral Management of Organizational Stakeholders," *Business Horizons*, 34 (July/August 1991), p. 42.

5. "Feds Eye Book Scans by Google," *The New York Post*, July 3, 2009 (http://www.nypost.com/seven/07032009/business/feds_eye_book_scans_by_google_177463.htm).

6. "Ethics and Business Conduct: How the Ethics Process Works at Lockheed Martin" (http://www.lockheedmartin.com/data/assets/corporate/documents/ethics/HowEthicsProcessWorks.pdf), accessed September 8, 2009.

7. These facts are from "Walmart Steps Up Efforts to Help Americans Manage Their Finances with $3 Rollback Price on Key Money Service," Walmart Press Release, February 18, 2009 (http://walmartstores.com/FactsNews/NewsRoom/8982.aspx); and "Walmart Foundation Teams Up with United Way and One Economy to Provide Free Tax Preparation and Filing Services," Walmart Press Release, February 10, 2009 (http://walmartstores.com/FactsNews/NewsRoom/8962.aspx).

8. "World Wildlife Fund, Coca-Cola Put Partnership in Action through Internships with University of Michigan's Erb Institute," World Wildlife Fund, April 10, 2008 (http://www.worldwildlife.org/who/media/press/2008/WWFPresitem8115.html).

9. These facts are from Salynn Boyles, "Kids' Cereals: Some are 50% Sugar," WebMD, October 1, 2008 (http://www.webmd.com/food-recipes/news/

20081001/kids-cereals-some-are-50-percent-sugar), accessed July 8, 2009; and Jennifer Mariani and Matt Schottmiller, "2009 Marketing and the Cereal Industry Case," The University of New Mexico.

10. These facts are from "Cohn & Wolf Financial Confidence Survey," Cohn & Wolf, January 20, 2009 (http://www.cohnwolfe.com/en/news/ new-us-consumer-survey-shows-high-distrust-financial-services-companies), accessed August 7, 2009; Sarah Marsh, "Economic Crisis Boosts Distrust of Business: Watchdog," *Reuters*, June 3, 2009 (http://www.reuters.com/article/ousiv/ idUSTRE5521LX20090603), accessed September 8, 2009; and "New U.S. Consumer Survey Shows High Distrust of Financial Services Companies," *Business Wire,* January 20, 2009 (http:// findarticles.com/p/articles/mi_m0EIN/is_2009_ Jan_20/ai_n31202849), accessed May 27, 2009.

11. Andrew Edgecliffe-Johnson, "Davos Confronted by Peak of Distrust," *Financial Times*, January 26, 2009 (http://www.ft.com/cms/s/0/91637254-ebc9-11dd-8838-0000779fd2ac.html), accessed July 20, 2009.

12. These facts are from Avon Foundation Website, http://www.avoncompany.com/women, accessed September 8, 2009; and "50 Most Powerful Women in Business," *Fortune,* October 13, 2008 (http://money.cnn.com/magazines/fortune/mostpo-werfulwomen/2008/full_list/index.html), accessed August 7, 2009.

13. "Worth Noting," *Business Ethics*, January/February 1999, p. 5.

14. Barry Newman, "An Ad Professor Huffs Against Puffs, But It's a Quixotic Enterprise," *The Wall Street Journal*, January 24, 2003, p. A1.

15. Benjamin Ikuta and Evan Moses, "Identifying, Avoiding and Remedying Employee Theft," *Lawdragon* (http://www.lawdragon.com/index.php/ newdragon/fullstory/identifying_avoiding_and_ remedying_employee_theft), accessed September 8, 2009.

16. These facts are from William T. Neese, Linda Ferrell, and O. C. Ferrell (2005), "An Analysis of Federal Mail and Wire Fraud Cases Related to Marketing," *Journal of Business Research*, pp. S8, 910–918; and "Snapshot," *USA Today*, October 3, 2002.

17. "FTC Order Bars Firm from Failing to Provide Timely Rebates," Federal Trade Commission, March 11, 2009 (http://www.ftc.gov/opa/2009/03/ ats.shtm), accessed August 7, 2009.

18. "National Restaurant Company Settles FTC Charges for Deceptive Gift Card Sales," Federal Trade Commission, April 3, 2007 (http://www .ftc.gov/opa/2007/04/darden.shtm), accessed August 7, 2009.

19. Carl Bialik, "In Ads, 1 Out of 5 Stats Is Bogus," *The Wall Street Journal*, March 11, 2009 (http://online .wsj.com/article/SB123672828150888771.html).

20. James Heckman, "Puffery Claims No Longer So Easy to Make," *Marketing News*, February 14, 2000, p. 6.

21. Traci Watson, "Eco-Friendly Claims Go Unchecked," *USA Today*, June 22, 2009, p. A1.

22. Linda Ferrell and O. C. Ferrell, *Ethical Business* (London: Dorling Kindersley Limited, 2009), pp. 38–39.

23. "FTC Releases List of Top Consumer Fraud Complaints in 2008," *Federal Trade Commission*, February 26, 2009 (http://www.ftc.gov/opa/2009/ 02/2008cmpts.shtm), accessed July 23, 2009.

24. "BBB Structure," *Better Business Bureau* (http:// www.bbb.org/us/BBB-Structure), accessed September 9, 2009.

25. These facts are from Greg Barr, "Stanford Files Appeal in Bond Decision," *Houston Business Journal,* July 10, 2009 (http://www.bizjournals.com/ houston/stories/2009/07/06/daily52.html), accessed July 10, 2009; Tim Elfrink, "The Rise and Fall of the Stanford Financial Group," *Houston Press*, April 9, 2009 (http://www.houstonpress. com/content/printVersion/1173931), accessed April 29, 2009; and Steve Stecklow, "Hard Sell Drove Stanford's Rise and Fall," *The Wall Street Journal*, April 3, 2009 (http://online.wsj.com/ article/SB123871796188984821.html), accessed April 29, 2009.

26. These facts are from Bob Curley, "FTC Supports Self-Regulation of Alcohol Industry Ads," *Join Together*, July 11, 2008 (http://www.jointogether.org/news/features/2008/ftc-supports-self-regulation.html), accessed August 7, 2009; and John Hechinger, "FTC Criticizes College-Themed Cans in Anheuser-Busch Marketing Efforts," *The Wall Street Journal*, August 25, 2009, pp. B1, B4.

27. Amie Vaccarro, "The White Dog Café: A Study of Social Business and Mission-Aligned Exit," Greenbiz.com, April 24, 2009 (http://www.greenbiz.com/blog/2009/04/24/white-dog-café), accessed July 9, 2009.

28. 2008–2009 Integrity Survey, KPMG LLP (http://www.kpmg.com/SiteCollectionDocuments/Integrity-Survey-2008-2009.pdf), p. 14, accessed September 8, 2009.

29. "Ethics Is the Cornerstone of TI," Texas Instruments Values and Ethics Statement (http://www.ti.com/corp/docs/csr/corpgov/statement.shtml), accessed September 9, 2009. Courtesy of Texas Instruments, Inc.

30. The TI Ethics Quick Test, http://www.ti.com/corp/docs/company/citizen/ethics/quicktest.shtml .Courtesy of Texas Instruments, Inc.

31. Debbie Thorne McAlister, O. C. Ferrell, and Linda Ferrell, *Business and Society: A Strategic Approach to Social Responsibility*, 3rd ed. (Mason, OH: Cengage, 2008).

32. Thomas A. Stewart, Ann Harrington, and Maura Griffin Sol, "America's Most Admired Companies: Why Leadership Matters," *Fortune*, March 3, 1998, pp. 70–71.

33. "LRN Ethics Study: Employee Engagement," LRN, 2007 (http://www.lrn.com/docs/lrn_ethics_study_employee_engagement.pdf), accessed August 7, 2009.

34. Diane E. Kirrane, "Managing Values: A Systematic Approach to Business Ethics," *Training and Development Journal*, 1 (November 1990), pp. 53–60.

35. O. C. Ferrell, Isabelle Maignan, and Terry Loe, "Corporate Ethics + Citizenship = Profits," *The Bottom Line: Good Ethics Is Good Business* (Tampa, FL: University of Tampa, Center for Ethics, 1997).

36. Terry Loe, "The Role of Ethical Climate in Developing Trust, Market Orientation, and Commitment to Quality," unpublished dissertation, University of Memphis, 1996.

37. Sarah Needleman, "Burger Chain's Health-Care Recipe," *The Wall Street Journal*, August 31, 2009 (http://online.wsj.com/article/SB125149100886467705.html), accessed September 3, 2009.

38. Isabelle Maignan and O. C. Ferrell, "Corporate Social Responsibility: Toward a Marketing Conceptualization," *Journal of the Academy of Marketing Science*, 32 (January, 2004), pp. 3–19.

39. "2009 World's Most Ethical Companies," Ethisphere (http://ethisphere.com/wme2009), accessed September 8, 2009.

40. These facts are from "Gap Inc. Partners on New 'Traceability' Program," Inside Gap Inc., May 2009 (http://www.gapinc.com/public/documents/GapWeb_Trace.pdf), accessed August 7, 2009; "2005–2006 Social Responsibility Report: What is a Company's Role in Society?" Gap Inc. (http://www.gapinc.com/public/documents/CSR_Report_05_06.pdf), accessed July 24, 2009; Factory Working Conditions, Gap. Inc. (http://www.gapinc.com/GapIncSubSites/csr/Goals/SupplyChain/SC_Factory_Working_Conditions.shtml), accessed August 7, 2009; and Supply Chain, Gap, Inc. (http://www.gapinc.com/GapIncSubSites/csr/Goals/SupplyChain/SC_Overview.shtml), accessed August 7, 2009.

41. Christine Moorman, Gerald Zaltman, and Rohit Deshpande, "The Relationship between Providers and Users of Market Research: The Dynamics of Trust within and between Organizations," *Journal of Marketing Research*, 29 (August 1993), pp. 314–328.

42. These facts are from "Cone Cause Evolution Study, 2007," Cause Marketing Forum, July 9, 2007 (http://www.causemarketingforum.com/page.asp?ID=583), accessed July 24, 2009; and Tim Wilson,

"Palm Oil Boycott Will Hurt Impoverished Farmers," ABC News, August 5, 2009 (http://www.abc.net.au/news/stories/2009/08/05/2646364.htm), accessed September 3, 2009.

43. "BBMG Study: Three-Fourths of U.S. Consumers Reward, Punish Brands Based on Social and Environmental Practices," CSR Wire, June 2, 2009 (http://www.csrwire.com/press/press_release/27052-BBMG-Study-Three-Fourths-of-U-S-Consumers-Reward-Punish-Brands-Based-on-Social-and-Environmental-Practices), accessed July 24, 2009.

44. These facts are from "Krispy Kreme Problems," *The Coloradoan*. August 11, 2005, D7; Carl Gutierrez, "Sour First Quarter for Krispy Kreme," *Forbes*, June 4, 2007 (http://www.forbes.com/2007/06/04/krispy-kreme-quarter-markets-equity-cx_cg_0604markets04.html), accessed July 23, 2009; and "Investor Relations," Krispy Kreme, July 23, 2009 (http://investor.krispykreme.com/releases.cfm?Year=&ReleasesType=&PageNum=4), accessed July 23, 2009.

45. "Reputations of the [60] Most Visible Companies," Harris Interactive (http://www.harrisinteractive.com/services/pubs/HI_BSC_REPORT_Annual RQ2008_SummaryReport.pdf), accessed September 3, 2009.

Chapter 4

1. These facts are from Parija Bhatnagar, "Home Depot Looking to Age Well," *CNNMoney*, January 17, 2006 (http://money.cnn.com/2006/01/17/news/companies/home_depot/index.htm); Alicia Clegg, "Mining the Golden Years," *BusinessWeek Online*, May 4, 2006 (http://www.businessweek.com/print/innovate/content/may2006/id20060504_612679.htm); Karen E. Klein, "Reaching Out to an Older Crowd," *BusinessWeek Online*, April 3, 2006 (http://www.businessweek.com/print/smallbiz/content/apr2006/sb20060403_549646.htm); Louise Lee, "Love Those Boomers," *BusinessWeek*, October 25, 2005; Janet Novak, "The Biggest Market Losers:

The Boomers," *Forbes Online*, May 14, 2009 (http://www.forbes.com/2009/05/14/stock-market-losses-survey-personal-finance-retirement-worried-baby-boomers.html); David Serchuk, "Boomers Leave the Table," *Forbes Online*, November 21, 2008 (http://www.forbes.com/2008/11/20/intelligent-investing-baby-boomer-retirement-Nov20-panel.html); and Ed Wallace, "The Boomers Stop Buying," *BusinessWeek Online*, February 26, 2009 (http://www.businessweek.com/lifestyle/content/feb2009/bw20090226_384582.htm).

2. These facts are from "MGA Asks Appeals Court to Halt Transfer of Bratz," *BusinessWeek Online*, May 27, 2009 (http://www.businessweek.com/ap/financialnews/D98ET0AG3.htm).

3. These facts are from Katrina Brooker, "The Pepsi Machine," *Fortune*, February 6, 2006, pp. 68–72.

4. Burt Helm, "Blowing Up Pepsi," *BusinessWeek Online*, April 23, 2009 (http://www.businessweek.com/magazine/content/09_17/b4128032006687.htm).

5. These facts are from Pamela Babcock, "America's Newest Export: White Collar Jobs," *HR Magazine* 49(4), April 2004; Nanette Byrnes, "The Jobs That Employers Can't Fill," *BusinessWeek Online*, May 29, 2009 (http://www.businessweek.com/careers/managementiq/archives/2009/05/the_jobs_that_e.html); and Robert J. Grossman, "The Truth About the Coming Labor Shortage," *HR Magazine*, 50(3), March 2005.

6. These facts are from Aaron Smith, "Time Warner to Split Off AOL," *CNN Money*, May 28, 2009 (http://money.cnn.com/2009/05/28/technology/timewarner_aol/index.htm).

7. These facts are from Shaun Rein, "China's Consumers Are Still Spending," *BusinessWeek Online*, March 25, 2009 (http://www.businessweek.com/globalbiz/content/mar2009/gb20090325_370224.htm).

8. These facts are from Ben Elgin and Brian Grow, "E-Waste: The Dirty Secret of Recycling Electronics," *BusinessWeek Online*, October 15, 2008

(http://www.businessweek.com/magazine/content/ 08_43/b4105000160974.htm); Olga Kharif, "E-Waste: Whose Problem Is It?" *BusinessWeek Online*, March 17, 2008 (http://www.businessweek .com/technology/content/mar2008/tc20080317_ 718350.htm); and Jessica Mintz, "Dell Bans E-Waste Export to Developing Countries," *BusinessWeek Online*, May 12, 2009 (http://www .businessweek.com/ap/tech/D9850TS80.htm).

9. Mary Ellen Pinkham, "20 Surprising Uses for Vinegar," http://www.ivillage.com/home/experts/ clean/articles/0258151_258168,00.html.

10. International Reciprocal Trade Association, "2004 Global Reciprocal Trade Statistics," http:// www.irta.com.

11. These facts are from "March of the Pinots" *BusinessWeek Online*, April 24, 2006 (http:// www.businessweek.com/magazine/content/06_17/ b3981101.htm); Mike Steinberger, "Not Such a G'Day," Slate, April 8, 2009 (http://www.slate.com/ id/2215153/); and W. Chan Kim and Renee Mauborgne, *Blue Ocean Strategy* (Boston, MA: Harvard Business School Press, 2005), 24–35.

12. These facts are from Aaron Smith, "'Ask Your Doctor' Ads in FDA Crosshairs," *CNNMoney*, October 31, 2005 (http://money.cnn.com/2005/ 10/31/news/fortune500/dtc/index.htm); and Arlene Weintraub, "More Frequent Dose of Dollars for Drug Ads," *BusinessWeek Online*, August 15, 2007 (http://www.businessweek.com/technol-ogy/content/aug2007/tc20070815_954771 .htm).

13. These facts are from Todd Wasserman and Kenneth Hein, "Gatorade Changes Up Its Game," *Brandweek*, December 29, 2008 (http://www. brandweek.com/bw/content_display/esearch/ e3i2f608e22d68972d48fe7df75c09b5a6a).

14. This definition of competitive intelligence is adapted from The Society of Competitive Intelligence Professionals, http://www.scip.org/ci/.

15. Ibid.

16. This information is from http:// www.inflationdata.com.

17. These facts are from Ken Jarboe, "Measuring Innovation and Intangibles," The *Intangible Economy*, Athena Alliance weblog, January 16, 2009 (http://www.athenaalliance.org/weblog/archives/ 2009/01/measuring_innovation_and_intangibles.html); Michael Mandel, "Why the Economy is a Lot Stronger Than You Think," *BusinessWeek Online*, February 13, 2006 (http://www.businessweek.com/magazine/content/06_07/ b3971001.htm); and Michael Mandel, "GDP: What's Counted, What's Not," *BusinessWeek Online*, February 13, 2006 (http://www.businessweek.com/magazine/content/06_07/ b3971010.htm).

18. These facts are from "Court to Review Anti-Fraud Law," *BusinessWeek Online*, May 18, 2009 (http:// www.businessweek.com/ap/financialnews/ D988NL482.htm); The Sarbanes-Oxley Act Community Forum (http://www.sarbanes-oxley-forum.com/); and Amey Stone, "SOX: Not So Bad After All?" *BusinessWeek Online*, August 1, 2005 (http://www.businessweek.com/bwdaily/dnflash/ aug2005/nf2005081_7739_db016.htm).

19. Kerry Capell, "Now, Will Europe Swallow Frankenfoods?" *BusinessWeek Online*, February 8, 2006 (http://www.businessweek.com/bwdaily/dnflash/ feb2006/nf2006028_3575_db039.htm); Germany Bans Monsanto's GMO Corn," *BusinessWeek Online*, April 16, 2009 (http://www.businessweek.com/ globalbiz/content/apr2009/ gb20090416_667169.htm); and "Greece Extends Ban on U.S. Biotech Corn Seeds," *BusinessWeek Online*, May 27, 2009 (http://www.businessweek.com/ap/financialnews/D98EL0TG2.htm).

20. These facts are from RFID Journal, http:// www.rfidjournal.com.

21. Administration on Aging Website, http:// www.aoa.gov.

22. "Hispanics Drive Minority Population Growth in the U.S.," *Hispanic Business*, May 14, 2009 (http:// www.hispanicbusiness.com/news/2009/5/14/ hispanics_drive_minority_population_growth_in. htm); *Minority Population Growth*: 1995 to 2050,

U.S. Department of Commerce, Minority Business Development Agency, September 1999, 1–3; and "More Diversity, Slower Growth," U.S. Census Bureau Press Release, March 18, 2004.

23. Ronald Grover, "U.S. Marketers Say Hola! to Hispanic Consumers," *BusinessWeek Online*, April 9, 2009 (http://www.businessweek.com/magazine/content/09_16/b4127076302996.htm).

24. Chip Walker and Elissa Moses, "The Age of Self-Navigation," *American Demographics*, September 1996.

25. The organizational descriptions of corporate affairs are taken from websites of these companies: Blue-Scope Steel (http://www.bluescopesteel.com/go/utilities-menu/contact-us/corporate-affairs/corporate-affairs-external-relations); Microsoft (http://members.microsoft.com/careers/careerpath/legal/default.mspx); Pfizer (http://www.pfizer.com/careers/working_for/corporate_functions.jsp); and Altria Group, Inc. (http://www.altria.com/responsibility/4_4_stakeholderengagement.asp).

Chapter 5

1. These facts are from Reena Jana, "Is Innovation Too Costly in Hard Times?" *BusinessWeek Online*, April 9, 2009 (http://www.businessweek.com/magazine/content/09_16/b4127046252968.htm?chan=magazine+channel_in%3A+inside+innovation); Matthew Maier, "Chewable Innovation," *Business 2.0*, April 20, 2006 (http://money.cnn.com/magazines/business2/business2_archive/2006/05/01/8375918/index.htm); and "The 50 Most Innovative Companies," *BusinessWeek Online*, April 9, 2009 (http://bwnt.businessweek.com/interactive_reports/innovative_50_2009/?chan=magazine+channel_in%3A+inside+innovation).

2. Nigel Piercy, *Market-Led Strategic Change* (Oxford, UK: Butterworth-Heineman Ltd., 1992), p. 257.

3. These facts are from Jena McGregor, "The World's Most Innovative Companies," *BusinessWeek*, April 24, 2006.

4. This list and most of this section are based on E. K. Valentin, "SWOT Analysis from a Resource-Based View," *Journal of Marketing Theory and Practice* 9 (Spring 2001), pp. 54–59.

5. Shelby D. Hunt, *A General Theory of Competition* (Thousand Oaks, CA: Sage Publications, 2000), pp. 67–68.

6. These facts are from the Bureau of Transportation Statistics, Airline Domestic Unit Costs (Cents per Mile), Tables 10 and 11, 4th Quarter 2008 (http://www.bts.gov/press_releases/2009/bts022_09/pdf/bts022_09.pdf); and "Airline Industry to Lose $4.7B in 2009," *CNNMoney*, March 24, 2009 (http://money.cnn.com/2009/03/24/news/international/airline_outlook_2009.reut/index.htm).

7. These facts are from Cora Daniels, "Mr. Coffee: The Man Behind the $4.75 Frappuccino Makes the 500," *Fortune*, April 14, 2003, pp. 139–140; and Starbucks Company Fact Sheet (http://www.starbucks.com/aboutus/Company_Factsheet.pdf).

8. George Stalk, Philip Evans, and Lawrence E. Shulman, "Competing on Capabilities: The New Rules of Corporate Strategy," *Harvard Business Review*, 70 (March-April 1992), pp. 57–69.

9. This information is based on editorial reviews of MP3 players at CNET.com, (http://reviews.cnet.com/mp3-player-buying-guide), accessed June 4, 2009.

10. Michael Treacy and Fred Wiersema, *The Discipline of Market Leaders* (Reading, MA: Addison-Wesley, 1995).

11. These facts are from Department Store Rankings, American Customer Satisfaction Index (http://www.theacsi.org/index.php?option=com_content&task=view&id=147&Itemid=155&i=Department+%26+Discount+Stores), accessed June 4, 2009; "Nordstrom Scores for Service," *Fortune, November* 15, 2005 (http://money.cnn.com/2005/11/15/news/fortune500/customer_service/index.htm); and the Nordstrom website (http://www.nordstrom.com).

12. These facts are from Michael Arndt, "3M's Seven Pillars of Innovation," *BusinessWeek Online*, May 10, 2006 (http://www.businessweek.com/innovate/content/may2006/id20060510_682823.htm); Charlotte Li, "3M: Years of Commitment to Green Business," *BusinessWeek Online*, May 14, 2009 (http://www.businessweek.com/magazine/content/09_21/b4132043810940.htm); and "Who We Are," 3M Company website (http://solutions.3m.com/wps/portal/3M/en_US/our/company/information/about-us/).

13. This material is based on Cornelis A. De Kluyver, *Strategic Thinking: An Executive Perspective* (Upper Saddle River, NJ: Prentice Hall, 2000), pp. 53–56; Philip Kotler, *A Framework for Marketing Management*, 2nd ed. (Upper Saddle River, NJ: Prentice Hall, 2003), p. 67; and Arthur A. Thompson, Jr. and A. J. Strickland, III, *Strategic Management: Formulation, Implementation, and Control*, 6th ed. (Boston: McGraw-Hill, 1997).

14. These facts are from Michael Felberbaum, "Altria Cites Smokeless Items as Key for Business," *BusinessWeek Online*, May 19, 2009 (http://www.businessweek.com/ap/financialnews/D989FBKG0.htm); and Altria Group's website (http://www.altria.com/about_altria/1_2_companiesandbrands.asp).

15. These facts are from David Goldman, "GM to Sell Saturn to Penske," *BusinessWeek Online*, June 5, 2009 (http://money.cnn.com/2009/06/05/news/companies/saturn_penske/index.htm).

16. These facts are from Alyssa Abkowitz, "Big Pharma's New Landscape," *CNNMoney*, March 12, 2009 (http://money.cnn.com/2009/03/11/news/companies/pharma.fortune/index.htm); Amy Barrett, "Why Merck Remains Unsettled," *BusinessWeek Online*, April 12, 2006 (http://www.businessweek.com/technology/content/apr2006/tc20060412_775867.htm); and Arlene Weintraub, "What Merck Gains by Settling," *BusinessWeek Online*, November 9, 2007 (http://www.businessweek.com/technology/content/nov2007/tc2007119_133486.htm).

17. The material in this section is adapted from W. Chan Kim and Renee Mauborgne, *Blue Ocean Strategy* (Boston, MA: Harvard Business School Press, 2005).

18. The strategy canvas for Southwest Airlines is from Kim and Mauborgne, *Blue Ocean Strategy*, p. 38.

19. Ibid, p. 39.

20. This information is from W. Chan Kim and Renee Mauborgne, *Blue Ocean Strategy* (Boston, MA: Harvard Business School Press, 2005), pp. 29–37.

21. See http://www.sears.com/shc/s/nb_10153_12605_NB_CSpricematch.

22. These facts are from the Home Depot Corporate Financial Overview, http://corporate.homedepot.com/en_US/Corporate/Public_Relations/Online_Press_Kit/Docs/Corp_Financial_Overview.pdf.

Chapter 6

1. These facts are from Stephen Baker, "What Data Crunchers Did for Obama," *BusinessWeek Online*, January 23, 2009 (http://www.businessweek.com/technology/content/jan2009/tc20090123_026100.htm); Stephen Baker, "Data Mining Moves to Human Resources," *BusinessWeek Online*, March 12, 2009 (http://www.businessweek.com/magazine/content/09_12/b4124046224092.htm); Tim Ferguson, "How Europeans Are Using Data Mining," *BusinessWeek Online*, May 17, 2009 (http://www.businessweek.com/globalbiz/content/may2009/gb20090517_529807.htm); "Math Will Rock Your World," *BusinessWeek*, January 23, 2006; and Chris Taylor, "Imagining the Google Future," *Business 2.0*, February 1, 2006 (http://money.cnn.com/magazines/business2/business2_archive/2006/01/01/8368125/index.htm).

2. These facts are from Robert Berner, "The Ethnography of Marketing," *BusinessWeek Online*, June 12, 2006 (http://businessweek.com/innovate/content/jun2006/id20060612_919537.htm); and Elizabeth Woyke, "Nokia Designs the Future," *Forbes Online*, November 11, 2008 (http://www.forbes.com/2008/

11/19/nokia-design-curtis-tech-wire-cx_ew_
1120nokia.html).

3. Peter Burrows, "How Microsoft Is Fighting Back," *BusinessWeek Online,* April 9, 2009 (http://www.businessweek.com/magazine/content/09_16/b4127063278613.htm).

4. These facts are from Marty Bernstein, "Will Honda's Fit Be a Hit?" *BusinessWeek Online,* April 27, 2006 (http://www.businessweek.com/autos/content/apr2006/bw20060427_337053.htm); and the Honda Fit website (http://automobiles.honda.com/fit/).

5. "Pret a Manger Founders Sitting Pretty," *Telegraph,* February 24, 2008 (http://www.telegraph.co.uk/finance/newsbysector/retailandconsumer/2784937/Pret-a-Manger-founders-sitting-pretty.html).

6. These facts are from Matthew Boyle, "Joe Galli's Army," *Fortune,* December 30, 2002, p. 135.

7. These facts are from Douglas MacMillan, "Online Marketers Wooing Minorities More," *BusinessWeek Online,* December 17, 2008 (http://www.businessweek.com/technology/content/dec2008/tc20081217_930574.htm); Esther Novak, "We the People: A Memo on Multiculturalism," *BusinessWeek Online,* December 9, 2008 (http://www.businessweek.com/bwdaily/dnflash/content/dec2008/db2008128_536371.htm); and Greg T. Spielberg, "Translation: An Ad Agency with Street Cred," *BusinessWeek Online,* February 28, 2009 (http://www.businessweek.com/bwdaily/dnflash/content/feb2009/db20090227_726516.htm).

8. Allison Van Dusen, "Is a Custom Gym Membership for You?" *Forbes Online,* September 9, 2008 (http://www.forbes.com/2008/09/29/custom-gym-popularity-forbeslife-cx_avd_0929health.html).

9. This discussion is based on information obtained from the VALS website, http://www.sric-bi.com/VALS/.

10. These facts are from the PRIZM$_{NE}$ website, http://www.claritas.com/MyBestSegments/Default.jsp.

11. This material is adapted from Charles W. Lamb, Jr., Joseph F. Hair, Jr., and Carl McDaniel, *Marketing,* 7th ed. (Mason, OH: South-Western, 2004),

pp. 228–231; and Philip Kotler, *A Framework for Marketing Management,* 2nd ed. (Upper Saddle River, NJ: Prentice-Hall, 2003), pp. 181–185.

12. These facts are from http://www.littmann.com.

13. These facts are from the Follett Corporation website, http://www.follett.com.

14. These facts are from W. Chan Kim and Renee Mauborgne, *Blue Ocean Strategy* (Boston, MA: Harvard Business School Press, 2005), pp. 109–110; and Allison Van Dusen, "The Price of a Perfect Smile," *Forbes.com,* January 17, 2008 (http://www.forbes.com/2008/01/16/health-smile-perfect-forbeslife-cx_avd_0117health.html).

Chapter 7

1. These facts are from Fred Mackerodt, "Defending a Brand Isn't Easy," *CEO Magazine,* April/May 2006, pp. 54–55; Maya Roney, "Steinway: Worth Much More Than a Song," *BusinessWeek Online,* March 6, 2007 (http://www.businessweek.com/bwdaily/dnflash/content/mar2007/db20070305_637888.htm); and Andy Serwer, "Happy Birthday, Steinway," *Fortune,* March 17, 2003, pp. 94–97.

2. The Hampton Inn Guarantee, http://hamptoninn.hilton.com/en/hp/brand/about.jhtml.

3. "Garmin to Sell Wireless Phone in Asia," *The Star Online* (via AP), June 8, 2009 [David Twiddy, "Garmin to Sell Wireless Phone in Asia," *BusinessWeek Online,* June 5, 2009 (http://www.businessweek.com/ap/financialnews/D98KP9QG0.htm)].

4. *New Products Management for the 1980s* (New York: Booz, Allen & Hamilton, 1982), p. 14.

5. These facts are from Moon Ihlwan, "Kia Motors' Cheap Chic," *BusinessWeek Online,* May 21, 2009 (http://www.businessweek.com/magazine/content/09_22/b4133058607966.htm).

6. These concepts are adapted from Jennifer Rice's Brand Blog, Mantra Brand Consulting, http://brand.blogs.com.

7. "Penney: Back in Fashion," *BusinessWeek Online,* January 9, 2006 (http://www.businessweek.com/magazine/content/06_02/b3966112.htm); and

Aarthi Sivaraman, "Buy or Sell—Will Penney Emerge Stronger from the Downturn?" *Forbes*, April 17, 2009 (http://www.forbes.com/feeds/afx/2009/04/17/afx6306069.html).

8. Andrew Ross Sorkin and Stephanie Saul, "J&J Buys Pfizer Unit for $16.6 Billion," *The New York Times*, June 26, 2006 (http://www.nytimes.com/2006/06/26/business/worldbusiness/26iht-pfizer.2057116.html).

9. David A. Aaker, *Managing Brand Equity: Capitalizing on the Value of a Brand Name* (New York: The Free Press, 1991).

10. Kia website, http://www.kia.com/#/warranty/.

11. "Beatles Lose Apple Court Battle," *BBC News*, May 8, 2006 (http://news.bbc.co.uk/2/hi/entertainment/4983796.stm).

12. These facts are from BIOTA Spring Water website (http://www.biotaspringwater.com/?q=bottle); Jessie Scanlon, "Coke's March towards Zero Waste," *BusinessWeek Online*, May 14, 2009 (http://www.businessweek.com/innovate/next/archives/2009/05/cokes_new_sugar.html); and Ariel Schwartz, "Can the PlantBottle Save the Bottled Water Industry?" *Fast Company*, May 15, 2009 (http://www.fastcompany.com/blog/ariel-schwartz/sustainability/can-plantbottle-save-bottled-water-industry).

13. "Lunchmeats Launch in Reusable PP Containers," http://www.packworld.com/cds_search.html?rec_id=14587&ppr_key=lunchmeat&sky_key=lunchmeat&term=lunchmeat, June 2, 2003.

14. These facts are from Stuart Elliott, "Tropicana Discovers Some Buyers Are Passionate About Packaging," *New York Times*, February 22, 2009 (http://www.nytimes.com/2009/02/23/business/media/23adcol.html); David Kiley, "Arnell Strikes Again: Orange You Glad You Hired Him Tropicana?" *BusinessWeek Online*, February 27, 2009 (http://www.businessweek.com/the_thread/brandnewday/archives/2009/02/arnell_strikes.html); David Kiley, "More Piling on Arnell's Tropicana Fiasco," *BusinessWeek Online*, March 18, 2009 (http://www.businessweek.com/the_thread/brandnewday/archives/2009/03/more_piling_on.html); and David Kiley, "Tropicana Fiasco From Arnell Is Gift That Keeps Giving," *BusinessWeek Online*, April 3, 2009 (http://www.businessweek.com/the_thread/brandnewday/archives/2009/04/tropicana_fiasc.html).

15. Eric Greenberg, "Drug Makers Not Preempted from Lawsuits," *Packworld*, April 17, 2009 (http://www.packworld.com/webonly-27416).

16. This material is adapted from Carol H. Anderson and Julian W. Vincze, *Strategic Marketing Management*, 2nd ed. (Boston: Houghton Mifflin Company, 2004), pp. 249–253.

17. Brian Morrissey, "Honda Touts Value Message," *Adweek*, April 6, 2009 (http://www.adweek.com/aw/content_display/esearch/e3iff50ba6951560a30c30555cab2e882ef).

18. Kopin Tan, "The New Consumer," *SmartMoney*, June 3, 2009 (http://www.smartmoney.com/Investing/Stocks/The-New-Consumer/).

19. Kenji Hall, "Sony Sharpens Its Focus," *BusinessWeek Online*, June 7, 2006 (http://www.businessweek.com/globalbiz/content/jun2006/gb20060607_941413.htm), and Kenji Hall, "Memo to Sony's SLR Group: What Took You So Long?" *BusinessWeek Online*, September 6, 2007 (http://www.businessweek.com/blogs/eyeonasia/archives/2007/09/memo_to_sonys_s.html).

20. See Napster's website, http://www.napster.com.

21. Zune website, http://www.zune.net/en-US/.

22. These facts are from Jia Lynn Yang, "Netflix Defies the Naysayers," *Fortune*, February 18, 2009 (http://money.cnn.com/2009/02/18/technology/netflix.fortune/index.htm).

23. "Open-Source Ad Campaigns," *Business 2.0*, April 2006, 92; and the Spread Firefox website (http://www.spreadfirefox.com), accessed June 30, 2009.

24. Corporate Design Foundation, "Branding That Speaks to the Eyes," *BusinessWeek Online*, March 16, 2006 (http://www.businessweek.com/innovate/content/mar2006/id20060316_504093.htm).

25. Kenji Hall, "Has Nintendo Peaked?" *BusinessWeek Online*, May 7 2009 (http://www.businessweek.com/globalbiz/content/may2009/gb2009057_844946.htm); Reena Jana, "Nintendo's New Brand Game," *BusinessWeek Online*, June 22, 2006 (http://www.businessweek.com/innovate/content/jun2006/id20060622_124931.htm); Sarah Lacy, "Social Gaming Scores in the Recession," *BusinessWeek Online*, April 30, 2009 (http://www.businessweek.com/technology/content/apr2009/tc20090429_963394.htm); "Miyamoto Faces the Future," *BusinessWeek Online*, May 11, 2006 (http://www.businessweek.com/innovate/content/may2006/id20060511_087395.htm); and Nintendo's Touch Generations website (http://us.touchgenerations.com).

26. Alex Taylor III, "Bankruptcy Baby: 2010 Chevrolet Camaro Coupe," *Fortune*, June 2, 2009 (http://thewheeldeal.blogs.fortune.cnn.com/2009/06/02/bankruptcy-baby-2010-chevrolet-camaro-coupe/); and Peter Valdes-Dapena, "Shelby Mustangs: $20,000 over Sticker," *CNNMoney.com* (Autos Section), May 19, 2006 (http://www.cnn.com/2006/AUTOS/05/17/shelby_over_sticker/index.html).

27. These facts are from Matthew Swibel, "Spin Cycle," *Forbes*, April 2, 2001, 118; and Randy Tucker, "Liquid Oxydol Aimed at Gen X," *Cincinnati Enquirer*, May 3, 2001 (http://www.enquirer.com/editions/2001/05/03/fin_liquid_oxydol_aimed.html).

Chapter 8

1. These facts are from Bruce Einhorn, "The World's Most Expensive Cities 2009," *BusinessWeek Online*, June 15, 2009 (http://images.businessweek.com/ss/09/06/0615_most_expensive_cities/index.htm); Diana Holden, "The World's 20 Cheapest Cities 2009," *BusinessWeek Online*, July 8, 2009 (http://images.businessweek.com/ss/09/07/0708_worlds_cheapest_cities/index.htm); and Simon Rogers, "The Top 50 Most Expensive Cities," *The Guardian (UK)*, July 7, 2009 (http://www.guardian.co.uk/news/datablog/2009/jul/07/global-economy-economics).

2. Information obtained from http://www.rivalwatch.com.

3. See (http://shopping.usairways.com/promotion/ESaver/Default.aspx) for further information.

4. Valarie A. Zeithaml, "Consumer Perceptions of Price, Quality, and Value: A Means-End Model and Synthesis of Evidence," *Journal of Marketing* 52 (July 1988), pp. 2–22.

5. This discussion is based on material from Charley Kyd, "Tempted to Cut Prices? It's Probably Time to *Raise* Them," *Today's Business*, Fall 2000, p. 3.

6. Material in this section is adapted from Mark M. Davis and Janelle Heineke, *Managing Services* (Boston: McGraw-Hill/Irwin, 2003), pp. 379–382.

7. For further information, see the Southwest Airlines Web site, http://www.southwest.com

8. Carol Vogel, "Picasso Musketeer Tops Sale by Sotheby's," *The New York Times*, June 24, 2009 (http://www.nytimes.com/2009/06/25/arts/design/25auction.html).

9. These facts are from Linda A. Johnson, "Drugmaker Pfizer's 2Q Profit Plunges 19 Percent," *BusinessWeek Online*, July 22, 2009 (http://www.businessweek.com/ap/financialnews/D99JLP680.htm); and Aaron Smith, "Zocor and Zoloft Face Patent Expiration," (*CNNMoney*), June 15, 2006 (http://money.cnn.com/2006/06/15/news/companies/zoloft_zocor/index.htm).

10. Olga Kharif, "Palm's Pre Is Trying to Live Up to the Hype," *BusinessWeek Online*, August 4, 2009 (http://www.businessweek.com/technology/content/aug2009/tc2009084_790176.htm).

11. These facts are from James Brightman, "Sony Expects Big Losses on PS3 Launch," *GameDaily*, May 1, 2006 (http://www.businessweek.com/innovate/content/may2006/id20060501_525587.htm); Eric Caoili, "iSuppli: Sony Still Losing $50 With Each PS3 Sold," *Gamasutra*, December 23, 2008 (http://www.gamasutra.com/php-bin/news_index.php?story=21657); Rachael Griffin, "Apple to Lose Money on iTunes Movie Releases,"

Infopackets.com, May 7, 2008 (http:// www.infopackets.com/news/business/apple/2008/ 20080507_apple_to_lose_money_on_itunes_ movie_releases.htm); Arik Hesseldahl, "Microsoft's Red-Ink Game," *BusinessWeek Online*, November 22, 2005 (http://www.businessweek.com/ technology/content/nov2005/tc20051122_ 410710.htm); Armando Rodriguez, "Biggest News of the Week: Microsoft Xbox 360 Division Loses $31 Million," *411Mania*, April 27, 2009 (http:// www.411mania.com/games/columns/103060/The- Good-the-Bad-and-the-Ugly-04.27.09:-Microsoft,- FFXIII,-Battlefield-1943-and-More.htm); and Christian Zibreg, "Opinion: Apple Should Open Up the iTunes Store," *(http://Geek.com)*, August 6, 2009 (http://www.geek.com/articles/mobile/ opinion-apple-should-open-up-the-itunes-store-2- 009086/).

12. eBay Fast Facts, *eBay Motors Backgrounder* (http:// news.ebay.com/common/download/download. cfm?companyid=EBAYPRESS&fileid=306112& filekey=ED6A01C7-AE1A-445F-8C44- 2AFD2B11AC25&filename=eBay_Motors_ Backgrounder.pdf), accessed August 5, 2009.

13. These facts are from "Sentencing in Archer Daniels Midland Price-Gouging Case," *The Agribusiness Examiner*, July 21, 1999; and Chris Kahn, "U.S. Issues Rule Policing Oil Price Manipulation," *BusinessWeek Online*, August 6, 2009 (http:// www.businessweek.com/ap/financialnews/ D99TGNI01.htm).

14. These facts are from Dan Fisher, "Blame the Spec- ulators!" *Forbes*, July 8, 2009 (http://www .forbes.com/2009/07/08/oil-cftc-speculators- business-energy-oil.html); Chris Kahn, "Oil Prices: Gauging the Speculator Impact," *BusinessWeek Online*, July 29, 2009 (http://www.businessweek .com/investor/content/jul2009/pi20090729_ 264394.htm); Steve LeVine, "Falling Oil Prices: Again, Blame Speculators," *BusinessWeek Online*, January 8, 2009 (http://www.businessweek.com/ bwdaily/dnflash/content/jan2009/db2009018_

370800.htm); and Ed Wallace, "Gas Prices Are Not Tied to Oil Prices," *BusinessWeek Online*, February 24, 2009 (http://www.businessweek .com/lifestyle/content/feb2009/bw20090224_ 273676.htm).

Chapter 9

1. Tom Andel, "Logistics @ Barnesandnoble.com," *Material Handling Management*, January 1, 2000, p. 39; "Barnes & Noble Implements 12 Solutions to Increase Distribution Center Efficiencies Nation- wide," *Canadian Corporate News*, May 8, 2001 (www.comtexnews.com); "Barnes & Noble Launches World's Largest eBookstore," Barnes & Noble Press Release (http://www.barnesand nobleinc.com/press_releases/2009_july_20_ ebookstore.html); "Barnes & Noble Reports 2008 Results," Barnes & Noble Press Release (http:// www.barnesandnobleinc.com/press_releases/ 2009_march_19_2008_earnings.html); "Barnes & Noble Selects Retek to Support Supply Chain Planning and Optimization," Barnes & Noble news release, January 10, 2001; and "Investor Relations," Barnes & Noble.com (http://www.barnesand nobleinc.com/for_investors/for_investors .html), accessed August 10, 2009.

2. Deborah Catalano Ruriani, "Inventory Velocity: All the Right Moves," *Inbound Logistics*, November 2005, p. 36.

3. James Watson, "Del Monte Foods Company," *Wikinvest* (http://www.wikinvest.com/stock/ Del_Monte_Foods_Company_%28DLM%29), accessed August 12, 2009.

4. These facts are from the PayPal website (https:// www.paypal-media.com/aboutus.cfm), accessed August 12, 2009.

5. These facts are from David Koenig, "Dell Recall Stems from Production Flaw," *BusinessWeek Online*, August 15, 2006 (http://www.businessweek .com/ap/financialnews/D8JH7QU80.htm).

6. These facts are from General Mills' 2009 Annual Report, p. 7; and Pallavi Gogoi, "General Mills'

Far-Flung Search for Efficiency Ideas," *BusinessWeek*, July 28, 2003, p. 74.

7. J.M. Smucker Company (http://www.smuckers. com/family_company/about_us/default.aspx), accessed August 12, 2009.

8. See Edward W. Davis and Robert E. Speckman, *The Extended Enterprise* (Upper Saddle River, NJ: Prentice-Hall Financial Times, 2004).

9. Ibid, p. 15.

10. Robert Dawson, *Secrets of Power Negotiation*, 2nd ed. (Franklin Lakes, NJ: Career Press, 1999).

11. Davis and Speckman, *The Extended Enterprise*, p. 161.

12. This information is adapted from "Collaborative SCM: Adversaries to Allies," *Inbound Logistics*, July 2000, p. 124.

13. Category Management Report ©1995 by the Joint Industry Project on Efficient Consumer Response.

14. Ibid.

15. U.S. Census Bureau, 2007 *E-commerce Multi-sector Report*, May 28, 2009 (http://www.census.gov/eos/www/2007/2007reportfinal.pdf), accessed August 12, 2009.

16. "What Is RFID?" *RFID Journal* (http://www.rfidjournal.com/article/articleview/1339/1/129/), accessed August 10, 2009.

17. These facts are from EcoSensa, "The Up and Down of Walmart RFID Implementation," *RFID Blog*, March 24, 2009 (http://ecosensa.com/rfidblog/2009/03/24/wal-mart-rfid-implementation/); Constance L. Hays, "What Walmart Knows About Customers' Habits," *The New York Times*, Nov. 14, 2004; John Johnson, "RFID Watch: Transmissions from the RFID Front Lines: How They Did It," *DC Velocity*, January 2006 (http://www.dcvelocity.com); Thomas Wailgum, "Walmart is Dead Serious About RFID," *CIO*, January 18, 2008 (http://www.cio.com/article/173702/Wal_Mart_Is_Dead_Serious_About_RFID); and Mary Hayes Weier, "Hewlett-Packard Data Warehouse Lands in Walmart's Shopping Cart," *Information Week*, August 4, 2007 (http://www.informationweek

.com/news/storage/showArticle.jhtml?articleID= 201203024).

18. The material in this section is based on Davis and Speckman, *The Extended Enterprise*, pp. 109–129.

19. These facts are from Nick Heath, "Banks: Offshoring, Not Outsourcing," *BusinessWeek Online*, March 10, 2009 (http://www.businessweek.com/globalbiz/content/mar2009/gb20090310_619247.htm).

20. Martin Murray, "3PL's Used by Three Quarters of the Fortune 500," *Martin's Logistics Blog*, January 28, 2009 (http://logistics.about.com/b/2009/01/28/3pls-used-by-three-quarters-of-the-fortune-500.htm), accessed August 12, 2009.

21. Ensenda website (http://www.ensenda.com/see.html), accessed August 12, 2009.

22. These facts are from Ben Levisohn, "Coinstar: Counting More Than Coins," *BusinessWeek Online*, February 8, 2008 (http://www.businessweek.com/investor/content/feb2008/pi2008028_098937.htm); Ryan Nakashima, "Whither Redbox? Hollywood Studios Are Conflicted," *The Seattle Times* (via AP), August 7, 2009 (http://seattletimes.nwsource.com/html/localnews/2009619612_apusredboxhollywood.html); Dorothy Pomerantz, "Red Menace," *Forbes*, March 6, 2009 (http://www.forbes.com/2009/03/06/redbox-blockbuster-rentals-business-media-rebox.html); and Paul Suarez, "Hollywood Hates Redbox's $1 DVD Rentals," *Macworld*, August 10, 2009 (http://www.macworld.com/article/142192/2009/08/redbox.html).

23. Bert Rosenbloom, *Marketing Channels: A Management View* (Hindsale, IL: Dryden, 1991), p. 103.

24. Attorney General of Washington (http://www.atg.wa.gov).

25. These facts are from Beth Bacheldor, "FDA Issues New 'Counterfeit Drug Task Force' Report," *RFID Journal*, June 9, 2006 (http://www.rfidjournal.com/article/articleview/2420/1/1/); and Jonathan Collins, "FDA Clears Way for RFID Tagging," *RFID Journal*, November 15, 2004 (http://www.rfidjournal.com/article/articleview/1238/1/1/).

Chapter 10

1. These facts are from Michael Bush, "DVR House-holds to Almost Double by 2014," *Advertising Age*, December 5, 2008 (http://adage.com/mediaworks/article?article_id=133047); Andrew Hampp, "How 'Top Chef' Cooks Up Fresh Integrations," *Advertising Age*, October 30, 2008 (http://adage.com/madisonandvine/article?article_id=132146); "The End of TV (As You Know It)," *BusinessWeek Online*, November 21, 2005 (http://www.businessweek.com/magazine/content/05_47/b3960075.htm); David Schatsky, "The Media Industry Is Falling to Pieces," *TelevisionWeek*, January 30, 2006, 10; and Rich Thomaselli, "How CBS Sports Can Use March Madness Success to Grow Online," March 11, 2009 (http://adage.com/digital/article?article_id=135186).

2. Enid Burns, "Marketers Push Toward Integrated Marketing Campaigns," *ClickZ Network*, June 14, 2006 (http://www.clickz.com/3613506), accessed September 8, 2009.

3. Emily Bryson York and Natalie Zmuda, "Top New Products of 2008: Gatorade G2 and Dunkin' Coffee," *Advertising Age*, March 25, 2009 (http://adage.com/article?article_id=135523).

4. These facts are from "Key News Audiences Now Blend Online and Traditional Sources," http://people-press.org/report/444/news-media, accessed April 8, 2009.

5. Jeffrey M. Humphreys, "The Multicultural Economy 2008," *Georgia Business and Economic Conditions* 68 (3), http://www.terry.uga.edu/selig/docs/executive_summary_2008.pdf, p. 8.

6. Carlotta Mast, "Latino Liftoff: Hispanic Consumares Targeted," *Denver Post*, August 2007 (http://www.denverpost.com/business/ci_6573828), accessed March 20, 2009.

7. "2009 U.S. National Edition Rates," *Time* (http://www.time.com/time/mediakit/1/us/timemagazine/rates/national/index.html), accessed April 10, 2009.

8. Ben Kunz, "Why Do Super Bowl Ads Cost 6 Times as Much?" *Thought Gadgets*, January 30, 2009 (http://www.thoughtgadgets.com/2009/01/why-do-super-bowl-ads-costs-6-times-as.html), accessed July 27, 2009.

9. Charisse Jones, "Winning Ad Made for Less than $2,000." *USA Today*, February 3, 2009, p. B1; Stuart Elliott, "Amateur TV Ad Makers are in the Chips." *The New York Times*, February 4, 2009 (http://tvdecoder.blogs.nytimes.com/2009/02/04/amateur-tv-ad-makers-are-in-the-chips).

10. These facts are from Jamin Brophy-Warren, "The New Examined Life," *The Wall Street Journal*, December 6-7, 2008, W1, W11; Tom Hayes and Michael S. Malone, "Marketing in the World of the Web," *The Wall Street Journal*, November 29-30, 2008, p. A13; Ann Meyer, "Facebook, Twitter, Other Social Media Help Drive Business for Firms," *Chicago Tribune*, April 27, 2009 (http://archives.chicagotribune.com/2009/apr/27/business/chi-mon-minding-social-media-042apr27); Jack Neff, "Few CEOs Think They Are Effectively Tracking Social Media, Word-of-Mouth," *Advertising Age*, January 26, 2009 (http://adage.com/cmostrategy/article?article_id=134085); and Randall Stoss, "Advertisers Face Hurdles on Social Networking Sites," *New York Times*, December 13, 2008 (http://www.nytimes.com/2008/12/14/business/media/14digi.html?pagewanted=1&_r=2&partner=rss&emc=rss).

11. New Belgium Brewery website, http://www.newbelgium.com.

12. "True North Nuts Help Homeless," *Cause Why Not?* February 24, 2009 (http://causewhynot.wordpress.com/2009/02/24/true-north-nuts-help-homeless), accessed April 2, 2009.

13. Andrew Hampp, "Turner Agrees to Pay Boston $2 Million," *Advertising Age*, February 5, 2007 (http://adage.com/mediaworks/article?article_id=114825); and Suzanne Smalley and Raja Mishra, "Froth, Fear, and Fury," *The Boston Globe*, February 1, 2007 (http://www.boston.com/news/local/massachusetts/articles/2007/02/01/froth_fear_and_fury).

14. These facts are from Jessi Hempel, "IBM's all-star salesman," *CNNMoney*, September 26, 2008 (http://money.cnn.com/2008/09/23/technology/hempel_IBM.fortune/index2.htm); "Challenges in OSS/BSS and Optimized Provisioning," *Sasken* (http://www.sasken.com/downloads/TGJ/issue3/challenges_in_oss_bss.htm), accessed on September 19, 2009; and Rajesh Mahapatra, "IBM Wins Order from Vodafone's India Arm," *The Washington Post*, December 10, 2007 (http://www.washingtonpost.com/wp-dyn/content/article/2007/12/10/AR2007121000473.html).

15. "100 Best Companies to Work for in 2009: #32 The Container Store" *Fortune*, February 2, 2009 (http://money.cnn.com/magazines/fortune/best-companies/2009/snapshots/32.html).

16. William C. Moncrief, Emin Babakus, David W. Cravens, and Mark W. Johnston, "Gender Differences in Sales Organizations," *Journal of Business Research* (September 2000), 245–257.

17. "Training Top 125," *Training Magazine*, February 2008 (http://www.managesmarter.com/managesmarter/images/pdfs/trg_20080201_top125ranking.pdf), accessed July 31, 2009.

18. "Training 2007 Industry Rep," *Training*, November/December 2007 (http://www.managesmarter.com/managesmarter/images/pdfs/trg_20071101_industry.pdf), accessed July 31, 2009.

19. Promotion Marketing Association, "State of the Promotion Industry Report," © 2005 Promotion Marketing Association (http://www.pmalink.org/resources/pma2005report.pdf).

20. Nathalie Zmuda, "Coke: Buy 1 Rival, Get our Brand Free," *Advertising Age*, March 9 and 16, 2009, pp. 1, 19; "Coke Promotion Gives Free Vault to Mountain Dew Customers," *Convenience Store News*, April 10, 2009, p. 1; "Coca Cola Brings Vault Drink Head to Head with Mtn Dew," *yumsugar*, March 11, 2009 (http://www.yumsugar.com/2912146), accessed April 11, 2009.

21. Tracy Turner, "Wendy's Newest Pitch Aimed at Online Crowd," *The Columbus Dispatch*, April 3, 2009 (http://www.columbusdispatch.com/live/content/business/stories/2009/04/03/wendys_bid.ART_ART_04-03-09_C10_8NDEO24.html), accessed September 19, 2009.

22. Sarah Skidmore, "New Generation of Coupons Means Users Clip Less," *ABC News* (via AP), August 27, 2009 (http://abcnews.go.com/Business/wireStory?id=8429206), accessed September 3, 2009.

23. These facts are from "For Our Members," Hallmark (https://portal.goldcrowncard.com/browse/hmkbenefits.html), accessed September 19, 2009; and Barry Silverstein, "Can Brand Loyalty Be Bought?" *Brandhome*, April 27, 2009 (http://www.brandchannel.com/features_effect.asp?pf_id=475#more), accessed September 19, 2009.

Chapter 11

1. These facts are from Green Mountain Coffee, 2008 Annual Report (http://www.gmcr.com/Investors/~/media/_IR/GMCR%20ANNUAL%20REPORT%202008.ashx), accessed August 13, 2009; Pallavi Gogoi, "Mickey D's New Brew," *BusinessWeek Online*, March 1, 2006 (http://www.businessweek.com/bwdaily/dnflash/mar2006/nf2006031_8259_db016.htm); "Green Mountain Coffee Roasters on the 200 Best Small Companies (2008)," *Forbes*, October 8, 2008 (http://www.forbes.com/entrepreneurs/lists/2008/23/biz_200smalls08_Green-Mountain-Coffee-Roasters_GMAE.html), accessed August 13, 2009; Green Mountain Coffee Roasters website (http://www.greenmountaincoffee.com); Hoover's Fact Sheet on Green Mountain Coffee (http://hoovers.com/green-mountain-coffee/--ID__45721--/free-co-factsheet.xhtml); "Learning on the Front Lines," *BusinessWeek Online*, July 10, 2006 (http://www.businessweek.com/magazine/content/06_28/b3992011.htm); and Ben Steverman, "The Stock Market's Coffee Craze," *BusinessWeek Online*, July 30, 2009 (http://www.businessweek.com/investor/content/jul2009/pi20090730_507221.htm).

2. Orville C. Walker, Jr., and Robert W. Ruekert, "Marketing's Role in the Implementation of Business Strategies: A Critical Review and Conceptual Framework," *Journal of Marketing*, 51 (July 1987), pp. 15–33.

3. Frank V. Cespedes, *Organizing and Implementing the Marketing Effort* (Reading, MA: Addison-Wesley, 1991), p. 19.

4. Robert Howard, "Values Make the Company: An Interview with Robert Haas," *Harvard Business Review*, 68 (September–October 1990), pp. 132–144.

5. See the New Belgium Brewery website, http://www.newbelgium.com.

6. Michael D. Hartline, James G. Maxham, III, and Daryl O. McKee, "Corridors of Influence in the Dissemination of Customer-Oriented Strategy to Customer Contact Service Employees," *Journal of Marketing*, 64 (April 2000), pp. 35–50.

7. Ibid.

8. Cespedes, *Organizing and Implementing the Marketing Effort*, pp. 622–623.

9. Robert W. Ruekert, Orville C. Walker, Jr., and Kenneth J. Roering, "The Organization of Marketing Activities: A Contingency Theory of Structure and Performance," *Journal of Marketing*, 49 (Winter 1985), pp. 13–25.

10. Hartline, Maxham, and McKee, "Corridors of Influence."

11. Michael Hammer and James Champy, *Reengineering the Corporation: A Manifesto for Business Revolution* (New York: Harper Business, 1993), p. 35.

12. Jena McGregor, "How Failure Breeds Success," *BusinessWeek Online*, July 10, 2006 (http://www.businessweek.com/magazine/content/06_28/b3992001.htm?chan=innovation_innovation+%2B+design_the+creative+corporation).

13. Myron Glassman and Bruce McAfee, "Integrating the Personnel and Marketing Functions: The Challenge of the 1990s," *Business Horizons*, 35 (May–June 1992), pp. 52–59.

14. Michael D. Hartline and O. C. Ferrell, "Service Quality Implementation: The Effects of Organizational Socialization and Managerial Actions on Customer-Contact Employee Behaviors," *Marketing Science Institute Working Paper Series*, Report No. 93–122 (Cambridge, MA: Marketing Science Institute, 1993).

15. Richard L. Oliver and Erin Anderson, "An Empirical Test of the Consequences of Behavior- and Outcome-Based Sales Control Systems," *Journal of Marketing*, 58 (October 1994), pp. 53–67.

16. Hartline, Maxham, and McKee, "Corridors of Influence."

17. Adam Lashinsky, "The Perks of Being a *Googler*," *Fortune* (*CNNMoney.com*) (http://money.cnn.com/galleries/2007/fortune/0701/gallery.Google_perks/), accessed August 13, 2009; and Dorian Wales, "How to Create the Environment of Organizational Commitment," *Helium* (http://www.helium.com/items/706133-how-to-create-the-environment-of-organizational-commitment), accessed August 13, 2009.

18. These facts are from Ram Charan, "The New (Recovery) Playbook," *Fortune* (CNNMoney.com), August 13, 2009 (http://money.cnn.com/2009/08/11/news/economy/new_rules_recovery.fortune/index.htm); Betsy Morris, "The New Rules," *Fortune*, July 24, 2006, pp. 70–87; and Betsy Morris, "Tearing Up the Jack Welch Playbook," *Fortune* (*CNNMoney.com*), July 11, 2006 (http://money.cnn.com/2006/07/10/magazines/fortune/rules.fortune/index.htm).

19. W. Chan Kim and Renee Mauborgne, *Blue Ocean Strategy* (Boston, MA: Harvard Business School Press, 2005).

20. The material in this section has been adapted from L. J. Bourgeois III and David R. Brodwin, "Strategic Implementation: Five Approaches to an Elusive Phenomenon," *Strategic Management Journal*, 5 (1984), pp. 241–264; and Steven W. Floyd and Bill Wooldridge, "Managing Strategic Consensus: The Foundation of Effective Implementation," *Academy of Management Executive*, 6 (November 1992), pp. 27–39.

21. These facts are from Emily Bryson York, "McD's Dollar-Menu Fixation Sparks Revolt," *Advertising Age*, 79 (June 2, 2008), pp. 1–2.

22. These facts are from "Brand-Led Marketing: Samsung Viewpoint," *Marketing Week*, July 2, 2009, p. 18; Patricia O'Connell, "Samsung's Goal: Be Like BMW," *BusinessWeek Online*, August 1, 2005 (http://www.businessweek.com/magazine/content/05_31/b3945107.htm); and Craig Smith, "Soaring Samsung Provides Proof of Marketing's Value," *Marketing*, September 25, 2003, p. 19.

23. Bourgeois and Brodwin, "Strategic Implementation: Five Approaches to an Elusive Phenomenon."

24. Hartline, Maxham, and McKee, "Corridors of Influence."

25. This information is from Mohammed Rafiq and Pervaiz K. Ahmed, "Advances in the Internal Marketing Concept: Definition, Synthesis and Extension," *Journal of Services Marketing*, 14 (2000), pp. 449–463.

26. Ibid.

27. Glassman and McAfee, "Integrating the Personnel and Marketing Functions."

28. Howard, "Values Make the Company."

29. Hartline and Ferrell, "Service Quality Implementation."

30. This section is based on material from Hartline, Maxham, and McKee, "Corridors of Influence"; and Bernard J. Jaworski, "Toward a Theory of Marketing Control: Environmental Context, Control Types, and Consequences," *Journal of Marketing*, 52 (July 1988), pp. 23–39.

31. These facts are from John D. Stoll, "At Saturn, a Split over Relying on the Penske Name," *The Wall Street Journal*, June 29, 2009, p. B1.

32. Ibid; and Brian P. Niehoff, Cathy A. Enz, and Richard A. Grover, "The Impact of Top-Management Actions on Employee Attitudes and Perceptions," *Group & Organization Studies*, 15 (September 1990), pp. 337–352.

33. Michael D. Hartline and O. C. Ferrell, "The Management of Customer-Contact Service Employees: An Empirical Investigation," *Journal of Marketing*, 60 (October 1996), pp. 52–70.

34. Ibid.

35. Ben M. Enis and Stephen J. Garfein, "The Computer-Driven Marketing Audit," *Journal of Management Inquiry* (December 1992), pp. 306–318; and Philip Kotler, William Gregor, and William Rodgers, "The Marketing Audit Comes of Age," *Sloan Management Review*, 30 (Winter 1989), pp. 49–62.

36. Jaworski, "Toward a Theory of Marketing Control."

37. Ibid.

38. Hartline, Maxham, and McKee, "Corridors of Influence.

39. These facts are from John Michael Farrell and Angela Hoon, "What's Your Company's Risk Culture?" *BusinessWeek Online*, May 12, 2009 (http://www.businessweek.com/managing/content/may2009/ca20090512_720476.htm); Kevin Kelly, "The Key to Risk: It's All About Emotion," *Forbes*, February 23, 2009 (http://www.forbes.com/2009/02/23/risk-culture-crisis-leadership-management_innovation.html); Karen E. Klein, "Using Risk Management to Beat the Downturn," *BusinessWeek Online*, January 9, 2009 (http://www.businessweek.com/smallbiz/content/jan2009/sb2009018_717265.htm); and Arvin Maskin, "Creating a Culture of Risk Avoidance," *BusinessWeek Online*, March 6, 2009 (http://www.businessweek.com/managing/content/mar2009/ca2009036_914216.htm).

40. Jack R. Meredith and Scott M. Shafer, *Introducing Operations Management* (New York: John Wiley and Sons, Inc., 2003), p. 458.

Chapter 12

1. These facts are from Mila D'Antonio, "Courting Customers," *1to1 magazine*, July/August 2006 (http://www.1to1media.com/Issues.aspx?Publication=9221); Barbara Ortutay, "Flower Shop Launches First Facebook Store," *USA Today*, July 29, 2009 (http://www.usatoday.com/tech/hotsites/2009-07-29-flowers-facebook_N.htm); and Rebecca Reisner, "Mixing Up the Bouquet at 1-800-Flowers.com," *BusinessWeek Online*, April 7, 2009

(http://www.businessweek.com/managing/content/apr2009/ca2009047_439174.htm).

2. Jill Dyché, *The CRM Handbook* (Boston, MA: Addison-Wesley, 2002), pp. 4–5.

3. Judy Strauss, Adel El-Ansary, and Raymond Frost, *E-Marketing,* 3rd ed. (Upper Saddle River, NJ: Prentice Hall, 2003), pp. 407–408.

4. Relationships Rule," *Business* 2.0, May 2000, pp. 303–319; and Strauss, El-Ansary, and Frost, *E-Marketing*, p. 406.

5. This information is taken from the Regions website (http://www.regions.com).

6. Cliff Edwards, "AMD + ATI: Imperfect Together?" *BusinessWeek Online*, July 25, 2006 (http://www.businessweek.com/technology/content/jul2006/tc20060725_893757.htm).

7. Adapted from Valarie Zeithaml, Mary Jo Bitner, and Dwayne Gremler, *Services Marketing*, 5th ed. (Boston: McGraw-Hill/Irwin, 2009), pp. 24–25.

8. This material is adapted from Valarie A. Zeithaml, A. Parasuraman, and Leonard L. Berry, *Delivering Quality Service: Balancing Customer Perceptions and Expectations* (New York: The Free Press, 2001).

9. These facts are from Brian Hindo, "Satisfaction Not Guaranteed," *BusinessWeek Online*, June 19, 2006 (http://www.businessweek.com/magazine/content/06_25/b3989041.htm); Jena McGregor, "Marvin Ellison: Home Depot's Mr. Fixit?" *BusinessWeek Online*, May 7, 2009 (http://www.businessweek .com/magazine/content/09_20/b4131054579392. htm); Jena McGregor, Aili McConnon, and David Kiley, "Customer Service in a Shrinking Economy," *BusinessWeek Online*, February 19, 2009 (http://www.businessweek.com/magazine/content/09_09/b4121026559235.htm); Erica Ogg, "A Modest Proposal to Fix Dell's Customer Service," *CNET News*, May 9, 2008 (http://news.cnet.com/8301-10784_3-9939821-7.html); and Harold L. Sirkin, "Serving Customers in a Downturn," *BusinessWeek Online*, July 31, 2009 (http://www.businessweek .com/managing/content/jul2009/ca20090731_913928.htm).

10. Information in this section is based on James H. Myers, *Measuring Customer Satisfaction* (Chicago: American Marketing Association, 1999); and Valarie A. Zeithaml, Leonard L. Berry, and A. Parasuraman, "The Nature and Determinants of Customer Expectations of Service," *Journal of the Academy of Marketing Science*, 21 (January 1993), pp. 1–12.

11. A. Parasuraman, Leonard L. Berry, and Valarie A. Zeithaml, "Understanding Customer Expectations of Service," *Sloan Management Review*, 32 (Spring 1991), p. 42.

12. These facts are from Andrea J. Ayers, "Executives Have No Idea What Customers Want," *Forbes*, March 10, 2009 (http://www.forbes.com/2009/03/10/consumers-executives-disconnect-leadership-managing-convergys.html); Kevin P. Coyne, "The Customer Satisfaction Survey Snag," *BusinessWeek Online*, June 19, 2009 (http://www.businessweek.com/managing/content/jun2009/ca20090619_272945.htm); and Timothy Keiningham and Lerzan Aksoy, "When Customer Loyalty Is a Bad Thing," *BusinessWeek Online*, May 8, 2009 (http://www.businessweek.com/managing/content/may2009/ca2009058_567988.htm).

13. Adapted from Strauss, El-Ansary, and Frost, *E-Marketing*, pp. 435–437.

Case 16

1. Helene M. Lawson and Kira Leck, "Dynamics of Internet Dating," *Social Science Computer Review*, Vol. 24, No. 2, Summer 2006, pp. 189–208, (http://ssc.sagepub.com/cgi/content/abstract/24/2/189), accessed November 2007.

2. "Finding true love: A look at the history of dating," (TODAYshow.com), February 17, 2005 (http://www.msnbc.msn.com/id/6967668/), accessed November 2007.

3. Meghan McNamara, "Tangled up in love: online dating," *The Post*, November 12, 2007 (http://www.thepost.ohiou.edu/Articles/2007/11/08/221-60/), accessed November 2007.

4. David Popenoe, "The State of Our Unions: The Social Health of Marriage in America," published by The National Marriage Project, Rutgers State University of New Jersey, 2007 (http://marriage.rutgers.edu/Publications/SOOU/TEXT-SOOU2007.htm), accessed October 2007.

5. "The frayed knot—Marriage in America," *The Economist,* May 26, 2007, p. 22, via ProQuest, ABI/Inform (www.proquest.com), accessed November 2007.

6. Frost, Jeana H., Zoe Chance, Michael I. Norton, and Dan Ariely. "People Are Experience Goods: Improving Online Dating with Virtual Dates." *Journal of Interactive Marketing* (forthcoming).

7. Mary Madden and Amanda Lenhart, "Online Dating: Americans who are seeking romance use the Internet to help them in their search, but there is still widespread public concern about the safety of online dating," Pew Internet & American Life Project, March 5, 2006.

8. Betsy Stevenson and Justin Wolfers, "Marriage and Divorce: Changes and their Driving Forces," *Journal of Economic Perspectives,*" 21, 2 (Spring 2007), via ProQuest, ABI/Inform (www.proquest.com), accessed November 2007.

9. Betsey Stevenson and Justin Wolfers, "Marriage and Divorce: Changes and their Driving Forces," *Journal of Economic Perspectives,*" 21, 2 (Spring 2007), via ProQuest, ABI/Inform (www.proquest.com), accessed November 2007.

10. Jeffrey Zaslow, "Moving On: Divorce Makes a Comeback—Poor Economy, Tense Times Prompt More Couples to Call It Quits," *The Wall Street Journal,* January 14, 2003, p. D1, via Factiva, accessed November 2007.

11. Betsy Stevenson and Justin Wolfers, "Marriage and Divorce: Changes and their Driving Forces," *Journal of Economic Perspectives,*" 21, 2 (Spring 2007), via ProQuest, ABI/Inform, (www.proquest.com), accessed November 2007.

12. Popenoe, "The State of Our Unions."

13. Liz Pulliam Weston, "Money isn't the culprit in most divorces," *MSN Money,* (http://articles.moneycentral.msn.com/CollegeAndFamily/SuddenlySingle/MoneyIsntTheCulpritInMostDivorces.aspx), accessed November 2007.

14. "Most People Make Only One Trip Down the Aisle, But First Marriages Shorter, Census Bureau Reports." Census Bureau press release (Washington, DC, September 19, 2007), (http://www.census.gov/PressRelease/www/releases/archives/marital_status_living_arrangements/010624.html), accessed October 2007; Rose M. Kreider, "Number, Timing, and Duration of Marriages and Divorces: 2001: Household Economic Studies," U.S. Census Bureau, February 2005, pp. 70–97 (http://www.census.gov/prod/2005pubs/p70-97.pdf), accessed November 2007; Jeffrey Zaslow, "Moving On: Divorce Makes a Comeback—Poor Economy, Tense Times Prompt More Couples to Call It Quits," *The Wall Street Journal,* January 14, 2003, p. D1, via Factiva, accessed November 2007.

15. "Finding true love: A look at the history of dating," (TODAYshow.com).

16. Wendi Gibson Richert, "All About Romance," *Roanoke Times & World News,* February 4, 1994, p. 1, via Factiva, accessed November 2007.

17. Karin Kapsidelis, "Surfing for love/Today's dating scene is undergoing a sea change," *The Richmond Times Dispatch,* January 27, 2008, p. G1, via Factiva, accessed March 2008.

18. Madden and Lenhart, "Online Dating."

19. Marcelle S. Fischler, "Online Dating Putting You Off? Try a Matchmaker," *The New York Times,* September 30, 2007, p. 20, via Factiva, accessed October 2007; Pete Barlas, "Dating Web Sites Get Cold Shoulder From More Users; The Attraction Is Diminishing; But study says percentage of visitors who end up as subscribers staying steady," *Investor's Business Daily,* February 12, 2007, p. A4, via Factiva, accessed October 2007.

20. Madden and Lenhart, "Online Dating."

21. Meghan McNamara, "Tangled up in love: online dating," *The Post,* November 12, 2007, (http://www.thepost.ohiou.edu/Articles/2007/11/08/221-60/), accessed November 2007; "National Vital

Statistics Reports—Births, Marriages, Divorces, and Deaths: Provisional Data for 2005," *U.S. Department of Health and Human Services*, Vol. 54, No. 20, July 21, 2006, (http://www.cdc.gov/nchs/) products Tralee Pearce, "Boomer seeks date, has PC skills; Midlifers have become the fastest-growing segment of the online dating world," *The Globe and Mail,* May 31, 2007, p. L1, via Factiva, accessed October 2007; Marcelle S. Fischler, "Online Dating Putting You Off? Try a Matchmaker," *The New York Times,* September 30, 2007, p. 20, via Factiva, accessed October 2007

22. Pete Barlas, "Dating Web Sites Get Cold Shoulder From More Users; The Attraction Is Diminishing; But study says percentage of visitors who end up as subscribers staying steady," *Investor's Business Daily,* February 12, 2007, p. A4, via Factiva, accessed October 2007.

23. Dale Buss, "Neil Warren: online passion," February 28, 2005, (brandchannel.com), (http://www.brandchannel.com/careers_profile.asp?-cr_id=53), accessed March 21, 2008.

24. Mark Wolf, "EHarmony Lets Lovelorn Click on Reality," *Rocky Mountain News,* June 22, 2002, p. 9F, via Factiva, accessed July 2007.

25. Janet Kornblum, "eHarmony: Heart and soul; Online dating service adheres to founder's moral values," *USA Today,* May 19, 2005, p. D1, via Factiva, accessed July 2007; Christopher Palmeri, "Dr. Warren's Lonely Hearts Club; EHarmony sheds its mom-and-pop structure, setting the stage for an IPO," *BusinessWeek,* February 20, 2006, p. 82, via Factiva, accessed July 2007.

26. "For 5000 Singles, eHarmony was the First Step Down the Aisle; Poll Reveals that 88% of Users are Looking for Life-Long Mate," Business Wire, March 8, 2004, via Factiva, accessed July 2007; "eHarmony Exceeds Growth Expectations with 3 Million Members; Milestone Demonstrates Leadership in Online Relationship Category," Business Wire, February 23, 2004, via Factiva, accessed July 2007.

27. "eHarmony Introduces eHarmony Marriage; New Marriage Wellness Program Offers Couples a New Approach to Strengthen Their Relationships," PR Newswire, February 6, 2006, via Factiva, accessed July 2007; Christopher Palmeri, "Dr. Warren's Lonely Hearts Club; EHarmony sheds its mom-and-pop structure, setting the stage for an IPO," *BusinessWeek*, February 20, 2006, p. 82, via Factiva, accessed July 2007; Hilary Potkewitz, "Internet Matchmaker Finds Tough Going to Find a Matching CEO," *Los Angeles Business Journal,* April 10, 2006, via Factiva, accessed July 2007; "New Research Find eHarmony Couples Are Significantly Happier in Their Marriages than Non-eHarmony Couples," *PR Newswire*, February 2, 2006, via Factiva, accessed July 2007.

28. "Probability of Finding Lasting Love Takes Quantum Leap Forward on Unusual New Web Site," *PR Newswire*, August 21, 2000, via Factiva, accessed July 2007; Janet Kornblum, "eHarmony: Heart and soul; Online dating service adheres to founder's moral values," *USA Today,* May 19, 2005, p. D1, via Factiva, accessed July 2007; "For 5000 Singles, eHarmony was the First Step Down the Aisle; Poll Reveals that 88% of Users are Looking for Life-Long Mate," Business Wire, March 8, 2004, via Factiva, accessed July 2007; Monica L. Haynes, "To eHarmony Couples Saying 'I Do' Couples Match Thanks To Popular Web Site Online Relationship Service Claims to Form More Perfect Unions," *Pittsburgh Post-Gazette,* December 28, 2004, p. B1, via Factiva, accessed July 2007. Janet Kornblum, "eHarmony: Heart and soul; Online dating service adheres to founder's moral values," *USA Today,* May 19, 2005, p. D1, via Factiva, accessed July 2007; Paul Farhi, "They Met Online, but Definitely Didn't Click," *The Washington Post,* May 13, 2007, p. D1, via Factiva, accessed July 2007.

29. Emily Parker, "The Weekend Interview with Greg Waldorf: The Matchmaker," *The Wall Street Journal,* February 10, 2007, p. A9, via Factiva, accessed July 2007.

30. Alex Mindlin, "On Niche Dating Sites, Many More Women," *The New York Times,* February 26, 2007, p. 3, via Factiva, accessed October 2007.

31. Hiawatha Bray, "Trying to set a fire under online dating; EHarmony tries science, and Match.com has Dr. Phil," *The Boston Globe,* February 14, 2007, p. 3, via Factiva, accessed July 2007; Gina Keating, "Web Dating Service Takes Scientific Approach to Love; If the "happily" has gone out of your "happily ever after," eHarmony wants to know all about it," *eWeek,* February 13, 2007, via Factiva, accessed July 2007; Sally Dadisman, "Love lab probes what's amore: California researchers try to unravel why couples click," *Edmonton Journal,* February 23, 2007, p. D6, via Factiva, accessed July 2007; Jessica E. Vascellaro, "Regulators Say Love Ain't 'Chemistry' After All—Scientific Claims By Dating Service Come Under Fire," *The Wall Street Journal,* September 17, 2007, p. B5, via Factiva, accessed October 2007.

32. "eHarmony Introduces eHarmony Marriage; New Marriage Wellness Program Offers Couples a New Approach to Strengthen Their Relationships," PR Newswire, February 6, 2006, via Factiva, accessed July 2007; Christopher Palmeri, "Dr. Warren's Lonely Hearts Club; EHarmony sheds its mom-and-pop structure, setting the stage for an IPO," *BusinessWeek,* February 20, 2006, p. 82, via Factiva, accessed July 2007; Hilary Potkewitz, "Internet Matchmaker Finds Tough Going to Find a Matching CEO," *Los Angeles Business Journal,* April 10, 2006, via Factiva, accessed July 2007; "New Research Find eHarmony Couples Are Significantly Happier in Their Marriages than Non-eHarmony Couples," PR Newswire, February 2, 2006, via Factiva, accessed July 2007.

33. "Over 90 Singles Marry Every Day on Average at eHarmony; Independent Research Shows Over 33,000 Members Married in One Year," PR Newswire, January 30, 2006, via Factiva, accessed July 2007.

34. John Tierney, "Hitting It Off, Thanks to Algorithms of Love," *The New York Times,* January 29, 2008, (http://www.nytimes.com/2008/01/29/science/29tier.html), accessed February 2008.

35. Max Freiert, "Love Doesn't Equal Loyalty: Online Dating in February 2007," March 29, 2007, (http://blog.compete.com/2007/03/29/online-dating-february-ranking/), accessed February 2008.

36. Josephine Marcotty, "Love at first site; They offer millions of psychological profiles and instant feedback. But can dating websites solve the mystery of what makes people click?" *Star-Tribune Metro,* February 14, 2007, p. 1E, via Factiva, accessed July 2007; "Chemistry.com Paints Rival as 'Heartbreak Hotel,'" *Brandweek,* April 30, 2007, via Factiva, accessed July 2007.

37. Raymond Fisman, Sheena S. Iyengar, Emir Kamenica, Itamar Simonson, "Gender Differences in Mate Selection: Evidence from a Speed Dating Experiment," *The Quarterly Journal of Economics,* May 2006, pp. 673–697.

38. Tierney, "Hitting It Off."

39. Jeana H. Frost, Zoe Chance, Michael I. Norton, and Dan Ariely, "People Are Experience Goods: Improving Online Dating with Virtual Dates," *Journal of Interactive Marketing* (forthcoming).

40. Gay Matchmaking sites find a growing market. San Francisco Chronicle, February 14, 2008; Mark Brooks, Niche Dating Sites Grow Steadily as Mainstream Ones Fail. (http://www.techcrunch.com /2008/04/24/nichedating-sites-grow-steadily-as-mainstream-ones-fail.), acessed May 2008. Num bers reported in the article were independently verified by the casewriters.

41. Joe Tracy, "Another Look: Starting an Online Dating Service," *Online Dating Magazine,* July 2007, (http://www.onlinedatingmagazine.com/columns/industry/2007/startinganonlinedatingservice.html), accessed October 2007.

42. "Jupiter Research Sees Steady Growth for Online Personals, Despite Explosion of Social Networking," *Jupiter Research,* February 11, 2008, (http://biz.yahoo.com/bw/080211/20080211005037.html?.v=1), accessed February 2008.

43. Vanessa L. Facenda, "Match.com Aims for 'Regular Folks' With New Campaign," Brandweek.com, December 20, 2007, (http://www.brandweek.com/bw/news/recent_display.jsp?vnu_content_id=1003687833), accessed February 2007.

44. IAC Annual 10-K Report 2007.

45. Vanessa L. Facenda, "Match.com Aims for 'Regular Folks' With New Campaign," *Brandweek.com,* December 20, 2007, (http://www.brandweek.com/bw/news/recent_display.jsp?vnu_content_id=1003687833), accessed February 2007. (http://www.bandt.com.au/news/ee/0c053eee.asp), accessed February 2008.

46. Josephine Marcotty, "Love at first site; They offer millions of psychological profiles and instant feedback. But can dating websites solve the mystery of what makes people click?" *Star-Tribune Metro,* February 14, 2007, p. 1E, via Factiva, accessed July 2007; "Chemistry.com Paints Rival as 'Heartbreak Hotel,'" *Brandweek,* April 30, 2007, via Factiva, accessed July 2007.

47. Rick Gershman, "Even eHarmony said no," *St. Petersburg Times,* June 16, 2007, p. 1, via Factiva, accessed July 2007.

48. Casewriters' estimates based on Yahoo! research analyst report by Bear Stearns, January 23, 2008, via Thompson Investext, accessed Feburary 2008.

Case 17

1. "Our History," Home Depot Company website, (http://www.corporate.homedepot.com), accessed January 23, 2008.

2. Brian Grow et al. "Out at Home Depot: Behind the flameout of controversial CEO Bob Nardelli," *BusinessWeek*, January 15, 2007, (http://www.businessweek.com/magazine/content/07_03/b4017001.htm) accessed November 29, 2007.

3. The Home Depot, 2001 Annual Report (Atlanta: The Home Depot, 2001), p. 2, (http://corporate.homedepot.com/en_US/Corporate/Investor_Relations/Annual_Reports/2001/complete_annualrpt.pdf), accessed March 6, 2008.

4. Grow et al. (January 15, 2007).

5. Ibid.

6. Ibid.

7. "How Nardelli Finally Helped the Stock," *BusinessWeek,* Stocks in the News, January 3, 2007, (www.businessweek.com), accessed January 15, 2008.

8. "DIY Retailing—US—March 2007," Mintel Oxygen, Mintel International Group Limited, via Investext [accessed January 18, 2008.

9. The Home Depot, "Welcome to The Home Depot, Inc. Corporate Web Site," The Home Depot Company Web site, (http://corporate.homedepot.com/wps/portal), accessed January 22, 2008.

10. Ibid.

11. Pallavi Gogoi, "Home Depot's Surprising Choice for CEO," *BusinessWeek,* January 4, 2007, (http://www.businessweek.com/bwdaily/dnflash/content/jan2007/db20070103_536329.htm), accessed January 15, 2008.

12. Pallavi (January 4, 2007).

13. Ibid.

14. The Home Depot, "Our History," The Home Depot Company Web site, (http://corporate.homedepot.com/wps/portal/!ut/p/.cmd/cs/.ce/7_0_A/.s/7_0_10D/_s.7_0_A/7_0_10D), accessed January 23, 2008.

15. "The Home Depot," *The New Georgia Encyclopedia*, (http://www.georgiaencyclopedia.org/nge/Article-Printable/jsp?id=h-1886), accessed January 23, 2008.

16. The Home Depot, "Our History," The Home Depot Company Web site, (http://corporate.homedepot.com/wps/portal/!ut/p/.cmd/cs/.ce/7_0_A/.s/7_0_10D/_s.7_0_A/7_0_10D), accessed January 23, 2008.

17. Ibid.

18. Ibid.

19. Ibid.

20. Ibid.

21. Charan (April 2006), p. 5.

22. The Home Depot, "Our History," The Home Depot Company Web site, (http://corporate.homedepot.

com/wps/portal/!ut/p/.cmd/cs/.ce/7_0_A/.s/7_0_
10D/_s.7_0_A/7_0_10D), accessed January 23,
2008.

23. The Home Depot, "Stores, Products, and Services,"
The Home Depot Company Web site, (http://
corporate.homedepot.com/wps/portal/!ut/p/c1/04-
_SB8K8xLLM9MSSzPy8xBz9CP0os3gDdwNHH0t-
DU1M3g1APR0N31xBjAwgAykfC5H1MzN0Mz-
DycDANMYdIGBHT7eeTnpuoX5EaUAwDOvP5h/
dl2/d1/L2dJQSEvUUt3QS9ZQnB3LzZfMEcw-
QUw5MTU1RjBVSEExR0NUMzAwMDAwMDA!),
accessed March 20, 2009.

24. Alex Biesada, "Home Improvement and Hardware
Retail—Industry Overview," Hoover's, Inc.,
(www.hoovers.com), accessed March 6, 2008.

25. "Industry Profile: Home Centers and Hardware
Stores," Hoover's, Inc., 2008, via Hoover's accessed
January 24, 2008.

26. "DIY Retailing—US—March 2007," Mintel Oxygen, Mintel International Group Limited, via
Investext, accessed January 18, 2008.

27. "Industry Profile: Home Centers and Hardware
Stores," Hoover's, Inc., 2008, via Hoover's,
accessed January 24, 2008.

28. Ibid.

29. Ibid.

30. Ibid.

31. Hardware Retailing, cited in "DIY Retailing—US—
March 2007," Mintel Oxygen, Mintel International
Group Limited, via Investext, accessed January 18,
2008.

32. "Lowe's Companies—Profile," Hoover's Online,
via Hoover's, accessed January 24, 2008.

33. The Home Depot, "Our History," The Home Depot
Company Web site, (http://corporate.homedepot
.com/wps/portal/!ut/p/.cmd/cs/.ce/7_0_A/.s/7_0_
10D/_s.7_0_A/7_0_10D), accessed January 23,
2008.

34. "Lowe's Companies—Profile," Hoover Online, via
Hoover's, accessed January 24, 2008.

35. Ibid.

36. Ibid.

37. Brian Hindo, "A Sharper Edge at Lowe's,"
BusinessWeek, January 15, 2007, (http://
www.businessweek.com/magazine/content/07_03/
b4017006.htm), accessed December 4, 2007.

38. Hindo (January 15, 2007).

39. Andrew Ward, "Quiet Achiever Led Lowe's to
Prosperity," FT.com, January 10, 2007, (http://
search.ft.com/ftArticle?queryText=Quiet+achie-
ver+led+Lowe%E2%80%99s+to+prosperity&y=
6&aje=false&x=13&id=070110009744&ct=0),
accessed December 4, 2007.

40. Ward (January 10, 2007).

41. Charan (April 2006), p. 2.

42. Ibid.

43. Ibid.

44. Grow et al. (March 6, 2006).

45. Dan Morse, "Under Renovation: A Hardware Chain
Struggles to Adjust to a New Blueprint," Wall Street
Journal, January 17, 2003, via Factiva, accessed
February 15, 2008.

46. Charan (April 2006), p. 8.

47. Ibid., p. 2.

48. Vanessa L. Facenda, "Cowboy Culture/GE Mentality: Bob Nardelli is trying to centralize operations
and rein in Home Depot's undisciplined past
without losing the entrepreneurial spirit in the
field," Retail Merchandiser, August 1, 2002, via
Factiva, accessed December 20, 2007.

49. Dan Morse, "Under Renovation: A Hardware Chain
Struggles to Adjust to a New Blueprint," Wall Street
Journal, January 17, 2003, via Factiva, accessed
February 15, 2008.

50. William A. Julian and Deidre Bane, "Home
Depot," Equity Research, Credit Suisse First Boston,
February 25, 2000, p. 3, via Investext, accessed
January 24, 2008.

51. Charan (April 2006), p. 2.

52. Dave Pennington, "Home Depot Leverages Enterprise Data to Increase Customer Satisfaction," DM
Review Magazine, January 2000, (http://www.
dmreview.com/issues/20000101/1784-1.html),
accessed February 29, 2008.

53. The Home Depot, 2000 Annual Report (Atlanta: Home Depot, 2001), p. 1, (http://corporate.homedepot.com/en_US/Corporate/Investor_Relations/Annual_Reports/2000/pdfs/hd2000.pdf), accessed December 2007.

54. The Home Depot, 2000 Annual Report (Atlanta: Home Depot, 2001), Founders' Letter, (http://corporate.homedepot.com/en_US/Corporate/Investor_Relations/Annual_Reports/2000/pdfs/hd2000.pdf), accessed December 2007.

55. William J Holstein, "Implementing Technology: IT Trials of a do-it-yourself enthusiast," *Financial Times*, September 29, 2004, via Lexis Nexis, accessed December 4, 2007.

56. J. P. Donlon, "Time Out Between Nardelli Meltdowns," January 9, 2007, (http://www.chiefexecutive.net), accessed January 7, 2008.

57. Donlon (2007).

58. Neil Buckley and Betty Liu, "Fixer puts the final touches to a DIY refit," *Financial Times*, July 8, 2003, p. 10, via Lexis-Nexus, accessed December 4, 2007.

59. Facenda (August 1, 2002).

60. William J Holstein, "Implementing Technology: IT Trials of a do-it-yourself enthusiast," *Financial Times*, September 29, 2004, via Lexis Nexis, accessed December 4, 2007.

61. Neil Buckley and Betty Liu, "Fixer puts the final touches to a DIY refit," *Financial Times*, July 8, 2003, p. 10, via Lexis-Nexus, accessed December 4, 2007.

62. Neil Buckley and Betty Liu, "Transcript of the interview with Robert Nardelli," *Financial Times*, July 7, 2003, via Factiva, accessed December 4, 2007.

63. The Home Depot, 2001 Annual Report (Atlanta: Home Depot, 2002), p. 4, (http://corporate.homedepot.com/en_US/Corporate/Investor_Relations/Annual_Reports/2001/complete_annualrpt.pdf), accessed December 2007.

64. "All Around the House," *HomeChannel News*, December 12, 2005, via Factiva, accessed February 15, 2008.

65. Ibid..

66. Patti Bond, "A revenue-building project, Home Depot has quietly expanded its wholesaling operations into a $12 billion unit," *Atlantic Journal Constitution*, August 6, 2006, via Factiva, accessed December 20, 2007.

67. From Betty Liu and Neil Buckley, "Transcript of the interview with Robert Nardelli," *Financial Times,* July 7, 2003, via Factiva, accessed December 4, 2007.

68. J. P. Donlon, "Time Out Between Nardelli Meltdowns," January 9, 2007, (http://www.chiefexecutive.net), accessed January 7, 2008.

69. From Betty Liu and Neil Buckley, "Transcript of the interview with Robert Nardelli," *Financial Times,* July 7, 2003, via Factiva, accessed December 4, 2007.

70. Renee Degross, "Five Years of Change: Home Depot's Results mixed under Nardelli," *The Atlanta Journal Constitution*, January 1, 2006, via Lexis-Nexus, accessed December 4, 2007.

71. "Home Depot Shifts it Merchandise Buying," *Wall Street Journal,* July 31, 2001, via Factiva, accessed December 20, 2007.

72. J. P. Donlon, "Time Out Between Nardelli Meltdowns," January 9, 2007, (http://www.chiefexecutive.net), accessed January 7, 2008.

73. John Caulfield, "Depot puts buying power in the hands of a dozen-Home Depot consolidates purchasing to regional," September 3, 2001, (http://findarticles.com/p/articles/mi_m0VCW/is_16_27/ai_78399495), accessed December 4, 2007.

74. Caulfield (September 3, 2001).

75. Ibid.

76. Ibid.

77. Tony Wilbert, "Home Depot implements another stop to cut costs," *Atlanta Journal-Constitution*, May 20, 2003, p. 12, via Lexis-Nexis, accessed December 4, 2007.

78. Wilbert (May 20, 2003), p. 12.

79. From Betty Liu and Neil Buckley, "Transcript of the interview with Robert Nardelli," *Financial Times,* July 7, 2003, via Factiva, accessed December 20, 2007.

80. Scott Larsen, "Heading in a Different Direction," *National Home Center News*, December 17, 2001, via Factiva, accessed December 20, 2007.

81. Grow et al. (January 15, 2007).

82. "Chain Store Age," *Digital Depot,* January 2004, via Factiva, accessed February 15, 2008.

83. Q3 2005 Home Depot Inc Earnings Conference Call—Final, *Voxant FD WIRE,* November 15, 2005.

84. The Home Depot, 2004 Annual Report (Atlanta: Home Depot, 2005), p. 2, (http://ir.homedepot.com/downloads/HD_2004_AR.pdf), accessed December 2007.

85. Much of this section was informed by Hal Plotkin, "Six Sigma: What it is and how to use it," *Harvard Management Update*, June 1999.

86. Plotkin (1999).

87. Ibid.

88. Ibid.

89. Ibid.

90. Ibid.

91. Harry R. Weber, "Home Depot retooling in face of challenge from Lowe's," November 26, 2003, *The San Diego Union-Tribune,* via Factiva, accessed February 15, 2008.

92. John Caulfield, "Making it Happen in the Field: District Managers take vanguard role in guiding store associates in the right direction," *National Home Center News*, December 17, 2001, via Factiva, accessed February 15, 2008.

93. Neil Buckley and Betty Liu, "Fixer puts the final touches to a DIY refit," *Financial Times*, July 8, 2003, p. 10, via Lexis-Nexus, accessed December 4, 2007.

94. Home Depot Inc. Analyst Meeting—Final, *FD Wire,* January 17, 2003, via Factiva, accessed February 27, 2008.

95. Dan Morse, "Under Renovation: A Hardware Chain Struggles to Adjust to a New Blueprint—Home Depot Chief Nardelli Tightens Central Control, and Employees Squawk—today he reveals more plans," *Wall Street Journal*, January 17, 2003, via Factiva, accessed December 4, 2007.

96. Home Depot Inc. Analyst Meeting—Final, *FD Wire,* January 17, 2003, via Factiva, February 26, 2008.

97. The Home Depot, 2002 Annual Report (Atlanta: Home Depot, 2003), p. 4, (http://ir.homedepot.com/downloads/HD_2002_AR.pdf), accessed December 2007.

98. Home Depot Inc. Analyst Meeting—Final, *FD Wire*, January 17, 2003, via Factiva, February 26, 2008.

99. Home Depot, 2004 Annual Report (Atlanta: Home Depot, 2005), p. 1, (http://ir.homedepot.com/downloads/HD_2004_AR.pdf), accessed December 2007.

100. Home Depot Inc. Analyst Meeting—Final, *FD Wire*, January 17, 2003, via Factiva, accessed February 27, 2008.

101. Home Depot Inc. Analyst Meeting—Final, *FD Wire*, January 17, 2003, via Factiva, accessed February 27, 2008.

103. Bond (December 8, 2002).

104. Grow et al. (March 6, 2006).

105. Bond (December 8, 2002).

106. Grow et al. (January 15, 2007).

107. Ibid.

108. Ibid.

109. Rebecca Zicarelli, "Home Depot's Hardware Warriors: The DIY store is drafting former military officers to lead the charge against rivals Wal-Mart and Lowe's," Fast Company, September 1, 2004, via Factiva, accessed February 27, 2008.

110. Martin Booe, "Reporting to the Depot," *Workforce Management,* January 1, 2005, via Factiva, accessed February 27, 2008.

111. Martin Booe, "Agent of Change," *Workforce Management*, January 1 2005, via Factiva, accessed February 27, 2008.

112. Grow et al. (March 6, 2006).

113. Ibid.

114. Terry C. Evans, "Home Depot management shift seen as healthy sign," October 8, 2001, (http://findarticles.com/p/articles/mi_m0VCW/is_18_27/ai_79353400), accessed December 4, 2007.

115. Grow et al. (March 6, 2006).

116. Ibid.

117. The Home Depot, 2002 Annual Report (Atlanta: Home Depot, 2003), p. 5, (http://ir.homedepot.com/downloads/HD_2002_AR.pdf), accessed December 2007

118. Home Depot, 2004 Annual Report (Atlanta: Home Depot, 2005), p. 1, (http://ir.homedepot.com/downloads/HD_2004_AR.pdf), accessed December 2007.

119. Scott Larsen, "Heading in a Different Direction," *National Home Center News*, December 17, 2001, via Factiva, accessed December 20, 2007.

120. Morse (January 17, 2003).

121. Ibid.

122. Grow et al. (March 6, 2006).

123. Facenda (August 1, 2002).

124. Budd Bugatch and Jessica Simmons, "Home Depot Incorporated," *Raymond James Equity Research*, February 11, 2002, p. 2, via Investext, accessed January 18, 2008.

125. Donald Trott, Jennifer Malone, and Timothy Allen, "Home Depot: Conquering New Worlds," Jeffries and Company, Inc., October 17, 2005, via Investext, accessed January 18, 2008.

126. Deborah L. Weinswig and Charmaine Tang, "Home Depot, Inc. Assuming Coverage: What Lies Beyond the Box," Citigroup, October 28, 2005, via Factiva, accessed January 18, 2008.

127. Facenda (August 1, 2002). .

128. Deborah L. Weinswig and Charmaine Tang, "Home Depot, Inc. Assuming Coverage: What Lies Beyond the Box," Citigroup, October 28, 2005, via Factiva, accessed January 18, 2008.

129. ISS US Proxy Advisory Services, "The Home Depot, Inc.," March 28, 2006.

130. Donald Trott, Jennifer Malone, and Timothy Allen, "Home Depot: Conquering New Worlds," Jeffries and Company, Inc., October 17, 2005, via Investext, accessed January 18, 2008.

131. Grow et al. (January 15, 2007).

132. Ibid.

133. Ibid.

134. Grow et al. (March 6, 2006).

135. Debbie Howell, "Nardelli nears five-year mark with riveting record," *DSN Retailing Today*, May 9, 2005, via Factiva, February 15, 2008.

136. Bond (December 8, 2002).

137. Patti Bond, "Nardelli Changing Culture," *Atlanta Journal-Constitution*, December 8, 2002, via Factiva, accessed December 20, 2007.

138. From Betty Liu and Neil Buckley, "Transcript of the interview with Robert Nardelli," *Financial Times,* July 7, 2003, via Factiva, accessed 20 December 2007.

139. Q2 2005 Home Depot Inc Earnings Conference Call-Final, *FD Wire,* August 16, 2005, via Factiva, accessed February 27, 2008.

140. Q1 2005 Home Depot Inc Earnings Conference Call-Final, *FD Wire*, May 17, 2005, via Factiva, accessed February 27, 2008.

141. Debbie Howell, "Nardelli nears five-year mark with riveting record," *DSN Retailing Today*, May 9, 2005, via Factiva, February 15, 2008.

142. Grow et al. (January 15, 2007).

143. Bond (December 8, 2002).

144. Grow et al. (March 6, 2006).

145. Patti Bond, "Home Depot Bumps up CFO," *Atlanta Journal-Constitution*, October 13, 2006, via Lexis Nexus, accessed December 4, 2007.

146. Q2 2006 Home Depot Inc Earnings Conference Call-Final, *Voxant FD Wire*, August 15, 2006, via Factiva, accessed February 27, 2008.

147. Patti Bond, "Q&A: Bob Nardelli, Home Depot Chairman and chief executive," *Atlanta Journal Constitution*, July 9, 2006, via Lexis Nexus, accessed December 4, 2007.

148. Bond (July 9, 2006).

Brands and Companies Index

NOTE: Company case studies are indicated by **bolded** page numbers.

Subject Index